Praise for *Alexander Hamilton*

"In *Alexander Hamilton*, Ron Chernow, author of *The House of Morgan, The Warburgs,* and *Titan* and a biography of John D. Rockefeller, has brought to vivid life the founding father who did more than any other to create the modern United States . . . [a] magisterial biography." —Michael Lind, *The Washington Post*

"Ron Chernow's new *Hamilton* could not be more welcome. This is grand-scale biography at its best—thorough, insightful, consistently fair, and superbly written. It clears away more than a few shopworn misconceptions about Hamilton, gives credit where credit is due, and is both clear-eyed and understanding about its very human subject. . . . The whole life and times are here in a genuinely great book." —David McCullough, author of *John Adams* and *Truman*

"Ron Chernow ranks as one of today's best writers of history and biography. Not only is his work compelling but, unusual among such writers, Chernow also has a sound understanding of finance and economics. These skills shined through in his previous books. . . . They are once again on full display in *Alexander Hamilton*." —Raymond J. Keating, *Newsday*

"Chernow's *Hamilton* is a success. Rarely does a biographer uncover so much new information about a long-dead, much-chronicled individual. Rarely does a biographer fill in the gaps with such incisive, justified speculation. Rarely does a biographer write narrative so well." —Steve Weinberg, *St. Louis Post-Dispatch*

"Ron Chernow has produced an original, illuminating, and highly readable study of Alexander Hamilton that admirably introduces readers to Hamilton's personality and accomplishments. Chernow penetrates more deeply into the mysteries of Hamilton's origins and family life than any previous biographer . . . Chernow's accounts of Hamilton's contributions to political theory, politics, and the law are compelling." —Walter Russell Mead, *Foreign Affairs*

"Like a few hundred thousand other people, I've been reading Ron Chernow's enthralling biography of Alexander Hamilton. It serves as a timely reminder that the era of the founding fathers, which we usually think of (correctly) as a time of high-minded philosophical discourse, was also full of venomous vituperation that has no parallel in modern America." —Max Boot, *Financial Times*

"A brilliant historian has done it again! The thoroughness and integrity of Ron Chernow's research shines forth on every page of his *Alexander Hamilton*. He has created a vivid and compelling portrait of a remarkable man—and at the same time he has made a monumental contribution to our understanding of the beginnings of the American republic." —Robert A. Caro, author of *The Power Broker* and *The Years of Lyndon Johnson*

"Fascinating." —*People*

"Chernow's gripping story sheds new light not only on Hamilton's legacy, but also on the conflicts that accompanied the republic's birth. . . . *Alexander Hamilton* is based on prodigious research, and it will likely prop up Hamilton's reputation in the same way David McCullough's biography bolstered John Adams's. . . . impressive detail."
—Matthew Dallek, *Washington Monthly*

"Magisterial. . . . Mr. Chernow has done a splendid job of capturing the backbiting political climate of Hamilton's times. . . . Mr. Chernow delivers a comprehensiveness that rivals Hamilton's . . . [and gives] the full measure of such a tireless, complex, and ultimately self-destructive man."—Janet Maslin, *The New York Times*

"A superb study. . . . Chernow's book is remarkable . . . for his unblinkered view of Hamilton's thought and behavior . . . Chernow's Hamilton is a whirlwind of a man, always in action, always in pursuit of a goal not quite within his grasp, and beset by the demons that have so often afflicted great minds. . . . It has been said that Hamilton was a great man but not a great American. Chernow's Hamilton is both."
—Edmund Morgan, *The New York Review of Books*

"Alexander Hamilton has been overshadowed by the founding fathers he served under, notably George Washington and Thomas Jefferson. Ron Chernow's magisterial new biography will certainly change that. . . . The first must-read biography of 2004."
—John Freeman, *TimeOut New York*

"A splendid new biography . . . Chernow unearths new information about Hamilton, but more importantly this beautifully written book recounts the formidable obstacles he surmounted to become, next to George Washington, the indispensable American founder. Chernow's *Alexander Hamilton* is the best biography of Hamilton ever written, and it is unlikely to be surpassed."
—Stephen F. Knott, *Claremont Review of Books*

"Superb . . . Chernow is a shrewd student of power, and he couldn't have chosen a more compelling subject."   —James Aley, *Fortune*

"Chernow writes beautifully and skillfully, and opens up aspects of Hamilton's life that others have not yet understood."   —Andrew Burstein, *Chicago Tribune*

"Now, Ron Chernow, whose previous books have chronicled the American Beauty roses and kudzu vines of mature American capitalism—*Warburgs*, Morgans, John D. Rockefeller, Sr.—examines the man who planted the seeds. . . . *Alexander Hamilton* is thorough, admiring, and sad—just what a big book on its subject should be."
—Richard Brookhiser, *Los Angeles Times*

"Terrific . . . Ron Chernow's magisterial *Alexander Hamilton* treats the first secretary of the treasury with the weight and gravitas of a nineteen-century novel."
—John Freeman, *The Atlanta Journal-Constitution*

"Powerful . . . Chernow's magisterial work combines a biography of Hamilton and a political history of the United States in the early years of the republic. Exhaustively researched and beautifully written, the volume tells us a great deal about the founding fathers and helps restore one of them to his rightful place in the pantheon." —Terry W. Hartle, *The Christian Science Monitor*

"Chernow has chosen an ideal subject. . . . No other founding father more richly deserves the modern-eye-on-the-colonial-guy treatment . . . electrifying . . . Chernow does an admirable job." —Justin Martin, *San Francisco Chronicle*

"[T]he life of Alexander Hamilton was 'so tumultuous that only an audacious novelist could have dreamed it up.' Such is the assessment of Ron Chernow in this splendid new biography of Hamilton." —Steve Raymond, *The Seattle Times*

"In this engaging new book, Ron Chernow reassesses the historical legacy of the brilliant founding father, political theorist, and politician Alexander Hamilton. . . . Lively and beautifully written." —Anne Lombard, *The San Diego Union-Tribune*

"*Alexander Hamilton* is a balanced portrait of the man and his many contradictions . . . Admirers of David McCullough's *John Adams* or Walter Isaacson's *Benjamin Franklin* will thoroughly enjoy this excellent book." —Roger Bishop, *BookPage*

"On July 11, 1804, on a ledge overlooking the Hudson River in Weehawken, New Jersey, Burr mortally wounded Hamilton . . . For thirty days, the city's residents wore black armbands. . . . The extraordinary and improbable career of Alexander Hamilton had come to and end, and here we have another fitting tribute to it: Ron Chernow's massively researched and beautifully written biography." —James Chace, *The New York Observer*

"Ron Chernow's absorbing, exhaustively researched *Alexander Hamilton* justifies his claim that Hamilton's was the most dramatic and improbable life among the founding fathers. . . . Chernow, who won the National Book Award for *The House of Morgan*, shows all Hamilton's complexity." —David Gates, *Newsweek*

"Chernow's splendid, thorough and brilliantly written biography of Hamilton gives us a new understanding of Hamilton's vital role during the war and immediately after as secretary of the treasury. . . . There have been other biographies of Hamilton, but Chernow's is far and away the most comprehensive and compelling of any I have read. It is a fitting tribute to the man who set the U.S. on the path that has made our nation the economic leader of the world." —Caspar W. Weinberger, former secretary of defense, and chairman of *Forbes*

"As Ron Chernow points out in this magnificent biography, Hamilton was the boy wonder of early American politics." —*The Economist*

"A splendid life of an enlightened and reactionary founding father . . . Literate and full of engaging asides. By far the best of the many lives of Hamilton now in print, and a model of the biographer's art." —*Kirkus Reviews* (starred)

"In *Alexander Hamilton*, his mammoth and comprehensive study of the nation's first treasury secretary, Chernow has captured the essence of the man. . . . Chernow is especially skillful at evoking a sense of time and place, an achievement that dominates *Alexander Hamilton*. He goes beyond the stick-figure characters that often emerge from most stories about the founders to present three-dimensional portrayals. . . . Now, with this carefully crafted revision of the record, Hamilton's accomplishments should be seen in a different light, one bright enough to show what he has meant for America." —Ray Locker, The Associated Press

"In this majestic and thorough biography, Chernow explores the conundrums and paradoxes of Hamilton's private and public life and gives the man his due." —John C. Chalberg, *Star Tribune* (Minneapolis)

"Ron Chernow's fascinating new biography of Alexander Hamilton is the best written about the man. . . . Chernow sorts out this period of history and humanizes Hamilton. . . . Chernow obviously believes Hamilton has not received much of the credit he deserves, but this book will help rectify the situation." —Larry Cox, *Tucson Citizen*

"In the first full-length biography of Alexander Hamilton in many years, Ron Chernow, known for his impressive work on the titans of American industry, has made an exceptional contribution to American history." —Dennis Lythgoe, *Deseret Morning News*

"Chernow's achievement is to give us a biography commensurate with Hamilton's character, as well as the full, complex content of his unflaggingly active life. . . . This is a fine work that captures Hamilton's life with judiciousness and verve." —*Publishers Weekly* (starred review)

"[Chernow's] sweeping narrative chronicles the complex and often contradictory life of Hamilton. . . . A first-rate life and excellent addition to the ongoing debate about Hamilton's importance in shaping America." —*Library Journal*

"Ron Chernow's altogether splendid, full-scale biography is a weighty and meticulously researched tome of more than 800 pages. It nonetheless reads like a great historical novel, because Chernow brings his central characters to such vivid life. This is a life not only of Hamilton the politician, lawyer, and technocrat, but of Hamilton the man." —John Steele Gordon, *American Heritage*

PENGUIN BOOKS

ALEXANDER HAMILTON

A graduate of Yale and Cambridge, Ron Chernow won the National Book Award in 1990 for his first book, *The House of Morgan*, which the Modern Library cites as one of the hundred best nonfiction books of the twentieth century. His second book, *The Warburgs*, won the Eccles Prize as the best business book of 1993. His biography of John D. Rockefeller, *Titan*, was a national bestseller and a National Book Critics Circle Award finalist. Both *Time* magazine and *The New York Times* listed it among the ten best books of 1998. Chernow lives in Brooklyn, New York.

AUTHOR'S NOTE

In order to make the text as fluent as possible and the founders less remote, I have taken the liberty of modernizing the spelling and punctuation of eighteenth-century prose, which can seem antiquated and jarring to modern eyes. I have also cured many contemporary newspaper editors of their addiction to italics and capitalized words. Occasionally, I have retained the original spelling to emphasize the distinctive voice, strong emotion, patent eccentricity, or curious education of the person quoted. I trust that these exceptional cases, and my reasons for wanting to reproduce them precisely, will be evident to the alert reader.

Alexander Hamilton

RON CHERNOW

ALEXANDER HAMILTON

PENGUIN BOOKS

PENGUIN BOOKS
Published by the Penguin Group
Penguin Group (USA) Inc., 375 Hudson Street, New York, New York 10014, U.S.A.
Penguin Group (Canada), 10 Alcorn Avenue, Toronto,
Ontario, Canada M4V 3B2 (a division of Pearson Penguin Canada Inc.)
Penguin Books Ltd, 80 Strand, London WC2R 0RL, England
Penguin Group Ireland, 25 St Stephen's Green, Dublin 2, Ireland (a division of Penguin Books Ltd)
Penguin Group (Australia), 250 Camberwell Road, Camberwell,
Victoria 3124, Australia (a division of Pearson Australia Group Pty Ltd)
Penguin Books India Pvt Ltd, 11 Community Centre, Panchsheel Park, New Delhi – 110 017, India
Penguin Books (NZ) cnr Airborne and Rosedale Roads, Albany,
Auckland 1310, New Zealand (a division of Pearson New Zealand Ltd)
Penguin Books (South Africa) (Pty) Ltd, 24 Sturdee Avenue,
Rosebank, Johannesburg 2196, South Africa

Penguin Books Ltd, Registered Offices:
80 Strand, London WC2R 0RL, England

First published in the United States of America by The Penguin Press,
a member of Penguin Group (USA) Inc. 2004
Published in Penguin Books 2005

39 40

Illustration credits appear on pages 789–90.

THE LIBRARY OF CONGRESS HAS CATALOGED THE HARDCOVER EDITION AS FOLLOWS:
Chernow, Ron.
Alexander Hamilton / Ron Chernow.
p. cm.
Includes bibliographical references and index.
ISBN 1-59420-009-2 (hc.)
ISBN 0 14 30.3475 8 (pbk.)
1. Hamilton, Alexander, 1757–1804. 2. Statesmen—United States—Biography.
3. United States—Politics and government—1783–1809. I. Title.
E3002.6.H2C48 2004
973.4'092—dc22
[B]
2003065641

Printed in the United States of America
Designed by Michelle McMillian

Contents

TO VALERIE,
best of wives and best of women

OBSERVATIONS BY ALEXANDER HAMILTON

I have thought it my duty to exhibit things as they are,
not as they ought to be.
—LETTER OF AUGUST 13, 1782

The passions of a revolution are apt to hurry
even good men into excesses.
—ESSAY OF AUGUST 12, 1795

Men are rather reasoning than reasonable animals,
for the most part governed by the impulse of passion.
—LETTER OF APRIL 16, 1802

Opinion, whether well or ill founded,
is the governing principle of human affairs.
—LETTER OF JUNE 18, 1778

THE OLDEST REVOLUTIONARY WAR WIDOW

In the early 1850s, few pedestrians strolling past the house on H Street in Washington, near the White House, realized that the ancient widow seated by the window, knitting and arranging flowers, was the last surviving link to the glory days of the early republic. Fifty years earlier, on a rocky, secluded ledge overlooking the Hudson River in Weehawken, New Jersey, Aaron Burr, the vice president of the United States, had fired a mortal shot at her husband, Alexander Hamilton, in a misbegotten effort to remove the man Burr regarded as the main impediment to the advancement of his career. Hamilton was then forty-nine years old. Was it a benign or a cruel destiny that had compelled the widow to outlive her husband by half a century, struggling to raise seven children and surviving almost until the eve of the Civil War?

Elizabeth Schuyler Hamilton—purblind and deaf but gallant to the end—was a stoic woman who never yielded to self-pity. With her gentle manner, Dutch tenacity, and quiet humor, she clung to the deeply rooted religious beliefs that had abetted her reconciliation to the extraordinary misfortunes she had endured. Even in her early nineties, she still dropped to her knees for family prayers. Wrapped in shawls and garbed in the black bombazine dresses that were de rigueur for widows, she wore a starched white ruff and frilly white cap that bespoke a simpler era in American life. The dark eyes that gleamed behind large metal-rimmed glasses—those same dark eyes that had once enchanted a young officer on General George Washington's staff—betokened a sharp intelligence, a fiercely indomitable spirit, and a memory that refused to surrender the past.

In the front parlor of the house she now shared with her daughter, Eliza Hamilton had crammed the faded memorabilia of her now distant marriage. When visitors called, the tiny, erect, white-haired lady would grab her cane, rise gamely from a black sofa embroidered with a floral pattern of her own design, and escort them to a Gilbert Stuart painting of George Washington. She motioned with pride to a silver wine cooler, tucked discreetly beneath the center table, that had been given to the Hamiltons by Washington himself. This treasured gift retained a secret meaning for Eliza, for it had been a tacit gesture of solidarity from Washington when her husband was ensnared in the first major sex scandal in American history. The tour's highlight stood enshrined in the corner: a marble bust of her dead hero, carved by an Italian sculptor, Giuseppe Ceracchi, during Hamilton's heyday as the first treasury secretary. Portrayed in the classical style of a noble Roman senator, a toga draped across one shoulder, Hamilton exuded a brisk energy and a massive intelligence in his wide brow, his face illumined by the half smile that often played about his features. This was how Eliza wished to recall him: ardent, hopeful, and eternally young. "That bust I can never forget," one young visitor remembered, "for the old lady always paused before it in her tour of the rooms and, leaning on her cane, gazed and gazed, as if she could never be satisfied."

For the select few, Eliza unearthed documents written by Hamilton that qualified as her sacred scripture: an early hymn he had composed or a letter he had drafted during his impoverished boyhood on St. Croix. She frequently grew melancholy and longed for a reunion with "her Hamilton," as she invariably referred to him. "One night, I remember, she seemed sad and absent-minded and could not go to the parlor where there were visitors, but sat near the fire and played backgammon for a while," said one caller. "When the game was done, she leaned back in her chair a long time with closed eyes, as if lost to all around her. There was a long silence, broken by the murmured words, 'I am so tired. It is so long. I want to see Hamilton.'"[1]

Eliza Hamilton was committed to one holy quest above all others: to rescue her husband's historical reputation from the gross slanders that had tarnished it. For many years after the duel, Thomas Jefferson, John Adams, and other political enemies had taken full advantage of their eloquence and longevity to spread defamatory anecdotes about Hamilton, who had been condemned to everlasting silence. Determined to preserve her husband's legacy, Eliza enlisted as many as thirty assistants to sift through his tall stacks of papers. Unfortunately, she was so self-effacing and so reverential toward her husband that, though she salvaged every scrap of his writing, she apparently destroyed her own letters. The capstone of her monumental labor, her life's "dearest object," was the publication of a mammoth authorized biography that would secure Hamilton's niche in the pantheon of the early republic. It was a long, exasperating wait as one biographer after another discarded the project or expired before its completion. Almost by default, the giant enterprise fell to her fourth son, John Church Hamilton, who belatedly disgorged a seven-volume history of his father's exploits. Before this hagiographic tribute was completed, however, Eliza Hamilton died at ninety-seven on November 9, 1854.

Distraught that their mother had waited vainly for decades to see her husband's life immortalized, Eliza Hamilton Holly scolded her brother for his overdue biography. "Lately in my hours of sadness, recurring to such interests as most deeply affected our blessed Mother . . . I could recall none more frequent or more absorbent than her devotion to our Father. When blessed memory shows her gentle countenance and her untiring spirit before me, in this one great and beautiful aspiration after duty, I feel the same spark ignite and bid me . . . to seek the fulfillment of her words: 'Justice shall be done to the memory of my Hamilton.'"[2] It was, Eliza Hamilton Holly noted pointedly, the imperative duty that Eliza had bequeathed to all her children: *Justice shall be done to the memory of my Hamilton.*

Well, has justice been done? Few figures in American history have aroused such visceral love or loathing as Alexander Hamilton. To this day, he seems trapped in a crude historical cartoon that pits "Jeffersonian democracy" against "Hamiltonian aristocracy." For Jefferson and his followers, wedded to their vision of an agrarian Eden, Hamilton was the American Mephistopheles, the proponent of such devilish contrivances as banks, factories, and stock exchanges. They demonized him as a slavish pawn of the British Crown, a closet monarchist, a Machiavellian intriguer, a would-be Caesar. Noah Webster contended that Hamilton's "ambition, pride, and overbearing temper" had destined him "to be the evil genius of this country."[3] Hamilton's powerful vision of American nationalism, with states subordinate to a strong central government and led by a vigorous executive branch, aroused fears of a reversion to royal British ways. His seeming solicitude for the rich caused critics to portray him as a snobbish tool of plutocrats who was contemptuous of the masses. For another group of naysayers, Hamilton's unswerving faith in a professional military converted him into a potential despot. "From the first to the last words he wrote," concluded historian Henry Adams, "I read always the same Napoleonic kind of adventuredom."[4] Even some Hamilton admirers have been unsettled by a faint tincture of something foreign in this West Indian transplant; Woodrow Wilson grudgingly praised Hamilton as "a very great man, but not a great American."[5]

Yet many distinguished commentators have echoed Eliza Hamilton's lament that justice has not been done to her Hamilton. He has tended to lack the glittering multivolumed biographies that have burnished the fame of other founders. The British statesman Lord Bryce singled out Hamilton as the one founding father who had not received his due from posterity. In *The American Commonwealth,* he observed, "One cannot note the disappearance of this brilliant figure, to Europeans the most interesting in the early history of the Republic, without the remark that his countrymen seem to have never, either in his lifetime or afterwards, duly recognized his splendid gifts."[6] During the robust era of Progressive Republicanism, marked by brawny nationalism and energetic government, Theodore Roosevelt took up the cudgels and declared Hamilton "the most brilliant American statesman who ever lived, possessing the loftiest and keenest intellect of his time."[7] His White House successor, William Howard Taft, likewise embraced Hamilton as "our greatest constructive statesman."[8] In all probability, Alexander Hamilton is the foremost political figure in American history who never attained the presidency, yet he probably had a much deeper and more lasting impact than many who did.

Hamilton was the supreme double threat among the founding fathers, at once thinker and doer, sparkling theoretician and masterful executive. He and James Madison were the prime movers behind the summoning of the Constitutional Convention and the chief authors of that classic gloss on the national charter, *The Federalist*, which Hamilton supervised. As the first treasury secretary and principal architect of the new government, Hamilton took constitutional principles and infused them with expansive life, turning abstractions into institutional realities. He had a pragmatic mind that minted comprehensive programs. In contriving the smoothly running machinery of a modern nation-state—including a budget system, a funded debt, a tax system, a central bank, a customs service, and a coast guard—and justifying them in some of America's most influential state papers, he set a high-water mark for administrative competence that has never been equaled. If Jefferson provided the essential poetry of American political discourse, Hamilton established the prose of American statecraft. No other founder articulated such a clear and prescient vision of America's future political, military, and economic strength or crafted such ingenious mechanisms to bind the nation together.

Hamilton's crowded years as treasury secretary scarcely exhaust the epic story of his short life, which was stuffed with high drama. From his illegitimate birth on Nevis to his bloody downfall in Weehawken, Hamilton's life was so tumultuous that only an audacious novelist could have dreamed it up. He embodied an enduring archetype: the obscure immigrant who comes to America, re-creates himself, and succeeds despite a lack of proper birth and breeding. The saga of his metamorphosis from an anguished clerk on St. Croix to the reigning presence in George Washington's cabinet offers both a gripping personal story and a panoramic view of the formative years of the republic. Except for Washington, nobody stood closer to the center of American politics from 1776 to 1800 or cropped up at more turning points. More than anyone else, the omnipresent Hamilton galvanized, inspired, and scandalized the newborn nation, serving as the flash point for pent-up conflicts of class, geography, race, religion, and ideology. His contemporaries often seemed defined by how they reacted to the political gauntlets that he threw down repeatedly with such defiant panache.

Hamilton was an exuberant genius who performed at a fiendish pace and must have produced the maximum number of words that a human being can scratch out in forty-nine years. If promiscuous with his political opinions, however, he was famously reticent about his private life, especially his squalid Caribbean boyhood. No other founder had to grapple with such shame and misery, and his early years have remained wrapped in more mystery than those of any other major American statesman. While not scanting his vibrant intellectual life, I have tried to gather anecdotal material that will bring this cerebral man to life as both a public and a private figure. Charming and impetuous, romantic and witty, dashing and headstrong, Hamilton offers the biographer an irresistible psychological study. For all his superlative mental gifts, he was afflicted with a touchy ego that made him querulous and fatally combative. He never outgrew the stigma of his illegitimacy, and his exquisite tact often gave way to egregious failures of judgment that left even his keenest admirers aghast. If capable of numerous close friendships, he also entered into titanic feuds with Jefferson, Madison, Adams, Monroe, and Burr.

The magnitude of Hamilton's feats as treasury secretary has overshadowed many other facets of his life: clerk, college student, youthful poet, essayist, artillery captain, wartime adjutant to Washington, battlefield hero, congressman, abolitionist, Bank of New York founder, state assemblyman, member of the Constitutional Convention and New York Ratifying Convention, orator, lawyer, polemicist, educator, patron saint of the *New-York Evening Post*, foreign-policy theorist, and major general in the army. Boldly uncompromising, he served as catalyst for the emergence of the first political parties and as the intellectual fountainhead for one of them, the Federalists. He was a pivotal force in four consecutive presidential elections and defined much of America's political agenda during the Washington and Adams administrations, leaving copious commentary on virtually every salient issue of the day.

Earlier generations of biographers had to rely on only a meager portion of his voluminous output. Between 1961 and 1987, Harold C. Syrett and his doughty editorial team at Columbia University Press published twenty-seven thick volumes of Hamilton's personal and political papers. Julius Goebel, Jr., and his staff added five volumes of legal and business papers to the groaning shelf, bringing the total haul to twenty-two thousand pages. These meticulous editions are much more than exhaustive compilations of Hamilton's writings: they are a scholar's feast, enriched with expert commentary as well as contemporary newspaper extracts, letters, and diary entries. No biographer has fully harvested these riches. I have supplemented this research with extensive archival work that has uncovered, among other things, nearly fifty previously undiscovered essays written by Hamilton himself. To retrieve his early life from its often impenetrable obscurity, I have also scoured records in Scotland, England, Denmark, and eight Caribbean islands, not to mention many domestic archives. The resulting portrait, I hope, will seem fresh and surprising even to those best versed in the literature of the period.

It is an auspicious time to reexamine the life of Hamilton, who was the prophet of the capitalist revolution in America. If Jefferson enunciated the more ample view of political democracy, Hamilton possessed the finer sense of economic opportunity. He was the messenger from a future that we now inhabit. We have left behind the rosy agrarian rhetoric and slaveholding reality of Jeffersonian democracy and reside in the bustling world of trade, industry, stock markets, and banks that Hamilton envisioned. (Hamilton's staunch abolitionism formed an integral feature of this economic vision.) He has also emerged as the uncontested visionary in anticipating the shape and powers of the federal government. At a time when Jefferson and Madison celebrated legislative power as the purest expression of the popular will, Hamilton argued for a dynamic executive branch and an independent judiciary, along with a professional military, a central bank, and an advanced financial system. Today, we are indisputably the heirs to Hamilton's America, and to repudiate his legacy is, in many ways, to repudiate the modern world.

ONE

THE CASTAWAYS

lexander Hamilton claimed Nevis in the British West Indies as his birthplace, although no surviving records substantiate this. Today, the tiny island seems little more than a colorful speck in the Caribbean, an exotic tourist hideaway. One million years ago, the land that is now Nevis Peak thrust up from the seafloor to form the island, and the extinct volcanic cone still intercepts the trade winds at an altitude of 3,200 feet, its jagged peak often obscured behind a thick swirl of clouds. This omnipresent mountain, looming over jungles, plunging gorges, and verdant foothills that sweep down to sandy beaches, made the island a natural fortress for the British. It abounded in both natural wonders and horrors: in 1690, the first capital, Jamestown, was swallowed whole by the sea during an earthquake and tidal wave.

To modern eyes, Nevis may seem like a sleepy backwater to which Hamilton was confined before his momentous escape to St. Croix and North America. But if we adjust our vision to eighteenth-century realities, we see that this West Indian setting was far from marginal, the crossroads of a bitter maritime rivalry among European powers vying for mastery of the lucrative sugar trade. A small revolution in consumer tastes had turned the Caribbean into prized acreage for growing sugarcane to sweeten the coffee, tea, and cocoa imbibed in fashionable European capitals. As a result, the small, scattered islands generated more wealth for Britain than all of her North American colonies combined. "The West Indians vastly outweigh us of the northern colonies," Benjamin Franklin grumbled in the 1760s.[1] After the French and Indian War, the British vacillated about whether to swap all of Canada for the island of Guadeloupe; in the event the French toasted their own diplomatic cunning in retaining the sugar island. The sudden popularity of sugar, dubbed "white gold," engendered a brutal world of overnight fortunes in which slavery proved indispensable. Since indigenous Caribbeans and Europeans balked at toiling in the sweltering canebrakes, thousands of blacks were shipped from slave-trading forts in West Africa to cultivate Nevis and the neighboring islands.

British authorities colonized Nevis with vagabonds, criminals, and other riffraff swept from the London streets to work as indentured servants or overseers. In 1727, the minister of a local Anglican church, aching for some glimmer of spirituality, regretted that the slaves were inclined to "laziness, stealing, stubbornness, murmuring, treachery, lying, drunkenness and the like." But he reserved his most scathing strictures for a rowdy white populace composed of "whole shiploads of pickpockets, whores, rogues, vagrants, thieves, sodomites, and other filth and cutthroats of society."[2] Trapped in this beautiful but godless spot, the minister bemoaned that the British imports "were not bad enough for the gallows and yet too bad to live among their virtuous countrymen at home."[3] While other founding fathers were reared in tidy New England villages or cosseted on baronial Virginia estates, Hamilton grew up in a tropical hellhole of dissipated whites and fractious slaves, all framed by a backdrop of luxuriant natural beauty.

On both his maternal and paternal sides, Hamilton's family clung to the insecure middle rung of West Indian life, squeezed between plantation aristocrats above and street rabble and unruly slaves below. Taunted as a bastard throughout his life, Hamilton was understandably reluctant to chat about his childhood—"my birth is the subject of the most humiliating criticism," he wrote in one pained confession—and he turned his early family history into a taboo topic, alluded to in only a couple of cryptic letters.[4] He described his maternal grandfather, the physician John Faucette, as "a French Huguenot who emigrated to the West Indies in consequence of the revocation of the Edict of Nantes and settled in the island of Nevis and there acquired a pretty fortune. [Revoked in 1685 by Louis XIV, the Edict of Nantes had guaranteed religious toleration for French Protestants.] I have been assured by persons who knew him that he was a man of letters and much of a gentleman."[5] Born ten years after his grandfather's death, Hamilton may have embellished the sketch with a touch of gentility. In the slave-based economy, physicians often attended the auctions, checking the teeth of the human chattel and making them run, leap, and jump to test whatever strength remained after the grueling middle passage. No white in the sugar islands was entirely exempt from the pervasive taint of slavery.

The archives of St. George's Parish in the fertile, mountainous Gingerland section of Nevis record the marriage of John Faucette to a British woman, Mary Uppington, on August 21, 1718. By that point, they already had two children: a daughter, Ann, and a son, John, the latter arriving two months before the wedding. In all likelihood, lulled by the casual mores of the tropics, the Faucettes decided to formalize their link after the birth of their second child, having lived until then as a common-law couple—an expedient adopted by Hamilton's own parents. In all, the Faucettes produced seven children, Hamilton's mother, Rachel, being the second youngest, born circa 1729.

A persistent mythology in the Caribbean asserts that Rachel was partly black, making Alexander Hamilton a quadroon or an octoroon. In this obsessively race-conscious society, however, Rachel was invariably listed among the whites on local tax rolls. Her identification as someone of mixed race has no basis in verifiable fact. (See pages 734–35.) The folklore that Hamilton was mulatto probably arose from the incontestable truth that many, if not most, illegitimate children in the West Indies bore mixed blood. At the time of Rachel's birth, the four thousand slaves on Nevis outnumbered whites by a ratio of four to one, making inequitable carnal relations between black slaves and white masters a dreadful commonplace.

Occupying a house in the southern Nevis foothills, the Faucettes owned a small sugar plantation and had at least seven slaves—pretty typical for the petite bourgeoisie. That Nevis later had a small black village named Fawcett, an anglicized version of the family name, confirms their ownership of slaves who later assumed their surname. The sugar islands were visited so regularly by epidemics of almost biblical proportions—malaria, dysentery, and yellow fever being the worst offenders—that five Faucette children perished in infancy or childhood, leaving only Rachel and her much older sister, Ann, as survivors. Even aided by slaves, small planters found it a tough existence. Skirting the volcanic cone, the Nevis hills were so steep and rocky that, even when terraced, they proved troublesome for sugar cultivation. The island steadily lost its economic eminence, especially after a mysterious plant disease, aggravated by drought, slowly crept across Nevis in 1737 and denuded it of much of its lush vegetation. This prompted a mass exodus of refugees, including Ann Faucette, who had married a well-to-do planter named James Lytton. They decamped to the Danish island of St. Croix, charting an escape route that Hamilton's parents were to follow.

Evidence indicates that the Faucette marriage was marred by perpetual squabbling, perhaps compounded by the back-to-back deaths of two of their children in 1736 and the blight that parched the island the next year. Mary Faucette was a pretty, socially ambitious woman and probably not content to dawdle on a stagnant island. Determined and resourceful, with a clear knack for cultivating powerful men, she appealed to the chancellor of the Leeward Islands for a legal separation from her husband. In the 1740 settlement, the Faucettes agreed to "live separately and apart for the rest of their lives," and Mary renounced all rights to her husband's property in exchange for an inadequate annuity of fifty-three pounds.[6] It is possible that she and Rachel traversed the narrow two-mile strait to St. Kitts, where they may even have first encountered a young Scottish nobleman named James Hamilton. Because her mother had surrendered all claims to John Faucette's money, sixteen-year-old Rachel Faucette achieved the sudden glow of a minor heiress in 1745 when her father died and left her all his property. Since Rachel was bright, beautiful, and strong willed—traits we can deduce from subsequent events—she must have been hotly pursued in a world chronically deficient in well-heeled, educated European women.

Rachel and her mother decided to start anew on St. Croix, where James and Ann Lytton had prospered, building a substantial estate outside the capital, Christiansted, called the Grange. The Lyttons likely introduced them to another newcomer from Nevis, a Dane named Johann Michael Lavien, who had peddled household goods and now aspired to planter status. The name *Lavien* can be a Sephardic variant of *Levine,* but if he was Jewish he managed to conceal his origins. Had he presented himself as a Jew, the snobbish Mary Faucette would certainly have squelched the match in a world that frowned on religious no less than interracial marriage.

From fragmentary evidence, Lavien emerges as a man who dreamed of plucking sudden riches from the New World but stumbled, like others, into multiple disappointments. The year before he met Rachel, he squandered much of his paltry capital on a minor St. Croix sugar plantation. On this island of grand estates, a profitable operation required fifty to one hundred slaves, something beyond the reveries of the thinly capitalized Lavien. He then lowered his sights appreciably and, trying to become a planter on the cheap, acquired a 50 percent stake in a small cotton plantation. He ended up deeply in hock to the Danish West India and Guinea Company. Beyond her apparent physical allure, Rachel Faucette must have represented a fresh source of ready cash for Lavien.

For Alexander Hamilton, Johann Michael Lavien was the certified ogre of his family saga. He wrote, "A Dane, a fortune hunter of the name of *Lavine* [Hamilton's spelling], came to Nevis bedizzened with gold and paid his addresses to my mother, then a handsome young woman having a *snug* fortune." In the eighteenth century, a "snug" fortune signified one sufficient for a comparatively easy life. Partial to black silk gowns and blue vests with bright gold buttons, Lavien was a flashy dresser and must have splurged on such finery to hide his threadbare budget and palm himself off on Mary Faucette as an affluent suitor. Hamilton rued the day that his grandmother was "captivated by the glitter" of Lavien's appearance and auctioned her daughter off, as it were, to the highest bidder. "In compliance with the wishes of her mother . . . but against her own inclination," Hamilton stated, the sixteeen-year-old Rachel agreed to marry the older Lavien, her senior by at least a dozen years.[7] In Hamilton's blunt estimation, it was "a hated marriage," as the daughter of one unhappy union was rushed straight into another.[8]

In 1745, the ill-fated wedding took place at the Grange. The newlyweds set up house on their own modest plantation, which was named, with macabre irony, Contentment. The following year, the teenage bride gave birth to a son, Peter, destined to be her one legitimate child. One wonders if Rachel ever submitted to further conjugal relations with Lavien. Even if Lavien was not the "coarse man of repulsive personality" evoked by Hamilton's grandson, it seems clear that Rachel felt stifled by her older husband, finding him crude and insufferable.[9] In 1748, Lavien bought a half share in another small sugar plantation, enlarging his debt and frittering away Rachel's fast dwindling inheritance. The marriage deteriorated to the point where the headstrong wife simply abandoned the house around 1750. A vindictive Lavien ranted in a subsequent divorce decree that while Rachel had lived with him she had "committed such errors which as between husband and wife were indecent and very suspicious."[10] In his severe judgment she was "shameless, coarse, and ungodly."[11]

Enraged, his pride bruised, Lavien was determined to humiliate his unruly bride. Seizing on a Danish law that allowed a husband to jail his wife if she was twice found guilty of adultery and no longer resided with him, he had Rachel clapped into the dreaded Christiansvaern, the Christiansted fort, which did double duty as the town jail.[12] Rachel has sometimes been portrayed as a "prostitute"—one of Hamilton's journalistic nemeses branded him "the son of a camp-girl"—but such insinuations are absurd.[13] On the other hand, that Lavien broadcast his accusations against her and met no outright refutation suggests that Rachel had indeed flouted social convention and found solace in the arms of other men.

Perched on the edge of Gallows Bay, Fort Christiansvaern had cannon that could be trained on pirates or enemy ships crossing the coral reef, as well as smaller artillery that could be swiveled landward and used to suppress slave insurrections. In this ghastly place, unspeakable punishments were meted out to rebellious blacks who had committed heinous crimes: striking whites, torching cane fields, or dashing off to freedom. They could be whipped, branded, and castrated, shackled with heavy leg irons, and entombed in filthy dungeons. The remaining cells tended to be populated by town drunks, petty thieves, and the other dregs of white society. It seems that no woman other than Rachel Lavien was ever imprisoned there for adultery. Rachel spent several months in a dank, cramped cell that measured ten by thirteen feet, and she must have gone through infernal torments of fear and loneliness. Through a small, deeply inset window, she could stare across sharpened spikes that encircled the outer wall and gaze at blue-green water that sparkled in fierce tropical sunlight. She could also eavesdrop on the busy wharf, stacked with hogsheads of sugar, which her son Alexander would someday frequent as a young clerk in a trading firm. All the while, she had to choke down a nauseating diet of salted herring, codfish, and boiled yellow cornmeal mush.

As an amateur psychologist, Lavien left something to be desired, for he imagined that when Rachel was released after three to five months this broken woman would now tamely submit to his autocratic rule—that "everything would be better and that she like a true wife would have changed her ungodly mode of life and would live with him as was meet and fitting," as the divorce decree later proclaimed.[14] He had not reckoned on her invincible spirit. Solitude had only stiffened her resolve to expel Lavien from her life. As Hamilton later philosophized in another context, "'Tis only to consult our own hearts to be convinced that nations like individuals revolt at the idea of being guided by external compulsion."[15] After Rachel left the fort, she spent a week with her mother, who was living with one of St. Croix's overlords, Town Captain Bertram Pieter de Nully, and supporting herself by sewing and renting out her three slaves.

Then Rachel did something brave but reckless that sealed her future status as a pariah: she fled the island, abandoning both Lavien and her sole son, Peter. In doing so, she relinquished the future benefits of a legal separation and inadvertently doomed the unborn Alexander to illegitimacy. In her proud defiance of persecution, her mental toughness, and her willingness to court controversy, it is hard not to see a startling preview of her son's passionately willful behavior.

When she left for St. Kitts in 1750, Rachel seems to have been accompanied by her mother, who announced her departure to creditors in a newspaper notice and settled her debts. Rachel must have imagined that she would never again set eyes on St. Croix and that the vengeful Lavien had inflicted his final lash. Alexander Hamilton may have been musing upon his mother's marriage to Lavien when he later observed, "'Tis a very good thing when their stars unite two people who are fit for each other, who have souls capable of relishing the sweets of friendship and sensibilities. . . . But it's a dog of [a] life when two dissonant tempers meet."[16] When the time came for choosing his own wife, he would proceed with special care.

Hamilton's other star-crossed parent, James Hamilton, had also been bedeviled by misfortune in the islands. Born around 1718, he was the fourth of eleven children (nine sons, two daughters) of Alexander Hamilton, the laird of Grange in Stevenston Parish in Ayrshire, Scotland, southwest of Glasgow. In 1711, that Alexander Hamilton, the fourteenth laird in the so-called Cambuskeith line of Hamiltons, married Elizabeth Pollock, the daughter of a baronet. As Alexander must have heard ad nauseam in his boyhood, the Cambuskeith Hamiltons possessed a coat of arms and for centuries had owned a castle near Kilmarnock called the Grange. Indeed, that lineage can be traced back to the fourteenth century in impeccable genealogical tables, and he boasted in later years that he was the scion of a blue-ribbon Scottish family: "The truth is that, on the question who my parents were, I have better pretensions than most of those who in this country plume themselves on ancestry."[17]

In 1685, the family took possession of ivy-covered Kerelaw Castle, set prominently on windswept hills above the little seaside town of Stevenston. Today just a mound of picturesque ruins, this stately pile then featured a great hall with graceful Gothic windows and came complete with its own barony. "The castle stands on the rather steep, wooded bank of a small stream, and overlooks a beautiful glen," wrote one newspaper while the structure stood intact.[18] The castle's occupants enjoyed a fine if often fogbound view of the island of Arran across the Firth of Clyde.

Then as now, the North Ayrshire countryside consisted of gently rolling meadows that were well watered by streams and ponds; cows and horses browsed on largely treeless hillsides. At the time James Hamilton grew up in Kerelaw Castle, the family estate was so huge that it encompassed not just Stevenston but half the arable land in the parish. Aside from a cottage industry of weavers and a small band of artisans who made Jew's harps, most local residents huddled in cold hovels, subsisted on a gruesome oatmeal diet, and eked out hardscrabble lives as tenant farmers for the Hamiltons. For all his storybook upbringing in the castle and highborn pedigree, James Hamilton faced uncertain prospects. As the fourth son, he had little chance of ever inheriting the storied title of laird of Grange, and, like all younger brothers in this precarious spot, he was expected to go off and fend for himself. As his son Alexander noted, his father, as "a younger son of a numerous family," was "bred to trade."

From the sketchy information that can be gleaned about James's siblings, it seems that he was the black sheep of the family, marked for mediocrity. While James had no formal education to speak of, two older and two younger brothers attended the University of Glasgow, and most of his siblings found comfortable niches in the world. Brother John financed manufacturing and insurance ventures. Brother Alexander became a surgeon, brother Walter a doctor and apothecary, and brother William a prosperous tobacco merchant, while sister Elizabeth married the surveyor of customs for Port Glasgow. Easygoing and lackadaisical, devoid of the ambition that would propel his spirited son, James Hamilton did not seem to internalize the Glaswegian ethos of hard work and strict discipline.

One has the impression that his eldest brother, John, now laird of Grange, was no country squire riding to hounds but an active, enterprising man who was intensely involved in the banking, shipping, and textile business revolutionizing Glasgow. This cathedral and university town, rhapsodized by Daniel Defoe in the 1720s as "the most beautiful little town in Britain," already breathed a lively commercial spirit of the sort that later appealed to Alexander Hamilton.[19] After the 1707 union with England, as Scottish trade with the North American and West Indian colonies boomed, merchant princes grew rich trafficking in sugar, tobacco, and cotton. In November 1737, John Hamilton took the affable but feckless James, then nineteen, and steered him into a four-year apprenticeship with an innovative Glasgow businessman named Richard Allan. Allan had executed a daring raid on Dutch industrial secrets (one that strikingly anticipates what Alexander Hamilton later attempted in bringing manufacturing to Paterson, New Jersey) and helped to pioneer the linen industry in Scotland with his Haarlem Linen and Dye Manufactory.

In 1741, John Hamilton teamed up with Allan and three Glasgow grandees—Archibald Ingram, John Glassford, and James Dechman—to form the Glasgow Inkle Factory, which produced linen tapes (inkles) that were used in making lace. Hamilton's partners were the commercial royalty of Glasgow, who drove about in fancy coaches, presided over landed estates, and dominated the River Clyde with their oceangoing vessels. For many years these men would tirelessly bail out the hapless James Hamilton from recurrent financial scrapes.

The onerous four-year contract that James Hamilton signed with Richard Allan in 1737 was a form of legal bondage that obligated him to work as both "an apprentice and servant."[20] John Hamilton paid Allan forty-five pounds sterling to groom his younger brother in the textile trade. In exchange, James would receive room, board, and fresh linen in the Allan household but no guaranteed holidays or free weekend time. John Hamilton must have thought that he was shepherding the wayward James into a promising new industry. In time, the linen industry indeed proved profitable, but during this start-up phase it was a dispiriting, money-draining proposition. So when the apprenticeship agreement expired in 1741, James Hamilton decided to test his luck in the West Indies.

Many young aristocrats flocked to the West Indian sugar islands, seduced by a common fantasy: they would amass a quick fortune as planters or merchants, then return to Europe, flush with cash, and snap up magnificent estates. The Glasgow countryside was studded with the country houses of winners in this sweepstakes. Great shiploads of sugar traveled from the West Indian islands to Glasgow's "boiling houses" or refineries, and its distilleries produced brandy from that sugar. Beyond the sugar trade, industrious Scots also operated stores that sold provisions to plantations and marketed their produce. One historian has noted, "Their emporiums were crammed with full lines of European and North American goods—hardware, draperies, clothing, shoes, and what not—and much resembled warehouses."[21] Of all the Caribbean islands, few enjoyed more intimate connections with Glasgow than St. Christopher in the Leeward Islands, commonly known as St. Kitts. More than half of the island's original land grants were awarded to Scots.

As the son of a Scottish laird, James Hamilton must have started out with a modicum of social cachet in St. Kitts, but it was never enhanced by money or business success. Trading sugar or plantation supplies in the West Indies was hazardous to those with skimpy capital. Clients demanded credit from these middlemen, who had to carry the risk for merchandise until it was resold in Europe; meanwhile, they had to pay the sugar duties. The slightest error in calculation or payment delay could swamp a trader in catastrophic losses. Some such fate probably overtook James Hamilton, who faltered quickly and had to be rescued repeatedly by his brother John and his Glasgow friends. "In capacity of a merchant he went to St. Kitts, where from too generous and too easy a temper he failed in business and at length fell into indigent circumstances," his son Alexander wrote in tactful tones.[22] He spoke of his father in a forgiving tone, tinged with pity rather than scorn. "It was his fault to have had too much pride and too large a portion of indolence, but his character was otherwise without reproach and his manners those of a gentleman."[23] In short, Hamilton saw his father as amiable but lazily inept. He inherited his father's pride, though not his indolence, and his exceptional capacity for work was its own unspoken commentary about his father's.

James Hamilton had little notion that his protective older brother was acting as his lender of last resort, for John exhorted his brother's creditors to mask his role, cautioning one creditor in 1749, "My brother does not know I am engaged for him."[24] From John Hamilton's letters, one senses that James was distant, even estranged, from his family. "The last letter his mother had from him was some time ago, where he writes he had bills but at that time they were not due," John disclosed in one letter to a business associate.[25] Perhaps embarrassed by his perennial bungling, James seems to have concealed the scope of his financial troubles.

That James Hamilton's career likely lay in ruins before Rachel Faucette Lavien materialized is suggested by the minutes of the St. Kitts Council meeting of July 15, 1748, which reported that he had taken the oath of either a watchman or a weigh man (insects have unfortunately eaten the middle letters) for the port of Basseterre, the island's capital.[26] So if his stint in the tropics was meant to be a fleeting, moneymaking interlude, it had begun to turn into a permanent trap instead. Many young European fortune seekers, expecting to return home, would take a temporary black or mulatto mistress and defer marriage until safely back on native soil. That his plans had drastically miscarried would have made James Hamilton more receptive to a romantic liaison with a separated European woman, now that he knew he was not going to see Scotland again any time soon.

By the time Rachel met James Hamilton for sure in St. Kitts in the early 1750s, a certain symmetry had shaped their lives. They were both scarred by early setbacks, had suffered a vertiginous descent in social standing, and had grappled with the terrors of downward economic mobility. Each would have been excluded from the more rarefied society of the British West Indies and tempted to choose a mate from the limited population of working whites. Their liaison was the sort of match that could easily produce a son hypersensitive about class and status and painfully conscious that social hierarchies ruled the world.

Divorce was a novelty in the eighteenth century. To obtain one in the Crown colonies was an expensive, tortuous affair, and this deprived James and Rachel of any chance to legitimize their match. Putting the best face on the embarrassing situation, Alexander sometimes pretended that his parents had married. Of Rachel's flight from St. Croix, he declared, "My mother afterwards went to St. Kitts, became acquainted with my father and a marriage between them ensued, followed by many years cohabitation and several children."[27] Since the relationship may have lasted fifteen years, it presumably took on the trappings of a marriage, enabling Alexander to maintain that his illegitimacy was a mere legal technicality and had nothing to do with negligent or profligate parents. Indeed, Hamilton's parents, though a common-law couple, presented themselves as James and Rachel Hamilton. They had two sons: James, Jr., and, two years later, Alexander. (Since Hamilton spoke of his mother's bearing "several children," other siblings may have died in childhood.)

The personalities of James and Rachel Hamilton evoked by Alexander's descendants have a slightly unreal, even sanitized, quality. Hamilton's own son John conjured up Rachel as "a woman of superior intellect, elevated sentiment, and unusual grace of person and manner. To her he was indebted for his genius."[28] Perhaps no less fanciful was the paternal portrait daubed by Hamilton's grandson Allan McLane Hamilton: "Hamilton's father does not appear to have been successful in any pursuit, but in many ways was a great deal of a dreamer, and something of a student, whose chief happiness seemed to be in the society of his beautiful and talented wife, who was in every way intellectually his superior."[29] Is this cozy domestic scene based on credible oral history or family public relations? The documentary record is, alas, mute. The one inescapable impression we have is that Hamilton received his brains and implacable willpower from his mother, not from his errant, indolent father. On the other hand, his father's Scottish ancestry enabled Alexander to daydream that he was not merely a West Indian outcast, consigned forever to a lowly status, but an aristocrat in disguise, waiting to declare his true identity and act his part on a grander stage.

Few questions bedevil Hamilton biographers more than the baffling matter of his year of birth. For a long time, historians accepted 1757, the year used by Hamilton himself and his family. Yet several cogent pieces of evidence from his Caribbean period have caused many recent historians to opt for 1755. In 1766, Hamilton affixed his signature as the witness to a legal document, a dubious honor if he was only nine. In 1768, a probate court in St. Croix reported his age as thirteen—highly compelling evidence, since it did not rely on his testimony but came from his uncle. When Alexander published a poem in a St. Croix newspaper in 1771, the aspiring bard informed the editor, "Sir, I am a youth about seventeen"—an adolescent's way of stating that he was sixteen, which would also tally with the 1755 date. The mass of evidence from the period after Hamilton's arrival in North America does suggest 1757 as his birth year, but, preferring the integrity of contemporary over retrospective evidence, we will opt here for a birthday of January 11, 1755.

From her father, Rachel had inherited a waterfront property on the main street in Charlestown, the Nevis capital, where legend proclaims that Alexander was born and lived as a boy. If so, he would have seen off to the left the town anchorage and a bright expanse of water, crowded with slave and cargo ships; off to the right lay the rugged foothills and dim, brown mountains of St. Kitts. Appropriately enough, this boy destined to be America's foremost Anglophile entered the world as a British subject, born on a British isle, in the reign of George II. He was slight and thin shouldered and distinctly Scottish in appearance, with a florid complexion, reddish-brown hair, and sparkling violet-blue eyes. One West Indian mentor who remembered Hamilton as bookish and "rather delicate and frail" marveled that he had mustered the later energy for his strenuous American exploits.[30] Like everyone in the West Indies, Hamilton had extensive early exposure to blacks. In this highly stratified society, with its many gradations of caste and color, even poor whites owned slaves and hired them out for extra income. In 1756, one year after Hamilton was born, his grandmother, Mary Faucette, now residing on the Dutch island of St. Eustatius, made out her final will and left "my three dear slaves, Rebecca, Flora and Esther" to her daughter Rachel.[31]

Hamiliton probably did not have formal schooling on Nevis—his illegitimate birth may well have barred him from Anglican instruction—but he seems to have had individual tutoring. His son later related that "rarely as he alluded to his personal history, he mentioned with a smile his having been taught to repeat the Decalogue in Hebrew, at the school of a Jewess, when so small that he was placed standing by her side upon a table."[32] This charming vignette squares with two known facts: elderly women in the Caribbean commonly tutored children, and Nevis had a thriving population of Sephardic Jews, many of whom had escaped persecution in Brazil and entered the local sugar trade. By the 1720s, they constituted one quarter of Charlestown's white population and created a synagogue, a school, and a well-kept cemetery that survives to this day. His French Huguenot mother may also have instructed Hamilton, for he was comfortably bilingual and later was more at ease in French than Franklin, Adams, Jefferson, and other American diplomats who had spent years struggling to master the tongue in Paris.

Perhaps from this exposure at an impressionable age, Hamilton harbored a life-long reverence for Jews. In later years, he privately jotted on a sheet of paper that the *"progress of the Jews* . . . from their earliest history to the present time has been and is entirely out of the *ordinary course* of human affairs. Is it not then a fair conclusion that the *cause* also is an *extraordinary one*—in other words that it is the effect of some great providential plan?"[33] Later on, in the heat of a renowned legal case, Hamilton challenged the opposing counsel: "Why distrust the evidence of the Jews? Discredit them and you destroy the Christian religion. . . . Were not the [Jews] witnesses of that pure and holy, happy and heaven-approved faith, converts to that faith?"[34]

For a boy with Hamilton's fertile imagination, Nevis's short history must have furnished a rich storehouse of material. He was well situated to witness the clash of European powers, with incessant skirmishes among French, Spanish, and English ships and swarms of marauding pirates and privateers. The admiralty court sat in Nevis, which meant that swaggering buccaneers in manacles were dragged into the local courthouse before proper hangings in Gallows Bay. While some pirates were just plain freebooters, many were discreetly backed by warring European nations, perhaps instructing Hamilton in the way that foreign powers can tamper with national sovereignty.

Periodically, cutthroats came ashore for duels, resorting to conventional pistols or slashing one another with heavy cutlasses—thrilling fare for any boy. Blood feuds were routine affairs in the West Indies. Plantation society was a feudal order, predicated on personal honor and dignity, making duels popular among whites who fancied themselves noblemen. As in the American south, an exaggerated sense of romantic honor may have been an unconscious way for slaveholders to flaunt their moral superiority, purge pent-up guilt, and cloak the brutish nature of their trade.

To the extent that dueling later entranced Hamilton to an unhealthy degree, this fascination may have originated in the most fabled event in Nevis in the 1750s. In 1752, John Barbot, a young Nevis lawyer, and Matthew Mills, a wealthy planter from St. Kitts, were bickering over a land deal when Mills lashed out at Barbot as "an impertinent puppy"—the sort of fighting words that prompted duels.[35] One day at dawn, elegantly clad in a silver laced hat and white coat, Barbot was rowed over to St. Kitts by a slave boy. At a dueling ground at Frigate Bay, he encountered Mills, lifted his silver-mounted pistol, and slaughtered him at close range.

At the sensational murder trial, it was alleged that Barbot had gunned down Mills before the latter even had a chance to grab his pistol from his holster. A star witness was Dr. William Hamilton (a possible relation of James Hamilton), who testified that Mills had been shot in the side and therefore must have been am-

bushed. Certain elements of this trial almost creepily foreshadow the fatal clash between Alexander Hamilton and Aaron Burr. Barbot, well bred yet debt ridden,
sneered at the softhearted notion that he had murdered the popular Mills, claiming
that he had "killed him fairly according to the notions of honour prevailing among
men."[36] Barbot insisted that Mills had aimed his pistol at him even as he absorbed
the fatal bullet. As was to happen with Aaron Burr, locals testified that Barbot, in
ungentlemanly fashion, had taken target practice in the preceding weeks. Barbot
was eventually convicted and packed off to the gallows. Nevis children such as
Hamilton, who was born three years later, would have savored every gory detail of
this history.

Violence was commonplace in Nevis, as in all the slave-ridden sugar islands. The
eight thousand captive blacks easily dwarfed in number the one thousand whites, "a
disproportion," remarked one visitor, "which necessarily converts all such white
men as are not exempted by age and decrepitude into a well-regulated militia."[37]
Charlestown was a compact town of narrow, crooked lanes and wooden buildings,
and Hamilton would regularly have passed the slave-auction blocks at Market Shop
and Crosses Alley and beheld barbarous whippings in the public square. The
Caribbean sugar economy was a system of inimitable savagery, making the tobacco
and cotton plantations of the American south seem almost genteel by comparison.
The mortality rate of slaves hacking away at sugarcane under a pitiless tropical sun
was simply staggering: three out of five died within five years of arrival, and slave
owners needed to replenish their fields constantly with fresh victims. One Nevis
planter, Edward Huggins, set a sinister record when he administered 365 lashes to a
male slave and 292 to a female. Evidently unfazed by this sadism, a local jury acquitted him of all wrongdoing. A decorous British lady who visited St. Kitts stared
aghast at naked male and female slaves being driven along dusty roads by overseers
who flogged them at regular intervals, as if they needed steady reminders of their
servitude: "Every ten Negroes have a driver who walks behind them, holding in his
hand a short whip and a long one . . . and you constantly observe where the application has been made."[38] Another British visitor said that "if a white man kills a
black, he cannot be tried for his life for the murder. . . . If a negro strikes a white
man, he is punished with the loss of his hand and, if he should draw blood, with
death."[39] Island life contained enough bloodcurdling scenes to darken Hamilton's
vision for life, instilling an ineradicable pessimism about human nature that infused all his writing.

All of the horror was mingled incongruously with the natural beauty of tur-
quoise waters, flaming sunsets, and languid palm fronds. In this geologically active
zone, the hills bubbled with high-sulfur hot springs that later became tourist mec-
cas. The sea teemed with lobster, snapper, grouper, and conch, while the jungles were

alive with parrots and mongooses. There were also monkeys galore, green vervets shipped from Africa earlier in the century. Many travelers prized the island as a secluded refuge, one finding it so "captivating" that he contended that if a man came there with his wife, he might linger forever in the "sweet recess" of Nevis.[40] It was all very pleasant and balmy, supremely beautiful and languid, if you were white, were rich, and turned a blind eye to the black population expiring in the canebrakes.

If Rachel thought that Johann Michael Lavien's appetite for revenge had been sated in Christiansted, she was sadly disabused of this notion in 1759. Nine years after Rachel had fled St. Croix, Lavien surfaced for one final lesson in retribution. Oppressed by debt, he had been forced to cede his most recent plantation to two Jewish moneylenders and support himself as a plantation overseer while renting out his little clutch of slaves. In the interim, he had begun living with a woman who took in washing to boost their income. It may have been Lavien's wish to marry this woman that abruptly prompted him to obtain an official divorce summons from Rachel on February 26, 1759.

In a document seething with outrage, Lavien branded Rachel a scarlet woman, given to a sinful life. Having failed to mend her ways after imprisonment, the decree stated, Rachel had "absented herself from [Lavien] for nine years and gone elsewhere, where she has begotten several illegitimate children, so that such action is believed to be more than sufficient for him to obtain a divorce from her."[41] Lavien noted bitterly that he himself "had taken care of Rachel's legitimate child from what little he has been able to earn," whereas she had "completely forgotten her duty and let husband and child alone and instead given herself up to whoring with everyone, which things the plaintiff says are so well known that her own family and friends must hate her for it."[42] After this vicious indictment, Lavien demanded that Rachel be denied all legal rights to his property. He warned that if he died before her, Rachel "as a widow would possibly seek to take possession of the estate and therefore not only acquire what she ought not to have but also take this away from his child and give it to her whore-children."[43] This was how Lavien designated Alexander and his brother: *whore-children*. He was determined to preserve his wealth for his one legitimate son, thirteen-year-old Peter.

Rachel was undoubtedly stunned by this unforeseen vendetta, this throwback to a nightmarish past. Summoned to appear in court in St. Croix, she must have feared further reprisals from Lavien and did not show up or refute the allegations. On June 25, Lavien received a divorce that permitted him to remarry, while Rachel was strictly prohibited from doing so. The Danish authorities took such decrees seriously and fined or dismissed any clergyman who married couples in defiance of such decisions. In one swiftly effective stroke, Lavien had safeguarded his son's inheritance and penalized Rachel, making it impossible for her two innocent sons ever to mitigate the stigma of illegitimacy. However detestable Lavien's actions, two things should be said in his defense. Rachel *had* relinquished responsibility for Peter and forced Lavien to bring the boy up alone. Also, Lavien subsequently witnessed legal documents for the Lyttons, Rachel's St. Croix in-laws, suggesting that her own family may have seen her life as less than blameless.

In view of this lacerating history, Rachel probably never imagined that she would return to St. Croix, but a confluence of events changed that. In the early 1760s, Lavien moved to Frederiksted, on the far side of St. Croix from Christiansted, and dabbled in real estate. Then, around 1764, Peter moved to South Carolina. So when James Hamilton received a business assignment in Christiansted in April 1765, he could have taken along Rachel and the two boys without fearing any untoward collisions with Lavien. James Hamilton had continued to feed off his brother's Glasgow business connections. He served as head clerk for Archibald Ingram of St. Kitts, the son of a Glasgow "tobacco lord" of the same name. The Ingrams asked James to collect a large debt due from a man named Alexander Moir, who was returning to Europe and denied owing them money; the resulting lawsuit was to drone on until January 1766. In the meantime, Rachel and the boys took up residence in Christiansted. Thrust back into the world of her former disgrace, Rachel lived blocks from the fort where she had been jailed and no longer had the liberty of posing as "Mrs. Hamilton." (On the St. Croix tax rolls, she shows up under misspelled variants of Faucette and Lavien.) Stripped of whatever cover of legitimacy had sheltered them, it would have become glaringly evident to Alexander and James, Jr., for the first time that they were "natural" children and that their mother had been a notorious woman.

James Hamilton scored an apparent victory in the Moir case, then left St. Croix and deserted his family forever. Why this sudden exit? Did Rachel's scandalous reputation cause a rift in their relationship? Did Lavien conduct a smear campaign and poison the air with innuendo? These scenarios seem unlikely given that James Hamilton never appeared on the St. Croix tax rolls, suggesting that he knew all along that he was a transient visitor. Alexander offered a forgiving but plausible reason for his father's desertion: he could no longer afford to support his family. Because James, Jr., twelve, and Alexander, ten, had attained an age where they could assist Rachel, James, Sr., may have believed that he could wash his hands of paternal duties without undue pangs of guilt. More in sorrow than malice, Alexander wrote a Scottish kinsman thirty years later, "You no doubt have understood that my father's affairs at a very early day went to wreck, so as to have rendered his situation during the greatest part of his life far from eligible. This state of things occasioned a separation between him and me, when I was very young."[44] Alexander probably never set eyes again on his vagabond father, who stayed in the Caribbean, either lured by the indolent tropic tempo or ground down by poverty. Father and son never entirely lost touch with each other, but a curious detachment, an estrangement as much psychological as geographical, separated them. As we shall see, there is a possible reason why James Hamilton may have felt less than paternal toward his son and Alexander less than filial toward him.

For a woman once hounded from St. Croix in disgrace, Rachel exhibited remarkable resilience upon her return. As she ambled about Christiansted in a red or white skirt, her face shaded by a black silk sun hat, this "handsome," self-reliant woman seems to have been fired by some inner need to vindicate herself and silence her critics. At this, she succeeded admirably, superseding James Hamilton as the family breadwinner. Already on August 1, 1765, her wealthy brother-in-law, James Lytton, had bought her six walnut chairs with leather seats and agreed to foot the bill for her rent. Alexander later testified to the Lyttons' indispensable largesse, saying that his father's departure "threw me upon the bounty of my mother's relations, some of whom were then wealthy."[45]

Rachel's return to St. Croix had probably been premised on support from Ann and James Lytton, a hope that never quite panned out, as her in-laws were themselves besieged by successive problems. As prominent sugar planters, the Lyttons had enjoyed a leisurely life at the Grange, occupying a stone "great house" with polished wooden floors, louvered blinds, paneled shutters, and chandeliers. Like many sugar plantations, it was a world in miniature, a compound that included slave quarters, a sugar mill, and a boiling house that produced molasses and brown sugar. Then, one by one, the Lytton children were overtaken by the curse that seemed to afflict everyone around Alexander Hamilton. Several years earlier, Ann and James's second son, James Lytton, Jr., had formed a partnership with one Robert Holliday. This business venture failed so abysmally that one summer night in 1764, the bankrupt James, Jr., and his wife climbed aboard the family schooner, herded twenty-two stolen slaves on board, and cast off for the Carolinas, while the less quick-witted Holliday was captured and jailed for nearly two years. Shattered by this scandal, James and Ann Lytton sold the Grange and in late 1765 moved back to Nevis, just months after Rachel and her two boys arrived in St. Croix from there. Within one year, Ann Lytton was dead, leaving Rachel as the last surviving Faucette.

Rachel took a two-story house on 34 Company Street, fast by the Anglican church and school. Adhering to a common town pattern, she lived with her two boys in the wooden upper floor, which probably jutted over the street, while turning the lower stone floor into a shop selling foodstuffs to planters—salted fish, beef, pork, apples, butter, rice, and flour. It was uncommon in those days for a woman to be a shopkeeper, especially one so fetching and, at thirty-six, still relatively young. One traveler to St. Croix remarked, "White women are not expected to do anything here except drink tea and coffee, eat, make calls, play cards, and at times sew a little."[46] In her enclosed yard, Rachel kept a goat, probably to provide milk for her boys. She bought some of her merchandise from her landlord, while the rest came from two young New York merchants, David Beekman and Nicholas Cruger, who had just inaugurated a trading firm that was to transform Hamilton's insecure, claustrophobic boyhood.

No less than in Nevis, slavery was all-pervasive on St. Croix—it was "the source from which every citizen obtains his daily bread and his wealth," concluded one contemporary account—with twelve blacks for every white.[47] A decade later, a census ascertained that Company Street had fifty-nine houses, with 187 whites and 427 slaves packed into breathless proximity. Since the neighborhood was zoned to incorporate free blacks and mulattoes, Alexander was exposed to a rich racial mélange. Because her mother had died, Rachel now owned five adult female slaves and supplemented her income by hiring them out. The slaves also had four children; Rachel assigned a little boy named Ajax as a house slave to Alexander and another to James. This early exposure to the humanity of the slaves may have made a lasting impression on Hamilton, who would be conspicuous among the founding fathers for his fierce abolitionism.

St. Croix had its picturesque side in its conical sugar mills, powered by windmills or mules, that crushed the sugarcane with big rollers. During harvesttime, the twilight glittered with fires from boiling houses that dotted the island. The coast around Christiansted was lined with soft, green hills and punctuated by secluded inlets and coves. Early idealized prints of the town show two distinct moods: a smart military precision down near the fort and wharf, with heaps of sugar barrels ready for export, and a slower, more sensual inland atmosphere, with black women balancing large bundles on their heads. Though house slaves donned shirts and skirts, it wasn't unusual for one or two hundred slaves to toil naked in a steaming field beneath the towering sugar stalks. By night, the whitewashed town of Christiansted, laid out in a formal grid by Danish authorities, erupted into a roaring, licentious bedlam of boisterous taverns and open brothels overflowing with rebels, sailors, and outlaws from many countries. So extensive was the sexual contact between whites and blacks that local church registers were thickly sprinkled with entries for illegitimate mulatto children.

If Alexander Hamilton was exposed to abundant savagery and depravity, he also snatched distant glimpses of an elegant way of life that might have fostered a desire to be allied with the rich. The local atmosphere was not likely to breed a flaming populist: poverty carried no dignity on a slave island. The big planters rode about in ornate carriages and shopped for imported watches, jewelry, and other European finery. Some oases of culture survived amid the barbarism. Two dancing schools gave lessons in the minuet, while the Leeward Islands Comedians served up a surprisingly varied fare of Shakespeare and Restoration comedy. Rachel tried to give her spartan household a patina of civility. From a later inventory, we know that she had six silver spoons, seven silver teaspoons, a pair of sugar tongs, fourteen porcelain plates, two porcelain basins, and a bed covered with a feather comforter.

Of most compelling interest to our saga, the upstairs living quarters held thirty-four books—the first unmistakable sign of Hamilton's omnivorous, self-directed reading. Many people on St. Croix would have snickered at his bookish habits, making him feel freakish and contributing to an urgent need to flee the West Indies. From his first tentative forays in prose and verse, we can hazard an educated guess about the books that stocked his shelf. The poetry of Alexander Pope must have held an honored place, plus a French edition of Machiavelli's *The Prince* and Plutarch's *Lives,* rounded off by sermons and devotional tracts. If Hamilton felt something stiflingly provincial about St. Croix, literature would certainly have transported him to a more exalted realm.

The boy could be forgiven his escapist cravings. In late 1767, Rachel, thirty-eight, uprooted her family and hustled them down the block to 23 Company Street. Then, right after New Year's Day, she dragged them back to number 34 and succumbed to a raging fever. For a week, a woman named Ann McDonnell tended Rachel before summoning a Dr. Heering on February 17; by that point, Alexander, too, had contracted the unspecified disease. Dr. Heering subjected mother and child to the medieval purgatives so popular in eighteenth-century medicine. Rachel had to endure an emetic and a medicinal herb called valerian, which expelled gas from the alimentary canal; Alexander submitted to bloodletting and an enema. Mother and son must have been joined in a horrid scene of vomiting, flatulence, and defecation as they lay side by side in a feverish state in the single upstairs bed. The delirious Alexander was probably writhing inches from his mother when she expired at nine o'clock on the night of February 19. Notwithstanding the late hour, five agents from the probate court hastened to the scene and sequestered the property, sealing off one chamber, an attic, and two storage spaces in the yard.

By the day of the funeral, Hamilton had regained sufficient strength to attend with his brother. The two dazed, forlorn boys surely made a pathetic sight. In a little more than two years, they had suffered their father's disappearance and their mother's death, reducing them to orphans and throwing them upon the mercy of friends, family, and community. The town judge gave James, Jr., money to buy shoes for the funeral and bought black veils for both boys. Their landlord, Thomas Dipnall, donated white bread, eggs, and cakes for the mourners, while cousin Peter

Lytton contributed eleven yards of black material to drape the coffin. As a divorced woman with two children conceived out of wedlock, Rachel was likely denied a burial at nearby St. John's Anglican Church. This may help to explain a mystifying ambivalence that Hamilton always felt about regular church attendance, despite a pronounced religious bent. The parish clerk officiated at a graveside ceremony at the Grange, the erstwhile Lytton estate outside of Christiansted, where Rachel was laid to rest on a hillside beneath a grove of mahogany trees.

There was to be no surcease from suffering for the two castaway boys, just a cascading series of crises. Heaps of bills poured in, including for the batch of medicine that had failed to save their mother. Less than a week after Rachel died, the probate officers again trooped to the house to appraise the estate. The moralistic tone of their report shows that Johann Michael Lavien meditated further revenge against Rachel at the expense of her two illegitimate sons. The court decided that it had to consider three possible heirs: Peter Lavien, whose father had divorced Rachel "for valid reasons (according to information obtained by the court) by the highest authority," and the illegitimate James and Alexander, the "obscene children born after the deceased person's divorce."[48] The whole marital scandal was dredged up again, only now at an age when Alexander and his brother could fully fathom its meaning. At a probate hearing, Lavien brandished the 1759 divorce decree and lambasted Alexander and James as children born in "whoredom," insisting that Peter merited the entire estate, even though Peter hadn't set eyes on his mother for eighteen years. Life had not improved for the embittered Lavien, who had remained on a steep economic slide and served as janitor of a Frederiksted hospital. His second wife had died just a month before Rachel, and the couple had already lost the two children they had together.

For a year after his mother's death, Alexander was held in painful suspense by the probate court and perhaps absorbed the useful lesson that people who manipulate the law wield the real power in society. While he was awaiting settlement of the small estate—principally Rachel's slaves and a stock of business supplies—the court auctioned off her personal effects. James Lytton considerately bought back for Alexander his trove of books. In light of Rachel's unhappy history with Lavien, the final court decision seems foreordained. Alexander and James Hamilton were disinherited, and the whole estate was awarded to Peter Lavien. In November 1769, no less implacably vengeful than his father, Peter Lavien returned to St. Croix and took possession of his small inheritance—an injustice that rankled Alexander for many years. Peter had fared sufficiently well in Beaufort, South Carolina, to be named a church warden—the chief financial and administrative officer—in St. Helena's Parish the previous year, yet he couldn't spare a penny for the two destitute half brothers orphaned by his mother's death.

One sidelight of Peter Lavien's return to St. Croix deserves attention because he did something shocking and seemingly inexplicable for a twenty-three-year-old church warden: he was quietly baptized. Why had he not been baptized before? One explanation is that Johann Michael Lavien had painstakingly concealed his Jewish roots but still did not want his son baptized. Peter's furtive baptism, as if it were something shameful, suggests that he felt some extreme need for secrecy.

After Rachel died, her sons were placed under the legal guardianship of their thirty-two-year-old first cousin Peter Lytton. Already a widower, Peter had stumbled through a string of botched business dealings, including failed grocery stores in Christiansted. His brother later insisted that Peter was "insane."[49] Life as a ward of Peter Lytton proved yet another merciless education in the tawdry side of life for Alexander Hamilton. Lytton had a black mistress, Ledja, who had given birth to a mulatto boy with the impressive name of Don Alvarez de Valesco. On July 16, 1769, just when the Hamilton boys must have imagined that fate couldn't dole out more horrors, Peter Lytton was found dead in his bed, soaked in a pool of blood. According to court records, he had committed suicide and either "stabbed or shot himself to death."[50] For the Hamilton boys, the sequel was equally mortifying. Peter had drafted a will that provided for Ledja and their mulatto child but didn't bother to acknowledge Alexander or James with even a token bequest. When a crestfallen James Lytton appeared to claim his son's estate, he tried to aid the orphaned boys but was stymied by legal obstacles resulting from the suicide. On August 12, 1769, less than one month after Peter's death, the heartbroken James Lytton died as well. Five days earlier, he had drafted a new will, which also made no provision for his nephews Alexander and James, who must have felt jinxed.

Let us pause briefly to tally the grim catalog of disasters that had befallen these two boys between 1765 and 1769: their father had vanished, their mother had died, their cousin and supposed protector had committed bloody suicide, and their aunt, uncle, and grandmother had all died. James, sixteen, and Alexander, fourteen, were now left alone, largely friendless and penniless. At every step in their rootless, topsy-turvy existence, they had been surrounded by failed, broken, embittered people. Their short lives had been shadowed by a stupefying sequence of bankruptcies, marital separations, deaths, scandals, and disinheritance. Such repeated shocks must have stripped Alexander Hamilton of any sense that life was fair, that he existed in a benign universe, or that he could ever count on help from anyone. That this abominable childhood produced such a strong, productive, self-reliant human being—that this fatherless adolescent could have ended up a founding father of a country he had not yet even seen—seems little short of miraculous. Because he maintained perfect silence about his unspeakable past, never exploiting it to puff his later success, it was impossible for his contemporaries to comprehend the exceptional nature of his personal triumph. What we know of Hamilton's childhood has been learned almost entirely during the past century.

Peter Lytton's death marked a fork in the road for Alexander and James, who henceforth branched off on separate paths. The latter was apprenticed to an aging Christiansted carpenter, Thomas McNobeny, which tells us much about his limited abilities. Most whites shied away from crafts such as carpentry, where they had to compete with mulattoes or even skilled slave labor. Had James shown any real promise or head for business, it is doubtful that he would have been relegated to manual work. By contrast, even before Peter Lytton's death, Alexander had begun to clerk for the mercantile house of Beekman and Cruger, the New York traders who had supplied his mother with provisions. It was the first of countless times in Hamilton's life when his superior intelligence was spotted and rewarded by older, more experienced men.

Before considering his first commercial experience, we must ponder another startling enigma in Hamilton's boyhood. While James went off to train with the elderly carpenter, Hamilton, in a dreamlike transition worthy of a Dickens novel, was whisked off to the King Street home of Thomas Stevens, a well-respected merchant, and his wife, Ann. Of the five Stevens children, Edward, born a year before Alexander, became his closest friend, "an intimate acquaintance begun in early youth," as Hamilton described their relationship.[51] As they matured, they often seemed to display parallel personalities. Both were exceedingly quick and clever, disciplined and persevering, fluent in French, versed in classical history, outraged by slavery, and mesmerized by medicine. In future years, Edward Stevens was wont to remind Hamilton of "those vows of eternal friendship, which we have so often mutually exchanged," and he often fretted about Hamilton's delicate health.[52]

If their personalities exhibited unusual compatibility, their physical resemblance bordered on the uncanny, often stopping people cold. Thirty years later, when Hamilton's close friend Timothy Pickering, then secretary of state, first set eyes on Edward Stevens, he was bowled over by the likeness. "At the first glance," recalled Pickering, "I was struck with the extraordinary similitude of his and General Hamilton's faces—I thought they must be *brothers.*" When Pickering confided his amazement to Stevens's brother-in-law, James Yard of St. Croix, the latter "informed me that the remark had been made a thousand times."[53] This mystery began to obsess the inquisitive Pickering, who finally concluded that Hamilton and Stevens *were* brothers. In notes assembled for a projected biography of Hamilton, Pickering wrote that "it was generally understood that Hamilton was an illegitimate son of a gentleman of [the] name" of Stevens.[54] This scuttlebutt resonated through the nineteenth century, so that in 1882 Henry Cabot Lodge could write that "every student of the period [is] familiar with the story, which oral tradition had handed down, that Hamilton was the illegitimate son of a rich West Indian planter or merchant, generally supposed to have been Mr. Stevens, the father of Hamilton's early friend and school-fellow."[55]

What to make of this extraordinary speculation? No extant picture of Edward Stevens enables us to probe any family resemblance. Nevertheless, in the absence of direct proof, the notion that Alexander was the biological son of Thomas Stevens instead of James Hamilton would clarify many oddities in Hamilton's biography. It might identify one of the adulterous lovers who had so appalled Lavien that he had hurled Rachel into prison. It would also explain why Thomas Stevens sheltered Hamilton soon after Rachel's death but made no comparable gesture to his brother, James. (In the eighteenth century, illegitimate children frequently masqueraded as orphaned relatives of the lord or lady of the house—a polite fiction understood and accepted by visitors.) This parentage would also explain why Hamilton formed an infinitely more enduring bond with Edward Stevens than with his own brother. It might suggest why James Hamilton, Sr., left his family behind, assumed no further responsibility for them, and took no evident delight in Alexander's later career. Most of all, it would account for the peculiar distance that later held Hamilton apart from both his father and his brother. As will be seen, Alexander Hamilton was an intensely loyal person, endowed with a deep streak of family responsibility. There is something telltale about the way that he, his father, and his brother let relations abruptly lapse, as if the three of them were in headlong flight from some harrowing shared secret.

TWO

HURRICANE

E ven in the languorous tropics, Hamilton, while clerking at Beekman and
Cruger, was schooled in a fast-paced modern world of trading ships and
fluctuating markets. Whatever his frustrations, he did not operate in an obscure corner of the world, and his first job afforded him valuable insights into
global commerce and the maneuvers of imperial powers. Working on an island first
developed by a trading company, he was exposed early on to the mercantilist policies that governed European economies.

Beekman and Cruger engaged in an export-import business that provided an
excellent training ground for Hamilton, who had to monitor a bewildering inventory of goods. The firm dealt in every conceivable commodity required by planters:
timber, bread, flour, rice, lard, pork, beef, fish, black-eyed peas, corn, porter, cider,
pine, oak, hoops, shingles, iron, lime, rope, lampblack, bricks, mules, and cattle.
"Amid his various engagements in later years," John C. Hamilton said of his father,
"he adverted to [this time] as the most useful part of his education."[1] He learned to
write in a beautiful, clear, flowing hand. He had to mind money, chart courses for
ships, keep track of freight, and compute prices in an exotic blend of currencies, including Portuguese coins, Spanish pieces of eight, British pounds, Danish ducats,
and Dutch stivers. If Hamilton seemed very knowing about business as a young
adult, it can partly be traced to these formative years.

Located above the harbor at the elevated intersection of King and King's Cross
Streets, Beekman and Cruger ran a shop and an adjoining warehouse. A pleasant
stroll down the sloping main street would have brought Hamilton, freshened by sea
breezes, to the hectic wharf area, where the firm maintained its own dock and ship.
While the clerk inspected incoming merchandise, some of it contraband, the air

was thick with the sweet fragrances of sugar, rum, and molasses, hauled in barrels
by horse-drawn wagons and ready for shipment to North America in exchange for
grain, flour, timber, and sundry other staples. The neutral Danish island served as a
transit point to the French West Indies, converting Hamilton's ease in French into a
critical business asset. As a rule, the merchants of St. Croix were natives of the
British Isles, so that English, not Danish, functioned as the island's lingua franca.

Beekman and Cruger furnished Hamilton with a direct link to his future home
in New York, which carried on extensive trade with St. Croix. Many Manhattan
trading firms dispatched young family members to the islands as local agents, and
Nicholas Cruger was a prime example. He came from one of colonial New York's
most distinguished families. His father, Henry, was a wealthy merchant, shipowner,
and member of His Majesty's Royal Council for the province. His uncle, John
Cruger, had been a long-standing mayor and a member of the Stamp Act Congress.
While this blue-blooded clan had distinct Anglophile tendencies, time was to expose a split. Nicholas's brother, also Henry, based in Britain, was elected a member
of Parliament from Bristol beside no less august a personage than Edmund Burke.
Nicholas himself was to side with the rebel colonists and revere George Washington. One wonders whether he functioned as Hamilton's first political tutor. He also
exposed Hamilton to a prosperous, civic-minded breed of New York businessmen,
who stood as models for the elite brand of Federalism he later espoused.

From the outset, the young Hamilton had phenomenal stamina for sustained
work: ambitious, orphaned boys do not enjoy the option of idleness. Even before
starting work, he must have developed unusual autonomy for a thirteen-year-old,
and Beekman and Cruger would only have toughened his moral fiber. Hamilton exuded an air of crisp efficiency and cool self-command. While his peers squandered
their time on frivolities, Hamilton led a much more strenuous, urgent life that was
to liberate him from St. Croix. He was a proud and sensitive boy, caught in the
lower reaches of a rigid class society with small chance for social mobility. His
friend Nathaniel Pendleton later said of his clerkship that Hamilton "conceived so
strong an aversion to it as to be induced to abandon altogether the pursuits of commerce."[2] On November 11, 1769, in his earliest surviving letter, the fourteen-year-
old Hamilton vented the blackest pent-up despair. Written in elegant penmanship,
the letter shows that the young clerk felt demeaned by his lowly social station and
chafed with excess energy. Already he sought psychic relief in extravagant fantasies
of fame and faraway glory. The recipient was his dear friend and lookalike Edward
Stevens, who had recently begun his studies at King's College in New York:

> To confess my weakness, Ned, my ambition is [so] prevalent that I contemn
> the grovelling and conditions of a clerk or the like to which my fortune &c.

condemns me and would willingly risk my life, tho' not my character, to exalt my station. I'm confident, Ned, that my youth excludes me from any hopes of immediate preferment, nor do I desire it, but I mean to prepare the way for futurity. I'm no philosopher, you see, and may be jus[t]ly said to build castles in the air. My folly makes me ashamed and beg you'll conceal it, yet Neddy we have seen such schemes successful when the projector is constant. I shall conclude [by] saying I wish there was a war. Alex. Hamilton.[3]

What prophetic aspirations Hamilton telescoped into this short letter! The boy hankering for heroism and martial glory was to find his war soon enough. He betrayed a stinging sense of shame that the adult Hamilton would studiously cloak behind an air of bravado. Of special interest are his intuitive fear that his outsized ambition might corrupt him and his insistence that he would never endanger his ethics to conquer the world. Despite some awkwardness in the writing, he appears surprisingly mature for fourteen and springs full-blown into the historical record.

He had ample opportunities to exercise his many talents. In 1769, David Beekman quit the business and was replaced by Cornelius Kortright—another New Yorker with another prestigious name—and the firm was reconstituted as Kortright and Cruger. In October 1771, for medical reasons, Nicholas Cruger returned to New York for a five-month stint and left his precocious clerk in charge.

A sheaf of revealing business letters drafted by Hamilton shows him, for the first time, in the take-charge mode that was to characterize his tumultuous career. With peculiar zeal, he collected money owed to the firm. "Believe me Sir," he assured the absent Cruger, "I dun as hard as is proper."[4] The bulk of the correspondence concerns a sloop called the *Thunderbolt,* partly owned by the Crugers, that carried several dozen miserable mules through churning seas in early 1772. Hamilton had to direct this cargo safely along the Spanish Main (South America's northwestern coast), then brimming with hostile vessels. Hamilton did not hesitate to advise his bosses that they should arm the ship with four guns. He said flatly to Tileman Cruger, who oversaw family operations in Curaçao, "It would be undoubtedly a great pity that such a vessel should be lost for the want of them."[5] When the ship docked with forty-one skeletal, drooping mules, Hamilton lectured the vessel's skipper in a peremptory tone that someday would be familiar to legions of respectful subordinates: "Reflect continually on the unfortunate voyage you have just made and endeavour to make up for the considerable loss therefrom accruing to your owners."[6] The adolescent clerk had a capacity for quick decisions and showed no qualms about giving a tongue-lashing to a veteran sea captain. So proficient and eager to lead was he that he must have been slightly deflated when Nicholas Cruger returned to St. Croix in March 1772.

Hamilton's apprenticeship provided many benefits. He developed an intimate knowledge of traders and smugglers that later aided his establishment of the U.S. Coast Guard and Customs Service. He saw that business was often obstructed by scarce cash or credit and learned the value of a uniform currency in stimulating trade. Finally, he was forced to ponder the paradox that the West Indian islands, with all their fertile soil, traded at a disadvantage with the rest of the world because of their reliance on only the sugar crop—a conundrum to which he was to return in his celebrated "Report on Manufactures." It may be that Hamilton's preference for a diversified economy of manufacturing and agriculture originated in his youthful reflections on the avoidable poverty he had witnessed in the Caribbean.

While Kortright and Cruger mostly brokered foodstuffs and dry goods, at least once a year the firm handled a large shipment of far more perishable cargo: slaves. On the slave ships, hundreds of Africans were chained and stuffed in fetid holds, where many suffocated. So vile were the conditions on these noisome ships that people onshore could smell their foul effluvia even miles away. On January 23, 1771, during Hamilton's tenure, his firm ran a notice atop the front page of the local bilingual paper, the *Royal Danish American Gazette:* "Just imported from the Windward Coast of Africa, and to be sold on Monday next, by Messrs. Kortright & Cruger, At said Cruger's yard, Three Hundred Prime SLAVES."[7] The following year, Nicholas Cruger imported 250 more slaves from Africa's Gold Coast and complained that they were "very indifferent indeed, sickly and thin."[8] One can only imagine the inhuman scenes that Hamilton observed as he helped to inspect, house, groom, and price the slaves about to be auctioned. To enhance their appearance, their bodies were shaved and rubbed with palm oil until their muscles glistened in the sunlight. Some buyers came armed with branding irons to imprint their initials on their newly purchased property. From the frequency with which Nicholas Cruger placed newspaper notices to catch runaway slaves, it seems clear that the traffic in human beings formed a substantial portion of his business.

By the time Hamilton arrived on St. Croix, the burgeoning slave population had doubled in just a decade, and the planters banded together to guard against uprisings or mass escapes to nearby Puerto Rico, where slaves could secure their freedom under Spanish rule. In this fearful environment, no white enjoyed the luxury of being a neutral spectator: either he was an accomplice of the slave system or he left the island. To remove any ambiguity in the matter, the government in Copenhagen issued a booklet, "The St. Croixian Pocket Companion," which spelled out the duties of every white on the island—duties that would have applied to Hamilton starting in 1771. Every male over sixteen was obligated to serve in the militia and attend monthly drills with his arms and ammunition at the ready. If the fort fired its guns twice in a row, all white males had to grab their muskets and flock there instantly.

On days when renegade slaves were executed at Christiansvaern, the white men formed a ring around the fort to prevent other slaves from interfering. Any slave who attacked a white person faced certain death by hanging or decapitation—death that probably came as a blessed relief after first being prodded with red-hot pokers and castrated. Punishments were designed to be hellish so as to terrorize the rest of the captive population into submission. If a slave lifted a hand in resistance, it would promptly be chopped off. Any runaway who returned within a three-month period would have one foot lopped off. If he then ran away a second time, the other foot was amputated. Recidivists might also have their necks fitted with grisly iron collars of sharp, inward-pointing spikes that made it impossible to crawl away through the dense underbrush without slashing their own throats in the effort.

It is hard to grasp Hamilton's later politics without contemplating the raw cruelty that he witnessed as a boy and that later deprived him of the hopefulness so contagious in the American milieu. On the most obvious level, the slave trade of St. Croix generated a permanent detestation of the system and resulted in his later abolitionist efforts. But something deeper may have seeped into his consciousness. In this hierarchical world, skittish planters lived in constant dread of slave revolts and fortified their garrison state to avert them. Even when he left for America, Hamilton carried a heavy dread of anarchy and disorder that always struggled with his no less active love of liberty. Perhaps the true legacy of his boyhood was an equivocal one: he came to detest the tyranny embodied by the planters and their authoritarian rule, while also fearing the potential uprisings of the disaffected slaves. The twin specters of despotism and anarchy were to haunt him for the rest of his life.

Like Ben Franklin, Hamilton was mostly self-taught and probably snatched every spare moment to read. The young clerk aimed to be a man of letters. He may already have had a premonition that his facility with words would someday free him from his humble berth and place him on a par with the most powerful men of his age. The West Indies boasted few stores that sold books, which had to be ordered by special subscription. For that reason, it must have been a godsend to the culture-starved Hamilton when the *Royal Danish American Gazette* launched publication in 1770. The paper had a pronounced Anglophile slant, reflecting the fact that King Christian VII of Denmark was both first cousin and brother-in-law to King George III of England. Each issue carried reverential excerpts from parliamentary debates in London, showcasing William Pitt the Elder and other distinguished orators, and retailed gossipy, fawning snippets about the royal household.

Having a potential place to publish, Hamilton began to scribble poetry. Once his verbal fountain began to flow, it became a geyser that never ceased. The refined wit and pithy maxims of Alexander Pope mesmerized the young clerk, and just as Pope wrote youthful imitations of the classical poets so Hamilton penned imitations of Pope. On April 6, 1771, he published a pair of poems in the *Gazette* that he introduced with a diffident note to the editor: "Sir, I am a youth about seventeen, and consequently such an attempt as this must be presumptuous; but if, upon perusal, you think the following piece worthy of a place in your paper, by inserting it you'll much oblige Your obedient servant, A. H." The two amorous poems that follow are schizophrenic in their contrasting visions of love. In the first, the dreamy poet steals upon his virgin love, who is reclining by a brook as "lambkins" gambol around her. He kneels and awakens her with an ecstatic kiss before sweeping her up in his arms and carrying her off to marital bliss, intoning, "Believe me love is doubly sweet / In wedlock's holy bands."[9] In the next poem, Hamilton has suddenly metamorphosed into a jaded rake, who begins with a shocking, Swiftian opening line: "Celia's an artful little slut." This launches a portrait of a manipulative, feline woman that concludes:

> So, stroking puss's velvet paws,
> How well the jade conceals her claws
> And purrs; but if at last
> You hap to squeeze her somewhat hard
> She spits—her back up—prenez garde;
> Good faith she has you fast.

The first poem seems to have been composed by a sheltered adolescent with an idealized view of women and the second by a world-weary young philanderer who has already tasted many amorous sweets and shed any illusions about female virtue. In fact, this apparent attraction to two opposite types of women—the pure and angelic versus the earthy and flirtatious—ran straight through Hamilton's life, a contradiction he never resolved and that was to lead to scandalous consequences.

The next year, Hamilton published two more poems in the paper, now recreating himself as a somber religious poet. The change in heart can almost certainly be attributed to the advent in St. Croix of a Presbyterian minister named Hugh Knox. Born in northern Ireland of Scottish ancestry, the handsome young Knox migrated to America and became a schoolteacher in Delaware. As a raffish young man, he exhibited a lukewarm piety until a strange incident transformed his life. One Saturday at a local tavern where he was a regular, Knox amused his tipsy companions with a mocking imitation of a sermon delivered by his patron, the Reverend John Rodgers. Afterward, Knox sat down, shaken by his own impiety but also moved by the sermon that still reverberated in his mind. He decided to study divinity at the College of New Jersey (later Princeton) under its president, Aaron Burr, an eminent divine and father of the man who became Hamilton's nemesis. It was almost certainly from Knox's lips that Alexander Hamilton first heard the name of Aaron Burr.

Ordained by Burr in 1755, Knox decided to propagate the gospel and was sent to Saba in the Dutch West Indies. This tiny island near Nevis measured five square miles, had no beaches, and was solitary enough to try the fortitude of the most determined missionary. Rough seas girded Saba's rocky shores, making it hazardous for ships to land there. As the sole clergyman, Knox resided in a settlement known as the Bottom, sunk in the elevated crater of an extinct volcano; it could be reached only by climbing up a stony path. Knox left a bleak picture of the heedless sinners he was assigned to save. "Young fellows and married men, not only without any symptoms of serious religion . . . but keepers of negro wenches . . . rakes, night rioters, drunkards, gamesters, Sabbath breakers, church neglecters, common swearers, unjust dealers etc."[10] An erudite man with a classical education, Knox was starved for both intellectual companionship and money. In 1771, he visited St. Croix and was received warmly by the local Presbyterians, who enticed him to move there. In May 1772, he became pastor at the Scotch Presbyterian church at a salary considerably beyond what he had earned inside his old crater.

After the lonely years in Saba, the forty-five-year-old Knox felt rejuvenated in St. Croix. Humane and tolerant, politically liberal (he was to fervently support American independence), opposed to slavery (though he owned some slaves), and later author of several volumes of sermons, he held a number of views that would have attracted Hamilton. In his earliest surviving letter, he defended his confirmed belief that illegitimate children should be baptized and argued that clergymen should rescue them from their parents instead of rejecting them. He departed from a strict Calvinist belief in predestination. Instead of a darkly punitive God, Knox favored a sunny, fair-minded one. He also saw human nature as insatiably curious and reserved his highest praise for minds that created "*schemes* or *systems* of truth."[11]

Then an illegitimate young clerk with an uncommon knack for systematic thinking stepped into his life. Knox must have marveled at his tremendous luck in discovering Hamilton. We do not know exactly how they met, but Knox threw open his library to this prodigious youth, encouraged him to write verse, and prodded him toward scholarship. An avuncular man with a droll wit, Knox worried that Hamilton was too driven and prone to overwork, too eager to compensate for lost time—a failing, if it was one, that he never outgrew. In later years, Knox liked to remind Hamilton that he had been "rather delicate & frail," with an "ambition to ex-

cel," and had tended to "strain every nerve" to be the very best at what he was doing.[12] Knox had an accurate intuition that this exceptional adolescent was fated to
accomplish great deeds, although he later confessed that Alexander Hamilton had
outstripped even his loftiest expectations.

Among his other gifts, the versatile Hugh Knox was a self-taught doctor and apothecary and a part-time journalist who occasionally filled in for the editor of the *Royal
Danish American Gazette*. It may have been at the newspaper office, not at the
church, that he first ran into Hamilton. That Knox moonlighted as a journalist
proved highly consequential for Hamilton when a massive hurricane tore through
St. Croix on the night of August 31, 1772, and carved a wide swath of destruction
through nearby islands.

By all accounts, the storm struck with unprecedented fury, the *Gazette* reporting
that it was the "most dreadful hurricane known in the memory of man." Starting at
sundown, the gales blew "like great guns, for about six hours, save for half an hour's
intermission. . . . The face of this once beautiful island is now so .calamitous and
disfigured, as it would beggar all description."[13] The tremendous winds uprooted
tall trees, smashed homes to splinters, and swept up boats in foaming billows and
flung them far inland. Detailed reports of the storm in Nevis, where the destruction
was comparable—huge sugar barrels were tossed four hundred yards, furniture
landed two miles away—confirm its terrifying power. Nevis had also been struck by
a severe earthquake that afternoon, and it seems probable that Nevis, St. Kitts, St.
Croix, and neighboring islands were deluged by a tidal wave up to fifteen feet high.
The devastation was so widespread that an appeal for food was launched in the
North American colonies to avert an anticipated famine.

On September 6, Hugh Knox gathered the jittery faithful at his church and delivered a consoling sermon that was published in pamphlet form some weeks later,
Hamilton must have attended and been inspired by Knox's homily, for he went
home and composed a long, feverish letter to his father, trying to convey the hurricane's horror. (It is noteworthy that Hamilton was still in touch with his father
more than six years after the latter's departure from St. Croix. That James Hamilton
resided outside the storm area suggests that he was in the southern Caribbean, possibly Grenada or Tobago.) In his melodramatic description of the hurricane, one
sees the young Hamilton glorying in his verbal powers. He must have shown the
letter to Knox, who persuaded him to publish it in the *Royal Danish American
Gazette*, where it appeared on October 3. The prefatory note to the piece, presumably written by Knox, explained: "The following letter was written the week after
the late hurricane, by a youth of this island, to his father; the copy of it fell by accident into the hands of a gentleman, who, being pleased with it himself, showed it to

others to whom it gave equal satisfaction, and who all agreed that it might not prove unentertaining to the public." Lest anyone suspect that an unfeeling Hamilton was capitalizing on mass misfortune, Knox noted that the anonymous author had at first declined to publish it—perhaps the last time in Alexander Hamilton's life that he would prove bashful or hesitant about publication.

Hamilton's famous letter about the storm astounds the reader for two reasons. For all its bombastic excesses, it does seem wondrous that a seventeen-year-old self-educated clerk could write with such verve and gusto. Clearly, Hamilton was highly literate and already had a considerable fund of verbal riches: "It seemed as if a total dissolution of nature was taking place. The roaring of the sea and wind, fiery meteors flying about it [*sic*] in the air, the prodigious glare of almost perpetual lightning, the crash of the falling houses, and the ear-piercing shrieks of the distressed, were sufficient to strike astonishment into angels."

But the description was also notable for the way Hamilton viewed the hurricane as a divine rebuke to human vanity and pomposity. In what sounded like a cross between a tragic soliloquy and a fire-and-brimstone sermon, he exhorted his fellow mortals:

Where now, oh! vile worm, is all thy boasted fortitude and resolution? What is become of thine arrogance and self sufficiency? . . . Death comes rushing on in triumph, veiled in a mantle of tenfold darkness. His unrelenting scythe, pointed and ready for the stroke . . . See thy wretched helpless state and learn to know thyself. . . . Despise thyself and adore thy God. . . . O ye who revel in affluence see the afflictions of humanity and bestow your superfluity to ease them. . . . Succour the miserable and lay up a treasure in heaven.[14]

Gloomy thoughts for a teenage boy, even in the aftermath of a lethal hurricane. The dark spirit of the storm that he summons up, his apocalyptic sense of universal tumult and disorder, bespeak a somber view of the cosmos. He also shows a strain of youthful idealism as he admonishes the rich to share their wealth.

Hamilton did not know it, but he had just written his way out of poverty. This natural calamity was to prove his salvation. His hurricane letter generated such a sensation—even the island's governor inquired after the young author's identity—that a subscription fund was taken up by local businessmen to send this promising youth to North America to be educated. This generosity was all the more remarkable given the island's dismal state. The hurricane had flattened dwellings, shredded sugarcane, destroyed refineries, and threatened St. Croix with prolonged economic hardship. It would take many months, maybe years, for the island to recover.

The chief sponsor of the subscription fund was likely the good-hearted Hugh

Knox, who later told Hamilton, "I have always had a just and secret pride in having advised you to go to America and in having recommended you to some [of] my old friends there."[15] The chief donors were probably Hamilton's past and present bosses—Nicholas Cruger, Cornelius Kortright, and David Beekman—plus his guardian, Thomas Stevens, and his first cousin, Ann Lytton Venton. Possibly aware of Hamilton's early (indeed, abiding) interest in medicine, the business community may have hoped to train a doctor who would return and treat the many tropical diseases endemic to the island. Doctors were perpetually scarce in the Caribbean, and Edward Stevens was already in New York preparing for such a career.

In the standard telling of his life, Hamilton boards a ship in October 1772 and sails off to North America forever. Yet a close study of the *Royal Danish American Gazette* and other documents raises questions about this usual chronology. Hamilton may have been the "Juvenis" who published a poem, "The Melancholy Hour," in the *Gazette* of October 11, 1772. This brooding work—"Why hangs this gloomy damp upon my mind / Why heaves my bosom with the struggling sigh"—reprises the theme of the hurricane as heavenly retribution upon a fallen world. On October 17, the *Gazette* ran an unsigned hymn in imitation of Pope that incontestably came from Hamilton's pen and was later cherished by his wife as proof of her husband's religious devotion. Entitled "The Soul Ascending into Bliss," it is a lovely, mystical meditation in which Hamilton envisions his soul soaring heavenward. "Hark! Hark! A voice from yonder sky / Methinks I hear my Saviour cry. . . . I come oh Lord, I mount, I fly / On rapid wings I cleave the sky." There is a third poem by Hamilton that has been overlooked and that appeared in the *Gazette* of February 3, 1773, under the heading: "Christiansted. A Character. By A. H." In this short, disillusioned verse, Hamilton evokes a sharp-witted fellow named Eugenio who manages inadvertently to antagonize all of his friends. The poem concludes: "Wit not well govern'd rankles into vice / He to his Jest his Friend will sacrifice!"[16] The discovery of this poem, possibly influenced by an event in the life of Molière, bolsters the supposition that Hamilton spent the winter of 1772–1773 in St. Croix, although he could have mailed Hugh Knox the verse from North America.

To understand this transitional moment in Hamilton's life, we must introduce yet another figure into the convoluted saga of his early years: his first cousin Ann Lytton Venton, later Ann Mitchell. So incalculable was Hamilton's debt to her that on the eve of his duel with Burr, as he contemplated his life, he instructed his wife: "Mrs. Mitchell is the person in the world to whom as a friend I am under the greatest obligations. I have [not] hitherto done my [duty] to her."[17] Why this guilt-ridden homage to a figure who has lingered in the historical shadows?

Twelve years older than Hamilton, Ann Lytton Venton was the oldest daughter of Rachel's sister, Ann. Like so many figures in Hamilton's family, she led a check-ered life. In her early teens, she married a poor Christiansted grocer, Thomas Hall-wood, and promptly had a son. After one year of marriage, Hallwood died. In 1759, Ann married the somewhat more prosperous John Kirwan Venton, who bought a small sugar estate. By 1762, his business had failed, and their home and effects were seized by creditors. The couple decamped to New York, leaving an infant daughter with Ann's parents. The Ventons evidently faltered in New York and were drawn back to St. Croix in 1770 after the suicide of Ann's brother Peter and the death of her father, James Lytton. If John Kirwan Venton hoped to lay hands on Ann's in-heritance, he was foiled by the foresight of his father-in-law, who left two-sevenths of his estate to Ann but specifically excluded Venton from the money, calling him "unfortunate in his conduct."

At this point, the Venton marriage dissolved in acrimony, with Ann and her daughter occupying Peter's house in Christiansted while John took refuge in Fred-eriksted. After the hurricane, John Venton filed for bankruptcy again and posted a notice to his creditors. No less mean-spirited than Johann Michael Lavien, Venton also placed the following threatening ad in the *Gazette* of May 15, 1773: "JOHN KIRWAN VENTON forbids all masters of vessels from carrying Ann Venton, or her daughter Ann Lytton Venton off this island."[18] Defying this warning, Ann Venton and her daughter fled to New York, a brave act that would have reminded Hamilton of his mother flouting the odious Lavien. To secure her inheritance, Ann entrusted the eighteen-year-old Hamilton with a power of attorney that allowed him to col-lect payments from her father's estate due on May 3 and 26 and June 3, 1773. It may well have been after receipt of this money that he boarded a vessel bound for Boston, leaving the West Indies forever. Perhaps in gratitude for his assistance or else plain affection for her exceedingly bright cousin, Ann Lytton Venton repaid Hamilton by becoming a benefactor—quite likely the *principal* benefactor—of his voyage to North America and subsequent education. If so, Hamilton repaid the fa-vor by aiding Ann financially in future years. He always felt under a more com-pelling obligation to her than to anyone else from his early years, and we may know only a fraction of the vital services that she rendered him.

What a world of scarred emotion and secret grief Alexander Hamilton bore with him on the boat to Boston. He took his unhappy boyhood, tucked it away in a men-tal closet, and never opened the door again. Beside the horrid memories, this young dynamo simply was not cut out for the drowsy, slow-paced life of slave owners on a tropical island, and he never evinced the least nostalgia for his West Indian boy-hood or voiced any desire to return. He wrote two years later, "Men are generally too much attached to their native countries to leave it and dissolve all their connexions, unless they are driven to it by necessity."[19] He chose a psychological strategy adopted by many orphans and immigrants: he decided to cut himself off from his past and forge a new identity. He would find a home where he would be accepted for what he did, not for who he was, and where he would no longer labor in the shadow of illegitimacy. His relentless drive, his wretched feelings of shame and degradation, and his precocious self-sufficiency combined to produce a young man with an insatiable craving for success. As a student of history, he knew the mutability of human fortune and later observed, "The changes in the human condition are uncertain and frequent. Many, on whom fortune has bestowed her favours, may trace their family to a more unprosperous station; and many who are now in obscurity, may look back upon the affluence and exalted rank of their ancestors."[20] He would be the former, his father no less unmistakably the latter.

As Alexander sailed north toward spectacular adventures, his father sank ever deeper into incurable poverty. Documents located in St. Vincent reveal that James Hamilton had wandered to the southern end of the Caribbean, almost to the coast of South America. On the tiny, secluded island of Bequia, located just south of St. Vincent, he had entered into a program set up by the British Crown to encourage impoverished settlers. Bequia is the northernmost of the Grenadine Islands, an isolated spot, seven square miles in size, of soft hills, jagged cliffs, and sandy beaches. On March 14, 1774, James Hamilton signed a contract that gave him twenty-five acres of free woodland property along the shore of Southeast Bay. In this lovely but menacing place, a stronghold of indigenous black and yellow Caribs and runaway slaves, James Hamilton chose a spot on public land reserved for a future fortification. Bequia was the sort of distant, godforsaken place that could have attracted only somebody who had exhausted all other options. The deed for James Hamilton's land purchase tells its own tacit tale of woe; it made clear that his twenty-five acres were "not adapted for sugar plantations" and had been set aside "for the accommodations of poor settlers."[21] Under the grant, James Hamilton didn't have to pay a penny for the first four years but had to stay on the island for at least one year. A 1776 survey shows him sharing seventy acres with a man named Simple, and they are the only two people listed on the roster of poor residents. There must have been days when it was hard for James to believe that he was the fourth son of a Scottish laird and had grown up in a fogbound castle. The descent of his life had been as stunning and irrevocable as the rise of his son in America was to seem almost blessedly inevitable.

THREE

THE COLLEGIAN

A lexander Hamilton never needed to worry about leading a tedious, un-
eventful life. Drama shadowed his footsteps. When his ship caught fire
during his three-week voyage to North America, crew members scrambled down ropes to the sea and scooped up seawater in buckets, extinguishing the
blaze with some difficulty. The charred vessel managed to sail into Boston Harbor
intact, and Hamilton proceeded straight to New York. This was a mandatory stop,
since he had to pick up his allowance at Kortright and Company, which managed
the subscription fund that financed his education. The New York firm owned seven
vessels that shuttled between New York and the West Indies and employed Kortright and Cruger as its St. Croix representative. Periodically, the subscription fund
was replenished by sugar barrels sent from St. Croix, with Hamilton pocketing a
percentage of the proceeds from each shipment. Hence, the education of this future
abolitionist was partly underwritten by sugarcane harvested by slaves.

When he came to New York, Hamilton was fortified with introductory letters
from Hugh Knox but otherwise did not know a soul except Edward Stevens. Yet this
young man from the tropics, who had probably never worn an overcoat or experienced a change of seasons, did not seem handicapped by his past and never struck
people as a provincial bumpkin. He seemed to vault over the high hurdles of social
status with ease. Smart, handsome, and outgoing, he marched with an erect military carriage, thrusting out his chest in an assertive manner. He had all the magnetic
power of a mysterious foreigner and soon made his first friend: a fashionable tailor
with the splendid name of Hercules Mulligan, whose brother was a junior partner
at Kortright and Company. Born in Ireland in 1740, the colorful, garrulous Mulligan was one of the few tradesmen Hamilton ever befriended. He had a shop and

home on Water Street, and Hamilton may have boarded with him briefly. With a sizable dollop of Irish blarney, Mulligan took full credit for introducing Hamilton into New York society: "Mr. H. used in the evenings to sit with my family and my brother's family and write doggerel rhymes for their amusement; he was always amiable and cheerful and extremely attentive to his books."[1] These soirees may have featured some subversive political content, for Hercules Mulligan had reputedly been one of the "Liberty Boys" involved in a skirmish with British soldiers on Golden Hill (John Street) six weeks before frightened British troops gunned down fractious colonists in the 1770 Boston Massacre. Later, during the British occupation of wartime New York, Mulligan was to dabble in freelance espionage for George Washington, discreetly pumping his foppish clients, mostly Tories and British officers, for strategic information as he taped their measurements.

Hamilton's early itinerary in America closely mirrored the connections of Hugh Knox. Through Knox, he came to know two of New York's most eminent Presbyterian clergymen: Knox's old mentor, Dr. John Rodgers—an imposing figure who strutted grandly down Wall Street en route to church, grasping a gold-headed cane and nodding to well-wishers—and the Reverend John M. Mason, whose son would end up attempting an authorized biography of Hamilton. Through another batch of Knox introductory letters, Hamilton ended up studying at a well-regarded preparatory school across the Hudson River, the Elizabethtown Academy. Like all autodidacts, Hamilton had some glaring deficiencies to correct and required cram courses in Latin, Greek, and advanced math to qualify for college.

Elizabethtown, New Jersey—today plain Elizabeth—was chartered by George II and ranked as the colony's oldest English community. It was a small, idyllic village graced with orchards, two churches, a stone bridge arching over the Elizabeth River, and windmills dispersed among the salt meadows outside of town. Located on the grounds of the Presbyterian church, the Elizabethtown Academy occupied a two-story building topped by a cupola. Its headmaster, Francis Barber, was a recent graduate of the College of New Jersey (henceforth called Princeton, its much later name) and was only five years older than Hamilton. He was a dashing figure, with a high forehead, heavy eyebrows, and a small, prim mouth. Steeped in the classics and with reform-minded political sympathies, he was in many ways an ideal preceptor for Hamilton. He would see combat duty on the patriotic side during the Revolution and would find himself at Yorktown, in a startling inversion, under the direct command of his West Indian pupil.

Because the Elizabethtown Academy supplied many students to Princeton, we can deduce something about Hamilton's preparatory studies from that college's requirements. Princeton applicants had to know Virgil, Cicero's orations, and Latin grammar and also had to be "so well acquainted with the Greek as to render any part of the four Evangelists in that language into Latin or English."[2] Never tentative about tackling new things and buoyed by a preternatural self-confidence, Hamilton proved a fantastically quick study. He often worked past midnight, curled up in his blanket, then awoke at dawn and paced the nearby burial ground, mumbling to himself as he memorized his lessons. (Hamilton's lifelong habit of talking sotto voce while pacing lent him an air of either inspiration or madness.) A copious note taker, he left behind, in a minute hand, an exercise book in which he jotted down passages from the *Iliad* in Greek, took extensive notes on geography and history, and compiled detailed chapter synopses from the books of Genesis and Revelation. As if wanting to pack every spare moment with achievement, he also found time to craft poetry and wrote the prologue and epilogue of an unspecified play performed by a local detachment of British soldiers.

Hamilton's attendance at the Elizabethtown Academy brought him into the immediate vicinity of the younger Aaron Burr, who had attended the same school several years earlier. Burr's brother-in-law, jurist Tapping Reeve, sat on the academy's board of visitors and had been a vital force behind the school's creation. By an extraordinary coincidence, Burr spent the summer of 1773 in Elizabethtown, right around the time Hamilton arrived. Hamilton might have seen this handsome, genial young man sauntering down the street, gliding by in a boat along the town's many inlets, or hunting in the nearby woods. As we shall see, they probably also met in the drawing rooms of mutual friends.

Hamilton always displayed an unusual capacity for impressing older, influential men, and he gained his social footing in Elizabethtown with surpassing speed, crossing over an invisible divide into a privileged, patrician world in a way that would have been impossible in St. Croix. Thanks to the letters from Hugh Knox, he had instant access to men at the pinnacle of colonial society in New Jersey. He met William Livingston and Elias Boudinot, well-heeled lawyers and luminaries in the Presbyterian political world, who exposed him to the heterodox political currents of the day. They were both associated with the Whigs, who sought to curb royal power, boost parliamentary influence, and preserve civil liberties.

Unquestionably the most vivid figure in Hamilton's new life was fifty-year-old Livingston, a born crusader, who had abandoned a contentious career in New York politics to assume the sedate life of a New Jersey country squire. As work proceeded on Liberty Hall, his 120-acre estate, Livingston took temporary quarters in town, and Hamilton may have lodged with him during this interlude. Livingston was the sort of contradictory figure that always enchanted the young Hamilton. A blue-blooded rebel and scion of a powerful Hudson River clan, Livingston had spurned an easy life to write romantic poetry, crank out polemical essays, and plunge into controversial causes. Tall and lanky, nicknamed "the whipping post," the voluble

Livingston tilted lances with royal authorities with such self-righteous glee that one Tory newspaper anointed him "the Don Quixote of the Jerseys."[3]

Like many Presbyterians, Livingston had gravitated to political dissent while opposing Tory efforts to entrench the Church of England in America. Two decades earlier, he had spearheaded a vitriolic campaign to block the establishment of an Anglican college in New York, which, he warned, would become "a contracted receptacle of bigotry" and an instrument of royal power.[4] After their campaign failed and the school received a royal charter as King's College in 1754, Livingston and his friends founded the New York Society Library to provide safe alternative reading matter for students. (Hamilton would take out books there.) An opponent of the Stamp Act and subsequent measures to saddle the colonies with oppressive taxes, Livingston was to attend the Continental Congress and the Constitutional Convention and become the first governor of an independent New Jersey in 1776.

A gregarious man, William Livingston conducted Hamilton into a much more glamorous society than the one he left behind. Though benefiting from Livingston largesse, Hamilton was never mistaken for the family help, and he befriended the Livingston children, including the cerebral Brockholst, who was later an eminent Supreme Court judge and already friendly with Aaron Burr. There were also dazzling Livingston daughters to ravish the eye. As one of Burr's friends observed of Elizabethtown at the time, "There is certainly something amorous in its very air."[5] Hamilton observed the courtship of the beautiful, high-spirited Sarah Livingston by a young lawyer named John Jay. (So regal was Sarah Livingston's presence that when she later attended the opera in Paris, some audience members mistook her for the queen of France.) A special rapport sprang up between Hamilton and another Livingston daughter, Catharine, known as Kitty. She was the type of woman Hamilton found irresistible: pretty, coquettish, somewhat spoiled, and always ready for flirtatious banter. Judging from a letter Hamilton wrote to her during the Revolution, one suspects that Kitty was his first romantic conquest in America:

> I challenge you to meet me in whatever path you dare. And, if you have no objection, for variety and amusement, we will even make excursions in the flowery walks and roseate bowers of Cupid. You know I am renowned for gallantry and shall always be able to entertain you with a choice collection of the prettiest things imaginable. . . . You shall be one of the graces, or Diana, or Venus, or something surpassing them all.[6]

It is hard to imagine that Alexander Hamilton slept under the same roof as Kitty Livingston and didn't harbor impure thoughts.

In this sociable world, Hamilton also befriended Livingston's brother-in-law,

William Alexander, a bluff, convivial man known as Lord Stirling because of his contested claim to a Scottish earldom. An extravagant spendthrift, he was already swamped with debt when he met Hamilton. A decade earlier, the handsome, round-faced Stirling had constructed a thousand-acre estate at Basking Ridge, adorned with stables, gardens, and a deer park in imitation of the country houses of British nobility. Like Livingston, Lord Stirling was a curious amalgam of reformer and self-styled aristocrat. He rode about in a coach emblazoned with the Stirling coat of arms and possessed a princely wardrobe of 31 coats, 58 vests, 43 pairs of breeches, 30 shirts, 27 cravats, and 14 pairs of shoes.

If Aaron Burr is to be trusted, Lord Stirling drank his way straight through the American Revolution as a brigadier general, plied by his aide-de-camp, James Monroe, who served as his faithful cupbearer: "Monroe's whole duty was to fill his lordship's tankard and hear, with indications of admiration, his lordship's long stories about himself."[7] Burr's barbed commentary doesn't do justice to the bibulous Lord Stirling, who would win renown in the battle of Brooklyn. He was a literate man with eclectic interests, including mathematics and astronomy (he published a monograph on the transit of Venus), and a cofounder of the New York Society Library. Of special relevance to Hamilton's future, he was a leading proponent of American manufactures. He bred horses and cattle, grew grapes and made wine, and produced pig iron and hemp. Lord Stirling had one final attraction for Hamilton: he also had enchanting daughters, especially the charming Catharine, always called "Lady Kitty." She was to marry William Duer, the most notorious friend in Hamilton's life.

The third and most enduring tie formed by Hamilton was with Elias Boudinot, a lawyer who later became president of the Continental Congress and who owned copper and sulfur mines. A balding man with a jowly face and a smile that radiated benign intelligence, Boudinot was an innkeeper's son and, like Hamilton, descended from French Huguenots. Such was his piety that he became the first president of the American Bible Society. As an organizer of the Elizabethtown Academy, he had pushed for the admission of "a number of free scholars in this town" and would have embraced heartily a poor but deserving youth such as Hamilton.[8]

As a regular visitor to Boudinot's mansion, Boxwood Hall, Hamilton was exposed to a refined world of books, political debate, and high culture. Boudinot's wife, Annie, wrote verse that George Washington complimented as "elegant poetry," and this bookish family gathered each evening to hear biographies and sacred histories read aloud.[9] Hamilton's friendship with the Boudinots was so intimate that when their infant daughter, Anna Maria, contracted a fatal illness in September 1774, Hamilton kept a vigil by the sickly child and composed an affecting elegy after she died. This poem highlights a notable capacity for empathy in Hamilton, who dared to write it in the voice of the grieving mother. Since Hamilton had at least one sibling who had died in infancy or childhood, the poem may have summoned up memories of his own mother's hardships:

> For the sweet babe, my doting heart
> Did all a mother's fondness feel;
> Careful to act each tender part
> And guard from every threatening ill.
>
> But what alas! availed my care?
> The unrelenting hand of death,
> Regardless of a parent's prayer
> Has stopped my lovely infant's breath—[10]

Later on, friends would comment on the almost maternal solicitude that Hamilton showed for friends or family members in distress.

As a young man in a constant rush, scarcely pausing for breath, Hamilton did not dally in Elizabethtown for more than six months. Nevertheless, this fleeting period may have left its imprint on his politics. He hobnobbed with wealthy, accomplished men who lived like English nobility even as they agitated for change. These men wanted to modify the social order, not overturn it—a fair description of Hamilton's future politics. At this juncture, Hamilton's New Jersey patrons rejected national independence as a rash option, favored reconciliation, and repeatedly invoked their rights as English subjects. Far from wanting separation from the British empire, they favored fuller integration into it. Britain remained their beau ideal, if a somewhat faded one. Hamilton later admitted to having had a "strong prejudice" for the British viewpoint while at Elizabethtown and apparently leaned toward monarchism. Like his mentors, he would always be an uneasy and reluctant revolutionary who found it hard to jettison legal forms in favor of outright rebellion.[11] Mingling with Presbyterians may also have influenced his politics. The denomination was associated with the Whig critique of the British Crown, while Anglicans tended to be Tories and more often supported British imperial policy toward the colonies and an established church.

As Hamilton contemplated his next educational step, there were only nine colleges in the colonies to consider. William Livingston and Elias Boudinot sat on Princeton's board of trustees—Livingston was such a trusted friend of the former president Aaron Burr that he had delivered his eulogy—and it would have been impolitic, not to say rude, for Hamilton to resist their entreaties to at least scout out the college. The school already had a contingent of West Indian students, and President John Witherspoon was so eager to augment their numbers (or tap the money of rich sugar planters for professorships) that he had issued a rousing newspaper appeal the previous year, an "Address to the Inhabitants of Jamaica and the Other West Indian Islands on Behalf of the College of New Jersey," wherein he discoursed "on the advantages of his college for the education of West Indian youth."[12] Founded in 1746 as a counterweight to the Church of England's influence, Princeton was a hotbed of Presbyterian/Whig sentiment, preached religious freedom, and might have seemed a logical choice for Hamilton. Hercules Mulligan contends that Hamilton told him that "he preferred Princeton to King's College because it was more republican."[13] Indeed, the school bubbled with such political ferment that it was denounced in Tory quarters as a nursery of political radicalism. President Witherspoon confessed that "the spirit of liberty" ran "high and strong" at Princeton.[14]

Little more than a coach stop between New York and Philadelphia, the rural hamlet of Princeton was hemmed in by thick forests. For Presbyterians eager to produce new ministers to fill rapidly expanding pulpits, this isolation was a protective measure that shielded students from urban temptations. The school stood in the throes of a religious revival when Hamilton applied. Hercules Mulligan said that he accompanied his young friend to this rustic outpost and introduced him to Witherspoon, but William Livingston and Elias Boudinot, as trustees, would have provided any needed introductions.

An eminent theologian, born in Edinburgh, Witherspoon was a husky man with an oddly shaped head that narrowed at the top and bulged out in the middle. Garry Wills has called him "probably the most influential teacher in the history of American education," and Princeton under his tutelage produced a bumper crop of politician alumni: a U.S. president, a vice president, twenty-one senators, twenty-nine congressmen, and twelve state governors.[15] He was to sign the Declaration of Independence and minister to the Continental Congress as its first clergyman. By no coincidence, Princeton outpaced all other colleges by sending nine alumni to the Constitutional Convention. Witherspoon could be intimidating on first encounter. Pugnacious and outspoken, he had an unsettling way of erupting in strange twitches and fidgets. Hamilton, with his rock-hard ego, held his ground with the college president. Witherspoon examined Hamilton orally and was impressed by his fully fledged intellect. Then Hamilton made an unconventional proposal. According to Hercules Mulligan, Hamilton informed Witherspoon that he wanted to enter the college and advance "with as much rapidity as his exertions would enable him to do. Dr. Witherspoon listened with great attention to so unusual a proposition from so young a person and replied that he had not the sole power to determine that but that he would submit the request to the trustees who would decide."[16] One feels here the vastly accelerated tempo of Hamilton's life, which was likely due to the chronic impatience fostered by his belated start in life.

When Witherspoon had taken over at Princeton a few years earlier, he had set about to stiffen its lax admissions requirements and might have frowned on Hamilton's special timetable for that reason. Mulligan blamed the trustees for rebuffing the proposal, saying that two weeks later Hamilton received a letter from Witherspoon "stating that the request could not be complied with because it was contrary to the usage of the college and expressing his regret because he was convinced that the young gentleman would do honor to any seminary at which he should be educated."[17] In fact, there had been a precedent for Hamilton's brash request: Aaron Burr had tried to enter Princeton at age eleven and was told he was too young. He had then crammed for two years and cheekily applied for admission to the *junior* class at age thirteen. In a compromise, he was admitted as a sophomore and graduated in 1772 at sixteen. Hamilton may have learned about this experience from Burr himself or through their mutual friend Brockholst Livingston.

In weighing Hamilton's demand, Witherspoon and his trustees may have been deterred by the recent experience of a young Virginia scholar who had entered as a sophomore in 1769 and worked himself into a state of nervous exhaustion by completing his bachelor's degree in two years instead of three. His name was James Madison, later Hamilton's illustrious collaborator on *The Federalist Papers*. Fond of Witherspoon and too weak to travel after graduation, Madison had lingered in Princeton for a year to study privately with "the old Doctor."[18] When Madison finally returned to Virginia in the spring of 1772, he was still so debilitated from his intense studies that he feared for his health.

While applying to Princeton Hamilton may have decided to "correct" his real age and shed a couple of years. If he was born in 1755, he would have been applying to college at eighteen, when fourteen or fifteen was often the standard minimum age for entrance—a highly uncomfortable state of affairs for a wunderkind. (Gouverneur Morris had entered King's College at age twelve.) Prodigies aren't supposed to be overaged freshmen. To be sure, Madison had entered Princeton at eighteen, but he was considered slightly old for a newcomer and skipped to sophomore status. If Hamilton trimmed two years from his age, one can sympathize with him. After all, while Aaron Burr was delivering a commencement speech at Princeton the year before, Hamilton, a year older, was still trying to figure out an escape route from Cruger's countinghouse on St. Croix. For a precocious young man in his predicament, lying about his age would have been a pardonable lapse.

Spurned at Princeton, Hamilton ended up at King's College. He did not lack sponsors. Lord Stirling, who had inherited a town house on Broad Street in lower Manhattan, had long sat on the college's governing board and raised money for it.

Hamilton's life was now set moving in a new direction. This nomadic, stateless boy found a home in the best possible city for a future treasury secretary, a city in which commerce always held an honored place. He was to be immersed in a heady world of business, law, and politics, and he made valuable contacts in the merchant community.

Had he gone to Princeton, Hamilton might well have been radicalized sooner in the revolt against Britain, but that is arguable. Instead of with Witherspoon, Hamilton studied under one of the most ardent Tories in the colonies, Dr. Myles Cooper, the president of King's. Attendance at King's placed Hamilton in a city with a vocal Tory population, the bastion of British colonial power. At the same time, being in New York was also to lead to firsthand contact with tremendous revolutionary ferment and exposure to some of the colonies' most eloquent agitators and outspoken newspapers. The virulent clash of Tories and Whigs in New York was to sharpen all of the conflicting feelings in Hamilton's nature, enabling him to sympathize with the views of both patriots and Loyalists. In fact, by rejecting Alexander Hamilton, President Witherspoon and his associates at Princeton unintentionally thrust the young West Indian straight into the thick of the combustible patriotic drama in a way that would have proved impossible in a sleepy New Jersey country town.

Set on an enormous tract of land that Trinity Church had received from Queen Anne early in the century, King's College stood on the northern fringe of the city, housed in a stately three-story building with a cupola that commanded a superb view of the Hudson River across a low, rambling meadow. This elevated campus is defined by today's West Broadway, Murray, Barclay, and Church Streets, a spot that one British visitor rhapsodized as the "most beautiful site for a college in the world."[19] President Cooper tried gamely to segregate his students from unwholesome external influences. "The edifice is surrounded by a high fence," he wrote, "which also encloses a large court and garden, and a porter constantly attends at the front gate, which is closed at ten o'clock each evening in the summer and at nine in the winter, after which hours, the names of all that come in are delivered weekly to the President."[20] This cloistered environment was modeled upon Oxford's and the students strode about in academic caps and gowns.

One reason that Cooper sought to sequester his students was that the college adjoined the infamous red-light district known as the Holy Ground, its name a satirical allusion to the fact that St. Paul's Chapel owned the land. As many as five hundred Dutch and English "ladies of pleasure" (equivalent to 2 percent of the city's entire population) patrolled these dusky lanes each evening, and the proximity of this haunt to susceptible young scholars troubled town elders. One dismayed Scot visitor wrote in 1774, "One circumstance I think is a little unlucky . . . is that the entrance to [King's College] is through one of the streets where the most noted prostitutes live."[21] The college promulgated rules that "none of the pupils shall frequent houses of ill fame or keep company with any persons of known scandalous behavior."[22] Women were strictly banned from the college grounds, along with cards, dice, and other subtle snares of the devil. In returning to the college before the curfew, did Hamilton sometimes linger in the Holy Ground to sample its profane pleasures?

In warding off outside temptations, President Cooper also looked askance at the political protests mounted nearby. King's College had evolved into the fortress of British orthodoxy that William Livingston and Presbyterian critics had feared, with the Anglican reverence for hierarchy and obedience breeding subservience to royal authority. (During the Revolution, the British Army was to take malicious pleasure in converting Presbyterian and Baptist churches into stables or barracks.) To President Cooper's consternation, King's College stood one block west of the Common (now City Hall Park), a popular spot for radicals to congregate in. During Hamilton's stay at the college, an eighty-foot pole towered over this grassy expanse, around the top of which spun a gilded weather vane with the single word *LIBERTY* on it. Hamilton's debut as a rabble-rousing orator was to take place in this very park.

With fewer than twenty-five thousand inhabitants, New York was already second in size among American colonial cities, behind Philadelphia but edging ahead of Boston. Founded as a commercial venture by the Dutch West India Company in 1623, the city already had a history as a raucous commercial hub, a boisterous port that blended many cultures and religions. Fourteen languages were spoken there by the time Hamilton arrived. Each year, its congested wharves absorbed thousands of new immigrants—mostly British, Scotch, and Irish—and Hamilton must have appreciated the city's acceptance of strangers carving out new lives. His friend Gouverneur Morris later observed that "to be born in America seems to be a matter of indifference at New York."[23]

The settled portion of the city stretched from the Battery up to the Common. Shaded by poplars and elms, Broadway was the main thoroughfare, flanked by mazes of narrow, winding streets. There were sights galore to enthrall the young West Indian. Fetching ladies promenaded along Broadway, handsome coaches cruised the streets, and graceful church spires etched an incipient skyline. Rich merchants had colonized Wall Street and Hanover Square, and their weekend pleasure gardens extended north along the Hudson shore. On his way to the Continental Congress in Philadelphia in 1774, John Adams admired the city's painted brick buildings and praised its streets as "vastly more regular and elegant than those in Boston and the houses are more grand as well as neat."[24] At the same time, the inhabitants already conformed to the eventual stereotype of fast-talking, sharp-elbowed, money-mad strivers. "They talk very loud, very fast, and all together," Adams protested. "If they ask you a question, before you can utter three words of your answer, they will break out upon you again and talk away."[25] The opulence made the poverty only more conspicuous. During the glacial winter of 1772–1773, the East River froze, and the municipal hospital was overrun with indigent patients. Crime was so pervasive that ground had recently been broken for Bridewell prison.

Hamilton must have entered King's in late 1773 or early 1774, because his stay overlapped with that of Edward Stevens, his St. Croix friend, and Robert Troup, both of whom graduated by the summer of 1774. President Cooper listed Hamilton among seventeen students who matriculated in 1774. Since the average King's student entered at fifteen, one again suspects that the nineteen-year-old Hamilton took the liberty of subtracting two years from his age. To gratify the youth's insistence upon rapid advancement, Cooper granted Hamilton status as a special student who took private tutorials and audited lectures but did not belong, at least initially, to any class. In September 1774, Hamilton contracted with Professor Robert Harpur to study math. Trained in Glasgow, Harpur probably introduced his new pupil to the writings of David Hume and other worthies of the Scottish Enlightenment. It took nine years for Hamilton to discharge his debt to Harpur, suggesting that even armed with his St. Croix subsidy Hamilton had to make do on a stringent budget and never quite forgot that he was a charity student.

There are no extant drawings of Hamilton at this age. From later descriptions, however, we know that he stood about five foot seven and had a fair complexion, auburn hair, rosy cheeks, and a wide, well-carved mouth. His nose, with its flaring nostrils and irregular line, was especially strong and striking, his jaw chiseled and combative. Slim and elegant, with thin shoulders and shapely legs, he walked with a buoyant lightness, and his observant, flashing eyes darted about with amusement. His later Federalist friend and ally Fisher Ames left some graphic impressions of Hamilton's appearance. Of his eyes, he said, "These were of a deep azure, eminently beautiful, without the slightest trace of hardness or severity, and beamed with higher expressions of intelligence and discernment than any others that I ever saw." Ames often bumped into Hamilton on his daily walks and said "he displayed in his manners and movements a degree of refinement and grace which I never witnessed in *any other man* . . . and I am quite confident that those who knew him intimately will cheerfully subscribe to my opinion that he was one of the most elegant of mortals. . . . It is impossible to conceive a loftier portion of easy, graceful, and polished movements than were exhibited in him."[26] Though Hamilton acquired greater urbanity later on, even as a young man, fresh from the islands, he had a dignified air of self-possession remarkable in a former clerk.

At first, Hamilton aspired to be a doctor and attended anatomy lectures given by

Dr. Samuel Clossy, a pioneering surgeon from Dublin. Upon arriving in New York in 1767, Clossy had acquired quick notoriety as a practitioner of the black art of snatching cadavers from local cemeteries for dissection. (The practice was not outlawed until 1789, after it sparked a massive riot.) Clossy's lectures stayed firmly embedded in Hamilton's retentive memory. Years later, Hamilton's physician, Dr. David Hosack, recalled, "I have often heard him speak of the interest and ardour he felt when prosecuting the study of anatomy" under Clossy. He further remarked of Hamilton that "few men knew more of the structure of the human frame and its functions."[27]

Though not an outstanding school, King's offered a solid classical curriculum of Greek and Latin literature, rhetoric, geography, history, philosophy, math, and science. Hamilton at once proved himself a student of incomparable energy, racing through his studies with characteristic speed. "I cannot make everybody else as rapid as myself," he was to one day write laughingly to his wife. "This you know by experience."[28] From his college essays, we can tell that he ransacked the library, poring over the works of Locke, Montesquieu, Hobbes, and Hume, as well as those of such reigning legal sages as Sir William Blackstone, Hugo Grotius, and Samuel von Pufendorf. He was especially taken with the jurist Emmerich de Vattel, whom he lauded as "the most accurate and approved of the writers on the laws of nations."[29] His education supplemented by voracious reading, Hamilton was able to compensate for his childhood deficiencies. After King's, he could rattle off the classical allusions and exhibit the erudition that formed parts of the intellectual equipment of all the founding fathers. Also, he would be able to draw freely on a stock of lore about Greek and Roman antiquity, providing essential material for the unending debates about the fate of republican government in America.

Hamilton was often spotted shortly after dawn, chattering to himself, as if unable to contain the contents of his bursting brain. He paced the Hudson River bank and rehearsed his lessons or walked along tree-shaded Batteau Street (later Dey Street). Based on a schedule that Hamilton later drew up for his son, we can surmise that he followed a tight daily regimen, rising by six and budgeting most of his available time for work but also allocating time for pleasure. His life was a case study in the profitable use of time. Hamilton showed little interest in student pranks and pratfalls, and his name does not appear in the college's Black Book, which recorded infractions against Myles Cooper's rules. Offending students were forced to memorize lines from Horace or translate essays from The Spectator into Latin.

When Hamilton was at King's, his friends were struck by his religious nature, though some of this may have stemmed from the school's requirements. There was obligatory chapel before breakfast, and bells chimed after dinner for evening prayers; on Sunday, students had to attend church twice. His chum at King's, Robert

Troup, was convinced that Hamilton's religious practice was driven by more than duty. He "was attentive to public worship and in the habit of praying on his knees night and morning. . . . I have often been powerfully affected by the fervor and eloquence of his prayers. He had read many of the polemical writers on religious subjects and he was a zealous believer in the fundamental doctrines of Christianity."[30]

The vivacious Hamilton never had trouble making friends; Troup, the son of a sea captain, was soon his warmest companion. At King's, Troup wrote, "they occupied the same room and slept in the same bed" and continued to live together for a time after Troup graduated.[31] Born in Elizabethtown in 1757, Troup had also become an orphan, his father having died in 1768 (the year Hamilton's mother died) and his mother the following year. As with Hamilton, some friends took responsibility for Troup's welfare. Adolescent hardship instilled in Troup a lasting sense of financial insecurity, and he was amazed that Hamilton worried so little about money. "I have often said that your friends would be obliged to bury you at their own expence," Troup wrote to Hamilton in later years, a statement that was to prove queasily prophetic.[32]

Was it pure happenstance that Troup and Hamilton roomed together, or did Myles Cooper guess that they would forge a secret bond among the more affluent boys? Where early sorrow had toughened Hamilton, hardening his self-reliance, it made Troup insecure and prone to hero worship. Bright and jovial, favored with an easy laugh, he idolized his gifted friends and came to enjoy the odd distinction of being a confidant of both Hamilton and Burr. In one letter, Burr referred to Troup fondly as "that great fat fellow" and said another time, "He is a better antidote for the spleen than a ton of drugs."[33] Both Hamilton and Burr were prey to depression and appear to have been buoyed by Troup's exuberant humor.

In Hamilton's first months at King's, he and Troup formed a club that gathered weekly to hone debating, writing, and speaking skills. The other members—Nicholas Fish, Edward Stevens, and Samuel and Henry Nicoll—rounded out Hamilton's first circle of intimates. Small literary societies were then a staple of college life, their members composing papers and reading them aloud for comment. Hamilton was the undisputed star. "In all the performances of the club," Troup said, Hamilton "made extraordinary displays of richness of genius and energy of mind."[34] As tension with England worsened, many discussions hinged on the question of royal-colonial relations. At first, Hamilton didn't differ much from the Loyalist views espoused by Myles Cooper and was "originally a monarchist," Troup asserted. "He was versed in the history of England and well acquainted with the principles of the English constitution, which he admired."[35] As Hamilton's views evolved, however, and he began to publish the outspoken anti-British pieces that made his reputation, he used the debating club at King's to preview his essays.

. . .

The colonial struggle against the Crown took a dramatic turn on the moonlit night of December 16, 1773, around the time that Hamilton entered King's College. A mob of two hundred men with soot-darkened faces, roughly costumed as Mohawk Indians, crept aboard three ships in Boston harbor, used tomahawks to smash open 342 chests of tea, and pitched the contents overboard. Another two thousand townspeople urged them on from the docks. "This is the most magnificent moment of all," John Adams cheered from Braintree, Massachusetts.[36] The Boston Tea Party expressed patriotic disgust at both violated principles and eroded profits. For a time, the colonists had acquiesced to a tea tax because they had been able to smuggle in contraband tea from Holland. After Parliament manipulated duties to grant a de facto tea monopoly to the East India Company in 1773, the smugglers were thwarted and rich Boston merchants—at least those not selected as company agents—suddenly decided to make common cause with the town radicals and protest the parliamentary measures.

Four days later, Paul Revere galloped breathlessly into New York with news of the Boston uprising. Troup contended that Hamilton rushed off to Boston to engage in firsthand reportage. This seems unlikely for a new student, but he may well have rushed into print. As a former clerk acquainted with import duties, contraband goods, and European trade policies, Hamilton was handed a tailor-made issue that wasn't entirely new to him: the West Indian islands had felt the distant repercussions of the Stamp Act protests and other thwarted attempts by Britain to tax the colonists. "The first political piece which [Hamilton] wrote," recalled Troup, "was on the destruction of the tea at Boston in which he aimed to show that the destruction was both necessary and politic."[37] This anonymous salvo may have been the "Defence and Destruction of the Tea" published in John Holt's New-York Journal. In Troup's telling, Hamilton assuaged the keen anxieties of merchants alarmed by the assault on property. Such reassurance was especially timely after New York hosted its own "tea party" on April 22, 1774, when a group of sea captains, led by Alexander McDougall and decked out in Mohawk dress, stormed the British ship London and chucked its tea chests into the deep.

The enraged British lost all patience with their American brethren after the Boston Tea Party and enacted punitive measures. One especially irate member of Parliament, Charles Van, said Boston should be obliterated like Carthage: "I am of the opinion you will never meet with that proper obedience to the laws of this country until you have destroyed that nest of locusts."[38] By May 1774, news arrived that England had retaliated with the Coercive or "Intolerable" Acts. These draconian measures shut down Boston's port until the colonists paid for the spilled tea.

They also curbed popular assemblies, restricted trial by jury, subjected Massachusetts to ham-handed military rule, and guaranteed that the Boston streets would be blanketed with British troops in an overpowering show of force. On May 13, General Thomas Gage, the new military commander, arrived in Boston with four regiments to enforce these acts, which dealt a crippling blow to the free-spirited maritime town. The British response triggered a still tenuous unity among colonists who balked at the notion that Parliament could impose taxes without their consent. Until this point, the colonies had been tantamount to separate countries, joined by little sense of common mission or identity. Now committees of correspondence in each colony began to communicate with one another, issuing calls for a trade embargo against British goods and summoning a Continental Congress in Philadelphia in September.

Even in rabidly Anglophile New York, the political atmosphere by late spring was "as full of uproar as if it was besieged by a foreign force," said one observer.[39] These were stirring days for Hamilton, who must have been constantly distracted from his studies by rallies, petitions, broadsides, and handbills. In choosing New York's delegates for the first Continental Congress, a feud arose between hard-line protesters, who favored a boycott of British goods, and moderate burghers who criticized such measures as overly provocative and self-defeating. To beat the drum for a boycott, the militant Sons of Liberty, members of a secret society first convened to flout the Stamp Act, gathered a mass meeting on the afternoon of July 6, 1774. It took place at the grassy Common near King's College, sometimes called The Fields, in the shadow of the towering liberty pole.

Alexander McDougall chaired the meeting and introduced resolutions condemning British sanctions against Massachusetts. The rich folklore surrounding this pivotal event in Hamilton's life suggests that his speech came about spontaneously, possibly prompted by somebody in the crowd. After mounting the platform, the slight, boyish speaker started out haltingly, then caught fire in a burst of oratory. If true to his later style, Hamilton gained energy as he spoke. He endorsed the Boston Tea Party, deplored the closure of Boston's port, endorsed colonial unity against unfair taxation, and came down foursquare for a boycott of British goods. In his triumphant peroration, he said such actions "will prove the salvation of North America and her liberties"; otherwise "fraud, power, and the most odious oppression will rise triumphant over right, justice, social happiness, and freedom."[40]

When his speech ended, the crowd stood transfixed in silence, staring at this spellbinding young orator before it erupted in a sustained ovation. "It is a collegian!" people whispered to one another. "It is a collegian!"[41] Hamilton, nineteen, looked young for his age, which made his performance seem even more inspired. From that moment on, he was treated as a youthful hero of the cause and recognized as such by Alexander McDougall, John Lamb, Marinus Willett, and other chieftains of the Sons of Liberty. It is worth remarking that at this juncture Hamilton sided with the radical camp, along with the artisans and mechanics, rather than with the more circumspect merchant class he later led. Hamilton had immigrated to North America to gratify his ambition and successfully seized the opportunity to distinguish himself. Both then and forever after, the poor boy from the West Indies commanded attention with the force and fervor of his words. Once Hamilton was initiated into the cause of American liberty, his life acquired an even more headlong pace that never slackened.

As rumors of the militant commotion at the Common filtered back to the college, Dr. Myles Cooper must have been appalled that the orphan whom he had treated so indulgently was now fraternizing with disreputable elements. Cooper maligned the Sons of Liberty as the "sons of licentiousness, faction, and confusion."[42] The situation was an awkward one for Cooper, who was tugging his forelock at royal authority while Hamilton was thumbing his nose at it. Exactly three months before, the college president had published an obsequious open letter to William Tryon, the departing royal governor, that was a classic of unctuous prose and that concluded, "We can only say, that as long as the society shall have any existence and wherever its voice can extend, the name of TRYON will be celebrated among the worthiest of its benefactors."[43]

Hamilton contended that he was "greatly attached" to Cooper, and in ordinary times he might have been a fond disciple.[44] Cooper was a witty published poet, a Greek and Latin scholar, and a worldly bachelor with epicurean tastes. In a portrait by John Singleton Copley, he has a smooth, well-fed face and stares sideways at the viewer in a smug, self-assured manner. On the tiny King's faculty, it was Cooper who likely tutored Hamilton in Latin, Greek, theology, and moral philosophy.

Cooper had been recommended for the King's presidency by the archbishop of Canterbury and was in many respects an outstanding choice. In little more than a decade, he had inaugurated a medical school, enlarged the library, added professors, and even launched an art collection. Like John Witherspoon, he boasted a roster of distinguished pupils, including John Jay, Robert R. Livingston, Gouverneur Morris, Benjamin Moore, and Hamilton. In 1774, Cooper had intensified the overriding quest of his presidency, for a charter that would convert King's College into a royal university. Then the Revolution blasted his hopes. He found the revolt at first an irritant, then an outrage, then a mortal threat to his ambitions. He could not afford to be a neutral bystander and began to flay the protesters in caustic essays, claiming that the tea tax was exceedingly mild. "The people of Boston are a crooked and perverse generation . . . and deserve to forfeit their charter," he wrote.[45] With such retrograde views, he became one of New York's most despised Loyalists and was increasingly assailed by his students. Samuel Clossy also grew disgusted with the turmoil and returned to the British Isles.

Colonial resistance began to assume a more organized shape. By late August 1774, all the colonies save Georgia had picked their delegates to the First Continental Congress. The New York delegates, among them John Jay and James Duane, departed for Philadelphia amid stirring fanfare. One newspaper reported, "They were accompanied to the place of their departure by a number of the inhabitants, with colours flying and music playing and loud huzzas at the end of each street."[46] It was not an assembly of dogmatic extremists who sat in Windsor chairs for six weeks in the red-and-black brick structure known as Carpenters' Hall. Far from being bent on fighting for independence, these law-abiding delegates offered up a public prayer that war might be averted. They reaffirmed their loyalty as British subjects, hoped for a peaceful accommodation with London, and scrupulously honored legal forms. Yet there were limits to their patience. The congress formed a Continental Association to enforce a total trade embargo—no exports, no imports, not even consumption of British wares—until the Coercive Acts were repealed. Every community was instructed to assemble committees to police the ban, and when New York chose its members that November, many of Hamilton's friends, including Hercules Mulligan, appeared among their numbers.

Even though John Adams had found Jay and Duane far too timid for his tastes, the Continental Congress's actions stunned Tory sentiment in New York. For Myles Cooper, the meeting had been a satanic den of sedition, which he acidly condemned in two widely read pamphlets. He informed the startled colonists that "subjects of Great Britain are the happiest people on earth."[47] Far from criticizing Parliament, he maintained that "the behavior of the colonies has been intolerable."[48] He then poured vitriol on the congress's initiatives: "To think of succeeding by force of arms or by starving the nation into compliance is a proof of shameful ignorance, pride, and stupidity."[49] Like many people, he scorned the notion that the colonies could ever defeat Britain's invincible military. "To believe America able to withstand England is a dreadful infatuation."[50]

Myles Cooper was not the only Anglican clergyman in New York to rail against the Continental Congress. He formed part of a Loyalist literary clique that included Charles Inglis, later rector of Trinity Church, and Samuel Seabury, the Anglican rector of the town of Westchester. Seabury was a redoubtable man of massive physique and learned mind. Educated at Yale and Oxford, he was very pompous and wrote prose that bristled with energetic intelligence. Because Westchester had been granted special privileges by a royal charter, local farmers felt especially threatened by the trade embargo. So after the Continental Congress adjourned, Seabury, with the full knowledge of Myles Cooper, launched a series of pamphlets under the pseudonym "A Westchester Farmer." (The title cunningly echoed John Dickinson's famous polemic against parliamentary taxation, *Letters from a Farmer in Pennsylvania.*) Seabury's blistering essays reviled the officers of the new Continental Association as "a venomous brood of scorpions" who would "sting us to death," and he suggested that they be greeted with hickory sticks.[51] He appealed cleverly to farmers by warning that they would be the major casualties of any trade boycott against Britain. If merchants could not import goods from Britain, would they not then hike their prices to farmers? As he wrote, "From the day the exports from this province are stopped, the farmers may date the commencement of their ruin. Can you live without money?"[52]

After the first installment of Seabury's invective was published by James Rivington in the *New-York Gazetteer,* the paper reported a febrile patriotic response, especially among Hamilton's newfound companions: "We can assure the public that at a late meeting of exotics, styled the Sons of Liberty," the "Farmer" essay was introduced, "and after a few pages being read to the company, they agreed . . . to commit it to the flames, without the benefit of clergy, though many, very many indeed, could neither write nor read."[53] To drive home the point, some copies were tarred and feathered and slapped on whipping posts. Nonetheless, the essay made a huge popular impression and demonstrated that the patriots were being outgunned by Tory pamphleteers and needed a literary champion of their own.

Seabury gave Hamilton what he always needed for his best work: a hard, strong position to contest. The young man gravitated to controversy, indeed gloried in it. In taking on Seabury, Hamilton might have suspected—and may well have *enjoyed*—the little secret that he was combating an Anglican cleric in Myles Cooper's inner circle. He had to tread stealthily and keep his name out of print. (Most political essays at the time were published anonymously anyway.) Eager to make his mark, Hamilton was motivated by a form of ambition much esteemed in the eighteenth century—what he later extolled as the "love of fame, the ruling passion of the noblest minds, which would prompt a man to plan and undertake extensive and arduous enterprises for the public benefit."[54] Ambition was reckless if inspired by purely selfish motives but laudable if guided by great principles. In this, his first great performance in print, Hamilton placed his ambition at the service of lofty ideals.

On December 15, 1774, the *New-York Gazetteer* ran an advertisement for a newly published pamphlet entitled "A Full Vindication of the Measures of the Congress" that promised to answer "The Westchester Farmer." The farmer's sophistry would be "exposed, his cavils confuted, his artifices detected, and his wit ridiculed."[55] This thirty-five-page essay had been written in two or three weeks by Hamilton, as he entered the fray with all the grandiloquence and learning at his disposal. He showed himself proficient at elegant insults, an essential literary talent at the time, and possessing a precocious knowledge of history, philosophy, politics, economics, and law. In retrospect, it was clear that he had found his calling as a fearless, swashbuckling intellectual warrior who excelled in bare-knuckled controversy.

By the time of "A Full Vindication," Hamilton had clearly assumed the coloring of his environment. Few immigrants have renounced their past more unequivocally or adopted their new country more wholeheartedly. "I am neither merchant, nor farmer," he now wrote, just a year and a half after leaving St. Croix. "I address you because I wish well to my country": New York.[56] Hamilton reviewed the Boston Tea Party and the punitive measures that had ensued in Boston, including "license [of] the murder of its inhabitants" by British troops.[57] Hamilton supported the Tea Party culprits and faulted the British for punishing the whole province instead of just the perpetrators. He voiced the increasingly popular complaints about taxation without representation and defended the trade embargo, insisting that England would suffer drastic harm. Sounding more like the later Jefferson than the later Hamilton, he evoked an England burdened by debt and taxes and corrupted by luxuries.

In many places, "A Full Vindication" was verbose and repetitive. What foreshadowed Hamilton's mature style was the lawyerly fashion in which he grounded his argument in natural law, colonial charters, and the British constitution. He already showed little patience with halfway measures that prolonged problems instead of solving them crisply. "When the political salvation of any community is depending, it is incumbent upon those who are set up as its guardians to embrace such measures as have justice, vigor, and a probability of success to recommend them."[58] Most impressive was Hamilton's shrewd insight into the psychology of power. Of the British prime minister, Lord North, he wrote with exceptional acuity:

> The Premier has advanced too far to recede with safety: he is deeply interested to execute his purpose, if possible. . . . In common life, to retract an error even in the beginning is no easy task. Perseverance confirms us in it and rivets the difficulty. . . . To this we may add that disappointment and opposition inflame the minds of men and attach them still more to their mistakes.[59]

After Seabury rebutted "A Full Vindication," Hamilton struck back with "The Farmer Refuted," an eighty-page tour de force that Rivington brought out on February 23, 1775. More than twice the length of its predecessor, this second essay betrayed a surer grasp of politics and economics. Seabury had mocked Hamilton's maiden performance and now suffered the consequences. "Such is my opinion of your abilities as a critic," Hamilton addressed him directly, "that I very much prefer your disapprobation to your applause."[60] As if Seabury were the young upstart and not vice versa, Hamilton taunted his riposte as "puerile and fallacious" and stated that "I will venture to pronounce it one of the most ludicrous performances which has been exhibited to public view during all the present controversy."[61] This slashing style of attack would make Hamilton the most feared polemicist in America, but it won him enemies as well as admirers. Unlike Franklin or Jefferson, he never learned to subdue his opponents with a light touch or a sly, artful, understated turn of phrase.

Like most colonists, Hamilton still hoped for amity with England and complained that the colonists were being denied the full liberties of British subjects. In justifying American defiance of British taxation, he elaborated the fashionable argument that the colonies owed their allegiance to the British king, not to Parliament. The point was critical, for if the colonies were linked only to the king, they could, theoretically, wriggle free from parliamentary control while creating some form of commonwealth status in the British empire. Indeed, Hamilton cast himself as "a warm advocate for limited monarchy and an unfeigned well-wisher to the present royal family."[62] In what became his trademark style, he displayed exhaustive research, tracing royal charters for North America back to Queen Elizabeth and showing that no powers had been reserved to Parliament. In one glowing passage, Hamilton invoked the colonists' natural rights: "The sacred rights of mankind are not to be rummaged for among old parchments or musty records. They are written, as with a sunbeam, in the whole *volume* of human nature by the hand of the divinity itself and can never be erased or obscured by mortal power."[63] These lines echo John Dickinson, who had written that the essential rights to happiness are bestowed by God, not man. "They are not annexed to us by parchments and seals."[64] Hamilton added beauty and rhythm to the expression.

Clearly, Hamilton was reading the skeptical Scottish philosopher David Hume, and he quoted his view that in framing a government "*every man* ought to be supposed a *knave* and to have no other end in all his actions but *private interests.*" The task of government was not to stop selfish striving—a hopeless task—but to harness it for the public good. In starting to outline the contours of his own vision of government, Hamilton was spurred by Hume's dark vision of human nature, which corresponded to his own. At one point, while talking about the advantages that England derived from colonial trade, he said, "And let me tell you, in this selfish, rapacious world, a little discretion is, at worst, only a *venial* sin."[65] That chilling aside—a "selfish, rapacious world"—speaks volumes about the darkness of Hamilton's upbringing.

With "The Farmer Refuted," the West Indian student became an eloquent booster of his chosen country and asserted the need for unity to resist British oppression. "If the sword of oppression be permitted to lop off one limb without opposition, reiterated strokes will soon dismember the whole body."[66] He already took the long view of American destiny, seeing that the colonies would someday overtake the mother country in economic power. "If we look forward to a period not far distant, we shall perceive that the productions of our country will infinitely exceed the demands, which Great Britain and her connections can possibly have for them. And as we shall then be greatly advanced in population, our wants will be proportionably increased."[67] Here, in embryonic form, is his vision of the vast, diversified economy that was to emerge after independence.

"The Farmer Refuted" was a bravura performance, flashing with prophetic insights. While the British disputed that America could win a war of independence, Hamilton accurately predicted that France and Spain would aid the colonies. The twenty-year-old student anticipated the scrappy, opportunistic military strategy that would defeat the British:

> Let it be remembered that there are no large plains for the two armies to meet in and decide the conquest. . . . The circumstances of our country put it in our power to evade a pitched battle. It will be better policy to harass and exhaust the soldiery by frequent skirmishes and incursions than to take the open field with them, by which means they would have the full benefit of their superior regularity and skills. Americans are better qualified for that kind of fighting which is most adapted to this country than regular troops.[68]

This was Washington's strategy, compressed into a nutshell and articulated even before the fighting broke out at Lexington and Concord. This was more than just precocious knowledge: this was intuitive judgment of the highest order.

As rumors went around that Hamilton had authored the two "Farmer" essays, many New Yorkers, Myles Cooper included, dismissed the notion as preposterous. "I remember that in a conversation I once had with Dr. Cooper," said Robert Troup, "he insisted that Mr. Jay must be the author[,] . . . it being absurd to imagine [that] so young a man" as Hamilton could have written it.[69] Others attributed the pieces to much more established figures, such as William Livingston. Hamilton must have been flattered by the fuss and his literary club deeply amused. In a city with a dearth of republican pamphleteers, Hamilton represented an important recruit to the cause. He had demonstrated inimitable speed (the two "Farmer" essays totaled sixty thousand words), supreme confidence in his views, and an easy, sophisticated grasp of the issues. He was to be a true child of the Revolution, growing up along with his new country and gaining in strength and wisdom as the hostilities mounted.

FOUR

THE PEN AND
THE SWORD

B y the time Hamilton wrote "The Farmer Refuted," the British Parliament
had declared Massachusetts to be in a state of rebellion and ratified the
king's unswerving determination to adopt all measures necessary to compel
obedience. On the night of April 18, 1775, eight hundred British troops marched
out of Boston to capture Samuel Adams and John Hancock and seize a stockpile of
patriot munitions in Concord. As they passed Lexington, they encountered a motley battalion of armed farmers known as Minutemen, and in the ensuing exchange
of gunfire the British killed eight colonists and then two more in Concord. As the
redcoats retreated helter-skelter to Boston, they were riddled by sniper fire that
erupted from behind hedges, stone walls, and fences, leaving a bloody trail of 273
British casualties versus ninety-five dead or wounded for the patriots.

The news reached New York within four days, and a mood of insurrection
promptly overtook the city. People gathered at taverns and on street corners to ponder events while Tories quaked. One of the latter, Judge Thomas Jones, watched exultant rebels storm by in the street "with drums beating and colours flying, attended
by a mob of negroes, boys, sailors, and pickpockets, inviting all mankind to take up
arms in defence of the 'injured rights and liberties of America,'" he said.[1] The newly
emboldened Sons of Liberty streamed down to the East River docks, pilfered ships
bound for British troops in Boston, then emptied the City Hall arsenal of its muskets, bayonets, and cartridge boxes, grabbing one thousand weapons in all.[2]

Armed with this cache, volunteer militia companies sprang up overnight, as they
did throughout the colonies. However much the British might deride these ragtag
citizen-soldiers, they conducted their business in earnest. Inflamed by the astonishing news from Massachusetts, Hamilton was that singular intellectual who picked

up a musket as fast as a pen. Nicholas Fish recalled that "immediately after the Battle of Lexington, [Hamilton] attached himself to one of the uniform companies of militia then forming for the defence of the country by the patriotic young men of this city under the command of Captain Fleming, in which he devoted much time, attending regularly all the parades and performing tours of duty with promptitude and zeal."[3] Fish and Troup were among the diligent cadre of King's College volunteers who drilled before classes each morning in the churchyard of nearby St. Paul's Chapel. Their drillmaster was Edward Fleming, who had served in a British regiment and married into the prominent De Peyster family but was still warmly attached to the American side. As a sturdy disciplinarian, Fleming was a man after Hamilton's own heart; Hamilton's son said that the fledgling volunteer company was named the Hearts of Oak, although military rolls identify the group as the Corsicans. The young recruits marched briskly past tombstones with the motto "Liberty or Death" stitched across their round leather caps. On short, snug green jackets they also sported, for good measure, red tin hearts that announced "God and Our Right."

Hamilton approached this daily routine with the same perfectionist ardor that he exhibited in his studies. Robert Troup stressed the "military spirit" infused into Hamilton and noted that he was "constant in his attendance and very ambitious of improvement."[4] Hamilton, never one to fumble an opportunity, embarked on a comprehensive military education. With his absorbent mind, he mastered infantry drills, pored over volumes on military tactics, and learned the rudiments of gunnery and pyrotechnics from a veteran bombardier. Despite the physical delicacy that Hugh Knox had observed, there was a peculiar doggedness about this young man, as if he were already in training for something far beyond humble infantry duty.

On April 24, a huge throng of patriots, some eight thousand strong, massed in front of City Hall. While radicals grew giddy with excitement, many terrified Tory merchants began to book passage for England. The next day, an anonymous handbill blamed Myles Cooper and four other "obnoxious gentlemen" for the patriotic deaths in Massachusetts and said the moment had passed for symbolic gestures, such as burning Tories in effigy. "The injury you have done to your country cannot admit of reparation," these five Loyalists were warned. "Fly for your lives or anticipate your doom by becoming your own executioners." This blatant death threat was signed, "Three Millions."[5] A defiant Myles Cooper stuck to his college post.

After a demonstration on the night of May 10, hundreds of protesters armed with clubs and heated by a heady brew of political rhetoric and strong drink descended on King's College, ready to inflict rough justice on Myles Cooper. Hercules Mulligan recalled that Cooper "was a Tory and an obnoxious man and the mob went to the college with the intention of tarring and feathering him or riding him upon a rail."[6] Nicholas Ogden, a King's alumnus, saw the angry mob swarming toward the college and raced ahead to Cooper's room, urging the president to scramble out a back window. Because Hamilton and Troup shared a room near Cooper's quarters, Ogden also alerted them to the approaching mob. "Whereupon Hamilton instantly resolved to take his stand on the stairs [i.e., the outer stoop] in front of the Doctor's apartment and there to detain the mob as long as he could by a harangue in order to gain the Doctor the more time for his escape," Troup later recorded.[7]

After the mob knocked down the gate and surged toward the residence, Hamilton launched into an impassioned speech, telling the vociferous protesters that their conduct, instead of promoting their cause, would "disgrace and injure the glorious cause of liberty."[8] One account has the slightly deaf Cooper poking his head from an upper-story window and observing Hamilton gesticulating on the stoop below. He mistakenly thought that his pupil was inciting the crowd instead of pacifying them and shouted, "Don't mind what he says. He's crazy!"[9] Another account has Cooper shouting at the ruffians: "Don't believe anything Hamilton says. He's a little fool!"[10] The more plausible version is that Cooper had long since vanished, having scampered away in his nightgown on Ogden's warning.

Hamilton likely knew he couldn't stop the intruders, but he won the vital minutes necessary for Cooper to clamber over a back fence and rush down to the Hudson. Afraid for his life, Cooper meandered along the shore all night. The next day, he boarded a man-of-war bound for England, where he resumed his tirades against the colonists from the safety of a study. Among other things, he published a melodramatic poem about his escape. He told how the rabble—"a murderous band"—had burst into his room, "And whilst their curses load my head / With piercing steel they probe the bed / And thirst for human gore."[11] This image of the president set upon by bloodthirsty rebels was more satisfying than the banal truth that he cravenly ran off half dressed into the night. Cooper never saw Hamilton again and wept copiously when England lost the Revolution. He could not resist grumbling in his will that "all my affairs have been shattered to pieces by this abominable rebellion."[12]

Of all the incidents in Hamilton's early life in America, his spontaneous defense of Myles Cooper was probably the most telling. It showed that he could separate personal honor from political convictions and presaged a recurring theme of his career: the superiority of forgiveness over revolutionary vengeance. Hamilton had shown exemplary courage. Beyond risking a terrible beating, he had taken the chance that he would sacrifice his heroic stature among the Sons of Liberty. But Hamilton always expressed himself frankly, no matter what the consequences. Most of all, the episode captured the contradictory impulses struggling inside this complex young man, a committed revolutionary with a profound dread that popular sentiment would boil over into dangerous excess. Even amid an insurrection that he supported, he fretted about the damage to constituted authority and worried about mob rule. Like other founding fathers, Hamilton would have preferred a stately revolution, enacted decorously in courtrooms and parliamentary chambers by gifted orators in powdered wigs. The American Revolution was to succeed because it was undertaken by skeptical men who knew that the same passions that toppled tyrannies could be applied to destructive ends. In a moment of acute anxiety a year earlier, John Adams had wondered what would happen if "the multitude, the vulgar, the herd, the rabble" maintained such open defiance of authority.[13]

For Hamilton and other patriotic New Yorkers, the late spring of 1775 was a season of pride, dread, hope, and confusion. When New England delegates to the Second Continental Congress swept through town en route to Philadelphia on May 6, thousands of New Yorkers jammed rooftops, stoops, and doorways to roar their approval above an incessant clanging of church bells. Since the old Loyalist assembly in New York had refused to send delegates to the First Continental Congress, it was disbanded and replaced by a New York Provincial Congress. This new body pieced together a slate of delegates to send to Philadelphia, including Philip Schuyler, Hamilton's future father-in-law, and George Clinton, his future political nemesis.

As the congress convened in the Pennsylvania State House (today's Independence Hall) on May 10, most colonists still prayed for a peaceful resolution of the standoff, though armed conflict now seemed inevitable. The Second Continental Congress lacked many of the prerequisites of an authentic government—an army, a currency, taxing power—yet it evolved in pell-mell fashion into the first government of the United States. Its most pressing task was to appoint a commander in chief. All eyes turned to a strapping, reticent Virginian who carried himself with unusual poise and wore a colonel's uniform to advertise his experience in the French and Indian War. One congressman said that George Washington was "no harum-scarum, ranting, swearing fellow, but sober, steady, and calm."[14] On June 15, Washington, forty-three, was named head of the Continental Army for reasons that transcended talent and experience. Since the fighting had thus far been restricted to New England, the choice of a Virginian signaled that this was a crusade of unified colonies, not some regional squabble. Also, with one-fifth of the population of the colonies, Virginia felt entitled to a leadership role, and the selection of Washington was the first of many efforts by the north to please and placate the south.

Two days later, at Bunker Hill—or, rather, Breed's Hill—north of Boston, a battle took place that hardly seemed at first like a patriotic victory. Americans were flushed from their elevated fortification, and more than four hundred were killed or wounded. Nevertheless, the patriotic soldiers showed great coolness under fire, and the British suffered more than one thousand casualties, including dozens of officers. "The dead lay as thick as sheep in a fold," said Colonel John Stark.[15] This first formal battle of the Revolution demolished the myth of British invincibility and raised, for the first time, the question of just how many deaths the mother country would tolerate to subjugate the colonies. The British were unhinged by the colonists' unorthodox fighting style and shocking failure to abide by gentlemanly rules of engagement. One scandalized British soldier complained that the American riflemen "conceal themselves behind trees etc. till an opportunity presents itself of taking a shot at our advance sentries, which done, they immediately retreat. What an unfair method of carrying on a war!"[16]

Following this battle, George Washington stopped in New York on his way to Cambridge, Massachusetts, to assume his command. On June 25, he crossed the Hudson on the Hoboken ferry, then proceeded along Broadway in a carriage pulled by a team of white horses, the triumphant procession moving grandly past King's College. On that glorious summer afternoon, Alexander Hamilton stood unnoticed among the delirious spectators, unaware that within two years he would serve as chief aide to the general he now observed for the first time. Probably accompanied by Major General Philip Schuyler, Washington sped by with a touch of magnificence, a purple sash across his blue uniform, and a ceremonial plume sprouting from his hat.

Hamilton had not been idle while the Second Continental Congress deliberated and urged Canadian colonists to join the fray. On the day that Washington was appointed top commander, Hamilton published the first of two letters in Rivington's paper assailing the Quebec Act, passed the previous year; the second article appeared just three days before Washington's visit. The act extended Quebec's boundaries south to the Ohio River and guaranteed full religious freedom to French-Canadian Catholics. For the patriots, this did not reflect British tolerance so much as the frightening imposition of French civil law and Roman Catholicism in a neighboring frontier area. Hamilton discerned a sinister intent behind Britain's bid to enlist the aid of the Roman Catholic clergy in Canada. "This act develops the dark designs of the ministry more fully than any thing they have done and shows that they have formed a systematic project of absolute power."[17] If Hamilton displayed some atavistic Huguenot fear of popery, he also sounded a theme that was to resonate straight through the Revolution and beyond: that the best government posture toward religion was one of passive tolerance, not active promotion of an established church.

On July 5, the Second Continental Congress made one final feeble effort to ward off further hostilities when it endorsed the Olive Branch Petition, urging a negotiated solution to the conflict with England. The document professed loyalty to the king and tactfully blamed his "artful and cruel" ministers.[18] When the haughty King George III did not deign to answer this conciliatory message, his frosty rigidity de-

moralized congressional moderates and guaranteed intensified military preparations. On August 23, the king issued a royal proclamation that his American subjects had "proceeded to open and avowed rebellion."[19] The world's most powerful
nation had now pledged itself, irrevocably, to breaking the resistance of its unruly
overseas colonists.

By coincidence, on that same night of August 23, Alexander Hamilton got his
first unforgettable taste of British military might. Everyone knew that Manhattan,
encircled by water, was vulnerable to the royal armada and would not be defensible
for long without a navy. So when the British warship *Asia* appeared in the harbor
that summer, it proved an effective instrument of terror. The New York Provincial
Congress worried that the two dozen cannon posted at Fort George at the tip of the
Battery might be seized by the British. Hamilton, joined by fifteen other King's College volunteers, signed up for a hazardous operation to drag the heavy artillery to
safety under the liberty pole on the Common. (College lore later claimed that two
of the salvaged cannon were buried under the campus green.) Lashing the cannon
with ropes, Hamilton and his fellow students rescued more than ten big guns before
a barge from the *Asia*, moored near the shore, began to strafe them with fire. The
patriots, possibly including Hamilton, returned fire as the barge darted back to the
Asia. The warship then let loose a thunderous broadside of grapeshot and cannonballs that blew a big hole in the roof of Fraunces Tavern and sent thousands of panicky residents fleeing from their beds and screaming into the streets.

As in his defense of Myles Cooper, the intrepid Hamilton displayed unusual
sangfroid. "The *Asia* fired upon the city," wrote Hercules Mulligan, "and I recollect
well that Mr. Hamilton was there, for I was engaged in hauling off one of the cannon when Mr. H. came up and gave me his musket to hold and he took hold of the
rope." After Hamilton disposed of his ordnance, he ran into Mulligan again and
asked for his musket back, only to be told that the tailor had left it down at the
Battery—the spot most exposed to fierce shelling from the *Asia*. "I told him where
I had left it," Mulligan continued, "and he went for it notwithstanding [that] the firing continued, with as much unconcern as if the vessel had not been there."[20]

During an autumn term that allowed little time for leisure, Hamilton found himself in a new predicament over the progressively more precarious situation of James
Rivington, the *New-York Gazetteer* publisher. The son of a prosperous London
bookseller, Rivington was an elegant but combative man who wore a silver wig.
When he inaugurated his newspaper in 1773 at the foot of Wall Street, he prided
himself on his political neutrality and swore that he would be receptive to all viewpoints. As shown by his relationship with Hamilton, he did not shrink from questioning Tory dogma.

Nevertheless, with the passage of time Tory opinion predominated in his paper. Rivington took an especially harsh tone toward the Sons of Liberty, with their rough-hewn, working-class followers, and singled out their leaders, Alexander Mc-Dougall and Isaac Sears, for special abuse. By September 1774, Sears retaliated with scathing letters to Rivington. "I believe you to be either an ignorant impudent pretender to what you do not understand," he wrote, "or a base servile tool, ready to do the dirty work of any knave who will purchase you."[21] Pretty soon, the rival *New-York Journal* ran lengthy lists of patriotic subscribers who felt so betrayed by Rivington that they had canceled their subscriptions to his paper. Rivington's days were numbered after Lexington and Concord. The same mob that chased Myles Cooper from King's proceeded to attack the petrified Rivington, who spent the next ten days in seclusion aboard the man-of-war *Kingfisher*. Though he returned to his print shop, his ordeal wasn't over. Later that summer, the New York Provincial Congress ruled that anyone aiding the enemy could be disarmed, imprisoned, or even exiled. Isaac Sears seized on this decision to be done with Rivington once and for all.

Though nicknamed the "king" of the New York streets, Sears was not a plebeian hero but a prosperous skipper who had worked the West Indian trade and amassed a small fortune as a privateer during the French and Indian War. On November 19, Sears gathered up a militia of nearly one hundred horsemen in Connecticut, kidnapped the Reverend Samuel Seabury, and terrorized his prisoner's family in Westchester before parading his humiliated Tory trophy through New Haven. Confined under military guard, Seabury refused to confess that he was the "Westchester Farmer" whose essays had provoked Hamilton's celebrated rebuttal. Sears's little army, turning south, then swooped down in a surprise raid on Rivington's print shop in Manhattan, planning to put it out of business. Because Hamilton poured out his anguish afterward in a letter to John Jay, this is one of the better-documented episodes of his King's College days. We also know about the fracas from another source. Probably encouraged by his old mentor, Hugh Knox, Hamilton seems to have mailed unsigned dispatches from New York to the *Royal Danish American Gazette*. These hitherto undiscovered articles give a more detailed glimpse of his life in the early days of the rebellion and fill major gaps in the sketchy documentary record of Hamilton's early career. In a report on Rivington, the anonymous correspondent wrote:

The contents of all last week's *New-York Gazetteer* occasioned Mr. Rivington, the printer, to be surprised and surrounded on the 23rd of November by 75 of the Connecticut Light horse, with firelocks and fixed bayonets, who burst into his house between twelve and one o'clock at noon, and totally destroyed all his types, and put an entire stop to his business, and reduced him at upwards of 50 years of age to the sad necessity of beginning the world again. The astonished citizens beheld the whole scene without affording the persecuted proscribed printer the least assistance. The printing of the *New-York Gazetteer* will be discontinued until America shall be blessed with the restoration of good government.[22]

Although the author of this dispatch was anonymous, who else but Hamilton would have filed such a dispatch to St. Croix? From Hercules Mulligan, we know that the one bystander who had the pluck to rise to Rivington's defense was Hamilton himself. "When Rivington's press was attacked by a company from the eastward, Mr. H., indignant that our neighbours should intrude upon our rights (although the press was considered a tory one), he went to the place, addressed the people present and offered if any others would join him to prevent these intruders from taking the type away."[23]

As with the mob assault against Myles Cooper, the scene at Rivington's became stamped on Hamilton's memory, and his horror at such mob disorder foreshadowed his fearful reaction to the French Revolution. Several days after Sears's men pillaged Rivington's shop, Hamilton wrote to John Jay and acknowledged that Rivington's press had been "dangerous and pernicious" and that the man himself was "detestable." Nevertheless, he felt obliged to condemn the lawless nature of the action:

In times of such commotion as the present, while the passions of men are worked up to an uncommon pitch, there is great danger of fatal extremes. The same state of the passions which fits the multitude, who have not a sufficient stock of reason and knowledge to guide them, for opposition to tyranny and oppression, very naturally leads them to a contempt and disregard of all authority. The due medium is hardly to be found among the more intelligent. It is almost impossible among the unthinking populace. When the minds of these are loosened from their attachment to ancient establishments and courses, they seem to grow giddy and are apt more or less to run into anarchy.[24]

Clearly, this ambivalent twenty-year-old favored the Revolution but also worried about the long-term effect of habitual disorder, especially among the uneducated masses. Hamilton lacked the temperament of a true-blue revolutionary. He saw too clearly that greater freedom could lead to greater disorder and, by a dangerous dialectic, back to a loss of freedom. Hamilton's lifelong task was to try to straddle and resolve this contradiction and to balance liberty and order.

The sequel to the print-shop raid deserves mention. James Rivington was temporarily put out of business, only to be resurrected as a "Printer to His Majesty the King" during Britain's wartime occupation of New York. Appearances could be deceiving. Even as he reviled the patriots in *The Royal Gazette,* Rivington was surreptitiously relaying British naval intelligence to Washington, sealed inside the covers of books he sold to patriotic spies. He was to be rewarded in the fullness of time.

While Rivington had been muzzled by his critics, Hamilton himself was still gripped by the publishing itch. For an ambitious young man of a broadly literary bent, polemical broadsides fired at the British ministry presented the surest road to fame. In early January 1776, a self-taught English immigrant, Thomas Paine, who had arrived in Philadelphia two years earlier, provided Hamilton with a perfect model when he anonymously published *Common Sense.* The onetime corset maker and excise officer issued a resounding call for American independence that sold a stupendous 120,000 copies by year's end.

By now, Hamilton had switched his journalistic allegiance to the stalwart republican paper of John Holt, the *New-York Journal.* He probably met Holt through William Livingston, who had cofounded the paper. In 1774, Holt had dropped the royal symbols from his masthead and replaced them with a well-known engraving that Ben Franklin had created to foster his Albany Plan of intercolonial union twenty years before: a copperhead snake sliced into segments and accompanied by the fighting slogan "Unite or Die." (In Franklin's version, "Join or Die.") Robert Troup said that Hamilton published many articles while at King's, "particularly in the newspaper then edited in New York by John Holt, who was a zealous Whig."[25] Nor had Hamilton given up on poetry. He constantly scribbled doggerel, rhyme, and satirical verse and gave Troup a thick sheaf of these poems, which the latter proceeded to lose during the Revolution.

Oddly, the otherwise thorough editors of Hamilton's papers have reprinted his essays published by the Tory Rivington but have omitted his collaborations with the dissident Holt. Hamilton's contemporaries knew him as the nameless scribe behind some of the *New-York Journal*'s most trenchant editorials. "I hope Mr. Hamilton continues busy," John Jay told Alexander McDougall on December 5, 1775. "I have not received Holt's paper these three months and therefore cannot judge of the progress he makes."[26] In fact, Hamilton's contributions were evident there. From November 9, 1775, to February 8, 1776, the *New-York Journal* ran fourteen installments of "The Monitor," probably the longest and most prominently featured string of essays that Holt printed before the Revolution. In this series, Hamilton recapitulated the central theme of his anti-"Farmer" essays that the colonies owed their fealty to the king, not to Parliament. Although Hamilton later retracted some of his more hot-blooded opinions, such as his opposition to standing armies, and though he may have regretted his withering mockery of statesmen, royalty, popes, and priests, many of the essays are vintage Hamilton.

In "The Monitor," Hamilton left many clues to his authorship. Echoing his 1769 letter to Edward Stevens, in which he bemoaned the "grovelling" life of a clerk, he now warned his comrades against "a grovelling disposition" that would degrade them "from the rank of freemen to that of slaves."[27] He expressed views of leadership that closely anticipate his later dicta about the need for decisive, unequivocal action: "In public exigencies, there is hardly anything more prejudicial than excessive caution, timidity and dilatoriness, as there is nothing more beneficial than vigour, enterprise and expedition."[28] At times, he repeated his anti-"Farmer" essays almost verbatim, saying of the British ministry, "They have advanced too far to retreat without equal infamy and danger; their honour, their credit, their existence as ministers, perhaps their life itself, depend upon their success in the present undertaking."[29] Like many prolific authors, Hamilton sometimes quoted himself unwittingly.

The "Monitor" essays reveal Hamilton as an anomalous revolutionary. At the outset, he shows the rousing optimism about the revolutionary future that is the stock-in-trade of radical prose. He delivers a paean to America's destiny as he prophesies that after the war the country will be elevated "to a much higher pitch of grandeur, opulence, and power than we could ever attain to by a humble submission to arbitrary rule."[30] Yet this hopefulness is hedged by a somber view of human affairs. Hamilton lauds the conduct of his countrymen but cannot refrain from saying sardonically that "it is a melancholy truth that the behaviour of many among us might serve as the severest satire upon the [human] species. It has been a compound of inconsistency, falsehood, cowardice, selfishness and dissimulation."[31] Hamilton also displays a swooning fascination with martyrdom, telling the colonists that they should vow either to "lead an honourable life or to meet with resignation a glorious death."[32] This idea so bewitched him that he ended one "Monitor" essay with a quote from Pope's *Iliad* that begins: "Death is the worst, a fate which all must try; / And, for our country, 'tis a bliss to die."[33]

Hamilton dashed off the "Monitor" essays at the frenetic pace of one a week—the more incredible as he was still a student and dutifully attending drills in the St. Paul's churchyard each morning. Even this did not exhaust the scope of his activities. This peerless undergraduate had begun preliminary legal studies and was combing the superb law library at King's, steeping himself in the works of Sir

William Blackstone and Sir Edward Coke. As he later said, by "steady and laborious exertion" he had qualified for a bachelor's degree and was able "to lay a foundation, by preparatory study, for the future profession of the law."[34] Hamilton probably spent little more than two years at King's and never formally graduated due to the outbreak of the Revolution. By April 6, 1776, King's College, tarred by its earlier association with Myles Cooper, was commandeered by patriot forces and put to use as a military hospital.

After Hamilton published his last "Monitor" installment on February 8, he parlayed his budding fame as a pamphleteer into a military appointment that perfectly suited his daydreams of martial glory. On February 18, he sent a personal dispatch to the *Royal Danish American Gazette* that announced he was joining the military. The unsigned letter was filled with grim forebodings of martyrdom: "It is uncertain whether it may ever be in my power to send you another line. . . . I am going into the army and perhaps ere long may be destined to seal with my blood the sentiments defended by my pen. Be it so, if heaven decree it. I was born to die and my reason and conscience tell me it is impossible to die in a better or more important cause."[35]

What prompted this declaration was that the Provincial Congress had decided to raise an artillery company to defend New York, providing another chance for the upwardly mobile West Indian to excel. Like most revolutions, this one made ample room for talented outsiders. Luckily for Hamilton, Alexander McDougall was in charge of forming New York's first patriotic regiment. A fiery, pugnacious Scot and former ship captain, McDougall was yet another Presbyterian protégé of William Livingston, who may have provided the introduction. While at King's, Hamilton borrowed political pamphlets from McDougall and was mortified when they were stolen from his room.

On February 23, the Provincial Congress reported that "Col. McDougall recommended Mr. *Alexander Hamilton* for Capt. of a Company of Artillery."[36] Robert Troup said that McDougall prodded John Jay (by this time William Livingston's son-in-law) to wrangle the coveted commission for Hamilton. After being examined, Hamilton received the assignment on March 14, 1776. When doubts arose about this student's fitness to lead an artillery company, McDougall and Jay persuasively overcame them. Right before Hamiliton received his appointment, he was approached by Elias Boudinot on behalf of Lord Stirling, who had been elevated to brigadier general and desired Hamilton as his military aide. The headstrong Hamilton shrank from being subordinate to anyone and rebuffed an offer that would have tempted his peers. Boudinot informed a disappointed Stirling that Hamilton had accepted an artillery command and "was therefore denied the pleasure of attending your Lordship's person as Brigade Major."[37]

Hercules Mulligan contended that Hamilton's appointment as artillery captain was premised on the condition that he would muster thirty men; Mulligan bragged that he and Hamilton recruited twenty-five the first afternoon alone. Hamilton assumed an almost paternal responsibility for the sixty-eight men who eventually came under his command. Some of them were illiterate and entered marks instead of signatures into the so-called pay book where Hamilton kept track of their food, clothing, pay, and discipline. According to tradition, he took money from his St. Croix subscription fund and used it to equip his company. He later wrote, "Military pride is to be excited and kept up by military parade. No time ought to be lost in teaching the recruits the use of arms."[38]

The twenty-one-year-old captain became a popular leader known for sharing hardships with his gunners and bombardiers. He was sensitive to inequities and lobbied to get the same pay and rations for his men as their counterparts in the Continental Army. As a firm believer in meritocracy, he favored promotion from within his company, a policy adopted by the New York Provincial Congress. His subordinates remembered him as tough but fair-minded. Years later, one of them retained Hamilton as a lawyer, even though he had become a vocal political enemy. When Hamilton questioned the wisdom of this, the ex-soldier replied, "I served in your company during the war and I know you will do me justice in spite of my rudeness."[39]

Throughout his career, Hamilton was fastidious about military dress, insisting that his men be properly attired. "Nothing is more necessary than to stimulate the vanity of soldiers," he later wrote. "To this end a smart dress is essential. When not attended to, the soldier is exposed to ridicule and humiliation."[40] His men wore blue coats with brass buttons and buff collars and white shoulder belts strapped diagonally across their chests. Within four months, he had secured seventy-five pairs of buckskin breeches for his men and personally advanced them money if needed. Hamilton's company looked and acted the part. "As soon as his company was raised," said Troup, "he proceeded with indefatigable pains to perfect it in every branch of discipline and duty and it was not long before it was esteemed the most beautiful model of discipline in the whole army."[41] Later on, as a major general, Hamilton instructed his officers on the need to be personally involved in drilling and training their men.

Hamilton betrayed none of the novice's typical air of slipshod indecision and made a profound impression on several senior military figures, who joined his swelling circle of admirers. One day, General Nathanael Greene, an ex-Quaker and former ironmonger from Rhode Island, was crossing the Common when Hamilton caught his eye. He was struck by how smartly this young man put his troops through their parade exercises and paused to chat with him. He then invited Hamilton to dinner and was thunderstruck by his immense military knowledge. The largely self-educated Greene was well placed to appreciate Hamilton's instant expertise, for his own military background was restricted to two years of militia duty. Most of what he knew about war was also gleaned from books. "His knowledge was intuitive," artillery chief Henry Knox later said of Greene. "He came to us the rawest and most untutored human being I ever met with, but in less than twelve months he was equal in military knowledge to any general officer in the army."[42] George Washington valued Nathanael Greene above all his other generals, and it was likely Greene who first touted Hamilton's merits to Washington. Like Lord Stirling, Greene may even have offered Hamilton a job as his military aide. If so, Hamilton again spurned a general's offer.

After Boston fell to the Continental Army in March—a shock for the British and a tonic to patriotic spirits—New York loomed as the next battlefront, and the city braced for impending invasion. Hamilton had already informed his distant St. Croix readers, "This city is at present evacuated by above one half of its inhabitants under the influence of a general panic."[43] Starting in March, Lord Stirling had supervised four thousand men who sealed off major streets and strung a network of batteries and earthworks across Manhattan from the Hudson to the East River. Hamilton's company constructed a small fort with twelve cannon on the high ground of Bayard's Hill, near the present-day intersection of Canal and Mulberry Streets.

In April, Washington came down from New England to oversee military preparations in New York and employed as his headquarters a Hudson River mansion called Richmond Hill, later the home of Aaron Burr. By a curious coincidence, Burr, fresh from the failed patriot assault on Quebec, visited Washington in June and accepted his offer to serve on his military staff, or "family," as it was known. By some accounts, the aristocratic young Burr had grandiose expectations and imagined that Washington would confer with him on grand matters of strategy. When he realized that he would be relegated to more prosaic duties, he quickly quit in disgust and sent a letter to Washington protesting that less-qualified men had been promoted ahead of him. He then went to work for Major General Israel Putnam. Something about Aaron Burr—his penchant for intrigue, a lack of sufficient deference, perhaps his insatiable chasing after women—grated on George Washington. Much of Burr's political future was shaped by his decidedly cool wartime relations with Washington, while other contemporaries, Hamilton being the prime example, profited from the general's approbation.

During this period, Washington was at least marginally aware of Hamilton. An exacting captain, Hamilton ordered the arrest of a sergeant, two corporals, and a private for "mutiny," and they received mild punishments in a court-martial. Washington pardoned the two principal offenders before issuing general orders for Hamilton to assemble his company on May 15, 1776, "at ten o'clock next Sunday morning upon the Common."[44] A month later, as we learn from the *Royal Danish American Gazette,* Hamilton gallantly led a nighttime attack of one hundred men against the Sandy Hook lighthouse outside New York harbor. "I continued the attack for two hours with fieldpieces and small arms," the war correspondent–cum–artillery captain reported, "being all that time between two smart fires from the shipping and the lighthouse, but could make no impression on the walls."[45] Hamilton did not lose any men and said the raid miscarried because he lacked sufficient munitions and because the enemy had been tipped off to the attack. With the speed of youthful dreams, Hamilton had moved from the fantasy to the reality of combat leadership.

Back in Manhattan, the young captain found a city engaged in a spree of wanton violence against Tory sympathizers. Many Loyalists were subjected to a harrowing ritual known as "riding the rail," in which they were carried through the streets sitting astride a sharp rail borne by two tall, strong men. The prisoners' names were proclaimed at each street corner as spectators lustily cheered their humiliation. One bystander reported, "We had some grand Tory rides in the city this week. . . . Several of them were handled very roughly, being carried through the streets on rails, their clothes torn off their backs and their bodies pretty well mingled with the dust. . . . There is hardly a Tory face to be seen this morning."[46]

Because New York had been a citadel of Tory sentiment, there was a pervasive fear of clandestine plots being hatched against Washington, whose capture or assassination would have been an inestimable prize to the British. Indeed, the former New York governor, William Tryon, tried to orchestrate just such a plan. On June 21, as Hamilton returned from Sandy Hook, a cabal to murder General Washington and recruit a Loyalist force to aid the British was laid bare. New York's Tory mayor, David Mathews, was charged "with dangerous designs and treasonable conspiracies against the rights and liberties of the United Colonies of America."[47] Others implicated in this shocking plot included several members of Washington's personal guard, especially Sergeant Thomas Hickey. Mayor Mathews admitted to having contact with the British and was imprisoned in Connecticut, but a defiant Hickey produced no witnesses at his court-martial and was sentenced to death.

Hamilton regaled his St. Croix readers with these dramatic events, telling them that "a most barbarous and infernal plot has been discovered among our Tories." He sketched a widespread conspiracy, the goal of which was to "murder all the staff officers, blow up the magazines, and secure the passes of the town."[48] On June 28, nearly twenty thousand spectators—virtually every person still in town, Hamilton included—turned out in a meadow near the Bowery to watch Thomas Hickey mount the gallows. The prisoner had remained unrepentant, and Washington decided to make an example of him. Hickey waived the presence of a chaplain, explaining that "they are all cutthroats."[49] He kept up his air of bravado until the hangman slipped the noose and blindfold over his head, at which point he briefly wiped away tears. Moments later, his body hung slack from the gallows. In his second dispatch on this sensational event, Hamilton applauded Washington's swift justice. "It is hoped the remainder of those miscreants now in our possession will meet with a punishment adequate to their crimes."[50] Hamilton might have ended his dispatch there. Instead, in a curious non sequitur, the future treasury secretary reported rumors that copper coins made with base metal alloys would be called in, possibly replaced by new continental copper coins of larger size. Evidently, the young captain was boning up on monetary policy.

Within days of Hickey's execution, King George III revealed just how far he was prepared to go to crush his refractory colonies. The world's foremost naval power began to gather a massive armada of battleships and transports at Sandy Hook, the prelude to the largest amphibious assault of the eighteenth century. An assemblage of military might was soon marshaled—some three hundred ships and thirty-two thousand men, including eighty-four hundred Hessian mercenaries—a fighting force designed expressly to intimidate the Americans and restore them to their sanity through a terrifying show of strength. The British had so many troops stationed aboard this floating city that they surpassed in numbers the patriotic soldiers and citizens left facing them in New York.

Entrenched in southern Manhattan, with fewer than twenty thousand inexperienced soldiers at his disposal and lacking even a single warship, Washington must have wondered how he could possibly defeat this well-oiled fighting machine. He was making "every preparation" for an imminent assault, he wrote, but conceded that his army was "extremely deficient in arms . . . and in great distress for want of them."[51] To remedy a grave shortage of ammunition, the New York Provincial Congress ordered that lead be peeled from roofs and windows and melted down to make bullets. So many trees had already been chopped down for firewood that New York resembled a ghost town. "To see the vast number of houses shut up, one would think the city almost evacuated," one fleeing Tory wrote. "Women and children are scarcely to be seen in the streets."[52]

On July 2, the British battle plan began to unfold as General William Howe directed ships commanded by his brother, Admiral Lord Richard Howe, to sail up through the Narrows. Thousands of redcoats disembarked on Staten Island. From Manhattan wharves and rooftops, Continental Army soldiers stared flabbergasted at the interminable procession of imposing vessels crowding into the harbor. Surveying a bay thick with British masts, one American soldier said that it resembled "a wood of pine trees." "I could not believe my eyes. I declare that I thought all London was afloat."[53] Captain Hamilton and his artillery company, posted at the Battery, had an unobstructed view of the enemy.

It seemed an inauspicious moment for the threatened colonies to declare independence, and yet that is exactly what they did. Faced with the military strength of the most colossal empire since ancient Rome, they decided to fight back. On July 2, the Continental Congress unanimously adopted a resolution calling for independence, with only New York abstaining. Two days later, the congress endorsed the Declaration of Independence in its final, edited form. (The actual signing was deferred until August 2.) There was nothing impetuous or disorderly about this action. Even amid a state of open warfare, these law-abiding men felt obligated to issue a formal document, giving a dispassionate list of their reasons for secession. This solemn, courageous act flew in the face of historical precedent. No colony had ever succeeded in breaking away from the mother country to set up a self-governing state, and the declaration signers knew that the historical odds were heavily stacked against them. They further knew that treason was a crime punishable by death, a threat that scarcely seemed abstract as reports trickled into Philadelphia of the formidable fleet bearing down on New York.

The Declaration of Independence did not achieve sacred status for many years and was not even officially inscribed on parchment for another two weeks. Instead, a Philadelphia printer, John Dunlap, ran off about five hundred broadsides that were distributed by fast riders throughout the colonies. On July 6, while Captain Hamilton wandered about trying to find a purse with money that he had lost—he sometimes had a touch of the absentminded genius—the local press announced independence. Two days later, Washington held a printed copy of the declaration in his hands for the first time. The next day, the New York Provincial Congress ratified the document, and at 6:00 P.M. Washington gathered all his troops on the Common—the very same Common where Hamilton had debuted as a speaker—to hear the stirring manifesto read aloud. As the rapt soldiers listened, they learned that "the United Colonies" of America had been declared "*Free and Independent States.*"[54]

The long-awaited words triggered a rush of patriotic exuberance. Militiamen and civilians barreled down Broadway, destroying every relic of British influence in their path, including royal arms painted on tavern signs. At Bowling Green, at the foot of Broadway, they mobbed a gilded equestrian statue of George III, portrayed in Roman garb, that had been erected to celebrate the repeal of the Stamp Act. John Adams had once admired this "beautiful ellipsis of land, railed in with solid iron, in the center of which is a statue of his majesty on horseback, very large, of solid lead, gilded with gold, on a pedestal of marble, very high."[55] Now, for reasons both symbolic and practical, the crowd pulled George III down from his pedestal, decapitating him in the process. The four thousand pounds of gilded lead was rushed off to Litchfield, Connecticut, where it was melted down to make 42,088 musket bullets. One wit predicted that the king's soldiers "will probably have melted majesty fired at them."[56]

The action boosted morale in the besieged city at a time of imminent peril. On July 12, the British decided to throw the fear of God into the rebels and test their defenses by sending the *Phoenix*, a forty-four-gun battleship, and the *Rose*, a twenty-eight-gun frigate, past southern Manhattan with guns blazing. Undeterred by fire from the Manhattan shore, the two ships raced up the Hudson, peppering several New York rooftops with cannonballs and sailing by unscathed. The din from the shelling was deafening. Hamilton commanded four of the biggest cannon in the patriotic arsenal and stood directly in the British line of fire. Hercules Mulligan recalled, "Capt. Hamilton went on the Battery with his company and his piece of artillery and commenced a brisk fire upon the *Phoenix* and *Rose* then sailing up the river, when his cannon burst and killed two of his men who . . . were buried in the Bowling Green."[57] Actually, Hamilton's exploding cannon may have killed as many as six of his men and wounded four or five others. Some critics blamed inadequate training for the mishap, but the general dissipation of troops addicted to whoring and drinking was more likely to blame. Lieutenant Isaac Bangs reported that many cannon at the Battery had been abandoned by troops who "were at their cups and at their usual place of abode, viz., on the Holy Ground."[58] Of the specific incident involving Hamilton's men, Bangs wrote that "by the carelessness of our own artillery men, six men were killed with our own cannon and several others very badly wounded. It is said that several of the company out of which they were killed were drunk and neglected to sponge, worm, and stop the vent and the cartridges took fire while they were ramming them down."[59] (In other words, the men hadn't swabbed out the sparks and powder after the previous firing.) That Hamilton was never reprimanded and that his military reputation only improved suggests that he was never faulted for the fatal mishap. However, crushed by the incident, he quickly learned that war was a filthy business.

By August 17, New York's population stood in such grave danger that Washington urged residents to evacuate immediately; only five thousand civilians of a prewar population of twenty-five thousand remained. With a condescension typical of the British command, Lord Howe's secretary, Ambrose Serle, snickered at the rebel forces as "the strangest that was ever collected: old men of 60, boys of 14, and blacks of all ages and ragged for the most part, compose the motley crew."[60] Washington had dispersed his tattered forces across Manhattan and Brooklyn. After crossing the East River to scout out the terrain, Hamilton doubted that the Continental Army could defend Brooklyn Heights against a concerted British onslaught. Hercules Mulligan recalled a dinner at his home at which Hamilton and the Reverend John Mason agreed on the need for a tactical retreat from Brooklyn, lest the Continental Army be wiped out. After they had "retired from the table, they were lamenting the situation of the army on Long Island and suggesting the best plans for its removal when Mr. Mason and Mr. Hamilton determined to write an anonymous letter to Gen[era]l Washington pointing out their ideas of the best means to draw off the army."[61] Mulligan transmitted this plan to one of Washington's aides, to no avail.

Hamilton proved dolefully accurate in his predictions. On August 22, the British began to transfer a huge invasion force across the Narrows from Staten Island to Brooklyn. Within a few days, British redcoats and Hessian mercenaries on Long Island numbered around twenty thousand, or more than twice the number of able-bodied Americans. Following a deceptive lull of several days, the British soldiers then advanced north through quaint Dutch and English farming villages. Moving through marsh and meadow, they leveled homes, flattened fences, uprooted crops in their paths, and slaughtered the inexperienced American soldiers. They took different routes, but their common objective was to reach and breach the patriotic fortifications erected on Brooklyn Heights. Although Washington rushed in reinforcements from Manhattan, the battle of Brooklyn turned into a full-blown fiasco with the patriots heavily outgunned. About 1,200 Americans were killed or captured, dwarfing British losses, and it looked as if Washington's army was now trapped in a vise, with the British Army in front and the East River at its back. The British had a chance to smash the revolt with one decisive blow.

It is commonly said that Hamilton took no part in the battle, yet an unnamed correspondent for the *Royal Danish American Gazette* submitted a narrative of his own involvement. One suspects the dispatch was Hamilton's handiwork, though the author identified himself only as a member of the "Pennsylvania troops." Along with Maryland and Delaware troops, these soldiers were commanded by Hamilton's hard-drinking former patron, Lord Stirling, and they displayed great valor. In the words of Stirling's biographer, "Neither he nor anyone else could have predicted that this overweight, rheumatic, vain, pompous, gluttonous inebriate would be so ardent in battle."[62] The St. Croix correspondent credited the bravery of Stirling's men, who defended a weak position with "but few cannon to defend them." He also explained the strategy behind Washington's famous nocturnal retreat across the East River on the night of August 29, saying that Washington feared that British men-of-war would sail upriver the next day and sever his access to Manhattan. The author told how in a cold, steady drizzle, "we received orders to quit our station about two o'clock this morning and had made our retreat almost to the ferry when General Washington ordered us back to that part of the line we were first at, which was reckoned to be the most dangerous post."[63] The reporter's company, stranded on a spit of land, crouched within easy musket-fire range of the dozing British troops but were screened by darkness and thick, rolling fog. At dawn, the author and his men scurried safely aboard one of the last ships to slide away from the Brooklyn shore. In an exemplary act of gallant leadership, Washington waited for one of the last boats before he himself crossed the river.

Despite this stealthy retreat, it seemed to the British that everything was proceeding according to schedule and that their amateurish American foes would crumble before force majeure. Instead of pursuing the rebels and pressing their advantage, the complacent British forces dawdled and botched an opportunity that might have ended the conflict. On Sunday, September 15, they tardily resumed their offensive with a sustained, earsplitting bombardment of American positions at Kip's Bay (approximately between Thirty-seventh and Thirty-eighth Streets today), on Manhattan's eastern shore. "So terrible and so incessant a roar of guns few even in the army and navy had ever heard before," said Lord Howe's secretary.[64]

As dozens of barges disgorged British and Hessian troops into the hilly, wooded area, the patriot forces lost their nerve and began to flee in undisguised terror, discarding any semblance of discipline. On horseback, an outraged Washington tried to stem the disorderly retreat. Though Washington was famous for his composure, his infrequent wrath was something to behold, and he cursed the panic-stricken troops and flailed at incompetent officers with his riding crop. Finally, he flung his hat on the ground in disgust and fumed, "Are these the men with whom I am to defend America?"[65] Since the British dragged their feet and failed to give chase to the Americans rushing northward, most of the patriots found sanctuary in the wilderness of Harlem Heights.

Hamilton stayed cool under fire. Again, the story comes from the garrulous Hercules Mulligan: "Capt[ain] H[amilton] commanded a post on Bunker Hill near New York and fought with the rear of our army."[66] Hamilton later confirmed this story indirectly when he testified, "I was among the last of our army that left the city."[67] Hamilton showed great fortitude and did not reach Harlem Heights until after dark, having walked the entire length of a thickly forested Manhattan in a drenching rain. He was very dispirited, later telling Mulligan that "in retiring he lost . . . his baggage and one of his cannon, which broke down."[68] He had surrendered his heavy guns, and his company's weaponry had now been whittled down to two mobile fieldpieces that could be pulled along by horse or hand.

As New York fell to the British, Hamilton and the ragged remnants of the Continental Army had little notion that they would be exiled from the city for seven years. Redcoats poured into Manhattan and went on a rampage, annihilating the hated vestiges of dissent. They slashed paintings and torched books at King's College, which they used for a hospital. After midnight on September 21, a fire started at the Fighting Cocks Tavern near the Battery, the flames leaping from house to house until this blazing conflagration consumed a quarter of the city's housing. Nobody ever solved the mystery of whether the culprit was nature or a renegade arsonist. The British, however, were convinced of rebel mischief and rounded up two hundred suspects, including an American spy, Captain Nathan Hale, who was hung from the gallows at a spot thought to be near the present Third Avenue and Sixty-sixth Street. Much of New York had been reduced to charred rubble. Despite this, thousands of desperate Tories flocked to the city for refuge, swelling its population and setting the stage for later conflicts with returning patriots.

After the humiliating loss of New York, Washington thought the craggy, wooded area of Harlem Heights would shelter his army as a natural fortress. He nearly yielded to despair as he bemoaned the drunkenness, looting, desertions in the ranks, and short-term enlistments. In pleading with Congress for a permanent army, he voiced arguments that were echoed by Hamilton and that united the two men in future years: "To place any dependence upon militia is assuredly resting on a broken staff."[69] According to Hamilton's son, it was at Harlem Heights that Washington first recognized Hamilton's unique organizational gifts, as he watched him supervise the building of an earthwork. It was also at Harlem Heights that Hamilton's company first came under the direct command of Washington, who "entered into conversation with him, invited him to his tent, and received an impression of his military talent," wrote John C. Hamilton.[70] It was yet another striking example of the instantaneous rapport that this young man seemed to develop with even the most seasoned officers.

In late October, Hamilton fought alongside Washington at White Plains in yet another bruising defeat for the patriots. The war was beginning to look like a farcical mismatch. The patriots were a slovenly, dejected bunch, while the redcoats, in their trim uniforms and brandishing polished bayonets, stepped smartly into battle to the inspirational strains of a military band. At White Plains, Washington posted the bulk of his troops on high ground while sending a separate detachment of about one thousand men to the west on Chatterton's Hill, above the Bronx River. John C. Hamilton says that his father planted his two fieldpieces upon a rocky ledge at Chatterton's Hill and sprayed Hessian and British columns with fire as they struggled to wade across the river. "Again and again Hamilton's pieces flashed," he wrote, sending "the ascending columns down to the river's edge."[71] Soon the British regrouped, forcing Hamilton and his comrades to abandon the hill and finally the entire area. Nevertheless, at White Plains, the British forces suffered larger losses than did the Americans, which provided a fillip to the dejected spirits of Washington's men.

After White Plains, the patriots, exposed to British seapower as well, had only a tenuous hold left on Manhattan. In the spring, they had built twin forts on opposite sides of the Hudson: Fort Washington on the Manhattan side and Fort Lee on the New Jersey side. On November 16, as he manned an observation post at Fort Lee, Washington gazed in dismay as a huge force of British and Hessian troops overran Fort Washington. Along with staggering losses of men, muskets, and supplies, the surrender of Fort Washington dealt another devastating, nearly mortal, blow to the fragile morale of the Continental Army. Washington was widely castigated for his failure to safeguard the men, not to mention all the cannon and gunpowder stored at the fort. Four days later, the patriots had to surrender Fort Lee hastily to Lord Cornwallis. With his army having dwindled to fewer than three thousand forlorn men, Washington had no choice but to retreat across New Jersey, with the vile epithets of his critics ringing in his ears.

FIVE

THE LITTLE LION

Plagued by foul weather and abysmal morale and with the British tailing his movements, George Washington led the bedraggled Continental Army across New Jersey. The losses he had sustained in New York strengthened his sense that he had to dodge large-scale confrontations that played to the enemy's strength. "We should on all occasions avoid a general action or put anything to the risk," he told Congress, "unless compelled by a necessity into which we ought never to be drawn."[1] Instead, he would opt for small-scale, improvisational skirmishes, the very sort of mobile, risk-averse war of attrition that Hamilton had expounded in his undergraduate article. Hamilton continued to believe in his theory. "By hanging upon their rear and seizing every opportunity of skirmishing," the situation of the British could "be rendered insupportably uneasy," he wrote.[2] The rugged terrain and dense forests of America would make it difficult for the British to wage conventional warfare.

Washington had occasion to marvel anew at Hamilton's prowess during the retreat. The general hoped to make a stand at the Raritan River, near New Brunswick, then decided that his straggling troops could not withstand an enemy offensive and decided to push ahead. Posted with guns high on a riverbank, Hamilton ably provided cover for the retreating patriots. According to Washington's adopted grandson, the commander "was charmed by the brilliant courage and admirable skill" Hamilton displayed as he "directed a battery against the enemy's advanced columns that pressed upon the Americans in their retreat by the ford."[3] In an early December letter to Congress, Washington, though not mentioning Hamilton by name, hailed the "smart cannonade" that allowed his men to escape.[4] In yet another blunder, General Howe occupied New Jersey but permitted Washington and his men to cross the Delaware River into Pennsylvania. As he pondered his scruffy, poorly clad men, Washington warned Congress on December 20, "Ten days more will put an end to the existence of our army."[5] With the enlistment periods of many soldiers about to expire, he needed to assay something daring to rally his despondent troops, who lacked winter clothing and blankets.

In his waning days as an artillery captain, Hamilton confirmed his reputation for persistence despite recurring health problems. He lay bedridden at a nearby farm when Washington decided to recross the Delaware on Christmas night and pounce on the besotted Hessians drowsing at Trenton. Hamilton referred vaguely to his "long and severe fit" of illness, but he somehow gathered up the strength to leave his sickbed and fight.[6] Through death and desertion, Hamilton's company had now been pared to fewer than thirty men. As part of Lord Stirling's brigade, they were summoned to move out after midnight, huddling in cargo boats caked with ice as they poled their way across the frigid Delaware.

After an eight-mile march through a thickening snowfall, Hamilton and his troops, equipped with two cannon, glimpsed the metal helmets and glinting bayonets of a Hessian detachment. When they exchanged fire, Hamilton narrowly escaped cannonballs, which whizzed by his ears. With snow muffling their footsteps, Washington and his men crept up on the main body of Hessians, groggy from their Christmas festivities the night before, and captured more than one thousand of them. The fire from Hamilton's artillery company helped to force the surrender of many enemy soldiers. Patriots everywhere rejoiced at the news, which had a psychological impact far out of proportion to its slim military significance.

Eager to capitalize on his triumph, Washington then attempted a stunning foray against British forces at Princeton on January 3, 1777—another minor but hugely inspiring triumph that revived faith in Washington's leadership. As his men rounded up two hundred British prisoners, an exultant Washington exclaimed, "It is a fine fox chase, my boys!"[7] A senior officer recalled Hamilton and his rump company marching into the village. "I noticed a youth, a mere stripling, small, slender, almost delicate in frame, marching beside a piece of artillery, with a cocked hat pulled down over his eyes, apparently lost in thought, with his hand resting on a cannon, and every now and then patting it, as if it were a favorite horse or a pet plaything."[8] A mythic gleam began to cling to the young captain. People had already noticed his special attributes during the retreat across New Jersey. "Well do I recollect the day when Hamilton's company marched into Princeton," said a friend. "It was a model of discipline. At their head was a boy and I wondered at his youth, but what was my surprise when that slight figure . . . was pointed out to me as that Hamilton of whom we had already heard so much."[9] Hamilton found himself back at the college that had spurned him a few years earlier, only this time one regiment of enemy troops occupied the main dormitory. Legend claims that Hamilton set up his cannon in the college yard, pounded the brick building, and sent a cannonball slicing through a portrait of King George II in the chapel. All we know for certain is that the British soldiers inside surrendered. Hamilton believed that the Continental Army had regained its esprit de corps, showing that green patriots could outwit well-trained British troops. He later referred to "the enterprises of Trenton and Princeton . . . as the dawnings of that bright day which afterwards broke forth with such resplendent luster."[10]

With these back-to-back victories, Washington saved Philadelphia from enemy forces and gained several months to restore his depleted army. He moved his three thousand men into winter quarters at Morristown, New Jersey, thirty miles from New York and cupped in a beautiful valley that formed a protective perimeter around his men. When a vacancy opened on Washington's staff, Hamilton was ideally suited to fill it. By now, the boy genius had been "discovered" by four generals—Alexander McDougall, Nathanael Greene, Lord Stirling, and Washington himself—any one of whom might have been responsible for his promotion. Robert Troup ascribed the foremost influence to Henry Knox, artillery commander of the Continental Army and Hamilton's nominal superior. A former Boston bookseller of Scotch-Irish ancestry, the three-hundred-pound Knox was a jolly fellow with a bulbous nose, a warm spirit, and an earthy sense of humor. He was already renowned for his heroism, having dragged artillery captured at Fort Ticonderoga across snow-covered expanses to defend Boston. Like many people Hamilton befriended in these years, the self-made Knox had known early hardship. His father died when he was twelve, and he had become his mother's sole support. Like Hamilton, Knox was a voracious reader who had tutored himself in warfare by digesting books on military discipline and quizzing British officers who visited his bookshop.

On January 20, 1777, slightly more than two weeks after the fighting at Princeton, Washington penned a note to Hamilton, personally inviting him to join his staff as an aide-de-camp. Five days later, *The Pennsylvania Evening Post* inserted this item: "Captain Alexander Hamilton, of the New York company of artillery, by applying to the printer of this paper, may hear of something to his advantage."[11] This cryptic sentence must have referred to Washington's note. The appointment was announced officially on March 1, and from that date Hamilton was jumped up to the rank of lieutenant colonel. By then, Hamilton was already encamped with Washington, who had set up his headquarters at Jacob Arnold's tavern on the village green at Morristown.

In fewer than five years, the twenty-two-year-old Alexander Hamilton had risen from despondent clerk in St. Croix to one of the aides to America's most eminent man. Yet Hamilton did not react with jubilation. Such was his craving for battlefield distinction that he balked at taking a job that would chain him to a desk, precluding a field command. Washington once wrote that those around him were "confined from morning to evening, hearing and answering . . . applications and letters."[12] More than twenty years later, when capable of much greater candor with Washington, Hamilton told him of his early disappointment on this score: "When in the year 1777 the regiments of artillery were multiplied, I had good reason to expect that the command of one of them would have fallen to me had I not changed my situation and this in all probability would have led further."[13] Hamilton may have underrated the signal importance of his promotion in March 1777, for that job won him the patronage of America's leading figure and ushered him into the presence of military officers who were later to form a critical sector of his political following. In many respects, the political alignments of 1789 were first forged in the appointment lists of the Revolution.

Still recuperating from illness, Hamilton was fortunate to take up his assignment with Washington at a slack moment in the campaign. The British fought at a leisurely pace, even though time worked to the Americans' advantage. Several weeks after reporting to Morristown, Hamilton told his New York associates of daily skirmishes but "with consequences so trifling and insignificant as to be scarcely worth mentioning."[14] He informed Hugh Knox in St. Croix that for several months after his appointment the war had produced "no military event of any great importance."[15] Yet if Hamilton sounded faintly bored at first, he took charge of Washington's staff with characteristic, electrifying speed. On March 10, he wrote to Brigadier General Alexander McDougall that Washington had been ill and that he had hesitated to disturb him. Now that Washington had recovered, Hamilton went on, "I find he is so much pestered with matters which cannot be avoided that I am obliged to refrain from troubling him on the occasion, especially as I conceive the only answer he would give may be given by myself."[16] How rapidly Hamilton had acquired the confidence to function as Washington's proxy! He already spoke in an authoritative voice and seemed to have few qualms about exercising his own judgment in Washington's absence.

The pause in the fighting that spring gave Hamilton plenty of time to study his new boss. The superficial contrast between the tall forty-five-year-old Virginian and his slight twenty-two-year-old aide was striking. Washington towered over Hamilton by at least seven inches. This physical contrast, among other things, belies the moldy canard that Washington had fathered the illegitimate Hamilton on a trip to Barbados in 1751, four years before Hamilton was actually born. Many events in Washington's early years might have engendered sympathy in him for Hamilton. Washington's patrician aura could be misleading. Though the son of a wealthy tobacco planter who died when George was only eleven, leaving him at the mercy of an imperious mother, Washington had limited formal schooling, never attended college, and had trained as a surveyor as an adolescent. Famous later on for granite self-control, he had been a hot-tempered youth. "I wish that I could say that he governs his temper," Lord Fairfax wrote to the mother of the sixteen-year-old Washington. "He is subject to attacks of anger and provocation, sometimes without just cause."[17]

As a teenager who knew the insecurities of an outsider and was eager to earn respect, Washington tried to advance into polished society through a strenuous program of self-improvement. He learned to dance and dress properly, read biographies and histories, and memorized rules of deportment from a courtesy manual. Like Hamilton, the young Washington saw military fame as his vehicle for ascending in the world. By age twenty-two, he was already a precocious lieutenant colonel in the Virginia militia, showing a brash courage during the French and Indian War. "I have heard the bullet's whistle," he said after experiencing battle, "and believe me there is something charming in the sound."[18] Sensitive to slights, Washington chafed under the British condescension toward colonial officers and never forgot his experience as aide-de-camp to the abusive, pigheaded General Edward Braddock. Early disappointments with people left Washington with a residual cynicism that was to jibe well with Hamilton's views.

By a swift, unforeseen series of events, Washington had been catapulted from frustrated young officer to prosperous planter. The death of his half brother Lawrence after their visit to Barbados eventually left him sole owner of the family estate, Mount Vernon. His prospects were further enhanced by marriage at twenty-six to the wealthy widow Martha Dandridge Custis. Though Custis had two surviving children from her previous marriage, she never had children with Washington, prompting speculation that he was sterile, possibly as a by-product of smallpox he contracted on the Barbados trip. Perhaps from unfulfilled paternal instincts, Washington had several surrogate sons during the Revolution, most notably the marquis de Lafayette, and he often referred to Hamilton as "my boy."

Washington proved an excellent businessman, first as a canny speculator in western lands, then as lord of Mount Vernon. Sometimes buying human cargo directly from the holds of slave ships, he came to own more than one hundred slaves by the Revolution and expanded his estate until it encompassed thirteen square miles. An innovative farmer, he invented a plough and presided over a small industrial village at Mount Vernon that included a flour mill and a shop for manufacturing cloth, an entrepreneurial bent that appealed to Hamilton. Washington also brought extensive political experience to his military command, having served for fifteen years in the Virginia House of Burgesses and having attended the First and

Second Continental Congresses. In a supreme act of patriotism, he refused to take a salary for his services during the Revolution, accepting money only for expenses.

The relationship between Washington and Hamilton was so consequential in early American history—rivaled only by the intense comradeship between Jefferson and Madison—that it is difficult to conceive of their careers apart. The two men had complementary talents, values, and opinions that survived many strains over their twenty-two years together. Washington possessed the outstanding judgment, sterling character, and clear sense of purpose needed to guide his sometimes wayward protégé; he saw that the volatile Hamilton needed a steadying hand. Hamilton, in turn, contributed philosophical depth, administrative expertise, and comprehensive policy knowledge that nobody in Washington's ambit ever matched. He could transmute wispy ideas into detailed plans and turn revolutionary dreams into enduring realities. As a team, they were unbeatable and far more than the sum of their parts.

Nonetheless, the two men had clashing temperaments and frequently showed more mutual respect than true affection. When Charles Willson Peale painted Washington in 1779, he presented a manly, confident figure with a quiet swagger and an easy air of command. In fact, Washington wasn't nonchalant and could be exacting and quick to take offense. While he had a dry wit, his mirth was restrained and seldom expressed in laughter. He did not encourage familiarity, fearing it would encourage laxity in subordinates, and held himself aloof with a grave sobriety that gave him power over other people. In addition, over time he became such a prisoner of his own celebrity that people couldn't relax in his presence. Gilbert Stuart noted the fierce temper behind the fabled self-control, and his later paintings of Washington show something hooded and wary in the hard, penetrating eyes. The self-control was something achieved, not inherited, and often masked combustible emotions that could explode in fury. "His temper was naturally irritable and high-toned, but reflection and resolution had obtained a firm and habitual ascendancy over it," Jefferson later said perceptively. "If ever, however, it broke its bonds, he was most tremendous in his wrath."[19]

Those who met Washington in social situations were usually taken with his gallantry and convivial charm. Abigail Adams fairly cooed when she met him, reassuring John that "the gentleman and soldier look agreeably blended in him."[20] Working with him in cramped quarters, however, Hamilton had many chances to see Washington's irritable side and sometimes ungovernable temper. Washington was extremely fond of Hamilton, preferring him to his other aides, but he did not express his affection openly. Hamilton always addressed him as "Your Excellency," and it irked him that he could not penetrate the general's reserve. But Lafayette noted that Hamilton, in turn, held something back. The notion that Hamilton was a surrogate son to Washington has some superficial merit but fails to capture fully the psychological interplay between them. If Hamilton was a surrogate son, some suppressed Oedipal rage entered into the mix. Hamilton was so brilliant, so coldly critical, that he detected flaws in Washington less visible to other aides. One senses that he was the only young member of Washington's "family" who felt competitive with the general or could have imagined himself running the army. It was temperamentally hard for Alexander Hamilton to subordinate himself to anyone, even someone with the extraordinary stature of George Washington. At the same time, he never doubted for an instant that Washington was a great leader of special gifts and the one irreplaceable personage in the early American pageant. He had the deepest admiration for Washington, even if he didn't wallow in hero worship. He had misgivings about Washington as a military leader—the general did lose the majority of battles he fought in the Revolution—but not about him as a political leader. Having hitched his star to Washington, Hamilton struck a bargain with himself that he honored for the remainder of his career: he would never openly criticize Washington, whose image had to be upheld to unify the country.

So diffident was George Washington in speech that John Adams described him as a great actor with "the gift of silence."[21] Washington knew that he lacked verbal flow, once writing, "With me it has always been a maxim rather to let my designs appear from my works than by my expressions."[22] Yet this taciturn man had to cope with an unending flood of paperwork as he dealt with Congress and state legislatures while also issuing orders and arbitrating disputes among deputies. All the managerial problems of a protracted war—recruiting, promotions, munitions, clothing, food, supplies, prisoners—swam across his desk. Such a man sorely needed a fluent writer, and none of Washington's aides had so facile a pen as did Hamilton.

Being Washington's chief secretary was much more than a passive, stenographic task. "At present my time is so taken up at my desk," Washington had written to Congress in September, "that I am obliged to neglect many other essential parts of my duty. It is absolutely necessary . . . for me to have persons that can think for me, as well as execute orders."[23] Washington further explained that his letters were drafted by aides, subject to his revision. Hamilton's advent was thus a godsend for Washington. He was able to project himself into Washington's mind and intuit what the general wanted to say, writing it up with instinctive tact and deft diplomatic skills. It was an inspired act of ventriloquism: Washington gave a few general hints and, presto, out popped Hamilton's letter in record time. Most of Washington's field orders have survived in Hamilton's handwriting. "The pen for our army was held by Hamilton and for dignity of manner, pith of matter, and elegance of style, General's Washington's letters are unrivalled in military annals," wrote Robert

Troup.[24] Hamilton was loath to admit that he served as a military adviser to Washington, lest this cast doubt on his boss's abilities, but he offered him opinions on many matters. Another aide, James McHenry, said that Hamilton "had studied military service, practically under General Washington, and his advice in many instances (a fact known to myself) had aided our chief in giving to the machine that perfection to which it had arrived previously to the close of the revolutionary war."[25]

Pretty soon, the twenty-two-year-old alter ego was drafting letters to Congress, state governors, and the most powerful generals in the Continental Army. Before long, he had access to all confidential information and was allowed to issue orders from Washington over his own signature. Timothy Pickering, then adjutant general, was later adamant that Hamilton was far more than the leading scribe at headquarters. "During the whole time that he was one of the General's aides-de-camp, Hamilton had to *think* as well as to *write* for him in all his most important correspondence."[26]

As Hamilton evolved from private secretary to something akin to chief of staff, he rode with the general in combat, cantered off on diplomatic missions, dealt with bullheaded generals, sorted through intelligence, interrogated deserters, and negotiated prisoner exchanges. This gave him a wide-angle view of economic, political, and military matters, further hastening his intellectual development. Washington was both military and political leader of the patriots, already something of a de facto president. He had to placate the Continental Congress, which insisted on supervising the army, and coordinate plans with thirteen bickering states. Both Washington and Hamilton came to think in terms of the general welfare, while many other officers and politicians got bogged down in parochial squabbles. In their mutual desire for a professional army and a strong central authority that would mitigate local rivalries, the two men felt the first stirrings of an impulse that would someday culminate in the Constitution and the Federalist party. Like Washington, Hamilton was scandalized by the dissension and cowardice, the backstabbing and avarice, of the politicians in Philadelphia while soldiers were dying in the field.

During his first weeks on Washington's staff, Hamilton began building a network that became the foundation of his future political base at home. He agreed to update New York politicians about military affairs and exchanged twice-weekly reports with a newly appointed body called the New York Committee of Correspondence, placing him in regular contact with leaders such as Gouverneur Morris, John Jay, and Robert R. Livingston. On April 20, 1777, when the New York State Constitution was approved, Hamilton expressed general satisfaction with it. In commenting to Morris, Hamilton foreshadowed his later views, arguing that the election for governor "requires the deliberate wisdom of a select assembly and cannot be safely lodged with the people at large." On the other hand, he still showed the radical influence of his student days when he worried that a separate senate, elected solely by propertied voters, will "degenerate into a body purely aristocratical."[27] In fact, the state's aristocratic landowners were hugely disappointed when General Philip Schuyler of Albany was defeated for governor by General George Clinton, the champion of the small farmers. Hamilton's future father-in-law was stung by the defeat, and, while expressing admiration for Clinton, Schuyler complained that "his family and connections do not entitle him to so distinguished a predominance."[28] One day, Hamilton was to inherit this Schuyler-Clinton feud as his own.

Shortly after Hamilton joined Washington's staff, Charles Willson Peale visited the New Jersey headquarters and executed the first portrait of Hamilton, a miniature on ivory. It shows him in a blue-and-buff uniform with gold epaulets and the green ribbon of an aide-de-camp. He has close-cropped hair and a long, sharp nose and fixes the viewer with an intense gaze. He had not yet acquired the urbane self-assurance that later marked his demeanor. There was something still lean and unformed about his face, which gradually widened with age and came to look almost too large for his trim, dapper body.

Quartered at Jacob Arnold's tavern, Hamilton lived in cheek-by-jowl intimacy with his new military family. So that he could summon his aides at any hour, Washington preferred to have them shelter under one roof. Sometimes, on frosty nights, the general would wrap himself in a blanket and lie thinking on a couch until interrupted by a sudden messenger on horseback. "The dispatches being opened and read," recalled his adopted grandson, "there would be heard in the calm deep tones of that voice . . . the command of the chief to his now watchful attendant, '*Call Colonel Hamilton.*'"[29]

The four to six young aides usually slept in one room, often two to a bed, then worked long days in a single room with chairs crowded around small wooden tables. Washington typically kept a small office off to the side. During busy periods, the aides sometimes wrote and copied one hundred letters per day, an exhausting grind relieved by occasional dances, parades, and reviews. At night, the aides pulled up camp stools to a dinner table and engaged in lively repartee. Hamilton, though the youngest family member, was nevertheless Washington's "principal and most confidential aide," as the general phrased it.[30] Instead of resenting him, the other aides treated Hamilton affectionately and nicknamed him "Ham" or "Hammie."[31] For an orphaned boy from the Caribbean, what better fate than to become part of this elite family?

Once again, the young immigrant had been transported to another sphere. Though past horrors would always lurk somewhere in his psyche, he spent the rest of his life in the upper stratum of American society, a remarkable transformation for someone with his rootless past. Unlike tradition-bound European armies, top-heavy with aristocrats, Washington's army allowed for upward mobility. Though not a perfect meritocracy, it probably valued talent and intelligence more highly than any previous army. This high-level service completed Hamilton's rapid metamorphosis into a full-blooded American. The Continental Army was a national institution and helped to make Hamilton the optimal person to articulate a vision of American nationalism, his vision sharpened by the immigrant's special love for his new country.

Hamilton won admirers for his sprightly personality as well as intelligence. General Nathanael Greene remembered his presence at headquarters as "a bright gleam of sunshine, ever growing brighter as the general darkness thickened."[32] Such comments were echoed by those who knew Hamilton in after years. Harrison Gray Otis, later a senator, wrote: "Frank, affable, intelligent and brave, young Hamilton became the favorite of his fellow soldiers."[33] Lawyer William Sullivan likewise found Hamilton eloquent, high-minded, and openhearted but also noted that he always had his fair share of detractors: "He was capable of inspiring the most affectionate attachment, but he could make those whom he opposed fear and hate him cordially."[34] With a ready tongue and rapier wit, Hamilton could wound people more than he realized, and he was so nimble in debate that even bright people sometimes felt embarrassingly tongue-tied in his presence.

Hamilton was surrounded by a congenial group of young aides for whom he felt a familial warmth. He shared correspondence with Robert H. Harrison of Alexandria, Virginia, a respected lawyer and a neighbor of Washington. Ten years older than Hamilton, Harrison treated him fondly and nicknamed him "the little Lion."[35] Another early comrade was Tench Tilghman, who started out with a light-infantry company in Philadelphia. For nearly five years, Washington said, Tilghman was his "faithful assistant," and he later applauded him as "a zealous servant and slave to the public" and as a man of "modesty and love of concord."[36] Richard Kidder Meade joined the staff around the same time as Hamilton and elicited warm praise from him: "I know few men estimable, fewer amiable and when I meet with one of the last description it is not in my power to withhold affection."[37]

The following year, James McHenry became an aide to Washington. Born and educated in Ireland, McHenry had studied medicine with Dr. Benjamin Rush of Philadelphia. He was able to minister to Hamilton's various maladies, including a malarial infection that recurred every summer, probably a legacy of his tropical boyhood. To correct Hamilton's constipation, McHenry instructed him to skip milk and go easy on the wine. "When you indulge in wine let [it] be sparingly—never go beyond three glasses—but by no means every day."[38] (That three glasses of wine was considered abstemious says much about the immoderate consumption of the day.) Warmhearted, with a touch of the poet, McHenry wrote heroic verse and often accompanied Hamilton in entertaining Washington's family with songs. Hamilton referred to "those fine sounds with which he and I are accustomed to regale the ears of the fraternity."[39]

From McHenry's diary, we can see that many of Washington's aides sneaked in romantic flings during inactive intervals that spring. In February, many wives of high-ranking officers—Mrs. Washington, Mrs. Knox, and Mrs. Greene, as well as Lady Stirling and her daughter, Lady Kitty—arrived and organized dainty little tea parties in the evening. One visitor, Martha Bland of Virginia, cast admiring eyes on the handsome young aides, finding them "all polite, sociable gentlemen who make the day pass with a great deal of satisfaction to the visitors."[40] One day, she joined a riding party headed by George and Martha Washington and was clearly taken with Hamilton, "a sensible genteel polite young fellow, a West Indian."[41] In this socially fluid situation, Hamilton could meet and court well-bred young women as social equals. Colonel Alexander Graydon recalled a self-possessed Hamilton surrounded by several adoring ladies at dinner, saying that he "acquitted himself with an ease, propriety and vivacity, which gave me the most favorable impression of his talents and accomplishments," as he displayed "a brilliancy which might adorn the most polished circles of society."[42]

One thing grew crystal clear at Morristown: Hamilton was girl crazy and brimming with libido. Throughout his career, at unlikely moments, he tended to grow flirtatious, almost giddy, with women. No sooner had he joined Washington's staff than he began to woo his old friend Catherine Livingston, daughter of his former patron, William Livingston, now the first governor of an independent New Jersey. In an April 11 letter to Kitty, Hamilton struck the note of badinage favored by young rakes of the day:

After knowing exactly your taste and whether you are of a romantic or discreet temper as to love affairs, I will endeavour to regulate myself by it. If you would choose to be a goddess and to be worshipped as such, I will torture my imagination for the best arguments the nature of the case will admit to prove you so. . . . But if . . . you are content with being a mere mortal, and require no other license than is justly due to you, I will talk to you like one [in] his sober senses.

That Hamilton was being more than playful with Kitty Livingston is shown in his declaration in the letter that the end of the Revolution would "remove those obstacles which now lie in the way of that most delectable thing called matrimony."[43]

When Hamilton received Livingston's belated reply to his rather forward letter, he passed it around among the other aides. "Hamilton!" one confided. "When you write to this divine girl, it must be in the style of adoration. None but a goddess, I am sure, could have penned so fine a letter!" In his response to Livingston, Hamilton made clear that some family members thought he was excessively preoccupied by the opposite sex. "I exercise [my pen] at the [risk] of being anathematized by grave censors for dedicating so much of my time to so trifling and insignificant a toy as—woman." Though Livingston, apparently, had spurned his advances—he chides her apathy—he concludes philosophically that "I shall probably be in a fine way" and tells her that "ALL FOR LOVE is my motto."[44] We can discern Hamilton's ambivalence toward fashionable young women as he alternately flatters and belittles Kitty. As in his first boyish love poems in St. Croix, Hamilton could fancy young women as chaste goddesses or naughty little vixens. Which type he ultimately preferred, he still may not have known.

In the late spring of 1777, Hamilton began the most intimate friendship of his life, with an elegant, blue-eyed young officer named John Laurens, who formally joined Washington's family in October. One portrait of Laurens shows a short, commanding figure in a pose of supreme assurance, with one arm akimbo and the other resting on the hilt of a long, curved sword. He was the son of one of South Carolina's most influential planters, Henry Laurens, who succeeded John Hancock as president of the Continental Congress that November. Hamilton and Laurens, both French Huguenot on one side of their families and English on the other, seemed like kindred spirits, spiritual twins. Both were bookish and ambitious, bold and enterprising, and hungered for military honor. Both were imbued with a quixotic sense that it was noble to die in a worthy cause. Like Hamilton, Laurens was so sure of himself that he could seem brusquely overbearing to those who disagreed with him. More than any friend Hamilton ever had, Laurens was his peer, and the two were long paired in the fond memories of many who fought in the Revolution.

Born in Charleston, South Carolina, a few months before Hamilton was born in Nevis, Laurens had a privileged upbringing on one of the state's biggest slave plantations. In 1771, while Hamilton toiled away as a clerk in St. Croix, Laurens's father enrolled him in a cosmopolitan school in Geneva, Switzerland. He was a versatile, accomplished student, who excelled in the classics, fenced, drew, and rode. While breathing in the republican atmosphere of Geneva, he prepared to become a barrister. In 1774, he studied law at the Middle Temple in London. This was a time of antislavery ferment, spurred by Lord Mansfield's legal decision that a slave became free by being brought to England. Laurens became a passionate convert to abolitionism, which was to create a strong ideological bond with Hamilton.

After Lexington and Concord, Laurens clamored to return home but was deterred by his fretful father, who worried about his son's youthful lust for combat. Henry Laurens always had a strange foreboding that his impetuous son would die in battle. After reading Thomas Paine's *Common Sense* in 1776, John Laurens grew ever more impatient to recross the Atlantic but remained trapped in England by an unexpected circumstance. He had impregnated a young woman, Martha Manning, whose wealthy father, William Manning, was a close friend of Henry Laurens. With his chivalric sense of honor, John Laurens married Manning in a clandestine ceremony in October 1776. Four months later, after Martha gave birth to a daughter, Laurens immediately boarded a ship back to Charleston. Not long after he returned, he signed on with the Continental Army and won the absolute trust of Washington, who invited him to join his family and gave him confidential missions "which neither time nor propriety would suffer me to commit to paper," Washington wrote.[45]

Hamilton and Laurens took an instant liking to each other and became inseparable. Hamilton later lauded his friend's "zeal, intelligence, enterprise."[46] As the war progressed, Hamilton wrote to Laurens with such unbridled affection that one Hamilton biographer, James T. Flexner, has detected homoerotic overtones in their relationship. Because the style of eighteenth-century letters could be quite florid, even between men, one must tread gingerly in approaching this matter, especially since Laurens's letters to Hamilton were warm but proper. It is worth noting here, however, how frequently people used the word *feminine* to describe Hamilton— the more surprising given his military bearing and virile exploits. When John C. Hamilton was preparing his father's authorized biography, he omitted a loose sheet that has survived in his papers and that describes the relationship between Hamilton and Laurens thus: "In the intercourse of these martial youths, who have been styled 'the Knights of the Revolution,' there was a deep fondness of friendship, which approached the tenderness of feminine attachment."[47] Hamilton had certainly been exposed to homosexuality as a boy, since many "sodomites" were transported to the Caribbean along with thieves, pickpockets, and others deemed undesirable. In all thirteen colonies, sodomy had been a capital offense, so if Hamilton and Laurens did become lovers—and it is impossible to say this with any certainty—they would have taken extraordinary precautions. At the very least, we can say that Hamilton developed something like an adolescent crush on his friend.

Hamilton and Laurens formed a colorful trio with a young French nobleman who was appointed an honorary major general in the Continental Army on July 31, 1777. The marquis de Lafayette, nineteen, was a stylish, ebullient young aristocrat inflamed by republican ideals and eager to serve the revolutionary cause. "The gay trio to which Hamilton and Laurens belonged was made complete by Lafayette," Hamilton's grandson later wrote. "On the whole, there was something about them rather suggestive of the three famous heroes of Dumas."[48] Lafayette always spoke of his two American friends in the most affectionate terms. Of Laurens, he wrote that "his openness, integrity, patriotism, and splendid gallantry have made me his devoted friend."[49] In describing Hamilton, Lafayette was still more effusive, calling him "my beloved friend in whose brotherly affection I felt equally proud and happy."[50] Eliza Hamilton confirmed that "the marquis loved Mr. Hamilton as a brother; their love was mutual."[51]

Portraits of Lafayette show a slender, handsome youth in a powdered wig with a long face, rosy lips, and delicately arched eyebrows. Like Hamilton's, his life was shadowed by early sorrow: his father had died when he was two, his mother when he was thirteen, making him an orphan at the same age as Hamilton. At sixteen, he had married the fourteen-year-old Adrienne de Noailles, the daughter of one of France's most august families, and he offered America invaluable contacts with the snobbish court of Louis XVI. His meteoric ascent in the Continental Army owed much to a letter that Benjamin Franklin wrote to George Washington from Paris, urging the political expediency of welcoming this well-connected young man. Lafayette agreed to serve without pay, brought a ship to America outfitted at his own expense, and spent lavishly from his own purse to clothe and arm the patriots.

Many people warmed to Lafayette, finding him full of poetry and fire and fine liberal sentiments. Franklin implored Washington to befriend "that amiable young nobleman" and expressed fear that people would take advantage of his goodness.[52] Franklin need not have worried about Washington's affections. When the young Frenchman was wounded in battle, Washington instructed the surgeon, "Treat him as though he were my son." For Lafayette, Washington became a revered paternal presence, and he named his only son George Washington Lafayette. Lafayette always had his quota of critics, who regarded him as vain, suspicious, and self-seeking. Thomas Jefferson pinpointed one especially flagrant fault: "His foible is a canine appetite for popularity and fame."[53] For all his love of Lafayette, even Hamilton mocked the "thousand little whims" to which the marquis was prey.[54] Whatever his flaws, however, Lafayette proved to be a valiant officer of surprisingly mature judgment and more than rewarded the faith of his admirers.

The bilingual Hamilton befriended Lafayette with the almost instantaneous speed of all his early friendships and was soon assigned to him as a liaison officer. As in the case of John Laurens, there was such unabashed ardor in Hamilton's relationship with the marquis that James T. Flexner has wondered whether it progressed beyond mere friendship. Did Hamilton's grandson mean much or little when he wrote, "There is a note of romance in their friendship, quite unusual even in those days, and Lafayette, especially during his early sojourn in this country, was on the closest terms with Hamilton"?[55] Late in the war, Lafayette wrote to his wife, "Among the general's aides-de-camp is a (young) man whom I love very much and about whom I have occasionally spoken to you. That man is Colonel Hamilton."[56] Where Hamilton was the more extravagant partner in corresponding with Laurens, Lafayette outshone Hamilton when it came to rapturous prose. "Before this campaign, I was your friend and very intimate friend agreeable to the ideas of the world," Lafayette wrote to him in 1780. But since returning from France, "my sentiment has increased to such a point the world knows nothing about."[57] Was this just a specimen of flowery French writing, voguish at the time, or something more? As with John Laurens, we will never know. But the breathless tone of the letters that Hamilton exchanged with Laurens and Lafayette is unlike anything in his later letters. This may simply have been a by-product of youth and wartime camaraderie. The broader point is that Alexander Hamilton, the outsider from the West Indies, had a rare capacity for friendship and was already attracting a circle of devoted, well-placed people who were to help to propel him to the highest political plateau.

In early July 1777, Fort Ticonderoga in upstate New York fell to the British, prompting King George III to clap his hands and exclaim, "I have beat them! Beat all the Americans."[58] It was a potential calamity for the patriots, since it opened a corridor for General John Burgoyne and his invading army from Canada to push south to New York City, slicing the rebel army in half and isolating New England—an overarching objective of British war policy. Livid at this defeat, Hamilton was unsparing in his censure of the commander held responsible, Philip Schuyler. "I have always been a very partial judge of General Schuyler's conduct and vindicated it frequently from the charges brought against it," he wrote to Robert R. Livingston, "but I am at last forced to suppose him inadequate."[59] Historians have proved more charitable toward Schuyler, who was weakened by desertions and the settled malice that his New England troops bore against him as a New York leader and a tough disciplinarian. The British had also pulled off a masterful plan by scaling the steep mountain that overlooked Ticonderoga, permitting its unlikely capture. After suffering many slurs, Schuyler was replaced as head of the army's Northern Department by Horatio Gates, whom he jeered at as the "idol" of the New Englanders.[60] Even though he was exonerated for the loss of Ticonderoga in a subsequent court-martial that he himself demanded, Schuyler never completely recuperated from the wounding debacle.

In Hamilton's upset over Ticonderoga one can see that this stateless young man had developed proprietary feelings toward New York. He told Livingston that he was disturbed by the threat to "a state which I consider, in a great measure, as my political parent. . . . I agree with you that the loss of your state would be a more affecting blow to America than any that could be struck by Mr. Howe to the southward."[61] The reference to "your state" suggests, however, that if Hamilton already identified with New York, he still had not committed himself irrevocably to any allegiance to it.

Hamilton already showed a solid grasp of military strategy. As he surveyed the British forces that summer, he hazarded several predictions that later sounded clairvoyant. First, he thought Burgoyne would be tempted to move down the Hudson toward New York—"The enterprising spirit he has credit for, I suspect, may easily be fanned by his vanity into rashness"—and that this would prove ruinous for him unless Sir William Howe rushed redcoats north from New York City to beef up his forces.[62] He didn't think Howe would be that smart, however, the British having "generally acted like fools." Instead, he prophesied, again with startling accuracy, that Howe would undertake "a bold effort against our main army" and rashly try to seize Philadelphia.[63]

In an era of primitive communications, even a massive armada could vanish at sea for long stretches. When General Howe departed from New York harbor in late July, commanding 267 ships and eighteen thousand soldiers, he dropped out of sight, materialized in Delaware Bay a week later, disappeared again, then resurfaced in the bay in late August. Hamilton was spoiling for a fight to thwart Howe's entrance into Philadelphia and told Gouverneur Morris in rousing tones, "Our army is in high health and spirits. . . . I would not only fight them, but I would attack them, for I hold it an established maxim that there is three to one in favour of the party attacking."[64] That Hamilton was much too sanguine became woefully evident on September 11 during a bloody clash between British and American troops at Brandywine Creek, outside of Philadelphia. Despite stouthearted resistance by the patriots, the savage fighting ended in a panic-stricken rout and terrible slaughter, with a final tally of 1,300 Americans killed, wounded, or captured—twice the losses inflicted on the British.

It now seemed futile to try to halt a British advance upon the capital. Washington dispatched Hamilton, Captain Henry "Light-Horse Harry" Lee (father of Robert E. Lee), and eight cavalrymen to burn flour mills on the Schuylkill River before they fell into enemy hands. While Hamilton and others were destroying flour at Daviser's (or Daverser's) Ferry, their sentinels fired a warning shot indicating the approach of British dragoons. To guarantee an escape route, Hamilton had moored a flat-bottomed boat at the river's edge. He and three comrades now leaped into the craft and pushed off from shore, while Lee and others took off on horseback. Lee recalled the British raking Hamilton's boat with repeated volleys from their carbines, killing one of Hamilton's men and wounding another. All the while, the intrepid Hamilton was "struggling against a violent current, increased by the recent rains."[65] Hamilton and his men finally dove from the boat into the swirling waters and swam to safety. Scarcely stopping for breath, Hamilton dashed off a message to

John Hancock that urged the immediate evacuation of the Continental Congress from Philadelphia. Just before Hamilton returned to headquarters, Washington received a letter from Captain Lee announcing Hamilton's death in the Schuylkill. There were tears of jubilation, as well as considerable laughter, when the sodden corpse himself sauntered through the door.

After the Continental Congress adjourned that night, John Hancock read Hamilton's letter predicting that the enemy might pounce on Philadelphia by daybreak. Many members decided to abandon the city and exited posthaste after midnight. In his diary, John Adams told of being awakened at 3:00 A.M. and informed of Hamilton's dire forecast. Adams grabbed his belongings, mounted his horse, and sped away with other congressmen before dawn. "Congress was chased like a covey of partridges from Philadelphia to Trenton, from Trenton to Lancaster," Adams wrote with his usual gift for evocative language.[66]

It turned out that Hamilton's warning had been premature, as the British stalled for more than a week before entering the city. Washington took advantage of this interlude to resupply his troops, who were desperately short of blankets, clothing, and horses. With reluctance, he invested Hamilton with tyrannical powers and placed one hundred men at his disposal, authorizing him to requisition supplies from Philadelphia residents. It was an assignment of the utmost gravity, and Washington feared that if it miscarried it would "involve the ruin of the army, and perhaps the ruin of America." As his orders to Hamilton specified:

> Painful as it is to me to order and as it will be to you to execute the measure, I am compelled to desire you immediately to proceed to Philadelphia and there procure from the inhabitants contributions of blankets and clothing and materials to answer the purposes of both. . . . This you will do with as much delicacy and discretion as the nature of the business demands.[67]

This extraordinary grant of power to his twenty-two-year-old aide demanded of him both exquisite tact and unyielding firmness. In a war being fought for democracy, the preservation of popular support was all-important. Hamilton had to impose discipline and importune citizens with sufficient tact to arouse sympathy instead of resentment. His training as a clerk helped him to keep careful accounts and issue receipts to residents. Washington wanted him to evacuate any horses that could be commandeered by the British, and Hamilton drew up a sensible list of the people who should be exempt from the edict: the poor, the transient, those about to leave the city, and those dependent on horses for their livelihood. Working at a nonstop pace for two days, Hamilton loaded up so many vessels with military stores and sent them up the Delaware "with so much vigilance, that very little public property fell with the city into the hands of the British general," wrote John Marshall, later chief justice of the Supreme Court.[68] Aided by these supplies, Washington engaged the British at Germantown on October 4. Although another thousand patriots were killed, wounded, or captured, General Howe was at least pinned down in Philadelphia and prevented from moving north to reinforce General Burgoyne.

In many ways, "Gentleman Johnny" Burgoyne—a dissolute, vainglorious man who was fond of mistresses and champagne and craved a knighthood—was more suited for the pleasures of peace than the arts of war. The renowned British actor David Garrick had starred in his play *The Maid of the Oaks* in Drury Lane. Burgoyne and his army marched down the Hudson Valley in early October 1777 with all the cumbersome pomp of royalty. As if proceeding to a coronation, not a battle, Burgoyne loaded up no fewer than thirty carts with his personal belongings, dragged by horses through fly-ridden bogs and swamps. Burgoyne epitomized the snobbery rife among the British officers. If anything, he believed that the British had shown too much clemency toward the American upstarts. "I look upon America as our child," he had said in 1774, "which we have already spoiled by too much indulgence."[69]

The original British battle plan for severing New England from other rebel colonies had envisioned Burgoyne's force from the north converging with those of Lieutenant Colonel Barrimore St. Leger from the west and General Howe from the south. Instead, with Howe in Philadelphia, Burgoyne found himself fighting alone, isolated in the upper Hudson Valley against patriot troops led by General Horatio Gates. Burgoyne's surrender of his entire army of 5,700 men at Saratoga in mid-October was the pivotal moment of the war: a victory so large, so thrilling, and so decisive that it emboldened the wavering France to enter the conflict on the patriotic side.

The victory meant that Washington could siphon off some of Gates's troops to strengthen his own shaky position to the south. The continental ranks had been thinned by the expiration of one-year enlistments—a recurring problem. Not long after receiving the wonderful news from Saratoga, Washington summoned a war council of five major generals and ten brigadiers, with Hamilton drafting the minutes. Word had begun to make the rounds that this young aide was far more than some docile clerk. Benjamin Rush, the radical Pennsylvania congressman, grumbled that Washington had allowed himself to be "governed by General Greene, General Knox, and Colonel Hamilton, one of his aides, a young man of twenty-one years."[70] At the meeting, the generals agreed that Gates must transfer a hefty chunk of his troops to Washington, since the Saratoga victory had drastically curtailed the British threat in New York. The emissary chosen to impart this most unwelcome piece of news to Gates was Alexander Hamilton.

It is remarkable that Washington would have drafted his young aide for such a tough assignment. After Saratoga, Horatio Gates was the hero of the day, the darling of New England politicians, and this only deepened the mutual antipathy between him and Washington. Gates had even snubbed Washington by refusing to inform him directly of his victory. Thus, Hamilton's mission was fraught with a multitude of perils. From a general at the zenith of his popularity, he had to pry loose a sizable number of troops and to do so, if possible, without issuing any orders. Hamilton would have to ride three hundred miles and then bargain with Gates without any further opportunity to consult with Washington. Clearly, the imperious Gates would feel demeaned by having to negotiate with a diminutive twenty-two-year-old. Hamilton would need to tap all the cunning and diplomacy in his nature.

To invest Hamilton with a suitable aura of power, Washington drafted a letter to Gates in which he introduced his aide and defined his mission: "to lay before you a full state of our situation and that of the enemy in this quarter. He is well informed . . . and will deliver my sentiments upon the plan of operations . . . now necessary."[71] The discretion delegated to Hamilton was impressive. If Hamilton found Gates using the requested troops in a manner that benefited the patriotic cause, "it is not my wish to give any interruption," Washington wrote. If that was not the case, however, "it is my desire that the reinforcements before mentioned . . . be immediately put in motion to join this army."[72] If there was a single moment during the Revolution when its outcome hinged on spontaneous decisions made by Alexander Hamilton, this was it.

Instructions in hand, Hamilton rode off to Albany at a furious pace, covering sixty miles a day for five consecutive days, riding like a man possessed. En route, he stopped on the eastern shore of the Hudson at Fishkill and lectured General Israel Putnam on the need for him to shift two brigades southward to help Washington. Hamilton did not shrink from exercising his own judgment. Acting on his own initiative, he induced Putnam to promise an additional seven hundred members of a New Jersey militia. He explained to Washington that "I concluded you would not disapprove of a measure calculated to strengthen you, though but for a small time, and have ventured to adopt it on that presumption." Eager to move on, he told Washington that a quartermaster was "pressing some fresh horses for me. The moment they are ready I shall recross the [Hudson] River in order to fall in with the troops on the other side and make all the haste I can to Albany to get the three brigades there sent forward."[73]

The instant Hamilton arrived in Albany on November 5, 1777, he arranged a hasty meeting with Horatio Gates. For Hamilton, it was Benedict Arnold, not Gates, who had merited the real laurels at Saratoga. He regarded Gates as a vain,

cowardly, inept general, and subsequent events were to bear out his scathing judgment. With gray hair and spectacles set low on his long, pointed nose—he was later
derided by his men as "Granny Gates"—the heavyset Gates was a much less imposing presence than Washington. The illegitimate son of a duke's housekeeper, he had
studied at British military academies and fought in the French and Indian War.
Now swollen with pride from his victory, Gates was reluctant to cede any of the
brigades under his command. Instead of listening meekly, Hamilton spoke to Gates
in a firm tone and told him how many troops he should spare. Gates retorted that
Sir Henry Clinton, the British commander in New York, might still march up the
Hudson and endanger New England. As a sop, Gates finally agreed to send Washington a single brigade, commanded by a General Patterson, instead of the three
Hamilton had stipulated. After the meeting, Hamilton snooped about and discovered that Patterson's six-hundred-man brigade was "by far the weakest of the three
now here," as he then wrote candidly to General Gates. "Under these circumstances,
I cannot consider it either as compatible with the good of the service or my instructions from His Excellency, General Washington, to consent that that brigade
be selected from the three to go to him."[74] Hamilton was careful to be neither too
forward nor too deferential as he skillfully blended his own opinions with those of
Washington. "I used every argument in my power to convince him of the propriety"
of sending troops, an exasperated Hamilton told Washington, "but he was inflexible in the opinion that two brigades at least of Continental troops should remain in
and near this place."[75] Hamilton later reproached Gates for "his impudence, his
folly and his rascality."[76]

It irked Gates that he had to negotiate with this cocksure, headstrong aide. In a
draft letter to Washington, Gates crossed out an allusion to Hamilton that showed
just how much he seethed over the situation: "Although it is customary and even
absolutely necessary to direct implicit obedience to be paid to the verbal orders of
aides-de-camp in action, or while upon the spot, yet I believe it is never practiced to
delegate that dictatorial power to one aide-de-camp sent to an army 300 miles distant."[77] In the end, Hamilton extracted a promise from Gates to surrender two of
the brigades he wanted. It was a bravura performance by Hamilton, who had shown
consummate political skill.

During the tense impasse with Gates, Hamilton tarried long enough in Albany
to see his old friend Robert Troup and dine at the mansion of Philip Schuyler. Having preceded Gates as head of the Northern Department, General Schuyler felt
cheated of the Saratoga triumph for which he had laid the groundwork. General
Nathanael Greene seconded this appraisal, calling Gates "a mere child of fortune"
and asserting that the "foundation of all the northern success was laid before his arrival there."[78] During this visit to Schuyler's mansion, Hamilton met for the first

time the general's second daughter, twenty-year-old Eliza, a relationship that was to resume more than two years later.

After his exhausting talks with Gates, Hamilton headed back down the Hudson, only to discover that his mission was not over. Having stopped at the home of New York governor George Clinton in New Windsor, he was taken aback to find that two of the brigades promised by General Israel Putnam had been withheld. A bluff, jowly farmer and former tavern keeper from Connecticut, Putnam was much beloved by his aide, Aaron Burr, who referred to him as "My good old general."[79] It was Putnam who supposedly told his men at Bunker Hill, "Don't fire until you see the whites of their eyes. Then, fire low."[80] When Hamilton saw that Putnam had reneged on his promise, he sent him a letter throbbing with anger. Hamilton cast aside the usual caution of an aide-de-camp and delivered a tongue-lashing to a veteran officer more than twice his age:

> Sir, I cannot forbear confessing that I am astonished. And alarmed beyond measure to find that all his Excellency's views have been hitherto frustrated and that no single step of those I mentioned to you has been taken to afford him the aid he absolutely stands in need of and by delaying which the cause of America is put to the utmost conceivable hazard. . . . My expressions may perhaps have more warmth than is altogether proper. But they proceed from the overflowing of my heart in a matter where I conceive this continent essentially interested.[81]

Hamilton had to issue direct orders to Putnam to send all of his Continental Army troops (that is, minus state militias) to Washington immediately. The fault was not entirely Putnam's, however, for the two brigades had not been paid in months and, mutinously, refused to march.

Having gone out on a limb, Hamilton expressed great trepidation in his reports to Washington that he might have exceeded his authority. It was therefore deeply gratifying when Washington sent him an unqualified endorsement of his work: "I approve entirely of all the steps you have taken and have only to wish that the exertions of those you have had to deal with had kept pace with your zeal and good intentions."[82] As in Philadelphia in September, Washington had given his wunderkind huge autonomy, and the gamble had paid off handsomely. The young aide-de-camp was revealed as a forceful personality in his own right, not just a proxy for the general. For Hamilton, his encounters with the two obdurate generals strengthened his preference for strict hierarchy and centralized command as the only way to accomplish things—a view that was to find its political equivalent in his preference for concentrated federal power instead of authority dispersed among the states.

The frantic rides up and down the Hudson damaged Hamilton's always fragile health. On November 12, he wrote to Washington from New Windsor to explain his delay in returning: "I have been detained here these two days by a fever and violent rheumatic pains throughout my body."[83] Despite his illness, Hamilton continued to direct the movement of troops slated to join Washington and went downriver to Peekskill to apply maximum pressure on Putnam's brigades. There, in late November, a haggard Hamilton climbed into bed at the home of Dennis Kennedy. It seemed uncertain whether he would recover. In a letter to Governor Clinton, Captain I. Gibbs wrote that he feared that the combined fevers and chills might prove mortal. On November 25, he reported that Hamilton "seemed to have all the appearance of drawing nigh his last, being seized with a coldness in his extremities, and he remained so for a space of two hours, then survived." On November 27, when the chill again invaded his legs from feet to knees, the attending physician thought he wouldn't last. However, "he remained in this situation for near four hours, after which the fever abated very much and from that time he has been getting much better." Hamilton had been so blistering in dealing with General Gates that not everyone welcomed his recovery. On December 5, Colonel Hugh Hughes wrote to his friend General Gates, "Colonel Hamilton, who has been very ill of a nervous disorder at Peekskill, is out of danger, unless it be from his own sweet temper."[84]

Right before Christmas, Hamilton set out to rejoin Washington, only to collapse again near Morristown. He was taken back in a hired coach for further rest in Peekskill, where he was nourished on a hearty diet of mutton, oranges, potatoes, quail, and partridge. Not until January 20, 1778, did Hamilton rejoin his colleagues at winter quarters in Valley Forge, near Philadelphia—a bleak place that could scarcely have elevated the spirits of the convalescing colonel.

Such was the inimitable luster of Horatio Gates after Saratoga that it was whispered in certain quarters that he ought to supplant Washington as commander in chief. The unhappiness with Washington was understandable. His military performance in New York and Philadelphia had been lackluster, and his setbacks at Brandywine and Germantown were fresher in people's memories than his spirited raids at Trenton and Princeton. The rivalry between Washington and Gates mirrored a political split in Congress. John and Samuel Adams, Richard Henry Lee, and others who wanted tighter congressional control over the war were sympathetic to Gates. In his diary that fall, John Adams had expressed dismay over Washington's generalship: "Oh, Heaven! grant us one great soul! . . . One active, masterly capacity would bring order out of this confusion and save this country."[85] Though he did not endorse Gates outright, Adams fretted that idolatry of Washington might end in military rule, and he was glad when the Saratoga victory cast something of a cloud over the commander in chief. Meanwhile, John Jay, Robert R. Livingston, Robert Morris, and other conservatives wanted to invest great executive power in the commander in chief and stood solidly arrayed behind Washington.

One of Gates's avid partisans was a moody Irishman named Thomas Conway, who had been educated in France, had served in the French Army, and had joined the Continental Army that spring. Hamilton made no secret of his contempt for the new brigadier general: "There does not exist a more villainous calumniator or incendiary," he wrote.[86] Conway aired freely to Gates his low opinion of General Washington's military talents and wrote to him after Saratoga, "Heaven has been determined to save your country or a weak general and bad counsellors would have ruined it."[87] Gates did not muzzle such treacherous talk. When a copy of this letter came into Washington's possession in November, he sent Gates a terse, angry note, quoting the line that referred to him and demanding an explanation.

Caught red-handed, Gates tried to deflect attention from his own disloyalty by searching out the culprit who had leaked the letter to Washington. His colleague Major James Wilkinson floated the idea that the conduit had been Robert Troup. Gates, recalling his testy exchanges with Hamilton, decided that Washington's young aide was the blackguard. "Colonel Hamilton was left alone an hour in this room," he told Wilkinson "during which time he took Conway's letter out of that closet and copied it and the copy has been furnished to Washington." Gates now embarked on a vendetta against Hamilton, still at this time recuperating in Peekskill. Gates said that he had adopted a plan "which would compel General Washington to give [Hamilton] up" so that "the receiver and the thief would be alike disgraced."[88]

On December 8, Gates wrote a tactless letter to Washington with a thinly veiled accusation against Hamilton. "I conjure your excellency to give me all the assistance you can in tracing out the author of the infidelity which put extracts from General Conway's letters to me into your hands. Those letters have been *stealingly copied,*" Gates informed Washington, stating that it was in his power to "do me and the United States a very important service by detecting a wretch who may betray me and capitally injure the *very operations under your immediate direction.*"[89]

It turned out that Hamilton was blameless and that the source of the disclosure was the raffish James Wilkinson, who had fingered Troup and Hamilton. While carrying dispatches to Congress, Wilkinson—a flamboyant character with an incurable weakness for liquor, intrigue, and bombast—had paused for alcoholic refreshment in Reading, Pennsylvania, and told an aide to Lord Stirling about the Conway letter to Gates. Lord Stirling then relayed the news to his friend Washington. Hamilton never forgot Gates's attempt to blacken his reputation: "I am his enemy personally," he wrote two years later, "for unjust and unprovoked attacks upon my character."[90]

Whether an actual conspiracy—the so-called Conway Cabal—ever existed with an explicit intention to displace Washington has long been fodder for historians. There was clearly some movement afoot, a loose network of critics, who wanted to replace Washington with Gates, even if they never entered into a formal pact. At first, it looked as if the cabal might succeed. In late November, Congress had appointed Horatio Gates president of the Board of War, which acquired new powers to supervise Washington. In mid-December, over Washington's protest, Conway was promoted to inspector general. Hamilton now believed that malevolent conspirators menaced Washington. "Since I saw you," he wrote to George Clinton, "I have discovered such convincing traits of the monster that I cannot doubt its reality in the most extensive sense."[91]

Countervailing forces had already begun to rein in the Conway conspirators. In early January 1778, Hamilton's dear friend John Laurens alerted his father to a design against Washington. Henry Laurens, now president of Congress, assured his son, "I will attend to all their movements and have set my face against every wicked attempt, however specious."[92] In the last analysis, Washington's popularity was unassailable, and the blatant scheming of his foes only solidified his reputation for integrity. By April 1778, Congress gladly accepted Conway's resignation as inspector general; Horatio Gates gradually lost his reputation on the battlefield. In the aftermath of the cabal, both Conway and Gates faced challenges to duels. James Wilkinson turned on his mentor and challenged Gates, but when the latter broke down and cried apologetically, the duel was called off. Because Conway persisted in maligning Washington, he was summoned to the dueling ground by General John Cadwalader, who fired a ball through Conway's mouth that came out the back of his head. Cadwalader showed no regret. "I have stopped the damned rascal's lying tongue at any rate," he observed as his opponent lay in agony on the ground.[93] Somehow, Conway managed to survive, but his career in the Continental Army was definitely over.

SIX

A FRENZY OF VALOR

W hen Hamilton, debilitated from illness, rejoined his comrades at Valley Forge in January 1778, he must have shuddered at the mud and log huts and the slovenly state of the men who shivered around the campfires. There was a dearth of gunpowder, tents, uniforms, and blankets. Hideous sights abounded: snow stained with blood from bare, bruised feet; the carcasses of hundreds of decomposing horses; troops gaunt from smallpox, typhus, and scurvy. Washington's staff was not exempt from the misery and had to bolt down cornmeal mush for breakfast. "For some days past there has been little less than a famine in the camp," Washington said in mid-February. Before winter's end, some 2,500 men, almost a quarter of the army, perished from disease, famine, or the cold.[1] To endure such suffering required stoicism reminiscent of the ancient Romans, so Washington had his favorite play, Addison's *Cato,* the story of a self-sacrificing Roman statesman, staged at Valley Forge to buck up his weary men.

That winter, Hamilton worked alongside Washington in the stone house of Isaac Potts, whose iron forge gave the area its name. Snappish and depressed over the Conway Cabal and unsettled by the wretched state of his men, Washington was more temperamental than usual. "The General is well but much worn with fatigue and anxiety," Martha Washington told a friend. "I never knew him to be so anxious as now."[2] Washington sometimes vented his rage at Hamilton, and tensions crept into their relationship. Hamilton yearned for a field command, but Washington could not afford to sacrifice his most valuable aide. It was Hamilton, after all, who wrote many of the pointed pleas to Congress asking for urgently needed provisions, and the young aide shared Washington's frustration. "For God's sake, my dear sir,"

Hamilton wrote to one colonel when authorizing him to collect wagons, "exert yourself upon this occasion. Our distress is infinite."[3]

Hamilton began to meditate on the deeper causes of the surrounding misery. Because the colonies had been forced to rely on England for textiles, the patriots lacked clothing. Because the colonies had relied on England for munitions, they lacked weapons. Hamilton also saw in graphic terms the inflationary dangers of printing too much paper money. Forced to accept at face value the depreciated paper issued by Congress and the states, farmers and merchants balked at selling food and clothing to the army and often ended up hawking their wares instead to the well-fed, well-clad redcoats carousing in Philadelphia. The situation at Valley Forge was scandalous: American soldiers were starving in the midst of fertile American farmland. Hamilton was also sickened by the bungling Commissary Department. He wrote to New York governor George Clinton in mid-February:

> At this very day, there are complaints from the whole line of having been three or four days without provisions. Desertions have been immense and strong features of mutiny begin to show themselves. It is indeed to be wondered at that the soldiers have manifested so unparalleled a degree of patience as they have. If effectual measures are not speedily adopted, I know not how we shall keep the army together or make another campaign.[4]

Hamilton cast a critical eye on the whole revolutionary effort. However upset by profiteering, he knew that the central weakness of the continental cause was political in nature. In his letter to Clinton, he scoffed at the rank favoritism shown by Congress in showering promotions on "every petty rascal who comes armed with ostentatious pretensions of military merit and experience."[5] Unable to enforce its requests for money and troops, an impotent Congress was reduced to begging from the states, which selfishly hoarded soldiers for their own home guards. The only way the Continental Army could lure soldiers was through expensive cash bounties and promises of future land. The republican partiality for state militias in lieu of a strong central army threatened to undermine the entire Revolution.

The disillusioned Hamilton also struggled to fathom why a Congress that had once boasted such distinguished figures was now glutted with mediocrities. Where had the competent members gone? Hamilton concluded that the talent had been drained off by state governments. "However important it is to give form and efficiency to your interior [i.e., state] constitutions and police," he told Clinton, "it is infinitely more important to have a wise general council. . . . You should not beggar the councils of the United States to enrich the administration of the several members."[6] Such statements presaged Hamilton's later nationalism. Ironically, George

Clinton became his bête noire, exemplifying the very parochial state power against which he inveighed.

Hamilton, just turned twenty-three, was already spouting civics lessons to state governors. His views were also solicited by his commander in chief. When Washington had to report to a congressional committee about a proposed army reorganization, he sought his aide's advice, and Hamilton enumerated a long list of abuses to be curbed. He urged that officers who overstayed their furloughs by ten days be court-martialed, recommended surprise inspections to keep sentries alert, and even prescribed the manner in which they should sleep: "Every man must have his haversack under his head and, if the post is dangerous, his arms in his hand." Hamilton also displayed an unbending sense of military discipline and seemed something of a martinet. Any dragoon who allowed another person to ride his horse without first notifying the inspector general should "receive one hundred lashes for such neglect."[7]

That Hamilton already contemplated America's political future was evident in March, when Washington assigned him to negotiate a prisoner exchange with the British. Having already questioned many British and Hessian deserters, Hamilton was a natural choice for the job and was joined by his former Elizabethtown mentor, Elias Boudinot, now the commissary general of prisoners. Some in Congress not only opposed negotiations but wanted them to fail so that Britain could be blamed. Shocked by this duplicity, Hamilton wrote to George Clinton, "It is thought to be bad policy to go into an exchange. But admitting this to be true, it is much worse policy to commit such frequent breaches of faith and ruin our national character."[8] Hamilton saw America's essential nature being forged in the throes of battle, and that made honest action imperative.

Shortly after Hamilton penned his report on army reorganization, a Prussian soldier with a drooping face and ample double chin appeared at Valley Forge. He billed himself as a German baron and acted the part with almost comical pomposity. Although the baron and the honorific "von" were likely fictitious, Frederick William August von Steuben came from a military family and had served as an aide to Frederick the Great. He came to America at his own expense and waived all pay unless the patriots triumphed. Washington appointed him a provisional inspector general, with a mandate to instill discipline in the army. Since Steuben's English was tentative at best, he relied on French as his lingua franca, bringing him into immediate contact with the bilingual Hamilton and John Laurens, who acted as interpreters. Though Steuben was forty-eight and Hamilton twenty-three, they became fast friends, united by French and their fondness for military lore and service.

Soon Steuben was strutting around Valley Forge, teaching the amateur troops to march in formation, load muskets, and fix bayonets and sprinkling his orders with colorful *goddamns* and plentiful polyglot expletives that endeared him to the troops. Wrote one young private: "Never before or since have I had such an impression of the ancient fabled god of war as when I looked on the baron. He seemed to me a perfect personification of Mars. The trappings of his horse, the enormous holsters of his pistols, his large size, and his strikingly martial aspect, all seemed to favor the idea."[9] Steuben overhauled the army's drill manual or "Blue Book" and created a training guide for company commanders, with Hamilton often recruited as editor and translator. Hamilton eyed the drillmaster with wry affection. "The Baron is a gentleman for whom I have a particular esteem," Hamilton said, though he chided his "fondness for power and importance."[10] He never doubted that Steuben had worked wonders for the élan of the Continental Army. " 'Tis unquestionably [due] to his efforts [that] we are indebted for the introduction of discipline in the army," he later told John Jay.[11] On May 5, 1778, Steuben was recognized for his superlative efforts and awarded the rank of major general.

During the winter encampments, Hamilton constantly educated himself, as if equipping his mind for the larger tasks ahead. "Force of intellect and force of will were the sources of his success," Henry Cabot Lodge later wrote.[12] From his days as an artillery captain, Hamilton had kept a pay book with blank pages in the back; while on Washington's staff, he filled up 112 pages with notes from his extracurricular reading. Hamilton fit the type of the self-improving autodidact, employing all his spare time to better himself. He aspired to the eighteenth-century aristocratic ideal of the versatile man conversant in every area of knowledge. Thanks to his pay book we know that he read a considerable amount of philosophy, including Bacon, Hobbes, Montaigne, and Cicero. He also perused histories of Greece, Prussia, and France. This was hardly light fare after a day of demanding correspondence for Washington, yet he retained the information and applied it to profitable use. While other Americans dreamed of a brand-new society that would expunge all traces of effete European civilization, Hamilton humbly studied those societies for clues to the formation of a new government. Unlike Jefferson, Hamilton never saw the creation of America as a magical leap across a chasm to an entirely new landscape, and he always thought the New World had much to learn from the Old.

Probably the first book that Hamilton absorbed was Malachy Postlethwayt's *Universal Dictionary of Trade and Commerce,* a learned almanac of politics, economics, and geography that was crammed with articles about taxes, public debt, money, and banking. The dictionary took the form of two ponderous, folio-sized volumes, and it is touching to think of young Hamilton lugging them through the chaos of war. Hamilton would praise Postlethwayt as one of "the ablest masters of political arithmetic."[13] A proponent of manufacturing, Postlethwayt gave the aide-de-camp a glimpse of a mixed economy in which government would both steer business activity and free individual energies. In the pay book one can see the future treasury wizard mastering the rudiments of finance. "When you can get more of foreign coin, [the] coin for your native exchange is said to be high and the reverse low," Hamilton noted.[14] He also stocked his mind with basic information about the world: "The continent of Europe is 2600 miles long and 2800 miles broad";[15] "Prague is the principal city of Bohemia, the principal part of the commerce of which is carried on by the Jews."[16] He recorded tables from Postlethwayt showing infant-mortality rates, population growth, foreign-exchange rates, trade balances, and the total economic output of assorted nations. Hamilton's notes from Postlethwayt showcase his exemplary discipline in undertaking private courses of study.

Like the other founding fathers, Hamilton rummaged through the wisdom of antiquity for political precedents. From the *First Philippic* of Demosthenes, he plucked a passage that summed up his conception of a leader as someone who would not pander to popular whims. "As a general marches at the head of his troops," so should wise politicians "march at the head of affairs, insomuch that they ought not to wait the *event* to know what measures to take, but the measures which they have taken ought to produce the *event*."[17] Nearly fifty-one pages of the pay book contain extracts from a six-volume set of Plutarch's *Lives*. Thereafter, Hamilton always interpreted politics as an epic tale from Plutarch of lust and greed and people plotting for power. Since his political theory was rooted in his study of human nature, he took special delight in Plutarch's biographical sketches. And he carefully noted the creation of senates, priesthoods, and other elite bodies that governed the lives of the people. Hamilton was already interested in the checks and balances that enabled a government to tread a middle path between despotism and anarchy. From the life of Lycurgus, he noted:

> Among the many alterations which Lycurgus made, the first and most important was the establishment of the senate, which having a power equal to the kings in matters of consequence did . . . foster and qualify the imperious and fiery genius of monarchy by constantly restraining it within the bounds of equity and moderation. For the state before had no firm basis to stand upon, leaning sometimes towards an absolute monarchy and sometimes towards a pure democracy. But this establishment of the senate was to the commonwealth what the ballast is to a ship and preserved the whole in a just equilibrium.[18]

Hamilton was especially attentive to the amorous stories and strange sexual customs reported by Plutarch. He registered in the pay book how in ancient Rome two naked young noblemen whipped young married women during the celebration of Lupercalia and "how the young married women were glad of this kind of whipping as they imagined it helped conception."[19] Hamilton was also intrigued that Lycurgus allowed a worthy man to ask permission of another husband to impregnate his wife, so that "by planting in a good soil he might raise a generous progeny to possess all the valuable qualifications of their parents."[20] This same Lycurgus tried to make the married women "more robust and capable of vigorous offspring" by allowing selected virgins and young men to "go naked and dance in their presence at certain festive occasions."[21]

For anyone studying Hamilton's pay book, it would come as no surprise that he would someday emerge as a first-rate constitutional scholar, an unsurpassed treasury secretary, and the protagonist of the first great sex scandal in American political history.

Restless at his desk, Hamilton longed to spring into combat, and he found a dramatic chance to do so in June 1778. The direction of the war had shifted in February when the French, heartened by the victory at Saratoga, decided to recognize American independence and signed military and commercial treaties with the fledgling nation. An ebullient John Adams spoke for many Americans when he exulted that Great Britain "is no longer mistress of the ocean."[22]

As part of their response to French entry into the war, the British replaced General Howe with Sir Henry Clinton as commander of their forces. Hamilton had been unimpressed by Howe's leadership. "All that the English need to have done was to blockade our ports with twenty-five frigates and ten ships of the line," Hamilton told a French visitor. "But, thank God, they did nothing of the sort."[23] If anything, he was even less dazzled by General Clinton. One day, Henry Lee broached to Washington an ingenious plan for kidnapping Clinton, who was quartered in a house on Broadway in New York. He had a large garden out back, overlooking the Hudson River, where he napped in a small pavilion each afternoon. Lee wanted to sneak men across the Hudson at low tide and snatch Clinton as he dozed. Hamilton spiked the plan with a cogent objection, telling Washington that if Clinton was taken prisoner "it would be our misfortune; since the British government could not find another commander so incompetent to send in his place."[24]

When General Clinton learned in mid-June that a French fleet had sailed for America, he feared that it might team up with the Continental Army and entrap his occupation force in Philadelphia. To avert this, he decided to evacuate the city and concentrate his troops in the more easily defensible New York. This meant that a huge British army of nine thousand men, laden with provisions filling fifteen hundred wagons—the baggage train stretched for twelve miles—would need to troop across New Jersey with perilous slowness. With supply lines stretched dangerously thin, these lumbering British forces would be exposed to the fire of the Continental Army. Washington saw an opportunity to score a telling blow against a vulnerable adversary and highlight the gains made by his men at Valley Forge under Steuben's vigorous stewardship.

Washington had survived the Conway Cabal only to have his authority challenged by General Charles Lee, an experienced officer who had been captured by the British in a tavern in late 1776 and had only recently been released after a fifteen-month captivity. Lee was a thin, quarrelsome, eccentric bachelor who spoke four foreign languages, had lost two fingers in an Italian duel, and traveled everywhere with his pack of dogs at his heels. He had briefly married an Indian woman, leading the Mohawks to nickname him, with good reason, Boiling Water. He was a talented but impossibly temperamental man who believed devoutly in his own military genius. Arrogant and indiscreet, he told Elias Boudinot that "General Washington was not fit to command a sergeant's guard."[25] He also ridiculed efforts made by Steuben and Hamilton to bring professional order to the army.

On June 24, 1778, Washington convened a council of war to debate whether to pounce on the retreating British Army. Hamilton took minutes. The opinionated Lee immediately poured scorn on Washington's plan, saying the Americans would be trounced by the superior Europeans and that it was foolhardy to court trouble when the French were soon to arrive. Hamilton—who dismissed Lee as "a driveler in the business of soldiership or something much worse"—writhed quietly.[26] To his astonishment, the officers agreed with Lee's views and in a manner, scoffed Hamilton, that "would have done honor to the most honorable society of midwives."[27] Washington preferred to operate by consensus, but he decided to override this vote and give orders to strike at the enemy "if fair opportunity offered."[28] Lee refused to serve as second in command for what he deemed a misguided maneuver. Only after Washington called his bluff and assigned the position to Lafayette did Lee back down and consent to ride out and take command of the advancing forces.

For the next few days, Hamilton, as a liaison officer to Lafayette, was constantly in motion, riding through muggy nights to reconnoiter enemy lines and convey intelligence among the officers. By the night of June 27, the British were encamped near Monmouth Court House in Freehold, New Jersey, with Lee and his soldiers lying only six miles away. Washington ordered Lee to attack in the early morning "unless there should be very powerful reasons to the contrary."[29] Washington, three miles farther back, would then bring up the rear with the army's main contingent. Hamilton drafted Washington's directive to Lee that night, telling the latter to "skirmish with [the enemy] so as to produce some delay and give time for the rest of the troops to come up."[30]

June 28, 1778, was to be an unforgettable day because of, among other things, the stifling heat. The thermometer reached the high nineties, and some soldiers rode naked from the waist up. During this day, horses and riders alike expired from heat prostration. The battle was supposed to start with Lee taking on the British rear guard. After hearing small-arms fire that morning, Hamilton was sent ahead by Washington to scout Lee's movements, and he was stunned by the tumult he found: far from engaging the enemy, as directed, Lee's men were in a full-blown retreat. Not a word of this had been communicated to Washington. Hamilton rode up to Lee and shouted, "I will stay here with you, my dear general, and die with you! Let us all die rather than retreat!"[31] Once again the young aide did not hesitate to talk to a general as a peer. Hamilton also spotted a threatening movement by a British cavalry unit and prevailed upon Lee to order Lafayette to charge them.

When Washington got wind of the chaotic flight of his troops, he galloped up to Lee, glowered at him, and demanded, "What is the meaning of this, sir? I desire to know the meaning of this disorder and confusion!"

Lee took umbrage at the peremptory tone. "The American troops would not stand the British bayonets," he replied.

To which Washington retorted, "You damned poltroon, you never tried them!"[32] Washington did not ordinarily use profanities, but, faced with Lee's insubordination that morning, he swore "till the leaves shook on the trees," said one general.[33]

America's idolatry of George Washington may have truly begun at the battle of Monmouth. One of America's most accomplished horsemen, Washington at first rode a white charger, given to him by William Livingston, now governor of New Jersey, in honor of his recrossing of the Delaware. This beautiful horse dropped dead from the heat, and Washington instantly switched to a chestnut mare. By sheer force of will, he stopped the retreating soldiers, rallied them, then reversed them. "Stand fast, *my boys*, and receive your enemy," he shouted. "The southern troops are advancing to support you."[34] Washington's steady presence had a sedative effect on the flying men. He summarily ordered Lee to the rear and goaded the troops into driving the British from the field. As he watched this legendary performance, Lafayette thought to himself, "Never had I beheld so *superb a man*."[35]

Hamilton, not prone to hero worship, was awed by Washington's unflinching courage and incomparable self-command. "I never saw the general to so much advantage," he told Elias Boudinot. "His coolness and firmness were admirable. He instantly took maneuvers for checking the enemy's advance and giving time for the army, which was very near, to form and make a proper disposition. . . . By his own good sense and fortitude he turned the fate of the day. . . . [H]e directed the whole with the skill of a master workman."[36]

Hamilton's bravery likewise left an enduring image. Famished for combat, he was in "a sort of frenzy of valor," Lee contended.[37] He seemed ubiquitous on the battlefield. When Hamilton found one brigade in retreat and feared the loss of its artillery, he ordered them to line up along a fence and then charge with fixed bayonets. Riding hatless in the sunny field, Hamilton was exhausted from the heat by the time his horse was shot out from under him. He toppled over, badly injured, and had to retire from the field. Aaron Burr and John Laurens also had horses shot from under them that day. So severe was Burr's sunstroke that it rendered him effectively unfit for further combat duty in the Revolution. Suffering from violent headaches, nausea, and exhaustion and probably irked by his lack of promotion under Washington, Burr took a temporary leave of absence in October.

Many people were struck by Hamilton's behavior at Monmouth, which showed more than mere courage. There was an element of ecstatic defiance, an indifference toward danger, that reflected his youthful fantasies of an illustrious death in battle. One aide said that Hamilton had shown "singular proofs of bravery" and appeared "to court death under our doubtful circumstances and triumphed over it."[38] John Adams later said that General Henry Knox told him stories of Hamilton's "heat and effervescence" at Monmouth.[39] At moments of supreme stress, Hamilton could screw himself up to an emotional pitch that was nearly feverish in intensity.

The battle of Monmouth was not an outright victory for the patriots, and the British Army escaped intact the next day. Most observers termed it a draw. Still, the ragtag continentals had killed or wounded more than one thousand troops—four times the number of American casualties—proving to naysayers that they could perform admirably against tip-top European soldiers. "Our troops, after the first impulse from mismanagement, behaved with more spirit and moved with greater order than the British troops," Hamilton rejoiced. "I assure you I never was pleased with them before this day."[40] Enraged that Lee had fumbled a tremendous opportunity, Hamilton applauded Washington when he arrested Lee for disobeying orders and making a shameful retreat. Hamilton was an eager witness against Lee during a court-martial that took place at New Brunswick in July under Lord Stirling's supervision. "Whatever a court-martial may decide," Hamilton warned Elias Boudinot, "I shall continue to believe and say his conduct was monstrous and unpardonable."[41] Among Charles Lee's sympathizers was Aaron Burr, who missed no chance to belittle Washington's military talents.

On July 4 and 13, Hamilton gave damaging testimony at the court-martial, recalling that Lee had taken no measures to stop the enemy's advance, even after being told to do so by Washington. He told of troops fleeing in wild disorder and of Lee's failure to notify Washington of this retreat. In a dramatic finale, Lee cross-examined Hamilton and accused him of having expressed in the field a contrary opinion of his conduct. "I did not," rejoined Hamilton. "I said something to you in the field expressive of an opinion that there appeared in you no want of that degree of self-possession, which proceeds from a want of personal intrepidity." Hamilton further informed the general that there had appeared in him "a certain hurry of spirits, which may proceed from a temper not so calm and steady as is necessary to support a man in such critical circumstances."[42] It was a curious clash indeed: the youthful aide pontificating to a veteran general on the ideal mental state of a field commander.

In the end, Charles Lee was found guilty on all counts but given a relatively lenient sentence: suspension from the army for one year. In October, the disgraced general assured Burr that he planned "to resign my commission, retire to Virginia, and learn to hoe tobacco."[43] But he did not let matters drop there, and he and his minions continued to vilify Washington and even Hamilton for having testified in the court-martial. In late November, Hamilton encountered Major John Skey Eustace, a worshipful young aide-de-camp to Lee and almost his adopted son. Hamilton tried to approach him in a conciliatory manner, even though Eustace was telling people that Hamilton had perjured himself in the court-martial. Eustace later described to General Lee his encounter with Hamilton:

> [Hamilton] advanced towards me, on my entering the room, with presented hand—I took no notice of his polite intention, but sat down without bowing to him. . . . He then asked me if I was come from camp—I said, *shortly, no,* without the usual application of Sir, rose from my chair—left *the room* and *him standing before the chair.* I could not treat him much more rudely—I've reported my *suspicions* of his *veracity on the trial* so often that I expect the son of a bitch will challenge me when he comes.[44]

In early December, Lee heaped further abuse upon Washington in print, and John Laurens urged Hamilton to rebut it. "The pen of Junius is in your hand and I think you will, without difficulty, expose . . . such a tissue of falsehood and inconsistency as will satisfy the world and put him forever to silence."[45] Perhaps because he was a party to the dispute, Hamilton, in a rare act of reticence, declined to lift his pen. Instead, Laurens challenged Lee to a duel to avenge the slurs against Washington. Hamilton agreed to serve as his second, the first of many such "affairs of honor" in which he participated.

Dueling was so prevalent in the Continental Army that one French visitor declared, "The rage for dueling here has reached an incredible and scandalous point."[46] It was a way that gentlemen could defend their sense of honor: instead of resorting to courts if insulted, they repaired to the dueling ground. This anachronistic practice expressed a craving for rank and distinction that lurked beneath the egalitarian rhetoric of the American Revolution. Always insecure about his status in the world, Hamilton was a natural adherent to dueling, with its patrician overtones. Lacking a fortune or family connections, he guarded his reputation jealously throughout his life, and affairs of honor were often his preferred method for doing so. The man born without honor placed a premium on maintaining his.

Late in the wintry afternoon of December 23, 1778, Hamilton accompanied John Laurens to the duel in a wood outside Philadelphia. Lee chose for his second Major Evan Edwards. By prearranged rules, Laurens and Lee strode toward each other and fired their pistols when they stood five or six paces apart. After Laurens shot Lee in the right side, Laurens, Hamilton, and Edwards rushed toward the general, who waved them away and requested a second round of fire. Neither Hamilton nor Edwards wanted Lee to continue, as they made clear in a joint account they issued the next day. "Col. Hamilton observed that unless the General was influenced by motives of personal enmity, he did not think the affair ought to be pursued any further. But as General Lee seemed to persist in desiring it, he was too tender of his friend's honor to persist in opposing it."[47] But no second round ensued. The duel ended with Lee declaring that he "esteemed General Washington" as a man and had never spoken of him in the abusive manner alleged.[48] For Laurens, this made sufficient amends, and the four men quit the woods. In their summary, Hamilton and Edwards praised the conduct of the two principals as "strongly marked with all the politeness, generosity, coolness, and firmness that ought to characterize a transaction of this nature."[49]

How was Hamilton affected by his first duel? He saw two gentlemen who had exhibited exemplary behavior and fought for ideals rather than just personal animosity. The object had not been to kill the other person so much as to resolve honorably a lingering dispute. Both Laurens and Lee walked away with their dignity more or less intact. Dueling may well have struck the young Hamilton less as a barbaric relic of a feudal age than as a noble affirmation of high honor. It was the last act of Charles Lee's military career. He withdrew from the scene and lived in seclusion with his beloved dogs, first in Virginia and then in Philadelphia, where he died of tuberculosis in October 1782.

One possible reason that Hamilton refrained from attacking Charles Lee in print that autumn was that he had just administered a stern rebuke to Maryland congressman Samuel Chase. A signer of the Declaration of Independence and later a

Supreme Court justice, Chase was a tall, ungainly man with a resemblance to Dr. Samuel Johnson and a face so broad and ruddy that he was dubbed "Bacon Face." He could be overbearing and blustered his way into controversies throughout his career.

Hamilton had published anonymous diatribes against Chase after noticing that the price of flour needed by the newly arrived French fleet had more than doubled. He claimed that Chase had leaked knowledge of a secret congressional plan to buy up flour for the French to his associates, who then cornered the market. To expose Chase, Hamilton resumed his acquaintance with *New-York Journal* publisher John Holt, who now printed a newspaper from Poughkeepsie during the British occupation of New York.

Using the pen name "Publius"—a lifelong favorite—Hamilton castigated Chase in three long letters in Holt's paper between October and November 1778. Chase didn't know the author was an adjutant to Washington. These essays belie the later caricature of Hamilton as a reflexive apologist for business, an uncritical exponent of the profit motive. After pointing to the punishment inflicted on traitors to the patriotic cause, he noted that "the conduct of another class, equally criminal, and, if possible, more mischievous has hitherto passed with that impunity. . . . I mean that tribe who . . . have carried the spirit of monopoly and extortion to an excess which scarcely admits of a parallel. When avarice takes the lead in a state, it is commonly the forerunner of its fall. How shocking is it to discover among ourselves, even at this early period, the strongest symptoms of this fatal disease?"[50]

The first "Publius" letter pointed out that greed can corrupt a state and that a public official who betrays his trust "ought to feel the utmost rigor of public resentment and be detested as a traitor of the worst and most dangerous kind."[51] In the second letter, Hamilton lapsed into gratuitous calumny against Chase. "Had you not struck out a new line of prostitution for yourself, you might still have remained unnoticed and contemptible," he hectored Chase. "It is your lot to have the peculiar privilege of being universally despised."[52] In the third letter, Hamilton gave a possible clue to his overwrought style: he was already thinking ahead. "The station of a member of C[ongre]ss is the most illustrious and important of any I am able to conceive. He is to be regarded not only as a legislator but as the founder of an empire."[53] Hamilton expected that someday the struggling confederation of states would be welded into a mighty nation, and he believed that every step now taken by politicians would reverberate by example far into the future.

It was fitting that Hamilton should have mused about America's future greatness in the fall of 1778, for the struggle with the British had expanded into a sweeping transatlantic conflict. Spain had entered the war on the colonial side after failing to regain control of Gibraltar from England. France had also decided to wage war on Britain for reasons having to do less with ideological solidarity with America—it scarcely behooved Louis XVI to encourage revolts against royal authority—than with a desire to subvert Britain and even the score after losing the French and Indian War. The French also sought better access to Caribbean sugar islands and North American ports. This early lesson in Realpolitik—that countries follow their interests, not their sympathies—was engraved in Hamilton's memory, and he often reminded Jeffersonians later on that the French had fought for their own selfish purposes. "The primary motives of France for the assistance which she gave us was obviously to enfeeble a hated and powerful rival by breaking in pieces the British Empire," he wrote nearly two decades later. "He must be a fool who can be credulous enough to believe that a despotic court aided a popular revolution from regard to liberty or friendship to the principles of such a revolution."[54]

According to his King's College classmate Nicholas Fish, Hamilton had a direct hand in prodding Lafayette to advocate bringing a French army to America. Before Admiral Jean Baptiste d'Estaing came with his fleet in July 1778, Hamilton played on Lafayette's vanity by touting the merits of having a French ground force with Lafayette as its commander. "The United States are under infinite obligations to [Lafayette] beyond what is known," Hamilton told Fish later, "not only for his valour and good conduct as major general of our army, but for his good offices and influence in our behalf with the court of France. The French army now here . . . would not have been in this country but through his means."[55]

Hamilton was posted to greet Admiral d'Estaing aboard his majestic flagship and became a frequent emissary to the French. He often served as interpreter for Washington, who did not speak the language and considered himself too old to learn. Hamilton also provided impeccable translations of diplomatic correspondence into French, with just the right dash of high-flown language. In this manner, the alliance with France further enhanced Hamilton's stature in the Continental Army.

Many French radicals who flocked to the Revolution were descended from nobility and were enchanted by Hamilton's social grace, ready humor, and erudition. J. P. Brissot de Warville recalled Hamilton as "firm and . . . decided[,] . . . frank and martial" and later had him named an honorary member of the French National Assembly.[56] The marquis de Chastellux marveled that such a young man "by a prudence and secrecy still more beyond his age than his information justified the confidence with which he was honored" by Washington.[57] The duc de La Rochefoucauld-Liancourt observed of Hamilton, "He united with dignity and feeling, and much force and decision, delightful manners, great sweetness, and was infinitely agreeable."[58] At the same time, the duke noticed that some things were so blindingly self-evident to Hamilton that he was baffled when others didn't grasp them quickly—an intellectual agility that could breed intolerance for less quick-witted mortals.

Though Hamilton was adored by the French officers in their royal blue-and-scarlet uniforms, he also nursed grievances against them. Familiarity bred contempt along with affection. Hamilton deplored many French aristocrats as vainglorious self-promoters who wanted to snatch a particle of fame from the Revolution and parlay it into a superior rank at home. He had to endure in silence insults from them about incompetent continentals. "The French volunteers, generally speaking, were men of ordinary talents and skills in the military arts," remarked Robert Troup, "and yet most of them were so conceited as to suppose themselves Caesars or Hannibals in comparison with the American officers."[59]

The self-made Hamilton was offended by favoritism shown toward the French, a situation that demoralized many in the continental ranks who fought at considerable personal sacrifice. "Congress in the beginning went upon a very injudicious plan with respect to Frenchmen," he informed one friend. "To every adventurer that came without even the shadow of credentials they gave the rank of field officers."[60] It often fell to Hamilton to smooth ruffled feelings between the allies, as when he arbitrated an early dispute between General John Sullivan and Admiral d'Estaing.

It was the bane of Hamilton's service that he had to draft numerous letters to Congress, requesting promotions for undeserving Frenchmen. If Congress spurned these requests, then he had to apply balm to the wounded suitors through oily compliments. Hamilton once told John Jay that he wrote these letters to shield Washington from the inevitable resentment of rejected Frenchmen. In private, nobody railed more against the preferential treatment of French aristocrats than Hamilton, who was later so freely branded an "aristocrat" by rivals. At the same time, he saw that an aristocratic class could contain progressive members and that republican wisdom wasn't a monopoly held by mechanics and tradesmen.

Though Hamilton often regarded the French allies as a royal nuisance, he never denied the decisive nature of their intervention. From the start, they had smuggled weapons and supplies to the patriots. Many were also fine soldiers, and Hamilton later paid tribute to the "ardent, impetuous, and military genius of the French."[61] By the spring of 1779, he could say categorically of these sometimes trying allies, "Their friendship is the pillar of our security."[62]

The status-conscious Hamilton was also sensitive to perceived inequities among Washington's staff, even when it pertained to his closest friend, John Laurens. In November 1778, just before Henry Laurens stepped down as its president, Congress tried to promote John Laurens to lieutenant colonel as a reward for valorous conduct. Laurens declined but accepted the offer when it was renewed in March 1779.

Hamilton didn't urge Laurens to reject the commission, but he was dismayed nonetheless. "The only thing I see wrong in the affair is this," Hamilton wrote to his friend. "Congress by their conduct . . . appear to have intended to confer a privilege, an honor, a mark of distinction . . . which they withhold from other gentlemen in the [military] family. This carries with it an air of preference, which, though we can all truly say we love your character and admire your military merit, cannot fail to give some of us uneasy sensations."[63]

Hamilton and Laurens shared an idealism about the Revolution that yoked them tightly together. They were both unwavering abolitionists who saw emancipation of the slaves as an inseparable part of the struggle for freedom as well as a source of badly needed manpower. "I think that we Americans, at least in the Southern col[onie]s, cannot contend with *a good grace* for liberty until we shall have enfranchised our slaves," Laurens told a friend right before the signing of the Declaration of Independence.[64] This represented a courageous stand for the son of a very significant South Carolina slaveholder. From the time he joined Washington's family, Laurens unabashedly championed a plan in which slaves would earn their freedom by joining the Continental Army. (About five thousand blacks eventually did serve alongside the patriots, though they were frequently relegated to noncombat situations; short of soldiers, Rhode Island raised a black regiment in 1778 by promising slaves their freedom.) Laurens offered more than lip service to his scheme, telling his father that he was willing to take his inheritance in the form of a black battalion, freed and equipped to defend South Carolina.

At the end of the year, Laurens's proposal acquired increased urgency as the British redirected their military operations southward, hoping to rouse Loyalist sympathies. By January 1779, they had captured both Savannah and Augusta and threatened South Carolina. Laurens resigned from Washington's family and returned to defend his home state, stopping in Philadelphia to solicit congressional approval for two to four black battalions for the Continental Army. Hamilton drafted an eloquent, supportive letter for his friend to deliver to John Jay, who had succeeded Henry Laurens as president of Congress. In the letter, Hamilton plainly revealed what he thought of the slave system that had surrounded him since birth: "I have not the least doubt that the negroes will make very excellent soldiers with proper management and I will venture to pronounce that they cannot be put in bettter hands than those of Mr. Laurens." Hamilton brushed aside the fallacies that slaves were not smart enough to turn into soldiers and were genetically inferior: "This is so far from appearing to me a valid objection that I think their want of cultivation (for their natural faculties are probably as good as ours) joined to that habit of subordination which they acquire from a life of servitude will make them sooner become soldiers than our white inhabitants."

In a typical Hamiltonian manner, he placed political realism at the service of a larger ethical framework, stressing that both humanity and self-interest argued for the Laurens proposal:

> The contempt we have been taught to entertain for the blacks makes us fancy many things that are founded neither in reason nor experience; and an unwillingness to part with property of so valuable a kind will furnish a thousand arguments to show the impracticability or pernicious tendency of a scheme which requires such a sacrifice. But it should be considered that if we do not make use of them in this way, the enemy probably will and that the best way to counteract the temptations they will hold out will be to offer them ourselves. An essential part of the plan is to give them their freedom with their muskets. This will secure their fidelity, animate their courage, and I believe will have a good influence upon those who remain by opening a door to their emancipation.[65]

Unfortunately, despite a supportive congressional resolution, Laurens's battle in the South Carolina legislature to enact his program proved futile. South Carolina had a special stake in the slave trade, with Charleston acting as the largest port of entry for slaves arriving in North America. As in many places, planters lived in dread of slave insurrections, constantly inspected slave quarters for concealed weapons, and sometimes themselves refused to serve in the Continental Army out of fear that in their absence their slaves might rise up and massacre their families.

The northern states were not about to override their southern brethren on the slavery issue. All along, the American Revolution had been premised on a tacit bargain that regional conflicts would be subordinated to the need for unity among the states. This understanding dictated that slavery would remain a taboo subject. There was also the ticklish matter that many slave owners had joined the Revolution precisely to *retain* slavery. In November 1775, Lord Dunmore, the royal governor of Virginia, had issued a proclamation offering freedom to slaves willing to defend the Crown—an action that sent many panicky slaveholders stampeding into the patriot camp. "How is it that we hear the loudest yelps for liberty from the drivers of Negroes?" Samuel Johnson protested from London.[66] Horace Walpole echoed this sentiment: "I should think the souls of the Africans would sit heavily on the swords of the Americans."[67]

Many on the patriot side recognized the hypocrisy of the American position. Even before the Declaration of Independence, Abigail Adams had bewailed the situation: "It always appeared a most iniquitous scheme to me—to fight for ourselves for what we are robbing and plundering from those who have as good a right to freedom as we have."[68] And yet, to the everlasting disgrace of the rebel colonists, it was General Sir Henry Clinton in June 1779 who promised freedom to runaway slaves defecting to the British side. The defeat of the Laurens plan left Hamilton utterly dejected. "I wish its success," he wrote to Laurens later in the year, "but my hopes are very feeble. Prejudice and private interest will be antagonists too powerful for public spirit and public good."[69]

After Laurens despaired of securing legislative action on his proposal, he turned to military service in South Carolina under Brigadier General William Moultrie. He was so fearless yet foolhardy in one rearguard action—without authority, he led his men across an exposed river position and suffered heavy casualties—that Moultrie later called Laurens "a young man of great merit and a brave soldier, but an imprudent officer. He was too rash and impetuous."[70] A story, perhaps apocryphal, says that when the British subsequently besieged Moultrie and his men at Charleston, Laurens vowed to run his sword through the first civilian who proposed surrendering the city and further refused to carry terms of capitulation to the enemy.

During Laurens's southern sojourn, Hamilton wrote to him some of the most personally revealing letters of his life. He knew the south was endangered by the British and that atrocities were being committed on both sides. Perhaps he wondered whether he would ever see his friend again. In one April 1779 letter, Hamilton expressed such open affection for Laurens that an early editor, presumably Hamilton's son, crossed out some of the words and scrawled across the top, "I must not publish the whole of this." Besides fondness for Laurens, the letter shows how much Hamilton, scarred by his past, was afraid to entrust his emotional security to anyone:

> Cold in my professions, warm in friendships, I wish, my dear Laurens, it m[ight] be in my power by action rather than words [to] convince you that I love you. I shall only tell you that till you bade us adieu, I hardly knew the value you had taught my heart to set upon you. Indeed, my friend, it was not well done. You know the opinion I entertain of mankind and how much it is my desire to preserve myself free from particular attachments and to keep my happiness independent of the caprice of others. You s[hould] not have taken advantage of my sensibility to ste[al] into my affections without my consent.[71]

Other letters that Hamilton wrote to Laurens betray the tone of a jealous, lovesick young man who was quick to chide his friend for failing to write frequently enough. "I have written you five or six letters since you left Philadelphia and I should have written you more had you made proper return," Hamilton wrote to Laurens in September. "But, like a jealous lover, when I thought you slighted my caresses, my affection was alarmed and my vanity piqued."[72]

Many things beyond the absence of Laurens troubled Hamilton that summer, especially the shortsighted failure of the states to grant mandatory taxing power to Congress in the Articles of Confederation, which had been approved as the new nation's governing charter on November 15, 1777, and submitted to the states for ratification. As a result, Congress had resorted to flimsy financial expedients—borrowing and printing reams of paper money—that were fast destroying America's credit. The paper currency was depreciating rapidly. Hence, for the first time, Hamilton began to fiddle with ideas for creating a national bank, through a mixture of foreign loans and private subscriptions.

Hamilton may have been more vocal in his criticism of Congress than he realized. In early July, he received a letter from a Lieutenant Colonel John Brooks, who reported derogatory comments that Congressman Francis Dana made about Hamilton at a Philadelphia coffeehouse. According to Brooks, Dana quoted Hamilton as saying "that it was high time for the people to rise, join General Washington, and turn Congress out of doors. To render this account in the highest degree improbable, he further observed that Mr. Hamilton could be no ways interested in the defence of this country and, therefore, was most likely to pursue such a line of conduct as his great ambition dictated."[73] These charges set an early pattern for future Hamilton controversies. People would assume that Hamilton, as an "outsider" or "foreigner," could not possibly be motivated by patriotic impulses. Hence, he must be power mad and governed by a secret agenda. In response, Hamilton would display a deep insecurity that he normally kept well hidden behind his confident demeanor. If struck, he tended to hit back hard.

Within days, Hamilton wrote to Dana and demanded either a retraction of the story or disclosure of its source. He intimated that he would demand a duel if the charges had actually been made, noting that "they are [of] so personal and illiberal a complexion as will oblige me to make them the subject of a very different kind of discussion from the present at some convenient season."[74] After a lengthy correspondence, Hamilton traced the rumor back to a critic of Washington named William Gordon, a Congregational minister in Jamaica Plains, Massachusetts. At first, Gordon pretended that he was merely repeating the story. He would name the source, he said, if Hamilton promised not to challenge him to a duel, a practice Gordon said he opposed on religious grounds. Even though Hamilton had served as a second for Laurens in the Charles Lee duel and had hinted at his own readiness to duel in the current matter, he told Gordon:

It often happens that our zeal is at variance with our understanding. Had it not been for this, you might have recollected that we do not now live in the days of chivalry and you would have judged your precautions, on the subject of duelling at least, useless. The good sense of the present times has happily found out that to prove your own innocence, or the malice of an accuser, the worst method you can take is to run him through the body or shoot him through the head. And permit me to add, that while you felt an aversion to duelling, on the principles of religion, you ought, in charity, to have supposed others possessed of the same scruples—of whose impiety you had no proofs.[75]

Aware that it clashed with his religious beliefs, Hamilton always retained some nagging reservations about dueling, which became more pronounced in later years. Hamilton never met Gordon on the field of honor, even though he did finally identify him as the source of the libel. Throughout the fall, he plied Gordon with combative letters, saying that he could not possibly have made the statements about Congress attributed to him. Yet Hamilton had been sniping at congressional ineptitude all year, and he may well have said something critical of Congress that was either misconstrued by his enemies or reported faithfully.

That September, Hamilton sent Laurens a letter that showed him steeped in inconsolable gloom. He told Laurens that he still yearned for the success of his virtuous scheme for black battalions but worried that private greed, indolence, and public corruption would undermine this good work. "Every [hope] of this kind my friend is an idle dream," he warned Laurens in a despairing tone that was to crop up throughout his life. He added, "There is no virtue [in] America. That commerce which preside[d over] the birth and education of these states has [fitted] their inhabitants for the chain and . . . the only condition they sincerely desire is that it may be a golden one."[76]

What a dark, weary view for a twenty-four-year-old fighting for glorious ideals. It was to be a recurring paradox of Hamilton's career that he grew enraged when accused of being an outsider and then sounded, in response, very much like the outsider evoked by his critics. The virulent charges made against him sometimes alienated him from his adopted country, leaving him feeling that perhaps his critics had a point after all.

SEVEN

THE LOVESICK COLONEL

The American Revolution unfolded in a leisurely enough manner to allow Hamilton a fairly rich social life amid the grim necessities of war. With a young man's need for diversion, he continued to flirt with the fashionable ladies who stopped by army headquarters—not for nothing did Martha Washington nickname her large, lascivious tomcat "Hamilton"—and they warmed to his high spirits, savoir faire, and dancing ability. The Continental Army had a sizable following of "camp ladies," and John Marshall was scandalized by the open debauchery that he encountered when visiting the army that September: "Never was I a witness to such a scene of lewdness," he complained to a friend.[1]

Hamilton once told a friend that a soldier should have no wife other than the military, yet he began to contemplate marriage in the spring of 1779, following the growing alliance with France, which improved the prospects of American victory. He knew that once the war ended, he had no family. That April, Hamilton composed a long letter to John Laurens, outlining his requirements for a wife. Probably from childhood experience, he thought that most marriages were unhappy, and he dreaded making the wrong choice. Parts of his letter were sophomoric, with Hamilton making bawdy references to the size of his nose—jocular eighteenth-century shorthand for his penis—but much of it was thoughtful, showing that Hamilton had given serious consideration to the elements of a stable marriage.

She must be young, handsome (I lay most stress upon a good shape), sensible (a little learning will do), well-bred (but she must have an aversion to the word *ton*), chaste and tender (I am an enthusiast in my notions of fidelity and fondness), of some good nature, a great deal of generosity (she must neither

love money nor scolding, for I dislike equally a termagant and an economist).
In politics, I am indifferent what side she may be of; I think I have arguments
that will easily convert her to mine. As to religion, a moderate streak will satisfy me. She must believe in god and hate a saint. But as to fortune, the larger
stock of that the better. You know my temper and circumstances and will
therefore pay special attention to this article in the treaty. Though I run no
risk of going to purgatory for my avarice, yet as money is an essential ingredient to happiness in this world—as I have not much of my own and as I am
very little calculated to get more either by my address or industry—it must
needs be that my wife, if I get one, bring at least a sufficiency to administer to
her own extravagancies.[2]

In describing his ideal wife, Hamilton sketches something of a self-portrait as he
tries to strike a balance between worldliness and morality. He frankly admits to a
desire for money yet is not a slave to greed. A believer in conventional morality and
marital fidelity, he nevertheless hates a prig. He likes religion in moderation.
Clearly, he dislikes fanaticism and sanctimony. And instead of a sex goddess or a
nubile coquette—types that had always titillated him—he opts for a solid, sensible,
reasonably attractive wife.

When Washington took his troops to winter headquarters at Morristown that
December, Hamilton had extra time to dwell on his future plans. Washington and
his staff occupied the mansion of the late Judge Jacob Ford, a stately white house
with green trim. Hamilton worked in a log office annexed to the mansion and slept
in an upstairs bedroom with Tench Tilghman and James McHenry. The elements
conspired against the Continental Army that winter, said to be the most frigid of
the century. In New York Bay, the ice froze so thick that the British Army was able
to wheel heavy artillery across it. Twenty-eight snowstorms pounded the Morristown headquarters, including a January blizzard that lasted three days, piling snow
in six-foot-high banks.

For Washington, it was the war's nadir, a winter even more depressing than the
one at Valley Forge. The snowstorms shut off roads and blocked provisions, leading
to looting among troops freezing in log huts. Men mutinied and deserted in large
numbers. On January 5, 1780, Washington sent Congress a dreary account: "Many
of the [men] have been four or five days without meat entirely and short of bread
and none but on very scanty supplies. Some for their preservation have been compelled to maraud and rob from the inhabitants and I have it not in my power to
punish or repress the practice."[3] These problems were compounded by the structural inability of Congress to tax the states or establish public credit. The memories
of Valley Forge and Morristown would powerfully affect the future political agen-

das of both Washington and Hamilton, who had to grapple with the defects of a weak central government.

In January, when Washington didn't allow Hamilton to join Laurens for a combat command in the south, Hamilton tumbled into the darkness of depression. "I am chagrined and unhappy, but I submit," he wrote to Laurens. "In short, Laurens, I am disgusted with everything in this world but yourself and *very* few more honest fellows and I have no other wish than as soon as possible to make a brilliant exit. 'Tis a weakness, but I feel I am not fit for this terrestrial country."[4] It was not the first time that Hamilton had glancingly alluded to suicide or emigration or suggested that he was miscast on the American scene.

Salvation, it turned out, was at hand, as the Morristown winter proved unexpectedly sociable. The marquis de Chastellux remembered one convivial dinner with George Washington at which the lively Hamilton doled out food, refilled glasses, and proposed gallant toasts. Sleighing parties full of pretty young women succeeded in crossing the snowdrifts to attend receptions. Hamilton subscribed to "dancing assemblies"—fancy-dress balls attended by chief officers—held at a nearby storehouse. Washington, in a black velvet suit, danced and cut a dashing figure with the ladies, while Steuben flashed with medals, and French officers glistened with gold braid and lace. In this anomalous setting, the women courted these revolutionaries in powdered hair and high heels. To the vast amusement of Washington's family, Hamilton was infatuated that January with a young woman named Cornelia Lott. Colonel Samuel B. Webb even wrote a humorous verse, mocking how the young conqueror had himself been conquered: "Now [Hamilton] feels the inexorable dart / And yields Cornelia all his heart!"[5] The fickle Hamilton soon moved on to a young woman named Polly.

On February 2, 1780, hard on the heels of Cornelia and Polly, Elizabeth Schuyler arrived in Morristown, accompanied by a military escort, to stay with relatives. She carried introductory letters to Washington and Steuben—"one of the most gallant men in the camp"—from her father, General Philip Schuyler.[6] The general's sister, Gertrude, had married a well-established physician, Dr. John Cochran, who had moved to New Brunswick, New Jersey, to have a safe, pleasant spot to inoculate people against smallpox. Not only was Cochran an excellent doctor—he also traveled with the army as Washington's personal physician, and Lafayette had dubbed him "good doctor Bones"—but he was later appointed director general of the army's medical department. During the winter encampment at Morristown, Cochran and his wife stayed at the neat white house of their friend Dr. Jabez Campfield, a quarter mile down the road from Washington's headquarters. So Schuyler found herself in close proximity to her future husband.

Hamilton's place on Washington's staff enabled him to socialize with Eliza Schuyler on equal terms. He had already met her on his flying visit to Albany in 1777 when he coaxed General Horatio Gates into surrendering troops to Washington. Even without this prior meeting, Hamilton would have met Schuyler because she came with their mutual friend, Kitty Livingston, long a favorite object of flirtation with Hamilton. Hamilton, twenty-five, was instantly smitten with Schuyler, twenty-two. Fellow aide Tench Tilghman reported: "Hamilton is a gone man."[7] Pretty soon, Hamilton was a constant visitor at the two-story Campfield residence, spending every evening there. Everyone noticed that the young colonel was starry-eyed and distracted. Although a touch absentminded, Hamilton ordinarily had a faultless memory, but, returning from Schuyler one night, he forgot the password and was barred by the sentinel. "The soldier-lover was embarrassed," recalled Gabriel Ford, then fourteen, the son of Judge Ford. "The sentinel knew him well, but was stern in the performance of his duty. Hamilton pressed his hand to his forehead and tried to summon the important words from their hiding-place, but, like the faithful sentinel, they were immovable."[8] Ford took pity on Hamilton and supplied the password.

By the time Hamilton left Morristown in early March to negotiate a prisoner exchange with the British in Amboy, New Jersey—scarcely more than a month after the courtship began—he and Schuyler had decided to wed. Hamilton must have been struck by the coincidence that his paternal grandfather, Alexander Hamilton, had also married an Elizabeth who was the daughter of a rich, illustrious man.

For Hamilton, Eliza formed part of a beautiful package labeled "the Schuyler Family," and he spared no effort over time to ingratiate himself with the three sons (John Bradstreet, Philip Jeremiah, and Rensselaer) and five daughters (Angelica, Eliza, Margarita, Cornelia, and the as yet unborn Catherine). The daughters in particular—all smart, beautiful, gregarious, and rich—must have been the stuff of fantasy for Hamilton. Each played a different musical instrument, and they collectively charmed and delighted all visitors to the Schuyler mansion in Albany. After spending a week with the family in April 1776, Benjamin Franklin expressed pleasure "with the ease and affability with which we were treated and the lively behaviour of the young ladies."[9] Tench Tilghman was likewise captivated: "There is something in the behavior of the gen[eral], his lady, and daughters that makes one acquainted with them instantly. I feel easy and free from restraint at his seat."[10] The daughters had enough spunky independence that four of the five eventually eloped, Eliza being the significant exception. Cornelia enacted the most colorful escape, later stealing off with a young man named Washington Morton by climbing down a rope ladder from her bedroom and fleeing in a waiting coach.

With fairy-tale suddenness, the orphaned Hamilton had annexed a gigantic and prosperous clan. After seeing pictures of Eliza's younger sister Margarita (always called Peggy), he sent her a long, rambling letter in which he poured out his love for her older sister:

> I venture to tell you in confidence that by some odd contrivance or other your sister has found out the secret of interesting me in everything that concerns her. . . . She is most unmercifully handsome and so perverse that she has none of those pretty affectations which are the prerogatives of beauty. Her good sense is destitute of that happy mixture of vanity and ostentation which would make it conspicuous to the whole tribe of fools and foplings. . . . She has good nature, affability, and vivacity unembellished with that charming frivolousness which is justly deemed one of the principal accomplishments of a *belle*. In short, she is so strange a creature that she possesses all the beauties, virtues, and graces of her sex without any of those amiable defects which . . . are esteemed by connoisseurs necessary shades in the character of a fine woman.[11]

In this letter, Hamilton endows Schuyler with traits exactly consistent with the list he had prepared for John Laurens ten months earlier: she was handsome, sensible, good-natured, and free from vanity or affectation. And since she was the daughter of one of New York's wealthiest, most powerful men, Hamilton would not have to choose between love and money.

Born on August 9, 1757, Elizabeth Schuyler—whom Hamilton called either Eliza or Betsey—remains invisible in most biographies of her husband and was certainly the most self-effacing "founding mother," doing everything in her power to focus the spotlight exclusively on her husband. Her absence from the pantheon of early American figures is unfortunate, since she was a woman of sterling character. Beneath an animated, engaging facade, she was loyal, generous, compassionate, strong willed, funny, and courageous. Short and pretty, she was utterly devoid of conceit and was to prove an ideal companion for Hamilton, lending a strong home foundation to his turbulent life. His letters to her reflected not a single moment of pique, irritation, or disappointment.

Everybody sang Eliza's praises. "A brunette with the most good-natured, lively dark eyes that I ever saw, which threw a beam of good temper and benevolence over her whole countenance," Tench Tilghman wrote in his journal.[12] She was no pampered heiress. An athletic woman and a stout walker, she moved with a determined spring in her step. On one picnic excursion, Tilghman watched her laughingly clamber up a steep hillside while less plucky girls required male assistance. The marquis de Chastellux liked her "mild agreeable countenance," while Brissot de Warville credited her with being "a delightful woman who combines both the charms and attractions and the candor and simplicity typical of American woman-hood."[13] Like others, James McHenry sensed intense passion throbbing beneath her restraint; she could be impulsive. "Hers was a strong character with its depth and warmth, whether of feeling or temper controlled, but glowing underneath, bursting through at times in some emphatic expression."[14]

In 1787, Ralph Earl painted a perceptive portrait of Eliza Hamilton. It shows her with strikingly alert black eyes—the feature that most attracted Hamilton—that glowed with inner strength. She flaunts one of the powdered bouffant hairdos so popular among society women at the time—what one of her friends called her "Marie Antoinette coiffure."[15] Her gaze is frank and open, as if she were ready to chat amiably with the viewer. Beneath her white silk taffeta dress, she has a shapely body but not a delicate femininity. Her makeup is so understated as to be scarcely noticeable. She seems robust and energetic, and one can imagine her having been a tomboy. All in all, she seems a cheerful, modest soul, blessed with gumption.

Schuyler's unassuming character is plain in her own admiring description of Martha Washington, whom she met at Morristown that winter:

She received us so kindly, kissing us both, for the general and papa were very warm friends. She was then nearly fifty years old, but was still handsome. She was quite short: a plump little woman with dark brown eyes, her hair a little frosty, and very plainly dressed for such a grand lady as I considered her. She wore a plain, brown gown of homespun stuff, a large white handkerchief, a neat cap, and her plain gold wedding ring, which she had worn for more than twenty years. She was always my ideal of a true woman.[16]

As soon as Schuyler arrived in Morristown, she gave Martha Washington a pair of cuffs as a gift, and the latter reciprocated with some powder. In time, the relationship between Schuyler and the older woman ripened into something akin to a mother-daughter bond.

Schuyler had received some tutoring but little formal schooling. Her spelling was poor, and she didn't write with the fluency of other Schuylers. One doesn't imagine her dipping into Hume or Hobbes or the weighty philosophers regularly consulted by her husband. On the other hand, as the daughter of a soldier and statesman, she was well versed in public affairs and had been exposed to many po-litical luminaries. At thirteen, she accompanied her father to a conclave of chiefs of the Six Nations at Saratoga and received an Indian name meaning "One-of-us."[17] She had been taught backgammon by none other than Ben Franklin in April 1776 when he visited General Schuyler en route to his diplomatic mission to Canada. Like Hamilton, Eliza was avidly interested in the world around her.

One intriguing question about Eliza Schuyler and Alexander Hamilton concerns their religious beliefs. An active member of the Dutch Reformed Church, Schuyler was a woman of such indomitable Christian faith that Tench Tilghman called her "the little saint" in one letter. Washington's staff was slightly taken aback that the rakish Hamilton chose this pious wife.[18] Hamilton had been devout when younger, but he seemed more skeptical about organized religion during the Revolution. Soon after meeting Schuyler, he wrote a letter of recommendation for a military parson, Dr. Mendy. "He is just what I should like for a military parson except that he does not whore or drink," Hamilton said. "He will fight and he will not insist upon your going to heaven, whether you will or not."[19] Eliza never doubted her husband's faith and always treasured his sonnet "The Soul Ascending into Bliss," written on St. Croix. On the other hand, Hamilton refrained from a formal church affiliation despite his wife's steadfast religiosity.

Hamilton wooed Schuyler that winter with all the verbal resources at his disposal. He even composed a romantic sonnet entitled "Answer to the Inquiry Why I Sighed." Its couplets included these lines: "Before no mortal ever knew / A love like mine so tender, true . . . No joy unmixed my bosom warms / But when my angel's in my arms."[20] Though Schuyler knew that Hamilton was a figure of awesome intelligence, he won her more with his kindly nature than with his intellect. She was to recollect fondly one of his favorite sayings: "My dear Eliza[,] . . . I have a good head, but thank God he has given me a good heart."[21] In later years, when harvesting anecdotes about her husband, Eliza Hamilton gave correspondents a list of his qualities that she wanted to illustrate, and it sums up her view of his multiple talents: "Elasticity of his mind. Variety of his knowledge. Playfulness of his wit. Excellence of his heart. His immense forbearance [and] virtues."[22]

When he wrote to John Laurens on March 30, 1780, Hamilton neglected to mention either Schuyler or his abrupt decision to marry her—a curious lack of candor. Then, on June 30, he broke down and confessed all to his friend: "I give up my liberty to Miss Schuyler. She is a good-hearted girl who, I am sure, will never play the termagant. Though not a genius, she has good sense enough to be agreeable, and though not a beauty, she has fine black eyes, is rather handsome, and has every other requisite of the exterior to make a lover happy." Hamilton knew that he sounded less than enraptured and that Laurens might suspect him of marrying Schuyler for her money, so he continued, "And believe me, I am [a] lover in earnest, though I do not speak of the perfections of my mistress in the enthusiasm of chivalry."[23] Lest Laurens experience a jealous pang, Hamilton added a few months later: "In spite of Schuyler's black eyes, I have still a part for the public and another for you," and he promised he would be no less devoted to his friend after marriage than before.[24]

. . .

Hamilton delighted in the company of all the Schuyler sisters. Eliza's younger sister Peggy was very beautiful but vain and supercilious. She married Stephen Van Rensselaer, six years her junior, the eighth patroon of Rensselaerswyck and the largest landowner in New York State. Starting with that first winter in Morristown, Hamilton was drawn almost magnetically to Eliza's married older sister, Angelica, and spent the rest of his life beguiled by both Eliza and Angelica, calling them "my dear brunettes."[25] Together, the two eldest sisters formed a composite portrait of Hamilton's ideal woman, each appealing to a different facet of his personality. Eliza reflected Hamilton's earnest sense of purpose, determination, and moral rectitude, while Angelica exhibited his worldly side—the wit, charm, and vivacity that so delighted people in social intercourse.

The attraction between Hamilton and Angelica was so potent and obvious that many people assumed they were lovers. At the very least, theirs was a friendship of unusual ardor, and it seems plausible that Hamilton would have proposed to Angelica, not Eliza, if the older sister had been eligible. Angelica was more Hamilton's counterpart than Eliza. James McHenry once wrote to Hamilton that Angelica "charms in all companies. No one has seen her, of either sex, who has not been pleased with her and she pleased everyone, chiefly by means of those qualities which made you the husband of her sister."[26]

John Trumbull's portrait of Angelica shows a fetching woman with a long, pale face, dark eyes, and a pretty, full-lipped mouth who is voguishly dressed and looks more sophisticated than Eliza. Angelica had a more mysterious femininity than her sister, the kind that often exerts a powerful hold on the male imagination. A playful seductress, she loved to engage in repartee, discuss books, strum the guitar, and talk about current affairs. She was to serve as muse to some of the smartest politicians of her day, including Thomas Jefferson, Robert R. Livingston, and, most of all, Hamilton. Angelica was one of the few American women of her generation as comfortable in a European drawing room as in a Hudson River parlor, and there was a gossipy irreverence about her that seemed very European. Unlike Eliza, she learned to speak perfect French. Where Eliza bowed reluctantly to the social demands of Hamilton's career, Angelica applauded his ambitions and was always famished for news of his latest political exploits.

For the next twenty-four years, Angelica expressed open fondness for Hamilton in virtually every letter that she sent to her sister or to Hamilton himself. Hamilton always wrote to her in a buoyant, flirtatious tone. Especially as his mind grew burdened with affairs of state, Angelica provided an outlet for his boyish side. To Eliza he wrote tenderly and lovingly, but seldom in the arch voice of gallantry. It is hard to escape the impression that Hamilton's married life was sometimes a curious ménage à trois with two sisters who were only one year apart. Angelica must have sensed that her incessant adoration of Hamilton, far from annoying or threatening her beloved younger sister, filled her with ecstatic pride. Their shared love for Hamilton seemed to deepen their sisterly bond. Ironically, Eliza's special attachment to Angelica gave Hamilton a cover for expressing affection for Angelica that would certainly have been forbidden with other women.

For a daring woman drawn to intellectual men, Angelica made a strange choice in marrying John Barker Church, a short man with shining eyes and thick lips who only grew fatter with the years. In 1776, he had been sent to Albany by Congress to audit the books of the army's Northern Department, then commanded by General Schuyler. While there, he managed both to woo Angelica and antagonize her father. John B. Church was then using the pseudonym of John B. Carter, and Schuyler scented something suspicious. Schuyler's instincts proved correct: Church had changed his name and fled to America, possibly after a duel with a Tory politician in London; some accounts have him on the lam from creditors after a bankruptcy brought on by gambling and stock speculation. Knowing that he would be denied parental consent, Church eloped with Angelica in 1777, and the Schuylers were predictably incensed.

Church amassed fantastic wealth during the Revolution. "Mr. Carter is the mere man of business," James McHenry told Hamilton, "and I am informed has riches enough, with common management, to make the longest life comfortable."[27] He and his business partner, Jeremiah Wadsworth, negotiated lucrative contracts to sell supplies to the French and American forces. Hamilton spoke highly of Church as "a man of fortune and integrity, of strong mind, very exact, very active, and very much a man of business."[28] Yet Church's letters present a cold businessman, devoid of warmth or humor. Very involved in politics, he could be tactless in expressing his opinions. One observer remembered him as "revengeful and false" after General Howe burned several American villages and towns. Church said he wanted to cut off the heads of the British generals and to "pickle them and to put them in small barrels, and as often as the English should again burn a village, to send them one [of] these barrels."[29] He lacked the intellectual breadth and civic commitment that made Hamilton so compelling to Angelica. On the other hand, he provided Angelica with the opulent, high-society life that she apparently craved.

Hamilton's relationship with his father-in-law was to be an especially happy part of his marriage to Eliza Schuyler. Tall and slim, with a raspy voice and bulbous nose, Philip Schuyler, forty-six, was already hobbled by rheumatic gout when he arrived in Morristown that April to investigate army reform as chairman of a congressional committee. It is testimony to Hamilton's gifts that he was readily embraced by someone with Schuyler's rigid sense of social hierarchy. "Be indulgent, my child, to your inferiors," Schuyler once advised his son John, "affable and courteous to your equals, respectful not cringing to your superiors, whether they are so by superior mental abilities or those necessary distinctions which society has established."[30] Yet this same status-conscious man enjoyed an instant rapport with the illegitimate young West Indian. Both Hamilton and Schuyler spoke French, were well-read, appreciated military discipline, and had a common interest in business and internal-development schemes, such as canals. They also shared a common loyalty to Washington and impatience with congressional incompetence, even though Schuyler was a member of the Continental Congress.

Descended from an early Dutch settler who arrived in New York in 1650 (the surname may have been German), Schuyler was counted among those Hudson River squires who presided over huge tracts of land and ruled state politics. The Schuylers had intermarried with the families of many patroons or manor lords. Philip Schuyler's mother was a Van Cortlandt. His elegant Georgian brick mansion, the Pastures, sat on an Albany hilltop, surrounded by eighty acres dotted with barns, slave quarters, and a smokehouse. The enterprising Schuyler also built a two-story house on the fringe of the Saratoga wilderness, where he created an industrial village with four water-power mills, a smithy, and storehouses that employed hundreds of people. (It evolved into the village of Schuylerville.) In all, this Schuyler estate extended for three miles along the Hudson, encompassing somewhere between ten and twenty thousand acres. As if this were not enough, Philip Schuyler had married Catherine Van Rensselaer, an heiress to the 120,000-acre Claverack estate in Columbia County.

The image of Philip Schuyler varied drastically depending upon the observer. His enemies viewed him as cold, arrogant, and petulant when people crossed him or when his pride was offended. Alexander Graydon left this unpleasant vignette of a Schuyler dinner during the Revolution: "A New England captain came in upon some business with that abject servility of manner which belongs to persons of the meanest rank. He was neither asked to sit or take a glass of wine, and after announcing his wants, was dismissed with that peevishness of tone we apply to a low and vexatious intruder."[31] Graydon admitted, however, that the man might have forced his way into Schuyler's presence.

Schuyler's friends, in contrast, found him courteous and debonair, a model of etiquette, and very amiable in mixed company. He could behave magnanimously toward his social peers. During the battle of Saratoga, General Burgoyne burned Schuyler's house and most other buildings on his property for military reasons.

When, after the surrender, Burgoyne apologized, Schuyler replied graciously that his conduct had been justified by the rules of war and that he would have done the same in his place. Baroness Riedesel, the wife of the Hessian commander Major General Friedrich von Riedesel, also recalled Schuyler's chivalry after the Saratoga debacle: "When I drew near the tents, a good looking man advanced towards me and helped the children from the calash and kissed and caressed them. He then offered me his arm and tears trembled in his eyes."[32] Schuyler invited the baroness, the defeated Burgoyne, and his twenty-member entourage to stay in his Albany mansion and furnished them with excellent dinners for days. At the time, Schuyler did not yet realize that Burgoyne's destruction of his Saratoga estate had dealt a crippling blow to his finances.

Hamilton knew that Schuyler could be a strict father to his sometimes rambunctious daughters and that John Barker Church had been ostracized for not obeying protocol in marrying Angelica. So while Hamilton negotiated a prisoner exchange, he patiently awaited the Schuylers' consent for their daughter's hand. In the meantime, he relished Eliza's letters. "I cannot tell you what ecstasy I felt in casting my eye over the sweet effusions of tenderness it contains," he said of one mid-March letter. "My Betsey's soul speaks in every line and bids me be the happiest of mortals. I am so and will be so."[33]

On April 8, 1780, Philip Schuyler sent Hamilton a businesslike letter, saying he had discussed the marriage proposal with Mrs. Schuyler, and they had accepted it. Hamilton was overjoyed. A few days later, he wrote to Mrs. Schuyler and thanked her for accepting his proposal, making sure to lay on the flattery with a trowel: "May I hope, madam, you will not consider it as a mere profession when I add that, though I have not the happiness of a personal acquaintance with you, I am no stranger to the qualities which distinguish your character and these make the relation in which I stand to you not one of the least pleasing circumstances of my union with your daughter."[34]

General Schuyler had taken a temporary house in Morristown and brought down Mrs. Schuyler from Albany. They stayed until the Continental Army decamped in June. Hamilton visited the Schuylers each evening, and the mutual affection between him and the family waxed steadily. In the end, the Schuylers felt flattered that the ex-clerk from the West Indies had chosen *them*. Two years later, Philip Schuyler sent Eliza a delighted report on her amazing husband:

Participate afresh in the satisfaction I experience from the connection you have made with my beloved Hamilton. He affords me happiness too exquisite for expression. I daily experience the pleasure of hearing encomiums on his virtue and abilities from those who are capable of distinguishing between real and pretended merit. He is considered, as he certainly is, the ornament of his country.[35]

The marriage to Eliza Schuyler was another dreamlike turn in the improbable odyssey of Alexander Hamilton, giving him the political support of one of New York's blue-ribbon families.

Thoughts of both love and money coursed through Hamilton's brain during that arctic winter in Morristown. The paper currency issued by the Continental Congress continued to sink precipitously in value, as inflation undercut the patriotic cause. During one ghastly period in 1779, the continental dollar shed half its value in three weeks. Silver coins disappeared, driven out by nearly worthless paper money, and state governments were also going broke. In March 1780, Congress tried to restore monetary order by issuing one new dollar in exchange for forty old ones, a move that wiped out the savings of many Americans. The need for financial reform had grown urgent. James Madison worried in a letter to Thomas Jefferson, "Believe me, sir, as things now stand, if the states do not vigorously proceed in collecting the old money and establishing funds for the credit of the new . . . we are undone."[36]

In his spare time, Hamilton pored over financial treatises. As Washington's aide, he was not at liberty to issue controversial plans that might jeopardize congressional relations, so he drafted a clandestine letter to an unidentified congressman and outlined a new currency regime. "The present plan," he started humbly, "is the product of some reading on the subjects of commerce and finance[,] . . . but a want of leisure has prevented its being examined in so many lights and digested so maturely as its importance requires."[37] If the recipient wished further explanation, Hamilton indicated that "a letter directed to James Montague Esqr., lodged in the post office at Morristown, will be a safe channel for any communications you may think proper to make and an immediate answer will be given."[38] "James Montague" may have been a name devised by Hamilton to cloak his own identity.

Hamilton's six-thousand-word letter attests to staggering precocity. He saw that inflation had originated with wartime shortages, which had led, in turn, to the waning value of money. Over time, the inflation had acquired a self-reinforcing momentum. Economic fundamentals alone could not account for this inflation, Hamilton noted, detecting a critical psychological factor at work. People were "governed more by passion and prejudice than by an enlightened sense of their interests," he wrote. "The quantity of money in circulation is certainly a chief cause of its decline. But we find it is depreciated more than five times as much as it ought to be. . . . The excess is derived from opinion, a want of confidence."[39]

How to remedy this want of confidence? Hamilton submitted a twelve-point program, a fully realized vision of a financial system that reflected sustained thinking. Congress should create a central bank, owned half by the government and half by private individuals, that could issue money and make public and private loans. Drawing on European precedents, Hamilton cited the Bank of England and the French Council of Commerce as possible models. Taxes and domestic loans could not finance the war alone, he argued, and he pressed for a foreign loan of two million pounds as the centerpiece of his program: "The necessity of a foreign loan is now greater than ever. Nothing else will retrieve our affairs."[40] He recognized that French and British political power stemmed from those countries' ability to raise foreign loans in wartime, and this inextricable linkage between military and financial strength informed all of his subsequent thinking.

For Hamilton the American Revolution was a practical workshop of economic and political theory, providing critical object lessons and cautionary tales that charted the course for his career. In May 1780, he had fresh cause to meditate on the failings of Congress when news came of a calamitous defeat: the British had taken Charleston, capturing an American garrison of 5,400 soldiers, including John Laurens. The year 1780 was to be a dismal one for the patriots. In August, Cornwallis inflicted a stinging loss on General Horatio Gates in Camden, South Carolina, killing nine hundred Americans and taking one thousand prisoners. For Hamilton, the terrible drubbings at Charleston and Camden drove home the need for longer enlistment periods and an end to reliance on state militias. He found some consolation in the fact that Gates had fled from Camden in terror, barely containing his glee at this sign of cowardice. "Was there ever an instance of a general running away, as Gates has done, from his whole army?" he gloated to New York congressman James Duane. "One hundred and eighty miles in three days and a half. It does admirable credit to the activity of a man at his time of life."[41] By October, General Nathanael Greene had replaced the disgraced Gates as commander of the Southern Army.

To the setbacks in South Carolina, Hamilton reacted with stoic resignation as well as schadenfreude. "This misfortune affects me less than others," he told Eliza Schuyler, "because it is not in my temper to repine at evils that are past but to endeavour to draw good out of them, and because I think our safety depends on a total change of system. And this change of system will only be produced by misfortune."[42] He did not mention that he had just rushed off a seven-thousand-word letter to James Duane that showed that the future American government was already fermenting in his hyperactive brain. He now subjected the Articles of Confederation to a searching critique. He thought the sovereignty of the states only enfeebled the union. "The fundamental defect is a want of power in Congress," he declared. He favored granting Congress supreme power in war, peace, trade, finance, and foreign affairs.[43] Instead of bickering congressional boards, he wanted strong executives and endorsed single ministers for war, foreign affairs, finance, and the navy: "There is always more decision, more dispatch, more secrecy, more responsibility where single men than when bodies are concerned. By a plan of this kind, we should blend the advantages of a monarchy and of a republic in a happy and beneficial union."[44] Hamilton was especially intent upon subjecting all military forces to centralized congressional control: "Without a speedy change, the army must dissolve. It is now a mob, rather than an army, without clothing, without pay, without provision, without morals, without discipline."[45] Then, in the most startling, visionary leap of all, Hamilton recommended that a convention be summoned to revise the Articles of Confederation. Seven years before the Constitutional Convention, Alexander Hamilton became the first person to propose such a plenary gathering. Where other minds groped in the fog of war, the twenty-five-year-old Hamilton seemed to perceive everything in a sudden flash.

At the end of the letter, Hamilton apologized to Duane for having written down his ideas so hastily. The wonder, of course, is that he had recorded them at all. In mid-July, a French fleet had arrived off Newport, Rhode Island, with an army of 5,500 men commanded by the short, stocky comte de Rochambeau. This was the French army that Hamilton had suggested to Lafayette as necessary to the war effort and that Lafayette had successfully urged at Versailles. As soon as the French arrived, Hamilton was worn down with tremendous duties. Before meeting with Rochambeau at Hartford in late September, Washington asked his aide-de-camp to draw up three scenarios for joint military operations with the French. Hamilton must have been exhausted as he scratched out his long letter to Duane by candlelight at day's end.

One might have thought that Hamilton, despite all the military uncertainty, would feel hopeful about his life. He was effectively Washington's chief of staff, was soon to be married to Elizabeth Schuyler, and was drafting high-level strategy papers and comprehensive blueprints for government. Yet, underneath his high spirits still lurked the pessimism from his West Indian boyhood, and he sometimes viewed the world with a jaundiced, even misanthropic, eye. Perhaps too much had happened too soon and it had all been disorienting. He was critical of his compatriots. "My dear Laurens," he had written to his friend that spring, "our countrymen have all the folly of the ass and all the passiveness of the sheep in their compositions."[46] As he became more outspoken in his views, he discovered his own capacity for making enemies. On September 12, he told Laurens that everybody was angry with him. Some people thought he was "a friend to military pretensions, however exorbitant," while others chided him for not being militant enough in defending army power: "The truth is I am an unlucky honest man that speaks my sentiments to all and with emphasis. I say this to you because you know it and will not charge me with vanity. I hate congress—I hate the army—I hate the world—I hate myself. The whole is a mass of fools and knaves. I could almost except you and [Richard Kidder] Meade. Adieu. A. Hamilton."[47]

Throughout his career, Hamilton had a knack for being present at historic moments; in September 1780, he was eyewitness to the treachery of General Benedict Arnold. Born in Norwich, Connecticut, Arnold had started out as a druggist and bookseller and expanded into speculative business ventures. A brave soldier and a student of military history, Arnold had distinguished himself in numerous clashes with the British and was wounded by a musket ball in the winter assault on Quebec. He fought so lustily at Saratoga, where he was injured again, that Hamilton and others had hailed him as the true, unacknowledged hero of the victory. As military governor of Philadelphia during the patriot occupation, however, Arnold was harried by charges of corruption, which he indignantly dismissed as "false, malicious, and scandalous."[48] He was exonerated of all but two minor charges by a court-martial and got off with a reprimand from Washington. Yet by this point, the embittered Arnold, increasingly dubious about American prospects, had decided to engage in treason, relaying secret information about troop movements to the British. After being named the new commandant of West Point, he colluded to deliver plans of the fortifications to the British, making the stronghold vulnerable to attack. In exchange, Arnold was promised money and a high-level appointment in the British Army.

Arnold took up his West Point command during the summer of 1780 and let its defenses fall into disrepair. On the morning of September 25, Washington and a retinue that included Hamilton and Lafayette were passing through the Hudson Valley as they returned from the conference in Hartford with the comte de Rochambeau. They planned to see Arnold and inspect West Point. Hamilton and James McHenry were sent ahead to prepare for Washington's reception at Arnold's headquarters in the Beverley Robinson house, a couple of miles downriver from West Point, on the east bank of the Hudson. During breakfast with the two aides, a flustered Arnold received a message indicating that a spy known as "John Anderson" had been seized north of New York City with descriptions of West Point's defenses tucked into his boot. Hamilton and McHenry were perplexed by Arnold's sudden agitation. Aghast that his plot had been foiled, Arnold raced upstairs to say good-bye to his wife, then slipped out of the house, hopped onto a barge, and fled downriver toward the British warship *Vulture*. Not long after, Washington showed up with his officers, noted Arnold's absence with puzzlement, had breakfast, then rowed across the Hudson for his West Point tour.

Hamilton stayed behind to sort through dispatches and was unnerved by intermittent shrieks from Mrs. Arnold upstairs. When Arnold's aide, Richard Varick, went up to investigate, he found her in a gauzy morning gown with disheveled hair. "Colonel Varick," the distraught woman demanded, "have you ordered my child to be killed?"[49] She then babbled on incoherently about hot irons being placed on her head. Twenty years younger than her husband, Margaret "Peggy" Shippen came from a Tory family in Philadelphia and had married Benedict Arnold at age eighteen the year before. She was a petite, ringleted blonde with small features and large social ambitions. When Hamilton went upstairs, he found her clutching her baby and accusing everyone in sight of wanting to murder her child.

Late in the afternoon, Washington returned to the house, befuddled by Arnold's absence from West Point and its negligent defenses. Hamilton gave Washington a thick packet of dispatches, including papers discovered on the captured "John Anderson." Hamilton then went off to confer with Lafayette. When the two young men returned, they found their usually composed commander fighting back tears. "Arnold has betrayed us!" Washington said with profound emotion. "Whom can we trust now?"[50] He sent Hamilton and McHenry off on horseback, careering down the Hudson for a dozen miles, in the futile hope that they could overtake Arnold before he reached the safety of British lines. They arrived too late: Arnold was already aboard the *Vulture* and had been whisked off to New York City.

On the spot, Hamilton displayed uncommon self-reliance. Aware that West Point lay in imminent peril, he sent directions to the Sixth Connecticut Regiment to reinforce the fortress. Once again, he did not seem bashful about bossing around generals. "There has been unfolded at this place a scene of the blackest treason," he wrote to General Nathanael Greene. "I advise you putting the army under marching orders and detaching a brigade immediately this way."[51]

Hamilton hurried to Washington a letter just received from Arnold in which he blamed American ingratitude for his betrayal and sought to exonerate his wife: "She is as good and as innocent as an angel and is incapable of doing wrong."[52] Mrs. Arnold was still behaving bizarrely. After Varick ushered Washington into the room, the sobbing woman refused to believe it was the general: "No, that is not General Washington. That is the man who was a-going to assist Colonel Varick in killing my child."[53] Washington sat by the bedside and tried to console the hysterical woman. Washington, Hamilton, and Lafayette were all duped by Peggy Arnold's command performance. They attributed her sudden raving to grief over her husband's traitorous behavior. To their gullible minds, this behavior was proof that she must be a blameless victim of Arnold's perfidy. In fact, she had been privy to the plot, having acted as conduit for some of her husband's correspondence with the British, and she played her mad scene to perfection.

For all his supposed sophistication about womanly wiles, Hamilton was completely hoodwinked by Mrs. Arnold's brazen charade. As always, he was hypersensitive to female charms, and well-bred ladies in distress especially brought out his chivalry. In a letter to Eliza that day, one can see how taken Hamilton was with Peggy Arnold:

> It was the most affecting scene I ever was witness to. She for a considerable time entirely lost her senses. . . . One moment she raved, another she melted into tears. Sometimes she pressed her infant to her bosom and lamented its fate, occasioned by the imprudence of its father, in a manner that would have pierced insensibility itself. All the sweetness of beauty, all the loveliness of innocence, all the tenderness of a wife and all the fondness of a mother showed themselves in her appearance and conduct. . . . She received us in bed with every circumstance that could interest our sympathy. Her sufferings were so eloquent that I wished myself her brother to have a right to become her defender.[54]

Hamilton was totally credulous in the face of this designing woman. Instead of being wary in a wartime situation, he converted Peggy Arnold's situation into a stage romance. His tenderness for an abandoned wife may have owed something to his boyhood sympathy for his mother, and this episode prefigured a still more damaging event in which he evinced misplaced compassion for a seemingly abandoned woman.

Washington issued a passport to Mrs. Arnold that allowed her to return home to Philadelphia. She made a stop in Paramus, New Jersey, where she stayed at the Hermitage, the home of Mrs. Theodosia Prevost, whose husband was a British colonel sent to the West Indies. Once the two women were alone, Mrs. Arnold told her friend how she had made fools of Washington, Hamilton, and the others and that she was tired of the theatrics she had been forced to affect. She expressed disgust with the patriotic cause and told of prodding her husband into the scheme to surrender West Point. The source of this story, printed many years later, was the man who was to be Theodosia Prevost's next husband: Aaron Burr.

That Hamilton adhered to a code of gentlemanly honor was confirmed in yet another sideshow of the Benedict Arnold affair: the arrest of Major John André, adjutant general of the British Army and Arnold's contact, traveling under the nom de guerre John Anderson. As he awaited a hearing to decide his fate, he was confined at a tavern in Tappan, New York. Though seven years younger than André, Hamilton developed a sympathy for the prisoner born of admiration and visited him several times. A letter that Hamilton later wrote to Laurens reveals his nearly worshipful attitude toward the elegant, cultured André, who was conversant with poetry, music, and painting. Hamilton identified with André's misfortune in a personal manner, as if he saw his own worst nightmare embodied in his fate:

> To an excellent understanding, well improved by education and travel, [André] united a peculiar elegance of mind and manners and the advantage of a pleasing person. . . . By his merit, he had acquired the unlimited confidence of his general and was making a rapid progress in military rank and reputation. But in the height of his career, flushed with new hopes from the execution of a project the most beneficial to his party that could be devised, he was at once precipitated from the summit of prosperity and saw all the expectations of his ambition blasted and himself ruined.[55]

Did Hamilton think that he, too, having attained such eminence, would suddenly plunge headlong back to earth?

The fate of Major André became the subject of a heated dispute between Hamilton and Washington over whether he had acted as a spy or as a liaison officer between the British command and Arnold. This semantic debate had practical significance. If André was a spy, he would hang from the gallows like a common criminal; whereas if he was merely an unlucky officer, he would be shot like a gentleman. Such distinctions mattered both to André and to Hamilton. Hamilton argued that André wasn't a spy, since he had planned to meet Arnold on neutral territory and was lured by Arnold behind patriotic lines against his intentions. A board of general officers convened by Washington disagreed, ruling that because André had come ashore secretly, assuming a fake name and civilian costume, he had functioned as a spy and should die like one. Washington certified the board's decision. He was adamant that André's mission could have doomed the patriotic cause and feared that anything less than summary execution would imply some lack of conviction about his guilt.

It may have been Hamilton who sent a secret letter to Sir Henry Clinton on September 30, proposing a swap of André for Arnold. The author tried to disguise his handwriting and signed the letter "A.B." (coincidentally, Aaron Burr's initials). But Clinton had no doubt of its provenance and scrawled across it, "Hamilton, W[ashington] aide de camp, received after A[ndré] death."[56] Clinton refused to consider a trade, which would have meant instant death for Arnold at the hands of vengeful patriots.

The decision to execute Major André was not the only time Hamilton regretted a choice by Washington, yet it was one time when he disagreed openly and consistently. "The death of André could not have been dispensed with," Hamilton conceded to Major General Henry Knox nearly two years later, "but it must still be viewed at a distance as an act of *rigid justice*."[57] Hamilton's dissent betrayed growing frustration with Washington's inflexibility, frustration that was presently to flare into open rebellion.

Major André faced his end with grace and valor. At five o'clock in the afternoon on the day after the board's decision, he was led to a hilltop gibbet outside of Tappan. When he saw the gallows, he reeled slightly. "I am reconciled to my death," he said, "though I detest the mode."[58] Unaided, he mounted a coffin that lay in a wagon drawn up under the scaffold. With great dignity, he tightened the rope around his own neck and blindfolded himself with his own handkerchief. Then the wagon bolted away, leaving André swinging from the rope. He was buried on the spot. Hamilton left a moving if romanticized description of his death:

> In going to the place of execution, he bowed familiarly as he went along to all those with whom he had been acquainted in his confinement. A smile of complacency expressed the serene fortitude of his mind. . . . Upon being told the final moment was at hand and asked if he had anything to say, he answered, "Nothing but to request you will witness to the world that I die like a brave man."[59]

Hamilton's description shows his abiding fascination with a beautiful, noble death. "I am aware that a man of real merit is never seen in so favourable a light as seen through the medium of adversity," he concluded in his letter to Laurens. "The clouds that surround him are shades that set off his good qualities."[60]

Major John André represented some beau ideal for Hamilton. The reverse side of this adulation, however, was a lacerating sense of personal inadequacy that the world seldom saw. However loaded with superabundant talent, Hamilton was a mass of insecurities that he usually kept well hidden. He always had to fight the residual sadness of the driven man, the unspoken melancholy of the prodigy, the wounds left by his accursed boyhood. Only to John Laurens and Eliza Schuyler did he confide his fears. Right after André's death, Hamilton wrote to Schuyler that he wished he had André's accomplishments.

I do not, my love, affect modesty. I am conscious of [the] advantages I possess. I know I have talents and a good heart, but why am I not handsome? Why have I not every acquirement that can embellish human nature? Why have I not fortune, that I might hereafter have more leisure than I shall have to cultivate those improvements for which I am not entirely unfit?[61]

It was a peculiar outburst: Hamilton was expressing envy for a man who had just been executed. Only in such passages do we see that Hamilton, for all his phenomenal success in the Continental Army, still felt unlucky and unlovely, still cursed by his past.

During the summer and fall preceding Hamilton's wedding in December 1780, he sometimes mooned about in a romantic haze, very much the lovesick swain. "Love is a sort of insanity," he told Schuyler, "and every thing I write savors strongly of it."[62] In frequent letters to "his saucy little charmer," he reassured her that he thought about her constantly.[63] "'Tis a pretty story indeed that I am to be thus monopolized by a little *nut brown maid* like you and [am] from a soldier metamorphosed into a puny lover."[64] He would steal away from crowds, he told her, and stroll down solitary lanes to swoon over her image. "You are certainly a little sorceress and have bewitched me, for you have made me disrelish everything that used to please me."[65]

As the wedding approached, Hamilton succumbed to anxieties about the future, and he sent Schuyler the most candid letters of his life. He was now optimistic about the war and thought the Continental Army, backed by French naval power, might yet snatch victory by year's end. Should the patriots lose, however, Hamilton suggested that they live in "some other clime more favourable to human rights" and suggested Geneva as a possibility. He then made a confession: "I was once determined to let my existence and American liberty end together. My Betsey has given me a motive to outlive my pride."[66] The sweet, retiring Schuyler would rescue him from the self-destructive fantasies that had long held sway over his imagination.

At the same time, the jittery Hamilton was beset by serious doubts about the wedding. All along, he had saluted Schuyler's beauty, frankness, tender heart, and good sense. Now he wanted more. "I entreat you, my charmer, not to neglect the charges I gave you, particularly that of taking care of yourself and that of employing all your leisure in reading. Nature has been very kind to you. Do not neglect to cultivate her gifts and to enable yourself to make the distinguished figure in all respects to which you are entitled to aspire."[67] As he tutored Schuyler in self-improvement, there was a Pygmalion dimension to his wishes, but he also worried that her love might cool and scuttle the wedding. In one letter, he related to her a dream he'd had of arriving in Albany and finding her asleep on the grass, with a strange gentleman holding her hand. "As you may imagine," he wrote, "I reproached him with his presumption and asserted my claim."[68] To his relief, Schuyler in the dream awoke, flew into his arms, and allayed his fears with a convincing kiss.

Those who saw Hamilton as shrewdly marrying into a great fortune would have been surprised that he did not count on the Schuyler money and beseeched Eliza to consider whether she could endure a more austere life. Referring to the subscription fund set up by his St. Croix sponsors, he lamented the "knavery" of those managing his money. "They have already filed down what was in their hands more than one half, and I am told they go on diminishing it." Thus, Schuyler should be prepared for anything: "Your future rank in life is a perfect lottery. You may move in an exalted, you may move in a very humble sphere. The last is most probable. Examine well your heart." Pressing the matter further, he then asked her:

> Tell me, my pretty damsel, have you made up your mind upon the subject of housekeeping? Do you soberly relish the pleasure of being a poor man's wife? Have you learned to think a homespun preferable to a brocade and the rumbling of a wagon wheel to the musical rattling of a coach and six? Will you be able to see with perfect composure your old acquaintances, flaunting it in gay life, tripping it along in elegance and splendor, while you hold a humble station and have no other enjoyments than the sober comforts of a good wife? . . . If you cannot, my dear, we are playing a comedy of all in the wrong and you should correct the mistake before we begin to act the tragedy of the unhappy couple.[69]

There is no hint here that Eliza was the daughter of a man whom Hamilton described as a gentleman of "large fortune and no less personal and public consequences."[70] Hamilton was too proud to sponge off the Schuylers—who would turn out, in any event, to be less affluent than legend held.

Hamilton's prenuptial letters to Schuyler hint at a young man exposed to deprivation at an early age. He had seen too much discontent to approach marriage optimistically. In one letter, he delivered a cynical view of both sexes and asked whether she could endure a hard life:

> But be assured, my angel, it is not a diffidence of my Betsey's heart but of a *female* heart that dictated the questions. I am ready to believe everything in favour of yours, but am restrained by the experience I have had of human nature and the softer part of it. Some of your sex possess every requisite to

please, delight, and inspire esteem, friendship, and affection. But there are too few of this description. We are full of vices. They are full of weaknesses[,] . . . and though I am satisfied whenever I trust my senses and my judgment that you are one of the exceptions, I cannot forbear having moments when I feel a disposition to make a more perfect discovery of your temper and character. . . . Do not, however, I entreat you, suppose that I entertain an ill opinion of all your sex. I have a much worse [opinion] of my own.[71]

Throughout this correspondence, George Washington's exacting presence hovered in the background. "I would go on, but the General summons me to ride," Hamilton ended one letter.[72] Since both he and Washington frowned on laxity during military campaigns, he refused to take a leave of absence to visit Schuyler. When Hamilton rode off to Albany in late November 1780 for the wedding, it was the first vacation he had taken in nearly five years of warfare.

Situated on a bluff above the Hudson River, Albany was still a rough-hewn town of four thousand inhabitants, about one-tenth of them slaves, and was enclosed by stands of virgin pine. Even as English influence overtook New York City, Albany retained its early Dutch character, reflected in the gabled houses. Dutch remained the chief language, and the Schuylers sat through long Dutch sermons at the Reformed Church every Sunday. In many respects, Eliza, who loved to sew and garden, was typical of the young Dutch women of her generation who were domestic and self-effacing, thrifty in managing households, and eager to raise large broods of children.

We have little sense of what Hamilton truly thought of his mother-in-law, Catherine Van Rensselaer Schuyler. Not long after marrying Philip Schuyler during the French and Indian War, she sat for a portrait that shows a striking, dark-eyed woman with a long, elegant neck and broad bosom. One contemporary described her as a "lady of great beauty, shape, and gentility."[73] By the time of Hamilton's wedding, however, she had settled into being a stout Dutch housewife. When the marquis de Chastellux visited the Schuylers that snowy December, he left with an indelible impression of Mrs. Schuyler as a dragoness who governed the house, intimidating her husband. The wary Frenchman decided that it was "best not to treat her in too cavalier a fashion" and concluded that General Schuyler was "more amiable when he is absent from his wife."[74] If Mrs. Schuyler, forty-seven, was less than hospitable, it may have been because she was seven months pregnant with her youngest daughter, Catherine, the last of twelve times she endured childbirth. She was visibly pregnant at the time of her daughter's wedding.

Hamilton had few people to invite to the wedding. His brother, James, was still alive, probably on St. Thomas, but he didn't come. Hamilton contacted his father, who was on Bequia in the Grenadines, but he didn't show up either, possibly because of problems posed by wartime travel for British subjects. Before the wedding, Alexander told Eliza:

> I wrote you, my dear, in one of my letters that I have written to our father but had not heard of him since. . . . I had pressed him to come to America after the peace. A gentleman going to the island where he is will in a few days afford me a safe opportunity to write again. I shall again present him with his black-eyed daughter and tell him how much her attention deserves his affection and will make the blessing of his gray hairs.[75]

Whether from shame, illness, or poverty, James Hamilton never met Eliza, the Schuylers, or his grandchildren, despite Alexander's sincere entreaties that he come to America.

At noon on December 14, 1780, Alexander Hamilton, twenty-five, wed Elizabeth Schuyler, twenty-three, in the southeast parlor of the Schuyler mansion. The interior of the two-story brick residence was light and airy and had a magnificent curving staircase with beautifully carved balusters. During the ceremony, the parlor was likely radiant with sunshine reflected from the snow outside. The ceremony followed the Dutch custom of a small family wedding in the bride's home. At the local Dutch Reformed Church, the clerk recorded simply: "Colonel Hamilton & Elisabeth [sic] Schuyler."[76] After the ceremony, the guests probably adjourned to the entrance hall, which was nearly fifty feet long and twenty feet wide and flanked by tall, graceful windows. Except for James McHenry, Hamilton's friends on Washington's staff were too busy with wartime duties to attend. For all the merriment and high spirits, few guests could have overlooked the mortifying contrast between the enormous Schuyler clan, with their Van Cortlandt and Van Rensselaer relatives, and the lonely groom, who didn't have a single family member in attendance.

The newlyweds spent their honeymoon at the Pastures and stayed through the Christmas holidays. They were joined by four French officers from Rochambeau's army who crossed the ice-encrusted Hudson and arrived in sleighs. Even the fussy French officers complimented the food, the Madeira, and the engaging company. Nothing marred the perfection of the experience for Hamilton. A few weeks later, he wrote to Eliza's younger sister Peggy, "Because your sister has the talent of growing more amiable every day, or because I am a fanatic in love, or both . . . she fancies herself the happiest woman in the world."[77]

Hamilton probably felt, for the moment, that he was the happiest man in the world. The wedding to Eliza Schuyler ended his nomadic existence and embedded him in the Anglo-Dutch aristocracy of New York. His upbringing, instead of making him resent the rich, had perhaps made him wish to reclaim his father's lost nobility. Through marriage, he acquired an important base in a state in which politics revolved around the dynastic ambitions of the foremost Hudson River families. For the first time in his life, Alexander Hamilton must have had a true sense of belonging.

His friendship with Philip Schuyler was to prove of inestimable value to Hamilton's career. At one point, when asking for Eliza's hand, Hamilton evidently told the general of his illegitimacy. "I am pleased with every instance of delicacy in those who are dear to me," Schuyler wrote in response, "and I think I read your soul on that occasion you mention."[78] Having come from opposite ends of the social spectrum, the two men had arrived at similar political conclusions and proved steadfast allies. Like Hamilton, Schuyler chafed at the impotence of Congress and the Articles of Confederation and wanted to invest George Washington with "dictatorial powers," if necessary, to win the war.[79] He distrusted the yeomen and artisans who had elected the populist George Clinton as New York's first governor instead of him. Having felt scapegoated for the fall of Fort Ticonderoga, Schuyler urged Hamilton to respond emphatically to personal attacks. "A man's character ought not to be sported with," he once wrote, "and he that suffers stains to lay on it with impunity really deserves none nor will he long enjoy one."[80] Such a man was not likely to curb Hamilton's predilection for feuds and duels.

Hamilton's wedding may have heightened the frustrations that he was quietly experiencing with Washington. The general could be a tetchy boss, and Hamilton witnessed the anger he choked down in public. One observer remarked, "The hardships of the revolutionary struggle . . . had shaken the masterly control Washington had gained over his passions, and the officers of his staff . . . had to suffer, not unfrequently, from the irritable temper and punctilious susceptibility of their commander."[81] Hamilton was too proud and gifted, too eager to advance in rank, to subordinate himself happily to anyone for four years, even to the renowned Washington.

Hamilton still hungered for a field command. He wanted fluttering flags, booming cannon, and bayonet charges, not a desk job. That October, as Lafayette prepared to mount a raid on Staten Island, he had asked Washington if Hamilton could lead a battalion. Washington vetoed the idea, saying he could not afford to give up Hamilton. Right before the wedding, Hamilton applied to lead a charge against British posts in northern Manhattan. "Sometime last fall when I spoke to your Excellency about going to the southward," he reminded Washington, "I explained to you candidly my feelings with respect to military reputation and how much it was my object to act a conspicuous part in some enterprise that might perhaps raise my character as a soldier above mediocrity."[82] Again, Washington spurned Hamilton.

Then Alexander Scammell tendered his resignation as adjutant general. Two generals—Nathanael Greene and the marquis de Lafayette—lobbied to have Hamilton replace him. Washington again balked, saying that he could not promote the young lieutenant colonel over full colonels. Washington's predicament was clear. He had plenty of combat officers, but nobody could match Hamilton's French or his ability to draft subtle, nuanced letters. After almost hourly contact with Washington for four years, Hamilton had become his alter ego, able to capture his tone on paper or in person, and was a casualty of his own success.

It would be a time rich in political disappointments for Hamilton. Right before his wedding, Congress decided to send an envoy extraordinary to the court of Versailles to join Benjamin Franklin in raising a substantial loan and expediting supply shipments. General John Sullivan nominated Hamilton, who had been a proponent of such a loan; Lafayette also took up the cudgels for him. Three days before Hamilton's wedding, John Laurens was unanimously chosen instead, even though he stubbornly maintained that Hamilton was better qualified. Laurens thought Hamilton's nomination faltered only because he was insufficiently known in Congress. Earlier in the year, when Laurens had tried to secure Hamilton a post as secretary to the American minister in France, Hamilton had analyzed his own rejection thus: "I am a stranger in this country. I have no property here, no connections. If I have talents and integrity . . . these are justly deemed very spurious titles in these enlightened days."[83] These disappointments only buttressed his belief in meritocracy, not aristocracy, as the best system for government appointments.

The day after Hamilton's wedding, Congressman John Mathews of South Carolina nominated him as minister to Russia. Again, he was passed over. Hamilton now feared that he would be shackled to his desk for the duration of the conflict—for him, a degrading form of drudgery. He wanted one last chance for battlefield honor, which would be a useful credential in the postwar political world. Perhaps the marriage to Eliza Schuyler emboldened Hamilton to challenge Washington and assert his independence. After all, he was no longer a penniless young immigrant, lacking in property and connections.

After Hamilton returned to military service in early January 1781, he hired a guide to lead him south through the narrow mountain passes to Washington's headquarters, now located at a Dutch farmhouse on the Hudson River at New Windsor. Eliza soon joined him, and they shared lodgings in the nearby village. The young bride often assisted Martha Washington in entertaining officers, and she observed George Washington in a vignette of domestic heroism that remained engraved on her memory. A fire broke out in a shed adjoining his headquarters, and Washington instantly bounded down the stairs from his second-floor office, grabbed a washtub full of suds from the farmer's wife, dumped the suds on the blaze, then dashed back and forth with other tubs until the fire was extinguished. Meanwhile, Eliza's new husband felt less than enamored of Washington. He had been snubbed over too many appointments and meditated an open break. He resolved that "if there should ever happen [to be] a breach between us," he was determined "never to consent to an accommodation."[84]

It was an inauspicious moment for Hamilton to clash with Washington. The Continental Army was experiencing another abominable winter. That January, mutinies erupted among Pennsylvania and New Jersey troops, who had not been paid for more than a year and protested the eternal shortages of clothing, shoes, horses, wagons, meat, flour, and gunpowder. Many wanted to return home at the expiration of their three-year enlistments but were prevented from doing so by their officers. So demoralized were these troops that some officers feared they might even defect to the British. Hamilton applauded when Washington took draconian steps to suppress the mutineers and refused to negotiate until they had laid down their weapons. On February 4, Hamilton wrote to Laurens that "we uncivilly compelled them to an unconditional surrender and hanged their most incendiary leaders."[85]

With this uprising quelled, Hamilton was now ready for a showdown with Washington, who remained edgy after the uprising of his men. On February 15, the two men worked till midnight as they readied dispatches for the French officers at Newport. The next day, a frazzled Hamilton was going downstairs in the New Windsor farmhouse as the general mounted the steps. Washington said curtly that he wanted to speak to Hamilton. Hamilton nodded, then delivered a letter to Tench Tilghman and paused to converse briefly with Lafayette on business before heading back upstairs. In a letter written to Philip Schuyler two days later, Hamilton narrated the confrontation that ensued:

> Instead of finding the General as usual in his room, I met him at the head of the stairs, where accosting me in a very angry tone, "Col[onel] Hamilton," (said he), "you have kept me waiting at the head of the stairs these ten minutes. I must tell you, sir, you treat me with disrespect." I replied without petulancy, but with decision "I am not conscious of it, sir, but since you have thought it necessary to tell me so, we part." "Very well, sir," (said he), "if it be your choice," or something to this effect and we separated. I sincerely believe my absence, which gave so much umbrage, did not last two minutes.[86]

Remarkably enough, it was Washington who made the largehearted, conciliatory gesture after this altercation and within an hour sent Tilghman to see Hamilton. Tilghman said that Washington regretted his fleeting temper and encouraged Hamilton to come and patch things up. Hamilton, now twenty-six, had the colossal courage, or colossal cheek, to turn down cold the commander in chief. Where others were awed by the godlike Washington, Hamilton knew too well his mortal foibles. "I requested Mr. Tilghman to tell him that I had taken my resolution in a manner not to be revoked; that as a conversation could serve no other purpose than to produce explanations mutually disagreeable, though I certainly would not refuse an interview if he desired it, yet I should be happy [if] he would permit me to decline it."[87] Washington reluctantly honored Hamilton's decision to leave his staff.

Hamilton knew these events would shock Philip Schuyler, Washington's warm friend, who had been thrilled to have the general's aide-de-camp as his son-in-law. Hamilton told Schuyler that he wanted to command artillery or light infantry, but he knew a fuller explanation was required. He had not acted rashly, he insisted. He had long hated the personal dependence that accompanied his position and had found Washington to be much more temperamental than his exalted reputation allowed. Their working relationship had done "violence to my feelings."[88] Then Hamilton made a stunning revelation: Washington had wanted to be closer all along. It was Hamilton who had rebuffed him:

For three years past, I have felt no friendship for him and have professed none. The truth is our own dispositions are the opposites of each other and the pride of my temper would not suffer me to profess what I did not feel. Indeed when advances of this kind [have been made] to me on his part, they were rec[eived in a manner] that showed at least I had no inclination [to court them, and that] I wished to stand rather upon a footing of m[ilitary confidence than] of private attachment. You are too good a judge of human nature not to be sensible how this conduct in me must have operated on a man to whom all the world is offering incense.[89]

The same day, Hamilton wrote to James McHenry in a more vindictive tone, showing that he was severely disillusioned with Washington and tired of feeling browbeaten. "The great man and I have come to an open rupture. . . . He shall, for once at least, repent his ill-humour. Without a shadow of reason and on the slightest ground, he charged me in the most affrontive manner with treating him with disrespect."[90] Hamilton acknowledged that Washington's popularity was necessary to the patriots, and he promised to keep their rift a secret, but he had no intention of revising his decision.

The rupture with Washington highlights Hamilton's egotism, outsize pride, and quick temper and is perhaps the first of many curious lapses of judgment and timing that detracted from an otherwise stellar career. Washington had generously offered to make amends, but the hypersensitive young man was determined to teach the commander in chief a stern lesson in the midst of the American Revolution. Hamilton exhibited the recklessness of youth and a disquieting touch of *folie de grandeur.* On the other hand, Hamilton believed that he had been asked to sacrifice his military ambitions for too long and that he had waited patiently for four years to make his mark. And he was only asking to risk his life for his country. If Hamilton were simply the brazen opportunist later portrayed by his enemies, he would never have risked this breach with the one man who would almost certainly lead the country if the Revolution succeeded.

Fortunately, Washington and Hamilton recognized that each had a vital role to play in the war and that this was too important to be threatened by petty annoyances. Despite their often conflicted feelings for each other, Washington remained unwaveringly loyal toward Hamilton, whom he saw as exceptionally able and intelligent, if sometimes errant; one senses a buried affection toward the younger man that he could seldom manifest openly. Where Hamilton had reservations about Washington as a general, he never underestimated his prudence, character, patriotism, and leadership qualities. In the last analysis, the durable bond formed between Hamilton and Washington during the Revolution was based less on personal intimacy than on shared experiences of danger and despair and common hopes for America's future. From the same situation, they had drawn the same conclusions: the need for a national army, for centralized power over the states, for a strong executive, and for national unity. Their political views, forged in the crucible of war, were to survive many subsequent attempts to drive them apart.

EIGHT

GLORY

For a month after their feud, Washington and Hamilton performed their charade admirably, pretending that nothing had happened between them. Hamilton requisitioned two horses—one for him, one for his baggage—and rode off with Washington in early March to perform his last stint as interpreter in a conference with the comte de Rochambeau and other French officers at Newport. On March 8, Washington, Hamilton, and their French counterparts rode out on horseback for a sunset review of the French fleet, and that same day Hamilton drafted his last letter under Washington's signature. A few days later, Washington departed for what he called "my dreary quarters at New Windsor," and Hamilton headed off to the Schuyler mansion in Albany.[1] One of the most brilliant, productive partnerships of the Revolution had ended.

If Washington expected relief from Hamilton badgering him for an appointment, he soon learned otherwise. Hamilton was fully prepared to become a pest. In mid-April, he found quarters for himself and Eliza in a brick-and-stone Dutch dwelling at De Peyster's Point on the east bank of the Hudson, by no coincidence opposite Washington's headquarters at New Windsor. He even ordered "a little boat which two people can manage" so that he could scoot back and forth on short notice.[2] No sooner was Hamilton unpacked than he told General Nathanael Greene that he was scouting for "anything that fortune may cast up. I mean in the military line."[3] Hamilton seemed ubiquitous in New Windsor. One evening, a New England visitor, Jeremiah Smith, found himself discussing topical events with strangers at a local tavern. "I was struck with the conversation, talents . . . and with the superior reasoning powers of one who seemed to take the lead. It exceeded anything I had before heard and even my conceptions. When the company retired, I found it was Colonel Hamilton I admired so much."[4]

On April 27, the amazingly persistent young colonel addressed a formal letter to Washington, requesting a position in the vanguard force to be sent south. Reminding Washington of his earlier exploits as artillery captain, he noted, "I began in the line and, had I continued there, I ought in justice to have been more advanced in rank than I now am."[5] One can almost feel Washington growing hot under the collar in his reply. He was still dealing with extreme discontent in the ranks; now he had to deal with Hamilton. "Your letter of this date has not a little embarrassed me," he replied, referring to the upheavals produced in the past when he had jumped junior officers above those of higher rank. Lest Hamilton suspect that his intransigence stemmed from their contretemps, Washington cautioned: "My principal concern arises from an apprehension that you will impute my refusal of your request to other motives than these I have expressed."[6]

While awaiting a military assignment, Hamilton, never idle, refined his thoughts about the financial emergency gripping the states. With the collapse of the continental currency, Congress conquered its fears of the centralized power that might be wielded by a finance minister. Power had begun to flow from congressional committees to individual department heads—for war, foreign relations, and finance—just as Hamilton had recommended to James Duane. General John Sullivan, now back in Congress, wanted to nominate Hamilton as the new superintendent of finance and sounded out Washington on his qualifications. However incredible it now seems, Washington confessed that he had never discussed finance with his aide, but he did volunteer: "This I can venture to advance from a thorough knowledge of him that there are few men to be found of his age who has [*sic*] a more general knowledge than he possesses, and none whose soul is more firmly engaged in the cause, or who exceeds him in probity and sterling virtue."[7] A glowing tribute from a man who had observed Hamilton at close range for four years.

In the end, Sullivan withheld Hamilton's nomination due to overwhelming congressional support for Robert Morris, who took office in May 1781. A native of Liverpool, Morris had served in the Continental Congress and reluctantly signed the Declaration of Independence. He was an impressive-looking man with a wide, fleshy face, an ample paunch, and the sharp, shrewd gaze of a self-made merchant prince. He lived in a sumptuous Philadelphia mansion, tended by liveried servants, and reputedly was the richest man in town. He brought a somewhat mixed legacy to the new post. Lacking federal taxing power and a central bank, the patriots had to rely on private credit, and Morris, more than anyone else, had sustained the cause by drawing on his own credit to pay troops and even government spies. On the other hand, critics had accused him of exploiting his government connections for personal gain.

A lowly figure beside the august Morris, Hamilton wanted to establish his intellectual bona fides with the new superintendent of finance. Before writing to him, Hamilton brushed up on money matters and had Colonel Timothy Pickering send him some primers: David Hume's *Political Discourses*, tracts written by the English clergyman and polemicist Richard Price, and his all-purpose crib, Postlethwayt's *Universal Dictionary of Trade and Commerce*. On April 30, 1781, Hamilton sent a marathon letter to Morris—it runs to thirty-one printed pages—that set forth a full-fledged system for shoring up American credit and creating a national bank. Portions of this interminable letter exist in Eliza's handwriting (complete with her faulty spelling), as if Hamilton's hand ached and he had to pass the pen to his bride at intervals. Hamilton started out sheepishly enough: "I pretend not to be an able financier. . . . Neither have I had leisure or materials to make accurate calculations."[8] Then he delivered a virtuoso performance as he asserted the need for financial reforms to complete the Revolution. "'Tis by introducing order into our finances—by restoring public credit—not by gaining battles that we are finally to gain our object."[9]

Hamilton forecast a budget deficit of four to five million dollars and doubted that foreign credit alone could trim it. His solution was a national bank. He traced the riches of Venice, Genoa, Hamburg, Holland, and England to their flourishing banks, which enhanced state power and facilitated private commerce. Once again, he plumbed the deep sources of British power. Where others saw only lofty ships and massed bodies of redcoats, Hamilton perceived a military establishment propped up by a "vast fabric of credit. . . . 'Tis by this alone she now menaces our independence."[10] America, he argued, did not need to triumph decisively over the heavily taxed British: a war of attrition that eroded British credit would nicely do the trick. All the patriots had to do was plant doubts among Britain's creditors about the war's outcome. "By stopping the progress of their conquests and reducing them to an unmeaning and disgraceful defensive, we destroy the national expectation of success from which the ministry draws their resources."[11] This was an extremely subtle, sophisticated analysis for a young man immersed in wartime details for four years: America could defeat the British in the bond market more readily than on the battlefield. Hamilton had developed a fine appreciation of English institutions while fighting for freedom from England. In the letter's finale, he contended that America should imitate British methods and exploit the power of borrowing: "A national debt, if it is not excessive, will be to us a national blessing. It will be powerful cement of our union."[12]

Clearly, Hamilton was in training to superintend American finance someday. In late May, Morris sent him a flattering reply, informing him that many of his opinions tallied precisely with his own. Congress had just approved Morris's plan for the Bank of North America, a merchant bank that he hoped would be expanded after the war to encourage commerce. This exchange of letters initiated an important friendship. During the next few years, Hamilton and Morris were kindred spirits in their efforts to establish American finance on a sound, efficient basis.

Hamilton continued to stew about the Articles of Confederation, which had been ratified belatedly by the last state on February 27, 1781. Hamilton thought this loose framework a prescription for rigor mortis. There was no federal judiciary, no guiding executive, no national taxing power, and no direct power over people as individuals, only as citizens of the states. In Congress, each state had one vote, and nine of the thirteen states had to concur to take significant actions. The Articles of Confederation promised little more than a fragile alliance of thirteen miniature republics. Hamilton had already warned that if the ramshackle confederacy fostered the illusion that Congress had sufficient power, "it will be an evil, for it is unequal to the exigencies of the war or to the preservation of the union hereafter."[13] Again, Hamilton appealed for a convention to bring forth a more durable government.

That the thirteen states would someday coalesce into a single country was far from a foregone conclusion. Indeed, the states had hampered many crucial war measures, such as long-term enlistments, from fear that their troops might shed their home-state allegiances. People continued to identify their states as their "countries," and most outside the military had never traveled more than a day's journey from their homes. But the Revolution itself, especially the Continental Army, had been a potent instrument for fusing the states together and forging an American character. Speaking of the effect that the fighting had on him, John Marshall probably spoke for many soldiers when he said, "I was confirmed in the habit of considering America as my country and Congress as my government."[14] During the war, a sense of national unity seeped imperceptibly into the minds of many American diplomats, administrators, congressmen, and, above all, the nucleus of officers gathered around Washington. These men had gotten many dismaying glimpses of the shortcomings of the Articles of Confederation, and many later emerged as confirmed advocates of a tight-knit union of the states.

As a member of Washington's family, Hamilton had stumbled upon the crowning enterprise of his life: the creation of a powerful new country. By dint of his youth, foreign birth, and cosmopolitan outlook, he was spared prewar entanglements in provincial state politics, making him a natural spokesman for a new American nationalism. As soon as he left Washington's staff, he began to convert his private opinions into cogently reasoned newspaper editorials. In July and August 1781, he published a quartet of essays in *The New-York Packet* entitled "The Continentalist" that were signed A.B.—the same initials as in the letter written to Sir Henry Clinton, proposing the trade of Major André for Benedict Arnold.

These four articles seem spirited precursors to *The Federalist Papers*. Instead of carping at problems in random fashion, Hamilton delivered a systematic critique of the current political structure. He introduced a critical theme: that the dynamics of revolutions differed from those of peacetime governance; the postwar world had to be infused with a new spirit, respectful of authority, or anarchy would reign: "An extreme jealousy of power is the attendant on all popular revolutions and has seldom been without its evils. It is to this source we are to trace many of the fatal mistakes which have so deeply endangered the common cause, particularly that defect which will be the object of these remarks, a want of power in Congress."[15] Where revolutions, by their nature, resisted excess government power, the opposite situation could be equally hazardous. "As too much power leads to despotism, too little leads to anarchy, and both eventually to the ruin of the people."[16]

Unless the central government's hand was strengthened, asserted Hamilton, the states would amass progressively more power until the union disintegrated into secessionist movements, smaller confederacies, or civil war. He especially feared that populous states would indulge in separatist designs and take advantage of commercial rivalries or boundary disputes as pretexts to wage war against smaller states. To avert this situation, Hamilton listed a litany of powers that Congress needed to strengthen the union, especially the powers to regulate trade, levy enforceable taxes on land and individuals, and appoint military officers of every rank. Only unity could wring from skittish foreign creditors the large loans necessary to conclude the war. In closing, Hamilton applauded the national bank proposed by Morris, which would wed the "interest of the monied men with the resources of government."[17] This alliance would help to prop up a shaky government.

Hamilton's life was to be all of a piece, and the kernel of many of his later theories first germinated in these essays. His views did not change greatly over time so much as expand in richness, depth, and scope. Vernon Parrington later observed of Hamilton, "Singularly precocious, he matured early; before his twenty-fifth year he seems to have developed every main principle of his political and economic philosophy, and thereafter he never hesitated or swerved from his path."[18] To a peculiar extent, his mind was already focused on the problems that were to dominate the postwar period.

During the spring and early summer of 1781, Hamilton never slackened in his efforts to wrest a field command from Washington. And yet he refused to admit his bulldog tenacity. In May, he told Washington, with no apparent irony, "I am incapable of wishing to obtain any object by importunity."[19] Eliza worried about his safety if he received a field command, while sister Angelica entered into Hamilton's elaborate ambitions. When Angelica's husband, John Barker Church, got wind of rumors that Hamilton might obtain an appointment, he coyly informed his brother-in-law that "a certain lady (who has not yet made her appearance this morning) is very anxious for your happiness and glory."[20]

In early July, still panting for a combat role, Hamilton tempted fate by sending Washington a letter containing his commission, thus tacitly threatening to resign if he didn't get his desired command. It says much about Washington's high esteem for Hamilton that instead of bridling at this effrontery, he sent Tench Tilghman to him in an accommodating spirit. "This morning Tilghman came to me in his [Washington's] name, pressed me to retain my commission, with an assurance that he would endeavor by all means to give me a command," Hamilton told Eliza, who had gone to stay with her family in Albany. "Though I know my Betsey would be happy to hear I had rejected this proposal, it is a pleasure my reputation would not permit me to afford her."[21] Finally, on July 31, Hamilton succeeded in his long-standing quest when he received command of a New York light-infantry battalion and chose Nicholas Fish, his King's College classmate, as his second in command. With the war nearing its climax, Hamilton knew that Washington had vouchsafed one last coveted chance for battlefield laurels.

If Eliza brooded about her husband's well-being, Hamilton returned the favor, especially after learning in late spring that Eliza was pregnant with their first child. The New York frontier around Albany had been plundered repeatedly by Tory and Indian raids—in one infamous massacre in 1778, they had mutilated and dismembered thirty-two patriots—and General Schuyler lamented to his son-in-law in May 1781 that the area was "one general scene of ruin and desolation."[22] Schuyler himself was especially vulnerable. He had overseen a spy network with such efficiency that the British were plotting to kidnap him at home, as he learned that spring, and he made special arrangements to have an Albany guard hasten to his aid in case of emergency.

On August 7, about twenty Tories and Indians barged into the Schuyler mansion, overpowered the sleeping guards, seized weapons in the cellar, and surrounded the house. (Angelica had removed some weapons to the cellar when she found her little boy playing with them.) General Schuyler retreated to an upstairs bedroom, where, using a prearranged signal, he fired his pistol out the window to summon help. Mrs. Schuyler and her daughters were so horrified—"some hanging on [General Schuyler's] arms and others embracing his knees in the most distressing terror and uncertainty," reported one eyewitness—that the general was trapped by his clinging family.[23] Then the women remembered that Mrs. Schuyler's infant daughter, Catherine, had been left in a cradle by the front door. Since both Eliza and

Angelica were pregnant, sister Peggy crept downstairs to retrieve the endangered child. The leader of the raiding party barred her way with a musket.

"Wench, wench! Where is your master?" he demanded.

"Gone to alarm the town," the coolheaded Peggy said.[24]

The intruder, fearing that Schuyler would return with troops, fled in alarm.[25] Legend maintains that one Indian hurled a tomahawk at Peggy's head as she trotted up the stairs with the baby in her arms; to this day the mahogany banister bears what are thought to be scars from the blade. Hamilton was shocked by the news: "I have received, my beloved Betsey, your letter informing me of the happy escape of your father. He showed an admirable presence of mind. . . . My heart . . . has felt all the horror and anguish attached to the idea of your being yourself and seeing your father in the power of ruffians."[26]

Until early August, Washington had been planning a siege of New York City, so Hamilton did not expect to be too distant from Eliza during her pregnancy. Then in mid-August, Washington learned that the comte de Grasse, admiral of the French fleet in the West Indies, planned to sail for Chesapeake Bay. This sensational piece of news dovetailed with another that promised a decisive military action: Lafayette informed him that General Cornwallis was now entrenched at Yorktown, surrounded by water on three sides. This made the spot, from one perspective, a perfect fortress—and from another a perfect trap. Washington had wanted to deal the coup de grâce to the British in New York and recoup his earlier losses by reclaiming Manhattan and Long Island. The comte de Rochambeau dashed this plan, citing problems posed by shallow waters outside New York harbor and the British fortifications on Manhattan. So with some reluctance, Washington agreed to hazard all by moving additional men to the Chesapeake to link up with Lafayette and de Grasse's fleet in choking off Cornwallis's army.

In late August, Hamilton informed Eliza indiscreetly that he and part of the army would be moving to Virginia. (The move was still a military secret.) He refused to quit his troops or request a leave to see his bride. "I must go without seeing you," he wrote three days after the New York troops began to march south. "I must go without embracing you. Alas I must go." He remained, however, the dreamy newlywed. "I am more greedy of your love" than a miser of his gold, he continued. "It is the food of my hopes, the object of my wishes, the only enjoyment of my life."[27] On September 6, he divulged to Eliza the army's destination—"tomorrow we embark for Yorktown"—and sounded confident of victory. In a poetic conceit that he often played with but never acted upon, he toyed with abandoning worldly pursuits to luxuriate in her company: "Every day confirms me in the intention of renouncing public life and devoting myself wholly to you. Let others waste their time and their tranquillity in a vain pursuit of power and glory. Be it my object to be happy in a quiet retreat with my better angel."[28] Like other founders and Enlightenment politicians, Hamilton could never quite admit the depth of his ambition, lest it cast doubts on his revolutionary purity. In the midst of such rarefied goals as freedom and independence, who could admit to baser motives or any thoughts of personal gain?

Washington had also balked at the Yorktown plan because he wondered how he could move his hungry, bedraggled troops long distances along muddy roads without advertising his intentions to the British. He solved this dilemma ingeniously, marching foot soldiers southward in parallel lines, at staggered intervals, to mislead the enemy about his intentions. Washington knew that he had a singular chance to strike a mortal blow against the British if he could coordinate the massive movements of men and ships. With unerring precision, he guided his two thousand men and de Rochambeau's four thousand so they would rendezvous in Virginia with twenty-nine large "ships of the line" and three thousand troops brought from the West Indies by Admiral de Grasse, supplemented by seven thousand Americans already in place under Lafayette. To Washington's jubilation, Admiral de Grasse showed up even before he did, a fact that made the reserved Washington literally jump for joy. When Washington boarded the admiral's flagship, the *Ville de Paris*—a resplendent triple decker with 120 guns—the Frenchman teased his towering American counterpart by calling him "Mon cher petit général!"[29]

In late September, Hamilton and his light infantry reached Williamsburg, the staging area for the Yorktown siege, where he enjoyed an exuberant reunion with a trio of old friends: Lafayette, then convalescing from malaria; John Laurens, just back from Paris with arms, ammunition, and a large French subsidy negotiated by Benjamin Franklin; and Lieutenant Colonel Francis Barber, his teacher from Elizabethtown days, who had been wounded at Monmouth and had fought valiantly throughout the war.

On September 28, Hamilton and his men trudged toward Yorktown, through deep woods that opened intermittently to reveal fields of corn and tobacco. When they arrived the next day, the siege had just commenced. Dug in on high ground, Cornwallis had been throwing up earthwork redoubts since early August, employing thousands of slaves who had defected to the British lines in expectation of earning their freedom. In all, he built ten outlying defensive strongholds; two would have caught the attention of Hamilton and his men at once: numbers nine and ten stood closer to allied troops than the others. It was here that Hamilton was finally to have his oft-postponed appointment with military glory.

By October 6, expert French engineers, aided by fine autumnal weather, began to carve out two deep, parallel trenches about six hundred yards from the British lines, to seal Cornwallis and his famished, fever-racked men inside a trap. Military custom dictated a small celebration when the first trench was completed. Hamilton and his men were drafted for this honor and had no sooner disappeared into the long ditch, amid swirling flags and thudding drums, than the British let loose cannon fire. With a bit of completely unnecessary bravado, Hamilton issued an outlandish order. Perhaps knowing his men were beyond the range of small-arms fire, he brought them out of the trench and onto exposed ground, where he put them through parade-ground drills before the flabbergasted British. Luckily, the British didn't—or couldn't—mow them down. Of this irresponsible performance, one subordinate, Captain James Duncan, wrote in his diary: "Colonel Hamilton gave these orders, and, although I esteem him one of the first officers in the American army, must beg in this instance to think he wantonly exposed the lives of his men."[30]

By October 9, the allies began to bombard Cornwallis, with Washington himself touching off the first volley of cannon fire. Day and night, the cannonade exploded with such unrelenting fury that one lieutenant in the Royal Navy said, "It seemed as though the heavens should split." As the din grew "almost unendurable," this British officer saw "men lying nearly everywhere who were mortally wounded, whose heads, arms, and legs had been shot off. The distressing cries of the wounded and the lamentable suffering of the inhabitants whose dwellings were chiefly in flames" added to an omnipresent sense of danger.[31]

By October 14, the second parallel trench had been nearly completed and only redoubts nine and ten needed to be overrun to complete it. These defenses bristled with sharpened trees poised to impale any invading troops. Addressing his men on horseback, Washington explained that the siege could not advance farther unless these two positions were taken by simultaneous bayonet attacks. Any delay would only enhance the likelihood that British rescue vessels might arrive in time to evacuate Cornwallis. Washington fraternally decided that one redoubt would be taken by a light-infantry brigade commanded by the French and the other by the Continental Army under Lafayette. Lafayette tapped his personal aide, Jean-Joseph Sourbader de Gimat, to spearhead the charge, a selection that scarcely produced the bipartisan Franco-American amity intended by Washington.

For Hamilton, who had envisioned this moment since his clerkship on St. Croix, Lafayette's choice of Gimat threatened to rob him of his last great chance to fight. Mustering all his fire and eloquence, he pleaded again with Washington by letter, pointing out that he had seniority over Gimat and that, as officer of the day projected for the attack, he enjoyed priority. At this point, Washington decided either that Hamilton was an implacable force or that Gimat was too French to represent the Continental Army. Nicholas Fish shared a tent with Hamilton at Yorktown and remembered his friend bursting in gleefully after visiting Washington. "We have it!" Hamilton shouted. "We have it!"[32] Hamilton was to command three battalions led by Gimat, Fish, and Laurens.

Hamilton's appointment at Yorktown has been shadowed by scurrilous gossip, mostly peddled by John Adams. Years later, Adams told his friend Benjamin Rush that Hamilton blackmailed Washington to get the command: "Hamilton flew into a violent passion and demanded the command of the party for himself and declared, if he had it not, he would expose General Washington's conduct in a pamphlet."[33] It is true that Hamilton sometimes spoke disparagingly about Washington's military abilities, but only in private. It is inconceivable that Hamilton would have resorted to threats against Washington or that the latter would have yielded to them or that their relationship would have survived such extortion for another eighteen years of the most intimate collaboration.

A portrait by Alonzo Chappell of Hamilton at the Yorktown siege presents him in an unexpected pose. He stands by a cannon in a plumed hat, sunk in thought, his arms folded, and his eyes downcast. More the man of thought than of action, he gives no clue to the theatrics he was shortly to perform in the frenzy of battle. Two days before exposing himself to enemy fire, Hamilton wrote to Eliza, now five months pregnant, a lighthearted letter that attempted to assuage her worries. He chided her for not matching his output of twenty letters in seven weeks and said she could make amends only one way: "You shall engage shortly to present me with *a boy.* You will ask me if a girl will not answer the purpose. By no means. I fear, with all the mother's charms, she may inherit the caprices of her father and then she will enslave, tantalize and plague one half [the] sex."[34]

To expedite the siege, Washington decided to seize redoubts nine and ten with bayonets instead of pounding them slowly into submission with cannon. French soldiers were to overrun the redoubt on the left while Hamilton's light infantry stormed the one on the right. After nightfall on October 14, the allies fired several consecutive shells in the air that brilliantly illuminated the sky. Hamilton and his men then rose from their trenches and raced with fixed bayonets toward redoubt ten, sprinting across a quarter-mile of landscape pocked and rutted from exploding shells. For the sake of silence, surprise, and soldierly pride, they had unloaded their guns to take the position with bayonets alone. Dodging heavy fire, they let out war whoops that startled their enemies. "They made such a terrible yell and loud cheering," said one Hessian soldier, "that one believed the whole wild hunt had broken out."[35] Hamilton and his men ran so fast that they almost overtook the sappers, who were snapping off the edges of the sharpened tree branches and opening a breach through which the infantry rushed. Hamilton, hopping on the shoulder of a kneeling soldier, sprang onto the enemy parapet and summoned his men to follow. Their password was "Rochambeau"—"a good one," said one American, because it "sounds like 'Rush-on-boys' when pronounced quick."[36]

Once inside the fallen redoubt, Hamilton assembled his men quickly in formation. The whole operation had consumed fewer than ten minutes. Hamilton had accomplished the capture handily, suffering relatively few casualties; the French brigade met stiffer resistance and suffered heavy losses. Hamilton was exemplary in his treatment of the enemy. Some of his men clamored for revenge against the captives, and one captain was about to run a British officer through the chest with a bayonet when Hamilton interceded to prevent any bloodshed. He later reported proudly, "Incapable of imitating examples of barbarity and forgetting recent provocations, the soldiers spared every man who ceased to resist."[37] Besides showing humanity, Hamilton in his leniency toward his prisoners expressed his belief that wars, like duels, were honorable rituals, conducted by gentlemen according to sacred and immutable rules.

The taking of the two redoubts enabled the allied troops to outfit them with howitzers and finish the second parallel trench. As Hamilton and Henry Knox inspected the captured redoubt, they engaged in an academic controversy that afforded a humorous interlude. Washington had given orders that whenever soldiers spotted a shell, they should exclaim, "A shell!" Hamilton didn't think this order soldierly, whereas Knox thought it reflected Washington's prudent regard for his men's welfare. Amid this learned dispute, two enemy shells burst inside the redoubt. The soldiers present screamed, "A shell! A shell!" Instinctively, Hamilton sought shelter by grabbing the obese Knox, who had to wrestle him off. "Now what do you think, Mr. Hamilton, about crying 'shell'?" Knox protested. "But let me tell you not to make a breastwork of me again!"[38]

Completion of the second trench snuffed out the last remnants of resistance among the British. Cornwallis had grown so desperate that he infected blacks with smallpox and forced them to wander toward enemy lines in an attempt to sicken the opposing forces. He knew that he lay in grave peril and wrote to Sir Henry Clinton, "My situation now becomes . . . critical. . . . [W]e shall soon be exposed to an assault in ruined works, in a bad position, and with weakened numbers."[39] After dark on October 16, Cornwallis tried to evacuate his men by sea, but a drenching midnight storm made that impossible. All the while, the allied artillery pummeled his position without mercy.

On the warm morning of October 17, a red-coated drummer boy appeared on the parapet, followed by an officer flapping a white handkerchief. The guns fell silent. Cornwallis had surrendered. "Tomorrow Cornwallis and his army are ours," Hamilton rejoiced to Eliza on October 18. "In two days after, I shall in all probability set out for Albany and I hope to embrace you in three weeks from this time."[40] Tens of thousands of onlookers gaped in amazement as the shattered British troops marched out of Yorktown and, to the tune of an old English ballad, "The World Turned Upside Down," moved between parallel rows of handsomely outfitted French soldiers and battered, ragged American troops.

Hamilton calmly surveyed the final ceremony on horseback. His chat with many defeated British soldiers left him with a bitter aftertaste. To the vicomte de Noailles he confided, "I have seen that army so haughty in its success[,] . . . and I observed every sign of mortification with pleasure." He was outraged by the British soldiers' taunts of future revenge against America: "Cruel in its vengeance, England will not believe that every project of conquest in America is vain."[41] Indeed, although the lopsided Franco-American victory at Yorktown put the eventual outcome of the war beyond dispute, the British still occupied New York City, fighting persisted in the West Indies, and the war was to drag on for another two years.

Within a week, Colonel Hamilton had sped off to join Eliza in Albany, riding so hard that he exhausted his horses and had to hire another pair. He was ill and fatigued from more than five years of fighting and spent much of the next two months recovering in bed. On January 22, 1782, Eliza rewarded him with a son, christened Philip in tribute to her father. "Mrs. Hamilton has given me a fine boy," Hamilton wrote jovially to the vicomte de Noailles, "whose birth, as you may imagine, was attended with all the omens of future greatness."[42] In case further heavy fighting should flare up, Hamilton did not resign from the army right away and got a furlough from Washington. Only after visiting Washington in Philadelphia in March did Hamilton retire; he preserved his rank yet surrendered "all claim to the compensations attached to my military station during the war or afterwards."[43] Among other things, Hamilton renounced a pension that ultimately was to equal five years of full pay. His motives were certainly laudable—he wanted to remove the slightest conflict of interest as the army was demobilized and its members' future compensation debated—but his widow and offspring were to one day rue his decision and work hard to reverse it.

Because of his valiant performance at Yorktown, Hamilton became a certified hero. Yet it rankled that Congress never honored his bravery as Louis XVI did the heroism of the Frenchman who seized the other redoubt. Though he lacked official recognition, Hamilton gained something infinitely more precious for his political future: legendary status. At Yorktown, Hamilton established his image as a romantic, death-defying young officer, gallantly streaking toward the ramparts. Take away that battle, and Hamilton would have gone down as the most prestigious of Washington's aides, but not a hero. And without that cachet, he might never have been appointed a major general later on.

The American Revolution transformed Hamilton from an insecure outsider to a consummate insider who was married to the daughter of General Schuyler and stood on easy terms with the leaders of the Continental Army. In a eulogy that he later delivered for General Nathanael Greene, Hamilton talked about the personal opportunities that accompany revolutions. He said of them that "it has very properly been ranked not among the least of the advantages which compensate for the evils they produce that they serve to bring to light talents and virtues which might otherwise have languished in obscurity or only shot forth a few scattered and wandering rays."[44] Who could doubt that the comment had an autobiographical ring?

NINE

RAGING BILLOWS

With the British still clinging to New York City after Yorktown, Hamilton adopted the Schuyler mansion in Albany as his temporary home for the next two years. His lifelong wanderings ended as he formally became a citizen of New York State in May 1782. As he rocked the cradle and dandled the infant Philip, the twenty-seven-year-old war veteran projected the image of a contented paterfamilias. "You cannot imagine how entirely domestic I am growing," he told ex–Washington aide Richard Kidder Meade.[1] In a letter veined with whimsy, Hamilton described Philip at seven months:

> It is agreed on all hands that he is handsome, his features are good, his eye is not only sprightly and expressive, but it is full of benignity. His attitude in sitting is by connoisseurs esteemed graceful and he has a method of waving his hand that announces the future orator. He stands however rather awkwardly and his legs have not all the delicate slimness of his father's. . . . If he has any fault in manners, he laughs too much. [2]

Hamilton so savored this unaccustomed domestic role that he informed Meade, "I lose all taste for the pursuits of ambition. I sigh for nothing but the company of my wife and my baby."[3] Meade must have known this was poppycock and that Hamilton's career would move forward with its own furious inner propulsion. He had lost time in the Caribbean, plus another five years in the Revolution, so as he resumed the legal studies suspended at King's he wanted to adhere to a speeded-up timetable. For Hamilton, the law arose as the shortest route to political power—the profession claimed thirty-four delegates at the Constitutional Convention—and it would enable him to make a tolerable, even lucrative, living. Ordinarily, the New York Supreme Court stipulated that would-be lawyers serve a three-year apprenticeship before appearing in court. However, responding to a petition from Aaron Burr that January, the rule was temporarily waived for returning veterans who had begun their law studies before the war. Having waded through the tomes of all the major legal sages at King's, Hamilton qualified for this exemption and set about mastering the law in short order.

Unlike other aspiring lawyers of the time, Hamilton declined to clerk under a practicing attorney and planned to instruct himself. After serving Washington, he probably did not wish to be subservient to another boss and could not bear the prospect of copying out legal documents for some self-styled mentor. He had access to the superlative law library in Albany owned by his friend James Duane, its shelves stocked with treatises on British law, which closely paralleled New York law. "In this state, our judicial establishments resemble more nearly than in any other those of Great Britain," Hamilton later wrote in *Federalist* number 83. For Hamilton and other New York law students, British thought crept into their minds in this subliminal fashion and exerted a conservative, Anglophile influence. Particularly influential were Sir William Blackstone's *Commentaries,* first published in America ten years earlier, which endowed British law with a more systematic coherence. Forrest McDonald has observed, "Blackstone taught Hamilton a reverential enthusiasm for the law itself. . . . Moreover, the law as Blackstone spelled it out resolved once and for all the tension Hamilton had felt between liberty and law."[4]

In that era, law students often cobbled together workbooks that arranged legal precedents, statutes, and procedures by category. John Marshall kept a digest that covered 238 manuscript pages, spanning more than seventy topics; he drew on it extensively in his practice. Hamilton prepared his own manual, entitled "Practical Proceedings in the Supreme Court of the State of New York." This compendium of 177 manuscript pages and thirty-eight topics is the earliest surviving treatise that captures New York law as it shifted away from British and colonial models. Hamilton did not just transcribe dry extracts; he poked fun at legal pretensions. In one place, he said facetiously that the courts had lately acquired "some faint idea that the end of suits at law is to investigate the merits of the cause and not to [get] entangle[d] in the nets of technical terms."[5] Later the source of famous proclamations about the law's majesty, Hamilton could also be quite waspish about his chosen profession, telling Lafayette that he was busy "rocking the cradle and studying the art of fleecing my neighbours."[6] "Practical Proceedings" was so expertly done, its copious information so rigorously pigeonholed, that it was copied by hand and circulated among New York law students for years until it was superseded by William Wyche's 1794 manual, *New York Supreme Court Practice,* which was itself based in part on Hamilton's outline. Even then, some attorneys continued to prefer Hamilton's seminal version.

Hamilton raced through his legal studies with quicksilver speed. By July, just six months after starting his self-education, he passed the bar exam and was licensed as an attorney who could prepare cases before the New York State Supreme Court. In October, he further qualified as a "counsellor" who could argue cases, a status akin to an English barrister. He had to sign an allegiance oath, which showed the extent to which states held sovereign sway under the Articles of Confederation: "I renounce . . . all allegiance to the King of Great Britain; and . . . will bear true faith and allegiance to the State of New York, as a free and independent state."[7]

In acquiring these credentials, Hamilton lagged six months behind Aaron Burr, who had opened an Albany law office in July 1782. Aside from having sacrificed time to warfare, both young men were rushing to set up practices because it was widely known that patriotic lawyers would inherit the lion's share of legal work after the peace. This had been confirmed in November 1781 when the New York legislature enacted a law barring Tory lawyers from state courts, a certain bonanza for republican attorneys. Even though Hamilton was to hotly contest anti-Tory bias, he and other young attorneys who had sided with the patriots profited from it during the more than four years that the law stayed in effect.

There is little doubt that Hamilton and Burr socialized a good deal in Albany. While Hamilton was still at Yorktown, Burr had shown up on the Schuyler doorstep with a letter of introduction from General Alexander McDougall: "This will be handed to you by Lieutenant Col. Burr, who goes to Albany, to solicit a license in our courts."[8] It was probably at this point that a pregnant Eliza first smiled and shook hands with her husband's future executioner. Hamilton's old classmate Robert Troup was studying for the bar in Albany with his friend Burr, and the two were licensed at the same time. During the summer of 1782, Troup resided at the Schuyler mansion, helping Hamilton with whatever legal tutoring he needed.

Thus, from the outset of their careers, Hamilton and Burr were thrust into close proximity and a competitive situation. Both were short and handsome, witty and debonair, and fatally attractive to women. Both young colonels had the self-possession of military men, liked to flaunt their titles, and seemed cut out to assume distinguished places at the New York bar. Yet in the political sphere, Burr already trailed his upstart acquaintance, who was now a hero of Yorktown and basked in the reflected aura of General Washington. Hamilton also inhabited the splendid Schuyler mansion, while Burr settled for a frugal life until he could build up a legal clientele. That July, Burr married Theodosia Prevost, the confidante of Peggy Shippen Arnold, in the Dutch Reformed Church frequented by the Schuylers. (Theodosia's husband, a British officer, had died in Jamaica the previous fall.) They had a daughter, also named Theodosia, the following year. The elder Theodosia was ten years older than Burr and was never mistaken for a beauty, but she was charming, pleasant, and conversant in both French and English literature. As much as any man of his day, Burr appreciated smart, accomplished women, which made his later roguish antics all the more inexplicable to admirers.

However impressive it was that Hamilton could compress three years of legal training into nine months, he juggled several other balls at once. After Yorktown, he wrote two more installments of the "Continentalist" essays, which he then lost or misplaced. "He has lately recovered them," *The New-York Packet* informed readers in April 1782 in introducing "The Continentalist No. V." The paper said he had published the essays "more to finish the development of his plan than from any hope that the temper of the times will adopt his ideas."[9] In a sweeping historical tour, Hamilton showed how the English government had fostered trade starting in the reign of Queen Elizabeth and how Louis Colbert had accomplished the like as Louis XIV's finance minister. He alluded to David Hume's essays in endorsing government guidance of trade, which he denied was self-regulating and self-correcting. Previewing his Treasury tenure, he advocated duties on imported goods as America's best form of revenue. For a nation still fighting a revolution over unjust duties on tea and other imports, this was, to put it mildly, a loaded topic. To those who feared oppressive taxes, Hamilton made an argument that anticipated "supply-side economics" of the late twentieth century, saying that officials "can have no temptation to abuse this power, because the motive of revenue will check its own extremes. Experience has shown that moderate duties are more productive than high ones."[10]

At the time, many states were loath to transfer control over their own import duties to Congress, and Hamilton feared that the resulting economic rivalries would threaten political unity. His qualms were shared by Robert Morris, who sketched the broad contours of a program—establishing a national bank, funding the war debt, and ending inflation—that was the forerunner of Hamilton's work as treasury secretary. To strengthen the central government, Morris decided to appoint a tax receiver in each state who would be free from dependence on local officials. On May 2, 1782, he asked Hamilton to become receiver of continental taxes for New York. As an inducement, he assured Hamilton that he could pocket one-quarter of 1 percent of any monies collected. Hamilton, feeling harried, turned him down flat. "Time is so precious to me that I could not put myself in the way of any interruptions unless for an object of consequence to the public or to myself," he replied.[11] Hamilton may have suspected that with five New York counties still in enemy hands, the job would not be that remunerative. In early June, Morris sweetened the pot by guaranteeing Hamilton a percentage of the money *owed*, not just collected.

This evidently persuaded Hamilton to accept the offer, and he further volunteered to lobby the state legislature for Morris's tax measures. Whether the self-taught Hamilton knew it or not—and one suspects that he very much did—he was now squarely positioned to succeed Robert Morris as America's preeminent financial figure.

The few months that Hamilton spent trying to gather taxes demonstrated anew the perils of the Articles of Confederation. States regarded their payments to Congress, in effect, as voluntary and often siphoned off funds for local purposes before making any transfers. This situation, combined with a lack of independent federal revenues, had forced the patriots to finance the Revolution by either borrowing or printing paper money. On July 4, in his sixth "Continentalist" essay, Hamilton, with a nod to Morris, applauded the appointment of federal customs and tax collectors to "create in the interior of each state a mass of influence in favour of the federal government."[12] This essay makes clear that, in the Revolution's waning days, Hamilton had to combat the utopian notion that America could dispense with taxes altogether: "It is of importance to unmask this delusion and open the eyes of the people to the truth. It is paying too great a tribute to the idol of popularity to flatter so injurious and so visionary an expectation."[13]

In mid-July, while still cramming for his next bar exam, Hamilton traveled to Poughkeepsie and pleaded successfully with state legislators to form a special committee to expedite tax collection. Working with Philip Schuyler, he got the legislature to adopt a set of resolutions (likely authored by Hamilton himself) calling for more congressional taxing power and a national conference to overhaul the Articles of Confederation—the first such appeal issued by a public body. Hamilton's determined pursuit of reform won plaudits from Morris, and in his correspondence with Hamilton, Morris let down his guard and confided his frustration at congressional ineptitude. Hamilton repaid the candor. "The more I see, the more I find reason for those who love this country to weep over its blindness," Hamilton wrote.[14] He recoiled at the cowardice and selfishness he saw rampant in the New York legislature. "The inquiry constantly is what will *please*, not what will *benefit* the people," he told Morris. "In such a government there can be nothing but temporary expedient, fickleness, and folly."[15] Increasingly Hamilton despaired of pure democracy, of politicians simply catering to the popular will, and favored educated leaders who would enlighten the people and exercise their own judgment.

Whatever his disdain for state legislators, Hamilton made a favorable impression at Poughkeepsie. Jurist James Kent recalled that "his animated and didactic conversation, far superior to ordinary discourse in sentiment, language, and manner, and his frank and manly deportment, interested my attention."[16] The legislators were so taken with Hamilton's presentation that he was chosen as one of five members of

New York's delegation to the Continental (or Confederation) Congress that was to convene in November. With typical dexterity, Hamilton had parlayed the technocratic job of tax collector into a congressional seat.

For Hamilton, nobody in his generation showed a more genuine love of country or more salient leadership traits than his friend John Laurens. In January 1782, at a time when the British still held Charleston and Savannah, Laurens had addressed the South Carolina legislature in a futile last bid for his star-crossed scheme to recruit black troops. That July, he wrote a warm letter to Hamilton, expressing hope that his friend would "fill only the first offices of the republic." (Once again, a portion of Laurens's letter is missing, perhaps sanitized by Hamilton's family.) The note concluded, "Adieu, my dear friend. While circumstances place so great a distance between us, I entreat you not to withdraw the *consolation* of your letters. You know the unalterable sentiments of your affectionate Laurens."[17] Hamilton believed fervently that, once the war ended, he and Laurens, like figures from classical antiquity, would embark jointly on a new political crusade to lay the foundations for a solid republican union. In mid-August, he told Laurens that the state legislature had named him to Congress. Striking an uplifting note, he made a stirring appeal for his old comrade to join him there. "Quit your sword my friend, put on the *toga,* come to Congress. We know each other's sentiments, our views are the same. We have fought side by side to make America free. Let us hand in hand struggle to make her happy."[18]

We do not know whether Laurens ever set eyes on this message. In late August 1782, a British expedition from Charleston was foraging for rice near the Combahee River when the impetuous Laurens flouted orders and tried to ambush them with a small force. The enemy was tipped off and squatted in the high grass waiting for him. Once they stood up to fire, Laurens began to charge and exhorted his men to follow. He was instantly cut down by a bullet. John Laurens was one of the last casualties of the American Revolution. Many thought he had foolishly risked his life and those of his men in a trivial action against a superior force after real hostilities had ended. His death vindicated Washington's judgment that the patriotic Laurens had only one serious fault: "intrepidity bordering on rashness."[19] He was mourned by many who thought he had had the makings of a fine leader. "Our country has lost its most promising character in a manner, however, that was worthy of the cause," John Adams consoled Henry Laurens.[20]

For Hamilton, the news was crushing. "Poor Laurens, he has fallen a sacrifice to his ardor in a trifling skirmish in South Carolina," he wrote sadly to Lafayette, the other member of their war triumvirate. "You know how truly I loved him and will judge how much I regret him."[21] The death deprived Hamilton of the political peer, the steadfast colleague, that he was to need in his tempestuous battles to consolidate the union. He would enjoy a brief collaboration with James Madison and never lacked the stalwart if often aloof patronage of George Washington. But he was more of a solitary crusader without Laurens, lacking an intimate lifelong ally such as Madison and Jefferson found in each other. On a personal level, the loss was even more harrowing. Despite a large circle of admirers, Hamilton did not form deep friendships easily and never again revealed his interior life to another man as he had to Laurens. He became ever more voluble in his public life but somehow less introspective and revelatory in private. Henceforth, his confessional remarks were reserved for Eliza or Angelica Church. After the death of John Laurens, Hamilton shut off some compartment of his emotions and never reopened it.

In late November 1782, Alexander Hamilton, after trotting on horseback all the way from Albany, arrived in Philadelphia to take up his place in the Confederation Congress. The city of forty thousand people that he encountered was larger and more affluent than New York or Boston. Having grown up in seaside towns, he must have found something pleasingly familiar about this seaport with its tall-masted ships and extensive wharves. Compared to the raucous commercial chaos of New York, Philadelphia was a more orderly place, abounding in elegant homes tucked tidily behind garden walls. On sunny days, fashionable ladies strolled with parasols. Many tree-shaded streets had brick sidewalks swept clean by a sanitation department and illuminated nightly by whale-oil lamps. Though Presbyterians and Baptists now outnumbered Quakers, a trace of their old austerity lingered. By 11:00 P.M., one young English visitor grumbled, "there is no city in the world, perhaps, so quiet. At that hour, you may walk over half the town without seeing the face of a human being, except the watchman."[22]

Hamilton had left Eliza and baby Philip behind but was still the starry-eyed newlywed and did not wander the streets in search of nocturnal adventure. He assured his wife several weeks after arriving that "there never was a husband who could vie with yours in fidelity and affection."[23] At first, he tolerated Eliza's absence well and did not yearn for her presence until early January, when he began arranging her trip to Philadelphia—then he could not wait to see her. "Every hour in the day I feel a severe pang on this account and half my nights are sleepless," he told her. "Come my charmer and relieve me. Bring my darling boy to my bosom."[24]

In Philadelphia, Hamilton found himself part of a Congress whose inadequacy he had long ridiculed. The whole jerry-built structure—the endless ad hoc committees, the voting rules that encouraged states to veto vital measures, the term limits that restricted congressmen to three one-year terms in a six-year period—guaranteed paralysis. As Hamilton complained, the undemocratic voting rules put

it in the power "of a small combination to retard and even to frustrate the most necessary measures."[25] For someone with his reverence for efficiency, it was an exasperating situation. The problems only worsened after November 30, 1782, when
American peace commissioners signed a provisional peace treaty with Great Britain, sapping incentives for further unity. Local leaders such as Sam Adams in Massachusetts and Patrick Henry in Virginia eloquently asserted the sovereignty of the
states. So magnetic was the allure of state governments that many members of Congress stayed home, making it difficult to muster quorums. The caliber of delegates
suffered accordingly, and their jealous discords infuriated Hamilton.

He was saved from despondency by a like-minded delegate who also foresaw a
mighty nation and had a richly furnished mind to match his own: James Madison.
They shared a continental perspective, enjoyed a congruent sense of missions, and
served together on numerous committees. Having been thrown on his own resources at an early age, Hamilton, twenty-seven, was far more worldly than Madison, thirty-one, who had led a cosseted life. On the other hand, Madison, laboring in
Congress since 1780, was already a seasoned legislator. He was so conscientious that
he set a congressional endurance record by scarcely missing a day during three years
of service. The French minister rated Madison "the man of soundest judgment in
Congress. . . . He speaks nearly always with fairness and wins the approval of his
colleagues."[26]

In many ways, Madison was a pivotal figure in Hamilton's career, their early collaboration and later falling-out demarcating distinct stages in Hamilton's life. People tended either to embrace Hamilton or to abhor him; Madison stands out for
having alternated between the usual extremes. Small and shy, James Madison had a
formidable mind, but he was unprepossessing in manner and appearance. He usually dressed in black, had the bookish pallor of a scholar, and cut a somber figure.
Seldom did he smile in public, and the wife of one Virginia politician chided him
for being "a gloomy stiff creature."[27] Another female observer found Madison entertaining in private but "mute, cold, and repulsive" in company.[28] He did not court
publicity and lacked the charismatic sparkle that made the brashly confident Hamilton a natural leader. If Hamilton seemed born to rule, then Madison seemed born
to reflect. Still, Madison's diffidence could be deceptive, and his indomitable force
showed when he opened his mouth. He was a queer mixture of intellectual assurance, bordering on conceit, and social timidity and awkwardness. Lacking Hamilton's social ease and fluency, he could also be funny and a superb raconteur among
warm companions, even telling the occasional bawdy tale. At the time they met,
Madison was a priggish bachelor and tight-lipped about his private affairs. No personal gossip ever smudged the severe rectitude of James Madison's image.

Madison came from a family that had lived comfortably in Virginia's Piedmont

region for a century and was related to many local landowners. Madison's grandfather owned 29 slaves, and his father boosted that number to 118, making him the
largest slaveholder in Orange County, Virginia. The family also owned up to ten
thousand acres in the county. Until age fifty, Madison, the oldest of ten children,
lived in economic dependence on his father and even in Congress fell back on income from the family plantation. Like Jefferson, he could not escape his dependence on slavery, whatever his private qualms, and told his father during his last
year in Congress that unless the delegates got a pay raise, "I shall be under the necessity of selling a Negro."[29]

Against an incongruous backdrop of black hands stooping in the fields, Madison
passed his cloistered childhood. Suffering from a nervous disorder reminiscent of
epilepsy, he was prone to hypochondria and, like many sickly children, took to
reading. He received a fine classical education: five years at a boarding school, followed by two years of private tutoring on his plantation. At Princeton, he absorbed
prodigious heaps of books and slept only four or five hours per night. President
Witherspoon, who had rejected Hamilton, remarked of Madison that "during the
whole time he was under [my] tuition [I] never knew him to do, or to say, an improper thing."[30] Madison retained the air of a perennial student and always immersed himself in laborious study before major political events.

Because of poor health, Madison served only briefly as a colonel in the Orange
County militia and then became a member of the Virginia House of Delegates and
the governor's Council of State before being named the youngest member of Congress in 1780. Hamilton and Madison represented a new generation of postwar
leaders whose careers were wholly identified with the new republic. At this juncture, they had a similar vision of the structural reforms needed by the government.
Madison favored a standing army, a permanent navy, and other positions later associated with the Hamiltonians. If anything, Madison was even more militant than
Hamilton in asserting central authority and wanted Congress to be able to apply
force against states that refused to pay their requested contributions.

Despite the thorny complexities, it was a heady time for these two young men
who saw themselves striving for mankind. As Madison phrased it in April 1783, the
rights for which America contended "were the rights of human nature," and its citizens were "responsible for the greatest trust ever confided to a political society."[31]
To galvanize the new country, Hamilton and Madison concentrated on the crying
need for revenue—a need alleviated only partially when John Adams had arranged
a large loan from Holland on June 11, 1782. They believed that Congress required
a permanent, independent revenue source, free from reliance on the capricious
whims of the states. Only then could Congress retire the huge war debt and stem a
nascent movement to repudiate it. Hamilton stressed this in a resolution that read

like a fervent trumpet blast: "*Resolved,* that it is the opinion of Congress that complete JUSTICE cannot be done to the creditors of the United States, nor restoration of PUBLIC CREDIT be effected, nor the future exigencies of the war provided for, but by the establishment of permanent and adequate funds to operate generally throughout the United States, *to be collected by Congress.*"[32]

Hamilton joined Madison in a campaign to introduce a federal impost—a 5 percent duty on all imports—that would finally grant Congress autonomy in money matters. For Hamilton, the overriding goal was to institute a federal power of taxation. The most heated opposition came from Rhode Island, and Hamilton and Madison sat on a committee that dealt with the maverick state. They issued a joint statement, almost entirely in Hamilton's handwriting, that reiterated his now standard plea of the importance of public credit to national honor. Then came a statement still more fraught with large consequences: "The truth is that no federal constitution can exist without powers that, in their exercise, affect the internal policy of the component members."[33]

Hamilton was throwing down a gauntlet: the central government had to have the right to enact laws that superseded those of the states and to deal directly with their citizens. In late January, he made a still more heretical speech: he wanted to assign federal tax collectors to the states as a way of "pervading and uniting" them.[34] Hamilton was now aiming openly not at a makeshift confederation of states but at a unitary nation. Taken aback by this excessive candor, Madison noted that some members "smiled at the disclosure" and gloated privately "that Mr. Hamilton had let out the secret."[35] The incident again showed that Hamilton, far from being a crafty plotter, often could not muzzle his opinions. He was not one to traffic in half-hearted measures—Congress was setting enduring precedents for peacetime—and he opposed a compromise bill in April that limited the scope of the imposts and left revenue collection to each state. Hamilton's quarrel with New York governor George Clinton over the impost was to blossom into full-blown mutual animosity and profoundly affect the rest of his career.

Money was needed urgently to mollify the disaffected officers of the Continental Army, who threatened to turn mutinous at their winter camp in Newburgh, New York. The provisional peace treaty raised the unsettling prospect that the army might disband without officers receiving either back pay—as much as six years owed, in some cases—or promised pensions. The officer corps buzzed with threats of mass resignations, and a three-man delegation went to Philadelphia to negotiate a solution. On January 6, 1783, they presented Congress with a petition that expressed festering grievances: "We have borne all that men can bear—our property is expended—our private resources are at an end."[36] Some soldiers had been left so indebted by the fighting and the devalued currency that they feared they would be jailed upon their discharge from the army. Hamilton and Madison met with the disgruntled officers and were assigned to a subcommittee to devise a solution. The two men seized the chance to admonish Congress to fund the entire national war debt and satisfy the soldiers along with other creditors. The sad reality was that, deprived of real taxing power, Congress could offer the soldiers little but rhetorical solace.

Hamilton held out slim hope that the states would replenish the general coffers and appease the officers' demands. With his pessimistic imagination, he dwelled on the dangers inherent in situations, and he feared that civil strife, even disunion, would follow peace with Britain. In mid-February, he wrote apprehensively to Governor Clinton, outlining a plan to resettle military officers in New York State: "I wish the legislature would set apart a tract of territory and make a liberal allowance to every officer and soldier of the army at large who will become a citizen of the state." As a leading "continentalist," Hamilton knew that such a suggestion might seem to counter his image. "It is the first wish of my heart that the union may last," he explained, "but feeble as the links are, what prudent man would rely upon it? Should a disunion take place, any person who will cast his eyes upon the map will see how essential it is to our state to provide for its own security."[37] In this case, Clinton heeded Hamilton's advice and handed out lucrative land grants in New York State to willing officers.

Hamilton knew that the final arbiter of the deadly stalemate between restive officers and an impotent Congress was George Washington, with whom he had not corresponded in more than a year. On February 13, presuming on their former trust, Hamilton addressed a confidential letter to him. Writing now as a peer, he dared to advise Washington on how to handle the threatened uprising. For Hamilton, such a threat had its uses if it could prod a lethargic Congress into bolstering national finances: "The claims of the army, urged with moderation but with firmness, may operate on those weak minds which are influenced by their apprehensions more than their judgments. . . . But the difficulty will be to keep a *complaining* and *suffering army* within the bounds of moderation."[38] For Washington to maintain his standing among both the army and the citizenry at large, Hamilton urged him to badger Congress through surrogates.

Hamilton was coaxing Washington to dabble in a dangerous game of pretending to be a lofty statesman while covertly orchestrating pressure on Congress. The letter shows Hamilton at his most devious, playing with combustible forces. (He wasn't alone in this strategy: Gouverneur Morris in Philadelphia was also writing to General Nathanael Greene that the states would never pay the army "unless the army be united and determined in the pursuit of it.")[39] Hamilton feared that the cautious Washington might be thrust aside by more militant officers and told him of whispering in the army that he did not uphold his soldiers' interests "with sufficient warmth. The falsehood of this opinion no one can be better acquainted with than myself, but it is not the less mischievous for being false."[40]

A week later, Hamilton and Madison met at the home of Thomas FitzSimons to discuss the growing officer militance. Madison's notes give us Hamilton's unexpurgated view of Washington at the time. It jibes with his earlier statements about Washington's sometimes irritable personality but absolute rectitude:

> Mr. Hamilton said that he knew Gen[era]l Washington intimately and perfectly, that his extreme reserve, mixed sometimes with a degree of asperity of temper, both of which were said to have increased of late, had contributed to the decline of his popularity. But that his virtue, his patriotism, and his firmness would . . . never yield to any dishonorable plans into which he might be called. That he would sooner suffer himself to be cut into pieces; that he (Mr. Hamilton), knowing this to be his true character, wished him to be the conductor of the army in their plans for redress in order that they might be moderated and directed to proper objects.[41]

On March 4, Washington thanked Hamilton for his frank letter and confessed that he had not fathomed the abysmal state of America's finances. He referred gravely to the "contemplative hours" he had spent on the subject of the soldiers' pay: "The sufferings of a complaining army on one hand, and the inability of Congress and tardiness of the states on the other, are the forebodings of evil." Washington then obliquely rebuffed Hamilton's misguided suggestion that he exploit army discontent to goad Congress into action on public finance, saying it might "excite jealousy and bring on its concomitants."[42] With unerring foresight, Washington perceived the importance of enshrining the principle that military power should be subordinated to civilian control.

The Newburgh situation grew only more incendiary. In the following days, two anonymous letters made the rounds in camp, fomenting opposition to Washington and rallying the officers to apply force against Congress. One document warned darkly, "Suspect the man who would advise to more moderation and longer forbearance."[43] It seemed as if the new nation might be lurching toward a military putsch. On March 12, Washington, alarmed by this state of affairs, told Hamilton that he would attend an officers' meeting on March 15 to stop them from "plunging themselves into a gulf of civil horror from which there might be no receding."[44] Washington kept his diplomatic balance, trying to head off rash action by his officers while pleading for timely congressional relief. "Let me beseech you therefore, my good sir," he told Hamilton, "to urge this matter earnestly and without further delay. The situation of these gentlemen, I do verily believe, is distressing beyond description."[45]

On March 15, Washington addressed the officers, determined to squash a reported scheme to march on Congress. For the first time, he confronted a hostile audience of his own men. Washington sternly rebuked talk of rebellion, saying it would threaten the liberties for which they had fought. An insurrection would only "open the floodgates of civil discord and deluge our rising empire in blood."[46] He then staged the most famous coup de théâtre of his career. He was about to read aloud a letter from a congressman when the words swam before his eyes. So he fished in his pockets for his glasses. "Gentlemen," he said, "you will permit me to put on my spectacles, for I have not only grown gray but almost blind in service to my country."[47] The mutinous soldiers, inexpressibly moved, were shamed by their opposition to Washington and restored to their senses. Washington agreed to lobby Congress on their behalf, and a committee chaired by Hamilton granted the officers a pension payment equivalent to five years' full pay. Whether Congress could really make good on such payments without its own taxing power was another question.

As soon as he heard of Washington's virtuoso performance, Hamilton applauded him: "Your Excellency has, in my opinion, acted wisely. The best way is ever not to attempt to stem a torrent but to divert it. You coincide in opinion with me on the conduct proper to be observed by yourself."[48] Washington had heeded Hamilton's advice in assuming a leadership role but had pointedly ignored his advice about inflaming the situation for political ends. Hamilton still clung to the notion that a convincing bluff of armed force could help spur congressional action, but that was as far as he would venture. "As to any combination of *force*," he observed, "it would only be productive of the horrors of a civil war, might end in the ruin of the country, and would certainly end in the ruin of the army."[49]

The feared mutiny at Newburgh deepened but also complicated relations between Hamilton and Washington. It reinforced their mutual conviction that the Articles of Confederation had to be revised root and branch and Congress strengthened. "More than half the perplexities I have experienced in the course of my command, and almost the whole of the difficulties and distress of the army, have their origin here," Washington wrote of congressional weakness.[50] At the same time, Washington saw a certain Machiavellian streak in Hamilton and bluntly told him of grumbling in the army about congressmen who tried to use the soldiers as "mere puppets to establish continental funds." He lectured Hamilton: "The army . . . is a dangerous instrument to play with."[51] Washington must have seen that Hamilton, for all his brains and daring, sometimes lacked judgment and had to be supervised carefully. On the other hand, Hamilton had employed his wiles in the service of ideals that Washington himself endorsed.

In the spring of 1783, Alexander Hamilton, twenty-eight, already stood near the pinnacle of national affairs. He chaired a military committee that hatched the first plan for a peacetime army under the aegis of the federal government. In early April, Congress named him chairman of the committee in charge of peace arrangements, equipped with a spacious mandate to investigate ways to "provide a system for foreign affairs, for Indian affairs, for military and naval peace establishments," in Madison's words. That month, Congress ratified the provisional peace treaty with Britain, marking an end to eight years of hostilities—news that only amplified the menacing clamor among soldiers who wanted to pocket their pay before going home. "And here, my dear Colo[nel] Hamilton," Washington wrote, "let me assure you that it would not be more difficult to still the raging billows in a tempestuous gale than to convince the officers of this army of the justice or policy of paying men in civil offices full wages when *they* cannot obtain a sixtieth part of their dues."[52] Even though Congress enacted a new system of import duties that April, Hamilton still feared that it would lack the requisite funds to pacify the army. When Robert Morris threatened to quit as superintendent of finance in May, Hamilton was among those enlisted to persuade him to stay until the army could be safely disbanded. He introduced an emergency resolution, asking the states to send money to the common treasury so the soldiers could be paid and demobilized.

In mid-June, the raging billows that Washington had warned about still surged and foamed. Rebellious troops in Philadelphia sent a petition to Congress, couched in threatening language, demanding their money. Two days later, word came that eighty armed soldiers were marching from Lancaster, Pennsylvania, to Philadelphia to pry loose the pay owed to them. Their surly ranks swelled as they advanced. Hamilton, now Congress's man for all seasons, was swiftly drafted into a three-man committee to fend off the threat. He and his colleagues appealed to Pennsylvania's Supreme Executive Council to send local militiamen to stop these soldiers before they reached Philadelphia and made common cause with troops in local barracks. Hamilton was irate when the state refused to act until some outrage was perpetrated. Unafraid to lead, he stepped into the void fearlessly and directed Major William Jackson, assistant secretary at war, to intercept the rowdy protesters before they reached the city line. "You will represent to them with coolness but energy the impropriety of such irregular proceedings," he instructed, "and the danger they will run by persisting in an improper conduct."[53]

The troops, brushing Jackson aside, poured into Philadelphia on June 20, banded together with fractious troops in city barracks, and seized control of several arsenals. The next day, Elias Boudinot, president of Congress and Hamilton's erstwhile sponsor, convened a special Saturday-afternoon session of Congress to deal with the worsening crisis. That morning, Boudinot heard reports that rebel troops might sack the local bank. The congressmen were scarcely seated when about four hundred rebel soldiers, bayonets stabbing the air, encircled the State House, where Congress and the state's Supreme Executive Council occupied separate chambers. Things looked ominous: the mutineers far surpassed in number loyal troops guarding the doors. The symbolism was especially troubling: a mob of drunken soldiers had besieged the people's delegates in the building where the Declaration of Independence had been signed.

The congressmen did not fear "premeditated violence," Madison reported, "but it was observed that spiritous drink from the tippling houses adjoining began to be liberally served out to the soldiers and might lead to hasty excesses."[54] The increasingly drunken troops sent a scolding petition to the delegates inside, insisting that they be allowed to choose their own officers and threatening to unleash an "enraged soldiery" unless their demands were met within twenty minutes. The delegates refused to submit to such blackmail, shorten their session, or negotiate with rabble.

After three hours, the embattled congressmen marched out of the State House to the sneers and taunts of rioters. As he emerged, Hamilton saw embodied his worst nightmare: a portion of the revolutionary army had broken down into a mob that was intimidating an enfeebled central government. Now it was Hamilton, like Washington three months before, who made a vigorous case for military subordination to civilian rule. "The licentiousness of an army is to be dreaded in every government," he later commented, "but in a republic it is more particularly to be restrained, and when directed against the civil authority to be checked with energy and punished with severity."[55] The situation made him again wonder how a spirited young democracy could generate the respect necessary for the rule of law to endure.

That evening, Elias Boudinot assembled congressmen at his home. They passed a defiant resolution, written by Hamilton, claiming that government authority had been "grossly insulted" by the rioters and demanding that "effectual measures be immediately taken for supporting the public authority."[56] If Pennsylvania persisted in its spineless inaction, Congress would relocate to Trenton or Princeton—by no coincidence, the scenes of famous patriotic victories. The next morning, Hamilton and Oliver Ellsworth delivered this blunt ultimatum to John Dickinson, now the president of the Supreme Executive Council. If Pennsylvania could not guarantee the safety of Congress, then it would suspend all further meetings in the city.

After his encounter with the council, Hamilton lost all hope that the state would send out the militia, and he submitted a chilling report to Congress. The mutineers, he noted, had selected their own officers to present their grievances and authorized them to use force, even threatening them "with death in case of their failing to execute their views."[57] Aghast at the "weak and disgusting" behavior of Pennsylvania's leaders at a moment demanding unequivocal action, Hamilton reluctantly concluded and Congress agreed that they should adjourn to Princeton by Thursday.[58]

In short order, Congress fled across the state line and set up a movable capital in Princeton. The delegates settled crankily into cramped, makeshift quarters, Madison sharing a bed with another delegate in a room scarcely larger than ten feet square. Most shocking to this bibliophile, it lacked a desk. "I am obliged to write in a position that scarcely admits the use of any of my limbs," he complained.[59] So primitive were the Princeton lodgings that one month later Congress, like a French medieval court in the hunting season, packed up again and moved to Annapolis, followed by Trenton one year later, then New York City in 1785. Of this runaway Congress, hounded from its home, Benjamin Rush said that it was "abused, laughed at, and cursed in every company."[60] True to Hamilton's prediction, the insurrection collapsed as soon as resolute action was undertaken. The Pennsylvania council tardily called up five hundred militiamen; once the mutineers learned of an approaching detachment, they laid down their arms, and the Lancaster contingent trudged back to its base.

A perpetual magnet for controversy, Hamilton was stung by charges that he had conspired to move the capital from Philadelphia as part of a plot to transfer it to New York. In fact, Hamilton had feared that if Congress decamped, it would dilute domestic respect for its authority and sully America's image abroad. On July 2, he seconded a resolution that Congress should return to Philadelphia and prodded Madison for a statement confirming that he had postponed the flight to Princeton until the very last instant. Like an attorney collecting affidavits in a lawsuit, Hamilton asked his colleague, "Did I appear to wish to hasten it, or did I not rather show a strong decision to procrastinate it?"[61] Madison obliged with a letter: yes, Hamilton had stalled until the last moment. Once again, the thin-skinned Hamilton was quick to refute insinuations of duplicity or self-interest. Convinced that appearances, not reality, ruled in politics, he never wanted to allow misimpressions to linger, however briefly, in the air.

The Philadelphia mutiny had major repercussions in American history, for it gave rise to the notion that the national capital should be housed in a special federal district where it would never stand at the mercy of state governments. For Hamilton, the episode only heightened his dismay over the Confederation Congress and the folly of relying on state militias. On the other hand, he thought Congress had been unfairly blamed for failing to fulfill its duties when it was consistently deprived of the means of doing so. Its flagrant weaknesses stemmed from its constitution, not from its administration.

By the time the Pennsylvania mutineers dispersed, Hamilton had endured seven weary months in Congress, a period that had taxed his energy and patience. That three of New York's five delegates had been absent much of the time only added to his heavy burden. He had concluded that the country was not ready to amend the risible Articles of Confederation, because local and state politics exerted too dominant an influence. "Experience must convince us that our present establishments are utopian before we shall be ready to part with them for better," he told Nathanael Greene.[62] While marking time in Princeton in July, Hamilton drafted a resolution that again called for a convention to revise the Articles of Confederation. This prescient document encapsulated many features of the 1787 Constitution: a federal government with powers separated among legislative, executive, and judicial branches, and a Congress with the power to levy taxes and raise an army. Hamilton again questioned the doctrine of free trade when he argued for federal regulation of trade so that "injurious branches of commerce might be discouraged, favourable branches encouraged, [and] useful products and manufactures promoted."[63] With his hyperactive mind, Hamilton was already fleshing out a rough draft of America's future government.

Yet with the war ending, many advocates of state sovereignty wanted Congress dismantled as a permanent body. They thought the current Congress was *too* strong. "The constant session of Congress cannot be necessary in times of peace," said Thomas Jefferson, who wanted to replace it with a committee.[64] Slowly but inexorably, the future battle lines were being drawn between those who wanted an energetic central government and those who wanted rights to revert to the states. When his draft resolution foundered, Hamilton saw no need to dawdle any longer in this dwindling, demoralized Congress. On July 22, he informed Eliza that once the definitive peace treaty arrived, he would join her: "I give you joy, my angel, of the happy conclusion of the important work in which your country has been engaged. Now, in a very short time, I hope we shall be happily settled in New York."[65]

Hamilton was dragooned into riding back to Albany with the dour Mrs. Schuyler, who insisted on making a detour through New York City. This stopover gave Hamilton a queasy foretaste of the tensions brewing between returning patriots and British sympathizers. He was scandalized by the flight of Tory businessmen—seven thousand had sailed for Nova Scotia in April alone—and feared the economic wreckage that might ensue from this large-scale exodus. When he got back to Albany, a shaken Hamilton wrote to Robert R. Livingston, "Many merchants of second class, characters of no political consequence, each of whom may carry away eight or ten thousand guineas have, I am told, applied for shipping to convey them away. Our state will feel for twenty years at least the effect of the popular frenzy."[66]

For more than a century, November 25, 1783, was commemorated in New York City as Evacuation Day, the blessed end to seven years of British rule and martial law. At the southern tip of Manhattan, in a spiteful parting gesture, sullen redcoats greased the fort's flagpole as the last British troops were ferried out to transport ships waiting in the harbor. Once the British had relinquished their hold over this last outpost of occupied soil, the procession of American worthies entered, led by General Henry Knox, who hoisted the American flag up a newly pitched pole. Cannon rattled off a thirteen-gun salute, flags flapped, and crowds cheered in delirium as George Washington and Governor George Clinton, guarded by Westchester light cavalry, rode side by side into the city, followed by throngs of citizens and soldiers marching eight abreast. The long, triumphant procession wound down to the Battery, taking in the roars of the ecstatic crowds packing the streets. America had been purged of the last vestiges of British rule. It had been a long and grueling experience—the eight years of fighting counted as the country's longest conflict until Vietnam—and the cost had been exceedingly steep in blood and treasure. Gordon Wood has noted that the twenty-five thousand American military deaths amounted to nearly 1 percent of the entire population, a percentage exceeded only by the Civil War.[67]

As Washington gazed at the crowds, he could observe on every street corner debris left by the war. The British had never rebuilt those sections of the town blighted by the giant conflagration of September 1776. The city was now a shantytown of tents and hovels, interspersed with skeletal ruins of mansions and hollowed-out dwellings. Cows roamed weedy streets rank with garbage. When the future mayor James Duane saw his old properties, he moaned that they "look as if they had been inhabited by savages or wild beasts."[68] To provide firewood for British troops, the city had been denuded of fences and trees, and the wharves stood rotting and decayed. "Noisome vapours arise from the mud left in the docks and slips at low water," said one visitor, "and unwholesome smells are occasioned by such a number of people being crowded together in so small a compass, almost like herrings in a barrel, most of them very dirty and not a small number sick of some disease."[69] Hamilton was already meditating a plan for removing this devastation. Instead of patching up derelict houses and building huts on vacant lots, he expressed hope that the city's mechanics and artisans would find "profitable and durable employment in erecting large and elegant edifices."[70]

Less apparent but no less momentous than the physical change was the huge demographic shift triggered by the approaching peace. As British hopes of victory faded, many Loyalists had crowded aboard convoys and escaped to Britain, Canada, and Bermuda. At the same time, there was a countervailing influx of patriots that doubled New York City's population from about twelve thousand on Evacuation Day to twenty-four thousand just two years later, making it a booming metropolis that surpassed Boston and Baltimore in size. The surge of new and returning residents drove up prices sharply for food, fuel, and lodging.

During his stay of a little more than a week in New York, Washington salvaged the reputations of several suspected Tories who had engaged in espionage for the patriots. Whether coincidentally or not, two were old acquaintances of Hamilton from King's College days. The morning after he entered New York, Washington breakfasted with the loquacious tailor, Hercules Mulligan, who had spied on British officers visiting his shop. To wipe away any doubts about Mulligan's true loyalties, Washington pronounced him "a true friend of liberty."[71]

Washington also strolled into the bookshop of the urbane printer James Rivington, who had been attacked by Isaac Sears and the Sons of Liberty when Hamilton was at King's. With the war over, Rivington tried to stay in business by deleting the world *Royal* from his newspaper's name and the British arms from its masthead, but he finally had to suspend publication. In reality, he had done yeoman's work for the patriots, having stolen the British fleet's signal book, which had been transmitted to Admiral de Grasse. Washington disappeared into a back room with Rivington under the guise of consulting some agricultural books and rewarded him with a bag of gold pieces.

On December 4, Washington made his tearful farewell to his officers at Fraunces Tavern at the corner of Broad and Pearl Streets, again underscoring that military officers were merely servants of the republic. Washington resisted all calls to become a king. There is no proof that Hamilton attended the historic valedictory, in spite of his having been at Washington's side for four years of war. His absence, which must have been noted, suggests that he still nursed some secret wound because of his treatment by Washington. Certainly Washington, of all people, would not have lacked the magnanimity to invite him. Afterward, trailed by speechless admirers, Washington strolled down Whitehall Street and boarded a barge that carried him to the New Jersey shore.

Just a few days earlier, Alexander and Eliza Hamilton, along with baby Philip, had begun to rent a house at 57 (later 58) Wall Street, not far from Fraunces Tavern. For the first time, the vagabond young man from the West Indies had a real hometown, a permanent address. By the standards of the day, Wall Street was a broad, elegant thoroughfare, and many of the best-known merchant families resided there. The Hamiltons lived on the less fashionable eastern end, which was full of shops and offices, while Aaron and Theodosia Burr lived at tony 3 Wall Street—"next door but one to the City Hall," at Wall and Broad, as Burr proudly put it.[72] The lives of Alexander Hamilton and Aaron Burr continued in parallel. Both had passed the bar in Albany at almost the same time, and they now occupied the same New York street and inaugurated their legal practices at almost the same time.

After so many years of war, Hamilton had a pressing need to earn money and tried to keep full-time politics at bay. A month after Evacuation Day, he spotted a newspaper item stating that he had been nominated for the New York Assembly. Hamilton politely but firmly deflected the honor. "Being determined to decline public office," he wrote to the paper, "I think it proper to declare my determination to avoid in any degree distracting the votes of my fellow citizens."[73] Local populists associated with the Sons of Liberty scored lopsided victories in the election, resulting in a spate of punitive measures against Tories. As a fierce opponent of such vengeance, Hamilton busied himself defending persecuted Tories and halting their banishment.

Perhaps no individual was identified more with the postwar resurgence of New York City—not to mention the city's future greatness—than Alexander Hamilton. He was destined to excel in what was to emerge as America's commercial and financial metropolis, and he articulated the most expansive vision of its future. Nonetheless his vision was imperfect. At a dinner party soon after Evacuation Day, Hamilton and some other educated young men fated to lead the city debated whether to invest in local real estate or unspoiled forestland upstate. Hamilton's son James told the tale:

> John Jay was in favor of New York and made purchases there and as his means enabled him to hold his lots. His speculation made him rich. . . . Some of the others, including my father, took the opposite view and invested in the lands in the northern counties of the state. The wild lands were purchased at a few cents an acre, but they were not settled very rapidly.[74]

This last sentence was a gross understatement. That Alexander Hamilton opted to purchase land in the far northern woods and bungled the chance to buy dirt-cheap Manhattan real estate must certainly count as one of his few conspicuous failures of economic judgment.

TEN

A GRAVE, SILENT, STRANGE
SORT OF ANIMAL

From the time he started out as a young lawyer in postwar New York, Hamilton presented a dashing figure in society. He was trim and stylish, though not showy in dress. His account books reflect a concern with fashion, as shown by periodic visits to a French tailor, and his sartorial elegance is confirmed in portraits. In one painting, he wears a double-breasted coat with brass buttons and gilt-edged lapels, his neck swathed delicately in a ruffled lace jabot. One French historian remarked, "He belonged to the age of manners and silk stockings and handsome shoe-buckles."[1] He was as fastidious as a courtier in caring for his reddish-brown hair, and his son James recorded his daily ritual with the barber: "I recollect being in my father's office in New York when he was under the hands of his hair-dress[er] (which was his daily course). His back hair was long. It was plaited, clubbed up, and tied with a black ribbon. His front hair was pomatumed [i.e., pomaded], powdered, and combed up and back from his forehead."[2] Many artists who painted Hamilton picked up the quiet smile that suffused his ruddy cheeks and shined in his close-set blue eyes, conveying an impression of mental keenness, inner amusement, and debonair insouciance. His strong, well-defined features, especially the sharply assertive nose and chin, made for a distinctive profile. Indeed, his family thought a profile—not a portrait—done by James Sharples the best likeness of him ever done.

Hamilton's friends liked to rhapsodize his charm. His Federalist ally Fisher Ames was to eulogize his great capacity for friendship by saying that he was "so entirely the friend of his friends . . . that his power over their affections was entire and lasted through his life."[3] For Judge James Kent, who often rendered him in superlatives, Hamilton "was blessed with a very amiable, generous, tender, and charitable disposition, and he had the most artless simplicity of any man I ever knew. It was impossible not to love as well as respect and admire him."[4] Yet close observers also detected something contradictory in the way the mobile features shifted quickly from gravity to mirth. Boston lawyer William Sullivan noted the contrasting expressions of his face: "When at rest, it had rather a severe and thoughtful expression, but when engaged in conversation, it easily assumed an attractive smile."[5] This mixture of the grave and the playful was the very essence of his nature. His grandson wrote that Hamilton's personality was "a mixture of aggressive force and infinite tenderness and amiability."[6]

In his early years, Hamilton drew much of his social sustenance from the small, clubby circle of New York lawyers. The New York Directory for 1786 listed approximately forty people under the rubric "Lawyers, Attorneys, and Notary-Publics." The departure of many Tory lawyers had cleared the path for capable, ambitious men in their late twenties and early thirties, including Burr, Brockholst Livingston, Robert Troup, John Laurance, and Morgan Lewis. They were constantly thrown together in and out of court. Much of the time they rode the circuit together, often accompanied by the judge, enduring long journeys in crude stagecoaches that jolted along bumpy upstate roads. They stayed in crowded, smoky inns and often had to share beds with one another, creating a camaraderie that survived many political battles.

To assist with a caseload of mostly civil but also criminal work, Hamilton struck a partnership with Balthazar de Haert, who was either his colleague or his office manager for three years. Though he had just passed the bar himself, Hamilton was swamped with requests to coach aspiring lawyers, and he trained the sons of many prominent men, including John Adams. Hamilton struck his young charges as an exacting boss. One early trainee, Dirck Ten Broeck, recruited straight from Yale, wrote a former classmate a mournful letter about clerking for the little dynamo: "But now, instead of all the happiness once so near to view, I am deeply engaged in the study of law, the attaining of which requires the sacrifice of every pleasure [and] demands unremitted application. . . . [H]eavy for the most part have been the hours to me."[7]

Notwithstanding later conspiracy talk that he had stashed away bribes from the British, Hamilton seemed relatively indifferent to money, and many contemporaries expressed amazement at his reasonable fees. The duc de La Rochefoucauld-Liancourt commented, "The lack of interest in money, rare anywhere, but even rarer in America, is one of the most universally recognized traits of Mr. Hamilton, although his current practice is quite lucrative. I've heard his clients say that their sole quibble with him is the modesty of the fees that he asks."[8] Robert Troup said that Hamilton rejected fees if they were larger than he thought warranted and generally favored arbitration or amicable settlements in lieu of lawsuits.

Hamilton's son James related two incidents that show his father's legal scruples. In one case, the executor of a Long Island estate tried to retain Hamilton to defend him against some heirs who were suing him. To soften him up, the man pushed a pile of gold pieces across Hamilton's writing table before stating his case. When he was done, "Hamilton pushed the gold back to him and said, 'I will not be retained by you in such a cause. Take your money, go home, and settle without delays with the heirs, as in justice you are bound to do.'"[9] Another time, he flatly refused the business of a certain Mr. Gouverneur after learning he had made disparaging remarks about the "attorneylike" way somebody had padded his bill. In a caustic note, Hamilton lectured Gouverneur that his behavior "cannot be pleasing to any man in the profession and [that it] must oblige anyone that has proper delicacy to decline the business of a person who professedly entertains such an idea of the conduct of this profession."[10]

As a lawyer in a humming seaport and financial hub, Hamilton dealt with innumerable suits over bills of exchange and maritime insurance. He also gravitated toward cases that established critical points of constitutional law. It would be a mistake, however, to think of Hamilton only as a cloud-wreathed, Olympian lawyer. He sometimes represented poor people in criminal cases on a pro bono basis or was paid with just a barrel of ham. He had an incorrigible weakness for aiding women in need. In December 1786, he defended a spinster, Barbara Ransumer, who was indicted for stealing fans, lace, and other costly items. "I asked her what defence she had," Hamilton recollected. "She replied that she had none."[11] Unlike many modern lawyers, Hamilton represented clients only if he believed in their innocence. But he disobeyed his personal rule with Ransumer. In a speech dripping with shameless pathos, he managed to persuade the jury of her innocence. "Woman is weak and requires the protection of man," Hamilton summed up. "And upon this theme, I attempted to awaken the sympathies of the jury and with such success that I obtained a verdict of 'not guilty.' I then determined that I would never again take up a cause in which I was convinced I ought not to prevail."[12] That same year, Hamilton represented George Turner, who was indicted as a "dueller, fighter, and disturber of the peace," again suggesting that Hamilton was perhaps less averse to dueling than he later intimated.[13]

Hamilton was regarded as one of the premier lawyers of the early republic and was certainly preeminent in New York. Judge Ambrose Spencer, who watched many legal titans pace his courtroom, pronounced Hamilton "the greatest man this country ever produced. . . . In power of reasoning, Hamilton was the equal of [Daniel] Webster and more than this could be said of no man. In creative power, Hamilton was infinitely Webster's superior."[14] A no less glowing encomium came from Joseph Story, a later Supreme Court justice: "I have heard Samuel Dexter, John Marshall, and Chancellor [Robert R.] Livingston say that Hamilton's reach of thought was so far beyond theirs that by his side they were schoolboys—rush tapers before the sun at noonday."[15]

Whence the source of this legendary reputation? Hamilton had a taste for courtroom theatrics. He had a melodious voice coupled with a hypnotic gaze, and he could work himself up into a towering passion that held listeners enthralled. In January 1785, jurist James Kent watched Hamilton square off against Chancellor Robert R. Livingston, who was representing himself in a lawsuit claiming additional land south of his vast estate on the Hudson. (The post of chancellor was one of the top judicial positions in the state.) A member of New York's most powerful family, Livingston was tall and confident and moved with the natural grace of a born aristocrat. In comparison, Hamilton's style seemed almost feverish. "He appeared to be agitated with intense reflection," Kent recalled. "His lips were in constant motion and his pen rapidly employed during the Chancellor's address to the court. He rose with dignity and spoke for perhaps two hours in support of his motion. His reply was fluent and accompanied with great earnestness of manner and emphasis of expression."[16]

In speech no less than in writing, Hamilton's fluency frequently shaded into excess. Hamilton had the most durable pair of lungs in the New York bar and could speak extemporaneously in perfectly formed paragraphs for hours. But it was not always advantageous to have a brain bubbling with ideas. Robert Troup complained that the prolix Hamilton never knew when to stop: "I used to tell him that he was not content with knocking [his opponent] in the head, but that he persisted until he had banished every little insect that buzzed around his ears."[17] Troup also speculated that Hamilton was so distracted by public matters later on that he never had the chance to become deeply read in the law. This was probably true. On the other hand, the myriad claims on his time forced Hamilton to avoid trivia and plumb the basic principles of a case. "With other men, law is a trade, with him it was a science," said Fisher Ames.[18] He forced other lawyers to fight on his turf, starting out with a painstaking definition of terms and then reciting a long string of precedents. He brought into court lengthy lists of legal authorities and Latin quotations he wished to cite. His sources were varied, esoteric, and unpredictable. His legal editor, Julius Goebel, Jr., has observed: "Hamilton's reading was not confined to English law, for in addition to citations to basic Roman law texts we find him proffering passages from exotics like the Frenchman Domat, the Dutchman Vinnius, and the Spaniard Perez."[19]

A good-natured legal rivalry arose between Alexander Hamilton and Aaron Burr. Sometimes they worked on the same team, more often on opposing sides. Hamilton did not drag political feuds into dinner parties and drawing rooms, and so he mingled with Burr cordially. Later on, Hamilton said that in their early relationship they had "always been opposed in politics but always on good terms. We set out in the practice of the law at the same time and took opposite political directions. Burr beckoned me to follow him and I advised him to come with me. We could not agree."[20] Burr's friend Commodore Thomas Truxtun verified this rapport in non-political matters: "I always observed in both a disposition when together to make time agreeable . . . at the houses of each other and of friends."[21] Burr and Hamilton supped at each other's homes, and Burr's wife, Theodosia, visited Eliza. In 1786, the two men helped to finance the Erasmus Hall Academy in Flatbush, the forerunner of Erasmus Hall High School, today the oldest secondary school in New York State.

Many weird coincidences stamped the lives of Hamilton and Burr, yet their origins were quite dissimilar. Burr embodied the old aristocracy, such as it then existed in America, and Hamilton the new meritocracy. Born on February 6, 1756, one year after Hamilton, Burr boasted an illustrious lineage. His maternal grandfather was Jonathan Edwards, the esteemed Calvinist theologian and New England's foremost cleric. Edwards's third daughter, Esther, married the Reverend Aaron Burr, a classical scholar and theologian who became president of Princeton.

The infant Burr was born into the most secure and privileged of childhoods, yet it was steeped in horror. At the time of Burr's birth, the college was moving from Newark to Princeton, and in late 1756 the family took up residence in the new president's house. Then came a nightmarish chain of events. In September 1757, Aaron Burr, Sr., died at forty-two and was replaced five months later as president by his father-in-law, Jonathan Edwards. Soon after arriving, Edwards was greeted with the news that his own father, a Connecticut clergyman, had died. Princeton had recently been struck by smallpox, which Edwards promptly contracted by inoculation, dying two weeks after settling in. Then Burr's mother, Esther, came down with smallpox and died two weeks after her father. Dr. William Shippen took Burr and his orphaned sister into his Philadelphia home. When Grandmother Edwards came to reclaim the children, she contracted virulent dysentery and died shortly afterward. Thus, by October 1758, two-year-old Aaron Burr had already lost a mother, a father, a grandfather, a grandmother, and a great-grandfather. Though he lacked any memory of these gruesome events, Burr was even more emphatically orphaned than Hamilton.

Raised in Stockbridge, Massachusetts, and Elizabethtown, New Jersey, by his uncle, the Reverend Timothy Edwards, Burr attended the same Presbyterian academy that later educated Hamilton. Entering Princeton at thirteen, he developed into a first-rate scholar and delivered a commencement speech entitled "Building Castles in the Air," in which he declaimed against frittering away energy on idle dreams.

Burr studied law with his brother-in-law, the Connecticut jurist Tapping Reeve, then fought courageously in the Revolution.

Like Hamilton, the impeccably tailored Burr made an elegant impression, with his lustrous dark eyes, full lips, and boldly arched eyebrows. He was witty, urbane, and unflappable and had a mesmerizing effect on men and women alike. Despite his later courtship of the Jeffersonians, Burr never shed a certain patrician hauteur, epicurean tastes, and a faint disdain for moneymaking activities. He believed that through self-control he could learn to control others. With his impervious aplomb, he was a better listener than talker. Hamilton was easy to ruffle, whereas Burr hid his feelings behind an enigmatic facade. When faced with confessions of wrongdoing, Burr said coolly, "No apologies or explanations. I hate them."[22] Unlike Hamilton, he could store up silent grievances over extended periods.

Throughout his career, Hamilton was outspoken to a fault, while Burr was a man of ingrained secrecy. He gloried in his sphinxlike reputation and once described himself thus in the third person: "He is a grave, silent, strange sort of animal, inasmuch that we know not what to make of him."[23] As a politician, Burr usually spoke to one person at a time and then in confidence. Starting in college, he wrote coded letters to his sister and classmates and never entirely discarded the self-protective habit. Nor did he commit ideas to paper. Senator William Plumer remarked, "Burr's habits have been never to trust himself on paper, if he could avoid it, and when he wrote, it was with great caution."[24] As Burr once warned his law clerk, "Things written remain."[25] This caution reflected Burr's principal quality as a politician: he was a chameleon who evaded clear-cut positions on most issues and was a genius at studied ambiguity. In his wickedly mordant world, everything was reduced to clever small talk, and he enjoyed saying funny, shocking things. "We die reasonably fast," he wrote during a yellow-fever outbreak in New York. "But then Mrs. Smith had twins this morning, so the account is even."[26] By contrast, Hamilton's writings are so earnest that one yearns for some frivolous chatter to lighten the mood.

It is puzzling that Aaron Burr is sometimes classified among the founding fathers. Washington, Jefferson, Madison, Adams, Franklin, and Hamilton all left behind papers that run to dozens of thick volumes, packed with profound ruminations. They fought for high ideals. By contrast, Burr's editors have been able to eke out just two volumes of his letters, many full of gossip, tittle-tattle, hilarious anecdotes, and racy asides about his sexual escapades. He produced no major papers on policy matters, constitutional issues, or government institutions. Where Hamilton was often more interested in policy than politics, Burr seemed interested *only* in politics. At a time of tremendous ideological cleavages, Burr was an agile opportunist who maneuvered for advantage among colleagues of fixed political views. Hamilton asked rhetorically about Burr, "Is it a recommendation to have *no theory*?

Can that man be a systematic or able statesman who has none? I believe not."[27] In a still more severe indictment, Hamilton said of Burr, "In civil life, he has never projected nor aided in producing a single measure of important public utility."[28]

Burr's failure to make any notable contribution in public policy is mystifying for such a bright, literate man. He was an omnivorous reader. The records of the New York Society Library show that in 1790 Burr read nine consecutive volumes of Voltaire. He then spent a year and a half poring over all forty-four volumes of *Modern Universal History.* How many men at the time both read and ardently recommended Mary Wollstonecraft's feminist tract, *A Vindication of the Rights of Woman?* "Be assured," he told his educated wife, Theodosia, "that your sex has in *her* an able advocate. It is, in my opinion, a work of genius."[29] Yet this same Burr could take cruel swipes at his wife, responding to one of her letters with the acid remark that her note had been "truly one of the most stupid I had ever the honour to receive from you."[30]

If not a deep thinker as a politician, Burr was a proficient lawyer who vied with Hamilton for standing at the New York bar. He knew that Hamilton was the better orator, despite his sometimes windy bombast. He also said that anyone who tried to compete with Hamilton on paper was lost.[31] Nevertheless, some of Burr's associates thought he was the superior lawyer, a man who went straight to the nub of the matter. "As a lawyer and as a scholar Burr was not inferior to Hamilton," insisted General Erastus Root. "His reasoning powers were at least equal. Their *modes* of argument were very different. . . . I used to say of them, when they were rivals at the bar, that Burr would say as much in half an hour as Hamilton in two hours. Burr was terse and convincing, while Hamilton was flowing and rapturous."[32] Hamilton smothered opponents with arguments, while Burr resorted to cunning ruses and unexpected tricks to carry the day.

Though Hamilton appreciated that Burr could be resourceful in court, he found something empty beneath the surface. "It is certain that at the bar he is more remarkable for ingenuity and dexterity than for sound judgment or good logic," he said.[33] On another occasion, Hamilton elaborated on this critique: "His arguments at the bar were concise. His address was pleasing, his manners were more—they were fascinating. When I analyzed his arguments, I could never discern in what his greatness consisted."[34] Hamilton venerated the law, while Burr often seemed mildly bored and cynical about it. "The law is whatever is successfully argued and plausibly maintained," he stated.[35]

That the competition between Hamilton and Burr originated in their early days in legal practice is confirmed by a tale told by James Parton, an early Burr biographer. The first time that the two men jointly defended a client, the question came up as to who would speak first and who would sum up. Protocol stipulated that the lead attorney would do the summation, and Hamilton wished to be the one. Burr was so offended by this patent vanity that in his opening speech he tried to anticipate all the points that Hamilton would likely make. Apparently, he was so effective at this that Hamilton, embarrassed, had nothing to say at the end. If the story is true, it was one of the few times that Alexander Hamilton was ever left speechless.[36]

As a New York lawyer, Hamilton was well positioned to help the country negotiate the passage from the rosy flush of revolution to the sober rule of law. The management of the peace, he knew, would be no less perilous a task than the conduct of the war. Could the fractious tendencies engendered by years of fighting be channeled in constructive directions? The Revolution had unified sharply disparate groups. Without the bonds of wartime comradeship, would the divisive pulls of class, region, and ideology tear the new country apart?

These questions took on special urgency in New York, the former citadel of the British Army. Even before the war, the enthusiasm for revolution had often seemed more tepid in New York than elsewhere, and the state had been occupied by British forces longer than any other. Hamilton knew that many New Yorkers had been fence-sitters or outright Tories during the war and regretted to see the British depart. To Robert Morris, Hamilton surmised of New Yorkers that at the war's outbreak "near one half of them were avowedly more attached to Great Britain than to their liberty. . . . [T]here still remains I dare say a third whose secret wishes are on the side of the enemy."[37]

Many patriots found it hard to sympathize with the Loyalists, who were often well-to-do Anglican merchants and members of the old social elite. To aggravate matters, New York City had witnessed many British atrocities. Hordes of American soldiers had been incarcerated aboard lice-ridden British prison ships anchored in the East River. A staggering eleven thousand patriots had perished aboard these ships from filth, disease, malnutrition, and savage mistreatment. For many years, bones of the dead washed up on shore. How could New Yorkers forgive such unspeakable deeds? During Hamilton's tour of the city in August 1783, street-corner scuffles were already commonplace as returning veterans demanded back rent or damage awards from residents who had occupied their properties during the war. For many patriots, the Tories were traitors, pure and simple, and they would fight anyone who sought to stop them from exacting revenge.

Alexander Hamilton became that brave, unfortunate target. His motives for such martyrdom have long stirred debate. Cynics scoffed that he had acquired a long list of rich Loyalist clients and peddled his soul for British gold. Another theory portrayed him as the pawn of patriotic landowners, who dreaded an upsurge of postwar radicalism and wanted to make common cause with conservative Tories.

After all, if the patriots could pounce on Tory estates, might not their own fiefdoms be next? Many Hudson River grandees had enjoyed social and business contacts with wealthy Loyalists before the war and viewed them as potential allies in the post-war era. And Hamilton did indeed later forge an alliance of progressive landowners and former Tories into the nucleus of the Federalist party in New York.

The full truth of Hamilton's motivation for defending loyalists is complex. He thought America's character would be defined by how it treated its vanquished enemies, and he wanted to graduate from bitter wartime grievances to the forgiving posture of peace. Revenge had always frightened him, and class envy and mob violence had long been his bugaboos. There were also economic reasons for his stand. He regretted the loss of capital siphoned off by departing Tories, and feared the sacrifice of trading ties vital to New York's future as a major seaport. He also maintained that the nation's survival depended upon support from its propertied class, which was being hounded, spat upon, and booted from New York.

Hamilton's crusade on behalf of injured Loyalists was also spurred by foreign-policy concerns. With the war over, he craved American respectability in Europe. "The Tories are almost as much pitied in these countries as they are execrated in ours," John Jay advised him from France. "An undue degree of severity towards them would therefore be impolitic as well as unjustifiable."[38] For Hamilton, the anti-Tory legislation in New York flouted the peace treaty with Britain, which stipulated that Congress should "earnestly recommend" to state legislatures that they make restitution for seized Tory property and refrain from future confiscations.[39] The treatment of the Tories sensitized Hamilton to the extraordinary danger of allowing state laws to supersede national treaties, making manifest the need for a Constitution that would be the supreme law of the land. For him, the vendetta against New York's Tories threatened the whole political, economic, and constitutional edifice that he visualized for America.

During the war, the New York legislature had passed a series of laws that stripped Tories of their properties and privileges. The 1779 Confiscation Act provided for the seizure of Tory estates, and the 1782 Citation Act made it difficult for British creditors to collect money from republican debtors. In March 1783, the legislature enacted the statute that most engrossed Hamilton: the Trespass Act, which allowed patriots who had left properties behind enemy lines to sue anyone who had occupied, damaged, or destroyed them. Other laws barred Loyalists from professions, oppressed them with taxes, and robbed them of civil and financial rights. Each of these acts had rabid constituencies. Those who had enriched themselves by buying Tory estates mouthed the rhetoric of liberty while profiting handsomely from their convictions. Revenge, greed, resentment, envy, and patriotism made for an inflammatory mix.

By early 1784, the city had erupted in a wave of reprisals against Tories, who were tarred and feathered. The patriotic press clamored that those who had stayed behind British lines during the war should leave the city voluntarily or be banished. Fearing a Tory stampede, Hamilton did what he always did in emergencies: he took up his pen and protested the anti-Tory legislation in his first "Letter from Phocion," published in *The New-York Packet*. In plucking the name Phocion from Plutarch, Hamilton cleverly alluded to his own life as well as to antiquity. Phocion was an Athenian soldier of murky parentage who came from another country and became an aide to a great general. Later, as a general himself, the iconoclastic Phocion favored reconciliation with the defeated enemies of Athens. In the essay, Hamilton said that, as a revolutionary veteran, he had "too deep a share in the common exertions of this revolution to be willing to see its fruits blasted by the violence of rash or unprincipled men, without at least protesting against their designs."[40] He railed against the baleful precedent that would be set if the legislature exiled an entire category of people without hearings or trials. If that happened, "no man can be safe, nor know when he may be the innocent victim of a prevailing faction. The name of liberty applied to such a government would be a mockery of common sense."[41]

Hamilton disputed the rhetoric of Tory baiters and said categorically that they were motivated by "little vindictive selfish mean passions." To those who thought to profit by driving out Tories, Hamilton cautioned that this strategy would backfire on merchants and workmen alike. "To the trader they say, 'You will be overborne by the large capitals of the Tory merchants'; to the mechanic, 'Your business will be less profitable, your wages less considerable by the interference of Tory workmen.'" In fact, Hamilton noted, traders would be denied credit once extended to them by Tory merchants, and mechanics would find that temporarily higher wages either drew more mechanics to New York or slashed demand for their services, returning wages to their former level. Hamilton insisted that the now-chastened Tories would prove faithful friends of the new government; time was to validate his optimism.

Many people were shocked that Alexander Hamilton, Washington's ex-adjutant, had taken up the Loyalist cause, even though Washington, too, preached mercy toward their former enemies. Hamilton's actions abruptly altered his image. He was accused of betraying the Revolution and tarnishing his bright promise, and it took courage for him to contest such frenzied emotion. An anonymous poem appeared in the papers that lampooned Hamilton as "Lysander, once most hopeful child of fame." The writer, a former admirer, lamented that after gallant wartime service Hamilton had stooped to become a lackey for the Loyalists:

Wilt thou LYSANDER, at this well earn'd height,
Forget thy merits and thy thirst of fame;

Descend to learn of law, her arts and slight,
And for a job to damn your honor'd name!

In spite of Hamilton's pleas for tolerance, the persecution of Tories intensified. At a huge meeting on the Common called by the revivified Sons of Liberty in March, speakers urged the massive crowd to expel all Tories by May 1 and asked the state legislature to approve a resolution denying restoration of their citizenship. Dismayed by this turmoil, Hamilton entered the lists again with a second "Letter from Phocion," reminding his fellow citizens that actions taken now would reverberate into the future: "'Tis with governments as with individuals, first impressions and early habits give a lasting bias to the temper and character." All mankind was watching the republican experiment: "The world has its eye upon America. The noble struggle we have made in the cause of liberty has occasioned a kind of revolution in human sentiment."[42] If America acted wisely, Hamilton believed, it had a historic opportunity to refute the skeptics of democracy and to doom despots everywhere. Unfortunately, the two Phocion articles did not halt the reign of vengeance. On May 12, 1784, the state legislature passed a law depriving most Loyalists of the vote for the next two years. For Hamilton, it was a horrifying breach of the peace treaty and boded ill for America's domestic harmony and relations abroad. But he was not intimidated into silence. The feisty Hamilton always reacted to controversy with stubborn grit and a certain perverse delight in his own iconoclasm. He never shrank from a good fight.

By the second "Phocion" letter, Hamilton was defending a rich Tory in a celebrated lawsuit that showed just how far he would go to champion an unpopular cause. He was not a politician seeking popularity but a statesman determined to change minds. In 1776, a patriotic widow, Elizabeth Rutgers, had fled the British occupation of New York, abandoning her family's large brewery and alehouse on Maiden Lane. As of then, the Rutgerses had parlayed their brewing fortune into a hundred-acre estate. Two years later, a couple of British merchants, Benjamin Waddington and Evelyn Pierrepont, took over the brewery at the prompting of the British Army and appointed Joshua Waddington its supervisor. By that time, the property had been so thoroughly scavenged that it was "stripped of everything of any value except an old copper [vessel], two old pumps, and a leaden cistern full of holes," Benjamin Waddington later testified.[43] To refurbish and reopen the idle brewery, the new operators spent seven hundred pounds for a new storehouse, stable, and woodshed, and they paid rent to the British Army after 1780. On November 23, 1783, two days before Washington entered New York, a fire had incinerated the brewery, causing nearly four thousand pounds in losses for its wartime owners.

Invoking the Trespass Act, Elizabeth Rutgers filed suit in the Mayor's Court of New York City, demanding eight thousand pounds in back rent from Joshua Waddington. As an aggrieved widow, Mrs. Rutgers aroused intense sympathy, and Hamilton was villainized as a turncoat and a crypto-Tory. But he thought the Rutgers lawsuit an ideal test case to challenge the legality of the Trespass Act. Unlike many Tory tenants who had vandalized properties during the war, Joshua Waddington had taken a crumbling property and restored it at considerable expense. When Mrs. Rutgers calculated the back rent Waddington owed her, she made no allowance for this investment. Also, Waddington had acted under the express authority of the British Army at a time when the city lay under martial law.

Arguments in *Rutgers v. Waddington* were presented on June 29, 1784, before five aldermen and two figures well known to Hamilton: Mayor James Duane and City Recorder (Vice Mayor) Richard Varick. John Adams described Duane as a man with "a sly, surveying eye, a little squint-eyed . . . very sensible, I think, and very artful."[44] A smart lawyer of Irish ancestry, Duane had married into the Livingston family, corresponded with Hamilton during the Revolution, and then given him the run of his law library. Richard Varick, tall and dignified, with a bald pate and keen eyes, had been an aide to Philip Schuyler and Benedict Arnold and had been with Hamilton when Mrs. Arnold performed her mad scene on the Hudson. If the odds seemed stacked in Hamilton's favor, especially with two competent cocounsels in Brockholst Livingston and Morgan Lewis, Mrs. Rutgers also fielded a distinguished legal team that included her nephew, Attorney General Egbert Benson, John Laurance, and Hamilton's King's College friend Robert Troup. Even in a crowd of six other outstanding lawyers, Hamilton gave a cogent exposition that "soared far above all competition," said James Kent, then a law clerk for Benson. "The audience listened with admiration for his impassioned eloquence."[45]

As he strode about James Duane's chamber, Hamilton articulated fundamental concepts that he later expanded upon in *The Federalist Papers,* concepts central to the future of American jurisprudence. In renting the property to Waddington, he declared, the British had abided by the law of nations, which allowed for the wartime use of property in occupied territory. New York's Trespass Act violated both the law of nations and the 1783 peace treaty with England, which had been ratified by Congress. In urging the court to invalidate the Trespass Act, Hamilton expounded the all-important doctrine of judicial review—the notion that high courts had a right to scrutinize laws and if necessary declare them void. To appreciate the originality of this argument, we must recall that the country still lacked a federal judiciary. The state legislatures had been deemed the most perfect expression of the popular will and were supposed to possess supreme power. Mrs. Rutgers's lawyers asserted state supremacy and said congressional action could not

bind the New York legislature. At bottom, *Rutgers v. Waddington* addressed fundamental questions of political power in the new country. Would a treaty ratified by
Congress trump state law? Could the judiciary override the legislature? And would
America function as a true country or a loose federation of states? Hamilton left no
doubt that states should bow to a central government: "It must be conceded that the
legislature of one state cannot repeal the law of the United States."[46]

When Duane delivered his verdict in mid-August, he commended Hamilton and
the other lawyers, applauding the arguments on both sides as "elaborate and the authorities numerous."[47] He handed down a split verdict that required Waddington to
pay back rent to Rutgers but only for the period *before* he started paying rent to the
British Army in 1780. Given the pent-up emotion surrounding the case, Hamilton
advised his client to negotiate a compromise with Rutgers, who settled for about
eight hundred pounds—much less than the eight thousand pounds she had initially sought. It was a smashing triumph for Hamilton, who had upheld the law of
nations. A mere nine months after Evacuation Day, he had won a real if partial victory for a rich British subject against a patriotic widow.

Hamilton knew the case would be a boon to his legal practice, which went full
throttle in defending Tories. During the next three years, he handled forty-five cases
under the Trespass Act and another twenty under the Confiscation and Citation
Acts. His victory also brought predictable notoriety in its wake. The radical press
fulminated against him for giving aid to "the most abandoned . . . scoundrels in the
universe," and rumors floated about of a cabal intent upon assassinating him. The
scandalmongering journalist James Cheetham later observed of Hamilton "that a
great majority of the loyalists in the state of New York owe the restoration of their
property solely to the exertions of this able orator."[48]

The tone of politics had rapidly grown very harsh. Some poison was released
into the American political atmosphere that was not put back into the bottle for a
generation. As after any revolution, purists were vigilant for signs of ideological
backsliding and departures from the one true faith. The 1780s and 1790s were to be
especially rich in feverish witch hunts for traitors who allegedly sought to reverse
the verdict of the war. For the radicals of the day, revolutionary purity meant a
strong legislature that would overshadow a weak executive and judiciary. For
Hamilton, this could only invite legislative tyranny. *Rutgers v. Waddington* represented his first major chance to expound the principle that the judiciary should enjoy coequal status with the other two branches of government.

If *Rutgers v. Waddington* made Hamilton a controversial figure in city politics in
1784, the founding of the Bank of New York cast him in a more conciliatory role.
The creation of New York's first bank was a formative moment in the city's rise as a

world financial center. Banking was still a new phenomenon in America. The first such chartered institution, the Bank of North America, had been started in Philadelphia in 1781, and Hamilton had studied its affairs closely. It was the brainchild of Robert Morris, and its two biggest shareholders were Jeremiah Wadsworth and Hamilton's brother-in-law John B. Church. These two men now cast about for fresh outlets for their capital. In 1783, John Church sailed for Europe with Angelica and their four children to settle wartime accounts with the French government. In his absence, Church named Hamilton as his American business agent, a task that was to consume a good deal of his time in coming years.

When Church and Wadsworth deputized him to set up a private bank in New York, Hamilton warmed to it as a project that could help to rejuvenate New York commerce. He was stymied by a competing proposal from Robert R. Livingston to set up a "land bank"—so called because the initial capital would be pledged mostly in land, an idea Hamilton derided as a "wild and impracticable scheme."[49] Since land is not a liquid asset and cannot be converted into ready cash in an emergency, Hamilton favored a more conservative bank that would conduct business exclusively in notes and gold and silver coins.

When Livingston solicited the New York legislature for a charter, the tireless Hamilton swung into action and mobilized New York's merchants against the effort. He informed Church that he had lobbied "some of the most intelligent merchants, who presently saw the matter in a proper light and began to take measures to defeat the plan."[50] Hamilton was more persuasive than he realized, and a delegation of business leaders soon approached him to subscribe to a "money-bank" that would thwart Livingston's land bank. "I was a little embarrassed how to act," Hamilton confessed sheepishly to Church, "but upon the whole I concluded it best to fall in with them."[51] Instead of launching a separate bank, Hamilton decided to represent Church and Wadsworth on the board of the new bank. Ironically, he held in his own name only a single share of the bank that was long to be associated with his memory.

On February 23, 1784, *The New-York Packet* announced a landmark gathering: "It appearing to be the disposition of the gentlemen in this city to establish a bank on liberal principles . . . they are therefore hereby invited to meet tomorrow evening at six o'clock at the Merchant's Coffee House, where a plan will be submitted to their consideration."[52] At the meeting, General Alexander McDougall was voted the new bank's chairman and Hamilton a director. Snatching an interval of leisure during the next three weeks, Hamilton drafted, singlehandedly, a constitution for the new institution—the sort of herculean feat that seems almost commonplace in his life. As architect of New York's first financial firm, he could sketch freely on a blank slate. The resulting document was taken up as the pattern for many subsequent bank charters and helped to define the rudiments of American banking.

In the superheated arena of state politics, the bank generated fierce controversy among those upstate rural interests who wanted a land bank and believed that a money bank would benefit urban merchants to their detriment. Within the city, however, the cause of the Bank of New York made improbable bedfellows, reconciling radicals and Loyalists who were sparring over the treatment of confiscated wartime properties. McDougall was a certified revolutionary hero, while the Scottish-born cashier, the punctilious and corpulent William Seton, was a Loyalist who had spent the war in the city. In a striking show of bipartisan unity, the most vociferous Sons of Liberty—Marinus Willett, Isaac Sears, and John Lamb—appended their names to the bank's petition for a state charter. As a triple power at the new bank—a director, the author of its constitution, and its attorney—Hamilton straddled a critical nexus of economic power.

One of Hamilton's motivations in backing the bank was to introduce order into the manic universe of American currency. By the end of the Revolution, it took $167 in continental dollars to buy one dollar's worth of gold and silver. This worthless currency had been superseded by new paper currency, but the states also issued bills, and large batches of New Jersey and Pennsylvania paper swamped Manhattan. Shopkeepers had to be veritable mathematical wizards to figure out the fluctuating values of the varied bills and coins in circulation. Congress adopted the dollar as the official monetary unit in 1785, but for many years New York shopkeepers still quoted prices in pounds, shillings, and pence. The city was awash with strange foreign coins bearing exotic names: Spanish doubloons, British and French guineas, Prussian carolines, Portuguese moidores. To make matters worse, exchange rates differed from state to state. Hamilton hoped that the Bank of New York would counter all this chaos by issuing its own notes and also listing the current exchange rates for the miscellaneous currencies.

Many Americans still regarded banking as a black, unfathomable art, and it was anathema to upstate populists. The Bank of New York was denounced by some as the cat's-paw of British capitalists. Hamilton's petition to the state legislature for a bank charter was denied for seven years, as Governor George Clinton succumbed to the prejudices of his agricultural constituents who thought the bank would give preferential treatment to merchants and shut out farmers. Clinton distrusted corporations as shady plots against the populace, foreshadowing the Jeffersonian revulsion against Hamilton's economic programs. The upshot was that in June 1784 the Bank of New York opened as a private bank without a charter. It occupied·the

Walton mansion on St. George's Square (now Pearl Street), a three-story building of yellow brick and brown trim, and three years later it relocated to Hanover Square. It was to house the personal bank accounts of both Alexander Hamilton and John Jay and prove one of Hamilton's most durable monuments, becoming the oldest stock traded on the New York Stock Exchange.

ELEVEN

GHOSTS

After the dreary saga of his own childhood, Hamilton wanted a large, buoyant clan, and Dr. Samuel Bard, the family physician, was kept in constant motion with Eliza bringing one little Hamilton after another into the world. On September 25, 1784, the Hamiltons had their first daughter, named Angelica in honor of Eliza's sister. Not until Hamilton's fourth and favorite child, James Alexander, came along in 1788 did they christen a baby in homage to the absentee grandfather in the Caribbean. Hamilton never named a child after his mother, Rachel, perhaps hinting at some residual bitterness toward her. In all, Alexander and Eliza produced eight children in a twenty-year span. As a result, Eliza was either pregnant or consumed with child rearing throughout their marriage, which may have encouraged Hamilton's womanizing.

After their third child, Alexander, was born on May 16, 1786, the Hamiltons performed an exceptional act of kindness that has long been overlooked: they added an orphan child to their burgeoning brood. Colonel Edward Antill, a King's College graduate and Revolutionary War veteran, had foundered as a lawyer and farmer after the war. When his wife died in 1785, he was grief-stricken and encumbered with six children. By 1787, after suffering a breakdown, he committed his two-year-old daughter, Fanny, to the Hamiltons, who took the bright, cheerful girl into their home. Edward Antill died two years later, so Alexander and Eliza kept the child until she was twelve, when she went to live with a married sister. "She was educated and treated in all respects as [Hamilton's] own daughter and married Mr. [Arthur] Tappan, an eminent philanthropist of New York," said son James.[1] From London, Angelica Church cheered on her saintly sister, telling Hamilton, "All the graces you have been pleased to adorn me with fade before the generous and benevolent action of my sister in taking the orphan Antle [*sic*] under her protection."[2] That Eliza married one orphan, adopted another, and cofounded an orphanage points up a special compassion for abandoned children that might explain, beyond his obvious merits, her initial attraction to Hamilton.

For ten years, the Hamiltons had a home at 57 (then 58) Wall Street. A sketch of this bygone Wall Street shows a prosperous thoroughfare lined with three-story brick buildings. Well-dressed people saunter down brick sidewalks and roll in carriages over cobblestones at a time when many lanes were still unpaved. The young couple lived comfortably enough and entertained often, although Hamilton's business records reveal numerous small loans from friends to tide them over. One of his first purchases after leaving the army bespoke the convivial host: he bought decanters, two ale glasses, and a dozen wineglasses. The vivacious Hamiltons stood high on the "supper and dinner list" compiled by Sarah and John Jay when they settled at 8 Broadway after returning from France in 1784. Very fond of drama, Alexander and Eliza were also frequently habitués of the Park Theater on lower Broadway.

Like her husband, Eliza was frugal and industrious, even if often appareled in the rich clothes of a society lady. Skilled in many domestic arts, she made handbags and pot holders, arranged flowers and wove table mats, designed patterns for furniture, cooked sweetmeats and pastry, and sewed undergarments for the children. She served plentiful meals of mutton, fowl, and veal, garnished with generous portions of potatoes and turnips and topped off with fresh apples and pears. The Hamiltons were treated to fresh produce shipped regularly from Albany by the Schuylers, and there were always demijohns of good wine on hand.

An acute disappointment of the Hamiltons' early married life was their constant separation from Angelica by the Atlantic Ocean. From 1783 to 1785, John Barker Church lingered in Paris while winding up his business affairs with the French government. Angelica never met a famous, intelligent man she didn't enchant, and she had soon befriended Benjamin Franklin. She prayed that Hamilton might someday sail to Europe and succeed him as American minister. Angelica was chagrined when her husband bought a town house on Sackville Street in London, then a regal country house near Windsor. During the summer of 1785, the Churches returned briefly to America and visited Hamilton, who was in Philadelphia on business, before returning to live in England. Afterward, Hamilton wrote forlornly to Angelica:

You have, I fear, taken a final leave of America and of those that love you here. I saw you depart from Philadelphia with peculiar uneasiness, as if foreboding you were not to return. My apprehensions are confirmed and, unless I see you in Europe, I expect not to see you again. This is the impression we all have. Judge the bitterness it gives to those who love you with the *love of nature* and to me who feel an attachment for you not less lively. . . . Your good and affectionate sister Betsey feels more than I can say on this subject.[3]

Outwardly, Angelica thrived in the tony salons of London and Paris and seemed a natural denizen of that risqué, rarefied world, yet she never overcame a certain homesick longing to get back to Eliza, Alexander, and her American roots.

With a perpetually busy husband, Eliza ran the household and supervised the education of the children when they were small. James Hamilton left a delightful vignette of how she taught them each morning. He remembered her "seated, as was her wont, at the head of the table with a napkin in her lap, cutting slices of bread and spreading them with butter for the younger boys, who, standing at her side, read in turn a chapter in the Bible or a portion of Goldsmith's *Rome*. When the lessons were finished, the father and the elder children were called to breakfast, after which the boys were packed off to school."[4] Like Martha Washington, Eliza was never politically outspoken and did not spur her husband's ambitions. At the same time, she never deviated from his beliefs, identified implicitly with his causes, and came to regard his political enemies as her own.

As a woman of deep spirituality, Eliza believed firmly in religious instruction for her children. On October 12, 1788, she and Alexander strolled with their children to the west end of Wall Street and had the three eldest—Philip, Angelica, and Alexander—baptized simultaneously at Trinity Church in the presence of the Schuylers, Baron von Steuben, and Angelica Church, who was visiting. After 1790, the Hamiltons rented pew ninety-two, and Alexander performed free legal work for the church, then the meeting ground for the city's Episcopalian blue bloods. He was now quite changed from the young man who had knelt twice daily in fervent prayer at King's College. Nominally Episcopalian, he was not clearly affiliated with the denomination and did not seem to attend church regularly or take communion. Like Adams, Franklin, and Jefferson, Hamilton had probably fallen under the sway of deism, which sought to substitute reason for revelation and dropped the notion of an active God who intervened in human affairs. At the same time, he never doubted God's existence, embracing Christianity as a system of morality and cosmic justice.

Hamilton's dark view of human nature never dampened his home life but only enhanced it. His eight children never appeared to utter a single unkind word about their father. Admittedly, his early death made such carping distasteful, but complaints don't even surface in private letters. The second he got home, he shed his office cares and entered into his children's imaginative world. Son James said, "His gentle nature rendered his house a most joyous one to his children and friends. He accompanied his daughter Angelica when she played and sang at the piano. His intercourse with his children was always affectionate and confiding, which excited in them a corresponding confidence and devotion."[5]

Hamilton read widely and accumulated books insatiably. The self-education of this autodidact never stopped. He preferred wits, satirists, philosophers, historians, and novelists from the British Isles: Jonathan Swift, Henry Fielding, Laurence Sterne, Oliver Goldsmith, Edward Gibbon, Lord Chesterfield, Sir Thomas Browne, Thomas Hobbes, Horace Walpole, and David Hume. Among his most prized possessions was an eight-volume set of *The Spectator* by Joseph Addison and Richard Steele; he frequently recommended these essays to young people to purify their writing style and inculcate virtue. He never stopped pondering the ancients, from Pliny to Cicero to his beloved Plutarch, and always had lots of literature in French on his creaking shelves: Voltaire and Montaigne's essays, Diderot's *Encyclopedia*, and Molière's plays. The politician who provoked a national furor with his firebreathing denunciations of the French Revolution paid tutors so that all his children could speak French.

From the outset of his New York residence, Hamilton contributed to many local institutions. In a quest to improve education in the state, he worked to create the Board of Regents and served on it from 1784 to 1787. In this capacity, he was also a trustee of his alma mater, now renamed Columbia College to banish any royal remnants, and received from it an honorary master-of-arts degree. He was involved in countless neighborhood projects, petitioning the Common Council to relocate a statue of William Pitt that obstructed Wall Street traffic or working to improve sanitation on the street by asking the council to raise "the pavements of the said street in the middle thereof so as to throw the water on each side of the street."[6]

Hamilton also performed innumerable small acts of benevolence for friends. One special recipient was Baron von Steuben, who had received a verbal pledge from Congress that he would be paid if the patriots won the Revolution. When Congress reneged on this promise, Hamilton took Steuben into his home and helped him to craft petitions to the legislature; Hamilton's papers are replete with entries for unpaid loans to the spendthrift baron, who was finally granted sixteen thousand acres in upstate New York. Alexander and Eliza also rescued a thirty-five-year-old painter, Ralph Earl, who had painted battle scenes of the Revolution and studied under Benjamin West in London. Upon returning to New York in 1786, Earl lost his money in dissolute habits and was tossed into debtors' prison. Moved by his plight, Hamilton induced Eliza "to go to the debtors' jail to sit for her portrait and she induced other ladies to do the same," wrote James Hamilton. "By this means, the artist made a sufficient sum to pay his debts."[7] To this thoughtful patronage we owe Earl's lifelike portrait of Eliza in a cushioned chair with gilded arms, which superbly captures the "earnest, energetic, and intelligent woman" that her son James evoked in his memoirs.[8]

By age thirty, Alexander Hamilton was a New York luminary and a stalwart member of the continental elite. He had traveled an almost inconceivable distance from his West Indian youth. Occasionally, his troubled past burst in upon him unexpectedly. After Yorktown, Hamilton was informed that his half brother Peter Lavien had died in South Carolina, leaving token bequests of one hundred pounds apiece to Hamilton and his brother, James. Lavien had been so estranged from his two illegitimate half brothers that in his will he referred to them as "Alexander & Robert [*sic*] Hamilton . . . now or late residents of the island of Santa Cruz in the West Indies."[9] Had Hamilton simply been the more vivid brother or had Lavien's memory been refreshed by reports that his bastard half brother was, miraculously, aide-de-camp to George Washington? Instead of being touched by this belated penance, such as it was, Hamilton noted scornfully that Peter Lavien had left the bulk of his assets—properties in South Carolina, Georgia, and St. Croix—to three close friends. From the way Hamilton broke the news to Eliza, we can see that she had long known the story of his being cheated of his inheritance. "You know the circumstances that abate my distress," he told her, "yet my heart acknowledges the rights of a brother. He dies rich, but has disposed of the bulk of his fortune to strangers. I am told he has left me a legacy. I did not inquire how much."[10] We can also learn much about Hamilton's attitude toward this bequest by legal work he performed on the will of Sir William Johnson, who, by coincidence, had a legitimate son named Peter and eight illegitimate children. Hamilton turned in an unsparing verdict: "I am of opinion that the survivors of the eight children were entitled" as well to the inheritance originally given to Peter alone.[11]

It must have distressed Hamilton to gaze backward, and he retained few acquaintances from his past. During the war, he had corresponded with his old St. Croix mentor, Hugh Knox, who doted proudly on his success, marveled at his proximity to Washington, and implored him to draft a history of the American Revolution. Then, in 1783, Knox sent Hamilton a plaintive letter, complaining that his former disciple had greeted his letters with silence for three years. He admitted to bruised feelings: "When you were covered with the dust of the camp and had cannonballs whistling thick about your ears, you used to steal an hour's converse with an old friend every 5 or 6 months; and now in a time of profound peace and tranquillity you cannot, it seems, find *two minutes* for this kind of office. . . . [A]re you grown too rich and proud to have a good memory? . . . Pray make haste to explain this strange mystery!"[12]

Hamilton rushed to mollify Knox, explaining that he had never received the letters. Knox then replied in ecstatic tones that "you have not only *answered*, but even far *exceeded* our most sanguine hopes and expectations."[13] He conjured up the frail but persistent adolescent he had befriended and beseeched Hamilton not to exhaust himself through overwork. Though Hamilton patched things up with Knox, the anomaly remains that he had not sent him a letter in three years. He displayed not the slightest interest in revisiting St. Croix or showing Eliza the scenes of his upbringing. Did he need some psychic distance from the West Indies to reinvent himself in America? When Knox died seven years later, Hamilton must have regretted that he had not seen his fond old mentor again. Knox was eulogized as a "universal lover of mankind" in Hamilton's old paper, the *Royal Danish American Gazette*.[14] He certainly had shown a special and abiding love for Hamilton.

In May 1785, Hamilton's brother, James, resurfaced with a letter begging for money. The envelope that Hamilton sent in reply shows that James had migrated to St. Thomas. (He probably died there the following year, from causes unknown.) Hamilton's reply is a shocking revelation of just how estranged he had grown from his carpenter brother and their father, notwithstanding his earlier efforts to stay in touch with them. Hamilton expressed surprise that James had not received a letter he sent him six months before and reproached him gently, saying this was only the second letter he had gotten from him in many years. We do not know what James thought of his wondrous brother, but how could he not have been envious? Forgiving his brother's failure to write, Hamilton addressed him with an affecting eagerness to help: "The situation you describe yourself to be in gives me much pain and nothing will make me happier than, as far as may be in my power, to contribute to your relief."[15] While Hamilton said that his own prospects were "flattering"—his sole, discreet reference to his own spectacular good fortune—he also said that he could not afford to lend him more at the moment, though he wanted in time to help settle him on a farm in America.

> My affection for you, however, will not permit me to be inattentive to your welfare and I hope time will prove to you that I feel all the sentiment of a brother. Let me only request of you to exert your industry for a year or two more where you are and at the end of that time, I promise myself to be able to invite you to a more comfortable settlement in this country. Allow me only to give you one caution, which is to avoid if possible getting in debt. Are you *married* or *single*? If the *latter*, it is my wish for many reasons it may be agreeable to you to continue in that state.[16]

That Hamilton didn't have the slightest notion of whether his brother was married or not and didn't assume that he would have been invited to any wedding suggests the wide gulf separating the two brothers. When Hamilton turned to the subject of their feckless father, his poignant letter grew more heartbreaking:

> But what has become of our dear father? It is an age since I have heard from him or of him, though I have written him several letters. Perhaps, alas! he is no more and I shall not have the pleasing opportunity of contributing to render the close of his life more happy than the progress of it. My heart bleeds at the recollection of his misfortunes and embarrassments. Sometimes I flatter myself his brothers have extended their support to him and that he now enjoys tranquillity and ease. At other times, I fear he is suffering in indigence. I entreat you, if you can, to relieve me from my doubts and let me know how or where he is, if alive; if dead, how and where he died. Should he be alive, inform him of my inquiries, beg him to write to me, and tell him how ready I shall be to devote myself and all I have to his accommodation and happiness.[17]

This letter confirms that Hamilton lacked any clear grasp of his wayward father's situation or even whether he was still alive. He did suspect, however, that his brother had maintained contact with him. The letter also makes manifest that he felt more tenderness and sorrow than anger toward his father.

There were only two figures from St. Croix with whom Hamilton remained in touch throughout his life. Hamilton's cousin Ann Lytton Venton, who had helped to bankroll his education at King's College, escaped a wretched marriage when her husband died in 1776. Four years later, she married a Scot, George Mitchell, who filed for bankruptcy the next year, forcing them to flee St. Croix. Three years after that, they moved to Burlington, New Jersey. It was a ghastly time for Ann Mitchell, who complained in 1796 that she and her daughter "have suffered and still suffer every hardship incident to poverty."[18] Hamilton sometimes met Mitchell in Philadelphia and tried to prop her up with financial and legal help, but he was later bothered by a nagging conscience that he had not done more to alleviate her struggles.

The only truly happy relationship that Hamilton sustained from boyhood was with his best friend, Edward Stevens. In 1777, Stevens had completed his medical studies in Edinburgh, publishing a dissertation in Latin on stomach digestion, inspired by the peculiar case of a man who made a living by swallowing stones to amuse street crowds. The following year, at age twenty-four, Stevens became the first junior president of the Royal Medical Society. Like Hugh Knox, he was thrilled by Hamilton's exploits under Washington, even slightly agog. "Who would have imagined, my friend," he wrote to Hamilton in French in 1778, "that a man of your *size*, of your delicacy of constitution, and your tranquillity would have shone so much and in such a short time on the Field of Mars, as you have done."[19] (The emphasis on Hamilton's "size" may well have been a bawdy allusion.) In 1783, Stevens returned to St. Croix, married, and started a medical practice. Like Hamilton, he seemed to succeed readily at everything he tried. "The doctor has an extensive and lucrative practice and is much and deservedly esteemed in his profession," Hugh Knox reported from the island. "He sometimes talks much of going to America and I believe would do exceedingly well there in one of the capitals, as he has a fine address and great merit and cleverness."[20] Hamilton and Stevens remained united by an indissoluble bond that seems conspicuously missing in Hamilton's relationships with his father and brother.

The memories of his West Indian childhood left Hamilton with a settled antipathy to slavery. During the war, Hamilton had supported John Laurens's futile effort to emancipate southern slaves who fought for independence. He had expressed an unwavering belief in the genetic equality of blacks and whites—unlike Jefferson, for instance, who regarded blacks as innately inferior—that was enlightened for his day. And he knew this from his personal boyhood experience.

Among many Americans, the Revolution had generated a backlash against slavery as a horrifying practice incompatible with republican ideals. In one abolitionist pamphlet, Samuel Hopkins had written, "Oh, the shocking, the intolerable inconsistence! . . . This gross, barefaced inconsistence."[21] As early as 1775, Philadelphia Quakers had launched the world's first antislavery society, followed by others in the north and south. Unfortunately, slavery itself had expanded in tandem with the rousing rhetoric of freedom that seemed to undercut its legitimacy.

Hamilton's marriage into the Schuyler family may have created complications in his stand on slavery. At times Philip Schuyler had as many as twenty-seven slaves tending his Albany mansion and his fields and mills near Saratoga. They labored at every branch of household work: cooking, cultivating gardens, grooming horses, mending shoes, as well as doing carpentry and laundry, and fishing. Eliza had direct contact with these domestic slaves, to the extent that her grandson surmised that she was "probably her mother's chief assistant in the management of the house and slaves."[22] The image is terribly jarring, for we know Eliza was a confirmed foe of slavery. There is no definite proof, but three oblique hints in Hamilton's papers suggest that he and Eliza *may* have owned one or two household slaves as well. Five months after his wedding, Hamilton wrote to Governor George Clinton that "I expect by Col. Hay's return to receive a sufficient sum to pay the value of the woman Mrs. H had of Mrs. Clinton."[23] Arguing that this transaction involved the hiring of a domestic servant, not the purchase of a slave, biographer Forrest McDonald has pointed out that the "sufficient sum" referred to back pay that Hamilton was slated to receive from Lieutenant Colonel Udny Hay, deputy quartermaster general—a sum that would have fallen far short of the money then requisite to buy a slave.[24] In 1795, Philip Schuyler informed Hamilton that "the Negro boy & woman are engaged for you." Apparently in payment, Hamilton debited his cashbook the next spring for $250 to his father-in-law "for 2 Negro servants purchased by him for me."[25] As we shall see, this purchase may have been made for John and Angelica Church and undertaken reluctantly by Hamilton. Ditto for the purchase of a Negro woman and child on May 29, 1797, which was explicitly charged to John B. Church. In 1804, Angelica noted regretfully that Eliza did not have slaves to assist with a large party that the Hamiltons were planning.

By no means confined to the south, slavery was well entrenched in much of the north. By 1784, Vermont, New Hampshire, Massachusetts, Pennsylvania, Rhode Island, and Connecticut had outlawed slavery or passed laws for its gradual extinction—at the very least, New England's soil did not lend itself to large plantations—but New York and New Jersey retained significant slave populations. New York City, in particular, was identified with slavery: it still held slave auctions in the 1750s and was also linked through its sugar refineries to the West Indies. Even in the 1790s, one in five New York City households kept domestic slaves, a practice ubiquitous among well-to-do merchants who wanted cooks, maids, and butlers and regarded slaves as status symbols. (After the Revolution, few Americans cared to work as servile bonded servants in this new, more egalitarian society.) Slaves tilled the farms of many Hudson River estates along with tenant farmers, one English visitor noting that "many of the old Dutch farmers . . . have 20 to 30 slaves[, and] to their care and management everything is left."[26]

The north never relied on slavery as much as the south, where it was inescapably embedded in the tobacco and cotton economies. When Thomas Jefferson drafted the Declaration of Independence, slaves constituted 40 percent of the population of his home state, Virginia. Slaves in South Carolina outnumbered whites. The magnitude of southern slavery was to have far-reaching repercussions in Hamilton's career. The most damning and hypocritical critiques of his allegedly aristocratic economic system emanated from the most aristocratic southern slaveholders, who deflected attention from their own nefarious deeds by posing as populist champions and assailing the northern financial and mercantile interests aligned with Hamilton. As will be seen, the national consensus that the slavery issue should be tabled to preserve the union meant that the southern plantation economy was effectively ruled off-limits to political discussion, while Hamilton's system, by default, underwent the most searching scrutiny.

Few, if any, other founding fathers opposed slavery more consistently or toiled harder to eradicate it than Hamilton—a fact that belies the historical stereotype that he cared only for the rich and privileged. To be sure, John Adams never owned a slave and had a good record on slavery, which he denounced as a "foul contagion in the human character."[27] Yet he did not always translate his beliefs into practice. According to biographer John Ferling, "As a lawyer he occasionally defended slaves, but as a politician he made no effort to loosen the shackles of those in bondage."[28] Fearing southern dissension, Adams opposed plans to emancipate slaves joining the Continental Army, contested the use of black soldiers, and opposed a bill in the Massachusetts legislature to abolish slavery. "There is no evidence that he ever spoke out on the issue of slavery in any national forum or that he ever entered into a dialogue on the subject with any of his southern friends," Ferling concluded.[29]

In his more radical later years, Benjamin Franklin was a courageous, outspoken president of Pennsylvania's abolition society. As a young and middle-aged man, however, he brokered slave sales from his Philadelphia print shop, ran ads for slaves, and bought and sold them for himself and others. At many times, he kept one or two household slaves. Biographer Edmund Morgan has noted of Franklin's involvement with slavery, "Not until late in life did it begin to trouble his conscience."[30]

The Virginia founders came to see the problem as intractable, since their economic security was so interwoven with slavery. By the time of the Revolution, George Washington was a mostly benevolent master of more than one hundred slaves at Mount Vernon, though he could be a stickler for reclaiming runaway slaves. While he did not criticize slavery publicly, he had an uneasy conscience and belatedly acted on his views. In 1786, when he owned more than two hundred slaves, he refused to break up families and swore not to buy another slave. "There is not a man living who wishes more sincerely than I do to see a plan adopted for the abolition" of slavery, he told Robert Morris.[31] Washington emancipated his slaves in his will and even set aside money to assist the freed slaves and their children.

As owner of about two hundred slaves at Monticello and other properties, Thomas Jefferson was acutely conscious of the discrepancy between high-minded revolutionary words and the bloody reality of slavery. Early in the Revolution, he endorsed a plan to stop importing slaves and was dismayed when Congress expunged a passage from the Declaration of Independence in which he blamed George III for the slave trade. In *Notes on the State of Virginia,* written in the early 1780s, he laid out a gradual scheme for ending slavery, with emancipated blacks relocated to the continent's interior. (As president, he preferred sending them to the West Indies.) In 1784, he proposed blocking slavery in the Northwest Territory, albeit with a sixteen-year grace period. Over time Jefferson yielded to a craven policy of postponing action on slavery indefinitely, constantly foisting the problem onto future generations, hoping vaguely that it would wither away. Unlike Washington,

Jefferson freed only a handful of his slaves, including the brothers of his apparent mistress, Sally Hemings.

Madison's views on slavery followed a pattern similar to Jefferson's. He was a relatively humane master for the nearly 120 slaves that he inherited, once instructing an overseer to "treat the Negroes with all the humanity and kindness consistent with their necessary subordination and work."[32] In the mid-1780s, he supported a bill in the Virginia Assembly to abolish slavery slowly but then began to duck the issue as a severe political liability. Madison never tried to defend the morality of slavery—at the Constitutional Convention, he called it "the most oppressive dominion ever exercised by man over man"—but neither did he distinguish himself in trying to eliminate it.[33] In the last analysis, biographer Jack Rakove has concluded, Madison "was no better prepared to live without slaves than [were] the other members of the great planter class to which his family belonged."[34] In his final years, he belonged to the American Colonization Society, which favored emancipation and resettlement of the former slaves in Africa. In the end, Madison's political survival in Virginia and national politics required endless prevarication on the slavery issue.

The issue surged to the fore with the peace treaty that ended the Revolution. At the prompting of Henry Laurens, article 7 placed a ban on the British "carrying away any Negroes or other property" after the war. This nebulous phrase was construed by slaveholders to mean that the British should return runaway slaves who had defected to the British lines or else pay compensation. The British, in turn, claimed that the former slaves had been freed when they crossed behind British lines. Conceding that Britain may have violated article 7 on technical grounds, Hamilton nevertheless refused to stand up for the slaveholders and invoked a higher moral authority:

> In the interpretation of treaties, things *odious* or *immoral* are not to be presumed. The abandonment of negroes, who had been induced to quit their masters on the faith of official proclamations, promising them liberty, to fall again under the yoke of their masters and into slavery is as *odious* and *immoral* a thing as can be conceived. It is odious not only as it imposes an act of perfidy on one of the contracting parties, but as it tends to bring back to servitude men once made free.[35]

This fierce defender of private property—this man for whom contracts were to be sacred covenants—expressly denied the sanctity of any agreement that stripped people of their freedom.

In New York, the dispute over article 7 had immediate practical repercussions.

After the war, slave owners from other states prowled New York's streets, hoping to spot and steal off with their fugitive slaves. Therefore, on January 25, 1785, nineteen people gathered at the home of innkeeper John Simmons to form a society that would safeguard blacks who had already secured their freedom and try to win freedom for those still held in bondage. The group was called the New York Society for Promoting the Manumission of Slaves. Its members were especially roiled by the rampant kidnapping of free blacks on New York streets, who were then sold into slavery. Robert Troup and Melancton Smith, a Poughkeepsie merchant and land speculator, were appointed to draw up the society's rules. Ten days later, an expanded group met at the Merchant's Coffee House, this time joined by Hamilton and Alexander McDougall. Though he owned five slaves, John Jay was voted chairman. Unless America adopted gradual abolition, Jay believed, "her prayers to heaven for liberty will be impious."[36] Robert Troup, who owned two slaves, read aloud a statement embellished with echoes of the Declaration of Independence:

> The benevolent creator and father of men, having given to them all an equal right to life, liberty, and property, no sovereign power on earth can justly deprive them of either. The violent attempts lately made to seize and export for sale several free Negroes, who were peaceably following their respective occupations in this city, must excite the indignation of every friend to humanity and ought to receive exemplary punishment.[37]

The New York Manumission Society, as it was known for short, conducted a wide-ranging campaign against slavery, sponsoring lectures, printing essays, and establishing a registry to prevent free blacks from being dragged back into slavery. It set up the African Free School to teach the basics to black students, drill discipline into them, and, paternalistically, keep them from "running into practices of immorality or sinking into habits of idleness."[38] The older boys were instructed in carpentry and navigation, the older girls in dressmaking and embroidery. At an early meeting, the society decided to petition the New York legislature for a gradual end to slavery; Aaron Burr, a member of the Assembly, agreed to help them. A pending bill proposed that all blacks born after a certain future date would automatically be considered free. To toughen the measure, Burr introduced language that would terminate all slavery after a certain date. When this radical amendment was defeated, Burr backed the diluted version. In the end, the legislature enacted a toothless, purely voluntary measure that permitted slaveholders to free slaves between twenty-one and fifty years of age.

Burr was no angel when it came to slavery: he always kept an entourage of four or five household slaves. Although he wrote about them with wry affection, his letters reflect no interest in freeing them. As he drifted into the Jeffersonian camp, Burr found it politically expedient to drop any pretense of being an abolitionist. As late as 1831 he tried to discourage William Lloyd Garrison, the publisher of *The Liberator*, from persisting in his antislavery crusade. Garrison recalled of Burr, "His manner was patronizing. . . . As he revealed himself to my moral sense, I saw he was destitute of any fixed principles."[39]

Burr was not the only abolition advocate in the mid-1780s who held slaves. In fact, the New York Manumission Society had to deal with the awkward fact that this contradiction was commonplace and that more than half of its own members owned slaves. As members of the society, these people wanted to cleanse themselves of this moral corruption, but how to do so and at what pace? At the February 4 meeting, Hamilton, Troup, and White Matlack were recruited as a ways-and-means committee to produce answers. The society minutes make clear that Hamilton was more than just a celebrity lending his prestige to a worthy cause. An activist by nature, he scorned timid measures and wanted to make a bold, unequivocal statement.

On November 10, 1785, Hamilton's committee presented its proposals on what members should do with their slaves. For many members, these suggestions were frighteningly abrupt and specific in their timetable. The plan proposed that slaves under twenty-eight should gain their freedom on their thirty-fifth birthday; those between twenty-eight and thirty-eight should be freed seven years hence; and those above forty-five should be freed immediately. It is hard to imagine that Hamilton would have advocated this uncompromising plan had he not contemplated releasing any house slaves he and Eliza might have owned. The members were also urged to emancipate their slaves, not to sell them, lest they be transported to harsher climes than New York.

Hamilton's committee threw down a gauntlet to the society, cleverly balancing immediate and future emancipation. Melancton Smith—who later emerged as a major proponent of states' rights and Hamilton's antagonist in the battle over the U.S. Constitution in New York—balked at such a precise timetable for freeing slaves. Instead, he scrapped Hamilton's plan by pushing a motion to defer the matter until the next quarterly meeting. Hamilton, Troup, and Matlack had produced a document too strong to be swallowed by their peers, and their committee was summarily disbanded. The successor committee faulted the earlier plan as likely to cause members to "withdraw their services and gradually fall off from the Society."[40] They recommended instead that members should remain free to emancipate their slaves as they saw fit, without any bothersome prompting from the society.

Despite this setback, Hamilton did not stride off in a huff. Three months later, in February 1786, he was added to the society's standing committee when it lobbied the state legislature to halt the export of slaves from New York. The committee deluged state and federal legislators with a pamphlet entitled "A Dialogue on the Slavery of the Africans etc." That March, Hamilton's name appeared on a petition that called upon the state legislature to end the New York slave trade and that deplored the plight of blacks exported "like cattle and other articles of commerce to the West Indies and the southern states." The petition demanded the termination of a practice "so repugnant to humanity and so inconsistent with the liberality and justice which should distinguish a free and enlightened people."[41]

This petition was signed by an illustrious cavalcade of dignitaries who would shortly be divided by bitter partisan wrangling over the Constitution and other issues. At this juncture, Hamilton, John Jay, and James Duane could still join hands in political amity with Robert R. Livingston, Melancton Smith, and Brockholst Livingston. In glancing at the signers of this petition, one is struck by how many would join the Federalist ranks in the 1790s and be roundly vilified as "aristocrats" by southern planters. One is further impressed by the sheer number of people in the Manumission Society who had been close to Hamilton since his arrival in America, among them Robert Troup, Nicholas Fish, Hercules Mulligan, William Livingston, John Rodgers, John Mason, James Duane, John Jay, and William Duer. The founding of the Manumission Society and antislavery societies in other states in the 1780s represented a hopeful moment in American race relations, right before the Constitutional Convention and the new federal government created such an overriding need for concord that even debating the divisive slavery issue could no longer be tolerated.

Even as Hamilton's involvement in the Manumission Society threw into relief his sympathy for the oppressed, his engagement in another society prompted accusations that he was conniving to foist a hereditary aristocracy on America. In the spring of 1783, General Henry Knox proposed creation of the Society of the Cincinnati for officers who had served with honor for at least three years. The fraternal society's name was a tribute to Cincinnatus, the general of ancient Rome who twice relinquished his sword after defending the republic and returned to his humble plow. The group had overriding political objectives (promoting liberty, a strong union of the states), charitable aims (providing for families of impoverished officers), and a social agenda (maintaining camaraderie among dispersed officers)—all of which seemed commendable enough, and George Washington was appointed the first president general. Having already left the army, Hamilton was not among the original signers, yet he soon became, with characteristic gusto, active in the New York branch headed by his friend Baron von Steuben.

The society stirred a hornet's nest of controversy because of a provision that eldest sons could inherit their fathers' memberships, as if they were receiving titles of nobility. For Americans still fuming against anything that smacked of decadent European courts, the Society of the Cincinnati raised the dreaded specter of a military cabal or a hereditary aristocracy. Samuel Adams, the Boston firebrand of the Revolution's early days and a second cousin of John Adams, was quick to declare that the society embodied "as rapid a stride toward a hereditary military nobility as was ever made in so short a time."[42] Reactions to the society exposed deep fissures among men who had cooperated to win the war and prefigured sharp cleavages in coming years. Franklin, Jay, Jefferson, and John Adams inveighed against the scheme as dangerous and preposterous.

Washington was so stung by the uproar that at the society's first general meeting in Philadelphia in May 1784 he prevailed upon the members to delete the provision for hereditary membership. The states balked at this and Hamilton was deputized by the New York chapter to formulate a response to these ideas. In December 1785, Washington wrote to him from Mount Vernon and pleaded "that if the Society of the Cincinnati mean to live in peace with the rest of their fellow citizens, they must subscribe to the alterations" adopted in Philadelphia.[43] The ever conciliatory Washington feared an outbreak of virulent partisanship and wanted to elevate the new society above political strife. Hamilton, by contrast, viewed the Cincinnati as a potentially useful tool for meshing the states into a stable union.

In July 1786, Baron von Steuben, president of the New York branch, and Philip Schuyler, its vice president, presided over two meetings. The first inducted new members and contained an extraordinary amount of nonsensical pomp. Baron von Steuben strutted into the room to a fanfare of kettledrums and trumpets. The treasurer and deputy treasurer stepped forth, bearing two white satin cushions, the first holding golden eagle insignias and the second parchments for new members. In his opening oration, Hamilton challenged the society's critics: "To heaven and our own bosoms, we recur for vindication from any misrepresentations of our intentions."[44] He insisted that the society existed only to maintain bonds of friendship and aid the families of fallen comrades. In the style of the day, innumerable toasts were raised and bumpers drained to honor the U.S. Congress, Louis XVI, and George Washington, while thirteen cannon boomed their approval after each toast. Toast number eight bore Hamilton's special imprint and showed that he had weightier political intentions in mind: "May the powers of Congress be adequate to preserve the general Union."[45]

At a second meeting at the City Tavern two days later, Hamilton delivered his report on the society's proposed changes. His speech contained remarks that would have surprised those who regarded him as a simpleminded agent of aristocracy or any form of favoritism. He admitted that he did not see how the society could survive without the hereditary feature. On the other hand, he opposed the use of primogeniture since it was "liable to this objection—that it refers to birth what ought to belong to merit only, a principle inconsistent with the genius of a society founded on friendship and patriotism."[46] As the second-born son in his family, Hamilton knew that the eldest son might not be the most able and was all too well acquainted with his father's sorry tale of being the fourth son of a Scottish laird. Somewhat paradoxically, he explicitly endorsed merit, not birth, as the motive force of the hereditary society and wanted to apply this operating principle to the larger society as well. As would often occur in the future, his avowed preference for an elite based on merit was misconstrued by enemies into a secret adoration of aristocracy.

TWELVE

AUGUST AND RESPECTABLE ASSEMBLY

A fter the Revolution, New York experienced a brief flush of prosperity that faded and then vanished in 1785, snuffed out by swelling debt, scarce money, and dwindling trade. Falling prices hurt indebted farmers, forcing them to repay loans with dearer money. As a Bank of New York director, Hamilton worried that defaulting debtors would also feign poverty and ruin their creditors. He later said of the deteriorating business climate, "confidence in pecuniary transactions had been destroyed and the springs of industry had been proportionably relaxed."[1]

In the coming months, Hamilton fell prey to lurid visions that the have-nots would rise up and dispossess the haves. Men of property would be held hostage by armies of the indebted and unemployed. Sensing a crisis on the horizon, he told one member of the Livingston family that "those who are concerned for the *security of property* or the prosperity of government" must "endeavour to put men in the legislature whose principles are not of the *levelling kind.*"[2] Despite his reservations about this rambunctious new democracy, Hamilton was not yet prepared to run for the legislature. When he came upon his name on a list of potential candidates for the state assembly published by *The New-York Packet* in April 1785, he hurriedly asked the publisher to strike his name from consideration "at the present juncture."[3] Reluctant to foreclose options, Hamilton did not rule out serving at a more auspicious time.

For Hamilton, the major threat to the state could now be summed up in three words: Governor George Clinton. As wartime governor, Clinton had emerged from the Revolution with unmatched popularity and had been reelected three times. He was a short, thickset man with broad shoulders and a protruding paunch. His coarse features—shaggy brows, unkempt hair, and fleshy jowls—gave him the brawny air of a fishmonger or stevedore. Everything about him suggested bull-headed persistence. For most of Hamilton's career, George Clinton was an immovable presence in New York, a craggy, forbidding mountain that loomed over the political landscape. If uncouth in appearance, he was a wily politician who clung tenaciously to power. Destined to serve seven terms as governor and two as vice president, Clinton represented what would become a staple of American political folklore: the local populist boss, not overly punctilious or savory yet embraced warmly by the masses as one of their own. As his biographer John Kaminski put it, "George Clinton's friends considered him a man of the people; his enemies saw him as a demagogue."[4]

The son of Scotch-Irish immigrants, George Clinton started out as a country lawyer from Ulster County and a rabble-rouser in the New York Assembly, followed by a period in the Continental Congress. As a brigadier general, he defended the Hudson Highlands during the war. He became the indomitable champion of the local yeomen, who saw him as a bulwark against the patrician families that had ruled colonial New York: the Livingstons, Schuylers, Rensselaers, and other Hudson River potentates. Theodore Roosevelt later observed, with the knowing eye of a veteran politician, that Clinton knew how to capitalize on the "cold, suspicious temper of small country freeholders" with their "narrow" jealousies.[5] Yet for all his aura of republican simplicity, Clinton was not the salt of the earth. He owned eight slaves and put together a fortune in office. If he lived frugally, it was less from lack of money than from notoriously miserly habits. During most of his time in office, this pooh-bah of the people sported the pretentious title "His Excellency George Clinton, Esquire, the Governor-General and Commander-in-Chief of all the militia, and Admiral of the Navy of the State of New-York."[6]

Hamilton and Clinton did not begin at loggerheads. Though Clinton was sixteen years older, he and Hamilton had kept up a friendly wartime correspondence and agreed on the need to bolster Congress. Hamilton applauded Washington's choice of Clinton to command American forces in the Hudson Valley. But when Hamilton married Eliza Schuyler, he inherited Clinton's special nemesis as his father-in-law. By 1782, while Hamilton still lauded Clinton as a "man of integrity," he had come to believe that Clinton pandered to popular prejudice "especially when a new election approaches."[7] As the decade progressed, Hamilton's critique of Clinton grew more venomous. He found the governor rude and petulant, his frank manner a cloak for infinite calculation. Clinton was "circumspect and guarded" and seldom acted "without premeditation or design."[8]

Alexander Hamilton was haunted by George Clinton for reasons that transcended his political style. Hamilton's besetting fear was that American democracy would be spoiled by demagogues who would mouth populist shibboleths to conceal their despotism. George Clinton, Thomas Jefferson, and Aaron Burr all came to incarnate that dread for Hamilton. Clinton also disapproved of banks, regarding them as devices to enrich speculators and divert money from hardworking farmers. Hamilton was further chagrined by Clinton's punitive postwar stance toward the Loyalists. One Tory chronicler said of Clinton: "He tried, condemned, imprisoned, and punished the Loyalists most unmercifully. They were by his orders tarred and feathered, carted, whipped, fined, banished, and in short, every kind of cruelty, death not excepted, was practised by this emissary of rebellion."[9]

Hamilton might have tolerated such flaws had it not been for one unforgivable sin: Clinton favored New York to the detriment of national unity. Clinton was well aware of Hamilton's ardent nationalist orientation. In time, he praised Hamilton as "a great man, a great lawyer, a man of integrity, very ambitious," but "anxious to effect that ruinous measure, a *consolidation of the states.*"[10] Much of Hamilton's cynicism about state politics can be traced to his growing disenchantment with George Clinton. At the governor's urging, New York State imposed a stiff duty on British goods entering from the West Indies, a tax that infuriated city merchants and shippers alike. Many of these imports ended up in neighboring New Jersey and Connecticut, but New York kept all of the taxes. New York also laid an "import" tariff on farm produce from New Jersey and lumber from Connecticut. Addicted to this financial racket and unwilling to share the booty, Governor Clinton had opposed the 5 percent federal tax on imports proposed by the Confederation Congress and supported by Hamilton.

So grave were the interstate tensions over trade that Nathaniel Gorham, named president of Congress in 1786, feared that clashes between New York and its neighbors might degenerate into civil war. Similarly acrimonious trade disputes erupted between other states with major seaports and neighbors who imported goods through them. The states were arrogating a right that properly belonged to a central government: the right to formulate trade policy. This persuaded Hamilton that unless a new federal government with a monopoly on customs revenues was established, disunion would surely ensue. As individual states developed interests in their own taxes, they would be less and less likely to sacrifice for the common good.

In April 1786, amid a worsening economic crisis, Hamilton agreed that the time had come to act and was elected to a one-year term in the New York Assembly. Later on, he told a Scottish relative that he had been involved in a lucrative legal practice "when the derangement of our public affairs by the feebleness of the general confederation drew me again reluctantly into public life."[11] His zeal for reform signaled anything but reluctance. He was seized with a crusading sense of purpose and had a momentous, long-term plan to enact. Hamilton told Troup he had stood for election because he planned to "render the next session" of the Assembly "subservient to the change he meditated" in the structure of the national government.[12] Indeed, his election to the Assembly was a preliminary step in an extended sequence of events that led straight to the Constitutional Convention.

The road leading to the Constitutional Convention was a long, circuitous one. It be-gan at Mount Vernon in 1785 when commissioners from Maryland and Virginia re-solved a heated dispute over navigation of the Potomac River. Virginia hoped this might serve as a pattern for settling other interstate disputes and in early 1786 called for a convention at Annapolis "for the purpose of framing such regulations of trade as may be judged necessary to promote the general interest."[13] The tutelary spirit, James Madison, was no less despondent than Hamilton about the trade and border disputes riling the states. In March 1786, Madison wrote to Jefferson, then the American minister in Paris, about "the present anarchy of our commerce" and described the way the predominant seaport states were fleecing their neighbors.[14] Appalled by selfish laws issuing from state legislatures, Madison warned Jefferson that they had become "so frequent and so flagrant as to alarm the most steadfast friends of republicanism."[15]

In May 1786, the New York legislature named six commissioners to the Annapo-lis conference; in the end, only Hamilton and his friend Egbert Benson, the state at-torney general, attended. This seemingly minor appointment was to have the most far-reaching ramifications for Hamilton. If he had missed Annapolis, he might not have attended the Constitutional Convention or ended up as the editorial impresa-rio of *The Federalist Papers.* Robert Troup later claimed that Hamilton knew that Annapolis would serve as the prelude to bigger things and had no interest in "a commercial convention otherwise than as a stepping stone to a general convention to form a general constitution."[16] Whether through luck, premeditation, or a knack for making things happen, Hamilton continued to demonstrate his unique flair for materializing at every major turning point in the early history of the republic.

On September 1, Hamilton set out for Annapolis, paying his own way. After his nomadic youth and wartime roaming, Hamilton had retained little wanderlust and now traversed scenery he had last viewed as a soldier. Ailing during the journey, he was relieved to arrive at Annapolis one week later. Eliza had recently given birth to their third child, Alexander, and Hamilton sorely missed his growing family. The moment he arrived in Maryland, he dashed off an affectionate note to Eliza, suf-fused with melancholy:

Happy, however, I cannot be, absent from you and my darling little ones. I feel that nothing can ever compensate for the loss of the enjoyments I leave at home or can ever put my heart at tolerable ease. . . . In reality, my attachments to home disqualify me for either business or pleasure abroad and the prospect of a detention here for eight or ten days, perhaps a fortnight, fills me with an anxiety which will best be conceived by my Betsey's own impatience. . . . Think of me with as much tenderness as I do of you and we cannot fail to be always happy.[17]

Clearly, the love between Alexander and Eliza had not cooled in the time since courtship and matrimony had tamed the libidinous young man into something of a homebody.

By choosing the relatively secluded town of Annapolis, Madison explained, the conference organizers had purposely bypassed the main commercial towns and congressional precincts to guard against any accusations that the commissioners were in the thrall of outside parties. They stayed at George Mann's City Tavern, a large, hundred-bed hostelry, and held working sessions in the old senate chamber at the State House. The turnout was meager—only twelve delegates showed up from five states—yet the paltry attendance proved a blessing, weeding out potential foes of a more centralized government. The intimacy of this group of nationalists allowed the talks to range far beyond commercial disputes to a richer, more trenchant critique of the crumbling Articles of Confederation.

Arriving at Annapolis several days before Hamilton, Madison approached the meeting with his matchless, professorial thoroughness. Jefferson had shipped him a "literary cargo" of treatises on politics and history, and his mind was already stuffed with precedents about republics and confederations. Hamilton probably had not seen his friend since their congressional days, Madison having studied law and served in the Virginia Assembly in the interim. He must have been pleased to renew ties with the small, bookish, balding man with the deep-set eyes and beetle brows. Though we know few details of the Annapolis sessions, it seems certain that Hamilton and Madison commenced the joint philosophical inquiries that yielded *The Federalist Papers* two years later. At this point, they were kindred spirits in their common distaste for the parochial tendencies of the states.

The Annapolis attendees soon agreed that the commercial disputes among the states were symptomatic of underlying flaws in the political framework, and they arrived at a breathtaking conclusion: they would urge the states to send delegates to a convention in Philadelphia the following May to amend the Articles of Confederation. Evidently, Hamilton wrote a hot-blooded first draft of this appeal, an indictment so scorching that Virginia governor Edmund Randolph asked him to tone it down. Hamilton flared up in righteous disagreement, and Madison had to take him aside and urge a tactical retreat. "You had better yield to this man," Madison cautioned, "for otherwise all Virginia will be against you."[18] Hamilton cooled off and consented.

In its final version, Hamilton's communiqué explained that the commissioners had ventured beyond their original commercial mandate because "the power of regulating trade is of such comprehensive extent" that fixing the problem required corresponding adjustments in other parts of the political system. Upon closer examination, the defects of the present system had been found "greater and more numerous" than previously imagined.[19] The Annapolis address, with its conception of the political system as a finely crafted mechanism, composed of subtly interrelated parts, had a distinctly Hamiltonian ring. It reflected his penchant for systemic solutions, his sense of the fine interconnectedness of things.

Madison and Hamilton had diametrically opposite experiences when their home states pondered the Annapolis resolution. The Virginia legislature gave it enthusiastic approval and tapped George Washington to head its delegation to the Constitutional Convention. By contrast, Governor George Clinton immediately played the spoilsport. He expressed "a strong dislike" for the idea, denied the need for reform, and affirmed "that the confederation as it stood was equal to the purposes of the Union."[20] For the next two years, George Clinton obstructed reform, even though many members of his own legislature welcomed the Annapolis appeal.

In 1776, John Adams had predicted accurately that "the most intricate, the most important, the most dangerous and delicate business" of the postwar years would be the creation of a central government.[21] Hamilton was now fully committed to that task, and after Annapolis he was strategically poised to pursue it. Paying homage to Hamilton's campaign for a closer union, Catherine Drinker Bowen later wrote in her classic account of the Constitutional Convention, "Among those who began early to work for reform three names stand out: Washington, Madison and Hamilton. And of the three, evidence points to Hamilton as the most potent single influence toward calling the Convention of '87."[22] Madison's admirers might respectfully beg to differ.

Money problems pervaded all others under the Articles of Confederation. America was virtually bankrupt as the federal government and state governments found it impossible to retire the gargantuan debt inherited from the Revolution. On European securities exchanges, investors expressed skepticism about America's survival by trading its securities at a small fraction of their face values. "The fate of America was suspended by a hair," Gouverneur Morris was to say.[23]

Many Americans were as debt-burdened as their legislatures. Even as the Annapolis conference unfolded, rural turmoil erupted in western Massachusetts as thousands of indebted farmers, struggling with soaring taxes and foreclosures on their lands, grabbed staves and pitchforks, shut down courthouses, and thwarted land seizures by force. As Hamilton had feared, after eight years of war violent protest against authority had become habitual. The farmers' uprising was dubbed Shays's Rebellion after one of its leaders, Daniel Shays, a former militia captain and suddenly a folk hero. At moments, it looked like a reprise of the American Revolution, now reenacted as a civil war. The rebels donned their old Continental Army uniforms and wore sprigs of hemlock in their hats in the spirit of '76. By February 1787, the state militia had quashed the disorder, but its influence lingered when Massachusetts passed debt-relief legislation. Many creditors and property owners were disturbed by the mounting power of state governments and dismayed by the impotent federal government, which had sold off its last warship and let its army shrink to an insignificant force of seven hundred soldiers.

Shays's Rebellion thrust to the fore economic issues—the very issues in which Hamilton specialized—as did an extremist movement in Rhode Island that beat the drum for abolishing debt and dividing wealth equally. The Massachusetts uprising shocked many who wondered just how far the rebels would go. "Good God!" Washington proclaimed of the rebellion, aghast that some protesters regarded America's land "to be the *common property* of all."[24] James Madison confessed to similar trepidation about the rebels to his father: "They profess to aim only at a reform of the constitution and of certain abuses in the public administration, but an abolition of debts public and private and a new division of property are strongly suspected in contemplation."[25] Where Madison thought a weak republic would only invite disorder, Jefferson reacted to the turmoil with aplomb. "I hold it that a little rebellion now and then is a good thing," he told Madison loftily from Paris, "and as necessary in the political world as storms in the physical."[26] To Colonel William Smith, Jefferson sent his famous reassurance: "The tree of liberty must be refreshed from time to time with the blood of patriots and tyrants."[27] While Hamilton feared that disorder would feed on itself, the more hopeful and complacent Jefferson thought that periodic excesses would correct themselves.

Ordinarily a veritable Niagara of opinion, Hamilton was initially mute about Shays's Rebellion. He kept silent because he sympathized with the farmers' grievances, however much he despised their methods. Hamilton wanted the federal government to take over state debts left from the war. Instead, Massachusetts, by trying to settle its own debt, had crushed the farmers with onerous taxes. "The insurrection was in a great degree the offspring of this pressure," he later wrote.[28] In *Federalist* number 6, he argued that "if Shays had not been a *desperate debtor,* it is much to be doubted whether Massachusetts would have been plunged into a civil war."[29] The rural uprising vindicated his sense that the federal government had to distribute the tax burden equitably across the states.

Many Americans wondered whether the fragile confederation could withstand the accumulating strains between rich and poor, creditors and debtors. In February 1787, Hamilton made a heroic stand in the New York Assembly to arrest the country's deteriorating finances, supporting the 5 percent import tax proposed by Congress. Hamilton was not sanguine about defeating the Clintonians, with their popular catchphrases about states' rights. Assemblyman Samuel Jones said of Hamilton's campaign, "He told me during the session that the citizens expected it of him and he thought he ought not to disappoint them, otherwise he did not think he should bring the question again before the Assembly."[30] Hamilton delivered a marathon speech of one hour and twenty minutes that unfurled a grim panorama of America under the confederation. He lashed out at Congress's reliance upon thirteen states for effectively voluntary payments and noted that some stingy states paid a fraction of their quotas or nothing at all. With the federal treasury empty, no surplus remained to service debt or establish American credit abroad. Domestic creditors might show patience, but foreign creditors would not. "They have power to enforce their demands," Hamilton warned, "and sooner or later they may be expected to do it."[31] Hamilton thought the warnings of inordinate federal power misplaced: "If these states are not united under a federal government, they will infallibly have wars with each other and their divisions will subject them to all the mischiefs of foreign influence and intrigue."[32]

Hamilton's masterly exposition met with stony stares from the Clintonians, who responded in insulting fashion. They demanded a vote on the issue without bothering to rebut Hamilton's speech. The federal tax was soundly defeated, as Hamilton had expected. His sustained eloquence left him bent over with exhaustion, though he was quickly buoyed by acclaim from supporters and recuperated sufficiently to attend the theater. "Hamilton went to the play after his famous speech in the House in favor of the impost," Margaret Livingston told her son, Chancellor Robert R. Livingston, "and when he came in he was called the great man. Some say he is talked of for G[overnor]."[33]

During his Assembly tenure that spring, Hamilton voted on two measures that suggested ambivalent feelings about his childhood. Oddly enough, he supported a bill making it impossible for people divorced due to adultery to remarry. Such a draconian statute in the Danish West Indies had prevented Hamilton's parents from legitimizing his birth. If this vote suggests some latent hostility toward his mother, another vote betokens tenderness for her. The Assembly was debating a bill that aimed to deter mothers of illegitimate children from killing them at birth. One controversial clause stipulated that if the child died, the unwed mother had to produce a witness who could corroborate that the child had been stillborn or died from natural causes. It bothered Hamilton that the mother would have to admit openly that she had given birth to an illegitimate child. One newspaper account showed Hamilton's empathy:

> Mr. Hamilton observed that the clause was neither politic or just. He wished it obliterated from the bill. To show the propriety of this, he expatiated feelingly on the delicate situation it placed an unfortunate woman in. . . . From the concealment of the loss of honor, her punishment might be mitigated and the misfortune end here. She might reform and be again admitted into virtuous society. The operation of this law compelled her to publish her shame to the world. It was to be expected therefore that she would prefer the danger of punishment from concealment to the avowal of her guilt.[34]

When Samuel Jones supported the measure, Hamilton refuted him "in terms of great cogency" and convinced the Assembly to side with him.[35] That Hamilton argued so strenuously for this measure hints at surviving hobgoblins from the Caribbean that still hovered uneasily in his mind.

Soon after Hamilton was trounced on the impost measure, he introduced a motion in the Assembly to send five delegates to the Constitutional Convention in Philadelphia. The general expectation was that the convention would simply tinker with the Articles of Confederation, not overhaul its basic machinery. Hamilton envisaged something far more audacious, hoping that a robust union would result. Two days later, the Clintonians boxed him into a corner by slashing the delegate count to three. Since Hamilton had been New York's chief catalyst for the convention, the Clintonians couldn't very well deny him a place; instead, they flanked him with two opponents of federal power who would smother his influence. Albany mayor John Lansing, Jr., was a prosperous landowner, and Robert Yates a pretentious judge on the New York Supreme Court. Both were vocal foes of efforts to endow Congress with independent taxing powers. They were a tightly knit pair for other reasons. The two men were related by marriage and the younger Lansing had clerked in Yates's law office as a teenager. So instead of leading a united delegation, Hamilton was demoted to being a minority delegate from a dissenting state.

Hamilton arrived in Philadelphia on May 18, 1787, and joined other delegates at the Indian Queen Tavern on Fourth Street. Madison had arrived days earlier to brace for battle, confiding to Washington his fears that the team of Lansing and Yates would be a fatal "clog" on their friend Hamilton.[36] Like other delegates, Madison had a sense of high drama, believing the document about to be drawn up would "decide forever the fate of republican government."[37] Lacking a quorum, the meeting did not convene officially for another week: against a patter of steady rain,

Washington was then unanimously elected president of the convention. Hamilton had helped to coax the reluctant general from his Mount Vernon retreat and convince him to attend. At the end of the Revolution, Washington had been no less perturbed than Hamilton by the weak central government and worried that "local or state politics will interfere too much with that more liberal and extensive plan of government which wisdom and foresight . . . would dictate."[38] Though Washington was taciturn at the convention, his preference for a more effective central government was well known.

Washington appointed Hamilton, George Wythe, and Charles Pinckney to a small committee that drew up rules and procedures for the convention. To free himself from the domination of Lansing and Yates, Hamilton wanted the votes of individual members recorded. Instead, the convention chose to proceed on a one-state, one-vote basis, which meant that Hamilton's vote would likely be nullified by his two fellow delegates. The committee prevailed in its general preference for secrecy. Preliminary votes were not recorded. To encourage candor, the committee also decided that "nothing spoken in the House be printed, or otherwise published, or communicated without leave."[39] Journalists and curious spectators were forbidden to attend, sentries were stationed at doors, and delegates, sworn to secrecy, remained tight-lipped to outsiders. The delegates even adjourned to the second floor of the State House to ensure confidentiality. During a sultry Philadelphia summer, in the face of thick swarms of tormenting flies, the blinds were often drawn and the windows shut to guarantee privacy. Even Madison's copious notes of the convention were not published until decades later.

Why such undemocratic rules for a conclave crafting a new charter? Many delegates believed they were enlightened, independent citizens, concerned for the commonweal, not members of those detestable things called factions. "Had the deliberations been open while going on, the clamours of faction would have prevented any satisfactory result," said Hamilton. "Had they been afterwards disclosed, much food would have been afforded to inflammatory declamation."[40] The closed-door proceedings yielded inspired, uninhibited debate and brought forth one of the most luminous documents in history. At the same time, this secrecy made the convention's inner workings the stuff of baleful legend, with unfortunate repercussions for Hamilton's later career.

The venue for the convention was the gunmetal-gray East Room of the redbrick State House, where the Declaration of Independence had been signed. It had the proper dignity and simplicity for these right-minded republicans. Delegates sat in Windsor chairs, arranged in fan-shaped rows in front of Washington's high-backed wooden chair, and jotted notes on tables covered with green baize. The tall windows were partly obscured by drooping green drapes. The room provided an intimate setting for these deliberations. Unlike orators in an amphitheater, the delegates met in a space cozy enough to enable speakers to make eye contact with every delegate and talk in a normal conversational voice.

Seated front-row center was James Madison, who staked out this pivotal spot to take minutes. "In this favorable position for hearing all that passed . . . I was not absent a single day, nor more than a casual fraction of an hour in any day, so that I could not have lost a single speech, unless a very short one."[41] One observer said that the diminutive Virginian, bent over his notes, had "a calm expression, a penetrating blue eye, and looked like a thinking man."[42]

Major William Pierce of Georgia filed the fullest portrait of Hamilton, finding him impressive, if a little too self-consciously the strutting young genius. "He is about 33 years old, of small stature, and lean," Pierce observed. "His manners are tinctured with stiffness and sometimes with a degree of vanity that is highly disagreeable." Hamilton's voice lacked the resonance of a great orator's, but he was eloquent and able and plumbed subjects to their roots: "When he comes forward, he comes highly charged with interesting matter. There is no skimming over the surface of a subject with him. He must sink to the bottom to see what foundation it rests on." Pierce captured Hamilton's mercurial personality, ponderous one moment, facetious the next. His "language is not always equal, sometimes didactic like Bolingbroke's, at others light and tripping like [Laurence] Stern[e]'s."[43]

Who were these solons rhapsodized by Benjamin Franklin as "the most august and respectable assembly he was ever in in his life"?[44] The fifty-five delegates representing twelve states—the renegade Rhode Island boycotted the convention—scarcely constituted a cross section of America. They were white, educated males and mostly affluent property owners. A majority were lawyers and hence sensitive to precedent. Princeton graduates (nine) trumped Yale (four) and Harvard (three) by a goodly margin. They averaged forty-two years of age, meaning that Hamilton, thirty-two, and Madison, thirty-six, were relatively young. As a foreign-born delegate, Hamilton wasn't alone, since nearly a dozen others had been born or educated abroad. Many delegates shared Hamilton's preoccupation with public debt. The majority owned public securities, the values of which would be affected dramatically by decisions taken here. During the next few months, Hamilton's attendance was spotty, but this wasn't atypical. Many delegates shuttled back to their home states on business, and only about thirty of the fifty-five delegates were present much of the time.

The convention gave Hamilton a fleeting brush with the one founder otherwise absent from his story: eighty-one-year-old Benjamin Franklin. The ancient Philadelphian, with his mostly bald head, lank strands of side hair, and double chin, was bedeviled by gout and excruciating kidney stones. He often discoursed to

Hamilton and other delegates under the canopy of a mulberry tree in his courtyard, sometimes with his fond grandson Benjamin Franklin Bache looking on. Legend has it that when the enfeebled Franklin first came to the convention, he was borne aloft on a sedan chair, toted by four convicts conscripted from the Walnut Street jail. Nevertheless, with exemplary dedication, he showed up for every session of the four-month convention, sometimes asking others to deliver statements for him. Hamilton's first act in Philadelphia paid homage to Franklin. The sage had opposed salaries for executive-branch officers, hoping such a measure would produce civic-minded leaders, not government officials feeding at the public trough. Others thought this would exclude all but the idle rich from holding office. Hamilton seconded Franklin's quixotic motion, likely from veneration for the man. Madison commented that the idea was "treated with great respect, but rather for the author of it than from any apparent conviction of its expediency or practicability."[45]

In theory, the convention had a mandate only to revise the Articles of Confederation. Any delegates who took this circumscribed mission at face value were soon rudely disabused. On May 30, Edmund Randolph presented a plan, formulated chiefly by Madison, that sought to scuttle the articles altogether and create a strong central government. This "Virginia Plan" made a clean break with the past and contained the basic design of the future U.S. government. It provided for a bicameral legislature, with both houses based on proportional representation. (As the most populous state, Virginia had a vested interest in this approach.) It concentrated extra power in the executive branch by calling for a one-person executive (i.e., a president) with a seven-year term, rather than the council favored by radicals. To heighten the separation of powers, it envisioned a national judiciary, crowned by a supreme tribunal. The Virginia Plan left little doubt that while the states would retain some sovereignty, they would be subservient to the federal government.

After Randolph's presentation, Hamilton confronted delegates with the core question of whether the new government should muddle on as a confederation or form a true nation. They should debate "whether the United States were susceptible to one government" or whether each state needed "a separate existence connected only by leagues."[46] Hamilton saw the vital importance of the national government possessing ultimate sovereignty. The positive reaction to his statement revealed that the delegates were ready to embark on vigorous reform, and the convention agreed overwhelmingly that "a national government ought to be established consisting of a supreme legislative, executive and judiciary."[47] Robert Yates at once exposed the irreparable split in the New York delegation by voting against Hamilton's motion. Had John Lansing, Jr., arrived by this time, he would surely have done likewise.

For many delegates, a separation of federal powers was one thing, a sharp diminution of state power quite another. Small states trembled at the thought of a bicameral legislature with both houses chosen by proportional representation. On June 15, William Paterson of New Jersey furnished the convention with a notably divergent vision. Instead of razing the old structure to erect a brand-new government, Paterson wanted to "correct" the Articles of Confederation and retain basic state sovereignty; instead of two houses of Congress, the New Jersey Plan envisioned one chamber, with each state casting one vote. It also retained the voluntary system of "requisitions" that had hobbled the country's finances. In place of a president, the plan contemplated an executive council that could be removed by a majority of the state governors. For obvious reasons, many large states gravitated toward the Virginia Plan, while smaller states coalesced around the New Jersey Plan.

Though a delegate from the fifth largest state, John Lansing expressed warm admiration for the New Jersey Plan, since it "sustains the sovereignty of the respective states." He chided the Virginia Plan: "The states willl never sacrifice their essential rights to a national government."[48] So visceral was Lansing's revulsion against Madison's plan that he said that if New York had suspected a new national government would be contemplated, it would never have sent delegates to Philadelphia. Lansing's speech confirmed Hamilton's minority status in his delegation, reducing his influence on the convention floor.

For those who knew Hamilton, his generally passive behavior during the first three weeks was mystifying. He had never been known to hug the sidelines. As the convention split over the Virginia and New Jersey plans, Hamilton stayed conspicuously aloof from both camps. Robert Yates noted on June 15, "Col. Hamilton cannot say he is in sentiment with either plan."[49] Madison recorded Hamilton as saying that he had been self-effacing partly because he did not wish to dissent from those "whose superior abilities, age, and experience rendered him unwilling to bring forward ideas dissimilar to theirs" and partly owing to the split in his delegation.[50]

It was predictable that when the wordy Hamilton broke silence, he would do so at epic length. Faced with a deadlock between large and small states, he decided to broach a more radical plan. On Monday morning, June 18, the thirty-two-year-old prodigy rose first on the convention floor and in the stifling, poorly ventilated room he spoke and spoke and spoke. Before the day was through, he had given a six-hour speech (no break for lunch) that was brilliant, courageous, and, in retrospect, completely daft. He admitted to the assembly that he would adumbrate a plan that did not reflect popular opinion. "My situation is disagreeable," he admitted, "but it would be criminal not to come forward on a question of such magnitude."[51] He said people were tiring in their enthusiasm for "democracy," by which he meant direct representation or even mob rule, as opposed to public opinion filtered through educated representatives. "And what even is the Virginia Plan," he asked, "but democracy checked by democracy, or pork with a little change of the sauce?"[52] Of all the founders, Hamilton probably had the gravest doubts about the wisdom of the masses and wanted elected leaders who would guide them. This was the great paradox of his career: his optimistic view of America's potential coexisted with an essentially pessimistic view of human nature. His faith in Americans never quite matched his faith in America itself.

It was typical of Hamilton's egotism, expansive imagination, and supernormal intellect that he refused to settle for refinements on somebody else's plan. His mind had minted an entire program for a new government, not just scattered aspects of it. In future years, he reminded critics that the deliberations had been kept secret precisely so that delegates could provoke debate and voice controversial ideas without fear of reprisals. Instead, his speech acquired diabolical status in the rumor mills of the early republic, providing gloating opponents with damning proof of his supposed political apostasy.

Though we have no written transcript of the speech, the sometimes conflicting notes left by Hamilton, Madison, Yates, Lansing, and Rufus King agree in most essentials. Ever since his September 1780 letter to James Duane, Hamilton had toyed with creating a new hybrid form of government that would have the continuity of a monarchy combined with the liberties of a republic, guarding against both anarchy and tyranny. He now suggested a president and Senate that would be elected but would then serve for life on "good behavior." Hamilton's chief executive differed from a hereditary monarch because he would be elected and, if he misbehaved, subject to recall. "It will be objected probably that such an executive will be an *elective monarch* and will give birth to the tumults which characterize that form of gov[ernmen]t," Madison scribbled as Hamilton declaimed. "He w[oul]d reply that *monarch* is an indefinite term. It marks not either the degree or duration of power."[53] It scarcely helped Hamilton's historical reputation that in his personal notes he observed of this monarch, "He ought to be hereditary and to have so much power that it will not be his interest to risk much to acquire more."[54] Hamilton edited this from his talk, however, and never openly advocated a hereditary monarchy, as evidenced by Madison's reference to an "*elective monarch.*" And nowhere else in Hamilton's vast body of work does he support a hereditary executive. Even here, in his most extreme statement, he called for a chief executive subject to ultimate legislative control. However atrociously misguided the idea was, it fell short of proposing a real monarchy, in which a king has permanent, autonomous, hereditary powers that supersede those of all other branches of government.

While Hamilton's Senate would be chosen for life by electors, his House of Representatives, by contrast, was exceedingly democratic, chosen directly by universal male suffrage every three years. Thus, the aristocratic element would be represented by the Senate, the common folk by the House. As prosperity widened income differentials in future years, Hamilton feared that the Senate and House might try to impose their wills on each other: "Give all power to the many, they will oppress the few. Give all power to the few, they will oppress the many."[55] The system needed an impartial arbiter to transcend class warfare and regional interests, and here Hamilton muddied the waters by using the dreaded word *monarch:* "This check is a monarch. . . . There ought to be a principle in government capable of resisting the popular current."[56] Fearing aristocrats as well as commoners, Hamilton wanted to restrain abusive majorities *and* minorities. "Demagogues are not always *inconsiderable* persons," he responded to one Madison speech. "Patricians were frequently demagogues."[57] To curb further abuse, Hamilton recommended a Supreme Court that would consist of twelve judges holding lifetime offices on good behavior. In this manner, each branch would maintain a salutary distance from popular passions. The House of Representatives would be the striking exception. Hamilton concluded, "The principle chiefly intended to be established is this—that there must be a permanent *will.*"[58]

No less inflammatory to some listeners was Hamilton's assessment of the former mother country. "In his private opinion," Madison recorded, "he had no scruple in declaring . . . that the British Gov[ernmen]t was the best in the world and that he doubted much whether anything short of it would do in America."[59] For future conspiracy theorists, this admission clinched the case: Hamilton was a dangerous traitor, ready to sell America back into bondage to Britain. In fact, admiration for the British political system was still widespread. At one point, Pierce Butler of South Carolina remarked that the delegates were "constantly running away with the idea of the excellence of the British parliament and with or without reason copying from them."[60] But Hamilton's detractors were to interpret his view as one of uniquely servile adoration for the British system, with a desire to import it to America.

When he finished, Hamilton received a polite smattering of applause. Perhaps the delegates were glad to escape the heat and head for their lodgings. Gouverneur Morris extolled Hamilton's speech as "the most able and impressive he had ever heard."[61] William Samuel Johnson of Connecticut said that Hamilton's speech "has been praised by everybody [but] . . . supported by none."[62] Years later, John Quincy Adams lauded the plan as one "of great ability" and even better in theory than the one adopted, however misplaced in an American setting.[63]

How had Hamilton blundered into this speech? That Hamilton had an abiding fear of mob rule did not distinguish him from most delegates. What did distinguish him was that his fears had triumphed so completely over his hopes. He was so busy clamping checks and balances on potentially fickle citizens that he did not stop to consider the potential of the electorate. Hamilton often seemed a man suspended between two worlds. He never supported a nobility, hereditary titles, or the other trappings of aristocracy. He never again uttered a kind word for monarchy. Still, he wondered whether republican government could withstand popular frenzy and instill the deep respect for law and authority that obtained in monarchical systems and that would safeguard liberties. Too often, his political vision harked back to a past in which well-bred elites made decisions for less-educated citizens. This contradicted the advanced economic thinking expressed in his vision of a fluid, meritocratic elite, open to talented outsiders such as himself.

Incorrigibly honest, Hamilton must have felt duty bound to provide an alternative to the Virginia and New Jersey plans, which he thought certain to fail. He must have believed that, if no consensus was reached, his speech would be dusted off and its merits belatedly better appreciated. Until then, he would rely on the secrecy of the proceedings. Hamilton wasn't the only delegate who offered harebrained ideas. At one point, Hugh Williamson of North Carolina claimed that it was "pretty certain that we should at some time or other have a king."[64] Four states even voted for Hamilton's proposal of a president serving "during good behavior," most notably the Virginia delegation that included James Madison, George Mason, and Edmund Randolph. When later taunted by the Jeffersonians, Hamilton was pleased to remind them that Madison, too, had favored such a president. If he was a monarchist, so was Madison. Madison also insisted upon giving the federal government a veto over state laws "as the King of Great Britain heretofore had."[65] Benjamin Franklin wanted a unicameral legislature and an executive council in lieu of a president. He also opposed a presidential veto on legislation, thinking it would lead to executive corruption "till it ends in monarchy."[66] John Dickinson wanted state legislatures to have the power to impeach the president. Elbridge Gerry wanted a three-man "presidency," with each member representing a different section of America. Though not a delegate, John Adams thought hereditary rule inevitable and prophesied, "Our ship must ultimately land on that shore."[67]

For the great majority of delegates, Hamilton's speech was just a daylong respite from the fierce infighting at hand. The next morning, nobody even took time to refute Hamilton. Madison feared that Hamilton's speech would alienate small states at a critical moment. In fact, Madison's Virginia Plan may have profited from Hamilton's speech because it now seemed moderate by comparison. (Some scholars have argued that this was the true intent of Hamilton's speech.) When Madison rose to speak, he made no reference to Hamilton's oratory and consigned it to temporary oblivion. Instead, he mercilessly dissected the New Jersey Plan.

Though Hamilton's plan was doomed, its effects were to linger long after the delegates had dispersed. Till the end of his days, opponents dredged up the speech, as if it embodied the *real* Hamilton, the *secret* Hamilton, as if he had blurted out the truth in a moment of weakness. In fact, nobody fought harder or more effectively for the new Constitution than Hamilton, who never wavered in his resolution to support it. The June 18 speech was to prove one of three flagrant errors in his career. In each case, he was brave, detailed, and forthright on a controversial subject, as if laboring under some compulsion to express his inmost thoughts. Each time, he was spectacularly wrongheaded and indiscreet, yet convinced he was right. Only one thing was certain: this verbose, headstrong, loose-tongued man made poor material for the conspirator conjured up by his enemies.

After his controversial speech, Hamilton lapsed into temporary silence as the large and small states squared off in a tense deadlock. It seemed the divided convention might collapse. When Franklin suggested on June 28 that each session start with a prayer for heavenly help, Hamilton countered that this might foster a public impression that "embarrassments and dissensions within the convention had suggested this measure."[68] According to legend, Hamilton also rebutted Franklin with the jest that the convention didn't need "foreign aid."[69] The Lord did not seem much in evidence at this point in the convention. One story, perhaps apocryphal, claims that when Hamilton was asked why the framers omitted the word *God* from the Constitution, he replied, "We forgot." One is tempted to reply that Alexander Hamilton never forgot anything important.

On June 29, Hamilton mustered the will to speak again, voicing grave anxiety over the stalemated convention: "It is a miracle that we [are] now here exercising our tranquil and free deliberations on the subject. It would be madness to trust to future miracles."[70] Hamilton seized the chance to enunciate his first major statement on foreign policy, noting that great nations follow their interests and contesting the chimerical view that America should concentrate on domestic tranquillity while disregarding its interests abroad: "No governm[en]t could give us tranquillity and happiness at home, which did not possess sufficient stability and strength to make us respectable abroad."[71] He also combated the fantasy that the Atlantic Ocean would protect America from future conflicts. With these fighting words, Hamilton splashed a cold dose of realism on the sentimental isolationism of the time.

After delivering these thoughts, Hamilton packed up and returned to New York the next day to attend to personal business. He was "seriously and deeply distressed" by the convention, he wrote to Washington. As he traveled back through New Jersey, he gathered impressions that reinforced his conviction that only tough, fearless measures could stem the country's chaos. "I fear that we shall let slip the golden opportunity of rescuing the American empire from disunion, anarchy, and misery," he informed Washington.[72]

The warring New York delegation shortly fell apart. By July 6, Robert Yates and

John Lansing, Jr., had expressed their disgust with the convention by also leaving Philadelphia. Members had come and gone before, but the two New York delegates were the first to depart irrevocably on principle. Washington, aggrieved, wrote to Hamilton: "I *almost* despair of seeing a favourable issue to . . . the Convention and do therefore repent having had any agency in the business." He inveighed against "narrow-minded politicians . . . under the influence of local views," who would selfishly block "a strong and energetic government" under the guise of protecting the people. Washington did not seem fazed by Hamilton's June 18 speech. "I am sorry you went away," he assured him. "I wish you were back."[73]

On July 16, the thick gloom finally lifted at Philadelphia when delegates agreed to a grand bargain, the so-called Connecticut Compromise, proposed by Roger Sherman of Connecticut and others. The major conflicts at the convention had perhaps hinged less on the question of federal versus state power than on how federal representation was apportioned among the states. The delegates solved this baffling riddle by deciding that all states would enjoy equal representation in the Senate (a sop to small states) while representation in the House of Representatives would be proportionate to each state's population (a sop to large states). This broke the deadlock, though the Senate's composition introduced a lasting political bias in American life in favor of smaller states.

Left in limbo by Yates and Lansing, Hamilton drifted back and forth between New York and Philadelphia that summer. "Yates and Lansing never voted *in one single instance* with Hamilton, who was so much mortified at it that he went home," George Mason told Thomas Jefferson. "When the season for courts came on, Yates, a judge, and Lansing, a lawyer, went to attend their courts. Then Hamilton returned."[74] With Yates and Lansing gone, Hamilton still could not vote because each state needed a minimum of two delegates present, so he became a nonvoting convention member. Yet he no longer had to appease delegates from his own state. Hamilton behaved civilly toward Yates and Lansing, telling them that "for the sake of propriety and public opinion" he would gladly accompany them back to Philadelphia.[75] Needless to say, neither ever took him up on the offer.

Having repudiated the convention, Yates and Lansing no longer felt bound by its gag rule and briefed Governor Clinton on what was being meditated in Philadelphia. "We must candidly confess that we should have been equally opposed to any system . . . which had in object the consolidation of the United States into one government."[76] Perceiving a threat to his power, Clinton stated publicly that the most likely effect of any new charter would be that "the country would be thrown into confusion by the measure," Hamilton recalled. Irate at this violation of the convention's confidentiality, Hamilton said that Clinton had not given the Philadelphia meeting a fair chance and had "clearly betrayed an intention to excite prejudices beforehand against whatever plan should be proposed by the Convention."[77]

Hamilton was spoiling for a fight as New York resounded with rumors about the events in Philadelphia. When a story appeared that delegates were colluding to bring the duke of York, George III's second son, from Britain to head an American monarchy, Hamilton traced this absurdity to a letter sent "to one James Reynolds of this city"—the first reference he ever made to the man whose wife would someday be his fatal enchantress.[78] On July 21, Hamilton took dead aim at Governor Clinton in New York's *Daily Advertiser*. In an unsigned article, he accused Clinton of poisoning the electorate's mind against the ongoing work in Philadelphia, contending that "such conduct in a man high in office argues greater attachment to his *own power* than to the *public good* and furnishes strong reason to suspect a dangerous predetermination to oppose whatever may tend to diminish the *former*, however it may promote the *latter*."[79] As so often in his career, Hamilton's assault on New York's most powerful man—the opening salvo in his protracted campaign to win New York's approval of the Constitution—seemed brave and foolhardy in equal measure.

In attacking Clinton, Hamilton went straight for the jugular. The Clintonians hit back hard, spreading smears about Hamilton. While Hamilton had chastised Clinton's character to illustrate the abuses of self-serving governors, his adversaries vilified his personal reputation. They knew that Hamilton enjoyed Washington's all-important patronage and tried to soil that association in the public's mind. In a piece signed "Inspector," one Clinton henchman wrote, "I have also known an upstart attorney palm himself upon a great and good man for a youth of extraordinary genius and under the shadow of such a patronage make himself at once known and respected. . . . [H]e was at length found to be a superficial, self-conceited coxcomb and was of course turned off and disregarded by his patron."[80]

Hamilton was deeply offended. This man born without honor was exceedingly sensitive to any slights to his political honor. As an outsider on the American scene, he did not believe that he could allow such slander to go unanswered, so he appealed to Washington to correct the distortion: "This, I confess, hurts my feelings, and if it obtains credit will require a contradiction," he told the general.[81] Friendly toward both Hamilton and Clinton, Washington was reluctant to take sides but confirmed to Hamilton that the charges against him were "entirely unfounded." He had no reason, he said, to believe that Hamilton had taken a single step to finagle an appointment to his military family. As for the confrontation that led to Hamilton's departure, "Your quitting [was] altogether the effect of your own choice."[82] Through the years, Hamilton was to exhaust himself in efforts to refute lies that grew up around him like choking vines. No matter how hard he tried to hack away at these myths, they continued to sprout deadly new shoots. These myths were perhaps the inevitable reaction to a man so brilliant, so outspoken, and so sure of himself.

Before returning to Philadelphia, Hamilton averted a duel between an English merchant friend, John Auldjo, and Major William Pierce, who happened to be a Georgia delegate to the Constitutional Convention. In a letter to Pierce's second, Hamilton pleaded for forgiveness of Auldjo's rude behavior in a business dispute and observed that "extremities ought then only to ensue when, after a fair experiment, accommodation has been found impracticable."[83] As was often the case, the prospect of a duel concentrated the minds of both parties, enabling them to reach a settlement without resort to bloodshed.

On August 6, the Philadelphia convention reconvened to begin the arduous task of refining the Constitution. Hamilton, back by August 13, dove into a debate that passionately engaged him: immigration. He opposed any attempt to restrict membership in Congress to native-born Americans or to stipulate a residency period before immigrants could qualify for it. He told the assembly that "the advantage of encouraging foreigners is obvious. . . . Persons in Europe of moderate fortunes will be fond of coming here, where they will be on a level with the first citizens. I move that the section be so altered as to require merely citizenship and inhabitancy."[84] This position again contradicts the image of Hamilton as indifferent to the plight of ordinary people. He was overruled: representatives would have a seven-year residency requirement, senators nine, the president fourteen. It has been speculated that Hamilton slipped a clause into the Constitution allowing him to become eligible for the presidency. The final document stated that the president had to be at least thirty-five and either native-born "or a Citizen of the United States, at the time of the Adoption of this Constitution." Since Hamilton was away from Philadelphia when a committee formulated this proposal, it seems unlikely that he had any influence upon it.

As Madison conceded, the specter of slavery haunted the convention, and he argued that "the states were divided into different interests not by their difference of size, but principally from their having or not having slaves. . . . [The conflict] did not lie between the large and small states. It lay between the northern and southern."[85] For many southerners, the slavery issue allowed no room for concessions, and they supported the Virginia Plan in exchange for protecting their peculiar institution. Charles Cotesworth Pinckney of South Carolina stated baldly, "South Carolina and Georgia cannot do without slaves."[86] The issue was so explosive that the word *slavery* did not appear in the Constitution, replaced by the euphemism of people "held to service or labor."

Slaveholding states wondered how their human property would be counted for congressional-apportionment purposes. Northern states finally agreed that five slaves would be counted as equivalent to three free whites, the infamous "federal ratio" that survived for another eighty years. The formula richly rewarded the southern states, artificially inflating their House seats and electoral votes and helping to explain why four of the first five presidents hailed from Virginia. This gross inequity was to play no small part in the eventual triumph of Jeffersonian Republicans over Hamiltonian Federalists. In exchange, southern states agreed that the importation of slaves might cease after 1808, feeding an illusory hope that slavery might someday just fade away. Without the federal ratio, Hamilton glumly concluded, "no union could possibly have been formed."[87] Indeed, the whole superstructure erected in Philadelphia rested on that unstable, undemocratic foundation.

Hamilton's upset over this tolerance of slavery may have been deeper than we know. There has always been some mystery as to his whereabouts after his August 13 statement on immigration. In fact, he had returned to New York for a meeting of the Manumission Society. Hamilton may have apprised members of the impending decision on slavery in Philadelphia, because they delivered a petition to the convention to "promote the attainment of the objects of this society."[88] After the slavery compromise in Philadelphia, Hamilton stepped up his involvement in the Manumission Society. The following year, even while pouring out fifty-one *Federalist* essays, serving in Congress, and campaigning to ratify the Constitution, he attended a meeting of the society that again protested the export of slaves from New York State and the "outrages committed in digging up and taking away the dead bodies of Negroes buried in the city."[89] Later in the year, Hamilton was appointed one of four counselors of the Manumission Society.

By September 6, Hamilton was back in Philadelphia, having made full peace with the new Constitution. Madison recorded Hamilton as telling delegates that "he had been restrained from entering into the discussion from his dislike of the scheme in general, but as he meant to support the plan . . . as better than nothing, he wished to offer a few remarks."[90] On September 8, Hamilton joined the Committee of Style and Arrangement, which would arrange the articles of the Constitution and polish its prose. The five-member committee, chaired by William Samuel Johnson, included Rufus King and James Madison but owed most of its success to Hamilton's friend Gouverneur Morris. Thanks to a carriage accident, Morris, thirty-five, had a wooden leg and walked with a cane, accoutrements that only enhanced his whimsically flamboyant presence. Like Hamilton, the blue-blooded Morris dreaded mob rule and had favored a Senate made up solely of great property owners. He considered slavery a "nefarious institution" that would summon the "curse of heaven on the states where it prevailed."[91] Although he represented Pennsylvania at the convention, he had grown up on Morrisania, the family estate in New York. Tall and urbane, he was a stout patriot with a biting wit and a cavalier twinkle in his eyes. He spoke a record 173 times at the convention, leading William Pierce to marvel at how "he charms, captivates, and leads away the senses of all who hear him."[92]

The polyglot Morris was a bon vivant who admitted that he had "naturally a taste for pleasure."[93] At King's College, he had composed essays on "Wit and Beauty" and on "Love." Like many flirtatious men who oozed charm, the "Tall Boy" was thought superficial, even decadent, by more austere observers. John Adams said he was a "man of wit and made pretty verses, but of a character *très légère.*"[94] In a similarly deprecatory vein, John Jay once wrote of the randy Morris, "Gouverneur's leg has been a tax on my heart. I am almost tempted to wish he had lost *something else.*"[95] Morris's peg leg did not seem to detract from his sexual appeal and may even have enhanced it.

Hamilton and Morris felt a mutual affinity, flavored with some hearty cynicism. Morris admired Hamilton's intellect even as he reproved him for being "indiscreet, vain, and opinionated."[96] Repaying the compliment, Hamilton called Morris "a man of great genius, liable however to be occasionally influenced by his fancy, which sometimes outruns his discretion."[97] On another occasion, Hamilton branded Morris "a native of this country, but by genius an exotic."[98]

There is a splendid, if unsubstantiated, story about Hamilton and Morris at the convention that rings true and conveys Morris's ironic, self-assured style. Hamilton and Morris were discussing how Washington signaled to people that they should maintain a respectful distance and not behave too familiarly with him. Hamilton wagered Morris that he would not dare to accost Washington with a friendly slap on the back. Taking up the challenge, Morris found Washington standing by the fireplace in a drawing room and genially cuffed him on the shoulder: "My dear general, how happy I am to see you look so well." Washington fixed Morris with such a frigid gaze that Morris was sorry that he had ever taken up Hamilton's dare.[99]

As a member of the style committee, Hamilton showed that, for all his misgivings about the Constitution, he could be cooperative and play a serviceable part. The convention showed good judgment in choosing him, given his literary gifts and rapid pen. It is hard to believe that the Committee of Style and Arrangement took only four days to burnish syllables that were to be painstakingly explicated by future generations. The objective was to make the document short and flexible, its language specific enough to constrain abuses but general enough to allow room for growth. As its chief draftsman, Morris shrank the original twenty-three articles to seven and wrote the great preamble with its ringing opening, "We the People of the

United States." Paying tribute to Morris's craftsmanship, Madison wrote, "The *finish* given to the style and arrangement fairly belongs to the pen of Mr. Morris."[100]

On September 17, 1787, after almost four months of hard-fought battles, the convention ended when thirty-nine delegates from twelve states signed the Constitution. By scrapping the Articles of Confederation and placing the states under a powerful central government, it represented a monumental achievement. Since Lansing and Yates remained stubborn holdouts, Hamilton ended up as the lone New York delegate to sign the charter. (The names of the states preceding the signatures appear in his handwriting.) It must have been with both relief and joy that Washington entered in his diary that night, "Met in Convention, when the Constitution received the unanimous assent of 11 States and Colo. Hamilton's from New York."[101] In the end, the headstrong Hamilton subordinated his ego to the common good. At the signing, he announced categorical support for the Constitution and appealed to the delegates for unanimous approval. Reported Madison:

> Mr. Hamilton expressed his anxiety [i.e., eagerness] that every member should sign. A few characters of consequence, by opposing or even refusing to sign the Constitution, might do infinite mischief by kindling the latent sparks which lurk under an enthusiasm in favor of the Convention, which may soon subside. No man's ideas were more remote from the plan than his were known to be. But is it possible to deliberate between anarchy and convulsion on one side and the chance of good to be expected from the plan on the other.[102]

After signing, the delegates adjourned to the City Tavern, which John Adams described as the "most genteel tavern in America," for a farewell dinner.[103] Behind the conviviality lurked unspoken fears, and Washington, for one, doubted that the new federal government would survive twenty years.

The delegates decided that the Constitution would take effect when nine state conventions approved it. For tactical and philosophical reasons, state legislatures were bypassed in favor of independent ratifying conventions. This would prevent state officials hostile to the new federal government from killing it off. Also, by having autonomous conventions approve the Constitution, the new republic would derive its legitimacy not from the statehouses but directly from the citizenry, enabling federal law to supersede state legislation.

With the possible exception of James Madison, nobody had exerted more influence than Hamilton in bringing about the convention or a greater influence afterward in securing passage of its sterling product. His behavior at the convention itself was another matter. It would long seem contradictory—and, to Jeffersonians, downright suspicious—that Hamilton could support a document that he had contested at such length. In fact, the Constitution represented a glorious compromise for every signer. This flexibility has always been honored as a sign of political maturity, whereas Hamilton's concessions have often been given a conspiratorial twist. For the rest of his life, Hamilton remained utterly true to his pledge that he would do everything in his power to see the Constitution successfully implemented. He never wavered either in public or in private. And there was a great deal in the document that was compatible with ideas about government that he had expressed since 1780. His reservations had less to do with the powers of the new government than with the tenure of the people exercising them. In the end, nobody would do more than Alexander Hamilton to infuse life into this parchment and make it the working mandate of the American government.

THIRTEEN

PUBLIUS

For all its gore and mayhem, the American Revolution had unified the thirteen states, binding them into a hopeful, if still restive, nation. The aftermath of the Constitutional Convention, by contrast, turned ugly and divisive, polarizing the populace. Four days after Hamilton affixed his signature to the Constitution, *The Daily Advertiser* gave New Yorkers their first glimpse of it, and many blanched in amazement. This charter went far beyond Congress's instructions to rework the Articles of Confederation: it brought forth a brand-new government. The old confederation had simply gone up in smoke. Marinus Willett, once a stalwart of the Sons of Liberty and now New York's sheriff, echoed the consternation among Governor Clinton's entourage when he lambasted the new Constitution as "a monster with open mouth and monstrous teeth ready to devour all before it."[1]

Amid great uproar and incessant debate, the country began to divide into two groups. Those in favor of the new dispensation and a dominant central government were called, somewhat illogically, federalists—a name ordinarily applied to supporters of a loose confederation. Opponents of the Constitution, who feared encroachments on state prerogatives, were now termed antifederalists. The two sides projected competing nightmares of what would happen if the other side prevailed. The federalists evoked disunion, civil war, and foreign intrigue, along with flagrant repudiation of debt and assaults on property. The antifederalists talked darkly of despotism and a monarchy, the ascendancy of the rich, and the outright abolition of the states. If both sides trafficked in hyperbole, we must remember how much was at stake. The Revolution had focused on independence from Britain and sidestepped the question of what sort of society America ought to be—a question that could no longer be postponed. Did the Revolution herald a new social order, or would it perpetuate something closer to the status quo ante? And didn't the new Constitution, by fostering a dominant central government, imitate the British model against which the colonists had rebelled? The brevity and generality of the Constitution made it susceptible to many interpretations. One could imagine almost anything about a government that existed only on paper. Paranoid thinking seems to be a legacy of all revolutions, with purists searching for signs of heresy, and the American experience was no exception.

Given the well-organized opposition in large states such as Virginia and New York, it seemed likely that it would be an uphill battle to get the Constitution ratified. As often incredulous citizens studied the document in taverns and coffeehouses, many rejected it at first blush. The convention's secrecy encouraged suspicions of a wicked cabal at work. Patrick Henry, for one, railed against "the tyranny of Philadelphia" and compared the new charter to "the tyranny of George III."[2] Objections to the Constitution ranged from the noble (insistence upon a bill of rights or the mandatory rotation of presidents) to the base (a desire to protect local politicians or preserve slavery from an intrusive federal government). The tariff issue held special force in New York, where state customs revenues made other taxes unnecessary. Under the new Constitution, customs collection would become a federal monopoly. By the fall of 1787, the debate over the new dispensation obsessed New Yorkers. In the words of one newspaper, "The rage of the season is . . . Jack, what are you, boy, federal or antifederal."[3]

The rancor ushered in a golden age of literary assassination in American politics. No etiquette had yet evolved to define the legitimate boundaries of dissent. Poison-pen artists on both sides wrote vitriolic essays that were overtly partisan, often paid scant heed to accuracy, and sought a visceral impact. The inflamed rhetoric once directed against Britain was now turned inward against domestic adversaries.

The Clintonians were still smarting over Hamilton's midsummer invective against the governor. Their animosity was further riled in early September when a newspaper scribe called "Rough Carver" ridiculed Clinton as the "thick-skulled and double-hearted chief" of those "who will coolly oppose everything which does not bear the marks of *self*."[4] For several weeks, a violent press battle raged between federalists and antifederalists. The Clintonian response to "Rough Carver" appeared under "A Republican" and took deadly aim at Hamilton and the "lordly faction" that wanted to "establish a system more favorable to their aristocratic views."[5] This led to a federalist rebuttal by "Aristides" that sketched a heroic portrait of Hamilton as a sublime human being "impelled from pure principles," who had sounded "a *noble* and *patriotic alarm*" against the dangers of the Articles of Confederation.[6]

Never one to dodge controversy, Hamilton admitted that he had written the anonymous summer attack on Clinton. But then, far from laying the feud to rest, he renewed the offensive. For Hamilton, Clinton epitomized the flaws of the old confederation, and he denounced "the pernicious intrigues of a man high in office to preserve power and emolument to himself at the expense of the union, the peace, and the happiness of America."[7] Hamilton presented himself as a paragon of virtue—a tactic that later came back to haunt him. Writing of himself in the third person, he issued this challenge to his opponents: "Mr. Hamilton can, however, defy all their malevolent ingenuity to produce a single instance of his conduct, public or private, inconsistent with the strict rules of integrity and honor."[8]

George Clinton responded to Hamilton's declaration of war on two levels. The governor almost certainly authored seven essays signed "Cato" that set forth reasoned objections to the Constitution. "Cato" wanted a stronger Congress, more members in the House of Representatives, and a weak president restricted to one term. Then a pair of newspaper articles styled "Inspector" showed just how vicious the calumny against Hamilton would be. Hamilton was portrayed as the uppity "Tom S**t" (Tom Shit) and introduced as a "mustee"—the offspring of a white person and a quadroon. This was the first time that Hamilton's opponents tried to denigrate him with charges of mixed racial ancestry. Tom Shit is mocked for his "Creolian" writing. In a soliloquy, Tom, a conceited upstart and British lackey, says, "My dear masters, I am indeed leading a very hard life in your service. . . . Consider the great sacrifices I have made for you. By birth a subject of his Danish Majesty, I quitted my native soil in the torrid zone and called myself a North American for your sakes." Tom is accused of having sent his "Phocion" essays, defending persecuted Tories, straight from the king's printer in England. After castigating Hamilton as a treacherous foreigner, the author refers to Washington as Hamilton's "immaculate daddy," a snide reference to Hamilton's illegitimacy.[9] Thus began the baseless mythology, which persists to this day, that Hamilton was Washington's "natural" child.

"Inspector" seemed to know all about Hamilton's notorious June 18 speech at the convention, but the secret nature of the deliberations made it impossible to print anything directly. So, in the next installment, he concocted an allegory in which a "Mrs. Columbia" asks Tom Shit how best to run her plantation. Tom replies that the plantation superintendent should be installed for life instead of for four-year terms. The author concludes, "Such strides [Tom] had already made in emerging from obscurity that he conceived nothing was beyond the reach of his good fortune."[10] Evidently, Clintonians thought the time had come to chop Hamilton down to size by jeering at his foreign birth, his supposed racial identity, his illegitimacy, and his putative links to the British Crown—attacks that set a pattern for the rest of Hamilton's career. Since critics found it hard to defeat him on intellectual grounds, they stooped to personal attacks.

In late September, Hamilton jotted down some unpublished reflections on the Constitution. He was guardedly hopeful that it would be ratified as men of property closed ranks to stop "the depredations which the democratic spirit is apt to make on property." He thought it would also be supported by creditors eager to see government debt repaid. On the other hand, it would be resisted by state politicians who feared a decrease in their power and citizens who dreaded new taxes. If the Constitution was not ratified, Hamilton expected a "dismemberment of the Union and monarchies in different portions of it" or else several republican confederacies. If civil war came, he foresaw a possible reversion to colonial status: "A reunion with Great Britain, from universal disgust at a state of commotion, is not impossible, though not much to be feared. [Presumably, Hamilton meant that it was not likely.] The most plausible shape of such a business would be the establishment of a son of the present [British] monarchy in the supreme government of this country with a family compact."[11]

Impelled by such fears, Hamilton flung himself into defending the Constitution. Throughout his career, he operated in the realm of the possible, taking the world as it was, not as he wished it to be, and he often inveighed against a dogmatic insistence upon perfection. Being a lawyer may have eased his transition from arch skeptic to supreme admirer of the Constitution, for he had the attorney's ability to make the best case for an imperfect client. He was not alone in making this transition: all the delegates at Philadelphia had adopted the final document in a spirit of compromise. They approached it as a collective work and championed it as the best available solution. What Jefferson said of George Washington could easily have applied to Hamilton: "He has often declared to me that he considered our new constitution as an experiment on the practicability of republic government . . . [and] that he was determined the experiment should have a fair trial and would lose the last drop of his blood in support of it. . . . I do believe that General Washington had not a firm confidence in the durability of our government."[12] Hamilton was no less hopeful, no less committed, and certainly no less skeptical.

By early October 1787, Hamilton conceived an ambitious writing project to help elect federalist delegates to the New York Ratifying Convention: a comprehensive explication of the entire document, written by New Yorkers for a New York audience. In early October 1787, James Kent encountered Hamilton at a dinner party at the Schuyler mansion in Albany, where Hamilton was attending the fall session of the state supreme court. Philip Schuyler expatiated on the need for a national revenue system while Hamilton listened quietly. "Mr. Hamilton appeared to be careless and desultory in his remarks," Kent recalled, "and it occurred to me afterwards . . . that he was deeply meditating the plan of the immortal work of *The Federalist*."[13]

Tradition claims that Hamilton wrote the first installment of the masterpiece known as *The Federalist Papers* in the cabin of a Hudson River sloop as he and Eliza returned to New York from Albany. Eliza recalled going upriver, not down, and said Hamilton laid out the contours of the project as they sailed: "My beloved husband wrote the outline of his papers in *The Federalist* on board of one of the North River sloops while on his way to Albany, a journey . . . which in those days usually occupied a week. Public business so filled up his time that he was compelled to do much of his studying and writing while traveling."[14] Whether he was sailing downriver or upriver, it is pleasant to picture Hamilton scratching out his plan as the tall, single-masted schooner slipped past the Hudson Highlands and the Palisades. This first essay appeared in *The Independent Journal* on October 27, 1787.

Hamilton supervised the entire *Federalist* project. He dreamed up the idea, enlisted the participants, wrote the overwhelming bulk of the essays, and oversaw the publication. For his first collaborator, he recruited John Jay, a tall, thin, balding man with a pale, melancholy face and a wary look in his deep-set gray eyes. Jay always looked austere, almost gaunt, in paintings, though he could show delightful flashes of wit. Descended from Huguenots, the son of a wealthy merchant, Jay had been the major draftsman of the New York State Constitution. Along with Franklin and Adams, he had negotiated the treaty that ended the Revolution and was a longtime secretary of foreign affairs under the Articles of Confederation. With his first-rate mind and unquestioned integrity, he was a superb choice to collaborate on the project.

Hamilton and Jay invited in three other authors. Madison wrote, "The undertaking was proposed by Alexander Hamilton to James Madison with a request to join him and Mr. Jay in carrying it into effect. William Duer was also included in the original plan and wrote two or more papers, which, though intelligent and sprightly, were not continued, nor did they make a part of the printed collection."[15] Hamilton courted Gouverneur Morris, who said he was "warmly pressed by Hamilton to assist in writing the Federalist" but was too harried by business to consent.[16] That Hamilton approached Morris and Madison shows that he wanted the anonymous essays to profit from detailed knowledge of the convention's inner workings. He always believed that the framers' intentions were important, though not decisive. He said the Constitution "must speak for itself. Yet to candid minds, the [contemporary] explanations of it by men who had had a perfect opportunity of knowing the views of its framers must operate as a weighty collateral reason for believing the construction agreeing with this explanation to be right, rather than the opposite one."[17]

Each author was assigned an area corresponding to his expertise. Jay naturally handled foreign relations. Madison, versed in the history of republics and confederacies, covered much of that ground. As author of the Virginia Plan, he also undertook to explain the general anatomy of the new government. Hamilton took those branches of government most congenial to him: the executive, the judiciary, and some sections on the Senate. Previewing things to come, he also covered military matters and taxation.

The *Federalist* essays first appeared in newspapers. The authors had to camouflage their identities behind a pseudonym, lest they be accused of betraying the confidentiality of the convention. At first, Hamilton planned to publish the pieces under the rubric of a "Citizen of New York" but changed it when James Madison of Virginia was recruited to the project. He then selected the pen name "Publius," which he had first used in 1778 when he berated Samuel Chase for wartime profiteering. It was an apposite choice: Publius Valerius had toppled the last Roman king and set up the republican foundations of government. Hamilton rushed a copy to Mount Vernon without identifying himself as its author. "For the remaining numbers of Publius," Washington responded, "I shall acknowledge yourself obliged, as I am persuaded the subject will be well handled by the author."[18] Jay wrote the next four numbers, then had to drop out because of a severe bout of rheumatism. In the final tally, *The Federalist Papers* ran to eighty-five essays, with fifty-one attributed to Hamilton, twenty-nine to Madison, and only five to Jay. Since Hamilton had not reckoned on Jay's illness and had expected to include Morris and Duer, he could never have anticipated that he and Madison would write so much in seven months—some 175,000 words in all—or that *The Federalist* would essentially settle down to a two-man enterprise. Thanks to the cooperation of Hamilton and Madison, New York emerged as the main arena of intellectual combat over the new plan of government.

The project's magnitude mushroomed tremendously from its origins, as indicated by Archibald McLean, the Hanover Square printer who published the bound version and felt beleaguered by the project. "When I engaged to do the work," he groused to Robert Troup, "it was to consist of twenty numbers, or at the most twenty-five."[19] Instead of one projected volume of two hundred pages, McLean complained, *The Federalist* ended up running to two volumes of about six hundred pages. To worsen matters, the luckless printer was stuck with several hundred unsold copies and grumbled that he didn't clear five pounds on the whole deal. For Archibald McLean, *The Federalist Papers* were a dreadful flop, an unfortunate publishing venture best forgotten.

To safeguard his anonymity, Hamilton sent the early essays to the newspapers via Robert Troup. If Hamilton was out of town, he sometimes sent them to Eliza, who may have then relayed them along to Troup. Later, as it became an open secret in New York political circles that Hamilton was the chief author, newspaper publisher

Samuel Loudon went straight to Hamilton's office for fresh copy. Many people knew that Hamilton, Madison, and Jay were the authors, but the trio proclaimed their authorship to only a chosen few and then mostly after the first bound volume was published in March 1788. Madison furnished Jefferson with the relevant names in code, while Hamilton sent Washington the book version and observed, "I presume you have understood that the writers . . . are chiefly Mr. Madison and myself, with some aid from Mr. Jay."[20] More sensitive was the question of who wrote what. Hamilton and Madison forged a pact that they would reveal this only by mutual agreement, initiating two centuries of scholarly disputation over the authorship of approximately fifteen of the essays. True to their pledge, Hamilton and Madison remained coy on the subject.

The Federalist has been extolled as both a literary and political masterpiece. Theodore Roosevelt commented "that it is on the whole the greatest book" dealing with practical politics.[21] Its achievement is the more astonishing for having been written under such fierce deadline pressure. The first of the staggered series of ratifying conventions was scheduled to start in late November, and this allowed Hamilton and Madison little opportunity for fresh research or reflection. They agreed to deliver four essays per week (that is, two apiece) at roughly three-day intervals, leaving little time for revision. The essays then appeared in four of the five New York newspapers. The constantly looming deadlines meant that the authors had to draw on information, ideas, and citations already stored in their minds or notes. Luckily, they had both been in training for several years. Madison explained to Jefferson, "Though [the publication is] carried on in concert, the writers are not mutually answerable for all the ideas of each other, there being seldom time for even a perusal of the pieces by any but the writer before they are wanted at the press, and sometimes hardly by the writer himself."[22] So excruciating was the schedule, Madison said, that often "whilst the printer was putting into type parts of a number, the following parts were under the pen and to be furnished in time for the press."[23] Very often, Hamilton and Madison first read each other's contributions in print.

Madison was aided by his convention notes and crib sheets from his preparatory reading. Without these scholarly crutches, he confessed, "the performance must have borne a very different aspect."[24] For Hamilton, it was a period of madcap activity. He was stuck with his law practice and had to squeeze the essays into breaks in his schedule, as if they were a minor sideline. Robert Troup noted of Hamilton's haste in writing *The Federalist:* "All the numbers written by [Hamilton] were composed under the greatest possible pressure of business, for [he] always had a vast deal of law business to engage his attention." Troup remembered seeing Samuel Loudon "in [Hamilton's] study, waiting to take numbers of *The Federalist* as they came fresh from" his pen "in order to publish them in the next paper."[25] During one prodigious burst after Madison returned to Virginia, Hamilton churned out twenty-one straight essays in a two-month period. On two occasions, he published five essays in a single week and published six in one spectacular week when writing on taxation.

Hamilton's mind always worked with preternatural speed. His collected papers are so stupefying in length that it is hard to believe that one man created them in fewer than five decades. Words were his chief weapons, and his account books are crammed with purchases for thousands of quills, parchments, penknives, slate pencils, reams of foolscap, and wax. His papers show that, Mozart-like, he could transpose complex thoughts onto paper with few revisions. At other times, he tinkered with the prose but generally did not alter the logical progression of his thought. He wrote with the speed of a beautifully organized mind that digested ideas thoroughly, slotted them into appropriate pigeonholes, then regurgitated them at will.

To understand Hamilton's productivity, it is important to note that virtually all of his important work was journalism, prompted by topical issues and written in the midst of controversy. He never wrote as a solitary philosopher for the ages. His friend Nathaniel Pendleton remarked, "His eloquence . . . seemed to require opposition to give it its full force."[26] But his topical writing has endured because he plumbed the timeless principles behind contemporary events. Whether in legal briefs or sustained polemics, he wanted to convince people through appeals to their reason. He had an incomparable capacity for work and a metabolism that thrived on conflict. His stupendous output came from the interplay of superhuman stamina and intellect and a fair degree of repetition.

Hamilton developed ingenious ways to wring words from himself. One method was to walk the floor as he formed sentences in his head. William Sullivan left an excellent vignette of Hamilton's intense method of composition.

> One who knew his habits of study said of him that when he had a serious object to accomplish, his practice was to reflect on it previously. And when he had gone through this labor, he retired to sleep, without regard to the hour of the night, and, having slept six or seven hours, he rose and having taken strong coffee, seated himself at his table, where he would remain six, seven, or eight hours. And the product of his rapid pen required little correction for the press.[27]

Since Hamilton's abiding literary sin was prolixity, the time and length constraints imposed by *The Federalist* may have given a salutary concision to his writing.

. . .

For all his charisma, Alexander Hamilton was essentially an intellectual loner who took perverse pride in standing against the crowd. All the more remarkable that his greatest literary triumph came in close collaboration with Madison and Jay. After leaving the convention in Philadelphia, Madison had returned to his lodgings at 19 Maiden Lane in Manhattan, where he resided with other Virginia delegates to the now almost moribund Confederation Congress. Later anointed "the Father of the Constitution," Madison had many reservations about the document, especially the equal representation of states in the Senate, and was content at first to let others take up the cudgels in its defense. He also thought it proper that others should assess the convention's work. But by late October, he was so upset by the grotesque distortions of the Constitution and the furor whipped up by the New York press that he agreed to work with Hamilton on *The Federalist*.[28]

Americans often wonder how this moment could have spawned such extraordinary men as Hamilton and Madison. Part of the answer is that the Revolution produced an insatiable need for thinkers who could generate ideas and wordsmiths who could lucidly expound them. The immediate utility of ideas was an incalculable tonic for the founding generation. The fate of the democratic experiment depended upon political intellectuals who might have been marginalized at other periods.

At this crossroads, Hamilton and Madison must have seemed an odd pair in the New York streets: Hamilton, thirty-two, the peacock, wearing bright colors and chattering gaily, and Madison, thirty-six, the crow in habitual black with a quiet, more reflective manner. When French journalist J. P. Brissot de Warville met them that year, it was the older Madison who resembled a pallid young scholar while Hamilton seemed older and more worldly. "This republican seems to be no more than thirty-three years old," the Frenchman wrote of Madison. "When I saw him, he looked tired, perhaps as a result of the immense labor to which he had devoted himself recently. His expression was that of a stern censor, his conversation disclosed a man of learning, and his countenance was that of a person conscious of his talents and of his duties."[29] Of Hamilton: "Mr. Hamilton is Mr. Madison's worthy rival as well as his collaborator. He looks thirty-eight or forty years old, is not tall, and has a resolute, frank, soldierly appearance. . . . [H]e has distinguished himself by his eloquence and by the soundness of his reasoning."[30]

Hamilton and Madison came to symbolize opposite ends of the political spectrum. At the time of the *Federalist* essays, however, they were so close in style and outlook that scholars find it hard to sort out their separate contributions. In general, Madison's style was dense and professorial, Hamilton's more graceful and flowing, yet they had a similar flair for startling epigrams and piercing insights. At this stage, Madison often sounded "Hamiltonian" and vice versa. Later identified as a "strict constructionist" of the Constitution, Madison set forth the doctrine of implied powers that Hamilton later used to expand the powers of the federal government. It was Madison who wrote in *Federalist* number 44, "No axiom is more clearly established in law or in reason than that wherever the end is required, the means are authorized."[31] At this juncture, they could make common cause on the need to fortify the federal government and curb rampant state abuses.

Both Hamilton and Madison were rational men who assumed that people often acted irrationally because of ambition and avarice. Madison wrote, "If men were angels, no government would be necessary."[32] The two shared a grim vision of the human condition, even if Hamilton's had the blacker tinge. They both wanted to erect barriers against irrational popular impulses and tyrannical minorities and majorities. To this end, they thought that public opinion should be distilled by skeptical, sober-minded representatives. Despite Hamilton's reputation as the elitist, the starting point of Madison's most famous essay, *Federalist* number 10, is that people possess different natural endowments, leading to an unequal distribution of property and conflicts of classes and interests. In a big, heterogeneous country, Madison argued, these conflicting interests would neutralize one another, checking abuses of power. "Let ambition counteract ambition," he wrote in *Federalist* number 51.[33]

If Madison displays a broader knowledge of theory and history in *The Federalist*, Hamilton betrays wider knowledge of the world. With his itinerant background, he brought commercial, military, and political expertise to bear. This was especially true in discussions of political economy, in which he outshone Madison. Madison showed more interest in constitutional curbs against tyrannical encroachments, whereas Hamilton lauded spurs to action. In sections of *The Federalist* dealing with the executive and judicial branches, Hamilton pressed his case for vigor and energy in government, a hobbyhorse he was to ride for the rest of his career. At the same time, he was always careful to reconcile the need for order with the thirst for liberty. Bernard Bailyn has written that "the Constitution, in creating a strong central government, *The Federalist* argued, did not betray the Revolution, with its radical hopes for greater political freedom than had been known before. Quite the contrary, it fulfilled those radical aspirations, by creating the power necessary to guarantee both the nation's survival and the preservation of the people and the states' rights."[34]

Let us pause to survey *The Federalist,* with special attention to Hamilton's contributions, for these essays testify to the extraordinary breadth of his thinking. As author of the opening salvo, Hamilton began with a flourish, addressing the series

"*To the People of the State of New York.* After an unequivocal experience of the inefficacy of the subsisting Federal Government, you are called upon to deliberate on a new Constitution for the United States of America." The main question was whether good governments could be created "from reflection and choice, or whether they are forever destined to depend for their political constitutions on accident and force."[35] One can almost see Hamilton declaiming as he announced that the outcome of the ratifying conventions would determine "the fate of an empire" and that rejection would be a "general misfortune of mankind."[36]

Hamilton questioned the motives of the Constitution's opponents and censured the two types who had populated his political nightmares: state politicians (read: George Clinton) who feared an erosion of their power, and demagogues who fed off popular confusion while proclaiming popular rights (Jefferson later took this starring role). Hamilton warned that "a dangerous ambition more often lurks behind the specious mask of zeal for the rights of the people than under the forbidding appearance of zeal for the firmness and efficiency of government."[37] Having set the stage, Hamilton outlined the general plan of the future essays but did not specify their number.

In the next four essays, John Jay showed how weak and vulnerable the confederation had been in foreign affairs. Then Hamilton devoted four essays to the pernicious domestic consequences that would ensue if the Articles of Confederation endured and states continued to bicker with one another. With his penchant for disaster scenarios, Hamilton cited dire precedents from ancient Greece to Shays's Rebellion. In *Federalist* number 6, he mocked as wishful thinking the notion that democratic republics would necessarily be peaceful: "Are not popular assemblies frequently subject to the impulses of rage, resentment, jealousy, avarice, and of other irregular and violent propensities?" This prophet of global trade also dismissed the pipe dream that commerce invariably unites nations: "Has commerce hitherto done anything more than change the objects of war? Is not the love of wealth as domineering and enterprising a passion as that of power or glory?"[38] Hamilton disputed that America would be an Eden governed by a special providence: "Is it not time to awake from the deceitful dream of a golden age and to adopt as a practical maxim for the direction of our political conduct that we, as well as the other inhabitants of the globe, are yet remote from the happy empire of perfect wisdom and perfect virtue?"

Starting with *Federalist* number 7, Hamilton reviewed the numberless things that states could squabble about without a strong union. The lack of fortifications and standing armies would only exacerbate wars among the states, tempting bigger states to behave in predatory fashion toward smaller ones. The resulting chaos would lead to the very despotic militarism that antifederalists feared, for in such a situation "the people are brought to consider the soldiery not only as their protec-tors, but as their superiors."[39] While conceding that republics had produced disor-ders in the past, Hamilton noted that progress in the "science of politics" had fostered principles that would prevent most abuses: the division of powers among departments, legislative checks and balances, an independent judiciary, and repre-sentation by elected legislators.[40] When Jay fell ill, Madison brilliantly leaped into the void with his celebrated *Federalist* number 10, the most influential of all the es-says, in which he took issue with Montesquieu's theory that democracy could sur-vive only in small states. Standing this argument on its head, Madison showed that in a more extensive republic, interest groups would counterbalance one another and avert tyrannical majorities.

In *Federalist* numbers 11–13, Hamilton displayed his practical, administrative bent as he explained the advantages of the new union for commerce as well as gov-ernment revenues and expenses. He revealed America's commercial destiny as he prophesied that envious European states would try to clip the wings "by which we might soar to a dangerous greatness."[41] With a powerful union, America would strike better commercial bargains and create a respectable navy. He offered an ex-pansive view of prosperous American merchants, farmers, artisans, and manufac-turers, all working together. In a sudden flash of economic foresight, he anticipated twentieth-century monetary theory: "The ability of a country to pay taxes must al-ways be proportioned, in a great degree, to the quantity of money in circulation and to the celerity [what economists now call velocity] with which it circulates."[42] Blessed with a potent union, the government would collect customs duties with greater efficiency, since it would not have to stop contraband among the states and need only patrol the Atlantic seaboard. Americans would likewise save money by having a single country rather than the separate confederacies that might stem from disunion. All this was a further rebuttal to Montesquieu's view that large re-publics could never survive.

In *Federalist* numbers 15–22, Hamilton and then Madison skewered the anar-chic state of the confederation. Pride and honor always loomed large in Hamilton's value system, both personal and political, and he mourned the national degrada-tion and loss of dignity after the Revolution. The United States had become a pariah country, sneered at by foreign states: "We have neither troops nor treasury nor gov-ernment."[43] Land and property values had plummeted, money had grown scarce, public credit had been destroyed—all because the central government lacked power. And it lacked that power because it had to rely for revenue upon the states, who competed to provide the least money to it.

Only if the federal government could deal directly with its citizens and not fear obstruction from the states could it be a true government. In number 17, Hamilton disagreed that national officials would be able to impose their wills on the states. State governments would always have superior claims on people's affections, and abuses of power would therefore more likely occur on the local level. Here Hamilton had planned a *tour d'horizon* of ancient and modern confederacies, showing how they tended to fall apart. When he learned that Madison had already undertaken this work, Hamilton handed him his notes for *Federalist* numbers 18–20. The resulting somewhat pedantic essays by Madison ended on a defensive note: "I make no apology for having dwelt so long on the contemplation of these federal precedents. Experience is the oracle of truth and where its responses are unequivocal, they ought to be conclusive and sacred."[44]

To round out his searching critique of the Articles of Confederation, Hamilton devoted two more essays to the central government's impotence in enforcing the law. Recalling Shays's Rebellion, he inquired, "Who can determine what might have been the issue of [Massachusetts's] late convulsions if the malcontents had been headed by a Caesar or a Cromwell?" (This and numerous other pejorative references to Caesar belie Jefferson's canard that Hamilton revered the Roman dictator.) He endorsed the need for federal regulation of commerce and allayed fears that the central government would levy oppressive customs fees: "If duties are too high, they lessen the consumption—the collection is eluded and the product to the treasury is not so great as when they are confined within proper and moderate bounds."[45] He also decried the confederation's lack of a federal judiciary: "Laws are a dead letter without courts to expound and define their true meaning and operation."[46] In typically categorical fashion, Hamilton ended by dismissing the Articles of Confederation as an abomination, "one of the most execrable forms of government that human infatuation ever contrived."[47]

In the next fourteen numbers (23–36), Hamilton undertook a point-by-point defense of the Constitution, making the case that an energetic government would require peacetime armies and taxation—both associated with British rule and hence anathema to radical populists. The new country would be so large, he contended, that only a mighty central government could govern it. To gain the requisite strength, that government would need the option of raising armies instead of relying on the much romanticized state militias: "War, like most other things, is a science to be acquired and perfected by diligence, by perseverance, by time, and by practice."[48] While others maintained that a wide ocean insulated America from European threats, Hamilton saw a country enmeshed in a shrinking world: "The improvements in the art of navigation have . . . rendered distant nations in a great measure neighbours."[49] Economic and military strength went hand in hand: "If we mean to be a commercial people . . . we must endeavour as soon as possible to have a navy."[50] As to fears that the federal government would amass excessive power,

Hamilton again reassured readers that "the general government will at all times stand ready to check the usurpations of the state governments and these will have the same disposition towards the general government."[51] Similarly, state militias would check potential abuses of any national army, safeguarding the balance of power between the federal and state governments.

Approaching the knotty subject of revenues in number 30, Hamilton described the power of taxation as "an indispensable ingredient in every constitution."[52] Without it, the confederation government "has gradually dwindled into a state of decay, approaching nearly to annihilation."[53] Not only would taxes underwrite operating expenses, but they would enable the country to pay off its debt, restore its credit, and raise large loans in wartime. From his reading of history, Hamilton concluded a few essays later that war was an inescapable fact of life: "the fiery and destructive passions of war reign in the human breast with much more powerful sway than the mild and beneficent sentiments of peace."[54]

Broaching the vital doctrine of implied powers in numbers 30–34, Hamilton asserted that in politics "the means ought to be proportioned to the end. . . . [T]here ought to be no limitation of a power destined to effect a purpose."[55] He wanted the Constitution to be a flexible document: "There ought to be a capacity to provide for future contingencies."[56] Making another critical distinction, Hamilton denied that the federal government would retain an exclusive taxing power. States would have concurrent power to tax their citizens because the Constitution "aims only at a partial Union or consolidation."[57] The sole exception would be the federal monopoly of customs duties, then the principal source of revenue and the leading source of existing tensions and inequities among the states.

At moments, it seems clear that while scribbling *The Federalist,* Hamilton was daydreaming about becoming treasury secretary. In number 35 he wrote, "There is no part of the administration of government that requires extensive information and a thorough knowledge of the principles of political economy so much as the business of taxation."[58] In the following essay, he inserted a statement with a patently autobiographical ring: "There are strong minds in every walk of life that will rise superior to the disadvantages of situation and will command the tribute due to their merit, not only from the classes to which they particularly belong, but from the society in general. The door ought to be equally open to all."[59] At the same time, Hamilton thought that a Congress composed mostly of landowners, merchants, and professionals could legislate effectively for the masses.

On January 11, 1788, Madison began to cover the general structure of the new union in a string of twenty essays, starting with number 37. Hamilton, now back in Albany, may have pitched in on the final ten. Until this point, Hamilton had scarcely said anything in *The Federalist* that he had not said repeatedly since his earliest wartime letters or in his "Continentalist" essays. Only as he touched upon such topics as elections in the later essays did he diverge from his own preferred beliefs, and even then he surrounded new positions with old arguments. Those who criticize Hamilton for having engaged in a propaganda exercise in *The Federalist* must reckon with the tremendous continuity that connects the *Federalist* essays to both his earlier and later writings.

As Madison reviewed the "compound character" of the federalist system in number 37, subtle but fateful differences with Hamilton began to emerge—differences that were to be enlarged over time. In number 41, Madison expressed reservations about standing armies and the onerous taxes needed to sustain them and was cynical about the corruption of the British Parliament. (In other places, however, he sounded like even more of a raging Anglophile than Hamilton.) Madison faulted the Articles of Confederation for their vague language and savored the Constitution's precision, which he hoped would circumscribe federal powers. Hamilton, in contrast, capitalized on what he saw as the document's general and elastic language to expand government power.

By numbers 59–61, Hamilton, returned to New York from Albany, took up the subject of congressional elections and regulations. Though identified with northern mercantile interests, Hamilton emphasized that in an agricultural society "the cultivators of land . . . must upon the whole preponderate in the government."[60] In *Federalist* number 60, he offered a vision of a House of Representatives dominated by landholders but also marked by diversity. Hamilton was careful to stress that, for the foreseeable future, manufacturing would play an auxiliary role in a predominantly agricultural society.

The five essays (62–66) on the Senate embody the *The Federalist*'s most collaborative section, with Madison handling the first two, Jay reappearing to take number 64, and Hamilton winding up the two concluding numbers. In number 62, Madison stated frankly that the balance struck between proportional representation in the House and equal representation in the Senate had come from political compromise, not ideal theory. In the next essay, he defended the small, elite Senate against charges that it would grow into "a tyrannical aristocracy" and sounded Hamiltonian when he stated that "liberty may be endangered by the abuses of liberty as well as by the abuses of power. . . . [T]he former rather than the latter is apparently most to be apprehended by the United States."[61] With this parting shot, Madison went back to Virginia in March to defend the Constitution in his home state. Once Jay wrote number 64 on the treaty powers of the Senate, Hamilton singlehandedly penned the next twenty-one essays (65–85), handling parts of the Senate as well as the entire commentary on the executive and judicial branches.

In his superb account of Senate impeachment powers in number 65, Hamilton visualized, with exceptional prescience, the problems that would occur when passions inflamed the country and partisanship split the Senate over an accused federal official. Since the impeached president or federal judge would remain liable to prosecution if removed from office, Hamilton showed the Constitution's wisdom in having the chief justice alone preside over the trial instead of the entire Supreme Court. The Senate would benefit from the chief justice's judicial knowledge while keeping the high court free for any future decisions related to the case. Acknowledging imperfections in the impeachment process, Hamilton stressed that the Constitution had produced the best compromise available: "If mankind were to resolve to agree in no institution of government until every part of it had been adjusted to the most exact standard of perfection, society would soon become a general scene of anarchy and the world a desert."[62]

In turning to the executive branch (67–77), Hamilton wrote about the part of government in which he had the keenest interest and which he considered the engine of the entire machinery. As he phrased it in number 70, "Energy in the executive is a leading character in the defintion of good government."[63] He mocked exaggerated fears of the powers bestowed on the president and said that in some respects he would have fewer powers than New York's governor. Hamilton drew freely on statements he had made at the Constitutional Convention to distinguish his "elective monarch" from a king. The British king, he pointed out, was hereditary, could not be removed by impeachment, had an absolute veto over the laws of both houses, and could dissolve Parliament, declare war, make treaties, confer titles of nobility, and bestow church offices. It clearly exasperated Hamilton that critics were drawing facile comparisons between the American president and the British king.

In his essays on the need for executive-branch vigor, Hamilton continually invoked the king of England as an example of what should be *avoided,* especially the monarch's lack of accountability. Every president "ought to be personally responsible for his behaviour in office."[64] In number 71, Hamilton presented his theory of presidents as leaders who should act for the popular good, even if the people were sometimes deluded about their interests. Hamilton made the argument that the separate branches of government were not intended only to curb one another but to afford independence to one another: "To what purpose separate the executive or the judiciary from the legislative if both the executive and the judiciary are so constituted as to be at the absolute devotion of the legislative?"[65]

Deviating from his convention speech, Hamilton now touted the merits of a four-year term for the president, who could run for additional terms. This would give occupants of the office an incentive to perform well and "secure to the government the advantage of permanency in a wise system of administration."[66] In reviewing presidential powers (73–77), Hamilton praised the presidential veto as a way to contain the legislature and offset popular fads. Where populists worried that the executive branch might overwhelm the legislature, Hamilton had a contrary fear of excessive legislative power. In number 74, he made a moving appeal for the presidential power to issue pardons: "Humanity and good policy conspire to dictate that the benign prerogative for pardoning should be as little as possible fettered or embarrassed. The criminal code of every country partakes so much of necessary severity that without an easy access to exceptions in favor of unfortunate guilt, justice would wear a countenance too sanguinary and cruel."[67] In this passage, he sounded reminiscent of the young Colonel Hamilton who pleaded with General Washington to show mercy for Major John André.

Notwithstanding his preference for a strong president, Hamilton applauded many checks on presidential power. To protect the country from a president corrupted by foreign ministries, Hamilton approved the provision requiring presidents to obtain two-thirds approval of the Senate to enact treaties. In a similar vein, he approved the presidential power to appoint ambassadors and Supreme Court judges, subject to Senate confirmation, which would check "a spirit of favoritism in the President."[68] In *The Federalist Papers,* Hamilton was as quick to applaud checks on powers as those powers themselves, as he continued his lifelong effort to balance freedom and order. In the final analysis, he thought that the federal government, not the states, would be the best guarantee of individual liberty.

In the last eight essays of *The Federalist* (78–85), written for the conclusion of the second bound volume, Hamilton dedicated the first six to the judiciary. Throughout his career, he showed special solicitude for an independent judiciary, which he thought the most important guardian of minority rights but also the weakest of the three branches of government: "It commands neither the press nor the sword. It has scarcely any patronage."[69] He was especially intent that the federal judiciary check any legislative abuses. In number 78, Hamilton introduced an essential concept, never made explicit in the Constitution: that the Supreme Court should be able to review and overturn legislation as unconstitutional. At Philadelphia, delegates had concentrated on the question of state versus federal courts, not whether courts could invalidate legislation. Here, Hamilton bluntly affirmed that "no legislative act . . . contrary to the constitution can be valid," laying the intellectual groundwork for the doctrine of judicial review later promulgated by Supreme Court justice John Marshall.[70] When Hamilton wrote these words, state judges had taken only the first tentative steps in nullifying laws passed by their assemblies.

Hamilton revered great judges and in the next essay pondered how the most highly qualified people could be recruited and retained by the courts. He argued for adequate salaries and against both age limits and the power to remove judges, except by impeachment. He then outlined the scope of the courts' jurisdiction and the separate bailiwicks of the Supreme Court and the appellate courts. In number 82, Hamilton tackled the vexed issue of how powers would be divided between state and federal courts, insisting that, in the last analysis, judicial power must rest with the federal courts. Though a believer in trial by jury, he dissented in the next essay from the fanciful idea that juries were universally applicable in civil as well as criminal cases. He was particularly alarmed at the prospect that juries would sit in cases involving foreign relations, where their ignorance of the law of nations might "afford occasions of reprisal and war" from the countries affected.[71]

Many foes of the Constitution were demanding a bill of rights as a precondition for ratification. In number 84, Hamilton said this would be superfluous and even potentially hazardous: "For why declare that things shall not be done which there is no power to do? Why, for instance, should it be said that the liberty of the press shall not be restrained when no power is given by which restrictions may be imposed?"[72] He also thought the Constitution had already guaranteed many rights ranging from habeas corpus to trial by jury. Where Hamilton often seems oracular in *The Federalist,* he was frightfully wide of the mark when it came to a bill of rights, one of his real failures of vision. We should note that in *Federalist* number 84, he supported with enthusiasm the Constitution's ban on titles of nobility: "This may truly be denominated the cornerstone of republican government, for so long as they are excluded, there can never be serious danger that the government will be any other than that of the people."[73]

In the final essay, number 85, Hamilton reminded readers that the Constitution was not a perfect document and cited Hume that only time and experience could guide political enterprises to completion. It would be folly to imagine that the framers could attain instant perfection. The final lines of *The Federalist* throbbed with high hopes but were also tinged with darkness. On a promising note, Hamilton said, "A nation without a national government is, in my view, an awful spectacle. The establishment of a constitution in [a] time of profound peace by the voluntary consent of a whole people is a prodigy, to the completion of which I look forward with trembling anxiety."[74] If Hamilton had ended on this uplifting note, he would not have been Hamilton. So he closed instead with the ominous warning that "I know that powerful individuals in this and in other states are enemies to a general national government in every possible shape."[75] Thus ended the most persuasive defense of the Constitution ever written. By the year 2000, it had been quoted no fewer than 291 times in Supreme Court opinions, with the frequency of citations rising with the years.

As the excruciating demands of *The Federalist* rendered Hamilton's life even more sedentary than usual, he was a prisoner of his desk. He had no relief from his labors or time for diversion. Reelected to Congress by the New York legislature on January 22, 1788, he didn't even have a chance to present his credentials until February 25. That spring, swept up in a political whirlwind, he apologized to Gouverneur Morris for having been incommunicado, saying, "The truth is that I have been so overwhelmed in avocations of one kind or another that I have scarcely had a moment to spare to a friend."[76] Amid his manifold labors, Hamilton kept a careful eye on the pregnant Eliza, who gave birth to their fourth child, James Alexander, on April 14. Eliza spent the summer with her family in Albany, attended by an unexpected visitor: Ann Venton Mitchell.

The Federalist is so renowned as the foremost exposition of the Constitution that it is easy to forget its original aim: ratification in Hamilton's home state. Printed in only a dozen papers outside of New York, its larger influence was spotty. In places where it did appear, the verbal avalanche of Hamilton, Madison, and Jay overwhelmed hapless readers. In mid-December, one embattled antifederalist in Philadelphia bewailed the never-ending onslaught of words: "Publius has already written 26 numbers, as much as would jade the brains of any poor sinner . . . so that in decency he should now rest on his arms and let the people draw their breath for a little."[77] Another antifederalist complained that Publius had "endeavored to force conviction by a torrent of misplaced words."[78] Supporters, however, had a bottomless appetite for the essays, and the authors' names began to leak out. When Edward Carrington of Virginia sent the first bound volume to Jefferson in Paris, he added, with suspiciously precise guesswork: "They are written, it is supposed, by Messrs. Madison, Jay and Hamilton."[79]

The Philadelphia convention had decided that the Constitution would take effect once it was ratified by nine state conventions. Hamilton had given the rationale for state conventions in *Federalist* number 22: "The fabric of American empire ought to rest on the solid basis of the consent of the people."[80] Delaware, Pennsylvania, and New Jersey approved the document in December 1787, Georgia and Connecticut in January, and Massachusetts by a slim majority in early February. *The Federalist* produced its greatest impact in the later stages of the ratification battle, especially after the first bound volume appeared on March 22. When New York selected convention delegates that April, Hamilton was among them. James Kent recalled that at one nomination meeting "the volumes were there circulated to the best of our judgments. . . . Col. Hamilton was very soon and very generally understood to be the sole or principal author."[81] Madison sent hundreds of copies to Virginia delegates, including John Marshall. *The Federalist*'s influence was to be especially critical in New York and Virginia, two large states indispensable to the union's long-term viability.

The state conventions were cunningly staggered so that a bandwagon effect might be created in favor of approval. This made the later gatherings scenes of high drama, as the tally of ratifying states approached the magic number nine. Though *The Federalist* was originally intended to sway delegate selection in New York, it failed in that intent. When the results were tabulated, the outlook appeared pretty ghastly for Hamilton and the federalists: they had attained a mere nineteen delegates in New York City and environs versus forty-six for an upstate antifederalist slate headed by Governor Clinton. For all the intellectual firepower marshaled in *The Federalist,* New York had a highly intelligent, well-oiled opposition to the Constitution.

By late May, Maryland and South Carolina had given their blessings to the Constitution, bringing the total of ratifying states to eight, just one shy of the number needed, but victory in some of the remaining states seemed questionable. North Carolina and Rhode Island both scorned the scheme, while New Hampshire vacillated. So the battle for the Constitution seemed to boil down to the contests in Virginia and New York, whose conventions began in June.

Fortunately for supporters, the second volume of *The Federalist* was published on May 28 and contained the eight new essays by Hamilton. These bonus essays appeared in the newspapers between June 14 and August 16, with a new one cropping up every few days as the New York delegates began to deliberate. Hamilton and Madison vowed to stay in touch as their respective conventions progressed. Because Virginia's started two weeks earlier, Hamilton had instructed Madison to relay to him immediately any favorable news, since passage in Virginia might prod reluctant New Yorkers to follow suit. "It will be of vast importance that an exact communication should be kept up between us at that period," Hamilton told Madison. "And the moment *any decisive* question is taken, if favourable, I request you to dispatch an express to me with pointed orders to make all possible diligence by changing horses & c."[82] In the same anxious tone, Hamilton arranged for swift riders to race from New Hampshire to New York with any encouraging news. In both cases, Hamilton promised to defray the expenses.

For all the high-toned language of *The Federalist,* Hamilton knew that the New York convention would come down to bare-knuckled politics. A prominent antifederalist had already warned him that "rather than to adopt the Constitution, I would risk a government of Jew, Turk or infidel."[83] Hamilton knew that such zealotry would not be amenable to persuasion, especially with George Clinton at the delegation's head. "As Clinton is truly the leader of his party and inflexibly obstinate, I count little on overcoming opposition by reason," Hamilton confided to Madison. "Our only chances will be the previous ratification by nine states, which may shake the firmness of his followers."[84]

Though eight states had already ratified, the final leg of the journey was anything but smooth. "The plot thickens fast," George Washington told the marquis de Lafayette in late May. "A few short weeks will determine the political fate of America."[85] As Hamilton gloomily surveyed the scene, he feared that New York might stall for another year before deciding whether to join the union, and he reiterated to Madison his perpetual fears of "an eventual disunion and civil war."[86]

Unlike upstate farmers, New York City merchants heartily supported the Constitution and gave a festive send-off to federalist delegates when they departed for the Poughkeepsie convention on June 14. Crowds waved, and thirteen cannon roared at the Battery as a delegation led by Mayor James Duane embarked on a Hudson River sloop for the seventy-five-mile journey upriver. This illustrious group included Hamilton, Jay, and Robert R. Livingston, and it made up in intelligence what it lacked in numbers. As the one person in Poughkeepsie who had signed the Constitution, Hamilton was to enjoy special prestige, but he knew it would be a tough, protracted struggle against George Clinton's fearsome political machine.

The convention was held at the Poughkeepsie courthouse, a two-story building with a cupola and gruesome dungeons below for prisoners. Governor Clinton was elected as the chairman. If dignified in mien, he was scarcely a neutral arbiter. In *Federalist* number 77, Hamilton had already blasted him for running "a despicable and dangerous system of personal influence."[87] Clinton feared that Hamilton wanted to obliterate the states, but he was confident he had sufficient votes to squash the Constitution in New York or encumber it with so many conditions as to make its acceptance impossible.

At the outset, Hamilton slipped a technical provision into the convention rules that was a tactical bonanza for the federalists: the Constitution had to be debated clause by clause before a general vote could be taken. It was a masterly stroke. Nobody could vie with Hamilton in close textual analysis, and this step-by-step approach would stall the proceedings, increasing the likelihood that riders from Virginia or New Hampshire would rush in with news that their state had ratified and force New York to follow suit.

Governor Clinton gathered several able antifederalist speakers, of whom the most adroit was Melancton Smith, who had a dry, plainspoken manner and an understated wit. He was a deceptively good debater who knew how to lure opponents into logical traps from which they found it hard to escape. Smith saw Hamilton as the cat's-paw of an aristocratic clique and told the assembly that he "thanked his God that *he* was a plebeian."[88] He had tremendous respect for Hamilton's abilities, however, even if he found him wordy and discursive. "Hamilton is the champion," he admitted to a friend. "He speaks frequently, very long, and very vehemently. He has, like Publius, much to say not very applicable to the subject."[89]

Hamilton's performance at the convention was an exhilarating blend of stamina, passion, and oratorical pyrotechnics. It was a lonely battle—"Our adversaries greatly outnumber us," he told Madison upon arriving—yet he showed unflagging courage as he stared down a large audience of hostile faces.[90] He spoke twenty-six times, far more than any other federalist, and soldiered on for six exhausting weeks. He must have operated on severely depleted reserves of energy. Since late October 1787 he had written fifty-one *Federalist* essays while juggling the considerable demands of his law practice.

Hamilton was implacable in his resolve to win against long odds. When a friend asked him what message he should convey to New York supporters, Hamilton retorted, "Tell them the convention shall never rise until the Constitution is adopted."[91] For spectators jammed into the courthouse galleries, Hamilton made an indelible impression. James Kent attended every session, later telling Eliza that her husband had been "prompt, ardent, energetic, and overflowing with an exuberance of argument and illustration. He generally spoke with much animation and energy and with considerable gesture." His mind was "filled with all the learning and precedents required for the occasion," enabling him to make numerous extemporaneous speeches.[92] He seduced the listeners with hope and provoked them with fear, leading one spectator to comment that "Hamilton's harangues combine the poignancy of vinegar with the smoothness of oil."[93]

During the first days at Poughkeepsie, Hamilton was constantly on his feet, reaching for high-flown eloquence. He denied that federalists exaggerated the weaknesses of the Articles of Confederation: "No, I believe these weaknesses to be real and pregnant with destruction. Yet, however weak our country may be, I hope we shall never sacrifice our liberties." He then cleverly disarmed opponents: "If therefore, on a full and candid discussion, the proposed system [the Constitution] shall appear to have that tendency, for God's sake, let us reject that!"[94]

On June 20, Hamilton made his first prolonged assault on opponents. Not relying on reason alone, he demonstrated how necessary it was for New York's security that it join the new union: "Your capital is accessible by land and by sea is exposed to every daring invader. And on the northwest, you are open to the inroads of a powerful foreign nation."[95] Under the new central government, he insisted, the tax burden would be shared much more evenly than before. He also reassured New Yorkers that state power would keep federal power in check. Hamilton spoke himself into a state of exhaustion and suddenly cut short his speech. "Many other observations might be made on this subject," he apologized, "but I cannot now pursue them, for I feel myself not a little exhausted. I beg leave therefore to waive for the present the further discussion of this question."[96]

The next day, Hamilton, buoyed by a second wind, disputed that the proposed House of Representatives, with sixty-five members, would have too few delegates and would be dominated by the rich. In his view, representative bodies did not need to mirror exactly those they represented; men of substance, wisdom, and experience could care for the common good. If they came more often from the wealthier, better-educated portion of the community, so be it. Hamilton did not think the rich were paragons of virtue. They had as many vices as the poor, he noted, except that their "vices are probably more favorable to the prosperity of the state than those of the indigent and partake less of moral depravity."[97] As creditors, they would acquire a special stake in perpetuating the new government, and their power would always be circumscribed by popular opinion. In "the general course of things, the popular views and even prejudices will direct the action of the rulers."[98]

That same day, Governor Clinton argued that the United States covered so vast a territory and possessed such a variety of peoples "that no general free government can suit" all the states.[99] In rebuttal, Hamilton outlined his vision of American nationalism, showing that a true nation, with a unified culture, had been fused from the diverse groups and regions of the original colonies. In all essential matters, "from New Hampshire to Georgia, the people of America are as uniform in their interests and manners as those of any established in Europe."[100] A national interest and a national culture now existed beyond state concerns. This was an assertion pregnant with significance, for if Americans already constituted a new political culture, they needed a new order to certify that reality. And the Constitution bodied forth that order.

For antifederalists who had traded whispered stories of Hamilton's infamous speech at the Constitutional Convention, he now sounded too reasonable, too plausible, as he spoke of the power of popular opinion. Clearly, he must be a brazen manipulator, a two-faced hypocrite, not someone making legitimate concessions for the sake of political compromise. "You would be surprised did you not know the man what an *amazing republican* Hamilton wishes to make himself be considered," Charles Tillinghast told another antifederalist caustically. "*But he is known.*"[101] The conviction that Hamilton must be dissembling became commonplace among his foes, who were bent upon unmasking the perfidious monarchist.

The proposed Senate was especially loathsome to Clintonians, who feared it would be an aristocratic conclave. They introduced an amendment allowing state legislatures to recall their senators. This idea touched a live wire in Hamilton, who saw the Senate as a check on fickle popular will and in need of political insulation. The proposal prompted him to make a speech on the dangers of maintaining a continuous revolutionary mentality in America. Hamilton believed that revolutions ended in tyranny because they glorified revolution as a permanent state of mind. A spirit of compromise and a concern with order were needed to balance the quest for liberty.

In the commencement of a revolution, which received its birth from the usurpations of tyranny, nothing was more natural than that the public mind should be influenced by an extreme spirit of jealousy. . . . The zeal for liberty became predominant and excessive. In forming our confederation, this passion alone seemed to actuate us and we appear to have had no other view than to secure ourselves from despotism. The object certainly was a valuable one and deserved our utmost attention. But, Sir, there is another object, equally important, and which our enthusiasm rendered us little capable of regarding. I mean a principle of strength and stability in the organization of our government and vigor in its operations.[102]

More than anyone else, Hamilton engineered the transition to a postwar political culture that valued sound and efficient government as the most reliable custodian of liberty. Calling such an effort "an object of all others the nearest and most dear to my own heart," he said that its attainment was "the most important study which can interest mankind."[103]

On the same day Hamilton said this, word arrived in Poughkeepsie that New Hampshire had become the ninth state to ratify the Constitution, meaning it would now be activated. This jolted the convention and abruptly transformed the debate from one about constitutional principles to the political expediency of New York's joining the union. The state now risked political estrangement if it stayed aloof. Nevertheless, the Clintonians continued to load crippling conditions on the Constitution, and Hamilton saw they would yield only if Virginia ratified. "We eagerly wait for further intelligence from you," he wrote urgently to Madison on June 27, "as our only chance of success depends on you."[104]

The next morning, all the pent-up emotions in Poughkeepsie gave way to rage. It grated on Hamilton that the Clintonians would enter the new union only under duress, while it galled the Clintonians that the national tide was now running against them. Hamilton made a superb speech about the powers that would be reserved to the states under the Constitution, showing, for instance, how the federal government could not make laws affecting the punishment of certain crimes, such as murder and theft. This was too much for John Lansing, Jr., Hamilton's fellow delegate at the Constitutional Convention, who accused him of saying one thing in Philadelphia and another in Poughkeepsie. In particular, he charged that Hamilton had argued earlier for abolishing the very states that he now held up as necessary foils to federal power.

This accusation produced a vivid confrontation. New York's entire delegation from the Constitutional Convention—Hamilton, Lansing, and Yates—dropped all show of decorum and began to denounce each other heatedly. *The Daily Advertiser*

reported that Hamilton described "Mr. Lansing's insinuation as improper, unbecoming, and uncandid. Mr. Lansing rose and with much spirit resented the imputation. He made an appeal to Judge Yates, who had taken notes in the Federal
Convention for a proof of Mr. Hamilton's expressions." Hamilton must have been
flabbergasted: Lansing was inviting Yates to breach the solemn oath of silence taken
at Philadelphia. On cue, Robert Yates flashed his notes and quoted Hamilton as
having stated in Philadelphia that to stop the states from encroaching on the federal
government, "they should be reduced to a smaller scale and be invested with only
corporate power."[105] At this point, Hamilton turned furiously on Yates and cross-
examined him in prosecutorial style. He asked point-blank: Did Yates not remember Hamilton saying that the states were useful and necessary? Did he not remember
him saying that the chief judges of the states ought to join with the chief justice of
the Supreme Court in a court of impeachments? Yates assented reluctantly.

Governor Clinton, realizing that he had to stop the quarreling, adjourned the
session. All of New York gossiped about the highly personalized altercation. One
member of Judge Yates's family reported that both Lansing and Hamilton "got extremely warm—insomuch that Lansing was charged by the other with want of candor and indecency."[106] Still another observer noted that bickering between Lansing
and Hamilton had shaded over from spirited repartee to such personal insults that
a duel might follow: "Personal reflections were thrown out by Mr. Lansing against
Mr. Hamilton, which were productive of serious disputation. It will be well if it
does not terminate seriously."[107] Two days later, the convention still seethed about
the matter.

As Hamilton tangled with Lansing, neither knew that Virginia had on June 25
become the tenth state to ratify the Constitution. Like their New York counterparts,
antifederalists there posed as plucky populists, even though their ranks included
many rich slaveholders. Patrick Henry, the leading antifederalist, warned delegates
who supported the Constitution, "They'll free your niggers."[108] George Washington
noted the hypocrisy of the many slaveholding antifederalists: "It is a little strange
that the men of large property in the South should be more afraid that the Constitution will produce an aristocracy or a monarchy than the genuine, democratical
people of the East."[109]

Shortly after noon on July 2, a rider rode up to the Poughkeepsie courthouse and
handed the doorkeeper a dispatch for Hamilton. Soon an excited murmur arose
that drowned out the voice of George Clinton. Hamilton read aloud a letter from
Madison with the dramatic announcement of Virginia's approval. It must have
been a deeply moving moment for Hamilton, the climax of his partnership with
Madison. Joyous federalists spilled out of the building and circled the courthouse in
celebration, accompanied by a fife and drum. If New York did not ratify the Con-

stitution, it would now be stranded and excluded from the newly formed union, lumped together with the outcast states of North Carolina and Rhode Island.

But the sparring now only intensified. At a Fourth of July parade in Albany, a riot broke out when a copy of the Constitution was publicly burned and federalist and antifederalist contingents collided, leaving one dead and eighteen wounded. Suddenly on the defensive, Clinton's forces tried to defeat the Constitution by demanding a bill of rights and other amendments. Hamilton thought this a tactical maneuver, and on July 12 he spoke at length in favor of unconditional adoption. In what one newspaper called "a most argumentative and impassioned address," Hamilton insisted that the convention lacked authority to make recommendations and gravely intoned that the delegates should "weigh well what they were about to do before they decided on a subject so infinitely important."[110]

Thus, in mid-July, the two sides remained unalterably apart. The point is worth stressing, since some historians have minimized Hamilton's bravura performance at Poughkeepsie by claiming that only approval by Virginia and New Hampshire tipped the scales in New York. Emotions, however, remained venomous even *after* ten states ratified the Constitution, and Governor Clinton still thought civil war possible. One member of the French diplomatic legation, Victor du Pont, wrote to Samuel du Pont de Nemours that if the Constitution faltered in New York, outraged federalists might pounce on Clinton and his retinue when they returned home and "smear them with tar, roll them in feathers, and finally walk them through the streets."[111] On July 17, Hamilton predicted that New York City might secede from the state if the Constitution was turned down; Clinton chided him from his chair for his "highly indiscreet and improper" warning.[112] Working himself up into a grand state of pathos, Hamilton summoned the ghosts of "departed patriots" and living heroes and with his words wrung tears from onlookers.[113]

Days later, Melancton Smith finally broke the deadlock when he endorsed the Constitution if Congress would promise to consider some amendments. Paying indirect tribute to Hamilton, Smith credited "the reasonings of gentlemen" on the other side for his changed vote.[114] On July 26, Smith and a dozen other antifederalists switched their votes to favor the Constitution, producing a wafer-thin majority. The final vote of thirty to twenty-seven was the smallest victory margin at any state convention and portended future political troubles for Hamilton. Governor Clinton would not budge but tolerated followers who changed their votes. Anticipating New York's approval, a huge rally had taken place in New York City three days earlier to express boisterous enthusiasm for the new government. It started at eight in the morning in light rain as five thousand representatives of sixty trades—from wig makers to bricklayers, florists to cabinetmakers—marched down Broadway amid a profusion of brightly colored floats and banners. The Constitution might be denounced as a rich man's plot upstate, but the city's artisans were now stouthearted federalists and crafted displays to illustrate the benefits that would flow from union. The bakers hoisted aloft a ten-foot "federal loaf," brewers pulled a three-hundred-gallon cask of ale, and coopers hauled barrels built with thirteen staves. Many of Hamilton's friends joined the crowd. Robert Troup marched alongside lawyers and judges, brandishing the new Constitution. Nicholas Cruger, his old employer from St. Croix, donned a farmer's costume and escorted a plow drawn by six oxen.

The parade apotheosized the hero of the hour, the man who had snatched victory from the antifederalist majority. So exuberant was the lionization of Alexander Hamilton that admirers wanted to rechristen the city "Hamiltoniana." It was one of the few times in his life that Hamilton basked in the warmth of public adulation. Sail makers waved a flag depicting a laurel-wreathed Hamilton bearing the Constitution while an allegorical figure representing Fame blew a trumpet in the air. This paled before the grandest tribute of all to Hamilton. Gliding down Broadway, pulled by ten horses, was a miniature frigate, twenty-seven feet long, baptized the "Federal Ship *Hamilton.*" The model ship rose above all other floats "with flowing sheets and full sails[,] . . . the canvas waves dashing against her sides" and concealing the carriage wheels moving the ship, noted one observer.[115] The cart men fluttered banners that proclaimed, "Behold the federal ship of fame / The Hamilton we call her name; / To every craft she gives employ; / Sure cartmen have their share of joy."[116] When the *Hamilton* arrived near the Battery, it was received by congressmen standing outside Bayard's Tavern. To represent the transition from the Articles of Confederation to the Constitution, the ship changed pilots amid a deafening cannonade. The parade marked the zenith of the federalist alliance with city artisans. Hamilton had never courted the masses, and never again was he to enjoy their favor to this extent. Riding high on the crest of the new Constitution, Hamilton and the federalists held undisputed sway in the city.

FOURTEEN

PUTTING THE MACHINE
IN MOTION

T he battle royal over the Constitution exposed such glaring rifts in the country that America needed a first president of unimpeachable integrity who
would embody the rich promise of the new republic. It had to be somebody of godlike stature who would seem to levitate above partisan politics, a symbol of national unity as well as a functioning chief executive. Everybody knew that
George Washington alone could manage the paradoxical feat of being a politician
above politics. Many people had agreed reluctantly to the new Constitution only
because they assumed that Washington would lead the first government.

Within weeks of the Poughkeepsie convention, Hamilton began to woo Washington for the presidency as determinedly as would a lover. Long ago, he had
hitched his career to the general's, and he needed George Washington as president
no less than America did. They had shared the same chagrin over the inept Congress and grasping state politicians and saw an assertive central government as the
indispensable corrective. In mid-August 1788, Hamilton broached the subject of
the presidency when he sent Washington the two-volume set of *The Federalist Papers*. He no longer had compunctions about revealing his authorship with Madison
and Jay. This was throat clearing for the letter's real intent: "I take it for granted, Sir,
you have concluded to comply with what will no doubt be the general call of your
country in relation to the new government. You will permit me to say that it is indispensable you should lend yourself to its first operations. It is to little purpose to
have *introduced* a system, if the weightiest influence is not given to its firm *establishment* in the outset."[1]

Washington replied that he had seen no better gloss on the Constitution than
The Federalist and predicted that "when the transient circumstances and fugitive

performance which attended this *crisis* shall have disappeared, that work will merit the notice of posterity." This tribute previewed things to come, since the first president would need constitutional experts in his cabinet to advise him on what actions were permissible. Washington approached the presidency gingerly. In the late eighteenth century, politicians tended to disclaim ambition and pretend that public service was purely sacrificial. So Washington closed the letter with a delicate statement that he would defer a decision on the presidency, intimating that he would rather stay at Mount Vernon: "For you know me well enough, my good Sir, to be persuaded that I am not guilty of affectation when I tell you it is my great and sole desire to live and die, in peace and retirement, on my own farm."[2]

Not since the Revolution had Washington and Hamilton spoken so candidly. Their bond, if sorely tested, had never frayed, and Washington seemed relieved to unburden himself about his future. Hamilton knew that the new republic would be on trial in the first administration, and he dreaded having a mediocrity at the top. If the first government miscarried, he warned Washington, "the blame will in all probability be laid on the system itself. And the framers of it will have to encounter the disrepute of having brought about a revolution in government without substituting anything that was worthy of the effort. They pulled down one Utopia, it will be said, to build up another."[3]

Far from bristling, Washington thanked Hamilton for his openness, which enabled him to assess the presidency without betraying unseemly ambition. In a confessional mode, Washington said that at the thought of being president he "always felt a kind of gloom" settle upon his mind and noted that if he became president, "the acceptance would be attended with more diffidence and reluctance than ever I experienced before in my life."[4] Sensing Washington's need for gentle prodding, Hamilton stressed that America's glorious destiny demanded him as president and that "no other man can sufficiently unite the public opinion or can give the requisite weight to the office in the commencement of the government."[5] Hearing this from others as well, Washington finally overcame his misgivings and agreed to stand for president.

While Hamilton endeared himself to Washington in this first election, he also antagonized John Adams, a man with an encyclopedic memory for slights. Returning from Europe in June 1788, Adams decided that any post less than vice president was "beneath himself," as wife Abigail phrased it.[6] As a favorite son of the New England states, with their hefty bloc of votes, Adams agreed to run for vice president. This created a ticklish predicament. Under the Constitution, the presidential electors cast two votes apiece, but they did not vote separately for president and vice president. Whoever garnered the most electoral votes became president and the runner-up vice president. The peril was manifest: there could be a tie vote, forcing the contest into the House of Representatives. Still worse, a vice presidential candidate might accidentally walk off with the presidency. "Everybody is aware of that defect in the constitution, which renders it possible the man intended for vice president may, in fact, turn up president," Hamilton told Pennsylvania federalist James Wilson in early 1789. If Adams received a unanimous vote and a few votes were "insidiously withheld" from Washington, Hamilton said, Adams might edge out Washington for the presidency.[7] Hamilton doubted that the sometimes irascible Adams could unite a divided country or give the new government its best chance of success. For Hamilton, the whole American experiment hinged upon having Washington as president. His worries were only compounded by the improbable presidential candidacy of George Clinton. As Hamilton maneuvered to wean electors away from Clinton, he feared they might turn to Adams instead of Washington. If so, Hamilton brooded, he might inadvertently help to defeat the one man he so desperately wanted as president.

In the fall of 1788, Hamilton and Adams had no personal relationship. Hamilton had become a major domestic figure during Adams's long diplomatic sojourn abroad. Adams knew of Hamilton's superlative reputation as a lawyer, but he would naturally have considered the younger man an upstart, a latecomer to the American Revolution. Hamilton, for his part, already felt ambivalent toward Adams. He could recall vividly the sympathy of the Massachusetts Adamses and the Virginia Lees with the nebulous Conway Cabal, which had encouraged the military pretensions of General Horatio Gates to supplant Washington. Hamilton told one Massachusetts ally, "The Lees and Adams[es] have been in the habit of uniting and hence may spring up a cabal very embarrassing to the executive and of course to the administration of the government."[8] At the same time, Hamilton credited Adams's indisputable patriotism, his "sound understanding," and his "ardent love for the public good," and he was certain he would not "disturb the harmony" of a Washington administration.[9] Hamilton confided to Madison that Adams was a trustworthy friend of the Constitution and as vice president would provide geographic balance with a Virginia president.

Nonetheless, Hamilton fretted that whether by chance or design Adams might sneak past Washington in the voting. So he approached two electors in Connecticut, two in New Jersey, and three or four in Pennsylvania and asked them to deny their votes to Adams to insure that Washington became president. As usual, Hamilton proved excessively fearful. When the sixty-nine electors met on February 4, 1789, they voted unanimously for Washington, who became the first president, and cast only thirty-four ballots for Adams, who came in second and thus became vice president. (The remaining thirty-five votes were split among ten candidates.) This relatively weak showing dealt a blow to the vanity of John Adams, who bemoaned it as a "stain" upon his character and even thought of declining the office out of wounded pride.[10] At this juncture, he did not know of Hamilton's efforts to deny him a handful of votes. When he learned of a "dark and dirty intrigue," apparently originating in New York, to deprive him of votes, he was incensed. "Is not my election to this office, in the scurvy manner in which it was done, a curse rather than a blessing?" he protested to Benjamin Rush.[11] Adams came to view Hamilton's actions as unforgivably duplicitous.

In fact, Hamilton had approached only seven or eight electors, so that his actions could have accounted for just a small fraction of Adams's thirty-five-vote deficit. And Hamilton had been motivated by a laudable desire to help Washington, not to harm Adams, whom he favored for vice president. Hamilton was thunderstruck when he learned that Adams had misread his actions as a calculated effort to humiliate him and lessen his public stature. Years later, he portrayed the episode as proof of Adams's "extreme egotism" and vanity: "Great was my astonishment and equally great my regret when afterwards I learned . . . that Mr. Adams had complained of unfair treatment in not having been permitted to take an equal chance with General Washington."[12] It was the first of many hurtful misunderstandings between these two giants of the early republic.

The true target of Hamilton's venom was Governor George Clinton, who had been in office for twelve years and ran again in the spring of 1789. Clinton had advocated the rotation of presidents in office but had no misgivings about converting the New York governorship into his personal fiefdom. Hamilton feared that Clinton would try to undermine the new government. Having waged a vigorous campaign to deny him the presidency, Hamilton now attempted to oust him as governor. Massachusetts federalist Samuel Otis informed a friend that Hamilton and Philip Schuyler planned to do everything in their power "to kill the governor politically."[13]

On February 11, 1789, Hamilton chaired an overflowing meeting at Bardin's Tavern on Broad Street, a business haunt, to anoint a candidate to challenge Clinton. The hundreds who showed up opted for a surprise choice: Judge Robert Yates. It was dramatic proof of Hamilton's resolve to unseat Clinton that he endorsed this erstwhile foe, whom he thought capable of assembling a winning coalition of downstate federalists and upstate antifederalist farmers. Yates had impressed him by his unswerving support for the Constitution once it was ratified in New York. Hamilton agreed to chair a correspondence committee to foster support for him. One of Yates's dearest friends, the antifederalist Aaron Burr, showed up at Bardin's Tavern and consented to join the group.

Once Hamilton had latched on to Yates, he was determined to strike hard at Clinton in the slashing style that was fast becoming his trademark—a combativeness that may well have been a legacy of his troubled upbringing. He advised one supporter, "In politics, as in war, the first blow is half the battle."[14] In customary fashion, Hamilton opened his campaign with a blistering series of sixteen anonymous letters printed in *The Daily Advertiser* under the initials "H. G." Like his *Federalist* essays, Hamilton wrote these letters in a titanic burst of energy, eight of them appearing in consecutive issues at the end of February 1789 alone.

Starting with the first "H. G." essay, Hamilton flung poisoned darts at Clinton. Reviewing the governor's political and military career, Hamilton accused him of "narrow views, a prejudiced and contracted disposition, a passionate and interested temper."[15] He questioned Clinton's bravery as a brigadier general during the Revolution: "After diligent enquiry, I have not been able to learn that he was ever more than once in actual combat."[16] In one letter, Hamilton differentiated between two types drawn to revolutions: those sincerely interested in the public good and "restless and turbulent spirits," such as Clinton, who sought to exploit unrest to become despots.[17] Upping the stakes, Hamilton accused Clinton of having stolen from Philip Schuyler the first governor's race, which was held during the Revolution, by forcing militiamen under his command to vote for him.

In later "H. G." letters, Hamilton occupied higher moral ground. He analyzed Clinton's unremitting opposition to the Constitution and found it unpardonable that the governor had maintained a course "replete with danger to the peace and welfare of this state and of the Union."[18] Hamilton wanted New York to continue as the nation's capital, as it had been since January 1785. He noted that Clinton had opposed it as the residence for Congress because he was afraid this would encourage dissolute behavior: "Every man of sense knows that the residence of Congress among us has been a considerable source of wealth to the state. And as to the idle tale of its promoting luxury and dissipation, I believe there has not been for a number of years past a period of greater frugality than that in which Congress have resided in this city."[19] More than just petty, power hungry, and stubborn, Clinton was cast by Hamilton as a boor devoid of good manners who had not even paid courtesy calls on the last two presidents of the Confederation Congress.

The federalists were overjoyed by these resounding blasts. "Never was anything read with more avidity and with greater success," wrote one Hamilton supporter.[20] Said another: "*Col. H*[amilton] has taken a very active part in favour of Judges Yates, from which circumstance much is expected. I believe old Clinton the *sinner* will get *ousted.*"[21] The old sinner did not rebut Hamilton with his own quill, preferring surrogates, and rejoinders soon glutted the press. In early March, one "Philopas" protested "the torrent of scurrility" from "H. G.".'s pen, which "would make an inhabitant of Billingsgate blush."[22] Another writer said the real issue in the election was that "an obscure *Plebeian*"—Clinton—had dared to oppose "the boundless ambition of *Patrician* families": the Schuylers.[23] If Yates beat Clinton, he predicted, he would be thrust aside at the next election so that the "F[athe]r and the S[o]n" could divide the fishes and loaves—a transparent reference to Philip Schuyler and his son-in-law Hamilton.[24] By making cutting personal remarks about Clinton, Hamilton had ensured that the retaliation would also be highly personal. That Hamilton could be so sensitive to criticisms of himself and so insensitive to the effect his words had on others was a central mystery of his psyche.

The invective grew uglier in late March when someone writing under "William Tell" branded Hamilton a Machiavellian and tarred him as a power-mad politician puffed up "by an expecting band of sycophants, a train of ambitious relations, and a few rich men." "William Tell" then leveled a charge against Hamilton more terrible than mere ambition: "Your private character is still worse than your public one and it will yet be exposed by your own works, for [you] will not be bound by the *most solemn of all obligations!********"[25] The seven asterisks must have signified the word *wedlock,* meaning that Hamilton was being charged, for the first time in print, with adultery. As we shall see, there was a reason why this charge surfaced at this time.

Like other founding fathers, Hamilton inhabited two diametrically opposed worlds. There was the Olympian sphere of constitutional debate and dignified discourse—the way many prefer to remember these stately figures—and the gutter world of personal sniping, furtive machinations, and tabloid-style press attacks. The contentious culture of these early years was both the apex and the nadir of American political expression. Such a contradictory environment was probably an inescapable part of the transition from the lofty idealism of Revolution to the gritty realities of quotidian politics. The heroes of 1776 and 1787 were bound to seem smaller and more hypocritical as they jockeyed for personal power and advantage in the new government.

For the remainder of the gubernatorial campaign, Hamilton issued open letters to the electorate, and at Clinton campaign rallies his essays were hurled under the table as marks of contempt. In shaping his final appeal to voters, Hamilton said that Clinton's most effective tactic was to single out the rich for abuse, and he warned that republicans scapegoated the rich to their detriment: "There is no stronger sign of combinations unfriendly to the general good than when the partisans of those in power raise an indiscriminate cry against men of property."[26]

The argument did not persuade voters: Governor Clinton solidly defeated Judge Yates. This vicious election left a trail of wounded feelings, removing any chance of a rapprochement between Hamilton and Clinton. New York remained a bitterly divided state, ripe for political manipulation. The wily Clinton knew that he had to shore up his base, so in September he offered the state attorney-general job to

Aaron Burr, whom he neither liked nor trusted. For the first time, Hamilton felt betrayed by Burr, who had campaigned for Yates. The political genius of Aaron Burr was to lie in figuring out endless ways to profit from the partisan wrangling in his home state. For three years, he had engaged in little political activity. Now his dormant ambition was beginning to awaken.

The new government was launched with all due pageantry and fanfare. On April 16, 1789, George Washington departed from Mount Vernon on an eight-day journey to New York that blossomed into a national celebration. Cannon saluted the president-elect as he approached each town. He passed under many triumphal arches and crossed a bridge in Trenton covered with flower petals strewn by thirteen young maidens cooing greetings. If this sometimes seemed like a royal procession, appearances could be misleading. Washington had fallen into debt and had to borrow heavily at exorbitant interest rates to make the trip. When he reached Elizabethtown, New Jersey, he boarded a sumptuous barge that transported him across the Hudson River to New York City. Shaded by a red canopy and tossed by brisk breezes, the barge was towed by thirteen pilots. At the foot of Wall Street, Governor Clinton and Mayor Duane welcomed the president-elect before masses of cheering people. Church bells chimed, ships in the harbor ran up their colors, and cannon fired a thirteen-gun salute before Washington made his way to his new residence, a three-story brick building at 10 Cherry Street. That night, with candles aglow in windows across the city, Governor Clinton hosted a state dinner for Washington. Hamilton smarted over the deference shown to the governor, but Washington wished to convey that he would be the leader of all the people.

Selected as temporary home of the new federal government, New York had devoted considerable expense to preparations. Hoping to become the permanent capital, the city had invested in some necessary improvements. The Common Council hired Major Pierre Charles L'Enfant, the French architect and engineer who was to later design Washington, D.C., to renovate City Hall at the corner of Broad and Wall. He transformed it into the elegant, neoclassical Federal Hall, surmounted by a glass cupola. Some money for the alterations came from local citizens and some from Hamilton's Bank of New York. When the new Congress first met there in early April, the flag from the "Federal Ship *Hamilton*" waved over the building, which had a depiction of an American eagle embedded in its facade.

On April 30, George Washington rose early, sprinkled powder on his hair, and prepared for his great day. At noon, accompanied by a legislative escort, he rode to Federal Hall in a fancy yellow carriage to take the oath of office. Ten thousand ecstatic New Yorkers squeezed into the surrounding streets to observe the historic moment. Hamilton, who had done as much as anyone to bring it about, looked on distantly from the balcony of his Wall Street home. From the outset, the fifty-seven-year-old Washington was determined to strike a happy medium between regal dignity and republican austerity. Resplendent with a ceremonial sword at his side, he also wore a plain brown suit of American broadcloth woven at a mill in Hartford. A special message for Hamilton's future was encoded in this outfit: that America should encourage manufactures, especially textiles, an industry dominated by Great Britain. Washington hoped it would soon "be unfashionable for a gentleman to appear" in any dress that was not of American origin.[27]

The strapping Virginian took the oath on the second-story balcony, flanked by columns against a backdrop of gold stars on a blue background. With John Adams standing beside him, Washington was sworn in by Chancellor Robert R. Livingston and then kissed the Bible brought on a crimson cushion. The moment was joyous but not flawless. When Washington read a brief inaugural address, probably drafted by James Madison, to Congress in the Senate chamber, he kept his left hand in one pocket and turned pages with the other, making an awkward impression. His nervous mumbling was scarcely audible. One observer said wryly of America's hero, Washington was more "agitated and embarrassed than ever he was by the leveled cannon or pointed musket."[28] Afterward, the first president and his entourage marched up Broadway to pray at St. Paul's Chapel, near where Hamilton had attended King's College.

Both Alexander and Eliza attended the first inaugural ball on May 7. Eliza was well placed to be a social ornament of the new regime and later looked back fondly on those days.

> As I was younger than [Martha Washington] I mingled more in the gaieties of the day. I was at the inauguration ball—the most brilliant of them all—which was given early in May at the Assembly Rooms on Broadway above Wall Street. It was attended by the President and Vice President, the cabinet officers, a majority of the members of the Congress, the French and Spanish Ministers, and military and civic officers, with their wives and daughters. Mrs. Washington had not yet arrived in New York from Mount Vernon and did not until three weeks later. On that occasion, every woman who attended the ball was presented with a fan prepared in Paris, with ivory frame, and when opened displayed a likeness of Washington in profile.[29]

As a close friend of Philip Schuyler and Hamilton, Washington enjoyed a warm rapport with Eliza and danced with her at the inaugural ball. Like Alexander, she was cordial with Washington but not too familiar, and she noted that even on the dance floor he never entirely relaxed or stopped being president. Present at many balls with Washington, she later described how "he would always choose a partner and walk through the figures correctly, but he never danced. His favorite was the minuet, a graceful dance, suited to his dignity and gravity."[30] This tallies with one observer's comment that Washington seldom laughed and that even when encircled by young belles his countenance "never softened nor changed its habitual gravity."[31]

Everything about Washington's administration assumed heightened importance, since he was setting precedents and establishing the tone of government. No sooner was he sworn in than questions of protocol provoked hairsplitting debates. How should a president be addressed? Should he receive visitors? Since many antifederalists were convinced that Hamilton and his circle meditated a monarchy, they followed such debates avidly for signs of incipient treachery. Though Hamilton opposed noble titles, he wondered what would substitute for courtly forms to inspire reverence for law. Other founders labored under a similar apprehension. In May 1789, Ben Franklin told Benjamin Rush, "We have been guarding against an evil that old states are most liable to, excess of power in the rulers. But our present danger seems to be defect of obedience in the subjects."[32]

The new vice president, John Adams, adopted an especially princely style that outraged republicans, and he was even mocked by Washington for his "ostentatious imitation [and] mimicry of royalty."[33] The Adamses rented the enchanting mansion known as Richmond Hill, which had splendid Hudson River views and was later home to Aaron Burr. Each morning, John Adams climbed into a costly coach, driven by a liveried servant, then presided over the Senate in a powdered wig. (He was often accompanied by his second son, Charles, just down from Harvard. Still unaware that Hamilton had worked to pare his electoral votes, Adams asked in July if Charles could study law with him; Hamilton accepted this flattering request.) In May, when a Senate committee took up the explosive issue of titles, Adams suggested that Washington be addressed as "His Highness, the President of the United States of America and Protector of their Liberties."[34] Adams provided fodder for contemporary wags and was promptly dubbed "His Rotundity" or the "Duke of Braintree." Adams wanted only to inspire respect for the new government, but his concern for decorum bred a belief in suspicious minds that he sought a hereditary monarch, with himself as king and son John Quincy groomed as his dauphin. In a slap at the Senate, the House of Representatives decided that the chief executive was to be referred to simply as "George Washington, President of the United States," and the Senate then concurred.

In early May, Washington asked Hamilton for his reflections on presidential etiquette. Like Adams, Hamilton thought the dignity of the office essential and recommended that Washington receive visitors at weekly "levees" but not stay longer than a half hour and never return visits. He thought private dinners with legislators and other officials should be limited to six or eight visitors and that the president should not linger at the table. In a revealing suggestion, he also advised Washington to be available to senators but not congressmen. Clearly, Hamilton wanted a president invested with a touch of grandeur and buffered from popular pressure.

Washington generally took Hamilton's advice, holding levees on Tuesday afternoons that proved exercises in tedium. Even at the best of times, Washington was not a blithe presence, and the strict reception rules hardened him into a waxwork. He materialized in a black velvet coat, yellow gloves, and black satin breeches, with a dress sword hanging in a scabbard. Then he circulated among guests with glacial slowness, bowing but not shaking hands, exchanging pleasantries with each. Guests must have stifled yawns and fought off drowsiness. Bewigged footmen stood by at lavish dinners that couldn't have been fun either. "The president seemed to bear in his countenance a settled aspect of melancholy," Senator William Maclay of Pennsylvania wrote of one occasion. "No cheering ray of convivial sunshine broke through the cloudy gloom of settled seriousness. At every interval of eating and drinking, he played on the table with a fork and knife, like a drumstick."[35] Both as a matter of temperament and policy, Washington was taciturn, once advising his adopted grandson, "It is best to be silent, for there is nothing more certain than that it is at all times more easy to make enemies than friends."[36] Such a circumspect president formed a striking contrast with the loquacious Hamilton.

Washington tried to be neither too lofty nor too casual and, according to Abigail Adams, succeeded admirably that spring: "He is polite with dignity, affable without formality, distant without haughtiness, grave without austerity, modest, wise, and good."[37] Still, antifederalists spied royal trappings galore, small but menacing concessions that portended a monarchy. When Washington rode out on public occasions, through unpaved streets teeming with wandering pigs, he often traveled in a buff-colored coach with two liveried postilions to guide him. The coach was pulled by six white horses that had been rubbed with lustrous white paste; their coats were brushed till they veritably gleamed in the dark. At the same time, to certify his republican credentials, Washington took daily walks at two o'clock each afternoon. To modern eyes, the most incongruous fact of all was that Washington had seven slaves shipped up from Mount Vernon to assist his white household servants.

There might have been less hand-wringing over social distinctions had it not been for an obvious and widening gap between the rich and poor in New York. After years of wartime austerity, local merchants flaunted their wealth. Brissot de Warville observed, "If there is a town on the American continent where the English luxury displays its follies, it is New York. . . . In the dress of the women, you will see the most brilliant silks, gauzes, hats, and borrowed hair. Equipages are rare but they are elegant."[38] Men of social distinction strode about in velvet coats and ruffled shirts, aping European nobility. For republicans afraid that the country would slip back into aristocratic ways, such foppery smacked of Old World decadence. They worried that if the capital stayed in New York, American innocence would be undone by urban hedonism. Many legislators led confined, threadbare lives and did not partake of the extravagance. Ralph Izard complained that the poorly paid senators were forced into "boardinghouses, lodged in holes and corners, associated with improper company, and conversed improperly so as to lower their dignity and character"—a situation that could only have heightened their resentment toward New York.[39]

Hamilton kept vigilant watch on the new Congress, aware that its early decisions were to affect profoundly American finance and the evolving structure of the executive and judiciary branches. Although scheduled to start in early March, the House and Senate took more than a month to muster quorums. In a significant piece of symbolism, the House met on the ground floor of Federal Hall and provided open galleries for visitors. At the inaugural session on April 1, 1789, Hamilton milled about among the onlookers. James Kent recalled, "Col. Hamilton remarked to me that as nothing was to be done the first day, such impatient crowds were evidence of the powerful principle of curiosity."[40] Meanwhile, the secretive Senate met upstairs in a chamber without a spectator section. For the first five years, senators conducted their business behind closed doors.

The Constitution had kept a tactful silence about the executive departments of government and made no mention of a cabinet. For months after his inauguration, George Washington *was* the executive branch. The administration was still a nebulous concept, not a tangible reality. Madison lamented, "We are in a wilderness without a single footstep to guide us."[41] The financial state of the new government was especially precarious. The United States had already suspended interest payments on much of its foreign and domestic debt, and American bonds continued to trade at steep discounts on European exchanges, suggesting little faith in the new government's ability to repay them. If this situation persisted, the government would have to pay extortionate interest rates to appease jittery creditors.

Despite shrieking vendors, tinkling cowbells, and rumbling carts on Wall Street that often drowned out speakers inside Federal Hall, the new government slowly took shape during the summer and early fall. In the House, James Madison helped to compress dozens of changes to the Constitution recommended by the state conventions into twelve amendments; the first ten, when ratified by the states, would be known as the Bill of Rights. And in the Senate, Oliver Ellsworth took the lead in drafting a judiciary act that provided for a six-member Supreme Court, buttressed by federal district and circuit courts. On May 19, Representative Elias Boudinot of New Jersey, Hamilton's old patron from Elizabethtown, proposed that Congress establish a department of finance. From the clamor that arose over what would become the Treasury Department, it was clear this would be the real flash point of controversy in the new government, the place where critics feared that European-style despotism could take root. Legislators recalled that British tax abuses had spawned the Revolution and that chancellors of the exchequer had directed huge armies of customs collectors to levy onerous duties. To guard against such concentrated power, Elbridge Gerry wanted to invest the Treasury leadership in a board, not an individual. It was Madison who insisted that a single secretary, equipped with all necessary powers, should superintend the department.

A tremendous hubbub accompanied the act outlining the treasury secretary's duties, including his need to report to Congress on matters in his bailiwick. Opponents did not see this duty as a welcome form of congressional oversight that would subject the secretary to the bright glare of scrutiny. Mindful of British precedent, they feared it would open the door to executive tampering with legislative affairs— a charge that was, in fact, to hound Hamilton throughout his tenure.

The spring of 1789 was a gratifying time for the patriotic Schuylers. Leaving behind her husband and four children, Angelica Church sailed from England and arrived in time to witness Washington's inauguration. She missed home terribly and was concerned about her gout-ridden father. Most of all, she yearned for the company of Alexander and Eliza. Hamilton remained smitten with his sister-in-law, never missing a chance to flatter or tease her with some arch message. With Angelica, he reverted to the high-spirited, chivalric young man. "I seldom write to a lady without fancying the relation of lover and mistress," he had told her after knocking off *Federalist* number 17. "It has a very inspiring effect. And in your case, the dullest materials could not help feeling that propensity."[42]

John Barker Church's political ambitions had subjected Angelica to a peculiarly uncomfortable fate: this daughter of an American general was about to become the wife of a member of the British Parliament. Trying to make the best of the situation, Angelica told Hamilton that she would happily have her husband in the House of Commons "if he possessed your eloquence."[43] Hamilton replied that he would rather have seen his brother-in-law elected to the new American Congress. Nevertheless, Church became an M.P. from Wendover Borough in 1790. At Down Place, their estate near Windsor Castle, the Churches surrounded themselves with luminous personalities from the literary, artistic, and political worlds. A visiting American cousin found the fashionable Angelica "an angel, all affectionate politeness towards a cousin who trudges out to her country seat on foot."[44] The Churches inhabited a social world in which excessive drinking, compulsive gambling, and discreet adultery were routine. At the center of their circle stood the Prince of Wales, later King George IV, who adored Angelica, and Charles James Fox, the Whig leader, who shared John Church's gambling passion and often borrowed immense sums from him to feed his habit. The Churches also kept a private box at the Drury Lane Theater and befriended the spendthrift playwright Richard Brinsley Sheridan, author of *The School for Scandal,* who once refused to satisfy his creditors on the grounds that "paying only encourages them."[45] The Churches also grew close to the American artist John Trumbull, lending him money so that he could study with Benjamin West in England and Jacques-Louis David in France.

For all the glamorous settings, Angelica was often lonely and melancholy in her European exile. In one later plaintive letter to Eliza, she described going to the theater and beholding the royal family there, then added, "What are Kings and Queens to an American who has seen a Washington!"[46] She went on to tell her sister: "I envy you the trio of agreeable men. You talk of my father and my Baron [von Steuben] and your Hamilton. What pleasant evenings, what agreeable chitchat, whilst my society must be confined to chill, gloomy Englishmen."[47] In another letter, heavy with homeward longing, Angelica wrote, "Adieu, my dear Eliza. Be happy and be gay and remember me in your mirth as one who deserves and wishes to partake of your happiness. Embrace Hamilton and the Baron."[48]

It may be more than coincidental that the first scandalous reference to Hamilton's marital infidelity occurred in late March 1789 just as Angelica Church returned to New York. The town was humming with social events marking the new government, and the mutual admiration between Hamilton and his sister-in-law, apparent at parties and dinners they attended, must have excited speculation. At one ball, Angelica dropped a garter that was swept gallantly off the floor by Hamilton. Angelica, who had a sly wit, teased him that he wasn't a Knight of the Garter. Angelica's sarcastic sister, Peggy, then remarked, "He would be a Knight of the Bedchamber, if he could."[49] This may all have been harmless banter, but such tales fed material to the local gossips.

Angelica stayed in New York till November, when she received a letter from John Church that some of their children had fallen sick. She promptly booked passage back to England. Whatever did—or did not—happen between Alexander and Angelica during her long stay in New York, Eliza was so distraught by her beloved sister's departure that she could not bear to see her off; she was consoled with difficulty by, among others, Baron von Steuben. Hamilton, his eldest son, Philip, and the baron escorted Angelica to the Battery and wistfully watched her vessel disappear from the harbor. The men gave way to extravagant emotions. "Imagine what we felt," Hamilton wrote to Angelica of this parting scene. "We gazed, we sighed, we *wept.*"[50] Even Steuben, hardened old warrior that he was, stood with tears brimming in his eyes. "Amiable Angelica!" Hamilton concluded. "How much you are formed to endear yourself to every good heart. . . . *Some* of us are and must continue inconsolable for your absence."[51] Alexander and Eliza seemed united, not divided, by their shared adoration of Angelica. "Betsey and myself make you the last theme of our conversation at night and the first in the morning," Hamilton told her.[52] Those gossips whose tongues wagged over the seeming flirtation of Alexander and Angelica might have been surprised to see Eliza's tender farewell note to her sister:

My very dear beloved Angelica: I have seated myself to write to you, but my heart is so saddened by your absence that it can scarcely dictate, my eyes so filled with tears that I shall not be able to write you much. But *remember, remember,* my dear sister, of the assurances of your returning to us and do all you can to make your absence short. Tell Mr. Church for me of the happiness he will give me in bringing you to me, not to me alone, but to fond parents, sisters, friends, and to my Hamilton, who has for you all the affection of a fond own brother. I can no more. Adieu, adieu. E. H.[53]

As if to symbolize the tenuous state of the new administration, George Washington developed a queer affliction in mid-June 1789 that nearly killed him. What started out as a fever was followed by a tenderness in his left thigh that soon progressed to painful swelling and a "malignant carbuncle." The president lost weight, could not sit up, and lay dangerously ill in bed for days. Few people outside the small presidential circle understood the extreme gravity of the illness, much less that it might prove fatal. Whether this was a product of anthrax, as diagnosed at the time, or a tumor, it was surgically excised without an anesthetic. (In a still rural America, it was not uncommon for farmers and planters to contract anthrax from infected animals.) The senior surgeon who presided over the procedure did so with seemingly sadistic gusto. "Cut away," he exclaimed. "Deep—deeper—deeper still. Don't be afraid. You will see how well he bears it!"[54] The president's health remained so uncertain that Mayor James Duane stopped carriages from passing Washington's residence and had straw spread on the sidewalk to muffle any sounds that might disturb him.

As he convalesced, Washington lacked the strength to attend a Fourth of July celebration conducted at St. Paul's Chapel by the Society of the Cincinnati. The ex–revolutionary officers forgathered at the City Tavern, then headed for the church, attended by an artillery regiment and martial band. As they passed the presidential residence, Washington, decked out in full regimental regalia, greeted them from the doorway. Martha Washington then joined the officers at St. Paul's for the most glittering assemblage of personalities since the inauguration. Vice President Adams attended with the Senate and House of Representatives in tow. With eagles pinned to their buttonholes, the bemedaled Cincinnati members occupied their own special section. The highlight of the program was Hamilton's memorial oration for his friend, General Nathanael Greene, who had died three years earlier. One newspaper noted that "a splendid assembly of ladies" gazed down from the galleries—doubtless to Hamilton's delight.[55]

The clean, airy chapel sparkled with cut-glass chandeliers and Corinthian columns and was a superb, if slightly ironic, setting for the occasion. Speakers stood at a hooded pulpit topped by a coronet of six feathers—the last surviving emblem of British rule in the city. Hamilton had once paid homage to Greene by saying that he lacked "nothing but an education to have made him the first man in the United States," and he now eulogized him with unfeigned affection.[56] Like Hamilton, Greene had risen from modest circumstances and taught himself the science of warfare. At moments, Hamilton's panegyric had autobiographical overtones:

It is an observation as just as it is common that in those great revolutions which occasionally convulse society, human nature never fails to be brought forward in its brightest as well as in its blackest colors. And it has very properly been ranked not among the least of the advantages which compensate for the evils they produce that they serve to bring to light talents and virtues which might otherwise have languished in obscurity or only shot forth a few scattered and wandering rays.[57]

As commander of the Southern Army late in the Revolution, harassing Cornwallis, Greene had been renowned for performing wonders with often meager forces. Probably with this in mind, Hamilton committed the faux pas of openly mocking the state militias that had served under Greene. In recounting his exploits, Hamilton deprecated the militias as "the mimickry of soldiership." As he told of fierce fighting in South Carolina, Hamilton said that front-line militia under Greene had buckled under fire and were rescued by a second line of brave, resolute Continentals.[58] Hamilton probably had scant notion that his passing comment on southern soldiers had mortally offended a congressman from South Carolina, Aedanus Burke, a bibulous, hot-tempered Irishman. At the time, Hamilton was not a federal official, and Burke did not make an open issue of the speech. Moreover, after the New York Ratifying Convention, Hamilton stood at the peak of his popularity, and Burke did not dare to challenge him. He later explained, "Mr. Hamilton was the hero of the day and the favorite of the people. And had I hurt a hair of his head, I'm sure I should have been dragged through the kennels of New York and pitched headlong into the East River."[59] As we shall see, Burke stewed about the episode and awaited a strategic moment to retaliate. He and other southerners perhaps also took umbrage at Hamilton's frank statement that patriotic operations in the south had been hampered "by a numerous body of slaves bound by all the laws of injured humanity to hate their masters."[60] Hamilton was admitting that masters *deserved* to be hated by their slaves and had behaved logically in sympathizing with the British or failing to cooperate with the patriots—sentiments that surely were anathema to the slaveholders.

Hamilton seemed to spark controversy at every turn. At the time of his July Fourth oration, New York still had not selected its first two senators. Under the Constitution, this decision fell to state legislatures, insuring that local mandarins would have a disproportionate say in the matter. As in the colonial period, New York politics was still largely governed by a few powerful families. In the felicitous words of one early Burr biographer, "The Clintons had *power*, the Livingstons had *numbers*, and the Schuylers had *Hamilton*."[61] As chieftain of his clan, General Philip Schuyler was a certain choice for one senatorial post. (One of Schuyler's other sons-in-law, the superrich Stephen Van Rensselaer, was elected to the New York Assembly that year.) Schuyler promised the rival Livingstons that he would support New York mayor James Duane, who had married into their family, for the other Senate seat. Had this alliance held, the Schuylers and the Livingstons might have shared power in New York and isolated George Clinton. They might even have thwarted the later Jeffersonian incursion into the state and altered the entire configuration of American politics.

This scenario never materialized, however, because Hamilton stumbled into a spectacular political blunder. Afraid that Duane's successor as mayor might be "some very unfit character" whose politics would prove "injurious to the city," Hamilton decided to oppose him for the second Senate seat.[62] In a blatant affront to the almighty Livingstons, Hamilton threw his weight behind his thirty-four-year-old friend Rufus King, a handsome, Harvard-educated lawyer from New England who had recently moved to New York. King had married a beautiful heiress, Mary Alsop, and the two socialized with the Hamiltons. A mellifluous orator and an impassioned critic of slavery, King had attended the Constitutional Convention as a Massachusetts delegate and served on the style committee with Hamilton. In a short period of time, King became a fixture in New York City society—"our King is as much followed and attended to by all parties as ever a new light preacher was by his congregation," Robert Troup told Hamilton[63]—and Hamilton induced Philip Schuyler to renege on his pledged support for Duane in favor of King. In a foolish and egotistical move, Hamilton was bent upon having both his father-in-law and his friend as New York's two senators.

With finely honed political instincts, George Clinton saw that Hamilton was overreaching, and he secretly aided King's candidacy in order to drive a wedge between the Schuylers and the Livingstons. When New York picked its second senator on July 16, 1789, Rufus King came out on top. Just as Clinton suspected, Chancellor Robert R. Livingston was irate and gradually moved into the governor's camp. The polished, graceful Livingston was accustomed to deference and felt stymied by the parvenu Hamilton. This weakened Hamilton in his home state, depriving him later of a vital springboard to the presidency. It also paved the way for Aaron Burr to work his peculiar mischief in state politics. Compounding the tension between Hamilton and Robert R. Livingston that summer was that both men had fixed their gaze on the same tantalizing prize: the job of treasury secretary, soon to be assigned by Washington and sure to be the most powerful spot in the first administration.

As George Washington mulled over his choice, he knew that fiscal bungling had led to the demise of the confederation, making this a critical appointment. He turned first to the man synonymous with patriotic finance, Robert Morris, the Philadelphia merchant who had pledged his personal credit on behalf of the Revolution. Washington's adopted grandson said that en route to the inauguration in April, the president-elect had stopped at Morris's opulent residence. "The treasury, Morris, will of course be your berth," Washington confided. "After your invaluable services as financier of the Revolution, no one can pretend to contest the office of the secretary of the treasury with you." Citing private reasons—Morris was already lurching down a long, slippery path that led to bankruptcy and debtors' prison—Morris politely declined the offer.

"But, my dear general," he reassured Washington, "you will be no loser by my declining the secretaryship of the treasury, for I can recommend to you a far cleverer fellow than I am for your minister of finance in the person of your former aide-de-camp, Colonel Hamilton."

Taken aback, Washington replied, "I always knew Colonel Hamilton to be a man of superior talents, but never supposed that he had any knowledge of finance."

"He knows everything, sir," Morris replied. "To a mind like his nothing comes amiss."[64] Another version of this story has Washington asking Morris what to do about the huge pile of public debt. Morris advised, "There is but one man in the United States who can tell you: that is, Alexander Hamilton."[65] Robert Morris served in the first U.S. Senate instead.

Even as Washington conferred with Morris, Hamilton was strolling down a New York street when he encountered Alexander J. Dallas, a Philadelphia lawyer. "Well, colonel, can you tell me who will be the members of the cabinet?" Dallas asked.

"Really, my dear sir," Hamilton answered, "I cannot tell you who will, but I can very readily tell you of one who will not be of the number and that one is your humble servant."[66]

Soon after being sworn in as president, Washington informed Hamilton that he planned to name him to the top financial spot. Hamilton must have daydreamed about this moment for years. Why else had he ploughed through dry economic texts during the war or perused the three-volume memoir of Jacques Necker, the French finance minister? For years, his mind had wrought detailed financial plans, as if he were rehearsing for the job. His ascent to the Treasury post seemed an almost inevitable next step in his headlong rush to fame. Clearly, he felt equal to the task and told Washington that he would accept if offered.

Friends cautioned him against heading the Treasury Department, the activities of which would arouse latent memories of British rule. When Gouverneur Morris assured him that the treasury secretary would be exposed to special calumny, Hamilton replied that "it is the situation in which I can do most good."[67] In debating the Constitution, Hamilton knew that the issue of federal taxation and tax collectors had provoked the biggest brouhaha. As chief tax collector, he would be the lightning rod for inevitable discontent. In fact, everything that Hamilton planned to create to transform America into a powerful, modern nation-state—a central bank, a funded debt, a mint, a customs service, manufacturing subsidies, and so on—was to strike critics as a slavish imitation of the British model.

After chatting with Washington, Hamilton informed Robert Troup of the momentous news and asked if he would assume his legal business. Troup was glad to oblige but thought Hamilton was committing a serious error. He noted the financial sacrifice entailed by the annual salary of $3,500, far less than Hamilton was then earning as a lawyer. Troup recalled he remonstrated with Hamilton "on the ground of the serious injury his quitting the practice of the law would work to his family. At that time [Hamilton's] fortune was very limited and his family was increasing." Hamilton told Troup that he understood the financial sacrifice, but "he thought it would be in his power in the financial department of the government to do the country great good and this consideration outweighed with him every consideration of a private nature."[68] A man of irreproachable integrity, Hamilton severed all outside sources of income while in office, something that neither Washington nor Jefferson nor Madison dared to do.

Later on, Hamilton acknowledged that the Treasury job was the logical culmination of his long campaign for the Constitution. Having been part of the system's gestation, "I conceived myself to be under an obligation to lend my aid towards putting the machine in some regular motion. Hence I did not hesitate to accept the offer of President Washington to undertake the office of Secretary of the Treasury."[69] Hamilton kept his appointment secret from all but a few friends while rivals maneuvered for the post. In late May, Madison told Jefferson that Robert R. Livingston coveted the Treasury job, but that Hamilton was "perhaps best qualified for that species of business" and stood a better chance.[70] After losing the Treasury job, Livingston lobbied to become chief justice of the United States and lost that battle to John Jay. When he added in his family's loss of the New York Senate seat, Livingston must have believed that Hamilton and Schuyler, if not the entire Washington administration, were unalterably hostile to his ambitions. In July, Hamilton recommended to Washington that Livingston be sent to negotiate a European loan, but this olive branch did not heal the breach between the two men.[71]

Throughout the summer, as word spread that Hamilton's appointment was imminent, it caused a flurry of excitement among admirers in New England and elsewhere. But the official announcement was deferred until Washington signed the bill creating the Treasury Department on September 2. Then, on Friday, September 11, 1789, thirty-four-year-old Alexander Hamilton was officially nominated for the job. The appointment was confirmed by the Senate the same day. Hamilton hit the ground running: the very next day, he arranged a fifty-thousand-dollar loan for the federal government from the Bank of New York. The day after that, a Sunday, he worked all day at the Treasury's new office on Broadway, just south of Trinity Church. He dashed off a plea to the Bank of North America in Philadelphia, asking for another fifty thousand dollars. Hamilton knew the symbolic value of rapid decision making and phenomenal energy. As he wrote during the Revolution, "If a Government appears to be confident of its own powers, it is the surest way to inspire the same confidence in others."[72] With support for the Constitution still tentative in some states, Hamilton knew that designing enemies lay in wait to destroy it. To succeed, the government had to establish its authority, and to this end he was prepared to move with exceptional speed. Alexander Hamilton never seemed to wander around in a normal human muddle. With preternatural confidence, he discerned clear solutions to the murkiest questions.

From the beginning, he faced pressure as wary creditors waited to see if the young treasury secretary could miraculously resurrect American credit. Only ten days after Hamilton was confirmed, the House of Representatives asked him to prepare a report on public credit, giving him a scant 110 days to respond. With this wind at his back, Hamilton took a giant, running leap in staking out his claim to leadership in Washington's administration.

No other moment in American history could have allowed such scope for Hamilton's abundant talents. The new government was a tabula rasa on which he could sketch plans with a young man's energy. Washington's administration had to create everything from scratch. Hamilton was that rare revolutionary: a master administrator and as competent a public servant as American politics would ever produce. One historian has written, "Hamilton was an administrative genius" who "assumed an influence in Washington's cabinet which is unmatched in the annals of the American cabinet system."[73] The position demanded both a thinker and a doer, a skilled executive and a political theorist, a system builder who could devise interrelated policies. It also demanded someone who could build an institutional framework consistent with constitutional principles. Virtually every program that Hamilton put together raised fundamental constitutional issues, so that his legal training and work on *The Federalist* enabled him to craft the efficient machinery of government while expounding its theoretical underpinnings.

Because the Constitution made no mention of a cabinet, Washington had to invent it. At first, this executive council consisted of just three men: Hamilton as secretary of the treasury, Jefferson as secretary of state, and Henry Knox as secretary of war. The first attorney general, thirty-six-year-old Edmund Randolph of Virginia, had no department and received an annual retainer of $1,500 for an essentially consultative role. Viewed as the government's legal adviser, the tall, handsome Randolph was expected to retain private clients to supplement his modest salary. Vice President John Adams was largely excluded from the administration's decision-making apparatus, a demotion in power that could only have sharpened his envy of young Hamilton.

The concept of a cabinet took some time to mature. During his first three years as president, Washington seldom assembled his secretaries for meetings—as Hamilton later told the British minister, "We have no cabinet and the heads of departments meet on very particular occasions only"—and preferred to solicit their views separately.[74] With only three executive departments, each secretary wielded considerable power. Moreover, departmental boundaries were not well defined, allowing each secretary to roam across a wide spectrum of issues. This was encouraged by Washington, who frequently requested opinions from his entire cabinet on an issue. It particularly galled Jefferson that Hamilton, with his keen appetite for power, poached so frequently on his turf. In fact, Hamilton's opinions were so numerous and his influence so pervasive that most historians regard him as having been something akin to a prime minister. If Washington was head of state, then Hamilton was the head of government, the active force in the administration.

As in the Revolution, Hamilton and Washington had complementary talents. Neither could have achieved alone what they did together. Sometimes emphasizing the ceremonial side of his job, Washington wanted to be a figure above the partisan fray, retaining his aura as an embodiment of the Revolution. His detached style left room for an assertive managerial presence, especially in financial matters, where Hamilton stepped willingly into the breach. If Washington lacked the first-rate intellect of Hamilton, Jefferson, Madison, Franklin, and Adams, he was gifted with superb judgment. When presented with options, he almost invariably chose the right one. Never a pliant tool in Hamilton's hands, as critics alleged, he often overrode his treasury secretary.

Washington and Hamilton also made an exceptional team because they offset each other's personal weaknesses. Washington could be hypersensitive to criticism and never forgot snubs, but he had learned to govern his emotions, making him a valuable foil to the volatile Hamilton. Hamilton could be needlessly tactless and provocative, while Washington was conciliatory, with an innate sense of decorum. Adams said that Washington possessed "the gift of taciturnity."[75] Hamilton's mind was so swift and decisive that it could lead him into rash decisions. Washington's management style was the antithesis of this. "He consulted much, pondered much, resolved slowly, resolved surely," Hamilton later said of the president.[76] Washington could weigh all sides of an issue and coolly appraise the political repercussions. "Perhaps the strongest feature in his character was prudence, never acting until every circumstance, every consideration, was maturely weighed; refraining if he saw a doubt, but, when once decided, going through with his purpose whatever obstacles opposed," said Jefferson.[77] Such a man could be counted on to temper his treasury secretary's excesses.

Perhaps the main reason that Washington and Hamilton functioned so well together was that both men longed to see the thirteen states welded into a single, respected American nation. At the close of the war, Washington had circulated a letter to the thirteen governors, outlining four things America would need to attain greatness: consolidation of the states under a strong federal government, timely payment of its debts, creation of an army and a navy, and harmony among its people. Hamilton would have written the identical list. The young treasury secretary gained incomparable power under Washington because the president approved of the agenda that he promoted with such tireless brilliance. Jefferson had it wrong when he charged that Hamilton manipulated Washington. On fundamental political matters, Washington was simply more attuned to Hamilton than he was to Jefferson. For that reason, Washington willingly served as the political shield that Alexander Hamilton needed as he became America's most influential and controversial man.

FIFTEEN

VILLAINOUS BUSINESS

As Alexander Hamilton began to stitch together his grand plan for a vigorous central government, the executive branch was still tiny and embryonic. On his first day at Treasury, Hamilton likely wandered through a set of empty rooms; he soon installed an elegant mahogany desk with caryatids—female figures—carved into its spindly legs. He was to perform an amazing amount of work on that desktop. Hamilton employed no ghostwriters for his countless speeches, articles, and reports, and almost all of his letters have come down to posterity in his own hand.

As master of Mount Vernon, George Washington presided over a larger staff than he did as president. From the outset, Hamilton supervised the biggest department, which soon had thirty-nine employees, compared to five for State, generating instant fears that he was building a large bureaucracy as his personal power base. The pace at Treasury was positively torrid compared to that at War. "When [Henry] Knox arrived in New York City and took up his official duties," notes biographer North Callahan, "he found little to do at first but become acquainted with his one secretary and one clerk, who at that time constituted the entire personnel of the War Department."[1] As the first treasury secretary, Hamilton had to devise rudimentary systems for bookkeeping, checking, and auditing, many of which endured for generations. Hamilton threw himself into the most mundane tasks, as if glorying in the managerial challenge. To pedestrians passing him in the street, the treasury secretary could seem an aloof, cerebral man, shut up inside his thoughts, seldom making eye contact with strangers. One New York newspaper joked that anyone hoping to be treasury secretary should "appear in the streets but seldom and then let him take care to look down on the pavement, as if lost in thought profound."[2]

Few intervals of leisure relieved the work pressure of these first months. After Angelica left for England, Eliza and the children retreated to Albany, leaving Hamilton alone in New York, trapped beneath piles of work. "I am a solitary lost being without you all," he wrote to Eliza, "and shall with increasing anxiety look forward to our reunion."[3] When Eliza returned later in the month, she and Alexander had the thrilling experience of going with George and Martha Washington to the John Street Theater to see Richard Brinsley Sheridan's comedy *The Critic*. As the politicians entered, the orchestra struck up the "President's March," and the audience gave them a standing ovation. Eliza always remembered with amusement another time when a Miss McIvers showed up at one of Martha Washington's receptions sporting an enormous headdress of ostrich feathers. When this fashion accessory caught fire from the chandelier, Major William Jackson, then an aide to the president, leaped to her side and extinguished the blaze by clapping the feathers between his hands.

Such outings were rare during Hamilton's harried first days in office. He had to create a customs service on the spot, for customs duties were to be the main source of government revenue. During his second day in office, he issued a circular to all customs collectors, demanding exact figures of the duties accumulated in each state. When they sent back suspiciously low numbers, Hamilton, who knew something about smuggling from St. Croix, suspected that it must be rife along the eastern seaboard, leading him to the next logical step. "I have under consideration the business of establishing guard boats," he told one correspondent in perhaps the first recorded allusion to what would turn into the Coast Guard.[4]

Hamilton's appetite for information was bottomless. To his port wardens, he made minute inquiries about their lighthouses, beacons, and buoys. He asked customs collectors for ship manifests so he could ascertain the exact quantity and nature of cargo being exported. The whole statistical basis of government took shape under his command. In a significant decision, he decided that customs revenues could be paid not just in gold and silver but with notes from the Bank of New York and the Bank of North America, an innovation that began to steer the country away from use of coins and toward an efficient system of paper money.

Hamilton had always been punctual—"I hate procrastination in business," he once said—and lost no time assembling a first-rate staff, imbued with a sense of public service.[5] On the day he was nominated, five assistants, including auditor Oliver Wolcott, Jr., of Connecticut, were confirmed as well. When Samuel Meredith of Pennsylvania was appointed treasurer, the hard-driving secretary lectured him, "I need not observe to you how important it is that you should be on the ground as speedily as possible."[6]

For his first assistant secretary, Hamilton picked his witty, elegant, vivacious friend William Duer, who had married Lord Stirling's daughter, Lady Kitty. The choice of Duer was to have grievous consequences for Hamilton, for he was an inveterate speculator, and his later scandals besmirched Hamilton's reputation. Duer had grown up in England and studied classics at Eton. After his father's death, he worked as a teenager for the East India Company in Bengal, where the climate injured his health. After spending time on a family plantation in Antigua, he bought land in upstate New York, not far from the Schuyler property in Saratoga, and sold lumber to the British Navy. Because he had befriended Myles Cooper in England, Duer came to know Hamilton while he was still studying at King's College.

The association with Duer became so supremely damaging to Hamilton that it later mystified many friends. But the two men were compatible in their political opinions and ebullient style, and Duer's résumé amply qualified him for the job. While still in England, he had been an outspoken Whig who championed the colonists' grievances and plumped for reforms to avert a revolt. During the Revolution, he supplied goods to the Continental Army, served in the Continental Congress, and attended the convention that drafted the New York State Constitution. He was smart enough that Hamilton had recruited him to write essays for *The Federalist,* only to reject his two submissions. At the time Hamilton picked him, Duer had just completed three years as secretary to the old Board of Treasury. In 1789, Hamilton cajoled him into staying on by creating the assistant secretary post expressly for him.

Unfortunately, William Duer suffered from a severe case of moral myopia and always found rather blurry the line between public service and private gain. That autumn, Hamilton was about to make decisions that would dramatically affect the value of outstanding government securities, so secrecy and integrity were obligatory among his colleagues. It later turned out that Duer had been assembling a huge stake in government securities for several years. Among other faults, the indiscreet Duer babbled to his cronies about Hamilton's scheme for funding government debt—the sort of priceless insider gossip that moves markets. Just a week after Hamilton took office, Noah Webster sent to a speculator in Amsterdam secret details of the treasury secretary's funding scheme, attributing them to "the outdoor talk of Col. Duer, the Vice-Secretary."[7] Senator William Maclay, a tireless if dyspeptic diarist, recorded rumors of congressmen speculating in state debt and said that "nobody doubts but all commotion originated from the Treasury. But the fault is laid on Duer."[8]

Unfortunately, Duer's actions fed unjust scuttlebutt that the new Treasury Department was a sink of corruption. In reality, as soon as he took office, Hamilton established high ethical standards and promulgated a policy that employees could not deal in government securities, setting a critical precedent for America's civil service.

Hamilton divested himself of any business investments that might create conflicts of interest. Even later, as a private citizen, he said that his own "scrupulousness" had prevented him from "being concerned in what is termed speculation."[9] This made his blindness to Duer's shameless machinations the more bewildering. Hamilton was an extremely perceptive judge of character, and William Duer was one of the few cases in which his acute vision seems to have been blinkered.

Because Jefferson hadn't yet arrived in New York to take up his duties as secretary of state, Hamilton wasn't shy about acting as his surrogate. A British diplomat named Major George Beckwith, an aide to the governor-general of Canada, sounded out Philip Schuyler about an unofficial meeting with the new treasury secretary. Hamilton's pro-British proclivities were well known. When Hamilton met secretly with Beckwith in October, they had to proceed cautiously, since Britain still lacked an official diplomatic presence in America. So the discussion qualified as unofficial, although Hamilton reassured Beckwith that his words reflected "the sentiments of the most enlightened men in this country. They are those of General Washington, I can confidently assure you, as well as of a great majority in the Senate."[10] For security reasons, Beckwith assigned Hamilton the code number "7" in reporting their talks back to London—a precaution that later led to preposterous charges that Hamilton was a British agent. In fact, Washington knew about some of these clandestine talks and received summaries from Hamilton.

In his wide-ranging chats with Beckwith, Hamilton touched upon the prospect of a commercial treaty with England and left little doubt about his sympathies: "I have always preferred a connection with you to that of any other country. *We think in English* and have a similarity of prejudices and of predilections."[11] He shared Beckwith's chagrin over proposals that Madison had submitted to Congress to discriminate against British shipping. "The truth is," Hamilton confided of Madison, "that although this gentleman is a clever man, he is very little acquainted with the world. That he is uncorrupted and incorruptible, I have not a doubt."[12]

Hamilton's projected vision of a commercial alliance between American and British commerce, far from being fawning, was laced with subtle threats and enticements. With his premonition of future American greatness, he made clear that Britain should reckon with American purchasing power: "I do think we are and shall be great consumers."[13] He foresaw that America, if now junior to Britain in status, would someday rival her as an economic power: "We are a young and growing empire with much enterprise and vigour, but undoubtedly are, and must be for years, rather an agricultural than a manufacturing people."[14] As a raw-materials producer, Hamilton noted, the United States currently formed a perfect fit with England, the manufacturing colossus. On the other hand, the northern states were making headway in manufacturing, and if Britain thwarted America, such threats to Britain's dominance would grow apace. If spurned by England, the United States could also forge an alliance with France that would threaten British possessions in the West Indies.

Far from being a pro-British lackey, much less a high-level spy, Hamilton stubbornly defended U.S. interests at every turn. He was bargaining with Beckwith, not groveling. He insisted that the United States should be able to trade with the British West Indies. He wanted England to heed the peace treaty and relinquish its western forts in the Ohio River valley. The one place where Hamilton deviated from official policy was in applauding Britain's refusal to hand over slaves who had defected during the Revolution. "To have given up these men to their masters, after the assurances of protection held out to them, was impossible," Hamilton told Beckwith.[15]

At the end of their talk, Hamilton hinted that the United States would soon send an emissary to England to continue talks about the matters discussed. On October 7, Washington discussed such an appointment with Hamilton and Jay and accepted Hamilton's suggestion that Gouverneur Morris go to England. Within weeks of his confirmation as treasury secretary, Hamilton had already staked out a position as the administration's most influential figure on foreign policy.

That Hamilton had time to worry about foreign policy is a wonder. The meeting with Beckwith was a fleeting respite from the giant task that engrossed him that fall: the report on public credit that Congress wanted by January. He had to sum up America's financial predicament and recommend corrective measures to deal with the enormous public debt left over from the Revolution. Hamilton solicited opinions, but his report was not the product of a committee. As with his fifty-one *Federalist* essays, he put in another sustained bout of solitary, herculean labor. Closeted in his study day after day, he scratched out a forty-thousand-word treatise—a short book—in slightly more than three months, performing all the complex mathematical calculations himself.

While other members of the revolutionary generation dreamed of an American Eden, Hamilton continued to ransack British and French history for ideas. He had inordinate admiration for Jacques Necker, the French finance minister who had argued that government borrowing could strengthen military prowess, but it was England that shone as Hamilton's true lodestar in public finance. Back in the 1690s, the British had set up the Bank of England, enacted an excise tax on spirits, and funded its public debt—that is, pledged specific revenues to insure repayment of its debt. During the eighteenth century, it had vastly expanded that public debt. Far from weakening the country, it had produced manifold benefits. Public credit had enabled England to build up the Royal Navy, to prosecute wars around the world,

to maintain a global commercial empire. At the same time, government bonds issued to pay for the debt galvanized the economy, since creditors could use them as
collateral for loans. By imitating British practice, Hamilton did not intend to make
America subservient to the former mother country, as critics claimed. His objective
was to promote American prosperity and self-sufficiency and make the country ultimately *less* reliant on British capital. Hamilton wanted to use British methods to
defeat Britain economically.

In preparing his report, Hamilton was eclectic in his sources. He had clearly
plumbed David Hume's *Political Discourses,* which admitted that public debt could
vitalize business activity. Montesquieu had stressed that states should honor financial obligations, "as a breach in the public faith cannot be made on a certain
number of subjects without seeming to be made on all."[16] Thomas Hobbes had emphasized the sacredness of contracts in transfers of securities, arguing that people
entered into such transactions voluntarily and must accept all the consequences—
a seemingly arcane point that shortly had explosive consequences for Hamilton's
career. During the Revolution, Hamilton had stuffed Malachy Postlethwayt's *Universal Dictionary of Trade and Commerce* into his satchel, and now he used it once
again. Postlethwayt stressed that no country could borrow money at attractive interest rates unless creditors could freely buy and sell its bonds: "Such is the nature
of public credit, that nobody would lend their money to the support of the state,
under the most pressing emergencies, unless they could have the privilege of buying and selling their property in the public funds, when their occasions required."[17]
Inviolable property rights lay at the heart of the capitalist culture that Hamilton
wished to enshrine in America.

As he toiled over the report, Hamilton queried several contemporaries, including John Witherspoon, the Princeton president who had rebuffed his request for accelerated study. Hamilton must have been amused by the educator's deferential
reply: "It is very flattering to me that you suppose I can render any assistance by advice in the important duties of your present station."[18] Aware that the American
Revolution had produced a nation averse to taxes, Hamilton asked Madison, "What
further taxes will be *least* unpopular?"[19] At this point, Hamilton and Madison still
shared a sense of political camaraderie. One lady remembered seeing them together
that summer "turn and laugh and play with a monkey that was climbing in a neighbor's yard."[20] But the letter that Madison now wrote to Hamilton gave the first
preview of a fateful schism between them. Madison did not want a long-term
government debt, fearing that such securities would fall into foreign hands: "As
they have more money than the Americans and less productive ways of laying it
out, they can and will pretty generally buy out the Americans."[21] When Madison

registered this muted dissent, Hamilton had no idea that such differences of opinion were soon to demolish their friendship.

Had Hamilton stuck to dry financial matters, his *Report on Public Credit* would never have attained such historic renown. Instead, he presented a detailed blueprint of the government's fiscal machinery, wrapped in a broad political and economic vision. From the opening pages, Hamilton reminded readers that the government's debt was the "price of liberty" inherited from the Revolution and had special claims on the public purse.[22] The states had balked at taxing citizens during a revolt against onerous taxes, and Congress had lacked the power to levy taxes, leaving borrowing as the only solution. The outstanding debt was now enormous: $54 million in national debt, coupled with $25 million in state debt, for a total of $79 million.

Hamilton argued that the security of liberty and property were inseparable and that governments should honor their debts because contracts formed the basis of public and private morality: "States, like individuals, who observe their engagements are respected and trusted, while the reverse is the fate of those who pursue an opposite conduct."[23] The proper handling of government debt would permit America to borrow at affordable interest rates and would also act as a tonic to the economy. Used as loan collateral, government bonds could function as money—and it was the scarcity of money, Hamilton observed, that had crippled the economy and resulted in severe deflation in the value of land. America was a young country rich in opportunity. It lacked only liquid capital, and government debt could supply that gaping deficiency.

The secret of managing government debt was to fund it properly by setting aside revenues at regular intervals to service interest and pay off principal. Hamilton refuted charges that his funding scheme would feed speculation. Quite the contrary: if investors knew for sure that government bonds would be paid off, the prices would not fluctuate wildly, depriving speculators of opportunities to exploit. What mattered was that people *trusted* the government to make good on repayment: "In nothing are appearances of greater moment than in whatever regards credit. Opinion is the soul of it and this is affected by appearances as well as realities."[24] Hamilton intuited that public relations and confidence building were to be the special burdens of every future treasury secretary.

How exactly the debt should be funded was to be the most inflammatory political issue. During the Revolution, many affluent citizens had invested in bonds, and many war veterans had been paid with IOUs that then plummeted in price under the confederation. In many cases, these upright patriots, either needing cash or convinced they would never be repaid, had sold their securities to speculators for as little as fifteen cents on the dollar. Under the influence of his funding scheme, with government repayment guaranteed, Hamilton expected these bonds to soar from their depressed levels and regain their full face value.

This pleasing prospect, however, presented a political quandary. If the bonds appreciated, should speculators pocket the windfall? Or should the money go to the original holders—many of them brave soldiers—who had sold their depressed government paper years earlier? The answer to this perplexing question, Hamilton knew, would define the future character of American capital markets. Doubtless taking a deep breath, he wrote that "after the most mature reflection" about whether to reward original holders and punish current speculators, he had decided against this approach as "ruinous to public credit."[25] The problem was partly that such "discrimination" in favor of former debt holders was unworkable. The government would have to track them down, ascertain their sale prices, then trace all intermediate investors who had held the debt before it was bought by the current owners—an administrative nightmare.

Hamilton could have left it at that, ducking the political issue and taking refuge in technical jargon. Instead, he shifted the terms of the debate. He said that the first holders were not simply noble victims, nor were the current buyers simply predatory speculators. The original investors had gotten cash when they wanted it and had shown little faith in the country's future. Speculators, meanwhile, had hazarded their money and should be rewarded for the risk. In this manner, Hamilton stole the moral high ground from opponents and established the legal and moral basis for securities trading in America: the notion that securities are freely transferable and that buyers assume all rights to profit or loss in transactions. The knowledge that government could not interfere retroactively with a financial transaction was so vital, Hamilton thought, as to outweigh any short-term expediency. To establish the concept of the "security of transfer," Hamilton was willing, if necessary, to reward mercenary scoundrels and penalize patriotic citizens. With this huge gamble, Hamilton laid the foundations for America's future financial preeminence.

As his report progressed, Hamilton tiptoed through a field seeded thickly with deadly political traps. The next incendiary issue was that some debt was owed by the thirteen states, some by the federal government. Hamilton decided to consolidate all the debt into a single form: federal debt. He wrote, "The Secretary, after mature reflection on this point, entertains a full conviction that an assumption of the debts of the particular states by the union and a like provision for them as for those of the union will be a measure of sound policy and substantial justice."[26] The repercussions of this decision were as pervasive as anything Alexander Hamilton ever did to fortify the U.S. government.

Why was this assumption of state debts by the federal government so crucial?

For starters, it would be more efficient, since there would be one overarching scheme for settling debt instead of many small, competing schemes. It also reflected a profound political logic. Hamilton knew that bondholders would feel a stake in preserving any government that owed them money. If the federal government, not the states, owed the money, creditors would shift their main allegiance to the central government. Hamilton's interest was not in enriching creditors or cultivating the privileged class so much as in insuring the government's stability and survival. Walter Lippmann later said of Hamilton, "He used the rich for a purpose that was greater than their riches."[27] On the other hand, he was naïve in thinking that the rich would always have a broader sense of public duty and would somehow be devoid of self-interest, instead of being captives to an even larger set of interests.

There was a further advantage to the assumption of state debt. The Constitution had granted the federal government an exclusive right to collect import duties. If states had to pay off debts, too, they might contest that monopoly and try to skim off money from their import duties, re-creating the chaos under the Articles of Confederation. Under his scheme, Hamilton believed, the states would lose incentive to compete with the federal government for major revenue sources.

Hamilton now had to decide whether state debt should be paid off at the original interest rates. He knew this would be impossible to accomplish without stiff taxes, which might precipitate a rebellion or impoverish the country. He also did not want to give *too* bountiful a reward to speculators who had rounded up state debt at cheap prices from small investors. So he decided that foreign debt, which bore interest rates of only 4 or 5 percent, was to be paid in full. Domestic debt, with a 6 percent interest rate, posed a greater dilemma.

To relieve financial pressure on the government, Hamilton decided on a partial repudiation of the domestic debt, though he certainly did not phrase it that way. He gambled that creditors would accept lower interest rates in exchange for rock-solid securities that could not be redeemed by the government if interest rates fell (in modern parlance, noncallable bonds). To entice domestic creditors, he offered a long list of voluntary options, only some of which were enacted. They could receive, for instance, part of their payment at the original 6 percent interest rate and part in western land, enabling them to participate in the appreciation of frontier property. Or they could take payment at a lower interest rate but stretched over a longer period. To enhance such choices, investors would be paid quarterly, not annually. Most significantly, creditors would be paid with taxes pledged for that express purpose. Hamilton's supporters praised the byzantine brilliance of this program; for his foes, it smacked of impenetrable mumbo jumbo, designed to hoodwink the public.

To make good on payments, Hamilton knew he would have to raise a substantial loan abroad and boost domestic taxes beyond the import duties now at his disposal. He proposed taxes on wines and spirits distilled within the United States as well as on tea and coffee. Of these first "sin taxes," the secretary observed that the products taxed are "all of them in reality luxuries, the greatest part of them foreign luxuries; some of them, in the excess in which they are used, pernicious luxuries."[28] Such taxation might dampen consumption and reduce revenues, Hamilton acknowledged, but he doubted this would happen, because "luxuries of every kind lay the strongest hold on the attachments of mankind, which, especially when confirmed by habit, are not easily alienated from them."[29]

In the report's final section, Hamilton reiterated that a well-funded debt would be a "national blessing" that would protect American prosperity. He feared this statement would be misconstrued as a call for a *perpetual* public debt—and that is exactly what happened. For the rest of his life, he was to express dismay at what he saw as a deliberate distortion of his views. His opponents, he claimed, neglected a critical passage of his report in which he wrote that he "ardently wishes to see it incorporated as a fundamental maxim in the system of public credit of the United States that the creation of debt should always be accompanied with the means of extinguishment." The secretary regarded this "as the true secret for rendering public credit immortal."[30] Three years later, Hamilton testily reminded the public that he had advocated extinguishing the debt "in the *very first* communication" which he "ever made on the subject of the public debt, in that *very report* which contains the expressions [now] tortured into an advocation [sic] of the doctrine that public debts are public blessings."[31] Indeed, in Hamilton's writings his warnings about oppressive debt *vastly* outnumber his paeans to public debt as a source of liquid capital. Five years after his first report, still fuming, he warned that progressive accumulation of debt "is perhaps the NATURAL DISEASE of all Governments. And it is not easy to conceive anything more likely than this to lead to great and convulsive revolutions of Empire."[32]

To make sure the debt was extinguished over time, Hamilton proposed the creation of a sinking fund, financed by post-office revenues and manned by the government's chief officers. (A sinking fund is a repository, set up apart from the general budget, for revenues to pay off debt.) It would sequester revenues from the sudden whims of grasping politicians who might want to raid the Treasury for short-term gain. The sinking fund would retire about 5 percent of the debt each year until it was paid off. Because outstanding bonds currently traded below their original face value, such purchases would benefit the government as the securities rose in price. Thus, the government would profit from rising prices alongside private investors. Hamilton concluded, "In the opinion of the Secretary . . . it ought to be the policy of the government to raise the value of stock to its true standard as fast as possible."[33] Little did he know how quickly he was to succeed or how much trouble this success was to bring in its wake.

Even as Hamilton compiled this magnum opus, the prices of government securities streaked upward in anticipation of its publication, the psychological effect being even more pronounced than Hamilton had expected. For the treasury secretary, it was a stunning affirmation of confidence in the new government. Interest rates were tumbling and faith in American credit was being restored.

The exact contents of Hamilton's report remained a mystery until mid-January. When Congress convened, so-called jobbers—or wealthy dealers in securities—swarmed around Federal Hall and buttonholed members, trying to ferret out details of Hamilton's program. Speculators could reap huge profits if they divined Hamilton's intentions correctly, and at New York dinner parties they hung on his every word. Many rich merchants had already posted agents to backwoods areas of the south to scoop up depreciated state debt that would become more valuable if the federal government assumed the debt. Amid this atmosphere of contagious greed, Hamilton deflected attempts to pry loose information from him. In November, his Virginia friend Henry Lee wrote to inquire if Hamilton could divulge any information about his plan. Lee said that he hoped his request was not improper. In response, Hamilton was the very model of a scrupulous treasury secretary:

I am sure you are sincere when you say you would not subject me to an impropriety. Nor do I know that there would be any in my answering your queries. But you remember the saying with regard to Caesar's wife. [That she should be beyond suspicion.] I think the spirit of it applicable to every man concerned in the administration of the finances of a country. With respect to the conduct of such men, *suspicion* is ever eagle-eyed and the most innocent things are apt to be misinterpreted.[34]

On the eve of filing his report, Hamilton succumbed to jitters. "Tomorrow I open the budget and you may imagine that today I am very busy and not a little anxious," he wrote to Angelica, who soon began to send him financial treatises from London bookshops.[35] Skittish and high-strung, Hamilton knew that his proposals would spark frenzied debate and that legislative foes were sharpening their knives. When he informed Congress that he was ready to deliver his report, a controversy flared over whether he should do so in person or on paper. So great was the residual fear of executive encroachment on the legislature that Hamilton was not allowed to present his text in person, so the fifty-one-page pamphlet was read aloud

to the House of Representatives on January 14. It was so lengthy that, by the end,
many representatives sat there in stupefied silence.

Much later, Daniel Webster rhapsodized about Hamilton's report as follows:
"The fabled birth of Minerva from the brain of Jove was hardly more sudden or
more perfect than the financial system of the United States as it burst forth from the
conception of Alexander Hamilton."[36] This was the long view of history and of
many contemporaries, but detractors were immediately vocal. They were befuddled
by the complexity of Hamilton's plan and its array of options for creditors. Opponents sensed that he was moving too fast, on too many fronts, for them to grasp all
his intentions. He had devised his economic machinery so cunningly that its cogs
and wheels meshed perfectly together. One could not tamper with the parts without destroying the whole. Hamilton later said of this ingenious structure, "Credit is
an *entire thing*. Every part of it has the nicest sympathy with every other part.
Wound one limb and the whole tree shrinks and decays."[37]

Perhaps the most settled prejudice Hamilton had to combat was a visceral sense
that any program even faintly resembling British practice was pernicious. It was not
just that a large funded debt seemed reminiscent of England's. It was also the fear
that Hamilton was switching the power balance in government, tilting it from the
House of Representatives, the "people's" branch, to the executive branch. Senator
William Maclay recorded his horror at Hamilton's program: "He recommends indiscriminate funding and in the style of a British minister has sent down his bill."[38]
Beyond this assertion of Treasury power, critics feared outright corruption of legislators by the executive. Maclay and others suspected that several congressmen dabbled in government securities. This "villainous business," Maclay concluded, will
"damn the character of Hamilton as a minister forever."[39] The myth of Alexander
Hamilton as the American Mephistopheles was being born. Maclay saw New York
financiers as satanic henchmen in collusion with Hamilton to foster "the most
abandoned system of speculation ever broached in our country."[40]

Hamilton denied that congressmen were speculating in government securities.
"As far as I know, there is not a member of the legislature who can properly be
called a stock-jobber or a paper dealer," he assured Washington. Of those who did
own such securities, most had held them since the war, and Hamilton saw nothing
wrong with this: "It is a strange perversion of ideas . . . that men should be deemed
corrupt and criminal for becoming proprietors in the funds of their country. Yet I
believe the number of members of Congress very small who have ever been considerably proprietors in the funds."[41]

Maclay scoffed at such claims and saw Congress in an unholy league with New
York speculators: "The whole town almost has been busy at it and, of course, all engaged in influencing the measures of Congress. Nor have the members [of Con-

gress] themselves kept their hands clean from this dirty work. . . . [H]enceforth we may consider speculation as a congressional employment."[42] Maclay was sincere in his misgivings and yet, like many of Hamilton's naysayers, basically ignorant of finance. When the sinking fund began buying up government debt later in the year, Maclay descried a plot to line the pockets of speculators. He didn't seem to realize that such market operations reduced debt and drove down interest rates, benefiting the entire economy. Maclay and other critics were correct that the Hamiltonian system didn't necessarily reward the just or the virtuous, yet they missed the larger social benefits that accrued to society.

Hamilton's *Report on Public Credit* had an electrifying effect. Securities began to change hands with a speed never before seen in America. Robert R. Livingston observed that the speculative craze "invaded all ranks of people," even infecting hardened antifederalists such as George Clinton and Melancton Smith.[43] Staggered by this rampant speculation, Congressman James Jackson dubbed the perpetrators "rapacious wolves seeking whom they may devour."[44] Jackson stood up on the House floor in late January to protest the "spirit of havoc, speculation, and ruin" that had followed Hamilton's report and charged that many speculators had profited from advance knowledge of it. He alleged that three vessels loaded with speculators had departed from New York within the past fortnight, bound for the south to sweep up state debt from unsuspecting investors who had not yet heard about Hamilton's program. "My soul arises indignant at the avaricious and immoral turpitude which so vile a conduct displays," he thundered.[45]

Another critic, Benjamin Rush of Philadelphia, exhibited the often untutored indignation that greeted Hamilton's plan. Making the exaggerated claim that Congress was now "legislating for British subjects," Rush objected not just to public debt but to *all* debt as harmful to society. "Let us not overvalue public credit," he warned. "It is to nations what private credit and loan offices are to individuals. It begets debt, extravagance, vice, and bankruptcy. . . . I sicken every time I contemplate the European vices that the Secretary's gambling report will necessarily introduce into our infant republic."[46]

Compounding Hamilton's problems was that his report crystallized latent divisions between north and south. There was a popular conception (to Hamilton, a gross misconception) that the original holders of government paper were disproportionately from the south and that the current owners who had "swindled" them were from the north. Hamilton denied that any such regional transfer took place, contending that the debt was now concentrated in northern hands only because much of the war had been fought there and more northern soldiers had received debt certificates. Still, the impression persisted that crooked northern merchants were hoodwinking virtuous southern farmers. It didn't help that many New Yorkers in Hamilton's own social circle—James Duane, Gouverneur Morris, William Duer, Rufus King—had accumulated sizable positions in government debt. Philip Schuyler alone had a sixty-seven-thousand-dollar stake and was reportedly so alarmed by Senate diatribes against Hamilton's plan that his hair stood "on end as if the Indians had fired at him."[47] And it didn't seem to occur to Hamilton that legislators, like Caesar's wife, should also be beyond suspicion. From the controversy over his funding scheme, we can date the onset of that abiding rural fear of big-city financiers that came to permeate American politics.

Hamilton knew that many current creditors who would profit from his measures were less than angelic. His vision, however, was fixed on America's future, not the partisan bickering of the moment. He was laying the groundwork for a great nation. "The general rules of property, and all those general rules which form the links of society, frequently involve in their ordinary operation particular hardships and injuries," he told Washington. "Yet the public order and the general happiness require a steady conformity to them. It is perhaps always better that partial evils should be submitted to than that principles should be violated."[48]

On February 8, 1790, the House of Representatives began to debate Hamilton's *Report on Public Credit*, which monopolized most of the second session of the First Congress. Maclay's diary tells us that the edgy Hamilton had started lobbying a week earlier, flitting from one member to the next: "Mr. Hamilton is very uneasy, as far as I can learn, about his funding system. He was here early to wait on the Speaker and I believe spent most of his time in running from place to place among the members."[49] Many congressmen experienced Hamilton's influence as an unrelenting pressure. To mental vigor, he added organizational bustle. A day after the House debate began, Maclay got a visit from another early Hamilton mentor, the theologian Dr. John Rodgers, who expounded Hamilton's system "as if he had been in the pulpit. . . . The [Society of the] Cincinnati is another of [Hamilton's] machines and the whole city of New York."[50] Before long, the disgruntled Maclay berated Hamilton's "tools" and "gladiators" for badgering him without remorse.[51] Americans had rejected a parliamentary system on the British model, forbidding executive officers from sitting in the legislature, but Hamilton's ubiquitous presence in Congress seemed to violate that understanding.

In fashioning his program, Hamilton had counted on loyal backing from James Madison, now a Virginia congressman. Ever since his inaugural address, President Washington had consulted regularly with Madison on matters ranging from etiquette to the selection of ambassadors. By dint of his seminal role at the Constitutional Convention, his Bill of Rights, and his work on *The Federalist Papers*, Madison was the most influential congressman.

If Hamilton thought Madison would support his plans, he was rudely undeceived on February 11, 1790, when the Virginian made a speech attacking the funding scheme. Madison was prepared to allow current holders of government debt to profit from past appreciation of their government securities. But as to future appreciation resulting from Hamilton's program, he wanted that windfall to go to the *original* holders, no matter how long ago they had sold off their securities. For Madison, these original holders had not surrendered faith in government, as Hamilton alleged, but had merely sold in desperation. He thought that blameless patriots were being victimized, and it disturbed his sense of justice that speculators were buying up debt from ignorant country folk. Madison saw a betrayal of the American Revolution in the making.

Hamilton was flabbergasted. He had laid out all the practical problems that made such "discrimination" unworkable, especially the missing documents that would be needed to trace original holders. And Madison's proposal would damage the invaluable principle that buyers of securities should reap all future dividends and profits. In Hamilton's view, government interference with this right amounted to confiscation of private property. Madison's arguments had a strong sentimental appeal to patriotic veterans, while Hamilton's contained a core of hardheaded practicality.

As the debate dragged on, the Federal Hall galleries filled with speculators wagering on the outcome, and tension built as a vote approached on Madison's proposal. On February 20, Abigail Adams told her sister that she was to attend the great debate on discrimination: "It is thought that tomorrow will be the decisive day with respect to that question. . . . On this occasion I am going for the first time to the House."[52] Hamilton had marshaled his forces effectively, whereas Madison had proven clumsy and inflexible. Madison's "pride seems of that kind which repels all communication," a disappointed Maclay wrote on February 22. "The obstinacy of this man has ruined the opposition" to Hamilton's plan.[53] That day, the House defeated Madison's motion by a thirty-six to thirteen vote. But in an ominous sign for Hamilton, nine of the thirteen dissenting votes came from Virginia, the most populous state.

Madison was beginning to drift away from Hamilton. Although he claimed that he objected only to parts of Hamilton's program, he admitted privately to more fundamental grievances, telling one correspondent, "I go on the principle that a public debt is a public curse."[54] Whereas the "Publius" team of Hamilton, Madison, and Jay had seen the supreme threat to liberty coming at the state level, Madison now began to direct his criticism at federal power lodged in the capable hands of the treasury secretary. John Adams, among others, seemed disillusioned with Madison as a legislator. "Mr. Madison is a studious scholar," the vice president told a friend in April, "but his reputation as a man of abilities is a creature of French puffs.

Some of the worst measures, some of the most stupid motions, stand on record to his infamy."[55]

For Hamilton, Madison's apostasy was a painful personal betrayal. One of Hamilton's supporters, minister-cum-speculator Manasseh Cutler, told a friend that Hamilton regarded Madison's opposition to his plan as "a perfidious desertion of the principles which [Madison] was solemnly pledged to defend."[56] This falling-out was to be more than personal, for the rift between Hamilton and Madison precipitated the start of the two-party system in America. The funding debate shattered the short-lived political consensus that had ushered in the new government. For the next five years, the political spectrum in America was defined by whether people endorsed or opposed Alexander Hamilton's programs.

Even as Madison flailed at Hamilton's funding scheme, a seemingly unrelated drama was being enacted in Congress over the slavery issue. Quakers from New York and Pennsylvania had submitted a petition to abolish the slave trade, while the Pennsylvania Society for Promoting the Abolition of Slavery, led by eighty-four-year-old Benjamin Franklin, filed a more aggressive petition to abolish slavery itself. On this sensitive issue, southern delegates flamed up in righteous anger. Aedanus Burke of South Carolina accused the Quakers of "blowing the trumpet of sedition" and asked that the galleries be cleared of spectators whose ears might be defiled by such heresy.[57] James Jackson of Georgia said that the Bible itself had approved slavery. The vehemence of southern legislators made plain that, on this issue, they would brook no compromise. William Loughton Smith of South Carolina reminded fellow legislators that southern states had ratified the Constitution on the proviso that it would not interfere with slavery. Any attempt to renege on this pledge would threaten the survival of the union.

This fracas was more than a footnote in the country's early history. Slavery was gradually fading away in many parts of the north, but with each passing year it became more deeply embedded in the southern economy. As Fisher Ames of Massachusetts complained to a friend of southern indignation, "Language low, indecent, and profane has been used. . . . The Southern gentry have been guided by their hot tempers and stubborn prejudices and pride in regard to Southern importance and negro slavery."[58]

The abolitionist petitions were referred to a House committee. When this group reported back in March, it cited the twenty-year grace period for the slave trade adopted by the Constitutional Convention, meaning that Congress lacked authority to eliminate the slave trade before 1808, much less to emancipate the slaves. Whether from reluctant pragmatism or outright cowardice, abolition was now officially dead. After the House committee report, Madison, who had just masterminded the Bill of Rights, told Edmund Randolph that the south should bury the slavery issue with benign neglect. "The true policy of the Southern members," he wrote approvingly, "was to let the affair proceed with as little noise as possible."[59] Madison was torn between intellectual sympathy for abolitionism and fear of irate southern reactions. Whether or not he was more motivated by a desire to save the union than to preserve slavery, his views would increasingly be colored by personal and regional self-interest as he curried favor with his Virginia constituents.

Tabling the slavery issue had been a precondition of union in 1787 and now again in 1790. Though a passionate slavery critic, Hamilton knew that this inflammatory issue could wreck the union. He couldn't be both the supreme nationalist *and* the supreme abolitionist. He certainly couldn't push through his controversial funding program if he stirred up the slavery question, which was probably a futile battle anyway. So this man of infinite opinions grew mute on that all-important matter, though he may have taken a secret swipe at slaveholders the following year. Historian Philip Marsh has argued that Hamilton, using the pen name "Civis" in a newspaper piece of February 23, 1791, penned the following telling sarcasm to Madison and Jefferson: "As to the negroes, you must be tender upon that subject. . . . Who talk most about liberty and equality . . . ? Is it not those who hold the bill of rights in one hand and a whip for affrighted slaves in the other?"[60] If Hamilton wrote this, he was updating a gibe by the English radical Thomas Day, who had written in 1776, "If there be an object truly ridiculous in nature, it is an American patriot, signing resolutions of independence with the one hand and with the other brandishing a whip over his affrighted slaves."[61]

The bipartisan decision to shelve the slavery issue had profound repercussions for Hamilton's economic measures, for it spared the southern economy from criticism. In the 1790s, America's critical energies were trained exclusively on the northern economy and the financial and manufacturing system devised by Hamilton. This became immediately apparent in the heated debate over his funding system, which allowed southern slaveholders to proclaim that northern financiers were the evil ones and that slaveholders were the virtuous populists, upright men of the soil. It was testimony to the political genius of Thomas Jefferson and James Madison that they diverted attention from the grisly realities of southern slavery by casting a lurid spotlight on Hamilton's system as the paramount embodiment of evil. They inveighed against the concentrated wealth of northern merchants when southern slave plantations clearly represented the most heinous form of concentrated wealth. Throughout the 1790s, planters posed as the tribunes of small farmers and denounced the depravity of stocks, bonds, banks, and manufacturing—the whole wicked apparatus of Hamiltonian capitalism.

When Congress returned to Hamilton's *Report on Public Credit* in March, after debating the abolitionist petitions, many southerners seemed more outraged over the powers that Hamilton planned to give the federal government. If the treasury secretary welded the states into a strong union through his assumption plan, might not that strengthen the federal power to meddle with slavery? And did it therefore not behoove the south to resist Hamilton's plan and shore up states' rights? The extent of southern ire that spring was shown dramatically in the erratic behavior of Aedanus Burke. Burke had a shock of thick, white hair, a long, pointed nose, and a piercing gaze that expressed his fiery nature. That spring, he found himself in a political bind because he supported Hamilton's assumption program even though many of his southern constituents opposed it.

To reclaim his political reputation, Burke pounced on a clever diversionary tactic. On March 31, 1790, he launched a tirade in the House against the July 4 eulogy that Hamilton had pronounced on General Nathanael Greene nine months earlier. From that speech, he plucked the line in which Hamilton referred to the militias as "the mimickry of soldiership." Burke found this reference insulting and countered that many southern militiamen had "sacrificed their lives at the holy altar of liberty. Their graves are to be seen scattered over our glades and woodlands, they are now no more."[62] Then casting his eyes on the visitors' gallery—since it was packed with pretty ladies, he supposed Hamilton sat among them—he blasted the treasury secretary in language that crossed the boundaries of political decorum: "In the face of this Assembly and in the presence of this gallery . . . I give the lie to Col. Hamilton."[63] This blatant affront was so shocking that congressmen interrupted Burke's outburst with loud calls for order.

Their main reason for alarm was that Burke, in branding Hamilton a liar, had violated his *personal* sense of honor. Like many contemporary politicians, Hamilton still inhabited two worlds: the modern world of constitutional law and the old feudal order based on honor and dignity. Unless retracted, any direct challenge to one's honor had to be settled outside the legal realm on the field of honor—the dueling ground. Senator William Maclay, who had stopped by the House to eavesdrop on the debate, noted in his diary "a violent personal attack on Hamilton by Judge Burke of South Carolina, which the men of the blade say must produce a duel."[64]

Some observers didn't take seriously Burke's insulting behavior. William Loughton Smith contended that Burke's "mode of speaking and his roughness only excite laughter."[65] Hamilton, however, wasn't laughing. Some members of the legislature did not yet know his irrepressible pugnacity or how fiercely he guarded his reputation. Fisher Ames observed that no man, "not the Roman Cato himself, was more inflexible on every point that touched, or only seemed to touch, integrity and honour" than Hamilton.[66] When Smith discussed the imbroglio with him, Hamilton drew a distinction between criticism of his policies and his person: "He said he should at all times disregard any observations applied to his public station as Secretary of the Treasury, but that *this* was not to be passed over."[67] Smith also noted that Burke was "amazingly intimate" with Governor George Clinton and reportedly courting one of his daughters. "Clinton hates Hamilton mortally and has probably set on Burke," he conjectured.[68]

The very next day, Hamilton sent off a short, heated letter to Burke. He claimed that the quote from the eulogy had been taken out of context and that the full sentence claimed that General Greene was "embarrassed by small fugitive bodies of volunteer militia, *the mimickry of soldiership.*" He had made a statement not about the South Carolina militia, but about irregular volunteers in the north: "Having thus, Sir, stated the matter in its true light, it remains for you to judge what conduct, in consequence of the explanation, will be proper on your part."[69]

Before the day was out, Burke replied to Hamilton in a manner that ratcheted up the pressure. In a letter designed for consumption back home, Burke lauded the bravery of the southern militias. He knew that he had to explain why he had waited nine months to broadcast his charges. To have done so at the time, he told Hamilton, "would have been downright madness," given Hamilton's popularity.[70] In the charged political atmosphere of the moment, the dispute now festered, and factions formed around the principals. "The town is much agitated about a duel between Burke and Hamilton," Maclay reported. "So many people concerned in the business may really make the fools fight."[71]

A party of six congressmen arbitrated an end to the dispute by securing two letters: one from Hamilton in which he insisted that he meant no dishonor to the southern militias, and a second from Burke in which he accepted this statement and apologized to Hamilton. It was all artfully orchestrated according to the unspoken rules of "affairs of honor." The uproar backfired on Burke, who found himself demoted in influence.

The affair wasn't altogether a victory for Hamilton. In his memorial speech for General Greene, he had taken gratuitous swipes at southern soldiers and had not paid sufficient attention to the pieties of democratic politics. Burke made him feel the sting of public opinion; it wasn't the last time Hamilton paid a price for needless indiscretion. The contretemps again demonstrated that beneath his invincible facade, Hamilton was still the hypersensitive boy from the West Indies. His combativeness was always more than just political calculation, for he brooded obsessively about slights to his honor. This supreme rationalist, who feared the passions of the mob more than any other founder, was himself a man of deep and often ungovernable emotions.

SIXTEEN

DR. PANGLOSS

On March 1, 1790, with Hamilton engulfed in conflict over his funding scheme, Thomas Jefferson set out from Monticello to assume his duties as the new secretary of state. He had sailed from Paris in October 1789, ending a five-year stint as American minister to France. Only when his ship docked in Norfolk, Virginia, in late November did he discover Washington's letter asking him to take the cabinet post. The Senate, still in its trusting infancy, had confirmed the nominee before he knew about the offer. Where the hyperthyroid Hamilton jumped at his assignment and sprang quickly into action, Jefferson dithered through the winter about taking the State Department job and did not accept until mid-February 1790.

Similarly, as Hamilton, Madison, and Jay had defended the Constitution in *The Federalist*, Jefferson had vacillated about America's new charter. At moments, he sounded as if he would have preferred a patched-up version of the Articles of Confederation. "There are very good articles in it and very bad," he declared of the new charter from Paris. "I do not know which predominate."[1] He confided to Madison that he liked the government's division into three branches but voiced grave doubts about his favorite bogeyman: executive power. In Philadelphia, Hamilton had espoused a lifetime president on good behavior, while Jefferson recoiled at any president who could serve additional four-year terms. "I own I am not a friend to a very energetic government," he told Madison. "It is always oppressive."[2] Such a man was bound to clash with Hamilton and have misgivings about serving in the new central government. When Congress first met in the spring of 1789, Jefferson was still equivocating about the Constitution. Asked whether he was a federalist or antifederalist, Jefferson evaded the issue and expressed opposition to all party labels.

"Therefore I protest to you that I am not of the party of the federalists," he explained to Francis Hopkinson, a Pennsylvania judge and signer of the Declaration of Independence. "But I am much further from that of the antifederalists."[3] So with a multitude of reservations, Thomas Jefferson cast his lot with the new government.

In 1789, French sculptor Jean Antoine Houdon executed a bust of Jefferson that shows a handsome man with a calm, self-confident air. Yet the vigilant eyes hint at someone who moved slowly, cautiously, taking everything in before acting. The tightly sealed lips convey something enigmatic beneath the patrician ease. Like Burr, Thomas Jefferson found strength in secrecy, in silence. Shy and aloof, he seldom made eye contact with listeners yet could be a warmly engaging presence among small groups of like-minded intimates. This laconic man knew how to sprinkle his conversation with brilliant aperçus that lingered in people's minds. With his quiet charm and courtly demeanor, he had a knack for winning people over at dinner parties distinguished by good food and eight varieties of wine.

Tall, lean, and freckled, with reddish hair and hazel eyes, Jefferson had one trait that the marble bust failed to capture: his slack-jointed movements. When William Maclay met the new secretary, his slouching figure seemed to lack ministerial dignity. Maclay groused, "He sits in a lounging manner, on one hip commonly, and with one of his shoulders elevated much above the other. . . . [H]is whole figure has a loose, shackling air."[4] His dress was casual, almost sloppy. The folksy air charmed people and allowed Jefferson to root out their secrets. The plain dress, mild manners, and unassuming air were the perfect costume for a crafty man intent upon presenting himself as the spokesman for the common people.

With an elite pedigree on both sides of his family, Jefferson was anything but common. His father, Peter, was a tobacco planter, a judge of the court of chancery, and a member of the Virginia House of Burgesses, while his mother, Jane Randolph, came from a prominent family. By the time Peter Jefferson died, he bequeathed to his children more than 60 slaves, 25 horses, 70 head of cattle, 200 hogs, and 7,500 acres; two-thirds of this bountiful legacy went to his eldest son, Thomas.

Peter Jefferson gave the boy a complete classical education. Tutored at home at age five, Jefferson went to a boarding school at age nine that afforded such thorough grounding in Greek and Latin that biographer Dumas Malone claims that for Jefferson "the heroes of antiquity were more real than either the Christian saints or modern historical figures."[5] He attended the College of William and Mary, which schooled the scions of the Virginia gentry, before being admitted to the bar. Like Hamilton, Jefferson was a fanatic for self-improvement. He rose before dawn each morning and employed every hour profitably, studying up to fifteen hours per day. Extremely systematic in his habits, Jefferson enjoyed retreating into the sheltered tranquillity of his books, and the spectrum of his interests was vast. He told his daughter, "It is wonderful how much may be done if we are always doing."[6] Whether riding horseback, playing the violin, designing buildings, or inventing curious gadgets, Thomas Jefferson seemed adept at everything. Like many accomplished people, he was seduced by this quest for self-perfection and not easily lured into public office. The self-sufficiency and philosophic repose made him an atypical politician. He once wrote, "The most effectual means of being secure against pain is to retire within ourselves and to suffice for our own happiness."[7]

This pampered life rested on a foundation of slavery. Jefferson's earliest memory was of being carried on a pillow by a slave on horseback. He never tried to justify slavery and said he eagerly awaited the day "when an opportunity will be offered to abolish this lamentable evil."[8] When the Virginia legislature rebuffed his bid to stop importing slaves into the state, he regretted that "the public mind would not bear the proposition."[9] However much Jefferson deplored the "moral and political depravity" of slavery, his own slaves remained in bondage to his career and his incorrigibly spendthrift ways.[10] When he commissioned his mountaintop home at Monticello, he seemed oblivious of the toll this would exact on his slaves, who had to hoist the building materials to such a height.

In 1769, while the fourteen-year-old Hamilton dreamed of escape from St. Croix, the twenty-six-year-old Jefferson was elected to Virginia's House of Burgesses. Jefferson belonged to an aristocracy with a clear path of advancement. At twenty-eight, he married a young widow, Martha Wayles Skelton, who inherited 135 slaves after her father's death. This loving ten-year marriage was marred by childhood mortality—only two of their six children reached maturity—and in September 1782 Martha herself died at thirty-four. Only thirty-nine at the time, Jefferson survived his wife by forty-four years but never remarried. Ensconced at Monticello with his books, inventions, and experiments, Jefferson became an unfathomable loner.

If the American Revolution had not supervened, Thomas Jefferson might well have whiled away his life on the mountaintop, a cultivated planter and philosopher. For Jefferson, the Revolution was an unwelcome distraction from a treasured private life, while for Hamilton it was a fantastic opportunity for escape and advancement. Like Hamilton, Jefferson rose in politics through sheer mastery of words—sunny, optimistic words that captured the hopefulness of a new country. Nobody gave more noble expression to the ideals of individual freedom and dignity or had a more devout faith in the wisdom of the common man. As chief draftsman of the Declaration of Independence, Jefferson took often commonplace ideas and endowed them with majestic form. When the new government was formed, the Declaration had not yet attained the status of American Scripture. (Jefferson's authorship remained largely anonymous until he found attribution politically convenient in the 1790s.) Thus, when Hamilton first met Jefferson in 1790, he did not see him as quite the revered figure that we do today.

Hamilton may have believed that Jefferson's contributions to the nation paled beside his own and not just because of his own work on behalf of the Constitution. Besides handling Washington's correspondence, Hamilton had spent five years in combat, exposing himself to enemy fire on many occasions. Jefferson had never set foot on a battlefield. Elected Virginia governor in 1779, he found the job irksome and wanted to resign, prompting Edmund Pendleton to complain to Madison, "It is a little cowardly to quit our posts in a bustling time!"[11] When the turncoat Benedict Arnold burned and pillaged Richmond in January 1781, the capital stood defenseless despite warnings from Washington to Jefferson. Governor Jefferson fled in the early hours, giving up Richmond without a shot and allowing munitions and government records to fall into British hands. In June, in Jefferson's waning hours as governor, the British pounced on Charlottesville and almost captured the Virginia Assembly gathered there. Then, when word came that a British cavalry was approaching Monticello, Jefferson scrambled off on horseback into the woods. He was accused of dereliction of duty and neglecting the transfer of power to his successor. Though the Virginia Assembly exonerated him of any wrongdoing, Hamilton wasn't the only one who suspected Jefferson of cowardice. He later wrote mockingly that when real danger appeared, "the *governor* of the *ancient dominion* dwindled into the *poor, timid philosopher* and, instead of rallying his brave countrymen, he fled for safety from a few light-horsemen and shamefully abandoned his trust!"[12]

The Revolution left Jefferson with an implacable aversion to the British, whom he regarded as a race of "rich, proud, hectoring, swearing, squabbling, carnivorous animals."[13] He had a long list of personal grievances beyond his distaste for Britain as a corrupt, monarchical society. Cornwallis had ravaged one of Jefferson's farms, butchering animals, torching crops, and snatching thirty slaves. Like many Virginia plantation owners, Jefferson was land rich but cash poor and chronically indebted to British creditors. He once said mordantly that the Virginia planters were "a species of property annexed to certain mercantile houses in London."[14] By the late 1780s, as tobacco prices plummeted, Virginia planters struggled to repay old debts to London creditors and demanded the return of slaves carried off by British troops. The steep payments he owed British bankers forced Jefferson to retain his enormous workforce of slaves despite his professed hatred for the institution. "The torment of mind I endure till the moment shall arrive when I shall owe not a shilling on earth is such really as to render life of little value," he told his American manager in 1787. But he would not sell land to pay his debts; "nor would I willingly sell the slaves as long as there remains any prospect of paying my debts with their labor."[15] The weight of that debt, created by his own extravagance, perhaps prevented Thomas Jefferson from being the person he would ideally like to have been. Even while secretary of state, he remained in hock to British creditors for an exorbitant seven thousand pounds. He carried these large debts until his death in 1826, necessitating the sale of 130 of his slaves at Monticello six months later. It was not the image that the philosopher of the common man would have preferred to leave to posterity.

When Jefferson went to France in 1784, succeeding Ben Franklin as U.S. minister— the word *ambassador* was still eschewed as a vestige of monarchy—he had firsthand experience of an absolutist government. "The truth of Voltaire's observation offers itself perpetually that every man here must be either the hammer or the anvil," he told a friend.[16] To George Washington, he expressed himself as unequivocally. "I was much an enemy to monarchy before I came to Europe. I am ten thousand times more so since I have seen what they are."[17] His French sojourn radicalized Jefferson and left him with a heightened suspicion of the damage that could be done by any aristocratic or monarchical sympathies in America—suspicions that were to crystallize around the figure of Alexander Hamilton.

All the while, Jefferson clung to a vision of France as America's fraternal ally. "Nothing should be spared on our part to attach this country to us," he wrote to Madison.[18] While scorning French political arrangements, Jefferson adored his life in that decadent society. He relished Paris—the people, wine, women, music, literature, and architecture. And the more rabidly antiaristocratic he became, the more he was habituated to aristocratic pleasures. Jefferson fancied himself a mere child of nature, a simple, unaffected man, rather than what he really was: a grandee, a gourmet, a hedonist, and a clever, ambitious politician. Even as he deplored the inequities of French society, he occupied the stately Hotel de Langeac on the Champs Elysées, constructed for a mistress of one of Louis XV's ministers. Jefferson decorated the mansion with choice neoclassical furniture bought from stylish vendors. The philosopher in powdered hair employed a coachman, a footman, a valet— seven or eight domestics in all, a household staff so complete that it included a *frotteur* whose job consisted solely of buffing the floors to a high gleam. Jefferson's colossal shopping sprees in Paris—he bought two thousand books and sixty-three paintings—betrayed a cavalier disregard for his crushing debts as well as the slaves whose labor serviced them. While Jefferson's Parisian life seems to contradict his politics, he was embraced by a group of Enlightenment aristocrats who exhibited the same exquisite contradictions.

For part of his Parisian stay, Jefferson was joined by his two daughters. The younger one, Polly, arrived in 1787 in the company of his light-skinned fourteen-year-old slave, Sally Hemings, who was called "Dashing Sally" at Monticello and was later described by another slave as "mighty near white" and "very handsome" with "long straight hair down her back."[19] Jefferson had inherited the Hemings family via his wife, and it is now presumed that Sally Hemings was her half sister. We do not know for certain whether Jefferson's apparent romance with Sally Hemings began at this time or after he returned to America. He was a widower who was highly susceptible to women. For all his paeans to married life, he had no qualms about flirtations with married women. In 1786, Jefferson, forty-three, squired around Paris a blond, coquettish British artist born in Italy, twenty-six-year-old Maria Cosway, whose husband, the painter Richard Cosway, was usually absent. Their dalliance lasted long enough to bring Jefferson into contact with Maria Cosway's closest friend, Angelica Church, who had recently incorporated the Cosways into her thriving salon.

When Jefferson first met Church in Paris in late 1787, she acted as a go-between for Mrs. Cosway, which tells us something about her own liberal views on extra-marital escapades. "Have you seen yet the lovely Mrs. Church?" Maria Cosway wrote to Jefferson that Christmas. "If I did not love her so much, I should fear her rivalship, but, no, I give you free permission to love her with all your heart."[20] Church brought Jefferson a little tea vase from her friend. He was as entranced by the worldly, seductive Church as Hamilton. Jefferson loved her warm vivacity and what he described as her "mild and settled" temperament.[21] When John Trumbull painted two miniatures of Jefferson, the American minister sent one copy to Maria Cosway, the other to Angelica Church. "The memorial of me which you have from Trumbull is the most worthless part of me," Jefferson confided to Church in an accompanying note. "Could he paint my friendship to you, it would be something out of the common line."[22] In an equally coquettish reply, Church said that she and Cosway were "extremely vain of the pleasure of being permitted to write him and very happy to have some share of his favorable opinion."[23] Though Angelica Church was married with four children, Jefferson persisted in his advances. In 1788, projecting a trip to America the following year, he invited her to visit him at Monticello, or else he would visit her in New York and they would travel to Niagara Falls. So close were Jefferson and Angelica Church at this time that Jefferson's copy of *The Federalist* displays this surprising dedication: "For Mrs. Church from her *Sister*, Elizabeth Hamilton."[24] Evidently, Church had given Jefferson the copy that Eliza rushed off to her in England.

In the end, Angelica Church spurned Jefferson's coy overtures, and nothing ever came of their flirtation. The feud beween Hamilton and Jefferson forced Church to choose between the two men, and, inevitably, she chose her brother-in-law. Yet the brief liaison may have had a political impact. During her 1789 stay in New York, Church doubtless told Hamilton about Jefferson's fling with Maria Cosway and his provocative suggestion that he and Church travel together in America. She may even have voiced some suspicions about Sally Hemings, whose son Madison later claimed that it was in Paris that "my mother became Mr. Jefferson's concubine, and when he was called home, she was *enceinte* by him."[25] Any such gossip about Jefferson in Paris would have given Hamilton an image of the new secretary of state strikingly different from the more ascetic one he wanted to project to the world. And when Hamilton later began a campaign to unmask what he saw as the real Jefferson, the closet sensualist, the knowledge of Jefferson's amorous ways, culled from Church's stories, may have colored his portrait. Both Hamilton and Jefferson came to see each other as hypocritical libertines, and this fed a mutual cynicism. Hamilton offered testimony of his own inexcusable lapses in this area, while the sphinx-like Jefferson was a man of such unshakable reticence that it took two centuries of sedulous detective work to provide partial corroboration of the story of his sexual liaison with Sally Hemings.

A congenital optimist, Jefferson was convinced that France, following America's lead, would cast off the shackles of despotism. Lafayette and other French aristocrats, he believed, after imbibing a love of liberty in America, would effect a comparable transformation in their own society. In November 1788, Jefferson wrote to Washington of a France buoyant with hope: "The nation has been awakened by our revolution, they feel their strength, they are enlightened, their lights are spreading, and they will not retrograde."[26] No less serenely, he told James Monroe that within two or three years France would have "a tolerably free constitution" without "having cost them a drop of blood."[27] As late as March 15, 1789, Jefferson seemed oblivious of the violent emotions churning in the breasts of the French populace, telling Madison, "France will be quiet this year, because this year at least is necessary for settling her future constitution."[28] By this point, desperate French peasants were looting grain wagons. The following month, the mere rumor that a wallpaper manufacturer was about to slash wages led workers to encircle his house, shouting, "Death to the rich, death to the aristocrats."[29] The subsequent crackdown on protesters left dozens, perhaps hundreds, dead.

It would be richly paradoxical that Jefferson, long an eyewitness to French politics, was blind to the murderous drift of events while Hamilton, who never set foot in Europe, was much more clear-sighted about the French Revolution. At first, Jefferson's exuberance was natural and understandable. In June 1789, the legislature was renamed the National Assembly, as Louis XVI seemed to accept a constitutional monarchy. On July 11, Lafayette presented to the assembly a declaration of rights that had been helpfully reviewed by Jefferson. Then came the gory atrocities that shadowed the Bastille's fall on July 14, 1789: severed heads propped on pikes, mutilated bodies dragged through the streets, corpses swinging from streetlamps. For those who cared to read the signs, the future of the Revolution was written in these bloodstained images. Simon Schama has noted that violence was, from the outset, part and parcel of the Revolution: "The notion that between 1789 and 1791, France basked in some sort of liberal pleasure garden before the erection of the guillotine is a complete fantasy."[30]

With his highly selective vision, Jefferson preferred to dwell on the hopeful aspects of the situation and filtered out the carnage. On August 3, 1789, he wrote to a friend:

> It is impossible to conceive a greater fermentation than has worked in Paris, nor do I believe that so great a fermentation ever produced so little injury in any other people. I have been through it daily, have observed the mobs with my own eyes in order to be satisfied of their objects and declare to you that I saw so plainly the legitimacy of them that I have slept in my house as quietly through the whole as I ever did in the most peaceable moments. . . . I will agree to be stoned as a false prophet if all does not end well in this country.[31]

To Maria Cosway, Jefferson hazarded a small joke about decapitating aristocrats— "The cutting off heads is become so much à la mode that one is apt to feel of a morning whether their own is on their shoulders"—and he left little doubt that the French Revolution was a worthy sequel to its American predecessor: "My fortune has been singular to see in the course of fourteen years two such revolutions as were never seen before."[32] Even as Jefferson departed from France that fall, thousands of poor, desperate women were swarming toward Versailles, determined to drag the royal family back to Paris.

Many Americans were flattered to think that their revolution had spawned a European successor with a similar respect for legal forms. All the more prophetic then the letter of October 6, 1789, that Hamilton sent to his old friend Lafayette, who had been appointed head of the national guard. Sitting in New York, slaving over his *Report on Public Credit,* the new secretary of the treasury peered deeper into French affairs than did Jefferson after five years in residence. "I have seen with a mixture of pleasure and apprehension the progress of the events which have lately taken place in your country," Hamilton began his carefully worded letter. "As a friend to mankind and liberty, I rejoice in the efforts which you are making to establish it, while I fear much for the final success of the attempts, for the fate of those I esteem who are engaged in it." Hamilton knew that Lafayette would wonder why he experienced "this foreboding of ill" and listed four reasons. The first three were the disagreements that would surface over the French constitution; the "vehement character" of the French people; and the resistance of the nobility to the sacrifices they would have to make. The fourth point was perhaps the most compelling: "I dread the reveries of your philosophic politicians who appear in the moment to have great influence and who being mere speculatists may aim at more refinement than suits either with human nature or the composition of your nation."[33]

The future secretary of state, now sailing home, was to strike Hamilton as just such a "philosophic politician" ignorant of human nature. Hamilton later explained to a political associate that Jefferson in Paris "drank deeply of the French philosophy in religion, in science, in politics. He came from France in the moment of a fermentation which he had had a share in exciting and in the passions and feelings of which he shared both from temperament and situation."[34] Fresh from the French Revolution, Jefferson was to be greeted by a most unexpected shock when he showed up in New York to assume his post.

On March 21, 1790, Jefferson moved into lodgings on Maiden Lane, where he was to live with something less than republican austerity. From Paris, he had shipped home eighty-six crates packed with costly French furniture, porcelain, and silver, as well as books, paintings, and prints. He had brought home 288 bottles of French wine. To appease his craving for French food, he also brought along one of his slaves, James Hemings (Sally's brother), who had studied fine cooking with a Parisian chef. While secretary of state, Jefferson maintained a household of five servants, four horses, and a maître d'hôtel imported from Paris.

In seeming contradiction to this patrician style, Jefferson cherished a vision of America as a place of arcadian innocence. "Indeed, madam, I know nothing as charming as our own country," he had written to Angelica Church from Paris. "The learned say it is a new creation and I believe them, not for their reasons, but because it is made on an improved plan. Europe is a first idea, a crude production, before the master knew his trade, or had made up his mind as to what he wanted."[35] Settled in his palatial Parisian residence, Jefferson lamented reports of unspoiled Americans succumbing to luxurious ways. "I consider the extravagance which has seized them as a more baneful evil than toryism was during the war," he told one correspondent.[36] Now he was eager to assess "the tone of sentiment" in America after his prolonged absence.[37]

In New York, Jefferson soon decided that America had been corrupted in his absence and that the Revolution stood in mortal danger. He concluded that "a preference of kingly over republican government was evidently the favorite sentiment" among affluent New Yorkers.[38] As he attended dinners, he was taken aback by the pro-British inclinations of many merchants and the sumptuous gowns and jewelry of their wives. The town struck him as infested with Tories and avaricious speculators in government securities, all looking worshipfully to Hamilton as their favorite. The heroes of 1776 had given way to those of 1787; as exemplified by Hamilton, they were a different, more conservative breed. Jefferson blamed the influence of British manners and manufactures for this decay of republican purity.

Twelve years Jefferson's junior, Hamilton had never met him before. Hamilton had been a lowly artillery captain at the time Jefferson was composing the Declaration of Independence, and Hamilton's incandescent rise had coincided with Jefferson's years abroad. Hamilton would have heard favorable things about Jefferson from Angelica Church and from James Madison, and the latter likely introduced them. That Hamilton and Jefferson were to become antagonists in a bloody, unrelenting feud would not have occurred to either man upon first meeting, and their relations started out amicably enough. Alexander and Eliza hosted a welcoming dinner for the newcomer, who showed up in a blue coat and crimson knee breeches and talked fondly of the French people and their desire to eliminate the monarchy. Jefferson got to know Eliza so well that he chided Angelica Church in June for not writing more often and sighed with mock despair, "I can count only on hearing from you thro' Mrs. Hamilton."[39] The new secretaries of state and treasury traded cordial notes.

Jefferson never underestimated Hamilton's superlative talents. After reading *The Federalist,* Jefferson pronounced it the "best commentary on the principles of government which ever was written."[40] Nor did he slight Hamilton's virtues. As he noted in later years, after their epic battles had faded into history, "Hamilton was indeed a singular character of acute understanding, disinterested, honest, and honorable in all private transactions, amiable in society, and duly valuing virtue in private life—yet so bewitched and perverted by the British example as to be under thorough conviction that corruption was essential to the government of a nation."[41] By *corruption,* Jefferson did not necessarily mean outright payments so much as unhealthy executive influence over legislators through honors, appointments, and other perquisites of office. A central tenet of the American Revolution had been that a corrupt British ministry had suborned Parliament through patronage and pensions and used the resulting excessive influence to tax the colonists and deprive them of their ancient English liberties. Jefferson always viewed Hamilton through the lens of this unsettling analogy.

By the time Jefferson arrived in New York, Madison had been trounced by Hamilton in the discrimination vote, and the treasury secretary was hurtling ahead with his funding scheme. Jefferson must have regretted having arrived so late. He had no doubt that the original holders of government paper had been cheated of rightful gains by speculators who were "fraudulent purchasers of this paper. . . . Immense sums were thus filched from the poor and ignorant and fortunes accumulated by those who had themselves been poor enough before."[42] Jefferson's objections to Hamilton's plan had philosophical roots. In his view, the smaller the government, the better the chances of preserving liberty. And to the extent that a central government was necessary, he wanted a strong Congress with a weak executive. Most of all, Jefferson wished to preserve state sovereignty against federal infringement. Since Hamilton's agenda was to strengthen the central government, bolster the executive branch at the expense of the legislature, and subordinate the states, it embodied everything Jefferson abhorred.

Jefferson feared that the funding scheme would create a fiercely loyal following for Hamilton among those enriched by it. He later told Washington that Hamilton had promoted a "regular system" of "interested persons" who were at the beck and call of the Treasury Department.[43] He was convinced that congressmen were investing in government securities and that "even in this, the birth of our government, some members were found sordid enough to bend their duty to their interests and to look after personal rather than public good."[44] Jefferson also did not believe that Hamilton really intended to pay off the government debt. "I would wish the debt paid tomorrow," Jefferson told Washington. "He wishes it never to be paid, but always to be a thing wherewith to corrupt and manage the legislature."[45] This idea of perpetual debt flew in the face of Hamilton's express words and turned his funding program into a blatant grab for power.

The ideological differences between Hamilton and Jefferson did not blaze into sudden, open enmity. In their early days in the cabinet, these erudite men held many private talks, with Jefferson hoarding statements by Hamilton that he later used against him. As a courtly gentleman of impeccable manners, Jefferson shrank from disagreement. Unlike Hamilton, a swashbuckler who reveled in debate, Jefferson hated controversy and was more guarded than Hamilton in exposing his thoughts. He suited his words to the occasion and catered to listeners' prejudices, saying what they wanted to hear. This kept his own views secret while encouraging others to speak. Hamilton—opinionated, almost recklessly candid—was incapable of this type of circumspection. Jefferson had learned the advantages of inscrutable silence. While serving with Jefferson in the Continental Congress, recalled John Adams, "I never heard him utter three sentences together."[46] On another occasion, Adams labeled the Virginian a "shadow man" and likened his character to "the great rivers, whose bottoms we cannot see and make no noise."[47] For Hamilton, unable to govern his tongue or his pen, his habit of self-exposure eventually placed him at the mercy of the tightly controlled Jefferson.

Jefferson's horror over the discrimination defeat led to the first major political alignment in the infant republic as Jefferson made common cause with Madison, now the House floor leader. Their partnership was to have ramifications for America's future as important as the earlier one beween Hamilton and Madison. Of the nearly mystic bond between Jefferson and Madison, John Quincy Adams said it was "a phenomenon, like the invisible and mysterious movements of the magnet in the physical world."[48] Since Hamilton's relationship with Madison had revolved around ideas, there was little personal chemistry to sustain their friendship when they fell out over politics. Madison's defection was a tremendous blow for Hamilton, who had consulted him in the early stages of his *Report on Public Credit*. So boundless was Hamilton's respect for Madison that he later said that he would never have accepted the Treasury post had he not believed that he could count on his general support.

Jefferson arrived in New York in the thick of the debate raging over assumption—Hamilton's plan to have the federal government assume the twenty-five million dollars of state debt. This venomous clash made the fight over discrimination look civilized, and Jefferson later categorized it as "the most bitter and angry contest ever known in Congress before or since the union of the states."[49] On February 24, 1790, Hamilton had been stunned when Madison, reversing his former position, contested assumption. Retreating from his old nationalist perspective, Madison complained that his home state and some other southern states had paid off most of their wartime debts and would be penalized if, "after having done their duty," they were forced "to contribute to those states who have not equally done their duty."[50] To Hamilton, it seemed that Madison spoke for his Virginia constituents and not, as in *The Federalist*, for the national good. (Of course, as treasury secretary, Hamilton enjoyed the luxury of a continental view.) Hamilton was blindsided by this backlash against his program; that Madison led it was an unkind cut. Hamilton plainly recalled discussing assumption with Madison during an "afternoon's walk" at the Constitutional Convention, and "we were perfectly agreed in the expediency and propriety of such a measure."[51]

Madison's physical appearance—his pale, unsmiling visage, his detached air and short stature—transmitted a superficial impression of timidity. And some fellow politicians believed that "Little Jemmy," as he was known, lacked the commanding, decisive air of a successful politician. His mental vigor, unlike Hamilton's, was not matched by a corresponding talent for translating thought into action. "His great fault as a politician appears to me a want of decision and a disposition to magnify his adversaries' strength," Congressman Edward Livingston told his brother, Robert R. Livingston. "He never determines to act until he is absolutely forced by the pressure of affairs and then regrets that he has neglected some better opportunity."[52] So powerful was this appearance of timidity that many observers were convinced that Madison, eight years younger than Jefferson, must have been dominated by his shrewd mentor. "Mr. Madison had always entertained an exalted opinion of the talents, knowledge and virtues of Mr. Jefferson," Hamilton later wrote. But he thought that, at bottom, each man stiffened the other's determination in opposing his funding program: "Jefferson was indiscreetly open in his approbation of Mr. Madison's principles upon his first coming to the seat of Government. I say indiscreetly because a gentleman in the administration of one department ought not to have taken sides against another in another department."[53]

The impression that Jefferson controlled Madison could be misleading, and not only because Madison deserted Hamilton before Jefferson even arrived in New York. Like Jefferson, Madison operated in the shadows and relied on subtle craft and indirection. His professorial air masked an iron will and a fanatical sense of conviction. Albert Gallatin, later treasury secretary under Jefferson and Madison, was to call Madison "slow in taking his ground, but firm when the storm rises."[54] If anything, Madison had a more supple and original mind than Jefferson and a deeper grasp of constitutional issues. If Madison in the 1780s was a philosopher king, Madison in the 1790s was a formidable practicing politician and so skillful at cutting deals that he was dubbed "the Big Knife." Hamilton's followers, who feared Madison's ability to marshal votes, later called him "the general" and Jefferson "the generalissimo."[55] Congressman Zephaniah Swift of Connecticut later confirmed that Madison's lack of Hamiltonian verve could be deceptive:

He has no fire, no enthusiasm, no animation, but he has infinite prudence and industry. [With] the greatest apparent candor, he calculates upon everything with the greatest nicety and precision. He has unquestionably the most personal influence of any man in the House of Representatives. I never knew a man that better understood [how] to husband a character and make the most of his talents. And he is the most artificial, studied character on earth.[56]

On four separate occasions between February and July 1790, the dexterous Madison thwarted attempts to enact assumption. People whispered into Hamilton's ear that Madison was jealous of his power, that Madison coveted his job. Time showed that political differences dwarfed personal considerations. Hamilton's funding plan brought state loyalties to the surface. Some states, such as Massachusetts and South Carolina, struggled with heavy debts and were glad to be relieved by the central government. Others, such as Virginia and North Carolina, had settled most of their debts and saw no reason to help. Such differences threatened to explode the brittle consensus that had been so arduous to reach at the Constitutional Convention.

In defending his plan, Hamilton did not speak just in arid technical terms. He talked of justice, equity, patriotism, and national honor. His funding system was premised upon a simple concept: that the debt had been generated by the Revolution, that all Americans had benefited equally from that revolution, and that they should assume collective responsibility for its debt. If state debts were unequal, so were the sacrifices made during the fighting. Praising the "immense exertions" of indebted Massachusetts, for instance, Hamilton stated, "It would not be too strong to say that they were in a great degree the pivot of the revolution."[57] Some states, he noted, had paid their debts by ignoble means. New York, for instance, had reneged on interest payments to drive down the market value of its debt, making it cheaper for the state to buy it back. Hamilton also made a subtle, sophisticated argument that without assumption, indebted states would have to raise their taxes, while healthy states would lighten their tax loads. This would trigger a dangerous exodus of people from high-tax to low-tax states, producing "a violent dislocation of the population of particular states."[58]

For Hamilton, assumption was his make-or-break issue, and the outlook seemed grim. Hamilton recalled, "It happened that Mr. Madison and some other distinguished characters of the South started in opposition to the assumption. The high opinion entertained of them made it be taken for granted in that quarter that the opposition would be successful."[59] Hamilton threw himself into battle with his accustomed impetuosity. In this exceptionally hard fight, Hamilton had to lead the charge without Washington. The president supported assumption but did not want to be accused of partisanship and so hesitated to express a public opinion. To aggravate the problem, Washington was laid low in May with an attack of pneumonia so debilitating that, Jefferson said, he was "pronounced by two of the three physicians present to be in the act of death. . . . You cannot conceive of the public alarm on this occasion."[60]

From May 10 to June 24, Washington was too feeble to record an entry in his diary, and Hamilton seemed to function as the de facto head of state. In unpublished comments on this period, Hamilton accused Jefferson of harboring presidential wishes during the interregnum:

> Mr. Jefferson fears in Mr. Hamilton a formidable rival in the competition for the presidential chair at a future period. . . . After he [Jefferson] entered on the duties of his station, the President was afflicted with a malady which while it created dismay and alarm in the heart of every patriot only excited the ambitious ardor of the secretary to remove out of his way every dangerous opponent. That melancholy circumstance suggested to him the probability of an approaching vacancy in the presidential chair and that he would attract the public attention as the successor to it were the more popular Secretary of the Treasury out of the way.[61]

Perhaps Hamilton decided to suppress this recollection because it revealed his own presidential fantasies as well as Jefferson's.

During Washington's illness, Hamilton and his minions, in a tremendous display of organizational skill, accosted congressmen and proselytized for assumption. The treasury secretary became a ubiquitous figure at Federal Hall, packing the gallery with supporters. Nobody was more offended than William Maclay. In his journal, he castigated Hamilton as "his Holiness" and on another occasion called him "a damnable villain."[62] (Hamilton got off easy: John Adams reminded Maclay of "a monkey just put into breeches.")[63] On account of his whirling energy, Hamilton encountered enormous resistance from congressmen fearful of a strong executive branch. His activities brought to mind Robert Walpole, Britain's chancellor of the exchequer in the 1720s, who achieved such omnipotence that he was the first to acquire the title of "prime" minister. In Philadelphia, Benjamin Rush deplored Hamilton's high-pressure lobbying: "I question whether more dishonourable influence has ever been used by a British Minister (bribery excepted) to carry a measure than has [been] used to carry the report of the Secretary. This influence is not confined to nightly visits, promises, compromises, sacrifices, and threats in New York."[64]

Alexander Hamilton was trying through his assumption plan to preserve the union, and yet nobody, for the moment, seemed to be widening its divisions more. If politics is preeminently the art of compromise, then Hamilton was in some ways poorly suited for his job. He wanted to be a statesman who led courageously, not a politician who made compromises. Instead of proceeding with small, piecemeal measures, he had presented a gigantic package of fiscal measures that he wanted accepted all at once.

As the newspaper war against Hamilton heated up, Madison's backers scented victory. On April 8, William Maclay gloated over the gloom of Hamilton's adherents: "I never observed so drooping an aspect, so turbid and forlorn an appearance as overspread the partisans of the Secretary in our House this afternoon. . . . [Rufus] King looked like a boy that had been whipped."[65] Maclay's exuberance was justified. On April 12, 1790, the House voted down Hamilton's assumption plan, thirty-one to twenty-nine, and two weeks later voted to discontinue all debate on the issue. By early June, it looked as if the assumption plan was heading for oblivion. So Hamilton began to search for a compromise that would salvage the linchpin of his economic program.

The issue that he seized on was the divisive question of where the national capital should be located. At the Constitutional Convention, the delegates had decided to create a federal district, ten miles square, in an unspecified location. This decision generated melodramatic speculation. Some people found the idea of a separate capital fraught with danger, fearing a privileged enclave. Governor George Clinton envisioned the ten-mile square as the scene of a presidential "court" disfigured by royal trappings and marked by "ambition with idleness, baseness with pride, the thirst of riches without labor . . . flattery . . . treason . . . perfidy, but above all the perpetual ridicule of virtue."[66]

The capital's location had already led to intensive lobbying and intrigue. It was a monumental decision for contestants, since it would confer massive wealth, power, and population upon the winning state. More important, it would affect the style of the federal government, which was bound to soak up some of the political atmosphere of the surrounding region. In a large country with poor transportation, the voices of local citizens would resonate loudly in the ears of federal legislators.

Complicating the debate was the expectation that there would first be a temporary capital, likely New York or Philadelphia, which would function as the makeshift seat of government while a permanent capital was readied. Notwithstanding his nationalist bent, Hamilton wanted New York to remain at least the temporary capital. In August 1788, he contacted his old mentor, Governor William Livingston of New Jersey, and expressed shock at reports that Livingston had capitulated to "the snares of Pennsylvania" and was leaning toward Philadelphia as temporary capital for the first Congress.[67] The northeastern states feared the enhanced power that would accrue to Pennsylvania if it housed the temporary capital, which might then prove permanent. Before Livingston, Hamilton dangled a tantalizing deal: if he supported New York City as temporary capital, Hamilton would endorse Trenton, New Jersey, as the long-term capital.

Hamilton's desire to have the capital in New York intensified as Washington's inauguration neared. In February 1789, he made a spirited campaign speech for his friend John Laurance, then running for Congress from New York City, and urged "that as the residence of Congress would doubtless be esteemed a matter of some import to the city of New York . . . *our representative* should be a man well qualified in oratory to prove that this city is the best station for that honorable body."[68] By January 17, 1790, with the uproar mounting over Hamilton's funding scheme, William Maclay believed that Hamilton, emboldened by his burgeoning power, was determined to retain New York as the capital: "I have attended in the minutest manner to the motions of Hamilton and the [New] Yorkers. Sincerity is not with them. They will never consent to part with Congress."[69]

In this tussle, New York was a controversial choice. It was becoming so associated with Hamilton that his enemies branded it "Hamiltonopolis." For many southerners, Jefferson in particular, New York City was an Anglophile bastion dominated by bankers and merchants who would contaminate the republican experiment. These critics equated New York with the evils of London. Benjamin Rush, a Philadelphia booster, told Madison, "I am satisfied that the influence of our city will be against the [Treasury] Secretary's system of injustice & corruption. . . . Philadelphia will be better ground to combat the system on than New York."[70]

The question of the capital served as a proxy for the question of whether America should assume an urban or agrarian character. Many southerners believed that a northern capital would favor the mercantile, monied urban interests and discriminate against agrarian life. Jefferson's pastoral dream of a nation of small, independent farms had a powerful appeal to the American psyche, however much it differed from the slaveholding reality of the south. Jefferson, Madison, and Washington wanted a permanent capital on the Potomac, not far from Mount Vernon. For Jefferson, this would plant the nation's capital in a bucolic setting, safe from abolitionist forces and the temptations "of any overgrown commercial city."[71] Madison and Henry Lee speculated in land on the Potomac, hoping to earn a windfall profit if the area was chosen for the capital.

There were other political questions to consider. Should the capital be near the population or the geographic center of America? New York was scarcely equidistant from the northern and southern tips of the country—sixteen of the twenty-four original senators came from south of the city—and this would present hardships for southern delegates who had to travel long distances. The choice of the capital was also seen as a referendum on America's future growth. For those who believed that the country would expand westward—a view especially prevalent in the southern states, whose western borders functioned as gateways to the frontier—a northeast capital would poorly serve America's future political landscape. All these simmering issues came to the surface during the ensuing debate.

During the spring of 1790, quarrels over assumption and the national capital grew so vitriolic that it didn't seem far-fetched that the union might break up over the issues. The south increasingly fired at Hamilton the same vituperative rhetoric once directed at the British. In writing to Madison, Henry Lee stated that the battle to stop assumption brought back memories of the Revolution: "It seems to me that we southern people must be slaves in effect or cut the Gordian knot at once."[72] Jefferson long remembered the sour mood that hung like a miasma over New York that spring: "Congress met and adjourned from day to day without doing anything, the parties being too much out of temper to do business together."[73]

Of the two policies that Hamilton wished to promote—the federal assumption of state debt and the selection of New York as the capital—assumption was incomparably more important to him. It was the most effective and irrevocable way to yoke the states together into a permanent union. So when he saw that Madison possessed the votes to block assumption, Hamilton considered bargaining away New

York as the capital in exchange for southern support for assumption. As early as May 16, glimmers of a deal emerged in a letter from Philip Schuyler to Stephen Van Rensselaer: "No motion has yet been brought forward to remove the seat [of] government, but we apprehend that, if the assumption is not carried, that the South Carolinians may (in order to obtain an object which is so important to them) negotiate with those who wish the removal."[74] Nine days later, William Maclay reported frantic negotiations: "The [New] Yorkers are now busy in the scheme of bargaining with the Virginians, offering the permanent seat on the Potomac for the temporary one in New York."[75]

On June 2, 1790, the House enacted Hamilton's funding bill without the assumption component. Hamilton knew he had to strike a deal quickly. Reluctant to surrender his reputation for uncompromising stands, he relied on deputies to make the conciliatory overtures. In the early republic, it was difficult for politicians to engage in legislative maneuvering that later became standard practice, so Hamilton dispatched emissaries to sound out Robert Morris, the Pennsylvania senator and a leading proponent of Philadelphia as the capital. "I did not choose to trust them," Morris said, "but wrote a note to Colonel Hamilton that I would be walking early in the morning on the Battery and if Colonel Hamilton had anything to propose to him he might meet him there."[76] To Morris's surprise, Hamilton was already at the rendezvous spot when he arrived. Hamilton's deal was simple: if Morris rounded up one vote in the Senate and five in the House for assumption, he would back Germantown or Trenton—both hard by Philadelphia—as the permanent capital. Hamilton had now tipped his hand as the master strategist behind the bargaining over the capital. Pennsylvania congressman Peter Muhlenberg told Benjamin Rush, "It is now established *beyond a doubt* that the Secretary of the Treasury guides the movements of the eastern phalanx."[77]

What likely scuttled Hamilton's deal was that the Pennsylvania and Virginia delegations had already reached an understanding: Philadelphia would become the temporary capital and the Potomac site the permanent capital. This was the very solution Hamilton had worked to avoid because it rejected a role for New York and placed the long-term capital in the south. The Pennsylvania legislators probably consented from a wishful hunch that the capital, once placed temporarily in Philadelphia, would be difficult to dislodge. By June 18, having surrendered hope of a permanent capital on the Delaware, Hamilton was slowly coming around to the Potomac site. That day, William Maclay reported that Hamilton "affects to tell Mr. Morris that the New England men will bargain to fix the permanent seat at the Potomac or at Baltimore."[78]

It was against this backdrop of an emerging consensus that one must evaluate the famous anecdote told by Jefferson about the dinner bargain that fixed the capital on the Potomac. According to Jefferson, the northern states were threatening "secession and dissolution" when he ran into a ragged Hamilton outside Washington's residence. Usually, Hamilton was dapper and polished; now, to Jefferson's amazement, he was despondent and unkempt: "His look was somber, haggard, and dejected. . . . Even his dress uncouth and neglected."[79] Hamilton seemed in despair.

> He walked me backwards and forwards before the President's door for half an
> hour. He painted pathetically the temper into which the legislature had been
> wrought; the disgust of those who were called creditor states; the danger of
> the *secession* of their members and the separation of the states. He observed
> that the members of the administration ought to act in concert; that though
> this question was not of my department, yet a common duty should make it
> a common concern . . . that the question having been lost by a small major-
> ity only, it was probable that an appeal from me to the judgment and discre-
> tion of some of my friends might effect a change in the vote.[80]

If assumption faltered, Hamilton hinted, he might have to resign. Jefferson blandly informed Hamilton that he "was really a stranger to the whole subject" of assumption—Jefferson was very adroit at presenting himself as a political naïf—when he had, in fact, followed the debate intently and had just written George Mason urging a compromise on the matter.[81] Doubtless with this in mind, he invited the treasury secretary to dine at his home the next day.

If we are to credit Jefferson's story, the dinner held at his lodgings on Maiden Lane on June 20, 1790, fixed the future site of the capital. It is perhaps the most celebrated meal in American history, the guests including Jefferson, Madison, Hamilton, and perhaps one or two others. For more than a month, Jefferson had been bedeviled by a migraine headache, yet he presided with commendable civility. Despite his dislike of assumption, he knew that the stalemate over the funding scheme could shatter the union, and, as secretary of state, he also feared the repercussions for American credit abroad.

Madison restated his familiar argument that assumption punished Virginia and other states that had duly settled their debts. But he agreed to support assumption—or at least not oppose it—if something was granted in exchange. Jefferson recalled, "It was observed . . . that as the pill would be a bitter one to the southern states, something should be done to soothe them."[82] The sedative measure was that Philadelphia would be the temporary capital for ten years, followed by a permanent move to a Potomac site. In a lucrative concession for his home state, Madison also seems to have extracted favorable treatment for Virginia in a final debt settlement with the central government. In return, Hamilton agreed to exert his utmost efforts to get the Pennsylvania congressional delegation to accept Philadelphia as the provisional capital and a Potomac site as its permanent successor.

The dinner consecrated a deal that was probably already close to achievement. The sad irony was that Hamilton, the quintessential New Yorker, bargained away the city's chance to be another London or Paris, the political as well as financial and cultural capital of the country. His difficult compromise testified to the transcendent value he placed on assumption. The decision did not sit well with many New Yorkers. Senator Rufus King was enraged when Hamilton told him that he "had made up his mind" to jettison the capital to save his funding system. For King, Hamilton's move had been high-handed and secretive, and he ranted privately that "great and good schemes ought to succeed not by intrigue or the establishment of bad measures."[83]

True to his dinner pledge, Hamilton applied his persuasive powers to the Pennsylvania delegation. Maclay's journal is again invaluable in tracking these closed-door deliberations. When he discovered that Hamilton had linked the "abominations" of his funding scheme with the Potomac capital, he berated Washington as a tool of Hamilton and "the dishclout of every dirty speculation."[84] In the Senate on June 23, Maclay noticed that Robert Morris was summoned from the chamber. "He at last came in and whispered [to] me: 'The business is settled at last. Hamilton gives up the temporary residence'" for New York.[85] The next day, the Pennsylvania congressional delegation bowed to the compromise that was to make Philadelphia the temporary capital for ten years.

To clinch the deal, Hamilton, Jefferson, and Secretary of War Knox dined with the Pennsylvanians on June 28. Maclay's recollections of that dinner are instructive. He found Jefferson stiff and formal, possessed of a "lofty gravity." He warmed more to the fat, easygoing Knox, who may have drunk to excess—Maclay calls him "Bacchanalian"—yet managed to project an aura of dignity. The description of Hamilton is suggestive: "Hamilton has a very boyish, giddy manner and Scotch-Irish people could well call him a 'skite.'"[86] The *Oxford English Dictionary* defines the Scottish word *skite* as meaning a vain, frivolous, or wanton girl. The choice of words hints at something feminine about Hamilton beneath the military bearing, an androgynous quality noted by others. The description also suggests that Hamilton had gone from abject despair to inexpressible elation as he won final backing for his funding scheme.

On July 10, 1790, the House approved the Residence Act, designating Philadelphia as the temporary capital and a ten-mile-square site on the Potomac as the permanent site. A disenchanted Maclay concluded that Hamilton was now all-powerful: "His gladiators . . . have wasted us months in this place. . . . Everything, even to the naming of a committee, is prearranged by Hamilton and his group of speculators."[87] On July 26, the House narrowly passed the assumption bill. The famous dinner deal had worked its political magic. Madison voted against Hamilton's measure but arranged for four congressmen from Virginia and Maryland to change their votes in favor of assumption.

In retrospect, it was a splendid moment for Hamilton, Madison, and Jefferson. They had devised a statesmanlike solution that averted disintegration of the union. In this idealistic dawn of the republic, however, such a compromise evoked howls of execration. Any backdoor deal savored of corruption, and legislators anxiously awaited the public response. Thomas FitzSimons of the Pennsylvania delegation feared "that stones would be thrown at him" in Philadelphia because he had gone along with a Potomac capital.[88] On the New York streets, the Pennsylvanians endured obscene epithets shouted by pedestrians disgusted at losing the temporary capital, New York City having already broken ground on a new presidential mansion. Among the most aggrieved New Yorkers was Philip Schuyler, who bewailed "a want of that decency which was due to a city whose citizens made very capital exertions for the accommodation of Congress."[89]

Jefferson would have to defend to posterity his complicity in a deal that weakened the states. He could have cited the peril to the union and left it at that. Instead, he decided to scapegoat Hamilton. Of his own part in passing the assumption bill, he later told Washington, "I was duped into it by the Secretary of the Treasury and made a tool for forwarding his schemes, not then sufficiently understood by me, and of all the errors of my political life this has occasioned me the deepest regret."[90] In 1818, Jefferson made the point still more graphically. Through assumption, Hamilton had thrown a lucrative sop "to the stock-jobbing herd. This added to the number of votaries of the Treasury and made its chief the master of every vote in the legislature which might give to the government the direction suited to his political views."[91] Jefferson traced the formation of the two main parties—to be known as Republicans and Federalists—to Hamilton's victory over assumption. For Jefferson, this event split Congress into pure, virtuous republicans and a "mercenary phalanx," "monarchists in principle," who "adhered to Hamilton of course as their leader in that principle."[92]

Why did Jefferson retrospectively try to downplay his part in passing Hamilton's assumption scheme? While he understood the plan at the time better than he admitted, he probably did not see as clearly as Hamilton that the scheme created an unshakable foundation for federal power in America. The federal government had captured forever the bulk of American taxing power. In comparison, the location of the national capital seemed a secondary matter. It wasn't that Jefferson had been duped by Hamilton; Hamilton had explained his views at dizzying length. It was simply that he had been outsmarted by Hamilton, who had embedded an enduring political system in the details of the funding scheme. In an unsigned newspaper article that September, entitled "Address to the Public Creditors," Hamilton gave away the secret of his statecraft that so infuriated Jefferson: "Whoever considers the nature of our government with discernment will see that though obstacles and delays will frequently stand in the way of the adoption of good measures, yet when once adopted, they are likely to be stable and permanent. It will be far more difficult to *undo* than to *do*."[93]

The dinner deal to pass assumption and establish the capital on the Potomac was the last time that Hamilton, Jefferson, and Madison ever cooperated to advance a common agenda. Henceforth, they found themselves in increasingly open warfare.

SEVENTEEN

THE FIRST TOWN
IN AMERICA

After passage of his funding program, Hamilton did not stop to take a breather from his work. This intensely driven man, always compensating for his deprived early years, had a mind that throbbed incessantly with new ideas. When it came to issues confronting America, he committed all the resources of his mind. Hamilton could not do things halfway: he cared too passionately, too personally, about the fate of his adopted country.

Inside his teeming brain, he found it hard to strike a balance between the grand demands of his career and the small change of everyday life. The endless letters that flowed from his pen are generally abstract and devoid of imagery. He almost never described weather or scenery, the clothing or manners of people he met, the furniture of rooms he inhabited. He scarcely ever alluded to days off, vacations, or leisure moments. In one letter, he told Angelica that his "favorite wish" was to visit Europe one day, but he never left the country and seldom ventured beyond Albany or Philadelphia.[1] Only rarely did he enliven letters with anecdotes or idle chatter. It was not so much that Hamilton was writing for the ages—though surely he knew his place in the larger scheme of things—as that his grandiose plans left scant space for commonplace thoughts.

Soon after Hamilton became treasury secretary, Philip Schuyler told Eliza a comical story about her husband's absentminded behavior in an upstate New York town where he once paused en route to Albany. Hamilton must have been composing a legal brief or speech in his mind, for he kept pacing in front of a store owned by a Mr. Rodgers. As one observer recalled:

Apparently in deep contemplation, and his lips moving as rapidly as if he was in conversation with some person, he entered the store [and] tendered a fifty-dollar bill to be exchanged. Rodgers refused to change it. The gentleman [Hamilton] retired. A person in the store asked Rodgers if the bill was counterfeited. He replied in the negative. Why, then, did you not oblige the gentleman by exchanging it? Because, said Rodgers, the poor gentleman has lost his reason. But, said the other, he appeared perfectly natural. That may be, said Rodgers, he probably has his lucid intervals. But I have seen him walk before my door for half an hour, sometimes stopping, but always talking to himself. And if I had changed the money and he had lost it, I might have received blame.[2]

As the main architect of the new American government, Hamilton was usually in harness to his work. A recurring theme among the Schuylers was that Eliza should coax her husband into getting some fresh air and exercise to relieve his overtaxed brain. In 1791, Henry Lee sent Hamilton a horse from Virginia so that, for health reasons, he could take "daily airings and short rides."[3] An excellent horseman who had ridden a great deal in the Revolution, Hamilton had asked Lee to send him an especially gentle horse. Hamilton still suffered from a recurring kidney ailment that one friend described as his "old nephritic complaint" and that made jolting carriage rides an agonizing experience.[4] Midway through Washington's first term, Angelica Church heard reports of Hamilton growing puffy from overwork. "Colonel Beckwith tells me that our dear Hamilton writes too much and takes no exercise and grows too fat," she complained to Eliza. "I hate both the word and the thing and you will take care of his health and good looks. Why, I shall find him on my return a dull, heavy fellow!"[5]

This man who worked with feverish, all-consuming energy could be the soul of conviviality after hours. William Sullivan left a verbal sketch of Hamilton that points up his incongruous blend of manly toughness and nearly feminine delicacy:

He was under middle size, thin in person, but remarkably erect and dignified in his deportment. . . . His hair was turned back from his forehead, powdered, and collected in a club behind. His complexion was exceedingly fair and varying from this only by the almost feminine rosiness of his cheeks. His might be considered, as to figure and color, an uncommonly handsome face.[6]

In describing one social gathering they attended, Sullivan said that Hamilton made a dramatic late entrance and was alternately the deep thinker and the witty conversationalist, especially when the ladies watched him adoringly:

When he entered the room, it was apparent from the respectful attention of the company that he was a distinguished individual. He was dressed in a blue coat with bright buttons; the skirts of his coat were unusually long. He wore a white waistcoat, black silk small clothes, white silk stockings. The gentleman who received him as a guest introduced him to such of the company as were strangers to him. To each he made a formal bow, bending very low, the ceremony of shaking hands not being observed. . . . At dinner, whenever he engaged in conversation, everyone listened attentively. His mode of speaking was deliberate and serious and his voice engagingly pleasant. In the evening of the same day, he was in a mixed assembly of both sexes and the tranquil reserve, noticed at the dinner table, had given place to a social and playful manner, as though in this he was alone ambitious to excel.[7]

Most people found Hamilton highly agreeable. Sullivan wrote, "Those who could speak of his manner from the best opportunities to observe him in public and private concurred in pronouncing him to be a frank, amiable, high-minded, open-hearted gentleman. . . . In private and friendly intercourse, he is said to have been exceedingly amiable and to have been affectionately beloved."[8] The few unflattering portraits of Hamilton's personality tend to stem, not surprisingly, from political enemies. Hamilton was a man of daunting intellect and emphatic opinions, and John Quincy Adams contended that it was hard to get along with him if you disagreed with him. Hamilton knew he had a dogmatic streak and once joked, writing about himself in the third person, "Whatever may be the good or ill qualities of that officer, much flexibility of character is not of the number."[9] John Adams perhaps saw in Hamilton the mirror of his own vanity, later telling Jefferson that he was an "insolent coxcomb who rarely dined in good company where there was good wine without getting silly and vaporing about his administration, like a young girl about her brilliants and trinkets."[10]

On the other hand, Hamilton had scores of faithful friends: Gouverneur Morris, Rufus King, Nicholas Fish, Egbert Benson, Robert Troup, William Duer, Richard Varick, Oliver Wolcott, Jr., Elias Boudinot, William Bayard, Timothy Pickering, and James Kent, to name but a few. Throughout his career, he accumulated companions "drawn to him by his humorous and almost feminine traits," his grandson observed.[11] James Wilkinson, who patched things up with Hamilton after their wartime clash, once told Hamilton that he missed his company because "I have never discovered in another [so much] matter to captivate the understanding and manner to charm the heart."[12] In view of the heartless image of Hamilton propagated by political opponents, it is worth noting the numerous acts of generosity strewn throughout his correspondence. Thanking him for an unspecified act of "disinterested friendship," Morgan Lewis told Hamilton, "Indeed, if my memory does not fail me, I may with truth assert the present [instance as] the only one I ever experienced."[13] After Hamilton bailed out James Tillary with a loan, the New York physician tipped his hat: "You lent me some money to serve me at a time when an act of friendship had embarrassed me, and I now return it to you with a thousand thanks."[14] Hamilton also did favors for humble people, as when he drolly recommended his barber, John Wood, to George Washington's secretary: "He desires to have the honor of dealing with the heads and chins of some of your family and I give him this line . . . to make him known to you."[15]

Given his imposing responsibilities, it is hard to imagine that Hamilton could have enjoyed a warm, happy social life without Eliza's support. They created an elegant but unostentatious home filled with lovely furniture, including chairs in Louis XVI style and a Federal mahogany sofa. Among other ornaments, they had a china snuffbox from Frederick the Great (courtesy of Baron von Steuben), a portrait of Louis XVI (a gift from the French ambassador), and, later on, a stately Gilbert Stuart painting of George Washington. From London, Angelica Church showered them with exquisite items, including gold-embossed porcelain tableware and blue-and-gold French flowerpots. Eliza would gladly have devoted herself to private life alone, but she submitted good-naturedly to the demands of her husband's career. She was always a sprightly presence at tea parties given by Martha Washington. She reminisced in old age:

> I had little of private life in those days. Mrs. Washington who, like myself, had a passionate love of home and domestic life, often complained of the "waste of time" she was compelled to endure. "They call me the first lady in the land and I think I must be extremely happy," she would say almost bitterly at times and add, "They might more properly call me the chief state prisoner." As I was younger than she, I mingled more in the gaieties of the day.[16]

Martha Washington's style of entertaining struck Eliza as possessing just the right amalgam of beauty, taste, and modesty. One of Eliza's few surviving personal effects is a pair of pink satin slippers that Martha Washington left at the Schuyler mansion and that Eliza gratefully inherited.

As energetic as her husband, Eliza never complained about family demands. By the time Hamilton became treasury secretary, she had already given birth to four of their eight children. Eliza was an excellent housekeeper who ably governed a large household. James McHenry once teased Hamilton about reports that Eliza "has as much merit as your treasurer as you have as treasurer of the wealth of the United States."[17] Hamilton appreciated her steady contributions to his life. In frequent letters to her, he constantly inquired about her in solicitous, protective tones. He seldom mentioned his work, as if wishing to shield her from the rough-and-tumble of politics.

The bulk of the child rearing fell to Eliza, a strict but loving mother. On one occasion, she told a family friend that there is a "hazard in young people having their evenings to themselves until they know there is a friend that will observe and advise them."[18] But even with his time-consuming career, Hamilton did not fob off all the parenting duties on Eliza. When they were in separate cities, he often kept one or two of the older boys with him, allowing them to share his bed at night, while the younger children remained with their mother. Hamilton was a chronic worrier about his family, an emotion perhaps held over from his childhood. Angelica once commented to Eliza about her brother-in-law, "His sensibility suffers from the least anxiety to you or your babies."[19]

Hamilton enjoyed tutoring his children. He had high expectations and wanted them to excel—he was, by nature, an exacting, ambitious person—but his handful of surviving letters to them also show patient affection. After his eldest son, Philip, went off at age nine to boarding school in Trenton in 1791, accompanied by Alexander, Jr., Hamilton received a letter from him, saying how contented he was. Hamilton replied:

Your teacher also informs me that you recited a lesson the first day you began, very much to his satisfaction. I expect every letter from him will give me a fresh proof of your progress, for I know you can do a great deal if you please. And I am sure you have too much spirit not to exert yourself that you may make us every day more and more proud of you.[20]

Hamilton did not assume that his children would emulate his outsize accomplishments and tailored his demands to their native endowments, gently molding their characters. When his daughter Angelica was nine and staying with Grandfather Schuyler in Albany, Hamilton took time from his duties to write this mildly didactic note:

I was very glad to learn, my dear daughter, that you were going to begin the study of the French language. We hope you will in every respect behave in such a manner as will secure to you the goodwill and regard of all those with whom you are. If you happen to displease any of them, be always ready to make a frank apology. But the best way is to act with so much politeness, good manners, and circumspection as never to have an occasion to make any apology. Your mother joins in best love to you. Adieu, my very dear daughter.[21]

The sensitivity and tact that Hamilton revealed as a father are the more remarkable considering the troubled circumstances of his own childhood, and he made it a point of honor never to break promises to his children.

Hamilton loved the arts and shared this interest with his children. Very musically inclined, he had Angelica Church search London for the best piano she could find for his daughter Angelica. Singing duets became their favorite pastime. Hamilton also had an appreciative eye for art. "I know Hamilton likes the beautiful in every way," Angelica Church once told Eliza. "The beauties of nature and of art are not lost on him."[22] Hamilton counseled Martha Washington on purchases of paintings and assembled his own collection of woodcuts and copper engravings, including works by Mantegna and Dürer. Just as he and Eliza had rescued Ralph Earl from debtors' prison in the 1780s, so they later scouted out work for William Winstanley, a British painter specializing in Hudson River scenes. Hamilton loaned money to the young artist and may have been responsible for two of his paintings that graced Martha Washington's drawing room.

Another leitmotif of Hamilton's private life was his constant support of educational and scholarly pursuits. On January 21, 1791, he was admitted to the American Philosophical Society, the country's oldest learned organization. Academic honors tumbled in on this man who had never officially finished college. Already a trustee of Columbia College, he now harvested a succession of honorary doctorates from Columbia, Dartmouth, Princeton, Harvard, and Brown, all before the tender age of forty.

Through his interest in educating native Americans, Hamilton's name came to adorn a college. During the Revolution, Philip Schuyler had negotiated with Indian tribes around Albany to guarantee their neutrality. For his translator and emissary, he often enlisted the cooperation of the Reverend Samuel Kirkland, a missionary to the six-nation Iroquois League. Especially close to the Oneida, Kirkland wooed them to the patriotic side. Hamilton had championed a humane, enlightened policy toward the Indians. When real-estate speculators had wanted to banish them from western New York, he warned Governor Clinton that the Indians' friendship "alone can keep our frontiers in peace. . . . The attempt at the total expulsion of so desultory a people is as chimerical as it would be pernicious."[23] He was often outraged by depredations perpetrated by frontier settlers against the Indians; in one later speech drafted for Washington, he wrote that government policy had been "inadequate to protect the Indians from the violences of the irregular and lawless part of the frontier inhabitants."[24] When problems with the Indians arose, he always favored reconciliation before any resort to force.

With such sympathy for the Indians' plight, Hamilton was receptive when Kirkland approached him in January 1793 to join the board of trustees of a new school in upstate New York to educate white and native American students. The latter would be taught both English and Indian languages. Kirkland wrote in his journal, "Mr. Hamilton cheerfully consents to be a trustee of the said seminary and will afford it all the aid in his power."[25] That same month, the New York legislature granted a charter for the Hamilton-Oneida Academy. The following year, Baron von Steuben, acting as Hamilton's ambassador, laid the school's cornerstone. Hamilton never actually visited the school, but his sponsorship was significant enough that the school was christened Hamilton College when it received a broad new charter in 1812.

The residence law that passed Congress in July 1790, establishing Philadelphia as the interim capital, dictated that all government offices relocate there by early December. The federal government did not decamp all at once but straggled off to Pennsylvania in a disorderly exodus. On August 12, 1790, Congress held its farewell session in Federal Hall; by the end of the month, President Washington had boarded a barge and waved his farewell to Manhattan. On September 1, surely with an audible sigh of relief, Jefferson and Madison fled the sinful haunts of Manhattan and began to roll south across New Jersey in a four-wheeled carriage. Abigail Adams, who did not set sail until November, seemed miffed by the enforced southward shift, swearing that she would try to enjoy Philadelphia but that "when all is done it will not be Broadway."[26]

In reality, Philadelphia was a cosmopolitan city, praised by a highborn British visitor as "one of the wonders of the world," "the first town in America," and one that "bids fair to rival almost any in Europe."[27] Larger than either New York or Boston, it supported ten newspapers and thirty bookshops. Largely through the civic imagination of Benjamin Franklin, it boasted an astounding panoply of cultural and civic institutions, including two theaters, a subscription library, a volunteer fire company, and a hospital.

As chieftain of the biggest government department, Hamilton executed the shift to Philadelphia with almost martial precision. In early August, he secured a two-story brick building on Third Street, between Chestnut and Walnut Streets. Though now headquarters of the most powerful government ministry, the building had a curiously makeshift air, as noted by the visitors Hamilton received between 9:00 and 12:00 each morning. One French caller, Moreau de St. Méry, was "astounded that the official lodgings of a minister could be so poor." He was surprised when a shuffling old retainer answered the front door. And of Hamilton's plain ground-floor office he wrote, "His desk was a plain pine table covered with a green cloth. Planks and trestles held records and papers, and at one end was a little imitation

Chinese vase and a plate with glasses on it. . . . In a word, I felt I saw Spartan customs all about me."[28]

From modest origins, the Treasury offices proliferated until they occupied the entire block. The 1791 city directory gives an anatomy of this burgeoning department, with 8 employees in Hamilton's office, 13 in the comptroller's, 15 in the auditor's, 19 in the register's, 3 in the treasurer's, 14 in the office for settling accounts between the federal government and the states, and 21 in the customs office on Second Street, with an additional 122 customs collectors and surveyors scattered in various ports. By the standards of the day, this represented a prodigious bureaucracy. For its critics, it was a monster in the making, inciting fears that the department would become the Treasury secretary's personal spy force and military machine. Swollen by the Customs Service, the Treasury Department payroll ballooned to more than five hundred employees under Hamilton, while Henry Knox had a mere dozen civilian employees in the War Department and Jefferson a paltry six at State, along with two chargés d'affaires in Europe. The corpulent Knox and his entire staff were squeezed into tiny New Hall, just west of the mighty Treasury complex. Inevitably, the man heading a bureaucracy many times larger than the rest of the government combined would arouse opposition, no matter how prudent his style.

The hardworking secretary informed merchant Walter Stewart that he wanted a house for his family "as near my destined office as possible." Reared in the tropics, he was now a confirmed resident of the northern latitudes and had taken on the identity of a New Yorker. "A cool situation and exposure will of course be a very material point to a New Yorker," he advised Stewart. "The house must have at least six rooms. Good dining and drawing rooms are material articles. I like elbow room in a yard. As to the rent, the lower the better, consistently with the acquisition of a proper house."[29] By October 14, Hamilton had taken a home at Third and Walnut, just down the block from his office, as if he wished to stumble from bed straight into his office. The move was indicative of how conscientious he was and how crowded his schedule.

History has celebrated his Treasury tenure for his masterful state papers, but probably nothing devoured more of his time during his first year than creating the Customs Service. This towering intellect scrawled more mundane letters about lighthouse construction than about any other single topic. This preoccupation seems peculiar until it is recalled that import duties accounted for 90 percent of government revenues: no customs revenue, no government programs—hence Hamilton's unceasing vigilance about everything pertaining to trade.

Congress had authorized Hamilton to keep "in good repair the lighthouses, beacons, buoys, and public piers in the several states," and he hired and supervised those assigned to care for them.[30] He also wielded huge patronage powers in award-ing contracts for these navigational aids. In creating a string of beacons, buoys, and lighthouses along the Atlantic seaboard, Hamilton reviewed each contract and got Washington's approval—an administrative routine that stifled the two men with maddening minutiae. On the day after the famous dinner deal on assumption and the nation's capital, Hamilton asked Washington to initial a contract "for timber, boards, nails and workmanship" for a beacon near the Sandy Hook lighthouse out-side New York harbor.[31] Hamilton became expert on such excruciating banalities as the best whale oil, wicks, and candles to brighten lighthouse beams.

Before the Revolution, smuggling had been a form of patriotic defiance against Britain, and colonists had cordially detested customs collectors. Now Hamilton had to correct these lawless habits. He asked Congress in April 1790 to commission a fleet of single-masted vessels called revenue cutters that would patrol offshore wa-ters and intercept contraband. By early August, Washington had signed a bill setting up this service, later known as the Coast Guard. Hamilton advised Washington to avoid regional favoritism by constructing the first ten revenue cutters in "different parts of the Union."[32] Previewing his upcoming industrial policy, he recommended using homegrown cloth for sails rather than foreign fabrics. Once again, an instinct for executive leadership, an innate capacity to command, surfaced in Hamilton. He issued directives of breathtaking specificity, requiring that each cutter possess ten muskets and bayonets, twenty pistols, two chisels, one broadax, and two lanterns. Showing a detailed knowledge of seafaring ways that surely dated back to his Caribbean days, he instructed customs collectors that since cutters might be blown off course "even to the West Indies, it will be always proper that they have salted meat with biscuit and water on board sufficient to subsist them in case of such an accident."[33]

In constructing the Coast Guard, Hamilton insisted on rigorous professionalism and irreproachable conduct. He knew that if revenue-cutter captains searched ves-sels in an overbearing fashion, this high-handed behavior might sap public sup-port, so he urged firmness tempered with restraint. He reminded skippers to "always keep in mind that their countrymen are free men and as such are impatient of everything that bears the least mark of a domineering spirit. [You] will therefore refrain . . . from whatever has the semblance of haughtiness, rudeness, or insult."[34] So masterly was Hamilton's directive about boarding foreign vessels that it was still being applied during the 1962 Cuban missile crisis.

Hamilton's power as head of customs extended beyond his legion of employees. Equally important was the comprehensive view of economic activity that he gained in a large country hobbled by primitive communications. Seven of every eight Trea-sury Department employees worked outside the capital, supplying Hamilton with an unending stream of valuable intelligence. One of Jefferson's chief political operatives, John Beckley, reviled this network as an "organized system of espionage through the medium of revenue officers."[35] To monitor government receipts, Hamilton insisted upon weekly reports from collectors, enabling him to track every ship passing through American ports. With his insatiable curiosity—he wanted to know the size, strength, and construction of ships, their schedules and trading routes and cargoes—he pioneered questionnaires to gather such data.

Hamilton also arbitrated innumerable disputes that arose with shippers, often wading into arcane legal issues. At one point, the Baltimore customs collector asked whether import duties should be levied on horses, and Hamilton decided that horses and livestock qualified as taxable objects of trade. He then made this further observation: "I think it, however, necessary to observe that I consider negroes to be exempted from duties on importation."[36] It is a sorry commentary that the question of imposing duties on horses immediately posed the question of how to treat slaves.

The Customs Service also invested Hamilton with huge influence over the monetary system, with tremendous sums passing through his hands. One apprehensive Virginian warned Madison, "I am not unacquainted personally with that *gentleman* at the head of that department of the revenue and . . . I tremble at the thought of his being at the head of such an immense sum as 86 millions of dollars—and the annual revenue of the Union."[37] In fact, Hamilton handled the cash flow in an impeccable manner.

Three quarters of the revenues gathered by the Treasury Department came from commerce with Great Britain. Trade with the former mother country was the crux of everything Hamilton did in government. To fund the debt, bolster banks, promote manufacturing, and strengthen government, Hamilton needed to preserve good trade relations with Great Britain. He understood the displeasure with Britain's trade policy, which excluded American ships from its West Indian colonies and allowed American vessels to carry only American goods into British ports. For Hamilton these irritating obstacles were overshadowed by larger policy considerations. America had decided to rely on customs duties, which meant reliance on British trade. This central economic truth caused Hamilton repeatedly to poach on Jefferson's turf at the State Department. The overlapping concerns of Treasury and State were to foster no end of mischief between the two men.

Hamilton hoped to diversify the revenue stream with domestic taxes. By the time he reported to Congress in December 1790 on the need for additional taxes, he feared that import duties were as high as they could reasonably go. The time had come to spread the pain more evenly, especially since import duties injured seaboard merchants who were part of Hamilton's social circle and political base in New York.

No immediate crisis spawned a need for fresh money. By late 1790, Hamilton had actually amassed a sizable government surplus. Government securities had tripled in value under his tutelage, and compared to the disarray under the Articles of Confederation his policies had produced a healthy burst of economic growth. One Boston correspondent said, "It appears to me that there never was a period when the United States had a brighter sunshine of prosperity. . . . It is pleasing indeed to see the general satisfaction which reigns among every class of citizens in this part of the Union. . . . [O]ur agricultural interest smiles, our commerce is blessed, our manufactures flourish."[38] But at Hamilton's urging the federal government had now assumed state debts, and Hamilton did not see how he could service them without a secondary source of income. He was boxed in, however, by the already ingrained American aversion to taxation. Direct taxation, whether of people or houses, was anathema to many, and, given the strength of agricultural interests and real-estate speculators, a land tax could never have been enacted. So what was there left to tax?

In December 1790, with other options foreclosed, Hamilton revived a proposal he had floated in his *Report on Public Credit:* an excise tax on whiskey and other domestic spirits. He knew the measure would be loathed in rural areas that thrived on moonshine, but he thought this might be more palatable to farmers than a land tax. Hamilton confessed to Washington an ulterior political motive for this liquor tax: he wanted to lay "hold of so valuable a resource of revenue before it was generally preoccupied by the state governments." As with assumption, he wanted to starve the states of revenue and shore up the federal government. Jefferson did not exaggerate Hamilton's canny capacity to clothe political objectives in technical garb. There *were* hidden agendas buried inside Hamilton's economic program, agendas that he tended to share with high-level colleagues but not always with the public.

To Hamilton's delight, Madison supported the excise tax on distilled spirits, agreeing that no plausible alternative existed. Madison averred that "as direct taxes would be still more generally obnoxious and as imports are already loaded as far as they will bear, an excise is the only resource and of all articles distilled spirits are least objectionable."[39] Madison thought the whiskey tax might even have collateral social benefits, since it would increase "sobriety and thereby prevent disease and untimely deaths."[40]

In perhaps the first distant rumble of the Whiskey Rebellion that flared up a few years later, the Pennsylvania House of Representatives passed a motion protesting Hamilton's tax. In the mountain hollows of western Pennsylvania, homemade brew was a time-honored part of local culture, and government interference was fiercely resented. As Hamilton worked to pass his liquor tax, William Maclay again saw him as the evil wizard of Congress, flitting from the House of Representatives on the first floor of Congress Hall to the Senate chamber on the second, dictating policy to his legislative myrmidons. When Maclay tried to present statistics on domestic stills to legislators, he found Hamilton there ahead of him: "I went to the door of the committee room . . . but finding Hamilton still with them, I returned."[41] When the Senate passed the excise tax, Maclay made a chillingly accurate prediction in his journal: "War and bloodshed are the most likely consequence of all this."[42] As he noted, even the Pennsylvania legislature had been unable to enforce excise taxes in the lawless hinterlands of the western counties.

Hamilton labored under no illusions about resistance to the whiskey tax and was prepared to equip a small army of inspectors with stiff enforcement powers. In his *Report on Public Credit,* he had outlined sweeping powers for such inspectors, including allowing them to enter homes and warehouses at any hour to seize hidden spirits. Dealers in spirits, even ramshackle one-man operations, would be required to present proper certificates and maintain accurate records. In a circular issued in May 1791, Hamilton promulgated rules that seemed excessively detailed, especially in a country with a congenital dislike of tax collectors. He wanted inspectors to visit all distilleries "*at least* twice a day" and file weekly reports, "specifying in these returns the name of each owner or manager of a distillery, the city, town or village . . . and the county in which such distillery is situated, the number of stills at each, and their capacity in gallons . . . the materials from which they usually distill, and the time for which they are usually employed."[43]

It did not take long for stirrings of revolt to crop up in western Pennsylvania. As soon as the tax took effect in July 1791, locals began to shun or even threaten inspectors. Hamilton imagined that he had been scrupulous in circumscribing the powers of inspectors—they "can't search and inspect *indiscriminately* all the houses and buildings of people engaged in the business"—but many distillers found their methods bullying and intrusive.[44] As discontent with the liquor tax increased, the protesters began to broaden their critique, taking aim at Hamilton's funding scheme and his entire gamut of policies.

Hamilton was caught on the horns of a dilemma. To prop up the federal government, he had to restore public credit. To restore public credit, he had to institute unpopular taxes, and this "gave a handle to its enemies to attack" the federal government, he later conceded.[45] Yet all of the alternatives to the liquor tax would have proved even more unpopular. As reports drifted back to Philadelphia of disturbances in western Pennsylvania, Hamilton did not lighten up on enforcement. He thought it his duty to implement unpopular but necessary policies, even if they detracted from his own popularity. Hamilton was not the sort to tolerate lawbreaking and was not finished with the lengthy list of controversial policies he planned to introduce.

EIGHTEEN

OF AVARICE
AND ENTERPRISE

O n December 14, 1790, one day after he jolted Congress with his call for an excise tax on liquor, Alexander Hamilton submitted another trailblazing report, this one a clarion call to charter America's first central bank. The country, still reeling from programs the treasury secretary had churned out in a mere fifteen months, was learning just how fertile Hamilton's brain was. He was setting in place the building blocks for a powerful state: public credit, an efficient tax system, a customs service, and now a strong central bank. Of all his monumental programs, his proposal for the Bank of the United States raised the most searching constitutional questions.

The American Revolution and its aftermath coincided with two great transformations in the late eighteenth century. In the political sphere, there had been a repudiation of royal rule, fired by a new respect for individual freedom, majority rule, and limited government. If Hamilton made distinguished contributions in this sphere, so did Franklin, Adams, Jefferson, and Madison. In contrast, when it came to the parallel economic upheavals of the period—the industrial revolution, the expansion of global trade, the growth of banks and stock exchanges—Hamilton was an American prophet without peer. No other founding father straddled both of these revolutions—only Franklin even came close—and therein lay Hamilton's novelty and greatness. He was the clear-eyed apostle of America's economic future, setting forth a vision that many found enthralling, others unsettling, but that would ultimately prevail. He stood squarely on the modern side of a historical divide that seemed to separate him from other founders. Small wonder he aroused such fear and confusion.

Over the past two centuries, Hamilton's reputation has waxed and waned as the country has glorified or debunked businessmen. Historian Gordon Wood has written, "Although late-nineteenth-century Americans honored Hamilton as the creator of American capitalism, that honor became a liability through much of the twentieth century."[1] All the conflicting emotions stirred up by capitalism—its bountiful efficiency, its crass inequities—have adhered to Hamilton's image. As chief agent of a market economy, he had to spur acquisitive impulses, accepting self-interest as the mainspring of economic action. At the same time, he was never a mindless business booster and knew how the desire for lucre could shade over into noxious greed. In *Federalist* number 12, when discussing how prosperity abets the circulation of precious metals, he referred to gold and silver as "those darling objects of human avarice and enterprise"—a phrase that sums up neatly his ambivalence about the drive to amass personal wealth.

In a nation of self-made people, Hamilton became an emblematic figure because he believed that government ought to promote self-fulfillment, self-improvement, and self-reliance. His own life offered an extraordinary object lesson in social mobility, and his unstinting energy illustrated his devout belief in the salutary power of work to develop people's minds and bodies. As treasury secretary, he wanted to make room for entrepreneurs, whom he regarded as the motive force of the economy. Like Franklin, he intuited America's special genius for business: "As to whatever may depend on enterprise, we need not fear to be outdone by any people on earth. It may almost be said that enterprise is our element."[2]

Hamilton did not create America's market economy so much as foster the cultural and legal setting in which it flourished. A capitalist society requires certain preconditions. Among other things, it must establish a rule of law through enforceable contracts; respect private property; create a trustworthy bureaucracy to arbitrate legal disputes; and offer patents and other protections to promote invention. The abysmal failure of the Articles of Confederation to provide such an atmosphere was one of Hamilton's principal motives for promoting the Constitution. "It is known," he wrote, "that the relaxed conduct of the state governments in regard to property and credit was one of the most serious diseases under which the body politic laboured prior to the adoption of our present constitution and was a material cause of that state of public opinion which led to its adoption."[3] He converted the new Constitution into a flexible instrument for creating the legal framework necessary for economic growth. He did this by activating three still amorphous clauses—the necessary-and-proper clause, the general-welfare clause, and the commerce clause—making them the basis for government activism in economics.

Washington's first term was devoted largely to the economic matters in which Hamilton excelled, and Woodrow Wilson justly observed that "we think of Mr. Hamilton rather than of President Washington when we look back to the policy of the first administration."[4] Hamilton had a storehouse of information that nobody else could match. Since the "science" of finance was new to America, Fisher Ames observed, "A gentleman may therefore propose the worst of measures with the best intentions."[5] Among the well-intentioned men who were woefully backward in finance, if forward-looking in politics, were Hamilton's three most savage critics of the 1790s: Jefferson, Madison, and Adams. These founders adhered to a static, archaic worldview that scorned banks, credit, and stock markets. From this perspective, Hamilton was the progressive figure of the era, his critics the conservatives.

As members of the Virginia plantation world, Jefferson and Madison had a nearly visceral contempt for market values and tended to denigrate commerce as grubby, parasitic, and degrading. Like landed aristocrats throughout history, they betrayed a snobbish disdain for commerce and financial speculation. Jefferson perpetuated a fantasy of America as an agrarian paradise with limited household manufacturing. He favored the placid, unchanging rhythms of rural life, not the unruly urban dynamic articulated by Hamilton. He wrote, "I think our governments will remain virtuous for many centuries as long as they are chiefly agricultural. . . . When they get piled upon one another in large cities, as in Europe, they will become corrupt as in Europe."[6] For Jefferson, banks were devices to fleece the poor, oppress farmers, and induce a taste for luxury that would subvert republican simplicity. Strangely enough for a large slaveholder, he thought that agriculture was egalitarian while manufacturing would produce a class-conscious society.

As a representative of New England's mercantile community, John Adams might have seemed a more likely candidate to sympathize with Hamilton's economic system, yet his views, too, harked back to simpler times. In later years, Adams told Jefferson that "an aristocracy of bank paper is as bad as the nobility of France or England." For Adams, a banking system was a confidence trick by which the rich exploited the poor. "Every bank in America is an enormous tax upon the people for the profit of individuals," he remarked, dismissing bankers as "swindlers and thieves."[7] "Our whole banking system I ever abhorred," he declared another time. "I continue to abhor and shall die abhorring . . . every bank by which interest is to be paid or profit of any kind made by the deponent."[8] Adams was too shrewd to think banks could be dispensed with altogether. Instead, he wanted a central bank with state branches but no private banks. Both Jefferson and Adams detested people who earned a living shuffling financial paper, and when Adams launched a bitter tirade in later years against the iniquitous banking system, Jefferson agreed that the business was "an infinity of successive felonious larcenies."[9] That banks could serve any economic purpose—that they could generate prosperity that might enrich the few but also lubricate the wheels of commerce—seemed alien to both men. So when they wrote about Hamilton in quasi-satanic terms, we must remember that they considered banking and other financial activities as so much infernal trickery.

Hamilton never doubted the urgent need for a central bank. Lacking a uniform currency acceptable in all states, still suffering from a hodgepodge of foreign coins, the country required an institution that could expand the money supply, extend credit to government and business, collect revenues, make debt payments, handle foreign exchange, and provide a depository for government funds. Hamilton stated flatly that anyone who served a single month as treasury secretary would develop a "full conviction that banks are essential to the pecuniary operations of the government."[10]

Hamilton was acquainted with private banks in Philadelphia, New York, and Boston, but homegrown institutions offered limited guidance in founding a central bank. Fortunately, he was steeped in European banking precedents, for amid the alarums and excursions of the American Revolution he had managed to become educated in financial history. In his astonishingly precocious letter to James Duane of September 1780, the twenty-five-year-old colonel had hit upon an insight that now informed his theory of central banks—the fruitful commingling of public and private money: "The Bank of England unites public authority and faith with private credit. . . . [T]he bank of Amsterdam is on a similar foundation. And why cannot we have an American bank?"[11] This hybrid character—an essentially private bank buttressed by public authority—was to define his central bank.

To tutor himself further about European central banks, Hamilton turned to Malachy Postlethwayt's *Universal Dictionary of Trade and Commerce* and Adam Smith's *Wealth of Nations,* the latter sent from London by Angelica Church. His main primer, however, was the charter of the Bank of England, established in 1694 under King William III. He kept a copy of it on his desk as a handy reference as he wrote his banking report, though he did not copy it uncritically and deviated in significant respects. Hamilton's bank would serve the government *and* invigorate the economy, and he constantly stressed the broader public benefits, lest the bank be misperceived as the iniquitous tool of a small clique of speculators.

From the outset of his report, Hamilton stressed his desire to catch up with European experience: "It is a fact well understood that public banks have found admission and patronage among the principal and most enlightened commercial nations. They have successively obtained in Italy, Germany, Holland, England, and France as well as in the United States."[12] Aware of the widespread prejudice against banks, Hamilton knew he needed to set out their advantages. Echoing Adam Smith, he showed how gold and silver, if locked up in a merchant's chest, were sterile. Deposit them in a bank, however, and these dead metals sprang to life as "nurseries of national wealth," forming a credit supply several times larger than the coins heaped in the bank's vaults.[13] In contemporary parlance, Hamilton wished to increase the money supply and the speed with which it circulated. Due to scarce money, many deals were being done as barter; in the south, warehouse receipts for tobacco often doubled as money. In contrast, a central bank would provide liquid capital that would promote the ease, freedom, and efficiency of commerce.

It speaks volumes about the prevalent detestation of banks that Hamilton dwelled so long on combating myths against them. For example, he had to contest that banks would invariably engender speculative binges in securities. The growing confidence in government, he asserted, would gradually reduce speculation in its bonds. At the same time, he admitted that speculative abuses are "an occasional ill, incident to a general good," that did not outweigh the overall advantages of bank lending: "If the abuses of a beneficial thing are to determine its condemnation, there is scarcely a source of public prosperity which will not speedily be closed."[14] Given the speculative mania about to break out, Hamilton's candor about it should be emphasized: "If banks, in spite of every precaution, are sometimes betrayed into giving a false credit to the persons described, they more frequently enable honest and industrious men of small or perhaps of no capital to undertake and prosecute business with advantage to themselves and to the community."[15]

For political and legal reasons, Hamilton had to address the loaded subject of paper money. The Constitution outlawed the issue of paper money by states; everybody remembered the worthless Continentals printed by Congress during the Revolution. Should the federal government now issue paper money? Fearing an inflationary peril, Hamilton scotched the idea: "The stamping of paper is an operation so much easier than the laying of taxes that a government in the practice of paper emissions would rarely fail in any such emergency to indulge itself too far."[16] As an alternative, Hamilton touted a central bank that could issue paper currency in the form of banknotes redeemable for coins. This would set in motion a self-correcting system. If the bank issued too much paper, holders would question its value and exchange it for gold and silver; this would then force the bank to curtail its supply of paper, restoring its value.

Hamilton wanted his central bank to be profitable enough to attract private investors while serving the public interest. He knew the composition of its board would be an inflammatory issue. Directors would consist of a "small and select class of men." To prevent an abuse of trust, Hamilton suggested mandatory rotation. "The necessary secrecy" of directors' transactions will give "unlimited scope to imagination to infer that something is or may be wrong. And this *inevitable* mystery is a solid reason for inserting in the constitution of a Bank the necessity of a change of men."[17] But who would direct this mysterious bastion of money? Its ten million dollars in capital would be several times larger than the combined capital of all existing banks, eclipsing anything ever seen in America. Hamilton, wanting the bank to remain predominantly in private hands, advanced a theory that became a truism of central banking—that monetary policy was so liable to abuse that it needed some insulation from interfering politicians: "To attach full confidence to an institution of this nature, it appears to be an essential ingredient in its structure that it shall be under a *private* not a *public* direction, under the guidance of *individual interest,* not of *public policy.*"[18]

At the same time, Hamilton worried that the bank would be so well buffered from public control that abuses might occur. To safeguard the public interest, the government would become a minority stockholder in the bank and able to vote for directors. Of the ten million dollars in capital, the president would be authorized to buy up to two million in bank stock—a stake presumably large enough to give the government substantial leverage, while not *so* large that it could dictate self-serving policies. The treasury secretary could also receive weekly reports on bank activities and retained the option of inspecting its books.

It was in the nature of Hamilton's achievement as treasury secretary that each of his programs was designed to mesh with the others to form a single interlocking whole. His central bank was no exception. Of the eight million of its capital that would be subscribed by private investors, three quarters would be paid in government securities. Thus Hamilton finely interwove his bank and public-debt plans, making it difficult to undo one and not the other. The byzantine, interrelated nature of his programs made him all the more the bane and terror of opponents.

On January 20, 1791, a bill to charter the Bank of the United States for twenty years virtually breezed through the Senate. At that point, nothing presaged the chasm about to yawn in American politics, one that was to create the first political parties. Only as the House mulled over the bank bill in early February did it become palpable that the amity between Hamilton and Madison, briefly restored by the excise tax, was about to shatter, this time irrevocably. Once again, Madison's dissent was partly local in origin. Some central-bank critics thought the institution would aggrandize northern merchants at the expense of southern agrarians, and Madison came from the largest rural state. Hamilton denied any urban bias, telling Washington that where banks had been established "they have given a new spring to agriculture, manufactures, and commerce."[19] Even if this were true, Hamilton had to reckon with the fact that farmers were debtors by nature and hence contemptuous of bankers and other creditors. Southern planters especially hated bankers. "Holding banking to be no more than the prostitution of money for illicit gain," historian

John C. Miller has written, "one Virginia planter swore that he would no more be caught going into a bank than into a house of ill fame."[20]

Hamilton wanted the new bank in Philadelphia. "It is manifest that a *large commercial city* with a great deal of *capital* and *business* must be the fittest seat of the Bank," he told Washington.[21] Madison fretted that placing the bank in Philadelphia might plant the national capital there permanently, reneging on the promised move to the Potomac. Congressman Benjamin Bourne of Rhode Island surmised that Madison might not have spoken against the bank had not "the gentlemen of the southward" viewed it as "adverse to the removal of Congress" to the Potomac.[22] For this and other reasons, Patrick Henry denounced Hamilton's economic program as a "constituent part of a system which I have ever dreaded—subserviency of southern to n[orther]n interests."[23]

Overshadowing this geographic split was the fundamental question of whether the Constitution allowed a central bank. While writing *The Federalist,* Madison had subscribed to an elastic interpretation of the charter. Now, speaking on the House floor, he made a dramatic turnabout, denying that the Constitution granted the federal government powers not specifically enumerated there: "Reviewing the Constitution . . . it was not possible to discover in it the power to incorporate a bank."[24] Hamilton turned to article 1, section 8, the catchall clause giving Congress the right to pass any legislation deemed "necessary and proper" to exercise its listed powers. Madison accused him of exploiting that power and "levelling all the barriers which limit the powers of the general government and protect those of the state governments."[25] Afraid that the agile Hamilton would dream up limitless activities and then rationalize them as "necessary and proper," Madison re-created himself as a strict constructionist of the Constitution.

For Madison, Hamilton was becoming the official voice of monied aristocrats who were grabbing the reins of federal power. He felt betrayed by his old friend. But it was Madison who had deviated from their former reading of the Constitution. To embarrass Madison, Elias Boudinot read aloud in Congress some passages about the "necessary and proper" clause from *Federalist* number 44, notably the following: "No axiom is more clearly established in law or in reason than wherever the end is required, the means are authorized; wherever a general power to do a thing is given, every particular power for doing it is included."[26] Hamilton probably tipped off his old friend that Madison had written these incriminating words.

On February 8, the House passed the bank bill by a one-sided thirty-nine to twenty, giving Hamilton a particularly sweet triumph. For a fleeting moment, his mastery of the government seemed complete, but the victory raised troublesome questions. Almost all congressmen from north of the Potomac had stood foursquare behind him, while their southern counterparts had almost all opposed him. As philosophical views increasingly dovetailed with geographic interests, one could begin to glimpse the contours of two parties taking shape. Individual issues were coalescing into clusters, with the same people lining up each time on opposite sides. In his *Life of Washington,* Chief Justice John Marshall traced the genesis of American political parties to the rancorous dispute over the Bank of the United States. That debate, he said, led "to the complete organization of those distinct and visible parties which in their long and dubious conflict for power have . . . shaken the United States to their center."[27]

Hamilton's seeming omnipotence unnerved Madison because it further skewed what the latter deemed the proper balance between executive and legislative power. For many delegates at Philadelphia in 1787, Congress was supposed to be the leading branch of government, the guardian of popular liberty that would prevent the restoration of British tyranny. That was why legislative duties were spelled out in article 1 of the Constitution. Consistent with this view, Madison thought the treasury secretary should serve as an adjunct to Congress, providing legislators with reports from which they would shape bills. Jefferson likewise balked at the way Hamilton both submitted reports and drafted bills based on them. Hamilton, in contrast, envisioned the executive branch as the main engine of government, the sole branch that could give force and direction to its policies, and time has abundantly vindicated his view.

Hamilton had not foreseen the looming constitutional crisis that his bank bill was to instigate. Jefferson and Madison grew fearful that Hamilton was not simply building a structure that dashed their principles but sculpting his creations in stone. His expansive vision of federal power filled them with foreboding. Precedents were being set that would be very hard to revoke later on. Hamilton admitted in retrospect that the new central bank represented his greatest stretch of federal power. The new government had reached a defining moment.

Madison wanted Washington to spike Hamilton's bank bill and cast the first veto in American history. To figure out whether the bill squared with the Constitution, Washington canvassed the members of his compact cabinet. First, he solicited the opinion of Attorney General Edmund Randolph, who wrote a weakly reasoned piece contending that the bank was unconstitutional. Washington then turned to Jefferson, who had long detested monopolies and chartered companies as privileges conferred by British kings; he could not reconcile a central bank with true republicanism. Jefferson was also increasingly irked by his relative impotence in Washington's cabinet and worried that the mercantile north, under Hamilton's auspices, was gaining the upper hand over the rural south. He told George Mason: "The only corrective of what is corrupt in our present form of government will be the augmentation of the numbers in the lower house so as to get a more agricultural representation, which may put that interest above that of the stock-jobbers."[28]

In a concise opinion, Jefferson blasted the Bank of the United States as unconstitutional on the grounds that Hamilton was perverting the necessary-and-proper clause. To pass the constitutional test, Jefferson said, a measure had to be more than just *convenient* in executing powers granted to the federal government: it had to be truly *necessary*—that is, indispensable. Taking literally the Constitution's recitation of congressional powers, he prophesied that "to take a single step beyond the boundaries thus specifically drawn . . . is to take possession of a boundless field of power, no longer susceptible of any definition."[29]

Just how vehemently Jefferson opposed the new bank can be inferred from a firebreathing letter he sent to Madison the following year. Governor Henry Lee wished to open a local bank in Virginia that would act as a counterweight to a branch of Hamilton's national bank. Jefferson worried about any measure that might confer legitimacy upon the central bank. From his letter, it is clear that he did not recognize the supremacy of federal over state law, a cardinal tenet of the Constitution:

> The power of erecting banks and corporations was not given to the general government; it remains then with the state itself. For any person to recognize a foreign legislature [Jefferson was talking about the U.S. Congress] in a case belonging to the state itself is an act of *treason* against the state. And whosoever shall do any act under color of the authority of a foreign legislature— whether by signing notes, issuing or passing them, acting as director, cashier or in any other office relating to it, shall be *adjudged guilty of high treason and suffer death accordingly* by the judgment of the state courts. This is the only opposition worthy of our state and the only kind which can be effectual. . . . I really wish that this or nothing should be done.[30] [Italics added.]

In other words, the principal author of the Declaration of Independence was recommending to the chief architect of the U.S. Constitution that any Virginia bank functionary who cooperated with Hamilton's bank should be found guilty of treason and executed.

Though inclined to support the bank, Washington was shaken by the negative verdicts rendered by Jefferson and Randolph, and on February 16 he rushed them to Hamilton for comment. Washington had ten days to sign or veto the measure. The document that Hamilton wrote in response, says one of his editors, is "the most brilliant argument for a broad interpretation of the Constitution in American political literature."[31] As always, Hamilton wanted to bury his foes beneath an avalanche of arguments. After gathering his thoughts, he consulted William Lewis, one of Philadelphia's foremost lawyers, and the two men spent an afternoon pacing Lewis's garden and reviewing Hamilton's arguments. In slightly more than a week, Hamilton, the human dynamo, elaborated a treatise of nearly fifteen thousand words that covers almost forty printed pages in his collected papers. On Monday the twenty-first, he reported back to Washington that he had "been ever since sedulously engaged" in preparing his defense and would send the results on Tuesday evening or Wednesday morning. With comical understatement, he said that he wanted to give the issue "a *thorough examination.*"[32] He went right down to the deadline with his treatise. Upon delivering it to Washington on Wednesday morning, a frazzled Hamilton noted that the final draft had "occupied him the greatest part of last night."[33]

Eliza Hamilton remembered the sleepless night when her husband gave immortal expression to a durable principle of constitutional law. As an ancient lady garbed in widow's weeds, she told the story to a young man who recorded it this way in his journal:

> Old Mrs. Hamilton . . . active in body, clear in mind . . . talks familiarly of Washington, Jefferson, and the fathers. I told her how greatly I was interested . . . on account of her husband's connection with the government. "He made your government," said she. "He made your bank. I sat up all night with him to help him do it. Jefferson thought we ought not to have a bank and President Washington thought so. But my husband said, 'We must have a Bank.' I sat up all night, copied out his writing, and the next morning, he carried it to President Washington and we had a bank."[34]

Hamilton's own allusion to staying up "the greatest part" of that night also attests to some electrifying finish, some final, brilliant burst of inspiration that completed his stupendous feat. As with many of his intellectual exploits, they were almost feats of athletic prowess as well.

Hamilton lent his opinion the erudition of a treatise and the warmth of a manifesto. The essence of it was that government must possess the means to attain ends for which it was established or the bonds of society would dissolve. To liberate the government from a restrictive reading of the Constitution, Hamilton refined the doctrine of "implied powers"—that is, that the government had the right to employ all means necessary to carry out powers mentioned in the Constitution.

In drafting his opinion, Hamilton claimed that minutes of the Constitutional Convention could provide "ample confirmation" of his liberal interpretation of the necessary-and-proper clause. Reluctant to break the convention's confidentiality oath—or perhaps afraid that Madison might play the same game—he then expunged the passage and let the Constitution speak for itself. He told Washington that, if adopted, "principles of construction like those espoused by the Secretary of State and the Attorney General would be fatal to the just and indispensable authority of the United States."[35] Then, in blazing italics, Hamilton trumpeted his main theme: "Now it appears to the Secretary of the Treasury that this *general principle* is *inherent* in the very *definition* of *government* and *essential* to every step of the progress to be made by that of the United States: namely that every power vested in a government is in its nature *sovereign* and includes by *force* of the *term* a right to employ all the *means* requisite and fairly *applicable* to the attainment of the *ends* of such power." If Jefferson's and Randolph's views were upheld, "the United States would furnish the singular spectacle of a *political society* without *sovereignty* or of a people *governed* without *government.*"[36]

Hamilton waved away complaints that the Constitution did not explicitly mention a bank: "It is not denied that there are *implied* as well as *express* powers and that the former are as effectually delegated as the latter."[37] To argue, as did Jefferson, that all government policies had to pass a strict test of being "absolutely necessary" to the performance of specified duties would paralyze government. How could one say with certainty what was absolutely necessary? Hamilton pointed out that, in setting up the Customs Service, he had overseen construction of lighthouses, beacons, and buoys, things not strictly necessary, but useful for society all the same. He was crafting a rationale for the future exercise of numerous forms of federal power.

The Bank of the United States would enable the government to make good on four powers cited explicitly in the Constitution: the rights to collect taxes, borrow money, regulate trade among states, and support fleets and armies. Jefferson wanted to deprive the federal government of the power to create *any* corporations, which Hamilton thought could cripple American business in the future. At the time, few corporations existed, and those mostly to build turnpikes. The farseeing Hamilton perceived the immense utility of this business form and patiently explained to Washington how corporations, with limited liability, were superior to private partnerships. In the end, his bank argument was predicated not only on his interpretation of the Constitution but on his reading of history: "In all questions of this nature, the practice of mankind ought to have great weight against the theories of individuals."[38]

After writing this magisterial defense, Hamilton packed it off to Washington before noon on Wednesday, February 23. The next day, Washington studied the opinion and, despite lingering doubts, was sufficiently impressed that he did not bother to send it to Jefferson. The day after that, he signed the bank bill.

Hamilton's plea for the bank had a continuing life in American history, partly from the influence it exerted upon Chief Justice John Marshall. When Daniel Webster made oral arguments for the Second Bank of the United States in the landmark case of *McCulloch v. Maryland* in 1819, he quoted Hamilton's 1791 memo to Washington on the necessary-and-proper clause. In words that distinctly echoed Hamilton's, Marshall said that *necessary* didn't mean *indispensable* so much as *appropriate.* Repeatedly in American history, Hamilton's flexible definition of the word *necessary* was to free government to handle unforeseen emergencies. Henry Cabot Lodge later referred to the doctrine of implied powers enunciated by Hamilton as "the most formidable weapon in the armory of the Constitution . . . capable of conferring on the federal government powers of almost any extent."[39] Hamilton was not the master builder of the Constitution: the laurels surely go to James Madison. He was, however, its foremost interpreter, starting with *The Federalist* and continuing with his Treasury tenure, when he had to expound constitutional doctrines to accomplish his goals. He lived, in theory and practice, every syllable of the Constitution. For that reason, historian Clinton Rossiter insisted that Hamilton's "works and words have been more consequential than those of any other American in shaping the Constitution under which we live."[40]

Among many arcane subjects that Hamilton had to master was the minting of coins. So laggard was America in this regard that after Washington took office, his daily expenses were still quoted in British pounds, shillings, and pence, even though the Confederation Congress had adopted the dollar as the currency unit. Businessmen in different states continued to assign differing values to the foreign coins that still circulated freely. So many gold and silver coins were adulterated with base metals that many merchants hesitated to do business for fear of being shortchanged. Counterfeiting was also widespread, and when Hamilton became treasury secretary it was still a crime punishable by death in New York State.

Somehow, even as he brought forth his bank report, Hamilton plowed through books about coinage in foreign nations, especially *Principles of Political Economy* by Sir James Steuart. He pored over tables that Isaac Newton, as master of the mint, had prepared for the British Treasury Board, specifying the pound's exact value in precious metals, and he ordered special assays of foreign coins to gauge the gold, silver, and copper content in their alloys.

On January 28, 1791, a week after the Senate approved his bank bill, Hamilton handed beleaguered legislators yet another hefty document. His *Report on the Mint* was studded with clever suggestions. "There is scarcely any point in the economy of national affairs of greater moment than the uniform preservation of the intrinsic value of the money unit," he intoned. "On this, the security and steady value of

property essentially depend."[41] He endorsed the dollar as the basic currency, divided into smaller coins on a decimal basis. Because many Americans still bartered,
Hamilton wanted to encourage the use of coins. As part of his campaign to foster a
market economy, Hamilton suggested introducing a wide variety of coins, including gold and silver dollars, a ten-cent silver piece, and copper coins of a cent or half
cent. He wasn't just thinking of rich people; small coins would benefit the poor "by
enabling them to purchase in small portions and at a more reasonable rate the nec-
essaries of which they stand in need."[42] To spur patriotism, he proposed that coins
feature presidential heads or other emblematic designs and display great beauty
and workmanship: "It is a just observation that 'The perfection of the coins is a
great safeguard against counterfeits.'"[43] With customary attention to detail, Hamilton recommended that coins should be small and thick instead of large and thin,
making it more difficult to rub away the metal.

As to whether coins should be minted from gold or silver, Hamilton caused no
end of mischief by opting for both, starting the vogue for "bimetallism" that was to
become the curse of American financial history. He stumbled into this decision because he feared that if he chose either gold or silver as the sole monetary metal, it
would "abridge the quantity of circulating medium" at a time when his primary
aim was to expand the money supply and stoke economic activity.[44] One major
problem that he sought to remedy was that the dollar had no fixed value in various
states. With typical exactitude, Hamilton tried to establish the quantity of precious
metal in each coin so that the silver dollar, for instance, would contain "370 grains
and 933 thousandth parts of a grain of pure silver."[45]

At the time Hamilton drafted his *Report on the Mint,* he and Jefferson still talked
civilly and exchanged ideas about money. Coinage was one of Jefferson's hobby-
horses, and he had reported on it to Congress the previous summer. In fact, Hamilton drew on that report in preparing his paper. For once, they seemed in agreement.
"I return your report on the mint, which I have read over with a great deal of satisfaction," Jefferson told Hamilton before the latter sent it to Congress.[46] While minister in Paris, Jefferson had visited the royal mint and marveled at a machine
concocted by the Swiss inventor Jean Pierre Droz, which could simultaneously
stamp images on both sides of a coin.

Hamilton long regretted that when the U.S. Mint was finally established by Congress in spring 1792 and began to produce the first federal coins, Washington
lodged it under Jefferson's jurisdiction at State. The mint was a pet interest of Jefferson, and Washington submitted to his prodding. The president also believed that
the treasury secretary was bowed beneath enough work. Unfortunately, Jefferson
ran the mint poorly. Hamilton later tried, in vain, to arrange a swap whereby the
post office would go to State in exchange for the mint coming under Treasury con-

trol, where it belonged. Despite this wobbly start, the mint became a Philadelphia fixture, and when the government moved to Washington, D.C., in 1800 it stayed behind in the interim capital.

That the Bank of the United States had sparked heated controversy and polarized the country must have seemed like forgotten history on July 4, 1791. On that memorable day in Philadelphia, the subscription to the stock of Hamilton's central bank was thrown open to an expectant public, and the public promptly went berserk. Speculaton was rife that the stock would pay rich dividends of 12 percent or more, and people had been flocking to the capital for a week in anticipation of this first offering. So lusty was the pent-up demand that mobs, dazzled by visions of riches, stormed the building, overwhelming the clerks. The heavily oversubscribed issue sold out within an hour, leaving many disgruntled investors empty-handed. Jefferson told James Monroe, "The bank filled and overflowed in the moment it was opened."[47]

Hamilton had expected an ebullient market in these publicly traded shares but nothing nearly this clamorous. By late June, reports flooded his office of large quantities of money flowing into the forthcoming subscription. "In all appearances, the subscriptions to the Bank of the United States will proceed with astonishing rapidity," Hamilton assured one congressman. "'Twill not be surprising if a week completes them."[48] Even Hamilton never dreamed that the response would be so giddy that it would take less than an hour to complete the offering.

When trading in shares commenced, prices promptly took off, buoyed by a money fever such as Americans had never witnessed. Investors did not purchase shares outright. To create a robust market and broaden share ownership, Hamilton agreed to sell the bank shares initially in the form of scrip. The system worked thus: investors made a twenty-five-dollar down payment and received a scrip that entitled them to buy a set number of shares at par and then pay off the balance over an eighteen-month period. So frenzied was the trading in scrip that many investors doubled their money within days, and the resulting madness was dubbed "scrippomania."

The contagion spread rapidly to other cities. Special couriers galloped off to New York to report prices rocketing upward in Philadelphia and Boston, and newspapers recorded each fresh spurt in shares. Madison happened to be in New York and watched with consternation as the trading mania descended on Manhattan. For this Virginia planter, the bedlam of speculation wasn't a pretty sight. On July 10, he informed Jefferson that "the Bank shares have risen as much in the market here as at Philadelphia" and castigated the booming market as "a mere scramble for so much public plunder."[49] Like Madison, Jefferson didn't view this "delirium of speculation" as a tribute to Hamilton's mystique so much as squandered money. He told Washington, "It remains to be seen whether in a country whose capital is too small to carry its own commerce, to establish manufactures, erect buildings, etc., such sums should have been withdrawn from these useful pursuits to be employed in gambling."[50]

Hamilton had brought the modern financial world to America, with all its unsettling effects. He had wanted to spread bank ownership widely, but he made a critical blunder that only ratified southern suspicions that he was the ringleader of a northern plot. Philadelphia had hosted the initial offering, and many investors had traveled there, lugging gold and silver, to make purchases. Hamilton had also arranged for Bostonians to buy scrip through the Bank of Massachusetts and New Yorkers through the Bank of New York. Hence, a disproportionate number of scrip holders resided in Philadelphia, Boston, and New York, which looked like arrant favoritism rather than a consequence of the fact that Boston and New York had banks to act as intermediaries. Hamilton regretted this ownership pattern, and his correspondence confirms that he *had* written to southerners, trying to entice them to buy bank shares.

The troubling preponderance of northeast investors combined with other factors to feed the impression of a northern oligarchy assiduously at work. Most subscribers were merchants and lawyers—part of Hamilton's political following—and some of the most visible speculators, especially William Duer, belonged to his entourage. With Jefferson and Madison poised to spot British-style corruption in the legislature, it did not help Hamilton's cause that at least thirty members of Congress and Secretary of War Knox subscribed to bank scrip.

Hamilton knew that a speculative binge on securities could tarnish his system. He welcomed enthusiasm but not crazed investors. "These extravagant sallies of speculation do injury to the government and to the whole system of public credit," Hamilton had warned earlier in the year.[51] He was never a hireling of monied interests; rather, he wanted to attach them to the new country's interests. Like many thinkers of his day, he thought that property conferred independent judgment on people and hoped that creditors would bring an enlightened, disinterested point of view to government. But what if they succumbed to speculation and disrupted the system they were supposed to stabilize? What if they engaged in destructive short-term behavior instead of being long-term custodians of the nation's interests? If that happened, it might undermine his whole political program.

As with any speculative bubble, it is hard to pin down the elusive moment when reasonable confidence in bank scrip bloomed into euphoria. As late as July 31, Fisher Ames wrote to Hamilton from Boston, praising the bank subscription: "People here are full of exultation and gratitude."[52] Then, in early August, prices soared upward in a vertical line. On August 8, Madison expressed shock to Jefferson: "The stock-jobbers will become the praetorian head of the Government, at once its tool and its tyrant, bribed by its largesses and overawing it by clamours and combinations."[53] Jefferson brooded about the harm to America's moral fiber: "The spirit of gaming, once it has seized a subject, is incurable. The tailor who has made thousands in one day, tho[ugh] he has lost them the next, can never again be content with the slow and moderate earnings of his needle."[54] Benjamin Rush reported the same money-mad bustle in Philadelphia. Everybody from merchants to clerks was forsaking everyday duties to wager on scrip: "The city of Philadelphia for several days has exhibited the marks of a great gaming house. . . . Never did I see so universal a frenzy. Nothing else was spoken of but scrip in all companies, even by those who were not interested in it."[55] Senator Rufus King later told Hamilton that New York City's economy had ground to a halt as people rushed off to gamble in bank shares: "The business was going on in a most alarming manner, mechanics deserting their shops, shopkeepers sending their goods to auction, and not a few of our merchants neglecting the regular and profitable commerce of the City."[56]

Finally, on August 11, 1791, came the first crash in government securities in American history. Bank scrip that had gone on sale for twenty-five dollars just over a month earlier had zoomed to more than three hundred dollars. The bubble was pricked when bankers refused to extend more credit to leading speculators. Then bears began to sell, and shares nose-dived. As the chief financial regulator, this market turbulence thrust Hamilton into a ticklish situation. He had no precedents to guide him. As a rule, he tried not to interfere with markets and thought it improper to register opinions on the value of government securities. But he also believed he had an obligation to protect the financial system, and so he improvised as he went along. On August 15, Rufus King informed Hamilton that speculators attempting to depress bank shares were quoting Hamilton's opinion that scrip was grossly overvalued: "They go further and mention prices below the present market as the value sanctioned by your authority."[57]

The rumors had some basis in truth. As Hamilton admitted to King, he did not ordinarily voice opinions about the suitable level of shares, but he *had* intimated that prices were too high: "I thought it advisable to speak out, for a bubble connected with my operations is, of all the enemies I have to fear, in my judgment the most formidable. . . . [T]o counteract delusions appears to me the only secure foundation on which to stand. I thought it therefore expedient to risk something in contributing to dissolve the charm."[58] In modern lingo, Hamilton subtly tried to "talk down" the market to avert a worse tumble later on. At the same time, he stressed that the price he had quoted as the proper level for scrip was not as low as the one being bandied about by speculators.

On August 16, Hamilton wrote confidentially to William Seton, cashier of the Bank of New York, instructing him to buy up $150,000 in government securities (what we would today call "open market operations"). Hamilton hoped that as these security prices rose, the beneficial effect would spill over into the market for bank shares. His strategy worked. What concerned Hamilton was not so much the harm to speculators as the risk to the financial system. He particularly feared that securities dealers, caught in a cash squeeze, might liquidate shares and precipitate a self-sustaining drop in prices. As he put it, "A principal object with me is to keep the stock from falling too low in case the embarrassments of the dealers should lead to sacrifices."[59]

Complicating matters was the uncomfortable fact that the most flamboyant New York speculator was Hamilton's boon companion from King's College days, William Duer. Duer had lasted seven months as assistant treasury secretary. After leaving office, he lost no time in capitalizing on his knowledge of Treasury operations and set about cornering state debt, sending teams of buying agents into the boondocks. Duer borrowed heavily to finance his enormous trading in bank scrip, and Hamilton knew this added extreme danger to the situation.

On August 17, Hamilton wrote a tough-minded letter to Duer, reproaching him for his maneuvers and invoking the South Sea Bubble of 1720. He told Duer that people were whispering that he and his associates were rigging the price of bank scrip through "fictitious purchases" to dupe a gullible public into buying more shares. While adding tactfully that he knew Duer would do no such duplicitous thing, Hamilton made clear that he took these reports seriously: "I will honestly own I had serious fears for you—for your *purse* and for your *reputation* and with an anxiety for both I wrote to you in earnest terms."[60] Hamilton's letter showed his usual integrity, displaying concern both for Duer as a friend and for the health of the securities market. Then Hamilton compromised himself by tipping his hand and suggesting to Duer an appropriate price for bank stock: "I should rather call it about 190 to be within bounds with hopes of better things and I sincerely wish you may be able to support it at what you mention."[61] It was one thing for Hamilton to employ the Bank of New York to prop up share prices and quite another to enlist a longtime friend and grand-scale speculator as his intermediary. Duer, of course, denied all wrongdoing. "Those who impute to my artifices the rise of this species of stock in the market beyond its true point of value do me infinite injustice," he pleaded.[62] Hamilton's letter could only have emboldened Duer to believe that he might profit from inside information, and he continued to flaunt his association with the treasury secretary, leading unsuspecting investors to believe he was privy to government plans.

For the moment, Hamilton's actions halted the slide in financial markets and averted a catastrophic break in prices. Scrip fell back to a more reasonable 110 share price before rallying to 145 in September. For the first time in American history, Hamilton had demonstrated how a financial regulator could steady a panicky market through deft, behind-the-scenes operations. Unfortunately, he had erred in confiding in William Duer, who remained deaf to Hamilton's admonition that he restrain his speculation.

For Hamilton's growing legion of critics, the financial mayhem showed the corrosive effect of his financial wizardry. New York merchant Seth Johnson deplored the behavior induced by prodigal trading in bank shares: "Those who gain play in hope of more, those who lose continue in hope of better fortune."[63] For Jefferson, scrippomania brought to the surface all his disgust for the Hamiltonian system, making imperative the need to preserve a pure, agrarian America. "Ships are lying at the wharves," he wrote that summer, "buildings are stopped, capitals are withdrawn from commerce, manufactures, arts, and agriculture to be employed in gambling, and the tide of public prosperity almost unparalleled in any country is arrested in its course and suppressed by the rage of getting rich in one day."[64] For Jefferson, Alexander Hamilton was more than just dead wrong in his prescriptions. He was becoming a menace to the American experiment, one who had to be stopped at all costs.

NINETEEN

CITY OF THE FUTURE

B y the summer of 1791, after his victories in his skirmishes with Jefferson and
Madison over public credit, assumption, and a central bank, Hamilton had
attained the summit of his power. Such stellar success might have bred an
intoxicating sense of invincibility. But his vigorous reign had also made him the enfant terrible of the early republic, and a substantial minority of the country was
mobilized against him. This should have made him especially watchful of his reputation. Instead, in one of history's most mystifying cases of bad judgment, he entered into a sordid affair with a married woman named Maria Reynolds that, if it
did not blacken his name forever, certainly sullied it. From the lofty heights of
statesmanship, Hamilton fell back into something reminiscent of the squalid world
of his West Indian boyhood.

Philadelphia had its quota of sensual pleasures. Though French visitors dismissed it as quaintly puritanical, it enjoyed a livelier reputation among Americans.
Hamilton and other government officials had access to a nocturnal medley of parties, balls, and plays. These social gatherings were often hosted by federalist merchants. The queen bee of local society was Anne Willing Bingham, wife of the
extremely rich William Bingham, who presided over banquets at their opulent
three-story mansion near Third Street and Spruce. Far from being prim, Philadelphia gatherings in the 1790s abounded in exposed arms and bosoms, if Abigail
Adams is to be trusted. She was shocked by all the female flesh on display at parties:
"The style of dress . . . is really an outrage upon all decency. . . . The arm naked almost to the shoulder and without stays or bodice. . . . Most [ladies] wear their
clothes too scant upon the body and too full upon the bosom for my fancy. Not

content with the *show* which nature bestows, they borrow from art and literally look like nursing mothers."[1]

The vivacious Alexander and Eliza Hamilton socialized with the Binghams and other affluent couples. Perhaps by that spring, Eliza had felt the strain of their social obligations and needed time to recuperate. In mid-May 1791, knowing that Hamilton was bogged down with work, Philip Schuyler begged Eliza and the four children (plus the orphaned Fanny Antill) to join him in Albany for the summer. To avoid epidemics, many people vacated Philadelphia and other large cities in sultry weather. "I fear if she remains where she is until the hot weather commences that her health may be much injured," Schuyler confided to Hamilton about Eliza. "Let me therefore entreat you to expedite her as soon as possible."[2] So due to Schuyler's tender concern, Eliza and the children left Philadelphia soon after the sensational offering of bank scrip on July 4 and stayed away for the rest of that torrid summer.

It was a dangerous moment for Eliza to abandon Hamilton. He was the cynosure of all eyes, and many people noted his enchantment with women. John Adams carped at his "indelicate pleasures," Harrison Gray Otis told his wife of Hamilton's "liquorish flirtation" with a married woman at a dinner party, and Benjamin Latrobe, later the surveyor of public buildings in Washington, branded him an "insatiable libertine."[3] Such descriptions, though hyperbolic, may have contained a grain of truth: Hamilton *was* susceptible to the charms of beautiful women. Like many people driven by their careers, he did not allow himself sufficient time for escape and relaxation. When Charles Willson Peale painted him in 1791, Hamilton had the air of a commanding politician, his mouth firm, his eyes narrowed with concentration. No trace of joy softened his serious face. He was a volatile personality encased inside a regimented existence.

Whenever he dealt with women, Hamilton shed his bureaucratic manner and reverted to the whimsy of bygone days. Right before the bank subscription, Hamilton received a volume of dramatic verse, *The Ladies of Castille*, from Mercy Warren, a Massachusetts poet, playwright, and historian. Hamilton sent a dashing note of thanks: "It is certain that in the 'Ladies of Castille,' the sex will find a new occasion of triumph. Not being a poet myself, I am in the less danger of feeling mortification at the idea that, in the career of dramatic composition at least, female genius in the United States has outstripped the male."[4] His wit with women was often flirtatious. When his friend Susanna Livingston inquired about Treasury certificates she owned, Hamilton apologized for his delay in responding and said that he held himself "bound by all the laws of chivalry to make the most ample reparation in any mode you shall prescribe. You will of course recollect that I am a married man!"[5]

As the son of a "fallen woman," Hamilton tended to be chivalric toward women in trouble. The day after he complimented Warren, he wrote to a Boston widow named Martha Walker who had petitioned Congress for relief, contending that her husband had sacrificed valuable property in Quebec to enlist in the Revolution. With countless petitions coming before Congress, it is noteworthy that Hamilton plucked this one from the pile, assuring Walker that "I shall enter upon the examination with every profession which can be inspired by favorable impression of personal merit and by a sympathetic participation in the distresses of a lady as deserving as unfortunate."[6] These letters to Warren and Walker, written right before Eliza left for Albany, suggest that Hamilton was more than receptive to overtures from women.

Six years later, Alexander Hamilton found himself transported back to that summer of 1791 as he told a flabbergasted public about his extended sexual escapade with twenty-three-year-old Maria (probably pronounced "Mariah") Reynolds, who must have been very alluring. She had arrived unannounced at his redbrick house at 79 South Third Street. He began his famous account thus: "Sometime in the summer of the year 1791, a woman called at my house in the city of Philadelphia and asked to speak with me in private. I attended her into a room apart from the family." Reynolds beguiled Hamilton with a doleful tale of a husband, James Reynolds, "who for a long time had treated her very cruelly, [and] had lately left her to live with another woman and in so destitute a condition that, though desirous of returning to her friends, she had not the means." Since Maria Reynolds came from New York and Hamilton was a New York citizen, Hamilton continued, "she had taken the liberty to apply to my humanity for assistance."[7] Her sudden listing in the 1791 city directory as the mysterious "Mrs. Reynolds"—she was virtually the only person to appear without a first name—seems to confirm her recent arrival in Philadelphia.

The thirty-six-year-old Hamilton never shrank from a maiden in distress, as Maria Reynolds must have known. He told her that her situation was "a very interesting one" and that he wished to assist her but that she had come at an inopportune moment (i.e., Eliza was at home). He volunteered to bring "a small supply of money" to her home at 154 South Fourth Street that evening. Hamilton recounted that meeting with a certain novelistic flair:

> In the evening, I put a bank bill in my pocket and went to the house. I inquired for Mrs. Reynolds and was shown upstairs, at the head of which she met me and conducted me into a bedroom. I took the bill out of my pocket and gave it to her. Some conversation ensued from which it was quickly apparent that other than pecuniary consolation would be acceptable.[8]

That encounter was the first of many times that Alexander Hamilton slipped furtively through the night to see Reynolds. Once Eliza had gone off to Albany, the coast was clear to bring his mistress home. After their first rendezvous, Hamilton recalled, "I had frequent meetings with her, most of them at my own house."[9] After a short period, Reynolds informed Hamilton of a sudden reconciliation with her husband, which Hamilton later claimed he had encouraged. But Maria Reynolds was no ordinary adulteress, and politics now entered into the picture. She informed Hamilton that her husband had speculated in government securities and had even profited from information obtained from Treasury Department sources.

When Hamilton met James Reynolds, the latter fingered William Duer as the source of this information. It is baffling that Hamilton, having worked to achieve a spotless reputation as treasury secretary, did not see that he was now courting danger and would be susceptible to blackmail. Maria Reynolds introduced Hamilton to her husband as her benevolent, disinterested savior during a time of desperation, and for this James Reynolds pretended gratitude. But when Reynolds said that he was going to Virginia, he asked whether Hamilton could secure a government job for him upon his return. Hamilton remained noncommittal.

In recollecting events, Hamilton admitted that the more he learned about the sleazy James Reynolds, the more he thought of ending the affair. He was in the midst of preparing his great *Report on Manufactures,* yet he was also in the grip of a dark sexual compulsion, and Maria Reynolds knew how to hold him fast in her toils by feigning love. "All the appearances of violent attachment and of agonizing distress at the idea of a relinquishment were played off with a most imposing art," he wrote. "This, though it did not make me entirely the dupe of the plot, yet kept me in a state of irresolution. My sensibility, perhaps my vanity, admitted the possibility of a real fondness and led me to adopt the plan of a gradual discontinuance rather than of a sudden interruption, at least calculated to give pain, if a real partiality existed."[10] As often is the case with addictions, the fanciful notion of a "gradual discontinuance" only provided a comforting pretext for more sustained indulgence.

In his later pamphlet, Hamilton was at pains to suggest that Maria Reynolds may have been sincerely smitten with him. His recounting of the affair suggests that at moments the relationship struck him as genuinely romantic. He could never make up his mind whether it had started honestly on her side and then turned to blackmail or whether she had conspired with James Reynolds all along. Perhaps, as Hamilton intimated, his vanity could not admit that he had been conned by a pair of lowlife tricksters. The man accused by his enemies of bottomless craft could be a most credulous dupe. Whenever his interest flagged, Maria Reynolds regained his sympathy by telling him that her husband was abusing her or, more pointedly, that he had threatened to spill the story to Eliza. For Hamilton, Maria Reynolds always remained a curious amalgam of tragicomic figure and confidence woman.

Whatever Maria Reynolds's initial intentions, Hamilton must have seemed elegant, charming, and godlike compared to her vulgarian husband. It is hard to imagine that some genuine feeling for Hamilton did not enter sporadically into her emotions. She wrote him numerous letters—Hamilton ruefully called her a "great scribbler"[11]—notable for atrocious grammar, spelling, and punctuation. Some letters seemed to consist of a single run-on sentence. In these missives, Maria Reynolds portrayed herself as a wretched, lovelorn creature, desperate to see Hamilton again and pining away with loneliness. While such letters may have persuaded Hamilton that her emotions were sincere, their hysterical excesses should have alerted him that he was dealing with a perilously unstable woman.

We know very little about the background of Maria Reynolds. She was born Mary Lewis in Dutchess County, New York, in 1768, married James Reynolds at fifteen, and two years later gave birth to a daughter named Susan. (At some point, she switched her name from Mary to Maria.) She told Hamilton that her sister Susannah had married Gilbert J. Livingston, which endowed her with respectable Hudson Valley connections. One Philadelphia merchant, Peter A. Grotjan, described her as smart, sensitive, and genteel, but this picture conflicts with an affidavit from Richard Folwell, whose mother was her first landlady in Philadelphia. Folwell etched a portrait of Maria Reynolds that tallies more closely with Hamilton's account of a mercurial personality prone to wild mood swings:

> Her mind at this time was far from being tranquil or consistent, for almost at the same minute that she would declare her respect for her husband, cry and feel distressed, [the tears] would vanish and levity would succeed, with bitter execrations on her husband. This inconsistency and folly was ascribed to a troubled, but innocent and harmless mind. In one or other of these paroxysms, she told me, so infamous was the perfidy of Reynolds, that he had frequently enjoined and insisted that she should insinuate herself on certain high and influential characters—endeavor to make assignations with them and actually prostitute herself to gull money from them.[12]

After leaving the Folwell residence, Maria and James Reynolds lived on North Grant Street, where they occupied separate beds (or even rooms) while Maria dabbled in prostitution. Gentlemen left letters in her entryway, Folwell said, and "at night she would fly off as was supposed to *answer* their contents."[13]

Folwell's testimony confirms both the sincerity and the patent insincerity of the mixed-up Maria Reynolds. There seems little question that she approached Hamilton as part of an extortion racket, delivering an adept performance as a despairing woman. It was also clear, however, that she was too flighty to stick to any script. Since she despised her husband, she may have nourished fantasies that Hamilton would rescue her even as she preyed upon him. Fact and fiction may have blended imperceptibly in her mind. Hamilton later concluded of his paramour, "The variety of shapes which this woman could assume was endless."[14]

Maria Reynolds was the antithesis of the sturdy, sensible, loyal Eliza. The more depressing then to survey the letters Hamilton sent to Eliza that summer to keep her at bay. On August 2, he expressed satisfaction that she had arrived safely in Albany and showed concern ("Take good care of my lamb") for their three-year-old son, James, who was ill. At the same time, Hamilton pressed her to stay in Albany: "I am so anxious for a perfect restoration of your health that I am willing to make a great sacrifice for it."[15] At one point, when Eliza seemed about to return on short notice, Hamilton, worried that he might be taken by surprise, exhorted her to "let me know beforehand your determination that I may meet you at New York."[16] In late August, when her return seemed imminent, Hamilton advised that "much as I long for this happy moment, my extreme anxiety for the restoration of your health will reconcile me to your staying longer where you are. . . . Think of me—dream of me—and love me my Bestsey as I do you."[17] Finally, in September, with Hamilton suffering from his old kidney ailment and taking warm baths to soothe it, Eliza decided to return with the children. One last time, Hamilton urged her, "Don't alarm yourself nor hurry so as to injure either yourself or the children."[18]

It is easy to snicker at such deceit and conclude that Hamilton faked all emotion for his wife, but this would belie the otherwise exemplary nature of their marriage. Eliza Hamilton never expressed anything less than a worshipful attitude toward her husband. His love for her, in turn, was deep and constant if highly imperfect. The problem was that no single woman could seem to satisfy all the needs of this complex man with his checkered childhood. As mirrored in his earliest adolescent poems, Hamilton seemed to need two distinct types of love: love of the faithful, domestic kind and love of the more forbidden, exotic variety.

In his later confessions, Hamilton tried to explain the mad persistence of this affair by citing his terror that James Reynolds might blurt out the truth to Eliza. As he phrased it, "No man tender of the happiness of an excellent wife could, without extreme pain, look forward to the affliction which she might endure from the disclosure, especially a *public disclosure,* of the fact. Those best acquainted with the interior of my domestic life will best appreciate the force of such a consideration upon me. The truth was that . . . I dreaded extremely a disclosure—and was willing to make large sacrifices to avoid it."[19] In the end, his desire to spare Eliza led him only to hurt her the more.

When Eliza returned to Philadelphia that fall, Hamilton could no longer receive Maria Reynolds at his residence and resorted to her home. (The Hamiltons had by now moved to Market Street, near the presidential mansion.) How he squeezed in time for these carnal interludes while compiling his *Report on Manufactures* is a wonder. That he inserted these trysts into such a tight schedule only strengthens the impression that Hamilton was ensnared by a sexual obsession. It was as if, after inhabiting a world of high culture for many years, Hamilton had regressed back to the sensual, dissolute world of his childhood. There is again a Dickensian quality to his story: the young hero escapes a tawdry life only to be lured back into it by a pair of unscrupulous swindlers.

If Hamilton thought he could commit adultery without paying a penalty, he learned otherwise when James Reynolds materialized again late that fall. During the Revolution, Reynolds had worked as a skipper on a Hudson River sloop and supplied provisions to patriotic troops, meeting William Duer and other purveyors. He then went to sea before settling in New York, and he had sought employment at the new Treasury Department in 1789. Though he wangled a reference letter from Robert Troup, he was rejected for a job, possibly giving him an extra motive for vengeance against Hamilton. The following year, some New York speculators sent Reynolds south to buy up claims that the government owed to veterans in Virginia and North Carolina.

On December 15, 1791, ten days after Hamilton submitted his *Report on Manufactures* to Congress, his earlier charade of friendship with James Reynolds abruptly ended. "One day, I received a letter from [Maria Reynolds] . . . intimating a discovery [of the sexual liaison] by her husband," Hamilton was to recall. "It was a matter of doubt with me whether there had been really a discovery by accident or whether the time for the catastrophe of the plot was arrived."[20] James Reynolds displayed a sure sense of timing: the hubbub over the manufacturing report made it an ideal moment to threaten Hamilton, who was much in the newspapers.

On the unforgettable afternoon of Thursday, December 15, 1791, Maria Reynolds warned Hamilton that her husband had written to him and that if he didn't receive a reply, "he will write Mrs. Hamilton." Maria, as usual, was overcome with emotion: "Oh my God I feel more for you than myself and wish I had never been born to give you so mutch unhappisness do not rite to him no not a Line but come here soon do not send or leave any thing in his power Maria."[21] Hamilton had indeed received a thinly veiled blackmail note from James Reynolds that began: "I am very sorry to find out that I have been so Cruelly trated by a person that I took to be my best friend instead of that my greatest Enimy. You have deprived me of every thing thats near and dear to me." A master of crude melodrama, Reynolds told

Hamilton that Maria had been weeping constantly, that this had made him suspicious, and that he had trailed a black messenger who carried one of her letters to Hamilton's home. Upon confronting Maria, "the poor Broken harted woman" had confessed to the affair. Here James Reynolds worked himself up into self-righteous wrath:

> instead of being a Friend. you have acted the part of the most Cruelist man in existence. you have made a whole family miserable. She ses there is no other man that she Care for in this world. now Sir you have bin the Cause of Cooling her affections for me. She was a woman. I should as soon sespect an angiel from heven. and one where all my happiness was depending. and I would Sacrefise almost my life to make her Happy. but now I am determed to have satisfation.[22]

Hamilton summoned Reynolds to his office that afternoon. He did not know whether Reynolds had proof of the affair or was bluffing, so he played it cagey. He later wrote that he neither admitted nor denied the affair, telling Reynolds "that if he knew of any injury I had done him, entitling him to satisfaction, it lay with him to name it. . . . It was easy to understand that he wanted money and to prevent an explosion, I resolved to gratify him. . . . He withdrew with a promise of compliance."[23] Hamilton was a rank amateur in adultery. By allowing James Reynolds to be seen in his office, he had given the blackmailer the upper hand.

On Saturday evening, December 17, James Reynolds wrote to Hamilton and charged him with alienating Maria's affections: "I find the wife always weeping and praying that I wont leve her. And its all on your account, for if you had not seekd for her Ruin it would not have happined."[24] Reynolds demanded some compensation for his ruined marriage and arranged to meet with Hamilton the next day. Hamilton was so alarmed that he sent a note to an unnamed correspondent stating, "I am this moment going to a rendezvous which I suspect may involve a most serious plot against me. . . . As any disastrous event might interest my fame, I drop you this line that from my impressions may be inferred the truth of the matter."[25]

At their meeting, Reynolds was very businesslike, and Hamilton asked him to name his price. The day after, Reynolds said that one thousand dollars would be a proper salve to his "wounded honor."[26] He contended that he could never regain his wife's love and that he planned to leave town with their daughter. Hamilton was forced to pay the now considerable blackmail money in installments, making one payment on December 22 and a second on January 3. James Reynolds, if poor at spelling, was able to fathom Hamilton's insatiable sexual appetite for his wife and his dread of exposure.

At this point, Hamilton tried to terminate the shabby affair, which formed such an odd counterpoint to the splendor of his public life. Briefly, he ceased all contact with Maria. This frightened James Reynolds, who saw future income fast fading away. On January 17, 1792, he wrote to Hamilton and urged him to visit the house and regard his wife as a "friend." Suddenly, he was no longer the wronged spouse but a philanthropist concerned with his wife's welfare, not a grief-stricken husband but a shameless pimp for his wife. It is hard to believe that at this juncture Hamilton did not abruptly end this hazardous affair. Of Reynolds's invitation, Hamilton wrote: "If I recollect rightly, I did not immediately accept the invitation, nor till after I had received several very importunate letters from Mrs. Reynolds." Subsequent letters from husband and wife were "a persevering scheme to spare no pains to levy contributions upon my passions on the one hand and upon my apprehensions of discovery on the other."[27]

Even as Hamilton had indulged his lust for Maria Reynolds, his imagination was conjuring up a futuristic industrial city, a microcosm of the manufacturing society that he envisioned to counter Jefferson's nation of citizen-farmers. At a time when nineteen of twenty Americans tilled the soil, Hamilton feared that if America remained purely agrarian, it would be relegated to eternally subordinate status vis-à-vis European societies.

It was already an age of scientific wonders that promised to reshape economies and boost productivity. From the first steam engine that James Watt built in Great Britain in the 1760s to the hot-air balloons that floated across French skies in the 1780s to Eli Whitney's invention of the cotton gin and the use of interchangeable parts in the 1790s, it was a time of technological marvels. No industry was being transformed more dramatically than British textiles. Sir Richard Arkwright had devised a machine called the water frame that used the power of rushing water to spin many threads simultaneously. By the time Hamilton was sworn in as treasury secretary, Arkwright's mills on the Clyde in Scotland employed more than 1,300 hands.

As much as the Bank of England, the British Exchequer, and the Royal Navy, these industrial breakthroughs had catapulted Britain to a leading position in the world economy. The British treated such economic discoveries as precious state secrets, which they guarded jealously against rival nations. Laws were passed to outlaw the export of textile machinery, and ships were stopped midocean if they contained such contraband cargo. Skilled mechanics who worked in textile factories were forbidden to emigrate upon pain of fine and imprisonment—for even if they couldn't smuggle out blueprints, they could memorize methods and peddle this valuable information abroad. All of this Hamilton watched with rapt fascination. "Certainly no other man in America saw so clearly the significance of the change that was taking place in English industrialism," Vernon Parrington wrote of Hamilton, "and what tremendous reservoirs of wealth the new order laid open to the country that tapped them."[28] The treasury secretary intuited that the future strength of nation-states would be proportionate to their industrial prowess, and he celebrated the early growth of American industry, whether it was entrepreneurs making wool hats or glass in Pennsylvania or watchmakers in Connecticut.

Contrary to his image as a tool of England, Hamilton enlisted early on in a scheme to challenge British supremacy in textiles. In January 1789, excited investors crowded into Rawson's Tavern on Wall Street to feast on wine and cake and consecrate the New York Manufacturing Society. Two months later, Hamilton's name appeared among charter subscribers investing in a new woolen factory scheduled to open on Crown Street (later Liberty Street) in lower Manhattan. In the end, the facility suffered from a fatal shortage of water power and closed a year or two later, but the experience initiated Hamilton into the mysteries of the new industrial order.

Around this time, a young man named Samuel Slater slipped through the tight protective net thrown by British authorities around their textile business. As a former apprentice to Sir Richard Arkwright, Slater had sworn that he would never reveal his boss's trade secrets. Flouting this pledge, he sailed to New York and made contact with Moses Brown, a Rhode Island Quaker. Under Slater's supervision, Brown financed a spinning mill in Rhode Island that replicated Arkwright's mill. Hamilton received detailed reports of this triumph, and pretty soon milldams proliferated on New England's rivers. With patriotic pride, Brown predicted to Hamilton that "mills and machines may be erected in different places, in one year, to make all the cotton yarn that may be wanted in the United States."[29]

Hamilton's policies were consistent with the drive for autarky and trade on equal terms with England that had fired the American Revolution in the first place. The colonists had rebelled against an imperial system that restricted their manufactures and forced them to hawk their raw materials to the mother country, stifling their economic potential. Before the Revolution, England had imposed a law banning the export to America of any tools that might assist in the manufacture of cotton, linen, wool, and silk. The British manufacturers of hats, nails, steel, and gunpowder had impeded American efforts to make comparable articles. It was Hamilton's vision of America as a manufacturing behemoth, not Jefferson's of a society of yeomen farmers, that threatened the British.

The shape of Hamilton's future industrial policy was foreshadowed in May 1790 when Tench Coxe replaced William Duer as assistant treasury secretary. The move possessed vast symbolic meaning, for Coxe was a well-known advocate of manufacturing and eager to raid Britain's industrial secrets. That February, he had written a long letter to Hamilton, praising America's maiden efforts at industry but citing a shortage of both capitalists and large-scale capital as retarding the introduction of labor-saving machinery. He regretted that because of Britain's pugnacious defense of her technological superiority in textiles the United States was not "yet in full possession of workmen, machines and secrets in the useful arts."[30]

Hamilton and Coxe teamed up in a daring assault on British industrial secrets. Coxe decided that the best way to achieve industrial parity with England was to woo knowledgeable British textile managers to America, even if this meant defying English law. Right before joining Treasury, he posted a man named Andrew Mitchell to England to snoop around factories and surreptitiously make models of textile machinery. Additionally, on January 11, 1790, Coxe had signed an agreement with a British weaver, George Parkinson, who also had studied at Arkwright's feet and bragged openly that he "possessed . . . the knowledge of all the secret movements used in Sir Richard Arkwright's patent[ed] machine."[31] In exchange for passage to Philadelphia, Parkinson agreed to provide Coxe with a working model of a flax mill that incorporated Arkwright's designs. On March 24, 1791, the U.S. government granted patents for Parkinson's flax mill, even though he had admitted that they were "improvements upon the mill or machinery . . . in Great Britain."[32] Clearly, the U.S. government condoned something that, in modern phraseology, could be termed industrial espionage. Building upon this precedent, Hamilton put the full authority of the Treasury behind the piracy of British trade secrets.

By April 1791, Hamilton had lent his prestige to Coxe's plan for a manufacturing society operated by private interests that would enjoy the general blessings of government. It would be a pilot project, a laboratory for innovation. The Society for Establishing Useful Manufactures (SEUM) was lauded by a later historian as "the most ambitious industrial experiment in early American history."[33] It was almost certainly Hamilton, with an assist from Coxe, who wrote the eloquent prospectus for the society that appeared on April 29. He left no doubt as to how he envisaged America's future, writing that "both theory and experiences conspire to prove that a nation . . . cannot possess much *active* wealth but as a result of extensive manufactures."[34]

The society intended to create more than a single mill. It projected an entire manufacturing *town*, with investors profiting from the factory's products and the appreciation of the underlying real estate. The prospectus listed a cornucopia of goods—including paper, sailcloth, cottons and linens, women's shoes, thread, worsted stockings, hats, ribbons, blankets, carpets, and beer—that the society might manufacture. Hamilton hoped that through the "spirit of imitation," the society would spawn comparable domestic businesses.[35] Thus far, the major hindrance to such enterprise had been "slender resources," but lack of capital had now been remedied by the government's funded debt. Once again, Hamilton used one program to advance the fortunes of another in an ever expanding web of economic activity. The society needed five hundred thousand dollars in seed capital, and the prospectus pointed out that it could be paid for partly in government bonds, promoting public debt and the industrial city at one stroke. "Here is the resource which has been hitherto wanted," Hamilton boasted.[36] That Hamilton was prepared to ransack European industrial secrets was made plain when the prospectus said that "means ought to be taken to procure from Europe skilful workmen and such machines and implements as cannot be had here in sufficient perfection."[37]

Hamilton did not lend his prestige to the scheme from afar. In July 1791—the same month investors gobbled up bank scrip and he began his dalliance with Maria Reynolds—he traveled to New York to drum up support for the society's first stock offering, which sold out instantly. He then attended the subscribers' inaugural meeting in New Brunswick, New Jersey, in August. In choosing directors later that year, Hamilton blundered by turning to his freewheeling companion, the speculator William Duer. He packed the board with local financiers—seven directors from New York, six from New Jersey—instead of striving for broad geographic representation. The board was also excessively crammed with financiers when men with industrial credentials were sorely needed.

Early on, Hamilton and Coxe settled on New Jersey as the optimal place for this venture. The state was densely populated, possessed cheap land and abundant forests, and enjoyed easy access to New York money. Most critically, it was well watered by rivers that could spin turbine blades and waterwheels. That August, Hamilton dispatched scouts to investigate these waterways. He and other society members were swamped with appeals from local landlords, touting the wonders of their riverside properties. It was later on concluded, largely at Duer's insistence, that the Great Falls of the Passaic in northern New Jersey offered "one of the finest situations in the world."[38]

Hamilton knew the secluded spot well. One day during the Revolution, he, Washington, and Lafayette had picnicked by the falls, enjoying a "modest repast" of cold ham, tongue, and biscuits in a sylvan setting that momentarily banished thoughts of war. The Great Falls mark a scenic bend in the Passaic River, the foaming water—up to two billion gallons per day—plunging seventy feet into a deep, narrow gorge of brownish-black basalt, blowing a rainbow-forming spray into the air. The society decided to call the new town Paterson to flatter Governor William Paterson. On November 22, 1791, the governor returned the favor, granting the society a charter (likely written by Hamilton) that gave it monopoly status and a ten-year tax exemption. The society bought seven hundred acres and carved it up into parcels, not just for factories but for a brand-new town—one that became the third largest city in New Jersey.

Incredibly, Hamilton, with his ever growing roster of projects, personally recruited supervisors for the first cotton spinning mill. This glorified adviser hired as foreman the same George Parkinson who had plundered British secrets for flax-spinning machinery; the Treasury subsidized Parkinson's living expenses. In July, Hamilton had received an extraordinary letter from another renegade employee of Sir Richard Arkwright, Thomas Marshall, who also came to America armed with British textile secrets. Having been superintendent at Arkwright's huge Derbyshire mill, he bragged to Hamilton that he had toured the mill again on a reconnaissance mission the previous fall: "I was all over his works and am consequently fully acquainted with every modern improvement." Marshall had no misgivings about snatching English mechanics for the society's projects and suggested that a "master of his business in the weaving branch and in possession of all or most of the fashionable patterns now worn in England will be very useful."[39] That August, Hamilton negotiated contract after contract with British textile refugees, including William Hall, who had learned to stain and bleach fabrics, and William Pearce, who had erected a Yorkshire cotton mill. That December, when the society's board met to consider personnel for the new operation, it rubber-stamped all of Hamilton's choices.

Hamilton wasn't content just to demonstrate the practicality of American manufacturing on a New Jersey riverbank. He felt compelled to make the theoretical case, which he did in his classic *Report on Manufactures,* submitted to Congress on December 5, 1791. The capstone of his ambitious state papers, it had fermented in his brain for some time. Nearly two years earlier, the House had asked him to prepare a report on how America might promote manufacturing. Hamilton now generated a full-blown vision of the many ways that the federal government could invigorate such economic activity. The report was the first government-sponsored plan for selective industrial planning in America, the tract in which, in the words of one Hamilton chronicler, he "prophesied much of post–Civil War America."[40]

The impetus for the report had been largely military and strategic in nature. Washington had admonished Congress that a "free people" ought to "promote such manufactories as tend to render them independent [of] others for essential, particularly for military supplies."[41] Remembering the scarcity of everything from gunpowder to uniforms in the Continental Army—a by-product of Britain's colonial monopoly on most manufacturing—Hamilton knew that reliance on foreign manufacturers could cripple America in wartime. "The extreme embarrassments of the

United States during the late war, from an incapacity of supplying themselves, are still matter of keen recollection," he noted in the report.[42]

To prepare for this study, the indefatigable Hamilton canvassed manufacturers and revenue collectors, quizzing them in detail about the state of production in their districts. As usual, he aspired to know everything: the number of factories in each district, the volume of goods produced, their prices and quality, the spurs and checks to production provided by state governments. To obtain a firsthand feel for American wares, he even wanted to touch them, to feel them. "It would also be acceptable to me," he told revenue supervisors, "to have samples in cases in which it could be done with convenience and without expence."[43] As he accumulated swatches—wool from Connecticut, carpets from Massachusetts—Hamilton, with a flair for showmanship, laid them out in the committee room of the House of Representatives, as if operating a small trade fair, an altogether new form of lobbying.

Hamilton's previous state papers had been purely the coinage of his own mind—he never employed ghostwriters—whereas he received critical assistance on the *Report on Manufactures* from Tench Coxe, who had drafted an early sketch urging American self-sufficiency in gunpowder, brass, iron, and other items. Eventually, Hamilton came to regard Coxe as a conceited, devious fellow who overrated his own talents. He later said, "That man is too cunning to be wise. I have been so much in the habit of seeing him mistaken that I hold his opinion cheap."[44] But at this juncture, Coxe's expertise was vital. Hamilton revised and elaborated Coxe's preliminary paper. He embroidered Coxe's proposals with esoteric economic theory and an assertive vision of American political might through manufacturing. Far more than just a technical document, the *Report on Manufactures* was a prescient statement of American nationalism.

In his advocacy of manufacturing, Hamilton knew that he would encounter stout resistance from those who feared that factories might hurt agriculture and menace republican government. His opponents cited abundant land and deficient capital and labor as reasons that America should remain a rural democracy. Jefferson, in particular, foresaw an enduring equation between American democracy and agriculture. Shortly before returning from France, he wrote that circumstances rendered it "impossible that America should become a manufacturing country during the time of any man now living."[45]

From the outset, Hamilton emphasized that he was not scheming to replace farms with factories and that agriculture had "*intrinsically a strong claim to preeminence over every other kind of industry.*" Far from wishing to harm agriculture, manufacturing would create domestic markets for surplus crops. All that he recommended was that farming not have "an exclusive predilection."[46] Since manufacturing and agriculture obeyed different economic cycles, a downturn in one could be offset by an upturn in another. Throughout the report, he contested the influence of the Physiocrats, the school of French economists that extolled agriculture as the most productive form of human labor and condemned government attempts to steer the economy. Hamilton refuted their belief that agriculture was inherently productive while manufacturing was "barren and unproductive."[47] Displaying an intimate familiarity with Adam Smith's *The Wealth of Nations,* Hamilton demonstrated that manufacturing, no less than agriculture, could increase productivity because it subdivided work into ever simpler operations and lent itself to mechanization. He also insisted that America's focus on agriculture was not just a natural by-product of geography but had been foisted on the country by European trading practices.

Hamilton evoked a thriving future economy that bore scant resemblance to the static, stratified society his enemies claimed he wanted to impose. His America would be a meritocracy of infinite variety, with a diversified marketplace absorbing people from all nations and backgrounds. Though slavery is nowhere mentioned in the report, Hamilton's ideal economy is devoid of the feudal barbarities of the southern plantations. Hamilton's list of the advantages of manufacuturing has a quintessentially American ring: "Additional employment to classes of the community not ordinarily engaged in the business. The promoting of emigration from foreign countries. The furnishing greater scope for the diversity of talents and dispositions which discriminate men from each other. The affording a more ample and various field for enterprise."[48] Manufacturers and laborers would flock to a country rich in raw materials and favored with low taxes, running streams, thick forests, and a democratic government. And that influx of workers would eliminate one of the most pressing obstacles to American manufacturing: high wages.

While Hamilton's emphasis on "diversity" may please modern ears, his stress on child labor is more jarring. Of the productive British cotton mills, he commented: "It is worthy of particular remark that, in general, women and children are rendered more useful, and the latter more early useful, by manufacturing establishments than they would otherwise be." In Britain's cotton mills, it was "computed that 4/7 nearly are women and children, of whom the greatest proportion are children and many of them of a very tender age."[49] Hamilton's approval of this may sound callous, and it is certainly fair to fault him for not foreseeing the brutality of nineteenth-century mills. On the other hand, child labor in farms and workshops was then commonplace—Hamilton himself had started clerking in his early teens, and his mother had worked. Hamilton didn't see himself as inflicting grim retribution upon the indigent so much as giving them a chance to earn decent wages. For Hamilton, a job could be an ennobling experience: "When all the different kinds of industry obtain in a community, each individual can find his proper element and can call into activity the whole vigour of his nature."[50] Hamilton did not equate child or female labor with exploitation.

In the best of all possible worlds, Hamilton preferred free trade, open markets, and Adam Smith's "invisible hand." He wrote late in life, "In matters of industry, human enterprise ought doubtless to be left free in the main, not fettered by too much regulation, but practical politicians know that it may be beneficially stimulated by prudent aids and encouragements on the part of the government."[51] At this early stage of American history, Hamilton thought aggressive European trade policies obligated the United States to respond in kind. He therefore supported temporary mercantilist policies that would improve American self-sufficiency, leading to a favorable trade balance and more hard currency. For a young nation struggling to find its way in a world of advanced European powers, Realpolitik trumped the laissez-faire purism of Adam Smith.

Reluctant to tinker with markets, Hamilton knew that he had to present a cogent brief for any government direction of investment. There was an obvious objection: wouldn't smart entrepreneurs spot profitable opportunities and invest capital without bureaucratic prompting? Yes, Hamilton agreed, entrepreneurs react to market shifts, but for psychological reasons they sometimes respond at a sluggish pace. "These," he wrote, "have relation to the strong influence of habit and the spirit of imitation; the fear of want of success in untried enterprises; the intrinsic difficulties incident to first essays toward a competition with those who have already attained to perfection in the business to be attempted."[52] Young nations had to contend with the handicap that other countries had already staked out entrenched positions. Infant industries needed "the extraordinary aid and protection of government."[53] Since foreign governments plied their companies with subsidies, America had no choice but to meet the competition.

After doing the intellectual spadework for government promotion of manufactures, Hamilton listed all the products he wanted to promote, ranging from copper to coal, wood to grain, silk to glass. He also enumerated policies, including premiums, bounties, and import duties, to protect these infant industries. Wherever possible, Hamilton preferred financial incentives to government directives. For instance, knowing that tariffs taxed consumers and handed monopoly profits to producers, Hamilton wanted them to be moderate in scale, temporary in nature, and repealed as soon as possible. He preferred bounties because they didn't raise prices. In some cases, he even wanted *lower* tariffs—on raw materials, for instance—to encourage manufacturing. And to speed innovation, he wanted to extend patent protection to inventors and adopt the sort of self-protective laws that Britain had used to try to hinder the export of innovative machinery.

For Hamilton, the federal government had a right to stimulate business and also, when necessary, to restrain it. As Arthur Schlesinger, Jr., has observed, "Hamilton's enthusiasm over the dynamics of individual acquisition was always tempered by a belief in government regulation and control."[54] In arguing, for instance, that government inspection of manufactured articles could reassure consumers and galvanize sales, he anticipated regulatory policies that were not enacted until the Progressive Era under Theodore Roosevelt: "Contributing to prevent fraud upon consumers at home and exporters to foreign countries—to improve the quality and preserve the character of the national manufactures—it cannot fail to aid the expeditious and advantageous sale of them and to serve as a guard against successful competition from other quarters."[55] He also recommended that the government inspect flour exports at all ports, "to improve the quality of our flour everywhere and to raise its reputation in foreign markets."[56] Endorsing still another form of government activism, Hamilton claimed that nothing had assisted Britain's industry more than its network of public roads and canals. He therefore touted internal improvements—what we would today call public infrastructure—to meld America's scattered regional markets into a single unified economy.

Even though he devoted only two skimpy paragraphs to the manufacture of gunpowder, Hamilton never lost sight that his *Report on Manufactures* was initially driven by the need for self-sufficiency in arms. Determined not to be caught shorthanded in case of war, Hamilton supported "an annual purchase of military weapons" to aid "the formation of arsenals."[57] So vital were supplies to national security that Hamilton did not rule out government-owned arms factories.

In closing, Hamilton made clear that the energetic programs he described were not suited to all countries at all times but were devised for an early stage of national development: "In countries where there is great private wealth much may be effected by the voluntary contributions of patriotic individuals. But in a community situated like that of the United States, the public purse must supply the deficiency of private resources."[58]

Hamilton's *Report on Manufactures* ultimately came to naught. Unlike his magnificent state papers on public credit, the mint, and the central bank, this report charted a general direction for the government, not solutions to specific, urgent problems. The House of Representatives shelved the report, and Hamilton made no apparent effort to resurrect it from legislative oblivion. For a document never translated into legislation, the report aroused exceptional apprehension because of its broad conception of federal power. As always, Hamilton cited constitutional grounds for his program, invoking the clause that gave Congress authority to "provide for the *common defence* and *general welfare*."[59] Owing in part to Hamilton's generous construction of this clause, it was to acquire enormous significance, allowing the government to enact programs to advance social welfare.

Madison was deeply alarmed by these arguments. Thus far, he said, those expounding a liberal interpretation of the Constitution had argued only for leeway in the *means* to attain ends spelled out in the Constitution. But no mention was made of manufacturing as an *end* of government. "If not only the *means*, but the *objects* are unlimited," Madison groaned, "the parchment had better be thrown into the fire at once."[60] Nor could Jefferson conceal his horror at the report, which called for an even more sweeping arrogation of power than had Hamilton's bank. In one postbreakfast talk with Washington, Jefferson mentioned Hamilton's latest position paper and wondered somberly whether Americans still lived under a limited government. He dreaded the powers that would accrue to government under his colleague's loose reading of the Constitution. He grumbled that "under color of giving *bounties* for the encouragement of particular manufactures," Hamilton was trying to insinuate that the "general welfare" clause "permitted Congress to take everything under their management which *they* should deem for the *public welfare*."[61] For Jefferson, this opened wide the floodgates to government activism.

When the craving for bank scrip had created a speculative bubble in the summer of 1791, Hamilton had cooled off the contagion before it got out of hand. The relief had proved short-lived. The very prosperity that his ebullient leadership engendered—reflected in rising exports, a booming demand for American bonds in Europe, and a rush of newly chartered companies—generated effervescent optimism that fed yet another mad scramble for government securities and bank scrip, pushing their prices to new highs during the winter of 1791–1792.

Once again, the main protagonist was Hamilton's old chum William Duer, always a restless soul beneath his bonhomie. Duer's wife, Lady Kitty, had long been chagrined by her husband's compulsive gambling. She once admonished him, "I fear . . . your mind will be too much harassed with the variety of business and speculations you undertake to allow you . . . inward quiet."[62] In a similar vein, Duer's friend, Samuel Chase of Maryland, pleaded with him to control his acquisitive impulses: "I know the activity of your soul and fear your views . . . and schemes are boundless. . . . I sincerely wish that you would set limits to your desires."[63]

Unfortunately, nobody could cure William Duer's speculative bent. He was now the colossus of New York financial markets and derisively crowned "King of the Alley" by Jefferson.[64] In late 1791, determined to corner the market in government bonds and bank shares, he formed a secret partnership with Alexander Macomb, a wealthy land speculator. Hamilton had just chosen Duer as governor of the Society for Establishing Useful Manufactures, where Macomb also served as a director. Now, to finance stock manipulation, the reckless Duer borrowed vast sums on his personal notes and drew other SEUM backers into an investing cabal nicknamed the Six Per Cent Club because of its plan to monopolize 6 percent government bonds.

In January 1792, Hamilton was monitoring financial markets in New York with foreboding when hectic trading in bank scrip received a sudden fillip from the announcement of three new banks being formed. Aside from the Bank of New York and a projected branch of the Bank of the United States, New York at this time had no other banks. The Million Bank was to be organized by Macomb and Hamilton's old adversary from the New York Ratifying Convention, Melancton Smith. At a time when banks had political colorings, the Million Bank was seen as a vehicle to boost the fortunes of Governor George Clinton. "The bank mania rages violently in this city," James Tillary told Hamilton, "and it is made an engine to help the governor's re-election."[65] When the bank's shares were floated on January 16, they were ten times oversubscribed within hours, as "bancomania" gripped the city. In rapid succession, proposals emerged for a State Bank and Merchants' Bank, culminating in a grand proposal to amalgamate the three new banks into one gigantic institution.

As treasury secretary, Hamilton had hoped to spur banking, but he rejected these new banks as so many brazen speculative vehicles. The instant he heard about the Million Bank, he wrote a vehement letter to William Seton of the Bank of New York, who had helped him to quell the panic the previous summer. Testifying to "infinite pain" at the news of this "dangerous tumour" in New York's economy, Hamilton warned, "These extravagant sallies of speculation do injury to the government and to the whole system of public credit by disgusting all sober citizens and giving a wild air to everything. . . . I sincerely hope that the Bank of New York will listen to no coalition with this newly engendered monster."[66] Seton replied that the "madmen" behind the Million Bank were trying to coerce the Bank of New York into an unwanted merger by unscrupulous means: withdrawing enough money from the bank to topple it. "The folly and madness that rages at present is a disgrace to us," he reported.[67] Hamilton wasn't blind to the speculative hazards of creating credit. "The superstructure of credit is now too vast for the foundation," he warned Seton. "It must be gradually brought within more reasonable dimensions or it will tumble."[68] Hamilton later conceded that share trading "fosters a spirit of gambling and diverts a certain number of individuals from other pursuits."[69] Yet this had to be weighed against the larger social benefits conferred by ready access to capital.

For Thomas Jefferson, bancomania wasn't an unavoidable flaw in an otherwise sound system but a canker at the heart of the Hamiltonian enterprise. He warned Washington that paper money was "withdrawing our citizens from . . . useful industry to occupy themselves and their capitals in a species of gambling, destructive of morality, and which had introduced its poison into the government itself."[70] Jefferson's fears were understandable, if often misplaced. He suspected Duer of trading on inside information and wrongly assumed that Hamilton was his constant, willing accomplice. When Jefferson wrote to Washington, accusing Hamilton of "the dealing out of Treasury-securities among his friends in what time and measure he pleases," he made a baseless charge that he and his political followers were to repeat ad nauseam.[71]

Buoyed by credit, the prices of government and bank securities soared to a peak in late January 1792, exceeding any sane levels of valuation. As Hamilton recalled, "The rapid and extraordinary rise . . . was in fact artificial and violent such as no discreet calculation of probabilities could have presupposed."[72] Then euphoria turned to doubt and doubt to despair as shares began a precipitate five-week slide. Duer desperately put up more money to cover his obligations and borrowed sizable sums from all quarters. He pried loose loans from wealthy New Yorkers and petty cash from butchers and shopkeepers and even took money from a "noted bawd, Mrs. McCarty," said one merchant.[73] He raised a half-million dollars on his personal notes. "Widows, orphans, merchants, mechanics, etc. are all concerned in the notes," Robert Troup informed Hamilton.[74] Scenting blood, Duer's creditors squeezed him with usurious interest rates that climbed as high as 6 percent per month. Duer had led a band of bulls betting on higher stock prices; three members of the Livingston family headed a counterclique of bears, who drove down share prices by yanking bank deposits and instigating a severe credit shortage that pushed interest rates to speculators to as high as 1 percent per day. This struck a fatal blow at the deeply indebted Duer. He began to jettison shares to repay loans, and this only worsened the downward spiral of bond prices.

On March 9, his resources exhausted, the embattled Duer stopped payment to some creditors. He owed so much money to so many people that his failure provoked financial mayhem. Twenty-five New York financiers went bust the next day as panic spread. Duer's undoing was money he owed the government. From his days as secretary to the old Board of Treasury, Duer had carried a huge outstanding debt of $236,000. On March 12, with Hamilton's blessing, Oliver Wolcott, Jr., comptroller of the treasury, wrote to New York's district attorney and ordered him to recover the money from Duer or file suit against him. As soon as Duer heard of this letter, he knew he was doomed unless he got it revoked. Distraught, he sent a hurried message to Hamilton: "For heaven's sake, use for once your influence to defer this [letter] till my arrival, when it will not be necessary. . . . Every farthing will be immediately accounted for. Of this I pledge my honor. If a suit should be brought on the part of the public . . . my ruin is complete."[75]

Hamilton waited to reply until March 14. In all likelihood he wanted to be able to inform Duer that Wolcott's instructions had been sent before he could recall them. In his note to Duer, Hamilton did nothing to impede the threatened lawsuit and refused to compromise his official integrity. In a spirit of friendship, he told Duer that he was "affected beyond measure" by his plight and had "experienced all the bitterness of soul on your account which a warm attachment can inspire." At the same time, he delivered this stern judgment: "Act with *fortitude* and *honor*. If you cannot reasonably hope for a favorable extrication, do not plunge deeper. Have the courage to make a full stop. Take all the care you can in the first place of institutions of public utility and in the next of all fair creditors."[76] The letter again refutes the caricature of Hamilton as a stooge for the monied interests. Meanwhile, Jefferson grumbled to his son-in-law that "the credit and fate of the nation seem to hang on the desperate throws and plunges of gambling scoundrels."[77]

Instead of bailing out Duer, Hamilton had the Treasury purchase large amounts of government securities in the marketplace. By doing so, he steadied the market and also bought back public debt at bargain prices. The money came from the sinking fund he had set up to redeem public debt. Sensitive to perceptions, Hamilton told William Seton to purchase the bonds piecemeal at the securities auctions held twice daily at the Merchant's Coffee House and "to keep up men's spirits by *appearing often*, though not much at one time."[78] He also wanted Seton to conceal the buyer's identity, allowing rumors to magnify the effect: "It will be very probably conjectured that you appear for the public. And the conjecture may be left to have its course but without confession."[79] Instinctively, Hamilton understood the creative ambiguity necessary for a central banker coping with a crisis. As was the case the previous summer, Hamilton had no training or tutors, yet he reacted with the sangfroid of an experienced central banker. He restored temporary calm to the marketplace, though milder gyrations continued through the fall.

The travail of William Duer was a public drama that transfixed New Yorkers for days. There were constant meetings at Duer's mansion to try to rescue him from creditors. "This poor man is in a state of almost complete insanity," Troup told Hamilton, "and his situation is a source of inexpressible grief to all his friends."[80] Duer portrayed himself as an innocent lamb, gored by his pitiless creditors. In an agitated, sometimes incoherent mood, he took refuge at Baron von Steuben's, where he vainly awaited a reprieve from Hamilton. With an invincible capacity for self-delusion, Duer assured one friend, "I am now secure from my enemies and feeling the purity of my heart I defy the world."[81] The day after he made this brave declaration, he was packed off to debtors' prison. Before long, Alexander Macomb failed and was also imprisoned.

By this point, Duer may have welcomed prison as a refuge from vengeful mobs howling that they wanted to disembowel him. Their animosity was so great that it was feared they might storm the jail and lynch him. On the night of April 18, hundreds of aggrieved creditors and investors ringed the jail and hurled stones at it. One newspaper wrote of the "frequent shouts and menaces" they uttered and said that many were "crying aloud, *We will have Mr. D[ue]r, he has gotten our money*"— words that "must have terrified the prisoner exceedingly and made him suppose that the vengeance of the injured citizens was immediately coming upon him."[82] Duer still expected to be freed by Hamilton's miraculous intervention. In fact, the treasury secretary had already decided to make an example of Duer, informing a friend, "There should be a line of separation between honest men and knaves, between respectable stockholders and dealers in the funds and mere unprincipled gamblers. Public infamy must restrain what the laws cannot."[83] Hamilton's letters to William Seton during these weeks mingle sadness and horror as he contemplated the plight of those destroyed by the panic.

Hamilton's critics gloated over these events as vindicating their critique of his system. For the slaveholding south, this was irrefutable proof of northern depravity. Jefferson inveighed against the "criminality of this paper system" and said people would now return to "plain unsophisticated common sense."[84] With a touch of schadenfreude, he computed that the five million dollars squandered by speculators equaled the combined value of all New York real estate. Madison observed with satisfaction, "The gambling system . . . is beginning to exhibit its explosions. D[uer] . . . the prince of the tribe of speculators has just become a victim of his enterprises."[85] Hamilton was appalled to learn of Madison's allegation that his purchases of government securities to steady the market had been made at high prices to benefit speculators. This complete misconception of his virtuoso performance was hard for Hamilton to stomach, and he told a Virginia friend it "left no doubt in anyone's mind that Mr. Madison was actuated by *personal* and political animosity."[86]

That Hamilton did not exaggerate the vindictive mood of Madison and the southern congressmen is confirmed in a letter Abigail Adams wrote about the panic to her sister: "The southern members are determined if possible to ruin the Secretary of the Treasury, destroy all his well-built systems, [and] if possible give a fatal stab to the funding system." Her husband, the vice president, had managed to "harmonize" the Senate, but this did not stem the regional rancor. "I firmly believe, if I live ten years longer, I shall see a division of the southern and northern states unless more candour and less intrigue, of which I have no hopes, should prevail," she wrote.[87]

William Duer's downfall exposed the magnitude of the securities market that Hamilton had opened up. It also showed how easily the market for government bonds could be rigged by swindlers planting false rumors and exploiting the auction system for stock trades. To provide more orderly markets, two dozen brokers gathered on May 17 under the shade of a buttonwood tree at 68 Wall Street and drew up rules to govern securities trading. This historic Buttonwood Agreement set a minimum for brokers' commissions and laid the foundations for what became the New York Stock Exchange. It attested to the extraordinary, if sometimes combustible, vigor of the capital markets that Hamilton had singlehandedly brought into being.

A year later, trading in government bonds grew so brisk that the Buttonwood group adjourned to an upstairs room of the new Tontine Coffee House, a three-story brick structure at Wall and Water Streets, right near Hamilton's New York home. Its first president was Archibald Gracie, whose East River mansion was to house New York mayors. Local wits christened the Tontine Coffee House "Scrip Castle" in honor of Hamilton's bank scrip, which had triggered expanded share trading. Henceforth, *Wall Street* would signal much more than a short, narrow lane in lower Manhattan. It would symbolize an industry, a sector of the economy, a state of mind, and it became synonymous with American finance itself.

On July 4, 1792, a full-length portrait of Hamilton, painted by John Trumbull on the commission of New York's grateful merchants, went up in City Hall. Lest he seem self-aggrandizing, Hamilton consented to the project with one caveat: that the painting "appear unconnected with any incident of my political life."[88] Trumbull painted Hamilton frequently—two original portraits and fifteen replicas—and captured him here in his prime, with only the slightest shadow of a double chin. The treasury secretary gazes off into the distance with visionary confidence. Very refined, he stands by his desk in a pale suit, his body slim and shapely, one bare hand poised on his desk, the other elegantly gloved and holding a second glove; his black cloak is draped over a nearby chair. In tribute to Hamilton's literary powers, a pen is dipped in an inkwell. With his face illuminated by a good-natured smile, he radiates a quiet, buoyant energy and seems ready for many more triumphs.

The 1792 financial panic came on the heels of the two great projects by which Hamilton hoped to excite the public with the shimmering prospects for American manufacturing: the Society for Establishing Useful Manufactures and submission of his *Report on Manufactures*. The outlook for both was badly damaged by the panic. Even a short list of the worst offenders in the share mania—William Duer, Alexander Macomb, New York broker John Dewhurst, Royal Flint—included so many SEUM directors that it almost sounded like a company venture. Duer's notoriety was especially detrimental since he had been SEUM governor, its largest shareholder, and its chief salesman in hawking securities. When Hamilton dispatched his friend Nicholas Low to sound out Duer in prison, the unyielding financier refused to resign as SEUM governor or account for the whereabouts of society funds. People who had pledged to purchase shares retreated in droves as the society's good name was muddied.

The remaining SEUM directors rummaged through its books to assess the damage and were dismayed to learn that Duer had emptied the society's bank accounts for his own use. "I trust they are not diverted," Hamilton had warned Duer in a letter. "The public interest and my reputation are deeply concerned in this matter."[89] When the panic had hit, Duer had had ten thousand dollars of society funds in his possession, and that money now simply vanished. It turned out he had taken a liberal fifty-thousand-dollar loan from the SEUM treasury (though much of this was recouped when shares he pledged as collateral were sold), and another fifty thousand to buy textile machinery had gone to John Dewhurst, who had absconded with the funds to Pennsylvania. When the society board held its quarterly meeting in New Brunswick, New Jersey, that April, the New York directors were so distracted by the mayhem that not a single one showed up. Deputy Governor Archibald Mercer appealed to Hamilton to "assist us in our operations as far as [it is] in your power."[90]

To revive the board's spirits, Hamilton promised to try to arrange loans for the society and suggested it hire needed workmen from Europe. What quickly became apparent was that the board was rife with financiers who were abysmally ignorant of industrial matters. "For my part, I confess myself perfectly ignorant of every duty relating to the manufacturing business," Mercer admitted to Hamilton while begging him to attend a special society meeting in mid-May. Intent upon salvaging the enterprise, Hamilton stole several days from his Treasury schedule to confer with the board.

How exactly would the SEUM, its coffers cleaned out by Duer, pay for its property on the Passaic River? Hamilton privately approached William Seton at the Bank of New York and arranged a five-thousand-dollar loan at a reduced 5 percent interest rate. He cited high-minded reasons, including the public interest and the advantage to New York City of having a manufacturing town across the Hudson, but more than the public interest was at stake: "To you, my dear Sir, I will not scruple to say *in confidence* that the Bank of New York shall suffer no diminution of its *pecuniary faculties* from any accommodations it may afford to the Society in question. I feel my reputation concerned in its welfare."[91] The SEUM's collapse, Hamilton knew, could jeopardize his own career. In promising Seton that he would see to it as treasury secretary that the Bank of New York was fully compensated for any financial sacrifice entailed by the SEUM loan, Hamilton mingled too freely his public and private roles.

For several days in early July 1792, Hamilton huddled with the society directors to hammer out a new program. "Perseverance in almost any plan is better than fickleness and fluctuation," he was to lecture one superintendent, with what could almost have been his personal motto.[92] Rewarding his efforts, the society approved wide-ranging operations: a cotton mill, a textile printing plant, a spinning and weaving operation, and housing for fifty workers on quarter-acre plots. Never timid about his own expertise, Hamilton pinpointed the precise spot for the factory at the foot of the waterfalls that had so impressed him with their strength and beauty during the Revolutionary War.

It was an index of the hope generated by Hamilton that the SEUM, at his suggestion, hired Pierre Charles L'Enfant, the architect who had just laid out plans for the new federal city on the Potomac River, to supervise construction of the society's buildings and plan the futuristic town of Paterson. At the same time, it was an index of Hamilton's persistent anxiety that he dipped into managerial minutiae befitting a factory foreman rather than an overworked treasury secretary. For instance, he instructed the directors to draw up an inventory of tools possessed by each worker and stated that, if any were broken, the parts should be returned and "a report made to the storekeeper and noted in some proper column."[93] With his reputation at stake, Hamilton even subsidized the venture with his own limited funds, advancing $1,800 to the mechanics. Despite the Duer fiasco, the SEUM commenced operations in spinning, weaving, and calico printing.

The subsequent society records make for pretty dismal reading, as Hamilton was beset by unending troubles. L'Enfant was the wrong man for the job. Instead of trying to conserve money for the cash-strapped society, he contrived extravagant plans for a seven-mile-long stone aqueduct to carry water. He was enthralled by the idea of creating a grand industrial city on the pattern of the nascent Washington, D.C., with long radiating avenues, rather than with building a simple factory. By early 1794, L'Enfant shucked the project and spirited off the blueprints into the bargain. To find qualified textile workers, the society sent scouts to Scotland and paid for the laborers' passage to America. Even the managers clamored for better pay, and SEUM minutes show that some disgruntled artisans personally hired by Hamilton began to sabotage the operation by stealing machinery. One of the saddest parts of the story relates to the employment of children. Whatever hopeful vision Hamilton may have had of children performing useful labor and being educated simultaneously, they had neither the time nor the money to attend school. To remedy the problem, the board hired a schoolmaster to instruct the factory children on Sundays—which, as Hamilton must have known, was scarcely a satisfactory solution.

By early 1796, with Hamilton still on the board, the society abandoned its final lines of business, discontinued work at the factory, and put the cotton mill up for sale. Hamilton's fertile dream left behind only a set of derelict buildings by the river. At first, it looked as if the venture had completely backfired. During the next two years, not a single manufacturing society received a charter in the United States. Hamilton's faith in textile manufacturing in Paterson was eventually vindicated in the early 1800s as a "raceway" system of canals powered textile mills and other forms of manufacturing, still visible today in the Great Falls Historic District. The city that Hamilton helped to found did achieve fame for extensive manufacturing operations, including foundries, textile mills, silk mills, locomotive factories, and the Colt Gun works. Hamilton had chosen the wrong sponsors at the wrong time. In recruiting Duer and L'Enfant, he had exercised poor judgment. He was launching too many initiatives, crowded too close together, as if he wanted to remake the entire country in a flash.

The SEUM's problems after the 1792 panic also occurred at a moment when Hamilton's political fortunes were starting to change. His never-ending reports and innovations were rattling the country. As one Jeffersonian writer said after Duer's comeuppance, Hamilton had "talked to them so much of imports . . . funds . . . banks . . . and . . . manufactures that they are considered as the cardinal virtues of the Union. Hence liberty, independence . . . have been struck out from the American vocabulary and the hieroglyphs of money inserted in their stead."[94] In September 1792, Elisha Boudinot—a Newark lawyer and brother of Elias—told Hamilton of rising political protests against the SEUM and warned that "a strong party" was forming in Philadelphia "against the Secretary of the Treasury." He reported that one unidentified Virginian was "very violent on the subject" and was trying to see what could be done "with regard to displacing" him.[95] For many Americans, the sheer profusion of Hamilton programs added up to a picture of America's future that frightened them.

The financial turmoil on Wall Street and the William Duer debacle pointed up a glaring defect in Hamilton's political theory: the rich could put their own interests above the national interest. He had always betrayed a special, though never reflexive or uncritical, solicitude for merchants as the potential backbone of the republic. He once wrote, "That valuable class of citizens forms too important an organ of the general weal not to claim every practicable and reasonable exemption and indulgence."[96] He hoped businessmen would have a broader awareness and embrace the common good. But he was so often worried about abuses committed *against* the rich that he sometimes minimized the skulduggery that might be committed *by* the rich. The saga of William Duer exposed a distinct limitation in Hamilton's political vision.

And what ever became of William Duer? After the 1792 panic, he lingered in prison for seven years—the remainder of his life. Until the end, he sent Hamilton heartrending notes, pleading for trifling loans of ten or fifteen dollars, which Hamilton granted. During one yellow-fever epidemic, Hamilton arranged for Duer to be transferred to another wing of the prison to protect him from the disease. Duer did not seem to blame his old friend for his imprisonment, and Hamilton seemed forgiving toward the man who had all but wrecked his manufacturing society and very nearly his reputation. Right before Duer died in 1799, he wrote movingly to Hamilton, "My affection for yourself and my sensibility for whatever interested your happiness has been ever sincere and I have felt with pain any appearance of your withdrawing from me."[97]

TWENTY

CORRUPT SQUADRONS

D espite financial panics and the setbacks of his manufacturing society, Alexander Hamilton's touch still seemed golden, his step nimble, and his position impregnable in Washington's administration. He was brimming with bold ideas and enacting them with singular panache. It petrified Jefferson and Madison that the one man in America willing and able to lead the country in precisely the wrong direction was Washington's right-hand man, who seemed to be virtually running the country.

As early as May 1791 Madison and Jefferson had begun to organize opposition to the treasury secretary's triumphal march. After Hamilton's success with the Bank of the United States, the two Virginians embarked on what seemed a harmless "botanizing tour" that led them through New York City, up the Hudson River to Lake George, then down through western New England—the heartland of Hamilton's support. As Jefferson observed, it was "from New England chiefly that these champions for a King, Lord, and Commons come."[1] Even though the two men registered copious notes about trees and floral specimens and pulled speckled trout from lakes, their activities thinly camouflaged a more serious agenda. As American politics split along regional lines, Jefferson knew that the south had to make northern inroads to stop the Hamiltonian juggernaut. "There is a vast mass of discontent gathered in the South and how and when it will break God knows," Jefferson told Robert R. Livingston on the eve of the trip.[2]

In New York, the two Virginians conferred with Livingston as well as Aaron Burr, who had replaced Philip Schuyler as one of New York's two senators. The alert Robert Troup suspected a plot to strip Hamilton of power in his own backyard. "There was every appearance of a passionate courtship between the Chancellor

[Livingston], Burr, Jefferson and Madison when the two latter were in town," he apprised Hamilton. "Delenda est Carthago, I suppose, is the maxim adopted with respect to you."[3] *Delenda est Carthago:* Carthage must be destroyed and obliterated. These fighting words, quarried from the pages of Roman history, signaled the start of interminable warfare between Hamilton and Jefferson, which was to tear apart Washington's cabinet and the country at large. The conflict went beyond the personal clash between Washington's two most gifted officials and contrasted two enduring visions of American government. "Of all the events that shaped the political life of the new republic in its earliest years," Stanley Elkins and Eric McKitrick wrote in their history of the period, "none was more central than the massive personal and political enmity, classic in the annals of American history, which developed in the course of the 1790s between Alexander Hamilton and Thomas Jefferson."[4] This feud, rife with intrigue and lacerating polemics, was to take on an almost pathological intensity.

As noted, Hamilton and Jefferson at first enjoyed cordial relations. "Each of us perhaps thought well of the other man," Jefferson recalled, "but as politicians it was impossible for two men to be of more opposite principles."[5] In combating Hamilton's cabinet influence, the courtly Jefferson, who hated confrontation, operated at a severe disadvantage. "I do not love difficulties," he once told John Adams. "I am fond of quiet, willing to do my duty, but [made] irritable by slander and apt to be forced by it to abandon my post."[6] By contrast, the bumptious Hamilton savored the cut and thrust of controversy. Fast on his feet, sure in his judgments, informed on every issue, he was as dazzling and voluble in debate as Jefferson was retiring. By early 1792, any pose of civility between the two secretaries disappeared, and Jefferson remembered them "daily pitted in the cabinet like two cocks." By the end of their tenure, the two adversaries could scarcely stand each other's presence.

Today we cherish the two-party system as a cornerstone of American democracy. The founders, however, viewed parties, or "factions" as they termed them, as monarchical vestiges that had no legitimate place in a true republic. Hamilton dreaded parties as "the most fatal disease" of popular governments and hoped America could dispense with such groups.[7] James Kent later wrote, "Hamilton said in *The Federalist,* in his speeches, and a hundred times to me that factions would ruin us and our government had not sufficient energy and balance to resist the propensity to them and to control their tyranny and their profligacy."[8] In many passages in *The Federalist,* Hamilton and Madison inveighed against malignant factions, although Hamilton conceded in number 26 that "the spirit of party, in different degrees, must be expected to infect all political bodies."[9] Hamilton associated factions with parochial state interests and imagined that federal legislators would be more broad-minded— "more out of the reach of those occasional ill humors or temporary prejudices and propensities which in smaller societies frequently contaminate the public councils," he said in number 27.[10]

Nevertheless, it was Hamilton, inadvertently, who became the flash point for the formation of the first parties. The searing controversy over his programs exploded idyllic fantasies that America would be free of partisan groupings. His charismatic personality and far-reaching policies unified his followers, who gradually became known as Federalists. By capitalizing the term used for supporters of the Constitution, the Federalists tacitly implied that their foes opposed it. The Federalists were allied with powerful banking and merchant interests in New England and on the Atlantic seaboard and were disproportionately Congregationalists and Episcopalians.

At the same time, the mounting fear of Hamilton among Jefferson, Madison, and their supporters cohered into an organized opposition that began to call itself Republican. Alluding to the ancient Roman republic, this was also a clever label, insinuating that Federalists were not real republicans and hence must be monarchists. Often Baptists and Methodists, Republicans drew their strength from rich southern planters and small farmers. They defined their beliefs, in large measure, by their dread of Hamilton's system and employed anti-Hamilton rhetoric as shorthand to express their solidarity. Jefferson distinguished the two parties by saying that Federalists believed that "the executive is the branch of our government which needs most support," while Republicans thought that "like the analogous branch in the English government, it is already too strong for the republican parts of the Constitution and therefore, in equivocal cases, they incline to the legislative powers."[11]

Elkins and McKitrick describe "the emergence of parties" as "the true novelty of the age" and date their onset to around 1792.[12] It is tempting but misleading to think of the Federalists as the patrician party and the Republicans as representing the commoners. "The controversy which embroiled the two champions was not basically concerned with the haves and the have-nots," James T. Flexner once wrote of the clash between Hamilton and Jefferson. "It was between rival economic systems, each of which was aimed at generating its own men of property."[13] In fact, the Federalist ranks had plenty of self-made lawyers like Hamilton, while the Republicans were led by two men of immense inherited wealth: Jefferson and Madison. Moreover, the political culture of the slaveholding south was marked by much more troubling disparities of wealth and status than was that of the north, and the vast majority of abolitionist politicians came from the so-called aristocrats of the Federalist party.

The sudden emergence of parties set a slashing tone for politics in the 1790s. Since politicians considered parties bad, they denied involvement in them, bristled at charges that they harbored partisan feelings, and were quick to perceive hypocrisy

in others. And because parties were frightening new phenomena, they could be easily mistaken for evil conspiracies, lending a paranoid tinge to political discourse.
The Federalists saw themselves as saving America from anarchy, while Republicans
believed they were rescuing America from counterrevolution. Each side possessed
a lurid, distorted view of the other, buttressed by an idealized sense of itself. No
etiquette yet defined civilized behavior between the parties. It also was not self-
evident that the two parties would smoothly alternate in power, raising the unsettling prospect that one party might be established to the permanent exclusion of
the other. Finally, no sense yet existed of a loyal opposition to the government in
power. As the party spirit grew more acrimonious, Hamilton and Washington regarded much of the criticism fired at their administration as disloyal, even treasonous, in nature.

One last feature of the inchoate party system deserves mention. The emerging
parties were not yet fixed political groups, able to exert discipline on errant members. Only loosely united by ideology and sectional loyalties, they can seem to
modern eyes more like amorphous personality cults. It was as if the parties were
projections of individual politicians—Washington, Hamilton, and then John Adams
on the Federalist side, Jefferson, Madison, and then James Monroe on the Republican side—rather than the reverse. As a result, the reputations of the principal figures formed decisive elements in political combat. For a man like Hamilton, so
watchful of his reputation, the rise of parties was to make him even more hypersensitive about his personal honor.

If, on the domestic side, Hamilton's bottomless chest of programs precipitated
the rise of parties, equally inflammatory were political convulsions in Europe—
specifically, whether U.S. policy should tilt toward England or France. Much of the
debate's fervor sprang from the fact that the colonists had fought a war against
England with France as their chief ally. Beyond this obvious backdrop, England
and France functioned as proxies in the domestic debate over what kind of society
America should be. For Jefferson and Madison, the problem was not simply that
Hamilton was pro-British but that his policies would replicate aspects of the British
government they loathed. And for Hamilton, the French Revolution was a bloody
cautionary tale of a revolution gone awry.

Jefferson possessed a long-standing grudge against Britain. Back in 1786, he had
received a glacial reception in London from British officials, and their insufferable
condescension had left a residue of implacable malice. "That nation hates us, their
ministers hate us, and their king more than all other men," Jefferson fulminated after two months in England.[14] It may be significant that Hamilton, who never visited
Europe or experienced firsthand the insolence that stung Jefferson and Franklin,

found it easier to warm to the British. Besides the dependence of Virginia tobacco planters upon British credit, Hamilton thought that some southern hostility toward Britain also dated from wartime experience: "It is a fact that the rigor with which the war was prosecuted by the British armies in our southern quarter had produced . . . there more animosity against the British Government than in the other parts of the United States."[15]

With evergreen memories of the Revolution, many Americans viewed Britain warily, and Hamilton had to preach the unpalatable truth that England was a more suitable trading partner for America than France, the clear sentimental favorite. The United States still had not escaped economic dependence on England, which consumed nearly half of American exports and accounted for three-quarters of American imports. Even that understated the dependence, since many British imports were articles of everyday use—cutlery, pottery, and the like—whereas France specialized in wine, brandy, women's hosiery, and other luxury goods. As an exponent of commercial realism in foreign affairs, Hamilton thought it better for America to operate temporarily as a junior partner in Britain's global trading system than to try to undercut Britain and align itself with France.

By virtue of his background, Hamilton may have been well disposed toward the British. His father, descended from Scottish nobility, had probably diverted his son with tales of the British Isles. The illegitimate boy may have identified with his father's lapsed patrician heritage. Nor would Hamilton have felt alone in his emotional affinity for England. The Revolution had been a family feud, with all the ambivalent feelings that implied. It had been their violated rights as *Englishmen* that had driven the colonists to revolt. Immigration soon diversified the population mix, but in the 1790s the country's Anglo-Saxon character remained largely intact.

Jefferson often told of a dinner discussion that he had about British politics with Adams, Knox, and Hamilton in Philadelphia in 1791. They were discussing the "corruption" of the British political system—the system of royal patronage and pensions, the unequal size of electoral districts, and so on—when the following exchange occurred:

Mr. Adams observed, "Purge that constitution of its corruption . . . and it would be the most perfect constitution ever devised by the wit of man." Hamilton paused and said, "Purge it of its corruption . . . and it would become an *impracticable* government. As it stands at present, with all its supposed defects, it is the most perfect government which ever existed."[16]

Jefferson gave this comment a sinister gloss, but Hamilton was merely saying that the Crown needed patronage to offset Parliament's power of the purse. In *Fed-*

eralist number 76, Hamilton had described the tendency of popular assemblies, in England and elsewhere, to encroach upon the executive branch. Admiration for Britain's unwritten constitution and representative government had been commonplaces of colonial rhetoric. John Marshall said of prerevolutionary America, "While the excellence of the English constitution was a rich theme of declamation, every colonist believed himself entitled to its advantages."[17] Only seven months before the Declaration of Independence, Jefferson wrote, "Believe me, dear Sir, there is not in the British empire a man who more cordially loves a union with Great Britain than I do."[18] During the fight to ratify the Constitution, Patrick Henry praised the British constitution as superior to the new American version. It was not illogical for patriots to see their new government as realizing British ideals that had been wantonly trampled on by the Crown. It was France, not England, that had long been associated with despotic government, and Hamilton's high praise for England was not as heretical as Jefferson pretended it was.

To Jefferson, it sometimes seemed that Hamilton wasn't just content to run the Treasury Department but wanted to annex the State Department to his domain. Some of this can be ascribed to Hamilton's ambition, some to the minute size of Washington's cabinet, and some to the fact that Hamilton's system hinged on customs duties from mostly British imports. The affairs of Treasury and State could not easily be pried apart. As mentioned earlier, even as Jefferson lobbied for closer trade ties with France in early 1791, Hamilton had launched freelance contacts with George Beckwith, an informal emissary of the British government.

Hamilton had told Beckwith that Britain could help her case by granting full diplomatic status to the United States and naming an official ambassador. Americans felt demeaned that Britain had sent no representative since the Revolution. Hamilton's hints bore fruit when the British sent twenty-eight-year-old George Hammond to Philadelphia in late 1791. Already a seasoned diplomat, Hammond commenced the first of many private chats with Hamilton. Hammond wrote to London, "I had a very long and confidential conversation with Mr. Hamilton . . . in the course of which the opinion I had entertained of that gentleman's just and liberal way of thinking was fully confirmed."[19] Hammond withheld his credentials from Washington, however, until the United States agreed to post an envoy to London.

George Hammond arrived at a critical juncture, with the United States and Britain still trading endless recriminations about which side had reneged on the peace treaty. America chided Britain for failing to surrender its northwest forts and not compensating planters for slaves it had spirited away, while Britain complained that America still had not paid off prewar debts to its creditors. Hamilton impressed upon Hammond the vital need for Britain to relinquish the forts and conceded the justice of British claims for repayment of old debts. The one issue that Hamilton again refused to push vigorously was compensation for emancipated slaves—a vital point for Jefferson. When Hammond downgraded the importance of this item, he noted with pleasure that Hamilton "seemed partly to acquiesce" in his reasoning.[20]

It is possible to fault Hamilton for poaching on Jefferson's turf with Hammond while also recognizing that he salvaged talks that Jefferson wanted to sabotage. Jefferson treated Hammond to a frigid reception such as he himself had received in London. Hammond complained of the secretary of state that "it is his fault that we are at a distance. He prefers writing to conversing and thus it is that we are apart."[21] Hamilton despaired when Jefferson dredged up stale arguments about the justice of the American Revolution, and he apologized to Hammond for "the intemperate violence of his colleague," assuring him that Jefferson's views were "far from containing a faithful exposition of the sentiments of this government."[22] Jefferson's pro-French bias prevented any real progress from being made in Anglo-American relations during his tenure at State. "When the British minister wanted to know whether a thing was or was not unreasonable," Elkins and McKitrick note, "he found the Secretary of the Treasury a better guide than the Secretary of State."[23] Hamilton, for his part, subverted moves by Jefferson to negotiate a commercial treaty with France. This internecine warfare between two ambitious, relentless politicians began to immobilize policy in the Washington administration.

On issue after issue, ranging from redemption of war debt to creating a national bank, Washington had sided with Hamilton against Jefferson and Madison. Washington shared many values with Hamilton, relied on his eclectic knowledge, and tended to be swayed by his judgments. This posed a dilemma for Republican critics of the administration because Washington was still America's hero and a political untouchable; to assail him outright was thought to be political suicide. Hamilton, vulnerable as Washington never could be, therefore became the necessary bogeyman.

How could Jefferson hound Hamilton from office without tipping his hand? A proficient political ventriloquist, Jefferson was skilled at using proxies while keeping his own lips tightly sealed. The mouthpiece he chose to broadcast his views was the poet Philip Freneau. The Republicans had been bedeviled by the *Gazette of the United States,* a paper edited by a former Boston schoolmaster, John Fenno, who was adoring in his treatment of Hamilton. Hamilton had urged Fenno to start the paper in 1789 and later raised money to rescue it from financial distress. It was a quasi-official paper, since Fenno did work for the federal government and was even listed in the 1791 Philadelphia directory as an officer of the U.S. government. Jefferson denounced the *Gazette* as "a paper of pure Toryism, disseminating the doctrines of monarchy, aristocracy, and the exclusion of the influence of the people."[24] Jefferson and Madison decided to groom Freneau as a foil to Fenno and make him editor of a Republican newspaper.

Educated at Princeton, Freneau had been a friend and classmate of James Madison before the Revolution. As a crew member on a revolutionary privateer, Freneau had been captured by the British and subjected to six harrowing weeks aboard a prison ship, leaving him with a lasting detestation of England. The so-called Poet of the Revolution, Freneau was known for his scathing ridicule of English royalty, including his caustic description of George III as "the Caligula of Great Britain."[25] He had also rhapsodized about Washington as "a second Diomede[s]" whose actions might have awed a "Roman Hero or a Grecian God."[26]

Three days after Washington signed Hamilton's bank bill on February 25, 1791, Jefferson, at Madison's behest, tried to lure Freneau to Philadelphia by offering him a job as State Department translator at a modest $250 annual salary. Freneau knew only one foreign tongue, French, and was poorly qualified for the post. In Hamilton's view, this sinecure disguised the real design. Indeed, Jefferson hinted to Freneau that the translation job "gives so little to do as not to interfere with any other calling the person may choose."[27] When Jefferson and Madison made their botanizing tour in 1791, they breakfasted with Freneau in New York and urged him to move to Philadelphia to launch an opposition paper. Jefferson volunteered to toss in small State Department jobs, such as printing legal notices, to give the paper extra income. (He later denied making any such promises.) In his acerbic account of these events, Hamilton observed of Jefferson, "He knows how to put a man in a situation calculated to produce all the effects he desires without the gross and awkward formality of telling him, 'Sir I mean to *hire* you for the purpose.'"[28] By July 1791, Freneau had agreed to take the job as State Department translator, and on October 31 the maiden issue of the *National Gazette* appeared. This freewheeling paper soon became the foremost Republican organ in America.

Like other newspapers of the 1790s, Freneau's *National Gazette* did not feign neutrality. With the population widely dispersed, newspapers were unabashedly partisan organs that supplied much of the adhesive power binding the incipient parties together. Americans were a literate people, and dozens of newspapers flourished. The country probably had more newspapers per capita than any other. A typical issue had four long sheets, crammed with essays and small advertisements but no drawings or illustrations. These papers tended to be short on facts—there was little "spot news" reporting—and long on opinion. They more closely resembled journals of opinion than daily newspapers. Often scurrilous and inaccurate, they had few qualms about hinting that a certain nameless official was embezzling money or colluding with a foreign power. "Nothing can now be believed which is seen in a newspaper," Jefferson later said. "Truth itself becomes suspicious by being put into that polluted vehicle."[29] No code of conduct circumscribed responsible press behavior.

Signed articles were relatively rare. Perhaps the era's most prolific essayist, Hamilton seldom published under his own name and drew on a bewildering array of pseudonyms. Such pen names were sometimes transparent masks through which the public readily identified prominent politicians. The fashion of allowing anonymous attacks permitted extraordinary bile to seep into political discourse, and savage remarks that might not otherwise have surfaced appeared regularly in the press. The brutal tone of these papers made politics a wounding ordeal. One contemporary critic said of newspaper publishers, "Like birds of game . . . they make sport to the public as their party prompts or supplies them with materials. By this practice our elective privileges are converted into a curse."[30]

Though Jefferson and Madison were the chief instigators of the *National Gazette*, Jefferson had to move cautiously, while Madison could be more open. Madison solicited friends to subscribe to the paper, explaining that he did so "from a desire of testifying my esteem and friendship to Mr. Freneau by contributing to render his profits as commensurate as possible to his merits."[31] That Madison held high partisan hopes for the *National Gazette* is evident from a letter to Attorney General Edmund Randolph in which he rhapsodized about Freneau as "a man of genius" and described the need for a newspaper that would be an "antidote to the doctrines and discourses circulated in favor of monarchy and aristocracy."[32] By now, *monarchy* and *aristocracy* were standard code words for Hamilton and the Federalists.

One of Jefferson's main weapons in discrediting Hamilton was his own insatiable appetite for political intelligence. After noteworthy discussions, Jefferson scribbled down the contents on scraps of paper. In 1818, he collected these snippets of political chatter into a scrapbook he called his "Anas"—a compendium of table gossip. In these pages, Hamilton figures as the melodramatic villain of the Washington administration, appearing in no fewer than forty-five entries. These horror stories about Hamilton have been regurgitated for two centuries and are now engraved on the memories of historians and readers alike. Unfortunately, these vignettes often cruelly misrepresent Hamilton and have done no small damage to his reputation. Jefferson understood very well the power of laying down a paper trail.

By coincidence or not, Jefferson recorded his first "Anas" item right after Freneau agreed to take the State Department job. Jefferson was credulous when it came to tales about Hamilton and believed implicitly in the Anglophile, royalist demon he conjured up. In the "Anas," he fingered Hamilton as the cat's-paw of a cabal that wished to defeat the Constitution and install a British-style monarchy—never mind that Hamilton had written the bulk of *The Federalist Papers* and almost sin-glehandedly gotten the Constitution ratified in New York. In his silent but lethal style, Jefferson stored up Hamilton's indiscretions. It was here that Jefferson re-corded the story of Hamilton and Adams singing the praises of the British consti-tution; of Hamilton supposedly raising a toast to George III at a St. Andrew's Society dinner in New York; and of Hamilton declaring at a dinner party that "there was no stability, no security in any kind of government but a monarchy."[33] The sus-pect nature of these stories can be seen in the anecdote Jefferson told of Hamilton visiting his lodging in 1791 and inquiring about three portraits on the wall. "They are my trinity of the three greatest men the world has ever produced," Jefferson replied: "Sir Francis Bacon, Sir Isaac Newton, and John Locke." Hamilton suppos-edly replied, "The greatest man that ever lived was Julius Caesar."[34] What makes the story suspect, if not downright absurd, is that Hamilton's collected papers are teeming with pejorative references to Julius Caesar. In fact, whenever Hamilton wanted to revile Jefferson as a populist demagogue, he invariably likened him to Julius Caesar. One suspects that if Hamilton was accurately quoted, he was joking with Jefferson.

The problem with the "Anas" isn't that Jefferson fabricated things. Sometimes he accepted secondhand gossip at face value. Sometimes he took a casual comment and blew it up into a monstrous portrait. Sometimes he missed nuances that would have cast matters in a different light. Take the references to Hamilton as an avowed monar-chist: Hamilton had always wondered whether the Constitution would be durable enough to protect society and feared that a constitutional monarchy might be nec-essary; on the other hand, he had sworn to do everything in his power to give the new government a fair chance. In one "Anas" entry of August 13, 1791, Jefferson got this emphasis right when he reported Hamilton as saying that the new republic "ought to be tried before we give up the republican form altogether, for that mind must be really depraved which would not prefer the equality of political rights which is the foundation of pure republicanism, if it can be obtained consistently with order."[35] At other times, however, Jefferson was not so careful, stating baldly that Hamilton "was not only a monarchist, but for a monarchy bottomed on corruption."[36]

The most damaging tale about Hamilton, however, came not from Jefferson but from a much later book called the *Memoir of Theophilus Parsons*. Parsons had been an attorney general appointed by John Adams; the book was published by his son in 1859—forty-six years after Theophilus Parsons died and fifty-five after Alexan-der Hamilton died. The author contends that at a New York dinner party, soon af-ter the Constitution was adopted, an unnamed guest was declaiming about the wisdom of the American people. Hamilton allegedly slammed his fist on the table and exclaimed, "Your people, sir—your people is a great beast!" The author added,

"I have this anecdote from a friend, to whom it was related by one who was a guest at the table."[37] As Stephen F. Knott has shown in *Alexander Hamilton and the Persistence of Myth,* this report of an event that occurred seventy-one years earlier, relayed by someone who heard it from someone else who heard it from someone else, has been trotted out at every opportunity by people seeking to smear Hamilton's reputation. In fact, the quote was derived from a populist poem by a Dominican friar, Tommaso Campanella (1568–1639), who argued that the people were a slumbering beast who should awaken to their own power. Hamilton was wont to say that the world was full of knaves and fools, but this particular comment, *if* he ever made it, may have had a very different tone or intent from what has been imputed to it.

On the afternoon of February 28, 1792, Jefferson sat down with Washington, ostensibly to discuss the post office. The real purpose was Jefferson's intention to warn Washington that Hamilton's Treasury Department was threatening to devour the government. Jefferson wanted the post office under his jurisdiction at State because "the department of the Treasury possessed already such an influence as to swallow up the whole executive powers and that even future presidents . . . would not be able to make head against this department."[38] As always, Jefferson piously disclaimed any political ambitions, said that he contemplated resigning his post, and noted glumly that Hamilton showed no signs of leaving. At breakfast the next day, Washington urged Jefferson to stay. Notwithstanding the general prosperity, Jefferson contended that the country's troubles arose from a single source, Hamilton's system, and he accused his colleague of luring the citizenry into financial gambling. Hamilton did not know about Jefferson's efforts to turn Washington against him.

Jefferson grew more sedulous in propagating defamatory charges against Hamilton. At one cabinet meeting in April, Hamilton said that he would try to accommodate congressional demands for internal Treasury Department documents but would reserve the right to withhold sensitive information. "They might demand secrets of a very mischievous nature," he explained. For Jefferson, this was all a cover story. "Here I thought [Hamilton] began to fear they would go on to examining how far their own members and other persons in the government had been dabbling in stocks, banks etc.," Jefferson wrote in his "Anas."[39] In May, Jefferson warned Washington that Philip Schuyler had advocated hereditary government at a dinner a few months earlier. That same month, Jefferson wrote a memo to Washington arguing that the "ultimate objective" of the Hamiltonian system was "to prepare the way for a change from the present republican form of government to that of a monarchy."[40] The incorruptible Washington had known Hamilton intimately for fifteen years and was smart enough to dismiss these charges.

Madison had become no less confirmed an opponent of Hamilton than had Jefferson and thought his diabolical foe must be stopped. As Garry Wills has observed,

"Madison tended to think that those who opposed what seemed to him the obvious truth must have evil motives."[41] Madison saw Hamilton grafting British-style corruption on America in preparation for a monarchy. Freneau's *National Gazette* provided a handy platform for Madison, and each month his anonymous blasts against Hamilton grew more withering. In February 1792, as Jefferson burrowed away at Hamilton from within the cabinet, Madison railed against "a government operated by corrupt influence, substituting the motive of private interest in place of public duty."[42] By March, Madison's critique of Hamilton had grown indiscriminate: Hamilton was coddling speculators, inflating the national debt, distorting the Constitution, and scheming to bring aristocracy to America.

A master legislative tactician, Madison was now recognized as the first opposition leader in House history and had most of the south lined up solidly behind him. Among other things, Madison may have resented that Hamilton had replaced him as Washington's confidential adviser. In an attempt to stymie Hamilton, Madison tried to exert legislative control over the Treasury's power to raise money for the army for an upcoming western expedition. Madison did not prevail, but Hamilton was aghast that his former friend tried to curtail his power so drastically. As he said afterward, Madison "well knew that if he had prevailed, a certain consequence was my *resignation.*"[43] Abigail Adams saw the anti-Hamilton campaign emanating from Virginia. "All the attacks upon the Secretary of the Treasury and upon the government come from that quarter," she told her sister, "but I think whilst the people prosper and feel themselves happy, they cannot be blown up."[44] Fisher Ames also saw systematic opposition to Hamilton coming from Virginia. "Virginia moves in a solid column," he told a friend, "and the discipline of the party is as severe as the Prussian. Deserters are not spared. Madison is become a desperate party leader."[45]

That spring, Hamilton closely monitored the *National Gazette.* While Freneau glorified Jefferson as the "illustrious patriot" and the "colossus of liberty," he presented Hamilton in satirical terms, mocking him as "Atlas."[46] In early May, he taunted Hamilton with this verse: "Public debts are public curses / In soldiers' hands! then nothing worse is! / In speculators' hands increasing, / Public debt's a public blessing!"[47] Nor did Freneau exempt Washington from his mockery. When Hamilton made an innocent proposal to place Washington's face on the new currency, Freneau saw royalist tendencies at work: "Shall Washington, my fav'rite child, / Be ranked 'mongst haughty kings?"[48]

That such antigovernment diatribes were being published by the paid translator for Jefferson's State Department was finally too much for Hamilton. He concluded that Jefferson and Madison had mounted a concerted effort to drive him from office. He wasn't being just criticized but crucified. With an imagination no less suspicious than Jefferson's, he saw a populist conspiracy out to destroy him. After years of restraint as treasury secretary, Hamilton's mind and emotions were now at full boil.

On May 26, 1792, he wrote a remarkable letter to Edward Carrington, a revenue supervisor in Virginia, that virtually declared war against Jefferson and Madison. Hamilton shed discretion and let his deepest feelings gush forth. He told Carrington that as early as the debates over his funding system, people had given him hints of Madison's enmity, but he had not believed them. Now the scales had dropped from his eyes. "It was not 'till the last session that I became unequivocally convinced of the following truth: *That Mr. Madison cooperating with Mr. Jefferson is at the head of a faction decidedly hostile to me and my administration and actuated by views in my judgment subversive of the principles of good government and dangerous to the union, peace and happiness of the country.*"[49] Of the "systematic opposition" of Jefferson and Madison, Hamilton declared, "My subversion, I am now satisfied, has been long an object with them."[50]

Hamilton seemed more anguished by Madison's betrayal than Jefferson's. By this point, Hamilton saw the mild-mannered Jefferson as a fanatic with a settled malice toward him, if not toward the federal government itself. Madison had always impressed him as the more brilliant and honorable man. Now he concluded that Madison had fallen under Jefferson's sway. "I cannot persuade myself that Mr. Madison and I, whose politics had formerly so much the *same point of departure,* should now diverge so widely in our opinions of the measures which are proper to be pursued," Hamilton told Carrington. "The opinion I once entertained of the candour and simplicity and fairness of Mr. Madison's character has, I acknowledge, given way to a decided opinion that *it is one of a peculiarly artificial and complicated kind.*"[51]

Not for the last time, Hamilton tried to refute the grotesque fantasy that he belonged to a "monarchical party" that meditated the downfall of republican government. He conceded that he and kindred spirits held less populist beliefs than Jefferson and Madison but that they would regard "as both *criminal and visionary* any attempt to subvert the republican system of the country." He wanted to give the Constitution every possible chance: "I am *affectionately* attached to the republican theory. I desire *above all things* to see the *equality* of political rights, exclusive of all *hereditary* distinction, firmly established by a practical demonstration of its being consistent with the order and happiness of society."[52]

If he had wanted to impose a monarchy upon America, Hamilton said, he would follow the classic path of a populist demagogue: "I would mount the hobbyhorse of popularity, I would cry out usurpation, danger to liberty etc. etc. I would endeavour to prostrate the national government, raise a ferment, and then ride in the whirlwind and direct the storm." He denied Madison was doing this but was doubtful about Jefferson, a "man of profound ambition and violent passions."[53] Lest Carrington consider these views confidential, Hamilton indicated that he had thrown down the gauntlet to both Jefferson and Madison: "They are both apprised indirectly from myself of the opinion I entertain of their views."[54] The period of covert skirmishing had ended. Open warfare had begun.

George Washington watched this feuding in his cabinet with dismay. He was no longer the swaggering young general of the Revolution but a craggy, aging man with parchment skin. His gray eyes seemed smaller, more deeply set in their sockets. He was plagued by rheumatism, and his painful dentures crafted from hippopotamus tusks rubbed agonizingly against his one remaining good tooth. William Maclay found his "complexion pale, nay, almost cadaverous. His voice hollow and indistinct, owing, as I believe, to artificial teeth before his upper jaw."[55]

Washington clung to an idealized image of the president as a citizen-king above partisanship. This pose was more and more difficult to maintain with a bitterly divided cabinet. Jefferson sniped privately at Washington as a vain, close-minded man, easily manipulated by flattery. "His mind has been so long used to unlimited applause that it could not brook contradiction or even advice offered unasked," Jefferson complained to a friend, adding that "I have long thought therefore it was best for the republican interest to soothe him, by flattering where they could approve the measures and to be silent when they disapprove."[56] Unable to believe that Hamilton won internal arguments on their merits, Jefferson concluded that Washington was being hoodwinked. If not an intellectual, Washington was fully capable of independent judgment and could not be tricked or coerced. When Jefferson later accused him of falling under Hamilton's influence, Washington reminded him irritably that "there were so many instances within [your] own knowledge of my having decided *against* as in *favor* of the opinions of the person evidently alluded to [Hamilton]."[57] By early July 1792, it was clear that George Washington would not have the option of silence or inaction in stemming the feud between Hamilton and Jefferson. He had probably waited too long to assert control. His fine, nonpartisan stance may have only intensified the partisan mischief between his two appointees.

The slanderous hyperbole of Philip Freneau's *National Gazette* now soared to a new pitch. To commemorate July 4, Freneau ran a front-page article listing the "rules for changing a limited republican government into an unlimited hereditary one" and mentioned Hamilton's programs as the most effective means for doing so.[58] Other articles followed with equally heavy-handed hints that Hamilton and his retinue planned to enslave America under a monarchy and an aristocracy. To provoke the president still further, Freneau had three copies of the *National Gazette* delivered to Washington each day.

Before leaving for Monticello for the rest of the summer, Jefferson again sat down with Washington to persuade him that a "corrupt squadron of voters in Congress" was in Hamilton's pocket and voted for his measures only because they owned bank stock or government paper.[59] Washington exhibited growing impatience with Jefferson's warnings of a royalist plot and stated flatly that he endorsed Hamilton's policies. Anyone who thought otherwise, he told Jefferson, must regard the president as "too careless to attend to them or too stupid to understand them."[60]

On July 25, Hamilton planted in Fenno's *Gazette of the United States* the opening shot in a sustained volley against Jefferson. Signed "T. L.," this letter posed a simple query about Freneau and his State Department stipend: "Whether this salary is paid him for *translations* or for *publications,* the design of which is to vilify those to whom the voice of the people has committed the administration of our public affairs . . . ?"[61] The letter was just one paragraph, yet it could not have been more momentous: the treasury secretary was making anonymous public accusations against the secretary of state. Hamilton had returned to his old career as a bare-knuckled polemicist, and Freneau relished the chance to retaliate. Three days later, he tarred John Fenno, his Federalist counterpart, as a "vile sycophant" who printed the journals of the U.S. Senate and received more money from the government than he did.[62]

Washington was upset by this extraordinary tumult. The nasty newspaper war was pushing things fast to the breaking point. On July 29, Washington sent Hamilton a letter from Mount Vernon, labeled "Private & Confidential," that enumerated twenty-one grievances about his administration that he had heard during his trip home. Everyone agreed that the country was prosperous and happy but voiced concern over specific measures. Although Washington pretended that George Mason was the principal voice of these concerns, Jefferson was clearly the source. Reluctant to offend Hamilton, Washington tactfully avoided mention that the twenty-one grievances all related to Hamilton's policies. The litany of complaints was by now familiar: the excise tax was oppressive, the public debt too high, speculation had drained capital from productive uses and corrupted Congress, and on and on. Finally, Washington told Hamilton of the rumor that the real intent of these initiatives was "to prepare the way for a change from the present republican form of government to that of a monarchy, of which the British Constitution is to be the model."[63]

By the time he received Washington's letter on August 3, Hamilton had already posted one to Mount Vernon, urging Washington to stand for reelection and warning him that failure to do so would be "deplored as the greatest evil that could befall the country at the present juncture."[64] Washington's letter must have reinforced Hamilton's fear that the government was encircled by enemies and that Jefferson was plotting his ouster. Before Hamilton replied, he published a stinging critique of Jefferson in the *Gazette of the United States.* Under the guise of "An American,"

Hamilton raised the stakes markedly by naming names. Freneau's newspaper, he alleged, had been set up to advance Jefferson's views, and Madison had been the intermediary in bringing Freneau to Philadelphia. Hamilton engaged in some wicked mockery, noting that the only foreign language the translator Freneau knew was French and that Jefferson was already acquainted with that language. He then directly accused Jefferson of disloyalty: "Is it possible that Mr. Jefferson, the head of a principal department of the government, can be the patron of a paper, the evident object of which is to decry the government and its measures?"[65] Many readers must have guessed the identity of the author hiding behind the mask of "An American."

Now in the fray, Hamilton published two more installments of "An American" on August 11 and 18, elaborating on the impropriety of Jefferson's relationship with Freneau: "It is a fact known to every man who approaches that officer . . . that he arraigns the principal measures of the government and, it may be added, with *indiscreet* if not *indecent* warmth."[66] Even as Hamilton fired these broadsides, he composed a fourteen-thousand-word letter to Washington, vindicating his Treasury tenure. He confessed to deep hurt at the false charges hurled against him. He could endure criticisms of his judgment but not of his integrity: "I feel that I merit them *in no degree* and expressions of indignation sometimes escape me in spite of every effort to suppress them."[67] Hamilton listed his economic feats in office. He talked of the steep drop in the interest rates that the United States had to pay for loans (from 6 percent to 4 percent) and the influx of foreign money that had financed commerce and agriculture. Abundant money was now available for legitimate business purposes. Even speculation had proved his system's soundness, for "under a bad system the public stock would have been too uncertain an article" for people to speculate in it.[68] Hamilton denied that any member of Congress "can properly be called a stock-jobber or a paper dealer," even if some had invested in government debt.[69] Many had bought bank stock *after* the founding of the Bank of the United States, and he saw nothing wrong with that. It irked Hamilton that Jefferson claimed a monopoly on morality, and he made the following retort to his adversary: "As to the love of liberty and country, you have given no stronger proofs of being actuated by it than I have done. Cease then to arrogate to yourself and to your party all the patriotism and virtue of the country."[70]

For all its brilliance, the zeal of Hamilton's letter must have heightened Washington's worries about the schism in his administration. In late August, he sent Hamilton a melancholy reply, pleading for mutual tolerance between him and Jefferson. Aware of the accusations they were trading in the press, Washington regretted these "wounding suspicions" and "irritating charges" and asked for "healing measures" to restore harmony.[71] The president feared that, if the acrimony continued, the union itself might dissolve.

This full-length portrait of Alexander Hamilton as treasury secretary in 1792 shows his trim physique and debonair style. Ensnared in controversy, Hamilton asked the artist, John Trumbull, to omit any allusions to his political life.

This 1768 portrait of Myles Cooper, an Anglican minister and second president of King's College, reflects the massive self-confidence of this unrepentant Tory. Hamilton helped save him from a patriotic mob in the early days of the Revolution.

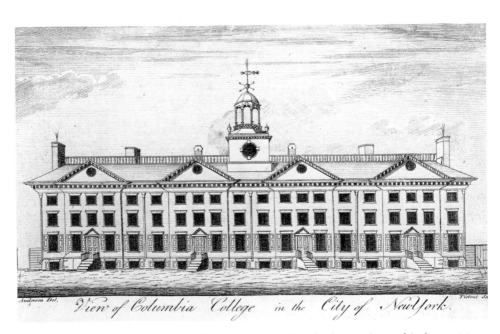

View of Columbia College in the City of New York.

In the eighteenth century, King's College (later Columbia) was situated in lower Manhattan and enjoyed a bucolic Hudson River vista.

George Washington at Princeton. This splendid Charles Willson Peale portrait conveys the graceful panache of the Revolutionary War general, so unlike the later stiffness of his presidential demeanor.

During the Revolution, Hamilton formed a gallant trio with the marquis de Lafayette, pictured below in military uniform in the early days of the French Revolution, and John Laurens. The Laurens miniature was probably a gift for Martha Manning, whom Laurens impregnated and then married during his prewar legal studies in London.

Prompted by her husband, Elizabeth Schuyler Hamilton visited a debtors' prison to pose for this portrait by the insolvent artist Ralph Earl. Despite her elaborate hairdo, Earl captured Eliza's lively, direct, and unpretentious nature.

Major General Philip Schuyler, a highly status-conscious man, embraced Hamilton as his son-in-law despite the latter's murky, illegitimate boyhood.

Angelica Church—bright, witty, and fashionable—captivated her brother-in-law Hamilton no less than she did Thomas Jefferson and other political notables of the day.

The elegant Schuyler mansion in Albany, the Pastures, was one of the few places where the high-strung, work-obsessed Hamilton allowed himself to relax.

This 1792 portrait of James Madison, painted a few years after his collaboration with Hamilton on *The Federalist*, testifies to his tough, combative nature as he tried to foil Hamilton's financial system in the House of Representatives.

For the Independent Journal.

The FŒDERALIST. No. I.

To the People of the State of New-York.

AFTER an unequivocal experience of the ineffi-cacy of the subsisting Fœderal Government, you are called upon to deliberate on a new Constitution for the United States of America. The subject speaks its own importance; comprehending in its consequen-ces, nothing less than the existence of the UNION, the safety and welfare of the parts of which it is com-posed, the fate of an empire, in many respects, the most interesting in the world. It has been frequent-ly remarked, that it seems to have been reserved to the people of this country, by their conduct and ex-ample, to decide the important question, whether so-cieties of men are really capable or not, of establish-ing good government from reflection and choice, or whether they are forever destined to depend, for their political constitutions, on accident and force. If there be any truth in the remark, the crisis, at which we are arrived, may with propriety be regarded as the æra in which that decision is to be made; and a wrong election of the part we shall act, may, in this view, deserve to be considered as the general misfortune of mankind.

This idea will add the inducements of philanthropy to those of patriotism to heighten the sollicitude, which all considerate and good men must feel for the event. Happy will it be if our choice should be de-cided by a judicious estimate of our true interests, unperplexed and unbiassed by considerations not con-nected with the public good. But this is a thing more ardently to be wished, than seriously to be expected. The plan offered to our deliberations, affects too ma-ny particular interests, innovates upon too many local institutions, not to involve in its discussion a variety of objects foreign to its merits, and of views, passi-ons and prejudices little favourable to the discovery of truth.

Among the most formidable of the obstacles which the new Constitution will have to encounter, may readi-ly be distinguished the obvious interest of a certain class of men in every State to resist all changes which may hazard a diminution of the power, emolument and consequence of the offices they hold under the State-establishments—and the perverted ambition of another class of men, who will either hope to aggrandise themselves by the confusions of their country, or will flatter themselves with fairer prospects of elevation from the subdivision of the empire into several par-tial confederacies, than from its union under one go-vernment.

The first newspaper installment of *The Federalist*. Hamilton turned out the essays in a white heat, publishing up to five or six "numbers" in a single week.

A wary, lugubrious John Jay depicted just before he teamed up with Hamilton on *The Federalist*. He finally had to drop the project because of severe rheumatism.

George Clinton, the seven-time governor of New York State, repeatedly clashed with Hamilton and came to personify for him the perils of state power.

The two faces of Thomas Jefferson. These portraits chart Jefferson's metamorphosis from the foppish aristocrat of his Parisian years to the seemingly more austere republican vice president under John Adams.

Philip Freneau. A celebrated poet and firebrand recruited by Jefferson and Madison to edit the *National Gazette*, Freneau baited both Hamilton and Washington with anti-administration polemics.

William Branch Giles, then a fervent young congressman from Virginia, harried Treasury Secretary Hamilton at every turn with resolutions and investigations.

James Monroe as American minister to France. Alexander and Eliza Hamilton devoutly believed that after the Federalists demanded Monroe's recall from Paris, he conspired to expose Hamilton's adulterous trysts with Maria Reynolds.

The flamboyant diplomacy of
Citizen Genêt in America
precipitated both frenzied
support and opposition
and split a nation already
deeply torn about the
French Revolution.

The wily Charles-
Maurice de Talleyrand-
Périgord thought that
Hamilton was arguably
the greatest political
figure of the age, while
Hamilton found the
French statesman bril-
liant but unprincipled.

This portrait of John Adams as vice president suggests formidable reserves of strength but also hints at his unyielding pugnacity.

The title page of Hamilton's 1800 pamphlet denouncing President Adams. Its publication was one of Hamilton's least inspired ideas and only hastened his political decline.

New York Historical Society from Gulian C. Ver
1009.

C.T
.A21
Box

LETTER

FROM

ALEXANDER HAMILTON,

CONCERNING

THE PUBLIC CONDUCT AND CHARACTER

OF

JOHN ADAMS, Esq.

PRESIDENT OF THE UNITED STATES.

NEW-YORK:

Printed for JOHN LANG, by GEORGE F. HOPKINS.

1800.

[Copy-right secured.]

Members of John Adams's cabinet, allegedly under the treacherous control of Alexander Hamilton:

Left: Timothy Pickering, secretary of state.

Bottom left: Oliver Wolcott, Jr., secretary of the treasury.

Bottom right: James McHenry, secretary of war.

Three stages in the protean career of Aaron Burr:

Left: As a young senator from New York, circa 1792, having replaced Philip Schuyler.

Bottom left: As vice president in 1802, two years before his fatal "interview" with Hamilton.

Bottom right: In 1834, two years before his death, the jaded Burr looked supremely cynical as he sat for his final portrait.

Recently graduated from
Columbia, nineteen-year-old
Philip Hamilton became embroiled
in a sudden dispute over his father's
reputation that resulted in his death
in November 1801.

This somber portrait
of Hamilton registers
profound grief after
his son's death and
reflects the sorrows
of his last years.

Eliza Hamilton outlived her husband by more than half a century. She was in her nineties when this delicate study was sketched in charcoal and chalk.

Until she died at ninety-seven, Eliza Hamilton doted on this marble bust of her beloved husband by Giuseppe Ceracchi.

Hamilton did not complete the Grange until two years before his death, but his widow and children continued to occupy the pastoral retreat for years afterward.

Political life in the young republic now presented a strange spectacle. The intellectual caliber of the leading figures surpassed that of any future political leadership in American history. On the other hand, their animosity toward one another has seldom been exceeded either. How to explain this mix of elevated thinking and base slander? As mentioned, both sides believed that the future of the country was at stake. By 1792, both political parties saw their opponents as mortal threats to the heritage of the Revolution. But the special mixture of idealism and vituperation also stemmed from the experiences of the founders themselves. These selfless warriors of the Revolution and sages of the Constitutional Convention had been forced to descend from their Olympian heights and adjust to a rougher world of everyday politics, where they cultivated their own interests and tried to capitalize on their former glory. In consequence, the founding fathers all appear to us in two guises: as both sublime and ordinary, selfless and selfish, heroic and humdrum. After the tenuous unity of 1776 and 1787, they had become wildly competitive and sometimes jealous of one another. It is no accident that our most scathing portraits of them come from their own pens.

Far from heeding Washington's call to desist from attacking Jefferson, Hamilton stepped up his efforts. Increasingly bitter, he was incapable of the forbearance Washington requested. The day before he replied to Washington on September 9, Hamilton found himself reeling from another fresh burst of articles against him. An author named "Aristides"—the name of an Athenian motivated by love of country, not mercenary gain—deified Jefferson as the "decided opponent of aristocracy, monarchy, hereditary succession, a titled order of nobility, and all the other mock-pageantry of kingly government." He implied that Hamilton had endorsed these abhorrent things when, in fact, he had always condemned them. Noting the anonymous nature of Hamilton's diatribes, the author likened the treasury secretary to "a cowardly assassin who strikes in the dark and securely wounds because he is unseen."[72] Freneau's *National Gazette* continued to lambaste the Federalists as the "monarchical party," the "monied aristocracy," and "monocrats"—none of this likely to induce a mood of remorse in Hamilton.

In his September 9 letter, Hamilton applauded Washington's attempts at reconciliation, then insisted that *he* hadn't started the feud, that *he* was the injured party, and that *he* was not to blame. He took the feud a step further by recommending that Jefferson be expelled from the cabinet: "I do not hesitate to say that, in my opinion, the period is not remote when the public good will require *substitutes* for the *differing members* of your administration."[73] As long as it had not undermined the government, Hamilton said, he had tolerated Jefferson's backstabbing. That was no longer the case: "I cannot doubt, from the evidence that I possess[,] that the *Na-*

tional Gazette was instituted by him [Jefferson] for political purposes and that one leading object of it has been to render me and all the measures connected with my department as odious as possible."[74] Hamilton thought it his duty to unmask this antigovernment coterie and "draw aside the veil from the principal actors. To this strong impulse . . . I have yielded."[75] In an astounding statement, Hamilton told Washington that he could not desist from newspaper attacks against Jefferson: "I find myself placed in a situation not to be able to *recede for the present*."[76]

Never before had Hamilton refused such a direct request from Washington, and not since quitting the general's wartime staff had he so willfully asserted his own independence. Even while telling Washington that he would try to abide by any truce, he was preparing his next press tirade. The furious exchanges between Hamilton and Jefferson had hardened into a mutual vendetta that Washington was powerless to stop.

Nor did Jefferson heed Washington's large-spirited plea for tolerance. In replying to the presidential request, he renewed his withering critique of Hamilton's system, which, he said, "flowed from principles adverse to liberty and was calculated to undermine and demolish the republic by creating an influence of his department over the members of the legislature." He charged Hamilton with favoring a king and a House of Lords at the Constitutional Convention—a misconstruction of what Hamilton had said. With greater justice, he grumbled about Hamilton's unauthorized meetings with British and French ministers, but he also displayed an ugly condescension toward Hamilton that he ordinarily concealed: "I will not suffer my retirement to be clouded by the slanders of a man whose history, from the moment at which history can stoop to notice him, is a tissue of machinations against the liberty of the country which has not only received him and given him bread, but heaped its honors on his head."[77] The comment smacked of aristocratic disdain for the self-made man. In fact, no immigrant in American history has ever made a larger contribution than Alexander Hamilton.

Hamilton seemed unhinged by the dispute. In the still secret Reynolds affair, he had shown a lack of private restraint. Now something compulsive and uncontrollable appeared in his public behavior. A captive of his emotions, he revealed an irrepressible need to respond to attacks. Whenever he tried to suppress these emotions, they burst out and overwhelmed him. Throughout that fall, the argumentative treasury secretary donned disguises and published blazing articles behind Roman pen names. Henceforth, he provided a running newspaper commentary on his own administration. Since he saw both his personal honor and the republic's future at stake, he fought with his full arsenal of verbal weapons. Again and again in his career, Hamilton committed the same political error: he never knew when to stop, and the resulting excesses led him into irremediable indiscretions.

In a new tack, Hamilton carried the battle into enemy territory: the pages of the *National Gazette* itself. Two days after telling Washington that he could not stop his polemics, he appeared twice in Freneau's paper. As "Civis," he warned of a Jeffersonian cabal trying to win power at the next election. In "*Fact* No. I," he corrected the continuing Jeffersonian distortions of his belief that a national debt could be a national blessing. He denied that government debt was a good thing at all times and held that "particular and temporary circumstances might render that advantageous at one time, which at another might be hurtful."[78] He also charged the Jeffersonians with hypocrisy for opposing both taxes and debt: "A certain description of men are for getting out of debt, yet are against all taxes for raising money to pay it off."[79]

Within a week, Hamilton had returned to his ideological home, Fenno's *Gazette of the United States,* publishing a new series under the name "Catullus." He had the cheek to praise himself handsomely, saying that the treasury secretary feared no scrutiny into his motives: "I mistake however the man . . . if he fears the strictest examination of his political principles and conduct."[80] As before, Hamilton limned Jefferson as a despot in disguise, masking political ambitions behind republican simplicity. He contended that Jefferson had first opposed the Constitution, then adopted it from expediency. Hamilton didn't stop with politics and now slashed at Jefferson's personal reputation. Hinting that he possessed darker knowledge of his subject's life, Hamilton intimated that Jefferson was a closet libertine: "Mr. Jefferson has hitherto been distinguished as the quiet, modest, retiring philosopher, as the plain simple unambitious republican. He shall not now for the first time be regarded as the intriguing incendiary, the aspiring, turbulent competitor." "Catullus" said that Jefferson's true nature had not been exposed before:

> But there is always "a *first time*" when characters studious of artful disguises are unveiled. When the vizor of stoicism is plucked from the brow of the Epicurean; when the plain garb of Quaker simplicity is stripped from the concealed voluptuary; when Caesar *coyly refusing* the proffered diadem is *seen* to be Caesar *rejecting* the trappings, but tenaciously gripping the substance of imperial domination.[81]

Hamilton was pointing to some deeper knowledge of Jefferson's private life, perhaps his knowledge of Jefferson's liaison with Sally Hemings, based on reports from Angelica Church. Notably, Hamilton again used Julius Caesar as an example of the worst sort of tyrant, not as history's greatest man.

In responding to Washington's call for toleration, the only difference between Hamilton and Jefferson was that Hamilton wielded his own pen while Jefferson employed proxies. Between September 26 and December 31, 1792, six essays entitled "Vindication of Mr. Jefferson" came out in the *American Daily Advertiser*. Jefferson's protégé from Virginia, Senator James Monroe, wrote five of them and Madison the sixth. The two men had conferred at length with Jefferson at Monticello, and Jefferson sent seven letters to Madison, which Monroe drew freely on in his articles. Monroe tried to exculpate Jefferson from charges that he had opposed the Constitution and wished to repudiate the national debt. In one essay, "A Candid State of Parties," Madison described the Hamiltonians as "more partial to the opulent than to the other classes of society" and said they wanted to conduct government by "the pageantry of rank, the influence of money and emoluments, and the terror of military force."[82] Before writing the article, Madison received word from John Beckley, clerk of the House of Representatives, that Hamilton had declared unequivocally that Madison was "his *personal* and *political* enemy."[83] Things had reached a frenzied state that would have been inconceivable to Hamilton and Madison five years earlier, when they started *The Federalist*.

Before breakfast on the morning of October 1, 1792, Jefferson met with George Washington at Mount Vernon and again tried to convince him that Hamilton headed a monarchist plot. According to Jefferson, Hamilton had told him that the "Constitution was a shilly-shally thing of mere milk and water, which could not last and was only good as a step to something better."[84] Washington now lost all patience with Jefferson and his obsessive belief in a nonexistent plot. He told him that "as to the idea of transforming this government into a monarchy, he did not believe there were ten men in the United States whose opinions were worth attention who entertained such a thought."[85] Washington also made it plain that he supported Hamilton's funding system because it had *worked*. "That for himself, he had seen our affairs desperate and our credit lost, and that this was in a sudden and extraordinary degree raised to the highest pitch," Jefferson later wrote.[86] Washington said that it did not bother him that some legislators owned government debt, because some self-interest was inescapable in any government.

Because the president sided with his much younger rival, Jefferson concluded grumpily that the president's brain must be enfeebled by age and that his opinions showed "a willingness to let others act and even think for him."[87] In despair, Jefferson repeated his intention to retire from the State Department at the end of Washington's first term (March 1793), though he was to linger until the end of that year. Hamilton had flowered in office and found his identity there, while Jefferson hated the paperwork, had wearied of contesting administration policies, and daydreamed about a return to more peaceful pursuits at Monticello. The job had trapped him among political enemies, and he knew it would be easier to build up his following outside of office. There was no longer any point in trying to convert George Washington. Alexander Hamilton had won.

TWENTY-ONE

EXPOSURE

The turbulent events of 1792—the rise of political parties, the newspaper wars, the furious intramural fights with Jefferson—should have made Alexander Hamilton extra vigilant about threats to his reputation. Now at the apex of his power, the thirty-seven-year-old treasury secretary had enemies ready to exploit his every failing. Despite this vulnerability, he continued his affair with Maria Reynolds and went on paying hush money to James Reynolds. His moral laxity and absurd willingness to risk exposure at such a moment remain a baffling conundrum.

Adding danger was the sudden appearance of a menacing new spectator: Jacob Clingman, a friend of James Reynolds and a former clerk of the erstwhile House Speaker Frederick Muhlenberg of Pennsylvania. Arriving at the Reynolds home one day, Clingman was stunned to discover Alexander Hamilton leaving. Several days later, Clingman beheld another dreamlike tableau. He was alone with Maria Reynolds when someone rapped at the door and the treasury secretary entered. Perhaps startled by Clingman's presence, Hamilton pretended, ridiculously, that he was delivering a message. He handed Maria a slip of paper, explaining that he had been "ordered" to give it to her by her husband, and left. The stupefied Clingman wondered how James Reynolds could boss around America's second most powerful man. Responding to his inquiries afterward, Maria Reynolds boasted that Hamilton had paid her husband "upwards of eleven hundred dollars."[1] James Reynolds likewise bragged to Clingman that he had gotten money from Hamilton for speculation. An archcritic of Hamilton's policies, Clingman was predisposed to see such payments as proof of Hamilton conniving with speculators in government securities. On one occasion, Clingman accompanied James Reynolds to visit Hamilton, waited outside, then watched his companion emerge with one hundred dollars. This certified his suspicion of Hamilton's venality.

Hamilton claimed that he had tried to terminate his liaison with Maria Reynolds. Whenever he told her that he wanted to break off the relationship, this femme fatale responded with sighs, groans, and weepy theatrics. She would beg to see him one last time and hint that, if denied her wishes, frightful consequences might ensue:

> Yes Sir Rest assuirred I will never ask you to Call on me again   I have kept my Bed those tow dayes and now rise from My pillow wich your Neglect has filled with the sharpest thorns I   no Longer doubt what I have Dreaded to no but stop I do not wish to se you to say any thing about my Late disappointments   No I only do it to Ease a heart wich is ready Burst with Greef   I can neither Eate or sleep   I have Been on the point of doing the moast horrid acts at I shuder to think where I might been what will Become of me. In vain I try to Call reason to aide me but alas there Is no Comfort for me[2]

Maria's maid was kept busy bustling through the night, relaying such erratic notes. One can only imagine Hamilton's cold sweats and unremitting horror at the thought of discovery by Eliza, who was now pregnant with their fifth child.

James Reynolds followed current events, and his threatening letters often coincided with key episodes in Hamilton's public life. Reynolds thought that Hamilton was an unscrupulous official who had given William Duer money for speculation and secretly made thirty thousand dollars from their illicit relationship—false information that he passed along to Clingman. So in late March 1792, as Hamilton grappled with financial panic in New York, James Reynolds forced him to grapple with turmoil in his private life. The day after Duer was imprisoned, both James and Maria Reynolds wrote to Hamilton and tightened the noose. They acted their roles to perfection: James, the strong but aggrieved husband, who had lost his wife's affections because of Hamilton; and Maria, the fickle, confused wife, hopelessly smitten with her lover, who gave way to operatic ravings and invocations of her cruel fortune. Did Hamilton find it poignant or merely grotesque that she still addressed him in writing as "Colonel Hamilton" and "Sir"?

In the letters sent after Duer's arrest, Maria Reynolds spouted poppycock about how she was "doomed to drink the bitter cup of affliction" and how "death now would be welcome." She renewed her pleas for another visit.[3] Simultaneously, James Reynolds told Hamilton that he had no wish to harm him but demanded satisfaction for his loss of domestic felicity. "I find when ever you have been with her. she is Chearful and kind," James Reynolds explained to Hamilton. "But when you have not in some time she is Quite to Reverse. and wishes to be alone by her self." This disturbed him, of course, as a loving husband. Maria had told Hamilton that her husband wished to meet him the next evening, so James Reynolds explained, with elaborate mock courtesy, that he hoped to convince Hamilton that "I would not wish to trifle with you And would much Rather add to the happiness of all than to disstress any."[4]

Whatever happened at this meeting, it only emboldened James Reynolds to demand more money. At first, he did so with a cringing humility. A week later, this master of malapropisms wrote to Hamilton, "Sir I hope you will pardon me in taking the liberty I do In troubling you so offen. it hurts me to let you Know my Setivation. I should take it as a protickeler if you will Oblige me with the loane of about thirty Dollars. . . . I want it for some little Necssaries of life for my family, sir."[5] To give a thin veneer of legality to his extortion, Reynolds pretended to be a proud family man who needed loans to tide him over tough times. He even gave Hamilton receipts and promised to repay the "loans." Four days later, Reynolds again requested money, this time forty-five dollars; the blackmailer was becoming more brazen. In a reply written without salutation or signature, Hamilton told Reynolds of his "scarcity of cash" and informed him with mounting anger, "Tomorrow what is requested will be done. 'Twill hardly be possible *today*."[6] The man who felt no need to placate Thomas Jefferson or James Madison had to grovel before the raffish James Reynolds, whom he later described bitterly as "an obscure, unimportant, and profligate man."[7] He was so frightened of Reynolds that he wrote to him in disguised handwriting, lest Reynolds use it as "the engine of a false credit or turn it to some other sinister use," Hamilton said.[8]

On April 17, 1792, Reynolds informed Hamilton that his adulterous romance with Maria had destroyed their marriage: "She has treated me more Cruel than pen cant paint out. and Ses that She is determed never to be a wife to me any more." In his most self-effacing mode, Reynolds said that he would not chide Hamilton: "I Freely forgive you and dont wish to give you fear or pain a moment on the account of it."[9] On the other hand, he continued, it lay in Hamilton's power to make some amends, and he said that he would come to Hamilton's office—which must have made the latter quake. Six days later, Reynolds demanded another thirty dollars and said he would await an answer at Hamilton's office.[10] In his letters, James Reynolds began to dispense with the fake, effusive professions of friendship and got straight down to business.

On May 2, 1792, James Reynolds sent Hamilton a letter that fully awakened him to the dire threat to his career. Hamilton already had political troubles enough: he was about to attend an emergency meeting to rescue the Society for Establishing Useful Manufactures from William Duer's embezzlement. In this letter, Reynolds explained that he had hoped Maria's infatuation for Hamilton would gradually subside. Since this had not happened, Reynolds declared, he would prohibit Hamilton from visiting her. Reynolds also reproached Hamilton for always sneaking in the back door of their house, as if he was ashamed to visit them. With a flamboyant show of self-pity, Reynolds asked, "am I a person of Such a bad Carector. that you would not wish to be seen in Coming in my house in the front way."[11] It now dawned on Hamilton belatedly that the blackmail scheme might have a political dimension: he remembered the "accidental" encounter with Jacob Clingman at the Reynolds house. Were his enemies trying to entrap him? Years later, Hamilton described the May 2 letter as a masterpiece: "The husband there forbids my future visits to his wife, chiefly because I was careful to avoid publicity. It was probably necessary to the project of some deeper treason against me that I should be seen at the house. Hence was it contrived, with all the caution on my part to avoid it, that [Jacob] *Clingman* should occasionally see me."[12] It is strange and almost inconceivable that a man of Hamilton's cynical worldliness should have taken so long to fathom this danger.

Sadly, it was the perceived threat to his career, not regret over his pregnant wife, that restored Hamilton to his senses. He finally mustered sufficient willpower and steeled himself against Maria Reynolds's further entreaties. Her last attempt came on June 2, 1792: "Dear Sir   I once take up the pen to solicit The favor of seing again oh Col hamilton what have I done that you should thus Neglect me."[13] This garbled note was followed by a fresh letter from James Reynolds, asking for three hundred dollars to invest in shares of the new Lancaster Turnpike.

Instead of appeasing Reynolds, Hamilton replied tersely, "It is utterly out of my power I assure you 'pon my honour to comply with your request. Your note is returned."[14] Rebuffed, Reynolds reduced his demand to fifty dollars and threw in a frightening new touch, saying that he would stop by Hamilton's house that evening. The treasury secretary paid up, but it was the last time Reynolds extorted money from him.

Hamilton probably thought the whole nightmarish episode had ended when it had only just begun. Incredibly, he had allowed this affair, enacted in the heart of the nation's capital, to proceed for almost a year. In a letter to a Federalist politician that September, Hamilton continued to present himself as a paragon of virtue, saying, "I pledge myself to you and to every friend of mine that the strictest scrutiny into every part of my conduct, whether as a private citizen or as a public officer, can only serve to establish the perfect purity of it."[15] The treasury secretary, it turned out, did protest too much.

During the summer of 1792, Hamilton was preoccupied with exposing Freneau's link with Jefferson and Madison and winning the internecine cabinet warfare. He had neither the time nor the inclination to dally with Maria Reynolds, and this ruined James Reynolds's plans. The blackmailing couple had moved to a large house on Vine Street, near the corner of Fifth, and hoped to cover costs by renting rooms to "genteel boarders," as James phrased it. The only snag was that they lacked cash to furnish the rooms.

As always, James Reynolds exhibited a keenly sadistic sense of timing. On August 22, Eliza Hamilton gave birth to the couple's fifth child, John Church Hamilton. "Mrs. Hamilton has lately given me another boy, who and the Mother are unusually well," Hamilton told Washington's secretary, Tobias Lear.[16] Perhaps James Reynolds thought that, with a newborn baby, Hamilton might be more easily coerced. On August 24, he wrote and tried to touch him for another two hundred dollars. A week later, he wrote again, lamenting that he had received no reply. Since Hamilton had stopped seeing his wife, James Reynolds seemed to have surrendered all power over him. Perhaps feeling guilty over Maria Reynolds, Hamilton stuck close to home, and in one letter that fall referred to his "growing and hitherto too much neglected family."[17]

The Reynolds affair might never have come to light if James Reynolds and Jacob Clingman had not been charged in mid-November with defrauding the U.S. government of four hundred dollars. The two swindlers had posed as executors of the estate of a supposedly deceased war veteran, Ephraim Goodenough, who had a claim against the government. In their scheme, Reynolds and Clingman prevailed upon one John Delabar to perjure himself and corroborate their story. Goodenough's name had been selected from a confidential list of soldiers owed money by the government—a list purloined from the Treasury Department. The man who prosecuted Reynolds and Clingman was Oliver Wolcott, Jr., who had been named comptroller of the treasury the previous year. An admirer of Wolcott's integrity and knowledge, Hamilton had persuaded Washington to appoint him over a competing candidate touted by Jefferson.

Reynolds and Clingman ended up in a Philadelphia jail. Because the Treasury Department filed the charges, James Reynolds suspected that Hamilton was engaged in a vendetta. He wrote to Hamilton twice, asking for help, but received no assistance. Hamilton then learned from Wolcott that Reynolds was insinuating loudly that he could "make disclosures injurious to the character of some head of a department."[18] Hamilton saw exactly where this was heading and advised Wolcott to keep Reynolds imprisoned until the accusations were cleared up.

Released on bail, Jacob Clingman turned to the most powerful man he knew: his former boss, Congressman Frederick Muhlenberg of Pennsylvania. The former House Speaker agreed to intercede on behalf of Clingman but not Reynolds, whom he had heard was a "rascal." He decided to speak with Hamilton in the company of

New York senator Aaron Burr. At the interview, a circumspect Hamilton agreed to do everything consistent with honor to aid Clingman. Muhlenberg persuaded Oliver Wolcott to strike a deal: if Clingman and Reynolds refunded the money defrauded from the government, returned the stolen list of soldiers, and identified the Treasury employee who had leaked the document, then charges against them might be dropped. Evidently, the two men met these conditions by early December 1792. "It was certainly of more consequence to the public to detect and expel from the bosom of the Treasury Department an unfaithful clerk to prevent future and extensive mischief than to disgrace and punish two worthless individuals," Hamilton later wrote.[19]

The matter might have ended there except that Clingman kept suggesting darkly to Muhlenberg that he harbored damning information about Hamilton. As Muhlenberg recalled, "Clingman, unasked, frequently dropped hints to me that Reynolds had it in his power, very materially, to injure the secretary of the treasury and that Reynolds knew several very improper transactions of his."[20] At first, Muhlenberg scoffed at this. Then Clingman told him that Hamilton was hip deep in speculation and had provided James Reynolds with money for that illicit purpose. What most impressed Muhlenberg was Reynolds's contention that "he had it in his power to hang the secretary of the Treasury."[21] Muhlenberg did not believe that he could hide such information, and on Wednesday morning, December 12, he turned to two other Republicans, Senator James Monroe and Representative Abraham B. Venable, both of Virginia. Monroe's entry into the drama was especially ominous for Hamilton, given his recent *National Gazette* pieces. It is not clear that Hamilton knew that Monroe was the author of these pieces, but he certainly knew of Monroe's intimacy with Jefferson and Madison.

Thanks to Maria Reynolds, Clingman had some unsigned notes sent by Hamilton to James Reynolds, which Muhlenberg now showed to Monroe and Venable. Hardly reluctant to pursue the charges, the Virginians went straight to see James Reynolds in his prison cell. The prisoner teased them with vague but tantalizing hints that "he had a person in high office in his power and has had a long time past." He further let drop that "Mr. Wolcott was in the same department" as this mystery person "and, he supposed, under his influence or control."[22] Though the allusion to Hamilton was patent, the wily Reynolds said that he would not divulge more information until he was freed.

Meanwhile, Maria Reynolds was scarcely idle. This artful twenty-four-year-old woman seemed able, on short notice, to secure appointments with high officials. She went to see Pennsylvania's governor, Thomas Mifflin, who expressed sympathy with her plight. Maria Reynolds told Mifflin about, among other things, her love affair with Hamilton. She also took advantage of the situation to visit her illustrious former lover, who was trying to walk a fine line between official propriety and self-protection. On the one hand, Hamilton echoed Wolcott's position that Clingman and James Reynolds should return the list of soldiers to the Treasury along with their ill-gotten money. On the other hand, according to Maria Reynolds, Hamilton also pressed her to burn his damaging letters to her husband. Fully aware of the value of these notes as an insurance policy, the siren of Philadelphia politics was smart enough to keep two or three.

Having no notion of any Hamiltonian adultery, Muhlenberg and Monroe visited Maria Reynolds at home on the evening of December 12, seeking more information about alleged financial collusion between Hamilton and her husband. At first, she was not communicative. Only gradually did she open up about business relations and about how she had burned a large number of signed notes that Hamilton had sent to James Reynolds. She said that Hamilton had promised to aid her and had urged her husband to "leave the parts, not to be seen here again . . . in which case, he would give [her] something clever." She piqued her visitors' curiosity by boasting that her husband "could tell something that would make some of the heads of departments tremble."[23] To boost her credibility, she showed them a letter she had received from Hamilton the week before.

It was an eventful day in the life of Alexander Hamilton, who knew that influential legislators had grilled James Reynolds that morning. At some time after midnight, having been freed from prison hours earlier, James Reynolds sent a young female messenger to Hamilton's house. Then he and Clingman paced outside, awaiting an answer. The girl emerged with a message that James Reynolds should call on Hamilton in the morning. Shortly after sunrise, Reynolds met Hamilton and left a vivid impression of the distraught treasury secretary, who "was extremely agitated, walking backward and forward [across] the room and striking, alternately, his forehead and thigh; observing to him that he had enemies at work, but was willing to meet them on fair ground and requested him not to stay long, lest it might be noticed."[24] Although any account from James Reynolds is suspect, the compulsive pacing and nervous gesticulations were typical of Hamilton. Once the interview was over, James Reynolds vanished from Philadelphia, fleeing either creditors or further prosecution. He had promised Monroe and Venable that he would reveal all at ten o'clock that morning, but the two Virginian legislators now discovered that he "had absconded or concealed himself."[25]

The flight of James Reynolds only heightened the suspicions of Muhlenberg, Monroe, and Venable that Hamilton was guilty of official misconduct. They were ready to present their shocking findings to Washington and had already drafted a letter to him. Before sending it, however, they thought it their duty to confront Hamilton with the allegations. On the morning of December 15, the three-man delegation filed into Hamilton's office, with Muhlenberg taking the lead. Hamilton recalled, "He introduced the subject by observing to me that they *had discovered a very improper connection* between me and a Mr. Reynolds. Extremely hurt by this mode of introduction, I arrested the progress of the discourse by giving way to very strong expressions of indignation."[26] Faced with Hamilton's wrath, the three legislators reassured him that they were not making any accusations but felt honor bound to discuss the matter with him before reporting to Washington. When they showed Hamilton his own handwritten notes to Reynolds, he instantly—and to their amazement—acknowledged their authenticity. He said that if they came to his house that evening, he would clear up the mystery by showing them written documents that would eliminate all doubt as to his innocence. Oliver Wolcott, Jr., was also invited to attend the meeting.

At home that evening, Alexander Hamilton treated the three Republican legislators to a salacious tale dramatically at odds with the scandalous one they had expected to hear. He had gathered a batch of letters from James and Maria Reynolds and recounted the history of his extramarital affair. Another man might have been brief or elliptical. Instead, as if in need of some cathartic cleansing, Hamilton briefed them in agonizing detail about how the husband had acted as a bawd for the wife; how the blackmail payments had been made; the loathing the couple had aroused in him; and his final wish to be rid of them. When the three legislators realized that the scandal involved marital infidelity, not government corruption, at least one of them "delicately urged me to discontinue it as unnecessary," Hamilton recalled. "I insisted upon going through the whole and did so."[27] They heard the impassioned, run-on letters from Maria Reynolds and the truculent demands for money from James Reynolds. It was as if Hamilton were both exonerating and flagellating himself at once.

The small delegation seemed satisfied with Hamilton's chronicle, if not a little flustered by the awkward situation. They apologized for having invaded his privacy. In retrospect, Hamilton detected subtle but perceptible differences in their reactions: "Mr. Muhlenberg and Mr. Venable, in particular, manifested a degree of sensibility on the occasion. Mr. Monroe was more cold, but entirely explicit."[28] In a memo the next day, Monroe wrote, "We left [Hamilton] under an impression our suspicions were removed. He acknowledged our conduct toward him had been fair and liberal—he could not complain of it."[29] Their accusatory letter to Washington was shelved. On the sidewalk afterward, Muhlenberg had drawn Wolcott aside and, with genuine sympathy for Hamilton, said that he wished he had not been present to watch his humiliating confession in such an intimate matter. In contrast, Monroe continued to meet with Jacob Clingman. In early January, Clingman complained to him that Hamilton had been exonerated of charges of official corruption. "He further observed to me," Monroe wrote afterward, "that he communicated the same to Mrs. Reynolds, *who appeared much shocked at it and wept immoderately.*"[30]

Muhlenberg, Monroe, and Venable had sworn they would keep the incident confidential. Given that the political world of the 1790s was one vast whispering gallery, Hamilton must have wondered if they would indeed honor their pledge. Two days later, upon reflection, he asked his three interlocutors for copies of the documents they had shown him. In allowing *them* to make the copies, Hamilton made a critical error, for Monroe entrusted the task to John Beckley, clerk of the House of Representatives. Beckley—the cunning, serviceable Jeffersonian loyalist who figured in so many intrigues against Hamilton—decided to preserve a set of papers for himself. For the rest of his life, Monroe refused to admit that he had violated his confidentiality pledge to Hamilton and provided the documents to Beckley. Thus, by December 17, 1792, Thomas Jefferson and James Madison knew about Hamilton's confrontation with the three legislators. Jefferson chose to misconstrue what had happened, interpreting the event as proof not just of Hamilton's love affair with Maria Reynolds but of his venal speculation in government securities—exactly what Hamilton had striven to refute. Beckley continued to ply Monroe and Jefferson with unsubstantiated rumors about the treasury secretary.

Equally unfortunate for Hamilton was that the man who retained the original papers was James Monroe. Later on, Monroe stated that he had "deposited the papers with a friend"—that friend being, in all likelihood, Thomas Jefferson.[31] On January 5, 1793, Monroe published his last installment of the "Vindication of Mr. Jefferson." He used the piece to telegraph a warning to Hamilton that he would not hesitate, if necessary, to exploit his knowledge of the Reynolds affair: "I shall conclude this paper by observing how much it is to be wished [that] this writer [i.e., Hamilton] would exhibit himself to the public view, that we might behold in him a living monument of that immaculate purity to which he pretends and which ought to distinguish so bold and arrogant a censor of others."[32] Hamilton knew what the snide reference to "immaculate purity" meant. For the rest of his time as treasury secretary, he was shadowed by the awareness that determined enemies had access to defamatory material about his private life. This sword of Damocles, perpetually dangling above his head, may provide one explanation of why he never made a serious bid to succeed Washington as president.

The marriage of Alexander and Eliza Hamilton survived the affair but the marriage between James and Maria Reynolds did not. In May 1793, Maria, reverting to Mary, filed for divorce in New York and hired as her lawyer, of all people, Aaron Burr. She now tagged James Reynolds as an unprincipled scoundrel and accused him of having committed adultery on July 10, 1792, with a woman named Eliza Flavinier of Dutchess County, New York. The date is intriguing, since it follows by a little more than a month Hamilton's refusal to pay more blackmail money to James Reynolds, suggesting that Maria may have outlived her usefulness to him. The same day that the divorce became official, Maria married Jacob Clingman. By representing Maria Reynolds in this case, Aaron Burr was vouchsafed a glimpse into the disorderly private affairs of Alexander Hamilton—a glimpse that might later have inflamed him when Hamilton raised questions about Burr's own misconduct.

And how did Hamilton react to the consequence of his execrable lack of judgment? We have no letters between Alexander and Eliza Hamilton that refer even obliquely to the scandal. But a close reading of Hamilton's writings offers his view of adultery in a most unlikely place: the middle of an unpublished essay, written months later, on the need for American neutrality in foreign affairs. In one passage, he reiterated his faith in marital fidelity and his knowledge that adultery damaged families and harmed the adulterer as well as the deceived spouse.

> A dispassionate and virtuous citizen of the U[nited] States will scorn to stand on any but purely *American* ground. . . . To speak figuratively, he will regard his own country as a wife to whom he is bound to be exclusively faithful and affectionate. And he will watch with a jealous attention every propensity of his heart to wander towards a foreign country, which he will regard as a mistress that may pervert his fidelity and mar his happiness. 'Tis to be regretted that there are persons among us who appear to have a passion for a foreign mistress, as violent as it is irregular—and who, in the paroxysms of their love seem, perhaps without being themselves sensible of it, too ready to sacrifice the real welfare of the political family to their partiality for the object of their tenderness.[33]

The Reynolds affair was a sad and inexcusable lapse on Hamilton's part, made only the more reprehensible by his high office, his self-proclaimed morality, his frequently missed chances to end the liaison, and the love and loyalty of his pregnant wife.

TWENTY-TWO

STABBED IN THE DARK

Even as their feud worsened, both Hamilton and Jefferson pleaded with Washington to stand for a second term as president. It may have been the sole thing that now united these sworn antagonists. Both men knew their personal warfare could wreck the still fragile union and thought Washington the one man who could hold it together. "North and South will hang together if they have you to hang on," Jefferson told the president.[1] Hamilton had additional motives for seeking a second term for Washington. The president had been his indispensable patron, the steadfast supporter of his policies, granting him preeminent status in the cabinet. (In drafting his annual address to Congress that autumn, Washington solicited suggestions from all cabinet members, then assigned the speech to Hamilton.) A second term for Washington would aid another Hamiltonian objective: to strengthen executive power. His fears of legislative tyranny had only increased as congressional opposition to him had gathered force.

Since Washington's victory seemed almost foreordained, the focus shifted to the vice presidential race. Unable to target the popular president directly, Republicans turned to the vice presidency as a referendum on Washington's first term. Hamilton never wavered in supporting John Adams as vice president, a fact obscured by their later row. (Even Abigail Adams, we have seen, cheered on Hamilton as treasury secretary.) Writing to a Federalist congressman in October 1792, Hamilton conceded that "Mr. Adams, like other men, has his faults and his foibles"—faults and foibles that Hamilton himself eventually exposed. He admitted they held some differing views. For all that, Adams was "honest, firm, faithful, and independent, a sincere lover of his country, a real friend to genuine liberty. . . . No man's private character can be fairer than his. No man has given stronger proofs than him of disinterested and intrepid patriotism."[2] Such glittering adjectives seldom flowed from Hamilton's captious quill.

By nature, Hamilton was a busybody and could not refrain from offering Adams unsolicited advice. The vice president was a Federalist more by default than conviction—he prided himself on his grumpy independence and freedom from "party virulence"—and saw no need to make common cause with Hamilton.[3] Distressed by rumors that Governor Clinton might challenge Adams for the vice presidency, Hamilton took it upon himself in June 1792 to warn Adams of "something very like a design to subvert the government."[4] Among Adams's many quirks was a penchant for extended absences from Philadelphia. By early September, Hamilton feared that Adams's prolonged sojourn at his home in Quincy, Massachusetts, might mar his reelection chances, and he sent him a tactfully worded note, urging him to return to the capital. His stay in Massachusetts "will give some handle to your enemies to misrepresent. And though I am persuaded you are very indifferent personally to the event of a certain election, yet I hope you are not so as it regards the cause of good government."[5]

Adams was far from indifferent to the election's outcome. John Ferling has noted, "There can be little doubt that Adams saw the vice-presidency as his best means by which to succeed President Washington. To further that end, he soon eschewed his powdered wig, ceremonial sword, and handsome coach."[6] Irked by Hamilton's advice, Adams did not rush back to Philadelphia. He was vain enough to tell Abigail that it was inconceivable that George Clinton, his inferior in knowledge and government service, could pose a serious political threat. Such was Adams's self-regard that he told son John Quincy during the campaign that his own life story had been one of "success almost without example."[7] But the election was to vindicate Hamilton's sense of urgency instead of Adams's complacency.

Shortly after Hamilton sent his missive to Adams, he was alerted to an even greater menace than George Clinton. Aaron Burr was letting it be noised about that he was prepared to challenge Adams as the Republican candidate for vice president. The thirty-six-year-old Burr had avid backers in the north, such as Benjamin Rush, who told him that "your friends everywhere look to you to take an active part in removing the monarchical rubbish of our government. It is time to *speak out* or we are undone."[8] For many in the south, Burr's entry into the race was an unwelcome intrusion. He lacked the depth and experience to oust someone of Adams's stature, and they had lined up regional support for Clinton. Burr's sudden trial balloon created suspicions among prospective southern allies that were to be confirmed nearly a decade later.

It was New York's other senator, Rufus King, who first informed Hamilton that Burr was rounding up key supporters in New England. King feared that Burr might shave ten votes from Adams's electoral total and that, with his delicate ego, Adams might then feel so degraded by the results that he would decline to serve. "If the enemies of the government are secret and united, we shall lose Mr. Adams," King warned Hamilton. "Nothing which has heretofore happened so decisively proves the inveteracy of the opposition."[9]

Hamilton was determined to have Washington *and* Adams back for a second term. Events of the previous year had taught him to cast a wary eye on Aaron Burr, whom Adams described as looking "fat as a duck and as ruddy as a roost cock."[10] Burr hadn't endeared himself to Hamilton by defeating Philip Schuyler for the Senate seat. And Burr was a lone operator, a protean figure who formed alliances for short-term gain. In the Senate, he was loosely allied with the Jeffersonians and was an enthusiast for the French Revolution—a stand that irked Hamilton. Then in early 1792, Burr had decided to test the waters for New York governor and challenge George Clinton's bid for a sixth term. His strategy was to enlist disaffected Clintonians and Federalists and reshuffle the political deck in New York. Afraid to adulterate his own party, Hamilton spiked this coalition and became an immovable obstacle in the path of Aaron Burr's ambitions—a position he was to occupy so frequently in future years that it finally drove Burr into a frenzy.

The New York gubernatorial contest in the spring of 1792 had been one of special venom. Once Burr saw that his attempt had miscarried, he switched back, without evident discomfort, to supporting Governor Clinton. On the other side, the Federalist ticket, likely crafted by Hamilton, consisted of Chief Justice John Jay for governor along with Stephen Van Rensselaer, Hamilton's brother-in-law, for lieutenant governor. The Federalist ticket was so identified with Hamilton that the race turned into something of a poll on his policies. The election culminated in a helpless stalemate. When votes in three upstate counties were disputed, Aaron Burr and Rufus King were asked to give opinions about the disputed ballots. Burr came down decisively on Clinton's side and handed him a controversial victory. Hamilton's friend Robert Troup was so irate that he called Burr a Clinton tool and denounced the "shameful prostitution of his talents. . . . The quibbles and chicanery made use of are characteristic of the man."[11] Such reports only reinforced Hamilton's sense of Burr as an unscrupulous opportunist eager to exploit popular turmoil.

In now opposing Burr's ambition to become vice president, Hamilton viewed him as a possible stalking horse for Governor Clinton and dispatched letters to dissuade people from backing him. Hamilton was a man of such deep, unalterable principles that Burr was bound to strike him as devoid of any moral compass. In writing to one correspondent, Hamilton even found sudden virtues in George Clinton, describing him as a "man of property" and "probity" in his private life. He couldn't say as much for Burr:

I fear the other gentleman [i.e., Burr] is unprincipled both as a public and private man. When the constitution was in deliberation . . . his conduct was equivocal. . . . In fact, I take it he is for or against nothing but as it suits his interest or ambition. He is determined, as I conceive, to make his way to be the head of the popular party and to climb . . . to the highest honors of the state and as much higher as circumstances may permit. . . . I am mistaken if it be not his object to play the game of confusion and I feel it a religious duty to oppose his career.[12]

Hamilton denounced Burr in language similar to that he employed against Jefferson, warning that "if we have an embryo-Caesar in the United States 'tis Burr."[13] But if Jefferson was a man of fanatical principles, he had principles all the same—which Hamilton could forgive. Burr's abiding sin was a total lack of principles, which Hamilton could *not* forgive.

Hamilton's anxieties about Burr proved premature. On October 16, a Republican caucus in Philadelphia bestowed unanimous approval upon George Clinton's candidacy for vice president. As a professional politician, Burr was ready to concede defeat and fight another day; he graciously stepped aside. Students of the period point to this meeting as one of the first examples of party organization in American elections, though the participants were skittish about calling themselves a party. But the group's multistate composition did reflect a new degree of political cohesion among like-minded politicians.

The ringleader was the seemingly omnipresent House clerk John Beckley. Soon after the Republican caucus, Beckley described to Madison Hamilton's growing influence in electoral politics. In the vice presidential race, Beckley said, the treasury secretary's efforts both "direct and indirect are unceasing and extraordinary. . . . [T]here is no inferior degree of sagacity in the combinations of this *extraordinary* man. With a comprehensive eye, a subtle and contriving mind, and a soul devoted to his object, all his measures are promptly and aptly designed and, like the links of a chain, depend on each other [and] acquire additional strength by their union."[14] Beckley retained an unwavering belief in Hamilton's wickedness and suggested to Madison that he had explosive new proof that might bring down the treasury secretary: "I think I have a clue to something far beyond mere suspicion on this ground, which prudence forbids a *present* disclosure of."[15] Beckley's letter hints at early knowledge of the Reynolds affair.

As always, Hamilton braced for attacks on his integrity and was prepared to squelch any slander. Early in the fall, he was advised that during a Maryland congressional campaign incumbent John F. Mercer had impugned his conduct in office. The son of a wealthy Virginia planter, Mercer had been a former aide-de-camp to General Charles Lee, the conceited general who had been court-martialed after the battle of Monmouth. A foe of strong central government, Mercer had been a voluble member of the Constitutional Convention (Jefferson described him as "afflicted with the morbid rage of debate") and had left Philadelphia without signing the document.[16]

In his campaign oratory, Mercer renewed every hoary charge ever leveled at Hamilton: Hamilton was the tool of the propertied class; had bought back government debt at inflated prices to enrich speculators; had dictated legislation to Congress; had rewarded William Duer with a lucrative contract to supply the Western Army; and had introduced the detestable excise tax on liquor. Mercer also revived a 1790 incident in which he had met Hamilton at the door of the Treasury building and asked to be reimbursed for horses shot from under him during the Revolution. Hamilton had replied facetiously that if Mercer voted for his assumption bill, he would pay for the horses from his own pocket. Mercer presented this passing jest as proof of Hamilton's corruption. Finally, he ridiculed Hamilton as an upstart, "a mushroom excrescence," who did not deserve the prominence he had gained.[17]

When it came to aspersions against his honor, Hamilton always had a hair-trigger temper. In language signaling a possible duel, Hamilton wrote testily to Mercer and asked him to disavow the charge that he had bought back government debt at inflated rates to help speculators. Mercer partially retracted his words and admitted that Hamilton had never bought government bonds for personal gain. On the other hand, he insisted that Hamilton *had* exerted his influence to attach "to your administration a monied interest as an engine of government."[18] Unable to let the matter drop, Hamilton knocked on Mercer's door in Philadelphia that December and demanded a further retraction. Hamilton got enough satisfaction—"I spoke nothing that could tend, in my opinion, to wound your honesty or integrity," Mercer conceded—that a possible duel was averted.[19] Hamilton may have opposed duels on principle, as he later claimed, but for such a hotheaded man these affairs of honor were expedient weapons in silencing his enemies. Whenever he was maligned, Hamilton aggressively sought retractions, persisting to the bitter end.

On December 5, 1792, members of the electoral college assembled in their respective states. The outcome gratified Hamilton and corresponded with his expectations. Washington was chosen unanimously as president. Adams received seventy-seven votes, enough to return him as vice president, while George Clinton gained a respectable fifty votes. In his "Anas"—always to be taken with a pound of salt—Jefferson reported that Senator John Langdon had commented to Adams on the closeness of his vote. According to Langdon, Adams gritted his teeth and exclaimed, "Damn 'em, damn 'em, damn 'em. You see that an elective government will not do."[20]

On the surface, the election seemed an impressive show of national unity, when it was just a passing truce in an ongoing war. For the last time, George Washington's prestige papered over growing differences between Hamiltonians and Jeffersonians. Three days after the electoral college met, James Monroe resumed his newspaper defense of Jefferson and slammed Hamilton as someone "suspected, with too much reason, to be attached to monarchy."[21] Far more noteworthy than such hackneyed tirades against Hamilton, however, were the first shots fired at Washington. No longer a sacred figure, immune to criticism, he was spattered with mud by Philip Freneau, who accused him of aping royalty in his presidential etiquette: "A certain *monarchical prettiness* must be highly extolled, such as *levees, drawing rooms, stately nods instead of shaking hands,* titles of office, seclusion from the people."[22] Given Washington's reluctance to serve a second term, this was an especially undeserved cut, and Adams lamented the "sour, angry, peevish, fretful, lying paragraphs" with which the press battered the government.[23]

Clearly, the political tone in Washington's second term was going to be even harsher than in the first. Right before Christmas, Hamilton wrote a despairing letter to John Jay. He was worn down by the interminable attacks against him and slander he felt powerless to stop. He told Jay that he was oppressed by the weight of official business and the need to track legislative maneuvers against him, but that his "burden and perplexity" had still more sinister origins: "'Tis the malicious intrigues to stab me in the dark, against which I am too often obliged to guard myself, that distract and harass me to a point which, rendering my situation scarcely tolerable, interferes with objects to which friendship and inclination would prompt me."[24] Hamilton wrote this cheerless assessment three days after meeting with Muhlenberg, Venable, and Monroe. He must have known the Maria Reynolds affair would have repercussions for many years to come.

As Washington's first term ended in early 1793, the president remained distraught over his bickering cabinet. He continued to admonish his headstrong secretaries of treasury and state that they should try to get along for the national good. Jefferson assured the president that he would strive for unity and that he had "kept myself aloof from all cabal and correspondence on the subject of the government."[25] In the next breath, however, he renewed his corrosive attacks on Hamilton. Washington's vaunted patience was giving way to petulant flashes of temper, and, according to Jefferson, he "expressed the extreme wretchedness of his existence while in office and went lengthily into the late attacks on him for levees."[26] This was an implicit rebuke of Jefferson, for it was Freneau who had accused Washington of holding royal "levees" or receptions.

Even as Jefferson mouthed sedative pledges of peace, he and Madison were secretly orchestrating the first concerted effort in American history to expel a cabinet member for official misconduct. They had come to regard Hamilton as a grave threat to republican government, a monarchist bent on destroying the republic— all without any proof. The *National Gazette* put it that Hamilton "fancies himself the great pivot upon which the whole machine of government turns, throwing out of view . . . the president, the legislature, and the Constitution itself."[27] Jefferson and Madison abandoned any residual restraint as they prepared to launch an all-out inquisition.

To disguise their efforts, they employed as their surrogate a fiery Virginia congressman, William Branch Giles, who later courted one of Jefferson's daughters. As early as the spring of 1792, Hamilton had suspected intrigue within the Virginia delegation and identified Madison as "the prompter of Mr. Giles and others, who were the open instruments of opposition."[28] The husky, often unkempt Giles was a Princeton graduate and noted Virginia lawyer. He shared his state's endemic hatred of banks and modern finance and thought a "northern faction" was out to destroy the union. As a frequent mouthpiece for Jefferson, he employed his pugnacious style for states' rights and did not spare anyone in the Federalist opposition. He even accused Washington of showing "a princely ignorance of the country," evidenced by the fact that "the wants and wishes of one part had been sacrificed to the interest of the other."[29]

Giles tried to discredit Hamilton over his use of money that the government had borrowed in Europe. This charge originated in a memo that Jefferson had prepared surreptitiously for Madison. Hamilton had wanted to use foreign loans to repay a government loan from the Bank of the United States—two million dollars that the bank had extended to the federal government to purchase stock in the bank itself. Partial as ever to the French Revolution, the Jeffersonians feared that this money would be diverted from American debt payments to France. In the past, Hamilton had applied foreign loans to the repayment of domestic debt—a technical violation of the law but one, he claimed, that had been approved verbally by Washington. The suspicion prevailed among critics, however, that he wanted to transfer borrowed funds from Europe to the national bank to aid speculators. And a small circle of opponents, including Jefferson and Madison, now also knew about the denouement of the Maria Reynolds affair, with its accusations of official wrongdoing by Hamilton. Twice in late December 1792, the House demanded from Hamilton a strict accounting of foreign loans. Distracted by the Reynolds probe, he still managed to crank out a detailed report by January 3. The beleaguered Hamilton felt the weight of unseen forces marshaled against him and feared he was now the target of a highly organized attempt to destroy his reputation.

Planning to exhaust Hamilton, Giles submitted five resolutions in the House on

January 23, calling for still more extensive information on foreign loans. By design, these resolutions made massive, nay overwhelming, demands on Hamilton. He had to furnish a complete reckoning of balances between the government and the central bank, as well as a comprehensive list of sinking-fund purchases of government debt. Some historians, including Giles's biographer, believe that Jefferson instigated these resolutions, with Madison drafting their language. Taking advantage of a short, four-month congressional session, the House gave Hamilton an impossible March 3 deadline. Republicans hoped that Hamilton's failure to comply would then be construed as prima facie evidence of his guilt; Federalists were equally convinced that he would prove to be incorruptible.

Hamilton's critics seriously underrated his superhuman stamina. He enjoyed beating his enemies at their own game, and the resolutions roused his fighting spirit. By February 19, in a staggering display of diligence, he delivered to the House several copious reports, garlanded with tables, lists, and statistics that gave a comprehensive overview of his work as treasury secretary. In the finale of one twenty-thousand-word report, Hamilton intimated that he had risked a physical breakdown to complete this heroic labor: "It is certain that I have made every exertion in my power, at the hazard of my health, to comply with the requisitions of the House as early as possible."[30] Hamilton's reports did not sway his opponents, who wanted to expose him, not engage him in debate. Every proof of his prodigious gifts made him seem only the more threatening.

Defying Washington's appeal for a truce with Hamilton, Jefferson intensified the combat at close quarters. On February 25, he proposed to Washington an official inquiry into Hamilton and the Treasury Department—a demand Washington spurned bluntly. Hamilton thought Jefferson should leave the cabinet and openly head the opposition, rather than subvert the administration from within. In response, Thomas Jefferson did something extraordinary: he drew up a series of resolutions censuring Hamilton and quietly slipped them to William Branch Giles. Jefferson now functioned as de facto leader of the Republican party. The great irony was that the man who repeatedly accused Hamilton of meddling with Congress and violating the separation of powers was now secretly scrawling congressional resolutions directed against a member of his own administration.

When Giles filed nine censure resolutions against Hamilton in late February, he did not disclose that they were based on Jefferson's rough draft. (The telltale document did not even surface until 1895.) Giles introduced his charges with what one spectator described as "a most pointed attack" on Hamilton.[31] The resolutions accused Hamilton of "indecorum" in dealing with Congress and of improperly mixing foreign and domestic loans. Giles omitted two of the more outlandish resolutions drawn up by Jefferson: a claim that Hamilton had attempted to benefit speculators and a demand that the treasurer's office be hived off from the rest of the Treasury Department. One Jefferson resolution exposed the true intent behind his vendetta: "*Resolved,* That the Secretary of the Treasury has been guilty of maladministration in the duties of his office and should, in the opinion of Congress, be removed from his office by the President of the United States."[32] By submitting these resolutions on the eve of the congressional recess, Giles intended to deprive Hamilton of adequate time to rebut the charges. Despite Madison's support, the House roundly voted down these resolutions. Jefferson anticipated this defeat but knew that the unsubstantiated accusations would float tantalizingly in the air. As he observed, the resolutions would enable people to "see from this the extent of their danger."[33]

The upshot of the abortive Republican campaign was an almost total vindication of Hamilton. All nine of the Virginian's resolutions were defeated on March 1. At worst, Hamilton was found guilty of excessive discretion in shifting money among accounts to insure that the government did not miss interest payments. He also was not always meticulous in matching specific loans to the laws authorizing them, but nobody ever proved that Alexander Hamilton had diverted a penny of public money for personal profit.

Federalists rejoiced that the Republican vendetta had backfired, and one Boston Federalist exclaimed, "The conquest to the cause of government and the reputation of Hamilton must be as glorious as it was unexpected."[34] Hamilton, however, foresaw further attacks. "There is no doubt in my mind," he told Rufus King, "that the next session will revive the attack with more system and earnestness."[35] By this point, harassment was exacting a terrible physical and mental toll on the exhausted Hamilton. Sometimes, he vented his rage in essays that he let molder in his drawer. In one unpublished essay, he railed against the Jeffersonians as "wily hypocrites" and "crafty and abandoned imposters."[36] He now viewed "hypocrisy and treachery" as "the most successful commodities in the political market. It seems to be the destined lot of nations to mistake their foes for their friends, their flatterers for their faithful servants."[37] He believed that he had made a huge but thankless sacrifice for his country.

Hamilton was correct that Jefferson and his cohorts had no intention of desisting from their attacks. He now discovered that Muhlenberg, Venable, or Monroe— or perhaps all three—had breached the vow of confidentiality in the Reynolds affair. In early May 1793, Hamilton's old friend from revolutionary days, Henry Lee, wrote from Virginia: "Was I with you, I would talk an hour with doors bolted and windows shut, as my heart is much afflicted by some whispers which I have heard."[38]

The vindication of Hamilton by Congress only strengthened the faith of the Jeffersonians that legislators could never exercise independent judgment when it came to him. Jefferson now asked John Beckley to provide him with a "list of paper-men"—

that is, congressmen who held bank stock or government bonds. The supposed conflicts of interest of these legislators gave Jefferson the all-purpose explanation he needed to account for Hamilton's acquittal. Madison, too, ascribed the defeated resolutions to corrupt congressmen who had profited from Hamilton's fiscal measures. At this stage, it grew more and more evident to Jefferson that he would have to perpetuate the struggle against the treasury secretary not from inside the government but from the safe haven of Monticello.

In the wake of their setback, Republicans seeking more damaging information about Hamilton latched on to a disgruntled former Treasury Department clerk named Andrew Fraunces. At first glance, he seemed like a magnificent find, an angry man with inside knowledge of Hamilton's official duties. He had labored at the Treasury Department from its formation in 1789 until he was fired in March 1793. After moving to New York City, Fraunces was short of money and longed to retaliate against Hamilton. In May 1793, he presented to the Treasury two warrants for redemption that dated back to the early confederation period. In the first days of the new government, Treasury officials had routinely honored these claims, but they later declined automatic payment as they discovered how slipshod had been the paperwork of their predecessors. As a onetime Treasury employee, Fraunces knew this history. Nonetheless, when his claims were denied, he protested that he was being penalized by the treasury secretary, and he pestered both Hamilton and Washington for payment.

In early June, Fraunces not only returned to Philadelphia but accosted Hamilton, who told him to renew his claim in writing. The stymied Fraunces now drifted into the twilight world of restless Hamilton haters. Pretty soon, he was meeting in New York with Jacob Clingman, the new husband of Maria Reynolds. He told Clingman, in boastful words reminiscent of those employed by James Reynolds six months earlier, that "he could, if he pleased, hang Hamilton."[39] Clingman was still trying to prove the preposterous notion that Hamilton had conspired with William Duer to rig the market in government securities, and Fraunces pretended that he had information linking Hamilton directly with Duer's ill-fated speculations.

Reports of talks between Clingman and Fraunces were relayed to John Beckley, who passed along this folderol to Jefferson. Beckley was prepared to believe any hearsay that defamed Hamilton, even the ludicrous notion that Hamilton had offered Fraunces two thousand dollars for papers showing his supposed financial ties to Duer. Fraunces went so far as to claim that he knew the couriers who had carried payments between the two men. Beckley was also intrigued by Clingman's assertion that Maria Reynolds was now prepared to tell everything she knew about her former husband's relations with Hamilton—as if the loose-tongued Maria had ever muzzled herself before.

Although Jacob Clingman knew that Andrew Fraunces was an unsavory character, this did not dent his belief in the man's story. Beckley recorded of Clingman's reaction: "He considers Fraunces as a man of no principle, yet he is sure that he is privy to the whole connection with Duer. . . . He tells me, too, that Fraunces is fond of drink and very avaricious and that a judicious appeal to either of those passions would induce him to deliver up Hamilton's and Duer's letters and tell all he knows."[40] Beckley was so famished for scandal about Hamilton that he traveled to New York and met with Fraunces "to unravel this scene of iniquity."[41] When Beckley tried to elicit documentation from Fraunces that would substantiate his wild allegations against Hamilton, the effort, as always, proved futile.

All of this raw gossip flowed straight to the secretary of state, who faithfully recorded every scrap in his diary, even though he had just received extreme proof of Beckley's bias. In his "Anas" for June 7, 1793, Jefferson noted Beckley's crackpot story that the British had offered Hamilton asylum if his plans for an American monarchy miscarried. About this fairy tale—allegedly gleaned from Britain's consul general in New York—Jefferson commented in the margin: "Impossible as to Hamilton. He was far above that." Jefferson then made this further observation on his chief source of political intelligence: "Beckley is a man of perfect truth as to what he affirms of his own knowledge, but too credulous as to what he hears from others."[42] Nonetheless, Jefferson added to his swelling dossier on Hamilton the farrago of stories that Beckley had taken down from Clingman and Fraunces.

By early July, Hamilton knew that enemies were tracking his movements and trying to extract information from Andrew Fraunces. He also knew that this spying operation was supervised by Jefferson's protégé Beckley. In early July, Hamilton took a potentially hazardous step by inviting Jacob Clingman to his office. We know roughly what Hamilton said because the dialogue was transmitted to Beckley. Like an attorney subtly probing a witness, Hamilton tried to draw Clingman out, asking if he knew Andrew Fraunces, had boarded at his house, had dined at his table, or had visited his office. Clingman admitted to one dinner and one office visit with Fraunces. Hamilton then told Clingman to discount what Fraunces said, "as he spoke much at random and drank."[43] Showing the accuracy of his suspicions, Hamilton then asked Clingman, point-blank, if he ever visited John Beckley. Clingman said he had run into Beckley at the home of Frederick Muhlenberg, his former boss. This information could only have validated Hamilton's worst fears.

Perhaps aware that Hamilton had been blackmailed with some success before, Fraunces wrote to him in early August and threatened to expose everything to "the people" if he did not get paid for his two warrants. Within hours, Hamilton sent back a furious reply. He was not about to repeat the mistake he made with James Reynolds: "Do you imagine that any menaces of appeal to the people can induce me to depart from what I conceive to be my public duty! . . . I set you and all your accomplices at defiance."[44] The next day, Hamilton did something out of character: he wrote a toned-down letter to Fraunces, apologized for his rash initial response, and merely protested the notion that he had failed to pay for the warrants because of "some sinister motives."[45] The change of tone apparently came about because Washington had received another letter from Fraunces and had asked Hamilton to comment on the case. This must have reminded Hamilton that he was dealing with official business, not just private threats. Hamilton explained the affair to Washington's satisfaction. At the same time, he sent a pointed letter to Fraunces's lawyer, warning of legal consequences if any fabricated documents were used against him.

Undeterred, in late August Fraunces published a pamphlet of his correspondence with Hamilton and Washington. On October 11, an irate Hamilton placed a notice in two New York newspapers, informing the public that he had repeatedly asked Fraunces for proof of his charges and that Fraunces had evaded the request. Hamilton called his former employee "contemptible" and a "despicable calumniator."[46] The next day, an unrepentant Fraunces retorted in a rival paper that "if I am a *despicable calumniator,* I have been, unfortunately, for a long time past a pupil of Mr. Hamilton's."[47] Fraunces kept up his diatribes, and Robert Troup and Rufus King gathered affidavits from prominent people attesting to Hamilton's innocence. It was testimony to the vile partisanship of the period that a disgruntled former government clerk, tainted by a well-known history of drinking, could sustain such a public assault upon Hamilton's character. It also testified to Hamilton's exaggerated need to free his name from the slightest stain that he felt obliged to trade public insults with such an obscure figure.

The Fraunces controversy ended when the former clerk appealed for justice to Congress, citing Hamilton's supposed mishandling of his warrants. The charges, as Hamilton knew, lacked merit. On February 19, 1794, Congress passed two resolutions rejecting Fraunces's claims and commending Hamilton's honorable handling of the matter.

TWENTY-THREE

CITIZEN GENÊT

On March 4, 1793, George Washington was sworn in for his second term as president. Unlike his talkative treasury secretary, the president believed in brevity and delivered a pithy inaugural address of two paragraphs. As he spoke in the Senate chamber, tension crackled below the surface of American politics that contrasted with the rapturous mood of the first inauguration. Fisher Ames, always a shrewd observer of the scene, mused that "a spirit of faction . . . must soon come to a crisis." He foresaw that congressional Republicans would discard their comparatively decorous criticism of Washington's first term: "They thirst for vengeance. The Secretary of the Treasury is one whom they would immolate. . . . The President is not to be spared. His popularity is a fund of strength to that cause which they would destroy. He is therefore rudely and incessantly attacked."[1]

Washington's second term revolved around inflammatory foreign-policy issues. The French Revolution forced Americans to ponder the meaning of their own revolution, and followers of Hamilton and Jefferson drew diametrically opposite conclusions. The continuing turmoil in Paris added to the caution of Hamiltonians, who were trying to tamp down radical fires at home. Those same upheavals encouraged Jeffersonians to stoke the fires anew. Americans increasingly defined their domestic politics by either their solidarity with the French Revolution or their aversion to its incendiary methods. The French Revolution thus served to both consolidate the two parties in American politics and deepen the ideological gulf between them.

Most Americans had applauded the French Revolution as a worthy successor to their own, a fraternal link renewed in August 1792 when the National Assembly in Paris bestowed honorary citizenship upon "Georges Washington," "N. Madison," and "Jean Hamilton."[2] When Hamilton received a letter from the French interior minister confirming this, he scribbled scornfully on the back: "Letter from government of French Republic, transmitting me a diploma of citizenship, mistaking the Christian name. . . . Curious example of French finesse."[3] But events in Paris had taken a bloody turn that horrified American representatives there. During the summer of 1792, William Short—Jefferson's former private secretary in Paris, now stationed in The Hague—wrote to Jefferson of "those mad and corrupted people in France who under the name of liberty have destroyed their own government." The Parisian streets, he warned, "literally are red with blood."[4] Short described to Hamilton mobs breaking into the royal palace and jailing King Louis XVI. In late August, a guillotine was erected near the Tuileries as Robespierre and Marat launched a wholesale roundup of priests, royalists, editors, judges, tramps, prostitutes—anyone deemed an enemy of the state. When 1,400 political prisoners were slaughtered in the so-called September Massacres, an intoxicated Robespierre pronounced it "the most beautiful revolution that has ever honored humanity."[5] "Let the blood of traitors flow," agreed Marat. "That is the only way to save the country."[6]

For a long time, Jeffersonians had dismissed these reports of atrocities as rank propaganda. Moved by the soul-stirring rhetoric of the French Revolution, they affected the title of "Jacobin" and saluted one another as "citizen" or "citizeness," in solidarity with their French comrades. After France declared itself a republic on September 20, 1792, American sympathizers feted the news with toasts, cannonades, and jubilation. When Jefferson replied to William Short's letter, he noted that the French Revolution had heartened American republicans and undercut Hamiltonian "monocrats." He regretted the lives lost in Paris, he said, then offered this chilling apologia: "The liberty of the whole earth was depending on the issue of the contest. . . . [R]ather than it should have failed, I would have seen half the earth desolated."[7] For Jefferson, it was not just French or American freedom at stake but that of the entire Western world. To his mind, such a universal goal excused the bloodthirsty means.

On January 21, 1793, more grisly events forced a reappraisal of the notion that the French Revolution was a romantic Gallic variant of the American Revolution. Louis XVI—who had aided the American Revolution and whose birthday had long been celebrated by American patriots—was guillotined for plotting against the Revolution. The death of Louis Capet—he had lost his royal title—was drenched in gore: schoolboys cheered, threw their hats aloft, and licked the king's blood, while one executioner did a thriving business selling snippets of royal hair and clothing. The king's decapitated head was wedged between his lifeless legs, then stowed in a basket. The remains were buried in an unvarnished box. England reeled from the news, William Pitt the Younger branding it "the foulest and most atrocious act the world has ever seen."[8] On February 1, France declared war against England, Holland, and Spain, and soon the whole continent was engulfed in fighting, ushering in more than twenty years of combat.

News of the royal beheading reached America in late March 1793, at an inopportune time for the Jeffersonians, who had stressed France's moral superiority over Britain. Would they condemn or rationalize the action? The answer became clear when Freneau's *National Gazette* published an article entitled "Louis Capet has lost his caput." The author qualified his levity in celebrating the king's death: "From my use of a pun, it may seem that I think lightly of his fate. I certainly do. It affects me no more than the execution of another malefactor."[9] The author said that the king's murder represented "a great act of justice," and anyone shocked by such wanton violence betrayed "a strong remaining attachment to royalty" and belonged to "a monarchical junto."[10] In other words, they were Hamiltonians. Once upon a time, Thomas Jefferson had lauded Louis XVI as "a good man," "an honest man."[11] Now, he asserted that monarchs should be "amenable to punishment like other criminals."[12]

Madison admitted to some qualms about "the follies and barbarities" in Paris but was generally no less militant than Jefferson in admiring the French Revolution, describing it as "wonderful in its progress and . . . stupendous in its consequences"; he denigrated its enemies as "enemies of human nature."[13] Madison agreed with Jefferson that if their French comrades failed it would doom American republicanism. Madison was not fazed by Louis XVI's murder. If the king "was a traitor," he said, "he ought to be punished as well as another man."[14] Like Jefferson, Madison filtered out upsetting facts about France and mocked as "spurious" newspaper accounts that talked about the king's innocence "and the bloodthirstiness of his enemies."[15]

One mordant irony of this obstinate blindness was that while Republicans rejoiced in the French Revolution and cited the sacred debt owed to French officers who had fought in the American Revolution, those same officers were being victimized by revolutionary violence. Gouverneur Morris, now U.S. minister to France, informed Hamilton after the king's execution, "It has so happened that a very great proportion of the French officers who served in America have been either opposed to the Revolution at an early day or felt themselves obliged at a later period to abandon it. Some of them are now in a state of banishment and their property confiscated."[16] With the monarchy's fall, the marquis de Lafayette was denounced as a traitor. He fled to Belgium, only to be captured by the Austrians and shunted among various prisons for five years. Tossed into solitary confinement, he eventually emerged wan and emaciated, a mostly hairless cadaver. Lafayette's family suffered grievously during the Terror. His wife's sister, mother, and grandmother were all executed and dumped in a common grave. Other heroes of the American Revolution succumbed to revolutionary madness: the comte de Rochambeau was locked up in the Conciergerie, while Admiral d'Estaing was executed.

If Republicans turned a blind eye to these events, the pro-British bias of the Federalists perhaps sharpened their vision. As early as March 1792, Jefferson groused in his "Anas" about Washington's "want of confidence in the event of the French revolution. . . . I remember when I received the news of the king's flight and capture, I first told him of it at his assembly. I never saw him so much dejected by any event in my life."[17] Washington was indeed sickened by the bloodshed in France, and this widened the breach between him and Jefferson. John Adams was quite prescient about events in France and regretted that many Americans were "so blind, undistinguishing, and enthusiastic of everything that has been done by that light, airy, and transported people."[18] He warned that "Danton, Robespierre, Marat, etc. are furies. Dragons' teeth have been sown in France and will come up as monsters."[19]

No American was to expend more prophetic verbiage in denouncing the French Revolution than Alexander Hamilton. The suspension of the monarchy and the September Massacres, Hamilton later told Lafayette, had "cured me of my goodwill for the French Revolution."[20] Hamilton refused to condone the carnage in Paris or separate means from ends. He did not think a revolution should cast off the past overnight or repudiate law, order, and tradition. "A struggle for liberty is in itself respectable and glorious," he opined. "When conducted with magnanimity, justice, and humanity, it ought to command the admiration of every friend to human nature. But if sullied by crimes and extravagancies, it loses its respectability."[21] The American Revolution had succeeded because it was "a *free, regular* and *deliberate* act of the nation" and had been conducted with "a spirit of justice and humanity."[22] It was, in fact, a revolution written in parchment and defined by documents, petitions, and other forms of law.

What threw Hamilton into despair was not just the betrayal of revolutionary hopes in France but the way its American apologists ended up justifying a "state of things the most cruel, sanguinary, and violent that ever stained the annals of mankind."[23] For Hamilton, the utopian revolutionaries in France had emphasized liberty to the exclusion of order, morality, religion, and property rights. They had singled out for persecution bankers and businessmen—people Hamilton regarded as agents of progressive change. He saw the chaos in France as a frightening portent of what could happen in America if the safeguards of order were stripped away by the love of liberty. His greatest nightmare was being enacted across the Atlantic—a hopeful revolution giving way to indiscriminate terror and authoritarian rule. His conclusion was categorical: "If there be anything solid in virtue, the time must come when it will have been a disgrace to have advocated the revolution of France in its late stages."[24]

Reports that France had declared war against England and other royal powers did not reach American shores until early April, when Hamilton informed Washington, then at Mount Vernon, "there seems to be no room for doubt of the existence of war."[25] Washington rushed back to Philadelphia to formulate policy. He inclined instantly toward neutrality and blanched at rumors that American ships were getting ready to wage war as pro-French privateers. Before Washington's arrival, Hamilton mulled over a neutrality proclamation and consulted with John Jay, not Thomas Jefferson, who was slowly being shunted aside in foreign policy. The day after his return on April 17, Washington asked his advisers to ponder thirteen questions for a meeting at his residence the next morning. The first question was the overriding one: Should the United States issue a proclamation of neutrality? The next twelve questions related to France, among them: Should America receive an ambassador from France? Should earlier treaties apply? Was France waging an offensive or defensive war? In these queries, with their implicit skepticism of France, Jefferson saw the handiwork of Hamilton, even though Washington had taken pains to write out the questions himself.

With his usual fierce certitude, Hamilton believed that neutrality was the only proper course and had already lectured Washington on the need for "a continuance of the peace, the desire of which may be said to be both universal and ardent."[26] This had less to do with scruples about war than with a conviction, shared by Washington, that the young country needed a period of prosperity and stability before it was capable of combat. The United States did not even possess a regular navy. At such a moment, Hamilton said, war would be "the most unequal and calamitous in which it is possible for a country to be engaged—a war which would not be unlikely to prove pregnant with greater dangers and disasters than that by which we established our existence as an independent nation."[27] Though Jefferson sympathized with France and Hamilton with Great Britain, they agreed that neutrality was the only sensible policy. The two secretaries differed on the form this should assume, however, and three days of spirited debate ensued.

At a dramatic session on April 19, Washington listened as Jefferson, eager to extract concessions from England, opposed an immediate declaration of neutrality, or perhaps any declaration at all. Why not stall and make countries bid for American neutrality? Aghast, Hamilton said that American neutrality was not negotiable. Drawing on his formidable powers of persuasion, he pummeled his listeners with authorities on international law: Grotius, Vattel, and Pufendorf. Hamilton carried the day, and the cabinet decided to issue a declaration "forbidding our citizens to take part in any hostilities on the seas with or against any of the belligerent powers."[28] Jefferson was horrified at suspending the 1778 treaties with France, sealed during the Revolution. But Hamilton argued that France had aided the American Revolution not from humanitarian motives but only to weaken England. He also argued that the French, having toppled Louis XVI, had traded one government for another, rendering their former treaties null and void. Predictably, he opposed a friendly reception for the French minister recently arrived in America, lest it commit the United States to the French cause. Nonetheless, Jefferson triumphed on the issue of accepting the new French minister without qualifications, as Washington demonstrated anew that he was not a puppet in Hamilton's hands.

On April 22, after days of heated rhetoric from Hamilton and Jefferson, Washington promulgated his Proclamation of Neutrality. Hamilton was the undisputed victor on the main point of issuing a formal, speedy executive declaration, but Jefferson won some key emphases. In particular, Jefferson had worried that the word *neutrality* would signal a flat rejection of France, so the document spoke instead of the need for U.S. citizens to be "friendly and impartial" toward the warring powers.[29] The proclamation set a vital precedent for a proudly independent America, giving it an ideological shield against European entanglements. Of this declaration, Henry Cabot Lodge later wrote, "There is no stronger example of the influence of the Federalists under the leadership of Washington upon the history of the country than this famous proclamation, and in no respect did the personality of Hamilton impress itself more directly on the future of the United States."[30] With the Neutrality Proclamation, Hamilton continued to define his views on American foreign policy: that it should be based on self-interest, not emotional attachment; that the supposed altruism of nations often masked baser motives; that individuals sometimes acted benevolently, but nations seldom did. This austere, hardheaded view of human affairs likely dated to Hamilton's earliest observations of the European powers in the West Indies.

The Neutrality Proclamation provoked another contretemps between Jefferson and Hamilton. The secretary of state opposed the form of this milestone in American foreign policy and expressed his indignation to Monroe: "Hamilton is panic-struck if we refuse our breech to every kick which Great Britain may choose to give it."[31] Madison, too, was enraged by the "anglified complexion" of administration policy and dismissed the proclamation as a "most unfortunate error." The executive branch, he thought, was usurping national-security powers that properly belonged to the legislature. Didn't Congress alone have the power to declare war and neutrality? He deplored Hamilton's effort to "shuffle off" the treaty with France as a trick "equally contemptible for the meanness and folly of it."[32] Madison favored Ameri-

can support for France and bemoaned that Washington had succumbed to "the unpopular cause of Anglomany." He still viewed the French Revolution as an inspirational fight for freedom and asked indignantly why George Washington "should
have anything to apprehend from the success of liberty in another country."[33]

On April 8, 1793, the new French minister to the United States sailed into
Charleston, South Carolina, aboard the frigate *Embuscade* and enjoyed a tumultuous reception from a giant throng. His name was Edmond Charles Genêt, but he
would be known to history, in the fraternal style popularized by the French Revolution, as Citizen Genêt. Short and ruddy, the thirty-year-old diplomat had flaming
red hair, a sloping forehead, and an aquiline nose. Gouverneur Morris sniffed that
he had "the manner and look of an upstart."[34] Though he often acted like a political amateur, he had an excellent résumé. Fluent in Greek at age six, the translator of
Swedish histories by twelve, he spoke seven languages, was an accomplished musi-
cian, and had already seen diplomatic service in London and St. Petersburg. He was
so closely associated with the moderate Girondists that, before the king's head was
severed, there had been speculation that Citizen Genêt might accompany the royal
family to America.

In social situations, the bustling young emissary could be charming and engaging, but he did not behave with the subtlety and prudence expected of a diplomat.
Indeed, if Hamilton had decided to invent a minister to dramatize his fears of the
French Revolution, he could have conjured up no one better than the vain, extravagant, and bombastic Genêt. The Frenchman was to swagger and bluster and wade
blindly into the warfare between Hamilton and Jefferson.

Citizen Genêt landed with a lengthy agenda. He wanted the United States to extend more funds to France and supply foodstuffs and other army provisions. Much
more controversially, he wanted to strike blows against Spanish and British possessions in North America and was ready to hire secret agents for that purpose. Jefferson became his clandestine accomplice when he furnished Genêt with a letter
introducing a French botanist named André Michaux to the governor of Kentucky.
Michaux planned to arm Kentuckians and stir up frontier settlements in Spanish
Louisiana. Jefferson's aid violated the policy of neutrality and made Hamilton's
unauthorized talks with George Beckwith seem like tame indiscretions in comparison.

What most roused Washington's and Hamilton's ire was that Genêt's satchel
bulged with some blank "letters of marque." These documents were to be distributed to private vessels, converting them into privateers. The marauding vessels
could then capture unarmed British merchant ships as "prizes," providing money
for the captors and military benefits for France. Genêt wanted to recruit American

and French seamen. Once settled in South Carolina, he chartered privateers to prey on British shipping from American ports and also assembled a sixteen-hundred-man army to invade St. Augustine, Florida. In Philadelphia, Hamilton condemned this mischief as "the height of arrogance" and divined its true intent: "Genêt came to this country with the affectation of not desiring to embark us in the war and yet he did all in his power by indirect means to drag us into it."[35] Hamilton was convinced that, far from acting alone, Genêt was executing official policy. His suspicions were to be vindicated.

Ten days after his arrival, Citizen Genêt began a prolonged journey north to Philadelphia to present his credentials to Washington. Acting more like a political candidate than a foreign diplomat, he was cheered at banquets, and his six-week tour acquired major political overtones. In many cities, Genêt's presence spawned "Republican" or "Democratic" societies whose members greeted and embraced each other as "citizens." These groups feared that once the European powers had overthrown the French Revolution, they would crush its American counterpart. Jittery Federalists worried that the new societies would mimic the radical Jacobin "clubs" that had provoked mayhem in Paris. As these groups forged links with one another, Hamilton thought they might replicate the methods of the Sons of Liberty chapters that helped spark the American Revolution. As a precaution, he advised his customs collectors to inform him of any merchant ships in their ports being pierced with loopholes for guns—a sign they were being converted into privateers.

With each day of his northward journey, the uproar over Genêt's activities mounted, and Federalist resentment vied with Republican adulation. While Genêt traveled, the *Embuscade* pounced upon the British ship *Grange* in American waters and hauled this prize to Philadelphia. George Hammond, the British minister, protested hotly to Thomas Jefferson, noting that such actions mocked Washington's Neutrality Proclamation. The secretary of state privately applauded these violations of U.S. law. When the *Grange* arrived in Philadelphia, Jefferson could not contain his joy. "Upon her coming into sight, thousands and thousands . . . crowded and covered the wharves," he told James Monroe. "Never before was such a crowd seen there and when the British colours were seen *reversed* and the French flag flying above them, they burst into peals of exultation."[36] Enchanted by Genêt, Jefferson informed Madison that he had "offered everything and asks nothing. . . . It is impossible for anything to be more affectionate, more magnanimous than the purport of his mission."[37]

This was all preamble to Citizen Genêt's triumphant landing at Philadelphia on May 16, 1793, when he was welcomed by Governor Thomas Mifflin amid repeated volleys of artillery fire. Republicans hoped that an outpouring of affection for

Genêt would cement Franco-American relations, and the two countries' flags flew side by side across the city. French sympathizers rented Philadelphia's biggest banquet hall for an "elegant civic repast," passed around "liberty caps," and roared out "The Marseillaise." The new ambassador even joined a Jacobin club in Philadelphia. Jefferson was jubilant. "The war has kindled and brought forward the two parties with an ardour which our own interests merely could never excite," he told Madison.[38] One Federalist writer could not believe the adoration heaped on Genêt: "It is beyond the power of figures or words to express the hugs and kisses [they] lavished on him. . . . [V]ery few parts, if any, of the Citizen's body, escaped a salute."[39]

Where others saw camaraderie and high spirits, Hamilton detected an embryonic plot to subvert American foreign policy. The organizers of Genêt's reception "were the same men who have been uniformly the enemies and the disturbers of the government of the U[nited] States."[40] Philadelphia was a stronghold of Republican sentiment, and leading figures flaunted their pro-French feelings. John Adams was appalled by daily toasts drunk to Marat and Robespierre, and he recalled one given by Governor Mifflin: "The ruling powers in France. May the United States of America, in alliance with them, declare war against England."[41] At times, Francophile passion was so unbridled that Adams feared violence against Federalists. "You certainly never felt the terrorism excited by Genêt in 1793," Adams chided Jefferson years later, "when ten thousand people in the streets of Philadelphia, day after day, *threatened to drag Washington out of his house* and effect a revolution in the government or compel it to declare war in favor of the French Revolution and against England."[42] Though vice president, Adams felt so vulnerable to attack that he had a cache of arms smuggled through back lanes from the war office to his home so that he could defend his family, friends, and servants. The new republic remained an unsettled place, rife with fears of foreign plots, civil war, chaos, and disunion.

In private talks with George Hammond, Hamilton promised that he would vigorously contest efforts to lure America into war alongside France. He also predicted that the United States would extend no large advances to the revolutionary government, and he delayed debt payments owed to France. In a dispatch to London, Hammond noted that Hamilton would defend American neutrality because "any event which might endanger the *external* tranquillity of the United States would be as fatal to the systems he has formed for the benefit of his country as to his . . . personal reputation and . . . his . . . ambition."[43] If Hamilton's unofficial meetings with Hammond showed gross disloyalty to Jefferson, the latter repaid the favor. Soon after arriving in Philadelphia, Genêt told his superiors in Paris of his candid talks with the secretary of state. "Jefferson . . . gave me useful notions of men in office and did not at all conceal from me that Senator [Robert] Morris and Secretary of the Treasury Hamilton, attached to the interests of England, had the greatest influence over the president's mind and that it was only with difficulty that he counterbalanced their efforts."[44]

Dubious about both the outcome and the legitimacy of the French Revolution, Hamilton recommended that Genêt be accorded a lesser diplomatic status. Washington overruled him and instructed Jefferson to receive the ambassador civilly, but with no real warmth, a reservation Jefferson interpreted as "a small sacrifice" by Washington to Hamilton's opinion.[45] When Genêt first arrived, Jefferson had resisted efforts to expel privateers in Charleston that Genêt had equipped with weapons. Everybody else in the cabinet—Washington, Hamilton, Knox, Randolph—regarded these actions as an affront to American sovereignty and sought to banish the ships. On June 5, Jefferson had to tell Genêt to stop outfitting privateers and dragooning American citizens to serve on them. At this point, Genêt again showed his inimitable cheek. Only ten days after Jefferson's warning, he began to transform a captured British merchant ship, the *Little Sarah*, into an armed privateer renamed *La Petite démocrate*. What made this additionally infuriating was that Genêt defied American orders in Philadelphia, "under the immediate eye of the Government," as Hamilton put it.[46] Hamilton and Knox wanted the ship returned to Britain or ordered from American shores; Washington adopted this latter course over Jefferson's dissent.

Amid this imbroglio, Hamilton wrote to Washington on June 21 that he wished to resign when the next congressional session ended in June 1794. He wanted enough time to enact the programs he had initiated and to clear his name in the ongoing inquiry led by William Branch Giles, but he was chafing under the restraints of office. He kept scribbling tirades against the French Revolution and then stashing them in the drawer.

The day after Hamilton drafted his letter to Washington, Citizen Genêt informed Jefferson that France had the right to outfit ships in American ports—and, what was more, the American people agreed with him. Hamilton, taken aback by this effrontery, termed the letter "the most offensive paper perhaps that ever was offered by a foreign minister to a friendly power with which he resided."[47] A few days later, Hamilton had a tense exchange with Genêt, telling him that France was the aggressor in the European war and that this freed America from any need to comply with their old defense treaty. When Hamilton defended Washington's right to declare neutrality, Genêt retorted that this misuse of executive power usurped congressional prerogatives. The scene had decided elements of farce: Citizen Genêt was lecturing the chief author of *The Federalist Papers* on the interpretation of the U.S. Constitution.

On July 6, Citizen Genêt committed a colossal blunder that dwarfed all previous gaffes. With Washington at Mount Vernon, Genêt took advantage of his absence to inform Alexander J. Dallas, the secretary of Pennsylvania, that he rejected the notion of American neutrality. He said that he planned to go above Washington's head and appeal directly to the American people, asking their assistance to rig French privateers in American ports. Genêt was doing more than just flouting previous warnings; he was clumsily insulting the U.S. government and slapping the face of the one man who could not be slapped: George Washington. Dallas related the story to Governor Mifflin, who passed it on to Hamilton and Knox, who passed it on to Washington. Suddenly, Jefferson's enchantment with Genêt disappeared. "Never, in my opinion, was so calamitous an appointment made as that of the present minister of France here," he protested to Madison. "Hotheaded, all imagination, no judgment, passionate, disrespectful, and even indecent toward the P[resident] in his written as well as verbal communications. . . . He renders my position immensely difficult."[48]

Hamilton was outraged, while also mindful that Genêt had handed him a blunt weapon to wield against France. On July 8, Hamilton, Jefferson, and Knox conferred at the State House to figure out what to do with *La Petite démocrate*. The absent Washington had already ruled that privateers armed in American ports should be stopped or forcibly seized. Hamilton and Knox wanted to post a militia and guns at a strategic spot called Mud Island, a few miles down the Delaware River, preventing the ship from escaping. Jefferson favored the milder course of dealing with American crew members rather than the ship itself. While not making promises, Genêt told Jefferson that the vessel wouldn't sail from Philadelphia before Washington returned. Hamilton, who did not trust Genêt, wanted forcible action to prevent *La Petite démocrate* from getting away. In a memo, he wrote, "It is a truth the best founded and of the last importance *that nothing is so dangerous to a government as to be wanting either in self confidence or self-respect.*"[49] But Hamilton could not prevail upon his colleagues to use force.

Washington returned to Philadelphia on July 11. *La Petite démocrate* managed to slip away and sail past Mud Island on July 12. On the spot, Hamilton proposed that the French government be asked to recall Genêt. Even Jefferson registered no protest. A few days, later *La Petite démocrate* was at sea.

As he watched Genêt's boorish behavior, Hamilton longed to broadcast his views to the public. He was not born to be a silent spectator of events. By late June, Hamilton could contain himself no longer and rushed into print. On June 29, 1793, a writer billing himself as "Pacificus" inaugurated the first of seven essays in the *Gazette of the United States* that defended the Neutrality Proclamation. Throughout

July, Hamilton's articles ran twice weekly, their impact enhanced by Citizen Genêt's intolerable antics.

In the first essay, Hamilton dealt with the objection that only Congress could issue a neutrality proclamation, since it alone had the power to declare war. Hamilton pointed out that if "the legislature have a right to make war, on the one hand, it is, on the other, the duty of the executive to preserve peace till war is declared."[50] Once again, Hamilton broadened the authority of the executive branch in diplomacy, especially during emergencies. He also speculated that the real reason behind the brouhaha over neutrality was the opposition's desire to weaken or remove Washington from office. In the second essay, he disputed that the Neutrality Proclamation violated the defensive alliance with France. That treaty, Hamilton noted, did not apply to offensive wars, and France had declared war against other European powers. In the third essay, Hamilton evoked the devastation that might result if America was dragged into war on France's side. Great Britain and Spain could instigate "numerous Indian tribes" under their influence to attack the United States from the interior. Meanwhile, "with a long extended sea coast, with no fortifications whatever and with a population not exceeding four millions," the United States would find itself in an unequal contest.[51]

In subsequent installments, Pacificus presented Louis XVI as a benevolent man and a true friend of America: "I am much misinformed if repeated declarations of the venerable Franklin did not attest this fact."[52] French support for the American Revolution, he argued, had emanated from the king and high government circles, not the masses: "If there was any kindness in the decision [to support America], demanding a return of kindness from us, it was the kindness of Louis the XVI. His heart was the depository of the sentiment."[53] It took courage for Hamilton, stigmatized as a cryptomonarchist, to express sympathy for a dead king. In the last "Pacificus" essay, he defended American neutrality on the grounds that a country "without armies, without fleets" was too immature to prosecute war.[54] To amplify his views, Hamilton organized rallies to demonstrate popular approval of the Neutrality Proclamation.

Hamilton was always fond of his "Pacificus" essays, which show the impassioned pragmatism that informed his foreign-policy views. He later incorporated them into an 1802 edition of The Federalist, proudly telling the publisher that "some of his friends had pronounced them to be his best performance."[55] Hamilton must have enjoyed bundling these essays with The Federalist, because they had provoked a venomous response from his main Federalist coauthor, James Madison. It was Jefferson who prodded Madison into taking on Hamilton over the Neutrality Proclamation. Jefferson had read the first few "Pacificus" essays with mounting dismay and decided once again to deploy a proxy to refute Hamilton. On July 7, he urged Madison to tilt lances with the treasury secretary: "Nobody answers him and his doctrines will therefore be taken for confessed. For God's sake, my dear Sir, take up your pen, select the most striking heresies, and cut him to pieces in the face of the public. There is nobody else who can and will enter the lists with him."[56]

Jefferson must have thought that Madison would leap at the chance to resist the expanded executive powers embodied in the Neutrality Proclamation. Instead, Madison balked. From his Virginia plantation, he complained to Jefferson that he lacked the necessary books and papers to refute "Pacificus," and he griped about the summer heat. He blamed hordes of houseguests who overstayed their welcomes. Did even Madison tremble at the thought of confronting Hamilton? When he had exhausted all excuses, he told Jefferson grudgingly, "I have forced myself into the task of a reply. I can truly say I find it the most grating one I ever experienced."[57]

In the end, Madison hammered away at Hamilton with five essays published under the name "Helvidius." The first essay reflected the deep animosity that had sprung up between the *Federalist* collaborators: "Several pieces with the signature of Pacificus were late published, which have been read with singular pleasure and applause by the foreigners and degenerate citizens among us, who hate our republican government and the French Revolution." Madison complained of "a secret Anglomany" behind "the mask of neutrality."[58] He flayed Hamilton as a monarchist for defending the Neutrality Proclamation. Such prerogatives, he said, were "*royal prerogatives in the British government and are accordingly treated as executive prerogatives by British commentators.*"[59]

In prose more pedestrian than Hamilton's, Madison brought the perspective of a strict constructionist to the neutrality issue. He wanted full authority over foreign policy to rest with Congress, not the president, except where the Constitution granted the chief executive specific powers. Madison was both edited and supplied with cabinet secrets by Jefferson, who seemed to have no reservations about abetting this assault on a presidential proclamation.

The instigator of many articles against his own administration, Jefferson knew that they were upsetting Washington. He felt sympathy for the president but also believed he was getting his just deserts. He wrote to Madison in June:

> The President is not well. Little lingering fevers have been hanging about him for a week or ten days and have affected his looks most remarkably. He is also extremely affected by the attacks made and kept on him in the public papers. I think he feels those things more than any person I ever yet met with. I am extremely sorry to see them. [Jefferson then indicated that Washington had

brought the attacks on himself.] Naked, he would have been sanctimoniously reverenced, but enveloped in the rags of royalty, they can hardly be torn off without laceration.[60]

During that eventful summer of 1793, administration infighting grew increasingly cutthroat. On July 23, Washington held a cabinet meeting that took on a surreal atmosphere. The president wanted to ask for Genêt's recall without offending France. This pushed Hamilton into an extended harangue on the crisis facing the government. He alluded to a "faction" that wanted to "overthrow" the government, and he said that to arrest its progress the administration should publish the story of Genêt's unseemly behavior; otherwise, people would soon join the "incendiaries."[61] What made this dramatic scene so unreal was that the spiritual leader of that faction was sitting right there in the room: Thomas Jefferson.

That summer, Jefferson found Hamilton both insupportable and inescapable. Besides his Treasury job, Hamilton conducted a full-time career as an anonymous journalist. In late July, the *American Daily Advertiser* printed his piece called "No Jacobin," the first of yet another nine essays that issued from Hamilton's fluent pen over a four-week period. He began by hurling a thunderbolt: "It is publicly rumoured in this city that the minister of the French republic *has threatened to appeal from The President of the United States to the People*."[62] The leak of this secret information about Genêt's insolent disrespect toward Washington had a pronounced effect on public opinion. In coming weeks, Hamilton continued to lash out at Genêt for meddling in domestic politics: "What baseness, what prostitution in a citizen of this country, to become the advocate of a pretension so pernicious, so unheard of, so detestable!"[63]

On August 1, Jefferson found himself trapped again in a cabinet meeting with Hamilton, the human word machine, who spontaneously spouted perfect speeches in every forum. The treasury secretary thundered on about the need to disclose the damaging correspondence with Citizen Genêt. From Jefferson's notes, we can see the highly theatrical manner that Hamilton assumed in Washington's small cabinet. "Hamilton made a jury speech of three quarters of an hour," a weary Jefferson told his journal, "as inflammatory and declamatory as if he had been speaking to a jury."[64] One senses the laconic Jefferson's perplexity in dealing with this inspired windbag. "Met again," Jefferson reported the next day. "Hamilton spoke again three quarters of an hour."[65] Hamilton repeated charges made by the royal European powers that France wanted to export its revolution to their countries. Jefferson inwardly reviled Hamilton as a traitor to republican government. "What a fatal stroke at the cause of liberty; *et tu Brute*," he wrote in his diary.[66]

At this point, Jefferson finally aired his own views. He predictably opposed public exposure of government dealings with Genêt and also warned of the futility of cracking down on "Democratic" societies that had sprung up since Genêt's arrival. If the government suppressed these groups, Jefferson argued, people would join them merely "to assert the right of voluntary associations."[67] His point was well taken, but he had squandered his credibility with the president, as he was about to discover in peculiarly dramatic fashion.

With heroic fortitude, Washington had tried to remain evenhanded with Hamilton and Jefferson, but he could no longer tolerate this dissension in his cabinet. A sensitive man of pent-up passion, he also could not endure the vicious abuse he had taken in Freneau's *National Gazette.* In May, Washington had asked Jefferson to fire Freneau from his State Department job after the editor wrote that Washington had signed the Neutrality Proclamation because the "Anglomen" threatened to cut off his head. Convinced that the *National Gazette* had saved the country from monarchy, Jefferson refused to comply with Washington's request. Now, in a cabinet session, Henry Knox happened to mention a tasteless satirical broadside called "The Funeral Dirge of George Washington," in which Washington, like Louis XVI, was executed by guillotine. This libel was thought to have been written by Freneau. Knox's reference lit a fuse inside Washington, and the seemingly phlegmatic president became a powder keg. In his "Anas," Jefferson described the unusual scene:

The President was much inflamed; got into one of those passions when he cannot command himself; ran on much on the personal abuse which has been bestowed on him; defied any man on earth to produce one single act of his since he had been in the government which was not done on the purest motives; [said] that he had never repented but once the having slipped the moment of resigning his office and that was every moment since; that *by God* he had rather be in his grave than in his present situation; that he had rather be on his farm than to be made *emperor of the* world; and yet they were charging him with wanting to be a king. That that *rascal Freneau* sent him three of his papers every day, as if he thought he would become the distributor of his papers; that he could see in this nothing but an impudent design to insult him. He ended in this high tone. There was a pause. Some difficulty in resuming our question.[68]

Jefferson scored few points in the cabinet that August. It was decided that America, as a neutral nation, could not allow belligerent powers to equip privateers in her ports or give them asylum. As head of the Customs Service, Hamilton was charged with punishing violators, fortifying his hand in foreign affairs. All the while, Jefferson conspired to strip Hamilton of his power. On August 11, he sent a confidential letter to Madison, noting that Republican representation would be stronger in the new House. The time had therefore ripened for weakening Hamilton with two measures: splitting the Treasury Department between a customs service and a bureau of internal taxes and severing all ties between the Bank of the United States and the government. If Jefferson could not diminish the man, he would try to diminish the office.

For all his growing dismay over the incorrigible Genêt, Jefferson still blocked cabinet efforts to release the full saga of Genêt's impertinent behavior.[69] He threatened to resign in late September, telling Washington that he hated having to socialize in the circles of "the wealthy aristocrats, the merchants connected closely with England, the new created paper fortunes," and he again cited steps being hatched to bring a monarchy to America.[70] Jefferson agreed to stay until year's end only after Washington agreed to keep confidential Genêt's obnoxious conduct. His cabinet colleagues continued to dissent. "Hamilton and Knox have pressed an appeal to the people with an eagerness I never before saw in them," Jefferson told Madison.[71]

Hamilton got the story out indirectly by prompting Senator Rufus King and Chief Justice John Jay to publish a revealing letter in a New York paper. An agitated Genêt protested to Washington, asking him urgently to "dissipate these dark calumnies."[72] His letter's intemperate tone would only have strengthened the suspicions he sought to allay, and Jefferson consequently had to draft a letter to France on August 16 asking for Genêt's recall.

Jefferson admitted that the tales told about Genêt were not Federalist fabrications. "You will see much said and gainsaid about G[enet's] threat to appeal to the people," Jefferson told Madison. "I can assure you it is a fact."[73] All through August, Madison and Monroe crafted resolutions thanking France for aiding the American Revolution. When Washington broke with Citizen Genêt, a crestfallen Madison stated that it "will give great pain to all those enlightened friends of the principles of liberty on which the American and French Revolution are founded."[74] Nor would Philip Freneau concede that the French Revolution had taken a vicious turn. In early September, to stress parallels between the two revolutions, he printed in succession the French Declaration of the Rights of Man and the American Constitution.

The situation in Paris, however, soon undermined this thesis. That spring had seen the creation of the Committee of Public Safety, soon the principal vehicle of revolutionary terror. In June, the moderate Girondist faction, to which Genêt belonged, was purged and placed under house arrest by radical Jacobins. This Jacobin triumph, Hamilton realized, had made French officials receptive to American requests to cashier the bumbling Genêt, whom they accused of offending a friendly power. Led by Robespierre, the Jacobins swept aside all obstacles to their Reign of

Terror. Nocturnal house searches and arbitrary arrests became routine by the fall. Priests were persecuted and churches vandalized in an anti-Christian campaign that led the cathedral of Notre-Dame to be renamed the Temple of Reason. On October 16, Marie Antoinette—or the "widow Capet," as she was designated—was pulled from her cell, stuck in a tiny farm cart, paraded through streets teeming with heckling citizens, and beheaded. The guillotine worked overtime: twenty-one Girondists were executed on October 31 alone.

As Hamilton got wind of the bloody fate that awaited Citizen Genêt in Paris, he urged Washington to allow him to remain in the United States, lest Republicans accuse Washington of having sent the brash Frenchman to his death. Washington agreed to give him asylum, and Citizen Genêt, ironically, became an American citizen. He married Cornelia Clinton, the daughter of Hamilton's nemesis Governor George Clinton, and spent the remainder of his life in upstate New York. In the end, Washington never submitted to Hamilton's wish to publicize a detailed account of Genêt's dealings with the administration. But Hamilton had gotten most of what he wanted in the Genêt affair, including the dearest bonus of all: the exit of Thomas Jefferson from the cabinet by year's end.

TWENTY-FOUR

A DISAGREEABLE TRADE

While Washington meditated the fate of Citizen Genêt that August, Philadelphia was beset by a threat far more fearsome than the French minister appealing to the American people. Some residents who lived near the wharves began to sicken and die from a ghastly disease that shook the body with chills and severe muscular pain. The red-eyed victims belched up black vomit from bleeding stomachs, and their skins turned a hideous jaundiced color. The onset of the yellow-fever epidemic, the worst to have befallen the young country thus far, has been traced to many sources. The disease had ravaged the West Indies that year, and an influx of refugees after the slave revolt in Santo Domingo may have introduced it to Philadelphia. A wet spring giving way to an uncommonly hot, dry summer may have helped to spread the disease. Sanitary conditions were atrocious in many parts of town, with residents dumping refuse into clogged, filthy gutters and drinking water from wells contaminated by outhouses.

By late August, twenty people per day were expiring from the epidemic, which was to claim more than four thousand lives, bringing government and commerce to a standstill. Coffin makers cried their wares in front of City Hall. People didn't understand that the disease was transmitted by mosquitoes but knew it could be communicated by contact with victims. People stopped shaking hands and stuck to the middle of the street to avoid other pedestrians. Some people covered their noses with vinegar-dipped handkerchiefs while others chewed garlic, releasing malodorous clouds that could be smelled several feet away. The safest course was to flee the city, and twenty thousand people did just that, thinning the ranks of government employees. By early September, six clerks in Hamilton's Treasury Department and seven in the Customs Service had the disease, as did three Post Office employees.

The city's preeminent physician was the indomitable Dr. Benjamin Rush—"a sprightly, pretty fellow," as John Adams described him—who scarcely slept during the pestilence, flitting bravely from house to house, treating rich and poor alike.[1] This required intestinal fortitude as carts rumbled across the cobblestones, carrying piles of cadavers, and residents were loudly exhorted, "Bring out your dead."[2] Rush had warning signs posted outside affected houses. In treating yellow fever, Rush adopted an approach that now sounds barbaric: he bled and purged the victim, a process frightful to behold. He emptied the patient's bowels four or five times, using a gruesome mixture of potions and enemas, before draining off ten to twelve ounces of blood to lower the pulse. For good measure, he induced mild vomiting. This regimen was repeated two or three times daily. Rush was a man of exemplary courage, but it is questionable whether he saved lives or only hastened deaths by weakening the body's natural defenses.

On September 5, 1793, Hamilton contracted a violent case of yellow fever. He and Eliza repaired to their summer residence, a mansion called Fair Hill that lay two and a half miles from town and was owned by Philadelphia merchant Joseph P. Norris. Their children were sequestered at an adjoining house. To calm them, Eliza would appear at a window and wave to them. Pretty soon, Eliza had the illness, and the children were evacuated to the Schuylers in Albany. In an astonishing storybook coincidence, Hamilton's boyhood friend from St. Croix, Edward Stevens, had turned up in Philadelphia and now attended to the couple. A prosperous, distinguished physician, Stevens had practiced in St. Croix for ten years until his wife, Eleonora, had died the previous year. He then married a rich widow named Hester Amory and moved to Philadelphia.

Having treated yellow-fever victims in the islands, Stevens dissented from the American dogma of bloodletting and bowel purges, which he thought only debilitated patients. He argued for remedies that were "cordial, stimulating, and tonic."[3] To strengthen patients, Stevens administered stiff doses of quinine called "Peruvian bark" as well as aged Madeira. He also submerged them in cold baths before giving them glasses of brandy topped with burned cinnamon. He sedated patients nightly with a tincture of opium (laudanum). To stop vomiting, patients quaffed an aromatic blend of camomile flowers, oil of peppermint, and lavender spirits.

When they learned of Hamilton's illness, George and Martha Washington sent sympathy notes and six bottles of vintage wine. "With extreme concern, I receive the expression of your apprehensions that you are in the first stages of the prevailing fever," the president wrote to Hamilton.[4] Quite different was the response of Thomas Jefferson, who wrote a misguided letter to Madison that accused Hamilton of cowardice, hypochondria, and fakery: "His family think him in danger and he puts himself so by his excessive alarm. He had been miserable several days before from a firm persuasion he should catch it. A man as timid as he is on the water, as timid on horseback, as timid in sickness, would be a phenomenon if his courage, of which he has the reputation in military occasions, were genuine. His friends, who have not seen him, suspect it is only an autumnal fever he has."[5] At one stroke, Jefferson heaped heartless abuse on a sick man and inverted reality. Not only did Hamilton have yellow fever, but he had shown outstanding valor during the Revolution while Jefferson, as Virginia governor, had cravenly fled into the woods before the advancing British troops.

Edward Stevens achieved spectacular results with Alexander and Elizabeth Hamilton, curing them within five days. Trusting a man who may have been Alexander's biological brother, the Hamiltons were saved while countless others perished. Ever since King's College, Hamilton had been interested in medicine; he had had his children inoculated against smallpox. He was not content to be a passive patient. No sooner had Stevens cured him than Hamilton wanted to proselytize for his approach. With Eliza responding well to treatment, he published an open letter to the College of Physicians, hoping to stop "that undue panic which is fast depopulating the city and suspending business both public and private."[6] Praising Stevens, he said his friend would gladly relate his methods to the medical faculty.

Hamilton's letter created a sensation. Even in illness, he was shadowed by controversy, since he had implicitly rebuked Benjamin Rush. Rush gave Stevens's methods a fair chance for several days, tossing buckets of cold water on patients and injecting quinine into their bowels, but he could not reproduce Stevens's results and reverted to the rigors of bleed-and-purge. Unfortunately, this legitimate clash of medical viewpoints took on political overtones. Rush was an abolitionist and a passionate, outspoken reformer who later published a groundbreaking treatise on mental illness. He was also a convinced partisan of Jefferson. So when Hamilton lauded Stevens's yellow-fever treatment as superior to the "standard" method, Rush was perhaps predisposed to take offense.

An unfortunate medical dispute erupted between the "Republican" method of Rush and the "Federalist" alternative of Stevens. Rush was not averse to casting the controversy in political terms. "Colonel Hamilton's remedies are now as unpopular in our city as his funding system is in Virginia and North Carolina," he declared.[7] He was persuaded that Hamilton's open letter betrayed political bias against him: "I think it probable that if the new remedies had been introduced by any other person than a decided democrat and a friend of Madison and Jefferson, they would have met with less opposition from Colonel Hamilton."[8] Rush, like Jefferson, refused to believe that Hamilton had had yellow fever and pooh-poohed it as an overblown cold. "Colonel Hamilton's letter has cost our city several hundred inhabitants," he told Elias Boudinot, asserting that the Hamiltons had suffered "nothing but common remitting fevers from cold instead of the malignant contagion."[9] Though Benjamin Rush blamed Alexander Hamilton for yellow-fever deaths, the public ended up blaming Rush. After a second yellow-fever epidemic in 1797 and more copious bloodletting, Rush lost so many patients that President Adams rescued him by appointing him treasurer of the U.S. Mint.

Alexander and Eliza eagerly awaited a reunion with their children in Albany. To make sure they were fully recovered, they relaxed and took carriage rides for two or three days before leaving Philadelphia on September 15. They set aside any garments that might have been infected and packed only fresh clothing. It was a long, wearisome trip. On the first leg, they stopped at a tavern packed with terrified refugees from Philadelphia, who refused to allow the Hamiltons to enter until the landlord insisted upon it. At town after town, they had to contend with barriers erected to keep out potentially contagious Philadelphians. Even New York posted guards at entrances to the city to deter fugitives from the plague-ridden capital.

The most unpleasant confrontation came in Albany. On September 21, the Albany Common Council passed a resolution forbidding ferrymen from transporting across the Hudson people who came from places infected with yellow fever. Philip Schuyler had to negotiate the Hamiltons' arrival with Albany's mayor, Abraham Yates, Jr. On September 23, Alexander and Eliza were stranded at a village directly across the Hudson from Albany. A delegation of physicians crossed over, examined them, and pronounced them fit. Leaving their servants and carriage on the east bank, the Hamiltons then crossed the Hudson and settled at the Schuyler mansion, as a hubbub arose over their arrival. One rumor said that, after embracing Eliza, Philip Schuyler had swabbed his mouth with vinegar disinfectant and then washed his face and mouth, as if she might still be contagious. Yates informed Schuyler of fears that the Hamilton carriage, baggage, servants, and clothing might transport yellow fever. He even wanted to station guards at the Schuyler mansion to avert contact between the Hamiltons and the local citizenry. Hamilton's political opponents must have enjoyed the symbolism of the treasury secretary spewing contamination wherever he went.

An offended Schuyler told Mayor Yates that the Hamiltons had brought neither clothes nor servants across the river and had taken all reasonable precautions. He promised that his family would not venture into the city and asked that a guard bring food out to the mansion, "for I am fully persuaded that it cannot be the intention . . . of my fellow citizens that I and my family shall be exterminated by famine."[10] Sarcastically, he suggested that the guard might want to deposit the food between the house and the main gate. Not until September 26 did Hamilton learn that his father-in-law had submitted to strict conditions to receive them. He then wrote in high dudgeon to Yates, insisting that he and Eliza had adhered to all safety measures and that it was "absolutely inadmissible" to cut off their access to town. Hamilton warned that he would go about his business, "which force alone can interrupt."[11]

During the following days, he and Eliza replenished their strength with fresh air and exercise. They learned from Washington's secretary that reports of Hamilton's death in New England had produced "deep regret and unfeigned sorrow," which had given way to "marks of joy and satisfaction" when the reports proved unfounded.[12] The controversy over Hamilton's presence ended when the Albany Common Council passed a resolution opening the city to anyone in good health who had been absent from Philadelphia for at least fourteen days. Having last been in Philadelphia more than two weeks earlier, the Hamiltons were free to move about.

Both Washington at Mount Vernon and Hamilton in Albany itched to resume the suspended work of government. Oliver Wolcott, Jr., who headed the Treasury Department in Hamilton's absence, had retreated to a large house on the Schuylkill River, leaving two or three clerks to soldier on in otherwise empty downtown offices fumigated with brimstone. Washington contemplated cabinet meetings in Germantown or some other spot free of fever near Philadelphia but was stumped by a constitutional conundrum: did he have the power to change the seat of government temporarily? Washington turned to his oracle on such matters, telling Hamilton that "as none can take a more comprehensive view and, I flatter myself, a less partial one on the subject than yourself . . . I pray you to dilate fully upon the several points here brought to your consideration."[13] Hamilton was very good at circumventing such legal roadblocks. The Constitution, he told Washington, allowed Congress to meet elsewhere only for specific, extraordinary purposes and "a contagion wouldn't qualify."[14] He solved the problem by a subtle semantic shift, saying that the president could *recommend* meeting elsewhere. And so Hamilton recommended Germantown as the ideal place.

Several Treasury clerks who had fled to New York for safety had ignored Wolcott's pleas to return to work. En route from Albany in mid-October, Hamilton collected these renegade employees. By October 26, he and Eliza arrived at Robert Morris's estate on the Schuylkill, the Hills. They stayed there for several weeks as isolated cases of yellow fever lingered in pockets of Philadelphia. For the first three weeks of November, the cabinet met in Germantown, until frost removed any danger of returning to downtown offices.

For some time after their brush with yellow fever, the Hamiltons experienced pronounced aftereffects. "Colonel Hamilton is indisposed and has sent to New York for Dr. Stevens," Benjamin Rush gloated on November 3. "He still defends bark and the cold bath in the yellow fever and reprobates my practice as obsolete in the West

Indies."[15] There were several days that November when the conscientious Hamilton skipped cabinet meetings and found his mind muddled—completely out of character for him. On December 11, he sent a totally atypical note to Jefferson: "Mr. Hamilton presents his compliments to Mr. Jefferson. He has a confused recollection that there was something agreed upon with regard to prizes about which he was to write to the collectors, but which his state of health at the time put out of his recollection. If Mr. Jefferson recollect it, Mr. H will thank him for information."[16] In late December, Hamilton told Angelica Church that he had mostly conquered the "malignant disease" that had left him prostrate: "The last vestige of it has been a nervous derangement, but this has nearly yielded to regimen, a certain degree of exercise, and a resolution to overcome it."[17]

Among the casualties claimed by the yellow-fever epidemic was John Todd, Jr., whose widow, Dolley Payne Todd, married James Madison the following year. Another victim was the *National Gazette*. The epidemic had cost the paper money, as had Freneau's rhapsodies about Citizen Genêt. On October 11, Freneau stepped down as State Department translator and two weeks later announced the suspension of his paper. The following month, Hamilton and Rufus King took up a collection to assist his competitor, John Fenno, and his ailing Federalist paper, the *Gazette of the United States*. Hamilton abused his position as treasury secretary by appealing for help to Thomas Willing, president of the Bank of the United States, who could scarcely rebuff a request from Hamilton. It was a hypocritical lapse for a man who had so often chided Jefferson for exploiting his office to assist Freneau.

It was perhaps fitting that the demise of the *National Gazette* preceded the year's most satisfying event for Hamilton: Thomas Jefferson's resignation as secretary of state on December 31, 1793. The Virginian had failed to eject Hamilton from the cabinet and had lost the contest for Washington's favor. For a long time, he had felt estranged from the cabinet and had labored "under such agitation of mind" as he had never known, he confided to his daughter.[18] To Angelica Church, Jefferson groaned about the dreary "scenes of business" in Philadelphia and commented, "Never was any mortal more tired of these than I am."[19] In returning to his beloved Monticello, he was to be "liberated from the hated occupations of politics and sink into the bosom of my family, my farm, and my books."[20] Jefferson proclaimed that he would now be a "stranger" to politics and would limit his statements to a single topic: "the shameless corruption of a portion" of Congress and "their implicit devotion to the treasury."[21]

Jefferson projected the image of a contemplative philosopher, yearning for his mountain retreat, but the magnitude of his ambition was sharply debated. It irked John Adams that Republicans considered Jefferson's resignation to be the sign of a pure, self-effacing man: "Jefferson thinks by this step to get the reputation as an humble, modest, meek man, wholly without ambition or vanity. . . . But if the prospect opens, the world will see and he will feel that he is as ambitious as Oliver Cromwell."[22] He thought Jefferson's resignation a shrewd tactical move to position him better for a later run at the presidency. Following Jefferson's departure from Philadelphia, he wrote to Abigail, "Jefferson went off yesterday and a good riddance of bad ware."[23]

Hamilton was no less convinced of Jefferson's hidden aspirations. In the spring of 1792, he had written, " 'Tis evident beyond a question, from every movement, that Mr. Jefferson aims with ardent desire at the presidential chair."[24] When Hamilton's son John wrote his father's biography, he left out one story that is contained in his papers. The authenticity of the anecdote cannot be verified, but it jibes with other things Hamilton said. According to this story, soon after Jefferson announced his plans to step down, Washington and Hamilton were alone together when Jefferson passed by the window. Washington expressed regret at his departure, which he attributed to his desire to withdraw from public life and devote himself to literature and agriculture. Staring at Washington with a dubious smirk, Hamilton asked, "Do you believe, Sir, that such is his only motive?" Washington saw that Hamilton was biting his tongue and urged him to speak. Hamilton explained that he had long entertained doubts about Jefferson's character but, as a colleague, had restrained himself. Now he no longer felt bound by such scruples. Hamilton offered this prediction, as summarized by his son:

> From the very outset, Jefferson had been the instigation of all the abuse of the administration and of the President; that he was one of the most ambitious and intriguing men in the community; that retirement was not his motive; that he found himself from the state of affairs with France in a position in which he was compelled to assume a responsibility as to public measures which warred against the designs of his party; that for that cause he retired; that his intention was to wait events, then enter the field and run for the plate; that if future events did not prove the correctness of this view of his character, he [Hamilton] would forfeit all title to a knowledge of mankind.

John C. Hamilton continued that in the late 1790s Washington told Hamilton that "not a day has elapsed since my retirement from public life in which I have not thought of that conversation. Every event has proved the truth of your view of his character. You foretold what has happened with the spirit of prophecy."[25] The story's likely veracity is bolstered by the fact that Jefferson exchanged no letters with Washington during the last three and a half years of the general's life.

. . .

For Hamilton, the triumph over Jefferson was a bittersweet victory that he scarcely had time to savor. He was besieged by enemies, worried about his health, and felt unappreciated by the public. In a letter to Angelica Church, Hamilton, nearly thirty-nine, struck again a world-weary note: "But how oddly are all things arranged in this sublunary scene. I am just where I do not wish to be. I know how I could be much happier, but circumstances enchain me."[26] In another letter, he said, "Believe me, I am heartily tired of my situation and wait only the opportunity of quitting it with honor and without decisive prejudice to the public affairs."[27]

The Republicans had captured majorities in the Congress that convened in December 1793 and that would render a final verdict over Hamilton's conduct as treasury secretary. He had already told Washington that he would stay in office only as long as it took to clear his name. In mid-December 1793, in a rare political spectacle, Hamilton asked House Speaker Muhlenberg to *resume* the Giles inquiry. While he had been exonerated by the first Giles investigation, the examination had been rushed by the short deadline, and Hamilton wanted to erase any last doubts about his probity. Whatever private melancholy he poured out to Angelica Church, he sounded buoyantly combative when he told Muhlenberg of the probe, "the more comprehensive it is, the more agreeable it will be to me."[28]

The Republicans were happy to oblige him. Even before Giles got down to business, Senator Albert Gallatin of Pennsylvania submitted resolutions asking for a comprehensive account of Treasury operations. He demanded reams of paper from Hamilton, ranging from a full statement of foreign and domestic debt to an itemized list of revenues. This oppressive investigation was scrapped when the foreign-born Gallatin lost his Senate seat after charges were made that he had not met the nine-year citizenship requirement. Hamilton, meanwhile, chafed at the dilatory tactics of Giles, who did not revive the Treasury inquiry until late February, even as Hamilton made threatening noises that he would resign.

Hamilton was being badgered from all sides. He was still deluged with questionable petitions, often marred by fraud or missing paperwork, from people claiming compensation for services provided during the Revolution. He felt so harassed by accusations of negligence from the Senate that on February 22 he complained to Vice President Adams in an anguished letter. Hamilton alluded to burdensome petitions, the disruptions of the yellow-fever epidemic, and eternal congressional studies of his conduct. As a conscientious public servant, he felt he should be spared petty censure over his handling of the petitions: "I will only add that the consciousness of devoting myself to the public service, to the utmost extent of my faculties and to the injury of my health, is a tranquillizing consolation of which I cannot be deprived by any supposition to the contrary."[29] Nine days later, Hamilton delivered to Congress his decisions on no fewer than thirty complex petitions for wartime compensation.

On February 24, the House assembled a select committee with sweeping powers to investigate the Treasury Department. Reflecting the new composition of Congress, the bulk of the committee was Republican. The members drew up an exhausting schedule to drain any energy Hamilton had left. Until their work was complete, they planned to meet every Tuesday and Thursday evening and Saturday morning. For three months, the committee stuck to this punitive schedule, and Hamilton testified at about half the sessions. Besides providing extensive official information, he had to disclose all of his *private* accounts with the Bank of the United States and the Bank of New York, as Republicans tried to prove that Hamilton had exploited his office to extort credits from the two banks.

The select committee, finding it hard to fix blame on Hamilton, fell back on the one charge that Giles had made stick: that he had exercised too much discretion in shifting government funds between the United States and Europe. When the committee asked Hamilton to cite his authority for transferring money abroad to the Bank of the United States, he cited both "verbal authority" and a letter from the president. The committee, suspecting a bluff, demanded proof, and Hamilton asked Washington for a letter to back up his assertions. Washington obliged Hamilton with a mealymouthed letter that was so bland—"from my general recollection of the course of proceedings, I do not doubt that it was substantially as you have stated it"—as to undercut Hamilton's position.[30] His enemies guffawed. "The letter from the P[resident] is inexpressibly mortifying to his [Hamilton's] friends," Madison wrote to Jefferson, "and marks his situation to be precisely what you always described it to be."[31]

As delicately as possible, a crestfallen Hamilton advised Washington that his letter might seem a lukewarm endorsement to cynics. He worried that "false and insidious men" would use it to "infuse doubts and distrusts very injurious to me."[32] In fact, Washington *was* beginning to balk at Hamilton's requests to transfer money in ways not tightly tied to specific legislative acts. Whether he thought the Jeffersonian arguments had merit or merely popular backing, Washington subtly distanced himself from Hamilton, insisting that he segregate funds from different sources. Once again, he proved that he was not a rubber stamp for Hamilton's policies. At the same time, he hardly wished to repudiate his treasury secretary and promised to help out with Congress. In the end, the select committee found no wrongdoing in the way Hamilton had used European loans for domestic purposes.

In its final report in late May, the Republican-dominated committee could not deliver the comeuppance it had craved. Instead, it confessed that all the charges lodged against Hamilton were completely baseless, as the treasury secretary had insisted all along. And what of the endless Jeffersonian insinuations that Hamilton had used public office to extract private credits? The report concluded that it appears "that the Secretary of the Treasury never has, either directly or indirectly, for himself or any other person, procured any discount or credit, from either of the said banks [Bank of New York and Bank of the United States] upon the basis of any public monies which, at any time, have been deposited therein under his direction."[33] The vindication was so resounding that Hamilton withdrew his long-standing resignation, and his cabinet position grew more impregnable than ever. Nevertheless, it frustrated him that after this exhaustive investigation his opponents still rehashed the stale charges of misconduct. He had learned a lesson about propaganda in politics and mused wearily that "no character, however upright, is a match for constantly reiterated attacks, however false." If a charge was made often enough, people assumed in the end "that a person so often accused cannot be entirely innocent."[34]

Once again, the best clue to Hamilton's mood comes from his confiding letters to Angelica Church, who still felt trapped in England by her husband's position in Parliament. In one letter, Hamilton offered Church a whimsical but rueful meditation on the nature of public office. This previously overlooked letter is contained in the papers of Hamilton's son James, who tore off and crossed out other portions, making one wonder whether it contained evidence of the long-rumored affair between Hamilton and his sister-in-law. Hamilton observed:

> Truly this trade of a statesman is but a sorry thing. It plagues a man more than enough and, when it obliges him to sacrifice his own pleasure, it is very far from fitting him the better to please other people. . . . I speak from experience. You will ask why I do not quit this disagreeable trade. How can I? What is to become of my fame and glory[?] How will the world go on without me? I am sometimes told very gravely it could not and one ought not, you know, to be very difficult of faith about what is much to our advantage. Besides, you would lose the pleasure of speaking of your brother[-in-law as] "The Chancellor of the Exchequer" if I am to give up the trade. . . . There is no fear that the minister will spoil the man. I find by experience that the man is every day getting the upper hand of the minister.[35]

TWENTY-FIVE

SEAS OF BLOOD

After Jefferson left the cabinet, Washington did not conduct a purge of Republicans. On the contrary, the unity-minded president turned to the foremost congressional Republican, James Madison, as his first choice as secretary of state. Only when Madison rejected the job did Washington hand it to Attorney General Edmund Randolph, who was succeeded in *his* post by William Bradford of Philadelphia. This sequence of events did not stop Jefferson and Madison from complaining that Washington was a captive of crafty, manipulative Federalists.

Jefferson's presence lingered in Congress through Madison. On the eve of his departure, Jefferson submitted a bulky report to the House on European trade policies toward America. He laid out a litany of charges—from unfair dominance of transatlantic shipping to the banning of American boats from the British West Indies—to buttress his claim that England discriminated against American trade. Based on this evidence, Jefferson advocated commercial reprisals against Britain coupled, not surprisingly, with expanded trade relations with France.

On January 3, 1794, Madison introduced seven congressional resolutions that converted Jefferson's brief into a tough anti-British trade policy. Ten days later, Federalist William Loughton Smith rebutted him in an eloquent speech of fifteen thousand words that adroitly picked apart Madison's arguments. Smith suggested that it would be suicidal for America to disrupt relations with the country that accounted for most of its trade. As soon as Jefferson scanned Smith's speech, he knew his old bête noire had struck again. "I am at no loss to ascribe Smith's speech to its true father," he told Madison. "Every letter of it is Hamilton's, except the introduction."[1]

Jefferson had guessed shrewdly: Hamilton either drafted Smith's speech or provided the information.

Responding to Madison's attempts to solidify relations with France, Hamilton lashed back in his time-tested manner. Under the disguise of "Americanus," he published two fervid newspaper essays about the horrors of the French Revolution. He condemned apologists for "the horrid and disgusting scenes" being enacted in France and branded Marat and Robespierre "assassins still reeking with the blood of murdered fellow citizens." Long before Napoleon came on the scene, he predicted that after "wading through seas of blood . . . France may find herself at length the slave of some victorious . . . Caesar."[2]

Unfortunately for Hamilton, even as he touted England as a law-abiding ally, the British evinced a bullying arrogance and stupidity toward America that surpassed the most acrid Jeffersonian caricatures. England refused to acknowledge the traditional doctrine "free ships make free goods"—i.e., that neutral vessels had a right to carry all cargo save munitions and enter the ports of belligerent countries. On November 6, 1793, William Pitt's ministry had decreed that British ships could intercept neutral vessels hauling produce to or from the French West Indies. Without further ado, the British fleet captured more than 250 American merchant ships, impounding more than half of them as war prizes. Britain also boarded American vessels at sea and dragged off sailors, claiming they were British seamen who had deserted. These high-handed actions kicked up such a ruckus in America that, for the first time since the Revolution, the prospect of a new war against Great Britain seemed a genuine possibility.

The Federalists felt shocked, betrayed, and embittered. "The English are absolute madmen," sputtered an indignant Fisher Ames. "Order in this country is endangered by their hostility no less than by French friendship."[3] When Hamilton heard about British depredations, he did not behave like a pawn of British interests. Rather, he drew up for Washington contingency plans to raise a twenty-thousand-man army to defend coastal cities and impose a partial trade embargo. "The pains taken to preserve peace," he told Washington, "include a proportional responsibility that equal pains be taken to be prepared for war."[4] Once again, Hamilton and Washington agreed that the executive branch should take the lead in a national emergency.

While continuing to meet with his dogged congressional investigators, the sorely taxed treasury secretary instructed customs collectors to fortify ports for a possible invasion, while Federalists presented plans to Congress for a provisional army. As word spread that the omnipresent Hamilton might supervise this new force, Republicans discerned another insidious power play. "You will understand the game behind the curtain too well not to perceive the old trick of turning every contingency into a resource for accumulating force in the government," Madison told Jefferson.[5] Madison and other Republicans opposed Federalist plans to form an army and increase taxes for national defense. When Federalists suggested that it was high time America had its own navy to combat the plunder of American shipping by Barbary pirates, Madison suggested, in all seriousness, that the United States hire the Portuguese navy instead.

Bent upon postponing war with Britain, influential Federalists gathered at the lodgings of Senator Rufus King. They agreed that Washington should send a special envoy to England and proposed Hamilton, who thought he was a splendid choice. As usual, the mere mention of his name sent Federalists into shivers of ecstasy: "Who but Hamilton would perfectly satisfy all our wishes?" asked Ames.[6] At first, Washington leaned toward Hamilton and grew resentful when Edmund Randolph interposed objections. Randolph thought Hamilton had been too vocal in criticizing France to enjoy credibility as an objective negotiator with Britain. Republicans joined this chorus of dissent and talked as if Washington were about to deputize the devil himself. Representative John Nicholas, brother-in-law of Senator James Monroe, told the president apropos of Hamilton that "more than half [of] America have determined it to be unsafe to trust power in the hands of this person. . . . Did it never occur to you that the divisions of America might be ended by the sacrifice of this one man?"[7] Jefferson detected yet another cabal to place "the aristocracy of this country under the patronage" of the British government, not to mention a convenient way to send Hamilton abroad and protect him "from the disgrace and public execrations which sooner or later must fall on the man."[8] In the end, Washington concluded that Hamilton lacked "the general confidence of the country" and wisely opted for a less partisan figure.[9]

On April 14, Hamilton composed a long, plaintive letter to Washington and removed himself from consideration for the post. Madison said that Hamilton was crushed and informed Jefferson that he had been turned down "to his great mortification."[10] Yet Hamilton must have known he would be a divisive choice. He also had reasons for staying close to home: he feared that, without him, Washington might submit to Republican influence; he was still committed to vindicating his reputation before the congressional investigating committee; and he wanted to deal with ominous protests now gathering force in western Pennsylvania against the excise tax he had imposed on liquor.

In his letter to Washington, Hamilton made some statements on foreign policy of lasting significance, especially the idea of war as a last resort. He said that he belonged to the camp that wanted "to preserve peace at all costs, consistent with national honor," resorting to war only if attempts at reparations failed. He warned that

Republicans wanted to poison relations with Britain, foster amity with France, and cancel debts owed to England. The British would then retaliate by blocking commodity exports to America, causing a catastrophic drop in customs duties. This would "bring the Treasury to an absolute stoppage of payment[,] . . . an event which would cut up credit by the roots."[11] Hamilton has often been extolled as the exponent of a rational foreign policy based on cool calculations of national self-interest. But his April 14 letter expressed his unswerving conviction that nations, transported by strong emotion, often *mis*calculate their interests: "Wars oftener proceed from angry and perverse passions than from cool calculations of interest."[12] War with Britain might unleash violent popular fantasies and set in motion "turbulent passions" that would lead to extremism on the French model, pushing America to "the threshold of disorganization and anarchy."[13] Like so many Hamilton polemics, the letter was a hot-blooded defense of a cool-eyed policy.

When he took himself out of the running for envoy, Hamilton recommended John Jay as the perfect substitute—"the only man in whose qualifications for success there would be thorough confidence and him whom alone it would be advisable to send."[14] As the first chief justice of the Supreme Court, Jay lacked Hamilton's conspicuous liabilities as a party head. Hamilton had always admired Jay, but with reservations. He once said of Jay that "he was a man of profound sagacity and pure integrity, yet he was of a suspicious temper."[15] In contrast to Hamilton's colorful exuberance, Jay often dressed in black, tended to be taciturn, and could be aloof, though Philip Schuyler once said that he numbered Jay among the few men for whom he had an affection approaching love.

Jay consented to undertake the mission to England without resigning as chief justice. Republicans found him more palatable than Hamilton but far from a neutral choice. In their eyes, he was another Federalist smitten with England. Nevertheless, the Senate approved him. To offset Jay's appointment, Washington decided to choose a Republican to succeed Gouverneur Morris as American minister to France and settled on James Monroe. Aaron Burr and some Republican colleagues suspected that Hamilton had induced Washington to veto Burr; for Burr, this was another of many times that Hamilton spiked his aspirations for office. But Washington continued to distrust Burr as a devious, prodigal man and needed no prodding from Hamilton.

If Hamilton could not go to London, he would engage in freelance diplomacy at home. Even before Jay was confirmed by the Senate, Hamilton met twice with the imperious George Hammond, Britain's minister to the United States. Once again, those who saw Hamilton as toadying to Britain would have been surprised by how vehemently he laced into Hammond. Hammond told superiors back in London that the treasury secretary "entered into a pretty copious recital of the injuries which the commerce of this country had suffered from British cruisers and into a defense of the consequent claim which the American citizens had on their government to vindicate their rights."[16] Hamilton wanted compensation for American vessels captured in the British West Indies, and Hammond was taken aback by the "degree of heat" Hamilton showed.[17]

At a meeting with Jay and Federalist senators and in a follow-up memo prepared for Washington, Hamilton sketched out Jay's instructions as envoy, making him the primary architect of the treaty that was to result. In addition to compensation, Hamilton wanted a settlement of outstanding issues from the 1783 peace treaty. The most controversial item on his agenda, however, was the forging of a new commercial alliance in which each nation would receive "most favored nation status" from the other—that is, the lowest possible duties on goods they traded with each other. Presumably, this would increase the volume of trade between the two countries. After some modification, Hamilton's instructions were adopted by the cabinet as Jay's marching orders. In frequent meetings with Jay before his departure, Hamilton made clear that he did not want to coddle the British. On the contrary, because of the outrage voiced by the American people, Hamilton wanted Jay to be tough and demand "*substantial* indemnification."[18] At the same time, he wanted Jay to woo the British with a compelling vision of the advantages of closer Anglo-American ties.

On May 12, a thousand New Yorkers cheered from the docks as Jay sailed to England, hoping to avert war. Notwithstanding Republican fears, Washington and Hamilton trod the fine line of neutrality that summer. The U.S. government protested renewed attempts by French privateers to seek asylum in American ports while building up American military strength in case of war with Britain. Washington gave orders to construct six frigates—the birth of the U.S. Navy—and Hamilton negotiated contracts for many naval components: cannon, shot and shells, iron ballast, sailcloth, live oak and cedar, and saltpeter for gunpowder.

Republicans watched Jay's mission with grave doubts. Madison had a nagging intuition that Jay would surrender too much to England and rupture Franco-American relations. The Republican press clung to the malicious fantasy that Jay would negotiate the sale of America back to the British monarchy. There were fresh rumors to boot that Hamilton was involved in a nefarious plot to make the duke of Kent, the fourth son of King George III, the new king of the United States. This prompted one Republican wag to opine that the royal family should adopt Alexander Hamilton to sire a new line in America. With Hamilton's well-known attraction to the ladies, the British monarchy would never need to worry about a shortage of heirs in America.

. . .

Even as the repression in France acquired a terrible new ferocity, Republicans could not shed their warm, fraternal attachment to the French Revolution. However upset by gory deeds committed in the name of liberty, Madison was heartened when Joseph Fauchet, Citizen Genêt's successor as French minister, declared "the revolution firm as a rock."[19] Jefferson still gazed at France through rose-colored glasses that magically transformed horrific events into a fresco of glowing colors. "I am convinced they will triumph completely," he said in May 1794 and blamed the excesses not on the French but on "invading tyrants" who had dared "to embroil them in such wickedness." Far from being repelled by bloodshed, Jefferson awaited the day when "kings, nobles, and priests" would be packed off to "scaffolds which they have been so long deluging with blood."[20] By early summer 1794, that blood ran in rivers, and executions in Paris reached a monstrous toll of nearly eight hundred per month. Nevertheless, when Jefferson's protégé James Monroe arrived in France, he embraced the president of the National Assembly and, to Jay's dismay, lauded the "heroic valor" of French troops.[21]

Where Jefferson dismissed these wholesale killings as regrettable but necessary sacrifices to freedom, Hamilton was traumatized by them. The burgeoning atheism of the French Revolution reawakened in him religious feelings that had lain dormant since King's College days. "The very existence of a Deity has been questioned and in some instances denied," he wrote in alarm about French attacks on Christianity. "The duty of piety has been ridiculed, the perishable nature of man asserted, and his hopes bounded to the short span of his earthly state. Death has been proclaimed an eternal sleep."[22] For Hamilton, the French Revolution had become a compendium of heretical doctrines, including the notion that morality could exist without religion or that human nature could be so refined by revolution that "government itself will become useless and society will subsist and flourish free from its shackles."[23]

Hamilton somehow managed to be worldly without having seen the world. He kept abreast of occurrences in France by subscribing to French newspapers and periodicals, and he polished his French through a Philadelphia tutor, M. Dornat. Equally important, he obtained eyewitness accounts of the French Revolution from the exodus of largely aristocratic refugees who flocked to America. At its peak, this refugee flood was so huge that one in every ten Philadelphians was French; one exile christened the capital "the French Noah's Ark."[24] Hamilton felt at home among these elegant, reform-minded aristocrats. "Mr. Hamilton spoke French fluently and, as we did not sympathize with the revolutionists who drove the exiles from their homes, he was a favorite with many of the cultivated émigrés," Eliza recalled.[25]

"He was small, with an extremely composed bearing, unusually small eyes, and something a little furtive in his glance," Moreau de St. Méry said of Hamilton. "He spoke French, but quite incorrectly. He had a great deal of ready wit, kept a close watch over himself, and was . . . extremely brave."[26] Nobody else ever faulted Hamilton's French. Another émigré, Madame de la Tour du Pin, said of Hamilton, "Although he had never been in Europe, he spoke our language like a Frenchman."[27]

Many French aristocrats were directed to Hamilton by Angelica Church, who had entertained them at her bountiful London table. She steered to him the vicomte de Noailles, Lafayette's brother-in-law, who had formed part of the brotherhood at Yorktown and knew Hamilton well. Like other refugees, de Noailles had been hopeful at the inception of the French Revolution, then recoiled in horror as it veered toward violence. Church also referred the duc de La Rochefoucauld-Liancourt to Hamilton. An enlightened aristocrat and social reformer who had set up a model farm and two factories, the melancholy duke had tried to protect the king from mobs in 1792 before seeking safety in England. In Philadelphia, he grew to adore Hamilton. "Mr. Hamilton is one of the finest men in America, at least of those I have seen," he later wrote. "He has breadth of mind and even genuine clearness in his ideas, facility in their expression, information on all points, cheerfulness, excellence of character, and much amiability."[28] Whatever his carping about the French, Hamilton invariably managed to charm them.

Most French refugees were in desperate straits, having suffered steep declines in status and wealth. Once well-to-do Frenchmen now scraped out livings by giving French lessons, becoming cooks, or opening small stores. "I wish I was a Croesus," Hamilton told Angelica Church. "I might then afford solid consolations to these children of adversity and how delightful it would be to do so. But now, sympathy, kind words, and occasionally a dinner are all I can contribute."[29] Both Alexander and Eliza Hamilton had a special feeling for the dispossessed and helped to raise money for indigent French émigrés. Beginning in 1793, Hamilton, touched as usual by the plight of distressed women, kept lists of French mothers marooned with their children in America. On one list, he wrote: "1 Madame Le Grand with two children lives near the little market at the house of Mr. Peter French hatter in the greatest indigence   2 Madame Gauvin second street North No. 83 with three children equally destitute." On the attached donor list, the biggest contributor stood out plainly: "Eliza Hamilton—20 dollars."[30] Eliza sent off bundles of food and clothing to refugee families, showing an activism that previewed her later dedication to the cause of widows and orphans in New York City.

Of all the French expatriates stranded in Philadelphia, none cut a more memorable figure than a French diplomat of unflappable composure who walked with a clubfoot from a childhood fall and who dissected the world with a sardonic eye:

Charles-Maurice de Talleyrand-Périgord, better known as Talleyrand. On the eve of the Revolution, the king had named him bishop of Autun, a reward for managing church finances, not for superior spirituality, but he did not allow the appointment to slow down his dissolute life. Gouverneur Morris described Talleyrand as "sly, cool, cunning, and ambitious."[31] He had an acerbic wit, and given his legions of enemies, he needed it. Mirabeau, the French revolutionary politician, once observed of Talleyrand that he "would sell his soul for money and he would be right, for he would be exchanging dung for gold."[32] Napoleon expressed this sentiment more concisely, calling Talleyrand "a pile of shit in a silk stocking."[33]

A man for all political seasons, Talleyrand had initially hoped the French Revolution would create a dynamic new state, based on law, order, and sound finance. He stuck with the Revolution until September 1792, when the overthrow of Louis XVI and the attendant massacres eliminated his last hopes. He sat out the subsequent Terror in England and was condemned in absentia for conspiring with the king. British Conservatives snubbed him, but he was welcomed by the opposition Whigs, led by Charles James Fox, and by the playwright Richard Brinsley Sheridan, the same social circle inhabited by John and Angelica Church.

In January 1794, Talleyrand, informed that he had five days to leave England or face deportation, decided to join other stateless émigrés in Philadelphia. The Churches subsidized the trip, and Angelica smoothed the way for Talleyrand and his traveling companion, the chevalier de Beaumetz, by writing to Eliza and introducing the two gentlemen as martyrs for "the cause of moderate liberty. . . . To your care, dear Eliza, I commit these interesting strangers. They are a loan I make you till I return to America, not to reclaim my friends entirely, but to share their society with you and dear Alexander the amiable."[34]

Angelica regretted that Eliza did not speak French nor Talleyrand English. Talleyrand's linguistic isolation in America made Hamilton's fluency an advantage. After Talleyrand arrived in April, Hamilton sounded out Washington discreetly about receiving him. Talleyrand himself ruled out an unofficial meeting. "If I cannot enter the front door," he declared, "I will not go in the back."[35] Talleyrand was still a pariah in revolutionary France, and Joseph Fauchet warned his Parisian superiors of "an infernal plan" being hatched by Talleyrand and Beaumetz, with Hamilton acting as their confederate. Fauchet let Washington know that France frowned upon his receiving Talleyrand, and the president declined a meeting, lest it cause a stir among his Republican detractors. "My wish is . . . to avoid offence to powers with whom we are in friendship by conduct towards their proscribed citizens which would be disagreeable to them," Washington told Hamilton, suggesting that private citizens take up the social burden of greeting Talleyrand.[36]

Talleyrand soon acquired a mulatto mistress, whom he squired openly through the Philadelphia streets. This bothered some priggish souls in polite society but not Hamilton, although Eliza may have been less forgiving. "He was notoriously misshapen, lame in one foot, his manners far from elegant, the tone of his voice was disagreeable, and in dress he was slovenly," she remembered as an old woman. "Mr. Hamilton saw much of him and while he admired the shrewd diplomat for his great intellectual endowments, he detested his utter lack of principle. He had no conscience."[37] Since Fauchet was already convinced that Hamilton was in league with Talleyrand, Hamilton suffered no political penalties in meeting with him. He and Talleyrand became companions with a mutual fascination, if not close friends.

During his two-year sojourn in America, Talleyrand cherished his time with Hamilton and left some remarkable tributes for posterity: "I consider Napoleon, Fox, and Hamilton the three greatest men of our epoch and, if I were forced to decide between the three, I would give without hesitation the first place to Hamilton. He divined Europe."[38] Of Hamilton he told one American travel writer that "he had known nearly all the marked men of his time, *but that he had never known one on the whole equal to him.*"[39] Hamilton savored the roguish diplomat's company and gave him, as a token of esteem, an oval miniature portrait of himself.

Hamilton and Talleyrand were both hardheaded men, disgusted with the utopian dreams of their more fanciful, radical compatriots. As one Talleyrand biographer put it, "They were both passionately interested in politics and both of them looked at politics from a realistic standpoint and despised sentimental twaddle whether it poured from the lips of a Robespierre or of a Jefferson."[40] Both men wanted to create strong nation-states, led by powerful executive branches, and both wanted to counter an aversion to central banks and stock markets. Oddly, Talleyrand agreed with Hamilton that Britain, not France, could best supply America with the long-term credit and industrial products it needed. Talleyrand recalled vividly how Hamilton asserted a passionate faith in America's economic destiny. In their talks, Hamilton said that he foresaw "the day when—and it is perhaps not very remote—great markets, such as formerly existed in the old world, will be established in America."[41] Talleyrand confessed to only one complaint about Hamilton: that he was overly enamored of the grand personages of the day and took too little notice of Eliza's beauty.

Talleyrand was grateful to Angelica Church for having opened the door to the Hamilton home, and he informed her of Eliza's kindness and Hamilton's unique mind and manners. This elicited from her a remarkable letter to Eliza about the man who had so long mesmerized them both. Angelica Church came close to an outright admission that she was more than just entranced by Hamilton. Socially ambitious, she had always dreamed of political glory for her brother-in-law and now gave full-throated expression to her adoration of him and her hopes for his future.

> I have a letter, my dear Eliza, from my worthy friend M. de Talleyrand, who expresses to me his gratitude for an introduction to you and my *Amiable*. By my Amiable, you know that I mean your husband, for I love him very much and, if you were as generous as the old Romans, you would lend him to me for a little while. But do not be jealous, my dear Eliza, since I am more solici-tous to promote his laudable ambition than any person in the world, and there is no summit of true glory which I do not desire he may attain, pro-vided always that he pleases to give me a little chit-chat and sometimes to say, I wish our dear Angelica was here. . . . Ah! Bess! you were a lucky girl to get so clever and so good a companion.[42]

TWENTY-SIX

THE WICKED INSURGENTS
OF THE WEST

Afriter being exculpated by the House investigating committee in late May 1794, Hamilton had informed George Washington that he would not resign after all, citing the prospect of war. In the end, he did go to war, not against European powers but against American frontier settlers. The Whiskey Rebellion in western Pennsylvania that year was an armed protest against the excise tax on domestic distilled spirits—the "whiskey tax," in common lingo—that Hamilton had enacted as part of his funding system. It may qualify as the first "sin tax" in American history, for in *Federalist* number 12, Hamilton had written reprovingly of liquor, "There is perhaps nothing so much a subject of national extravagance as these spirits."[1]

The whiskey tax was doomed to be unpopular, inevitably reminding Americans of the Stamp Act and the whole hated apparatus of British tax collecting. Nonetheless, the tax constituted the second largest source of federal revenues and was indispensable to Hamilton. If deprived of that crucial tax, he would have to raise tariffs, which would encourage more smuggling and tax evasion and spur commercial retaliation abroad. The government also needed money to finance military expeditions against the Indians—expeditions that were especially popular in the affected frontier communities, such as those of western Pennsylvania.

Shortly after the whiskey tax was passed, federal collectors were shunned, tarred, feathered, blindfolded, and whipped. In May 1792, Hamilton had tried to pacify opponents by lowering the rates, but this conciliatory action did not appease them. That summer, Philip Freneau printed inflammatory letters that likened Hamilton's taxes to those imposed arbitrarily under British rule: "The government of the United States, in all things wishing to imitate the corrupt principles of the court of

Great Britain, has commenced the disgraceful career by an excise law."[2] In August 1792, embodying Hamilton's worst nightmare of mob rule, protesters terrorized Captain William Faulkner, who had rented his house to a whiskey-tax inspector, Colonel John Neville. Hamilton received hair-raising reports of the incident: "They drew a knife on him, threatened to scalp him, tar and feather him, and finally to reduce his house and property to ashes if he did not solemnly promise them to prevent the office of inspection from being there."[3] The next day, thirty armed men on horseback, their faces blackened, burst into Faulkner's house, hoping to seize and throttle Neville.

Around this time, a mass meeting in Pittsburgh tried to lend a patina of legitimacy to this open lawlessness. The gathering's clerk was a Swiss-born member of the Pennsylvania Assembly, Albert Gallatin, who had taught French at Harvard and spoke with an unmistakable Gallic accent. A tall, skinny man with a narrow face and hooked nose, Gallatin was a notoriously slovenly character. It was probably Gallatin who drafted a resolution saying the protesters would persist in every "legal measure that may obstruct the operation of the [excise] law until we are able to obtain its total repeal." In the meantime, tax collectors would be treated with the "contempt they deserve."[4] Gallatin later portrayed his part in this meeting as "my only political sin," but Hamilton had a long memory for such transgressions.[5] Moreover, as we have seen, when sworn in as a U.S. senator in late 1793, Gallatin had quickly emerged as an unremitting Hamilton critic.

Refusing to tolerate illegal behavior and not finding the violent protests as colorful as did some later commentators, Hamilton appealed to Washington for "vigorous and decisive measures," or else "the spirit of disobedience will naturally extend and the authority of the government will be prostrate."[6] Hamilton was being typically decisive. He worried that federal authority was still suspect in the backcountry and needed to be firmly established—ideally by consent, if necessary by force. He wanted Washington to issue a proclamation warning tax evaders to desist and, if they refused, to send in troops. Washington reacted in a more temperate fashion. He issued a call for obedience to the law, but he regarded using soldiers as a last resort and hesitated to deploy troops against domestic opponents. If he dispatched troops, he told Hamilton, critics would only exclaim, "The cat is let out. We now see for what purpose an army was raised."[7] It was an accurate prediction.

The mostly Scotch-Irish frontiersmen of western Pennsylvania, who regarded liquor as a beloved refreshment, had the highest per-capita concentration of homemade stills in America. In places, whiskey was so ubiquitous that it doubled as money. The rough-hewn backwoods farmers grew abundant wheat that they couldn't transport over the Allegheny Mountains, which were crossed only by narrow horse paths. They solved the problem by distilling the grain into whiskey, pouring it into kegs, and toting them on horseback across the mountains to eastern markets. Some whiskey was also shipped down the Mississippi. Local farmers believed they unfairly bore the economic brunt of Hamilton's excise tax and also resented any interference with their recreational consumption of homemade brew.

Trouble flared anew in western Pennsylvania during the summer of 1794 just as Hamilton was bedeviled by family problems. His fifth child, John Church Hamilton, who was almost two, became gravely ill, upsetting the again pregnant Eliza. Although Hamilton scarcely ever took a vacation, he beseeched Washington for "permission to make an excursion into the country for a few days to try the effect of exercise and change of air upon the child."[8] When Eliza and "beloved Johnny" failed to improve after a week, Hamilton extended his leave and escorted them partway to the Schuyler mansion in Albany. The diligent Hamilton apologized to Washington, saying he hoped that "when the delicate state of Mrs Hamilton's health is taken in connection with that of the child, I trust they will afford a justification of the procrastination."[9] After Maria Reynolds, the guilt-ridden Hamilton continued to be a doting paterfamilias.

While Hamilton nursed his family, whiskey protesters blasted the stills of their neighbors who had honored the tax. They again terrorized Colonel John Neville, the long-suffering whiskey inspector. A Revolutionary War veteran who had served writs on those evading the tax, Neville issued an emergency summons for militia assistance after angry farmers surrounded his house. About a dozen soldiers tried to hold at bay five hundred rebels who fired at Neville's house for an hour while torching his crops, barn, stables, and fences. They also kidnapped David Lenox, the U.S. marshal for the district, who was released after swearing that he would serve no more papers on tax evaders. Lenox and Neville finally fled the region "by a circuitous route to avoid personal injury, perhaps assassination," Hamilton told Washington.[10]

On August 1, six thousand rebels converged on Braddock's field outside Pittsburgh as extemporaneous violence took on a more systematic character. An organizer named Bradford, having feasted on news of the French Revolution in the *Pittsburgh Gazette*, touted Robespierre as a splendid model for the crowd. He urged creation of a "committee of public safety" along Jacobin lines and several weeks later exhorted his comrades to erect guillotines. To obtain weapons, the rebels decided to attack the government garrison at Pittsburgh, with Bradford boasting, "We will defeat the first army that comes over the mountains and take their arms and baggage."[11]

Always haunted by the hobgoblins of disorder, Hamilton saw more than mass disobedience: he saw signs of treasonous plots against the government. The man who seldom wavered sent Washington a 7,500-word account, reviewing the thuggish punishments meted out to revenue officers since the excise tax was introduced. Hamilton wished to strip these violations of any veneer of acceptable "civil disobedience" and showed they had been massive, vicious, and premeditated. He was not alone in perceiving a more general threat. Attorney General William Bradford regarded the western upheaval as a "formed and regular plan for weakening and perhaps overthrowing the general government," while Secretary of War Knox wanted to combat the unrest with "a superabundant force."[12] Regarding the uprising as a direct threat to constitutional order, Washington asked Supreme Court Justice James Wilson to declare a state of anarchy around Pittsburgh.

When it came to law enforcement, Hamilton believed that an overwhelming show of force often obviated the need to employ it: "Whenever the government appears in arms, it ought to appear like a *Hercules* and inspire respect by the display of strength. The consideration of expence is of no moment compared with the advantages of energy."[13] Meeting with state officials on a blazing day in early August, Hamilton advised them to send troops to the western part of the state. He recommended that Washington assemble a multistate militia of twelve thousand men to suppress an uprising estimated at seven thousand armed men. Secretary of State Edmund Randolph advised against sending troops, fearing it would only unify the protesters, and called instead for a "spirit of reconciliation"—a position echoed by Pennsylvania officials.[14]

Washington contrived a statesmanlike compromise between Hamilton's truculence and Randolph's civility. He issued a proclamation telling the insurgents to desist by September 1, or the government would send in a militia. At the same time, he announced that a three-man commission would confer with citizens. William Bradford was picked as one of the three commissioners, and before the attorney general headed west Hamilton, later accused of lusting for a showdown with the rioters, told him that he was prepared to enact "any reasonable alterations" to make the excise tax more palatable. "For in truth," he told Bradford, "every admissible accommodation in this way would accord with the wishes of this department."[15] This lenient approach, unfortunately, only emboldened the rebels. On August 17, the three commissioners met with concerned Pittsburgh residents, who contended that extremists both "numerous and violent" had resolved to resist the excise tax "at all hazards." The commissioners reluctantly concluded that enforcing compliance with the law would require "the physical strength of the nation."[16]

As the use of force loomed, Knox told Washington that he had to go to Maine to deal with some pressing real-estate problems, though he said he could postpone the trip if necessary. Remarkably enough, Washington let Knox go at this critical moment, which meant that temporary responsibility for the War Department fell upon Hamilton's slim shoulders. This once more provided emphatic proof of

Washington's faith in Hamilton's varied abilities and of Hamilton's perennial eagerness to exercise power.

Hamilton found himself in an agonizing predicament. He was immersed in urgent business—"I have scarcely a moment to spare," he had told Eliza—as he assigned contracts to military vendors for a possible operation in western Pennsylvania.[17] He was ordering horses, tents, and other military stores and did not feel he could vacate his post. But the news he received from Eliza in Albany made him heartsick: little Johnny, despite treatment with laudanum and limewater, was losing ground, and Eliza's pregnancy was precarious. As he tore open each letter, Hamilton trembled that it might announce his son's death. "Alas my charmer, great are my fears, poignant my distress," he told Eliza. "I feel every day more and more how dear this child is to me and I cease not to pray heaven for his recovery."[18] Hamilton's letters show both love for his family and an encyclopedic medical knowledge. He gave Eliza minute instructions on what to do if the baby's situation worsened:

> If he is worse, abandon the laudanum and try the cold bath—that is, abandon the laudanum by degrees, giving it overnight but not in the morning, and then leaving it off altogether. Let the water be put in the kitchen overnight and in the morning let the child be dipped in it head foremost, wrapping up his head well and taking him again immediately out, put in flannel and rubbed dry with towels. Immediately upon his being taken out, let him have two teaspoons full of brandy, mixed with just enough water to prevent its taking away his breath. Observe well his lips. If a glow succeeds, continue the bath. If a chill takes place, forbear it.[19]

This sounds like more than book knowledge. Somewhere along the way, possibly as a boy or in the army, he had learned a considerable amount about nursing the sick and did so with a touching solicitude. By the end of the month, John Church Hamilton had started to recover, and Hamilton sent his wife and child to New York City, where they remained under the watchful care of Nicholas Fish and Elisha Boudinot. All the while, events in western Pennsylvania lurched toward an open confrontation with the government.

On the morning of August 23, 1794, subscribers to the *American Daily Advertiser* of Philadelphia read an impassioned warning from a writer called "Tully." For this apprehensive author, the tumult in western Pennsylvania was a thinly veiled pretext for tearing down the constitutional order. The foes of the federal government were too cunning to attack it directly, he argued, so they feigned moderation and exploited issues such as the excise tax. Despite ailing health, Hamilton wrote three more "Tully" letters during the next nine days. As always, his easily alarmed mind dwelled on dire outcomes: "There is no road to *despotism* more sure or more to be dreaded than that which begins at *anarchy*."[20] In Hamilton's opinion, the most sacred duty of government was an "inviolable respect for the Constitution and laws."[21] He believed the supreme test of the new government's strength was at hand.

Scarcely had "Tully" spoken than the three commissioners returned from western Pennsylvania and offered Washington's cabinet a bleak assessment. During a marathon eight-hour session, Washington, Hamilton, and Randolph decided to call up Virginia's militia under Governor Henry Lee and muster an additional force of up to fifteen thousand troops for possible action. After the meeting, Hamilton swung into action to line up additional supplies.

Like Hamilton, Washington feared that a disruptive faction wanted to pull down the government, and he was prepared to defend the Constitution at all costs. Still, with his finely honed instincts, he delayed dispatching troops. The more assertive Hamilton gave Washington evidence of militia colonels who had abetted the rioters and of judges who had defended resistance to the tax. There had not been a single instance, he alleged, where a Pennsylvania official had punished someone for flouting the whiskey tax. Especially upsetting was the fear that the upheaval might be spreading to other states. When Maryland summoned its militia to enforce the tax, soldiers turned on their officers and set up a liberty pole in the courthouse square. Rumor claimed that the rebels were about to pillage the state armory for weapons.

By September 9, Washington had had enough. "If the laws are to be trampled upon with impunity," he said, "and a minority is to dictate to the majority, there is an end put at one stroke to republican government."[22] Worried about the advent of cold weather, he ordered troops to march to western Pennsylvania. Since Pennsylvania had been reluctant to quash the insurrection, militias from New Jersey, Maryland, and Virginia were recruited instead. Hamilton was in constant motion as he bore the burdens of both the Treasury and War Departments. With his inexhaustible capacity for work, he outfitted an entire army, ordering shoes, blankets, shirts, coats, medicine chests, kettles, rifles, and muskets. As was his wont, he specified everything in great detail, especially when it came to uniforms. "The jackets ought to be made of some of the stuffs of which sailors jackets are usually made," he ordered, "and, like them, without skirts, but of sufficient length of body to protect well the bowels. The trousers, or rather overalls, ought also to be of some strong coarse cheap woolen stuff."[23]

Though the natural leader of the western expedition, Washington wanted to limit his participation. "The President will be governed by circumstances," Hamilton told Rufus King. "If the thing puts on an appearance of magnitude, he goes. If not, he stays." Hamilton himself had never outgrown his love of martial glory and yearned to participate: "If *permitted,* I shall at any rate go."[24] As author of the excise tax, Hamilton assured Washington, it would be good for him to accompany the army: "In a government like ours, it cannot but have a good effect for the person who is understood to be the adviser or proposer of a measure, which involves danger to his fellow citizens, to partake in that danger."[25] Washington acceded to Hamilton's wishes. Secretary of State Randolph then felt obliged to remind Washington "how much Colonel Hamilton's accompanying him was talked of out of doors and how much stress was laid upon the seeming necessity of the Commander-in-Chief having him always at his elbow."[26]

Hamilton remained in a state of trepidation about Eliza's pregnancy. The day before departing for western Pennsylvania, he tried to reassure his children with breezy words: "For by the accounts we have received here, there will be no fighting and, of course, no danger. It will only be an agreeable ride, which I hope will do me good."[27] On the morning of September 30, Washington and Hamilton set off quaintly for war: they climbed into a carriage on Market Street and headed west to join the troops. Soon, they rolled through peaceful farmland. If this carriage ride seems less than epic in nature, we must recall that Washington, sixty-two, could no longer endure long days in the saddle. Hamilton made the travel arrangements for the president and scrupulously declared that if the president stayed in any private homes, he would insist upon paying; otherwise, he would take rooms at local taverns. With Hamilton tending to Washington's needs, the general and his former aide-de-camp must have experienced a queer sense of déjà vu. Hamilton was back serving his general. On the other hand, Hamilton, thirty-nine, had become a mighty figure in his own right. It was far less remarkable that Washington had been elevated to the presidency than that his former aide had risen to become America's second most powerful man.

By October 4, the two men reached their rendezvous with troops at Carlisle, Pennsylvania, in the state's southern tier, about halfway to Pittsburgh. They reviewed a throng of three thousand soldiers, an army that finally swelled to twelve thousand men. The superefficient Hamilton bristled when he discovered that shipments of clothing and ammunition had not arrived and gave a tongue-lashing to the person responsible: "For heaven sake, send forward a man that can be depended upon on each route to hasten them. My expectations have been egregiously disappointed."[28] While Washington and Hamilton camped at Carlisle, emissaries from western Pennsylvania, led by Congressman William Findley, a former weaver, tried to persuade them to turn back. They reported that people in the west country would now submit to the excise tax without coercion. Washington replied that if no shots were fired at his troops, no force would be used, but that he would not desist. Hamilton was even more unyielding. When Findley mentioned one individual who was supposedly restoring order in the area, Hamilton "answered us that that very man, if he was met with, would be skewered, shot, or hanged on the first tree."[29] Seeing the expedition as a major test of government will, Hamilton was in no mood to back down.

While the army was at Carlisle, a young man named David Chambers brought messages from Governor Henry Lee. He later left this telling vignette of Hamilton and Washington:

> As soon as it was known that dispatches had arrived from General Lee, they were taken possession of and earnestly perused by Col. Hamilton, who seemed to be the master spirit. The President remained aloof, conversing with the writer in relation to roads, distances etc. Washington was grave, distant, and austere. Hamilton was kind, courteous, and frank. Hamilton in person prepared answers to the dispatches and, with the most insinuating and easy familiarity, encouraged the writer to carry out the purpose of the mission with dispatch and fidelity. At the same time [he] bestowed a douceur from his purse.[30]

Later, crossing the Alleghenies, Chambers again encountered Hamilton, who gave him a tour of the troops "with all the familiarity and kindness of a father."[31]

Hamilton always found bracing the manly atmosphere of a military camp. Setting up an elegant tent for himself, he strode about and swapped stories of the Revolution with soldiers. Never a martinet, Hamilton did insist on discipline and condoned no lapses. Often, he roamed the camp after dark, surprising sentries at their posts. Finding one wealthy young sentry seated lazily with his musket by his side, Hamilton reproached his laxity. After the youth complained of a soldier's hard life, "Hamilton shouldered the musket, and pacing to and fro, remained on guard until relieved," John Church Hamilton later wrote. "The incident was rumored throughout the camp, nor did the lesson require repetition."[32] Hamilton's experience with this amateurish militia reinforced his long-held conviction that the central government needed a standing army. "In the expedition against the western insurgents," he later said, "I trembled every moment lest a great part of the militia should take it into their heads to return home rather than go forward."[33] A larger federal army was exactly what Republicans feared, and Madison reported to Jefferson that "fashionable language" was now being heard in Philadelphia that a standing army might soon be "necessary for enforcing the laws."[34]

Washington decided that, if the army's situation looked favorable, his own involvement would terminate at Carlisle. So at the end of October, he returned to Philadelphia and left Hamilton and Virginia governor Henry Lee in charge of an army larger than the one he had usually headed in the Revolution. The soldiers marched west along muddy roads in soaking rain. Despite these conditions, Hamilton's health was restored by the campaign, and he even wrote playfully to Angelica Church about his exploits. In a letter marked "205 Miles Westward of Philadelphia," he told his sister-in-law, "I am thus far, my dear Angelica, on my way to attack and subdue the wicked insurgents of the west. But you are not to promise that I shall have any trophies to lay at your feet. A large army has cooled the courage of those madmen and the only question seems now to be how to guard best against the return of the frenzy."[35]

Once Washington left Hamilton in charge of one wing of the army, the imagination of the Republican press ran riot. The Whiskey Rebellion conjured up their favorite bogeyman of Hamilton as the Man on Horseback, the military-despot-in-waiting. Now that Freneau's paper had folded, the principal source of anti-Hamilton bile was Benjamin Franklin Bache, a grandson of Benjamin Franklin and editor of a newspaper soon known as the *Aurora*. As Hamilton rode the soggy, rutted roads of western Pennsylvania, Bache saw devilry in his leadership: "By some it is whispered that he is with the army without invitation and by many it is shrewdly suspected his conduct is a first step towards a deep laid scheme, not for the promotion of the country's prosperity, but the advancement of his private interests."[36] Washington, unfazed, sent this screed to Hamilton, who replied that "it is long since I have learnt to hold popular opinion of no value."[37]

The military expedition met little overt resistance in the mutinous regions. Many delinquent distillers were rounded up, and others either surrendered or fled into the mountains. At times, the behavior of the rowdy, heavy-drinking soldiers was more worrisome than that of the whiskey rebels, and at least two innocent civilians were killed by militia. Washington set an important precedent by having these soldiers tried in civilian, not military, courts.

Hamilton was appalled by his meetings with disaffected elements, which convinced him that revolutionary tendencies had to be extirpated root and branch. He wanted the culprits to lose their homes or even be deported—the beginning of a major shift in his tolerant views on immigration. "This business must not be skinned over," he told Rufus King. "The political putrefaction of Pennsylvania is greater than I had any idea of."[38] He was especially disturbed by the involvement of elected officials in the uprising.

Federal action in suppressing the Whiskey Rebellion left behind a trail of controversy. William Findley believed that Hamilton had welcomed this chance to prove the government's power. He left a one-sided chronicle of events that gives a glimpse of Hamilton's tough, prosecutorial tactics in interrogating prisoners. Hamilton was especially harsh toward those he deemed the leaders. In one case, he questioned a Major Powers about Albert Gallatin's role at insurgent rallies. When Powers answered grudgingly, Hamilton advised him to take an hour to refresh his memory. Findley claims that Powers was flung into a room with other prisoners with a bayonet at his head. An hour later, with Hamilton "suddenly assuming all his terrors, [he] told Major Powers that he was surprised at him, that having the character of an honest man he would not tell the truth, asserting that he had already proofs sufficient of the truth of what he knew he could testify."[39] Powers was held in military custody for eight days, then released as innocent of all charges.

Another suspect, Hugh Henry Brackenridge, was questioned by Hamilton, who struck him as courteous if severe. He "was willing to treat me with civility, but was embarrassed with a sense that, in a short time, I must probably stand in the predicament of a culprit and be in irons."[40] Hamilton asked Brackenridge bluntly if he had planned to overthrow the government, at which point the prisoner recounted his actions. Hamilton scribbled detailed notes during this two-day interrogation, then freed Brackenridge, saying he had been misrepresented. Hamilton's behavior here would seem exemplary—the treasury secretary had taken two days to weigh a man's innocence—but William Findley talked only of the "terrors" that Hamilton had "dispensed" to Brackenridge.[41] Brackenridge himself believed that the show of force orchestrated by the federal government had made its use unnecessary, just as Hamilton had predicted.

Findley told of his own interrogation at the hands of Hamilton, who believed that Findley had published thirteen anonymous newspaper pieces against him. According to Findley, Hamilton snapped at him "that he would never forgive me, because I had told or wrote lies about him." Hamilton was irate that Findley and Gallatin, both elected representatives, had abetted the troublemakers: "He expressed much surprise and indignation at their reposing so much confidence in foreigners, that Gallatin and I were both foreigners and therefore not to be trusted."[42] Findley, who had been born in Ireland, found it scandalous that Hamilton of all people should object to his immigrant background: "I say for secretary Hamilton to object to such a man as a foreigner must be astonishing to those who have any knowledge of his own history."[43]

Public opinion applauded the way Washington balanced firmness and clemency in suppressing the Whiskey Rebellion. There had been very few deaths. Washington and Hamilton had brought new prestige to the government and shown how a democratic society could handle popular disorder without resort to despotic methods. Contrary to European wisdom, democracies did not necessarily degenerate into lawlessness. Hamilton wanted to make an example of some perpetrators, but Henry Lee issued an amnesty proclamation that exempted from prosecution all but about 150 prisoners alleged to have committed "atrocities." Although two insurrectionists were accused of treason and convicted, Washington, with his usual magnanimity, pardoned them. Hamilton feared that this clemency would only encourage lawless elements.

In a public postmortem on the rebellion, Washington blamed the Democratic-Republican societies that had sprouted in the wake of Citizen Genêt's arrival. This presidential message to Congress infuriated James Madison, who rated it "perhaps the greatest error" of Washington's political career and further proof that he was the tool of Alexander Hamilton.[44] "The game was to connect the democratic societies with the odium of insurrection—to connect the Republicans in Congress with those societies—[and] to put the President ostensibly at the head of the other party in opposition to both," Madison fumed.[45] He saw the Whiskey Rebellion as the prelude to the establishment of a standing army that would constrain American liberties. Like Madison, Jefferson regarded the uprising as another instance of Hamilton's vainglorious desire to exercise power and of his fiendish control over Washington's mind. Jefferson had never liked the "infernal" excise tax and had the temerity to label the episode "Hamilton's insurrection."[46] Jefferson likened Washington to an aging "captain in his cabin" who dozed while "a rogue of a pilot has run them into an enemy's port."[47]

Hamilton's friend Timothy Pickering later observed that the excise tax remained "particularly odious to the whiskey drinkers" and that Jefferson's pledge to repeal the tax did much to boost his popularity: "So it may be said, with undoubted truth, that the whiskey drinkers made Mr. Jefferson the President of the United States."[48]

Enough rancor toward Hamilton remained in western Pennsylvania that he required a special escort of six soldiers on horseback when he left Pittsburgh in late November. Tired and weather-beaten from almost two months on the road, he galloped toward Philadelphia with an urgent need to see Eliza, who still struggled with a difficult pregnancy and felt alone without him. Even Angelica Church in London knew about the strained situation. "During his absence I know, my love, that you have been very unhappy and I have often thought of you with more than common tenderness," she wrote to Eliza.[49] On November 24, Henry Knox told Hamilton of Eliza's earnest prayers for his return: "It seems that she has had, or has been in danger of a miscarriage, which has much alarmed her." The guardian angel of the Hamilton household, Edward Stevens, who seemed to appear at providential moments, now tended Eliza and reassured her that she was in no danger. Nevertheless, Knox informed Hamilton that she was "extremely desirous of your presence [and] in order to tranquilize her this note is transmitted by the President's request."[50]

It turned out that Eliza *did* have a miscarriage, and Hamilton flagellated himself for this misfortune. "My dear Eliza has been lately very ill," he wrote to Angelica

Church in early December, sidestepping direct mention of the miscarriage. "Thank God, she is now quite recovered, except that she continues somewhat weak. My absence on a certain expedition was the cause. . . . You will see, notwithstanding your disparagement of me, I am still of consequence to her."[51] Ever since the Maria Reynolds fiasco, Hamilton had tried to be attentive to his family, but the ceaseless demands of public life had often denied him the necessary time, and now his absence had yielded dreadful results.

Hamilton now believed that his great opportunities lay behind him. On December 1, 1794, the day he returned to Philadelphia, he told Washington that he would surrender his Treasury post in late January. One wonders whether Eliza's miscarriage affected this snap decision. With her selfless love for Hamilton, she didn't care for the blood sport that passed for politics and was disgusted by the unceasing attacks on her husband. It pained her to see the scant appreciation for his sacrifices. Angelica Church wrote to Eliza with mixed emotions when she heard of Hamilton's rumored resignation, "The country will lose one of her best friends and you, my dear Eliza, will be the only person to whom this change can be either necessary or agreeable. I am inclined to believe that it is your influence [that] induces him to withdraw from public life."[52] Church knew Hamilton's fun-loving side and agreed that Hamilton needed a respite from politics, telling Eliza that "when you and I are with him, he shall not talk politics to us. A little of his *agreeable nonsense* will do us more good."[53]

The news of Hamilton's departure was a watershed for Washington, who had made him the master builder of the new government. When John Marshall later read through Washington's correspondence for his authorized biography, he expressed "astonishment at the proportion of it" from Hamilton's pen.[54] In acknowledging Hamilton's resignation, Washington penned one of his loftiest tributes.

> In every relation which you have borne to me, I have found that my confidence in your talents, exertions, and integrity has been well placed. I the more freely render this testimony of my approbation, because I speak from opportunities of information w[hi]ch cannot deceive me and which furnish satisfactory proof of your title to public regard. My most earnest wishes for your happiness will attend you in retirement.[55]

The letter shows why Washington tended to discount the Jeffersonian invective against Hamilton. Both as general and president, Washington had numberless chances to observe Hamilton and had seen only competence, dedication, and integrity. In yet another tribute to Hamilton, Washington replaced him with his deputy at Treasury, Oliver Wolcott, Jr.

Hamilton was eager to leave office with an unscarred reputation and immediately informed House Speaker Muhlenberg of his planned resignation. He wanted to give the select investigating committee time to pursue any last-minute inquiries so that nobody would ever intimate that he had ducked questions. It was not Hamilton's style to fade away quietly, and he mustered the strength for one last voluminous report on government finance, which he submitted to the House on January 19, 1795. He wanted to chart a wide-ranging course for the future. Washington had recently asked Congress for plans to retire the public debt and "prevent that progressive accumulation of debt which must ultimately endanger all government."[56] Congress had debated piecemeal proposals instead of a comprehensive plan. For a long time, Hamilton had chafed at the distorted perception that he invariably viewed a public debt as a public blessing; in many circumstances, he knew, a public debt could be a public curse. "The debt of France brought about her revolution," he wrote. "Financial embarrassments led to those steps which led to the overthrow of the government and to all the terrible scenes which have followed."[57] Despite such disclaimers, Hamilton could not shake the pernicious stereotype that he always favored a large public debt. Jefferson told a friend about the public debt, "The only difference . . . between the two parties is that the republican one wish it could be paid tomorrow and the fiscal [Federalist] party wish it to be perpetual, because they find in it an engine for corrupting the legislator."[58]

Debt was a legitimate concern, with an astounding 55 percent of federal expenditures being siphoned off to service it. Hamilton's parting shot to Congress, his *Report on a Plan for the Further Support of Public Credit,* called the bluff of Republican opponents and laid out a program for extinguishing the public debt within thirty years. He wanted new taxes passed and old ones made permanent, and he showed painstakingly that he had striven to reduce debt as speedily as possible. He could not resist tweaking the whiskey insurgents by pointing out that any surplus produced by the excise tax on liquor was explicitly pledged to reducing public debt.

Hamilton's proposals were rolled into a bill passed by Congress within little more than a month of his departure as treasury secretary. He was bothered by amendments proposed by Aaron Burr and others that he thought violated the spirit of his scheme. He told Rufus King that he was "haunted" by the action and railed against this "abominable assassination of the national honor."[59] He wondered why he cared so desperately about the fate of his adopted country and others seemingly so little.

To see the character of the government and the country so sported with, exposed to so indelible a blot, puts my heart to the torture. Am I then more of an American than those who drew their first breath on American ground? Or what is it that thus torments me at a circumstance so calmly viewed by almost everybody else? Am I a fool, a romantic Quixote, or is there a constitutional defect in the American mind? Were it not for yourself and a few others, I . . . would say . . . there is something in our climate which belittles every animal, human or brute. . . . I disclose to you without reserve the state of my mind. It is discontented and gloomy in the extreme. I consider the cause of good government as having been put to an issue and the verdict against it.[60]

In this melodramatic letter, Hamilton again gave way to despair about the American prospect. No longer constrained by the decorum of public life, he drew on this deep well of anger more often. There was a radical alienation inside Hamilton, a harrowing sense that he remained, on some level, a rootless outsider in America. In the end, Congress enacted Hamilton's bill largely intact, rejecting the amendments proposed by Burr. Hamilton's response had been disproportionate to the threat and showed a depressive streak, a chronic tendency to magnify problems. For a man so involved in public life, he was curiously unable to develop a self-protective shell.

Whatever his disappointments, Hamilton, forty, must have left Philadelphia with an immense feeling of accomplishment. The Whiskey Rebellion had been suppressed, the country's finances flourished, and the investigation into his affairs had ended with a ringing exoneration. He had prevailed in almost every major program he had sponsored—whether the bank, assumption, funding the public debt, the tax system, the Customs Service, or the Coast Guard—despite years of complaints and bitter smears. John Quincy Adams later stated that his financial system "operated like enchantment for the restoration of public credit."[61] Bankrupt when Hamilton took office, the United States now enjoyed a credit rating equal to that of any European nation. He had laid the groundwork for both liberal democracy and capitalism and helped to transform the role of the president from passive administrator to active policy maker, creating the institutional scaffolding for America's future emergence as a great power. He had demonstrated the creative uses of government and helped to weld the states irreversibly into one nation. He had also defended Washington's administration more brilliantly than anyone else, articulating its constitutional underpinnings and enunciating key tenets of foreign policy. "We look in vain for a man who, in an equal space of time, has produced such direct and lasting effects upon our institutions and history," Henry Cabot Lodge was to contend.[62] Hamilton's achievements were never matched because he was present at the government's inception, when he could draw freely on a blank slate. If Washington was the father of the country and Madison the father of the Constitution, then Alexander Hamilton was surely the father of the American government.

TWENTY-SEVEN

SUGAR PLUMS
AND TOYS

A fter Hamilton and his family left Philadelphia in mid-February 1795,
they rented lodgings in New York City for several days before proceeding
to the Schuyler residence in Albany for a long-overdue rest. Hamilton
found it hard to retrieve his privacy. He was lionized by New York's merchant community, which treated him to a hero's homecoming. In late February, the Chamber
of Commerce feted him at a huge dinner attended by two hundred people, "the
rooms not being large enough to accommodate more," one newspaper noted.[1] It
was a merry, boisterous affair, with toasts offered impartially to both commerce and
agriculture. Hamilton received nine cheers, compared to three apiece for Washington and Adams. With New York about to overtake Philadelphia and Boston as
America's main seaport, Hamilton was saluted as the patron saint of local prosperity. In his toast, Hamilton paid homage to local businessmen: "The merchants of
New York: may they never cease to have honor for their commander, skill for their
pilot, and success for their port."[2] Two weeks later, Mayor Richard Varick awarded
Hamilton the freedom of the city—a form of honorary citizenship. In the manner
of many immigrants who found thriving new identities in New York City, Hamilton had developed a special feeling for his adopted home. "Among the precious tes-
timonies I have received of the approbation of my immediate fellow citizens," he
told Varick, "none is more acceptable or more flattering to me than that which I
now acknowledge."[3]

After Hamilton left the government, the English artist James Sharples did a sensitive pastel of him in profile that shows that, despite his tireless exertions in
Philadelphia and the lethal broadsides hurled by the Jeffersonians, he still exuded
good humor. Sharples captured an alert man with keenly observant eyes and an

amused air of high spirits. He has a pointed chin, a long, slightly irregular nose, and a receding hairline. Whatever the underlying depths of despair, Hamilton was still very much in his prime and able to project a long career ahead of him.

The news of his resignation unleashed speculation about his future. Cynics perceived deep cunning in his stepping down as treasury secretary, a desire to succeed Washington as president. Detractors and admirers could not conceive that he intended to try private life for a while. When Governor Clinton announced in January that he would not run for reelection, the press pegged Hamilton as a gubernatorial prospect, maybe with his old boss Nicholas Cruger as lieutenant governor. Hamilton instructed Philip Schuyler to dampen this speculation, much of it, he thought, motivated by a wish to present him as a man of irrepressible ambition. When one New York attorney asked Hamilton if he could float his name for governor, he did not answer but appended his own private memo to the message: "This letter was probably written with some ill design. I keep it *without answer* as a clue to future events. A. H."[4] This self-protective action says much about the suspicious atmosphere of the day.

The plain truth was that Hamilton was indebted and needed money badly. This alone refuted accusations that he had been a venal official. If Hamilton had a vice, it was clearly a craving for power, not money, and he left public office much poorer than he entered it. Having taken care of the nation's finances, he had told Angelica Church, "I go to take a little care of my own, which need my care not a little."[5] He planned "to resign my political family and set seriously about the care of my private family."[6] As treasury secretary, Hamilton had made $3,500 per year, which fell far short of the expenses of his burgeoning family and of what he might have earned as an attorney. He owned little more than his household furniture and estimated it would take five or six years of steady work to repay his debts and replenish his finances. Because such indebtedness did not square with Jeffersonian orthodoxy, it had to be denied. After Hamilton resigned, Madison wrote to Jefferson, saying peevishly of Hamilton, "It is pompously announced in the newspaper that poverty drives him back to the bar for a livelihood."[7]

Hamilton was frank about his financial travails. George Washington Parke Custis, the president's adopted grandson, told how Hamilton appeared at the presidential mansion after tendering his resignation. Washington's staff was there when Hamilton smilingly entered. "Congratulate me, my good friends," he announced, "for I am no longer a public man. The president has at length consented to accept my resignation and I am once more a private citizen." Hamilton, noting their dismay, explained, "I am not worth exceeding five hundred dollars in the world. My slender fortune and the best years of my life have been devoted to the service of my adopted country. A rising family hath its claims." Hamilton then picked up a slim volume on the table and turned it over in his hands. "Ah, this is the constitution," he said. "Now, mark my words. *So long as we are a young and virtuous people, this instrument will bind us together in mutual interests, mutual welfare, and mutual happiness. But when we become old and corrupt, it will bind us no longer.*"[8] This queasy view of America's future guaranteed that Hamilton wouldn't just bask in the afterglow of his Treasury success and would return to politics.

Having grown up with insecurity, Hamilton was not immune to the attractions of wealth and wanted to live comfortably, but he had no desire to acquire a fortune by unethical means and gave dramatic proof of this after leaving office. When he returned to New York, he was contacted by his old classmate Robert Troup, who had been "in the habit of lending him [Hamilton] small sums of money to answer current family calls" while he was treasury secretary.[9] The affable Troup had prospered as an agent for a leading real-estate promoter, Charles Williamson, who represented some wealthy British investors in American land. In late March 1795, Troup urged Hamilton to join a scheme for purchasing property in the old Northwest Territory: "No event will contribute more to my happiness than to be instrumental in making a man of fortune—I may say—a gentleman of you. For such is the present insolence of the world that hardly any man is treated like a gentleman unless his fortune enables him to live at his ease."[10] Troup then added that the law would wear down Hamilton and leave him, a decade later, unable to support his family.

If Hamilton lusted for money, here was his chance: a dear friend fairly panted to make him rich by legitimate means. Instead, though touched by Troup's concern, Hamilton wrote him a gracious letter and declined the invitation. That Williamson represented foreigners weighed in his decision because he foresaw "a great crisis in the affairs of mankind" and wanted to be free of any overseas involvement. Hamilton feared that the terrors of the French Revolution might soon be visited upon America, guillotines and all, and that he himself might be condemned by a revolutionary tribunal. "The game to be played may be a most important one," he told Troup. "It may be for nothing less than true liberty, property, order, religion and, of course, *heads*. I will try Troup, if possible, to guard yours and mine." He didn't need to live "*in splendor* in town" if he could "at least live in *comfort* in the country and I am content to do so."[11] Thus Hamilton renounced his chance at fortune. He did accept a legal retainer from Charles Williamson but did not take part in the land deal.

Hamilton spent most of that spring with Eliza and the children in Albany, while shuttling back and forth to a small temporary home and office at 63 Pine Street in Manhattan. He had fleeting reveries about making his first trip to Europe—it would have been his first outside the country since arriving in North America—but opted to spend this precious time with his family. Liberated from official duties, he seemed more lighthearted than he had in years and took an insouciant tone with Eliza. One day, when he failed to book the stagecoach to Albany in time, he told her, "I must therefore take my chance by water, which I shall do tomorrow and must content myself with praying for a fair wind to waft me speedily to the bosom of my beloved."[12] In May, Hamilton even took a weeklong vacation, riding with his friend Henry Glen all the way from Schenectady, New York, to the Susquehanna River and back. Hamilton could not relax for long, however, and by summer he was back in the city, attending to a blue-ribbon clientele that included many eminent New York names. From this base in lower Manhattan, Hamilton would not be as distant from national politics in Philadelphia as geography alone might have suggested.

Hamilton's vacation from American politics was so transient that few people could have noticed. While taking on a full legal calendar, he did not slacken the pace of his essay writing and dove into the first great controversy following his resignation: the furor over the Jay Treaty. No sooner had John Jay arrived in London the previous summer than Hamilton's personal ambassador, Angelica Church, had taken him in hand and invited him to her soirees. Like other powerful males, Jay was taken with Church, telling Hamilton, "She certainly is an amiable, agreeable woman."[13] As he made the social rounds and received a cordial reception, Jay knew that the treaty he would negotiate could ignite a firestorm back home. He warned Hamilton that "we must not make a delusive settlement that would disunite our people and leave seeds of discord to germinate."[14]

Hamilton was still in office when the draft of the so-called Jay Treaty with England arrived in Philadelphia. Jefferson claimed that when Hamilton first set eyes on it, he criticized it privately as "execrable" and "an old woman's treaty."[15] Whether true or not, Hamilton gave the draft treaty a coolly perspicacious review and protested to Secretary of State Edmund Randolph that article 12 placed too many restrictions on American trade with the British West Indies.

Jay signed the final version on November 19, 1794. Refusing to brave the North Atlantic in winter, he remained in England until the spring, while the official version of his treaty preceded him to Philadelphia on March 7, 1795. It was not the sort of document calculated to gladden American hearts, and Washington decided to cloak it in "impenetrable secrecy," as Madison termed it.[16] Possibly because he was an ardent abolitionist, Jay had not pressed England to make good on compensation for slaves carried off at the close of the Revolution. Nor did he obtain satisfaction for American sailors abducted by the British Navy. Americans had expected him to uphold the traditional prerogatives of a neutral power in wartime, but he seemed to have bargained this away too. Most heinous of all to Republicans, Jay had granted British imports most-favored-nation status, while England made no equivalent concessions for American imports. Jay *had* secured some small but notable victories. Britain agreed to evacuate its northwest forts, to allow arbitration for American merchants whose cargo had been seized, and to grant limited access to the West Indies for small American ships. For the Jeffersonians, the Jay Treaty represented, in its rawest form, a Federalist capitulation to British hegemony and a betrayal of the historic alliance with France.

From the Federalist perspective, however, Jay had attained something of surpassing importance. He had won peace with Britain at a time when war seemed suicidal for an ill-prepared America. By aligning the country's fortunes with the leading naval power, Jay had also guaranteed access to overseas markets for American trade. Joseph Ellis has written of the treaty, "It linked American security and economic development to the British fleet, which provided a protective shield of incalculable value throughout the nineteenth century."[17]

Soon after Jay returned to America in late May, Washington summoned a special session of the Senate to debate his treaty behind closed doors. Hamilton expressed extreme anxiety about the outcome. "The common opinion among men of business of all descriptions," he told Rufus King, "is that a disagreement to the treaty would greatly shock and stagnate pecuniary plans and operations in general."[18] Rather than renewing negotiations with England, Hamilton wanted the Senate to predicate approval on deleting the noxious article 12. Senate opposition was spearheaded by Aaron Burr, who wanted "the value of the Negroes and other property" carried off after the Revolution to "be paid for by the British government."[19] He indicated objections to ten other articles as well. Overriding Burr, the Senate narrowly passed the Jay Treaty on June 24 with the proviso that article 12 be partly suspended.

Worried about popular reaction to the treaty, Washington still withheld the text from public scrutiny. Hamilton was eager for it to be printed, if only to allay exaggerated fears, and so advised Washington. On July 1, the full text, leaked by a Republican senator, appeared in a Philadelphia newspaper and created a hullabaloo such as American politics had never seen. Madison said the galvanic effect was "like an electric velocity" imparted "to every part of the Union."[20] Jay surfaced as the new scapegoat for Republican wrath. He had just resigned as first chief justice of the Supreme Court—Hamilton rebuffed an overture to replace him—and had been elected, in absentia, New York's governor, with Hamilton's brother-in-law, Stephen Van Rensselaer, as lieutenant governor. Jay was attacked with peculiar venom. Near his New York home, the walls of a building were defaced with the gigantic words, "Damn John Jay. Damn everyone that won't damn John Jay. Damn everyone that won't put up lights in the windows and sit up all night damning John Jay."[21]

The Jay Treaty resurrected the vengeful emotions called forth by the Citizen

Genêt contretemps two years earlier. "No international treaty was ever more passionately denounced in the United States," Elkins and McKitrick have written, "though the benefits which flowed from it were actually considerable."[22] The popular fury that swept city after city again disclosed the chasm separating the two main political factions. On the Fourth of July, Jay was burned in effigy in so many cities that he said he could have walked the length of America by the glow from his own flaming figure. For Hamilton, these protests confirmed his premonition that Jeffersonians were really Jacobin fanatics in disguise. On July 14, Charleston citizens celebrated Bastille Day by dragging the Union Jack through the streets then setting it ablaze in front of the British consul's house.

The capital was shaken by raucous demonstrations reminiscent of revolutionary Paris, albeit without royalist heads skewered on pikes. Oliver Wolcott, Jr., recorded one such scene: "The treaty was thrown to the populace, who placed it on a pole. A company of about three hundred then proceeded to the French minister's house before which some ceremony was performed. The mob then went before Mr. [George] Hammond's house and burned the treaty with huzzahs and acclamations."[23] John Adams was aghast and later recollected Washington's residence being "surrounded by an innumerable multitude from day to day, buzzing, demanding war against England, cursing Washington, and crying success to the French patriots and virtuous Republicans."[24]

Thus far, Hamilton had generally hesitated to intrude upon his former cabinet colleagues and kept a salutary distance. Now his views were solicited by Washington—with his encyclopedic knowledge of trade and other issues, Hamilton was not easily replaced. Fully aware that the Jay Treaty was bound to be unpopular among Republicans, Washington at least wished to be convinced of its merits in his own mind and know how best to defend it. On July 3, he had sent Hamilton a letter marked "Private and perfectly confidential," asking him to evaluate the treaty. He laid on the flattery pretty thick, praising Hamilton for having studied trade policy "scientifically upon a large and comprehensive scale."[25] Washington apologized for distracting Hamilton from his law practice and said he should refuse the request if he was too busy. Washington must have smiled as he wrote this, knowing Hamilton would deliver a formidable critique at the earliest opportunity. Indeed, on July 9, 10, and 11, Hamilton shipped to Washington, in three thick chunks, a detailed analysis of the treaty. He approved of the first ten articles, dealing with issues from the 1783 peace treaty. He again condemned article 12, restricting American trade with the West Indies, and reserved harsh words for article 18, with its absurdly long list of contraband goods that could be seized by Britain from American ships. The overwhelming message of the Jay Treaty, however, was benign and irresistible: peace for America. "With peace, the force of circumstances will enable us to make our way sufficiently fast in trade. War at this time would give a serious wound to our growth and prosperity."[26]

Washington was thunderstruck when he received Hamilton's treatise so promptly. He expressed sincere thanks, adding, "I am really ashamed when I behold the trouble it has given you to explore and to explain so fully as you have done."[27] Washington quibbled with Hamilton on one or two points but otherwise stood in perfect agreement. His letter to Hamilton again corroborates what the Jeffersonians found difficult to credit: that Washington never shied away from differing with the redoubtable Hamilton but agreed with him on the vast majority of issues.

After Alexander Hamilton left the Treasury Department, he lost the strong, restraining hand of George Washington and the invaluable sense of tact and proportion that went with it. First as aide-de-camp and then as treasury secretary, Hamilton had been forced, as Washington's representative, to take on some of his decorum. Now that he was no longer subordinate to Washington, Hamilton was even quicker to perceive threats, issue challenges, and take a high-handed tone in controversies. Some vital layer of inhibition disappeared.

This was first seen in Hamilton's crusade for the Jay Treaty. Despite Senate passage, Washington had not yet affixed his signature to it. The battle over the treaty became more than a routine political clash for Hamilton. He fought as if it were a political Armageddon that would decide America's fate. That summer he saw himself as in the midst of a quasi-revolutionary atmosphere in New York. The French tricolor even flapped above the Tontine Coffee House, gathering place of the merchant elite. In his more fearful moments, Hamilton envisaged Jeffersonian tumbrels carting him and other Federalists off to homegrown guillotines. "We have some cause to suspect, though not enough to believe, that our Jacobins meditate serious mischief to certain individuals," Hamilton wrote confidentially to Oliver Wolcott, Jr. "It happens that the militia of this city, from the complexion of its officers in general, cannot be depended on. . . . In this situation, our eyes turn as a resource in a sudden emergency upon the military now in the forts."[28]

It was increasingly difficult for Hamilton to trust the sincerity of his opponents, whom he viewed as a malignant force set to destroy him. Early in the spring, Commodore James Nicholson—the father-in-law of Albert Gallatin, a friend of Aaron Burr, and the former president of New York's Democratic club—had leveled vicious accusations against him. Nicholson claimed that Hamilton, as treasury secretary, had stashed away one hundred thousand pounds sterling in a London bank—the clear insinuation being that Hamilton had both profited from public office and connived with the British. One of Hamilton's friends, taking umbrage at this slander, demanded proof. The unruffled Nicholson replied that he would disclose his source only if Hamilton called upon him. "No call has, however, been made from that time to this," John Beckley informed Madison, as if this constituted proof of Hamilton's guilt. "Nicholson informed me of these particulars himself and added that, if Hamilton's name is at any time brought up as a candidate for any public office, he will instantly publish the circumstance."[29] That Republicans could swallow such nonsense as gospel truth suggests that Hamilton did not entirely dream up the conspiracies ranged against him.

The altercation with Nicholson formed the backdrop to some extraordinary events that unfolded in mid-July 1795. For several days, New York City was saturated with handbills urging citizens to gather at City Hall (Federal Hall) at noon on July 18 "to deliberate upon the proper mode of communicating to the President their disapprobation of the English treaty."[30] Boston citizens had issued a blanket condemnation of the Jay Treaty, and Hamilton feared a bandwagon effect. Already leaders of the Democratic clubs were delivering heated antitreaty speeches on Manhattan street corners. To devise ways to blunt the gathering, the business community summoned a meeting at the Tontine Coffee House on the night of the seventeenth at which Hamilton and Rufus King endorsed the Jay Treaty. They appealed to supporters to show up at City Hall the next day and stage a counterdemonstration.

As the clock tolled twelve the next day, Hamilton took up a position on the stoop of an old Dutch building on the west side of Broad Street, right across from City Hall. More than five thousand people had squeezed into the intersection where George Washington had taken the oath as president in 1789. But the scene of concord six years earlier now witnessed one of the uglier clashes in the early republic. From his stoop, Hamilton shouted out and demanded to know who had convened the meeting. The irate crowd shouted back in response, "Let us have a chairman."[31] Colonel William S. Smith, John Adams's son-in-law, was chosen and presided from the balcony of City Hall. Peter R. Livingston began to speak against the Jay Treaty, but he was brusquely interrupted by Hamilton, who questioned his right to speak first. When a vote was taken, the vast majority of those present favored Livingston, who resumed his oration. But there was so much heckling, such a tremendous din of voices, that Livingston could not be heard, and he suggested to treaty opponents that they move down Wall Street toward Trinity Church.

Not all treaty critics drifted away, however, and about five hundred listened in a surly mood as Hamilton began his ringing defense. According to one newspaper, Hamilton stressed "the necessity of a *full discussion* before the citizens could form their opinions. Very few sentences, however, could be heard on account of hissings, coughings, and hootings, which entirely prevented his proceeding."[32] This was a remarkable spectacle: the former treasury secretary had descended from Mount

Olympus to expose himself to street hecklers. John Church Hamilton contends that when his father asked the demonstrators to show respect, he was greeted "by a volley of stones, one of which struck his forehead. When bowing, he remarked, 'If you use such knock-down arguments, I must retire.'"[33] Federalist Seth Johnson confirmed the tale: "Stones were thrown at Mr. Hamilton, one of which grazed his head," while another indignant Federalist said that the "Jacobins were prudent to endeavour to knock out Hamilton's brains to reduce him to an equality with themselves."[34] Before long, treaty opponents stormed down to the Battery, formed a circle, and ceremonially burned a copy of the Jay Treaty. When Jefferson heard about Hamilton being stoned in the street, he didn't react with horror or sadness; rather, he was elated, telling Madison that "the Livingstonians appealed to stones and clubs and beat him and his party off the ground."[35] Evidently, Jefferson thought this would delight the author of the Bill of Rights.

For a man of his stature, Hamilton had suffered the ultimate indignity. The opposition had turned into the faceless rabble he had feared. On the other hand, his own behavior had been provocative and unbecoming. When he told "friends of order" to follow him down the block, only a small number complied. It was at this moment that Hamilton and his entourage came upon a shouting match in the street between a Federalist lawyer, Josiah Ogden Hoffman, and the same Commodore James Nicholson who had smeared Hamilton months earlier. When Hamilton intervened to stop the quarrel, he was insulted anew by Nicholson, who called him an "abettor of Tories" and told him he had no right to interrupt them. Hamilton tried to herd the feuding men indoors. Nicholson then said that he didn't need to listen to Hamilton and accused him of having once evaded a duel. These were incendiary words for any gentleman. "No man could affirm that with truth," Hamilton retorted, and he "pledged himself to convince Mr. Nicholson of his mistake" by calling him to a duel at a more suitable time and place.[36]

Hamilton wasn't through with his swaggering performance. After leaving Nicholson, he and his followers stopped by the front door of Edward Livingston—the youngest brother of Chancellor Robert R. Livingston, a later mayor of New York, and a man Hamilton called "rash, foolish, intemperate, and obstinate"—where Hoffman and Peter Livingston were locked in a nasty verbal scuffle over the Jay Treaty.[37] The discussion grew more heated until Edward Livingston and Rufus King begged the men to settle their quarrel elsewhere. "Hamilton then stepped forward," Edward Livingston later said, "declaring that if the parties were to contend in a personal way, he was ready, that he would fight the whole party one by one. I was just beginning to speak to him on the subject [of] this imprudent declaration when he turned from me, threw up his arm and declared that he was ready to fight the whole '*detestable faction*' one by one."[38] Livingston thought Hamilton must have been "mortified at his loss of influence before he would descend [to] language that would have become a street bully."[39] This was truly amazing behavior: Hamilton was prepared to descend into outright fisticuffs in the streets with his opponents, as if he were a common ruffian. Maturin Livingston, Peter's brother, coolly told Hamilton that he was ready to take up his offer and duel him "in half an hour where he pleased."[40] Hamilton confessed that he already had another duel on his hands but would get around to Livingston once he had disposed of Nicholson. Evidently, Hamilton had no concerns about issuing two deadly challenges in quick succession. Vigilant as ever about his reputation, he knew how to exploit such affairs of honor to face down his enemies.

The Republican newspaper, *The Argus,* called for another large protest rally against the Jay Treaty two days later. This huge meeting passed a resolution against the treaty, an action duplicated by protest rallies in Philadelphia, Baltimore, and Charleston. It was a horrendously busy week for Hamilton, who was supposed to defend before the Supreme Court the legality of a tax on carriages that he had instituted as treasury secretary. (In the end, the case wasn't argued until February.) Two days after their encounter, Hamilton stung Commodore Nicholson with a letter proposing a duel a week later: "The unprovoked rudeness and insult which I experienced from you on Saturday leaves me no option but that of a meeting with you, the object of which you will readily understand."[41] Hamilton didn't leave room for an apology and proceeded straight to a challenge. His old friend Nicholas Fish, drafted as his second, delivered the letter to Nicholson. Within minutes, the impulsive Nicholson scratched out a reply, accepting the duel and asking that it take place the next morning. He claimed that his family would be upset by any delay and that word might leak out. In a series of faintly mocking replies—"I should hope that it will be easy for you to quiet the alarm in your family"—Hamilton insisted that he was too busy to duel before the following Monday.[42] He adopted the brisk tone of an important man irritated by having to negotiate with an inferior. From the tone of this exchange, one can tell that Hamilton felt fully in charge and free to needle Nicholson at will.

For several days, their seconds scurried back and forth, trying to work out a settlement. In all likelihood, Hamilton thought Nicholson was bluffing and would back down. But Hamilton took the prospect of a duel seriously enough that he named Troup executor of his estate and wrote him a letter that would serve as a revised will. Hamilton was especially concerned about a sheaf of personal papers that he had stowed in a leather trunk and marked "JR. *To be forwarded to Oliver Wolcott Junr. Esq.*"[43] Presumably, the "JR" referred to James Reynolds, with Wolcott charged if need be with the safekeeping of the correspondence related to the Reynolds affair.

The 1795 will sheds light on other mysteries, including Hamilton's relationship with his father, who had moved to St. Vincent five years earlier. They had never entirely lost touch and now exchanged stilted, intermittent letters through couriers. James Hamilton ended one letter to his famous son with his "respectful compliments to Mrs. Hamilton and your children," whom he had still never met.[44] James Hamilton had borrowed seven hundred dollars from his son. Hamilton now worried that, if he died in a duel, his creditors might seek to recover money from his aging father. Hamilton told Troup that he had considered giving his father special protection from creditors, then decided against it:

> I hesitated whether I would not also secure a preference to the drafts of my father. But these, as far as I am concerned, being a merely voluntary engagement, I doubted the justice of the measure and I have done nothing. I regret it lest they should return upon him and increase his distress. Though, as I am informed, a man of respectable connections in Scotland, he became bankrupt as a merchant at an early day in the West Indies and is now in indigence. I have pressed him to come to me, but his great age and infirmity have deterred him from the change of climate.[45]

Hamilton seemed to repress some unspoken hostility here—there is pity but no warmth in the description—as he leaves his father to the tender mercies of his creditors. Though now free of Treasury duties, Hamilton never expressed a wish to visit his aging father in St. Vincent.

The will again belies Jeffersonian fantasies that Hamilton had reaped a fortune from government service and had salted away embezzled funds in a British bank. Hamilton told Troup that he owed five thousand pounds to his brother-in-law, John Barker Church, and that he feared he was insolvent: "For after a life of labor, I leave my family to the benevolence of others, if my course shall happen to be terminated here."[46] In the event that he died in debt, Hamilton said that he trusted to the "friendship and generosity" of John Barker Church.[47]

In the end, Hamilton tinkered with the apology that he wanted Nicholson to make, and Nicholas Fish got him to sign it pretty much verbatim. As for the second duel that Hamilton broached on July 18, he got Maturin Livingston to deny that he had ever cast aspersions on his manhood or accused him of cowardice. Hamilton had prevailed in the two affairs of honor arising from the Jay Treaty protests, but at what price? He had shown a grievous lack of judgment in allowing free rein to his combative instincts. Without Washington's guidance or public responsibility, he had again revealed a blazing, ungovernable temper that was unworthy of him and rendered him less effective. He also revealed anew that the man who had helped to forge a new structure of law and justice for American society remained mired in the old-fashioned world of blood feuds. When it came to intensely personal conflicts, New York's most famous lawyer still turned instinctively not to the courtroom, but to the dueling ground.

Four days after confronting his Jay Treaty foes in the streets, Hamilton took to the public prints. Republicans had chipped away at the treaty behind Roman names—whether Robert R. Livingston writing as "Cato" or Brockholst Livingston as "Decius" and "Cinna"—and Hamilton commenced a ferocious counterattack called "The Defence." Over a period of nearly six months, he published twenty-eight glittering essays, strengthening his claim as arguably the foremost political pamphleteer in American history. As with *The Federalist Papers*, "The Defence" spilled out at a torrid pace, sometimes two or three essays per week. In all, Hamilton poured forth nearly one hundred thousand words even as he kept up a full-time legal practice. This compilation, dashed off in the heat of controversy, was to stand as yet another magnum opus in his canon.

Like *The Federalist*, "The Defence" was conceived as a collaboration. Hamilton planned to handle the first section of the Jay Treaty, which dealt with violations of the 1783 peace treaty, writing twenty-eight articles in all. Rufus King contributed another ten on the commercial and maritime articles. Governor Jay stayed in touch with both men but refrained from adding to their output. "Jay was also to have written a concluding peroration," John Adams told Abigail, "but being always a little lazy, and perhaps concluding that it might be most politic to keep his name out of it, and perhaps finding that the work was already well done, he neglected it. This I have from King's own mouth."[48]

Hamilton employed a daring strategy used before, publishing the first twenty-one essays deep in enemy territory: the pages of *The Argus*, which had printed Robert R. Livingston's "Cato" essays. For his nom de guerre, Hamilton picked "Camillus," from Plutarch's *Lives*. This Roman general was a perfect symbol: a wise, virtuous man who was sorely misunderstood by his people, who did not see that he had their highest interests at heart. The fearless Camillus expressed unpalatable truths and was finally exiled for his candor. He was vindicated when he was recalled from banishment to rescue his city, which was endangered by the Gauls. The choice of pen name tells us much about how Hamilton viewed himself and what he perceived as a lack of appreciation by his fellow citizens.

As usual, Hamilton wrote like a man possessed, showing drafts to James Kent, who marveled that even under deadline pressure Hamilton did not stint on scholarship: "Several of the essays of *Camillus* were communicated to me before they were printed and my attention was attracted . . . to the habit of thorough, precise, and authentic research which accompanied all his investigations. He was not content, for instance, with examining Grotius and taking him as an authority in any other than the original Latin."[49]

In his first essay on July 22, Hamilton attacked the motives of the Jay Treaty opponents—what he saw as their desire to subvert the Constitution, embroil the United States in war on France's side, and install one of their own as president: "There are three persons prominent in the public eye as the successor of the actual president of the United States in the event of his retreat from the station: Mr. Adams, Mr. Jay, Mr. Jefferson."[50] By discrediting the treaty, Hamilton averred, Republican critics hoped to destroy Jay as a presidential candidate. Since Adams was also a Federalist, Hamilton clearly implied that the hue and cry over the treaty was a stratagem to further Jefferson's presidential ambitions. Interestingly enough, after reading this first issue, Washington wrote an approving note from Mount Vernon: "To judge of this work from the first number, which I have seen, I augur well of the performance, and shall expect to see the subject handled in a clear, distinct, and satisfactory manner."[51]

Washington had complained of the treaty being distorted by "tortured interpretation" and "abominable misrepresentations," and so Hamilton reviewed each article in turn.[52] First, however, he wanted to address the larger political context. The specter of war with Britain was real, and Hamilton dreaded the demolition of his economic program. "Our trade, navigation, and mercantile capital would be essentially destroyed" if war came, he warned.[53] He excoriated the Republicans as "our war party" and pleaded that the young nation required an interval of peace. The United States was "the embryo of a great empire," and the European powers, if given half a chance, would happily stamp out this republican experiment: "If there be a foreign power, which sees with envy or ill will our growing prosperity, that power must discern that our infancy is the time for clipping our wings."[54] Better to negotiate than to engage in premature war with England. In the "Defence" essays, we see the restrained, pacific side of Hamilton, who turned to war only as a last resort in case of direct aggression or national humiliation.

Hamilton was not content to write as Camillus alone. Two days after his second essay appeared, he began to publish, in the same paper, a parallel series as "Philo Camillus." For several weeks, Philo Camillus indulged in extravagant praise of Camillus and kept up a running attack on their Republican adversaries. The prolific Hamilton was now writing pseudonymous commentaries on his own pseudonymous essays. He also tossed in two trenchant essays under the name "Horatius" in which he accused Jeffersonians of "a servile and criminal subserviency to the views of France."[55] During this frenetic period, Hamilton found time to stop by political gatherings. At one meeting at the Assembly Room on William Street, he warned his followers that "unless the treaty was ratified, we might expect a *foreign war*, and if it is ratified, we might expect a *civil war*."[56] Hamilton was not alone in worrying that civil turmoil could erupt. From Philadelphia, Treasury Secretary Wolcott reported, "I think we shall have no dangerous riots, but one month will determine the fate of our country."[57] In the third "Defence," Hamilton portrayed his opponents in the blackest colors: "If we suppose them sincere, we must often pity their ignorance; if insincere, we must abhor the spirit of deception which it betrays."[58] Contrary to his usual image, Hamilton paid homage to the ability of the common people to resist such deceptions and said that they would disappoint those "who, treating them as children, fancy that sugar plums and toys will be sufficient to gain their confidence and attachment."[59]

In reviewing the 1783 peace treaty, Hamilton noted that the Jay Treaty would create a bilateral commission to arbitrate disputes over debt, the British seizure of American ships, and the boundaries between America and Canada. He claimed that the only article that Britain refused to honor was payment of compensation for nearly three thousand former slaves, and he thought it foolish to risk the treaty over this issue. This uncompromising abolitionist wrote that "the abandonment of negroes, who had been promised freedom, to bondage and slavery would be odious and immoral."[60] Hamilton also made the courageous but still taboo argument that the United States as well as England had violated the peace treaty. As to whether the Jay Treaty would create an "alliance" with Great Britain, Hamilton described this as "an insult to the understandings of the people to call it by such a name."[61] He was being disingenuous, however, when he said that the treaty would not bind the United States more closely to Great Britain and suggested that a commercial treaty lacked political implications. There was a deeply emotional coloring to Hamilton's pro-British views that he could not admit and that often clashed with his image as the cool-eyed exponent of Realpolitik. In much the same way, his detestation of France was fueled by moral outrage as well as a sober assessment of U.S. interests. Madison was certain that the treaty would undercut U.S. neutrality: "I dread in the ratification . . . an immediate rupture with France. . . . I dread a war with France as a signal for a civil war at home."[62]

Critics said that Jay had given away everything in his treaty and gotten little in return. Hamilton countered that Britain had made significant concessions, modifying her old "system of colonial monopoly and exclusion" and granting concessions to America that no other country had won.[63] He thought these would lead to a burst of American trading abroad. Bold, cosmopolitan, and self-confident, Hamilton thought the United States had nothing to fear from commercial engagement with the rest of the planet. "The maxims of the U[nited] States have hitherto favoured a free intercourse with all the world," he wrote. "They have conceived that

they had nothing to fear from the unrestrained competition of commercial enterprise and have only desired to be admitted to it upon equal terms."[64]

By the time Hamilton completed eight "Defence" and three "Philo Camillus" essays, President Washington had signed the Jay Treaty in mid-August 1795 despite a
steady drumbeat of press criticism. At first the treaty's prospects had looked poor,
but the American economy was booming from British trade while French trade had
dropped by more than half since the Bastille was stormed in 1789. With the treaty
approved, Hamilton did not rest his pen. If anything, its passage gave his "Defence"
essays extra weight as an authoritative exposition.

Hamilton had become the treaty's undisputed champion. Fisher Ames thought
he was so far superior to his Republican critics that he had squandered his talents
in writing "The Defence": "Jove's eagle holds his bolts in his talons and hurls them,
not at the Titans, but at sparrows and mice."[65] Though of a different political persuasion, Jefferson agreed that the Republicans had provided no effective antidote to
Hamilton's poison. It was a difficult time for Jefferson, who was suffering from
rheumatism at Monticello. He was reading the "Defence" series, forwarded to him
by John Beckley, with mounting upset. He feared that Hamilton was winning the
argument, and by September 21 he could stand it no longer. Once again, he turned
to Madison as his proxy. In so doing, Jefferson gave voice to the sheer terror that
Hamilton's intellect inspired in him and paid his foe one of the supreme left-
handed tributes in American history. He told Madison:

> Hamilton is really a colossus to the anti-republican party. Without numbers,
> he is an host [i.e., an army or multitude] within himself. They have got them-
> selves into a defile, where they might be finished. But too much security
> on the Republican part will give time to his talents and indefatigableness
> to extricate them. We have had only middling performances to oppose to
> him. In truth, when he comes forward, there is nobody but yourself who can
> meet him.[66]

Before Jefferson requested his aid, Madison had been cocky in his critique of
Hamilton's performance, stating that "Camillus . . . if I mistake not will be betrayed
by his anglomany into arguments as vicious and vulnerable as the treaty itself."[67]
Now that Jefferson asked him to rebut those arguments, Madison beat a hasty retreat from the challenge.

While Madison shrank from verbal jousting with Hamilton, he continued to wage
a vigorous legislative campaign against the Jay Treaty. He did so by pouncing upon
an interpretation of the Constitution so unorthodox as to provoke a full-blown

constitutional crisis. Back in the distant days when they had coauthored *The Federalist Papers,* Madison and Hamilton had jointly explained why the Constitution gave the Senate—with its long terms, learned members, and institutional memory—the sole power to ratify treaties. Now Madison found it expedient to argue that approval of the Jay Treaty fell within the bailiwick of the House of Representatives as well, because it had the power to regulate commerce. Of this astonishing proposition, biographer Garry Wills has noted that it was more than a "loose construction" of the Constitution: "It amounted to reversal of its plain sense."[68]

Once upon a time, Jefferson had applauded the notion that the populist House would retain power over money matters while foreign affairs would be assigned to the more patrician Senate. Eager to scotch the treaty, he now altered his position: "I trust the popular branch of our legislature will disapprove of it and thus rid us of this infamous act."[69]

Hamilton considered the legislative threat to the Jay Treaty as tantamount to a House veto—something that would fundamentally alter the balance of power in the American system. Fortunately, Hamilton was in an excellent position to resume his protreaty crusade. Rufus King had just completed his "Defence" essays dealing with the commercial side of the treaty, allowing Hamilton to cap the series by tackling the new constitutional issues. In early January, he devoted the last two essays of "The Defence" to exposing the absurdity of letting the House scrap a treaty. If such a precedent was established, the "president, with the advice and consent of the Senate, can make neither a treaty of commerce nor alliance and rarely, if at all, a treaty of peace. It is probable that, on minute analysis, there is scarcely any species of treaty which would not clash, in some particular, with the principle of those objections."[70] If Madison's novel argument stood, the federal government would be unable to manage relations with foreign countries and would have to cede such authority to a squabbling, pontificating Congress.

The young country seemed to face another clash on basic governance issues, another battle over the true meaning of the Constitution. Led by Madison, the Republicans seemed willing to hazard all to kill the treaty. John Adams told Abigail that the "business of the country . . . stands still. . . . [A]ll is absorbed by the debates." If the Republicans remained "desperate and unreasonable," he warned, "this Constitution cannot stand. . . . I see nothing but a dissolution of government and immediate war."[71] Under the shadow of this impasse, business slowed, prices fell, and imports declined.

In pushing the treaty, the major asset that the Federalists possessed was still George Washington, the unifying figure in American life. For Jefferson, Federalism was a spent force sustained only by the president's unique stature. Hence, Republicans decided that the time had come to shatter the taboo about criticizing Washington, and they declared open season on him. Once again, the Republican press drew a facile equation between executive power and the British monarchy. On December 26, 1795, Philip Freneau wrote that Washington wanted to enact the Jay Treaty to elevate himself to a king: "His *wishes* (through the treaty) will be gratified with a hereditary monarchy and a House of Lords."[72] This sort of vicious abuse, once reserved for Alexander Hamilton, was now directed at the venerable Washington. The president heard rumors that Jefferson was leading a whispering campaign that portrayed him as a senile old bumbler and easy prey for Hamilton and his monarchist conspirators. Jefferson kept denying to Washington that he was the source of such offensive remarks. Joseph Ellis has commented, however, "The historical record makes it perfectly clear, to be sure, that Jefferson *was* orchestrating the campaign of vilification, which had its chief base of operations in Virginia and its headquarters at Monticello."[73]

In the early days of Washington's presidency, James Madison had been his most trusted adviser and confidant. Now in early March 1796, Madison risked an unalterable break with Washington by supporting a congressional demand that the president turn over the private instructions given to Jay to guide his negotiations—instructions that Hamilton had largely assembled. Hamilton, outraged, urged Washington to protect the confidentiality of these executive discussions; being Hamilton, he listed thirteen compelling reasons for such executive privilege. If Madison prevailed, it would set a precedent that "will be fatal to the negotiating power of the government, if it is to be a matter of course for a call of either House of Congress to bring forth all the communications, however confidential."[74] Hamilton's position toughened in coming weeks, and by late March he advised Washington that he should send no reply whatever to the House and "resist in totality."[75] If the House gained the power to nullify a treaty, Hamilton warned, it would destroy executive power and erect "upon its ruins a legislative omnipotence."[76] Hamilton and Madison were again pitted in a fundamental contest over whether the executive or legislative branch would run American foreign policy.

Hamilton was relieved when Washington denied Congress the treaty instructions. With this request spurned, Madison and House Republicans vowed to starve the treaty by blocking appropriations needed to implement it. Hamilton wanted Washington to deliver a solemn protest to Congress, citing "the certainty of a deep wound to our character with foreign nations and essential destruction of their confidence in the government."[77] Partly at Hamilton's instigation, the Federalists organized meetings of merchants and circulated petitions to promote the treaty. "We must seize and carry along with us the public opinion," Hamilton told Rufus King.[78] A tremendous outpouring of popular feeling arose on both sides of the issue, and mass rallies in many cities culminated in pro or con resolutions. When a demonstration against the treaty was called for the Common in New York City—the same public space where Hamilton had made his dramatic debut as a student orator—he sent a broadside to be distributed to those attending. He invoked the glorious wartime service of Washington, Jay, and others who now stood accused of selling their souls to England: "Can you, I ask, believe that all these men have [of] a sudden become the tools of Great Britain and traitors to their country?"[79]

At first, Madison had been energized by the sense of a congressional majority backing him, but the Federalist campaign slowly whittled down this strength. Adams noted the toll on a shaken Madison. "Mr. Madison looks worried to death. Pale, withered, haggard."[80] On April 30, 1796, Federalists eked out a razor-thin victory of fifty-one to forty-eight in the House to make money available for the Jay Treaty. Hamilton's "Defence" essays may well have tipped the balance. Biographer Broadus Mitchell concluded, "It is a fair inference that Hamilton's arguments for the treaty made the difference between acceptance and rejection."[81] For Madison, the vote confirmed Washington's power and the success of scare tactics employed by the Federalists. Always searching for sinister cabals, Madison also believed that northern merchants and banks had bought the vote, though it was probably the general prosperity spawned by trade with England that enlisted the sympathies of ordinary citizens.

Wrangling over the Jay Treaty cost Madison his friendship with Washington. Washington was so indignant at what he regarded as Madison's duplicity that he unearthed the secret minutes from the Constitutional Convention and showed how the framers, Madison included, had refused to give the House the power to thwart the executive branch in making treaties. Madison was sure that Hamilton had goaded Washington into this "improper and indelicate act," though it was actually Washington's own doing.[82] Washington never forgave Madison, never sought his counsel again, and never invited him back to Mount Vernon. It was a crushing defeat for the short, erudite Republican leader. Federalist pamphleteer William Cobbett gloated of Madison, "As a politician he is no more. He is absolutely deceased, cold, stiff and buried in oblivion for ever and ever."[83] Jefferson likewise refused to concede that the treaty had passed on its merit or because of Hamilton's inspired advocacy; he credited the Federalist victory to the prestige of Washington, "the one man who outweighs them all in influence over the people."[84]

Increasingly disillusioned with both Jefferson and Madison, Washington felt a corresponding warmth toward Hamilton. Even though he was no longer in the cabinet, Hamilton was still the one who helped Washington to reconcile political imperatives with constitutional law. The two men had won a great victory together: they had established forever the principle of executive-branch leadership in foreign policy. Shortly before the House vote on the treaty, Washington thanked Hamilton "for the pains you have been at to investigate the subject" and assured him of "the warmth of my friendship and of the affectionate regard" in which he held him.[85] Washington had never expressed friendship for Hamilton so fervently before. For Hamilton, the Jay Treaty victory represented the culmination of his work with Washington. By settling all outstanding issues left over from the Revolution, the treaty removed the last impediments to improved relations with England and promised sustained prosperity.

TWENTY-EIGHT

SPARE CASSIUS

As demonstrated by his leadership on the Jay Treaty, Hamilton was more than just the principal theorist of the Federalists. He was also their chief tactician and organizer, mobilizing the faithful through numberless letters, speeches, and writings. Most astounding of all, his political work formed just one portion of his demanding life, and perhaps not the most time-consuming one. "I am overwhelmed in professional business and have scarcely a moment for anything else," he told Rufus King two years after leaving office.[1] By common consent, he was New York's premier lawyer, with an elite clientele that included the city of Albany and the state of New York. "He was employed in every important and every commercial case," noted James Kent. "He was a very great favorite with the merchants of New York."[2] With so much lucrative work, he now earned three or four times his Treasury salary, but he did not aim to maximize his income. As Attorney General William Bradford once teased him, "I hear that . . . you will not even pick up money when it lies at your feet. . . . You were made for a statesman and politics will never be out of your head."[3]

Often the political and legal sides of Hamilton's life dovetailed. He handled many maritime-insurance cases stemming from the seizure of American ships by foreign powers. He also argued notable constitutional cases, finally traveling to Philadelphia in early 1796 to defend before the Supreme Court the constitutionality of the carriage tax he had introduced as treasury secretary. "He spoke for three hours," said one newspaper, "and the whole of his argument was clear, impressive and classical."[4] The court approved Hamilton's argument that this excise tax was legal and that Congress had power "over every species of taxable property, except exports."[5] The decision in *Hylton v. United States* not only endorsed Hamilton's broad view of federal taxing power but represented the first time the Supreme Court ever ruled on the constitutionality of an act of Congress.

With his life engrossed by work, Hamilton had little leisure time left over for the scientific, scholarly, and artistic pursuits that embellished the days of Jefferson. He was chronically overworked and increasingly absentminded. Months after leaving office, he wrote to the Bank of the United States and admitted that he did not know his account balance because he had lost his bank book—this from the man who had created the bank. He did allow himself some vacation time. During the summer of 1795, he made a three-week journey to meet with Indian tribes at Cayuga Lake in upstate New York. From a sketchy journal he kept, it appears this was basically a business trip involving a land sale, enlivened by ceremonial meetings with tribal leaders. In the autumn of 1796, Hamilton spent five days hunting and riding horseback on Long Island with two friends, a trip that may have been therapy for medical problems. His old kidney disorder had flared up, forcing Hamilton to renounce champagne forever. "We got a few grouse and the ride restored Hamilton's digestion," reported his friend John Laurance. "He was not well."[6] This was the extent of Hamilton's wanderlust. It is odd that the man who melded the nation so closely together through his fiscal policies never arranged a pleasure trip through the United States.

Hamilton's failure to travel to Europe or even the south is explained partially by his workload, but his attachment to family may have been no less important. After his Long Island adventure, he rushed off to Albany to argue a case and wrote to Eliza from the Schuyler mansion, "I need not add that I am impatient to be restored to your bosom and to the presence of my beloved children. 'Tis hard that I should ever be obliged to quit you and them. God bless you my beloved. . . . Y[ou]rs. with unbounded Affec[tion] A Hamilton."[7] Hamilton wrote dozens of such tender notes to Eliza. Whatever his imperfections, he was a caring father and husband who often seemed anxious about the health and welfare of his family. Once the Maria Reynolds affair ended, he was not eager to leave Eliza and the children alone.

Alexander and Eliza continued their longtime practice of sheltering orphans. On October 1, 1795, George Washington Lafayette, son of the marquis, appeared incognito with a tutor in New York. Hamilton had never lost his affection for Lafayette, who he thought would recover his popularity in France after the Revolution faded, but the arrival of Lafayette's son posed a thorny situation for George Washington. The marquis was still imprisoned by the Austrians at the Olmütz fortress, and young Lafayette wanted American help in freeing him. With his paternal regard for Lafayette, Washington dearly wanted to embrace his son, but the Jay Treaty furor made this a vexed question. Washington already stood accused of anti-

French bias, and Lafayette, while a certified hero of the American Revolution, had been branded a traitor to the French one.

For Washington, suspended between his personal feelings and political necessity, it was an exquisitely painful predicament. Though he was inclined to have Hamilton send the two young men to Philadelphia, Hamilton thought it prudent to postpone this, and he took the two young Frenchmen into his home. "The President and Mrs. Washington would gladly have received them into their family," Eliza recalled, "but state policy forbade it at that critical time. The lad and his tutor passed a whole summer with us."[8] Actually, it was the whole winter. For six months, the Hamiltons tried to cheer up the gaunt, melancholy youth before he was finally allowed to see Washington in April 1796 as the Jay Treaty crisis waned.

It was to be more than a year before Lafayette was released from prison and wrote to Washington after what he described as "five years of a deathlike silence from me."[9] Both thrilled and relieved, Hamilton wrote at length to Lafayette, assuring him that their friendship would "survive all revolutions and all vicissitudes. . . . No one feels more than I do the motives which this country has to love you, to desire and to promote your happiness. And I shall not love it, if it does not manifest the sensibility by unequivocal acts." If Lafayette ever needed asylum in America, he would receive a cordial reception: "The only thing in which our parties agree is to love you."[10] Alexander Hamilton seldom used the word *love* three times in one letter.

The Republican demonizing of Alexander Hamilton only intensified after he left the Treasury Department. To opponents, he seemed able to manipulate the government from New York. That Hamilton came to exercise profound influence over the distant cabinet members is patent from his extensive correspondence with them. What is equally clear, however, is that he did not obtrude in some power-hungry, ham-handed fashion but was gradually invited into their deliberations.

A case in point is Hamilton's relationship with his Treasury successor, Oliver Wolcott, Jr. As early as April 1795, Hamilton did volunteer to tutor Wolcott on how to maintain American credit, saying, "Write me as freely as you please."[11] Government expenses were growing, the deficit yawned wider, and Republicans grumbled. Hamilton was glad to retain this hidden influence, but it was Wolcott who solicited advice, as if Hamilton had never stopped being his boss, and he plied him with technical questions about everything from French privateers to government loans. In a single letter on June 18, Wolcott asked Hamilton seven complicated questions about fiscal management. He could not quite emerge from Hamilton's shadow and at times struck an almost plaintive note: "Will you reply briefly to a few questions I lately stated. I care not how briefly. Your ideas upon a system projected essentially by you will enable me to proceed with less hesitation. Indeed I need some help. There is no comptroller here."[12] In another letter, Wolcott confessed, "The public affairs are certainly in a critical state. I do not clearly see how those of the Treasury are to be managed. . . . [I]ntimations from you will always be thankfully rec[eive]d."[13] Based on these queries, Hamilton may well have fancied himself an ex officio member of the administration. He was uniquely poised to render authoritative opinions on how policies had evolved in the new government.

In September 1795, Hamilton wrote deferentially to Washington, "I beg, Sir, that you will at no time have any scruple about commanding me."[14] Washington took full advantage of the offer. In late October, he asked Hamilton to help prepare his annual address to the opening session of Congress, and Hamilton drafted a speech as if he remained on the government payroll.

The crux of the problem was that Washington's second generation of cabinet members was decidedly inferior to the first. Federalist William Plumer compared Hamilton and Wolcott: "The first was a prodigy of genius and of strict undeviating integrity. The last is an honest man, but his talents are immensely beneath those of his predecessor."[15] The same could be said of other cabinet officers. There was simply a dearth of qualified people for Washington to consult. The plague of partisan recriminations had already diminished the incentives for people to serve in government. Washington told Hamilton a woeful tale of trying to replace Edmund Randolph. "What am I to do for a Secretary of State?" he asked forlornly, noting that four people had already rejected the post. "I ask frankly and with solicitude and shall receive kindly any sentiments you may express on the occasion."[16] Washington asked Hamilton to sound out Rufus King, who became the fifth person to turn down the State Department job. Hamilton reported that King declined because of "the foul and venomous shafts of calumny" constantly shot at government officials.[17]

In the end, Washington settled upon his seventh pick, the crusty Timothy Pickering, a stern Federalist and unabashed Hamilton admirer. Like Wolcott, Pickering solicited Hamilton's opinion regularly. When the secretary of war job descended to James McHenry, Hamilton's old friend from Washington's military family, Hamilton suddenly had three steadfast admirers in the cabinet. Its uniformly Federalist cast was no accident. Washington told Pickering that it would be "political suicide" to recruit anyone into his administration who was not prepared to support his programs wholeheartedly.[18] He had learned his lesson with Jefferson and discarded the naïve belief that he could straddle both political factions. He was now more solidly aligned with the Federalists, and few of the prominent ones stood entirely outside of Hamilton's extended social and intellectual coterie. James Madison, observing the stout phalanx of Hamiltonians surrounding the president, asked Jefferson rhetorically, "Through what official interstice can a ray of republican truths now penetrate to the President?"[19]

Washington was probably glad to be spared any further rays of Republican truth. In portraits done during his final years in office, he looks moody and irritable, devoid of serenity. His energy seems spent, his eyes are dully glazed, and his military carriage sags. He was suffering from an aching back, bad dentures, and rheumatism; visitors noted his haggard, careworn look. Scarred by Republican attacks, Washington found it hard to contain his rage. One reason that he decided to return to private life was that he no longer wished to be buffeted "in the public prints by a set of infamous scribblers."[20]

Washington's decision to forgo a third term was momentous. He wasn't bound by term limits, and many Americans expected him to serve for life. He surrendered power in a world where leaders had always grabbed for more. Stepping down was the most majestic democratic response he could have flung at his Republican critics. Toward the end of his first term, he had asked James Madison to draft a farewell address and then stashed it away when he decided on a second term. Now, in the spring of 1796, he unearthed that draft. As at the close of the American Revolution, Washington wanted to make a valedictory statement that would codify some enduring principles in American political life. To update Madison's draft, he turned to Hamilton. Washington no longer felt obliged to restrain his affection for his protégé and now sent Hamilton handwritten notes marked "Private." He increasingly treated him as a peer and warm friend, and Hamilton responded with gratitude.

There was piquant irony in Washington asking Hamilton—who had espoused a perpetual president at the Constitutional Convention—to draft the farewell address. Hamilton would now help to embed in American politics a tradition of presidents leaving office after a maximum of two terms, a precedent that remained unbroken until Franklin Roosevelt. In mid-May 1796, Washington sent Hamilton a rough draft, which consisted of Madison's speech and a section that Washington had appended to reflect the "considerable changes" wrought by the past four years, especially in foreign affairs.[21] He invited Hamilton, if he thought it best, to discard the old speech and "to throw the *whole* into a different form."[22] Washington wanted Hamilton to make the style plain and avoid personal references and controversial expressions. The goal was to create a timeless document that would elevate Americans above the partisan sniping that had disfigured public life. Usually the hotheaded one, Hamilton deleted some splenetic lines that Washington had slipped in about newspapers filled "with all the invective that disappointment, ignorance of facts, and malicious falsehoods could invent to misrepresent my politics."[23]

Hamilton tackled the task with exemplary energy, giving depth and scope and sterling expression to the overarching themes listed by Washington. That summer, he prepared two documents for Washington. One was a reworking of the Madison-Washington draft and the other his own version of the speech. Washington preferred the latter, which became the basis of the final product. But the president was bothered by the length of Hamilton's draft; he had envisioned something elegant and concise, which could fit into a newspaper. "All the columns of a large gazette would scarcely, I conceive, contain the present draught," he told Hamilton.[24] By now a seasoned ghostwriter, Hamilton speedily pruned his draft to a more compact size. Washington and Hamilton honed and polished the speech until it had a uniformly authoritative voice. Occasionally, Hamiltonian thunder rumbled through the prose, as in the ranting line that factions can become "potent engines, by which cunning, ambitious, and unprincipled men will be enabled to subvert the power of the people and to usurp for themselves the reins of government."[25] In general, however, their two voices blended admirably together. The result was a literary miracle. If Hamilton was the major wordsmith, Washington was the tutelary spirit and final arbiter of what went in. The poignant opening section in which Washington thanked the American people could never have been written by Hamilton alone. Conversely, the soaring central section, with its sophisticated perspective on policy matters, showed Hamilton's unmistakable stamp.

It is difficult to disentangle the contributions of Washington and Hamilton because their ideas overlapped on many issues. Both men were still smarting over the Jay Treaty dispute and livid at reports that France might send an envoy and a fleet to demand its immediate repeal. Were it not for domestic acrimony over the treaty, Washington told Hamilton, he would tell the French bluntly, "We are an independent nation and act for ourselves. Having fulfilled . . . our engagements with other nations and having decided on and strictly observed a neutral conduct towards the belligerent powers . . . we will not be dictated to by the politics of any nation under heaven farther than treaties require of us."[26] The farewell address sprang from this recent experience.

As its centerpiece, the farewell address called for American neutrality, shorn of names and party labels. Hamilton's words, however, were saturated with arguments that he had used to promote the Jay Treaty. Beneath its impartial air, the farewell address took dead aim at the Jeffersonian romance with France. When Hamilton implied that it was folly for one nation to expect disinterested favors from another, he restated an old argument against Jefferson: that France had aided America during the Revolution only to harm England. When Hamilton sounded the great theme that the United States should steer clear of permanent foreign alliances—"That nation which indulges towards another a habitual hatred or a habitual fondness is in some degree a slave"—he echoed his earlier statements about Republicans betraying a reflexive hatred of England and adoration of France.[27] Even his comments on the need for religion and morality, slightly altered in the final version, arose from his horror at the "atheistic" French Revolution: "Religion and morality are essential props. In vain does that man claim the praise of patriotism who labours to subvert or undermine these great pillars of human happiness."[28]

The domestic portion of the address was a digest of ideas that Hamilton had advanced under Washington's aegis. Hamilton expressed an urgent plea for preserving the union and enumerated various threats. He cited the danger of domestic factions, which could become vehicles for unscrupulous men; urged a vigorous central government to protect liberty; stressed public credit and the need to control deficits; and invoked the sacred duty of obeying the Constitution. In a country riven by quarrels, Hamilton produced a vision of harmonious parts. Agriculture and commerce were mutually beneficial. North and south, the western frontier and the eastern seaboard, enjoyed complementary economies. The only thing needed to capitalize on these strengths was national unity.

The farewell address was meant to be printed, not spoken, and Washington consulted Hamilton about the optimal time and place for publication. On September 19, 1796, it appeared in *Claypoole's American Daily Advertiser,* and it was then reprinted in newspapers across the country. It can be read two ways: as a dispassionate statement of American principles and as a thinly disguised attack on the Republicans. With consummate artistry, Washington and Hamilton had extracted general themes from particular debates about the Jay Treaty, the Whiskey Rebellion, and other events and endowed them with universal meaning. Over time, the underlying events have faded away, lending the aphorisms an oracular quality. The arguments for neutrality and a foreign policy based on national interests became especially influential. "It was the first statement, comprehensive and authoritative at the same time, of the principles of American foreign policy," Felix Gilbert has written.[29] A century later, as the document evolved into a canonical text, Congress read the speech aloud each year on Washington's birthday.

Though contemporary Americans hailed the address, the Republican reaction was venomous and unwittingly underscored its urgent plea for unity. One newspaper denounced Washington's words as "the loathings of a sick mind."[30] In the *Aurora,* Benjamin Franklin Bache dredged up the old wives' tale that Washington had conspired with the British during the Revolution. Bache also gave prominent play to an open letter to Washington from Thomas Paine, the author of *Common Sense,* expressing the hope that Washington would die and telling him that "the world will be puzzled to decide whether you are an apostate or an impostor, whether you have abandoned good principles or whether you ever had any."[31]

Though never humble, Hamilton could be self-effacing in serving Washington and his country. Only a handful of intimates—Eliza, Robert Troup, and John Jay among them—knew that he had crafted the president's address. Fired by a sense that Hamilton had been denied credit, Eliza often recollected the composition of the address. More than forty years later, she testified that Hamilton had written it

> principally at such time as his office was seldom frequented by his clients and visitors and during the absence of his students to avoid interruption; at which times he was in the habit of calling me to sit with him that he might read to me as he wrote, in order, as he said, to discover how it sounded upon the ear and making the remark, "My dear Eliza, you must be to me what Moliere's old nurse was to him." [Molière was popularly reported to have tested dramatic speeches on his old nurse to get her reaction.] The whole or nearly all the "Address" was read to me by him as he wrote it and a greater part, if not all, was written by him in my presence.[32]

After the farewell address appeared, it was sold widely in pamphlet form. Eliza cherished the memory of strolling down Broadway with her husband when an old soldier accosted them and tried to sell them a copy. After buying one, Hamilton said laughingly to Eliza, "That man does not know he has asked me to purchase my own work."[33]

Hamilton's central role also stayed a well-kept secret because Washington's admirers feared its disclosure might detract from the ex-president's Olympian stature. They perhaps succeeded too well. After Hamilton's death, his draft of the farewell address and all related correspondence with Washington were entrusted to Rufus King. In the 1820s, Eliza and her sons had to file a lawsuit to retrieve the documents from King, who relinquished them only reluctantly. Later, Eliza recorded her memories of the events surrounding the farewell address so "that my children should be fully acquainted with the services rendered by their father to our country and the assistance given by him to General Washington during his administration for the one great object: the independence and stability of the government of the United States."[34]

For all the strife surrounding his time in office, historians now routinely rank George Washington with Abraham Lincoln and Franklin Roosevelt as one of the three outstanding American presidents. Washington left a legacy of prosperity, neutrality, sound public credit, stable government, and a viable constitution. As the resident policy genius of the administration, Hamilton deserves a large share of the accolades. Why, then, was he not a presidential candidate in 1796 or beyond? He had the advantage of being a major Federalist—perhaps *the* major Federalist—at a time when party elites chose presidential candidates. Nevertheless, Hamilton gave no hint that he or anybody else envisioned him as Washington's successor, and he never received a single electoral vote in a presidential contest.

How to explain the paradox that a man of such unbounded talent and ambition never attained the top office or even made a covert run for it? Surely he must have wanted to be president. The conundrum can be solved partly by noting that the political stars were never suitably aligned for Hamilton. Obviously, he could not have challenged Washington for the presidency, and, as John Adams correctly told Abigail, "I am the heir apparent."[35] Hamilton himself had stated that Adams, Jefferson, and Jay, by virtue of their seniority, were seen as presumptive presidential contenders. Also, Hamilton left the government determined to repair his finances and refurbish his legal practice. Moreover, by then he was so controversial, so divisive, that the mere mention of his name could trigger debates. Adored by his followers, he was seen as cocky, conceited, and swaggering by his enemies.

Other reasons account for Hamilton's failure to snatch the prize. Though blessed with a great executive mind and a consummate policy maker, Hamilton could never master the smooth restraint of a mature politician. His conception of leadership was noble but limiting: the true statesman defied the wishes of the people, if necessary, and shook them from wishful thinking and complacency. Hamilton lived in a world of moral absolutes and was not especially prone to compromise or consensus building. Where Washington and Jefferson had a gift for voicing the hopes of ordinary people, Hamilton had no special interest in echoing popular preferences. Much too avowedly elitist to become president, he lacked what Woodrow Wilson defined as an essential ingredient for political leadership: "profound sympathy with those whom he leads—a sympathy which is insight—an insight which is of the heart rather than of the intellect."[36] Alexander Hamilton enjoyed no such mystic bond with the American people. This may have been why Madison was so adamant that "Hamilton *never* could have got in" as president.[37]

A baser reason may explain Hamilton's reluctance to stand for the presidency. During the 1796 election, Noah Webster, then a Federalist editor, suggested in his newspaper, *The Minerva,* that Hamilton might be an appropriate presidential candidate. According to scandalmonger James T. Callender, an unnamed Republican saw this and dispatched an emissary to New York, who confronted Hamilton to "inform him that if Webster should in future print a single paragraph on that head," the Maria Reynolds papers would instantly "be laid before the world. It is believed the message was delivered to Mr. Hamilton for the *Minerva* became silent."[38]

While Hamilton knew he would not succeed Washington, he wasn't about to play a passive role in 1796, the first contested presidential race in American history and the first dominated by parties. At the time, it was still considered crass for candidates to campaign or violate the charade of passivity, and this magnified the influence of party leaders. Madison began to agitate for Jefferson, who let his friend carry the burden. Similarly, the Federalist front-runner, John Adams, declared, "I am determined to be a silent spectator of the silly and wicked game."[39]

At first, Hamilton told a correspondent that his one overriding goal was to stop Thomas Jefferson from becoming president: "All personal and partial considerations must be discarded and everything must give way to the great object of excluding Jefferson."[40] He even toyed with backing Patrick Henry, who had grown estranged from Virginia Republicans and might erode support for Jefferson in the south, where Federalists were weak. When Henry refused to run, Hamilton turned to another dark-horse southerner, Thomas Pinckney, a wartime hero and former governor of South Carolina, who had served as an American diplomat in Spain and England.

Hamilton's support for Pinckney's candidacy set him on a collision course with Adams, who regarded himself as the legitimate successor to the presidency. There was a vague understanding among Federalists that Adams would be the presidential and Pinckney the vice presidential candidate. Hamilton's unspoken preference for Pinckney was not immediately apparent because under the old constitutional rules electors did not distinguish between their votes for president and vice president. Some Federalists planned to withhold votes from Pinckney to insure that Adams became president, leaving Hamilton with a haunting fear that Jefferson might accidentally become president or vice president. (We recall his similar fear that Washington might be denied the first presidency by accident.) As a party chieftain, Hamilton stuck to his official position that Federalist electors should cast their votes equally for Adams *and* Pinckney. This surface neutrality, however, was really a stratagem to elect Pinckney as president. Since Pinckney was the stronger candidate in the south, if he managed to tie Adams in the north, he would roll up more total votes.

Hamilton bet on the wrong horse, a mistake that would haunt the rest of his career. As treasury secretary, he had only limited contact with John Adams, who was excluded from the inner policy circle. The two men had maintained a wary distance. Hamilton later said that by the time Washington left office, "men of principal influence in the Federal party" began to "entertain serious doubts about [Adams's] fitness" for the presidency because of his temperament. Yet Adams's "pretensions in several respects were so strong that, after mature reflection, they thought it better to indulge their hopes than to listen to their fears."[41]

George Washington, who "consulted much, pondered much, resolved slowly, resolved surely," was Hamilton's ideal of presidential temperament.[42] John Adams, by contrast, was fiery and dyspeptic, as volatile as Washington was steady. Hamilton contrasted Pinckney's "far more discreet and conciliatory" personality to "the disgusting egotism, the distempered jealousy, and the ungovernable discretion" of John Adams.[43] These observations, written later, probably expressed reservations that Hamilton harbored in more muted form at the time.

At first, Adams did not suspect Hamilton's duplicity in the campaign. He told friends that Hamilton genuinely feared that his own weakness as a presidential candidate might elect Jefferson and that Hamilton supported Pinckney as an alternative only in case he himself could not win. When Jefferson wrote to warn Adams that "you may be cheated of your succession by a trick worthy [of] the subtlety of your arch-friend of New York," Madison persuaded Jefferson not to send the letter, lest it be interpreted as a crude effort to stir up dissension among Federalists.[44] In late December, however, Elbridge Gerry presented Adams with evidence from Aaron Burr, the self-promoting Republican favorite for vice president, that exposed Hamilton's quiet efforts to elect Pinckney ahead of Adams. Both John and Abigail Adams were shocked. "'Beware that spare Cassius' has always occurred to me when I have seen that cock sparrow," Abigail told her husband of Hamilton. "I have ever kept my eye on him."

"I shall take no more notice of his puppyhood," John replied, "but return to him the same conduct that I always did—that is, to keep him at a distance."[45] This was Adams's opening volley in an unending stream of abuse against Hamilton, whom he termed "as great a hypocrite as any in the U.S. His intrigues in the election I despise."[46] He thought Hamilton had championed Pinckney as somebody more pliant to his own ambitions, someone who would create "an army of horse and foot with Mr. Hamilton at their head."[47] Madison likewise thought that Hamilton feared that someone such as Adams was "too headstrong to be a fit puppet" for his "intrigues behind the screen."[48] Adams's wrath against Hamilton was understandable, but he immediately stooped to personal insults and called Hamilton a "Creole bastard."[49] Such scurrilous comments about Hamilton persisted throughout Adams's presidency and inflamed the already tense situation between the two men.

On October 15, 1796, John Beckley, the House clerk, alerted James Madison to a string of essays launched under the signature "Phocion" in the *Gazette of the United States*. Beckley divined that Hamilton was the author and guessed his dual intent: to denigrate Jefferson as a presidential candidate and tepidly endorse Adams. Between October 14 and November 24, the voluble Phocion published twenty-five installments of election commentary. Although John Adams also identified Hamilton as the author, these essays have inexplicably been omitted from Hamilton's collected papers and biographies. They are not only unmistakably Hamiltonian in style— mocking, brilliant, prolix, bombastic, sometimes hairsplitting—but also characteristic in their obsession with Jefferson and the sanguinary turmoil of the French

Revolution. Hamilton made little effort to conceal his identity, quoting earlier things he had written almost verbatim—a rare case of Hamilton cannibalizing his own work. For instance, writing as Catullus on September 29, 1792, Hamilton had called Jefferson a "Caesar *coyly refusing* the proferred diadem" and said he was "tenaciously grasping the substance of imperial domination."[50] Now, Phocion likened Jefferson to a proto-Caesar who had "coyly refused the proffered diadem" while "tenaciously grasping the substance of imperial domination."[51] Once again, Hamilton portrayed Jefferson as a closet voluptuary hiding behind the garb of Republican simplicity.

Phocion reviewed Jefferson's career from the time when, as Virginia governor, he had fled from British troops. Hamilton detected similar cowardice in Jefferson's departure from Washington's cabinet at a moment of national danger. "How different was the conduct of the spirited and truly patriotic HAMILTON?" Hamilton asked, almost advertising his presence. "He wished to retire as much as the philosopher of Monticello. He had a large family and his little fortune was fast melting away in the expensive metropolis. But with a Roman's spirit he declared that, much as he wished for retirement, yet he would remain at his post as long as there was any danger of his country being involved in war."[52]

The Phocion essays contain the most withering critique that Hamilton ever leveled at Jefferson as a slaveholder, and they hint heavily at knowledge of the Sally Hemings affair. Visitors to Monticello noted the many light-skinned slaves in residence, especially the Hemings family. One such visitor in 1786, the comte de Volney, expressed astonishment in his journal: "But I was amazed to see children as white as I was called blacks and treated as such."[53] In theory, Jefferson could have fathered all of Sally Hemings's children. Fawn M. Brodie has written, "Jefferson was not only not 'distant' from Sally Hemings but in the same house nine months before the births of each of her seven children and she conceived no children when he was not there."[54] Jefferson freed only two slaves in his lifetime and another five in his will, and all belonged to the Hemings family, though he excluded Sally. On her deathbed, Sally Hemings told her son Madison that he and his siblings were Jefferson's children. In 1998, DNA tests confirmed that Jefferson (or some male in his family) had likely fathered at least one of Sally Hemings's children, Eston. Reading between the lines of "Phocion," one surmises that Hamilton knew all about Sally Hemings, quite possibly from Angelica Church.

In the first "Phocion" essay, Hamilton listed eight virtues claimed for Jefferson and demolished each in turn. Was Jefferson a good moral philosopher? Hamilton replied with sarcasm: "If it can be shown that he has disapproved of the *cruelties* which have stained the French revolution . . . his qualities as a good moral philosopher would be valuable ingredients in the character of the President of the United

States."[55] Had Jefferson made discoveries in the useful arts? Hamilton drolly evoked an airy philosopher at Monticello "impaling butterflies and insects and contriving turn-about chairs *for the benefit of his fellow citizens and mankind in general.*"[56] But Hamilton was just warming up for his real indictment of Jefferson as a hypocritical slaveholder. He observed that in *Notes on the State of Virginia,* written in the early 1780s, Jefferson had argued for emancipating Virginia's slaves and shipping them elsewhere—"exported to some less friendly region where they might all be murdered or reduced to a more wretched state of slavery."[57] He ridiculed Jefferson's pseudoscientific belief that blacks were genetically inferior to whites. In *Notes,* Jefferson had said of blacks, "They secrete less by the kidneys and more by the glands of the skin, which gives them a very strong and disagreeable odour."[58] Hamilton further quoted him: "The first difference which strikes us is that of colour: whether the black of the negro resides in the reticular membrane between the skin and the scarf skin [epidermis], or in the scarf skin itself. Whether it proceeds from the colour of the blood or the colour of the bile or from that of some other secretion, the difference is fixed in nature and is as real as if the cause were better known to us."[59]

Hamilton taunted Jefferson about holding contradictory beliefs on race, saying that he could not make up his mind whether slaves belonged to the human race or not, with the result that he ranked blacks as "a peculiar race of animals below *man* and above the *orangutan . . .* a high kind of brute hitherto undescribed."[60] This referred to a passage in *Notes* in which Jefferson said that blacks favored the beauty of whites over their own kind and cited "the preferences of the Orangutan for the black woman over those of his own species."[61] (*Orangutan* also denoted the "wild man of the woods" in the Malay language.) Hamilton then touched on the subject that he must have known Jefferson would dread above all others: sexual relations between masters and slaves.

> At one moment he [Jefferson] is anxious to emancipate the blacks to vindicate the liberty of the human race. At another he discovers that the blacks are of a different race from the human race and therefore, when emancipated, they must be instantly removed beyond the reach of mixture lest he (or she) should *stain the blood* of his (or her) master, not recollecting what from his situation and other circumstances he ought to have recollected—that this *mixture* may take place while the negro remains in slavery. He must have seen all around him sufficient marks of this *staining of blood* to have been convinced that retaining them in slavery would not prevent it.[62]

It is this last suggestion that seems to betoken knowledge of Sally Hemings.

Until this point, one can applaud Hamilton for satirizing Jefferson's bigotry and raising taboo issues about his sexual behavior that were otherwise to slumber for two centuries. Unfortunately, the further one digs into the "Phocion" essays, the more apparent it becomes that Hamilton was engaging in devious manipulation of the southern vote. He was trying to turn southern slaveholders against Jefferson by asking whether they wanted a president who "promulgates his approbation of a speedy emancipation of their slaves."[63] Hamilton was trying to have it both ways. As an abolitionist, he wanted to expose Jefferson's disingenuous sympathy for the slaves. As a Federalist, he wanted to frighten slaveholders into thinking that Jefferson might act on that sympathy and emancipate their slaves.

When Phocion turned to John Adams, the Massachusetts patriot appeared to great advantage compared to Jefferson. Hamilton paid Adams a mighty compliment, describing him as "a citizen pre-eminent for his early, intrepid, faithful, persevering, and comprehensively useful services, a man pure and unspotted in private life, a patriot having a high and solid title to the esteem, the gratitude, and the confidence of his fellow citizens."[64] (In September 1792, Hamilton had written as Catullus that Adams was "preeminent for his early, intrepid, faithful, persevering, and comprehensively useful services to his country, a man pure and unspotted in private life, a citizen having a high and solid title to the esteem, the gratitude and the confidence of his fellow citizens.)[65] He cited thirty years of unblemished public conduct and said the Jeffersonian press had distorted Adams's political writings, trying to convert him into a monarchist. "For my own part," Hamilton concluded, "were I a Southern planter, owning negroes, I should be ten thousand times more alarmed at Mr. Jefferson's ardent wish for *emancipation* than at Mr. Adams's system of checks and balances."[66]

At first glance, Hamilton's paean to Adams suggests an unqualified endorsement and seems fully consistent with Hamilton's stated position that Federalists should vote equally for Adams and Pinckney. Nonetheless, one wonders whether there was not a subtle strategy here to sabotage Adams. Hamilton knew that if he could prompt southern slaveholders to desert Jefferson over emancipation, they would opt not for Adams, an abolitionist, but for Thomas Pinckney of South Carolina. There was no way that invoking the slavery issue could assist Adams in the south, where he needed the votes.

When the ballots were counted in February 1797, the outcome was a split ticket. Adams became president with seventy-one electoral votes and Jefferson vice president with sixty-eight. Pinckney received fifty-nine votes and Burr, making a miserable showing in the south, only thirty. Renegade electors in New England had reversed Hamilton's strategy and denied Pinckney eighteen votes. The New England states had voted solidly for Adams, while the south went for Jefferson. Adams had been prepared to resign if he was only reelected as vice president or subjected to the indignity of a tie vote that threw the election into the House of Representatives. He regarded his thin victory as also a blow to his pride, however, and blamed it on followers of Hamilton and Jefferson. "As both parties despaired of obtaining their favorite," he later wrote with self-pity, "Adams was brought in by a miserable majority of one or two votes, with the deliberate intention to sacrifice him at the next election. His administration was therefore never supported by either party, but vilified and libelled by both."[67] He blamed Hamilton more than Jefferson for this slim margin and spent the next four years trying to punish him.

Jefferson did not especially mind winning second place. Since resigning as secretary of state, he had been in isolation at his mountain fastness at Monticello. "From 1793 to 1797, I remained closely at home, saw none but those who came there, and at length became very sensible of the ill effect it had on my own mind. . . . [I]t led to an anti-social and misanthropic state of mind," he told his daughter.[68] With his unerring sense of timing, Jefferson did not think the moment auspicious for a Republican president. Troubles were still brewing with France, and he was happy to let Adams bear the brunt. Sure that the wheel of history would soon turn in his favor, the prescient Jefferson counseled patience to Madison.

Many Republicans preferred President Adams to Washington, if only because of his distance from Hamilton. The Jeffersonian *Aurora* celebrated Adams's anticipated victory with an implicit swipe at Washington and Hamilton: "There can be no doubt that Adams would not be a *puppet*—that having an opinion and judgment of his own, he would act from his own impulses rather than the impulses of others."[69] Similarly, Jefferson welcomed an Adams presidency as "perhaps the only sure barrier against Hamilton's getting in."[70] Though currently estranged from Adams, Jefferson had been dear friends with him and Abigail in Paris, and once the election was over he sought to ingratiate himself with the president-elect and turn him against Hamilton by dwelling on the latter's election machinations. "There is reason to believe that [Adams] is detached from Hamilton and there is a possibility he may swerve from his politics," he told one confidant.[71] Hamilton studiously monitored the attempted rapprochement between Adams and Jefferson. "Mr. Adams is President, Mr. Jefferson Vice President," he reported to Rufus King, now the American minister in London. "Our Jacobins say they are well pleased and that the *lion* and the *lamb* are to lie down together."[72] Hamilton was skeptical about this truce, seeing Jefferson as too wedded to ideology to make compromises.

Hamilton received fair warning that Adams intended to retaliate for his disloyalty during the election. That January, Hamilton was laid up with an injured leg that resulted from serving on nocturnal patrols that sought to stop a rash of mysterious fires in New York—fires that may have been related to slave revolts. Stephen

Higginson of Boston told Hamilton that the "blind or devoted partisans of Mr. Adams" were accusing him of leading a cabal that had tried to swing the election for Thomas Pinckney. "At the head of this junto, as they call it, they place you and Mr. Jay and they attribute the design to him and you of excluding" Adams from the presidency.[73] Hamilton thus went from unmatched access to President Washington to total exclusion from President Adams. Given his belief in Hamilton's treachery, Adams made the seemingly contradictory decision to retain Washington's cabinet, which was filled with Hamilton's friends, admirers, and former colleagues. Adams was to come to regret that decision as much as any other he made in office.

TWENTY-NINE

THE MAN IN THE
GLASS BUBBLE

It was ironic that John Adams, like Hamilton, was denigrated as a monarchist, because he grew up without the patrician comforts enjoyed by Jefferson and Madison, who were the quickest to apply the epithet against him. He was born in Braintree, Massachusetts, to a father who toiled as a farmer in summer and as a shoemaker in winter. Though his family lacked wealth, it boasted a proud ancestry, tracing its roots back to Puritans who had emigrated from England in the 1630s: "My father, grandfather, great grandfather, and great, great grandfather were all inhabitants of Braintree and all independent country gentlemen."[1]

Adams was schooled in the ascetic virtues of Puritan New England: thrift, hard work, self-criticism, public service, plain talk, and a morbid dread of ostentation. As a young man, he wrote, "A puffy, vain, conceited conversation never fails to bring a man into contempt, although his natural endowments be ever so great and his application and industry ever so intense."[2] Much of his life's drama arose from the intense, often fitful, sometimes tormenting struggle to measure up to his own impossibly high standards, and he never entirely made peace with his own craving for fame and recognition.

After a formal education that began at age six, Adams entered Harvard at fifteen, the first in his family to attend college. He briefly taught school in Worcester, then turned to law as the most promising career route. In 1764, he married Abigail Smith, a smart, sharp-tongued minister's daughter with a passion for politics and books. Abigail Adams tended the farm and raised the children while John roamed the world on diplomatic missions. Before Hamilton had arrived in North America, Adams had fought against the Stamp Act and defended British soldiers accused of killing five colonists in the so-called Boston Massacre of 1770. This legal work dis-

played a perverse streak of independence in Adams that ranked among his most attractive qualities. He was a born gadfly, always skeptical of reigning orthodoxy. Like
Hamilton, he was an ambivalent revolutionary, appalled by the repressive measures
of the British Crown but unsettled by the disorder of the rebel colonists. He always
had a vivid sense of how easily righteous causes could degenerate into mob excess.
Before independence, he asked himself what "the multitude, the vulgar, the herd,
the rabble, the mob" would do if the colonists flouted royal authority. "I feel unutterable anxiety," he confessed to his diary.[3]

At the Continental Congress, John Adams emerged as the most impassioned
voice for independence, leaping to his feet in rich bursts of oratory. All the while,
this feisty, rough-hewn lawyer brooded about potential anarchy. "There is one
thing, my dear sir, that must be attempted and most sacredly observed or we are
all undone," he told a friend in 1776. "There must be decency and respect and
veneration introduced for persons of authority of every rank."[4] His dedication
in Congress was prodigious: he sat on ninety congressional committees, chairing
twenty-five of them. He also laid claim to having been the main talent scout of the
Revolution, touting Washington as commander of the Continental Army and recruiting Jefferson to write the Declaration of Independence. Somehow, Adams
also found time to draft a constitution for Massachusetts and publish a pamphlet,
Thoughts on Government, which influenced other state constitutions.

Adams served his country with sustained diplomatic assignments in London,
Paris, and Amsterdam. In 1782, he coaxed the Dutch into recognizing the United
States and cajoled a two-million-dollar loan from Amsterdam bankers. His Paris
stay brought him into close contact with both Franklin and Jefferson. Adams could
not match their social graces and was "quite out of his element," fretted his friend
Jonathan Sewall: "He cannot dance, drink, game, flatter, promise, dress, swear with
the gentlemen, and talk small talk or flirt with the ladies."[5] In addition, Franklin's
blithe hedonism offended the austere New England soul of John Adams. "His whole
life has been one continued insult to good manners and to decency," Adams complained.[6] Franklin's fame in France was a blow to Adams's amour propre, his sense
that he was the superior man.

Franklin himself captured Adams with a penetrating epigram: "He means well
for his country, is always an honest man, often a wise one, but sometimes, and in
some things, absolutely out of his senses."[7] Franklin was one of the first to spot the
paranoid streak that came to mar Adams's career. In 1783, he grumbled about the
"ravings" of Adams, who suspected him and the comte de Vergennes, the French
foreign minister, "of plots against him which have no existence but in his own troubled imaginations."[8] In a similar vein, Bernard Bailyn later observed of Adams:
"Sensitive to insults, imaginary and real, he felt the world was generally hostile, to

himself and to the American cause, which was the greatest passion of his life. There were enemies on all sides."[9]

The prickly Adams developed a tender affection for Jefferson, albeit one mingled with an uneasy sense of his unfathomable mystery. No less than Hamilton, Adams perceived that Jefferson, behind the facade of philosophic tranquillity, was "eaten to a honeycomb" with ambition.[10] Jefferson, in turn, detected traces of the curmudgeon in Adams. "He hates Franklin, he hates Jay, he hates the French, he hates the English," he told Madison from Paris. "To whom will he adhere? His vanity is a lineament in his character which had entirely escaped me."[11] Four years later, Jefferson sent Madison a more potent version of this same critique, calling Adams "*vain, irritable, and a bad calculator* of the force and probable effect of the motives which govern men."[12] For all that, Jefferson appreciated Adams as a warmhearted, convivial spirit, a fascinating conversationalist, and a man of bedrock integrity. Their relationship had foundered in 1791 when Jefferson lauded *The Rights of Man* by Thomas Paine by drawing an invidious contrast to the "political heresies which have sprung up among us"—a cutting reference to Adams's *Discourses on Davila*, which Jeffersonians read as a plea for a hereditary presidency.[13] After Jefferson stepped down as secretary of state, he and Adams seldom corresponded during the next three years.

John Adams was an unprepossessing man. Short and paunchy with a round, jowly face and a pale complexion, he had piercing eyes that protruded from behind thick lids. He had an exceedingly active mind, always bubbling with words. Images welled up spontaneously from his imagination, as in his extraordinary description of Thomas Paine as "the satyr of the age . . . a mongrel between pig and puppy, begotten by a wild boar on a butch wolf."[14] Because he bared his psyche in diaries and letters, we know him more intimately than any other founder. One can summon up an army of adjectives for John Adams—crotchety, opinionated, endearing, temperamental, frank, erudite, outspoken, generous, eccentric, restless, petty, choleric, philosophical, plucky, quirky, pugnacious, fanciful, stubborn, and whimsical—and scarcely exhaust the possibilities. His life was a kaleidoscope of constantly shifting moods. Charles Francis Adams summed up his mercurial grandfather well when he wrote that he could be very warm and engaging in ordinary conversation but "extremely violent" when provoked.[15]

Adams was a mass of psychosomatic symptoms, his nervous tics and tremors often betraying extreme inner tension. "My constitution is a glass bubble," he once said, and he had a medical history of headaches, fatigue, chest pains, failing eyesight, and insomnia to prove it.[16] In 1776, he etched this self-portrait: "My face is grown pale, my eyes weak and inflamed, my nerves tremulous."[17] He seems to have undergone some form of nervous breakdown during his time in Amsterdam, suffering from periods of withdrawal from society and flashes of temper. Later on, he complained of "quivering fingers" and lost several teeth from pyorrhea, forcing him to speak with a lisp. By the time he became president, the sixty-one-year-old John Adams looked like a pudgy, toothless old man.

But it was Adams's vanity, not premature aging, that most detracted from his image. "Vanity, I am sensible, is my cardinal vice and cardinal folly," he admitted as a young man.[18] At least thirty times, he posed for portraits and quibbled with the results. From some underlying insecurity, he spent inordinate time brooding about his place in history. He worried that rivals would overshadow him or steal credit that he deserved. This vanity made him feel unappreciated. In 1812, he told Benjamin Rush, "From the year 1761, now more than fifty years, I have constantly lived in an enemies' country."[19] Biographer Joseph Ellis has observed of Adams, "Lurking in his heart was a frantic and uncontrollable craving for personal vindication, a lust for fame that was so obsessive, and so poisoned by his accurate awareness that history would not do him justice, that he often appeared less like a worthy member of the American gallery of greats than a beleaguered and pathetic madman."[20]

This insecurity fostered envy of other founders. He even bemoaned the "impious idolatry" of Washington, dubbing him Old Muttonhead, and seemed bothered by all the adulation he received.[21] He thought Washington better at striking heroic poses than providing leadership. In later writings, he faulted Washington's intelligence, said he "could not write a sentence without misspelling some word," and took him to task for being "but very superficially read in the history of any age, nation, or country."[22] Relatedly, by the time he became president, Adams found Alexander Hamilton flamboyant, lascivious, and egotistical, a conceited, conniving upstart who had been unfairly catapulted above him in Washington's government.

In considering Adams's presidency, two or three traits should be emphasized because they formed the burden of Hamilton's critique of him. Adams could be thin-skinned and hypersensitive, as he himself acknowledged. "My temper, in general, has been tranquil except when any instance of extraordinary madness, deceit, hypocrisy, ingratitude, treachery or perfidy has suddenly struck me," Adams once confided. "Then I have always been irascible enough."[23] He did not handle pressure very well. He tended to store up anger until his patience had been tested long enough; then he would explode. He told Benjamin Rush there had "been very many times in my life when I have been so agitated in my own mind as to have no consideration at all of the light in which my words, actions, and even writings would be considered by others."[24] His combative spirit did not always lend itself to presidential decorum, social lies, or useful flattery. In old age, he said that as a public figure, "I refused to suffer in silence. I sighed, sobbed, and groaned, and sometimes screeched and screamed. And I must confess to my shame and sorrow that I sometimes swore."[25]

Had they been more alike in style and temperament, Hamilton and Adams might have embraced as political comrades, since their views tallied on so many issues. Consider this statement from Adams: "Popularity was never my mistress, nor was I ever or shall I ever be a popular man. . . . But one thing I know: a man must be sensible of the errors of the people and upon his guard against them and must run the risk of their displeasure sometimes or he will never do them any good in the long run."[26] This was Hamilton's credo as well. Like Hamilton, Adams had sufficient faith in the people to want liberty for them but enough doubts to want to constrain their representatives with an ironclad system of checks and balances. Both men were staunch nationalists; admired the British system; were averse to utopian thinking; rejected romantic notions that human nature could be purified by democracy; and thought the masses could be no less tyrannical than kings. Both also feared the French Revolution as a possible portent for America. For Adams, events in France reeked of "blood and horror, of murder and massacre, of ambition and avarice."[27]

On the other hand, Adams lacked Hamilton's financial acumen. He favored a nation of small farmers and expressed grave reservations about aspects of Hamilton's economic program, thinking that it was informed by the "mercenary spirit of commerce."[28] He detested banks and believed that Hamilton's system would "swindle" the poor and release the "gangrene of avarice" into the American atmosphere.[29] Most important for his presidency, John Adams did not care for standing armies or closer relations with Great Britain—both views that were to lead to severe clashes with Hamilton.

Whatever the congruence of their political views, Hamilton and Adams had contrasting personalities. Smoothly artful in society, Hamilton could have been a European courtier. He was much more worldly than Adams. As a young man, notes biographer David McCullough, "Adams often felt ill at ease, hopelessly awkward. He sensed people were laughing at him, as sometimes they were, and this was especially hurtful."[30] Where the young Adams dreaded the mockery of others, the young Hamilton was uplifted by an encouraging sense of destiny. It is easy to see why Adams resented Hamilton as a preening, uppity young man: he had missed the formative struggles of the American Revolution dating back to the 1760s. Fisher Ames noted that Adams tended to hold cheap any reputation that wasn't "founded and topped off" during the Revolution.[31] By this standard, Hamilton was an intruder, a bumptious latecomer to the restricted honor roll of American founders. Adams ended up regarding Hamilton as someone "in a delirium of ambition. He had been blown up with vanity by the Tories, had fixed his eye on the highest station in America, and he hated every man young or old who stood in his way."[32]

For all his fundamental decency, patriotism, and good heart, John Adams struck the lowest blows against Alexander Hamilton. He was preoccupied with Hamilton's illegitimacy and foreign birth and could be quite heartless on the subject. He characterized Hamilton as being born "on a speck more obscure than Corsica, from an original not only contemptible but infamous, with infinitely less courage and capacity than Bonaparte."[33] On one occasion, borrowing a line from Jonathan Swift, he vilified Hamilton as "the bastard brat of a Scotch pedlar." At other times, Hamilton became "the Scottish Creolian of Nevis" or the "Creole bastard."[34] As a foreigner, Adams alleged, Hamilton was devoid of knowledge of the American character or true appreciation of the Revolution's patriots and "could scarcely acquire the opinions, feelings, or principles of the American people."[35] Adams found nothing admirable in the extraordinary saga of this self-made man from the tropics. "Hamilton had great disadvantages," he told Benjamin Rush. "His original was infamous; his place of birth and education were foreign countries; his fortune was poverty itself."[36] Adams made these misfortunes sound like so many personal failings.

A disproportionate number of references to Hamilton's womanizing come from the straitlaced Adams. "Hamilton I know to be a proud, spirited, conceited, aspiring mortal, always pretending to morality," said Adams, "but with as debauched morals as old Franklin, who is more his model than anyone I know."[37] Hamilton, he said, had "a superabundance of secretions which he could not find whores enough to draw off."[38] "His fornications, adulteries and his incests [an apparent insinuation that he had slept with Angelica Church] were propagated far and wide."[39] In time, Adams came to detest Hamilton so much that he fell victim to sheer credulity. Surely Adams was the only person ever to accuse Hamilton of slacking off at Treasury or of lazily fobbing off work onto subordinates so that he could frolic in Philadelphia society. In one particularly bizarre letter, Adams intimated that Hamilton might have owed his eloquence to drug usage. In his last years, he informed a friend, with a straight face, "I have been told by Parson Montague of Dedham, though I will not vouch for the truth of it, that General Hamilton never wrote or spoke at the bar or elsewhere in public without a bit of opium in his mouth."[40] Despite these absurd aspersions against Hamilton, Adams continued to see himself as a man who always turned the other cheek. "I never wrote a line of slander against my bitterest enemy," he told Mercy Warren, "nor encouraged it in any other."[41]

Adams had spent most of his vice presidency exiled in the Senate, casting a record thirty-one tiebreaking votes. Of the number-two post, he said wearily but indelibly that it was "the most insignificant office that ever the invention of man contrived or his imagination conceived."[42] Washington seldom consulted him, banishing him to the distant wings of power.

When John Adams was sworn in as the second president on March 4, 1797, he had on a gray suit and had powdered his hair and brandished a ceremonial sword at his side. Washington exuded the serenity of a successful, outgoing president, while Adams seemed more unsure of himself and told Abigail later that he had been afraid he would faint. Upon leaving Congress Hall, Washington, Adams, and Jefferson executed a delicate little minuet of etiquette, with Washington magnanimously insisting that Adams and Jefferson precede him.

Shy in many ways, Adams disliked the trappings of power. "I hate speeches, messages, addresses and answers, proclamations, and such affected, studied, contraband things," he told Abigail. "I hate levees and drawing rooms. I hate to speak to a thousand people to whom I have nothing to say."[43] Beyond the unenviable task of succeeding Washington, Adams had several handicaps to overcome. Despite long years in politics, he had never exercised executive power at the state or federal level. And he detested political parties at a time when America was being torn asunder by factions. As president, Adams was the nominal head of the Federalists, yet he dreamed of being a nonpartisan president. Hence, he effectively abdicated the role of partisan leader, which Hamilton, with his taste for power, was only too glad to assume. In later years, Adams conceded that in holding himself apart from Hamilton, "the sovereign pontiff of Federalism," he knew he would cause all of Hamilton's "cardinals to excite the whole church to excommunicate and anathematize me."[44] During his presidency, Adams was often stranded between the Federalists and the Republicans and accepted by neither. It was to prove a rare case in American history of the president hesitating to function as the de facto party leader.

This first transfer of presidential power naturally awakened fears of civil war, despotism, and foreign intrigue. To soothe worries about an orderly succession and placate the Federalists, Adams took the statesmanlike step of retaining the core of Washington's cabinet: Timothy Pickering at State, Oliver Wolcott, Jr., at Treasury, and James McHenry at War, the "triumvirate" that he came to loathe as traitors.[45] All three men were identified with Hamilton and the rabidly Anglophile wing of the party known as High Federalists. Why did Adams submit to a situation that seems in retrospect fraught with trouble? "Washington had appointed them and I knew it would turn the world upside down if I removed any one of them," he explained. "I had then no particular objection to any of them."[46] As he developed objections to his cabinet members, he portrayed himself as their helpless captive, duped by Hamilton and his minions. Hamilton did not think Adams could sidestep responsibility so lightly: "As the President nominates his ministers and may displace them when he pleases, it must be his own fault if he be not surrounded by men who for ability and integrity deserve his confidence."[47]

John Adams told two stories of his presidency that never quite jibed. In one, he claimed to be an innocent bystander, long oblivious of Hamilton's influence over his cabinet members. He had no idea until the end, he said, that they were receiving guidance from his foe; when he belatedly discovered the plot, he moved swiftly to purge the culprits. In another version, Adams claimed that he had known all along that Hamilton controlled the cabinet, because he had already controlled it under Washington: "The truth is, Hamilton's influence over [Washington] was so well known that no man fit for the office of State or War would accept either." For this reason, Washington "was driven to the necessity of appointing such as would accept. And this necessity was, in my opinion, the real cause of his retirement from office. For you may depend upon it, that retirement was not voluntary."[48] According to Adams, Washington was merely the titular president, a "viceroy under Hamilton."[49] Furthermore, wrote Adams, "I could not name a man who was not devoted to Hamilton without kindling a fire. . . . I soon found that if I had not the previous consent of the heads of departments and the approbation of Mr. Hamilton, I ran the utmost risk of a dead negative [veto] in the Senate."[50]

After Adams was inaugurated, Hamilton inadvertently ruffled the new president by sending him an unsolicited memorandum, suggesting policies for the new administration. This "long, elaborate letter," Adams said, contained "a whole system of instruction for the conduct of the President, the Senate and the House of Representatives. I read it very deliberately and really thought the man was in a delirium. . . . I despised and detested the letter too much to take a copy of it."[51] The sort of advice that Washington had so valued, Adams chose to resent. Not surprisingly, Hamilton wanted to maintain the intellectual preeminence he had enjoyed under Washington. Once again, he tried to be the one-man brain trust, promiscuously dispensing his opinions, and he was probably assaying what access he would enjoy under Adams. Hamilton was not the sort to surrender his proximity to power. Having mastered many arcane issues, he aspired to be the shadow president of the Federalists. In his endless missives to Pickering, Wolcott, and McHenry, one can feel Hamilton's frustration that he no longer held the levers of power.

Washington had always shown great care and humility in soliciting the views of his cabinet. Adams, in contrast, often disregarded his cabinet and enlisted friends and family, especially Abigail, as trusted advisers. His cabinet members found him aloof and capricious and prone to bark out orders instead of asking opinions. Oliver Wolcott, Jr.—who had one of the warmer relationships with Adams—gave this sarcastic description of the administration: "Thus are the United States governed, as Jupiter is represented to have governed Olympus. Without regarding the opinions of friends or enemies, all are summoned to hear, reverence, and obey the unchangeable fiat."[52]

The friction between Adams and his cabinet was exacerbated by the president's puzzling retreats to his home in Quincy, Massachusetts. As a member of the Continental Congress and a diplomat in Europe, Adams had been ideally diligent and self-sacrificing, enduring separations from Abigail of as long as five years. Especially during John's later years as vice president, Abigail often suffered from rheumatism and was forced to stay in Massachusetts. Adams became an absentee official, spending as many as nine months per year away from Philadelphia. During one foreign-policy crisis, Washington complained to his cabinet about his truant vice president: "Presuming that the vice president will have left the seat of government for Boston, I have not requested his opinion to be taken. . . . Should it be otherwise, I wish him to be consulted."[53]

As president, Adams stuck to a similarly peculiar schedule and frequently seemed to be absent from his own administration. During his first year in office, he spent four months in Quincy, twice as long a period as Washington had ever left the capital. At times, Adams seemed to be in headlong flight from his own government, spending up to seven months at a stretch in Massachusetts and trying to run the government by dispatch. Washington, mystified by this behavior, groaned that it "gives much discontent to the friends of government, while its enemies chuckle at it and think it a favorable omen for them."[54] Adams, of course, blamed Hamilton for his loss of control over his cabinet and said bitterly that "I was as president a mere cipher."[55] But it is hard to separate Adams's absences from the disloyalty of his cabinet. David McCullough has observed, "Adams's presence at the center of things was what the country rightfully expected and could indeed have made a difference."[56]

It was an inauspicious situation for the Federalists. The Republican leaders, Jefferson and Madison (the latter having now retired from Congress to Montpelier, his Virginia plantation), exhibited remarkable discipline and discretion. The two Virginians were shrewd men with an imperviously close bond and an impressive degree of patience and self-control. Meanwhile, the Federalists, united for two terms under Washington, were about to degenerate into a fractured party, led by two brilliant and unstoppable windbags, Adams and Hamilton, who cordially detested each other. Both were hasty, erratic, impulsive men and capable of atrocious judgment. And both had blazing gifts for invective, which they eventually turned against each other.

THIRTY

FLYING TOO
NEAR THE SUN

That spring, Hamilton received a long overdue letter from Scotland—several decades overdue, in fact—that afforded him profound satisfaction. It came from William Hamilton, one of his father's younger brothers, who amiably related news of his Scottish relatives. This marked the first time that Hamilton, forty-two, had any contact with his paternal family. Despite a lack of direct dealings with them, he had valued his Scottish ancestry, serving as an officer of the St. Andrew's Society of New York State.

In a cordial reply, Hamilton included the only thumbnail sketch of his life that he ever set down. It provided the contours of his life without shading; as so often in personal matters with Hamilton, the letter was essentially evasive. He assumed that his uncle knew about his father's early mishaps in the West Indies and the separation it had caused in the family. But Hamilton's letter confirms that James Hamilton had subsequently lost touch with his family, since Alexander had to inform his uncle that James still languished on St. Vincent: "I have strongly pressed the old gentleman to come to reside with me, which would afford him every enjoyment of which his advanced age is capable. But he has declined it on the ground that the advice of his physicians leads him to fear that the change of climate would be fatal to him."[1] Hamilton gave the impression of being a worldly man, secure in his station, who could afford to downplay his own exploits. He struck a mellow note of personal contentment: "It is impossible to be happier than I am in a wife and I have five children, four sons and a daughter, the eldest a son somewhat past fifteen, who all promise well as far as their years permit and yield me much satisfaction."[2] He told of the pecuniary sacrifice that went with public office and the baneful spirit of faction that had weakened executive authority: "The union of these motives, with the reflections of prudence in relation to a growing family, determined me as soon as my plan had attained a certain maturity to withdraw from office."[3]

Hamilton seemed eager to stay in touch with his reclaimed relatives. This eagerness has a certain pathos, for Hamilton did not fathom the self-interested nature of the sudden overture from Uncle William. The Scottish Hamiltons had never tried to rescue Alexander from an impoverished, orphaned state and had never congratulated him on his amazing ascent in the world. The only reason William now wrote to Hamilton was for selfish purposes. He had been a successful tobacco and sugar merchant, but his business had gone awry, and he needed help. Pretty soon, Hamilton had the odd sensation of receiving a reverential letter from his first cousin Alexander Hamilton, a Sanskrit scholar who had returned from India because of his father's business troubles. The following year, the Scottish Alexander Hamilton disclosed the true reason behind the correspondence: the family had to find work for his brother, a sailor named Robert, who was prepared to become a naturalized American citizen if he could obtain an assignment with the U.S. Navy. The willingness of the Scottish Hamiltons to exploit their American cousin's eminence seems shameless. Nevertheless, having lacked a family and suffered the taint of illegitimacy, Hamilton took Robert Hamilton into his home for five months, squired his young relative around New York, and landed him an appointment as a lieutenant in the U.S. Navy. The grateful Scottish kinsmen hung a portrait of Hamilton above their mantel—sweet vindication for a man who had started out as a castaway of the islands—but they never made an effort to aid Hamilton's father on St. Vincent or showed the least curiosity about him. Hamilton continued to do favors for his Scottish relatives, who had never done any favors for him.

Even more satisfying than this new rapport with his Scottish clan was the return of John and Angelica Church to New York. For years, Angelica had yearned to return home and was held back only by her husband's parliamentary career. "You and my dear Hamilton will never cross the Atlantic," she lamented to Eliza. "I shall never leave this island and, as to meeting in heaven, there will be no pleasure in that."[4] After Hamilton resigned from the Treasury and set up house with Eliza in New York at 26 Broadway, he implored his sister-in-law to come home. "You know how much we all love you," he wrote with accustomed gallantry. "'Tis impossible you can be so well loved where you are. And what is there can be put in competition with the sweet affections of the heart?"[5] Hamilton was preaching to the converted. Angelica wanted to rejoin the Hamiltons, reassuring Eliza that "I hope to pass with you the remainder of my days, that is, if you will be so obliging as to permit my brother [Hamilton] to give me his society, for you know how much I love and admire him.

We will see each other every day."[6] Eliza advised Angelica on the fashions that she would find de rigueur in New York: "Remember that your waist must be short, your petticoats long, your headdress moderately high, and altogether *à la Grec.*"[7]

The Churches' move to New York was slower than anticipated. In late 1795, they drafted Hamilton to scout luxurious mansions. Harried by a thousand duties, Hamilton found time to reconnoiter local real estate and bought his in-laws several lots on Broadway. "I am sensible how much trouble I give you," Angelica wrote, "but you will have the goodness to excuse it when you know that it proceeded from a persuasion that I was asking from one who promised me his love and attention if I returned to America."[8] Angelica still wrote to Hamilton in a coquettish style, anointing him "the arbiter of wit and elegance," and he gladly reciprocated.[9] "How do you manage to charm all that see you?" he asked her. "While naughty tales are told to you of us, we hear nothing but of your kindness, amiableness, agreeableness &c."[10] For all his intimacy with Angelica, Hamilton was a bond that still seemed to unite the sisters instead of divide them. As he awaited Angelica's appearance in New York, Hamilton told her that the only rivalry he and Eliza had "is in our attachment to you and we each contend for preeminence in this particular. To whom will you give the apple?"[11] (This intriguing image alludes to the Trojan prince Paris, who had to hand an apple to the fairest of three goddesses.) Eliza would never have harbored deep affection for her sister or allowed Hamilton to write to her so freely if she had been aware of any real transgressions. In one revealing letter, Hamilton said that Eliza "consents to everything, except that I should love you *as well as herself* and this you are too reasonable to expect."[12] Angelica was always careful to incorporate them both into a triangle of family love. "Embrace my dear Hamilton with all my heart," she wrote to Eliza during the summer of 1796. "Give me leave to love you both affectionately in spite of my being sometimes a little saucy."[13]

After years of frustrating delays, the Churches at last moved to New York in May 1797. John Barker Church soon established himself as a personage of staggering wealth and New York's foremost insurance underwriter. "His equipage and style of living are several degrees beyond those of any other man amongst us," Robert Troup marveled.[14] Angelica began to throw extravagant parties at which guests dined on plates of polished silver. She usually glittered with diamonds and captivated many socialites. There was something racy about the Churches that seemed more reminiscent of London society than New York. Angelica scandalized local matrons by introducing risqué European fashions, while John was a compulsive gambler who often played cards into the wee hours. The Churches' parties featured whist, loo, and games of chance. A guest at these soirees, Hamilton probably drew the attention of gossips who saw him mooning around Angelica's adoring gaze.

This was not the only whiff of scandal that followed Hamilton during that sum-

mer of 1797. For four and a half years, the Maria Reynolds affair had remained
a well-kept secret confined to Republican rumor mills and what Hamilton called
"dark whispers."[15] By a curious coincidence, the Churches returned to New York
just as that scandal was about to burst into print, so any gossip about Hamilton and
Angelica would only have heaped fuel on the flames. In late June, Hamilton saw a
newspaper advertisement for a series of pamphlets, subsequently published in book
form, with the innocuous title *The History of the United States for 1796.* The notice
promised that the series would publish documents pertaining to Hamilton's conduct as treasury secretary. Hamilton soon laid his hands on pamphlet number five,
which rehashed old charges of official misconduct and cited documents from James
Reynolds and Jacob Clingman. On July 8, Hamilton published a letter in the *Gazette
of the United States* and admitted the authenticity of the papers but pointed out that
their charges were false and misleading: "They were the contrivance of two of the
most profligate men in the world to obtain their liberation from imprisonment for
a serious crime by the *favor of party spirit.*"[16] No copies of these pamphlets have
survived, but number five or six brought the additional charge of adultery against
Hamilton.

The author of this malice was the Scottish-born James Thomson Callender, an
ugly, misshapen little man who made a career of spewing venom. He was a hack
writer who had fled from Edinburgh a few years earlier after being charged with
sedition by the British government. Having denounced Parliament as "a phalanx of
mercenaries" and the English constitution as "a conspiracy of the rich against the
poor," he was fated to whirl into Republican circles in America and write for Benjamin Franklin Bache's *Aurora.*[17] In later years, Jefferson condemned Callender as
"a poor creature . . . hypochondriac, drunken, penniless, and unprincipled."[18] But
at this time, when Callender flung his darts at the Federalists, Jefferson glorified
him as "a man of genius" and "a man of science fled from persecution."[19] In late
June 1797, Jefferson was so pleased with Callender's handiwork that he stopped by
his lodgings to congratulate him and to buy copies of his scandalous *History.*

In the bound volume, Callender sneaked up on the Reynolds scandal, first reviewing other events of 1796 before pouncing on Hamilton: "We now come to a
part of the work more delicate perhaps than any other."[20] Callender said that he was
incensed by the way that Federalists and Hamilton in particular—the "prime mover
of the federal party"—had treated James Monroe, who had just returned to Philadelphia after being recalled as American minister to France.[21] Hamilton, among others, had pleaded with Washington to recall Monroe for his unabashed favoritism
toward the French Revolution. Back home, Monroe had huddled with Jefferson,
Burr, and Albert Gallatin and expressed indignation over his dismissal. "The unfounded reproaches heaped on Mr. Monroe form the immediate motive to the

publication of these papers," Callender declared.[22] Indeed, Monroe's connivance in Callender's project was clear to Alexander and Eliza Hamilton, who became unalterably convinced that Monroe had reneged on his confidentiality vow and leaked the Reynolds documents.

Callender promised readers that he would debunk Hamilton's pretensions to superior virtue, stating that "we shall presently see this great master of morality, although himself the father of a family, confessing that he had an illicit correspondence with another man's wife."[23] For posterity, the Callender disclosures were associated with Hamilton's exposure as a libertine. For Callender, however, this was merely a collateral benefit. His real aim was to resurrect the shopworn myth, discredited by the Giles investigations, that Hamilton had secretly enriched himself as treasury secretary through improper speculation in government securities. In fact, Callender blithely repeated the very error that had initially misled Muhlenberg, Venable, and Monroe in December 1792: that the money Hamilton had paid to James Reynolds related to official misconduct, not to infidelity.

Callender's diatribe had a specious air of deep research. He published the entire trove of papers that Hamilton had entrusted to Muhlenberg, Venable, and Monroe. "So much correspondence could not refer exclusively to wenching," stated Callender. "No man of common sense will believe that it did. . . . Reynolds and his wife affirm that it respected certain speculations."[24] Callender scorned the very idea of a romantic liaison: "Even admitting that . . . [Maria Reynolds] was the favourite of Mr. Hamilton, for which there appears no evidence but the word of the Secretary, this conduct would have been eminently foolish. Mr. Hamilton had only to say that he was sick of his amour and the influence and hopes of Reynolds at once vanished."[25] Callender denied the authenticity of Maria Reynolds's billets-doux to Hamilton and conjectured that Hamilton had forged them, filling them with spelling errors to make them seem plausible. Quite understandably, Callender could not conceive that someone as smart and calculating as Hamilton could have stayed so long in thrall to an enslaving passion. Hamilton could not have been stupid enough to pay hush money for sex, Callender alleged, so the money paid to James Reynolds *had* to involve illicit speculation. In fairness to Callender, it *is* baffling that Hamilton submitted to blackmail for so long.

The mystery of why Callender and his cronies disclosed the Reynolds scandal that summer is a tantalizing one. Callender mentioned the recall of James Monroe, but there were other reasons as well. The infamous exposé might never have been published if Washington had still been in office. For Republican pamphleteers, it was now open season on the Federalists. Callender wanted to prevent Hamilton from exercising the same influence over Adams that he'd had over Washington. He also wanted to besmirch Washington's reputation by demonstrating that he had been a puppet mouthing words scripted by Hamilton. Callender contended that Hamilton had received private parcels from Washington with speeches for rewriting: "'After opening such a parcel,' said Mr. Hamilton, 'what do you think were the contents?' 'DEAR HAMILTON, *put this into style for me.*' [Then Hamilton supposedly commented:] 'Some speech or letter has been enclosed, which I wrote over again, sent it back, and then the OLD DAMNED FOOL gave it away as *his own.*'"[26] Evidently, Callender was aware of scuttlebutt that Hamilton had ghostwritten most of Washington's farewell address.

Another compelling explanation for the timing of Callender's exposé relates to Hamilton's "Phocion" essays the previous fall, which had delved openly for the first time into Jefferson's private life. On October 15, 1796, we recall, Hamilton had seemed to make reference to Sally Hemings. On October 19, indulging in more heavy breathing, Hamilton said that Jefferson's "simplicity and humility afford but a flimsy veil to the *internal* evidences of aristocratic splendor, sensuality, and epicureanism."[27] Then on October 23, the Jeffersonian *Aurora* had published an anonymous response that referred discreetly, for the first time, to the Reynolds affair. The message was addressed to Treasury Secretary Wolcott and asked whether he had not been privy in December 1792 to "the circumstances of a certain enquiry of a very suspicious aspect, respecting real malconduct on the part of his friend, patron and predecessor in office, which ought to make him extremely circumspect on the subject of investigation . . . ?"[28] The author threatened to cite specifics: "Would a publication of the circumstances of that transaction redound to the honour or reputation of the parties and why has the subject been so long and carefully smothered up?"[29] Hamilton got the message. In subsequent installments of "Phocion," he fell silent abruptly on the subject of Jefferson's sex life.

The man making these menacing noises in the *Aurora* may have been John Beckley, recently ousted as clerk of the House of Representatives. Perhaps he leaked the Reynolds documents to Callender as revenge against the Federalists, or maybe he no longer felt morally bound to silence after resigning his job. Monroe himself fingered Beckley as the culprit. "You know, I presume, that Beckley published the papers in question," Monroe told Aaron Burr.[30] It should be recalled, however, that Monroe had given the papers to Beckley in the first place, so Monroe was admitting to Burr that he had not insured the secrecy of documents entrusted to him and had known all along that confidentiality had been breached. In holding James Monroe responsible, Alexander and Eliza were not off the mark.

A shadowy operative, adept at intrigue, Beckley continued to move stealthily in the background of Republican party politics. He is a type familiar in political history: the aide who lurks in the cloakrooms of power, listening and absorbing valuable information. Beckley had started out as clerk of the Virginia House of

Delegates; Jefferson, then the governor, called him the ablest clerk in the country. As first clerk of the House of Representatives, Beckley was a protégé of House Speaker Frederick Muhlenberg, which may also explain how he was drawn into the Reynolds scandal. Beckley's humble title did not capture the enormous power he wielded. Madison, Monroe, William Branch Giles, and other powerful Republicans gathered for talks at his lodgings. According to Hamilton's son, they once drank a mean-spirited toast to Hamilton when he was sick: "A speedy immortality to Hamilton."[31]

Beckley had an unslakable thirst for political intelligence. Benjamin Rush said of Beckley that "he possesses a fund of information about men and things and, what is more in favor of his principles, he possesses the confidence of our two illustrious patriots, Mr. Jefferson and Mr. Madison."[32] Beckley was constantly trying to dig up derogatory information to satisfy the Republican fantasy that Hamilton and Washington headed a pro-British monarchical conspiracy. Jefferson never shed his intense admiration for Beckley. When elected president himself, he restored Beckley as clerk of the House of Representatives and, loading him down with still more honors, appointed him the first librarian of Congress.

Hamilton thought that Jefferson was one of the conspirators behind the Callender exposé. Jefferson's secretary, William A. Burwell, said that around the time of the Maria Reynolds revelation, Hamilton had threatened Jefferson with public exposure of a shameful episode many years earlier in which Jefferson had repeatedly tried to seduce Betsey Walker, the wife of his friend and Virginia neighbor John Walker. Perhaps for this reason, the conflicted Jefferson both subsidized Callender and also urged him to refrain from further attacks on Hamilton. Callender reported that Jefferson "advised that the [Reynolds] papers should be suppressed . . . but his interposition came too late."[33]

Once Callender's charges were published, Hamilton faced an agonizing predicament: should he ignore the accusations as beneath his dignity or openly rebut them? Friends recommended tactful silence. Wolcott urged Hamilton to defer a response, telling him of the "indignation against those who have basely published this scandal."[34] Jeremiah Wadsworth thought any defense would be fruitless, warning that "it will be easy to invent new calumnies and you may be kept continually employed in answering."[35] Deaf to such advice, Hamilton decided to respond at length. When it came to major decisions, he always trusted to his inner promptings. Ordinarily, he told associates, he would have ignored the slander, but Callender was insinuating that Muhlenberg, Venable, and Monroe had refused to believe him in 1792 when he said that his payments to James Reynolds involved adultery and extortion. Callender upped the stakes by warning Hamilton that if he printed only extracts from his correspondence with those three men, he would be accused of shading the truth. In an open letter on July 12, he taunted Hamilton by saying the public "have long known you as an eminent and able statesman. They will be highly gratified by seeing you exhibited in the novel character of a lover."[36]

Hamilton now reverted to lifelong practice: he would drown his accusers with words. In mid-July, he holed up in a Philadelphia boardinghouse with his friend Congressman William Loughton Smith of South Carolina among the tenants. As he confessed his sins, Hamilton probably did not want to face his family. One pictures him stooped over his desk, scratching away at a furious pace. According to Smith, Hamilton wrote with zest and a vengeful glee. He "was in excellent health and in very excellent spirits, considering his complicated situation."[37] Months earlier, Hamilton had complained to Smith of feeble health. Now, he burst forth in fighting trim, striking a note of bravado as he confronted his enemies.

This writing spree resulted in a ninety-five-page booklet: thirty-seven pages of personal confessions, supplemented by fifty-eight pages of letters and affidavits. The volume is usually referred to as "the Reynolds pamphlet," but the full title was *Observations on Certain Documents Contained in No. V & VI of "The History of the United States for the Year 1796," In Which the Charge of Speculation Against Alexander Hamilton, Late Secretary of the Treasury, Is Fully Refuted. Written by Himself.*[38] Before examining the specific charges against him, Hamilton placed Callender's pamphlets in a political context, identifying the true enemy as the "spirit of Jacobinism." To accomplish its evil deeds, American Jacobinism had descended to calumny so that "the influence of men of upright principles, disposed and able to resist its enterprises, shall be at all events destroyed."[39] Thus Hamilton tried to elevate his personal defense into another apocalyptic crusade to save the nation.

After years of monetary sacrifices in public office, Hamilton again found it ruefully funny that he was accused of avarice. He said that his character had been marked "by an indifference to the acquisition of property rather than an avidity for it."[40] Then he got to the nub of the matter in the frankest confession yet uttered by an American public official: "The charge against me is a connection with one James Reynolds for purposes of improper pecuniary speculation. My real crime is an amorous connection with his wife, for a considerable time with his privity and connivance, if not originally brought on by a combination between the husband and wife with the design to extort money from me."[41] Even at this late date, Hamilton wavered as to whether Maria Reynolds had colluded with her husband from the outset or only over time. If he *had* been a venal official, Hamilton jeered, he would have chosen a more important accomplice than James Reynolds: "It is very extraordinary, if the head of the money department of a country, being unprincipled enough to sacrifice his trust and his integrity, could not have contrived objects of profit sufficiently large to have engaged the cooperation of men of far greater importance than Reynolds."[42] And if he had conspired with Reynolds, he would not have passed along relatively petty sums of fifty dollars.

Hamilton's strategy was simple: he was prepared to sacrifice his private reputation to preserve his public honor. He knew this would be the most exquisite torture for Eliza. Hadn't he just told William Hamilton that he could not be happier in a wife? And now here he was subjecting her to a nightmarish narrative of his betrayal. He wrote angrily of his accusers, "With such men, nothing is sacred. Even the peace of an unoffending and amiable wife is a welcome repast to their insatiate fury against the husband."[43] We do not know whether Hamilton discussed his pamphlet with Eliza beforehand. After admitting to adultery, he made the following statement: "This confession is not made without a blush. . . . I can never cease to condemn myself for the pang which it may inflict in a bosom eminently entitled to all my gratitude, fidelity, and love. But that bosom will approve that even at so great an expence, I should effectually wipe away a more serious stain from a name which it cherishes with no less elevation than tenderness."[44]

The steadfast Eliza may have sympathized with Hamilton's wish to cleanse his name. Yet readers of the pamphlet must have wondered why, instead of settling for a brief apology and a convincing mea culpa, Hamilton insisted upon telling the story in almost picaresque detail. He described Maria Reynolds coming to his door during the summer of 1791, of going around to her house that evening, and of being invited into her bedroom. Such descriptive touches, however much they gratified public curiosity, could only have mortified Eliza. All of Hamilton's breast-beating—"I have paid pretty severely for the folly and can never recollect it without disgust and self condemnation"—could not disguise that he was exposing Eliza to public humiliation.[45]

Why did Hamilton make this long, rambling confession? He was disgusted by the monstrous slurs upon his character and decided he would expose them once and for all. He intended to construct an account that would encompass all known facts and remove any room for misinterpretation by enemies. Moreover, Callender had already warned of the danger of publishing only extracts of the story. Far from being the subtle Machiavellian of Jeffersonian legend, Hamilton again suffered from excessive openness. "No man ever more disdained duplicity or carried *frankness* further than he," Fisher Ames said.[46] Hamilton was incapable of a wise silence. He probably imagined that the best way to prove the philandering and refute the corruption charges was to overwhelm his readers with details. As in all political battles, Hamilton was seized by an overmastering compulsion to counterattack with all the verbal weapons at his command. He viewed himself less as the guilty party than as the righteous one, unfairly maligned by scheming opponents, and he decided to turn the tables on his adversaries.

Hamilton's antics had dazzled and appalled the country for years, and never more so than with the Reynolds pamphlet. His friends were agog at his faulty judgment. "Humiliating in the extreme," was the verdict of Henry Knox.[47] Robert Troup observed that Hamilton's "ill-judged pamphlet has done him inconceivable injury."[48] William Loughton Smith thought Hamilton had rebutted Callender, "yet it is afflicting to see so great a man dragged before the public in such a delicate situation and compelled to avow a domestic infidelity to an unfeeling world."[49] Noah Webster wondered why someone of Hamilton's stature would "publish a history of his private intrigues, degrade himself in the estimation of all good men, and scandalize a family to clear himself of charges which no man believed."[50] Small wonder that Hamilton's family later tried to buy up and destroy all copies of the pamphlet left on the market.

The Republican press had a field day with the pamphlet and battened off it for years. Henceforth, Hamilton would be viewed as the oversexed treasury secretary. Callender rejoiced at Hamilton's indiscretion, telling Jefferson, "If you have not seen it, no anticipation can equal the infamy of this piece. It is worth all that fifty of the best pens in America could have said ag[ains]t him."[51] Drawing on this material, Callender wrote mockingly that the "whole proof in this pamphlet rests upon an illusion. 'I am a rake and for that reason I cannot be a swindler.'"[52] The *Aurora* responded similarly when it paraphrased Hamilton as saying, "I have been grossly . . . charged with . . . being a *speculator,* whereas I am only *an adulterer.* I have not broken the *eighth* commandment. . . . It is only the *seventh* which I have violated."[53]

In sacrificing his private virtue, Hamilton had imagined he would at least preserve a spotless public record. He would have been disheartened by Jefferson's reaction. Writing to John Taylor, a Virginia politician, the circumspect Jefferson said that Hamilton's "willingness to plead guilty to adultery seems rather to have strengthened than weakened the suspicions that he was in truth guilty of the speculations."[54] Madison's reaction was more perceptive: "The publication . . . is a curious specimen of the ingenious folly of its author. Next to the error of publishing it at all is that of forgetting that simplicity and candor are the only dress which prudence would put on innocence."[55]

For John and Abigail Adams, who already considered Hamilton a debauchee, their suspicions were fully confirmed. Before the pamphlet appeared, Abigail told her husband of Hamilton, "Oh, I have read his heart in his wicked eyes. The very devil is in them. They are lasciviousness itself."[56] Timothy Pickering, the secretary of state, recalled that soon after Adams became president, Abigail called on Mrs. Pickering and "took her to ride with her in her carriage. . . . [M]y wife afterwards told me that Mrs. Adams dwelt on the licentiousness of Hamilton's character in regard to the female sex."[57] When the scandal broke, the Adamses were probably less shocked at Hamilton's behavior than at his candor in admitting it. After they returned to Philadelphia in November 1797, fresh from a four-month absence, Abigail wrote of the Reynolds pamphlet, "Alas, alas, how weak is human nature."[58] John Adams traced Hamilton's roguish deeds back to his days on Washington's staff, followed by "debaucheries in New York and Philadelphia" at which he had made "his audacious and unblushing attempts upon ladies of the highest rank and purest virtue."[59]

It is difficult to figure out if the charges of sexual profligacy made against Hamilton all trace back, ultimately, to Maria Reynolds. There are only scattered references to his amorous ways in contemporary documents between the time of the affair (1791–1792) and its exposure (1797), then a tremendous increase after Callender performed his dirty work. That Hamilton loved the ladies and had a high libido seems clear. But was his adult life really a rake's progress of sexual conquests? For all the innuendoes about adultery, he did not engage in indiscriminate sex, and we can connect him with only Maria Reynolds for certain. There was plenty of understandable speculation about Angelica Church, but she was mostly abroad between 1783 and 1797, and we will never know whether her mutual enchantment with Hamilton was sexually consummated. One strong argument against such outright adultery was that Eliza and the entire Schuyler family adored Hamilton until the day he died. Would they have tolerated Hamilton if he had been sleeping with Eliza's sister? After Hamilton's death, the ever vigilant John Beckley referred to Hamilton as a "double adulterer"—presumably referring to Maria Reynolds and Angelica Church—but he named no one else.[60] Alexander Hamilton was the most controversial public figure of his era. If he had other women, why didn't the scandal-loving Republican press refer to these other romances? It seems unlikely that, if other women abounded, their identities would have been so well concealed for two centuries. And why, if Hamilton was so promiscuous, did he father no illegitimate children that we know of?

For all the tongue clucking and finger wagging at Hamilton, the Reynolds scandal diminished but scarcely destroyed his political stature. Though the Reynolds pamphlet provided the Jeffersonian press with fodder for satire, it did not lead to a wholesale abandonment of Hamilton by the Federalists. As David Cobb, a Federalist judge from Massachusetts, told Henry Knox, "Hamilton is fallen for the present, but if he fornicates with every female in the cities of New York and Philadelphia, he will rise again, for purity of character after a period of political existence is not necessary for public patronage."[61] In later years, John Adams conducted a revealing exchange of letters with William Cunningham, who said that Hamilton's friends had not abandoned him for straying from his wife. He offered an analogy from Roman history, the patriot Cato:

Cato valued himself on his integrity and was, it is said, addicted to intemperance. But the friends of Cato prized him so highly for his main excellence that they looked upon his occasional intoxication with indulgence. Thus I have understood it of Hamilton. He set the estimation made of his uprightness against that which might be formed from the confession of his lewdness and he determined that the weight of his cardinal virtues would preponderate over every defect and forever keep that scale immovably down.[62]

Perhaps the most telling reaction to Hamilton's troubles came from Washington, who knew Hamilton better than any other public figure. On August 21, from out of the blue, he sent his beleaguered friend a gift along with a note that made no reference to the scandal.

Not for any intrinsic value the thing possesses, but as a token of my sincere regard and friendship for you and as a remembrance of me, I pray you to accept a wine cooler for four bottles. . . . I pray you to present my best wishes, in which Mrs. Washington joins me, to Mrs. Hamilton and the family, and that you would be persuaded that with every sentiment of the highest regard, I remain your sincere friend and affectionate honorable servant.[63]

The letter was eloquent for what it did not say. It confirmed that Washington thought Hamilton was being persecuted and that he wanted to express solidarity with him. The wine cooler would always be treasured by Eliza Hamilton. That she cherished this gift so much tells us something about her view of the Maria Reynolds scandal.

For Hamilton and his descendants, the villain of the piece was always James Monroe. Hamilton's grandson blamed the exposure of the Reynolds affair on "the mean traps laid for him, principally by Monroe."[64] During the summer of 1797, Hamilton figured out pretty quickly that Monroe had made the Reynolds papers available to John Beckley in 1792. In *The History of the United States for 1796*, Callender had reproduced a statement by Muhlenberg, Venable, and Monroe about their dramatic confrontation with Hamilton on December 15, 1792, but now quoted them as saying that they had left Hamilton that evening "*under an impression our suspi-*

cions were removed."[65] This implied that they had not really believed Hamilton. Still more damaging was a private memo, published by Callender, that Monroe had written on January 1, 1793. It reported on a meeting at which Jacob Clingman told Monroe that the putative romance between Hamilton and Maria Reynolds was a mere "fabrication" to cover up Hamilton's wrongdoing at Treasury. By reporting this conversation without comment, Monroe seemed to lend tacit credence to its contents.

Now Hamilton promptly wrote and asked the three legislators to repudiate Callender's interpretation of the December 1792 meeting. Muhlenberg sent a friendly reply, regretted publication of the Reynolds papers, and confirmed that he had trusted Hamilton's account at the time. Venable's response, if a bit testier, agreed that the trio had accepted Hamilton's explanation. He also imparted the key piece of information that the Reynolds documents had been entrusted to James Monroe: "I do not know any means by which these papers could have got out unless by the person who copied them [i.e., John Beckley]."[66]

Monroe received Hamilton's letter just as he was preparing to visit his New York in-laws, the Kortrights. Before replying, Monroe wanted to huddle with Muhlenberg and Venable. Miffed by what he saw as stalling, Hamilton flew into a rage when he heard that Monroe was staying near him, on Wall Street. On July 10, he sent Monroe a terse note: "Mr. Hamilton requests an interview with Mr. Monroe at any hour tomorrow forenoon which may be convenient to him. Particular reasons will induce him to bring with him a friend to be present at what may pass. Mr. Monroe, if he pleases, may have another."[67] Beyond its cold formality, the note's reference to bringing witnesses signified the potential onset of an affair of honor. Faced with this challenge, Monroe consented to have Hamilton come to his lodgings at ten o'clock the next morning. It was to be one of the most emotional encounters of Hamilton's tumultuous life.

James Monroe was a tall, handsome man with piercing blue eyes and a rather awkward manner. Unlike the quick-witted Hamilton, Monroe was a plodding speaker and a middling intellect. Jefferson and other companions valued his sincerity. "Turn his soul wrong side outwards and there is not a speck on it," Jefferson once told Madison.[68] Like Hamilton, Monroe, a carpenter's son who had fought courageously in the Revolution, came from humble origins. He had crossed the Delaware with Washington, and his lung had been pierced by a bullet at the battle of Trenton. By war's end, Monroe was a protégé of Jefferson, who urged him to study law and enter politics. The two Virginians shared a belief that emancipation should be postponed, with the freed slaves someday transplanted to Africa. As a member of the Confederation Congress in the early 1780s, Monroe drew close to Madison but voted against ratifying the Constitution at the Virginia convention.

In the Senate, Monroe had exhibited special fervor in the Republican cause, just as Madison did in the House. He dismissed Britain as a corrupt, tottering state, saw the Federalists as their spineless lackeys—he denounced Hamilton's programs as "calculated to elevate the government above the people"—and favored an outright military alliance with France.[69] For Monroe, the "enemies of the French Revolution" were likewise "partisans for monarchy" in America.[70] Five days after Monroe arrived in Paris as American minister, Robespierre was executed, but all the carnage did not cool Monroe's infatuation for the Revolution. He frequently sided with the French government, advised it to ignore Washington as an "Angloman," and opposed the Jay Treaty. After two years of such disloyal bungling, Monroe was recalled by Washington and chastised as "a mere tool in the hands of the French government."[71]

Hamilton arrived on the morning of July 11 with John B. Church, while Monroe invited along David Gelston, a New York merchant and Republican politician. Gelston left a graphic account of the showdown between the ex–treasury secretary and the future president. From the second he entered the room, Hamilton seemed beside himself with rage. In Gelston's words, he "appeared very much agitated" and launched into an extended monologue about the December 1792 meeting. Even in Gelston's neutral chronicle, one can feel the extreme tension throbbing in the air. The two antagonists were visibly offended by each other. Hamilton pointed out that he had written to Monroe, Muhlenberg, and Venable and had "expected an immediate answer to so important a subject in which his character, the peace and reputation of his family were so deeply interested." Monroe replied that if Hamilton "would be temperate or quiet for a moment . . . he would answer him candidly."[72]

Hamilton asked if Monroe had leaked the Reynolds papers or failed to guarantee their security. Monroe replied that he thought the documents had "remained sealed" with a Virginia friend, that he had not intended to publish them, and knew nothing of their appearance until his return from Europe.[73] At this, Hamilton dropped any pose of civility and chastised Monroe, saying "your representation is totally false."[74] According to Gelston, the two men rose instantly. Monroe called Hamilton a "scoundrel," whereupon Hamilton immediately adopted the ritual language of dueling, saying, "I will meet you like a gentleman." To which Monroe retorted, "I am ready, get your pistols."[75]

The two men, like a pair of squabbling schoolboys, nearly came to blows, and Gelston and Church had to pry them apart, urging moderation. Although they soon sat down, Gelston observed that Hamilton was still "extremely agitated," while Monroe adopted an icy tone of contempt, telling Hamilton he would explain what he knew if the latter would just calm down.[76] Gelston brought the hourlong meeting to a close by saying that Hamilton should wait until Monroe met with Venable and Muhlenberg in Philadelphia. Hamilton agreed reluctantly.

This began an interminable correspondence between Hamilton and Monroe that lasted the rest of the year and never gave Hamilton satisfaction. After Monroe conferred with Muhlenberg in Philadelphia (Venable having left for Virginia), the two men drafted a joint letter to Hamilton. They agreed that in December 1792 they had credited his story about Maria Reynolds and had dropped their suspicions about Treasury misconduct. This letter removed one bone of contention and took Muhlenberg out of the picture. But it left Hamilton brooding about another piece of evidence: the January 1, 1793, statement in which Monroe seemed to endorse Jacob Clingman's wild allegation. Hamilton followed Monroe to Philadelphia and peppered him with brief, pointed letters, trying to get him to renounce that statement. "Alexander Hamilton has favored this city with a visit," the *Aurora* reported with hearty pleasure. "He has certainly not come for the benefit of the fresh air."[77] Because Monroe had been responsible for the documents surfacing, Hamilton lectured him that it was incumbent upon him "as a man of honor and sensibility to have come forward in a manner that would have shielded me completely from the unpleasant effects brought upon me by your agency. This you have not done." Hamilton then employed language that again presaged a duel: "The result in my mind is that you have been and are actuated by motives towards me malignant and dishonorable."[78]

Monroe was enraged by Hamilton's truculence. He told Hamilton that if he wanted to convert this dispute into a personal affair—in other words, a duel—he was fully prepared to oblige him. He took refuge behind a hairsplitting distinction. He said that while he had recorded Clingman's statement without comment, he had not endorsed it. In a stinging rejoinder, Hamilton pointed out that for Monroe to have "recorded and preserved in secret" this accusatory statement was scarcely a friendly action. At this juncture in late July, Hamilton was weighing whether or not to publish his pamphlet. Monroe's obstinacy apparently pushed him over the edge. "The public explanation to which I am driven must decide, as far as public opinion is concerned, between us," Hamilton told him. "Painful as the appeal will be in one respect, I know that in the principal point it must completely answer my purpose."[79]

In early August, the feud between Hamilton and Monroe took on the formality of an affair of honor. Both men denied wanting to duel but stood ready if necessary. What are we to make of all this blowing and bluster? In their endless exchange of letters that summer, Monroe could have let Hamilton off the hook by stating that the veracity of the Clingman memo rested on Clingman's credibility alone. But Monroe was still smarting over his ignominious recall from Paris and did not wish to make life easy for Hamilton. On the other hand, it is equally noteworthy that

Hamilton was intransigent and made it hard for Monroe to compromise without losing face.

On August 6, Monroe sent Aaron Burr a copy of his correspondence with Hamilton and tried to enlist his aid to avert a duel. Obviously, he thought Burr was friendly enough with Hamilton to act as a mediator. Monroe made it plain that while he would not shrink from a duel, he would gladly avoid one if done "with propriety."[80] Just as Hamilton thought Monroe was motivated by partisan purposes, so Monroe thought Hamilton goaded on by "party friends." "In truth I have no desire to persecute this man," Monroe told Burr, "though he justly merits it. . . . I had no hand in the publication, was sorry for it, and think he has acted, by drawing the public attention to it and making it an aff[ai]r of more consequence than it was in itself, very indiscreetly."[81] Monroe did not understand just how upset the illegitimate Hamilton was about anything that affected his reputation. In a letter delivered by Burr, Monroe told Hamilton that he had no intention of challenging him to a duel. At this, Hamilton temporarily backed down, saying that any further action on his own part would be improper.

The most fair-minded advice in the dispute came from Aaron Burr, who seemed devoid of the petty, vindictive spirit that actuated the chief adversaries. Unlike the Jeffersonians, he did not doubt Hamilton's integrity. That August, he told Monroe that he hoped his correspondence with Hamilton would be burned. "If you and Muhlenberg really believe, as I do and think you must, that H[amilton] is innocent of the charge of any concern in speculation with Reynolds, it is my opinion that it will be an act of magnanimity and justice to say so in a joint certificate. . . . Resentment is more dignified when justice is rendered to its object."[82] Had he already hated Hamilton, Burr could have egged on Monroe and engineered a duel in which Hamilton might have died. Instead, he had the grace and decency to plead for fairness toward Hamilton. He was the one upright actor in the whole affair.

In late August, the appearance of Hamilton's *Observations* pamphlet revived the feud with Monroe, which sputtered on for months. After poring over the pamphlet, Madison reassured Monroe that it did not threaten his honor. Monroe would not listen. In early December, he reactivated the dormant feud by sending a provocative letter to Hamilton. "In my judgment," he told Hamilton, "you ought either to have been satisfied with the explanations I gave you or to have invited me to the field [of honor]."[83] Burr was authorized to act as a second in any duel but let the matter quietly lapse. Among other things, Burr did not think that Hamilton would actually fight, a misperception that may have influenced his later decisions in his own encounter with Hamilton. In fact, Hamilton drafted a letter to Monroe in January 1798, accepting a duel if necessary. Fortunately, the confrontation petered out, and Hamilton never sent the note. As a result of this and other dealings with him, Burr came away with a lower opinion of Monroe. When Monroe's name later surfaced as a possible presidential candidate, Burr jotted down this scathing assessment of him:

> Naturally dull and stupid; extremely illiterate; indecisive to a degree that would be incredible to one who did not know him; pusillanimous and, of course, hypocritical; has no opinion on any subject and will be always under the government of the worst men; pretends, as I am told, to some knowledge of military matters, but never commanded a platoon nor was ever fit to command one. . . . As a lawyer, Monroe was far below mediocrity.[84]

The first advertisement for Hamilton's pamphlet appeared in the *Gazette of the United States* on July 31, yet it was not actually published until August 25. Why this curious hiatus after Hamilton had rushed to complete his defense? Some time may have elapsed as Hamilton rounded up affidavits, but the paramount reason was probably simpler: Eliza was pregnant with their sixth child. Because of her earlier miscarriage, it would be their first child in five years. Hamilton must have dreaded that exposure of his actions might provoke another miscarriage, as had occurred when he rode off to the Whiskey Rebellion three years earlier. Hamilton's delay in issuing his pamphlet gave Eliza the necessary reprieve. On August 4, 1797, she gave birth to a healthy baby, William Stephen Hamilton, who was baptized by the Reverend Benjamin Moore at Trinity Church. "Mrs. Hamilton has lately added another boy to our stock," Hamilton told Washington in late August, after receiving the wine cooler. "She and the child are both well."[85] The name may have celebrated Hamilton's new rapport with his Scottish uncle and paid tribute to his brother-in-law, Lieutenant Governor Stephen Van Rensselaer, then grieving over the death of his eldest daughter.

The Republican press made the Reynolds exposé as hellish as possible for Eliza. "Art thou a wife?" the *Aurora* asked her. "See him, whom thou has chosen for the partner of this life, lolling in the lap of a harlot!!"[86] Eliza never commented publicly on the Reynolds scandal, but we can deduce her general reaction from several snippets of information. On July 13, while Hamilton was in Philadelphia, John Barker Church sent him a letter that described Eliza's response to the open letter just published by Callender: "Eliza is well. She put into my hand the newspaper with James Thomson Callender's letter to you, but it makes not the least impression on her, only that she considers the whole knot of those opposed to you to be [scoundrels]."[87] This drives home several points: that Eliza was outraged at Hamilton's critics; that she agreed that a conspiracy was afoot; and that her faith in her husband's integrity was unshaken. Of course, at this point Hamilton had not yet published his own pamphlet, spilling out lurid details of his adultery. The *Aurora* later screamed, "He acknowledges . . . that he violated the sacred sanctuary of his own house, by taking an unprincipled woman during the absence of his wife and family to his bed."[88] But already Eliza showed flashes of the militant loyalty to her husband that was to distinguish her widowhood. Church also mentioned to Hamilton that Angelica was sick: "My Angelica is not very well. She complains that her throat is a little sore. I hope it will not be of long duration."[89]

While Hamilton was pouring out his confessions in Philadelphia, he showed a special solicitude for Eliza. He knew that his pamphlet, at least temporarily, would shatter her heroic image of him, and he must have trembled with apprehension. He wrote to Eliza that he eagerly looked forward "to her embrace and to the company of our beloved Angelica. I am very anxious about you both—you for an obvious reason and her because Mr. Church mentioned in a letter to me that she complained of *a sore throat*. Let me charge you and her to be well and happy, for you comprise all my felicity. Adieu angel."[90] Two days later, Hamilton wrote again and said he would return to New York the next day. "Love to Angelica & Church," he wrote. "I shall return full freighted with it for my dear brunettes."[91]

Eliza decided to have the baby in Albany. A guilt-ridden Hamilton escorted her to the sloop that transported her up the Hudson, but he did not join her. Probably his presence was then too distressing. Angelica saw Hamilton right after he returned from the boat, and she sent Eliza a consoling note. Angelica always wrote to her as the worldly, protective older sister, often calling her "my dear child." She knew Eliza was pure hearted and easily wounded. On the other hand, Angelica was willing to make allowances for her brother-in-law.

> When [Hamilton] returned from the sloop, he was very much out of spirits and you were the subject of his conversation the rest of the evening. Catherine [Angelica's daughter] played at the harpsichord for him and at 10 o'clock he went home. Tranquillize your kind and good heart, my dear Eliza, for I have the most positive assurance from Mr. Church that the dirty fellow who has caused us all some uneasiness and wounded your feelings, my dear love, is effectually silenced. Merit, virtue, and talents must have enemies and [are] always exposed to envy so that, my Eliza, you see the penalties attending the position of so amiable a man. All this you would not have suffered if you had married into a family less *near the sun*. But then [you would have missed?] the pride, the pleasure, the nameless satisfactions.[92]

Angelica signed the note, "With all my heart and redoubled tenderness."[93] Eliza did not buckle under the strain. One imagines that she had tolerated some discreet philandering from Hamilton before but not such open scandal. Did she see life with

Hamilton the way Angelica did—that marriage to such an exceptional man entailed a large quota of pain and suffering that was abundantly compensated by his love, intelligence, and charm? The rest of her life suggests that this was indeed the case. The publication of Hamilton's pamphlet must have been inexpressibly mortifying to Eliza when she discovered how vulgar and uneducated Maria Reynolds was and how breezily Hamilton had deceived her during the affair, urging her to stay in Albany for her health. Whatever pain she suffered, however, Eliza never surrendered her conviction that her husband was a noble patriot who deserved the veneration of his countrymen and had been crucified by a nefarious band. Her later work for orphans, the decades spent compiling her husband's papers and supervising his biography, her constant delight in talking about him, her pride in Washington's wine cooler, her fight to stake Hamilton's claim to authorship of the farewell address—these and many, many other things testify to unflinching love for her husband. And the most convincing proof of all was the undying hatred that she bore for James Monroe.

Just a couple of weeks after Hamilton published the Reynolds pamphlet, he experienced a medical scare with his eldest son, Philip, that may have seemed like heavenly retribution for his wayward conduct. The fifteen-year-old Philip, an uncommonly handsome and intelligent boy, was the most promising of the children. In early September, he "was attacked with a severe, bilious fever, which soon assumed a typhus character," said Dr. David Hosack, a professor of medicine and botany at Columbia College, who was summoned to attend the boy.[94] Hamilton had to leave for Hartford, Connecticut, to represent New York State in a case in federal court. As soon as he reached Rye, thirty miles north of New York City, he wrote to his wife in a state of distress: "I am arrived here, my dear Eliza, in good health, but very anxious about my dear Philip. I pray heaven to restore him and in every event to support you." He recommended a cold-bath treatment not unlike the one used by Edward Stevens to cure him of yellow fever: "Also, my Betsey, how much do I regret to be separated from you at such a juncture. When will the time come that I shall be exempt from the necessity of leaving my dear family? God bless my beloved and all my dear children. AH."[95]

As Philip's condition worsened, Hosack began to despair of his survival. Eliza grew so distraught that the good doctor banished her to another room so "that she might not witness the last struggles of her son."[96] He sent an express courier to fetch Hamilton from Hartford so he would arrive before the boy died. Meanwhile, Philip grew delirious, lost his pulse, and became comatose. Hosack managed to revive him by immersing him in hot baths of Peruvian bark and rum, then wrapping him in warm, dry blankets. Hosack later described Hamilton's return as one of his most gratifying moments as a physician:

> In the course of the night, General Hamilton arrived at his home under the full expectation that his son was no more. But to his great joy he still lived. When the father knew what had been done and the means that had been employed . . . he immediately came to my room where I was sleeping, and although I was then personally unknown to him, awakened me and taking me by the hand, his eyes suffused with tears of joy, he observed, "My dear Sir, I could not remain in my own house without first tendering to you my grateful acknowledgment for the valuable services you have rendered my family in the preservation of my child."[97]

Hosack paid tribute to the "tender feeling" and "exquisite sensibility" that Hamilton showed as he assumed the role of maternal care. In tending his son, Hamilton was both nurse and physician, leaving the doctor amazed by both his medical knowledge and his tenderness toward his children.[98] Hosack recalled, "From that moment, he devoted himself most assiduously to the care of his son, administering with his own hand every dose of medicine or cup of nourishment that was required. I may add that this was his custom in every important case of sickness that occurred in his family."[99] This was not a family that Hamilton was prepared to abandon, and whether from penance for the Reynolds affair or from his usual paternal dedication, he was very attentive to Eliza and the children in the coming years.

THIRTY-ONE

AN INSTRUMENT
OF HELL

One reason that Hamilton so feared the repercussions of the Reynolds affair was a premonition that the United States might soon be at war with an imperious France. If this conflict came about, Hamilton intended to assume a major position and could not afford any hint of scandal. As many Republicans had predicted, the French had retaliated against the Jay Treaty by allowing their privateers to prey on American ships carrying contraband cargo bound for British ports. With Napoleon emerging as the new French military strongman, Hamilton had little doubt that his troops would spread despotism across Europe. Writing under "Americus," Hamilton had warned early in 1797 that the "specious pretence of enlightening mankind and reforming their civil institutions is the varnish to the real design of subjugating" other nations.[1] Hamilton predicted that France would become "the terror and the scourge of nations."[2]

Soon after being sworn in as president, John Adams learned that the Directory, the five-member council now ruling France, had expelled the new American minister, Charles Cotesworth Pinckney, and promulgated belligerent new orders against America's merchant marine. By spring, the French had seized more than three hundred American vessels. To lift domestic morale, Hamilton suggested to Secretary of State Pickering a day of prayer "to strengthen religious ideas in a contest" that might pit Americans "against atheism, conquest, and anarchy."[3] Not trusting to the Lord alone, Hamilton also recommended more muscular measures, principally a new naval force and a twenty-five-thousand-man provisional army. Far from being a reflexive warmonger, Hamilton wanted to explore first every diplomatic option. "My opinion is to exhaust the expedients of negotiation and at the same time to prepare *vigorously* for the worst," he advised Oliver Wolcott, Jr.[4] "*Real firmness* is good for everything. *Strut* is good for nothing."[5] He told William Loughton Smith, "My plan ever is to combine *energy* with *moderation*."[6]

President Adams decided to pursue a two-pronged strategy: maintaining American neutrality through negotiations while simultaneously expanding the military in case talks with France miscarried. He entertained the anodyne hope that he could thread a neat path between Federalist Anglophiles and Republican Francophiles. Like Adams, Hamilton wanted to preserve peace with France through diplomacy and possibly even negotiate a commercial treaty on the Jay Treaty model. In a high-minded mode, he urged that a bipartisan three-man commission that included an old political rival be sent to France. "Unless Mr. Madison will go, there is scarcely another character that will afford advantage," he said.[7] Despite heated protests from some Federalists, Hamilton thought that any delegation lacking a prominent Republican would forfeit all credibility with the French. He also yearned to call the Republicans' bluff and show that the Federalists had done everything possible to conserve peace. Nevertheless, the three members of Adams's cabinet under Hamilton's supposed dominion—Pickering, Wolcott, and McHenry—steadfastly opposed the choice of a Republican. Wolcott did more than just defy Hamilton's wishes: he threatened to resign if Adams executed such a policy. As Hamilton suspected, Madison, who had a deathly fear of transatlantic travel, turned down the chance to join the delegation to France, as did Jefferson.

Starting with this first crisis of the Adams administration, Hamilton answered interminable queries from the secretaries of state, treasury, and war, who sought his guidance and shared with him internal cabinet documents. Ensconced in his Manhattan law office, Hamilton was apprised of everything happening in Philadelphia. Adams knew nothing of these contacts. At first, Hamilton did not denigrate Adams or his cabinet and behaved in exemplary fashion. "I believe there is no danger of want of firmness in the executive," he told Rufus King. "If he is not ill-advised, he will not want prudence."[8] Vice President Jefferson, by contrast, was already in the thick of a secret campaign to sabotage Adams in French eyes. The French consul in Philadelphia, Joseph Létombe, held four confidential talks with Jefferson in the spring of 1797—talks no less unorthodox than the ones Hamilton had held with British minister George Hammond—and informed his superiors in Paris, paraphrasing Jefferson, that "Mr. Adams is vain, suspicious, and stubborn, of an excessive self-regard, taking counsel with nobody."[9] Jefferson predicted to Létombe that Adams would last only one term and urged the French to invade England. In the most brazen display of disloyalty, he advised the French to stall any American envoys sent to Paris: "Listen to them and then drag out the negotiations at length and mollify them by the urbanity of the proceedings."[10] Jefferson and other Republicans encouraged the French to believe that Americans sided with them overwhelmingly, and this may have toughened the tone that the Directory adopted with the new administration.

On May 16, 1797, President Adams delivered a bellicose message to Congress, denouncing the French for ejecting Charles Cotesworth Pinckney and stalking American ships and chiding them for having "inflicted a wound in the American breast."[11] He also announced plans to expand the navy and bolster the militias. For the *Aurora,* this suggested too much belligerence. After a pacific inaugural speech, editorialized the paper about Adams, "we see him gasconading like a bully, swaggering the hero, and armed cap-a-pie, throwing the gauntlet to the most formidable power on earth." Ergo, Adams must be a British agent: "We behold him placing himself the file-leader of a British faction and marshalling his forces as if he were the representative of George the Third, instead of the chief magistrate of the American people."[12]

Dashing this Republican stereotype, Adams made a conciliatory overture and announced plans to dispatch a diplomatic mission to Paris. The three-man delegation was to include two southern Federalists, John Marshall and Charles Cotesworth Pinckney, and a northern Republican, Elbridge Gerry of Massachusetts, who had been a partisan of the French Revolution. "The French are no more capable of a republican government," Adams advised Gerry, "than a snowball can exist a whole week in the streets of Philadelphia under a burning sun."[13] Quite unlike the cabinet members he reputedly controlled, Hamilton applauded Adams with gusto. "I like very well the course of executive conduct in regard to the controversy with France," he told Wolcott.[14] But he had reservations about the likely outcome of the mission. He believed that Adams had erred by not sending a southern Republican, a move that would have convinced the French that the deck was not stacked against them. He also doubted that French officials would treat the American envoys respectfully and fulminated against them as "the most ambitious and horrible tyrants that ever cursed the earth," rebuking Republicans who would "make us lick the feet of her violent and unprincipled leaders."[15]

When the American commissioners arrived in France in August 1797, they were greeted by a lame minister of foreign affairs who had been a pariah a few years earlier: Charles Maurice de Talleyrand-Périgord, who had befriended Hamilton in Philadelphia. With the end of the Terror, Talleyrand had been rehabilitated and returned to France. Hamilton knew that he was avaricious and regarded public office as a means of obtaining money. The cynical Frenchman once told a mutual friend that "he found it very strange that a man of his [Hamilton's] quality, blessed with such outstanding gifts, should resign a ministry in order to return to the practice of law and give as his reason that as a minister he did not earn enough to bring up his eight children."[16] After Hamilton returned to New York, Talleyrand was en route to a dinner party one night when he glimpsed Hamilton toiling by candlelight in his law office. "I have seen a man who made the fortune of a nation laboring all night to support his family," he said, shocked.[17] After becoming French foreign minister in July 1797, he rejoiced at the plunder placed at his fingertips. "I'll hold the job," he confided to a friend. "I have to make an immense fortune out of it, a really immense fortune."[18] He proceeded to scoop up an estimated thirteen to fourteen million francs during his first two years as foreign minister alone.

By the time the three Americans showed up in Paris, Napoleon had crushed the Austrian army in Italy. Then, in early September, the Directory staged a veritable coup d'état, arresting and deporting scores of deputies and shutting down more than forty newspapers in a wholesale purge of moderate elements. John Marshall sent a gloomy assessment to Pickering: "All power is now in the undivided possession of those who have directed against us those hostile measures of which we so justly complain."[19] Corruption, long endemic among French officials, had only worsened under the Directory. When Talleyrand received the three American commissioners in October, he treated them civilly during a fifteen-minute audience, but they did not hear from him again for another week. The tone then turned frigid as Talleyrand explained that the Directory was "excessively exasperated" by statements made about France by President Adams in his May 16 address to Congress. Talleyrand then forced the three Americans to deal with three minions—Jean Conrad Hottinguer, Pierre Bellamy, and Lucien Hauteval—who were to become infamous in American history through the three coded letters, *X, Y,* and *Z,* that identified them in diplomatic dispatches sent to Philadelphia. Through these underlings, Talleyrand imposed a series of insufferable demands: that President Adams retract the controversial passages of his truculent speech; extend a large loan to France; and even pay for damage inflicted on American ships by French privateers! Talleyrand's lieutenants further insisted that the Americans fork over a considerable bribe as the prelude to any negotiations. Playing a cat-and-mouse game, Talleyrand deferred meetings with the American envoys, allowing extra time for his intermediaries to extort money.

John Marshall and Charles Cotesworth Pinckney were disgusted and wanted to terminate the negotiations at once—"No! No! Not a sixpence!" Pinckney spluttered in protest—while the Francophile Elbridge Gerry counseled patience. Marshall began drafting two long accounts to Timothy Pickering that chronicled the indignities they had endured. Due to the absence of winter traffic across the North Atlantic, the dispatches did not arrive in Philadelphia until the spring. While Adams awaited the results, Jefferson continued to make mischief by urging France to put off talks with the American delegation. "The Vice-President still argues that the Directory has everything to gain here by temporizing and he repeats to me incessantly that Machiavelli's maxim, *Nil repente* [nothing suddenly], is the soul of great affairs," Létombe told his French bosses.[20]

Not until March 4, 1798, did Marshall's explosive narratives land on President Adams's desk. Once decoded, they made for shocking reading. The mission had been a disaster, nothing short of a grand national humiliation. After receiving an account of Talleyrand's chicanery, Hamilton advised Pickering, "I wish to see a *temperate,* but *grave, solemn,* and *firm* communication from the president to the two houses on the result of the advices from our commissioners."[21] Still willing to leave the door to talks open, Hamilton laid out an ambitious program for an enlarged army: "The attitude of *calm defiance* suits us," he told Pickering.[22]

At first, President Adams made a politic speech to Congress that announced that the mission had foundered while omitting the notorious circumstances that would have riled the public. He asked for a broad array of military preparations. In a serious miscalculation, the Republicans branded Adams a warmonger and claimed that France had behaved far better than the president was allowing. Vice President Jefferson referred privately to Adams's speech as an "insane message."[23] On March 29, 1798, Hamilton's old foe William Branch Giles of Virginia intimated that Adams was suppressing documents that would show France in a more flattering light. When he and other Republicans demanded the release of the communiqués, the House agreed. Hamilton was pleased that France would now be shown in its true colors. Americans "at large should know the conduct of the French government towards our envoys and the abominable corruption of that government together with their enormous demands for *money.* These are so monstrous as to shock every reasonable man when he shall know them."[24]

When the XYZ papers were published, they proved a bonanza for the Federalists, and John Adams attained the zenith of his popularity as president. Although he had no military background, he now began to appear in military regalia, exhorting his followers to adopt a "warlike character."[25] After Adams dined with a delegation of patriotic admirers from New York in late May, Abigail gave each visitor a black cockade—a knot of ribbons—which became the emblem of support for the administration. "The act has produced the most magical effects," Robert Troup said after the XYZ dispatches appeared. "A spirit of warm and high resentment against the rulers of France has suddenly burst forth in every part of the United States."[26] Congress rushed through a program for fortifying eastern seaports and augmenting the army and navy.

The Republicans contrived ways to rationalize what had happened. Jefferson complained to Madison that Adams had perpetrated "a libel on the French government" as part of his "swindling experiment."[27] He conceded that Talleyrand might have organized an extortion plot, but "that the Directory knew anything of it is neither proved nor provable."[28] Jefferson's conviction that the XYZ Affair was a Federalist hoax only grew with time. The whole brouhaha was "a dish cooked up by [John] Marshall, where the swindlers are made to appear as the French government."[29] Nor did the XYZ Affair lead Madison to reevaluate the French Revolution. After hearing of Talleyrand's conduct toward the American envoys, Madison could not believe that the French minister had behaved so stupidly. He thought President Adams, not the Directory, "the great obstacle to accommodation" and accused the Federalists of resorting to "vile insults and calumnies" to foment war with France.[30]

Some Republican papers had the temerity to blame the XYZ Affair on Hamilton. The *Aurora* said the whole fiasco resulted from his relationship with Talleyrand: "Mr. Talleyrand is notoriously anti-republican. . . . [H]e was the intimate friend of Mr. Hamilton . . . and other great Federalists[,] and . . . it is probably owing to the determined hostility which he discovered in them towards France that the government of that country consider us only as objects of plunder."[31] This must have been hard for Hamilton to swallow. For years, he had accused France of being a faithless friend. Now that the XYZ dispatches had vindicated his judgment, the Republicans chided him instead of admitting their own errors.

As was his wont, Hamilton charged into print with a seven-part newspaper series entitled "The Stand," in which he advocated the formation of a large army to face down French aggression. When it had been a question of a possible war with Great Britain a few years earlier, Hamilton had been willing to make concessions and negotiate at length to avoid hostilities. But his foreign-policy views frequently varied with the situation, and he now adopted a much tougher tone when France was the potential belligerent power.

In writing "The Stand," Hamilton took dead aim against Republicans who had become apologists for French misbehavior: "Such men merit all the detestation of their fellow citizens and there is no doubt that with time and opportunity they will merit much more from the offended justice of the laws."[32] Hamilton mocked Jefferson's claim that Talleyrand, not the Directory, was to blame for the XYZ Affair. He noted that Talleyrand was the world's "most circumspect man" and would never have acted without the direct support of the Directory.

> The recourse to so pitiful an evasion betrays in its author a systematic design to excuse France at all events, to soften a spirit of submission to every violence she may commit, and to prepare the way for implicit subjection to her will. To be the pro-consul of a despotic Directory over the United States, degraded to the condition of a province, can alone be the criminal, the ignoble aim of so seditious, so prostitute a character.[33]

Hamilton's indignation with Jefferson was warranted, but the idea that he wanted to reduce the United States to a French province or that his ideas were criminal was cruelly overblown and reminiscent of the most malicious nonsense heaved at Hamilton himself.

The strident tone of "The Stand" reflects the polarization that had gripped America over the French crisis. Feelings ran so high that Jefferson told one correspondent, "Men who have been intimate all their lives cross the street to avoid meeting and turn their heads another way, lest they should be obliged to touch hats."[34] Hamilton thought that America was in an undeclared civil war that had segregated the country into two warring camps. At first, the XYZ Affair seemed a windfall for the Federalists, and their fortunes improved sharply in elections that autumn. Having been strong in the patrician Senate, they now made sweeping gains in the House and even picked up southern seats. But this sudden flush of power in time proved perilous for the Federalists, for they were henceforth to lack the self-restraint necessary to curtail their more dogmatic, authoritarian impulses, thus paving the way for abuses of power.

As he braced for potential conflict with France, President Adams had to cope with the ambivalent emotions Americans brought to the vexed subject of war. As colonists, they had been antagonized by the need to quarter and provision redcoats and remembered the arrogance of the standing armies sent to enforce hated laws. Among the fanciful dreams fostered by American independence was the fond hope that America would be spared wars and the need for a permanent military presence. "At the close of our revolution[ary] war," wrote Hamilton, "the phantom of perpetual peace danced before the eyes of everybody."[35] Gordon Wood has observed, "Since war was promoted by the dynastic ambitions, the bloated bureaucracy, and the standing armies of monarchies, then the elimination of monarchy would mean the elimination of war itself."[36] Hamilton, by contrast, believed that war was a permanent feature of human societies.

Many Republicans deplored standing armies as tools used by oppressive kings to subdue popular legislatures. The Declaration of Independence had protested standing armies kept in the colonies in peacetime. At the Constitutional Convention, Elbridge Gerry had bawdily likened standing armies to a tumescent penis: "An excellent assurance of domestic tranquillity, but a dangerous temptation to foreign adventure."[37] Jefferson wanted to ban standing armies in the Bill of Rights. He thought state militias and small gunboats sufficient to guard American shores. Republican orthodoxy declared that citizen-soldiers could defend the nation and obviate the need for a permanent military. Jeffersonians also feared that war would engender the powerful central government favored by Hamilton. In Madison's view, "War is the parent of armies; from these proceed debts and taxes; and armies and debts and taxes are the known instruments for bringing the many under the domination of the few."[38] Unlike many Federalists, John Adams thought a navy and militia would suffice to guard the country and feared a large standing army as a "many bellied monster."[39] Hobbled by this aversion to a federal military, the country was reduced to a regular army of just a few thousand troops when Washington left office.

During the Revolution, Hamilton had despaired of reliance on militias and learned to respect the superiority of trained soldiers. During the war scare with France, he saw a chance to promote a robust national defense and advanced a pet project for a fifty-thousand-man army: twenty thousand regulars joined by thirty thousand auxiliaries. The president reacted with contempt. "The army of fifty thousand men . . . appeared to me to be one of the wildest extravagances of a knight errant," Adams later wrote, harping again on Hamilton's foreign birth. "It proved to me that Mr. Hamilton knew no more of the sentiments and feelings of the people of America than he did of those of the inhabitants of one of the planets."[40] As far as Adams was concerned, "Hamilton's hobby was the army."[41]

Hamilton's blood boiled as France grew more audacious in attacking American ships. In May 1798, a French privateer captured American vessels outside New York harbor. "This is too much humiliation after all that has passed," Hamilton protested to Secretary of War McHenry. "Our merchants are very indignant. Our government [is] very prostrate in the view of every man of energy."[42] That month, amid growing fears of an imminent French invasion, Congress decided to create a separate Navy Department with twelve new frigates and a "Provisional Army" of ten thousand men. The euphemistic language was significant: a permanent or standing army was anathema. In July, Congress provided for an "Additional Army" of twelve infantry regiments and six cavalry companies. These numbers exceeded what Adams wanted, though they fell short of Hamilton's fantasies. Adams, who sometimes portrayed himself as a passive spectator of his presidency, blamed Hamilton for pushing through this larger army: "Such was the influence of Mr. Hamilton in Congress that, without any recommendation from the President, they passed a bill to raise an army."[43] As war hysteria grew, trade with France was embargoed, and American naval vessels were empowered to pounce on any French ships threatening American trade. The so-called Quasi-War with France was under way.

It proved impossible to separate the war from partisan domestic wrangles. Republicans feared that the unacknowledged agenda behind this burgeoning military establishment was not to defend America from France so much as to save America for the Federalists and stifle domestic dissent. Sometimes, Hamilton had trouble keeping the issues apart in his mind because he thought that, if France invaded, many Jeffersonians would aid the interlopers and "flock to the standard of France to render it easy to quell the resistance of the rest."[44]

Hamilton hovered in a queer limbo during this period. He felt both powerful and powerless. He was a private citizen and lawyer, yet alleged by some to be more influential than the president himself. He certainly had unparalleled access to Adams's cabinet and often sent them letters that they repeated verbatim in memos for the president, without identifying Hamilton as the source. At the same time, Hamilton struggled to redeem his reputation after the disclosure of his assignations with Maria Reynolds. Writing to Rufus King, Robert Troup noted the paradox that Hamilton's legal practice was "extensive and lucrative" but that he was still under siege from the scandal. "For this twelvemonth past this poor man—Hamilton I mean—has been most violently and infamously abused by the democratical party. His ill-judged pamphlet has done him incomparable injury."[45]

One might have thought that Hamilton would crow in triumph after Congress approved a new army. Surely he was slated for a commanding position. Instead, in personal letters to Eliza, he again seemed weary of public life and hankered for a more retired existence. When Eliza went off to Albany in early June 1798, leaving him with the older boys, Hamilton seemed incurably lonesome. "I always feel how necessary you are to me," he wrote to her. "But when you are absent, I become still more sensible of it and look around in vain for that satisfaction which you alone can bestow."[46] More than at any time since their courtship, Hamilton showed his deep emotional dependence upon his wife. She provided a psychological anchor for this turbulent man who was disenchanted with public life. "In proportion as I discover the worthlessness of other pursuits," he wrote to Eliza, "the value of my Eliza and of domestic happiness rises in my estimation."[47] One suspects that Alexander and Eliza had slowly repaired the harm done by the Reynolds affair, that she had begun to forgive him, and that they had recaptured some earlier intimacy. Perhaps it took this scandal for Hamilton to recognize just how vital his wife had been in providing solace from his controversial political career.

By 1798, many people were trying to woo Hamilton back into public life. When one of New York's two senators resigned, Governor John Jay offered the post to Hamilton. "If after well considering the subject, you should decline an appointm[en]t," he told Hamilton obligingly, "be so good as to consult with some of our most judicious friends and advise me as to the persons most proper to appoint."[48] Congressman Robert G. Harper, a South Carolina Federalist, dangled before Hamilton the prospect of becoming secretary of war, hinting that he had sounded out President Adams on the subject. Both times, Hamilton declined, for he was stalking bigger game. For someone of his vaulting ambition, the leadership of the new army was a shiny, irresistible lure, especially with the presidency foreclosed. Fisher Ames said that the only distinction that Hamilton devoutly craved was not money or power but military fame. "He was qualified beyond any man of the age to display the talents of a great general."[49] Many Federalists assumed that if France attacked America, Washington would head the war effort with Hamilton loyally at his side, in a rousing reenactment of the Revolution. "The old *chief* is again furbishing his sword," Robert Troup reported excitedly to Rufus King. "If there be a conflict and he is invited, he will take the field. And so will Hamilton."[50]

On military matters, John Adams was often adrift. For all his dogged committee work in the Continental Congress and sturdy promotion of an American fleet, he had not experienced combat and perhaps felt deprived of some essential glory. "Oh, that I was a soldier!" he had written in 1775. "I will be. I am reading military books. Everybody must and will and shall be a soldier."[51] The fraternal bond that knit Washington and his former officers into an elite caste excluded Adams. In matters of war, nobody could possibly measure up to the exalted Washington, who would be needed to confer legitimacy on any new army.

After Congress authorized the provisional army, Hamilton beseeched Washington to take the lead. He again exhibited perfect pitch in addressing his mentor. "You ought also to be aware, my dear Sir," Hamilton told him, "that in the event of an open rupture with France, the public voice will again call you to command the armies of your country." Washington's friends were reluctant to summon him from retirement, "yet it is the opinion of all those with whom I converse that you will be compelled to make the sacrifice."[52]

Now somewhat infirm at sixty-six, Washington thought the military required an able man in his prime. Should he agree to serve, he confided to Hamilton, "I should like previously to know who would be my coadjutors and whether you would be disposed to take an active part if arms are resorted to."[53] Washington signed the letter, "Your affectionate friend and obed[ien]t ser[van]t"—a style that underscored their new peer relationship. So, without prompting, Washington made Hamilton's cooperation a precondition for heading the new army.

On June 2, Hamilton informed Washington that he would join the army only if given the number-two post: "If you command, the place in which I should hope to be most useful is that of Inspector General with a command in the line. This I would accept."[54] The inspector general would be the second spot, carrying the rank and pay of major general. Since Washington expected any French invasion force to be far more mobile and daring than the stodgy British armies he had fought during the Revolution, he thought the inspector general should be an energetic young man. And Hamilton was his undisputed choice.

During the next few weeks, Hamilton sent a flurry of messages to Adams's cabinet about war preparations. He tossed off stiffly worded dispatches, as if he were the president in absentia. Flashing, as usual, with a surplus of ideas, he told Treasury Secretary Wolcott that the United States should boost taxes, take out a large loan, and establish "an academy for naval and military instruction."[55] He furnished a precise description of the new navy he envisioned: six ships of the line, twelve frigates, and twenty small vessels. Hamilton was typically quick, clear, and decisive in his recommendations. It is easy to understand why Adams's cabinet warmed to his executive prowess and equally easy to understand why Adams resented his highhanded intrusion. The flinty Timothy Pickering later recounted three testy exchanges with Adams as to who should supervise the new army:

A[dams]: "Whom shall we appoint Commander-in-Chief?"
P[ickering]: "Colonel Hamilton."
Then on a subsequent day:
A: "Whom shall we appoint Commander-in-Chief?"
P: "Colonel Hamilton."
Then on a third day:
A: "Whom shall we appoint Commander-in-Chief?"
P: "Colonel Hamilton."
A: "Oh no! It is not his turn by a great deal. I would sooner appoint Gates or Lincoln or Morgan."[56]

Adams preferred these three senior veterans of the battle of Saratoga. Pickering explained wearily to Adams that the ailing Daniel Morgan had "one foot in the grave," that Horatio Gates was "an old woman," and that Benjamin Lincoln was "always asleep." Pickering later drew the moral for Hamilton's son: "It was from these occurrences that I first learned Mr. Adams's extreme aversion to or hatred of your father."[57] Such petulant talks occurred two years before Adams's "discovery" of Hamilton's influence over his cabinet.

On June 22, President Adams sent an ambiguously worded inquiry to Washington, asking for advice about leadership of any new army: "In forming an army, whenever I must come to that extremity, I am at an immense loss whether to call out the old generals or to appoint a young set."[58] Adams told Washington that he hoped to consult him periodically. In a striking example of political gaucheness, Adams then nominated Washington to command the new army before he had a chance to register an opinion. On July 3, the Senate hastily approved the choice. With a few conspicuous exceptions, Hamilton had always treated Washington with punctilious courtesy and was taken aback that Adams had made the appointment without first securing Washington's consent. On July 8, he wrote to the first president from Philadelphia, "I was much surprised on my arrival here to discover that your nomination had been without any previous consultation of you." Yet he urged Washington to accept: "Convinced of the goodness of the motives, it would be useless to scan the propriety of the step."[59]

To ensure Washington's acceptance, Adams dispatched James McHenry on a three-day mission to Mount Vernon. The secretary of war toted a batch of communiqués, including Washington's commission and a letter from the president. Unbeknownst to Adams, McHenry also bore a message from Hamilton that was anything but friendly toward the president and faulted his expertise in military affairs: "The President has no *relative* ideas and his prepossessions on military subjects in reference to such a point are of the wrong sort. . . . Men of capacity and exertion in the higher stations are indispensable."[60] Because of his advancing age, Washington did not intend to take the field until a war actually arrived, so his chief deputy would be the effective field commander. Both McHenry and Pickering knew of Adams's dislike of Hamilton and schemed behind their boss's back to get Washington to choose Hamilton. As it happened, Washington did not need coaching, telling McHenry that he would entertain only Hamilton or Charles Cotesworth Pinckney as his deputy. In a confidential letter, Washington bluntly advised Pickering that Hamilton's "services ought to be secured at *almost* any price."[61] Before McHenry returned to Philadelphia, Washington slipped him a sheet naming the three men he wished to see as his major generals, listed in order: Alexander Hamilton, Charles Cotesworth Pinckney, and Henry Knox. Writing to Adams, Washington made the appointment of his general officers a precondition for accepting the commanding post.

What a world of trouble was packed into the seemingly inoffensive list. John Quincy Adams later identified the feud over this list as the "first decisive symptom" of a schism in the Federalist party.[62] Ideally, Washington wanted the three men ranked in exactly the order he had given—that is, with Hamilton given precedence as his second in command. There were complications aplenty, however, not the least that Adams wished to reverse the order and have Knox and Pinckney supersede the upstart Hamilton. For Adams, this was a straightforward assertion of presidential prerogative. After all, Washington had not named his own subordinates during the Revolution. To Washington, however, it seemed a rough slap in the face and violated his basic conditions for taking the assignment.

Though Washington rated Hamilton's abilities above those of Knox and Pinckney, he knew they had some legitimate claims to preference. During the Revolution, Knox had been a major general and Pinckney a brigadier general, while Hamilton had been a lowly lieutenant colonel. Washington claimed that this outdated hierarchy no longer counted. This was a touchy matter for the hearty, affable Henry Knox.

The three-hundred-pound former secretary of war had been a brigadier general when Hamilton was a mere collegian and captain of an artillery company. Knox had been an early booster of Hamilton, perhaps even instrumental in getting him the job on Washington's staff, and Hamilton told McHenry how pained he was by any conflict with Knox, "for I have truly a warm side for him and a high value for his merits."[63] All the same, their relative stations had shifted in the intervening years. It was Hamilton who had been preeminent in Washington's cabinet and Hamilton who had overseen the military campaign during the Whiskey Rebellion when Knox was distracted by real-estate dealings in Maine. Afterward, Knox had thanked Hamilton profusely: "Your exertions in my department during my absence will never be obliterated."[64] Nevertheless, Knox was stung to learn that Washington now planned to demote him below Hamilton and Pinckney. Washington laid greater stress on the recruitment of Charles Cotesworth Pinckney of South Carolina. He calculated that the French might invade the south, hoping to gain the support of local Francophiles and arm the slave population. He thought it politic to have a southerner and worried that Pinckney might refuse a place inferior to Hamilton.

Adams seemed dazed, infuriated, and plain befuddled by the frantic jockeying around him. On July 18, 1798, he submitted the nominations for general officers to the Senate in the order Washington had noted them, but he hoped their relative ranks would be reversed. Within a week, when Hamilton accepted appointment as inspector general, Republicans were aghast. The *Aurora* loudly ridiculed Adams's religion and morality in promoting the self-confessed lover of Maria Reynolds: "He has appointed Alexander Hamilton inspector general of the army, the same Hamilton who published a book to prove that he is AN ADULTERER. . . . Mr. Adams ought hereafter to be silent about *French* principles."[65]

Adams fled to Quincy and stayed there for the rest of the controversy, then complained that his cabinet had plotted behind his back to foist Hamilton on him. He saw himself as a decent, helpless man, tangled in byzantine plots dreamed up by the devious mind of Alexander Hamilton. The controversy simmered throughout the summer. Henry Knox, refusing to be subordinated to Hamilton, complained to McHenry on August 8: "Mr. Hamilton's talents have been estimated upon a scale of comparison so transcendent that all his seniors in rank and years of the late army have been degraded by his elevation."[66] Fuming, Adams informed McHenry in mid-August that, even though the three nominations had been confirmed, he wanted Knox to take the lead: "General Knox is legally entitled to rank next to General Washington and no other arrangement will give satisfaction." For good measure, he added that Pinckney "must rank before Hamilton."[67] In early September, Oliver Wolcott, Jr., reminded Adams that Washington had made Hamilton's appointment his prerequisite for taking command and concluded that "the opinion of General Washington and the expectation of the public is that General Hamilton will be confirmed in a rank second only to the commander in chief."[68]

In his reply to Wolcott, Adams let all his bile gush to the surface in a tirade against Hamilton. Even though Hamilton had tendered more than twenty years of outstanding service to his country, he was still blackballed in Adams's eyes for being foreign born. The president daubed him in demonic colors:

> If I should consent to the appointment of Hamilton as a second in rank, I should consider it as the most [ir]responsible action of my whole life and the most difficult to justify. He is not a native of the United States, but a foreigner and, I believe, has not resided longer, at least not much longer, in North America than Albert Gallatin. His rank in the late army was comparatively very low. His merits with a party are the merits of John Calvin—
>
> *"Some think on Calvin heaven's own spirit fell,*
> *While others deem him [an] instrument of hell."*
>
> I know that Knox has no popular character, even in Massachusetts. I know, too, that Hamilton has no popular character in any part of America.[69]

Adams was ventilating his frustration and decided, on second thought, not to send the unfair letter. What he actually wrote to James McHenry was: "Inclosed are the commissions for the three generals signed and all dated on the same day."[70] It was a victory for Hamilton and a humiliating surrender for Adams, who later griped, "I was no more at liberty than a man in prison."[71]

By this point, Washington was smarting at how badly Adams had botched things. He told Adams pointedly, "You have been pleased to order the last to be first and the first to be last."[72] Addressing the question of whether Hamilton's former service entitled him to high military position, he remarked that, as his principal wartime aide, Hamilton had "the means of viewing everything on a larger scale than those who have had only divisions and brigades to attend to, who know nothing of the correspondences of the commander in chief or of the various orders to or transactions with the general staff of the army."[73] In other words, Hamilton had been his chief of staff, not a high-ranking secretary. Adams's patent displeasure with Hamilton afforded Washington an opportunity to pay his protégé a huge compliment. Washington said that some people considered Hamilton "an ambitious man and therefore a dangerous one. That he is ambitious I readily grant, but it is of that laudable kind which prompts a man to excel in whatever he takes in hand. He is enterprising, quick in his perceptions, and his judgment intuitively great." In sum, Hamilton's loss would be "irreparable."[74] Far from weakening Washington's faith in Hamilton, Adams had drawn the two old allies closer together. On October 15, Adams yielded grudgingly to the appointment of Hamilton as inspector general. Knox refused to serve under him, but Charles Cotesworth Pinckney agreed and praised Hamilton. "I knew that his talents in war were great," he told McHenry, "that he had a genius capable of forming an extensive military plan, and a spirit courageous and enterprizing, equal to the execution of it."[75]

Adams's defeat over Hamilton's appointment only added to his dislike of the younger man, and the incident never ceased to rankle. To be sure, Hamilton had been cunning, quick-footed, and manipulative and had placed Adams in an awkward spot. But Adams had made the classic mistake of committing his presidential prestige to a fight he could not win. He could not accept that most observers, from Washington to Jay, thought Hamilton the most highly qualified man for the job.

While trying to fend off Hamilton as inspector general, Adams became correspondingly unyielding in his desire to name his son-in-law, Colonel William Smith, a brigadier general, a rank one rung below major general. The handsome young colonel had given John and Abigail Adams no end of grief. He was chronically indebted from speculation and a year earlier had temporarily abandoned their daughter, Nabby. Smith had mostly survived on sinecures doled out by President Washington. Later on, he was imprisoned twice: once for debt and once for enlisting in a scheme to liberate Venezuela. Despite Smith's irresponsible shenanigans, Adams now wanted to fob him off on America as a brigadier general, and Washington was flabbergasted. "What in the name of military prudence could have induced the appointment of [William Smith] as brigadier?" Washington asked Secretary of State Pickering. "The latter never was celebrated for anything that ever came to my knowledge except the murder of Indians."[76]

At first, Pickering tried to dissuade Adams from this disastrous choice, but the stubborn president "pronounced his son-in-law a military character far, very far, superior to Hamilton!!!" Pickering recalled.[77] Dusting off an old proverb, Pickering said, "Mr. Adams has always *thought his own geese swans.*"[78] Pickering secretly lobbied the Senate to veto the appointment—another instance of disloyalty, if a pardonable one. When the Senate duly rejected Smith, Abigail Adams detected "secret springs at work" and thought some senators were "tools of they knew not who."[79] Pickering contended that Adams's disdain for him dated from that event.

Two years later, Adams again tried to elevate his son-in-law to a regimental command. Hamilton chided him, as gingerly as possible, that the appointment might look like favoritism: "There are collateral considerations affecting the expediency of the measure, which I am sure will not escape your reflection. . . . I trust this remark will not be misunderstood."[80]

Adams wrote back blind with rage: "I see no reason or justice in excluding him from all service, while his comrades are all ambassadors or generals, merely because he married my daughter. I am, Sir, with much regard your most obedient and humble Servant   John Adams."[81]

John Adams had a long memory when it came to slights. On May 9, 1800, Benjamin Goodhue, a Federalist senator from Massachusetts, found himself in an unforgettable tête-à-tête with an apoplectic president. Adams returned to the Senate's rejection of William Smith for brigadier general and blamed Goodhue, Pickering, and Hamilton. As Goodhue related this remarkable outburst, Adams claimed that "we had killed his daughter [metaphorically] by doing this; that rejection originated with Hamilton, and from him to Pickering, who he said (with extreme agitation and anger) influenced me and others to reject him; that Col. Smith was a man of the first military knowledge in the U.S. and was recommended to the appointment by Genl. Washington." (Washington's letter directly belies this assertion.) Goodhue went on to state that Adams's "resentment appeared implacable towards the conduct of the Senate in those instances which resulted, as he said, with no other view than to wound his feelings and those of his *family.*" Throughout the discussion, Goodhue said, Adams exhibited "a perfect rage of passion that I could not have expected from the supreme executive."[82] Many such stories circulated among the Federalists about Adams's incontinent wrath.

Another intricate appointment battle involved Aaron Burr, who had left the U.S. Senate the year before and returned to the New York Assembly. To appease the Republicans, Adams wanted to name Burr a brigadier general. Hamilton was pushing measures to defend seaports against French incursions and sat on a local military committee with Burr to improve New York City's defenses. For the moment, the mutable Burr was flirting with the Federalists, and Robert Troup was agog that Burr, an enthusiast for the French Revolution, was now helping to equip the city against a possible French assault. Troup told Rufus King that Burr's "conduct [is] very different from what you would imagine. Some conjecture that he is changing his ground."[83] Burr and Hamilton were more openly amicable than they had been for some time.

Hamilton was skeptical that Burr would abandon his Republican comrades but was content to see what would happen. He must have been grateful that Burr had used his good offices the previous fall to cool off his confrontation with Monroe. When one military man appeared in New York that summer, he asked if Hamilton would take it amiss if he visited Burr. "Little Burr!" exclaimed Hamilton cheerily, explaining that they had always been on good terms despite political differences. "I fancy he now begins to think he was wrong [in politics] and I was right."[84] So Hamilton took seriously the idea that Burr might be mulling over a switch in party affiliation, and he wished to encourage it cautiously.

Burr mirrored Hamilton in his military daydreams, and he was attracted by an appointment to the new army. This may explain his short-lived political rapport with Hamilton. "I have some reasons for wishing that the administration may manifest a cordiality to him," Hamilton wrote guardedly to Wolcott when Burr set out for Philadelphia in late June 1798. "It is not impossible he will be found a useful co-operator. I am aware there are different sides, but the case is worth the experiment."[85] Around this time, Hamilton chatted with Burr about an appointment. Aware of bad blood between him and Washington, Hamilton asked Burr whether he could serve faithfully under the general. Burr unhesitatingly replied that "he despised Washington as a man of no talents and one who could not spell a sentence of common English."[86]

Having tussled with Washington over Hamilton and William Smith, Adams compounded his mistake by asking the former president to take on Burr as a brigadier general despite their well-known history of friction. Washington refused, pulling no punches: "By all that I have known and heard, Colonel Burr is a brave and able officer, but the question is whether he has not equal talents at intrigue?"[87]

Years later, Adams still spluttered with emotion at this retort: "How shall I describe to you my sensations and reflections at that moment. [Washington] had compelled me to promote over the heads of Lincoln, Clinton, Gates, Knox, and others and even over Pinckney . . . the most restless, impatient, artful, indefatigable, and unprincipled intriguer in the United States, if not in the world, to be second in command under himself and now dreaded an intriguer in a poor brigadier."[88] In retirement, Adams mused that if Burr had become a brigadier general in 1798, it might have tethered him to the Federalists and assured his own reelection in 1800. Indeed, Adams was right in one respect: Washington blundered by recruiting only Federalists to top military positions, while Adams had wished to include two Republicans—Burr and Frederick Muhlenberg—as brigadiers. Had the army taken on a more bipartisan complexion, it might well have been more popular.

Alexander Hamilton was now addressed as General Hamilton and was so listed in the New York City directory. With his congenital weakness for uniforms, he allowed a painter from the British Isles, P. T. Weaver, to capture him in dazzling military dress, braided with epaulettes. A hardness now sharpened Hamilton's features—his profile was finer, his gaze more direct than in other pictures—yet he complimented the portrait and, in a sentimental gesture, gave it to his old friend from St. Croix, Edward Stevens.

Ever the master administrator, Hamilton flung himself into the gargantuan task of organizing an army with unflagging energy. For five weeks in November and December 1798, he conferred in Philadelphia with Washington, who made his first resplendent return to the capital in twenty months, appearing in uniform on horseback. Charles C. Pinckney and Secretary of War McHenry joined the planning sessions. Hamilton sketched out this phantom force in microscopic detail, producing comprehensive charts for regiments, battalions, and companies. In a typical passage, Hamilton was to write, "A company is subdivided equally into two platoons, a platoon into two sections and a section into two squads, a squad consisting of four files of three or six files of two."[89] He assigned ranks to officers, set up recruiting stations, stocked arsenals with ammunition, and drew up numerous regulations.

For the moment, Washington delegated plenary power to him. Hamilton told one general, since Washington had "for the present declined actual command, it has been determined . . . to place the military force everywhere under the superintendence of Major General Pinckney and myself."[90] Not just the new army but the old one stationed on the western frontier came under Hamilton's direct command, while Pinckney oversaw the southern troops. Hamilton exercised his far-flung authority from a small office at 36 Greenwich Street in Manhattan. From the outset, his work was often thankless. He drew no salary until November and then earned only $268.35 a month, one-quarter of what he had taken home as a lawyer. More than half of his legal clients, fearing distractions, dropped him when he was made inspector general. Hamilton could not resist government service but could never quite reconcile himself to the pecuniary sacrifice. In pleading for more money with McHenry, he said, "It is always disagreeable to speak of compensations for one's self, but a man past 40 with a wife and six children and a very *small* property beforehand is compelled to wa[i]ve the scruples which his nicety would otherwise dictate."[91]

Frequently laid up with poor health that winter, Hamilton had to conjure up an entire army aided by a single aide-de-camp, twenty-year-old Captain Philip Church, Angelica's eldest son. He was so exceedingly good-looking that Hamilton told Eliza that his presence "gives great pleasure to the ladies who wanted a *beau*."[92] This Anglo-American young man had led an improbable life. Educated at Eton with young noblemen and trained as a legal apprentice at the Middle Temple in London, he was now handling clerical work for a major general in the U.S. Army. Contemptuous of President Adams for touting his inept son-in-law, Hamilton engaged here in some minor nepotism of his own. He admitted to the president that Church's appointment was "a personal favour to myself" and added, "Let me at the same time beg you to be persuaded, Sir, that I shall never on any other occasion place a recommendation to office on a similar footing."[93] Nevertheless, he pressed James McHenry to name several Schuyler relatives as lieutenants.

A chronic stickler for etiquette, Hamilton entered into the minutiae of protocol and dress, showing an unrestrained love of military matters. The most fastidious tailor could not have dictated more precise instructions for Washington's uniform: "A blue coat without lapels, with lining collar and cuffs of buff, yellow buttons and gold epaulettes of double bullion tag with fringe, each having three stars. Collar cuffs and pocket flaps to have full embroidered edges and the button holes of every description to be full embroidered." For Washington's hat: "A full cocked hat, with a yellow button gold loop, a black cockade with a gold eagle in the center and a white plume." For his boots: "Long boots, with stiff tops reaching to the center of the knee pan, the whole of black leather lined above with red morocco so as just to appear."[94] Hamilton's descriptions of other uniforms were no less meticulous.

His mind percolating with ideas, Hamilton also designed huts for each rank. The huts for lieutenant colonels had to measure fourteen by twenty-four feet, while majors were given fourteen by twenty-two feet: "It is contemplated that the huts be roofed with boards, unless where slabs can be had very cheap."[95] After learning the value of training manuals from Steuben during the Revolution, the indefatigable inspector general devised one for drill exercises. What, for instance, should a soldier do when a commander barked "Head right"? Hamilton answered: "At the word 'right,' the soldier turns his head to the right, briskly but without violence, bringing his left eye in a line with the buttons of his waistcoat and with his right eye looking along the breasts of the men upon his right."[96] He signed up the German-born John De Barth Walbach to test cavalry systems used in Prussia, France, and Great Britain and to figure out which would work best in an American setting. To identify the ideal length and speed of the marching step, he conducted experiments using pendulums that vibrated at 75, 100, and 120 times per minute.

So encyclopedic was Hamilton's grasp of military affairs that he laid down the broad outlines of the entire military apparatus. He viewed the new army as the kernel of a permanent military establishment that would free the country from reliance on state militias. To foster a corps of highly trained officers, he pursued an idea that he and Washington had discussed: establishing a military academy. Contrary to many of his compatriots, Hamilton thought America had much to learn from Europe about military affairs. "Self-sufficiency and a contempt of the science and experience of others are too prevailing traits of character in this country," he wailed to John Jay.[97] (This attitude was of a piece with his dismay over the Jeffersonian faith that Americans had much to teach the world but little to learn from it.) He had already pressed a leading French military authority to present him with "a digested plan of an establishment for a military school. This is an object I have extremely at heart."[98] For a military academy, Hamilton wanted a site on navigable water, with easy access to cannon foundries and small-arms manufacturers. A few weeks later, he galloped off to tour the fortress at West Point.

Hamilton's elaborate plans contemplated five schools specializing in military science, engineering, cavalry, infantry, and the navy. With Hamiltonian thoroughness, he listed the necessary instructors right down to two drawing masters, an architect, and a riding master. He was no less directive when it came to curricula, declaring that the engineering school should teach "fluxions, conic sections, hydraulics, hydrostatics, and pneumatics."[99] Before Adams left office, Hamilton and McHenry had introduced in the House of Representatives "A Bill for Establishing a Military Academy." Ironically, the academy at West Point was to come into being during the presidency of Thomas Jefferson, who had rejected the idea as unconstitutional during Washington's administration.

Hamilton also devised plans for military hospitals and something very like a veterans' administration that would tend men wounded in battle and their families: "Justice and humanity forbid the abandoning to want and misery men who have spent their best years in the military service of a country or who in that service had contracted infirmities which disqualify them to earn their bread in other modes."[100]

Hamilton had a plethora of ideas, but implementing them was tough, partly because of the mediocrity of his old friend James McHenry. From the start, Oliver Wolcott, Jr., had warned Hamilton that if he became inspector general he would have to double as secretary of war because McHenry's "good sense, industry, and virtues are of no avail without a certain address and skill in business which he has not and cannot acquire."[101] Washington chimed in that McHenry's "talents were unequal to great exertions or deep resources."[102] The new army was plagued by bureaucratic problems, and Hamilton ended up lecturing McHenry on how to run a cabinet department. "I observe you plunged in a vast mass of detail," he told McHenry, admonishing him to delegate more authority. As an old friend of McHenry, Hamilton did not wish to shunt him aside, but his incompetence was too glaring to overlook. Hamilton advised Washington confidentially that "my friend McHenry is wholly insufficient for his place, with the additional misfortune of not having himself the least suspicion of the fact!"[103]

Hamilton constantly issued directives to the hapless McHenry. That he accepted such guidance from Hamilton makes one suspect that he lacked confidence in his abilities and welcomed the guidance. But McHenry was not a quick pupil, and Hamilton wearied of trying to educate him. Before long, a querulous tone crept into Hamilton's letters. He opened a back channel to Wolcott, telling his Treasury successor how he might assist McHenry in managing the War Department. All this intrigue thrust Hamilton ever deeper into the inner workings of John Adams's cabinet. But this wasn't simply a case of Hamilton's trying to control the cabinet or alienate it from President Adams; rather, he needed a capable bureaucrat at the helm of the War Department. There was painful irony in the fact that Hamilton was quietly feuding with one of the very people whom Adams would shortly accuse him of controlling.

As Hamilton assembled his army in 1799, the bureaucratic snags only worsened, and recruits began to desert. At moments, Hamilton seemed to be reliving the anguish of the Revolution, when an inefficient Congress seemed deaf to the pleas of the Continental Army. Hamilton complained to McHenry about the lack of pay for his soldiers, the shortage of clothing, his fear that dissatisfied troops might mutiny. But the difficulties went deeper than administrative inadequacy on McHenry's part; the real problems were political and far more intractable.

Republicans had long viewed Hamilton as a potential despot, but so long as he worked in harness to George Washington these fears had been totally baseless. As a member of Washington's wartime family and then his cabinet, Hamilton operated within strict bounds. Now, Washington was retreating to a more passive role. As Hamilton drifted away from Washington's supervision and felt more exasperated by Adams's undisguised hostility toward him, he began to indulge in wild flights of fantasy and to resemble more the military adventurer of Republican mythology or the epithets that Abigail Adams pinned to him: "Little Mars" and "a second Bonaparty."[104] This martial fervor was most apparent in Hamilton's woefully misguided dream of liberating European colonies in North and South America. If an open break with France came, he wanted to collude with Britain to take over Spanish territory east of the Mississippi, while wresting Spanish America from Spain. "All on this side [of] the Mississippi must be *ours*, including both Floridas," he had already argued to McHenry in early 1798.[105]

This imperialist escapade traced its origins back to a man named Francisco de Miranda. Born in Venezuela, he had fought against the British in the American Revolution along with Spanish forces. Stopping in New York in 1784, he had wooed a wary Hamilton with plans to emancipate Venezuela. A womanizer with a taste for luxury, Miranda had droned on with rapid, impassioned eloquence, pacing the room with long strides. Hamilton had given him a list of American officers whose interest might be piqued by his plan. In the years that followed, the nomadic Miranda lived in England and tried to dragoon Britain into inciting revolution in Latin America. Thwarted, he crossed the Channel and became a lieutenant general in the French Army. Then he became disillusioned with the French Revolution, telling Hamilton it had been taken over by crooks and ignoramuses in the name of liberty. In early 1798, upon leaving France, he resumed his crusade to have England and America jointly expel Spain from Latin America.

Miranda was a close friend of Adams's son-in-law, William Smith, and perhaps imagined he would find a sympathetic ear in America. In London, he held secret talks with the U.S. minister, Rufus King, who relayed the contents to Timothy Pickering. Miranda also wrote about his plans to Hamilton, who did not answer the letter and scrawled on top of it: "Several years ago this man was in America, much heated with the project of liberating S[outh] Am[erica] from the Spanish domination. . . . I consider him an intriguing adventurer."[106] Only after becoming inspector general did Hamilton reply to Miranda's letters and then cautioned him that nothing could be done unless the project was "patronized by the government of this country."[107] Nevertheless, Hamilton endorsed the plan in his letter, foresaw a combined British fleet and American army, and noted that he was raising an army of twelve thousand men. Hoping that the project would mature by winter, he told Miranda he would then "be happy in my official station to be an instrument of so good a work."[108] In sending this reply, Hamilton took a bizarre precaution to preserve secrecy, enlisting his six-year-old son, John Church Hamilton, as secretary so the letter would not bear his own handwriting. The boy also copied out a letter to Rufus King in London, supporting Miranda's harebrained plot and hoping that the projected land force would be completely American. "The command in this case would very naturally fall upon me and I hope I should disappoint no favourable anticipation," said Hamilton.[109]

Like the Reynolds pamphlet, these clandestine messages signal a further deterioration in Hamilton's judgment once he no longer worked under Washington's wise auspices and was left purely to his own devices. His actions were wrongheaded on several counts. Outwardly, he was professing neutrality toward Britain and France, while secretly contemplating an invasion with Britain. He was also mustering an army intended to defend America against a French threat while meditating its use in the southern hemisphere. He was also encouraging Miranda by private diplomatic channels rather than taking the matter directly to President Adams, with whom he seldom communicated. The projected mission, with Hamilton as its self-styled commander, gave him a vested interest in perpetuating the new army and resisting any accommodation with France. Drafting a letter for Washington in December 1798, Hamilton said the new army should be retained because there "may be imagined enterprises of very great moment to the permanent interests of this country, which would certainly require a disciplined force."[110]

By early 1799, Hamilton advocated the South American operation far more openly, telling Harrison Gray Otis, who chaired the House committee on defense, "If universal empire is still to be the pursuit of France, what can tend to defeat the purpose better than to detach South America from Spain, which is only the channel th[r]ough which the riches of *Mexico* and *Peru* are conveyed to France? The executive ought to be put in a situation to embrace favorable conjunctures for effecting that separation."[111] As it happened, the chief executive rightly thought the whole plan an unspeakable piece of folly that would tear the country apart. "I do not know whether to laugh or weep," Adams said of the intended scheme. "Miranda's project is as visionary, though far less innocent, than . . . an excursion to the moon in a cart drawn by geese."[112] Adams then extrapolated a legitimate concern into a full-fledged conspiracy theory, telling Elbridge Gerry that "he thought Hamilton and a party were endeavoring to get an army on foot to give Hamilton the command of it and then to proclaim a regal government, place Hamilton at the head of it, and prepare the way for a province of Great Britain."[113] Adams later swore that he would have resigned before approving the Miranda plan, which would have produced "an instantaneous insurrection of the whole nation from Georgia to New Hampshire."[114]

Hamilton believed that the United States should preemptively seize Spanish Florida and Louisiana, lest they fall into hostile French hands. To accomplish this, he directed General James Wilkinson to assemble an armada of seventy-five riverboats. The son of a Maryland planter, the hard-drinking Wilkinson was always ready for any mayhem. It later turned out that he had pocketed stipends from the Spanish government to incite a transfer of the Kentucky Territory to Spain. John Randolph of Roanoke called Wilkinson "the mammoth of iniquity. . . . [T]he only man I ever saw who was from the bark to the very core a villain."[115] The plump, ruddy Wilkinson made a showy appearance, wearing medals and gold buttons on his braided uniform. Even in the backwoods, he rode around in gold stirrups and spurs while seated on a leopard saddlecloth. He was happy to assist Hamilton in his expansionist plans. Wilkinson wanted to create a string of forts along the western edge of American settlement—measures that even Hamilton thought excessive. "The imbecility of the Spanish government on the Mississippi is as manifest as the ardor of the French fanatics of Louisiana is obvious," Wilkinson told Hamilton.[116] Hamilton never carried out his plans for Louisiana or Florida, much less for Spanish America. As the original rationale for his army—defense against a French invasion—was increasingly undercut by peace negotiations, such plans seemed increasingly pointless, preposterous, and irrelevant. Still, the episode went down as one of the most flagrant instances of poor judgment in Hamilton's career.

THIRTY-TWO

REIGN OF WITCHES

The period of John Adams's presidency declined into a time of political savagery with few parallels in American history, a season of paranoia in which the two parties surrendered all trust in each other. Like other Federalists infected with war fever, Hamilton increasingly mistook dissent for treason and engaged in hyperbole. In one newspaper piece, he blasted the Jeffersonians as "more *Frenchmen* than Americans" and declared that to slake their ambition and thirst for revenge they stood ready "to immolate the independence and welfare of their country at the shrine of France."[1] Republicans behaved no better, interpreting policies they disliked as the treacherous deeds of men in league with England and bent on bringing back George III. The indiscriminate use of pejorative labels—"Jacobins" for Republicans, "Anglomen" for Federalists—reflected the rancorously unfair emotions. During this melancholy time, the founding fathers appeared as all-too-fallible mortals.

An episode at Congress Hall in January 1798 symbolized the acrimonious mood. Representative Matthew Lyon of Vermont, a die-hard Republican, began to mock the aristocratic sympathies of Roger Griswold, a Federalist from Connecticut. When Griswold then taunted Lyon for alleged cowardice during the Revolution, Lyon spat right in his face. Griswold got a hickory cane and proceeded to thrash Lyon, who retaliated by taking up fire tongs and attacking Griswold. The two members of Congress ended up fighting on the floor like common ruffians. "Party animosities have raised a wall of separation between those who differ in political sentiments," Jefferson wrote sadly to Angelica Church.[2]

The publication of the XYZ dispatches led to an even more militant atmosphere in Philadelphia. Violent clashes arose between roving bands of Federalists, sporting black cockades, and Republicans wearing French tricolor cockades. Actors singing "The Marseillaise" were booed off one stage. A Federalist gang descended upon the Republican newspaper the *Aurora* and not only smashed the windows of editor Benjamin Franklin Bache but smeared a statue of his revered grandfather with mud. As rumors gathered that French saboteurs might torch the city, John Adams stationed guards outside the presidential residence and laid in a store of arms.

The low point of his presidency came in June and July 1798. While Adams wrestled with Hamilton over the ranking of Washington's major generals, Congress enacted four infamous laws designed to muzzle dissent and browbeat the Republicans into submission. They were known as the Alien and Sedition Acts. The Naturalization Act, passed on June 18, lengthened from five to fourteen years the period necessary to become a naturalized citizen with full voting rights. The Alien Act of June 25 gave the president the power to deport, without a hearing or even a reasonable explanation, any foreign-born residents deemed dangerous to the peace. The Alien Enemies Act of July 6 granted the president the power to label as enemy aliens any residents who were citizens of a country at war with America, prompting an outflow of French émigrés. Then came the capstone of these horrendous measures: the Sedition Act of July 14, which rendered it a crime to speak or publish "any false, scandalous, or malicious" writings against the U.S. government or Congress "with intent to defame . . . or to bring them . . . into contempt or disrepute."[3] If found guilty, the perpetrators could face up to two thousand dollars in fines and two years in prison.

The Federalist-controlled Congress was maneuvering for partisan advantage and betraying an unbecoming nativist streak. Federalists wanted to curb an influx of Irish immigrants, who were usually pro-French and thus natural adherents to the Republican cause. Congressman Harrison Gray Otis of Boston set a strident tone when he declared that America should no longer "wish to invite hordes of wild Irishmen, nor the turbulent and disorderly parts of the world, to come here with a view to disturb our tranquillity after having succeeded in the overthrow of their own governments."[4]

Another grievance rife among Federalists was reckless press behavior. During the 1790s, as the number of American newspapers more than doubled, many partisan sheets specialized in vituperative character attacks. Jefferson acknowledged the strategic power of these papers for Federalists and Republicans alike. "The engine is the press," he told Madison. "Every man must lay his purse and his pen under contribution."[5] John Adams had learned to loathe many members of the Republican press. After Benjamin Franklin Bache died at twenty-nine in September 1798 in a yellow-fever epidemic (which also claimed the life of Federalist rival John Fenno),

Adams described Bache as a "malicious libeller" and said "the yellow fever arrested him in his detestable career and sent him to his grandfather, from whom he inherited a dirty, envious, jealous, and revengeful spite against me."[6]

Embittered by published screeds against her husband, Abigail Adams wrote perfervid letters in support of the Alien and Sedition Acts. Until Congress passed a sedition bill, she warned her sister-in-law, nothing would halt the "wicked and base, violent and calumniating abuse" of the Republican papers.[7] She added that in "any other country, Bache and all his papers would have been seized long ago."[8] She hoped the Alien Act would be invoked to oust the Swiss-born Albert Gallatin, the House Republican leader after Madison's departure. She considered Gallatin and his Jeffersonian colleagues little more than "traitors to their country."[9] She also distrusted immigrants, averring that "a more careful and attentive watch ought to be kept over foreigners."[10]

Of course, the supreme bugaboo of Republican scribes was Alexander Hamilton. On May 21, 1798, William Keteltas, a Republican lawyer in New York, chastised him for ingratitude to a nation that had embraced him as a young man. Keteltas likened him to Caesar: "But like Caesar, you are ambitious and for that ambition to enslave his country, Brutus slew him. And are ambitious men less dangerous to American than Roman liberty?"[11] Replying in the same newspaper the next day, Hamilton drew a dire inference about the author. "By the allusion to *Caesar* and *Brutus,* he plainly hints at assassination."[12]

John Adams always tried to sidestep responsibility for the Alien and Sedition Acts, the biggest blunder of his presidency. He did not shepherd these punitive laws through Congress, but they were passed by a Federalist-dominated Congress during his tenure and with his tacit approval. After Hamilton was dead, Adams did not hesitate to blame *him* for these unfortunate measures. Upon taking office in 1797, Adams maintained, he had gotten a memo from Hamilton recommending an alien and sedition law. Embroidering this recollection in 1809, Adams thumped his chest proudly at his principled rejection of Hamilton's advice: "I recommended no such thing in my speech. Congress, however, adopted both these measures. I knew there was need enough of both and therefore consented to them. But as they were then considered as war measures and intended altogether against the advocates of the French and peace with France, I was apprehensive that a hurricane of clamour" might be raised against them.[13] Adams straddled two positions here, presenting himself as both prescient critic and reluctant advocate of the Alien and Sedition Acts. The truth is that Hamilton never espoused any such laws in the memos he drew up after Adams's inauguration.

So what *did* Hamilton think of the notorious laws? Fearing an American fifth column, he now wanted to throttle the flow of immigration. "My opinion is that the mass [of aliens] ought to be obliged to leave the country"—a disappointing stance from America's most famous foreign-born citizen and once an influential voice for immigration. He did argue for exceptions, however, and admonished Pickering, "Let us not be cruel or violent."[14] In contrast, he was stunned by his first glance at the Sedition Act, protesting to Treasury Secretary Wolcott, "There are provisions in this bill which according to a cursory view appear to me highly exceptionable and such as more than anything else may endanger civil war. . . . I hope sincerely the thing may not be hurried through. Let us not establish a tyranny. Energy is a very different thing from violence."[15]

Unfortunately, once they were amended, Hamilton supported the Alien and Sedition Acts. Among other things, he was still outraged by the cutthroat behavior of the Scottish-born James T. Callender, who had exposed the Reynolds scandal. By late 1799, Hamilton exhorted Senator Jonathan Dayton to prosecute such foreign-born journalists, claiming that "in open contempt and defiance of the laws they are permitted to continue their destructive labours. Why are they not sent away? Are laws of this kind passed merely to excite odium and remain a dead letter?"[16] Hamilton was never an automatic press critic, however much he deplored its abuses. And he justly applauded one meritorious idea buried in the Sedition Act: that in libel cases, the truth of an allegation should be allowed as a defense. Before, it had been necessary for the prosecution to prove only that the charges were defamatory, not that they were true. Hamilton would have much more to say about this issue in a dramatic legal case that was to expand press freedom in the United States. For this reason, he later said that "the sedition law, branded indeed with epithets the most odious[,] . . . will one day be pronounced a valuable feature in our national charac-ter."[17] For Republicans, however, the most salient feature of the Sedition Act was that it violated the First Amendment of the Constitution.

Republicans knew the unashamedly partisan nature of the new bills. "The Alien bill proposed in the Senate is a monster that must forever disgrace its parents," Madi-son told Jefferson, who quickly agreed that it was "a most detestable thing."[18] So he would not have to preside over a Senate enacting legislation that he found hateful, Jefferson slipped away from Philadelphia and took refuge at Monticello for four and a half months. Beyond indignation, Jefferson professed a serene faith that the common sense of the people would rectify such errors. He told a fellow Virginian, "A little patience and we shall see the reign of witches pass over, their spells dis-solved, and the people, recovering their true sight, restoring their government to its true principles."[19] He would not rely upon patience alone. He believed that Wash-ington had checked the most harmful tendencies of the Federalists but that under

Adams the party had "mounted on the car of state and, free from control, like Phaethon on that of the sun, drove headlong and wild."[20]

Often amazingly accurate in his predictions, Jefferson saw the country approaching a political crossroads. The Federalists were displaying insufferable arrogance and using federal power to snuff out the opposition. In so doing, he concluded, they would relinquish the advantages they had won through the XYZ dispatches. Perhaps suffering from fatigue after almost a decade in power, the Federalists were governed more by fear than by hope. They had helped to build a durable government but did not trust the strength of the institutions they had so well created. Ironically, it was Jefferson, searing in his criticism of Federalist measures, who surveyed the future with habitual optimism. The Alien and Sedition Acts unified the Republican party while unchecked warfare between the Adams and Hamilton wings of the Federalist party was inwardly eroding its strength.

Many Republicans thought it best to sit back and let the Federalists blow themselves up. As James Monroe put it, the more the Federalist party was "left to itself, the sooner will its ruin follow."[21] Jefferson and Madison were not that patient, especially after Hamilton became inspector general of the new army. Jefferson thought the Republicans had a duty to stop the Sedition Act, explaining later that he considered that law "to be a nullity as absolute and as palpable as if Congress had ordered us to fall down and worship a golden image."[22] With Federalists in control of the government, this political magician decided that he and Madison would draft resolutions for two state legislatures, declaring the Alien and Sedition Acts to be unconstitutional. The two men operated by stealth and kept their authorship anonymous to create the illusion of a groundswell of popular opposition. Jefferson drafted his resolution for the Kentucky legislature and Madison for Virginia. The Kentucky Resolutions passed on November 16, 1798, and the Virginia Resolutions on December 24. Jefferson's biographer Dumas Malone has noted that the vice president could have been brought up on sedition charges, possibly even impeached for treason, had his actions been uncovered at the time.

In writing the Kentucky Resolutions, Jefferson turned to language that even Madison found excessive. Of the Alien and Sedition Acts, he warned that, "unless arrested at the threshold," they would "necessarily drive these states into revolution and blood."[23] He wasn't calling for peaceful protests or civil disobedience: he was calling for outright rebellion, if needed, against the federal government of which he was vice president. In editing Jefferson's words, the Kentucky legislature deleted his call for "nullification" of laws that violated states' rights. The more moderate Madison said that the states, in contesting obnoxious laws, should "interpose for arresting the progress of the evil."[24] This was a breathtaking evolution for a man who had pleaded at the Constitutional Convention that the federal government should possess a veto over state laws. In the Kentucky and Virginia Resolutions, Jefferson and Madison set forth a radical doctrine of states' rights that effectively undermined the Constitution.

Neither Jefferson nor Madison sensed that they had sponsored measures as inimical as the Alien and Sedition Acts themselves. "Their nullification effort, if others had picked it up, would have been a greater threat to freedom than the misguided [alien and sedition] laws, which were soon rendered feckless by ridicule and electoral pressure," Garry Wills has written.[25] The theoretical damage of the Kentucky and Virginia Resolutions was deep and lasting. Hamilton and others had argued that the Constitution transcended state governments and directly expressed the will of the American people. Hence, the Constitution began "We the People of the United States" and was ratified by special conventions, not state legislatures. Now Jefferson and Madison lent their imprimatur to an outmoded theory in which the Constitution became a compact of the states, not of their citizens. By this logic, states could refrain from complying with federal legislation they considered unconstitutional. This was a clear recipe for calamitous dissension and ultimate disunion. George Washington was so appalled by the Virginia Resolutions that he told Patrick Henry that if "systematically and pertinaciously pursued," they would "dissolve the union or produce coercion."[26] The influence of the doctrine of states' rights, especially in the version promulgated by Jefferson, reverberated right up to the Civil War and beyond. At the close of that war, James Garfield of Ohio, the future president, wrote that the Kentucky Resolutions "contained the germ of nullification and secession, and we are today reaping the fruits."[27]

For Hamilton, the Virginia and Kentucky Resolutions threatened to undo his lifelong goal of molding the states into a single, indivisible nation. Rejecting as a "gangrene" the idea that states could arbitrarily disobey certain federal laws, he asserted categorically that this would "change the government."[28] He inquired of Theodore Sedgwick, a High Federalist, "What, my dear Sir, are you going to do with Virginia? This is a very serious business, which will call for the wisdom and firmness of the government."[29] Hamilton wanted the Virginia and Kentucky Resolutions submitted to a special congressional committee, which would expose how they would destroy the Constitution and afford evidence "of a regular conspiracy to overturn the government."[30] Just as Jefferson believed that Republicans could turn the Alien and Sedition Acts to advantage, so Hamilton thought the Federalists could capitalize on the misconceived Kentucky and Virginia Resolutions. "If well managed," he told Rufus King, "this affair will turn to good account."[31]

Of the quartet of laws intended to silence dissent, the Sedition Act proved the most pernicious; indictments were brought against Republican editors based on flimsy, trumped-up charges. Some people were hauled into court for the heinous crime of setting up a liberty pole with the banner: "No Stamp Act; no Sedition, no Alien-Bill; no Land Tax; Downfall to the Tyrants of America; Peace and Retirement to the President."[32] One Republican editor made the mistake of calling Hamilton's projected army a "standing army" and paid a steep price: a two-hundred-dollar fine plus two months in prison, where he could ponder his linguistic error. Another editor earned eighteen months behind bars for daring to print the heresy that the government allowed the wealthy to benefit at the expense of commoners. Congressman Matthew Lyon of Vermont got four months in jail for criticizing the president's "unbounded thirst for ridiculous pomp, foolish adulation, and selfish avarice."[33] The most outlandish case involved the prosecution of Luther Baldwin of New Jersey, who, under the spell of strong drink, wished that the ceremonial cannon fire greeting President Adams had landed in his backside. Five of the six most influential Republican papers were ultimately prosecuted under the new laws by a Federalist-dominated judiciary.

During the reign of the Alien and Sedition Acts, Hamilton, long embattled by slander, instigated a libel suit against New York's leading Republican newspaper, *The Argus.* After the death of publisher Thomas Greenleaf in September 1798, his widow, Ann, perpetuated the paper's crusade against the Adams administration. Backed by the Sedition Act, Secretary of State Pickering—nicknamed "the Scourge of Jacobinism" for exploiting the government's new prosecutorial powers—asked New York district attorney Richard Harison to monitor *The Argus* for "audacious calumnies against the government."[34] This led to a sedition prosecution against Ann Greenleaf for her paper's contention that "the federal government was corrupt and inimical to the preservation of liberty."[35] Her problems were exacerbated on November 6, 1799, when the paper reprinted an article alleging that Hamilton had tried to squash the Philadelphia-based *Aurora* by offering to buy it for six thousand dollars from the widow of Benjamin Franklin Bache. (The sum was supposedly Hamilton's share of a joint Federalist bid.) Margaret Bache claimed that she had rebuffed Hamilton's offer in high dudgeon, insisting that she would never dishonor her husband's memory by selling to Federalists. Aside from the small detail that he had never made such a bid, what irked Hamilton was that the *Aurora* had spun a tangled skein of speculation as to where he might have gotten the six thousand dollars. How, the *Aurora* queried, could Hamilton afford this when he had made so much of his inability to pay James Reynolds ("the reputed husband of the *dear Maria*") one thousand dollars? The *Aurora* author served up a ready-made answer: the funds came from "British secret service money. . . . One would have supposed Mr. Hamilton might have fallen upon a better plan to suppress the *Aurora,* for it is a bungling piece of work at best."[36]

For years, Hamilton had tried ceaselessly to stamp out slander and preserve his reputation. Now, he was convinced that it was all part of a well-organized plot to overthrow the government, as evidenced by the Kentucky and Virginia Resolutions. The same day that *The Argus* ran its offending piece about him, he composed an angry letter to Josiah Ogden Hoffman, New York's attorney general, asking for criminal prosecution of the perpetrators on libel charges. He cast his grievance in cosmic terms, saying that he had long been subject to "the most malignant calumnies" but had refrained from libel suits, "repaying hatred with contempt." He continued: "But public motives now compel me to a different conduct. The design[s] of that faction to overturn our government . . . become every day more manifest and have of late acquired a degree of system which renders them formidable. One principal engine for effecting the scheme is by audacious falsehoods to destroy the confidence of the people in all those who are in any degree conspicuous among the supporters of the government."[37] The next day, Cadwallader Colden, the assistant attorney general, visited Ann Greenleaf to apprise her of the prosecution. When she pleaded that she had merely reprinted the questionable article from another paper, Colden pointed out that under the Sedition Act her paper was still liable. Greenleaf then tried another line of defense: she had played no part in running the paper.

The suit was therefore filed against the editor, David Frothingham, who tried to dodge prosecution by billing himself as a journeyman printer in *The Argus* office. Despite his demanding duties as inspector general, Hamilton sat in on the trial, itching to testify. According to one newspaper account, the attorney general told the court that Hamilton's "reputation depended in a great measure on the verdict then to be given. This was dearer to the witness than property or life."[38] (In retrospect, this statement has an eerily true ring.) Falling back on the common law, the court did not allow Hamilton to testify as to the truth or falsity of the charges leveled against him—a situation that may have firmed his resolve to establish this principle in American libel law. He did testify to general circumstances about the articles and said he had never made any offer for the *Aurora*. Asked whether the *Aurora* was hostile to the U.S. government, Hamilton fired back a resounding yes. Frothingham was convicted, fined one hundred dollars, and incarcerated in Bridewell prison for four months.

For the Republican press, the Frothingham conviction had one inestimable virtue: it allowed a full-scale reprise of the Maria Reynolds affair, a subject of which readers never tired. With heavy sarcasm, Hamilton was now styled "the *amorous general*."[39] Both *The Argus* and the *Aurora* cast him as a heartless scamp who had gone from a dalliance with Maria Reynolds, under the guise of protecting her, to the callous prosecution of the Widow Bache. The *Aurora* taunted this "distinguished man of *gallantry*" and added that "the heart of this man must be formed of peculiar *stuff.*"[40] Another Republican paper suggested that Hamilton's pursuit of *The Argus* had been revenge for the Reynolds exposé, saying of Hamilton that "it is very likely his ire has been provoked against the press for publishing to the world what a good friend he has been to female distress; how like the angel of charity he has poured the balm of consolation on the wounds of a poverty-struck matron; that he deigned to stoop from his then high and important station to console the sorrows and to relieve the woes of an afflicted fair one."[41] If Hamilton's aim had been to crush *The Argus,* he succeeded. The following year, Ann Greenleaf shut down the paper and sold its equipment, depriving the Republicans of a key party organ on the eve of national elections.

Hamilton's tough action against *The Argus* involved a legitimate case of libel. Far more questionable was the use he wished to make of the new army to deal with domestic disturbances. All along, Republicans had worried that his soldiers would pounce on them instead of Napoleon. The *Aurora,* as usual, sounded the alert: "The *echoes* of our ministerial *oracles* assert that the army of mercenaries contemplated to be raised are entirely for *home* service."[42] In some respects, the threat from Hamilton was exaggerated. His army remained more hypothetical than real, and he never commanded a large force. He would also have required the approval of President Adams for any domestic use of force.

But the record shows that the inspector general did have domestic as well as foreign enemies on his mind, especially after passage of the Kentucky and Virginia Resolutions. In a letter he sent to Harrison Gray Otis on December 27, 1798, he argued against any force reduction by noting that "with a view to the possibility of internal disorders alone, the force authorised is not too considerable."[43] From William Heth, a Federalist customs collector in Virginia, he received disturbing reports of a possible armed insurrection against the federal government. "You ask, 'What do[es] the [Republican] faction in your state aim at?'" Heth reported. "I answer—nothing short of disunion and the heads of John Adams and Alexander Hamilton and some few others perhaps."[44] Heth misled Hamilton with an erroneous report that the Virginia legislature had decided to buy arms to combat the federal government.

By this point, Hamilton thought it might be necessary to put down subversion in Virginia, and this became integral to his rationale for a national army instead of state militias. "Whenever the experiment shall be made to subdue a *refractory* and powerful *state* by militia," he told Theodore Sedgwick, "the event will shame the advocates. When a clever force has been collected, let them be drawn towards Virginia for which there is an obvious pretext—and then let measures be taken to act upon the laws and put Virginia to the test of resistance."[45] Jefferson watched Hamilton warily, telling one ally that "our Bonaparte" might "step in to give us political salvation in his own way."[46]

The violent resistance to federal law foreseen by Hamilton cropped up in eastern Pennsylvania instead of Virginia. The opposition was centered in three counties north of Philadelphia—Bucks, Northampton, and Montgomery—with dense concentrations of German immigrants. They were generally uneducated and easily misled by rumors, such as the notion that President Adams planned a wedding between one of his sons and a daughter of George III. Local residents were so upset by federal property taxes, imposed to finance the Quasi-War with France, that they resisted new property assessments. The ringleader of this obstruction was a cooper, auctioneer, and former militia captain named John Fries, who had ten children. After marshals arrested a group of tax protesters, Fries stormed the Bethlehem jail along with 150 armed militiamen to free the prisoners. President Adams decided to send in troops to squash the rebellion and on March 12, 1799, issued a proclamation ordering the army to put down "combinations too powerful to be suppressed by the ordinary course of judicial proceedings."[47] Having declared this emergency, Adams left Philadelphia the same day for Quincy, Massachusetts.

Since Hamilton was de facto commander of the army, he had to handle the disorder, which became known as Fries's Rebellion. He was handicapped by the lack of presidential leadership. "I get nothing very precise about the insurrection," he complained to Washington. "But everything continues to wear the character of feebleness in respect to the measures for suppressing it."[48] Treasury Secretary Wolcott, despondent over the president's improbable absence in the midst of a crisis, wrote to Hamilton from Philadelphia: "I am grieved when I think of the situation of the gov[ernmen]t. An affair which ought to have been settled at once will cost much time and perhaps be so managed as to encourage other and formidable rebellions. We have no Pres[iden]t here and the appearance of languor and indecision are discouraging to the friends of government."[49]

To deal with the rebellion, Hamilton assembled a force that blended state militia and federal regulars. Believing, as always, that psychology was half the battle, Hamilton decided to stage a tremendous show of force. As in the Whiskey Rebellion, the army he sent into eastern Pennsylvania seemed disproportionately large and heavy-handed compared to the threat, which had already begun to wane. The troops took sixty prisoners back to Philadelphia, where the chief instigators were tried and convicted of treason. In the spring of 1800, against the unanimous advice of his cabinet, President Adams reversed position and pardoned Fries and two other convicted protesters, calling them "obscure, miserable Germans, as ignorant of our language as they were of our laws."[50] Adams thought treason too strong a charge to apply to the Pennsylvania rioters. The action was reminiscent of Washington's clemency after the Whiskey Rebellion, though it may have been influenced by Adams's fears that the German population would defect to the Republicans in the 1800 presidential election. Hamilton was dismayed by the pardon.

Adams worried increasingly about the militaristic tendencies and authoritarian side that had emerged in the frustrated, restless Hamilton's behavior. He justly observed, "Mr. Hamilton's imagination was always haunted by that hideous monster or phantom so often called a crisis and which so often produces imprudent measures."[51] In later years, he congratulated himself that he had restrained Hamilton, who "save for me would have involved us in a foreign war with France and a civil war with ourselves."[52] What Adams could not admit was that he had failed to exercise strong leadership and had allowed the feud with Hamilton and his cabinet to fester. Escaping to his home in Quincy was not the most effective way to deal with intramural clashes.

THIRTY-THREE

WORKS GODLY
AND UNGODLY

On June 3, 1799, James Hamilton died on the small, volcanic island of St. Vincent, having left the even tinier nearby island of Bequia nine years earlier. He would have been about eighty years old. The fortunes of the elder Hamilton had never improved, and he ended up trapped on a bloody island that had witnessed terrible atrocities during the previous four years. Starting in 1795, native Caribs conspired with French inhabitants to spark an uprising on the British island. Many settlers were massacred and sugar plantations burned before British troops brutally put down the insurrection. This must have provided a frightening backdrop for the last years of the feeble, aging Hamilton. Alexander's failure to see James Hamilton during the last thirty-four years of his life raises anew the question of whether he was really Alexander's biological father or whether Alexander simply felt alienated from a deeply flawed parent who had deserted the family and left him orphaned after his mother's death. Perhaps Hamilton was too busy for a trip back to the islands. Whatever the truth of this fathomless story, Hamilton had dutifully provided his father with financial aid, approximately two remittances per year, right up until his last payment at Christmas 1798.

Like many self-invented immigrants, Hamilton had totally and irrevocably repudiated his past. He never evinced the slightest desire to revisit the haunts of his early life, and his upbringing remained a taboo topic. Yet childhood scenes may have continued to color the way he saw things, especially slavery. By the time he left the Treasury in 1795, slavery had begun to recede in New England and the mid-Atlantic states. Rhode Island, Vermont, Massachusetts, New Hampshire, Pennsylvania, and Connecticut had decided to abolish it. Conspicuously missing were New

York and New Jersey. So in January 1798, Hamilton resumed his association with the New York Manumission Society, his personal affiliation having lapsed during his Philadelphia years. Elected one of its four legal advisers, he helped defend free blacks when slave masters from out of state brandished bills of sale and tried to snatch them off the New York streets.

In 1799, the society enjoyed a magnificent victory when the largely Federalist Assembly, voting along party lines, decreed the gradual abolition of slavery in New York State by a vote of sixty-eight to twenty-three. (Aaron Burr, though he retained his own slave entourage for many years, defected to the Federalist majority.) By 1804, New Jersey had followed New York's example, assuring that the north would extirpate the practice over the next generation, helping to set the stage for the Civil War. In the southern states, with their fast-growing slave population and the invention of the cotton gin, slavery became more ineradicable. Those founders bewitched by the fantasy that slavery would slowly fade away were being proved wrong. Twenty years after New York decided to end slavery, Jefferson, Madison, and Monroe still clung to such rationalizations, saying, for instance, that if slavery were extended into the new western states, it would weaken and die.

Hamilton's name cropped up unexpectedly in the Manumission Society minutes for its March 1799 meeting. The society was trying to win the freedom of a slave named Sarah, who had been brought to New York from Maryland. It turned out, to Hamilton's embarrassment, that she belonged to his brother-in-law John Barker Church. The minutes flagged this awkward circumstance without editorial comment: "A[.] Hamilton was agent for Church in the business."[1] John and Angelica Church had pressed Hamilton to purchase slaves for them before their return to New York. At the next meeting, it was reported that the Churches had suddenly given Sarah her freedom. This incident strengthens the hunch that one or both of the apparent references to slave purchases in Hamilton's cashbooks for 1796 and 1797 referred to purchases for the Churches, not for himself. By late 1795, we recall, Hamilton was already hunting for housing for his returning relatives.

The Manumission Society's work was far from over. It ran a school for one hundred black children, teaching them spelling, reading, writing, and arithmetic. It also protested an increasingly common practice: New York slaveholders were circumventing state laws by exporting slaves to the south, from where they were transferred to the West Indian sugar plantations that Hamilton had known as a boy. Hamilton refused to drop his involvement in the Manumission Society even as his renown grew and his commitments vastly multiplied. He kept up his connection as a legal adviser until his death. Was this perhaps his personal way of acknowledging the past by rectifying the injustice that had surrounded his early years?

. . .

Hamilton's antislavery work in the late 1790s was paralleled by Eliza's growing activism on behalf of marginal and downtrodden people, work that was to dominate the last half century of her life. Because Eliza Hamilton was a modest, self-effacing woman who apparently destroyed her own letters and tried to expunge her presence from the history books, the force of her personality and the magnitude of her contribution have been overlooked. Her son Alexander, Jr., once described her as "remarkable for sprightliness and vivacity."[2] Her pioneering work to relieve the suffering of the poor has been all but forgotten. "She was a most earnest, energetic, and intelligent woman," said her son James. "Her engagements as a principal of the Widows Society and Orphan Asylum were incessant."[3]

The story of Eliza Hamilton's charitable work is inseparable from that of a remarkable Scottish widow named Isabella Graham, who came to New York in 1789 after her husband died of yellow fever in Antigua. A devout Presbyterian with three daughters, Graham decided to dedicate her life to "godly work" and befriended two clergymen in the Wall Street area who had stood among Hamilton's first American contacts, John Rodgers and John Mason.[4] Aided by these church leaders, Graham set up a school to inculcate Christian virtues and a sound education in fashionable young women. She was assisted by her daughter Joanna, who then married a well-to-do merchant, Richard Bethune. This marriage freed Graham from the need to run her school and enabled her to consecrate her efforts to the poor. In December 1797, mother and daughter launched a groundbreaking venture, the Society for the Relief of Poor Widows with Small Children. This missionary society, composed of Christian women from various denominations, may rank as the first all-female social-service agency in New York City. Bearing food parcels and medicine to indigent widows, the Widows Society volunteers saved almost one hundred women from the poorhouse during its first winter of operation alone. Eliza appeared on the membership rolls as "Mrs. General Hamilton," and the Widows Society served as her entryway into a broader universe of evangelical social work. Joanna Bethune's son remembered Eliza thus: "Her person was small and delicately formed, her face agreeable and animated by her brilliant black eyes, showing and radiating the spirit and intelligence so fully exhibited in her subsequent life."[5]

In the late 1790s, the unceasing demands of a growing family prevented Eliza from a full-scale commitment to Christian charity work. On November 26, 1799, she gave birth to her seventh child, Eliza, but she continued to shelter strays and waifs, a practice that she and Alexander had started in adopting Fanny Antill. In 1795, Eliza's brother, John Bradstreet Schuyler, had died, leaving a son, Philip Schuyler II. During the week, the boy attended school on Staten Island with the

Hamilton boys and then spent weekends with Uncle Alexander and Aunt Eliza. So Eliza's home was always bursting with youngsters demanding attention.

Eliza was never allowed to forget the Reynolds affair, since the Republican press refreshed the public's memory at every opportunity. In December 1799, the *Aurora* pointed out gleefully that General Hamilton had arrived in Philadelphia after some recent sightings of his former mistress, implying that the affair continued: "Mrs. Reynolds, alias *Maria,* the sentimental heroine of the memorable *Vindication,* is said to be in Philadelphia once more. In the early part of last year, she was in town and had the imprudence to intrude herself on women of virtue with a relation of her story that she was *the* Maria."[6] In fact, Hamilton had never again set eyes on his quondam mistress. The ever-shifting Maria Reynolds had re-created herself as a widow named Maria Clement. In an attempt to gain respectability in Philadelphia, she ran the household of a French doctor. Nevertheless, the Republican papers continued to ride their favorite hobbyhorse, intimating that her romance with Hamilton still flourished.

Hamilton found increasing pleasure at home at 26 Broadway. One senses that he and Eliza clung to each other with a deep sense of mutual need. "I am well aware how much in my absence your affectionate and anxious heart needs the consolation of frequently hearing from me and there is no consolation which I am not very much disposed to administer to it," he told Eliza in one letter. "It deserves everything from me. I am much more in debt to you than I can ever pay, but my future life will be more than ever devoted to your happiness."[7] The more despairing he became about politics and human nature—and his worldview was never very rosy to begin with—the more he appreciated his sincere, unpretentious wife. From Philadelphia, he wrote to her, "You are my good genius of that kind which the ancient philosophers called a *familiar* and you know very well that I am glad to be in every way as familiar as possible with you." He concluded: "Adieu best of wives and best of mothers."[8] Even a rugged soldier's life, once his sovereign remedy for all ills, no longer possessed its curative powers. "I discover more and more that I am spoiled for a military man," he told Eliza. "My health and comfort require that I should be at home—at that home where I am always sure to find a sweet asylum from care and pain in your bosom."[9]

Hamilton never stopped doting on Angelica Church. During one stay with his in-laws in Albany, he found himself seated at dinner opposite a John Trumbull portrait of her and her son Philip. Hamilton sent Angelica a witty letter, describing how he had dined in the mute presence of a special lady friend:

> I was placed directly in front of her and was much occupied with her during the whole dinner. She did not appear to her usual advantage and yet she was

very interesting. The eloquence of silence is not a common attribute of hers, but on this occasion she employed it *par force* and it was not considered as a fault. Though I am fond of hearing her speak, her silence was so well placed that I did not attempt to make her break it. You will conjecture that I must have been myself dumb with admiration.[10]

Hamilton was approaching his mid-forties and perhaps feeling his age. His high-pressure life was still packed with plenty of responsibilities. As inspector general, he bore single-handedly the weight of an entire army, while trying to retain his restive legal clients. "The law has nearly abandoned him or rather he has forsaken it," Robert Troup told Rufus King. "The loss he sustains is immense!"[11] Hamilton's life began to lose some of its clockwork precision, and the darkness of depression again invaded his mind. While staying with Oliver Wolcott, Jr., in November 1798, Hamilton watched the emaciated Mrs. Wolcott wasting away from a terminal disease. He confessed to Eliza that he was haunted by despondent thoughts that he could not shake: "I am quite well, but I know not what impertinent gloom hangs over my mind, which I fear will not be entirely dissipated until I rejoin my family. A letter from you telling me that you and my dear children are well will be a consolation."[12] During one trip, he told Angelica Church of "a sadness which took possession" of his heart after leaving New York.[13] These confessional remarks leap off the page because Hamilton seldom admitted to anxiety in this candid manner and tended to shield his innermost thoughts.

Now an invalid crippled by gout and abdominal troubles, Philip Schuyler worried about the punishing demands that his son-in-law made on himself. In early 1799, he again exhorted Hamilton to relax.

Mrs. Church writes me that you suffer from want of exercise, that this and unremitted attention to business injures your health. I believe it is difficult for an active mind to moderate an application to business but, my dear sir, you must make some sacrifice to that health which is so precious to all who are dear to you and to that country which rever[e]s and esteems you. Let me then entreat you to use more bodily exercise and less of that of the mind.[14]

Schuyler discreetly exhorted Eliza to saddle Hamilton's horse every day and get him to ride in the fresh air.

Hamilton did engage in some outdoor recreation. He had recently bought a rifle and liked to go out hunting with a retriever dog named Old Peggy. With his "fowling piece" in hand—a light gun with "A. Hamilton, N.Y." carved into its stock—he sometimes roamed the Harlem forests, searching for birds to shoot. At other times, he prowled the Hudson, fishing for striped bass.[15] He was still a habitué of the theater, whether classical tragedies or lighter fare, and he attended the Philharmonic Society concerts at Snow's Hotel on Broadway. Hamilton's problem was never a shortage of interests so much as the time to cultivate them.

On occasion, Hamilton gave evidence of a prankish spirit at odds with the image of the sober public man. While on a visit to Newark, Hamilton's aide Philip Church met a Polish poet, Julian Niemcewicz, a friend of General Tadeusz Kosciuszko. Niemcewicz insisted that Kosciuszko had entrusted him with a magic secret that permitted him to summon up spirits from the grave. Hamilton, intrigued, invited the Polish poet to a Friday-evening soiree. To give conclusive proof of his black art, Niemcewicz asked Hamilton to step into an adjoining room so that he could not see what was going on. Then one guest wrote down on a card the name of a dead warrior—the baron de Viomenil, who had seen action at Yorktown—and asked the Polish poet to conjure up his shade. Niemcewicz uttered a string of incantations, accompanied by a constantly clanging bell. When it was over, Hamilton strode into the room and "declared that the Baron [de Viomenil] had appeared to him exactly in the dress which he formerly wore and that a conversation had passed between them wh[ich] he was not at liberty to disclose," related Peter Jay, the governor's son.[16] That Hamilton had communed with a fallen comrade attracted exceptional attention in New York society, so much so that he had to admit that it was all a hoax he had cooked up with Philip Church and Niemcewicz "to frighten the family for amusement and that it was never intended to be made public."[17]

The yellow-fever epidemic of 1798 that had claimed the lives of Benjamin Franklin Bache and John Fenno had also given fresh urgency to the work of the Widows Society, as many women lost their family breadwinners. "None but eyewitnesses," Isabella Graham wrote, "could have imagined the sufferings of so many respectable, industrious women who never thought to ask bread of any but of God."[18] This same scourge led the more profane Aaron Burr to create quite a different sort of institution in New York: the Manhattan Company.

To understand this pivotal moment between Aaron Burr and Alexander Hamilton, one must fathom the severity of the epidemic that had struck the city that autumn. In September, as many as forty-five victims perished per day, and Hamilton and his family even briefly took rooms several miles from town. Robert Troup described the terrifying paralysis that gripped New York: "Our courts are shut up, our trade totally stagnant, and we have little or no appearance of business. . . . I call in once a day at Hamilton's and we endeavour to fortify each other with philosophy to bear the ills we cannot cure."[19] Wealthier residents escaped to rural outskirts, while the poor were exposed to a disease spread by mosquitoes that multiplied around the many swamps and stagnant ponds. Almost two thousand New Yorkers died, and a fresh potter's field was consecrated in what is now Greenwich Village.

Aaron Burr's brother-in-law, Dr. Joseph Browne, blamed contaminated water for the recurrent outbreaks of yellow fever—the city still depended on often polluted wells—and submitted a plan to the Common Council for drawing fresh water from the Bronx River. Browne's plan contemplated the creation of a private water corporation chartered by the state legislature. The piped water was also hailed as a panacea for other civic needs, ranging from fighting fires to washing filthy streets. Although the Common Council applauded the basic concept of a water company, it countered with a proposal for a *public* company to conduct this business.

In reality, Browne's plan was a ruse concocted by Burr, who had no interest whatever in pure water but considerable interest in setting up a Republican bank. Among the many putative advantages Hamilton and his Federalist associates enjoyed in New York politics was a virtual monopoly over local banking. At the start of 1799, both of the banks in New York City happened to be the brainchildren of Alexander Hamilton: the Bank of New York and the local branch of the Bank of the United States. Republican businessmen nursed a perennial grievance that these banks discriminated against them, one Republican journalist charging that "it became at length impossible for men engaged in trade to advocate republican sentiments without sustaining material injury. . . . As the rage and violence of party increased, directors became more rigorous in enforcing their system of *exclusion*."[20] It is not clear that Republicans were actually penalized, but the suspicion was certainly abroad. Hamilton opposed the vogue for state banks that proliferated in the 1790s, less from narrow political motives than from a fear that competition among banks would dilute credit standards and invite imprudent lending practices as bankers vied for clients.

Now a member of the New York Assembly, Burr knew that any politician who smashed the Federalist monopoly in local banking would attain heroic status among Republicans—at least those who did not regard banks as diabolical instruments. Easy access to a bank also appealed to an incorrigible spendthrift such as Burr, who had ongoing money problems. In early 1797, toward the end of his term in the U.S. Senate, his financial troubles had grown so acute that he had neglected his legislative duties. To establish a New York bank, he had to scale a very high hurdle. The state legislature conferred bank charters, and it was currently under Federalist sway; in those days, every New York corporation engaged in business needed a legislative charter. As the crafty Burr cast about for a stratagem that would let him sneak a bank charter past the opposition party, he hit upon the unlikely subterfuge of using the proposed water company as a blind.

In a cunning political sleight of hand, Burr lined up a bipartisan coalition of six luminaries—three Republicans and three Federalists—to approach the Common Council as sponsors of his proposal for a private water company. For his Federalist phalanx, he recruited Gulian Verplanck, president of the Bank of New York; John Murray, president of the Chamber of Commerce; and his greatest prize, Major General Alexander Hamilton. Why did Hamilton go along with Burr? Burr had recently flirted with the Federalists and had cooperated with Hamilton to fortify New York City against a French invasion. For the moment, the two men stood on a relatively good footing. Hamilton had survived yellow fever and would have favored a project to save the city from further epidemics. Hamilton may also have been investigating a business opportunity for John B. Church. Angelica had prodded her husband to give up his parliamentary career and return to America, but now Church seemed bored, if fabulously prosperous, in New York. Hamilton noted, "He has little to do [and] time hangs heavy on his hands."[21] Church emerged as a director of the Manhattan Company, which may have been a precondition for Hamilton's participation. "Whatever Hamilton's motives," one Burr biographer has written, "no member of the committee of six worked harder [than Hamilton] to make possible Aaron Burr's upcoming triumph in the New York legislature."[22]

On February 22, 1799, Hamilton and Burr marched into the office of Mayor Richard Varick to plead the water company's case. After conferring with an English canal engineer, Hamilton drew up an impressive memo that went far beyond waterworks to a systematic plan for draining city swamps and installing sewers. Persuaded by Hamilton, the Common Council ceded the final decision to the state legislature. Burr must have savored the situation: he was exploiting Alexander Hamilton and enlisting his foe's mighty pen in a clandestine Republican cause. It was exactly the sort of joke that the drolly mysterious Burr treasured. He also got Hamilton to prepare a memo for the state legislature in support of a private water company. In late March, obliging state legislators approved the creation of the Manhattan Company, and on April 2 an unsuspecting Governor John Jay signed this act into law. Earlier promises about the company providing free water to combat fires and repair city streets damaged by laying pipes—standard features of water-company contracts in other states—had been quietly deleted by Burr from the final bill.

As usual, the devil lay in the details. At the final moment, with many legislators having departed for home and others too lazy to examine the fine print, Burr embedded a brief provision in the bill that widened immeasurably the scope of future company activities. This momentous language said "that it shall and may be lawful for the said company to employ all such surplus capital as may belong or accrue to the said company in the purchase of public or other stock or in any other monied transactions of operations."[23] The "surplus capital" loophole would allow Burr to use the Manhattan Company as a bank or any other kind of financial institution. The Federalists had dozed right through this deception because they knew of the Republican antipathy for banks and also because Burr had cleverly decorated the board with eminent Federalists.

Burr, it turned out, was too smart for his own good. If some Republicans admired his finesse, the general electorate did not. At the end of April, as he faced a re-election campaign for his Assembly seat, voters grasped the magnitude of his deception and shunned the ticket he headed. Once Hamilton realized that Burr had hoodwinked him, he was livid. He later complained of Burr, "I have been present when he has contended against banking systems with earnestness and with the same arguments that Jefferson would use. . . . Yet he has lately by a trick established a *bank,* a perfect monster in its principles, but a very convenient instrument of *profit and influence.*"[24] Even some stalwart Republicans shuddered at Burr's machinations. Of Burr's discredited slate, Peter R. Livingston commented that "it would hardly be a wonder if they *did* lose the election, for they had such a *damn'd ticket* that no decent man could hold up his head to support it."[25] Burr's editor, Mary-Jo Kline, has observed that the Manhattan Company scheme "was so baldly self-serving that it temporarily halted Burr's political career and lost him the public office that had served him so well."[26]

On April 22, when Manhattan Company shares went on sale, they were instantly snapped up. In early September, dropping any pretense that it was principally a water company, the company opened with great fanfare its new "office of discount and deposit" on Wall Street. This bank immediately posed a competitive threat to the Bank of New York, now housed in an elegant two-story building down the block at Wall and William Streets. By its wondrously vague charter—a magic carpet of corporate possibilities—the Manhattan Company was allowed to raise two million dollars, operate anywhere, and go on in perpetuity, whereas the Bank of New York had less than one million in capital, was restricted to operations in the city, and had a charter that expired in 1811. To purchase the favor of all political cliques, Burr shrewdly parceled out the company's twelve directorships, dispensing nine to Republicans (with places carefully allocated for Clintonians, Livingstons, and Burrites) and three to Federalists, including John Barker Church.

Perhaps the least of Aaron Burr's sins in organizing the Manhattan Company was his having gulled Hamilton and state legislators into granting a bank charter under false pretenses. Far more grievous were the fraudulent claims he had made for a water company. The plan set forth by Joseph Browne to rid the city of yellow fever by delivering fresh water proved a sham in Burr's nimble hands. In July 1799, the betrayed Browne wrote pathetically to Burr, "I expect and hope that enough will be done to satisfy the public and particularly the legislature that the institution is not a speculating job [but] an undertaking from whence will result immediate and incalculable advantages to the City of New York."[27] The doctor was swiftly disabused. The Manhattan Company promptly scrapped plans to bring water from the Bronx River—the directors had already raided its "surplus capital" for the bank—and instead drew impure water from old wells, pumping it through wooden pipes. That summer, yellow fever returned to New York with a vengeance. Not only had Burr's plan failed to provide pure water but it had thwarted other sound plans afoot, including those for a municipal water company.

The day after the Manhattan Company inaugurated business on Wall Street, two of its directors, Aaron Burr and John Barker Church, celebrated the event in idiosyncratic fashion: with a duel. A staunch Federalist, Church was an opinionated, quarrelsome man who never shrank from a good fight and was not averse to duels. One theory of why he had fled from England to America on the eve of the Revolution, adopting the pseudonym of John B. Carter, was that he had killed a man during a London duel.

The present feud arose from "unguarded language" that Church used about Burr "at a private table in town," as one New York newspaper daintily put it.[28] Church's comments referred to illicit services performed by Burr for the Holland Company, which speculated in American property on behalf of Dutch banks. The Holland Company felt hobbled by restrictions placed on New York land owned by foreigners and retained Burr as a lobbyist to deal with this impediment. Never one to idealize human nature, Burr recommended to his client that it sprinkle five thousand dollars around the state legislature to brighten the prospects for corrective legislation. The money worked wonders, and the consequent Alien Landowners Act removed the legal obstacles. On the Holland Company's ledgers, the payment to Burr appeared not as a bribe but as an unpaid loan. As an attorney for the Holland Company, Hamilton would have known about this seamy affair and likely conveyed his findings to John Barker Church.

In discussing Burr's behavior, John Barker Church made the unpardonable error of employing the word *bribery* in mixed company. Troup reported in early September, "A day or two ago, Mr. Church in some company intimated that Burr had been bribed for his influence whilst in the legislature to procure the passing of the act permitting the Holland Company to hold their lands."[29] The allegation against Burr, Troup added, was widely believed. The instant Burr heard about Church's derogatory remarks, he called him to a duel. Church was a quick, decisive personality—in Hamilton's words a man "of strong mind, very exact, very active, and very much a man of business"—and forthwith took up the challenge.[30] Burr's actions could only have aggravated Hamilton's fury about the Manhattan Company fiasco.

Burr's challenge to John B. Church seems rash until one realizes that he was eyeing the presidential election the following year. His short-lived flirtation with the Federalists had ended. After his humbling setback in the Assembly race due to the Manhattan Company, he had to remove this fresh blemish from his reputation, and a duel with Hamilton's brother-in-law promised to embellish his image in Republican circles. The speed with which Burr entered the duel suggests that, unlike in his later confrontation with Hamilton, he had no murderous intent and went through the ritual purely for political effect. It was a very different affair of honor from one the previous year after Republican Brockholst Livingston had been attacked by Federalist James Jones as he ambled along the Battery. Jones pounced on him, thrashed him with a cane, and gave his nose a good twist. Livingston, in revenge, summoned him to a dueling ground in New Jersey and shot him dead.

On September 2, 1799, Burr and Church rowed across the Hudson for a sunset duel. Burr chatted affably with Church and sauntered about "the field of honor" with sangfroid. One observer said there was "not the least alteration in his [Burr's] behavior on the ground from what there would have been had they met on friendly terms."[31] Church chose Abijah Hammond, former treasurer of the Society for Establishing Useful Manufactures, for his second, while Burr turned to Hamilton's old nemesis Aedanus Burke. That Burr's second came from South Carolina heightens the suspicion that he was trying to woo southern Republicans with the duel.

Contrary to legend, the encounter was not fought with pistols owned by Church and later used in the Hamilton-Burr affair. We know that the pistols belonged to Burr because of a comic mishap. Burr had explained privately to Burke that the bullets he had brought were too small for the pistols and needed to be wrapped in greased chamois leather. As the duel was about to begin, Burr saw Burke trying to tamp the bullet into the barrel by tapping the ramrod with a stone. Burke whispered an apology to Burr: "I forgot to grease the leather. But you see he [Church] is ready, don't keep him waiting. *Just take a crack as it is and I'll grease the next!*"[32] In his coolly unruffled style, Burr told Burke not to worry: if he missed Church, he would hit him the second time. Burr then took the pistol, bowed to Burke, and measured off ten paces with Church. That Burr would fight with an imperfectly loaded weapon suggests that the mood at Hoboken was hardly homicidal on either side. It also would have been poor advertising for the Manhattan Company if one of its directors had murdered another during its gala opening week.

The two men raised their pistols and fired simultaneously. Church's shot clipped a button from Burr's coat while Burr's missed Church altogether. As the two seconds stoked the pistols with fresh shot, Church stepped forward and apologized to Burr for his statements. According to Troup, "Church declared he had been indiscreet and was sorry for it."[33] This was not a retraction or outright admission of error, but it indicated that Church knew that he had no definitive proof of the bribery charge. As if eager to terminate the duel, Burr professed satisfaction at this sop. The two men shook hands, ending the duel, and the principals and seconds rowed back to Manhattan in high spirits.

The Church-Burr duel forms an instructive contrast with the later Hamilton-Burr duel. It was hastily arranged and devoid of the often torturous negotiations that attended more serious affairs of honor. It was halted at an early opportunity, with both sides seemingly keen to quit and hurry back to Manhattan. It was Church who proved the expert shot, while Burr did not even wing his opponent, or perhaps did not try to. Most important, the duel did not throb with the uncontainable passion, hatred, and high drama that was to shadow the encounter in Weehawken nearly five years later. One wonders whether Hamilton formed any lasting impressions of Burr based on this duel. If so, they would all have been wrong, for Burr had come off as both a poor shot and a reasonable man, not as a skilled marksman who might arrive at the field of honor prepared to shoot with deadly intent.

THIRTY-FOUR

IN AN EVIL HOUR

The mighty provisional army that Alexander Hamilton was trying to muster was based on a simple premise: that a hostile France, having spurned negotiations with the United States, might embark on war. That premise seemed far more questionable during the winter of 1798–1799. The French realized they had blundered in the XYZ Affair and did not wish to antagonize President Adams any further. After John Marshall and Charles Cotesworth Pinckney returned from France, the delegation's third member, Elbridge Gerry, dawdled in Paris. Like most Republicans, Gerry worried that war with France would drive America into Great Britain's embrace. Gerry was a notoriously cranky personality. Small, squint-eyed, and argumentative, hindered by a stutter in debate, he had a talent for both offending and mystifying people. (He favored two capitals, for instance, with a dazed Congress shuttling between them.) "Poor Gerry always had a wrong kink in his head," Abigail Adams observed.[1] For all his crotchety eccentricity, however, Elbridge Gerry had a warm admirer in John Adams, who felt oppressed by the mounting cost of military preparations and public disquiet over the property taxes enacted to pay for them. So when Gerry told Adams in October 1798 that the French desired peace, Adams took him seriously.

Hamilton and his confederates in the Adams cabinet tended to brush aside such tidings as cynical, tactical maneuvers by the French. "Such inveterate prejudice shocked me," Adams later wrote, though he himself had earlier been skeptical of French overtures. "I said nothing, but was determined I would not be the slave of it. I knew the man [Gerry] infinitely better than all of them." Adams had no doubt who was leading the campaign to discredit Gerry: "No man had a greater share in propagating and diffusing these prejudices against Mr. Gerry than Hamilton."[2]

In early December 1798, with both Washington and Hamilton present, Adams made a somewhat conciliatory address to Congress, declaring that the French government had "in a qualified manner declared itself willing to receive a minister from the United States for the purpose of restoring a good understanding."[3] Many Federalists were aghast that Adams held out an olive branch to France, while many Republicans still found the president too hawkish. As architect of an army designed to rebuff the French menace, Hamilton was naturally ambivalent about anything that appeared to lessen the danger. He insisted that if the French threat had subsided, it was only because of military efforts undertaken thus far. Hamilton told Harrison Gray Otis that if negotiations did not take place in earnest by August, the president should be given authority to declare war against France. Nonetheless, Adams leaned toward a diplomatic solution, and Secretary of War McHenry apprised Hamilton that in reviewing the new army's progress with Adams the president "seemed to insinuate the affair need not be hurried."[4] Hamilton saw that sluggishness in organizing the army stemmed from Adams himself and told Washington that "obstacles of a very peculiar kind stand in the way of an efficient and successful management of our military concerns."[5]

Because the new army was headed by his rivals, Washington and Hamilton, it brought out all of Adams's competitive instincts, suspicions, and unappeasable vanity. One day in early February 1799, Theodore Sedgwick, the incoming Federalist Speaker of the House, raised with Adams the seemingly innocuous question of whether Washington should bear the title *General* in the new army. This ignited a temper tantrum in the president. "What, are you going to appoint him general over the president?" Adams asked, his voice rising. "I have not been so blind but I have seen a combined effort, among those who call themselves the friends of government, to annihilate the essential powers given by the president."[6] These outbursts were transmitted back to Hamilton.

Then, on February 18, 1799, President Adams stirred up a still greater political tempest by taking what David McCullough has justly praised as "the most decisive action of his presidency."[7] He sent a messenger to Vice President Jefferson, who read aloud in the Senate a short but startling note from the president. Having decided to give diplomacy a second chance, Adams had nominated William Vans Murray, the American minister at The Hague, as minister plenipotentiary to France. It was a typical Adams decision: solitary, impulsive, and quirky. Before springing this decision, he had not conferred with his cabinet, who had previously warned him that such a move would be an "act of humiliation."[8] "I beg you to be assured that it is wholly *his own act* without any participation or communication with any of us," Secretary of State Pickering told Hamilton.[9] Time was to vindicate the enlightened nature of Adams's decision, but the manner of making it only aggravated tensions with his cabinet members. When they proved skeptical about French peace over-tures, Adams decided to question their loyalty. "He began to suspect a dark treach-ery within his cabinet, a cabal that sought nothing less than the annihilation of his constitutional powers," wrote biographer John Ferling.[10] Yet Adams stuck with his strange decision to both retain and ignore his unreliable cabinet when he should have either consulted them or fired them.

Adams's decision also shattered any semblance of unity between many Federal-ists and the president. When a thunderstruck delegation of senators asked Adams to explain the Murray appointment, he grew brusquely combative. As Pickering re-lated, the moment they announced the purpose of their visit, "Mr. Adams burst into a violent passion and, instead of giving any explanation, he upbraided the committee as stepping out of their proper sphere in making the enquiry."[11] Theodore Sedgwick and the president ended up shouting at each other, with Sedgwick at-tributing Adams's decision to "the wild and irregular starts of a vain, jealous, and half frantic mind."[12] After these wounding confrontations, Adams beat a hasty re-treat to Quincy and stayed there for seven months, sometimes buried in the col-lected works of Frederick the Great. Federalist Robert G. Harper of South Carolina said that he hoped that, en route to Quincy, the president's horses might run wild and break their master's neck.

Adams's diplomatic initiative threatened plans for a grand new army, and Hamil-ton said tartly that it "would astonish if anything from that quarter could aston-ish."[13] Both the style and substance of the presidential turnabout bothered him. He thought the decision came not from careful forethought but from "the fortuitous emanations of momentary impulses."[14] He believed that Adams should have con-sulted his cabinet and that any negotiations should have occurred on American soil.

Hamilton had a low opinion of William Vans Murray, a Maryland lawyer. "Murray is certainly not strong enough for so immensely important a mission," Hamilton stated, and he lobbied to have him incorporated into a three-man com-mission.[15] Hamilton prevailed, and Adams agreed grudgingly to have two envoys accompany Murray: Oliver Ellsworth, chief justice of the Supreme Court, and William Davie, the Federalist governor of North Carolina. For loyalty's sake, the Federalists supported this commission, but the damage to party unity was severe. Adams had again flouted the Federalists in his cabinet and in Congress and had jet-tisoned the one issue that had united the party: the threat of Jacobinism. Hence-forth, it was no longer self-evident that Adams would enjoy unanimous Federalist backing in his 1800 reelection campaign. Troup echoed many Federalists when he said, "The late nomination of the President for the purpose of renewing negotia-tions with France has given almost universal disgust. . . . There certainly will be se-rious difficulties in supporting Mr. Adams at the next election if he should be a candidate."[16] Rumors made the rounds about the president's erratic behavior, with some even questioning his sanity.

In another shift that boded ill for Hamilton, George Washington cooled perceptibly in his enthusiasm for the new armed force. Had the army been raised right after the outcry over the XYZ dispatches, he told Hamilton, there would have been no trouble gathering recruits. "*Now* the measure is not only viewed with indifference, but deemed unnecessary by that class of people" who might have served.[17] With each new letter to Hamilton, Washington sounded more dubious, beginning one message on this pessimistic note: "In the present state of the army (or, more properly, the embryo of one, for I do not perceive from anything that has come to my knowledge that we are likely to move beyond this) . . ."[18]

Despite his dismay, Hamilton persisted with plans for his army, however bleak the chances it would ever materialize. He worried that Napoleon might attempt a sneak attack on an American port and that the country would be caught off guard. He got bogged down in bickering about petty details, telling McHenry that he was "disappointed and distressed" by a shipment of cocked hats ordered for one regiment. He lectured him pedantically that cocked hats must be cocked on *all three* sides: "But the hats received are only capable of being cocked on one side and the brim is otherwise so narrow as to consult neither good appearance nor utility. They are also without cockades and loops."[19]

The depression that had afflicted Hamilton the previous fall worsened, and he turned moody and snappish with McHenry about his procurement of supplies. Ever the perfectionist, Hamilton complained that he was starved for funds and felt plunged back into the worst days of the Continental Army. Aside from Philip Church, he had only one secretary and had to handle much of the correspondence by himself. What was unusual for Hamilton was the haughty, almost sadistic, tone that he took when writing to his longtime friend McHenry. These bilious outbursts make for painful reading, with Hamilton sounding like a stern schoolmaster fed up with a doltish pupil. "The fact is that the management of your agents as to the affair of supplies is ridiculously bad," Hamilton told him in one letter.[20] He constantly pointed out errors in McHenry's procedures and never spared his feelings.

Complicating matters was the reluctance of Treasury Secretary Wolcott to provide money for equipping the army. McHenry told Hamilton that he and Pickering had "not been able to remove any one of the prejudices entertained by the Secretary of the Treasury against the augmentation of the army."[21] "It is a pity, my dear sir, and a reproach, that our administration have no general plan," Hamilton replied. He made clear that he still meditated assorted military adventures: "Besides eventual security against invasion, we ought certainly to look to the possession of the Floridas and Louisiana and we ought to squint at South America."[22] Once upon a time, Hamilton had encouraged the cabinet to defer to Adams. Now he broke ranks and encouraged outright resistance. "If the chief is too desultory," he told McHenry, "his ministers ought to be the more united and steady and well settled in some reasonable system of measures."[23] As if competitive with Adams and blatantly envious of his power, Hamilton became more zealous in pushing his views and interfering in internal cabinet politics. By late June 1799, he told McHenry more or less openly that if the president did not hold correct opinions, he should be ignored.

If Hamilton incontestably betrayed Adams, the reverse was also true. Congress had authorized the president to boost the army by more than ten thousand men. Yet Adams had scarcely lifted a finger to help Hamilton raise these new regiments, and a scant two thousand men were enlisted by summer's end in 1799. Hamilton never reached even half the number that he was legally authorized to muster. By October, many troops had not been paid for six months, and a shortage of money threatened to halt recruiting efforts.

As if such setbacks weren't enough, Hamilton had personal money problems. Despite his low pay, he had been unable to take on lucrative new legal clients. "I cannot be a general and a practicer of the law at the same time without doing injustice to the government and myself," he told McHenry.[24] He laid out money for fuel and servants for his army office but did not think he should have to pay for the new office that he needed. "You must not think me rapacious," he told McHenry. "I have not changed my character. But my situation as commanding general exposes me to much additional expence in entertaining officers." To this he added the consideration "of a wife and 6 children whose maintenance and education are to be taken care of."[25] Hamilton felt demeaned, ignored, and unappreciated during his military service under Adams.

Escaping from his duties to Quincy, Adams was also morose and irritable during the spring and summer of 1799. It is hard to comprehend the length of his marathon stay. Adams was tending an ailing, rheumatic Abigail—the previous year he had worried that the affliction might prove mortal—but as president he did not enjoy the luxury of nursing his wife for seven months. Biographer Joseph Ellis has speculated that Adams may have wanted to stall the peace mission until conditions had sufficiently improved in France. Whatever the case, the president's appetite was poor, he lost weight, and his patience grew short. John Ferling has given this vivid portrait of how overwrought Adams became during this period:

> At times he was so irascible that Abigail thought it unwise even to permit him to see state documents. He acted the perfect curmudgeon, snapping at his wife and the hired help and treating old acquaintances and well-wishers in a contemptible and uncivil manner. When General Knox and two others called

on him, he refused to engage in conversation, reading the newspaper instead while they stared uncomfortably at one another. One morning a group of naval officers and Harvard students rode out from Boston hoping for an appearance, and, if they were lucky, a few brief remarks by the president. He did appear at his front door, but only to tongue-lash them for their insolence at coming to his estate without an invitation. The men were mortified at the president's conduct, Abigail wrote, and she was embarrassed for him.[26]

Prior to the fall of 1799, Hamilton and Adams had managed to avoid a showdown partly by steering clear of each other. Their paths converged in a fateful way that fall. Navy Secretary Benjamin Stoddert implored Adams to terminate his self-imposed exile and return to the capital, where "artful designing men" were trying to subvert his peace initiative with France.[27] Adams finally headed south in early October. On his way, he tarried in New York for a harrowing encounter with his son Charles, who had succumbed to alcoholism and bankruptcy. Adams had once chided his son as "a madman possessed of the devil" and dismissed him to Abigail as "a mere rake, buck, blood and beast."[28] Now he vowed to Charles that he would never see him again, and he was to remain true to his word.[29] This unfortunate episode could only have darkened the president's mood before his encounter with Hamilton.

Another yellow-fever epidemic in Philadelphia had sent the government scurrying into temporary exile in Trenton, crowding the little town with government employees and military men. Suffering from a bad cold, President Adams lodged in a boardinghouse and made do with a small bedroom and sitting room. He arrived in Trenton hoping to break a logjam that had developed over the French peace mission. At first, he had been disturbed by evidence of fresh intrigue in the Directory that summer, telling Pickering, "The revolution in the Directory and the revival of the clubs and private societies in France . . . seem to warrant a relaxation of our zeal for the sudden and hasty departure of our envoys."[30] On October 15, however, in a session that lasted until nearly midnight, Adams gathered his cabinet to confer final approval upon the peace commission. The next morning, he ordered the three envoys to sail by early November. Hamilton decided to hazard one last frantic effort to change the president's mind, a confrontation that neither ever forgot.

In recounting the origins of this stormy session, Adams claimed that Hamilton had been training his troops at Newark when he learned of the cabinet decision. He said that Hamilton had ridden for two days and galloped unannounced into Trenton in a churlish breach of etiquette. Hamilton's appearance "was altogether unforeseen, unrequested, and undesired. It was a sample of his habitual impudence."[31] Hamilton's correspondence shows, however, that by October 8 he was already in

Trenton on War Department business to confer with General Wilkinson about western fortifications, and he may well have stayed there. Hamilton denied Adams's insinuation that he was there as part "of some mischievous plot against his independence."[32] While in Trenton, he heard about the cabinet decision to dispatch the peace mission to France. As commanding general of an army created to ward off a French invasion, he naturally wanted to consult with the president. And as the de facto leader of the president's own party and a man with a considerable ego, he thought he was entitled to the president's ear. Adams thought Hamilton was being pushy and overbearing. He regarded his intervention as a breach of presidential prerogative and dangerous meddling with civilian policy by a military man. He also worried that Hamilton wanted to use his new army against his southern foes. Abigail Adams went so far as to fear that Hamilton might stage a coup d'état against her husband's administration.

The climactic encounter between Adams and Hamilton probably unfolded in a parlor of the boardinghouse where the president was staying. The conversation dragged on for hours. If Adams's account is accurate, "the little man," as he called Hamilton, spoke with vehement eloquence and was "wrought up . . . to a degree of heat and effervescence."[33] Adams probably did not exaggerate: during this period, Hamilton was often agitated, despondent, and gripped by strong emotions. Adams recalled that he reacted calmly to Hamilton, as if indulging a madman: "I heard him with perfect good humor, though never in my life did I hear a man talk more like a fool."[34] Hamilton tried to persuade Adams that changes in the Directory presaged a possible restoration of Louis XVIII to the French throne by Christmas. Adams replied caustically: "I should as soon expect that the sun, moon and stars will fall from their orbs as events of that kind take place in any such period."[35] Adams was correct: Louis XVIII was not to reign for another fifteen years. On the other hand, Adams erred in thinking that a European peace would prevail by winter. "I treated him throughout with great mildness and civility," Adams concluded, "but after he took leave, I could not help reflecting in my own mind on the total ignorance he had betrayed of every thing in Europe, in France, England, and elsewhere."[36]

Hamilton was stunned by Adams's altered stance toward France. Within the space of a month, the president had seemed to go from deep concern about the changed government in Paris to cavalier indifference. "The President has resolved to send the commissioners to France notwithstanding the change of affairs there," he told George Washington. "All my calculations lead me to regret the measure."[37] When Hamilton noted that Adams had not consulted his war or treasury secretary, Washington sounded equally critical. "I was surprised at the *measure,* how much more so at the manner of it?" he told Hamilton. "This business seems to have commenced in an evil hour and under unfavourable auspices."[38]

After his meetings in Trenton, Hamilton returned to New York, pausing en route to review his troops at their winter quarters in Scotch Plains, New Jersey. With envoys setting out for France, Hamilton must have wondered how long his inchoate army would last. He blamed Adams's diplomacy for this threat to his army, but it also lacked the broad-based public support necessary in a democracy. The electorate did not want to pay new taxes or borrow money to maintain an expensive army and feared the uses to which Hamilton might put the troops. Even Hamilton's most ardent supporters detected waning enthusiasm. Theodore Sedgwick worried that "the army everywhere to the southward is very unpopular and is growing daily more so."[39] Treasury Secretary Wolcott told Fisher Ames that nothing "is more certain than that the army is unpopular even in the southern states for whose defence it was raised. . . . The northern people fear no invasion or if they did, they perceive no security in a handful of troops."[40] While Hamilton wove fantasies around his army, the American people were fast losing interest in any military preparations. When Adams addressed a joint session of Congress in early December, he issued no new appeals for soldiers or sailors.

The confrontation between Hamilton and Adams in Trenton effectively ended their relationship. Adams could not bear to be hectored by Hamilton, who could not bear to be patronized by Adams. These two vain, ambitious men seemed to bring out the worst in each other. Instead of curtailing his plans, Hamilton reacted with more extravagant dreams. He now gazed at the world through a lens that magnified threats and obscured the chances for peace with France. He composed a long, nearly apocalyptic letter to Senator Jonathan Dayton of New Jersey, setting forth a new Federalist political agenda. This document shows a total loss of perspective by Hamilton, the nadir of his judgment. Some ideas were vintage Hamilton: the establishment of a military academy, new factories to manufacture uniforms and other army supplies, and canals to improve interstate commerce. Other ideas, however, reflected a morbidly exaggerated fear of disorder. He believed his Virginia foes were plotting to dissolve the union and that the country was in jeopardy of civil war. He wanted more taxes to build ships and introduce longer army reenlistment periods. Showing waning faith in the good sense of the public, he wanted to strengthen state militias so they could be called out "to suppress unlawful combinations and insurrections."[41] Formerly skeptical about aspects of the Alien and Sedition Acts, he now gave them full-throated support and ranted about the need to punish people, especially the foreign born who libeled government officials: "Renegade aliens conduct more than one of the most incendiary presses in the U[nited] States and yet in open contempt and defiance of the laws they are permitted to continue their destructive labours. Why are they not sent away?"[42] To reduce the power wielded by Virginia, Hamilton even came up with a crackpot scheme to break up large states into smaller units: "Great states will always feel a rivalship with the common head [and] will often be disposed to machinate against it. . . . The subdivision of such states ought to be a cardinal point in the Federal policy."[43]

It is difficult to separate this dark, vengeful letter from the setbacks in Hamilton's recent political life. Under President Washington, he had grown accustomed to great power and deference. President Adams had destroyed this sense of entitlement, and Hamilton never forgave him. The bitter face-off with Adams at Trenton confirmed that Hamilton had lost all direct influence with the president. There had been the further humiliation of the Reynolds scandal, which had mocked Hamilton's pretensions to superior private morality. He had also been greatly embittered by the pitiless censure of his enemies. His vision now appeared to be so steeped in gloom that one wonders how much depression warped his judgment in later years. The ebullient hopefulness of his early days as treasury secretary seemed to be in eclipse.

By contrast, in these final years of the century, the abiding respect between Hamilton and Washington had ripened into real affection. On December 12, 1799, Washington sent Hamilton a letter applauding his outline for an American military academy: "The establishment of an institution of this kind . . . has ever been considered by me as an object of primary importance to this country."[44] It was the last letter George Washington ever wrote. After riding in a snowstorm, he developed a throat infection and died two days later. Washington did not live to see the government transferred to the new capital that was to bear his name. Haunted by a fear of being buried alive, he left instructions that his interment in a Mount Vernon vault should be held up for a few days after his death.

Washington departed the planet as admirably as he had inhabited it. He had long hated slavery, even though he had profited from it. Now, in his will, he stipulated that his slaves should be emancipated after Martha's death, and he set aside funds for slaves who would be either too young or too old to care for themselves. Of the nine American presidents who owned slaves—a list that includes his fellow Virginians Jefferson, Madison, and Monroe—only Washington set free all of his slaves.

Washington's death dealt another devastating blow to Hamilton's aspirations. For twenty-two years, their careers had been yoked together, and Hamilton had never needed Washington's sponsorship more urgently than now. Hamilton confided to Charles C. Pinckney after Washington's death, "Perhaps no friend of his has more cause to lament on personal account than myself. . . . My imagination is gloomy, my heart sad."[45] To Washington's secretary, Tobias Lear, Hamilton wrote, "I have been much indebted to the kindness of the general. . . . [H]e was an aegis very essential to me. . . . If virtue can secure happiness in another world, he is happy."[46] Not wishing to intrude upon her mourning, Hamilton waited nearly a month before writing to Martha Washington: "No one better than myself knows the greatness of your loss or how much your excellent heart is formed to feel it in all its extent."[47] Hamilton's heartfelt sadness over Washington's death only thickened the shadows that surrounded him in his final years.

Briefly, the partisan squabbling ceased as the nation paid homage to its foremost founder. On December 26, 1799, Hamilton marched in a somber procession of government dignitaries, soldiers, and horsemen that escorted a riderless white horse from Congress Hall to the German Lutheran Church, where Henry "Light-Horse Harry" Lee of Virginia eulogized Washington as "first in war, first in peace, first in the hearts of his countrymen."[48] The members of Hamilton's army would wear crepe armbands in the coming months. Though Vice President Jefferson presided over the Senate in a chair draped in black, he had been alienated from Washington and boycotted the memorial service. The envious Adams found excessive the posthumous glorification of Washington and later faulted the Federalists for having "done themselves and their country invaluable injury by making Washington their military, political, religious and even moral Pope and ascribing everything to him."[49]

Adams was right about one thing: the Federalists *had* relied too much on Washington to heal the fratricidal warfare in their party, and this made them vulnerable after his death, especially with a presidential election in the offing. Many High Federalists around Hamilton wanted to discard Adams; Gouverneur Morris had drafted a letter to Washington right before he died, asking that he run again. Hamilton knew that Washington's death could destroy the unstable Federalist coalition: "The irreparable loss of an inestimable man removes a control which was felt and was very salutary."[50] The Hamiltonian Federalists faced a knotty dilemma: whether to acquiesce in administration policies they detested or to risk a schism in the party.

Washington's death left vacant the post of commanding officer of the army, and Hamilton thought he had earned the right to it. "If the President does not nominate" Hamilton, said Philip Schuyler, "it will evince a want of prudence and propriety . . . for I am persuaded that the vast majority of the American community expect that the appointment will be conferred on the general."[51] Hamilton had struggled tirelessly and at great personal sacrifice to create a new army with six cavalry companies and twelve infantry regiments. But having regretted naming Hamilton to the number-two position, Adams was not about to cede the top position to him, which therefore remained unfilled. Hamilton did succeed Washington as president general of the Society of the Cincinnati.

Time ran out on Hamilton's military ambitions. By February 1800, Congress halted enlistments for the new army that he was assembling and that had monopolized his valuable time. That same month, Americans learned that Napoleon Bonaparte had eliminated the Directory in November and pronounced himself first consul, in precisely the turn to despotism that Hamilton had long prophesied for France. The fulfillment of his prediction, however, left him stranded in an awkward situation. Napoleon's coup marked the end of the French Revolution and thereby weakened the case for military preparations against a country that the Federalists had identified with Jacobinism.[52] Hamilton saw his vision of a brand-new army evaporate: "It is very certain that the military career in this country offers too few inducements and it is equally certain that my *present* station in the army *cannot* very long continue under the plans which seem to govern," he told a friend.[53]

But as spring arrived, Hamilton still could not surrender his daydreams for the American military. With his hyperactive mind, he drafted a bill for a military academy encompassing the navy as well as the army and another for an army corps of engineers. He refined his guidelines for infantry training right down to the correct pace for marching—75 steps per minute for the *common* step, 120 per minute for the *quick* step. Hamilton was spinning his wheels. When Congress gave Adams the power in mid-May to disband most of the new army, he quickly exercised it. By this point, Adams thought Hamilton's army an abomination and later recalled that it "was as unpopular as if it had been a ferocious wild beast let loose upon the nation to devour it."[54] Adams quipped grimly that if the venturesome Hamilton had been given a free hand with the army, he would have needed a second army to disband the first.[55]

Hamilton tried to keep up a brave face, but he was heartbroken over his ill-fated corps. He told Eliza that he had to play "the game of good spirits but . . . it is a most artificial game and at the bottom of my soul there is a more than usual gloom."[56] He was unaccustomed to failure, and here he had devoted a year and a half of his life to an aborted army. On May 22, 1800, he emerged from his tent at Scotch Plains to review his troops one last time before they were demobilized in mid-June. Abigail Adams was present and, despite her dislike of Hamilton, was impressed by his troops. "They did great honor to their officers and to themselves," she told her sister.[57] At the beginning of July, Hamilton shut up his New York headquarters, notified the secretary of war of his departure, and ended his military service. The taxing, dispiriting episode was over in every respect but one: he had not yet discharged his full store of bitterness against the president whom he held responsible for this inglorious end.

THIRTY-FIVE

GUSTS OF PASSION

Even while carrying out his duties as inspector general of a nascent army, Hamilton made time for the occasional legal case. He had seldom gravitated to criminal cases, preferring civil cases with substantial constitutional issues or commercial cases that generated adequate fees. On those infrequent occasions when he took criminal cases, he usually defended the underdog on a pro bono basis—evidence that once again challenges the historic stereotype of Hamilton as an imperious snob. Such a case arose in the spring of 1800 when he thought a likable young carpenter named Levi Weeks was being unjustly accused of murder. As in the postwar Loyalist cases, Hamilton was disturbed whenever public opinion howled for bloody revenge.

In the annals of New York crime, the Levi Weeks case is often called the Manhattan Well Tragedy, and it forms yet another chapter in the convoluted relationship of Hamilton and Aaron Burr. At first glance, the case seemingly involved an innocent maiden betrayed by an unfeeling cad. On the snowy evening of December 22, 1799, Gulielma Sands, about twenty-two, left her boardinghouse on Greenwich Street, which was operated by her respectable Quaker relatives, Catherine and Elias Ring. It was believed that she had gone off to marry her fiancé, Levi Weeks, who was also a tenant and was seen chatting with her before her departure. Later that night, Weeks returned to the Ring household alone, inquired if Sands had gone to bed, and was shocked to discover that she was not there. On January 2, her fully dressed corpse was fished from a wooden well owned by the Manhattan Company. Perhaps because he had founded the company, Aaron Burr joined with Hamilton and Brockholst Livingston to defend Levi Weeks against a murder charge.

The corpse of Gulielma Sands was mottled and swollen and badly bruised around the face and breasts. The public was riveted by these gory details, and hand-bills insinuated that she had been impregnated and then murdered by Weeks. Elias and Catherine Ring egged on this speculation, with Elias recalling that when Weeks came home on the evening of Sands's disappearance "he appeared as white as ashes and trembled all over like a leaf."[1] The Rings even engaged in some macabre show-manship at their boardinghouse. They displayed Sands's body in a coffin for three days and then placed it for a day on the pavement outside, allowing people to gratify their ghoulish curiosity and decide whether she had been pregnant. (The inquest said she had not.) As the uproar against Levi Weeks reached a crescendo—"Scarcely anything else is spoken of," said one local diarist—gossips whispered of ghostly apparitions at the Manhattan well.[2] The prosecution of Weeks assumed the vengeful mood of a witch-hunt. The indictment said that, "not having the fear of God before his eyes, but being moved and seduced by the instigation of the devil," Weeks had "beat[en] and abused" Sands before murdering her and stuffing her down the well.[3]

The People v. Levi Weeks began on March 31 at the old City Hall on Wall Street, the Federal Hall of Washington's first inauguration. Such a huge throng showed up that constables had to empty the courtroom of "superfluous spectators."[4] Levi Weeks could hear crowds outside chanting for his blood: "Crucify him! Crucify him!"[5] The case holds a special place in Hamilton's legal practice because William Coleman, a court clerk and later editor of the *New-York Evening Post,* provided an almost complete stenographic transcript—a novelty in those days. Unfortunately, Coleman did not specify which defense lawyer spoke at any given moment, though we can make some educated guesses. For instance, the grandiloquent lawyer who opened the defense case spoke in a florid style reminiscent of Hamilton rather than the more succinct Burr.

> I know the unexampled industry that has been exerted to destroy the reputation of the accused and to immolate him at the shrine of persecution without the solemnity of a candid and impartial trial. . . . We have witnessed the extraordinary means which have been adopted to inflame the public passions and to direct the fury of popular resentment against the prisoner. Why has the body been exposed for days in the public streets in a manner the most indecent and shocking? . . . In this way, gentlemen, the public opinion comes to be formed unfavourably and long before the prisoner is brought to his trial he is already condemned.[6]

It seems mystifying that Levi Weeks could have assembled a team composed of the three preeminent lawyers in New York. Hamilton could scarcely have warmed to Burr after the Manhattan Company sham and was likely motivated by his friend-ship with Ezra Weeks, Levi's brother, whom he had hired to construct a weekend home north of the city. Another likely reason why Hamilton collaborated with Burr is that the trial occurred on the eve of local elections that were to have profound national implications. None of the three lawyers could afford to miss a chance to publicize his talents in a spectacular criminal case.

The trial unfolded with a speed that seems unimaginable today. Fifty-five wit-nesses testified in three days, each day's testimony lasting well past midnight. The rigorous defense team established a credible alibi for Levi Weeks, claiming that he had dined with Ezra on the night in question. During that dinner, John B. Mc-Comb, Jr., the architect hired for Hamilton's new home, arrived and found a cheer-ful Levi stowing away a hearty dinner. From medical experts, the defense elicited helpful opinions that the marks on Gulielma Sands's body might have been pro-duced by drowning or by the autopsy itself, opening up the possibility of suicide. (The coroner's inquest had established drowning, not beating, as the cause of death.) The defense lawyers also discredited the testimony of Elias and Catherine Ring, showing that Elias Ring had probably slept with Gulielma Sands and that Sands, no innocent damsel, had a little weakness for laudanum. The image of the Ring household evolved from a scene of violated gentility into something closer to a sedate brothel.

As the trial proceeded, the defense cast suspicion on a Richard Croucher, a shady salesman of ladies' garments, who had zealously stirred up malice against Levi Weeks. Croucher had arrived from England the year before and was yet another raffish lodger at the steamy Ring premises. As principal witness for the prosecution, he seemed too eager to retail stories about sexual liaisons between Levi Weeks and Gulielma Sands. The defense lawyers damaged Croucher's credibility by getting him to confess that he had quarreled with Weeks.

It has become part of Hamiltonian legend that when Croucher testified, Hamil-ton placed candles on both sides of his face, giving his features a sinister glow. "The jury will mark every muscle of his face, every motion of his eye," Hamilton is said to have declaimed. "I conjure you to look through that man's countenance to his conscience."[7] Croucher supposedly confessed on the spot. Oddly enough, Aaron Burr later claimed that *he* had grabbed two candelabra from the defense table, held them toward Croucher, and declared theatrically, "Behold the murderer, gentle-men!"[8] Traumatized by this exposure, the guilty Croucher was alleged to have bolted in terror from the courtroom. Coleman's transcript shows when the famous moment may have occurred. One witness was testifying to Croucher's unsavory character when, Coleman noted, "*here one of the prisoner's counsel held a candle close to Croucher's face, who stood among the cro[w]d and asked the witness if it was he and he said it was.*"[9] Hamilton or Burr may have flicked the candle toward Croucher in a rapid gesture that made him appear to cringe guiltily in the glare of a burning taper. The lodger never confessed to the crime. The likelihood that Croucher, not Weeks, was the culprit increased three months later when he was convicted of raping a thirteen-year-old girl at the racy Ring boardinghouse.

The protracted case ended at 1:30 in the morning on April 2, 1800. The bleary-eyed prosecutor had not slept for forty-four hours, and Hamilton noted that everyone was "sinking under fatigue." Hamilton therefore waived the right to a summation, saying he would "rest the case on the recital of the facts" by the bench. Hamilton felt confident that the case required no "laboured elucidation."[10] He and his colleagues had convincingly shown that Levi Weeks had a watertight alibi, that the evidence against him was circumstantial, and that he possessed no motive for butchering his fiancée. The jury agreed. William Coleman ended his transcript: "*The jury then went out and returned in about five minutes with a verdict*—NOT GUILTY."[11] It was a triumph for the defense and a hideous embarrassment for Elias and Catherine Ring. As Hamilton strode from the courtroom, Catherine Ring waved a fist in his face and shouted, "If thee dies a natural death, I shall think there is no justice in heaven."[12]

While Hamilton and Burr bestrode the Wall Street courtroom, they knew that local elections for the state legislature in late April might affect much more than New York politics: they might determine the next president of the United States. With John Adams certain to run strongly in New England and Thomas Jefferson equally so in the south, the election would hinge on pivotal votes in the mid-Atlantic states, particularly New York, which had twelve electoral votes. The Constitution gave each state the right to choose its own method for selecting presidential electors, and New York picked its by a joint ballot of the two houses of the legislature, both now with Federalist majorities, yet with the upstate counties evenly split between Republicans and Federalists. The New York City elections that spring could tip the balance of the legislature one way or the other. Thus, as New York City went, so went the state, and possibly the nation.

Jefferson realized this and advised Madison in early March that "if the city election of N[ew] York is in favor of the Republican ticket," then the national winner might be Republican.[13] Within Hamilton's Federalist coterie, the April elections arose as the best chance to blunt John Adams's reelection bid and substitute a more congenial Federalist candidate. Robert Troup wrote to Rufus King, "This election will be all important . . . and particularly so as there is a *decided and deep rooted disgust* with Mr. Adams on the part of his *best old friends.*"[14]

The centrality of the New York City elections presented an unprecedented opportunity for that most dexterous opportunist, Aaron Burr, who knew that the Republicans wanted to achieve geographic balance on their national ticket by having a northern vice presidential candidate. If he could deliver New York into the Republican camp, he might parlay that feat into a claim on the second spot under Jefferson. In the polarized atmosphere of American politics, Burr knew that a northern renegade aligned with southern Republicans could provide a critical swing factor. This was Alexander Hamilton's recurring nightmare: an electoral deal struck between Virginia and New York Republicans.

In the New York City elections that spring, Hamilton and Burr descended from the lofty heights to spar in the grit and bustle of lower Manhattan ward politics. On April 15, Hamilton met with his Federalist adherents at the Tontine City Hotel and drew up a largely undistinguished slate of candidates for the state Assembly. It was composed of an atypical (for the Federalists) cross-section of New Yorkers, with a potter, a mason, a ship chandler, a grocer, and two booksellers. This may have been a strategy to outflank the Republicans, or it may have reflected the reluctance of many wealthy Federalists to put in time as poorly paid state legislators, especially with the state capital now transferred to Albany. Burr, with his customary craft, waited for Hamilton to present his slate before revealing his own. When Burr scanned a sheet naming the Federalist candidates, he "read it over with great gravity, folded it up, put it in his pocket, and . . . said, 'Now I have him all hollow,'" said John Adams.[15]

The suave Burr packed his slate with gray eminences. He cajoled the perennial ex-governor, George Clinton, out of retirement and added the aging Horatio Gates, still feeding off his wartime victory at Saratoga, as well as Brockholst Livingston, his recent cocounsel. An early master of the art of coalition politics, Burr made common cause with Clintonians and Livingstons to present a redoubtable united front. Hamilton thought Burr had engaged in deceptive window-dressing by padding his slate with luminaries who had no real intention of serving in the state legislature and cared only about the selection of Republican electors in the presidential race.

Unlike other contemporary politicians, Burr enjoyed the nitty-gritty of such campaigns and embraced the electioneering they disdained. No other member of the founding generation would have explained his fondness for elections by stating that they provided "a great deal of fun and honor and profit."[16] That spring, Burr ran a campaign that, with its exhaustive toolbox of techniques, previewed modern political methods. Federalists had benefited from a requirement that voters needed to own substantial real estate. To bypass this, Burr exploited a legal loophole that enabled tenants to pool their properties and claim that their *combined* values qualified them to vote. He sent German-speaking orators into German-speaking areas. Burr also infused his passionate young followers with uncommon zeal at a time of haphazard campaigning. They drew up lists of voters in the city, with long columns of names accompanied by thumbnail sketches of the voter's political bent, finances, health, and willingness to volunteer. With his campaign workers knocking on doors to solicit funds, Burr dispensed canny tips about potential donors. "Ask nothing of this one," he would say. "If we demand money, he'll be offended and refuse to work for us. . . . Double this man's assessment. He'll contribute generously if he doesn't have to work."[17] However aristocratic his lineage, Burr was a proponent of the hard sell and shrewdly sized up his targets. He also scented victory on several topical issues, denouncing the Alien and Sedition Acts and the unpopular taxes levied to finance Hamilton's army. "Burr's generalship, perseverance, industry, and execution exceeds all description," Commodore James Nicholson told Albert Gallatin. He was as "superior to the Hambletonians as a man is to a boy."[18]

That April, New Yorkers out for a stroll could have stumbled upon either Alexander Hamilton or Aaron Burr addressing crowds on street corners, sometimes alternating on the same platform. They treated each other with impeccable courtesy. Neither seemed to have any hesitation about soliciting voters individually or in small groups. One Republican paper could scarcely believe Hamilton's strenuous campaigning as he rallied the faithful like a general marshaling men for battle: "Hamilton harangues the astonished group. Every day he is seen in the street, hurrying this way and darting that. Here he buttons a heavy-hearted fed[eralist] and preaches up courage, there he meets a group and he simpers in unanimity. . . . [H]e talks of perseverance and (God bless the mark) of virtue!"[19] The Federalist papers professed similar shock at seeing the patrician Burr working the Manhattan sidewalks, one paper asking how a would-be vice president could "stoop so low as to visit every corner in search of voters?"[20] Burr opened his home to his workers, serving refreshments and scattering mattresses on the floor to allow quick naps. One New York merchant recorded in his diary: "Col. Burr kept open house for nearly two months and committees were in session day and night during that whole time at his house."[21]

Burr displayed similar professional stamina during the three-day polling period. To guard against any Federalist vote tampering, he assigned poll watchers to voting stations and kept a ten-hour vigil at one venue. A local congressman told James Monroe, "Burr is in charge, to his exertions we owe much. He attended the [polling] places within the city for 24 hours without sleeping or resting."[22] To turn out the vote, he organized a cavalcade of "carriages, chairs and wagons" to transport Republican sympathizers to the polls. For three days, Hamilton was no less assiduous, mounting his horse and riding from place to place, mobilizing supporters and enduring shouts of "scoundrel" and "villain" in Republican precincts.[23]

By midnight on May 1, 1800, the local political world learned the result of this fierce election, one that portended a fundamental realignment in American politics: the Republican slate had swept New York City, converting Hamilton's own home turf from a Federalist to a Republican stronghold. This meant that Jefferson could now count on twelve electoral votes where he had received none in 1796. Since he had lost to Adams then by only three votes, this shift was a real thunderbolt. Burr took justifiable pride in his triumph, explaining to one downcast Federalist that "we have beat[en] you by superior *management*."[24] Theodore Roosevelt later interpreted Burr's victory as that of the skillful ward politician, with a "mastery of the petty political detail," over the statesmanlike Hamilton, but Hamilton had not hesitated to dip into the humble mechanics of politics.[25]

A shaken Hamilton and fellow Federalists attended a May 4 caucus that was infiltrated by the Republican press. The *Aurora* said that the "despondency" of those assembled verged on "the melancholy of despair."[26] Those present were so petrified at the thought of Jefferson as president that they considered desperate measures. Led by Hamilton, they decided to appeal to Governor Jay and have him convene the outgoing state legislature to impose new rules for choosing presidential electors. They now wanted the electors chosen through popular voting by district. Most shocking of all, they wanted this new system applied retroactively, to overturn the recent election. In heated arguments over the proposition, the *Aurora* noted that "when it was urged that it might lead to a civil war . . . a person present observed that a civil war would be preferable to having Jefferson."[27]

Hamilton's appeal may count as the most high-handed and undemocratic act of his career. A year earlier, Burr had championed a proposal in the state legislature to scrap the existing method for selecting presidential electors: instead of having the legislature elect them, they would be elected by the people on a district-by-district basis. The Federalists had hooted this down, but now Hamilton had the gall to revive the idea. On May 7, he warned Jay that the recent election would probably install Jefferson—"an *atheist* in religion and a *fanatic in politics*"—as president.[28] He portrayed the Republican party as an amalgam of dangerous elements, some favoring "the overthrow of the government by stripping it of its due energies, others . . . a revolution after the manner of Buonaparte."[29] Hamilton acknowledged that Republicans would unanimously oppose his measure but that "in times like these in which we live, it will not do to be overscrupulous. It is easy to sacrifice the substantial interests of society by a strict adherence to ordinary rules."[30] This from a man who had consecrated his life to the law. Henry Cabot Lodge said of this irreparable blot on Hamilton's career, "The proposition was, in fact, nothing less than to commit under the forms of law a fraud, which would set aside the expressed will of a majority of voters in the state."[31] Hamilton seemed oblivious of the contradiction in asking Jay to resort to extralegal means to conserve the rule of law. A politician of strict integrity, Jay was dumbstruck by Hamilton's letter, which he tabled and never answered. On the back, he wrote this deprecating description: "Proposing a measure for party purposes which it would not become me to adopt."[32] Jay's silence was an apt expression of scorn.

How had Hamilton justified this disgraceful action to himself? He believed that Jefferson's support for the Constitution had always been lukewarm and that, once in office, he would dismantle the federal government and return America to the chaos of the Articles of Confederation. This was not entirely paranoid thinking on Hamilton's part, for Jefferson made statements that sounded as if he wanted an annulment or radical recasting of the Constitution. "The true theory of our Constitution," Jefferson told Gideon Granger, was that "the states are independent as to everything within themselves and united as to everything respecting foreign nations."[33] The application of this theory would have canceled out much of Hamilton's domestic system. Yet by this point Hamilton should have known that Jefferson's rhetoric tended to outpace reality and that a wily, pragmatic politician lurked behind the sometimes overheated ideologist.

Within days of the New York election, Burr felt within his grasp the prize he coveted: the Republican nomination for vice president. As a reward for the New York victory, a congressional caucus in Philadelphia decided that the party's vice presidential candidate should come from that state. Although consideration was given briefly to George Clinton and Robert R. Livingston, Burr had masterminded the victory, and his followers exacted their due. A heavy load of mutual distrust between Jefferson and Burr was temporarily set aside. Burr remembered that during the previous presidential campaign, Virginia Republicans had pledged to support him and then given him only lackluster backing. For his part, Jefferson later admitted that he had employed Burr as a (slippery) tool to further his ambitions in 1800. "I had never seen Colonel Burr till he came as a member of [the] Senate," he would write. "His conduct very soon inspired me with distrust. I habitually cautioned Mr. Madison against trusting him too much."[34] Only Burr's bravura performance in the New York elections had secured his place on the ticket. "When I destined him for a high appointment," Jefferson continued, "it was out of respect for the favor he had obtained with the republican party by his extraordinary exertions and successes in the New York election in 1800."[35] Jefferson had no true respect for Burr, much less affection. Their partnership was to last as long as it served their mutual interests and not a second longer.

Hamilton always believed that the Federalist defeat in New York City in the spring of 1800 had thrown John Adams into such a fright about his reelection prospects that he decided to purge his cabinet of Hamilton loyalists in order to court Repub-

lican votes. On May 3, the day the news arrived, Jefferson saw that the election results had indeed dealt a horrendous blow to Adams. "He was very sensibly affected,"
Jefferson reported, "and accosted me with these words, 'Well, I understand that you
are to beat me in this contest and I will only say that I will be as faithful a subject as
any you will have."[36]

John Adams later claimed that in May 1800 he had experienced a sudden epiph-
any and discovered Hamilton's malevolent control over his cabinet. But he had
harbored such thoughts all along, and rumors of impending cabinet firings had
flitted about since the previous summer. George Washington had handled cabinet
infighting in a forceful, dignified fashion, as when he tried in vain to impose a truce
in the anonymous newspaper war between Hamilton and Jefferson. By contrast,
Adams had sputtered and railed and done nothing. "Adams was contemplative and
something of a loner," wrote John Ferling, "whereas Washington was an aggressive,
energetic businessman-farmer who read relatively little and was happiest when he
was physically active."[37] Washington had a command over his subordinates, and a
subtle knowledge of their true nature that Adams never managed to achieve.

Increasingly, Adams had accused Pickering and McHenry of being tools of Great
Britain who opposed his French peace initiatives, and he excoriated them openly.
Treasury Secretary Wolcott told a colleague in December 1799 that President Adams
"considers Col. Pickering, Mr. McHenry, and myself as his enemies; his resentments
against General Hamilton are excessive; he declares his belief at the existence of a
British faction in the United States."[38] With his selective memory, Adams sometimes forgot having made such defamatory remarks. Federalist George Cabot told
Wolcott that the president "denies that he ever called us [a] 'British faction.' . . .
[H]e does not recollect these intemperances and thinks himself grossly misunderstood or misrepresented."[39] House Speaker Sedgwick supplied Hamilton with similar anecdotes of the president belittling his Federalist colleagues and subordinates:
"He everywhere denounces the men . . . in whom he confided at the beginning of
his administration as an oligarchish faction." Adams noisily upbraided his cabinet,
Sedgwick said, telling them that "they cannot govern him" and that "this faction
and particularly Hamilton its head . . . intends to drive the country into a war with
France and a more intimate . . . union with Great Britain."[40] Fisher Ames said that
Adams went on in this vein "like one possessed."[41]

The image of a wrathful Adams, prone to temper tantrums, was not the invention of Alexander Hamilton, and he was far from alone in finding Adams agitated,
intemperate, and subject to violent fits. Congressman James A. Bayard of Delaware
told Hamilton that Adams was "liable to gusts of passion little short of frenzy,
which drive him beyond the control of any rational reflection. I speak of what I
have seen. At such moments the interest of those who support him or the interest

of the nation would be outweighed by a single impulse of rage."[42] The Republicans disseminated a similarly unflattering view of an irascible Adams. Jefferson recalled how Adams shouted profanities at his cabinet while storming around the room and "dashing and trampling his wig on the floor."[43] And Jefferson's tool, James T. Callender, assailed Adams in a string of essays collected into a book entitled *The Prospect Before Us:* "The reign of Mr. Adams has been one continued tempest of malignant passions. As president, he has never opened his lips or lifted his pen without threatening and scolding."[44] Callender got nine months in jail for his tirade, which had been modestly subsidized by Jefferson. The latter denied any involvement until Callender later publicized a clutch of telltale letters that Jefferson had written to him.

Many High Federalists who constituted Hamilton's wing of the party preferred Charles Cotesworth Pinckney as their presidential standard-bearer. An Oxford-educated lawyer from South Carolina—a southern state with a significant merchant class—Pinckney had risen to brigadier general during the Revolution and later attended the Constitutional Convention. His candidacy possessed powerful symbolic value, on account of his role in the XYZ Affair and his position as Hamilton's senior partner in the recent army. Pinckney's admirers, however, knew that they could hardly dump a sitting president and would have to settle for him as vice president. After Federalist congressmen caucused in Philadelphia on May 3, 1800, they decided that to "support *Adams and Pinckney,* equally, is the only thing that can possibly save us from the fangs of *Jefferson,*" as Hamilton wrote.[45] But if Pinckney received more votes than Adams in his native South Carolina, he could easily become president instead of vice president on the Federalist ticket. Adams saw the Pinckney boomlet as a thinly veiled ploy by Hamilton to replace him with someone more tractable to his wishes. Hamilton now regarded Adams as unstable and thought Pinckney had a more suitable temperament for the presidency. His preference for Pinckney was a risky strategy, since Adams was an incumbent president, and Americans were scarcely clamoring for Charles Cotesworth Pinckney.

So when Adams inaugurated his cabinet purge on May 5, 1800, it was not so much that he had just "discovered" Hamilton's control over his cabinet in a flash of light. Rather, he was alarmed by the realization of his own weakness as a candidate, as evidenced by the New York elections that week. One can scarcely fault Adams for cleansing his cabinet of mediocre or disloyal men, and he should have fired them a lot earlier. But he conducted the firings in an autocratic manner that led to a political bloodbath, widened the discord in Federalist ranks, and confirmed Hamilton's doubts about his unbecoming behavior.

The firings started on May 5 when Adams summoned the unwitting James McHenry from a dinner party. The Irish-born McHenry had been an inept secretary of war. He was a sensitive, mild-mannered man who wrote poetry and retained a lilt in his voice. As a cabinet member, McHenry had been unnerved by the president's mercurial moods and capricious judgment. He once said that whether Adams was "sportful, playful, witty, kind, cold, drunk, sober, angry, easy, stiff, jealous, cautious, confident, close, open," it was "almost always in the *wrong place* or to the *wrong persons.*"[46]

At first, Adams pretended that he had yanked McHenry from the dinner party to discuss some inconsequential War Department business. Then, as McHenry was leaving, Adams erupted in a furious monologue about Hamilton and the New York election and accused McHenry of conspiring against him. Against all evidence, Adams accused the indefatigable Hamilton of having sought a Federalist defeat in the New York election. A dumbfounded McHenry said, "I have heard no such conduct ascribed to General Hamilton and I cannot think it to be the case." To which Adams replied, "I know it, Sir, to be so and require you to inform yourself and report."[47] Then Adams unleashed a memorable volley:

> Hamilton is an intriguant—the greatest intriguant in the world—a man devoid of every moral principle—a bastard and as much a foreigner as Gallatin. Mr Jefferson is an infinitely better man, a wiser one, I am sure, and, if President, will act wisely. I know it and would rather be vice president under him or even minister resident at the Hague than indebted to such a being as Hamilton for the Presidency. . . . You are subservient to Hamilton, who ruled Washington and would still rule if he could. Washington saddled me with three secretaries who would control me, but I shall take care of that.[48]

This monologue went on and on. Adams faulted McHenry for not having forewarned him that Hamilton would materialize in Trenton the previous fall, charged him with incompetence in running his department, and mocked the notion that McHenry might know something about foreign affairs. "You cannot, sir, remain longer in office," he concluded.[49]

McHenry was shocked less at being sacked than by Adams's "indecorous and at times outrageous" behavior. He told his nephew that the president sometimes spoke "in such a manner of certain men and things as to persuade one that he was actually insane."[50] McHenry had just bought an expensive home in Washington, D.C., the federal district where the government would shortly move, and the firing cost him dearly. Nonetheless, he fell on his sword and resigned the next day.

Adams later expressed remorse at having "wounded the feelings" of McHenry, but Hamilton knew that McHenry was not the only one who felt the president's anger. "Most, if not all, his ministers and several distinguished members of the two houses of Congress have been humiliated by the effects of these gusts of passion," Hamilton wrote.[51] For years, McHenry licked his wounds. Later on, upon reading Adams's defense of his administration, he commented to Pickering, "Still in his own opinion the greatest man of the age, I see [Adams] will carry with him to the grave his vanity, his weaknesses, and follies, specimens of which we have so often witnessed and always endeavored to veil them from the public."[52]

Five days after expelling McHenry, Adams wrote to Timothy Pickering and tried to induce the secretary of state to tender his resignation. A former adjutant general in the Continental Army, the Harvard-educated Pickering was too ornery to be controlled by anyone, even Hamilton, who acknowledged something "warm and angular in his temper."[53] He had tenaciously supported the Alien and Sedition Acts and proved an unyielding opponent of the Paris peace mission. Abigail Adams described Pickering as a man "whose temper is sour and whose resentments are implacable," while her husband found him shifty eyed and ruthless, "a man in a mask, sometimes of silk, sometimes of iron, and sometimes of brass."[54] For Adams, Pickering had been Hamilton's main henchman in his cabinet and an object of special detestation. As a confirmed abolitionist, Pickering so admired Hamilton that he later tried his hand at an authorized biography of him. "Mr. Pickering would have made a good collector of the customs, but, he was not so well qualified for a Secretary of State," said Adams. "He was so devoted an idolater of Hamilton that he could not judge impartially of the sentiments and opinions of the President of the U[nited] States."[55] When Pickering received Adams's note, he refused to give him the satisfaction of resigning, so Adams cashiered him in an act he called "one of the most deliberate, virtuous and disinterested actions of my life."[56]

After three years of dealing with Adams at close quarters, Pickering circulated many stories about the president's unreserved venom for Hamilton. "Once when Col. Hamilton's name was mentioned to Mr Adams (who hated him) Adams said, 'I remember the young bastard when he entered the army.' "[57] Adams complained to Pickering that in accepting Hamilton as inspector general, the Senate had "crammed Hamilton down my throat."[58] Pickering believed that Adams feared Hamilton as a rival of superior talents and intelligence. Adams's loathing of Hamilton grew so visceral, Pickering said, that the mere mention of his name "seemed to be sufficient to rouse his sometimes dormant resentments. And it is probable that he hoarded up all the gossiping stories of Hamilton's amorous propensities."[59]

Adams's ouster of the two Hamiltonians produced jubilation among Republicans and led some Federalists to wonder whether that wasn't the real point of the exercise. Pickering thought the clumsy firings were part of a deal that Adams cut with Republican opponents who would "support his re-election to the presidency, provided he would make peace with France and remove Mr. McHenry and me from office."[60] The Federalist press echoed this theme, with *The Federalist* of Trenton explaining Adams's conduct as "the result of a political arrangement with Mr. Jefferson, an arrangement of the most mysterious and important complexion."[61]

The repercussions of Adams's firings were enduring. Combined with his simultaneous disbanding of the new army, Adams's actions touched off a vindictive, mean-spirited mood in Hamilton, who now said of the president, "The man is more mad than I ever thought him and I shall soon be led to say as wicked as he is mad."[62] Beyond his own injured vanity and thwarted ambition, Hamilton regarded Adams as playing a duplicitous game, and he preferred an honest enemy to a dishonest friend. "I will never more be responsible for [Adams] by my direct support, even though the consequence should be the election of *Jefferson*," Hamilton told Theodore Sedgwick. "If we must have an enemy at the head of the government, let it be one whom we can oppose and for whom we are not responsible."[63] Hamilton was congenitally incapable of compromise. Rather than make peace with John Adams, he was ready, if necessary, to blow up the Federalist party and let Jefferson become president.

The stream of personal abuse directed by Adams at Hamilton only made a bad situation worse. On June 2, McHenry sent Hamilton a confidential letter giving the unexpurgated version of his May 5 confrontation with Adams, complete with presidential references to Hamilton's bastardy and foreign birth. Hamilton was as sensitive as ever about his illegitimacy, especially after a Republican newspaper in Boston warned him that "the mode of your descent from a dubious father, in an English island," would bar any pretensions he might have to the presidency.[64] Hamilton must have winced at this and quickly drafted a letter to an old wartime comrade, Major William Jackson. "Never was there a more ungenerous persecution of any man than of myself," Hamilton began. "Not only the worst constructions are put upon my conduct as a public man but it seems my birth is the subject of the most humiliating criticism."[65] Hamilton then furnished the only account he ever left of his parentage, telling of his father's chronic business troubles and his mother's marriage to Johann Michael Lavien and subsequent divorce. He lied pathetically when he said that his parents had married but that the union was rendered technically illegal by the terms of his mother's earlier divorce. With more than a dash of wounded pride, he added, "The truth is that on the question who my parents were, I have better pretensions than most of those who in this country plume themselves on ancestry."[66]

Instead of sending the statement to Jackson, Hamilton showed it to James McHenry, who gave him wise advice:

> I sincerely believe that there is not one of your friends who have paid the least attention to the insinuations attempted to be cast on the legitimacy of your

birth or who would care or respect you less were all that your enemies say or impute on this head true. I think it will be most prudent and magnanimous to leave any explanation on the subject to your biographer and the discretion of those friends to whom you have communicated the facts.[67]

That someone of Hamilton's elevated stature felt obligated to defend his birth at this stage of his career suggests how harrowing it must have been to hear of Adams's constant digs at his upbringing.

After McHenry and Pickering were dismissed, Hamilton was emboldened to go further with his plans to strip Adams of the presidency. Most Federalists balked at opposing Adams, but some warmed to the idea of dropping a vote for him here and there and giving the edge to his running mate, Charles Cotesworth Pinckney. That June, Hamilton sounded out Federalist opinion during a three-week tour that he made to New England under the guise of saying adieu to his crumbling army. In reality, it was a vote-getting campaign for Pinckney. In Oxford, Massachusetts, Hamilton reviewed a brigade and "expressed an unequivocal approbation of the discipline of the army and beheld with pleasure the progress of subordination and attention to dress and decorum," a Boston paper reported.[68] At moments, the tour seemed a sentimental version of Washington's farewell from the Continental Army. At Oxford, under a flag-draped colonnade, with a backdrop of martial music, Hamilton threw a dinner for his outgoing officers. After toasting Washington's memory, Hamilton gave a talk that "suffused every cheek" and showed "the agitation of every bosom."[69]

Hamilton's progress was tracked by a watchful Republican press. The *Aurora* told readers that Hamilton was traveling with "well-known aristocrats," and when their carriage broke down in Boston the paper construed this mishap as a portent of "the downfall of aristocracy in the U[nited] States."[70] Hamilton must have felt he was riding high when he was honored by an adulatory dinner in Boston that included almost every Federalist of importance in the state. "The company was the most respectable ever assembled in this town on a similar occasion," said one paper.[71] Everywhere he went, Hamilton conjured up disturbing images of a French-style revolution in America, even telling one listener that it did not matter who became the next president because "he did not expect his head to remain four years longer upon his shoulders unless it was at the head of a victorious army."[72] This sounded like scare talk, but Hamilton actually believed these overblown fantasies of impending Jacobin carnage in America.

Spending the summer and early fall in Quincy, John and Abigail Adams understood the political agenda behind Hamilton's mission. Quite understandably, John

Adams became so consumed by anger against Hamilton, said Fisher Ames, that he was "implacable" against him and used language that was "bitter even to outrage and swearing."[73] Abigail disparaged Hamilton as "the little cock sparrow general" and described his trip as "merely an electioneering business to feel the pulse of the New England states and impress those upon whom he could have any influence to vote for Pinckney."[74] For Abigail, Hamilton was "impudent and brazen faced," an upstart next to her husband.[75] She derided Hamilton and his followers as "boys of yesterday who were unhatched and unfledged when the venerable character they are striving to pull down was running every risk of life and property to serve and save a country of which these beings are unworthy members."[76] This seemed to overlook Hamilton's valor on many Revolutionary War battlefields. Increasingly, John and Abigail Adams pinned a new conspiratorial tag on Hamilton and his followers, branding them the Essex Junto. These supposed plotters, many of them born in Essex County, Massachusetts, included Fisher Ames, George Cabot, Benjamin Goodhue, Stephen Higginson, John Lowell, and Timothy Pickering.

As Hamilton's trip progressed, it was something less than the triumphal tour he had expected. He declared snobbishly that the "first class men" were for Pinckney and the "second class men" for Adams, but he encountered more of the latter than he bargained for.[77] Many Adams supporters told Hamilton bluntly that if he persisted in trying to elect Pinckney, they would withhold votes from him to guarantee an Adams victory. Bruised by his brushes with Adams, Hamilton was deaf to these warnings. An incomparable bureaucrat and master theoretician, he had no comparable gift for practical politics.

The most striking example of Hamilton's maladroit approach came when he lobbied Arthur Fenner, the Rhode Island governor. Fenner said that Hamilton showed up at his home, grandly surrounded by a retinue of colonels and generals, and instantly broached the topic of the presidential election. Hamilton stressed that only Pinckney would have broad support in both the north and south and that Adams couldn't be reelected. Fenner turned on him hotly: "I then asked him what Mr. Adams had done that he should be tipped out of the tail of the cart."[78] Fenner lauded the peace mission to France and praised the comeuppances of McHenry and Pickering. "Adams is out of the question," Hamilton insisted to Fenner. "It is Pinckney and Jefferson."[79] After years of painting Thomas Jefferson as the devil incarnate, Hamilton suddenly preferred him to John Adams, again showing that both Hamilton and Adams had lost all perspective in their rages against each other.

Impervious to criticism, Hamilton had embarked on a mad escapade to elect Pinckney, and it was bootless for friends to warn him that he had started a dangerous vendetta. Visiting Rhode Island that July, John Rutledge, Jr., a Federalist congressman from South Carolina, heard nasty scuttlebutt about Hamilton. Many

Rhode Island residents, Rutledge informed Hamilton, are "jealous and suspicious of you in the extreme, saying . . . that your opposition to Mr. A[dams] has its source in private pique. If you had been appointed commander in chief on the death of Gen[era]l W[ashington] you would have continued one of Mr A[dams]'s partisans. . . . [Y]ou are endeavoring to give success to Gen[era]l P[inckney]'s election because he will administer the government under your direction."[80] Although several associates warned Hamilton that his lobbying campaign was backfiring, he did not heed them. He had drawn all the wrong lessons from his peregrinations through New England and decided that he would have to enlighten benighted voters to the manifold failings of John Adams. And he would do so by the method that he had employed throughout his career at critical moments: a blazing polemic in which he would lay out his case in crushing detail.

THIRTY-SIX

IN A VERY
BELLIGERENT HUMOR

I n writing an intemperate indictment of John Adams, Hamilton committed a
form of political suicide that blighted the rest of his career. As shown with "The
Reynolds Pamphlet," he had a genius for the self-inflicted wound and was
capable of marching blindly off a cliff—traits most pronounced in the late 1790s.
Gouverneur Morris once commented that one of Hamilton's chief characteristics
was "the pertinacious adherence to opinions he had once formed."[1]

Hamilton found it hard to refrain from vendettas. He would be devoured by dislike of someone, brood about it, then yield to the catharsis of discharging his venom
in print. "The frankness of his nature was such that he could not easily avoid the expression of his sentiments of public men and measures and his extreme candor in
such cases was sometimes productive of personal inconveniences," observed friend
Nathaniel Pendleton.[2] Even Eliza in after years conceded that her adored husband
had "a character perhaps too frank and independent for a democratic people."[3]

So long as Hamilton was inspector general, he had stifled his pent-up anger
against Adams, but by July 1800 his military service had ended and he could gratify
his need to lash out at the president. He would repay all the snubs and slurs he had
suffered, all the galling references to his bastardy. Once McHenry and Pickering
were fired, Hamilton did not simply commiserate with them but encouraged them
to preserve internal papers that would expose the president. "Allow me to suggest,"
he told Pickering, "that you ought to take with you copies and extracts of all such
documents as will enable you to *explain* both *Jefferson and Adams*."[4] Pickering encouraged the project that Hamilton meditated: "I have been contemplating the importance of a bold and frank exposure of A[dams]. Perhaps I may have it in my

power to furnish some facts."[5] Suspecting that Adams and Jefferson had sealed a secret election pact, Hamilton told McHenry, "Pray favour me with as many circumstances as may appear to you to show the probability of coalitions with Mr. Jefferson[,] . . . which are spoken of."[6]

Hamilton ended up with the cooperation of the discontented cabinet members, including the one member of the triumvirate who had avoided the purge, Oliver Wolcott, Jr., the capable if unimaginative treasury secretary. Even though Adams thought Wolcott more loyal than McHenry and Pickering, Wolcott considered the president a powder keg. Of Adams, he told Fisher Ames, "We know the temper of his mind to be revolutionary, violent and vindictive. . . . [H]is passions and selfishness would continually gain strength."[7] Wolcott deprecated Adams's peace overtures to France as a mere "game of diplomacy" designed to court votes.[8] At moments, however, Wolcott grew ambivalent about the idea of Hamilton exposing Adams, arguing that "the people [already] believe that their president is crazy."[9] In the end, though, convinced that Adams would ruin the government, Wolcott told Hamilton that somebody had to write a "few paragraphs exposing the folly" of those who had idealized Adams as a noble, independent spirit.[10]

Thus, in his massive indictment of Adams, Hamilton drew on abundant information provided by McHenry, Pickering, and Wolcott about presidential behavior behind closed doors. Hamilton knew that the three would be charged with treachery by Adams, but he thought his pamphlet would forfeit all credibility without such documentation. Stories about Adams's high-strung behavior, if legion in High Federalist circles, were little known outside of them. Hamilton also wanted to stress the mistreatment of cabinet members, lest readers dismiss his critique of Adams as mere personal pique over the disbanded army. Adams was duly shocked by the confidences that his ex–cabinet members betrayed. "Look into Hamilton's pamphlet," he told a friend. "Observe the pretended information of things which could only have passed between me and my cabinet."[11] In these revelations, Adams saw patent "treachery and perfidy."[12]

By early August, Hamilton was in a fighting mood. On July 12, the *Aurora* printed yet another article accusing him—"the *morally chaste* and *virtuous* head" of the Treasury Department—of having devised a "corrupt system" of controlling the press and government employees while in office.[13] Hamilton was so offended by this interminable nonsense that he told Wolcott he might institute a libel suit: "You see I am in a very belligerent humor."[14]

Just how belligerent was already clear on August 1, 1800, when the hotheaded Hamilton composed an extraordinary letter to the president. All summer, Hamilton had chafed at reports that Adams was branding him a British lackey. Now he wrote to the president in peremptory terms.

It has been repeatedly mentioned to me that you have on different occasions asserted the existence of a *British Faction* in this Country, embracing a number of leading or influential characters of the *Federal Party* (as usually denominated) and that you have named me . . . as one of this description of persons. . . . I must, Sir, take it for granted that you cannot have made such assertions or insinuations without being willing to avow them and to assign the reasons to a party who may conceive himself injured by them.[15]

Hamilton demanded the evidence behind these statements. As Adams would have known from the phraseology, Hamilton was, implausibly, commencing an affair of honor with the president of the United States. Many duels began with such imperious demands for explanations of purported slander. Adams did not answer the letter because of its insolent tone; perhaps he also knew that it would be difficult to substantiate his accusations. Hamilton, too, must have realized that he would be rebuffed by Adams. On October 1, he sent a follow-up note to Adams, calling the allegations against him "a base, wicked, and cruel calumny, destitute even of a plausible pretext to excuse the folly or mask the depravity which must have dictated it."[16] This was shockingly offensive language to use with a president and terminated all possibility of future contact between the two men.

Once launched upon a course of action, the combative Hamilton could never stop. As Federalists speculated about his upcoming open letter, prominent party members had misgivings. George Cabot told Hamilton that a careful, well-tempered critique of Adams might tip the balance toward Pinckney, but he thought it was too late for the Federalists to abandon Adams altogether. He feared that Hamilton would go to extremes and only excite jealousy and discord. "Although I think some good [may] be derived from an exhibition of Mr Adams's misconduct," Cabot wrote, "yet I am well persuaded that you may do better than to put your name to it. This might give it an interest with men who need no such interest, but it will be converted to a new proof that you are a *dangerous man*."[17] The wavering Wolcott also warned Hamilton that his letter might breed divisions among Federalists, but he pressed on undeterred.

Hamilton did not seem to foresee that his anti-Adams pamphlet would prove so sensational. At first, he conceived of it as a private letter that would circulate among influential Federalists in New England and especially South Carolina, where he hoped electors might give the edge to Pinckney over Adams. What he did not anticipate was that his letter would soon be purloined and excerpted by the *Aurora* and other hostile Republican papers.

How did they gain access to Hamilton's circular letter? Historians have tended to finger Burr, who obtained a copy and provided extracts to selected newspapers. In fact, the ubiquitous John Beckley, who leaked the Maria Reynolds pamphlet, may have been the conduit to the *Aurora*. Republicans knew that publishing Hamilton's letter would deepen the rift in the Federalist party. Beckley gloated over Hamilton's faulty judgment and hoped his letter would deal the coup de grâce to his career. "Vainly does he essay to seize the mantle of Washington and cloak the moral atrocities of a life spent in wickedness and which must terminate in shame and dishonor," Beckley told a friend.[18] The president's nephew, William Shaw, confirmed that the pamphlet had been "immediately sent to Beckley at Philadelphia, the former clerk of the House of Rep[resentative]s, who caused extracts to be reprinted in the *Aurora*, through which medium it was first made known to the public."[19]

The appearance of juicy passages in the *Aurora* and other Republican papers forced Hamilton to revise his plans and publish his letter openly in pamphlet form. He preferred that people read the entire document rather than portions selectively culled by his enemies. Among other things, Hamilton's pamphlet was his riposte to Adams's failure to acknowledge his challenging letter. So, contrary to his usual practice of anonymous publishing, Hamilton knew that, as a man of honor, he had to sign his name boldly to the document. The fifty-four-page pamphlet was published on October 24, 1800, while Hamilton was arguing a case before the New York Supreme Court in Albany. Instead of the letter being restricted to specific localities, it was now broadcast to a national audience.

In "The Reynolds Pamphlet," Hamilton had exposed only his own folly. In the Adams pamphlet, he displayed both his own errant judgment *and* Adams's instability. An elated Madison wrote to Jefferson, "I rejoice with you that Republicanism is likely to be so *completely* triumphant."[20] William Duane, the *Aurora* editor, exulted that the "pamphlet has done more mischief to the parties concerned than all the labors" of his paper.[21] The Federalists were no less staggered by Hamilton's folly. Noah Webster said that Hamilton's "ambition, pride, and overbearing temper" threatened to make him "the evil genius of this country."[22] Condemnation of the pamphlet echoed down the generations even among the most admiring Hamiltonians. Henry Cabot Lodge labeled the open letter "a piece of passionate folly," which coming on "the eve of a close and doubtful contest for the presidency was simple madness."[23]

The bulk of the *Letter from Alexander Hamilton, Concerning the Public Conduct and Character of John Adams, Esq. President of the United States* is a petulant survey of John Adams's life and presidency. The author presented a tale of growing disenchantment with a man he once admired: "I was one of that numerous class who had conceived a high veneration for Mr. Adams on account of the part he acted in the first stages of our revolution."[24] However, in the early 1780s, while Hamilton served in Congress, Adams had shed his halo as he displayed "the unfortunate foibles of a vanity without bounds and a jealousy capable of discoloring every object."[25] He described the Adams presidency as "a heterogeneous compound of right and wrong, of wisdom and error."[26] While granting that Adams was a fair theorist, he criticized his handling of the peace mission to France, told how he routinely overrode cabinet members, and recounted the "humiliating censures and bitter reproaches" meted out to James McHenry.[27]

Not content to catalog wrongs done to administration members, Hamilton made the mistake of reviewing his own personal grievances. He complained that the president had not named him commander in chief after Washington's death and cited sources that "Mr. Adams has repeatedly indulged himself in virulent and indecent abuse of me . . . has denominated me a man destitute of every moral principle . . . [and] has stigmatized me as the leader of a British Faction."[28] Such special pleading made Hamilton appear petty and vengeful, more a self-absorbed man seeking personal vindication than an upstanding party leader.

The final section of the pamphlet seemed particularly absurd. Having pummeled Adams for dotty behavior, he then endorsed him for president and advised electors to vote equally for Adams and Pinckney. If Federalists stayed united behind these two men, he predicted, they would "increase the probability of excluding a third candidate of whose unfitness all sincere Federalists are convinced"—namely, Jefferson.[29] For a man of Hamilton's incomparable intellect, the pamphlet was a crazily botched job, an extended tantrum in print.

In his sketch of Adams, it must be said, Hamilton only repeated what he had seen and heard. Adams certainly was not "mad," as Hamilton alleged, but he *had* given way to numerous instances of profane and inappropriate behavior. There had been raving and cursing, indecent comments, and loss of self-control. Hamilton reiterated criticisms that Jefferson, Franklin, and others had made privately about Adams and synthesized them with observations from cabinet members and other Federalists who had witnessed the president's oddly changeable behavior. Joseph Ellis has written that, despite Hamilton's political prejudices, "he effectively framed the question that has haunted Adams's reputation ever since: how was it that one of the leading lights in the founding generation seemed to exhibit such massive lapses in personal stability?"[30]

Some Federalists certified the accuracy of the Adams portrait. Benjamin Goodhue of Massachusetts saluted Hamilton's courage: "We have been actuated by a pernicious policy in being so silent respecting Mr. A[dams]. The public have been left thereby to form opinions favorable to him and of course unfavorable to those who were the objects of his mad displeasure."[31] Charles Carroll, a former senator from Maryland, likewise sang the letter's praises: "The assertions of the pamphlet, I take it for granted, are true. And, if true, surely it must be admitted that Mr Adams is not fit to be president and his unfitness should be made known to the electors and the public. I conceive it a species of treason to conceal from the public his incapacity."[32] Still other Federalists, such as William Plumer of New Hampshire, said sotto voce what Hamilton had the temerity to trumpet in print: "Mr. Adams's conduct in office, in many instances, has been very irregular and highly improper. The studied neglect and naked contempt with which he has treated the heads of departments afford strong evidence of his being governed by caprice or that age has enfeebled his mental faculties."[33]

Those siding with Hamilton composed a small minority of politicos. Most Federalists and all Republicans understood that the extended tirade against Adams made Hamilton look hypocritical and woefully indiscreet, especially when combined with the Maria Reynolds pamphlet. Robert Troup said that Hamilton's letter had been universally condemned: "In point of imprudence, it is coupled with the pamphlet formerly published by the general respecting himself and not a man in the whole circle of our friends but condemns it. . . . Our enemies are universally in triumph."[34] Only something "little short of a miracle" could now stop Jefferson from becoming president, Troup feared, and he had little doubt that the pamphlet would sharply erode Hamilton's influence among the Federalist faithful.[35] At the other end of the political spectrum, Jefferson also believed that the tract dealt a mortal blow to Adams's chances for reelection.

At first, Hamilton was caught off guard by news that his private letter would be widely circulated, but then he professed pleasure. Like Adams, he was blinded by pride. George Cabot told Hamilton that even his most "respectable friends" faulted him for displaying "egotism and vanity" in the publication.[36] When Troup said he dreaded the impact on the Federalist cause, Hamilton insisted that it was being read with "prodigious avidity" and would be "productive of good."[37] Hamilton had departed so far from common sense that he solicited "new anecdotes" from McHenry and Pickering for a revised, expanded edition, even though McHenry had been shocked to see Hamilton print his stories without permission.[38] Oliver Wolcott, Jr., was so alarmed about the projected update that he goaded McHenry into writing a letter that "pointedly advised" Hamilton against any such move.[39] Hamilton reconsidered, and no new edition appeared.

Without question, Adams was correct in not dignifying the pamphlet with a response. "This pamphlet I regret more on account of its author than on my own because I am confident it will do him more harm than me," he told a friend, while reviving his bizarre accusation that Hamilton had tried to blackmail Washington by threatening to publish "pamphlets upon his character and conduct."[40] For Adams to have responded publicly on the eve of national elections would only have aggravated turmoil in Federalist ranks. Abigail Adams privately mocked Hamilton with epithets often applied to her husband and derided his "weakness, vanity and ambitious views."[41]

Adams did compose a refutation of Hamilton's *Letter* but then let it gather dust in the drawer. He was no more capable of long-term silence than Hamilton, however, though he waited until after Hamilton's death. The manner of Hamilton's dying did not faze Adams, who said that he would not permit his "character to lie under infamous calumnies because the author of them, with a pistol bullet through his spinal marrow, died a penitent."[42] In 1809, Adams undertook an elaborate justification of his presidency in *The Boston Patriot*. The series continued almost weekly for three years, and Adams proved every bit as volatile as Hamilton had long ago alleged. He rejected Hamilton's pamphlet as being "written from his mere imagination, from confused rumors, or downright false information."[43] He was not content to undo the work of the pamphlet and again stooped to personal characterizations as spiteful as anything Hamilton had written against him. He again criticized him for being foreign born, for knowing nothing of the American character, for not being a *real* patriot, for being an incorrigible rake, for being immature, for lacking military knowledge, even for being a shiftless treasury secretary who spent his time scribbling "ambitious reports" while underlings carried out the real departmental business. Like most people, Hamilton and Adams were preternaturally sensitive to flaws in the other that they themselves possessed.

For all their fratricidal warfare, the Federalists ran a surprisingly close race for the presidency. Jefferson and Burr tied with seventy-three electoral votes apiece, while Adams and Pinckney trailed with sixty-five and sixty-four votes respectively. As expected, New England unanimously backed Adams, while Jefferson captured virtually the entire south. The New York City elections in April 1800, which had pitted Hamilton against Burr in riveting political drama, had the expected decisive influence. New York cast its twelve electoral votes in a solid bloc for the Republican ticket, giving it the edge. David McCullough has noted the rich irony that "Jefferson, the apostle of agrarian America who loathed cities, owed his ultimate political triumph to New York."[44]

But John Adams never doubted that Hamilton's pamphlet had dealt a fatal blow to his candidacy. He later said, "if the single purpose had been to defeat the President, no more propitious moment could have been chosen."[45] On another occasion, Adams said that Hamilton and his band had "killed themselves and . . . indicted me for the murder."[46] Scholars have questioned the pamphlet's direct impact on the vote. In many of the sixteen states, electors had been chosen by state legislatures whose composition had been determined long before Hamilton perpetrated his pamphlet. And the results in states that had not yet selected their electors did not deviate significantly from earlier predictions. Hamilton had hoped that his efforts might boost Charles C. Pinckney in his native South Carolina, but Republicans swept the state.

Many observers thought Hamilton had frittered away his prestige and that his letter had backfired. "I do not believe it has altered a single vote in the late election," Robert Troup remarked, adding that it had exposed Hamilton's character, not Adams's, as *radically deficient in discretion.*"[47] The Federalists had not dropped votes for Adams to install Pinckney as president, as Hamilton had urged—a precipitate fall from grace for Hamilton, who had lost his luster and once unchallenged power over Federalist colleagues. However peripheral in the election, Hamilton's letter almost certainly hastened the collapse of the Federalists as a national political force. Adams was sure that Hamilton's "ambition, intrigues, and caucuses have ruined the cause of federalism."[48] The Federalists lingered for another decade or two, but outside of New England they were a spent force. Their decline eliminated any chance that Hamilton would ever regain a top post, much less the presidency.

Why did Hamilton contribute to this disarray among the Federalists? As usual, he thought the country was careening toward a national emergency, either a French invasion or a civil war, and was convinced that Adams would adulterate federalism. Better to purge Adams and let Jefferson govern for a while than to water down the party's ideological purity with compromises. "If the cause is to be sacrificed to a weak and perverse man," Hamilton said of Adams's leadership of the Federalists, "I withdraw from the party and act upon my own ground."[49] Doubtless Hamilton thought that he could pick up the pieces of a shattered Federalist party. What he overlooked was that in trying to wreck Adams's career, he would wreck his own and that the Federalists would never be resurrected from the ashes.

The personal recriminations of the 1800 election can obscure the huge ideological shift that reshaped American politics and made the Republicans the majority party. In races for the House of Representatives, where Hamilton's *Letter* played no part, the Republicans took control by a more lopsided margin—sixty-five Republicans to forty-one Federalists—than in their presidential victory. The people had registered their dismay with a long litany of unpopular Federalist actions: the Jay Treaty, the Alien and Sedition Acts, the truculent policy toward France, the vast army being formed under Hamilton and the taxes levied to support it. The 1800 elections revealed, for the first time, the powerful centrist pull of American politics—the electorate's tendency to rein in anything perceived as extreme.

The stress placed upon the Adams-Hamilton feud pointed up a deeper problem in the Federalist party, one that may explain its ultimate failure to survive: the elitist nature of its politics. James McHenry complained to Oliver Wolcott, Jr., of their adherents, "They write private letters to each other, but do nothing to give a proper direction to the public mind."[50] The Federalists issued appeals to the electorate but did not try to mobilize a broad-based popular movement. Hamilton wanted to lead the electorate and provide expert opinion instead of consulting popular opinion. He took tough, uncompromising stands and gloried in abstruse ideas in a political culture that pined for greater simplicity. Alexander Hamilton triumphed as a doer and thinker, not as a leader of the average voter. He was simply too unashamedly brainy to appeal to the masses. Fisher Ames observed of Hamilton that the common people don't want leaders "whom they see elevated by nature and education so far above their heads."[51]

The intellectual spoilsport among the founding fathers, Hamilton never believed in the perfectibility of human nature and regularly violated what became the first commandment of American politics: thou shalt always be optimistic when addressing the electorate. He shrank from the campaign rhetoric that flattered Americans as the most wonderful, enlightened people on earth and denied that they had anything to learn from European societies. He was incapable of the resolutely uplifting themes that were to become mandatory in American politics. The first great skeptic of American exceptionalism, he refused to believe that the country was exempt from the sober lessons of history.

Where Hamilton looked at the world through a dark filter and had a better sense of human limitations, Jefferson viewed the world through a rose-colored prism and had a better sense of human potentialities. Both Hamilton and Jefferson believed in democracy, but Hamilton tended to be more suspicious of the governed and Jefferson of the governors. A strange blend of dreamy idealist and manipulative politician, Jefferson was a virtuoso of the sunny phrases and hopeful themes that became staples of American politics. He continually paid homage to the wisdom of the masses. Before the 1800 election, Federalist Harrison Gray Otis saw Jefferson's approach as "a very sweet smelling incense which flattery offers to vanity and folly at the shrine of falsehood."[52] John Quincy Adams also explained Jefferson's presidential triumph by saying that he had been "pimping to the popular passions."[53] To Jefferson we owe the self-congratulatory language of Fourth of July oratory, the evangelical conviction that America serves as a beacon to all humanity. Jefferson told John Dickinson, "Our revolution and its consequences will ameliorate the condition of man over a great portion of the globe."[54] At least on paper, Jefferson possessed a more all-embracing view of democracy than Hamilton, who was always frightened by a sense of the fickle and fallible nature of the masses.

Having said that, one must add that the celebration of the 1800 election as the simple triumph of "progressive" Jeffersonians over "reactionary" Hamiltonians greatly overstates the case. The three terms of Federalist rule had been full of dazzling accomplishments that Republicans, with their extreme apprehension of federal power, could never have achieved. Under the tutelage of Washington, Adams, and Hamilton, the Federalists had bequeathed to American history a sound federal government with a central bank, a funded debt, a high credit rating, a tax system, a customs service, a coast guard, a navy, and many other institutions that would guarantee the strength to preserve liberty. They activated critical constitutional doctrines that gave the American charter flexibility, forged the bonds of nationhood, and lent an energetic tone to the executive branch in foreign and domestic policy. Hamilton, in particular, bound the nation through his fiscal programs in a way that no Republican could have matched. He helped to establish the rule of law and the culture of capitalism at a time when a revolutionary utopianism and a flirtation with the French Revolution still prevailed among too many Jeffersonians. With their reverence for states' rights, abhorrence of central authority, and cramped interpretation of the Constitution, Republicans would have found it difficult, if not impossible, to achieve these historic feats.

Hamilton had promoted a forward-looking agenda of a modern nation-state with a market economy and an affirmative view of central government. His meritocratic vision allowed greater scope in the economic sphere for the individual liberties that Jefferson defended so eloquently in the political sphere. It was no coincidence that the allegedly aristocratic and reactionary Federalists contained the overwhelming majority of active abolitionists of the period. Elitists they might be, but they were an open, fluid elite, based on merit and money, not on birth and breeding—the antithesis of the southern plantation system. It was the northern economic system that embodied the mix of democracy and capitalism that was to constitute the essence of America in the long run. By no means did the 1800 election represent the unalloyed triumph of good over evil or of commoners over the wellborn.

The 1800 triumph of Republicanism also meant the ascendancy of the slaveholding south. Three Virginia slaveholders—Jefferson, Madison, and Monroe—were to control the White House for the next twenty-four years. These aristocratic exponents of "democracy" not only owned hundreds of human beings but profited from the Constitution's least democratic features: the legality of slavery and the ability of southern states to count three-fifths of their captive populations in calculating their electoral votes. (Without this so-called federal ratio, John Adams would have defeated Thomas Jefferson in 1800.) The Constitution did more than just tolerate slavery: it actively rewarded it. Timothy Pickering was to inveigh against "Negro presidents and Negro congresses"—that is, presidents and congresses who owed their power to the three-fifths rule.[55] This bias inflated southern power against the north and disfigured the democracy so proudly proclaimed by the Jeffersonians. Slaveholding presidents from the south occupied the presidency for approximately fifty of the seventy-two years following Washington's first inauguration. Many of these slaveholding populists were celebrated by posterity as tribunes of the common people. Meanwhile, the self-made Hamilton, a fervent abolitionist and a staunch believer in meritocracy, was villainized in American history textbooks as an apologist of privilege and wealth.

THIRTY-SEVEN

DEADLOCK

Hamilton, Adams, and other Federalists had proved far more realistic about the course of the French Revolution than their credulous Republican counterparts. On dozens of occasions, Hamilton had prophesied that the revolutionary chaos would culminate in a dictatorship. This forecast had been borne out on November 9, 1799, when Napoleon Bonaparte grabbed power in a coup d'état that made him first consul of the French Republic. When Talleyrand, the eternal foreign minister, declared that it was time to settle differences with America, Napoleon agreed.

On October 3, 1800, the American envoys concluded a treaty with France at Château Môrtefontaine, ending the Quasi-War, which had so bedeviled the Adams presidency. Most Americans had grown tired of the undeclared war and were happy to close this chapter. The diplomatic breakthrough was not reported in American newspapers until November, and the treaty itself arrived at the Senate in mid-December. Unlike many die-hard Federalists, Hamilton favored the treaty, or at least realized the futility of opposing it, telling Gouverneur Morris that "it will be of consequence to the Federal cause in future to be able to say, 'The Federal Administration steered the vessel through all the storms raised by the contentions of Europe into a peaceable and safe port.'"[1] Hamilton was, shall we say, a belated convert to this more peaceable approach to the conflict.

For John Adams, who had defied the High Federalists and stuck to his policy, it was a stunning vindication of his stubborn faith in diplomacy against Hamilton's saber rattling. He established a vital precedent that timely, well-executed diplomacy can forestall the need for military force. In fact, Adams had won such a major diplomatic victory that many historians have tended to condone the antic, unreasonable behavior that preceded it. Even Hamilton biographer Broadus Mitchell has called Adams "the hero of the piece. His annoying inconsistencies drop away because when resolution was needed he was right. He saved the country from war with France as Hamilton and others had saved it shortly before from war with Britain."[2] Adams described the preservation of peace during his presidency as the "most splendid diamond in my crown" and requested that the following words be incised on his tombstone: "Here lies John Adams, who took upon himself the responsibility of peace with France in the year 1800."[3] Adams later cited the "diabolical intrigues" of Hamilton and his colleagues, contending that he had pursued negotiations with France "at the expense of all my consequence in the world and their unanimous and immortal hatred."[4]

Adams's success came too late to sway the presidential election and therefore bore a bittersweet flavor. The bad timing only exacerbated his sense of being unlucky, unloved, and unappreciated. His admirers have echoed his view that he had acted in a noble, self-sacrificing manner, but his motives were not entirely saintly. He had adopted a hawkish stance toward France when that was popular early in his administration and then taken a more conciliatory posture to curry favor with Republicans as the 1800 election beckoned. By that point, his moderation was popular with electors in some critical states. George Clinton said that Adams having "sent a special mission to France and effected a peace came very near preventing the election of Mr. Jefferson to the Presidency. If the Republicans had not already named Jefferson for president, we should have supported Mr. Adams."[5] The peace mission to France was unquestionably the supreme triumph of the Adams presidency, but it testifies to political agility as well as wisdom.

By mid-December 1800, it was evident that Jefferson and Burr would garner an equal number of electoral votes, throwing the presidential contest into a lame-duck House of Representatives that was still dominated by Federalists. While no constitutional mechanism differentiated between the votes for president and vice president, it had been understood among Republicans that Jefferson was the presidential candidate. Afraid of jeopardizing Burr's chances for the vice presidency, Jefferson had held back from asking Republican electors to drop a few votes for Burr to insure that he himself would come out on top. At first, Burr reacted to the tie vote in a gracious, honorable way, just as Jefferson had expected. He wrote to Republican Samuel Smith and renounced the sacrilegious thought of challenging Jefferson for the presidency: "It is highly improbable that I shall have an equal number of votes with Mr. Jefferson, but if such should be the result, every man who knows me ought to know that I should utterly disclaim all competition."[6]

At least one knowledgeable observer doubted that Burr's intentions were quite so benign. Hamilton was privy to rumors that Federalists in Congress might prefer Burr to Jefferson. So when he learned of the projected tie vote, he fired off a letter to Oliver Wolcott, Jr., to nip trouble in the bud:

> As to *Burr,* there is nothing in his favour. His private character is not de-
> fended by his most partial friends. He is bankrupt beyond redemption, except
> by the plunder of his country. His public principles have no other spring or
> aim than his own aggrandizement. . . . If he can, he will certainly disturb our
> institutions to secure to himself *permanent power* and with it *wealth*. He is
> truly the *Catiline* of America.[7]

This was a powerful indictment: in ancient Rome, Catiline was notorious for his personal dissipation and treacherous schemes to undermine the republic. In order to stop Burr, Hamilton decided to back his perpetual rival, Thomas Jefferson, telling Wolcott that Jefferson "is by far not so dangerous a man and he has pretensions to character."[8] He also thought that Jefferson was much more talented than the overrated Burr and that the latter was "far more cunning than wise, far more dexterous than able. In my opinion he is inferior in real ability to Jefferson."[9] Hamilton's endorsement of Jefferson was the most improbable reversal in an improbable career. Nobody enjoyed Hamilton's embarrassing predicament in having to choose between his two enemies more than John Adams. "The very man— the very two men—of all the world that he was most jealous of are now placed above him," Adams said with pardonable gloating.[10]

Even in the thick of the campaign that summer, Hamilton had noted Burr's electoral intrigues in New Jersey, Rhode Island, and Vermont and surmised that he was only feigning deference to Jefferson. Burr alone had engaged in open electioneering, while Jefferson, Adams, and Pinckney stuck to the gentlemanly protocol of avoiding the stump. The alliance between Burr and Jefferson had been a marriage of convenience to pull New York into the Republican camp. "I never indeed thought him an honest, frank-dealing man," Jefferson later said of Burr, "but considered him as a crooked gun or other perverted machine, whose aim or shot you could never be sure of."[11] That Jefferson twice recruited this crooked gun for his running mate indicates just how cynical he could be. Burr, in turn, still believed that he had been betrayed by Jefferson in the 1796 election, when he got only one vote in Virginia. "As to my Jeff," he wrote with mordant whimsy, "after what happened at the last election (et tu Brute!) I was really averse to having my name in question . . . but being so, it is most obvious that I should not choose to be trifled with."[12]

Despite Burr's declaration that he would yield the presidency to Jefferson, Federalist leaders pelted Hamilton with letters about the expediency of supporting Burr and ending Virginia's political hegemony. Because Burr lusted after money and power, they thought they could strike a bargain with him. They worried less about Burr's loose morals than about what they perceived as Jefferson's atheism (clergymen were telling their congregations that if Jefferson became president, they would need to hide their Bibles) and his doctrinaire views. Better an opportunist than a dangerous ideologue, many Federalists thought. Fisher Ames feared that Jefferson was "absurd enough to believe his own nonsense," while Burr might at least "impart vigor to the country."[13] John Marshall and others thought Burr a safer choice than Jefferson, who might try to recast the Constitution to conform to his "Jacobin" tenets.

If forced to choose, Hamilton preferred a man with wrong principles to one devoid of any. "There is no circumstance which has occurred in the course of our political affairs that has given me so much pain as the idea that Mr. Burr might be elevated to the Presidency by the means of the Federalists," Hamilton told Wolcott. If the party elected Burr, it would be exposed "to the disgrace of a defeat in an attempt to elevate to the first place in the government one of the worst men in the community."[14] Hamilton had never spoken about Adams and Jefferson in these terms. "The appointment of Burr as president would disgrace our country abroad," he informed Sedgwick. "No agreement with him could be relied upon."[15] Unlike other Federalists, Hamilton did not think Burr would be a harmless, lackadaisical president. "He is sanguine enough to hope everything, daring enough to attempt everything, wicked enough to scruple nothing," Hamilton told Gouverneur Morris.[16] From his legal practice, Hamilton knew that Burr had exorbitant debts and might be susceptible to bribes from foreign governments. He briefed Federalists about the scandals involving Burr and the Holland Company and the gross trickery behind the Manhattan Company.

While inspector general, Hamilton had had a disturbing conversation with Burr that he now repeated to Robert Troup and two other friends. "General, you are now at the head of the army," Burr had told him. "You are a man of the first talents and of vast influence. Our constitution is a miserable paper machine. You have it in your power to demolish it and give us a proper one and you owe it to your friends and the country to do it." To which Hamilton said he replied, "Why Col. Burr, in the first place, the little army I command is totally inadequate to the object you mention. And in the second place, if the army were adequate, I am too much troubled with that thing called morality to make the attempt." Reverting to French, Burr poohpoohed this timidity: "General, all things are moral to great souls!"[17]

So unalterably opposed was Hamilton to Burr that he told Federalist friends that he would withdraw from the party or even from public life if they installed Burr as president. By endorsing Burr, he warned, the Federalists would be "signing their own death warrant."[18] Hamilton feared that Burr might supplant him as de facto party head or might even foster a third party composed of disenchanted elements from the other two. Either way, Hamilton feared he would be shunted aside. Had he risked his career to block Adams's reelection only to have Aaron Burr fill the void?

By late December 1800, as Hamilton had forewarned, Burr changed his mind: he would not seek the presidency, but neither would he reject it if the House chose him over Jefferson. Burr told Samuel Smith that he was offended by the presumption that he should resign if elected president. It bothered him that Republicans, who had embraced him for expediency as vice president, now blanched at him becoming president. By adopting this defiant stand, Burr pushed the situation to the brink of crisis. In early January, Hamilton heard of a Burr bandwagon gaining force among Federalists. By late January, his sources were saying that the Federalists were decidedly, even unanimously, in favor of Burr over Jefferson.

Faced with this terrifying vision of a Burr presidency, Hamilton was forced to come up with his most candid, fair-minded, and perceptive appraisal of Jefferson. During the 1800 campaign, Federalists had vilified Jefferson as a coward, a spend-thrift, and a voluptuary, not to mention a potential demagogue wedded to noxious dogmas. Federalist Robert G. Harper mocked Jefferson as fit to be "a professor in a college or president of a philosophical society . . . but certainly not the first magis-trate of a great nation."[19] Now Hamilton had to combat rooted notions that he himself had helped to propagate.

In one letter, Hamilton confessed to having said many unflattering things about Jefferson: "I admit that his politics are tinctured with fanaticism[,] . . . that he is crafty and persevering in his objects, that he is not scrupulous about the means of success, nor very mindful of truth, and that he is a contemptible hypocrite."[20] At the same time, he admitted that Jefferson was often more fervent in rhetoric than in ac-tion and would be a more cautious president than his principles might suggest. He predicted, accurately, that Jefferson's penchant for France, once it was no longer po-litically useful, would be discarded. (In an abrupt volte-face, on January 29, 1800, Jefferson, after learning that Napoleon had made himself dictator, wrote, "It is very material for the . . . [American people] to be made sensible that their own charac-ter and situation are materially different from the French."[21] Hamilton had been saying this for a decade.) Hamilton was also dubious about Jefferson's past prefer-ence for congressional power. He shrewdly noted that, whenever it suited his views, Jefferson had supported executive power, as if he knew he would someday inherit the presidency and did not wish to weaken the office. Hamilton told James A. Bay-ard of Delaware, "I have more than once made the reflection that viewing himself as the reversioner [i.e., one having a vested right to a future inheritance], he was solicitious to come into possession of a good estate."[22]

The fierce debates about Jefferson and Burr took place amid a welter of reports that the Federalists would refuse to yield power. One Republican scenario hypothesized that desperate Federalists would prevent *both* Republican candidates from being elected and that President Adams would choose a Federalist successor to head an interim government. One of Hamilton's adversaries from the Whiskey Rebellion, Hugh Henry Brackenridge, envisioned Hamilton descending upon the capital with an army that would seize control of the government during the deadlock. Governor Thomas McKean of Pennsylvania swore that if Republicans were denied their victory, the Pennsylvania militia, twenty thousand strong, would march upon the capital and arrest any congressman who named someone other than Jefferson or Burr as president. Burr concurred that any Federalist attempt to subvert the election should be met by "a resort to the sword."[23]

Nobody was more upset by talk of extralegal schemes than Hamilton, who thought that any interference with the election would be "most dangerous and unbecoming."[24] The Federalists nourished their own fantasies of Republican plots, and Hamilton himself later claimed that Republican groups had colluded to "cut off the leading Federalists and seize the government" if Jefferson did not make it to the presidency.[25] One Federalist newspaper quoted Jefferson's partisans as issuing shrill threats that, if Burr became president, "we will march and *dethrone him as an usurper.*" If Federalists dared to "place in the presidential chair any other than the philosopher of Monticello . . . ten thousand republican *swords will instantly leap from their scabbards* in defence of the violated rights of the people!!!"[26] This hysterical atmosphere only intensified as congressmen tried to resolve the stalemate between Jefferson and Burr.

It was not until February 11, 1801, that votes cast by presidential electors in the various states were actually opened in the Senate chamber, confirming what was already common knowledge: that Jefferson and Burr had tied with seventy-three votes apiece. It was a snowy day in the brand-new capital. The helter-skelter site was a swampy, ramshackle village with a few boardinghouses clustered around an unfinished Capitol (Henry Adams quipped that it had "two wings without a body"), as well as some houses and stores near an unfinished executive mansion.[27] The north wing of the Capitol still lacked a roof, and Pennsylvania Avenue was studded with tree stumps. Quail and wild turkey abounded, and the sharp reports of hunters' guns punctuated construction sounds. It was very much a southern town, with ten thousand white citizens, seven hundred free blacks, and three thousand slaves. As a result, the majority of the six hundred workers who erected the White

House and the Capitol were slaves whose wages were garnisheed by their masters. The federal government was still so small that when it had moved from Philadelphia the previous year, the complete executive-branch archives fit neatly into eight packing cases.

Once the ballots were counted, the high drama moved to the House of Representatives. Each of the sixteen states was allowed a single vote for president, reflecting the majority sentiment of its delegation, and the winner would need a simple majority of nine votes. Since Federalists had dominated the outgoing Congress, their preference for Burr might have seemed conclusive. But matters were more complicated, since the Federalist votes were so concentrated in New England. On the first ballot, six states voted for Burr versus eight for Jefferson, who fell one vote short of winning. The delegations of the two remaining states, Vermont and Maryland, were evenly divided and therefore cast no votes. Since neither Jefferson nor Burr had nine votes, an impasse ensued that opened the door to further mischief, and rumors flew about that the Virginia militia was preparing to march on Washington.

After Hamilton's infamous Adams pamphlet, his power over the Federalists had dwindled. His judgment was now suspect, his actions imputed to personal pique. The first ballot deadlock confirmed his sense of his own waning power. Robert Troup reported, "Hamilton is profoundly chagrined with this prospect! He has taken infinite pains to defeat Burr's election but he believes in vain. . . . Hamilton declared that his influence with the federal party was wholly gone, that he could no longer be useful."[28] Nonetheless, Hamilton was not one to give up easily. He had already told Gouverneur Morris that he could support Jefferson with a clear conscience *if* the latter provided "assurances on certain points: the maintenance of the present system, especially on the cardinal articles of public credit, a *navy, neutrality.* Make any discreet use you think fit of this letter."[29] Jefferson had seemed to resist any deal. In the early republic, secret agreements behind closed doors were regarded as distasteful relics of monarchical ways. Nevertheless, the outlines of Hamilton's deal were to linger and ultimately prevail.

It was a long, hard road to the final ballot at the Capitol. The first session, which droned on for twenty hours, did not adjourn until 9:00 the next morning. Refreshments were brought to parched members at their seats. Some dozed in overcoats or lay down on the floor. One sick legislator who had not been present at first was carried through the snow and set down on a cot in an adjoining room, ready to vote if necessary. For five grueling days, the legislators suffered through thirty-five ballots that continued to replicate the original eight-to-six vote for Jefferson. The tedious pace only fostered concerns that disappointed Federalists would stall the vote until after the March 4 inauguration date and then anoint their own candidate as president.

Afterward, both Jefferson and Burr swore that they had chastely refrained from politicking during the thirty-five ballots. Recent scholarship has tended to exonerate Burr from charges that he did anything untoward, and he certainly did not bargain outright. In the weeks before the balloting, his romantic liaisons seemed to bulk far larger in his correspondence than the presidential contest. (His wife, Theodosia, had died of stomach cancer in 1794.) Besides his amorous intrigues, Burr was busy with parochial New York politics and preparing for the wedding of his only child, his beloved daughter, Theodosia. Nonetheless, Burr's behavior was not as passive as it seemed, for his silence and inaction stated eloquently that he was willing to defy the intentions of Republican electors and accept the presidency. Joanne Freeman has written that Burr made "one fundamental mistake: he did nothing to hide his interest in the office."[30] Hamilton had little doubt that Burr was maneuvering for the presidency. "Hamilton has often said he could prove it to the satisfaction of any court and jury," Robert Troup told Rufus King.[31]

The situation was tailor-made for Jefferson, who specialized in subtle, roundabout action. He denied stoutly that he had compromised to break the deadlock and told James Monroe, "I have declared to [the Federalists] unequivocally that I would not receive the government on capitulation, that I would not go into it with my hands tied."[32] That Jefferson believed his own version is certain. He did not lie to others so much as to himself. John Quincy Adams later observed of Jefferson that he had "a memory so pandering to the will that in deceiving others he seems to have begun by deceiving himself."[33] He now stuck by the serviceable fiction that he had refused to negotiate with the Federalists.

The man who helped to rescue the representatives from their misery was James A. Bayard, a Delaware Federalist. A thickset lawyer known for sartorial elegance, Bayard was under heavy Federalist pressure to vote for Burr and did so for thirty-five ballots. As the lone representative of a tiny state, he was in a unique position. If he changed his vote, Delaware changed its vote. For two months, Hamilton bombarded him with letters, spelling out Burr's flaws and heretical positions. "I have heard him speak with applause of the French system as unshackling the mind and leaving it to its natural energies and I have been present when he has contended against banking systems with earnestness." Burr lacked any fixed principles, Hamilton argued, and played instead on "the floating passions of the multitude."[34]

Though Bayard did not like the deadlocked vote, it was hard to resist the tide of Federalist support for Burr. When he suggested at one party caucus that he might vote for Jefferson to save the Constitution, he was hooted down with jeers of

"Deserter!"[35] But after the caucus, Bayard huddled with two friends of Jefferson: John Nicholas of Virginia and Samuel Smith of Maryland. Quite possibly influenced by Hamilton's barrage of letters, Bayard set forth some Federalist prerequisites for supporting Jefferson: he would have to preserve Hamilton's financial system, maintain the navy, and retain Federalist bureaucrats below cabinet level. After talking to Jefferson, Smith relayed to Bayard the candidate's opinion that the Federalists need not worry about the points mentioned. This smelled like a deal, and Bayard interpreted it as such, but Jefferson, ever the consummate politician, blandly called his chat with Smith a private tête-à-tête of no political consequence. Everybody involved kept up an air of perfect innocence. Timothy Pickering alleged that certain congressmen had "*sold* their votes to Mr. Jefferson and *received their pay* in appointment to public offices. Had Burr been at the seat of government and made similar promises of appointments to offices," he would have been president instead of Jefferson.[36]

Perhaps softened up by Hamilton's diatribes, Bayard later claimed he had doubted Burr's Federalist credentials all along. On the thirty-sixth round of voting in the House, he submitted a blank ballot and withdrew Delaware's vote from the Burr column. Simultaneously, Federalist abstentions in Vermont and Maryland gave Jefferson ten votes and a clear-cut victory. Burr, cut loose by both parties, was left in a political limbo for the rest of his life. While his second-place finish earned him the vice presidency, it simultaneously earned him the enmity of President-elect Jefferson. Jefferson probably owed his victory to Hamilton as much as to any other politician. Hamilton's pamphlet had first dealt a blow to Adams, though not a mortal one, and he had then intervened to squelch Burr's chances for the presidency, paving the way for a Federalist deal with Jefferson.

As the first incumbent president in American history defeated for reelection, John Adams had a chance to set a precedent and end his tenure with dignity. But during his final days in office, he brooded alone and grieved over the recent death of his alcoholic son, Charles, whom he had refused to see again. On March 4, 1801, the day of Jefferson's inauguration, Adams—now a balding, toothless, cantankerous old man—climbed into a stagecoach at four o'clock in the morning and left for Massachusetts eight hours before Thomas Jefferson was sworn into office. He thus became the first of only three presidents in American history who chose to boycott their successors' inaugurations. "The golden age is past," mourned Abigail Adams. "God grant that it may not be succeeded by an age of terror."[37]

At ten o'clock that morning, Aaron Burr was sworn in as vice president in the Senate chamber and then retreated to the seat from which he would oversee the Senate for the next four years. Jefferson showed up around noon, accompanied by

Adams's cabinet. To radiate republican simplicity, the new president wore plain clothes and marched behind a modest militia detachment. Secure in his victory, Jefferson believed that he embodied the will of the American people and could afford to be magnanimous in his inaugural address. He struck a conciliatory note when he remarked in a soft, almost inaudible voice, "We have called by different names brethren of the same principle. We are all Republicans, we are all Federalists."[38] As Joseph Ellis has noted, in his handwritten draft of the speech, Jefferson did not capitalize *Republicans* and *Federalists,* making the famous statement a little less generous than it seemed. Jefferson sounded quite a different note when he said in a private letter that he would "sink federalism into an abyss from which there shall be no resurrection."[39]

In New York, Hamilton monitored the inaugural speech for compliance with the tacit deal that Jefferson had made with the Federalists. He was pleased to see that Jefferson promised to honor the funding system, the national debt, and the Jay Treaty. Hamilton wrote, "We view it as virtually a candid retraction of past misapprehensions and a pledge to the community that the new President will not lend himself to dangerous innovations, but in essential points will tread in the steps of his predecessors."[40] This grandly bipartisan tone wouldn't last for long.

Hamilton had intuited rightly that Jefferson, once in office, would be reluctant to reject executive powers he had deplored in opposition. Madison was appointed secretary of state and Albert Gallatin secretary of the treasury. Gallatin had been a persistent critic of Hamilton, publishing a pamphlet during the campaign claiming that Hamilton had enlarged the public debt instead of shrinking it. But as treasury secretary, he discovered merits in Hamilton's national bank, which he had lambasted as a congressman. Hamilton, meanwhile, began his long retreat to the status of a prophet without honor.

THIRTY-EIGHT

A WORLD FULL
OF FOLLY

Once Jefferson became president, Hamilton, forty-six, began to fade from public view, an abrupt fall for a man whose rise had been so spectacular, so incandescent. If stripped of his former political standing, however, he remained at the pinnacle of the legal profession, exerting influence over a wide range of New York institutions. He drew up a will for a wealthy retired seaman, Robert Richard Randall, who wanted to set up a sanctuary for retired American merchant sailors. The resulting home on Staten Island was called Sailors' Snug Harbor. Hamilton also tendered legal advice to the Church of St. Mark's in the Bowery as it sought independent status within the Trinity Church parish.

But no legal fame or fortune could offset the painful decline of his political stature. From the time of his first newspaper essays at King's College, Hamilton had shown a steady knack for being near the center of power. He had gravitated to Washington's wartime staff, the Confederation Congress, the Constitutional Convention, and the first government. Now he was exiled from the main political action, a great general with no army marching behind him.

In his more despairing moments, Hamilton had long toyed with the fantasy of retiring to a tranquil rural life, especially as Philip Schuyler continued to badger him about his cerebral, sedentary labors. But something had held him back. Part of the problem was that Hamilton was a quintessentially urban man, who preferred to commune with books, not running brooks. The other founders—Washington, Jefferson, Madison, Adams—had plantations or substantial farms from which they had drawn financial and spiritual sustenance, while Hamilton had remained a city dweller, harnessed to his work.

This began to change in the late 1790s as Hamilton found increasing solace in his family. Away on a business trip, he chided Eliza mildly for not having written about their sick infant, Eliza: "It is absolutely necessary to me when absent to hear frequently of you and my dear children. While all other passions decline in me, those of love and friendship gain new strength. It will be more and more my endeavor to abstract myself from all pursuits which interfere with those of affection. 'Tis here only I can find true pleasure."[1]

To fulfill his pledge of spending more time with his family, Hamilton formed a "sweet project" to build a country house nine miles north of lower Manhattan.[2] He told a friend laughingly, "A disappointed politician is very apt to take refuge in a garden."[3] During the fall of 1799, he and Eliza rented a country house along with the Churches in the vicinity of Harlem Heights. This decision probably owed something to the yellow-fever epidemics that visited the city each autumn. Hamilton knew the area well. On fishing expeditions up the Hudson, he sometimes moored his boat to a dock owned by pharmacist Jacob Schieffelin, who had a lovely summer house on a nearby hilltop. Hamilton was so enraptured by the exquisite vista from this house that he tried to buy it. Instead, in August 1800 Schieffelin sold him an adjoining fifteen-acre parcel with a two-hundred-foot elevation with views of the Hudson River on one side and the Harlem River and East River on the other. From physician Samuel Bradhurst, Hamilton bought an additional twenty acres. The combined property was picturesquely wooded and watered by two streams that converged in a duck pond. It had outlying buildings, including stables, barns, sheds, gardens, orchards, fences, and a chicken house. The property was bisected by Bloomingdale Road (today Hamilton Place), which provided a fast, direct connection by stagecoach or carriage to Manhattan or Albany.

Hamilton called his retreat the Grange, a name that paid homage to both the ancestral Hamilton manse in Scotland and the plantation of uncle James Lytton in St. Croix. It was to be the only surviving residence linked to Hamilton's memory and the only one we know for certain that he owned. Its name suggested both pride in his Scottish ancestry and a more relaxed attitude toward his Caribbean origins. One day, Hamilton was riding up to Albany to visit Eliza's ailing sister Peggy and had to choose between bringing her a pie or a basket of crabs. Upon reflection, he told Eliza, he had opted for crabs: "Perhaps as a *Creole,* I had some sympathy with them."[4] Twenty years before, Hamilton would never have hazarded such a flippant remark about his boyhood.

The Hamiltons used the existing farmhouse as a temporary residence until they completed a new structure. For this home, Hamilton drafted a man whom he had once hired at Treasury to design lighthouses: John McComb, Jr., then the most prominent New York architect and soon to be in charge of constructing the new City Hall. The main contractor was Ezra Weeks, brother of Levi, whom Hamilton had defended in the Manhattan Well Tragedy case. From his sawmills at Saratoga, Philip Schuyler shipped planks and boards down the Hudson along with hand-carved timber, still rough with bark, to decorate the children's attic. He also sent enormous bushels of potatoes and wheels of cheese. Hamilton brimmed with so much nervous energy that he could not remain aloof from any project for long and collaborated with McComb on everything from the design of the tall chimneys to the Italian-marble fireplaces. Like all new homeowners, he had scouted other residences for ideas. On one journey to Connecticut, he told Eliza, "I remark as I go along everything that can be adopted for the embellishment of our little retreat, where I hope for a pure and unalloyed happiness with my excellent wife and sweet children."[5]

The two-story Federal house that McComb and Weeks completed by the summer of 1802 occupied a spot near the corner of present-day West 143rd Street and Convent Avenue. (It was later moved south for preservation purposes.) The neat, handsome structure had a yellow-and-ivory frame exterior, topped by classical balusters. With six rooms upstairs and eight fireplaces to warm the family in winter, it was clearly designed with Hamilton's brood of seven children in mind. As elegantly meticulous as Hamilton himself, the house was small for a man of his fame, though marked with mementos of his past power. Visitors entering the doorway under a delicate fanlight glimpsed a Gilbert Stuart painting of George Washington, a gift from Washington himself. Ironically, the Anglophile Hamilton furnished the parlor with a Louis XVI sofa and chairs. The centerpiece of the house was two octagonal rooms that stood side by side, one serving as parlor, the other as dining room. When the doors were thrown open, they created a single, continuous space in which to entertain guests. The mirrored doors that covered three sides of the parlor reflected the leafy landscape seen through the high French windows. Further blending the living room with the sylvan setting, the windows opened onto a balcony with panoramic river views. Incapable of total relaxation—Hamilton had probably never experienced an indolent day in his life—he commandeered for his study a tiny room to the right of the entryway and fitted it out with a beautiful roll-top desk that he called "my secretary at home."[6] This compulsive bibliophile packed the Grange with up to one thousand volumes.

Perhaps the aspect of this hideaway that most captivated Hamilton was landscaping it and growing fruit and vegetable gardens. As a newcomer to the bucolic life, he humbly sought assistance from friends and country neighbors. "In this new situation, for which I am as little fitted as Jefferson [is] to guide the helm of the U[nited] States, I come to you as an adept in rural science for instruction," he wrote to Richard Peters, an agricultural expert.[7] He also drew on the expertise of his friend and physician, David Hosack, who also served as a renowned botany professor at Columbia College. Hosack had just established a botanical garden with greenhouses and tropical plants where Rockefeller Center stands today. En route to or from the Grange, Hamilton surveyed Hosack's flowers and frequently rode off with cuttings, bulbs, and seeds. He even communicated a political message through his gardening. Among the many shade trees that he dispersed around the grounds, he planted to the right of the front door a row of thirteen sweet gum trees meant to symbolize the union of the original thirteen states.

We know about Hamilton's supervision of the grounds because he was often away on business and left detailed instructions for Eliza, who oversaw much of the day-to-day development. Hamilton was enchanted by an ornamental bed of tulips, lilies, and hyacinths that Hosack had devised, and he sent a drawing of it to Eliza. With his usual exactitude, he told her, "The space should be a circle of which the diameter is eighteen feet and there should be nine of each sort of flowers. . . . They may be arranged thus: wild roses around the outside of the flower garden with laurel at foot. . . . A few dogwood trees, not large, scattered along the margin of the grove would be very pleasant."[8] Hamilton also planted strawberries, cabbages, and asparagus and constructed an icehouse covered with cedar shingles.

Eliza kept close tabs on outlays for the Grange, which proved an extravagance for a couple with seven children. Always a tightwad compared to Jefferson, Hamilton began to spend with an open hand and lavished about twenty-five thousand dollars, or twice his annual income, on the house and grounds. Since the property itself cost fifty-five thousand, the cumulative expense dragged Hamilton into debt. He was aware that his liberal spending was outstripping his wealth but anticipated that his growing legal practice would defray future bills. In the past, Hamilton had been somewhat cavalier about collecting legal fees, but he now demanded payment from clients in arrears. When he asked one client to pay for a will drawn up many years earlier, he explained, "As I am building, I am endeavouring to collect my outstanding claims."[9]

For Alexander and Eliza Hamilton, the country house ushered in a new stage of their lives with a mellow, autumnal tone. The Grange did double duty as both rustic refuge and posh venue for dinner parties. The Hamiltons functioned as a complete, stable family as they seldom had before. Both Alexander and Eliza had been upset that his career had so often separated them and caused the children to be split up between them. Her life's greatest sacrifice, Eliza once said, was "that of being one half the week absent from him [Hamilton] to take care of the younger while he took care of the elder children."[10] For someone with Hamilton's early family history, these separations must have carried an extra burden of anxiety and frustration.

Hamilton made more and more time for his children. On one occasion, when

Eliza went to Albany, he wrote to her from the Grange, "I am here, my beloved Betsey, with my two little boys, John and William, who will be my bedfellows tonight. . . . The remainder of the children were well yesterday. Eliza pouts and plays and displays more and more her ample stock of caprice."[11] He liked to sing with the family and gather them in the gardens on Sunday mornings to read the Bible aloud. Hamilton's children tended to remember their father at the Grange, partly because they were older then and partly because it was there that they had the full attention of a man whose life had been hectic and distracted by controversy.

The new squire was no passive spectator of the national scene and followed avidly the fortunes of Aaron Burr. Once Jefferson entered the White House, Burr was no longer just expendable to the president: he was an outright hindrance. After betraying Jefferson's trust during the electoral tie, Burr knew he would probably be dropped as vice president when Jefferson sought reelection, and in the meantime he was pointedly excluded from the president's counsels. "We are told and we believe that Jefferson and [Burr] hate each other and Hamilton thinks that Jefferson is too cunning to be outwitted by him," Robert Troup reported to Rufus King.[12] As Burr became a pariah in Washington, he realized that he had to shore up his political base at home.

By coincidence, an acrimonious race for New York governor followed the electoral stalemate in Washington. That old Republican warhorse George Clinton decided to seek yet another term as governor. When John Jay declined to run for reelection, the Federalists turned to thirty-six-year-old Stephen Van Rensselaer, the incumbent lieutenant governor and Hamilton's brother-in-law. That Hamilton would get involved was further assured when Burr began to meddle on behalf of Clinton. For Hamilton, this exposed the shameless deceit behind Burr's flirtation with the Federalists during the tie election. He said in sarcastic tones to Eliza, "Mr. Burr, as a proof of his conversion to Federalism, has within a fortnight taken a very active and officious part against [Van] Rensselaer in favour of Clinton."[13]

Hamilton had a compelling personal motive for entering the fray. Eliza's younger sister Peggy was married to Stephen Van Rensselaer (Hamilton crowned her with the comic nickname "Mrs. Patroon") and had been gravely ill for two years. For a time, doctors plied her with oxygen that helped to revive her. Then, in early March 1801, while Hamilton was waylaid in Albany on legal business, Peggy's health deteriorated. Hamilton visited her bedside often and kept Eliza posted on developments. When Hamilton finished his court work, Peggy asked him to stay for a few days, and he complied with her wishes. In mid-March, Hamilton had to send Eliza a somber note: "On Saturday, my dear Eliza, your sister took leave of her sufferings and friends, I trust, to find repose and happiness in a better country. . . . I long to come to console and comfort you, my darling Betsey. Adieu my sweet angel. Remember the duty of Christian resignation."[14] Peggy's funeral at the Patroon's manor house was attended by all of his many tenants, marching in mourning.

So aside from wanting to thwart Burr and Clinton, Hamilton must have felt compelled to assist young Stephen Van Rensselaer, who had been widowed at the advent of his gubernatorial race. In a blizzard of articles and speeches, Hamilton credited the Federalists with producing peace and prosperity. He also tried to convert the election into a referendum on the Republican infatuation with France, evoking the "hideous despotism" of Napoleon that was "defended by the bayonets of more than five hundred thousand men in disciplined array."[15] After Jefferson's victory, the New York Federalists were desperate to resuscitate their party. As he campaigned with verve, Hamilton felt the full fury of vengeful Republicans, who were giddy with their recent triumph. "At one of the polls, General Hamilton, with impunity by the populace, was repeatedly called a thief and at another poll, with the same impunity, he was called a rascal, villain, and everything else that is infamous in society!" Robert Troup reported. "What a commentary is this on republican virtue?"[16]

To restore some civility, Hamilton suggested at one Federalist rally that both candidates appoint supporters to conduct a calm, reasoned debate on the issues. Republican papers turned on him harshly and accused him of "haranguing the citizens of New York in different wards in his usual style of imprecation and abuse against the character of the venerable Clinton." The same paper suggested that Hamilton should be "obscure and inactive," since he had been "detected in his illicit amours with his lovely Maria, on whose supposed chastity rested the happiness of her husband and family."[17] Burr watched amusedly as Hamilton squirmed. "Hamilton works day and night with the most intemperate and outrageous zeal," he told his son-in-law, "but I think wholly without effect."[18] Indeed, in an especially ominous sign for Hamilton, Clinton regained the governorship by a landslide.

But Clinton's return augured poorly for Burr as well. As Hamilton had predicted, President Jefferson gloried in the exercise of power and now moved to sweep Federalist officeholders from New York posts. The president blatantly snubbed Burr and showered most New York appointments on the Livingstons and Clintons. In trying to prop up his base in New York, Burr saw that he would indeed have to cobble together a new coalition of disaffected Republicans and free-floating Federalists. Such a strategy also threatened any comeback meditated by Hamilton and promised sharp future clashes between the two men.

Jefferson had not captured the presidency by a wide margin over Adams, but he was an agile politician with a sure sense of populist symbolism.[19] A handsome man of sometimes unkempt appearance, Jefferson eliminated the regal trappings of the Washington and Adams administrations and brilliantly crafted an image of himself as a plain, unadorned American. The various Jeffersons served up by Hamilton in his essays—the epicurean Jefferson, the spendthrift Jefferson, the patrician Jefferson, the indebted Jefferson, the slave-owning, lovemaking Jefferson—were blotted out by one of history's most impressive image makers. For two weeks after his inauguration, Jefferson stayed at his boardinghouse near the Capitol and supped at the common table. Once in the White House, the folksy president (who had been a fashion plate in Paris) galloped through Washington on horseback, dispensed with wigs and powdered hair, shuffled around in slippers, fed his pet mockingbird, and answered the doorbell himself. (When William Plumer first visited the executive mansion, he mistook the president for a servant.) Only Jefferson could have turned frumpy clothing into a resonant political statement.

Jefferson endowed his election with cosmic significance, later saying that "the revolution of 1800 was as real a revolution in the principles of our government as that of 1776 was in its form," and the Republican press cheered his victory as a liberation from British tyranny.[20] In fact, Jefferson proved a more moderate president than either he or Hamilton cared to admit. The Virginian no longer had the luxury of being in opposition and could not denounce every assertion of executive power as a rank betrayal of the Revolution. A group of purists calling themselves Old Republicans protested that the turncoat Jefferson had violated his former principles by refusing to dismantle Hamilton's system, including the national bank. Jefferson intended to cut taxes and public debt, contract the navy, and shrink the central government—a swollen bureaucracy of 130 employees!—to "a few plain duties to be performed by a few servants," but many changes were less than revolutionary.[21] He made the mistake of scuttling much of the navy, which was to leave the country appallingly vulnerable during the War of 1812. In the end, however, Jefferson often devised variants of Hamilton programs, stressing household manufactures over factories for instance. On the other hand, he overturned some bad Federalist policies and allowed the Alien and Sedition Acts to lapse.

Jefferson's more extreme impulses were restrained by his treasury secretary, the balding, Geneva-born Albert Gallatin, who broke the shocking news to him that it was too soon to abolish all internal taxes. He educated Jefferson that the national bank and Customs Service did help reduce the national debt. "It mortifies me to be strengthening principles which I deem radically vicious," the president replied, but he agreed that Gallatin was probably right "that we can never completely get rid of [Hamilton's] financial system." Indeed, Hamilton had deliberately shaped his policies so as to make it difficult to extirpate them.

The new president relished the chance to rifle through Treasury files and corroborate his suspicions of Hamilton. He asked Gallatin to browse through the archives and uncover "the blunders and frauds of Hamilton." Having tangled with Hamilton over the years, Gallatin undertook the task "with a very good appetite," he admitted, but he failed to excavate the findings Jefferson wanted. Years later, he related the president's crestfallen reaction: "'Well Gallatin, what have you found?' [Jefferson asked]. I answered: 'I have found the most perfect system ever formed. Any change that should be made in it would injure it. Hamilton made no blunders, committed no frauds. He did nothing wrong.' I think Mr. Jefferson was disappointed."[22] Gallatin complimented Hamilton by saying that he had done such an outstanding job as the first treasury secretary that he had turned the post into a sinecure for all future occupants. As for the First Bank of the United States, once denounced by Jeffersonians as a diabolical lair, Gallatin proclaimed that it had "been wisely and skillfully managed."[23] Republicans still found it hard to accept the need for the central bank. As president, James Madison allowed the bank's charter to expire, and American finances suffered as a result during the War of 1812. When a chastened Madison then sponsored the Second Bank of the United States, critics inveighed that he "out-Hamiltons Alexander Hamilton."[24]

Hamilton still feared that Jefferson would weaken presidential power, since he had long contended that a strong executive branch would revert to monarchical methods. "A preponderance of the executive over the legislative branch cannot be maintained but by immense patronage, by multiplying offices, making them very lucrative, by armies, navies, which may enlist on the side of the patron all those whom he can interest and all their families and connections," Jefferson had written.[25] Hamilton should have trusted his election prediction that Jefferson in office would discover the joys of presidential power. Jefferson resolved his ideological dilemma by showing outward deference to Congress while subtly steering congressional leaders at private dinners that he held three times per week at the presidential residence.

One area where Hamilton perceived a legitimate threat to the Federalist legacy was the judiciary, the last redoubt of party power. Right before Adams left office, Congress had enacted the Judiciary Act, which created new courts and twenty-three new federal judgeships so as to spare Supreme Court justices the onerous task of riding the circuit. The high court's justices had spent more time negotiating muddy roads than deciding cases in Philadelphia. At the end of his term, President Adams rushed through appointments for these judges, offending Republicans who thought he should have allowed the new president to choose. Worse, Adams made baldly partisan selections for a judiciary already packed with Federalists. His appointment of the so-called midnight judges rubbed old Republican wounds. "The Federalists have retired into the judiciary as a stronghold and from that battery all the works of republicanism are to be beaten down and erased," Jefferson declared.[26] William Branch Giles agreed with Jefferson that "the revolution is incomplete so long as the judiciary" was possessed by the enemy.[27] Thus the battle was joined between triumphant Republicans and defeated Federalists over Republican efforts to repeal the Judiciary Act. Hamilton and other High Federalists feared that Republicans would thereby destroy judicial independence.

Republican ire about the Federalist dominance of the judiciary became especially strident after Adams nominated John Marshall as chief justice of the Supreme Court in late January 1801. Marshall, forty-five, was a tall, genial man with penetrating eyes and a shock of unruly hair. He now rivaled, perhaps even superseded, Hamilton as the leading Federalist and had contempt for his distant cousin, Jefferson, whom he mocked as "the great lama of the mountain."[28] Historian Henry Adams said of Marshall, "This excellent and amiable man clung to one rooted prejudice: he detested Thomas Jefferson."[29] Jefferson reciprocated the animosity, especially since the new chief justice revered Hamilton, having once observed that next to the former treasury secretary he felt like a mere candle "beside the sun at noonday."[30] After reading through George Washington's papers, Marshall pronounced Hamilton "the greatest man (or one of the greatest men) that had ever appeared in the United States."[31] Marshall considered Hamilton and Washington the two indispensable founders, and it therefore came as no surprise that Jefferson looked askance at the chief justice as "the Federalist serpent in the democratic Eden of our administration."[32]

During thirty-four years on the court, John Marshall, more than anyone else, perpetuated Hamilton's vision of both vibrant markets and affirmative government. When he became chief justice, the Supreme Court met in the Capitol basement in a less-than-magisterial setting. Hamilton had always regarded the judiciary as the final fortress of liberty and the most vulnerable branch of government. John Marshall remedied that deficiency, and many of the great Supreme Court decisions he handed down were based on concepts articulated by Hamilton. In writing the decision in *Marbury v. Madison* (1803), Marshall established the principle of judicial review—the court's authority to declare acts of Congress unconstitutional—drawing liberally on Hamilton's *Federalist* number 78. His decision in the landmark case of *McCulloch v. Maryland* (1819) owed a great deal to the doctrine of implied powers spelled out by Hamilton in his 1791 opinion on the legality of a central bank.

The scalding debate over repeal of the Judiciary Act prompted Hamilton to lambast Jefferson in a series of eighteen essays entitled "The Examination." Reviving themes from *The Federalist Papers,* he explained why the judiciary was destined to be the weakest branch of government. It could "ordain nothing. Its functions are not active but deliberative. . . . Its chief strength is in the veneration which it is able to inspire by the wisdom and rectitude of its judgments."[33] For Hamilton, Jefferson's desire to overturn the Judiciary Act was an insidious first step toward destroying the Constitution: "Who is so blind as not to see that the right of the legislature to abolish the judges at pleasure destroys the independence of the judicial department and swallows it up in the impetuous vortex of legislative influence?"[34] Without an independent judiciary, the Constitution was a worthless document. "Probably before these remarks shall be read," he concluded, the "Constitution will be no more! It will be numbered among the numerous victims of democratic frenzy."[35] Despite the ink that Hamilton copiously expended and his warning before the New York bar that the law's cancellation would trigger civil war, the Republicans managed to repeal the Judiciary Act in March 1802 without incident.

The repeal and other Jeffersonian innovations had spurred Hamilton and his friends to found a new Federalist paper, the *New-York Evening Post,* now the oldest continuously active paper in America. Robert Troup complained at the time, "We have not a paper in the city on the federal side that is worth reading."[36] Newspaper editor Noah Webster had turned against Hamilton after the Adams pamphlet, depriving him of an outlet for his views. Marginalized but far from eliminated as a force in national affairs, Hamilton hoped the *Post* would chart a path for other Federalist newspapers and breathe life into a nearly moribund party. Of the ten thousand dollars of start-up capital, Hamilton likely contributed one thousand. Tradition has it that the decision to launch the *Post* was made in the mansion of merchant Archibald Gracie.

For chief editor, Hamilton plucked one of his most colorful disciples, thirty-five-year-old William Coleman, an engaging man with a broad, florid face and a nimble wit. Born to an impecunious Boston family, Coleman had been serving in the Massachusetts House of Representatives when Hamilton toured New England in 1796 and Coleman fell promptly under his spell. He considered Hamilton "the greatest statesman beyond comparison of the age" and later dated his professional success from the time of their meeting.[37] After moving to New York, Coleman practiced law with Aaron Burr, a decision he regretted and quickly reversed. Attracted to writers, he joined a literary society called the Friendly Club, where he mingled with Hamilton's Federalist associates. Coleman was wrestling with financial problems when Hamilton got him the coveted clerkship of the circuit court, where he employed his shorthand skills to produce the comprehensive transcript of the Manhattan Well Tragedy case.

William Coleman was such an unreconstructed Federalist that one Republican journalist crowned him "The Field Marshall of Federal Editors."[38] After Jefferson's election, Coleman sent the new president a bombastic epistle, accusing him of pulling down the old temple of morality and religion and erecting in its place "a foul and filthy temple consecrated to atheism and lewdness."[39] He threw himself so wholly into Stephen Van Rensselaer's gubernatorial campaign that a Republican paper predicted that this "seller of two-pence halfpenny pamphlets, this sycophantic messenger of Gen. Hamilton[,] . . . will at one time or another receive a due reward."[40] Coleman was a casualty of the back-to-back victories of Thomas Jefferson and George Clinton. After the governor's nephew De Witt Clinton emerged as the reigning figure of the all-powerful Council of Appointments, he purged Federalist officeholders and ejected Coleman from his clerkship.

Hamilton and his partners set up Coleman in a brick house on Pine Street. When the newspaper's first issue appeared on November 16, 1801, it sounded a patrician note, promising "to diffuse among the people correct information on all interesting subjects, to inculcate just principles in religion, morals, and politics, and to cultivate a taste for sound literature."[41] It made no bones about soliciting the backing of local merchants, announcing it would write about whatever relates to "that large and respectable class of our fellow-citizens."[42] While openly admitting its Federalist pedigree, it also noted that "we disapprove of that spirit of dogmatism which lays exclusive claim to infallibility and . . . believe that honest and virtuous men are to be found in each party."[43] The paper soon won plaudits for its legible print, high-quality paper, and lucid, trenchant writing. None other than James T. Callender bestowed kind words upon Hamilton's publication: "This newspaper is, beyond all comparison, the most elegant piece of workmanship that we have seen either in Europe or America."[44]

The *Post* immediately became Hamilton's newspaper of choice for assailing Jefferson, and all eighteen installments of "The Examination" appeared there under the name Lucius Crassus. Hamilton was no hands-off investor, and Coleman candidly described his pervasive influence on the paper: "Whenever anything occurs on which I feel the want of information, I state matters to him, sometimes in a note. He appoints a time when I may see him, usually a late hour in the evening. He always keeps himself minutely informed on all political matters. As soon as I see him, he begins in a deliberate manner to dictate and I to note down in shorthand. When he stops, my article is completed."[45] Coleman's vignette confirms that Hamilton had a lawyer's ability to organize long speeches in his head and often dictated his essays. Otherwise, the sheer abundance of his writing is hard to comprehend.

In a macabre coincidence, the *New-York Evening Post* had its first major story on its hands just one week after its maiden issue: a duel involving Hamilton's eldest son. With his high forehead, luminous eyes, and Roman nose, Philip Hamilton, nearly twenty, was exceedingly handsome. Smart and with a winning manner, he had followed a career path that replicated his father's: he had graduated the year before from Columbia College with high honors, was a fine orator, and studied to be a lawyer. "Philip inherits his father's talents," Angelica Church told Eliza. "What flattering prospects for a mother! You are, my dear sister, very happy with such a husband and such promise in a son."[46] One of Eliza's friends asked whimsically if she could notify the "renowned Philip" that she had heard he had "outstripped all his competitors in the race of knowledge" and daily gained "new victories by surpassing himself."[47]

Hamilton regarded Philip as the family's "eldest and *brightest* hope" and was grooming him for major accomplishments.[48] In Robert Troup's opinion, Hamilton held "high expectations of his future greatness" and likely expected him to perpetuate his own work.[49] Like Hamilton, Philip was partial to ornate rhetoric and once complained to his father that the Columbia president had made him strike this purple patch from a speech: "*Americans, you have fought the battles of mankind, you have enkindled that sacred fire of freedom.*"[50] Like his father when he was younger, Philip had a wayward streak—Troup called him a "sad rake"—and drifted into escapades that required gentle paternal reprimands.[51] Strict but loving, Hamilton had recently prepared a daily schedule for Philip that included reading, writing, church attendance, and recreation, governing all his waking moments from 6:00 A.M. to 10:00 P.M. Nevertheless, Hamilton showed some amused tolerance for his son's antics, ending one letter to Eliza in October 1801 with the words, "I am anxious to hear from Philip. Naughty young man."[52]

Philip's duel originated in a speech given by a committed young Republican lawyer, George I. Eacker, during a Fourth of July celebration that year. As principal draftsman of the Declaration of Independence, President Jefferson had a personal stake in whipping up patriotic fever on the holiday, and New York's festivities were especially exuberant. Bells chimed, cannon belched thunder and smoke, and militia marched up Broadway to the Brick Church, where the Declaration was read aloud. Then Captain Eacker, in his late twenties, addressed the crowd with partisan gusto. Instead of blaming the XYZ Affair or French privateering for the Quasi-War with France, he blamed Britain and suggested that Hamilton's army had been designed to cow Republicans. "To suppress all opposition by fear, a military establishment was expressly created under pretended apprehension of a foreign invasion," he told the crowd.[53] He credited Jefferson with chasing a Federalist aristocracy from the government and saving the Constitution. When the speech was published, Philip Hamilton pored indignantly over the references to his father.

Probably by chance, Philip spotted Eacker at the Park Theater in Manhattan on Friday evening, November 20, 1801. The two young men scarcely knew each other. The theater was presenting a comedy entitled *The West-Indian* when the son of

America's most celebrated West Indian, along with a friend named Price, barged into a box where Eacker was enjoying the show with a male companion and two young ladies. The two interlopers began taunting Eacker about his Fourth of July oration. At first he tried to ignore them, but the growing commotion drew stares from the audience. Eacker asked the two men to step into the lobby. As they did so, Eacker muttered, "It is too abominable to be publicly insulted by a set of rascals." Philip Hamilton and Price retorted, "Who do you call damn'd rascals?"[54] *Rascal* was a loaded word and often the prelude to a duel. When Eacker grabbed Philip by the collar, the antagonists nearly came to blows. They retired to a tavern, where Eacker reiterated that he considered them both rascals. As he left to return to the play, Eacker said, "I expect to hear from you." Philip and Price blurted out in chorus, "You shall."[55] Events then moved swiftly. By the time Eacker left the theater, he had a letter from Price challenging him to a duel, and he accepted the offer.

That same night, Philip Hamilton consulted his friend David S. Jones, a young lawyer and former private secretary to Governor Jay. Jones decided to take no further steps until he had conferred with John Barker Church, the Schuyler family authority on dueling. Church advised the young men that Eacker's insulting behavior demanded a response. On the other hand, he noted that Philip, having given first offense, should try to resolve his differences amicably with Eacker. That Sunday afternoon, Eacker and Price fought a hastily arranged duel in New Jersey. They exchanged four shots without injury and declared the matter closed. Afterward, John Church and David Jones tried to negotiate a truce for Philip Hamilton with Eacker's second. Among other things, they feared the political ramifications of a bloody encounter between Alexander Hamilton's son and a young Jeffersonian. Since Eacker blamed Philip Hamilton more than Price for the theater incident, he would not retract the word *rascal* even if Philip apologized for his rudeness. The negotiations foundered, and the two sides agreed to duel at 3:00 P.M. the following afternoon at Paulus Hook, New Jersey (today Jersey City). The dueling ground was located on a sandbar that was attached to the mainland only at low tide, affording privacy to the antagonists.

Where was Alexander Hamilton in all this? The *New-York Evening Post* coverage shielded his involvement and conveyed the impression that Philip arranged the duel before his unsuspecting father knew what was afoot. In fact, Hamilton knew all about it but hovered in the background while applauding his brother-in-law's efforts to stave off bloodshed. Hamilton was trapped in a dilemma that later plagued him with Burr. He believed in rebuking insults to one's integrity and abiding by the gentlemanly code of honor, but he grew increasingly critical of dueling as he returned to the religious fervor of his youth. During the mustering of his army, he had even issued a circular to his men to curb the practice. Hamilton's feelings were further complicated by the knowledge that his son was blameworthy and wished to make amends.

Grappling with these contradictory feelings, Hamilton devised a compromise response that previewed his own duel with Burr. He thought that Philip should throw away his shot on the field of honor, a maneuver that French duelists styled a *delope*. The idea was that the duelist refused to fire first or wasted his shot by firing in the air. If his opponent then shot to kill him, honorable men would regard it as murder. One of Philip's former classmates, Henry Dawson, confirmed this: "On Monday before the time appointed for the meeting . . . General Hamilton heard of it and commanded his son when on the ground to reserve his *fire* till after Mr E[acker] had shot and then to discharge his pistol in the air."[56] Of course, there was no guarantee that one's opponent would not shoot to kill.

At the duel, Philip Hamilton heeded his father's advice and did not raise his pistol at the command to fire. Eacker followed suit, and for a minute the two young men stared dumbly at each other. Finally, Eacker lifted his pistol, and Philip did likewise. Eacker then shot Philip above the right hip, the bullet slashing through his body and lodging in his left arm. In what might have been a spasmodic, involuntary discharge, Philip fired his pistol before he slumped to the ground. Both sides agreed that Philip's dignity and poise had been exemplary. "His manner on the ground was calm and composed beyond expression," the *Post* reported. "The idea of his own danger seemed to be lost in anticipation of the satisfaction which he might receive from the final triumph of his generous moderation."[57] The wounded young man was rushed back across the river to Manhattan. Henry Dawson wrote that he was "rowed with the greatest rapidity to this shore where he was landed near the state prison. All the physicians in town were called for and the news spread like a conflagration."[58]

Once Alexander Hamilton learned that negotiations had foundered, he raced to the home of Dr. David Hosack to inform him that his professional services might be needed. Hosack later recalled that Hamilton "was so much overcome by his anxiety that he fainted and remained some time in my family before he was sufficiently recovered to proceed."[59] In fact, Hosack already knew about the duel and had hurried to the home of John and Angelica Church, where Philip had been brought. When Hamilton afterward arrived, he gazed at his son's ashen face and tested his pulse. Then, Hosack related, "he instantly turned from the bed and, taking me by the hand, which he grasped with all the agony of grief, he exclaimed in a tone and manner that can never be effaced from my memory, 'Doctor, I despair.'"[60] Then came the horror-struck Eliza, three months pregnant with their eighth child. A month earlier, when she had gotten sick, Hamilton had feared another miscarriage.

"The scene I was present at when Mrs. Hamilton came to see her son on his deathbed . . . and when she met her husband and son in one room beggars all description!" said Robert Troup.[61]

Alexander and Eliza clung to their groaning son through a dreadful night. Henry Dawson recorded this wrenching tableau: "On a bed without curtains lay poor Phil, pale and languid, his rolling, distorted eyeballs darting forth the flashes of delirium. On one side of him on the same bed lay his agonized father, on the other his distracted mother, around [him] his numerous relatives and friends weeping and fixed in sorrow."[62] After professing faith in Christ, Philip Hamilton died at five in the morning, some fourteen hours after receiving the mortal wound. He was buried on a rainy day, with an enormous throng of mourners in attendance. As he approached the grave, the faltering Hamilton had to be propped up by friends. By all accounts, he behaved bravely in the face of calamity. "His conduct was extraordinary during this trial," Angelica Church wrote.[63] For a long time, Eliza was inconsolable. Despite the feared miscarriage, her eighth and final child was born at the Grange on June 2, 1802, and christened Philip in memory of his deceased brother. (Often he was called "Little Phil.") Philip Schuyler expressed the entire family's hopes when he wrote to Eliza, "May the loss of one be compensated by another Philip."[64]

The aftermath of the duel had eerie parallels to Hamilton's later confrontation with Burr. Philip's partisans told of his noble but ultimately suicidal resolution not to fire first, and they cursed the rival who had failed to respond in kind. Even the debate over whether Philip had discharged his weapon deliberately or in a spasm of pain was recapitulated later. Since Philip had been killed after withholding his fire for the sake of honor, Hamilton's reaction to his son's death tells us how he might have appraised his own fatal encounter. Many contemporaries believed that Hamilton collaborated with William Coleman on the *New-York Evening Post* articles about the duel, casting Eacker as the aggressor. These sanitized articles did not mention that Philip and Price had invaded Eacker's box, and they claimed that the two young men had teased Eacker in a spirit of "levity."[65] The episode was depoliticized, with the *Post* making no mention that the crux of the dispute was Eacker's Fourth of July oration about Hamilton. The paper further suggested that, if Eacker had been as conciliatory as Philip during the negotiations, the duel might never have occurred. The strongest blast directed at Eacker was that he had "murdered" Philip Hamilton by firing at someone who had no intention of firing back. This offended Eacker's friends, who pointed out that Philip had agreed to the duel, had come armed, and had pointed his gun at Eacker.

When the *Post* editorialized on the need to outlaw dueling, it may have been Hamilton himself who wrote, "Reflections on this horrid custom must occur to every man of humanity, but the voice of an individual or of the press must be ineffectual without additional, strong, and pointed legislative interference."[66] George Eacker was never prosecuted for Philip Hamilton's death. The young Jeffersonian lawyer died two years later of consumption.

One of the casualties of Philip's death was the Hamiltons' seventeen-year-old daughter Angelica, a lively, sensitive, musical girl who resembled her beautiful aunt. When Hamilton was treasury secretary, Martha Washington had taken Angelica to dancing school twice a week with her own children. Having been exceedingly close to her older brother, Angelica was so unhinged by his death that she suffered a mental breakdown. That fall, Hamilton did everything in his power to restore her health at the Grange and catered to her every wish. He asked Charles C. Pinckney to send her watermelons and three or four parakeets—"She is very fond of birds"—but all the loving attention did not work, and her mental problems worsened.[67] James Kent tactfully described the teenage girl as having "a very uncommon simplicity and modesty of deportment."[68] She lived until age seventy-three and wound up under the care of a Dr. Macdonald in Flushing, Queens. Only intermittently lucid, consigned to an eternal childhood, she often did not recognize family members. For the rest of her life, she sang songs that she had played on the piano in duets with her father, and she always talked of her dead brother as if he were still alive. In her will, Eliza entreated her children to be "kind, affectionate, and attentive to my said unfortunate daughter Angelica."[69] In 1856, Angelica's younger sister, Eliza, contemplating Angelica's expected death, wrote, "Poor sister, what a happy release will be hers. Lost to herself a half century!!"[70]

After Philip's death, Hamilton tumbled into a bottomless despair. Though no stranger to depression, he had never lapsed into the lethargy that usually accompanies it. No matter how grief stricken in the past, he still pumped out papers and letters with almost mechanical ease. Now the well-oiled machinery of his life ran down. He returned to political writing but was too disconsolate to discuss Philip's death. "Never did I see a man so completely overwhelmed with grief as Hamilton has been," Robert Troup wrote two weeks after the duel.[71] Having been abandoned by his own father, Hamilton must have regretted keenly his failure to protect his son. Four months passed before he could even acknowledge the many sympathy notes he had received. His replies reflect deep grief over his son's loss, his own disenchantment with life, and an aching need for religious consolation. Replying to Benjamin Rush, he wrote that Philip's death was "beyond comparison the most afflicting of my life. . . . He was truly a fine youth. But why should I repine? It was the will of heaven and he is now out of the reach of the seductions and calamities of a world full of folly, full of vice, full of danger, of least value in proportion as it is best known. I firmly trust also that he has safely reached the haven of eternal repose and felicity."[72]

Hamilton was an altered man after Philip died. He even looked different. Troup said that his face was "strongly stamped with grief," and this changed condition was captured on canvas by an Albany painter, Ezra Ames.[73] A frequent guest at the Schuyler mansion, Ames produced a remarkable portrait of the bereaved Hamilton that illuminates his abrupt emotional decline. In earlier portraits, Hamilton had looked buoyantly into the distance, touched with youthful ardor, or had stared at the viewer with an urbane confidence. Ames captured Hamilton looking troubled and introspective, as if lost in thought and staring into an abyss. The ebullient wit had fled, and the eyes were fixed downward in a melancholy gaze. Some new, impenetrable darkness had engulfed his mind.

THIRTY-NINE

PAMPHLET WARS

The popularity of President Jefferson further darkened Hamilton's pessimistic outlook. Fortified by Republican majorities in the House and Senate, Jefferson presided over a united government that his two predecessors would have envied, as he purged Federalist officeholders. Thanks to Washington and Hamilton, the American economy flourished; thanks to Adams, the Quasi-War with France had receded to a memory. Inheriting domestic prosperity and international peace, Jefferson benefited from exceptional good fortune as America settled down for the first time since the Revolution.

Jefferson soon adopted a relatively reclusive style as an administrator. He almost never made speeches and communicated with cabinet officers largely through memos. But he took daily horseback rides through Washington and perfected his populist image. "He has no levee days, observes no ceremony, often sees company in an undress, sometimes with his slippers on, always accessible to, and very familiar with, the sovereign people," said Robert Troup.[1] Jefferson cultivated rapport with the common people, while Hamilton stuck with his dated, paternalistic view of politics. The Federalists found themselves on the wrong side of a historical divide, associated with well-bred gentlemen, while Republicans appealed to a more democratic, rambunctious populace.

With Jefferson triumphant, Hamilton imagined that his own achievements would be scorned or soon forgotten. Republican journalist James Cheetham revived the hoary story that Hamilton had advocated a monarchy at the Constitutional Convention. Forced again to refute this propaganda, Hamilton sent a famously bleak letter to Gouverneur Morris in late February 1802:

Mine is an odd destiny. Perhaps no man in the U[nited] States has sacrificed or done more for the present Constitution than myself. And contrary to all my anticipations of its fate, as you know from the very beginning, I am still labouring to prop the frail and worthless fabric. Yet I have the murmur of its friends no less than the curses of its foes for my rewards. What can I do better than withdraw from the scene? Every day proves to me more and more that this American world was not made for me.[2]

Written during the period of mourning after Philip's death, the letter is tremendously revealing about Hamilton's deep sense of estrangement from American politics. He hewed to a tragic view of life in which virtue was seldom rewarded or vice punished.

If given to dispirited musings, Hamilton could never completely withdraw from politics. His dismay over Jefferson's success only added urgency to his desire to reverse the Republican tide. In "The Examination" essays, Hamilton undertook a broad-gauge assault on Jefferson's program. The tone was captious and lacked the large-minded generosity that had distinguished his earlier work. Jefferson wanted to abolish the fourteen-year naturalization period for immigrants, and Hamilton insinuated that foreigners, not real Americans, had voted the Virginian into office; he predicted that "the influx of foreigners" would "change and corrupt the national spirit."[3] Most amazing of all, this native West Indian published a diatribe against the Swiss-born treasury secretary, Albert Gallatin. "Who rules the councils of our own ill-fated, unhappy country?" Hamilton asked, then replied, "*A foreigner!*"[4] Throughout his career, Hamilton had been an unusually tolerant man with enlightened views on slavery, native Americans, and Jews. His whole vision of American manufacturing had been predicated on immigration. Now, embittered by his personal setbacks, he sometimes betrayed his own best nature.

After Philip's death, Hamilton's views seemed to emanate from some gloomy recess of his mind. He stood on more solid ground when he took Jefferson to task for favoring repeal of the whiskey tax and all other revenues except import duties. It galled him that Jefferson, who had accused him of wanting a perpetual debt, now canceled taxes that might have extinguished the federal debt more rapidly. In the end, Jefferson proved lucky: through a trade-induced boom in tariff revenues, he was able to cut taxes and produce a budget surplus.

As he pondered an amorphous comeback—he never spelled it out—Hamilton struggled with the conundrum that while Republicans might be "wretched impostors" with "honeyed lips and guileful hearts," they had won the public's affection.[5] How could this be? Hamilton thought that Republicans appealed to emotion, while Federalists relied too much on reason. "Men are rather reasoning than reasonable animals, for the most part governed by their passion," he told James Bayard, and his controversial solution was something called the Christian Constitutional Society.[6] The charge of atheism had been a leitmotif of Hamilton's critiques of Jefferson and the French Revolution. Now he hoped that by publishing pamphlets, promoting charities, and establishing immigrant-aid societies and vocational schools, this new society would promote Christianity, the Constitution, and the Federalist party, though not necessarily in that order of preference. By signing up God against Thomas Jefferson, Hamilton hoped to make a more potent political appeal. The society was an execrable idea that would have grossly breached the separation of church and state and mixed political power and organized religion. Hamilton was not honoring religion but exploiting it for political ends. Fortunately, other Federalists didn't cotton to the idea. As he drifted into more retrograde modes of thought, Hamilton seemed to rage alone in the wilderness, and few people listened.

It is striking how religion preoccupied Hamilton during his final years. When head of the new army, he had asked Congress to hire a chaplain for each brigade so that soldiers could worship. Although he had been devout as a young man, praying fiercely at King's College, his religious faith had ebbed during the Revolution. Like other founders and thinkers of the Enlightenment, he was disturbed by religious fanaticism and tended to associate organized religion with superstition. While a member of Washington's military family, he wrote that "there never was any mischief but had a priest or a woman at the bottom."[7] As treasury secretary, he had said, "The world has been scourged with many fanatical sects in religion who, inflamed by a sincere but mistaken zeal, have perpetuated under the idea of serving God the most atrocious crimes."[8]

The atheism of the French Revolution and Jefferson's ostensible embrace of it (Jefferson was a deist who doubted the divinity of Christ, but not an atheist) helped to restore Hamilton's interest in religion. He said indignantly in his 1796 "Phocion" essays, "Mr. Jefferson has been heard to say since his return from France that the men of letters and philosophers he had met with in that country were generally *atheists*."[9] He thought James Monroe had also been infected by godless philosophers in Paris and pictured the two Virginians dining together to "fraternize and philosophize against the *Christian religion* and the absurdity of *religious worship*."[10] For Hamilton, religion formed the basis of all law and morality, and he thought the world would be a hellish place without it.

But did Hamilton believe sincerely in religion, or was it just politically convenient? Like Washington, he never talked about Christ and took refuge in vague references to "providence" or "heaven." He did not seem to attend services with Eliza, who increasingly spoke the language of evangelical Christianity, and did not belong formally to a denomination, even though Eliza rented a pew at Trinity Church. He showed no interest in liturgy, sectarian doctrine, or public prayer. The old discomfort with organized religion had not entirely vanished. On the other hand, Eliza was a woman of such deep piety that she would never have married someone who did not share her faith to some degree. Hamilton believed in a happy afterlife for the virtuous that would offer "far more substantial bliss than can ever be found in this checkered, this ever varying, scene!"[11] He once consoled a friend in terms that left no doubt of his overarching faith in a moral order: "Arraign not the dispensations of Providence. They must be founded in wisdom and goodness. And when they do not suit us, it must be because there is some fault in ourselves which deserves chastisement or because there is a kind intent to correct in us some vice or failing of which perhaps we may not be conscious."[12] How then did Hamilton interpret God's lesson after the death of Philip?

The papers of John Church Hamilton provide fresh evidence of his father's genuine religiosity in later years. He said that Hamilton experienced a resurgence of his youthful fervor, prayed daily, and scribbled many notes in the margin of the family Bible. A lawyer by training, Hamilton wanted logical proofs of religion, not revelation, and amply annotated his copy of *A View of the Evidences of Christianity,* by William Paley. "I have examined carefully the evidence of the Christian religion," he told one friend, "and if I was sitting as a juror upon its authenticity, I should rather abruptly give my verdict in its favor."[13] To Eliza, he said of Christianity, "I have studied it and I can prove its truth as clearly as any proposition ever submitted to the mind of man."[14] John Church Hamilton believed that the time his father spent at the Grange, strolling about the grounds, broadened his religious awareness. During his final months, he was walking with Eliza in the woods and speaking of their children when he suddenly turned to her and said in an enraptured voice, "I may yet have twenty years, please God, and I will one day build for them a chapel in this grove."[15]

The one grim consolation that Hamilton derived from Jefferson's administration was that Aaron Burr's ostracism only worsened with time. The vice president's contacts with the president were confined to fortnightly dinners, and he met with the cabinet once a year. Burr gave a satiric picture of his exclusion from power when he told his son-in-law, "I . . . now and then meet the [cabinet] ministers in the street."[16] One senator said that Burr presided over the Senate "with great ease, dignity and propriety," yet it says much about Burr's estrangement from Jefferson that his most notable achievements came in the legislature.[17] John Adams had experienced the same frustration as vice president but not the same hostility from Washington's administration.

Burr kept up a loyal air to Jefferson until he broke ranks with other Republicans over repeal of the Judiciary Act. With this, Burr knew that he had signed his death warrant with the party and had to curry favor with the Federalists. Burr was now "completely an insulated man in Washington," declared Theodore Sedgwick, "wholly without personal influence."[18] Just how far Burr would go to woo Federalists became evident on February 22, 1802, when party legislators gathered at Stelle's Hotel to honor Washington's birthday, with Gouverneur Morris hosting the festivities. At the end of the dinner, guests heard a modest tapping at the door and were amazed when the vice president slipped into the room and asked if he was intruding. Having been invited by the organizers, he was received civilly, and he offered a bipartisan toast to a "*union* of all *honest* men."[19] With that deft gesture, Burr effectively severed ties with Jefferson. Pondering Burr's appearance, Hamilton asked, "Is it possible that some new intrigue is about to link the Federalists with a man who can never [be] anything else than the bane of a good cause?"[20]

As Federalists entered a game of mutual manipulation with the vice president, Hamilton did not dismiss Burr's overture outright, thinking that the best way to engineer Jefferson's downfall was to drive a wedge between him and Burr and divide Republicans. "As an *instrument*, the person will be an auxiliary of *some* value," Hamilton wrote of Burr, while noting that "as a chief, he will disgrace and destroy the party."[21] For Hamilton, this strategy was fraught with peril, for Burr might try to replace him as the Federalist chieftain. Thus, a situation arose in which Alexander Hamilton and Aaron Burr, two desperate politicians with fading careers, regarded each other as insuperable obstacles to their respective political revivals.

As Burr eyed a New York comeback—either by taking control of the local Republican party, infiltrating the Federalists, or patching together a coalition of defectors from both parties—press attacks erupted among local factions in what historians have labeled the Pamphlet Wars. After Burr became vice president, a mysterious handbill entitled "A Warning to Libellers" appeared on the walls of New York coffeehouses, accusing him of "abandoned profligacy." This anonymous sheet claimed that "numerous unhappy wretches" had been victimized by this seasoned "debauchee."[22] It also listed the initials of courtesans whom Burr had left "the prey of disease, of infamy, and [of] wretchedness."[23] Some contemporaries drew parallels between the sexual exploits of Hamilton and those of Burr. Architect Benjamin Latrobe observed that "both Hamilton and Burr were little of stature and both inordinately addicted to the same vice."[24] But the innumerable references to women in Burr's letters attest to the exotic variety and frequency of his affairs. In comparison, Hamilton was a mere choirboy.[25]

The unsigned broadside against Burr may have originated with De Witt Clinton, the governor's rangy, strong-willed nephew, who now controlled state patronage, earning him the unsavory title of "father of the spoils system."[26] Adept at the bare-knuckled style, Clinton was the moving force behind the *American Citizen,* started in 1801 and edited by a former hatter and rabble-rousing English journalist named James Cheetham. It soon became necessary for every New York faction to possess its own newspaper. Hamilton had countered with William Coleman and the *New-York Evening Post.* Burr and his cohorts started the *Morning Chronicle,* which was edited by Peter Irving, the older brother of Washington Irving.

Far more vexing to Burr than exposure of his love affairs was scrutiny of his electoral tie with Jefferson in 1801. James Cheetham and the *American Citizen* pounced on the theme of Burr's electoral duplicity and drove it home with obsessive frequency. The moment Burr was nominated, Cheetham contended, "he put into operation a most extensive, complicated, and wicked scheme of intrigue to place himself in the presidential chair."[27] At first, Burr reacted to these charges with typical phlegm, but as Cheetham and others stepped up their campaign, he began to sulk about a conspiracy to destroy him. As the Clintonians heaped more abuse on Burr, Robert Troup reported, "The high probability is that Burr is a gone man and that all his cunning, enterprise, and industry will not save him."[28]

Not content to smear Burr alone, Cheetham also reviled Hamilton as a traitor to the American Revolution who had reverted to his aristocratic roots. To make this far-fetched claim, Cheetham had to re-create Hamilton's father as "a merchant of some eminence."[29] The reality of a self-made, enterprising orphan did not suit Cheetham's needs: "Mr. Hamilton, unfortunately, was a native of that part of the civilized world where tyranny and slavery prevail in a manner even unknown to the despots of Europe. It was utterly impossible that the habits and prejudices he contracted in infancy could ever have been eradicated."[30] Having emigrated from England in 1798, Cheetham knew little and cared less about Hamilton's abolitionist activities. Cheetham's main thesis was that Burr planned to run on the *Federalist* ticket in 1804 along with Charles Cotesworth Pinckney: "Viewing the matter then in this light . . . Mr. Hamilton is evidently in his [Burr's] way!!"[31] In fact, after the Reynolds fiasco and Adams pamphlet, Hamilton would not have been a strong contender for president in 1804 and never implied that he planned to run.

As stunning as the verbal abuse in New York politics was the physical violence. Duels became fashionable for settling political quarrels: historian Joanne Freeman has counted sixteen such affairs of honor between 1795 and 1807, though not all resulted in duels.[32] When John Swartwout, a Burr protégé, denounced Cheetham as the mouthpiece of De Witt Clinton, Clinton denounced Swartwout as "a liar, a scoundrel, and a villain."[33] Accordingly, Clinton and Swartwout exchanged rounds of gunfire at the dueling ground in Weehawken, New Jersey. After Swartwout took two bullets in the leg, Clinton strode from the field and would not fire again. Newspaper editors, too, traded bullets as well as words. After James Cheetham accused

William Coleman of siring a mulatto child, the two men almost fought a duel before being legally restrained from confronting each other. This did not stop a certain Captain Thompson, a Jeffersonian harbormaster, from accusing Coleman of cowardice and fighting a twilight duel with him in Love Lane (now Twenty-first Street), in which Thompson suffered a mortal wound. After killing his adversary, the unruffled Coleman returned to the *Post* "and got out the paper in good style, although half an hour late," said a subsequent editor.[34] In yet another political fracas, Coleman received a caning that left him paralyzed from the waist down.

President Jefferson was not immune to the gutter journalism that thrived in these years. He and the Republicans had championed James T. Callender, who had criticized President Adams and thus been slapped with a nine-month jail term and a two-hundred-dollar fine under the Sedition Act. Once out of jail, Callender appealed to the president to help pay his fine and solicited an appointment as postmaster of Richmond, Virginia. When Jefferson gave him only a niggardly fifty dollars, the vengeful, heavy-drinking Callender defected to the Federalist camp. Editing a Federalist newspaper in Richmond, he revealed that Jefferson, while vice president, had subsidized him to malign Adams and Hamilton. When Jefferson denied this, Callender published documents showing that Jefferson had sent him money in 1799 and 1800 to assist with publication of *The Prospect Before Us,* in which Hamilton had been denigrated as "the son of a camp-girl."[35] The embarrassed Jefferson lamely described these payments as prompted by "mere motives of charity."[36]

Then, on September 1, 1802, Callender broke a story that he had learned about in jail and that was to reverberate down through American history: Jefferson's scandalous romance with Sally Hemings: "It is well known that the man *whom it delighteth the people to honor,* keeps and for many years has kept, as his concubine, one of his slaves. Her name is Sally. . . . By this wench Sally, our President has had several children. There is not an individual in the neighborhood of Charlottesville who does not believe the story, and not a few who know it. . . . The African Venus is said to officiate as housekeeper at Monticello."[37] Callender mentioned that "Dusky Sally" had five mulatto children and that her son Tom ("yellow Tom") bore a decided resemblance to Jefferson. Merciless toward his ex-comrades, Callender now referred to the Republicans as the "mulatto party."[38] He also said that he was ready to confront the president in a court of law and debate the truth of his relationship with "the black wench and her mulatto litter."[39]

Jefferson preserved a tactful silence on the issue, though he complained to Robert Livingston that "the federalists have opened all their sluices of calumny. Every decent man among them revolts at [Callender's] filth."[40] James Madison denounced the Sally Hemings story as "incredible," but Federalist wags whooped with delight and exhorted the president in verse to repent: "Thy tricks, with *sooty Sal,* give o'er. / Indulge thy body, Tom, no more. / But try to save thy *soul*."[41] Another Federalist editor claimed that he had verified that Sally Hemings "has a room to herself at Monticello in the character of a seamstress to the family, if not as house-keeper" and was "treated by the rest of his house as one much above the level" of the other servants.[42] Abigail Adams believed that Jefferson had gotten his due and wrote with barely concealed glee to him, "The serpent you cherished and warmed bit the hand that nourished him."[43] John Adams implied that he thought the story was true, while conceding that "there was not a planter in Virginia who could not reckon among his slaves a number of his children."[44] For Adams, the situation was "a natural and almost unavoidable consequence of that foul contagion in the human character—Negro slavery."[45]

Hamilton and his family were irate that Jefferson had paid Callender to libel him. "If Mr Jefferson has really encouraged that wretch Callender to vent his calumny against you and his predecessors in office, the head of the former must be abominably wicked and weak," Philip Schuyler complained to his son-in-law.[46] As early as his 1796 "Phocion" essays, Hamilton had suggested that he knew about the Sally Hemings affair. Now, having seen his own love life merchandised in print, he urged Federalist editors to ignore the scandal and stick to the high road in political matters. In the *New-York Evening Post* he declared that his editorial sentiments were "adverse to all personalities not immediately connected with public considerations."[47] This did not stop the *Post* from calling Callender "a reptile" and running a twelve-part series entitled "Jefferson and Callender."[48] The Jeffersonians also accused Hamilton of leaking to the *Gazette of the United States* the musty charge that the twenty-five-year-old Jefferson had tried to seduce Betsey Walker, the wife of his friend and neighbor, John Walker. Callender picked up this story and sensationalized it to the point where John Walker felt obliged to challenge Jefferson to a duel.

In July 1803, James T. Callender died in an abrupt, murky manner that has fed speculation for two centuries. The Jeffersonian press had begun to issue death threats against him, and he had also been accused of sodomy. Meriwether Jones of the *Richmond Examiner* editorialized, "Are you not afraid, Callender, that some avenging fire will consume your body as well as your soul?"[49] In another open letter to Callender, Jones imagined Callender drowning: "Oh, could a dose of James River, like Lethe, have blessed you with forgetfulness, for once you would have neglected your whiskey."[50] After Callender spent a night in heavy drinking, his sodden corpse was found bobbing in three feet of water in the James River on July 17, 1803. A coroner's jury concluded that it was the accidental death of an inebriated man. Yet such was the venomous atmosphere of the day that more than one Federalist wondered if Callender had been bludgeoned by vindictive Jeffersonians, then dumped in the river.

FORTY

THE PRICE OF TRUTH

Alexander Hamilton experienced conflicting moods in his final, bitter-sweet years. At moments, he seemed engrossed by his political future. At other times, he was so dismayed by Jefferson's triumph that he seemed ready to make good on his recurrent pledge to retire to the country and forget all about politics. No longer regarded as the Federalist leader, he had acquired the uncomfortable status of a glorified has-been. He still had a law office in lower Manhattan—in 1803, he moved it from 69 Stone Street to 12 Garden Street—and maintained a pied-à-terre at 58 Partition Street (now Fulton Street), but he spent as much time as possible drinking in the tranquillity of the Grange. In November 1803, Rufus King recorded this impression of Hamilton's new rustic life and state of mind:

> Hamilton is at the head of his profession and in the annual rec[eip]t of a handsome income. He lives wholly at his house nine miles from town, so that on an average he must spend three hours a day on the road going and re-turning between his house and town, which he performs four or five days each week. I don't perceive that he meddles or feels much concerning politics. He has formed very decided opinions of our system as well as of our admin-istration and, as the one and the other has the voice of the country, he has nothing to do but to prophesy![1]

Hamilton concentrated on law and political theory rather than everyday poli-tics. He initially balked at a project to publish *The Federalist Papers* in book form, telling the publisher that he was sure he could outdo it. "*Heretofore* I have given the people *milk; hereafter* I will give them *meat.*"[2] In the end, Hamilton cooperated with the project, proofreading and agreeing to the corrections in the new bound edition that appeared in 1802. He showed little interest in identifying the authors of the various essays, even though he had composed the bulk of them. When Judge Egbert Benson asked him to do so, Hamilton responded in a curiously indirect fashion, as if discomfited by the request. Stopping at Benson's office one morning, he inserted without comment the desired list in a sheaf of legal papers. Madison left his own, sometimes contradictory, list, spawning a future cottage industry of scholars.

Hamilton's intellectual ambitions were still far from sated. Chancellor James Kent recalled the grave thoughts that preoccupied his host during a visit to the Grange in the spring of 1804. Hamilton's house stood on high ground and was struck by a storm so furious that it "rocked like a cradle," Kent said.[3] Perhaps stirred by this tempestuous setting, Hamilton embarked upon "a more serious train of reflections on his part than I had ever before known him to indulge. . . . [He] viewed the temper, disposition, and passions of the times as portentous of evil and favorable to the sway of artful and ambitious demagogues."[4] Hamilton disclosed to Kent his plans for a magnum opus on the science of government that would surpass even *The Federalist.* He wished to survey all of history and trace the effects of governmental institutions on everything from morals to freedom to jurisprudence. As with *The Federalist,* Hamilton planned to function as general editor and assign separate volumes to six or eight authors, including John Jay, Gouverneur Morris, and Rufus King. The Reverend John M. Mason might write one on ecclesiastical history and Kent another on law. Then Hamilton would compose a grand synthesis of the preceding books in a prodigious, climactic volume. "The conclusions to be drawn from these historical reviews," Kent said, "he intended to reserve for his own task and this is the imperfect scheme which then occupied his thoughts."[5]

On this visit, Kent was struck by a new mildness in Hamilton. He noted the affectionate father, the tenderly solicitous host: "He never appeared before so friendly and amiable. I was alone and he treated me with a minute attention that I did not suppose he knew how to bestow."[6] It was probably on this visit that Hamilton performed a small courtesy that Kent never forgot. Feeling poorly, Kent retired early to bed. Anxious about his guest, Hamilton tiptoed into his room with an extra blanket and draped it over him delicately. "Sleep warm, little judge, and get well," Hamilton told him. "What should we do if anything should happen to you?"[7]

Hamilton was increasingly plagued by ailments, especially stomach and bowel problems, and his mind could not escape thoughts of mortality. For years, he had experienced all the self-imposed pressures of the prodigy, the autodidact, the self-made man. At moments, his life had seemed one fantastic act of overcompensation for his deprived upbringing. No longer was he the cocky wunderkind from the

Caribbean, and he sounded older and more subdued. Alexander and Eliza had already suffered terrible tribulations: the death of Philip, the attendant madness of Angelica, and the death of Eliza's younger sister, Peggy. Much more suffering lay ahead. On March 7, 1803, Eliza's mother, Catherine Van Rensselaer Schuyler, died of a sudden stroke and was buried at the family grave in Albany. Philip Schuyler, a dashing major general when Hamilton first met him, had turned into a sad, hypochondriacal man, pestered by gout. Eliza stayed in Albany to comfort her father while Hamilton took care of the children at the Grange. "Now [that] you are all gone and I have no effort to make to keep up your spirits, my distress on his account and for the loss we have all sustained is very poignant," Hamilton wrote to her.[8] A few days later, he added stoically, "Arm yourself with resignation. We live in a world full of evil. In the later period of life, misfortunes seem to thicken round us and our duty and our peace both require that we should accustom ourselves to meet disasters with Christian fortitude."[9]

However inconsistent his judgment and somber his mood in later years, Hamilton's mental faculties remained razor sharp. Robert Troup, now a district-court judge, had watched his friend since King's College days and marveled to another friend that Hamilton "seems to be progressing to greater and greater maturity. Such is the common opinion of our bar and I may say with truth that his powers are now enormous!"[10] He was besieged by clients and preferred cases that enabled him to harry President Jefferson. The two men now clashed in an unexpected arena: freedom of the press. Jefferson had long flaunted his respect for newspapers. As president, he had pardoned Republican editors jailed under the Sedition Act and stressed his tolerance for the ferocious barbs flung at him by Federalist editors. When a Prussian minister discovered a hostile Federalist newspaper in the president's anteroom, Jefferson told him, "Put that paper in your pocket, Baron, and should you ever hear the reality of our liberty, our freedom of the press questioned, show them this paper and tell them where you found it."[11] Jefferson was not quite the saintly purist that he pretended. He wrote to Pennsylvania's governor that he favored "a few prosecutions" that "would have a wholesome effect in restoring the integrity of the presses," and by the end of his presidency he was squawking about the newspapers' "abandoned prostitution to falsehood."[12]

Jefferson conducted two high-profile prosecutions of Federalist editors. One was Harry Croswell of Hudson, New York, whose defense Hamilton undertook. Croswell edited a Federalist newspaper called *The Wasp* that had a crusading motto emblazoned across its masthead: "To lash the rascals naked through the world."[13] Writing under the pseudonym "Robert Rusticoat," Croswell had snickered at Jefferson's claim that he had assisted James T. Callender's *The Prospect Before Us* solely out of "charitable" motives. In the summer of 1802, Croswell said of Callender: "He is precisely qualified to become a tool, to spit the venom and scatter the malicious poisonous slanders of his employer. He, in short, is the very man that a dissembling patriot, pretended 'man of the people,' would employ to plunge the dagger or administer the arsenic."[14] In another article, Croswell said, "Jefferson paid Callender for calling Washington a traitor, a robber, and a perjurer; for calling Adams a hoary-headed incendiary; and for most grossly slandering the private characters of men whom he well knew were virtuous."[15] These comments tested Jefferson's reverence for press freedom. The concerns he had expressed about libel prosecutions brought by the federal government against Republican editors under the Sedition Act seemed to vanish when state governors so prosecuted Federalist editors.

In January 1803, a grand jury in Columbia County, New York, indicted Harry Croswell for seditious libel against President Jefferson. The case generated intense political heat, as Federalists flocked to Croswell's banner. Ambrose Spencer, New York attorney general and a recent convert to the Jeffersonian persuasion, personally handled the prosecution. Although Croswell wanted Hamilton as his lawyer, the latter was committed to other cases and could not participate in the early stages of the defense. Philip Schuyler informed Eliza that a dozen Federalists had called upon him, hoping he would use his influence to enlist Hamilton's services. Schuyler sympathized with them, telling Eliza that Jefferson "disgraces not only the place he fills, but produces immorality by his pernicious example."[16] By the time the circuit court convened in the small brick courthouse at Claverack, New York, in July, Hamilton had agreed to join the defense team. Because the case touched on two momentous constitutional issues, freedom of the press and trial by jury, he waived any fee.

The gist of Hamilton's argument was that the truth of the claims made by an author should be admissible evidence for the defense in a libel case. The standard heretofore had been that plaintiffs in libel cases needed to prove only that statements made against them were defamatory, not that they were false. Both Hamilton and Croswell wanted to delay the trial until they could transport James T. Callender to the courtroom to testify about Jefferson's patronage of his writing. Whether coincidentally or not, Callender met his watery death a few weeks before the trial began. Hamilton was tempted to subpoena Jefferson or at least extract a deposition from him. However, the presiding judge, Morgan Lewis, reverted to common-law doctrine and informed the jury that they "were judges of the fact and not of the truth or intent of the publication."[17] In other words, the jury's job was simply to determine whether Harry Croswell had published the libelous lines about Jefferson, not whether they were true and sincerely meant. Bound by these instructions, the jurors had no choice but to find Croswell guilty.

In mid-February 1804, Hamilton journeyed to Albany and pleaded for a new trial before the state supreme court. On the bench, Hamilton had a friend and Federalist ally in James Kent but otherwise faced three Republican judges. Hamilton's speech was so eagerly awaited that the Senate and Assembly chambers emptied out when he spoke. The lawmakers were drawn to the courtroom by more than curiosity: they had under consideration a bill that would allow truth as a defense in libel trials. Hamilton did not disappoint his expectant spectators in his six-hour speech. In arguing for a new trial, Hamilton highlighted the principle at stake, the protection of a free press: "The liberty of the press consists, in my idea, in publishing the truth from good motives and for justifiable ends, [even] though it reflect on the government, on magistrates, or individuals."[18] As a victim of repeated press abuse, Hamilton did not endorse a completely unfettered press: "I consider this spirit of abuse and calumny as the pest of society. I know the best of men are not exempt from attacks of slander. . . . Drops of water in long and continued succession will wear out adamant."[19] Hence the importance of truth, fairness, and absence of malice in reportage.

Only a free press could check abuses of executive power, Hamilton asserted. He never mentioned Jefferson directly, but the president's shadow flickered intermittently over his speech. In describing the need for unvarnished press coverage of elected officials, Hamilton reminded the judges "how often the hypocrite goes from stage to stage of public fame, under false array, and how often when men attained the last objects of their wishes, they change from that which they seemed to be." In case any auditors missed the allusion, Hamilton added that "men the most zealous reverers of the people's rights have, when placed on the highest seat of power, become their most deadly oppressors. It becomes therefore necessary to observe the actual conduct of those who are thus raised up."[20]

By spotlighting the issue of intent, Hamilton identified the criteria for libel that still hold sway in America today: that the writing in question must be false, defamatory, and malicious. If a published piece of writing "have a good intent, it ought not to be a libel for it then is an innocent transaction."[21] Hamilton showed how truth and intent were inextricably linked: "Its being a truth is a reason to infer that there was no design to injure another."[22] He conceded, however, that truth alone was not a defense and that libelers could use "the weapon of truth wantonly."[23] And he did not argue that the truth should be conclusive, only that it should be admissible; if a journalist slandered his target accurately but maliciously, then he was still guilty of libel. He noted that the Sedition Act, "branded indeed with epithets the most odious," contained one redeeming feature: it allowed the alleged libeler to plead both truth and intent before a jury.[24] In deciding intent in libel cases, Hamilton also stressed the need for an independent jury instead of a judge appointed by the executive branch, lest the American judiciary revert to the tyranny of the Star Chamber.

In a ringing summation, Hamilton sounded again like the young firebrand from King's College days and spoke freely from the heart: "I never did think the truth was a crime. I am glad the day is come in which it is to be decided, for my soul has ever abhorred the thought that a free man dared not speak the truth."[25] The issue of press freedom was all the more important because the spirit of faction, "that mortal poison to our land," had spread through America. He worried that a certain unnamed party might impose despotism: "To watch the progress of such endeavours is the office of a free press. To give us early alarm and put us on our guard against the encroachments of power. This then is a right of the utmost importance, one for which, instead of yielding it up, we ought rather to spill our blood."[26]

People who heard Hamilton's speech that day, which distilled so many themes of his varied career, never forgot his spellbinding message or the mood he cast over the hushed courtroom. James Kent slid a hastily scribbled note to a friend: "*I never heard him so great.*"[27] New York merchant John Johnston wrote afterward, "It was indeed a most extraordinary effort of human genius. . . . [T]here was not, I do believe, a dry eye in court." Another observer, Thomas P. Grosvenor, confirmed that Hamilton's speech "drew tears from his eyes and . . . from every eye of the numerous audience."[28] Chancellor Kent, always an insightful observer of Hamilton's courtroom prowess, singled out the Croswell speech for his highest encomium.

I have always considered General Hamilton's argument in that cause as the greatest forensic effort that he ever made. There was an unusual solemnity and earnestness on the part of General Hamilton in this discussion. He was at times highly impassioned and pathetic. His whole soul was enlisted in the cause and in contending for the rights of the jury and a free press, he considered that he was establishing the surest refuge against oppression.[29]

Even Hamilton's adversary, Attorney General Spencer, lavished praise on Hamilton's legal powers, calling him "the greatest man this country has produced. . . . In creative power, Hamilton was infinitely [Senator Daniel] Webster's superior."[30]

Hamilton, ironically, lost the case. Because the four judges were evenly split, with Chief Justice Morgan Lewis opposing him, Croswell could not win a retrial, but neither was he sentenced. As a reward for shielding President Jefferson, Lewis was lionized by Republicans and nominated as the party's candidate for New York governor six days later. But Hamilton's arguments in the case prevailed over the long term. In April 1805, the New York legislature passed a new libel law that incorporated the features he had wanted. With this new law in place, the state supreme court granted Harry Croswell a new trial that summer—a belated triumph that Hamilton did not live to see.

In April 1803, President Jefferson reached the zenith of his popularity with the Louisiana Purchase. For a mere pittance of fifteen million dollars, the United States acquired 828,000 square miles between the Mississippi River and the Rocky Mountains, doubling American territory. Hamilton was ruefully amused that Jefferson, the strict constructionist, committed a breathtaking act of executive power that far exceeded anything contemplated in the Constitution. The land purchase dwarfed Hamilton's central bank and others measures once so hotly denounced by the man who was now president. After considering a constitutional amendment to sanctify the Louisiana Purchase, Jefferson settled for congressional approval. "The less we say about the constitutional difficulties respecting Louisiana, the better," he conceded to Madison. To justify his audacity, the president invoked the doctrine of implied powers first articulated and refined by Alexander Hamilton. As John Quincy Adams remarked, the Louisiana Purchase was "an assumption of implied power greater in itself, and more comprehensive in its consequences, than all the assumptions of implied powers in the years of the Washington and Adams administrations."[31] When it suited his convenience, Jefferson set aside his small-government credo with compunction.

At first, Hamilton had denied that Napoleon would ever sell the territory. "There is not the most remote probability that the ambitious and aggrandizing views of Bonaparte will commute [i.e., exchange] the territory for money," he observed.[32] Hamilton thought the United States should simply seize New Orleans and *then* negotiate a purchase of the territory with a France bankrupted by war. Perhaps Hamilton was slipping back into the old reveries of military glory that he had nursed under President Adams. Then, envious of Jefferson's easy windfall, Hamilton belittled the significance of the Louisiana Purchase, contending that any settlement in this vast wilderness "appears too distant and remote to strike the mind of a sober politician with much force."[33]

In the end, Hamilton was one of the few Federalists to support the action, which squared neatly with his nationalistic vision. Swapping roles with Republicans, however, many Federalists emerged as strict constructionists and denied that the Constitution permitted the purchase. Beyond legal reservations, they worried that this new American territory would weaken Federalist power, sealing their doom. The new western terrain would be preponderantly Republican and agricultural, and slavery might flourish there. In fact, every state that entered the Union between 1803 and 1845 as a result of the purchase turned out to be a slave state, further tipping the political balance toward the south. Fearful of being overshadowed by an expanding Republican slave empire in the west, some New England Federalists began to talk of secession from the union. Such plans formed part of the context for the Hamilton-Burr duel. If any such secessionist movement occurred, Hamilton, ever the passionate nation builder, wanted to retain the sterling reputation necessary to counter it with all his might.

Where Hamilton saw a threat to the Union in the incipient secession movement, Aaron Burr beheld a chance to rehabilitate his flagging political career. As the 1804 presidential election approached, Burr knew that Jefferson would drop him from the Republican ticket. This assumption was reinforced on January 20, 1804, when Governor George Clinton, citing age and ill health, informed Jefferson that he would not run again for New York governor. Jefferson began to muse upon Clinton's strengths as a running mate—not least among them that he was too old to pose any competitive threat to himself and would leave the door open for James Madison to succeed him as the next president.

On January 26, Burr hazarded one last meeting with Jefferson to determine whether he had any future in the national Republican party. Knowing it would be fruitless to ask Jefferson to keep him on as vice president, he abased himself to solicit "a mark of favor" from Jefferson that he could transmit to the world as evidence that he was leaving office with the president's confidence.[34] Mixing flattery with self-pity, Burr complained that the Livingstons and Clintons, abetted by Hamilton, had launched "calumnies" against him in New York and asked Jefferson to help defend his name.[35] Jefferson held out no hope of political redemption. In his evasive style, he said that he never meddled with elections and had no plans to do so now. As for press attacks against Burr, Jefferson waved them away blithely, saying that he "had noticed it but as the passing wind."[36] Clearly, as far as Jefferson was concerned, Aaron Burr was persona non grata in the Republican party.

Burr concluded that his political salvation lay in New York. He would try to exchange places with George Clinton and run for New York governor, backed by a coalition of Federalists and disgruntled Republicans. Hamilton feared that Burr might try to unite New York with New England in a breakaway confederacy, courting Federalist votes in the process. With his talent for subtle suggestions, Burr had already dined with New England Federalist legislators, who had probed his views on the subject. Congressman Roger Griswold of Connecticut said that Burr spoke "in the most bitter terms of the Virginia faction and of the necessity of a union at the northward to resist it. But what the ultimate objects are which he would propose, I do not know."[37] Without committing himself, the inscrutable Burr kept alive hopes that, as New York governor, he might encourage state residents to forge a union with the New England states.

In essaying a New York comeback, Burr had to contend with two willful opponents: thirty-four-year-old De Witt Clinton, now New York's handsome, overbearing mayor, and the damaged but still resourceful Hamilton. The resulting political battle was to be brutal even by the savage standards of the day. The *American Citizen,* Clinton's mouthpiece, was to play an especially provocative role. To discredit Burr among Republicans, editor James Cheetham disinterred old charges that Burr had colluded with Federalists in the 1801 tie election. He took special pleasure in quoting Hamilton that Burr was a "Catiline" or traitor. This only aggravated tensions between Hamilton and Burr.

In hindsight, several Burr confidants blamed Cheetham for goading the two men into a duel. The editor "had done everything in his power to set Burr and Hamilton to fighting," claimed Charles Biddle.[38] Indeed, Cheetham exploited every opportunity to bait the two men. On January 6, 1804, he had jeered openly at Hamilton in print: "Yes, sir, I dare assert that you attributed to Aaron Burr one of the most atrocious and unprincipled of crimes. He has not called upon you. . . . Either he is guilty or he is the most mean and despicable bastard in the universe."[39] Cheetham also prodded Burr, asking him if he was "so degraded as to permit even General Hamilton to slander him with impunity?"[40] Now an embattled, lonely figure, Burr was as hypersensitive to attacks on his character as Hamilton. If he could not redeem his personal reputation, then he could not salvage his career. So that February he filed a libel suit against Cheetham, one of thirty-eight that the sleazy editor faced in his brief career. Cheetham mischievously responded that he was merely reiterating allegations that Hamilton had made against Burr: "I repeat it. General Hamilton believes him guilty and has said so a thousand times—and will say so and *prove* him so whenever an opportunity offers."[41] By stoking this animosity, Cheetham was playing a lethal game.

The Federalists had been so debilitated in New York by the Jeffersonians that they could not even field a viable gubernatorial candidate. It therefore became a question of which Republican or independent candidate to support. Sensing the futility of any Federalist candidacy, Rufus King rebuffed Hamilton's entreaty that he run. In February, Hamilton and other leading Federalists caucused at the City Tavern in Albany to decide on a Republican candidate to back. (Hamilton was in Albany to deliver his summary remarks in the Croswell case.) Disconcerted by what he saw as a diabolical plot to dismember the union, Hamilton combated Burr with special intensity. In notes prepared for his speech, Hamilton said that Burr was an "adroit, able, and daring" politician and skillful enough to combine unhappy Republicans and wavering Federalists. But Burr, he said, yearned to head a new northern confederacy, and "placed at the head of the state of New York no man would be more likely to succeed."[42]

Aware of Hamilton's strenuous efforts to stop him, Burr informed his daughter, Theodosia, that "Hamilton is intriguing for any candidate who can have a chance of success against A[aron] B[urr]."[43] A few months later, Burr pretended that he had had no idea of the true opinion that Hamilton entertained of his private character and summoned Hamilton to a duel on that basis. Yet on March 1, 1804, the *American Citizen* reported that Hamilton had criticized Burr for both his public *and* his private character: "General Hamilton did not oppose Mr. Burr because he was a *democrat* . . . but because HE HAD NO PRINCIPLE, either in morals or in politics. The sum and substance of his language was that no *party* could trust him. He drew an odious, but yet I think a very just picture of the little Colonel."[44]

In the end, Hamilton endorsed for governor one of his earliest political foes, John Lansing, Jr., whom he had first tangled with as a fellow New York delegate at the Constitutional Convention. Hamilton thought Lansing would be a weak governor who would erode Republican unity. After Lansing declined the nomination, Republicans rallied around Chief Justice Morgan Lewis, who had married into the Livingston clan. This was a terrible blow to Hamilton, who did not think Lewis could win and feared that Federalists would now defect to Burr. "Burr's prospect has extremely brightened," he lamented.[45] Indeed, on February 18, a caucus of disaffected Republicans nominated Burr for governor. Just as Hamilton foresaw, prominent Federalists, from John Jay to his own brother-in-law Stephen Van Rensselaer, lined up behind Burr. In disgust, Hamilton told Philip Schuyler that he would not get involved in the election, but he was incapable of inaction. He ended up campaigning for Lewis to the point that one Burr lieutenant wrote, "General Hamilton . . . opposed the election of Colonel Burr with an ardor bordering on fanaticism. The press teemed with libels of the most atrocious character."[46]

As groups statewide endorsed Burr—"Burr is the universal, I mean the general, cry," exclaimed one exuberant observer—Hamilton fell into a despondent state.[47] In this mood, he lashed out at any efforts to impugn his character. On February 25, one week after Burr was nominated, Hamilton went to the Albany home of Judge Ebenezer Purdy to confront him with reports that he had revived an old canard: that before the Constitutional Convention Hamilton had secretly plotted with Britain to install a son of George III as an American king in exchange for Canada and other territories. To emphasize the gravity of the visit, Hamilton took along another judge, Nathaniel Pendleton, a Virginia native and later his second in the duel with Burr. With Pendleton taking notes, Purdy refused to disclose the source for his story, admitting only that the man lived in Westchester and had seen the telltale British letter in Hamilton's office. The source, in fact, was Pierre Van Cortlandt, Jr., who had clerked for Hamilton in the mid-1780s before becoming a Republican politician. More to the point, Van Cortlandt was now the son-in-law of George Clinton.

Hamilton told Purdy that he was determined to trace the slander. Purdy mentioned that Governor Clinton had a copy of the British letter, and Hamilton decided to contact his old bogeyman. That same day, Clinton was nominated by the Republicans as Jefferson's running mate for vice president. Hamilton demanded of his longtime foe "a frank and candid explanation of so much of the matter as relates to yourself."[48] Clinton said that a General Macomb had shown him a copy of the letter around the time of the Constitutional Convention. Hamilton insisted that Clinton send him the letter, if he retained it in his files, so that he could hunt down its source. Clinton sent a blunt, unrepentant reply, saying that he could not find the letter but precisely recollected its contents: "It recommended a government for the United States similar to that of Great Britain. . . . The [American] House of Lords was to be composed partly of the British hereditary nobility and partly of such of our own citizens as should have most merit in bringing about the measure."[49] Clinton clearly gave credence to this nonsensical fairy tale, and he no longer felt any need to defer to Hamilton, who had lost his power and could now be bullied. In a guarded response, Hamilton expressed hope that if Clinton found the letter, he would hand it over to him. For fifteen years, Hamilton had tried to run down the sources of the lies told about him. The effort had left him weary and dispirited, but he still could not shed the fantasy that, if only he went after slander with sufficient persistence, he could vanquish his detractors once and for all.

To fathom the full bitterness of Aaron Burr in the spring of 1804, one must dip into the hateful campaign literature spewed forth by his opponents during the gubernatorial race. Few elections in American history have trafficked in such personal defamation. Undeterred by Burr's libel suit, Cheetham's *American Citizen* engaged in ever more reckless sallies against him. Cheetham advised readers that his staff had assembled a list of "*upwards of twenty women of ill fame* with whom [Burr] has been connected." Another list in his possession, he said, cited married ladies who were divorced due to Burr's seductions as well as "chaste and respectable ladies whom he has attemped to *seduce*."[50] The most infamous Cheetham tale concerned a "nigger ball" that Burr allegedly threw at his Richmond Hill estate to woo free black voters.[51] Supervised by his slave Alexis—described by an early Burr biographer as "the black factotum of the establishment"—this party was said to have featured Burr dancing with a voluptuous black woman, whom he then seduced.[52] This election coverage set a new low for Cheetham, which is saying something.

While being battered by the press, Burr had to fend off a wave of anonymous broadsides in the streets, his well-known profligacy forming the theme of many of them. Cheetham wrote some of them, including one claiming that the father of a young woman deflowered by Burr had arrived in New York to seek revenge. One by "Sylphid" warned, "Let the disgraceful debauchee who permitted an infamous prostitute to insult and embitter the dying moments of his injured wife—let him look home."[53] Another handbill, signed "A Young German," accused Burr of looting the estate of a Dutch baker to relieve his own indebtedness of six thousand dollars.[54] "An Episcopalian" informed readers that Burr "meditates a violent attack upon the *rights of property.*"[55] Some broadsides even got around to dealing with politics. "The Liar, Caught in His Own Toils" reiterated the familiar refrain that Burr had tried to swipe the 1800 election from Jefferson and now planned to dismember the union.[56]

At his late January meeting with Jefferson, Burr had identified Hamilton as the author of unsigned broadsides against him, but no evidence of this exists. Even in private letters, Hamilton never referred to specific carnal acts committed by Burr; in that sense, he was quite discreet. Yet Burr may have thought that Hamilton secretly contributed to Federalist slander, even though most of the offensive handbills echoed articles in the *American Citizen* and probably originated with Republicans. From his campaign literature, it was clear that Burr, like Hamilton, felt persecuted by slander and powerless to stop it. One broadside said indignantly, "Col. Burr has been loaded with almost every epithet of abuse to be found in the English language. He has been represented as a man totally destitute of political principle or integrity."[57]

Burr feigned indifference to the "new and amusing libels" published against him, as if nothing could shake his perfect aplomb.[58] Unlike his opponents, he ran a clean, if aggressive, campaign from his John Street headquarters. He fought with his usual zest and charm, and his criticisms of Morgan Lewis fell within the bounds of propriety. Criticizing nepotism among the Livingstons and Clintons, he lent his campaign a populist tinge by styling himself "a plain and unostentatious citizen" who ran for office "unaided by the power of innumerable family connections."[59] To elevate Burr in Federalist eyes, his broadsides likened him to Hamilton. One sheet described him as a first-rate lawyer who stood on a par "with Hamilton in point of sound argument, polished shafts and manly nervous eloquence, impressive and convincing reasoning."[60]

Despite the propaganda barrage directed against him, Burr thought the race was winnable, and his followers remained sanguine as the April vote approached. Oliver Wolcott, Jr., considered it "most probable that Colo. Burr will succeed. It is certain that he commands a numerous and intrepid party who are not to be intimidated or subdued."[61] Days before the election, Hamilton sounded mournful about the outcome. "I say nothing on politics," he confided to his brother-in-law Philip Jeremiah Schuyler, "with the course of which I am too much disgusted to give myself any future concern about them."[62] As usual, Hamilton proved too pessimistic. When the votes were counted in late April, Burr had narrowly won New York City, but he was outvoted so heavily upstate that he lost the race by a one-sided margin of 30,829 to 22,139.

This stunning, unexpected defeat seemed to deal a mortal blow to Burr's career. He had ten months left as vice president, but then what? Hounded from Washington and the Republican party, he had failed to recoup lost ground in New York. Was Hamilton responsible for his loss in the gubernatorial race? Hamilton's friend Judge Kent dismissed this view, noting that most Federalists had voted for Burr, while the "cold reserve and indignant reproaches of Hamilton may have controlled a few."[63] It is highly unlikely that Hamilton's waning influence could have made the difference in a landslide election. John Quincy Adams observed that New York Federalists were now "a minority, and of that minority, only a minority were admirers and partisans of Mr. Hamilton."[64] Far more decisive in the outcome was President Jefferson. After assuring Burr that he never intruded in elections, he intimated to two New York congressmen that Burr was officially excommunicated from the Republican party. This view, reported in the New York papers, stigmatized Burr among Republican loyalists.

Nonetheless, Burr's admirers were adamant that Alexander Hamilton had destroyed his career. "If General Hamilton had not opposed Colonel Burr, I have very little doubt but he would have been elected governor of New York," wrote Burr's friend Charles Biddle.[65] This view was repeated by an early Burr biographer, who said that Burr had won "the confidence of the more moderate Federalists and nothing but Hamilton's vehement opposition had prevented that party's voting for him en masse."[66] This theory ignores the awkward fact that Burr had fared very well indeed among New York Federalists. Burr's editor, Mary-Jo Kline, has written, "By the week before the election . . . there were signs that the Federalist organization had given A[aron] B[urr] full, if clandestine, support."[67] After the loss, Burr kept up his usual unflappable air. Once the election results were in, he sent a letter full of fake bravado to his daughter, Theodosia, in which he recounted his recent love life. He had been unable to visit a certain mistress named Celeste, he said, but had made time for his New York "inamorata," identified as "La G." He praised the latter for being "good-tempered and cheerful" but also faulted her for being "flat-chested." Then, almost as an afterthought, he mentioned the governor's race, saying that the "election is lost by a great majority: *tant mieux* [so much the better]."[68] This glib insouciance reflected Burr's lifelong self-protective pose of aristocratic disdain and indifference. Under this urbanity, however, grew a murderous rage against Hamilton. In his eyes, Hamilton had blocked his path to the presidency by supporting Jefferson in 1801. Now Hamilton had blocked his path to the New York governorship. Alexander Hamilton was a curse, a hypocrite, the author of all his misery. At least that's how Aaron Burr saw things in the spring of 1804.

During the campaign, Hamilton had been troubled by new secession threats among Federalists. Nothing was more antithetical to his conception of Federalism. A friend, Adam Hoops, recalled running into Hamilton in Albany in early March and asking him about the secession rumors. "The idea of disunion he could not hear of without impatience," recalled Hoops, "and expressed his reprobation of it *using strong* terms."[69] In a tremendous visionary leap, Hamilton foresaw a civil war between north and south, a war that the north would ultimately win but at a terrible cost: "The result must be destructive to the present Constitution and eventually the establishment of separate governments framed on principles in their nature hostile to civil liberty."[70] Hamilton was so appalled by this specter that he and Hoops talked of it for more than an hour: "The subject had taken such fast hold of him that he could not detach himself from it until a professional engagement called him into court."[71] Hamilton continued to worry about the "bloody anarchy" and the overthrow of the Constitution that might result from Jefferson's policies.[72]

That spring, Timothy Pickering, the ex–secretary of state and now a senator from Massachusetts, made the rounds of Federalist leaders in New York, trying to drum up support for a runaway northern confederacy "exempt from the corrupt and corrupting influence and oppression of the aristocratic Democrats of the South."[73] Without support from the two large mid-Atlantic states, New York and New Jersey, such a federation would be stillborn. Pickering and the so-called Essex Junto hoped to recruit leading local Federalists. Though many New York Federalists feared the dominance of Virginia and the expansion of slavery after the Louisiana Purchase, both Hamilton and Rufus King solidly opposed any secessionist movement. Soon after Pickering's visit, Major James Fairlie asked Hamilton if he had been approached about the northern confederacy. Fairlie recalled that Hamilton "said that he had been applied to in relation to that subject by some persons from the eastward." Hamilton then added, "You know there cannot be any political confidence between Mr. Jefferson and his administration and myself. But I view the suggestion of such a project with *horror*."[74]

The secession campaign had matured to the point that its instigators planned a Boston meeting late that fall, after Jefferson's presumed reelection. Hamilton agreed to attend, undoubtedly to dissuade participants from this self-destructive act. Some detractors tried to cast Hamilton as a confederate in the plot, when it flew in the face of his life's overwhelming passion: the strength and stability of the union. Even Jefferson later referred to "the known principle of General Hamilton never, under any views, to break the Union."[75] Hamilton's dismay about the secessionist threat preoccupied him during the weeks leading up to the duel. His son John Church Hamilton told of one dinner party at the Grange just a week before the fatal encounter. "After dinner, when they were alone, Hamilton turned to [John] Trumbull, and looking at him with deep meaning, said: 'You are going to Boston. You will see the principal men there. Tell them from ME, at MY request, for God's sake, to cease these conversations and threatenings about a separation of the Union. It must hang together as long as it can be made to."[76] Since 1787, Hamilton had never wavered in his belief that the Constitution must be preserved as long as possible, nor in his commitment to do everything in his power to make it work. He was not about to change that view now.

FORTY-ONE

A DESPICABLE OPINION

Sometime in March 1804, Hamilton dined in Albany at the home of Judge John Tayler, a Republican merchant and former state assemblyman who was working for the election of Morgan Lewis. Both Judge Tayler and Hamilton expressed their dread at having Aaron Burr as governor. "You can have no conception of the exertions that are [being made] for Burr," Tayler had told De Witt Clinton. "Every artifice that can be devised is used to promote his cause."[1]

This private dinner on State Street triggered a chain of events that led inexorably to Hamilton's duel with Burr. Present at Tayler's table was Dr. Charles D. Cooper, a physician who had married Tayler's adopted daughter. Contemptuous of Burr, Cooper was delighted to sit back and listen to two of New York's most illustrious Federalists, Hamilton and James Kent, denounce him bluntly at the table. So exhilarated was Cooper by this virulent talk that on April 12 he dashed off an account to his friend Andrew Brown, telling him that Hamilton had spoken of Burr "as a dangerous man and one who ought not to be trusted."[2] Cooper asked a friend to deliver the letter; he later claimed it was purloined and opened. This may have been a cover story, though people often pored over private letters at local inns that served as post offices; it was not uncommon for letters to be intercepted and then turn up unexpectedly in print.

Before Cooper knew it, excerpts from his letter had appeared in the *New-York Evening Post.* Editor William Coleman evidently thought Cooper's words had been published in a handbill and needed to be refuted. He reminded readers that Hamilton had "repeatedly declared" his neutrality in the race between Burr and Lewis.[3] To drive home the point, Coleman ran a letter from Philip Schuyler repeating Hamilton's pledge to stay aloof from the race and saying that he could never have made the statement attributed to him about Burr. By writing this letter, Schuyler, unwittingly, became the agent of his cherished son-in-law's death.

Cooper took umbrage at Schuyler's insinuation that he had invented the story and on April 23 wrote a second letter, this time to Schuyler, substantiating his claim that Hamilton had traduced Burr: "Gen. Hamilton and Judge Kent have declared, in substance, that they looked upon Mr. Burr to be a dangerous man and one who ought not to be trusted with the reins of government."[4] Cooper noted that in February Hamilton had said as much publicly when Federalists met at the City Tavern in Albany to choose a gubernatorial candidate. But it was Cooper's next assertion that pushed relations between Hamilton and Burr past the breaking point. Far from being irresponsible, said Cooper, he had been "unusually cautious" in recounting the dinner at Tayler's, "for really, sir, I could detail to you a still more despicable opinion which General Hamilton has expressed of Mr. Burr."[5] This letter, which changed so many lives, appeared in the *Albany Register* on April 24, 1804.

On June 18, seven weeks after his election defeat, Burr received a copy of the upstate paper with Cooper's letter. Whether it was sent by an irate friend or a malicious enemy, we do not know. In his cool, disdainful style, Burr had prided himself on sloughing off allegations and not dignifying them with responses. But now, banished to the political wilderness, Burr was no longer immune to criticism, and he flew into a rage. Like many people who hide hostility behind charming facades, Burr was, at bottom, a captive of his temper. With his insatiable appetite for political gossip, he knew that Hamilton had been maligning him for years. On two previous occasions, they had nearly entered into affairs of honor over Hamilton's statements. During his feverish efforts to prevent Burr from becoming president during the 1801 election tie, Hamilton had called him profligate, bankrupt, corrupt, and unprincipled and had accused him of trying to cheat Jefferson out of the presidency. In October 1802, Hamilton had averted a duel over this by admitting that he had "no *personal knowledge*" of such machinations.[6] Burr later told a friend:

> It is too well known that Genl. H[amilton] had long indulged himself in illiberal freedoms with my character. He had a peculiar talent of saying things improper and offensive in such a manner as could not well be taken hold of. On two different occasions, however, having reason to apprehend that he had gone so far as to afford me fair occasion for calling on him, he anticipated me by coming forward voluntarily and making apologies and concessions. From delicacy to him and from a sincere desire for peace, I have never mentioned these circumstances, always hoping that the generosity of my conduct would have some influence on his.[7]

Some Burr admirers have noted that while Hamilton made scathing comments about Burr, he never responded in kind. This may say less about Burr's ethics than his style. Where Hamilton was outspoken in denunciations of people, the wily Burr tended to cultivate a wary silence, a studied ambiguity, in his comments about political figures.

When Burr set eyes on Cooper's letter, he was still smarting from his election defeat and the apparent collapse of his career. Before 1800, he could not have acted against Hamilton because of the latter's immense influence in the Washington and Adams administrations. Then as vice president under Jefferson, Burr knew that his political fate might rest with the Federalists and that he could not antagonize Hamilton. Now, Hamilton was fair game. He still bore the famous name but without the power that once made it so fearsome. Joanne Freeman has written, "Burr was a man with a wounded reputation, a leader who had suffered personal abuse and the public humiliation of a lost election. A duel with Hamilton would redeem his honor and possibly dishonor Hamilton."[8] Sometime that spring, Burr told Charles Biddle that "he was determined to call out the first man of any respectability concerned in the infamous publications concerning him," recalled Biddle. "He had no idea then of having to call on *General Hamilton.*"[9] Burr was, however, laboring under the misimpression that Hamilton had drafted anonymous broadsides against him. Perhaps Cooper's letter confirmed his hunch that Hamilton had been making mischief behind the scenes.

The great mystery behind Burr's challenge to Hamilton lies in what exactly Charles Cooper meant when he said he could detail a "still more despicable opinion" that Hamilton had spouted against Burr. The question has led to two centuries of speculation. Gore Vidal has titillated readers of fiction with his supposition that Hamilton accused Burr of an incestuous liaison with his daughter, Theodosia. But Burr was such a dissipated, libidinous character that Hamilton had a rich field to choose from in assailing his personal reputation. Aaron Burr had been openly accused of every conceivable sin: deflowering virgins, breaking up marriages through adultery, forcing women into prostitution, accepting bribes, fornicating with slaves, looting the estates of legal clients. This grandson of theologian Jonathan Edwards had sampled many forbidden fruits. To give but one recent example of scandal: six months before the dinner at Tayler's, Burr had received a letter from a former lover, Mrs. Hayt, that politely requested hush money. She explained that she was "in a state of pregnancy and in want. . . . [O]nly think what a small sum you gave me, a gentleman of your connections." She did not wish to expose him, she promised, "but I would thank you if you would be so kind as to send me a little money."[10] If Burr did not pay her, Hayt may have made good on her threat to expose him; if so, New York society would have been abuzz with the story. In the last analysis, however, the specific charge that Cooper had in mind was unimportant, for Burr was now poised to exploit any pretext to strike at Hamilton. Their affair of honor was less about slurs and personal insults than politics and party leadership.

On Monday morning, June 18, after digesting the Cooper letter, Burr asked his friend William P. Van Ness to come immediately to Richmond Hill, his home overlooking the Hudson. Burr was suffering from an ague, and his neck was wrapped in scarves. Many people, Burr told Van Ness, had informed him that "General Hamilton had at different times and upon various occasions used language and expressed opinions highly injurious to [my] reputation."[11] Thus, it was clearly a catalog of *cumulative* insults, rather than the Cooper letter alone, that had provoked Burr to action. By eleven o'clock that morning, Van Ness materialized at Hamilton's law office with a letter from Burr, sternly demanding an explanation of the "despicable" act alluded to in Cooper's letter. Both the tone and substance of Burr's letter telegraphed to Hamilton that Burr was commencing an affair of honor.

Everything in Alexander Hamilton's life pointed to the fact that he would not dodge a duel or negotiate a compromise. He was incapable of turning the other cheek. With his checkered West Indian background, he had predicated his career on fiercely defending his honor. No impulse was more deeply rooted in his nature. This outspoken man was always armed for battle and vigilant in deflecting attacks on his integrity. On six occasions, Hamilton had been involved in the duel preliminaries that formed part of affairs of honor, and three times he had been attached to duels as a second or an adviser. Yet he had never actually been the principal in a duel. His editor, Harold C. Syrett, has observed that, until the summer of 1804, Hamilton "was obsessed with dueling in the abstract, but not with duels in fact."[12]

The dueling cult was still widespread, though far from universal. Jefferson and Adams opposed dueling, and Franklin had deplored it as a "murderous practice."[13] Dueling was especially prevalent among military officers, who prided themselves on their romantic sense of honor and found this ritualized violence the perfect way to express it. Both Hamilton and Burr had been schooled in this patrician culture. Military men always feared that if they ducked a duel they might be branded cowards, drastically impairing their future ability to command troops. Since he envisioned a host of bloody possibilities in America's immediate future—a civil war, anarchy, a secessionist revolt—and thought he might lead an army to deal with them, Hamilton dwelled on the implications for his courage in accepting or declining Burr's challenge. Courage was inseparable from his conception of leadership. Said one contemporary of Hamilton: "He was a *soldier* and could not bear the imputation of wanting spirit. Least of all could he bear the supercilious vaunting of Aaron Burr that he had been called by him to account and shrunk from the call."[14]

Dueling was de rigueur among those, like Burr and Hamilton, who identified with America's social elite—Burr by birth, Hamilton by marriage and accomplishment. If a social inferior insulted you, you thrashed him with your cane. If you traded insults with a social equal, you selected pistols and repaired to the dueling ground. In theory, Burr could have sued Hamilton for libel, but it was thought infra dig for a gentleman to do so. Hamilton said loftily that he had largely refrained from libel suits because he preferred "repaying hatred with contempt."[15]

Politicians were among the most ardent duelists. Many duels arose from partisan disputes and, as Joanne Freeman has shown in *Affairs of Honor*, they often followed contested elections, as losers sought to recoup their standing. Political parties were still fluid organizations based on personality cults, and no politician could afford to have his honor impugned. Though fought in secrecy and seclusion, duels always turned into highly public events that were covered afterward with rapt attention by the press. They were designed to sway public opinion and shape the images of the adversaries.

Duels were also elaborate forms of conflict resolution, which is why duelists did not automatically try to kill their opponents. The mere threat of gunplay concentrated the minds of antagonists, forcing them and their seconds into extensive negotiations that often ended with apologies instead of bullets. Experience had taught Hamilton that if he was tough and agile in negotiations he could settle disputes without resort to weapons. In the unlikely event that a duel occurred, the antagonists frequently tried only to wound each other, clipping an arm or a leg. If both parties survived the first round of a duel, they still had a chance to pause and settle their dispute before a second round. The point was not to exhibit deadly marksmanship; it was to demonstrate courage by submitting to the duel. Further militating against a mortal ending was that many states had levied harsh penalties for dueling. Although these laws were seldom applied, especially when social luminaries were involved, the possibility of prosecution always existed. Even if no legal action was taken, the culprit might still be ostracized as a bloodthirsty scoundrel, defeating his purpose in having dueled.

Hamilton could thus have assumed that he would likely emerge alive, though not unscathed, from his affair of honor with Burr. At the same time, he faced a situation in many ways unlike anything he had ever experienced. In previous affairs, Hamilton had been on the offensive, taking opponents by surprise and briskly demanding apologies and retractions. He was a past master at using this technique to muzzle specific people who had slandered him. Now he found himself on the receiving end, deprived of the righteous wrath and moral authority of being the wronged party. He could not take an aggressive, high-minded tone, since it was he who stood accused of slander.

Ordinarily, Hamilton might have assumed that the worldly Burr would see that he had nothing to gain and everything to lose by murdering him. They had been colleagues for twenty years and had enjoyed each other's company. That spring, Hamilton had told a mutual friend that political disputes were more civilized in New York than in Philadelphia and that they "never carried party matters so far as to let it interfere with their social parties." He even mentioned that he and Colonel Burr "always behaved with courtesy to each other."[16] Yet Hamilton knew that Burr's career had been damaged, even ruined, and he feared that he was in a homicidal mood. Hamilton told his friend the Reverend John M. Mason that "for several months past he had been convinced that nothing would satisfy the malice of Burr but the sacrifice of his life."[17] At every step, Hamilton proceeded with a sense of gravity that suggested his awareness of the possibility of his impending death.

Throughout his affair with Burr, Hamilton evinced ambivalence about dueling. In light of his extensive history of affairs of honor, it may seem disingenuous for Hamilton to have stated that he did not believe in duels. But with his son Philip's death and his own growing attention to religion, Hamilton *had* developed a principled aversion to the practice. By a spooky coincidence, in the last great speech of his career Hamilton eloquently denounced dueling. During the Harry Croswell case, he argued that it was forbidden "on the principle of natural justice that no man shall be the avenger of his own wrongs, especially by a deed alike interdicted by the laws of God and man."[18] In agreeing to duel with Burr, Hamilton claimed to be acting contrary to his own wishes in order to appease public opinion. As his second, Nathaniel Pendleton, later wrote, dueling might be barbarous, but it was "a custom which has nevertheless received the sanction of public opinion in the refined age and nation in which we live, by which it is made the test of honor or disgrace."[19] In 1804, Alexander Hamilton did not think he could afford to flunk that test, though many friends would fault him for bowing to this popular prejudice.

It is hard to escape the impression that in the early stages of negotiations it was the headstrong Hamilton, not Burr, who was the intransigent party. The letter that William P. Van Ness carried to Hamilton's law office on June 18 demanded a "prompt and unqualified acknowledgment or denial" of any expression that might have justified Charles Cooper's use of the term *despicable.*[20] Hamilton could have mollified Burr by saying that he had no personal quarrel with him and offering a bland statement of apology or regret. Instead, he adopted the slightly irritated tone of a busy man being unjustly harassed. In niggling, hairsplitting style, Hamilton objected that Burr's charge against him was too general and that "if Mr. Burr would refer to any *particular expressions,* he would recognize or disavow them."[21]

Technically, Hamilton was correct. In affairs of honor, the aggressor was sup-posed to pinpoint his accusations and do so as soon after the event as possible. In his own experiences, Hamilton had cited chapter and verse about the charges. Now Burr was dragging up dinner-party chatter from three months ago and resting everything on an adjective. For a man with Hamilton's full schedule, it was difficult, if not impossible, to recollect old table talk, and he had legitimate grounds to protest. Yet he must have suspected that Burr was trying to coax him into a duel to satisfy political purposes as well as rage. If so, he played into Burr's hands by be-having in a haughty, inflexible manner.

When Van Ness said that he found his response inadequate, Hamilton promised that he would review the *Albany Register*—he had never even seen the Cooper quote—as well as Burr's letter and get back to him later in the day. At 1:30 P.M., Hamilton stopped by Van Ness's home and pleaded a "variety of engagements," while assuring him of a response by Wednesday. He told Van Ness that "he was sorry Mr Burr had adopted the present course, that it was a subject that required some deliberation, and that he wished to proceed with justifiable caution and cir-cumspection."[22]

On Wednesday evening, June 20, Hamilton dropped off his response at Van Ness's home. Instead of applying balm to Burr's wounds, Hamilton struck a didac-tic tone and quibbled over the word *despicable.* "'Tis evident that the phrase 'still more despicable' admits of infinite shades from very light to very dark. How am I to judge of the degree intended?"[23] A defensive tone crept into his prose: "I deem it in-admissible on principle to consent to be interrogated as to the justness of the *infer-ences* which may be drawn by *others* from whatever I may have said of a political opponent in the course of a fifteen years competition."[24] He stood ready to avow or disavow specific charges, but he would not give Burr a blanket retraction. Then he curtly added lines that committed him to a duel: "I trust, on more reflection, you will see the matter in the same light with me. If not, I can only regret the circum-stance and must abide the consequences."[25]

In his acerbic reply the next day, Burr only hardened his position. He thought Hamilton had patronized him with a pedantic discourse. "The question is not whether [Cooper] has understood the meaning of the word or has used it accord-ing to syntax and with grammatical accuracy," Burr wrote, "but whether you have authorised this application either directly or by uttering expressions or opinions derogatory to my honor." Far from being appeased, Burr resolved to proceed with his challenge: "Your letter has furnished me with new reasons for requiring a defi-nite reply."[26]

At noon on Friday, June 22, Van Ness delivered Burr's message to Hamilton, who read it in his presence. Hamilton seemed perplexed and said that Burr's letter "con-

tained several offensive expressions and seemed to close the door to all further reply. . . . [H]e had hoped the answer he had returned to Col. Burr's first letter would
have given a different direction to the controversy."[27] As if this were a legal debate
or a tutorial in logic, Hamilton could not see why Burr would expect him to make
a specific disavowal to a general statement. He did not appreciate the need for personal delicacy. Eager to defuse the controversy, Van Ness fairly dictated language to
Hamilton that would have ended the matter. He said that if Hamilton replied to
Burr that "he could recollect the use of no terms that would justify the construction
made by Dr Cooper it would . . . have opened a door for accommodation."[28] But
Hamilton, turning a deaf ear, repeated his original objection to a broad disavowal.
Since Hamilton had refused to reply, Van Ness returned to Richmond Hill and in-
formed Burr that he "must pursue such [a] course as he should deem most proper."[29]
In a shockingly brief span, the two men had moved to the brink of a duel and were
ready to lay down their lives over an adjective.

After talking with Hamilton, Van Ness consulted with Nathaniel Pendleton. At
first, Pendleton could not understand why Hamilton refused to repudiate any statement he might have made. "Mr. Pendleton replied that he believed General Hamilton would have no objections to make such [a] declaration and left me for the
purpose of consulting him," Van Ness recalled.[30] Pendleton was chastened by his
visit with Hamilton, who called Burr's letter "rude and offensive" and unanswer-
able.[31] Later in the day, Pendleton told Van Ness that he had not appreciated "the
whole force and extent" of Hamilton's feelings and his profound difficulty in complying with Burr's request.[32] In a new letter, Hamilton gave Burr a good tongue-
lashing, describing his expressions as "indecorous and improper" and making
compromise ever more elusive.[33] He tried to turn the tables on Burr, seize the moral
high ground, and cast himself as the victim. It clearly bothered him that he was being asked to make amends to Burr, whom he regarded as his intellectual, political,
and ethical inferior.

Judge Nathaniel Pendleton was a confidant of Hamilton who had fought in the
Revolution before becoming a U.S. district-court judge in Georgia. Even though he
suspected Pendleton of Republican leanings, Hamilton had developed such high
respect for him that he had recommended him to President Washington as a candidate for secretary of state: "Judge Pendleton writes well, is of respectable abilities,
and [is] a gentlemanlike, smooth man."[34] In 1796, Pendleton moved to New York to
escape the Georgia climate, which was harming his health, and he quickly established himself as a distinguished jurist.

The courteous, dignified Pendleton was dismayed by Hamilton's rigidity. "The
truth is that General Hamilton had made up his mind to meet Mr. Burr before he
called upon me, provided he should be required to do what his first letter declined,"

Pendleton later told a relative. "And it was owing to my solicitude and my efforts to prevent extremities that the correspondence was kept open from 23 June to the 27th."[35] Burr, it must be said, proved no less obdurate. George Clinton later told one senator that "Burr's intention to challenge was known to a certain club . . . long before it was known to Hamilton. . . . [T]his circumstance induced many to consider it more like an assassination than a duel."[36] Between Hamilton's combative psychology and Burr's need to solve his political quandary, there was little room for the seconds to hammer out a deal.

In replying to Hamilton's unyielding second letter, Burr obeyed the inexorable logic of an affair of honor. He wrote to Hamilton and regretted that he lacked "the frankness of a soldier and the candor of a gentleman" and quoted Hamilton's ominous phrase that he was ready to meet the consequences. "This I deemed a sort of defiance," said Burr. "Thus, sir, you have invited the course I am about to pursue and now by your silence impose it upon me."[37] Aaron Burr and Alexander Hamilton had moved from frosty words to a mutual and irreversible commitment to a duel.

Hamilton spent that weekend at the Grange and did not set eyes on Burr's letter until June 26. Over the weekend, Pendleton met several times with Van Ness, trying to arbitrate a solution. If Hamilton had been the more recalcitrant one at first, it was now Burr's turn to throw up insurmountable obstacles. Pendleton thought he saw a way out of the impasse. If Burr asked Hamilton to specify whether there had been "any impeachment of his *private* character" (italics added) during the Albany dinner, Hamilton could disclaim such a statement.[38] But Burr had drawn up truculent instructions for Van Ness that precluded any such harmonious resolution. For a long time, he said, he had endured Hamilton's insults "till it approached to humiliation," and he concluded that Hamilton had "a settled and implacable malevolence" toward him.[39] By this point, Burr was clearly spoiling for a fight. On Monday, Pendleton asked Hamilton to recount what had been said at the Albany dinner. Hamilton's recollections were fuzzy, and he remembered only that he had spoken of "the political principles and views of Col. Burr . . . without reference to any particular instance of past conduct or to private character."[40]

By this point, Burr had gone far beyond the Cooper slur and upped the stakes dramatically. Van Ness told Pendleton that Burr now wanted Hamilton to make a *general* disavowal of any previous statements that might have conveyed "impressions derogatory to the honor of Mr. Burr," and he made clear that "more will now be required than would have been asked at first."[41] Burr was deliberately making impossible demands, asking Hamilton to deny that he had *ever* maligned Burr, at any time or place, in his public or private character. Hamilton could not sign such a document, which would have been untrue and which Burr might have brandished in future elections as an endorsement. Hamilton must have feared that such a concession would strip him of standing in Federalist eyes and make military leadership difficult. Burr's provocation only adds to the suspicion that the "despicable" statement was just a transparent pretext to pounce on Hamilton. After discussing the latest demands with Hamilton, Pendleton reported back to Van Ness that Hamilton now perceived "predetermined hostility" on Burr's part.[42]

At this point, a confrontation was unavoidable. On Wednesday, June 27, Van Ness delivered to Pendleton a formal duel request. Henceforth, Burr would entertain no further letters from Hamilton, and all communication would take place between the seconds. Duels tended to occur posthaste to prevent the secret from leaking out. But this duel was scheduled at a relatively distant date, July 11, for reasons that speak well of Hamilton. The New York Supreme Court was holding its final session in Manhattan on Friday, July 6, and Hamilton felt duty bound to satisfy clients who had lawsuits pending. His sense of professional responsibility was impeccable. He told Pendleton, "I should not think it right in the midst of a circuit court to withdraw my services from those who may have confided important interests to me and expose them to the embarrassment of seeking other counsel who may not have time to be sufficiently instructed."[43] He also needed time to put his personal affairs in order. For the next two weeks, Hamilton hid the situation from Eliza and the children, as Burr did from his daughter, Theodosia. Only a handful of politically well-connected people in New York knew of the unfolding drama.

Once a duel was agreed upon, Hamilton had to reconcile the two glaringly incompatible elements of the situation: his need to fight to preserve his political prestige and his equally powerful need to remain true to his avowed opposition to dueling. He opted for a solution chosen by honorable duelists before him: he would throw away his fire—that is, purposely miss his opponent. This was the strategy Hamilton's son Philip had disastrously followed in his duel. It was likely Hamilton himself, writing in the *New-York Evening Post,* who gave this description of Philip's approach: "[A]verse in principle to the shedding of blood in private combat, anxious to repair his original fault, as far as he was able without dishonor, and to stand acquitted to his own mind, [he] came to the determination to reserve his fire, receive that of his antagonist, and then discharge his pistol in the air."[44] Only after Philip threw his fire away was his second supposed to announce his reason for doing so and try to resolve the dispute.

Aside from Pendleton, Hamilton confided his plan to waste his shot to Rufus King, the former minister to Great Britain and "a very moderate and judicious friend," who tried several times to talk him out of it.[45] King found dueling abhorrent but told Hamilton that "he owed [it] to his family and the rights of self-defence to fire at his antagonist."[46] King sneaked out of town the morning of the encounter, leading to criticism that he had acted cravenly when he could have headed off the catastrophe. King said that even though Hamilton had the "most capacious and discriminating" mind he had ever known, he rigidly followed the rules known as the "code duello."[47] Pendleton was likewise horrified at Hamilton's decision to throw away his shot and exhorted him not to "decide lightly, but take time to deliberate fully."[48] Hamilton would not listen. As so often in his career—the Reynolds and Adams pamphlets spring to mind—he became possessed by a notion and would not let it go. In this frame of mind and in spite of his son's experience, he was impervious to reason.

Hamilton's decision has given rise to speculation that he was severely depressed and that the duel was suicidal. Henry Adams phrased it, "Instead of killing Burr, [Hamilton] invited Burr to kill him."[49] Historian Douglas Adair has evoked a guilt-ridden Hamilton who planned to atone for his sins by exposing himself to Burr's murderous gunfire. In 1978, four psychobiographers studied the duel and also concluded that it was a disguised suicide.

It is indisputable that in Hamilton's final years he was seriously depressed by personal and political setbacks, and his judgment was often spectacularly faulty. Long beguiled by visions of a glorious death in battle, he had also never lost a certain youthful ardor for martyrdom. Yet in the duel with Burr, he obeyed the antique logic of affairs of honor. Because he followed a script lost to later generations, his actions seem lunatic rather than merely rash and wrongheaded. "He did not think of this course of action as suicidal," Joseph Ellis has written, "but as another gallant gamble of the sort he was accustomed to winning."[50] While the duel shocked many contemporaries, Hamilton and Burr partisans understood its logic, even if they did not endorse it. Attorney David B. Ogden said that his friend Hamilton knew that if he did not duel, "it would in a great measure deprive him of the power of being hereafter useful to his country."[51] Likewise, William P. Van Ness said that Burr had to defend his honor, for if he "tamely sat down in silence and dropped the affair, what must have been the feelings of his friends?"[52]

Hamilton gambled that Burr would not shoot to kill. He knew that Burr had nothing to gain by murdering him. Burr would be denounced from every pulpit as an assassin, and it would destroy the remnants of his career. Since he had provoked the duel to rehabilitate his career, it did not make sense for him to kill Hamilton. Hamilton calculated (correctly, it turned out) that Burr could not kill him without committing political suicide at the same time. This did not rule out the possibility, of course, that Burr might kill him accidentally or that he might submit to a murderous rage that overrode his political interests. If Burr did kill him, Hamilton knew, he would at least have the posthumous satisfaction of destroying Burr's alliance with the Federalists. On the other hand, Hamilton never wavered in his belief that if he did not face Burr's fire, he would lose standing in the political circles that mattered to him. With an exalted sense of his place in history, he viewed himself as a potential savior of the republic. He once told a friend, "Perhaps my sensibility is the effect of an exaggerated estimate of my services to the U[nited] States, but on such a subject every man will judge for himself."[53]

The antagonists approached their rendezvous in starkly different personal situations. Hamilton had a large family of dependents: Eliza and seven children ranging in age from two to nearly twenty. Some observers criticized Hamilton for having recklessly jeopardized his family to salvage his reputation. Burr, by contrast, was a widower with a daughter, Theodosia, who had married into the wealthy Alston family of South Carolina; he did not need to worry about the financial aftermath of his death.

Deeply conflicted about the duel, Hamilton displayed a fatalistic passivity. When King told Hamilton that Burr undoubtedly meant to murder him and that Hamilton should prepare as best he could, Hamilton replied that he could not bear the thought of taking another human life, to which King retorted, "Then, sir, you will go like a lamb to be slaughtered."[54] The day before the duel, Pendleton begged Hamilton to study the pistols and handed him one. "He quickly raised it to a line," said Robert Troup, "but, dropping his arms as quickly, he returned the pistol to Pendleton and this constituted the whole of his preparation to fight an antagonist very adroit in firing with pistols. I verily believe that Hamilton had not fired a pistol since the termination of the revolutionary war."[55]

Quite different was the diligent preparation of Aaron Burr, a superb marksman who had killed several enemy soldiers during the Revolution. After the duel with Hamilton, the press was awash with rumors that Burr had engaged in intensive target practice. One Federalist paper quoted a Burr friend as admitting "that for three months past, he had been in the constant habit of practicing with pistols."[56] The Reverend John M. Mason insisted that "Burr went out determined to kill" Hamilton and for a long time had been "qualifying himself to become a '*dead shot.*'"[57] John Barker Church later said that he had reason to believe that Burr "had been for some time practising with his pistols for this purpose."[58] Burr's friend Charles Biddle disputed this, saying that Burr "had no occasion to practice, for perhaps there was hardly ever a man could fire so true and no man possessed more coolness or courage."[59] So commonplace was the accusation that Burr had taken repeated target practice that it is probably more than mere Federalist mythology. George W. Strong, Eliza's lawyer in later years, visited Burr's home right before the duel. "He went out once to Burr's place at Richmond Hill on business," recalled his son, John

Strong, "and there he saw the board set up and perforated with pistol balls, where the infernal, cold-blooded scoundrel had been practicing."[60]

At least outwardly, Hamilton and Burr continued to mingle in New York society, pretending that nothing was amiss. Charles Biddle told of an acquaintance who "dined in company with Hamilton and Burr the week before the duel. He has since told me he had not the most distant idea of there being any difference between them."[61] Their final encounter before the duel occurred on the Fourth of July. Since Washington's death, Hamilton had been president general of the Society of the Cincinnati, the order of retired Revolutionay War officers that had aroused suspicions of hereditary rule. Hamilton could not skip the group's festivities without drawing notice, and he and Burr shared a banquet table at Fraunces Tavern. The year before, Burr had joined the society when courting the Federalist vote.

Burr sat morose and taciturn among the other members, averting his eyes from Hamilton. As John Trumbull recalled, "The singularity of their manner was observed by all, but few had any suspicions of the cause. Burr, contrary to his wont, was silent, gloomy, sour, while Hamilton entered with glee into the gaiety of a convivial party."[62] At first, Hamilton could not be induced to sing, then submitted. "Well, you shall have it," he said, doubtless to cheers from the veterans.[63] Some have said his valedictory song was a haunting old military ballad called "How Stands the Glass Around," a song reputedly sung by General Wolfe on the eve of his battlefield death outside Quebec in 1759. Others said that it was a soldiers' drinking song called "The Drum." Both tunes expressed a common sentiment: a soldier's proud resignation in the face of war and death. One version of the evening has Hamilton standing on a table, lustily belting out his ballad. As he delivered this rendition, Burr is said to have raised his eyes and watched his foe with fixed attention.

During this strange period of concealment, Hamilton continued to perform his fatherly duties. His son James, now a student at Columbia College, asked him to review a speech he had written. James was mystified by his father's response and only later understood its import. "My dear James," Hamilton began, "I have prepared for you a thesis on discretion. *You may need it.* God Bless you. Your affectionate father. A.H."[64] In retrospect, this homily sounds like the confessions of a man who had never learned to be discreet himself. Hamilton told his son: "A prudent silence will frequently be taken for wisdom and a sentence or two cautiously thrown in will sometimes gain the palm of knowledge, while a man well informed but indiscreet and unreserved will not uncommonly talk himself out of all consideration and weight." Someone without discretion, Hamilton added, was apt to have "numerous enemies and is occasionally involved by it in the most [difficul]ties and dangers."[65]

Did Hamilton here give vent to tacit regret for the loose language he had employed toward Burr?

By the spring of 1804, Alexander and Eliza had completed their retreat, the Grange, and begun entertaining on a grander scale. In May, they had hosted a dinner for Jérôme Bonaparte, Napoleon's youngest brother, who had just married Elizabeth Patterson of Baltimore. Then, in the week preceding the duel, Hamilton invited seventy people to the Grange for a lavish ball that included John Trumbull, Robert Troup, Nicholas Fish, and William Short, Jefferson's onetime secretary in Paris. Hamilton was fascinated by the French *fête champêtre,* the elegant alfresco parties held in wooded surroundings, favored by the French aristocracy. In the woods, Hamilton had planted a small cluster of unseen musicians, so that guests caught faint strains of a horn and clarinet as they strolled. John Church Hamilton left a sketch of his father at this dinner that conveys his social magnetism:

> Never was the fascination of his manner more remarked, gay and grave as was the chanced topic. . . . Never did he exhibit more the safe softness with the man of society. Eloquent feelings, sportive genius, graceful narrative—all spoke the charm of a generous, rich, and highly cultivated nature. Even at this time, amid the brilliant circle, he brought forward the son of a deceased friend, commended him to the attention of an influential friend, then took him aside and conferred with him as to his plans for the future. This was one of the last sunny days of Hamilton's short life.[66]

Hamilton devoted considerable time to arranging his affairs and drawing up farewell letters. The solemnity with which he performed these duties seems to bespeak some premonition that he might die. On July 1, he drew up a statement of assets and liabilities that showed him with a comfortable net worth. Yet he acknowledged that, if death prompted a forced sale of his property, the proceeds might not suffice for his fifty-five thousand dollars in debt. Most of the money had been spent on the Grange, so he needed to defend this splurge: "To men who have been so much harassed in the busy world as myself, it is natural to look forward to a comfortable retirement in the sequel of life as a principal desideratum. This desire I have felt in the strongest manner and to prepare for it has latterly been a favourite object."[67] Hamilton had expected to retire his debts with his twelve thousand dollars in annual income. Now he had to reckon on the chance that Eliza might be deprived of this money. Trying to console himself, he computed that Eliza stood to inherit some money from her recently deceased mother, and "her father is understood to possess a large estate."[68] He further noted that the Grange, "by the progressive rise of property on this island and the felicity of its situation," would "become more and more valuable."[69] Unfortunately, Hamilton's estimates were to prove grossly optimistic, so that the man who had so ably managed the nation's finances left his own family oppressed with debts.

Aware of the duel's political dimensions, Hamilton labored over a statement that would justify his conduct to the public. He admitted that he might have injured Burr, even though he had spoken only the truth. As a result, he wrote, he planned "to *reserve* and *throw away* my first fire and I *have thoughts* even of *reserving* my second fire and thus giving a double opportunity to Col Burr to pause and to reflect."[70] The wording here is significant. Hamilton assumed that Burr would have two such opportunities. Thus, Hamilton would have to signal to Burr his intention to waste his shot. He could either, as Philip had, fail to lift his pistol, or fire first and very wide of the mark.

In the statement, Hamilton acknowledged the grievous pain he might cause his family and even the harm he would do to his creditors. Writing for public consumption, Hamilton sounded more statesmanlike toward Burr than he probably felt. It is hard to take at face value his contention that he bore "no *ill-will* to Col Burr distinct from political opposition."[71] He saw that while he had much to lose by refraining from the duel, he had precious little to gain by facing it: "I shall hazard much and can possibly gain nothing by the issue of the interview."[72] Why then did he fight? To maintain his sense of honor and capacity for leadership, he argued, he had to bow to the *public's* belief in dueling: "The ability to be in future useful, whether in resisting mischief or effecting good, in those crises of our public affairs which seem likely to happen would probably be inseparable from a conformity with public prejudice in this particular."[73] In other words, he had to safeguard his career to safeguard the country. His self-interest and America's were indistinguishable. For Burr, Hamilton's letter reeked of sanctimony. When he later read it, he reacted with coldhearted contempt: "It reads like the confessions of a penitent monk."[74]

FORTY-TWO

FATAL ERRAND

In his last days, Hamilton seemed wistful but not distraught. He seems to have made peace with his decision to duel and elected to savor his remaining hours with his family. On Sunday morning, July 8, he, Eliza, and the children wandered the shady grounds of the Grange in the morning coolness. Back at the house, encircled by his family, he "read the morning service of the Episcopal church," recalled John Church Hamilton.[1] Then, later in the day, "gathering around him his children under a near tree, he laid with them upon the grass until the stars shone down from the heavens."[2]

On Monday morning, July 9, Hamilton left Eliza at the Grange and rode down to lower Manhattan, where he drafted a will at his last Manhattan town house at 54 Cedar Street. He named John B. Church, Nicholas Fish, and Nathaniel Pendleton as executors. In this document, he again stated, with more hope than true conviction, that his assets would extinguish his debts: "I pray God that something may remain for the maintenance and education of my dear wife and children."[3] As a man devoted to property rights and the sanctity of contracts, he also fretted about the fates of his creditors: "I entreat my dear children, if they or any of them shall ever be able, to make up the deficiency."[4] And again he expressed the tentative hope that the Schuyler fortune would save Eliza: "Probably her own patrimonial resources will preserve her from indigence."[5] That the methodical Hamilton left dangling the critical question of Eliza's future solvency seems shockingly out of character.

More than Hamilton, Burr found waiting for the duel unbearable, telling William Van Ness that he preferred an afternoon duel and did not care to "pass over" another day of delay. "From 7 to 12 is the least pleasant [time], but anything so we *but* get on," he moaned.[6] A surgeon usually attended duels, and Hamilton

proposed his friend Dr. David Hosack. Burr seemed inclined to skip medical attention, appending this curious postscript to Van Ness: "H[osack] is enough and even
that unnecessary."[7] Does this signify that Burr planned to kill Hamilton, making a
surgeon superfluous? Did he hope that, if wounded, Hamilton would simply bleed
to death? Or did he think that nobody would be injured? We'll never know. On the
afternoon of July 9, Van Ness and Pendleton finalized plans for the duel, which would
take place at dawn on Wednesday, July 11, across the river in Weehawken, New Jersey.

Right up until the end, Hamilton comported himself with stoic gallantry, giving
no hint of what was to come. He spent the afternoon and evening of July 9 with
his old Treasury protégé, Oliver Wolcott, Jr., who found Hamilton "uncommonly
cheerful and gay."[8] On his last workday, July 10, Hamilton ran into a family friend
and client on Broadway, Dirck Ten Broeck, who reminded him that he had forgotten to deliver a promised legal opinion. Afterward, Ten Broeck reflected with astonishment on Hamilton's reaction: "He was really ashamed of his neglect, but [said]
that I must call on him the next day, Wednesday—(*the awful fatal day*)—at 10
o'clock, when he would sit down with me, lock the door, and then we would finish
the business."[9] This represents, again, extraordinary proof of Hamilton's sense of
responsibility. Far from being suicidal, Hamilton planned to go straight from the
early-morning duel to his office to catch up on work—hardly the behavior of a depressed man meditating suicide. Nobody who saw Hamilton right before the duel
reported any special symptoms of gloom.

During Hamilton's final day at his Garden Street (today Exchange Place) law office, his clerk, Judah Hammond, observed nothing untoward in his demeanor:
"General Hamilton came to my desk in the *tranquil* manner usual with him and
gave me a business paper with his instructions concerning it. I saw no change in his
appearance. These were his last moments in his place of business."[10] Hamilton
drafted an elaborate opinion in a legal matter. Late in the afternoon, he made a last
stop on his itinerary, one that must have carried sentimental meaning. For weeks,
his King's College chum Robert Troup had lain bedridden with a grave illness that
Hamilton feared might prove mortal. When he dropped by to visit Troup, Hamilton did not mention the duel and overflowed with medical suggestions. "The General's visit lasted more than half an hour," said Troup, "and after making particular
inquiries respecting the state of my complaint, he favored me with his advice as to
the course which he thought would best conduce to the reestablishment of my
health. But the whole tenor of the General's deportment during the visit manifested
such composure and cheerfulness of mind as to leave me without any suspicion of
the rencontre that was depending."[11]

On the eve of the duel, Nathaniel Pendleton stopped by Hamilton's town house and made a last-ditch effort to dissuade him from his resolution to squander his first shot. Once again, Hamilton insisted he would fire in the air. When Pendleton protested, Hamilton indicated that his mind was made up. "My friend," he told Pendleton, "it is the effect of a religious scruple and does not admit of reasoning. It is useless to say more on the subject as my purpose is definitely fixed."[12]

Hamilton dedicated his last night to the activity that had earned him such lasting fame: framing words. Since one purpose of the duel was to prepare to head off a secessionist threat, he wrote a plea to Theodore Sedgwick of Massachusetts, warning against any such movement among New England Federalists: "I will here express but one sentiment, which is that dismemberment of our empire will be a clear sacrifice of great positive advantages without any counterbalancing good."[13] The secession movement would provide no "relief to our real disease, which is democracy"—by which he meant unrestrained, disruptive popular rule.[14]

That evening, in surveying his life, Hamilton was evidently transported back to his West Indian boyhood and the near-miraculous escape that he had made from St. Croix more than three decades earlier. His mind turned to his cousin, Ann Mitchell, who had rescued him with money for his education. At ten o'clock, Hamilton took up his quill and wrote to Eliza, "Mrs. Mitchell is the person in the world to whom as a friend I am under the greatest obligations. I have [not] hitherto done my [duty] to her."[15] Ann Mitchell was struggling in impoverished circumstances, and Hamilton expressed a fervent wish that his estate might "render the evening of her days comfortable." Should that prove impossible, he told Eliza, "I entreat you to . . . treat her with the tenderness of a sister."[16] He also told Eliza that he could not bear to kill another human being and that the "scruples of a Christian" had convinced him to expose his life to Burr: "This must increase my hazards and redoubles my pangs for you. But you had rather I should die innocent than live guilty. Heaven can preserve me and [I humbly] hope will, but in the contrary event, I charge you to remember that you are a Christian."[17] In contemplating the duel, Hamilton may have miscalculated, may have been egregiously foolish, may have talked himself into the mad and elliptical logic of dueling, but he definitely was not in a suicidal state of mind.

Many thoughts swirled through Aaron Burr's brain in his last days, and some of the most vexing pertained to money. The profligate Burr was more than short of cash: he was dead broke. The previous fall, he had contemplated selling his Richmond Hill estate to ward off demanding creditors. That he faced financial as well as political ruin may help to explain his almost palpable mood of desperation while seeking a duel with Hamilton. According to John Church Hamilton, in the period immediately preceding the duel (presumably before the challenge was issued) Burr was so harried by debt that he appealed even to Hamilton for help. Hamilton's son related this incredible tale that Eliza told her children:

> Hamilton was at his country seat and, soon after the early summer sun had arisen, was awakened by a violent ringing at the bell of his front door. He arose, descended, and found Burr at the door. With great agitation, he related circumstances which rendered immediate pecuniary assistance absolutely necessary to him. On returning to his bed, Hamilton relieved the anxiety of his wife caused by his early call. "Who do you think was at the door? Colonel Burr. He came to ask my assistance."[18]

With astonishing generosity, Hamilton solicited money from John Church Barker, who had dueled with Burr, and other friends to raise ten thousand dollars in cash. Burr also scrambled to scrounge up another $1,750 for an unforgiving creditor who had demanded sudden repayment.

Burr had always doted on his daughter, Theodosia, playing a Pygmalion role as he molded her into his image of womanly perfection. In so doing, he converted her into one of America's most literate young women. Burr wrote to his daughter in an intimate shorthand, chockful of clever jokes and gossipy references to his various amours. He gave her critical appraisals of the faces and figures of his many lovers. On June 23, the day after writing the defiant letter to Hamilton that guaranteed the duel, he celebrated his daughter's birthday at Richmond Hill in her absence, telling her the next day how the guests "laughed an hour and danced an hour and drank her health."[19] (Theodosia was then in South Carolina.) He advised her to study history, botany, and chemistry and gave her tips on how to form a first-class library. In these letters, Burr kept hinting at some unspoken crisis but never mentioned the duel. While Hamilton's last days were crammed with family and friends, Burr spent much of his time in solitude. On July 1, he told his daughter that he was sitting alone by the library fire at sundown, shivering from a sudden chill in the summer heat.

Burr had taken a personal interest in educating his slaves, though he never planned to free them. The night before the duel, he jotted down a sheet of instructions dictating their fates. It showed that the previous fall, this so-called abolitionist was still buying slaves, in this case a black boy named Peter, whom he hoped to groom as a valet for his grandson. Burr spoke kindly of a slave named Peggy and hoped Theodosia would retain her ownership, but the other servants were not nearly so lucky. "Dispose of Nancy as you please," he told his daughter. "She is honest, robust, and good-tempered."[20] Having married into a large South Carolina slave-owning family, Theodosia scarcely required more servants, making Burr's refusal to free his slaves the more inexcusable.

The final letters written by Hamilton and Burr provide an instructive comparison. As the two men contemplated eternity, Hamilton feared for America's future and the salvation of the union, while Burr worried about incriminating letters he had written to his mistresses, urging Theodosia to "burn all such as . . . would injure any person. This is more particularly applicable to the letters of my female correspondents."[21] Long reviled as an archconspirator by the Jeffersonians, Hamilton had nothing whatsoever to conceal and did not ask that any personal papers be destroyed. Burr, by contrast, wanted to incinerate many worrisome documents, telling Theodosia to burn one small bundle of letters tied with red string and another wrapped in a white handkerchief. Since he made these last-minute arrangements, Burr must have imagined, at least in theory, that he could die in the duel. This confirms that he had no idea that Hamilton planned to withhold his fire at Weehawken.

The night before the duel, Burr lost no sleep and dozed off quickly on the couch in his library. His slumber was neither fitful nor agitated. "Mr. Van Ness told me that the morning of the duel when he went to Colonel Burr, he found him in a very sound sleep," reported Charles Biddle. "He was obliged to hurry on his clothes to be ready at the time appointed for the meeting."[22] Burr donned a black silk coat that was to provide grist for interminable speculation. James Cheetham described its fabric as "impenetrable to a ball"—a sort of eighteenth-century equivalent of a bulletproof vest.[23] Burr partisans portrayed their hero as simply garbed in a bombazine coat and cotton pants. Burr was escorted to a boat awaiting him at a Hudson River dock by the most trusted lieutenants of his recent campaign—John Swartwout, Matthew L. Davis, and others—as if they were sending him off to a rousing election rally.

After Hamilton completed his valedictory note to Eliza in his upstairs study at 54 Cedar Street, he went downstairs and entered a bedroom where a boy was reading a book. This must have been the orphaned boy who had attended the recent outdoor party at the Grange. In an unpublished fragment that may have embroidered the truth, John Church Hamilton reveals that his father entered the room, gazed pensively at the boy, and asked if he would share his bed that night. Hamilton "soon retired, and placing [the boy's] little hands on his own, he repeated with him the Lord's Prayer."[24] The child then fell asleep in his arms. This image of Hamilton sleeping with his arms wrapped around an orphaned youth during his last night on earth is inexpressibly poignant and makes one think that his own tormented boyhood weighed on his mind that night. At three o'clock in the morning, Hamilton awoke one of his sons and asked the drowsy boy to light a candle. He made up a story that his four-year-old sister, Eliza, who had stayed at the Grange with her mother, had been taken ill and that he had to head up there with Dr. Hosack. In the dim candlelight, Hamilton composed a beautiful hymn to Eliza that was to become one of her sacred heirlooms.

By the time he finished, Nathaniel Pendleton and Dr. Hosack had arrived, ready to accompany him to Weehawken, and they all went off in a carriage. To avoid detection, Pendleton and Van Ness had worked out a precise timetable, with both parties scheduled to depart from separate Manhattan docks around 5:00 A.M. Each boat was to be rowed by four weaponless oarsmen whose identities would remain secret, sparing them any legal liability. The pistols were secreted in a leather case so that the boatmen could later swear under oath that they had never set eyes on any guns. Aside from the oarsmen, only the duelist, his second, and his surgeon were allowed on each boat.

Instead of the usual muggy July weather, the day dawned fine and cool on the water. Weehawken then stood far north of the city, so the seconds had allotted two hours for the journey upriver. (The dueling ground stood opposite today's West Forty-second Street.) Hamilton's boat departed from the vicinity of Greenwich Village. As the boat pushed north across a brightening river, Hamilton seemed relaxed and reiterated to Pendleton his vow "that he should not fire at Col. Burr as he had not the most distant wish to kill him."[25] At one point, Hamilton glanced back at the raucous, lively city that had given this outcast of the West Indies a home. During the past decade, New York's population had doubled to eighty thousand, and the vacant downtown lots had disappeared. The sight of the growing city apparently touched something in Hamilton, for "he pointed out the beauties of the scenery and spoke of the future greatness of the city," wrote his son.[26]

Because New York law dealt severely with dueling, local residents frequently resorted to New Jersey, where the practice was also banned but tended to be treated more leniently. At Weehawken, the Hudson Palisades form a steep cliff rising nearly two hundred feet from the water, and they were overgrown by thick woods and tangled brush. From afar, the cliff looked like a straight drop to the water, an impenetrable wall of rock clothed with dense vegetation. But at low tide, a little beach appeared down below. If the duelists pushed aside the bushes and tramped up a narrow path, they came upon a rocky ledge twenty feet above the Hudson that was well screened by trees. Idyllic and secluded, it faced an uninhabited stretch of Manhattan shoreline. Flanked by boulders and an old cedar tree, this level shelf was about twenty-two paces long and eleven paces wide—just large enough to accommodate a duel. The property was owned by Captain William Deas, who resided atop the cliff and was frustrated that his ledge was constantly used for duels. He heard the pistol reports, but could not see the duelists.

Vice President Burr arrived at 6:30 A.M. He and Van Ness stepped from their boat, ascended the dirt path, and began to sweep away underbrush and other debris from the dueling space. The rising sun began to shine down and they peeled off their jackets as they worked. Shortly before 7:00, the second barge arrived with Hamilton and Pendleton, who clambered up to the ledge and left Dr. Hosack down below. This was to protect the surgeon and boatmen from any legal consequences. The surgeon was expected to be close enough to the duel to heed cries for help but far enough away to profess ignorance, if necessary, of the whole transaction.

Thus, at 7:00 A.M. on July 11, 1804, Alexander Hamilton and Aaron Burr stood face-to-face, ready to settle their furious quarrel. Both gentlemen followed strict etiquette and "exchanged salutations."[27] Twenty-three days had elapsed since the onset of their clandestine imbroglio. For two decades, they had met in New York courtrooms and salons, election meetings and legislatures, and had preserved an outward cordiality. Had it not been for their political rivalry, they might have been close friends. Both entered the duel from weak positions, hoping to reap some measure of political rehabilitation. To judge from a final painting of him by John Trumbull, Hamilton retained his keen, steady gaze, but melancholy clouded his face. And to judge from a John Vanderlyn painting done two years earlier, Burr had receding hair, graying at the edges, and a hint of anger darkened his expression. He was handsome and elegantly attired, however, and fearless on the field of honor.

In businesslike fashion, Pendleton and Van Ness marked out ten paces for the duel and drew lots to choose positions for their principals. When Pendleton won, he and Hamilton oddly decided that Hamilton would take the northern side. Because of the way the ledge was angled, this meant that Hamilton would face not just the river and the distant city but the morning sunlight. As Burr faced Hamilton, he would have the advantage of peering deep into a shaded area, with his opponent clearly visible under overhanging heights.

As the challenged party, Hamilton had picked the weapons and chosen flintlock pistols. Pendleton and Van Ness had drawn up guidelines specifying that the barrels could not extend more than eleven inches and had to be smoothbore. (Smoothbore pistols were unreliable; by contrast, if the pistol barrels were rifled, the inner grooves made possible greater accuracy.) Hamilton brought the brace of dueling pistols owned by John Barker Church, the same pistols used by Philip Hamilton and George Eacker in 1801. Hamilton might have wanted to use these pistols in homage to his dead son. More likely, he needed to confine knowledge of the duel to a tiny circle of confidants. John Barker Church was a trusted, intimate friend, possibly the only one with a pair of dueling pistols, though many fashionable gentlemen of the day owned such pistols. Though he often had recourse to affairs of honor, Hamilton himself possessed no such pistols, underscoring that he had used these affairs to silence critics, not to harm them. The Church pistols had been man-ufactured by a celebrated London gunsmith, Wogden, in the mid-1790s. They were long, slim, and elegant, with lacquered walnut handles, ornamental designs, and gold mountings along their brass barrels. While they looked light and easy to han-dle, they weighed several pounds apiece, and their large lead bullets weighed an ounce apiece. It took practice to handle these unwieldy guns with speed and finesse.

During an examination of the pistols for the 1976 bicentennial celebration, ex-perts discovered an optional hair-trigger mechanism, which, when set, allowed a much lighter squeeze than if the regular trigger was used. Some commentators have found something suspect about Hamilton's choice of these pistols, as if this hidden feature unmasked his true intention to fire at Burr. Yet historians have always known about the hair trigger. When Pendleton handed Hamilton his weapon on the dueling ground, he asked "if he would have the hair spring set" and Hamilton replied, "Not this time."[28] Thus, even if Hamilton had intended to conceal the hair trigger from Burr, he decided not to exploit it. Hamilton's reply shows that he was still vacillating over whether to throw away his fire on the second shot as well.[29]

Pendleton and Van Ness again drew lots, and it fell to Pendleton to supervise the duel. The seconds loaded the pistols in each other's presence, then handed them, al-ready cocked, to Hamilton and Burr, who took up their assigned places. Pendleton recited the rules. He would ask them if they were ready. If they agreed, he would say "Present," at which point they could fire. If one party fired and the other did not, the duelist who had fired had to wait for the opposing second to say, "One, two, three, fire," giving his foe a chance to return fire. If the opponent refused to do so, then the sides would confer to see whether the dispute could be settled verbally or whether a second round was required.

Fanned by a light morning breeze, Hamilton and Burr now assumed sideways poses, presenting the slim silhouettes preferred by duelists. The sun was rising fast, and when Pendleton asked if they were ready, Hamilton, unnerved by light bounc-ing off the river, called out, "Stop. In certain states of the light one requires glasses."[30] He lifted his pistol and took several sightings, something that might have misled Burr about his intentions. Then he fished in his pocket for spectacles, put them on with one hand, and aimed the pistol in several directions. Burr and Van Ness later made much of the fact that Hamilton aimed the pistol once or twice at Burr. "This will do," Hamilton finally said, apologizing for the delay. "Now you may proceed."[31] That Hamilton put on his glasses has been given a sinister meaning by some com-mentators, but he may have wanted to ensure that he *didn't* hit Burr. We also know that he had not ruled out firing accurately on a second round.

Van Ness later confirmed that Burr had no idea of Hamilton's vow to fire into the woods. Hamilton did not have the option of standing there with his arms slackly at his sides. To have done so would have been interpreted as a cowardly refusal to duel, detracting from the heroic aura that Hamilton wished to project and defeating the whole purpose of submitting to the duel. So as Burr glared at Hamilton, he saw a guilt-ridden malevolence that did not exist. "When he stood up to fire," Burr later said of Hamilton, "he caught my eye and quailed under it. He looked like a convicted felon."[32] On another occasion, Burr said that Hamilton "looked as if oppressed with the horrors of conscious guilt."[33] Hamilton gave no evidence to anyone else of being bowed down by guilt.

Hamilton and Burr now braced for the event that Henry Adams later described as "the most dramatic moment in the early politics of the Union."[34] When Pendleton asked if they were ready, they both answered yes, and he then uttered the word *Present.* Hamilton lifted his pistol, as did Burr. Both guns were discharged with explosive flashes, separated by a split second or perhaps several seconds. Pendleton was adamant that Burr had fired first and that Hamilton's shot was merely "the effect of an involuntary exertion of the muscles produced by a mortal wound," a terrible blow in the abdominal area above his right hip, Pendleton wrote.[35] Hamilton rose up on his toes, writhing violently and twisting slightly to the left before toppling headlong to the ground. Hamilton seemed to know that his wound was mortal and proclaimed instantly, "I am a dead man."[36] Pendleton called for Hosack, who came charging up the path. In Pendleton's recollection, Burr started toward the fallen Hamilton in a manner "expressive of regret," until Van Ness warned him that Hosack and the boatmen were approaching. From a legal standpoint, Van Ness feared this would place Burr at the crime scene in full view of witnesses, and the two men therefore withdrew as Van Ness tried to shield Burr's face with an umbrella. Right before they stepped onto their boat, Burr said to Van Ness of Hamilton, "I must go and speak to him!"[37] Van Ness counseled him that this was ill-advised. To placate Burr, Van Ness ran up the footpath himself and reported back on Hamilton's condition before they pushed off from shore.

Van Ness never deviated from his insistent claim that Hamilton had fired first. "That Gen[era]l Hamilton fired first, I am as well persuaded as I ever was of any fact that came under my observation," he said.[38] He recalled this distinctly, he contended, because as soon as he heard the first shot, he swiveled around to see if Burr had been struck by Hamilton's bullet. For a moment, he even imagined that Burr had been hit because he seemed to falter. Afterward, Burr told Van Ness that he had stumbled on a stone or branch in front of him and sprained his ankle. He also explained that he had paused several seconds before firing back at Hamilton because the breeze had swirled the smoke from Hamilton's pistol in obscure eddies before his face and he was waiting for the smoke to clear.

Neither Burr nor Van Ness ever explained why, if Hamilton shot first, he missed his target by so wide a margin. When Pendleton returned to the scene the next day, he tracked down Hamilton's bullet and discovered that it had smashed the limb of a cedar tree more than twelve feet off the ground. The spot was also approximately four feet to the side of where Burr had stood—in other words, nowhere in his vicinity. (Pendleton sawed off the limb and gave it to John Barker Church, as either legal evidence or a memento.) If Hamilton had shot first, he had wasted his fire, exactly as foretold. And if Burr had fired first, as Pendleton alleged, then Hamilton seems to have squeezed the trigger in a reflexive spasm of agony and shot involuntarily into the trees. In neither scenario did Hamilton aim his gun at Aaron Burr.

Curiously enough, twenty-five years later, apparently without realizing the significance of his own statement, Burr himself confirmed that Hamilton's bullet had hit the tree overhead. In his seventies, he returned to the dueling ground with a young friend and relived the dramatic encounter. Of Hamilton's shot, he remembered that "he heard the ball whistle among the branches and saw the severed twig above his head."[39] Burr thus corroborated that Hamilton had honored his pledge and fired way off the mark. In other words, Burr *knew* that Hamilton had squandered his shot before he returned fire. And how did he react? He shot to kill, even though he had a clear shot at Hamilton and could have just wounded him or even stopped the duel. The most likely scenario is that Hamilton *had* fired first but only to show Burr that he was throwing away his shot. How else could he have shown Burr his intentions? As he had written the night before, he wanted to give Burr a chance "to pause and to reflect." He must have assumed that, once he fired, Burr would be too proud or too protective of his own political self-interest to try to kill him.

Once Hamilton had been shot, Pendleton propped him up on a reddish-brown boulder that is still preserved at Weehawken, the sole relic of the duel to survive other than the pistols. Hosack found his friend sitting on the grass, his face livid and ghastly. "His countenance of death I shall never forget," Hosack wrote. "He had at that instant just strength to say, 'This is a mortal wound, Doctor,' when he sunk away and became to all appearance lifeless."[40] Hosack slit away Hamilton's blood-stained clothes and examined the dying man. The bullet had fractured a rib on the right side, ripped through Hamilton's liver and diaphragm, and splintered the second lumbar vertebra, coming to rest in his spine. Hamilton was so weak that Hosack could not locate a pulse or detect any breathing and feared that his friend was dead. The only hope, he thought, was to get Hamilton out on the water. Assisted by the oarsmen, Pendleton and Hosack lifted Hamilton and carried the bleeding man down the footpath. They spread him out in the bottom of the boat and departed immediately for Manhattan, as Hosack administered ammonia-based smelling salts to his unconscious friend: "I now rubbed his face, lips, and temples with spirits of hartshorne, applied it to his neck and breast and to the wrists and palms of his hands, and endeavoured to pour some into his mouth."[41]

As they crossed the Hudson, Hamilton was revived by the river breeze and suddenly blinked open his eyes. "My vision is indistinct," he said, and his gaze appeared to wander.[42] Hamilton spotted the pistol he had used in the duel and, apparently convinced that he had never fired it, said, "Take care of that pistol. It is undischarged and still cocked. It may go off and do harm. Pendleton knows that I did not intend to fire at him."

"Yes, I have already told Dr. Hosack that," Pendleton rejoined.[43]

It was a very characteristic moment for Hamilton: the instinctive sense of responsibility, the fear of violence and disorder, the mental lucidity and self-possession even in his greatest agony. Hamilton's comments also suggest that Burr may have fired first and that his own unremembered shot had been a spasmodic reaction. Trying to conserve his ebbing energy, Hamilton again shut his eyes. He informed Hosack that he had lost all feeling in his legs, and the doctor verified this total paralysis. When the boat approached William Bayard's dock on the Manhattan shore, Hamilton told the doctor, "Let Mrs. Hamilton be immediately sent for. Let the event be gradually broken to her, but give her hopes."[44] Eliza, still at the Grange, knew nothing of what had happened, and it would take time to bring her downtown.

Notified by his servant that Hamilton and Pendleton had pushed off toward New Jersey at dawn, apparently from his own dock, the waiting William Bayard later said that "too well he conjectured the fatal errand and foreboded the dreadful result."[45] Bayard, a rich merchant and Bank of New York director, watched the incoming boat with trepidation and burst into tears when he saw Hamilton lying at the bottom. Servants brought a cot down to the water and gently transported Hamilton across Bayard's garden to his mansion, which stood at what is now 80–82 Jane Street. Taken to a large, second-floor bedroom, Alexander Hamilton was never to emerge from the house.

Soon after Hamilton was deposited in the upstairs room, word of what had occurred spread with electrifying speed. At the Tontine Coffee House, watering hole for the city's business elite, a sensational bulletin was posted: "GENERAL HAMILTON WAS SHOT BY COLONEL BURR THIS MORNING IN A DUEL. THE GENERAL IS SAID TO BE MORTALLY WOUNDED."[46] As onlookers absorbed this shocking news, they blanched with horror. Dirck Ten Broeck, threading his way through the streets en route to his scheduled appointment with Hamilton, encountered a friend who told him of the duel. "I was thunderstruck," he said, "but alas the report was true."[47] Pretty soon, knots of anxious New Yorkers gathered on street corners to discuss the still fragmentary reports. As the hours passed, the frenetic life of the city that Hamilton had enriched so immeasurably ground to a halt. "This is indeed a sad day," wrote Hamilton's associate David Ogden. "All business seems to be suspended in the city and a solemn gloom hangs on every countenance."[48] Throughout the day came bulletins on the dying man's state, and a mass of people congregated before the Bayard mansion. Some French ships anchored in New York harbor sent surgeons specially trained in treating gunshot wounds to see if they could resuscitate Hamilton.

At first, Hamilton suffered such exquisite pain that Dr. Hosack did not strip off his bloody garments but just plied him with weak wine and water. When Hamilton complained of acute back discomfort, Hosack and other attendants took off his clothes, darkened the room, and began to administer sizable doses of laudanum to dull the ache. Despite the pain, Hamilton reacted to the situation with stoic fortitude and an impressive regard for others, worrying constantly about the plight of Eliza and the children. Following his advice, Eliza had been summoned from the Grange but was told at first only that her husband was suffering from "spasms." Initially she trusted this fiction, Oliver Wolcott, Jr., wrote, and nobody dared to tell her the truth because it was "feared she would become frantic."[49] The concern for Eliza's mental health was not misplaced. When she discovered the horrid truth, she grew "half-distracted" and gave way to "frantic grief," said Hosack.[50] To comfort her, Hamilton kept intoning the one refrain he knew would soothe her troubled spirit above all others: "*Remember, my Eliza, you are a Christian.*"[51]

For those packed into the Bayard household, the scene of grief was unbearable. David Ogden watched as Eliza sat devotedly at her husband's bedside, fanning his feverish face. Ogden wrote a friend that "it is but two years since her eldest son was killed in the same manner. Gracious God! What must be her feelings?"[52] Angelica Church hastened to succor the man who had been her obsession for so many years. Gouverneur Morris would remember an inconsolable Angelica "*weeping her heart out.*"[53] She expressed her profound admiration for Eliza in the face of such intolerable adversity. "My dear sister bears with saintlike fortitude this affliction," she told their brother Philip.[54]

Aside from his strongly protective feelings toward his family, Hamilton was preoccupied with spiritual matters in a way that eliminates all doubt about the sincerity of his late-flowering religious interests. It is not certain that Hamilton was as eloquent on his deathbed as his friends later attested, but their accounts corroborate one another and are remarkably consistent. No sooner was he brought to the Bayard house than he made it a matter of urgent concern to receive last rites from the Episcopal Church. He asked to see the Reverend Benjamin Moore, who was the rector of Trinity Church, the Episcopal bishop of New York, and the president of

Columbia College. The eminent Moore balked at giving Hamilton holy communion as he wrestled with two nagging reservations. He thought dueling an impious practice and did not wish to sanction the confrontation with Burr. He also knew that Hamilton had not been a regular churchgoer. As a result, Bishop Moore could not, in good conscience, comply with Hamilton's wishes.

In desperation, Hamilton turned to a dear friend, the Reverend John M. Mason, the pastor of the Scotch Presbyterian Church, which stood near the Hamilton home on Cedar Street. A Columbia College graduate and trustee and a confirmed Federalist, Mason revered Hamilton's talents, and the latter reciprocated the affection. "He is in every sense a man of *rare merit*," Hamilton once said.[55]

When Mason entered the chamber, he took Hamilton's hand, and the two men exchanged a "melancholy salutation" before they studied each other in mournful silence.[56] Hamilton asked if Mason would administer communion to him. The abashed pastor said that it gave him "unutterable pain" to receive from Hamilton any request to which he could not accede, but in the present instance any compliance would be incompatible with his obligations. He explained that "it is a principle in our churches never to administer the Lord's Supper privately to any person under any circumstances."[57] Hamilton respected Mason's candor and prodded him no further.

Mason tried to console Hamilton by saying that all men had sinned and were equal in the Lord's sight. "I perceive it to be so," Hamilton said. "I am a sinner. I look to His mercy."[58] Hamilton also stressed his hatred of dueling: "I used every expedient to avoid the interview, but I have found for some time past that my life *must* be exposed to that man. I went to the field determined not to take *his* life."[59] As Mason told how Christ's blood would wash away his sins, Hamilton grasped his hand, rolled his eyes heavenward, and exclaimed with fervor, "I have a tender reliance on the mercy of the Almighty, through the merits of the Lord Jesus Christ."[60] Hamilton, struggling for breath, promised that if he survived he would repudiate dueling.

Rebuffed by Mason, Hamilton redirected his hopes of communion to the skittish Benjamin Moore. The bishop now faced considerable pressure to appease Hamilton, whose friends thought it heartless to refuse a dying man's last wish. "This refusal was cruel and unjustifiable," wrote David Ogden. "Why deny a man the consolation and comforts of our holy religion in his last moments?"[61]

Willing to reconsider, the stern prelate with the bald pate and long, grave face returned to the scene at one o'clock that afternoon. As befits a great orator, Hamilton roused himself for one last burst of persuasion. "My dear Sir," he told Moore, "you perceive my unfortunate situation and no doubt have been made acquainted with the circumstances which led to it. It is my desire to receive the communion at your hands. I hope you will not conceive there is any impropriety in my request." Then he added, "It has for some time past been the wish of my heart and it was my intention to take an early opportunity of uniting myself to the church by the reception of that holy ordinance."[62] Hamilton expressed his faith in God's mercy. When Moore termed dueling a "barbarous custom," Hamilton assured him, too, that he would renounce it if he lived.[63] Lifting his hands beseechingly, he said, "I have no ill will against Col. Burr. I met him with a fixed resolution to do him no harm. I forgive all that happened."[64] At that point, Moore relented and gave holy communion to Hamilton, who then lay back serenely and declared that he was happy.

The next morning, Hamilton's mind was still clear, though his strength was depleted and his body motionless. He could speak only with difficulty. Except for one heartbreaking moment, he managed to maintain his exceptional composure. Eliza had not allowed the children into their father's presence the previous day, but she now realized that the time had come for Hamilton to bid them farewell. She held up their two-year-old boy, Philip, to his lips for a final kiss. Then Eliza lined up all seven children at the foot of the bed so that Hamilton could see them in one final tableau, a sight that rendered him speechless. According to Hosack, "he opened his eyes, gave them one look, and closed them again till they were taken away."[65]

In Hamilton's last hours, more than twenty friends and family members pressed into his chamber, most praying on their knees with their eyes fixed on Hamilton's every expression. David Ogden said they gave way to "a flood of tears" and "implored heaven to bless their friend."[66] For some, the deathwatch became insupportable. "The scene is too powerful for me," Gouverneur Morris wrote. "I am obliged to walk in the garden to take breath."[67] Morris later recalled the scene around Hamilton, "his wife almost frantic with grief, his children in tears, every person present deeply afflicted, the whole city agitated, every countenance dejected."[68] Hamilton alone seemed resigned as the end neared. At one point, speaking of politics, he said, "If they break this union, they will break my heart."[69] He could have left no more fitting political epitaph.

Hamilton repeated to Bishop Moore that he bore no malice toward Burr, that he was dying in a peaceful state, and that he was reconciled to his God and his fate. His faculties stayed intact until about fifteen minutes before the end. Then, at 2:00 P.M. on Thursday, July 12, 1804, thirty-one hours after the duel, forty-nine-year-old Alexander Hamilton died gently, quietly, almost noiselessly. After a frenzied life of passion and drama, of incomparable heights and depths, it proved a mercifully easy transition. "Thus has perished one of the greatest men of this or any age," Oliver Wolcott, Jr., wrote to his wife.[70] A large bloodstain soaked into the Bayards' floor where Hamilton expired, and for many years the family refused to expunge this sacred spot.

Eliza snipped a lock of hair from her husband's head and commenced the long rites of widowhood. She was tortured with grief. "The poor woman was almost distracted [and] begged uncle Gouverneur Morris might come into her room," said David Ogden. "She burst into tears, told him he was the best friend her husband had, begged him to join her in prayers for her own death, and then to be a father for her children."[71] Normally a witty, cosmopolitan man and bon vivant, the peg-legged Morris could only stare at Eliza with tears streaming down his cheeks.

We do not know when Eliza first saw the hymn that Hamilton had written for her in the early-morning hours before the duel. Nor do we know when she tore open the envelope and read the farewell letter that Hamilton had composed for her on July 4, the day he attended the bittersweet banquet of the Society of the Cincinnati. At some moment during the next few days, a tearful Eliza sat down and read the lines that her dead husband had prepared for her:

> This letter, my very dear Eliza, will not be delivered to you unless I shall first have terminated my earthly career to begin, as I humbly hope from redeeming grace and divine mercy, a happy immortality.
>
> If it had been possible for me to have avoided the interview, my love for you and my precious children would have been alone a decisive motive. But it was not possible without sacrifices which would have rendered me unworthy of your esteem. I need not tell you of the pangs I feel from the idea of quitting you and exposing you to the anguish which I know you would feel. Nor could I dwell on the topic lest it should unman me.
>
> The consolations of religion, my beloved, can alone support you and these you have a right to enjoy. Fly to the bosom of your God and be comforted. With my last idea, I shall cherish the sweet hope of meeting you in a better world.
>
> Adieu best of wives and best of women. Embrace all my darling children for me.
>
> Ever yours
> A H[72]

FORTY-THREE

THE MELTING SCENE

When a handwritten notice of Hamilton's death went up at the Tontine Coffee House, the city was transfixed with horror. "The feelings of the whole community are agonized beyond description," Oliver Wolcott, Jr., told his wife.[1] New Yorkers of the era never forgot the extravagant spectacle of sadness, the pervasive grief. Even Burr's friend Charles Biddle conceded that "there was as much or more lamentation as when General Washington died."[2] As with Washington, this mass communal sorrow provoked reflections on the American Revolution, the Constitutional Convention, and the founding of the government. Unlike at Washington's death, however, the sorrow was laced with shock and chagrin at the senselessness of Hamilton's demise.

Because of Hamilton's relative youth, his large bereaved family, his extended service to his country, and his woeful end, he achieved in death what had so often eluded him in life: an emotional outpouring of sympathy from all strata of New York society. This reaction was repeated in other former Federalist strongholds, with one Boston cleric telling of streets crowded "with those who carry badges of mourning because the first of their fellow citizens has sunk in blood."[3] In Philadelphia, muffled church bells sounded, and newspapers dressed their columns with funereal borders. For the rest of its term, the New York Supreme Court draped its bench in black fabric, while the Bank of New York building was also sheathed in black. For thirty days, New Yorkers wore black bands on their arms.

Everybody in New York knew that the city had lost its most distinguished citizen. As statesman Edward Everett later said, Hamilton had set the city on the path to becoming "the throne of the western commercial world."[4] The evening of Hamilton's death, New York's leading merchants exhorted one another to shutter their shops for a state funeral hastily arranged for Saturday, July 14. "The corpse is already putrid," Gouverneur Morris wrote that Friday, "and the funeral procession must take place tomorrow morning."[5] Mourners assembled on Saturday morning in front of 25 Robinson Street (today Park Place), the home of John and Angelica Church. The New York Common Council, which paid for the funeral, issued a plea that all business in the city should halt out of respect for Hamilton. It was the grandest and most solemn funeral in the city's history to date.

That Saturday morning, guns fired from the Battery, church bells rang with a doleful sound, and ships in the harbor flew their colors at half-mast. Around noon, to the somber thud of military drums, New York militia units set out at the head of the funeral procession, bearing their arms in reversed position, their muzzles pointed downward. Numerous clergymen and members of the Society of the Cincinnati trooped behind them. Then came the most affecting sight of all. Preceded by two small black boys in white turbans, eight pallbearers shouldered Hamilton's corpse, set in a rich mahogany casket with his hat and sword perched on top. Hamilton's gray horse trailed behind with the boots and spurs of its former rider reversed in the stirrups. Then came Hamilton's four eldest sons and other relatives, followed by representatives of every segment of New York society: physicians, lawyers, politicians, foreign diplomats, military officers, bankers, merchants, Columbia College students and professors, ship captains, mechanics, and artisans. Collectively, they symbolized the richly diversified economic and political mosaic that Hamilton had envisaged for America. Conspicuously missing were the female victims of the calamity: Eliza, Angelica Church, and Hamilton's nineteen-year-old daughter, Angelica. Four-year-old Eliza and two-year-old Philip also stayed behind with their mother.

As the funeral procession wound east along Beekman Street, then down Pearl Street and around Whitehall Street to Broadway, the sidewalks were congested with tearful spectators, and onlookers stared down from every rooftop. There were no hysterical outbursts, only a shocked hush that deepened the gravity of the occasion. "Not a smile was visible, and hardly a whisper was to be heard, but tears were seen rolling down the cheeks of the affected multitude," wrote one newspaper.[6] So huge was the throng of mourners that the procession streamed on for two hours before the last marchers arrived at Trinity Church. "The funeral was the most solemn scene I ever witnessed," wrote David Ogden. "Almost every person was in tears, even the rabble of boys and negroes who filled the streets seemed to partake of the general grief. . . . The windows were crowded with females who were, almost without exception, weeping at the fate of their departed friend."[7]

A private drama enacted that day previewed the historical ambivalence that Hamilton was to inspire. Gouverneur Morris had delivered the funeral oration for

Washington at St. Paul's Chapel and was drafted to do the same honor for Hamilton. He was so shaken by Hamilton's death that friends thought he might not bear the strain of the address, but his real problems were of an altogether different nature. Instead of rushing to eulogize his friend, Morris first succumbed to a host of doubts and anxieties. In part, he was alarmed by the vengeful outcry against Burr and decided to omit all mention of the duel, lest the vast assembly fly into an uncontrollable fury. "How easy it would have been to make them, for a moment, absolutely mad!" he said.[8] But that problem was manageable compared to how to depict his brilliant but controversial and imperfect friend. For starters, there was the problem of his origins. "The first point of his biography is that he was a stranger of illegitimate birth," Morris confessed to his diary. "Some mode must be contrived to pass over this handsomely."[9] And what about Maria Reynolds? "I must not either dwell on his domestic life. He has long since foolishly published the avowal of conjugal infidelity."[10] And then Hamilton had never been guilty of modesty: "He was indiscreet, vain, and opinionated. These things must be told or the character will be incomplete and yet they must be told in such a manner as not to destroy the interest."[11] Perhaps most problematic was the controversial bargain that Alexander Hamilton had struck with the Constitution, dedicating his life to what he deemed a flawed document. "He was on principle opposed to republican and attached to monarchical government," Morris wrote.[12] Morris distorted and exaggerated Hamilton's views no less than his Republican enemies, but he identified a genuine, abiding conflict inside Hamilton as to whether republican government could achieve the proper balance between liberty and order.

Under the towering portico of Trinity Church, the funeral organizers had erected a carpeted stage with two chairs at the center: one for Gouverneur Morris, the other for John Barker Church. Hamilton's casket rested on a bier in front of the stage. The sprawling crowd was so massive that when Morris spoke his voice seemed to fade away in the vast space, turning his speech into an unintended dumb show for many of those squeezed onto lower Broadway. In his oration, Morris was more just and generous toward Hamilton than in his grudging diary notes. He applauded Hamilton's bravery in the Revolution; cited his legitimate doubts as to whether the Constitution could avert anarchy and despotism; and noted that Hamilton, far from being artful or duplicitous, was in most ways excessively frank: "Knowing the purity of his heart, he bore it, as it were, in his hand, exposing to every passenger its inmost recesses. This generous indiscretion subjected him to censure from misrepresentation. His speculative opinions were treated as deliberate designs and yet you all know how strenuous, how unremitting, were his efforts to establish and to preserve the Constitution."[13]

Morris sensed that the crowd was disappointed with his talk. The indignant spectators wanted to hoot and jeer lustily at Burr, who was never even mentioned. Moreover, the impact of Morris's words paled beside the arresting vignette of family grief presented to the spectators. Four of Hamilton's sons—Alexander (eighteen), James (fourteen), John (eleven), and William (six)—sat weeping on the stage beside Morris. One paper recorded: "The scene was impressive and what added unspeakably to its solemnity was the mournful group of tender boys, the sons, the once hopes and joys of the deceased, who, with tears gushing from their eyes, sat upon the stage, at the feet of the orator, bewailing the loss of their parent! It was too much. The sternest powers, the bloodiest villain, could not resist the melting scene."[14]

Once Morris had finished his speech, the casket was transferred to a grave site in the Trinity churchyard, not far from where Hamilton had studied and lived, practiced law and served his country. With Bishop Moore officiating, Hamilton's remains were deposited in the heart of the district that was to become the center of American finance. At the close, troops gathered around his grave, formed a neat square, and fired three volleys at intervals into the air. Hamilton was laid to rest with full honors in a martial style that would have gratified the most florid fantasies of the adolescent clerk on St. Croix who had once prayed for a war to prove his valor. "This scene was enough to melt a monument of marble," said Hamilton's *New-York Evening Post*.[15] Thus ended the most dramatic and improbable life among the founding fathers.

Because of his untimely death at forty-nine, Hamilton has retained a freshness in our historical memory. He never lived to grow gray or acquire the stiff dignity of an elder statesman. "Somehow it is impossible to imagine Hamilton as an old man," Catherine Drinker Bowen once wrote. "Even his hardheadedness and relentless skepticism showed a quality not of caution but of youthful daring, careless defiance."[16] The brilliance of his life was matched only by its brevity. The average life expectancy was then about fifty-five, so the dying Hamilton did not seem as young to his contemporaries as he does today, but many obituaries portrayed him as cut down by a bullet in his prime. Perhaps our impression of Hamilton's youthfulness has been magnified by the longevity of the first eight American presidents, who lived an average of nearly eighty years, with only Washington failing to reach his seventieth birthday. Hamilton's relatively short life robbed him not only of any chance for further accomplishment but of the opportunity to mold his historical image. Jefferson and Adams took advantage of the next two decades to snipe at Hamilton and burnish their own exploits through their lengthy correspondence and other writings. With his prolific pen and literary gifts, Hamilton would certainly have left voluminous and convincing memoirs.

In death as in life, the assessment of Hamilton's historical worth was sharply divided. His friends believed that a protean genius and rare spirit had exited the American scene. The Reverend John M. Mason thought him the "greatest statesman in the western world, perhaps the greatest man of the age. . . . He has left none like him—no second, no third, nobody to put us in mind of him."[17] His staggering catalog of achievements, compressed into a thirty-year span, has been matched by few Americans. But not everyone mourned his departure. In after years, John Adams grumbled of the duel, "No one wished to get rid of Hamilton in *that* way."[18] Adams complained to Jefferson that Hamilton's death had been marked by "a general grief," while Samuel Adams and John Hancock had died in "comparative obscurity."[19] In his autobiography, Adams took another potshot at Hamilton's death: "Vice, folly, and villainy are not to be forgotten because the guilty wretch repented in his dying moments."[20]

James Madison seemed less concerned with Hamilton's death than the exploitation of it by his Federalist opponents. Writing to James Monroe, he noted that "the newspapers which you receive will give you the adventure between Burr and Hamilton. You will easily understand the different uses to which the event is turned."[21] Jefferson reacted to Hamilton's death in the oblique style that Hamilton knew only too well. Three days after the funeral, almost as an afterthought in a letter to his daughter, Jefferson appended a postscript: "I presume Mr. Randolph's newspapers will inform him of the death of Colo. Hamilton, which took place on the 12th." Even now, Jefferson insisted on demoting General Hamilton back to a colonel. Aside from another fleeting reference to some "remarkable deaths lately," Jefferson made no mention of the man who had been the bane of his political life for fourteen years.[22]

After returning from Weehawken, Aaron Burr's boat docked at the foot of Canal Street, and he had proceeded on horseback to Richmond Hill with the blithe insouciance of a man who had just taken the morning air. Made of indestructible stuff, the vice president of the United States was not one to be tormented by guilt or unduly disturbed by some bloodshed. According to his early biographer James Parton, a young Connecticut relative dropped by Richmond Hill unannounced and found Burr in his library. Every inch the cordial host, Burr neglected to mention that he had shot Alexander Hamilton two hours earlier. While his antagonist was dying a half mile to the north, Burr breakfasted with his cousin and exchanged pleasantries about mutual friends. After the young relative left at about ten o'clock, he was walking down Broadway when a friend accosted him with astonishing news: "Colonel Burr has killed General Hamilton in a duel this morning."

"Why, no, he hasn't," said Burr's incredulous cousin. "I have just come from there and taken breakfast with him."

"But I have this moment seen the news on the bulletin," his friend insisted.[23]

Many such anecdotes circulated after the duel, portraying the bloodless composure and macabre humor with which Burr reacted to Hamilton's death. Some reports spoke of revelry at Richmond Hill, while others said that Burr expressed regret only for not having shot Hamilton straight in the heart. Some of these tales were doubtless fabricated and rightly dismissed as Federalist propaganda. William Van Ness insisted that Burr, "far from exhibiting any degree of levity or expressing any satisfaction at the result of the meeting" with Hamilton, had shown only "regret and concern."[24] Indeed, right after the duel, Burr asked Dr. Hosack to stop by Richmond Hill and update him on Hamilton's condition. But that about sums up the extent of Aaron Burr's concern for Hamilton. For the rest of his life, he never uttered one word of contrition for having killed a man with a wife and seven children and behaved as if Hamilton's family did not exist.

The rumors of this sangfroid surfaced in so many quarters and so perfectly coincide with the tone of Burr's own letters as to inspire a certain credibility. On the day of Hamilton's death, Dirck Ten Broeck wrote to his father, "Col. Burr is at his house, seemingly perfectly at ease and from report seemingly in perfect composure."[25] A Federalist paper, *The Balance and Columbian Repository,* conjured up a man "flushed with his victory" who cantered home after the duel and stopped to greet a married lady of his acquaintance, telling her "with gaiety that it was a fine morning."[26] The paper identified Burr's breakfast companion that morning as not his cousin but his broker, Nathaniel Prime, summoned for an amiable business chat. The paper stated that it took "a circle of half a dozen gentlemen" to convince Prime afterward that Burr had fired a lethal shot at Alexander Hamilton that morning.

If Burr reacted initially in cavalier fashion to the duel's outcome, it may have been because he did not yet know that Hamilton had informed both Pendleton and Rufus King of his plan to throw away his shot. To make this critical point stick, Hamilton repeated it several times on his deathbed and worked it into his farewell letters. As an artful lawyer, he had left behind a consistent trail of evidence for his posthumous vindication. Within a week, both Pendleton and Van Ness had published separate accounts of the duel and the correspondence leading up to it, sparking a hue and cry against Burr. Critics accused Burr of a premeditated plot to kill Hamilton, and overwrought citizens threatened to burn down his house. James Parton observed, "It was from that hour that Burr became a name of horror. The letters, for a person ignorant of the former history, were entirely damning to the memory of the challenger. They present Burr in the light of a revengeful demon, burning for an innocent victim's blood."[27] Many Hamilton partisans believed that Burr had done more than just try to vindicate his honor and that he had gunned down Hamilton in cold blood. One New York newspaper said that Hamilton had fallen "by the hand of a BASE ASSASSIN!"[28]

Thus, Hamilton triumphed posthumously over Burr, converting the latter's victory at Weehawken into his political coup de grâce. Burr's reputation perished along with Hamilton, exactly as Hamilton had anticipated. Both the Jeffersonian and Federalist press canonized Hamilton and vied in detestation of Burr. "We find the direful blow to have been the entire consequence and fixed purpose of [Burr's] own subtle, premeditated, fiend-like rancor," thundered a Maryland editorial.[29] An editor in Charleston, South Carolina, speculated that Burr's heart must have been stuffed with "cinders raked from the fires of hell."[30] Burr scoffed at such reactions. He believed that he had suffered Hamilton's slander for an unusually long period, had obeyed the standard dueling conventions, and was being persecuted by Hamilton's hypocritical friends. "General Hamilton died yesterday," Burr told his son-in-law on July 13. "The malignant federalists or tories and the embittered Clintonians unite in endeavouring to excite public sympathy in his favour and indignation against his antagonist. Thousands of absurd falsehoods are circulated with industry."[31] It especially irked Burr that New York Republicans who had berated Hamilton for years were suddenly kneeling and genuflecting before his martyred image.

The thick-skinned Burr probably could have faced down the sullen New York crowds. Then he learned that the city coroner had convened a jury to probe Hamilton's death. He knew that if he was indicted for murder, he might not be allowed to post bail, and so he began to mull over plans to leave town for several weeks. Ordinarily, gentlemen were not prosecuted for duels, and, since the duel had occurred in New Jersey, Burr did not think New York even had jurisdictional authority. "You can judge what chance I should have in our courts on a trial for my life, though there is nothing clearer to a dispassionate lawyer than that the courts of this state have nothing to do with the death of Genl. H[amilton]," he told Charles Biddle.[32] In plotting his next moves, Burr also had to contend with the fact that he was bankrupt. Just one day after Hamilton died, Burr wrote forlornly to William Van Ness, "Can you aid me?"[33]

Burr refused to allow duels, debts, or death threats to slow the racy tempo of his love life. On the night of July 20, he made time for a parting tryst with his new love interest, "La G," and boasted to Theodosia that she had shown "a degree of sensibility and attachment toward him" which pleased him very much.[34] That he had killed Hamilton nine days earlier did not seem to affect his sexual appetite and may even have enhanced it. The following evening, under cover of dark and attended by his fifteen-year-old slave, Peter, Burr boarded a barge in the Hudson and fled from any retribution in New York and New Jersey. By July 24, the fugitive vice president had arrived in Philadelphia, where he stayed on Chestnut Street with Charles Biddle, whose son Nicholas Biddle was one day to become president of the Second Bank of the United States. Even if he was a pariah, Burr was determined to enjoy his quota of fun. He contacted a favorite mistress, Celeste, and then told Theodosia wryly, "If any male friend of yours should be dying of ennui, recommend him to engage in a duel and a courtship at the same time."[35] Such ghoulish humor was Burr's stock-in-trade. Despite assassination threats, he stayed with Biddle for two and a half weeks and took only minimal precautions. Undeterred by hostile stares, he moved freely about the city. One paper reported, "Colonel Burr, the man who has covered our country with mourning, was seen walking with a friend in the streets of this city in open day."[36] All the while, Burr received reports from New York that the coroner's jury was pursuing his friends and had clapped his close associate Matthew Davis into jail for not answering questions.

On August 2, 1804, the coroner's jury delivered the verdict Burr had dreaded: that "Aaron Burr, Esquire, Vice President of the United States, was guilty of the murder of Alexander Hamilton, and that William P. Van Ness and Nathaniel Pendleton were accessories."[37] Arrest warrants were issued, but the situation was not nearly as dire for Burr as it seemed, as New York governor Morgan Lewis protested Burr's prosecution as "disgraceful, illiberal, and ungentlemanly."[38] Nonetheless, Burr feared that the governor might be coerced into ordering his extradition from Pennsylvania, and he made plans to flee farther south. He was convinced that, in the end, the charges would not stick, but he had to wait for the public hubbub to subside. Indeed, on August 14, a New York grand jury dropped the original murder indictment and replaced it with a lesser charge. Burr, Van Ness, and Pendleton were now accused of violating the law by sending a challenge to a duel.

For his temporary hideaway, Burr chose a large slave plantation on St. Simons Island, off the Georgia coast, an estate owned by his foppish friend Pierce Butler, the son of a baronet and a former senator. Before sailing south, Burr dabbled in the sort of secessionist mischief that Hamilton had feared, though of an even more treacherous nature. He held a secret meeting with British ambassador Anthony Merry and assured him that he would cooperate in any British attempt "to effect a separation of the western part of the United States from that which lies between the Atlantic and the mountains in its whole extent."[39] Inasmuch as Burr was now a political outcast, rejected by both parties, and a reprobate into the bargain, Merry considered the situation promising.

Burr passed several luxurious weeks on St. Simons with Peter and a young friend, twenty-one-year-old Samuel Swartwout. Outside of South Carolina, southerners tended to sympathize with someone who had slain Alexander Hamilton, and

Burr was showered with presents by the islanders. In early September, he toured the Spanish-controlled Floridas, posing as a London merchant and surveying the territory for a possible secessionist plot. Then he started his journey northward under the pseudonym "R. King." In many towns, his transparent disguise was quickly penetrated, and he was received royally, especially in the Jeffersonian stronghold of Virginia. He may have imagined that he was on the road to political rehabilitation, only to learn in late October that a grand jury in Bergen County, New Jersey, had indicted him for murder. The indictment was later tossed out because Hamilton had died in New York. Burr was taking no chances, however, and continued to steer clear of both New Jersey and New York. With irreverent humor, he wondered to Theodosia which state "shall have the honour of hanging the vice president."[40] The indebted Burr had another motive for boycotting New York: his creditors had seized his assets, auctioned his furniture, and sold Richmond Hill to John Jacob Astor, who was to subdivide it into four hundred small parcels and make a fortune. Now seven or eight thousand dollars in debt, Burr would face legal proceedings from local creditors if he crossed the state line. For the moment, the safest place in America for the vice president was the nation's capital, where he could preside safely over the Senate.

At the opening of Congress on November 4, 1804, it was more than a trifle startling for some legislators to see Aaron Burr settling into his chair on the Senate dais. Federalist William Plumer rubbed his eyes in disbelief: "The man whom the grand jury in the county of Bergen, New Jersey have recently indicted for the murder of the incomparable Hamilton appeared yesterday and today at the head of the Senate! . . . It certainly is the first time—and God grant it may be the last—that ever a man, so justly charged with such an infamous crime, presided in the American Senate."[41] An acute observer, Plumer noted that Burr had dropped his nonchalant veneer: "He appears to have lost those easy, graceful manners that beguiled the hours away [in] the last session. He is now uneasy, discontented, and hurried."[42]

Frozen out of Jefferson's administration for four years, Burr found a new warmth and hospitality in the wake of the duel. The president invited him to dine at the White House several times, and both Secretary of State Madison and Treasury Secretary Gallatin received him with newfound camaraderie. This may have expressed tacit contempt for Hamilton, but it also reflected another factor: as president of the Senate, Burr was to preside over the impeachment trial of Samuel Chase, an arch-Federalist and associate justice of the Supreme Court who had derided the "mobocracy" of the Jefferson administration.[43] Chase had been charged, among other things, with unbecoming conduct in the trial of James T. Callender under the Sedition Act. The trial was part of Jefferson's continuing assault on the

Federalist-dominated judiciary. And the president's confidence was only bolstered when he and George Clinton trounced Charles C. Pinckney and Rufus King in a landslide victory in the 1804 election.

In his final vendetta against Hamilton, Senator William Branch Giles of Virginia, who had harassed Hamilton with hostile resolutions as a congressman a decade earlier, organized a group of eleven Republican colleagues who appealed to New Jersey governor Joseph Bloomfield to terminate Burr's prosecution. Notwithstanding his later denials, Burr instigated this lobbying effort. The senators argued that "most civilized nations" refused to treat dueling deaths as "common murders" and pointed to the absence of penalties in previous New Jersey duels.[44] Senator Plumer was disgusted by what he saw as the Republicans' two-faced embrace of Burr: "I never had any doubts of their joy for the death of Hamilton. My only doubts were whether they would manifest that joy by caressing his murderer."[45] Governor Bloomfield spurned the appeal, and three years passed before New Jersey dismissed the indictment.

William Plumer wasn't the only person who gagged at Burr's incongruous presence in the Senate when the Chase impeachment trial started on February 4, 1805. One newspaper registered its shock thus: "What a page will that be in the history of the present democratic administration . . . that a man under an indictment for MURDER presided at the trial of one of the justices of the Supreme Court of the United States, accused of a petty misdemeanor!"[46] Chase was acquitted of all charges, while Burr was universally praised for his evenhanded conduct of the trial. For the moment, things were looking brighter for Burr. Before he stepped down as vice president, one Republican senator defended his duel by citing David and Goliath and claiming that Burr was controversial "only because *our* David had slain the Goliath of Federalism."[47] On March 2, Burr delivered a celebrated farewell speech to the Senate in which he praised the institution as a "sanctuary and a citadel of law, of order, of liberty."[48] His words possessed such poignant eloquence—the speech was his farewell to public life—that they wrung tears from many colleagues.

After leaving the vice presidency, Burr suffered instant political exile. He had outlived his brief usefulness for the Republicans and his courtship of the Federalists had ended with him gunning down the party's erstwhile leader. He was now bankrupt and stateless, a wanted man, even if he flippantly dismissed the New Jersey indictment. "You treat with too much gravity the New Jersey affair," he lectured Theodosia. "It should be considered a farce and you will yet see it terminated so as to leave only ridicule and contempt to its abettors."[49] Beneath his inveterate banter, Burr was worried: "In New York, I am to be disfranchised and in New Jersey hanged. Having substantial objections to both, I shall not, for the present, hazard either but shall seek another country."[50] As a result of Hamilton's death, many reformers were denouncing dueling, though the archaic institution survived well into the nineteenth century, counting Andrew Jackson, Henry Clay, John Randolph, Stephen Decatur, Sam Houston, Thomas Hart Benton, August Belmont, and Jefferson Davis among its practitioners.

With the restless spirit that had long perturbed Hamilton, Burr roamed through the Ohio and Mississippi River valleys, where frontier settlers tended to tolerate duels and despise Federalists. He explored various cabals with England to seize portions of American soil, including Louisiana and other territories west of the Appalachians, in order to forge a new empire. This would-be conquistador also meditated an auxiliary plot to march into Mexico and liberate it from Spanish rule. His admirers hailed Burr as a visionary patriot, bent upon adding Spanish colonies to America, while detractors, including Jefferson, detected an evil plan to detach territory from the union. In 1807, Burr was arrested for treason and for trying to incite a war against Spain. He was acquitted by Chief Justice John Marshall, who applied a strict definition of treason. The acquittal only sharpened Jefferson's contempt for "the original error of establishing a judiciary independent of the nation."[51]

For four years, the disgraced Burr traveled in Europe, resorting occasionally to the pseudonym H. E. Edwards to keep creditors at bay. Sometimes he lived in opulence with fancy friends and at other times languished in drab single rooms. This aging roué sampled opium and seduced willing noblewomen and chambermaids with a fine impartiality. All the while, he cultivated self-pity. "I find that among the great number of Americans here and *there* all are hostile to A.B.—All—What a lot of rascals they must be to make war on one whom they do not know, on one who never did harm or wished harm to a human being," he recorded in his diary.[52] He befriended the English utilitarian philosopher Jeremy Bentham and spoke to him with remarkable candor. "He really meant to make himself emperor of Mexico," Bentham recalled. "He told me I should be the legislator and he would send a ship of war for me. He gave me an account of his duel with Hamilton. He was sure of being able to kill him, so I thought it little better than murder."[53] Always capable of irreverent surprises, Burr gave Bentham a copy of *The Federalist*. The shade of Alexander Hamilton rose up to haunt Burr at unexpected moments. In Paris, he called upon Talleyrand, who instructed his secretary to deliver this message to the uninvited caller: "I shall be glad to see Colonel Burr, but please tell him that a portrait of Alexander Hamilton always hangs in my study where all may see it."[54] Burr got the message and left.

By the time Burr sailed home in 1812 as "Mr. A. Arnot," all charges had been dropped against him. To get back on his feet in New York, he borrowed a law library from Robert Troup and tried to revive his practice. A solitary figure who had relinquished interest in politics, he soon lost the last emotional props of his life. That summer, his adored grandson, Aaron Burr Alston, died at age ten. He still had his beloved Theodosia, however, whose portrait he had toted around Europe, cradling it in his lap during stagecoach trips. Though her husband was now governor of South Carolina, gossip claimed that he was abusing her. At the end of 1812, the morose Theodosia sailed for New York to join her father, but she never made it. She died at sea, age twenty-nine, the victim of either a storm or pirates. It was the heaviest blow that Burr ever weathered, so crushing that he described himself as "severed from the human race."[55] Four years later, his son-in-law, Joseph Alston, died at thirty-seven. This rash of calamities recapitulated the stunning sequence of deaths that Burr had suffered as a child. Already a ghost of times past, Burr became a famous recluse, occasionally pointed out on the New York streets. He seldom socialized beyond a small circle of people.

As for the duel with Hamilton, Burr almost never showed any remorse. Soon after returning to America, he visited his aunt, Rhoda Edwards, who worried about his immortal soul and warned him, "You have committed a great many sins against God and you killed that great and good man, Colonel Hamilton. I beseech you to repent and fly to the blood and righteousness of the Redeemer for pardon." Burr found this rather quaint: "Oh, aunt, don't feel too badly," he replied. "We shall both meet in heaven."[56]

One day, Burr was walking down Nassau Street in New York when Chancellor James Kent happened to see him. Kent lost all control, swooped down on Burr, and started flailing at him with his cane. "You are a scoundrel, sir!" Kent shouted. "A scoundrel!" His legendary aplomb intact, Burr tipped his hat and said, "The opinions of the learned Chancellor are always entitled to the highest consideration."[57] Then he bowed and walked away.

Burr never lost his sense of humor about having killed Hamilton and made facetious references to "my friend Hamilton, whom I shot."[58] Once, in the Boston Athenaeum, Burr paused to admire a bust of Hamilton. "There was the poetry," he said, tracing creases in Hamilton's face with his finger.[59] Another time, Burr paused at a tavern to refresh his horses and wandered over to a traveling waxworks exhibition. He suddenly came upon a tableau that represented him and Hamilton in the duel. Underneath ran this verse: "O Burr, O Burr, what has thou done? / Thou hast shooted dead great Hamilton. / You hid behind a bunch of thistle, / And shooted him dead with a great hoss pistol."[60] In relating the story, Burr roared with laughter. Only once did Burr betray any misgivings about killing Hamilton. While reading the scene in Laurence Sterne's *Tristram Shandy* in which the tenderhearted Uncle Toby picks up a fly and delicately places it outside a window instead of killing it,

Burr is said to have remarked, "Had I read Sterne more and Voltaire less, I should have known the world was wide enough for Hamilton and me."[61]

Burr lingered on for twenty-four years after he returned to America. In 1833, age seventy-seven, he mustered enough strength or cynicism for one final romance and married a fabulously wealthy widow, fifty-eight-year-old Eliza Jumel, who occupied a mansion in Washington Heights. (Improbable legend claims that Hamilton once had a fling with her.) Née Betsey Bowen, she had started life as a courtesan and had borne an illegitimate son before marrying the rich wine merchant Stephen Jumel. Burr, as usual, behaved like a scamp and frittered away Madame Jumel's money while being unfaithful. A year later, she filed for divorce and accused her incorrigible husband of adultery. Why had she expected Burr to reform at this late hour? On September 14, 1836, he died in a Staten Island hotel after two strokes and was buried in Princeton near his father and grandfather. The death mask of Aaron Burr is haunting and unforgettable, with the nose twisted to the left, the mouth crooked, and the expression grotesque, as if all the suppressed pain of his life were engraved in his face by the end. John Quincy Adams left this epitaph of the man: "Burr's life, take it all together, was such as in any country of sound morals his friends would be desirous of burying in profound oblivion."[62]

ELIZA

For Eliza Hamilton, the collapse of her world was total, overwhelming, and remorseless. Within three years, she had had to cope with four close deaths: her eldest son, her sister Peggy, her mother, and her husband, not to mention the mental breakdown of her eldest daughter. Because the news of Hamilton's death further weakened the already precarious health of Philip Schuyler, Eliza stayed in Albany to nurse him. As his gout flared up anew, he hobbled about in tremendous pain and became bedridden. "I trust that the Supreme Being will prolong my life that I may discharge the duties of a father to my dear child and her dear children," Philip Schuyler told Angelica Church. Eliza "knows how tenderly I loved my dear Hamilton, how tenderly I love her and her children."[1] The Supreme Being, alas, had other plans for the ailing general. On November 18, 1804, four months after his son-in-law slumped to the ground in Weehawken, Philip Schuyler died and was buried in the Albany Rural Cemetery.

How did Eliza soldier on after these dreadful events that came thick and fast upon her? A month after the duel, she answered a sympathy note from Colonel William S. Smith, who had written to inform her that the Society of the Cincinnati would erect a monument to Hamilton in Trinity Church. In her letter, Eliza alluded to the forces that would sustain her. Suffering from "the irreparable loss of a most amiable and affectionate husband," she prayed for "the mercies of the divine being in whose dispensations" all Christians should acquiesce. Beyond religious solace, she drew strength from sympathetic friends and family members and the veneration paid to her husband. She wrote, "The wounded heart derives a degree of consolation from the tenderness with which its loss is bewailed by the virtuous, the wise, and humane" and "that high honor and respect with which the memory of the dear deceased has been commemorated."[2]

Eliza's fierce, unending loyalty to Hamilton certifies that their marriage had been deeply rewarding, albeit marred by Maria Reynolds and other misadventures. Blessed with a forgiving heart, Eliza made ample allowance for her husband's flaws. Two months after the duel, she described Hamilton to Nathaniel Pendleton as "my beloved, sainted husband and my guardian angel." She thought that God, in snatching Hamilton away, had balanced the ledgers of her life, inflicting exquisite pain equal to her matchless joy in marriage: "I have remarked to you that I have had a double share of blessings and I must now look forward to grief. . . . For such a husband, his spirit is in heaven and his form in the earth and I am nowhere any part of him is."[3] She pored so frequently over his letters to her that they began to crack and crumble into dust. Around her neck, she wore a tiny bag containing brittle yellow scraps of the love sonnet that Hamilton had given to her during their courtship in Morristown—the scraps were sewn together as the paper decomposed—and the intimate farewell letter he had prepared for her on the eve of the duel.

Eliza retained boundless affection for "her Hamilton," even though he had left her stranded in a terrible financial predicament. Hamilton died illiquid, if not insolvent. This mocked the hardy Republican fairy tale that he had enriched himself as treasury secretary and colluded with British paymasters. The secret London bank account that legend said awaited him when the monarchy returned to America—a staple of Jeffersonian lore—had never existed. America's financial wizard earned comparatively little in his lifetime, and his executors feared that any distress sale of his assets—chiefly the Grange and some land in western New York and the Ohio River valley—would slash their value. Gouverneur Morris was appalled by the magnitude of Hamilton's debts and confided to Rufus King,

> Our friend Hamilton has been suddenly cut off in the midst of embarrassments which would have required years of professional industry to set straight—a debt of between fifty thousand and sixty thousand dollars hanging over him, a property which in time may sell for seventy or eighty thousand, but which, if brought to the hammer, would not, in all probability, fetch forty.[4]

Philip Schuyler had already disposed of a considerable portion of his wealth among his eight children and their descendants—his entire estate of thirty-five thousand dollars could not have covered Hamilton's debts—so Eliza's inheritance fell dreadfully short of Hamilton's more sanguine expectations. She inherited farmland around Albany and Saratoga that yielded a paltry $750 in annual income and did not begin to defray her expenses. Heavily indebted from abortive business ventures, Philip Schuyler died land rich but cash poor. The aura of Schuyler-family wealth had outdistanced reality.

To keep the family afloat, Gouverneur Morris organized a secret subscription fund among Hamilton's friends. He had to conquer an automatic assumption that the Hamilton children, with their rich grandfather, would never know want. Morris and more than one hundred other subscribers poured in about eighty thousand dollars, while New England Federalists donated Pennsylvania land as well. This fund was such a closely guarded secret that Hamilton's children did not know of it for a generation, and the Bank of New York managed to keep its existence confidential until 1937.

The executors did not dare to dispossess Eliza from the Grange, so they bought it for thirty thousand dollars and sold it back to her at half price, ensuring that she could stay there indefinitely. If such generosity preserved Eliza from indigence, it did not spare her incessant anxiety about money and the humiliating need to cadge small loans. Three years after the duel, she appealed to Nathaniel Pendleton for an emergency handout, telling him that "as I am nearly out of cash, I take the liberty to ask you to negotiate a loan of three hundred dollars."[5] Eliza, though never prodigal, had grown up in comfort and now learned to cultivate thrift. Notwithstanding her financial plight, she heeded one sacred injunction in Hamilton's farewell letter: to take care of his now blind, poor cousin, Ann Mitchell. Eliza invited her to stay at the Grange for extended periods and bailed her out with a $630 gift in 1810.

Eliza never wavered in her belief that the government owed substantial debts, financial and intangible, to her husband. At the end of the Revolution, Hamilton had waived the pension to which he was entitled as an army officer. From "scruples of delicacy" as a member of Congress, he had sought to eliminate any personal conflict of interest as he pondered the vexed question of veterans' compensation.[6] In a similarly high-minded spirit, he had waived his right to the "bounty" lands awarded to other officers. No amateur when it came to political timing, Eliza bided her time until Jefferson left the White House in 1809 and then immediately lobbied the apparently more forgiving President Madison for relief. By the time Madison left office, the persistent Eliza Hamilton had prevailed upon Congress to award her the cash equivalent of 450 acres in bounty lands plus five years' worth of full army pay—about ten thousand dollars.

It was a huge struggle for Eliza to educate her children on a modest, fluctuating income. She bemoaned having to raise them in a world of "disastrous events" and "evil passions," but she did a creditable job.[7] Her five surviving sons gravitated to careers in the Hamiltonian mold: law, government, and the military. The second son, Alexander, graduated from Columbia weeks after his father's duel. Eliza said that it was the wish "of my beloved, departed husband that his son Alexander should be placed in a countinghouse to be bred a merchant."[8] But when Stephen Higginson invited Alexander to apprentice in his Boston firm, Eliza could not bear losing her eldest surviving son to another city. "Unnerved by affliction and broken down by distress," she told Higginson, "what can be my wishes but to have the children of the best, the tenderest husband always with me."[9] Alexander became a lawyer, fought abroad in the duke of Wellington's army, returned to America as an infantry captain during the War of 1812, and wound up as a U.S. district attorney in New York. With fine irony, he represented Eliza Jumel when she divorced the unfaithful Aaron Burr.

The third son, James Alexander Hamilton, graduated from Columbia, served as an officer in the War of 1812, was an acting secretary of state under President Andrew Jackson (and as such favored the abolition of the Second Bank of the United States), and became a U.S. attorney for the southern district of New York. An easygoing, fast-talking man, he published a newspaper and developed a close friendship with Martin Van Buren, sometimes regarded as a "natural child" of Aaron Burr. At first, James A. Hamilton defended slavery as constitutional, then during the Civil War proved an early supporter of emancipation. In homage to his father's birthplace, he created a home called "Nevis" on the Hudson.

The fourth son, John Church Hamilton, was a lawyer, also fought in the War of 1812, and devoted decades to writing a many-volumed life of his father and sorting through his labyrinthine papers. The fifth son, William Stephen, was charming, handsome, and eccentric. After studying at West Point, he fought in the Black Hawk War, surveyed public lands in Illinois, and enjoyed a bachelor's free-spirited life on the western frontier. In 1849, he flocked to the California gold rush and opened a store in Sacramento to sell supplies to miners. He died there of cholera in 1850, the only child other than the elder Philip to predecease Eliza. The sixth son, "Little Phil," was a kindhearted, sensitive man. He married the daughter of Louis McLane, secretary of the treasury and secretary of state under Andrew Jackson. Phil served as an assistant U.S. attorney under his brother James but leaned toward altruistic pursuits and developed a reputation as "the lawyer of the poor."[10] The eldest daughter, Angelica, lingered on under a physician's care and remained "the sad charge" of Eliza's "bleeding heart," according to a friend.[11] She died in 1857. The younger daughter, Eliza Hamilton Holly, assumed the burden of caring for her mother in her later years.

For ten years after the duel, Eliza clung to the indispensable support of her sister Angelica, her strongest bond to the past and to her fallen husband. A fixture of New York society, Angelica kept busy attending balls and parties until the end. In 1806, her son, Philip, took a large tract of land that he had inherited in upstate New York and established the town of Angelica in her honor. In March 1814, Angelica Church died at fifty-seven and was buried in the same Trinity Churchyard that held the brother-in-law who had so lastingly captivated her. John Barker Church returned to England and died in London in April 1818.

In her first decades of widowhood, Eliza had to endure an endless parade of presidents—Jefferson, Madison, Monroe, and John Quincy Adams—who had crossed swords with her husband and had no desire to gild his memory. As "Federalism" became a term of abuse, she embarked on a single-minded crusade to do justice to her husband's achievements. After the Reverend John M. Mason, Timothy Pickering, and others failed to produce the major biography that she craved, she turned to her son, John Church Hamilton, to edit Hamilton's papers and produce a massive history that would duly glorify the patriarch. Eliza buttonholed elderly politicians and peppered them with detailed questionnaires, soliciting their recollections of her husband. She traveled to Mount Vernon and borrowed letters that Hamilton had written to Washington. She knew that she was racing against the clock, against mortality, against the vanishing trove of mementos of the revolutionary years. "I have my fears I shall not obtain my object," she wrote to her daughter Eliza of the seemingly jinxed project in 1832. "Most of the contemporaries of your father have also passed away."[12] The immense biographical project was not completed until seven years after Eliza's death.

The decades that she devoted to conserving her husband's legacy made Eliza only more militantly loyal to his memory, and there was one injury she could never forget: the exposure of the Maria Reynolds affair, for which she squarely blamed James Monroe. In the 1820s, after Monroe had completed two terms as president, he called upon Eliza in Washington, D.C., hoping to thaw the frost between them. Eliza was then about seventy and staying at her daughter's home. She was sitting in the backyard with her fifteen-year-old nephew when a maid emerged and presented the ex-president's card. Far from being flattered by this distinguished visitor, Eliza was taken aback. "She read the name and stood holding the card, much perturbed," said her nephew. "Her voice sank and she spoke very low, as she always did when she was angry. 'What has that man come to see me for?'" The nephew said that Monroe must have stopped by to pay his respects. She wavered. "I will see him," she finally agreed.[13]

So the small woman with the upright carriage and the sturdy, determined step marched stiffly into the house. When she entered the parlor, Monroe rose to greet her. Eliza then did something out of character and socially unthinkable: she stood facing the ex-president but did not invite him to sit down. With a bow, Monroe began what sounded like a well-rehearsed speech, stating "that it was many years since they had met, that the lapse of time brought its softening influences, that they both were nearing the grave, when past differences could be forgiven and forgotten."[14]

Eliza saw that Monroe was trying to draw a moral equation between them and apportion blame equally for the long rupture in their relationship. Even at this late date, thirty years after the fact, she was not in a forgiving mood. "Mr. Monroe," she told him, "if you have come to tell me that you repent, that you are sorry, *very* sorry, for the misrepresentations and the slanders and the stories you circulated against my dear husband, if you have come to say this, I understand it. But otherwise, no lapse of time, no nearness to the grave, makes any difference."[15] Monroe took in this rebuke without comment. Stunned by the fiery words delivered by the elderly little woman in widow's weeds, the ex-president picked up his hat, bid Eliza good day, and left the house, never to return.

Because Eliza Hamilton tried to erase herself from her husband's story, she has languished in virtually complete historical obscurity. To the extent that she has drawn attention, she has been depicted as a broken, weeping, neurasthenic creature, clinging to her Bible and lacking any identity other than that of Hamilton's widow. In fact, she was a woman of towering strength and integrity who consecrated much of her extended widowhood to serving widows, orphans, and poor children. On March 16, 1806, less than two years after the duel, Eliza and other evangelical women cofounded the New York Orphan Asylum Society, the first private orphanage in New York. Perhaps nothing expressed her affection for Hamilton more tenderly than her efforts on behalf of orphans. If Eliza did not draft the society's constitution, she endorsed its credo that "crime has not been the cause" of the orphan's misery and "future usefulness may yet be the result of [his or her] protection. God himself has marked the fatherless as the peculiar subjects of His divine compassion."[16] Surely some extra dimension of religious fervor had entered into Eliza's feelings toward her husband because of his boyhood. She possessed "her own pitying, loving nature, blended with a rare sense of justice," said her friend Jessie Benton Frémont. "All these she dedicated to the care of orphan children."[17]

For many years, Eliza was a mainstay of the orphanage board and held the position of second directress, or deputy director. She was present in 1807 when the cornerstone was laid for its two-story wooden headquarters in Greenwich Village. In 1821, Eliza was elevated to first directress with the chief responsibility for the 158 children then housed and educated in the asylum. For the next twenty-seven years, with a tenacity that Hamilton would have savored, she oversaw every aspect of the orphanage work. She raised money, leased properties, visited almshouses, investigated complaints, and solicited donations of coal, shoes, and Bibles. She often gave the older orphans jobs in her home and helped one gain admittance to West Point. With a finesse reminiscent of her husband's, she handled the society's funds on the finance committee. After obtaining a state charter for the society, she lobbied the state legislature for annual grants. "Mamma, you are a sturdy beggar," her son once teased her. "My dear son," she retorted, "I cannot spare myself or others. My Maker has pointed out this duty to me and has given me the ability and inclination to perform it."[18] She was still first directress in 1836 when the cornerstone was laid for an imposing new orphanage at Seventy-third Street and Riverside Drive. Eliza led the organization cheerfully, willingly, aided by her dear friend Joanna Bethune. "My mother's regard and esteem for this venerable lady continually increased," George Bethune said of his mother's warm friendship with Eliza. "Both were of determined disposition. . . . Mrs. Bethune was the more cautious, Mrs. Hamilton the more impulsive, so that occasions of dispute did occur. But it was charming to see how affectionately these temporary altercations soon terminated in mutual embraces."[19]

Like her evangelical colleagues, Eliza believed passionately that all children should be literate in order to study the Bible. In 1818, she returned to the state legislature and won a charter for the Hamilton Free School, which was the first educational institution in the Washington Heights section of Manhattan. It stood on land Eliza donated on Broadway between 187th and 188th Streets in upper Manhattan and was established in honor of her husband's memory.

A painting of Eliza from later years shows a woman with a strong but kindly face and a firm, determined mouth. Her silver hair was parted down the middle under her widow's cap, and her dark eyes were still large and girlishly bright. "Her face is delicate but full of nerve and spirit. The eyes are very dark and hold the life and energy of the restraining face," said Jessie Benton Frémont, who marveled at Eliza's unabated vigor.[20] "When I first lived on the Hudson River, quite near her son's home, it was still remembered how the old lady, past eighty, would leave the train at a way station and climb two fences in her shortcut across meadows, rather than go on to the town where the carriage could meet her."[21] Her willpower and spunk surprised people. At one anniversary celebration of the Orphan Asylum Society, Eliza, then in her nineties, materialized, to everyone's amazement—"a very small, upright little figure in deep black, never altered from the time her dark hair was first framed by the widow's cap, until now the hair was white as the cap."[22] Frémont noted how she "retains in an astonishing degree her faculties and converses with much of that ease and brilliancy which lent so peculiar a charm to her younger days."[23]

In 1848, the ninety-one-year-old Eliza moved to Washington, D.C., to live with her younger daughter, Eliza, who was now widowed after the death of her husband, Sidney Augustus Holly. At their H Street residence near the White House, Eliza Hamilton cherished her status as a relic of the American Revolution. Like her husband, she was a committed abolitionist who delighted in entertaining slave children from the neighborhood, and she referred derisively to the slaveholding states as the "African States." Always busy knitting or making mats, she was an irresistible curiosity to visitors and a coveted ornament at White House dinners. "Mrs. General Hamilton, upon whom I waited at table, is a very remarkable person," President James K. Polk reported in his diary after one such dinner in February 1846. "She retains her intellect and memory perfectly, and my conversation with her was highly interesting."[24] Eliza aided her friend Dolley Madison in raising money to construct the Washington Monument and remained sharp and alert until the end. When historian Benson J. Lossing interviewed her when she was ninety-one, he found her anything but tearful or morose: "The sunny cheerfulness of her temper and quiet humor . . . still made her deportment genial and attractive."[25]

During the winter of 1852–1853, Eliza and her daughter enjoyed the company of a young relative named Elizabeth Hawley, who was startled by the constant stream of visitors who showed up at their doorstep. On the morning of New Year's Day 1853, the young woman was disheartened by the gray skies and the apparent paucity of gentleman callers. But before noon, "the sky cleared and the tide of visitors flowed in," she wrote to her aunt. "The rooms were crowded all day and we received several hundred call[er]s. . . . Gentlemen brought their children to see Mrs. Hamilton, many called who went to no other place, and as you are fond of hearing all, I wish I had room to tell you the names of the most distinguished senators, members, etc." General Winfield Scott showed up, looking dashing in his uniform, followed by New York senator William H. Seward. Then the dense throng parted, and, to the young woman's amazement, President Millard Fillmore advanced across the room toward Eliza. "I had heard he was thinner than when I saw him, but I never saw him looking stouter or handsomer. He sat with Mrs. Hamilton some time and asked her to appoint some time to dine with him."[26] When the ninety-five-year-old Eliza dined at the White House a month later, she made a grand entrance with her daughter. President Fillmore fussed over her, and the first lady gave up her chair to her. Everybody was eager to touch a living piece of American history.

A devout woman, Eliza never lost her faith that she and Hamilton would be gloriously reunited in the afterlife. She prized a small envelope that Hamilton had once sent her, with a romantic inscription emblazoned across the back: "I heal all wounds but those which love hath made."[27] For Eliza, those wounds had never healed. On November 9, 1854—a turbulent year in which the Kansas-Nebraska Act was enacted and the union that Hamilton had done so much to forge stood gravely threatened—Elizabeth Schuyler Hamilton died at age ninety-seven. Her widowhood had lasted fifty years, or slightly longer than her life before the duel. She was buried where she had always longed to be: right beside her Hamilton in the Trinity Churchyard.

Acknowledgments

Any biographer foolhardy enough to attempt an authoritative life of Alexander Hamilton must tread a daunting maze of detail. Matters that at first seem susceptible to easy solution prove slippery indeed. Hence, my special gratitude to the generous people who provided guidance. During the early stages of my research, I had a part-time assistant, Daniel Wein, who extracted countless articles and book excerpts and was a delightful, stimulating luncheon companion. After that period, I enlisted research assistants only for isolated projects that would have required extensive travel.

The most opaque portion of Hamilton's life is obviously his myth-shrouded boyhood on Nevis and St. Croix, where the intrepid biographer must cope with brown, brittle documents and ledgers devoured by illiterate insects. Many pertinent eighteenth-century documents have also been obliterated by hurricanes, war, neglect, and other mishaps.

To track down those elusive phantoms James Hamilton and Rachel Faucette Lavien, I drew on the help of many people. In St. Croix, I am especially indebted to William Cissel, a first-class historian and park ranger at the Christiansvaern fort, who identified the prison cell that had held Hamilton's mother and also served up a graphic account of her misery. My thanks as well to Carol Wakefield and Barbara Hagan-Smith at the Whim Library of the St. Croix Landmarks Society. It was there that I stumbled upon Hamilton's prolific freelance journalism for the *Royal Danish American Gazette*. Patricia Ramirez assisted me at the Florence A. S. Williams Library in Christiansted, while Edgar Lake and William Wallace jogged my imagination as to the lasting impact upon Hamilton of his Caribbean origins. Elizabeth A. Armstrong and Barbara Armstrong Jamieson supplied me with some island history.

In Nevis, I enjoyed the hospitality of Joan Robinson of the Museum of Nevis

History (the re-created Alexander Hamilton house), Lornette Hanley of the Nevis Historical and Conservation Society, and Mova David in the local registrar's office. On neighboring St. Kitts, I was able to search the government archives thanks to Victoria Borg O'Flaherty and her daughter, Tamara. Beverly Smith helped at the Von Scholten Collection of the Enid M. Baa Library and Archives on St. Thomas. My friend and special emissary Emily Altman volunteered for research duty on Trinidad and Tobago, where Nadia Gajadhar also rendered assistance.

Perhaps the most surprising finds came in a distant corner of the Caribbean: St. Vincent and the Grenadines. Through the courteous cooperation of Eldon Millington and Dr. Earl Kirby on St. Vincent, I was able to locate the deed that documented the impoverished existence of James Hamilton on Bequia. The Bequia Tourism Association steered me to two local historians, Rodger Durham and Nolbert Simmons, who alerted me to the 1776 map in the Library of Congress that pinpointed the exact location of James Hamilton's property.

To extend my Caribbean research, I hired Tim Guest, a young English writer, who reviewed numerous colonial papers at the Public Record Office at Kew, while Rikke Vindberg, a history student at the University of Copenhagen, pored over papers related to St. Croix in the Danish national archives. (Judith Goldstein and Bo Lidegaard provided entrée in Denmark.) Paul Jenkins and M. H. Kaufman of the Royal Medical Society in Edinburgh contributed information about Hamilton's childhood friend Edward Stevens. Thanks to the combined efforts of three people in South Carolina—Liz Newcombe of the Charleston County Public Library, Carey Lucas Nikonchuk of the South Carolina Historical Society, and Judge Kenneth Fulp of the Beaufort County Probate Court—I was able to locate the will of Hamilton's half brother, Peter Lavien. Carol Kahn Strauss and Dana Ledger at the Leo Baeck Institute in New York helped me ponder the intriguing question of whether Johann Michael Lavien was of Jewish ancestry.

To probe the Scottish background of James Hamilton, I traveled to Glasgow and was able to verify his early trade apprenticeship in the Division of Business Records and Family History at the splendid Mitchell Library. At the North Ayrshire Archives in Ardrossan, Jill McColl, Elizabeth Bell, Peggy O'Brien, and John Millar plied me with local lore and directed me to the ruins of Kerelaw Castle, where James Hamilton grew up.

It is impossible to discuss Hamilton's West Indian boyhood without encountering the subject of his racial identity. Despite an absence of evidence, the presumption remains widespread among many in the Caribbean and the African-American community that Hamilton, as an illegitimate West Indian orphan, must have been partly black. So formidable a black scholar as W. E. B. DuBois referred to him proudly as "our own Hamilton." Far from resisting this thesis, I was eager to test it and either confirm it or lay it to rest. I consulted two of the world's top geneticists—Dr. Victor McKusick of The Johns Hopkins School of Medicine and Sir Alec J. Jeffreys of the University of Leicester—to determine whether a surviving lock of Hamilton's hair might yield up secrets about his racial ancestry. They persuaded me that genetic testing wouldn't furnish conclusive answers, and I decided it might only confuse the issue. I then discovered that a retired professor at Pennsylvania State University, Gordon Hamilton (no descendant of Alexander), was coordinating a Hamilton DNA Project intended to trace genetic linkages among the extended Hamilton family. Hoping that such a project might provide answers about Hamilton's paternity—specifically, whether he was the son of James Hamilton or of Thomas Stevens—I offered to pay for the genetic testing of any direct Hamilton descendants. The results are pending.

Another will-o'-the-wisp during my research was whether Hamilton had fathered an illegitimate mulatto child. This extraordinary tale was first brought to my attention by Donald Yacovone, an assistant editor of *The Black Abolitionist Papers*, who pointed out that William Hamilton (1773–1836), a free black carpenter and a noted journalist and abolitionist before the Civil War, claimed to be Hamilton's son. I explored this prospect with several well-qualified parties—Roy Finkenbine, director of the Black Abolitionist Archives of the University of Detroit Mercy; Robert F. Gibson of the New York Genealogical and Biological Society; W. E. B. DuBois biographer David Levering Lewis; Christopher Moore and Howard Dodson of the Schomburg Center in Harlem; and Brent Staples of *The New York Times*, who has written on racial identity in American history. While I remain dubious about William Hamilton's claim—he was born in 1773, the hectic year that Hamilton escaped from St. Croix and began intense preparation for college in Elizabethtown, New Jersey—the paucity of evidence makes it impossible to deliver a final verdict. The matter seemed too tenuous to merit inclusion in the text.

As a New York resident, I found myself in fertile territory for Hamilton research. The Rare Book and Manuscript Library of the Butler Library at Columbia University holds massive Hamilton resources. While compiling the collected papers for Columbia University Press, Harold Syrett and his team gathered a vast trove of Hamilton-related documents. In addition, many Hamilton family members deposited papers there, permitting discoveries in private letters and on old scraps of paper. My thanks to Jean Ashton and the library's pleasant, efficient staff. Marilyn Pettit, the director of University Archives at the Columbiana Library, alerted me to her useful doctoral dissertation, which situates Eliza Hamilton in the milieu of evangelical women activists in early-nineteenth-century New York. Poul Jensen, president of Graham Windham Services, the successor organization to the Orphan Asylum Society cofounded by Eliza, allowed me to delve into the organization's early records, with the assistance of Susan Gunn of the Graham School.

The highly professional staffs of the New-York Historical Society and the New York Public Library shepherded me through numerous manuscript collections, including those relating to the duel. The New-York Historical Society houses the papers of both Hamilton's second, Nathaniel Pendleton, and Burr's second, William P. Van Ness, permitting a fully rounded view of events from firsthand sources. The society's superb collection of historical newspapers permitted my discovery of Hamilton's undergraduate "Monitor" essays as well as his 1796 "Phocion" essays with their eye-opening comments on Adams, Jefferson, and slavery. Valerie Komor provided much-appreciated help in tracking down historical images. Besides Hamilton and Schuyler family papers, the New York Public Library has abundant pamphlets showing the ample stock of slurs made against Burr in the 1804 election and revealing just how many "despicable opinions" Hamilton could have drawn upon. I also want to thank the staffs of the Schuyler Mansion State Historic Site in Albany and the Schuyler House in Schuylerville, New York.

In pursuit of fresh materials about the duel, I approached J. P. Morgan Chase, which owns the brace of dueling pistols with the best claim to authenticity. Jean Elliott and Shelley M. Diamond allowed me to sift through bank documents pertaining to the purchase of the pistols and also arranged for me to lift and aim them. (Nobody, luckily, was killed.) An unexpectedly good source on the duel was the Weehawken Free Public Library, where Eric Negron supplied me with two fascinating folders of articles on the history of the local dueling ground.

Christine McKay, consulting archivist at the Bank of New York, made available bank records concerning the secret trust fund set up for Hamilton's family. She also passed along the revelatory letter written by Dirck Ten Broeck that shows Hamilton's positive frame of mind the day before the duel. Brian Thompson and Meg Ventrudo at the Museum of American Financial History furnished me with early newspaper articles that I hadn't found elsewhere. Eugene Tobin, president of Hamilton College in Clinton, New York, was a consistently cheerful supporter of this project. At Trinity Church, archivist Gwynedd Cannan trawled through baptismal records and pew rentals and provided key information on Hamilton's religious life. Christopher Keenan and John Daskalakis, park rangers at the Hamilton Grange National Memorial, responded patiently to questions, as did Judith Mueller and Kathy Hansen at the Federal Hall National Memorial on Wall Street. At the New York Society Library, Mark Piel, Edmee B. Reit, and Sara Holliday helped with the reading habits of Hamilton and Burr. Steven Wheeler at the New York Stock Exchange responded to questions about its early history.

Finally, to round out my New York sources, I would like to thank Fred Bassett, senior librarian at the New York State Library in Albany; Darwin Stapleton and Tom Rosenbaum at the Rockefeller Archive Center, which owns Schuyler papers; Vin Montuori, vice president of marketing for the *New York Post;* Roy Fox, curator of the King Manor Museum in Jamaica, Queens; and the staff of the Morris-Jumel Mansion in Washington Heights.

In New Jersey, Kathy Grimshaw at the Passaic County Historical Society in Paterson, New Jersey, helped me unearth revealing documents of the Society for Establishing Useful Manufactures. James Lewis of the New Jersey Historical Society provided background on Hamilton's first American teacher, Francis Barber. I profited from a trip to the Morristown National Historical Site and the Joint Free Public Library of Morristown and Morris Township, as well as a tour of the Schuyler Hamilton House in Morristown, conducted by Phyllis R. Sanftner. At Princeton University, three eminent classicists—Edmund Keeley, Robert Fagles, and Edward Champlin—tried to unravel the thorny riddle of what Hamilton meant when he coined the code name "Savius" for Burr in 1792. They convinced me that the name probably didn't refer to an extremely obscure figure in Roman history, Saevius Plautus, who is identified in St. Jerome's "Chronicle" as having defiled his son and then committed suicide during the subsequent trial. This story has led some recent writers to claim that Hamilton, in making his "despicable" charge against Burr, accused him of incest with his daughter, Theodosia—a hypothesis originated by Gore Vidal in his entertaining novel *Burr.* To my mind, the Savius mystery remains unsolved.

The Library of Congress contains the largest haul of Hamilton papers, including many of the letters printed in his collected papers. I would like to thank the staff of the Manuscript Division, especially Jeffrey M. Flannery. Ditto for Nicholas Graham and the staff of the Massachusetts Historical Society, another source of original papers. I am further indebted to the Historical Society of Pennsylvania, and to Rob Cox and Roy Goodman of the American Philosophical Society. At the Christ Church Preservation Trust, I had an illuminating chat about Hamilton's religion with Neil Ronk. At Yale University, Ellen Cohn, chief editor of the Benjamin Franklin Papers, was kind enough to survey Franklin's still-unpublished papers for any stray references to Hamilton. In England, Valerie Cromwell of the History of Parliament Trust sketched in background information about John Barker Church. David Hildebrand of the Colonial Music Institute provided lyrics and learned commentary on the songs that Hamilton might have sung right before the duel.

Fellow historians were generous in responding to my queries. My special thanks to David McCullough, who graciously encouraged me to undertake this project. Two knowledgeable Hamilton hands, Joanne Freeman of Yale and Carol Berkin of Baruch College and the CUNY Graduate Center, responded to miscellaneous questions with alacrity. James F. Gaines of Mary Washington College regaled me with a wonderful disquisition on Molière's nurse. Others who provided support, suggestions, or research materials include Joseph McCarthy, who has made a documentary film about Lord Stirling; Leon Friedman, a First Amendment expert and an aficionado of *The Federalist Papers;* Schuyler Chapin, a direct descendant of General Philip Schuyler; Walter Russell Mead, who has analyzed Hamiltonian foreign policy at the Council on Foreign Relations; Roxana Robinson, who showed me an unpublished Hamilton document; Scott P. Lindsay, president of the Alexander Hamilton Historical Society; and two people who offered help with Hamilton family genealogy: Alexander Hamilton (no direct descendant of the treasury secretary) and Louis Auchincloss. My thanks as well to Hamilton descendants John Rhinelander, Mary Rhinelander McCarl, and Tony Rhinelander.

It was my longtime agent, Melanie Jackson, who saw, with a touch of clairvoyance, that Hamilton should be my next biographical subject and that I should give a breather to the tycoons of the Gilded Age. She has been an indispensable figure in my career, a matchless business manager, literary adviser, and trusted friend, all rolled into one. Her assistant, Andrea Schaefer, ably fielded many questions these past few years.

My editor, Ann Godoff, performed an astonishing feat of acrobatics as she kept this project moving along smoothly despite her departure from Random House and her creation of The Penguin Press. Never once did I feel adrift: the good ship *Hamilton* continued to sail along, protected by Ann from the smallest ripples. Her editorial comments, as usual, were invaluable and her dedication to the book exemplary. During this busy start-up period, I benefited from the good-natured support of her assistant, Meredith Blum. I feel lucky to have again secured the copyediting services of the meticulous Timothy Mennel, assisted by senior production editor Bruce Giffords, and to have Lynn Goldberg, Mark Fortier, Tracy Locke, and Rachel Rokicki aboard for publicity. Gabriele Wilson created a beautiful cover that captures the mood of the book with uncanny precision. Sandra J. Markham provided knowing assistance with the picture section, as did Amanda Dewey, and Michelle McMillian created the interior design. I thank Sigrid Estrada for the excellent jacket photo.

It will come as no surprise to readers of my previous books that at this point I will pause and genuflect to my selfless wife, Valerie. She has shared all of my exhilaration and despair, trooped along on research trips, suffered tropical heat and inedible food, listened to me read aloud every line of the book, and functioned as a perceptive surrogate editor. Whatever her own private woes, she refused to let them interfere with the completion of this book. For a comparable case of love and loyalty, one would have to turn to Eliza Hamilton.

Notes

Abbreviations

CU-DWCP   Columbia University, New York, N.Y., De Witt Clinton Papers

CU-FFP   Columbia University, Fish Family Papers

CU-HFP   Columbia University, Hamilton Family Papers

CU-HPPP   Columbia University, Hamilton Papers Publication Project

CU-JCHP   Columbia University, John Church Hamilton Papers

LC-AHP   Library of Congress, Washington, D.C., Alexander Hamilton Papers

LC-WPP   Library of Congress, William Plumer Papers

LPAH   The Law Practice of Alexander Hamilton. Ed. Julius Goebel, Jr., et al. 5 vols. New York: Columbia University Press, 1964–1981.

MHi-TPP   Massachusetts Historical Society, Boston, Timothy Pickering Papers

NYHS-DGFP   New-York Historical Society, New York, N.Y., De Groot Family Papers

NYHS-MM   New-York Historical Society, Miscellaneous Microfilms

NYHS-NPP   New-York Historical Society, Nathaniel Pendleton Papers

NYHS-NYCMS   New-York Historical Society, New York City Manumission Society Papers

NYHS-RTP   New-York Historical Society, Robert Troup Papers

NYHS-WVNP   New-York Historical Society, William Van Ness Papers

NYPL-AYP   New York Public Library, Abraham Yates, Jr., Papers

NYPL-JAHP   New York Public Library, James A. Hamilton Papers

NYPL-KVB   New York Public Library, Pamphlet Collection for New York election, spring 1804

NYPL-PSP   New York Public Library, Philip Schuyler Papers

NYSL   New York State Library, Albany, N.Y.

PAH   The Papers of Alexander Hamilton. Ed. Harold C. Syrett et al. 27 vols. New York: Columbia University Press, 1961–1987. (Unless otherwise stated, all letters cited are written either to or from Alexander Hamilton. Documents written neither by nor to Hamilton are cited only by volume and page number.)

Prologue: The Oldest Revolutionary War Widow

1. *Atlantic Monthly,* August 1896.
2. CU-HFP, box 3, letter from Elizabeth Hamilton Holly to John C. Hamilton, February 27, 1855.
3. Cooke, *Alexander Hamilton,* p. vii.
4. Malone, *Jefferson and His Time,* vol. 2, p. 271.
5. Cooke, *Alexander Hamilton,* p. 149.
6. *The Political Science Quarterly,* March 1890.
7. Knott, *Alexander Hamilton and the Persistence of Myth,* p. 87.
8. Ibid., p. 259.

One: The Castaways

1. Van Doren, *Benjamin Franklin,* p. 312.
2. Hubbard, *Swords, Ships, and Sugar,* p. 40.
3. Ibid., p. 33.
4. *PAH,* vol. 25, p. 88, letter to William Jackson, August 26, 1800.
5. Ibid.
6. Flexner, *Young Hamilton,* p. 9.

7. *PAH,* vol. 25, p. 89, letter to William Jackson, August 26, 1800.
8. Ramsing, *Alexander Hamilton's Birth and Parentage,* p. 4.
9. Hamilton, *Intimate Life of Alexander Hamilton,* p. 11.
10. Ramsing, *Alexander Hamilton's Birth and Parentage,* p. 8.
11. *The American Genealogist,* January 1945.
12. Mitchell, *Alexander Hamilton: Youth to Maturity,* p. 7.
13. Schachner, *Alexander Hamilton,* p. 1.
14. *The American Genealogist,* January 1945.
15. *PAH,* vol. 16, p. 276, letter to George Washington, April 14, 1796.
16. Ibid., vol. 2, p. 539, letter to Margarita Schuyler, January 21, 1781.
17. Ibid., vol. 25, p. 88, letter to William Jackson, August 26, 1800.
18. *Kilmarnock Standard,* April 5, 1924.
19. Castle, *John Glassford of Douglaston,* pp. 22–23.
20. LC-AHP, reel 29, "Agreement of November 11, 1737."
21. Ragatz, *Fall of the Planter Class in the British Caribbean,* pp. 16–17.
22. *PAH,* vol. 25, p. 89, letter to William Jackson, August 26, 1800.
23. Ibid.
24. LC-AHP, reel 29, letter from John Hamilton to Thomas Reid, 1749 [n.d.].
25. Ibid.
26. St. Kitts Archives, Government of St. Kitts and Nevis, Basseterre, St. Kitts.
27. *PAH,* vol. 25, p. 89, letter to William Jackson, August 26, 1800.
28. Hamilton, *Life of Alexander Hamilton,* vol. 1, p. 42.
29. Hamilton, *Intimate Life of Alexander Hamilton,* p. 13.
30. *PAH,* vol. 3, p. 573, letter from Hugh Knox, July 28, 1784.
31. Schachner, *Alexander Hamilton,* p. 8.
32. Hamilton, *Life of Alexander Hamilton,* vol. 1, p. 42.
33. *PAH,* vol. 26, p. 774, "Comments on Jews," n.d.
34. Hamilton, *Life of Alexander Hamilton,* vol. 7, pp. 710–11.
35. *London Magazine,* August 1753.
36. Ibid.
37. Brookhiser, *Alexander Hamilton,* p. 14.
38. Andrews, *Journal of a Lady of Quality,* p. 127.
39. Nevis Historical and Conservation Society, RG MG 2.25, Charlestown, Nevis.
40. Emery, *Alexander Hamilton,* p. 13.
41. *The William and Mary Quarterly,* April 1952.
42. Ramsing, *Alexander Hamilton's Birth and Parentage,* p. 8.

43. Ibid.
44. *PAH,* vol. 21, p. 77, letter to William Hamilton, May 2, 1797.
45. Ibid.
46. Ibid., vol. 22, p. 223.
47. Tyson and Highfield, *Kamina Folk,* p. 46.
48. Flexner, *Young Hamilton,* p. 31.
49. *PAH,* vol. 20, p. 458, "From Ann Mitchell" [1796].
50. Ramsing, *Alexander Hamilton's Birth and Parentage,* p. 28.
51. *PAH,* vol. 15, p. 331, "To the College of Physicians," September 11, 1793.
52. Ibid., vol. 1, p. 369, letter from Edward Stevens, December 23, 1777.
53. MHi-TPP, reel 51.
54. Ibid.
55. Lodge, *Alexander Hamilton,* p. 286.

Two: Hurricane

1. Hamilton, *Life of Alexander Hamilton,* vol. 1, p. 44.
2. NYHS-NPP, "Draft Obituary Notice for Hamilton," n.d.
3. *PAH,* vol. 1, p. 4, letter to Edward Stevens, November 11, 1769.
4. Ibid., p. 21, letter to Nicholas Cruger, late 1771 or early 1772.
5. Ibid., p. 23, letter to Tileman Cruger, February 1, 1772.
6. Ibid., p. 24, letter to Captain Newton, February 1, 1772.
7. *Royal Danish American Gazette,* January 23, 1771.
8. Flexner, *Young Hamilton,* p. 39.
9. *PAH,* vol. 1, p. 7.
10. *Proceedings of the New Jersey Historical Society,* vol. 69, April 1951.
11. Knox, *Letter to the Rev. Mr. Jacob Green,* p. 48.
12. *PAH,* vol. 3, p. 573, letter from Hugh Knox, July 28, 1784.
13. *Royal Danish American Gazette,* September 9, 1772.
14. Ibid., October 3, 1772.
15. *PAH,* vol. 3, p. 573, letter from Hugh Knox, July 28, 1784.
16. *Royal Danish American Gazette,* February 3, 1773.
17. *PAH,* vol. 26, p. 307, letter to Elizabeth Hamilton, July 10, 1804.
18. *Royal Danish American Gazette,* May 15, 1773.
19. *PAH,* vol. 1, p. 147, "The Farmer Refuted," February 23, 1775.
20. Ibid., vol. 5, p. 125, "New York Ratifying Convention, Third Speech," June 28, 1788.
21. St. Vincent Registry, deed book for 1784–1787, entered at Grenada on May 27, 1786, but first signed on March 14, 1774.

Three: The Collegian

1. *The William and Mary Quarterly,* April 1947.
2. *The American Historical Review,* January 1957.
3. Bowen, *Miracle at Philadelphia,* p. 65.
4. Burrows and Wallace, *Gotham,* p. 180.
5. Davis, *Memoirs of Aaron Burr,* vol. 1, p. 37.
6. Flexner, *Young Hamilton,* p. 150.
7. Davis, *Memoirs of Aaron Burr,* vol. 2, p. 434.
8. Mitchell, *Alexander Hamilton: Youth to Maturity,* p. 42.
9. Bobrick, *Angel in the Whirlwind,* p. 468.
10. *PAH,* vol. 1, p. 43.
11. Flexner, *Young Hamilton,* p. 56.
12. Schachner, *Alexander Hamilton,* p. 25.
13. Mitchell, *Alexander Hamilton: Youth to Maturity,* p. 50.
14. Ketcham, *James Madison,* p. 38.
15. Wills, *Explaining America,* p. 15.
16. *The William and Mary Quarterly,* April 1947.
17. Ibid.
18. Ketcham, *James Madison,* p. 38.
19. Humphreys, *Catherine Schuyler,* p. 103.
20. *The Columbia Monthly,* February 1904.
21. Burrows and Wallace, *Gotham,* p. 214.
22. Van Amringe and Smith, *History of Columbia University,* p. 53.
23. *PAH,* vol. 25, p. 560, letter from Gouverneur Morris, March 11, 1802.
24. Parton, *Life and Times of Aaron Burr,* p. 142.
25. Ibid., pp. 143–44.
26. New York *Mirror,* n.d. Copy in LC-AHP, reel 31.
27. *PAH,* vol. 25, p. 436.
28. Ibid., vol. 22, p. 340, letter to Elizabeth Hamilton, December 10, 1798.
29. Ibid., vol. 7, p. 40, letter to George Washington, September 15, 1790.
30. Hamilton, *Life of Alexander Hamilton,* vol. 1, p. 47.
31. LC-AHP, reel 30, "Memo of Robert Troup on the Conway Cabal, October 26, 1827."
32. Tripp, "Robert Troup," p. 167.
33. Davis, *Memoirs of Aaron Burr,* vol. 1, p. 307, and Tripp, "Robert Troup," p. 64.
34. *The William and Mary Quarterly,* April 1947.
35. Flexner, *Young Hamilton,* p. 63.
36. Wood, *American Revolution,* p. 37.
37. LC-AHP, reel 31, "Robert Troup Memoir of General Hamilton, March 22, 1810."
38. Hibbert, *George III,* p. 144.
39. Burrows and Wallace, *Gotham,* p. 216.
40. Mitchell, *Alexander Hamilton: Youth to Maturity,* p. 63.
41. Hamilton, *Life of Alexander Hamilton,* vol. 1, p. 56.
42. Callahan, *Royal Raiders,* p. 139.
43. *New-York Gazetteer,* March 30, 1774.
44. Mitchell, *Alexander Hamilton: Youth to Maturity,* p. 53.

45. *Columbia University Quarterly,* September 1899.
46. *New-York Journal; or, The General Advertiser,* September 8, 1774.
47. Van Amringe and Smith, *History of Columbia University,* p. 46.
48. *Columbia University Quarterly,* September 1899.
49. Tyler, *Literary History of the American Revolution,* p. 394.
50. *Columbia University Quarterly,* September 1899.
51. Miller, *Alexander Hamilton,* p. 9.
52. Callahan, *Royal Raiders,* p. 143.
53. *New-York Gazetteer,* January 12, 1775.
54. *PAH,* vol. 4, p. 613.
55. *New-York Gazetteer,* December 15, 1774.
56. *PAH,* vol. 1, p. 65, "A Full Vindication of the Measures of Congress," December 22, 1774.
57. Ibid., p. 68.
58. Ibid., p. 48.
59. Ibid., p. 50.
60. Ibid., p. 86, "The Farmer Refuted," February 23, 1775.
61. Ibid., p. 82.
62. Ibid., p. 164.
63. Ibid., p. 122.
64. Bobrick, *Angel in the Whirlwind,* p. 201.
65. *PAH,* vol. 1, p. 125, "The Farmer Refuted," February 23, 1775.
66. Ibid., pp. 135–36.
67. Ibid., p. 128.
68. Ibid., pp. 157–58.
69. *The William and Mary Quarterly,* April 1947.

Four: The Pen and the Sword

1. Bobrick, *Angel in the Whirlwind,* p. 119.
2. Burrows and Wallace, *Gotham,* p. 223.
3. CU-FFP, box 1818–1828, letter from Nicholas Fish to Timothy Pickering, December 26, 1823.
4. *The William and Mary Quarterly,* April 1947.
5. Van Amringe and Smith, *History of Columbia University,* p. 48.
6. O'Brien, *Hercules Mulligan,* p. 184.
7. LC-AHP, reel 31, letter from Robert Troup to Timothy Pickering, March 27, 1828.
8. Ibid.
9. *The Columbia Monthly,* February 1904.
10. Callahan, *Royal Raiders,* p. 139.
11. *Gentleman's Magazine,* July 1776.
12. "The Presidents of Columbia," Columbia University Archives, New York, N.Y.
13. Ferling, *John Adams,* p. 98.
14. Wood, *American Revolution,* p. 75.
15. Bobrick, *Angel in the Whirlwind,* p. 142.
16. Wood, *American Revolution,* p. 74.
17. *PAH,* vol. 1, p. 174, "Remarks on the Quebec Bill," June 15, 1775.
18. Wood, *American Revolution,* p. 53.
19. Maier, *American Scripture,* p. 24.

20. O'Brien, *Hercules Mulligan,* p. 182.
21. *New-York Journal; or, The General Advertiser,* September 1, 1774.
22. *Royal Danish American Gazette,* April 10, 1776.
23. O'Brien, *Hercules Mulligan,* p. 184.
24. *PAH,* vol. 1, pp. 176–77, letter to John Jay, November 26, 1775.
25. LC-AHP, reel 31, "Robert Troup Memoir of General Hamilton, March 22, 1810."
26. Schachner, *Alexander Hamilton,* p. 32.
27. "The Monitor No. I," *New-York Journal; or, The General Advertiser,* November 9, 1775.
28. "The Monitor No. VII," *New-York Journal; or, The General Advertiser,* December 21, 1775.
29. Ibid.
30. "The Monitor No. I," *New-York Journal; or, The General Advertiser,* November 9, 1775.
31. "The Monitor No. VIII," *New-York Journal; or, The General Advertiser,* December 28, 1775.
32. "The Monitor No. I," *New-York Journal; or, The General Advertiser,* November 9, 1775.
33. "The Monitor No. III," *New-York Journal; or, The General Advertiser,* November 23, 1775.
34. *PAH,* vol. 21, p. 77, letter to William Hamilton, May 2, 1797.
35. "Extract of a Letter from a Gentleman in New York, Dated February 18th," *Royal Danish American Gazette,* March 20, 1776.
36. Mitchell, *Alexander Hamilton: Youth to Maturity,* p. 79.
37. Valentine, *Lord Stirling,* p. 170.
38. *PAH,* vol. 23, p. 122, letter to James McHenry, May 18, 1799.
39. Hamilton, *Reminiscences of James A. Hamilton,* p. 11.
40. *PAH,* vol. 23, p. 122, letter to James McHenry, May 18, 1799.
41. *The William and Mary Quarterly,* April 1947.
42. Bobrick, *Angel in the Whirlwind,* p. 150.
43. "Extract of a Letter from a Gentleman in New York, Dated February 18th," *Royal Danish American Gazette,* March 20, 1776.
44. Flexner, *Young Hamilton,* p. 92.
45. "NEW YORK. Sandy Hook, June 21, 1776," *Royal Danish American Gazette,* August 14, 1776.
46. Callahan, *Royal Raiders,* p. 69.
47. Ibid., p. 73.
48. "Extract of a Letter from New York, June 24," *Royal Danish American Gazette,* August 14, 1776.
49. Callahan, *Royal Raiders,* p. 74.
50. "Extract New York, July 1," *Royal Danish American Gazette,* August 28, 1776.
51. Maier, *American Scripture,* p. 44.
52. Burrows and Wallace, *Gotham,* p. 227.
53. Ibid., p. 231.
54. Bobrick, *Angel in the Whirlwind,* p. 203.

55. Parton, *Life and Times of Aaron Burr,* p. 143.
56. *The New York Times,* July 4, 2003.
57. O'Brien, *Hercules Mulligan,* p. 183.
58. Schecter, *Battle for New York,* p. 104.
59. Ibid.
60. Bobrick, *Angel in the Whirlwind,* p. 208.
61. Ibid.
62. Schecter, *Battle for New York,* p. 150.
63. "Extract of a Letter from New York, August 30," *Royal Danish American Gazette,* December 14, 1776.
64. McCullough, *John Adams,* p. 158.
65. Flexner, *Washington,* p. 83.
66. O'Brien, *Hercules Mulligan,* p. 183.
67. Hamilton, *Life of Alexander Hamilton,* vol. 1, p. 126.
68. *The William and Mary Quarterly,* April 1947.
69. McCullough, *John Adams,* p. 159.
70. Hamilton, *Life of Alexander Hamilton,* vol. 1, p. 128.
71. Ibid., p. 133.

Five: The Little Lion

1. Wood, *American Revolution,* p. 78.
2. Brookhiser, *Alexander Hamilton,* p. 32.
3. Custis, *Recollections and Private Memoirs of Washington,* p. 344.
4. Mitchell, *Alexander Hamilton: Youth to Maturity,* p. 96.
5. Bobrick, *Angel in the Whirlwind,* p. 229.
6. *PAH,* vol. 1, p. 200, letter to the Convention of the Representatives of the State of New York, March 6, 1777.
7. Bobrick, *Angel in the Whirlwind,* p. 235.
8. Hamilton, *Life of Alexander Hamilton,* vol. 1, p. 137.
9. Ibid.
10. Flexner, *Young Hamilton,* p. 132.
11. *PAH,* vol. 1, p. 195.
12. Brookhiser, *Alexander Hamilton,* p. 29.
13. *PAH,* vol. 22, p. 37, letter to George Washington, July 29[–August 1], 1798.
14. Ibid., vol. 1, p. 209, letter to the New York Committee of Correspondence, March 20, 1777.
15. Ibid., vol. 2, p. 359, letter to Hugh Knox, July 1[–28], 1777.
16. Ibid., vol. 1, p. 202, letter to Alexander McDougall, March 10, 1777.
17. Smith, *Patriarch,* p. 4.
18. *The Wall Street Journal,* February 10, 2000.
19. Custis, *Recollections and Private Memoirs of Washington,* p. 214.
20. Ferling, *John Adams,* p. 136.
21. McCullough, *John Adams,* p. 593.
22. Smith, *Patriarch,* p. 8.
23. Mitchell, *Alexander Hamilton: Youth to Maturity,* p. 108.

24. Hamilton, *Life of Alexander Hamilton*, vol. 1, p. 177.
25. Steiner, *Life and Correspondence of James McHenry*, p. 572.
26. MHi-TPP, reel 51, p. 189.
27. *PAH*, vol. 1, p. 255, letter to Gouverneur Morris, May 19, 1777.
28. Kaminski, *George Clinton*, p. 21.
29. Custis, *Recollections and Private Memoirs of Washington*, pp. 345–46.
30. Flexner, *Young Hamilton*, p. 143.
31. Ibid., p. 146.
32. Ibid., p. 148.
33. Otis, *Eulogy on Alexander Hamilton*, p. 7.
34. Graydon, *Memoirs of His Own Time*, p. 276.
35. Hamilton, *Life of Alexander Hamilton*, vol. 1, p. 170.
36. Graydon, *Memoirs of His Own Time*, p. 277.
37. *PAH*, vol. 3, p. 150, letter to Richard Kidder Meade, August 27, 1782.
38. Ibid., vol. 1, p. 551, letter from James McHenry, September 21, 1778.
39. Ibid., vol. 2, pp. 53–54, letter to John Laurens, May 22, 1779.
40. Flexner, *Young Hamilton*, p. 149.
41. Ibid.
42. Ibid.
43. *PAH*, vol. 1, p. 225, letter to Catharine Livingston, April 11, 1777.
44. Ibid., p. 259, letter to Catharine Livingston, May 1777.
45. Wallace, *Life of Henry Laurens*, p. 470.
46. *PAH*, vol. 2, p. 17, letter to John Jay, March 14, 1799.
47. CU-JCHP, box 20.
48. Hamilton, *Intimate Life of Alexander Hamilton*, p. 245.
49. Lafayette, *Lafayette in the American Revolution*, vol. 3, p. 302.
50. Emery, *Alexander Hamilton*, p. 244.
51. Baxter, *Godchild of Washington*, p. 225.
52. Van Doren, *Benjamin Franklin*, p. 578.
53. Wilson and Stanton, *Jefferson Abroad*, p. 123.
54. *PAH*, vol. 2, p. 321.
55. Hamilton, *Intimate Life of Alexander Hamilton*, p. 245.
56. Lafayette, *Lafayette in the American Revolution*, vol. 3, p. 310.
57. Flexner, *Young Hamilton*, p. 316.
58. Bobrick, *Angel in the Whirlwind*, p. 253.
59. Flexner, *Young Hamilton*, pp. 166–67.
60. Gerlach, *Proud Patriot*, p. 309.
61. *PAH*, vol. 1, p. 314, letter to Robert R. Livingston, August 18, 1777.
62. Ibid., p. 285, letter to John Jay, July 5, 1777.
63. Ibid., p. 300, letter to Hugh Knox, July 1777.
64. Ibid., p. 321, letter to Gouverneur Morris, September 1, 1777.
65. Ibid., pp. 326–27.
66. Ellis, *Passionate Sage*, p. 111.
67. *PAH*, vol. 1, p. 330, letter from George Washington, September 21, 1777.
68. Mitchell, *Alexander Hamilton: Youth to Maturity*, p. 121.
69. Bobrick, *Angel in the Whirlwind*, p. 244.
70. Flexner, *Young Hamilton*, p. 185.
71. *PAH*, vol. 1, p. 347, letter from George Washington, October 30, 1777.
72. Ibid.
73. Ibid., p. 350, letter to George Washington, November 2, 1777.
74. Ibid., p. 351, letter to Horatio Gates, November 5, 1777.
75. Ibid., p. 353, letter to George Washington, November 6, 1777.
76. Ibid., vol. 2, p. 36, letter to John Laurens, April 1779.
77. Mitchell, *Alexander Hamilton: Youth to Maturity*, p. 138.
78. Gerlach, *Proud Patriot*, p. 304.
79. Lomask, *Aaron Burr: The Years from Princeton to Vice President*, p. 45.
80. Burrows and Wallace, *Gotham*, p. 236.
81. *PAH*, vol. 1, p. 356, letter to Israel Putnam, November 9, 1777.
82. Ibid., p. 365, letter from George Washington, November 15, 1777.
83. Ibid., pp. 360–61, letter to George Washington, November 12, 1777.
84. Flexner, *Young Hamilton*, pp. 204–5.
85. McCullough, *John Adams*, p. 173.
86. Flexner, *Young Hamilton*, p. 210.
87. Mitchell, *Alexander Hamilton: Youth to Maturity*, p. 149.
88. Ibid., p. 150.
89. Ibid., p. 151.
90. *PAH*, vol. 2, p. 420, letter to James Duane, September 6, 1780.
91. Ibid., vol. 1, p. 428, letter to George Clinton, February 13, 1778.
92. Wallace, *Life of Henry Laurens*, p. 267.
93. Bobrick, *Angel in the Whirlwind*, p. 306.

Six: A Frenzy of Valor

1. Bobrick, *Angel in the Whirlwind*, p. 291.
2. Ibid., p. 287.
3. *PAH*, vol. 1, p. 435, letter to Henry E. Lutterloh, February 1778.
4. Ibid., p. 426, letter to George Clinton, February 13, 1778.
5. Ibid.
6. Ibid., p. 427.
7. Ibid., vol. 1, p. 418, memo to George Washington, January 29, 1778.
8. Ibid., p. 440, letter to George Clinton, March 12, 1778.

9. Bobrick, *Angel in the Whirlwind,* p. 333.
10. *PAH,* vol. 1, pp. 497–98, letter to William Duer, June 18, 1778.
11. Ibid., vol. 3, p. 588, letter to John Jay, December 7, 1784.
12. Lodge, *Alexander Hamilton,* p. 241.
13. *PAH,* vol. 3, p. 101, "The Continentalist No. VI," July 4, 1782.
14. Ibid., vol. 1, p. 411, "Pay Book of the State Company of Artillery."
15. Ibid., p. 373.
16. Ibid., p. 381.
17. Ibid., p. 390.
18. Ibid., p. 397.
19. *The American Historical Review,* January 1957.
20. *PAH,* vol. 1, p. 400.
21. Ibid., pp. 399–400.
22. Ferling, *John Adams,* p. 206.
23. Hamilton, *Intimate Life of Alexander Hamilton,* p. 295.
24. Hamilton, *Reminiscences of James A. Hamilton,* p. 11.
25. Rosenfeld, *American Aurora,* p. 356.
26. *PAH,* vol. 1, p. 510, letter to Elias Boudinot, July 5, 1778.
27. Flexner, *Washington,* p. 120.
28. Ibid.
29. Ibid., p. 121.
30. *PAH,* vol. 1, pp. 507–8, "Proceedings of a General Court-Martial for the Trial of Major General Charles Lee, July 4, 1778."
31. Flexner, *Young Hamilton,* p. 231.
32. Bobrick, *Angel in the Whirlwind,* p. 345.
33. Ibid.
34. Custis, *Recollections and Private Memoirs of Washington,* p. 220.
35. Ibid., p. 221.
36. *PAH,* vol. 1, p. 512, letter to Elias Boudinot, July 5, 1778.
37. Ibid.
38. Custis, *Recollections and Private Memoirs of Washington,* pp. 232–33.
39. *PAH,* vol. 23, pp. 546–47.
40. Ibid., vol. 1, p. 513, letter to Elias Boudinot, July 5, 1778.
41. Ibid.
42. Lee, *Charles Lee Papers,* p. 62.
43. Davis, *Memoirs of Aaron Burr,* vol. 1, p. 135.
44. Lee, *Charles Lee Papers,* p. 393.
45. *PAH,* vol. 1, p. 593, letter from John Laurens, December 5, 1778.
46. *Journal of the Early Republic,* spring 1995.
47. *PAH,* vol. 1, p. 603, "Account of a Duel Between Major General Charles Lee and Lieutenant Colonel John Laurens," December 24, 1778.
48. Lee, *Charles Lee Papers,* p. 285.
49. *PAH,* vol. 1, p. 603, "Account of a Duel Between Major General Charles Lee and Lieutenant Colonel John Laurens," December 24, 1778.
50. Ibid., pp. 562–63, first "Publius" letter, October 16, 1778.
51. Ibid.
52. Ibid, p. 569, second "Publius" letter, October 26, 1778.
53. Ibid., p. 580, third "Publius" letter, November 16, 1778.
54. *PAH,* vol. 19, p. 521, "Relations with France," [1795–1796].
55. Hamilton, *Life of Alexander Hamilton,* vol. 1, p. 563.
56. Kennedy, *Burr, Hamilton, and Jefferson,* p. 103.
57. Hamilton, *Life of Alexander Hamilton,* vol. 2, p. 36.
58. Mitchell, *Alexander Hamilton: Youth to Maturity,* p. xv.
59. LC-AHP, reel 30, "Robert Troup Memo on the Conway Cabal," October 26, 1827.
60. *PAH,* vol. 1, pp. 246–47, letter to William Duer, May 6, 1777.
61. Ibid., vol. 20, p. 509, "The Warning No. II," February 7, 1797.
62. Ibid., vol. 2, p. 53, letter to John Laurens, May 22, 1779.
63. Ibid., p. 35, letter to John Laurens, April 1779.
64. Wallace, *Life of Henry Laurens,* p. 474.
65. *PAH,* vol. 2, pp. 17–18, letter to John Jay, March 14, 1779.
66. McCullough, *John Adams,* p. 133.
67. Bobrick, *Angel in the Whirlwind,* p. 101.
68. Ibid., p. 102.
69. *PAH,* vol. 2, p. 166, letter to John Laurens, September 11, 1779.
70. McDonough, *Christopher Gadsden and Henry Laurens,* p. 240.
71. *PAH,* vol. 2, pp. 34–35, letter to John Laurens, April 1779.
72. Ibid., p. 165, letter to John Laurens, September 11, 1779.
73. Ibid., p. 91, letter from John Brooks, July 4, 1779.
74. Ibid., p. 99, letter to Francis Dana, July 11, 1779.
75. Ibid., p. 154, letter to William Gordon, September 5, 1779.
76. Ibid., p. 167, letter to John Laurens, September 11, 1779.

Seven: The Lovesick Colonel

1. Smith, *John Marshall,* p. 68.
2. *PAH,* vol. 2, p. 37, letter to John Laurens, April 1779.
3. Rosenfeld, *American Aurora,* p. 377.
4. *PAH,* vol. 2, p. 255, letter to John Laurens, January 8, 1780.
5. Ibid., p. 261.
6. Brooks, *Dames and Daughters of Colonial Days,* p. 237.

7. Mitchell, *Alexander Hamilton: Youth to Maturity,* p. 198.
8. Lossing, *Hours with the Living Men and Women of the Revolution,* p. 140.
9. Van Doren, *Benjamin Franklin,* p. 544.
10. Humphreys, *Catherine Schuyler,* p. 136.
11. *PAH,* vol. 2, p. 270, letter to Margarita Schuyler, February 1780.
12. Flexner, *Young Hamilton,* p. 277.
13. Chastellux, *Travels in North America,* p. 375, and Warville, *New Travels in the United States of America,* p. 148.
14. Hamilton, *Intimate Life of Alexander Hamilton,* p. 105.
15. Ibid., p. 106.
16. Baxter, *Godchild of Washington,* p. 222.
17. *Atlantic Monthly,* August 1896.
18. *The William and Mary Quarterly,* January 1955.
19. *PAH,* vol. 2, p. 354, letter to Anthony Wayne, July 6, 1780.
20. Hamilton, *Intimate Life of Alexander Hamilton,* p. 126.
21. CU-HFP, box 1, letter from Elizabeth Hamilton to Philip Church, n.d.
22. LC-AHP, reel 30, letter from Elizabeth Hamilton to Mrs. Cochran, October 25, 1819.
23. *PAH,* vol. 2, p. 348, letter to John Laurens, June 30, 1780.
24. Ibid., p. 431, letter to John Laurens, September 16, 1780.
25. Ibid., vol. 21, p. 177, letter to Elizabeth Hamilton, July 21, 1797.
26. Steiner, *Life and Correspondence of James McHenry,* p. 45.
27. Ibid.
28. *PAH,* vol. 21, p. 481, letter to Oliver Wolcott, Jr., June 2, 1798.
29. Riedesel, *Letters and Memoirs Relating to the War of American Independence,* p. 196.
30. Humphreys, *Catherine Schuyler,* p. 88
31. Graydon, *Memoirs of His Own Time,* p. 144.
32. Gerlach, *Proud Patriot,* p. 320.
33. *PAH,* vol. 2, pp. 286–87, letter to Elizabeth Schuyler, March 17, 1780.
34. Ibid., pp. 309–10, letter to Catherine Schuyler, April 14, 1780.
35. Hamilton, *Life of Alexander Hamilton,* vol. 2, p. 336.
36. Ketcham, *James Madison,* p. 90.
37. *PAH,* vol. 2, p. 250, "Letter on Currency," December 1779–March 1780.
38. Ibid.
39. Ibid., p. 242.
40. Ibid., p. 237.
41. Emery, *Alexander Hamilton,* p. 48.
42. *PAH,* vol. 2, p. 422, letter to Elizabeth Schuyler, September 6, 1780.
43. Ibid., p. 401, letter to James Duane, September 3, 1780.
44. Ibid., p. 405.
45. Ibid., p. 406.
46. Ibid., p. 347, letter to John Laurens, May 12, 1780.
47. Ibid., p. 428, letter to John Laurens, September 12, 1780.
48. Bobrick, *Angel in the Whirlwind,* p. 412.
49. Van Doren, *Secret History of the American Revolution,* p. 346.
50. Flexner, *Young Hamilton,* p. 308.
51. *PAH,* vol. 2, pp. 440–41, letter to Nathanael Greene, September 25, 1780.
52. Ibid., p. 439, letter from Benedict Arnold to George Washington, September 25, 1780.
53. Flexner, *Young Hamilton,* p. 314.
54. *PAH,* vol. 2, p. 442, letter to Elizabeth Schuyler, September 25, 1780.
55. Ibid., p. 467, letter to John Laurens, October 11, 1780.
56. Van Doren, *Secret History of the American Revolution,* p. 366.
57. *PAH,* vol. 3, p. 92, letter to Henry Knox, June 7, 1782.
58. Bobrick, *Angel in the Whirlwind,* p. 420.
59. *PAH,* vol. 2, p. 468.
60. Ibid., p. 467.
61. Ibid., p. 449, letter to Elizabeth Schuyler, October 2, 1780.
62. Ibid., p. 474, letter to Elizabeth Schuyler, October 13, 1780.
63. Ibid., p. 385, letter to Elizabeth Schuyler, August 31, 1780.
64. Ibid., p. 455, letter to Elizabeth Schuyler, October 5, 1780.
65. Ibid., p. 374, letter to Elizabeth Schuyler, August 8, 1780.
66. Ibid., p. 422, letter to Elizabeth Schuyler, September 6, 1780.
67. Ibid., p. 351, letter to Elizabeth Schuyler, July 2–4, 1780.
68. Ibid., p. 493, letter to Elizabeth Schuyler, October 27, 1780.
69. Ibid., p. 398, letter to Elizabeth Schuyler, August 1780.
70. Ibid., vol. 21, p. 78, letter to William Hamilton, May 2, 1797.
71. Ibid., vol. 2, p. 418, letter to Elizabeth Schuyler, September 3, 1780.
72. Ibid., p. 374, letter to Elizabeth Schuyler, August 8, 1780.
73. Rogow, *Fatal Friendship,* p. 59.
74. Gerlach, *Proud Patriot,* pp. 437–38.
75. *PAH,* vol. 2, p. 350, letter to Elizabeth Schuyler, June–October 1780.
76. Ibid., p. 521.

77. Ibid., p. 539, letter to Margarita Schuyler, January 21, 1781.
78. Mitchell, *Alexander Hamilton: Youth to Maturity,* p. 202.
79. Gerlach, *Proud Patriot,* p. 403.
80. Ibid., p. 191.
81. Mitchell, *Alexander Hamilton: Youth to Maturity,* p. 568.
82. *PAH,* vol. 2, p. 509, letter to George Washington, November 22, 1780.
83. Ibid., p. 255, letter to John Laurens, January 8, 1780.
84. Ibid., p. 565, letter to Philip Schuyler, February 18, 1781.
85. Ibid., p. 549, letter to John Laurens, February 4, 1781.
86. Ibid., pp. 563–64, letter to Philip Schuyler, February 18, 1781.
87. Ibid., p. 564.
88. Ibid., p. 565.
89. Ibid., pp. 566–67.
90. Ibid., p. 569, letter to James McHenry, February 18, 1781.

Eight: Glory

1. "Hamilton's Quarrel with Washington, 1781," *The William and Mary Quarterly,* April 1955.
2. Flexner, *Young Hamilton,* p. 338.
3. *PAH,* vol. 2, p. 595, letter to Nathanael Greene, April 19, 1781.
4. Hamilton, *Life of Alexander Hamilton,* vol. 2, p. 191.
5. *PAH,* vol. 2, p. 601, letter to George Washington, April 27, 1781.
6. Ibid., p. 602, letter from George Washington, April 27, 1781.
7. Ibid., p. 235.
8. Ibid., p. 606, letter to Robert Morris, April 30, 1781.
9. Ibid., p. 605.
10. Ibid., p. 618.
11. Ibid., p. 631.
12. Ibid., p. 635.
13. Ibid., p. 554, letter to the marquis de Barbé-Marbois, February 7, 1781.
14. Smith, *John Marshall,* p. 5.
15. *PAH,* vol. 2, p. 650, "The Continentalist No. I," July 12, 1781.
16. Ibid., p. 651.
17. Ibid., p. 674, "The Continentalist No. IV," August 30, 1781.
18. Cooke, *Alexander Hamilton,* p. 136.
19. *PAH,* vol. 2, p. 636, letter to George Washington, May 2, 1781.
20. Ibid., p. 641, letter from John B. Church, May 18, 1781.
21. Ibid., p. 647, letter to Elizabeth Hamilton, July 10, 1781.
22. Kaminski, *George Clinton,* p. 40.
23. NYPL-PSP, reel 17.
24. Cunningham, *Schuyler Mansion,* p. 205.
25. NYPL-PSP, reel 17.
26. *PAH,* vol. 2, p. 666, letter to Elizabeth Hamilton, August 16, 1781.
27. Ibid., p. 667, letter to Elizabeth Hamilton, August 22, 1781.
28. Ibid., p. 675, letter to Elizabeth Hamilton, September 6, 1781.
29. Tuchman, *First Salute,* p. 267.
30. Flexner, *Young Hamilton,* p. 357.
31. Tuchman, *First Salute,* p. 281.
32. McDonald, *Alexander Hamilton,* p. 25.
33. Rosenfeld, *American Aurora,* p. 420.
34. *PAH,* vol. 2, p. 678, letter to Elizabeth Hamilton, October 12, 1781.
35. Flexner, *Young Hamilton,* p. 364.
36. Bobrick, *Angel in the Whirlwind,* p. 461.
37. Hamilton, *Life of Alexander Hamilton,* vol. 2, p. 270.
38. Bobrick, *Angel in the Whirlwind,* p. 461.
39. Mitchell, *Alexander Hamilton: Youth to Maturity,* p. 259.
40. *PAH,* vol. 2, p. 683, letter to Elizabeth Hamilton, October 18, 1781.
41. Ibid., vol. 26, p. 421, letter to the vicomte de Noailles, November–December 1781.
42. Ibid., pp. 424–25, letter to the vicomte de Noailles, April 4, 1782.
43. Mitchell, *Alexander Hamilton: Youth to Maturity,* p. 261.
44. *PAH,* vol. 5, p. 348, "Eulogy for Nathanael Greene, July 4, 1789."

Nine: Raging Billows

1. *PAH,* vol. 3, p. 69, letter to Richard Kidder Meade, March 1782.
2. Ibid., pp. 150–51, letter to Richard Kidder Meade, August 27, 1782.
3. Ibid., pp. 69–70, letter to Richard Kidder Meade, March 1782.
4. McDonald, *Alexander Hamilton,* pp. 60–61.
5. *LPAH,* vol. 1, p. 52.
6. *PAH,* vol. 3, p. 192, letter to the marquis de Lafayette, November 3, 1782.
7. Ibid., p. 471.
8. NYPL-PSP, reel 17, letter from Alexander McDougall to Philip Schuyler, October 12, 1781.
9. *The New-York Packet and the American Advertiser,* April 18, 1782.
10. *PAH,* vol. 3, p. 78, "The Continentalist No. V," April 18, 1782.

11. Ibid., p. 89, letter to Robert Morris, May 18, 1782.
12. Ibid., p. 105, "The Continentalist No. VI," July 4, 1782.
13. Ibid., p. 102.
14. Ibid., p. 169, letter to Robert Morris, September 28, 1782.
15. Ibid., p. 135, letter to Robert Morris, August 13, 1782.
16. LC-AHP, reel 30, letter from James Kent to Elizabeth Hamilton, December 20, 1832.
17. *PAH*, vol. 3, p. 121, letter from John Laurens, July 1782.
18. Ibid., p. 145, letter to John Laurens, August 15, 1782.
19. Wallace, *Life of Henry Laurens*, p. 489.
20. McDonough, *Christopher Gadsden and Henry Laurens*, p. 262.
21. *PAH*, vol. 3, p. 192, letter to the marquis de Lafayette, November 3, 1782.
22. Bowen, *Miracle at Philadelphia*, p. 97.
23. *PAH*, vol. 3, p. 226, letter to Elizabeth Hamilton, December 18, 1782.
24. Ibid., p. 238, letter to Elizabeth Hamilton, January 8, 1783.
25. Ibid., p. 424, memo of July 1783.
26. Ketcham, *James Madison*, p. 112.
27. Wills, *James Madison*, p. 19.
28. Brodie, *Thomas Jefferson*, p. 301.
29. Wills, *James Madison*, p. 20.
30. Ibid., p. 35.
31. Ketcham, *James Madison*, p. 119.
32. *The American Historical Review,* January 1957.
33. *PAH*, vol. 3, p. 216, "Continental Congress Report on a Letter from the Speaker of the Rhode Island Assembly," December 16, 1782.
34. Elkins and McKitrick, *Age of Federalism*, p. 102.
35. *The American Historical Review,* January 1957.
36. Mitchell, *Alexander Hamilton: Youth to Maturity*, p. 292.
37. *PAH*, vol. 3, p. 256, letter to George Clinton, February 14, 1783.
38. Ibid., p. 254, letter to George Washington, February 13, 1783.
39. Brookhiser, *Gentleman Revolutionary*, p. 72.
40. *PAH*, vol. 3, p. 254, letter to George Washington, February 13, 1783.
41. Ibid., p. 264, James Madison notes on the conversation on the evening of February 20, 1783.
42. Ibid., p. 278, letter from George Washington, March 4, 1783.
43. Bobrick, *Angel in the Whirlwind*, p. 474.
44. *PAH*, vol. 3, p. 286, letter from George Washington, March 12, 1783.
45. Ibid., p. 287.
46. Flexner, *Washington*, p. 174.
47. Ellis, *Founding Brothers*, p. 130.
48. *PAH*, vol. 3, p. 291, letter to George Washington, March 17, 1783.
49. Ibid., p. 293.
50. Ibid., p. 310, letter from George Washington, March 31, 1783.
51. Flexner, *Young Hamilton*, p. 412.
52. *PAH*, vol. 3, p. 335, letter from George Washington, April 22, 1783.
53. Ibid., p. 397, letter to William Jackson, June 19, 1783.
54. Ketcham, *James Madison*, p. 142.
55. *PAH*, vol. 3, p. 451, letter to John Dickinson, September 25–30, 1783.
56. Ibid., p. 401, "Continental Congress Resolutions on Measures to Be Taken in Consequence of the Pennsylvania Mutiny," June 21, 1783.
57. Ibid., p. 406, "Continental Congress Report of a Committee Appointed to Confer with the Supreme Executive Council of Pennsylvania on the Mutiny," June 24, 1783.
58. Ibid., p. 407, letter to George Clinton, June 29, 1783.
59. Ketcham, *James Madison*, p. 142.
60. Malone, *Jefferson and His Time*, vol. 1, p. 404.
61. *PAH*, vol. 3, p. 412, letter to James Madison, July 6, 1783.
62. Ibid., p. 376, letter to Nathanael Greene, June 10, 1783.
63. Ibid., "Continental Congress Unsubmitted Resolution Calling for a Convention to Amend the Articles of Confederation," July 1783.
64. Wood, *American Revolution*, p. 148.
65. *PAH*, vol. 3, p. 413, letter to Elizabeth Hamilton, July 22, 1783.
66. Ibid., p. 431, letter to Robert R. Livingston, August 13, 1783.
67. Wood, *American Revolution*, p. 87.
68. *LPAH*, vol. 1, p. 223.
69. Bobrick, *Angel in the Whirlwind*, p. 421.
70. *PAH*, vol. 3, p. 492, "Letter from Phocion," January 1784.
71. Schecter, *Battle for New York*, p. 377.
72. Lomask, *Aaron Burr: The Years from Princeton to Vice President*, p. 82.
73. *PAH*, vol. 3, p. 481, letter to Samuel Loudon, December 27, 1783.
74. King, *Life and Correspondence of Rufus King,* vol. 4, p. 407.

Ten: A Grave, Silent, Strange Sort of Animal

1. Hamilton, *Intimate Life of Alexander Hamilton,* p. 240.
2. NYPL-JAHP, box 1.
3. Ames, *Sketch of the Character of Alexander Hamilton,* pp. 7–8.

4. Kent, *Memoirs and Letters of James Kent,* p. 228.
5. Sullivan, *Public Men of the Revolution,* p. 260.
6. Hamilton, *Intimate Life of Alexander Hamilton,* p. 37.
7. *LPAH,* vol. 1, p. 46.
8. King, *Life and Correspondence of Rufus King,* vol. 3, p. 460.
9. NYPL-JAHP, box 1.
10. Ibid.
11. Hamilton, *Reminiscences of James A. Hamilton,* p. 6.
12. Ibid.
13. *LPAH,* vol. 1, p. 689.
14. McDonald, *Alexander Hamilton,* p. 63.
15. Ibid., p. 314.
16. LC-AHP, reel 30, letter from James Kent to Elizabeth Hamilton, December 20, 1832.
17. Ibid., letter from Robert Troup to Timothy Pickering, March 31, 1828.
18. Ames, *Sketch of the Character of Alexander Hamilton,* p. 10.
19. *LPAH,* vol. 1, p. 7.
20. *PAH,* vol. 26, p. 239.
21. Parton, *Life and Times of Aaron Burr,* p. 368.
22. Lomask, *Aaron Burr: The Years from Princeton to Vice President,* p. 14.
23. Ibid., p. 97.
24. LC-WPP, reel 1, diary entry of January 22, 1807.
25. *The New York Review of Books,* February 2, 1984.
26. Hamilton, *Intimate Life of Alexander Hamilton,* p. 427.
27. *PAH,* vol. 25, p. 321, letter to James A. Bayard, January 16, 1801.
28. Ibid., p. 296, letter to John Rutledge, Jr., January 4, 1801.
29. Rogow, *Fatal Friendship,* p. 91.
30. Ibid., p. 93.
31. Lodge, *Alexander Hamilton,* p. 188.
32. Parton, *Life and Times of Aaron Burr,* p. 153.
33. *PAH,* vol. 25, p. 298, letter to John Rutledge, Jr., January 4, 1801.
34. LC-WPP, reel 1, diary entry, January 22, 1807.
35. Brookhiser, *Alexander Hamilton,* p. 150.
36. Parton, *Life and Times of Aaron Burr,* p. 149.
37. *PAH,* vol. 3, p. 141, letter to Robert Morris, August 13, 1782.
38. Ibid., p. 459, letter from John Jay, September 28, 1783.
39. Bobrick, *Angel in the Whirlwind,* p. 481.
40. *PAH,* vol. 3, p. 484, "Letter from Phocion," January 1784.
41. Ibid., p. 485.
42. Ibid., p. 556, "Second Letter from Phocion," April 1784.
43. Hamilton, *Intimate Life of Alexander Hamilton,* p. 152.
44. *LPAH,* vol. 1, p. 307.

45. Brookhiser, *Alexander Hamilton,* p. 58.
46. Hamilton, *Intimate Life of Alexander Hamilton,* p. 153.
47. *LPAH,* vol. 1, p. 301.
48. Cheetham, *Narrative of the Suppression by Col. Burr,* p. 55.
49. *PAH,* vol. 3, p. 524, letter to Gouverneur Morris, March 21, 1784.
50. Ibid., p. 521, letter to John B. Church, March 10, 1784.
51. Ibid.
52. Ibid., p. 514, "Constitution of the Bank of New York."

Eleven: Ghosts

1. Hamilton, *Reminiscences of James A. Hamilton,* p. 3.
2. *PAH,* vol. 4, p. 279, letter from Angelica Church, October 2, 1787.
3. Ibid., vol. 3, p. 620, letter to Angelica Church, August 3, 1785.
4. Ibid., pp. 3–4.
5. Ibid., p. 3.
6. Ibid., vol. 4, p. 120.
7. Menz, *Historic Furnishing Report,* pp. 70–71.
8. Hamilton, *Reminiscences of James A. Hamilton,* p. 65.
9. Original Will Transcript Book of South Carolina, 1780–1783, "Will of Peter Lavien." Copy in the South Carolina Room, Charleston County Public Library, Charleston, S.C.
10. *PAH,* vol. 3, p. 235, letter to Elizabeth Hamilton, 1782.
11. Hamilton, *Intimate Life of Alexander Hamilton,* p. 184.
12. *PAH,* vol. 3, p. 474, letter from Hugh Knox, October 27, 1783.
13. Ibid., p. 573, letter from Hugh Knox, July 28, 1784.
14. *Proceedings of the New Jersey Historical Society,* April 1951.
15. *PAH,* vol. 3, p. 617, letter to James Hamilton, June 22, 1785.
16. Ibid.
17. Ibid.
18. Ibid., vol. 20, p. 459, "From Ann Mitchell," [1796].
19. Ibid., vol. 1, p. 484, letter from Edward Stevens, May 8, 1778.
20. Ibid., vol. 3, p. 574, letter from Hugh Knox, July 28, 1784.
21. Bailyn, *Ideological Origins of the American Revolution,* p. 244.
22. Hamilton, *Intimate Life of Alexander Hamilton,* p. 96.
23. *PAH,* vol. 2, p. 642, letter to George Clinton, May 22, 1781.

24. McDonald, *Alexander Hamilton,* p. 373.
25. *PAH,* vol. 19, p. 204, letter from Philip Schuyler, August 31, 1795; *LPAH,* vol. 5, p. 409, cashbook entry for March 23, 1796.
26. William-Myers, *Long Hammering,* p. 23.
27. McCullough, *John Adams,* p. 134.
28. Ferling, *John Adams,* p. 172.
29. Ibid., p. 173.
30. Morgan, *Benjamin Franklin,* p. 105.
31. *The New York Review of Books,* November 4, 1999.
32. Ketcham, *James Madison,* p. 374.
33. Rakove, *James Madison and the Creation of the American Republic,* p. 144.
34. Ibid., pp. 144–45.
35. *PAH,* vol. 18, p. 519, "The Defence No. III," July 29, 1795.
36. Brookhiser, *Gentleman Revolutionary,* p. 34.
37. NYHS-NYCMS, reel 1, February 4, 1785.
38. Burrows and Wallace, *Gotham,* p. 286.
39. Lomask, *Aaron Burr: The Conspiracy and Years of Exile,* p. 403.
40. NYHS-NYCMS, reel 2, [ca. August–September 1786].
41. Ibid., [ca. March 1786].
42. Wood, *American Revolution,* p. 120.
43. *PAH,* vol. 3, p. 639, letter from George Washington, December 11, 1785.
44. *Extract from the Proceedings of the New-York State Society, of the Cincinnati,* p. 6.
45. Ibid., p. 10.
46. Ibid., p. 12.

Twelve: August and Respectable Assembly
1. *PAH,* vol. 25, p. 479, "The Examination," no. 5; *New-York Evening Post,* December 29, 1801.
2. Ibid., vol. 3, p. 609, letter to Robert Livingston, April 25, 1785.
3. *The New-York Packet,* April 7, 1785.
4. Kaminski, *George Clinton,* p. 107.
5. Knott, *Alexander Hamilton and the Persistence of Myth,* p. 87.
6. Kaminski, *George Clinton,* p. 246.
7. *PAH,* vol. 3, pp. 137–38, letter to Robert Morris, August 13, 1782.
8. Ibid., vol. 5, p. 290, "H. G. Letter XI," March 6, 1789.
9. Kaminski, *George Clinton,* p. 18.
10. LC-WPP, reel 1, diary entry, March 15, 1806.
11. *PAH,* vol. 21, pp. 77–78, letter to William Hamilton, May 2, 1797.
12. *The William and Mary Quarterly,* April 1947.
13. Kaminski, *George Clinton,* p. 115.
14. Mitchell, *Alexander Hamilton: Youth to Maturity,* p. 356.
15. Wood, *American Revolution,* p. 152.
16. Hamilton, *Federalist,* pp. lviii–lix.

17. *PAH,* vol. 3, p. 684, letter to Elizabeth Hamilton, September 8, 1786.
18. Wills, *Explaining America,* p. 12.
19. *PAH,* vol. 3, p. 687, "Address of the Annapolis Convention," September 14, 1786.
20. Mitchell, *Alexander Hamilton: Youth to Maturity,* p. 367.
21. Cooke, *Alexander Hamilton,* p. xviii.
22. Bowen, *Miracle at Philadelphia,* p. 5.
23. Brookhiser, *Gentleman Revolutionary,* p. 80.
24. Ferling, *John Adams,* p. 309.
25. Wills, *Explaining America,* p. 7.
26. Wilson and Stanton, *Jefferson Abroad,* p. 120.
27. McCullough, *John Adams,* p. 371.
28. *PAH,* vol. 19, p. 18, "The Defence of the Funding System," July 1795.
29. Ibid., vol. 4, p. 312, "The Federalist No. 6," November 14, 1787.
30. LC-AHP, reel 30, letter from Samuel Jones to Elizabeth Hamilton, June 1, 1818.
31. *PAH,* vol. 4, p. 86, speech to New York Assembly, February 1787.
32. Ibid., pp. 89–90.
33. CU-HPPP, box 261, letter from Margaret Livingston to Robert R. Livingston, March 3, 1787.
34. *The Daily Advertiser,* February 10, 1787.
35. Ibid.
36. Kaminski, *George Clinton,* p. 119.
37. "Hamilton and Washington: The Origins of the American Party System," *The William and Mary Quarterly,* April 1955.
38. Bobrick, *Angel in the Whirlwind,* p. 488.
39. Ketcham, *James Madison,* p. 195.
40. *PAH,* vol. 12, p. 355, "Amicus," *National Gazette,* September 11, 1792.
41. Bowen, *Miracle at Philadelphia,* p. 30.
42. Ibid., p. 236.
43. Butzner, *Constitutional Chaff,* p. 162.
44. Ketcham, *James Madison,* p. 195.
45. Bowen, *Miracle at Philadelphia,* p. 61.
46. Ketcham, *James Madison,* p. 196.
47. Ibid.
48. Bowen, *Miracle at Philadelphia,* pp. 104–5.
49. *PAH,* vol. 4, p. 178, "Constitutional Convention Speech on a Plan of Government."
50. Ibid., p. 187, Madison's notes, June 18, 1787.
51. Ibid., p. 195, Robert Yates notes, June 18, 1787.
52. Bowen, *Miracle at Philadelphia,* p. 113.
53. *PAH,* vol. 4, p. 194, Madison's notes, June 18, 1787.
54. Ibid., p. 186, Hamilton's notes, June 18, 1787.
55. Ibid., p. 192, Madison's notes, June 18, 1787.
56. *The Mississippi Valley Historical Review,* March 1950.
57. *PAH,* vol. 4, p. 165, "Notes Taken in the Federal Convention."

58. Ibid., p. 186, Hamilton's notes, June 18, 1787.
59. Ibid., p. 192, Madison's notes, June 18, 1787.
60. Bowen, *Miracle at Philadelphia,* p. 101.
61. Mitchell, *Alexander Hamilton: Youth to Maturity,* p. 391.
62. Ibid.
63. Bowen, *Miracle at Philadelphia,* p. 114.
64. Ibid., p. 188.
65. Ibid., p. 14.
66. Rosenfeld, *American Aurora,* p. 471.
67. Ferling, *John Adams,* p. 309.
68. Isaacson, *Benjamin Franklin,* p. 451.
69. *The William and Mary Quarterly,* 1955.
70. *PAH,* vol. 4, p. 221, "Remarks on Equality of Representation of the States in the Congress," June 29, 1787.
71. Ibid.
72. Ibid., pp. 224–25, letter to George Washington, July 3, 1787.
73. Ibid., p. 225, letter from George Washington, July 10, 1787.
74. Jefferson, *Anas of Thomas Jefferson,* p. 87.
75. *PAH,* vol. 4, p. 235, letter to Rufus King, August 20, 1787.
76. Bowen, *Miracle at Philadelphia,* p. 311.
77. *PAH,* vol. 5, p. 289, "H.G. Letter XI," March 6, 1789.
78. Mitchell, *Alexander Hamilton: Youth to Maturity,* p. 407.
79. *The Daily Advertiser,* July 21, 1787.
80. *New-York Journal,* September 20, 1787.
81. *PAH,* vol. 4, p. 280, letter to George Washington, October 11–15, 1787.
82. Ibid., p. 284, letter from George Washington, October 18, 1787.
83. Ibid., p. 226, letter to Nathaniel Mitchell, July 20, 1787.
84. Bowen, *Miracle at Philadelphia,* p. 208.
85. Ellis, *Founding Brothers,* p. 91.
86. Ibid., p. 92.
87. Ibid., p. 201.
88. NYHS-NYCMS, reel 1, August 1787.
89. Ibid., January 26, 1788.
90. Emery, *Alexander Hamilton,* p. 103.
91. Berkin, *Brilliant Solution,* p. 113.
92. Brookhiser, *Gentleman Revolutionary,* p. 88.
93. Ibid., p. 60.
94. Bowen, *Miracle at Philadelphia,* p. 42.
95. Fleming, *Duel,* p. 22.
96. Brookhiser, *Alexander Hamilton,* p. 7.
97. *PAH,* vol. 7, p. 72, "Conversation with George Beckwith," September 25–30, 1790.
98. Elkins and McKitrick, *Age of Federalism,* p. 317.
99. Bowen, *Miracle at Philadelphia,* p. 195.
100. Brookhiser, *Gentleman Revolutionary,* p. 26.
101. Bowen, *Miracle at Philadelphia,* p. 263.
102. *PAH,* vol. 4, p. 253, "Remarks on Signing the Constitution," September 17, 1787.
103. Colimore, *The* Philadelphia Inquirer's *Guide to Historic Philadelphia,* p. 9.

Thirteen: Publius

1. Kaminski, *George Clinton,* p. 131.
2. Bowen, *Miracle at Philadelphia,* p. 271.
3. Burrows and Wallace, *Gotham,* p. 289.
4. Kaminski, *George Clinton,* p. 125.
5. Ibid.
6. Ibid., p. 127.
7. *The Daily Advertiser,* September 15, 1787.
8. Ibid.
9. *New-York Journal,* September 20, 1787.
10. Ibid., October 4, 1787.
11. *PAH,* vol. 4, p. 276, "Conjectures About the New Constitution," September 17–30, 1787.
12. Custis, *Recollections and Private Memoirs of Washington,* p. 215.
13. Kent, *Memoirs and Letters of James Kent,* pp. 301–2.
14. Baxter, *Godchild of Washington,* p. 219.
15. *PAH,* vol. 4, p. 288.
16. Ibid.
17. Ibid., vol. 25, p. 558, "The Examination," no. 15, *New-York Evening Post,* March 3, 1802.
18. *PAH,* vol. 4, p. 308, letter from George Washington, November 10, 1787.
19. CU-HPPP, box 261, letter from Archibald McLean to Robert Troup, October 14, 1788.
20. Mitchell, *Alexander Hamilton: Youth to Maturity,* p. 418.
21. Knott, *Alexander Hamilton and the Persistence of Myth,* p. 89.
22. Mitchell, *Alexander Hamilton: Youth to Maturity,* p. 417.
23. Bailyn, *To Begin the World Anew,* p. 102.
24. Madison, *Papers of James Madison,* vol. 10, p. 260.
25. *The William and Mary Quarterly,* April 1947.
26. NYHS-NPP.
27. Sullivan, *Public Men of the Revolution,* p. 261.
28. Ketcham, *James Madison,* p. 236.
29. Warville, *New Travels in the United States of America,* p. 147.
30. Ibid.
31. Scigliano, *Federalist,* p. 290.
32. Ibid., p. 331.
33. Ibid.
34. Bailyn, *To Begin the World Anew,* p. 113.
35. *PAH,* vol. 4, p. 301, "The Federalist No. 1," October 27, 1787.
36. Ibid.
37. Ibid., p. 304.

38. Ibid., p. 313, "The Federalist No. 6," November 14, 1787.
39. Ibid., p. 331, "The Federalist No. 8," November 20, 1787.
40. Ibid., p. 333, "The Federalist No. 9," November 21, 1787.
41. Ibid., p. 340, "The Federalist No. 11," November 24, 1787.
42. Ibid., p. 347, "The Federalist No. 12," November 27, 1787.
43. Ibid., p. 356, "The Federalist No. 15," December 1, 1787.
44. Ibid., p. 395, "The Federalist No. 20," December 11, 1787.
45. Ibid., p. 400, "The Federalist No. 21," December 12, 1787.
46. Ibid., p. 409, "The Federalist No. 22," December 14, 1787.
47. Ibid.
48. Ibid., p. 426, "The Federalist No. 25," December 21, 1787.
49. Ibid., p. 420, "The Federalist No. 24," December 19, 1787.
50. Ibid., p. 421.
51. Ibid., p. 439, "The Federalist No. 28," December 26, 1787.
52. Ibid., p. 450, "The Federalist No. 30," December 28, 1787.
53. Ibid., p. 451.
54. Ibid., p. 472, "The Federalist No. 34," January 5, 1788.
55. Ibid., p. 456, "The Federalist No. 31," January 1, 1788.
56. Ibid., p. 472, "The Federalist No. 34," January 5, 1788.
57. Ibid., p. 461, "The Federalist No. 32," January 2, 1788.
58. Ibid., p. 482, "The Federalist No. 35," January 5, 1788.
59. Ibid., p. 483, "The Federalist No. 36," January 8, 1788.
60. Ibid., p. 548, "The Federalist No. 60," February 23, 1788.
61. Ibid., p. 567, "The Federalist No. 63," March 1, 1788.
62. Ibid., p. 575, "The Federalist No. 66," March 7, 1788.
63. Ibid., p. 599, "The Federalist No. 70," March 15, 1788.
64. Ibid., p. 605.
65. Ibid., p. 609, "The Federalist No. 71," March 18, 1788.
66. Ibid., p. 612, "The Federalist No. 72," March 19, 1788.
67. Ibid., p. 625, "The Federalist No. 74," March 25, 1788.
68. Ibid., p. 636, "The Federalist No. 76," April 1, 1788.
69. Ibid., vol. 25, p. 550, "The Examination," no. 14, *New-York Evening Post,* March 2, 1801.
70. Ibid., vol. 4, p. 658, "The Federalist No. 78," May 28, 1778.
71. Ibid., p. 697, "The Federalist No. 83," May 28, 1788.
72. Ibid., p. 706, "The Federalist No. 84," May 28, 1788.
73. Ibid., p. 705.
74. Ibid., p. 721, "The Federalist No. 85," May 28, 1788.
75. Ibid.
76. *PAH,* vol. 4, p. 650, letter to Gouverneur Morris, May 19, 1788.
77. Wills, *Explaining America,* p. xvi.
78. Bailyn, *To Begin the World Anew,* p. 101.
79. Jefferson, *Papers of Thomas Jefferson,* vol. 13, p. 156.
80. *PAH,* vol. 4, p. 409, "The Federalist No. 22," December 14, 1787.
81. LC-AHP, reel 30, letter from James Kent to Elizabeth Hamilton, December 20, 1832.
82. *PAH,* vol. 4, pp. 649–50, letter to James Madison, May 19, 1788.
83. NYPL-AYP.
84. *PAH,* vol. 4, p. 649, letter to James Madison, May 19, 1788.
85. Bowen, *Miracle at Philadelphia,* p. 293.
86. *PAH,* vol. 5, p. 3, letter to James Madison, June 8, 1788.
87. Ibid., vol. 4, p. 641, "Federalist No. 77," April 2, 1788.
88. Hamilton, *Intimate Life of Alexander Hamilton,* p. 49.
89. *The William and Mary Quarterly,* July 1967.
90. *PAH,* vol. 5, p. 10, letter to James Madison, June 19, 1788.
91. Cooke, *Alexander Hamilton,* p. 15.
92. LC-AHP, reel 30, letter from James Kent to Elizabeth Hamilton, December 20, 1832.
93. Burrows and Wallace, *Gotham,* p. 292.
94. *PAH,* vol. 5, p. 16, speech of June 19, 1788.
95. Ibid., p. 18, speech of June 20, 1788.
96. Ibid., p. 26.
97. Ibid., p. 43, speech of June 21, 1788.
98. Ibid., p. 37.
99. Kaminski, *George Clinton,* p. 151.
100. Ibid.
101. *The William and Mary Quarterly,* July 1967.
102. *PAH,* vol. 5, p. 68, speech of June 24, 1788.
103. Ibid., p. 67.
104. Ibid., p. 91, letter to James Madison, June 27, 1788.
105. *The Daily Advertiser,* July 4, 1788.
106. NYPL-AYP.

107. NYHS-MM, reel 4, letter from Abraham Bancker to Evert Bancker, June 28, 1788.
108. Smith, *John Marshall*, p. 119.
109. Berkin, *Brilliant Solution*, p. 188.
110. *The Daily Advertiser*, July 12, 1788.
111. Kaminski, *George Clinton*, p. 166.
112. Burrows and Wallace, *Gotham*, p. 293.
113. *The William and Mary Quarterly*, July 1967.
114. Ibid.
115. Burrows and Wallace, *Gotham*, p. 293.
116. Brookhiser, *Alexander Hamilton*, p. 74.

Fourteen: Putting the Machine in Motion

1. *PAH*, vol. 5, p. 202, letter to George Washington, August 13, 1788.
2. Ibid., p. 207, letter from George Washington, August 28, 1788.
3. Ibid., p. 221, letter to George Washington, September 1788.
4. Ibid., p. 223, letter from George Washington, October 3, 1788.
5. Ibid., p. 234, letter to George Washington, November 18, 1788.
6. Ferling, *John Adams*, p. 298.
7. *PAH*, vol. 5, p. 248, letter to James Wilson, January 25, 1789.
8. Ibid., p. 225, letter to Theodore Sedgwick, October 9, 1788.
9. Ibid., p. 231, letter to Theodore Sedgwick, November 9, 1788.
10. Ferling, *John Adams*, p. 299.
11. McCullough, *John Adams*, p. 409.
12. *PAH*, vol. 25, p. 191, *Letter from Alexander Hamilton*, October 24, 1800.
13. Kaminski, *George Clinton*, p. 178.
14. *PAH*, vol. 26, p. 479, letter to Isaac Ledyard, February 18, 1789.
15. Ibid., vol. 5, p. 263, "H. G. Letter I," *The Daily Advertiser*, February 20, 1789.
16. Ibid., p. 265, "H. G. Letter II," *The Daily Advertiser*, February 21, 1789.
17. Ibid., p. 269, "H. G. Letter IV," *The Daily Advertiser*, February 24, 1789.
18. Ibid., p. 292, "H. G. Letter XI," *The Daily Advertiser*, March 7, 1789.
19. Ibid., p. 298, "H. G. Letter XIII," *The Daily Advertiser*, March 9, 1789.
20. Kaminski, *George Clinton*, p. 182.
21. Ibid., p. 187.
22. Ibid., p. 182.
23. Ibid., p. 186.
24. Ibid., p. 187.
25. Mitchell, *Alexander Hamilton: The National Adventure*, p. 560.
26. *PAH*, vol. 5, pp. 321–22, letter of April 7, 1789, to the New York State Electors.
27. Burrows and Wallace, *Gotham*, p. 297.
28. Ketcham, *James Madison*, p. 283.
29. Baxter, *Godchild of Washington*, p. 224.
30. Ibid.
31. Sullivan, *Public Men of the Revolution*, p. 117.
32. Van Doren, *Benjamin Franklin*, p. 772.
33. Ferling, *John Adams*, p. 302.
34. Elkins and McKitrick, *Age of Federalism*, p. 48.
35. Hamilton, *Intimate Life of Alexander Hamilton*, p. 315.
36. Smith, *Patriarch*, p. 291.
37. McCullough, *John Adams*, p. 413.
38. Hamilton, *Intimate Life of Alexander Hamilton*, p. 208.
39. Freeman, *Affairs of Honor*, p. 40.
40. LC-AHP, reel 30, letter from James Kent to Elizabeth Hamilton, December 20, 1832.
41. Freeman, *Affairs of Honor*, p. 9.
42. *PAH*, vol. 4, p. 375, letter to Angelica Church, December 6, 1787.
43. Ibid., p. 279, letter from Angelica Church, October 2, 1787.
44. Humphreys, *Catherine Schuyler*, p. 201.
45. Foreman, *Georgiana*, p. 45.
46. CU-HPPP, box 264, letter from Angelica Church to Elizabeth Hamilton, January 23, 1792.
47. Ibid.
48. Ibid., June 3, 1792.
49. Emery, *Alexander Hamilton*, p. 126.
50. *PAH*, vol. 5, p. 501, letter to Angelica Church, November 8, 1789.
51. Ibid.
52. Ibid.
53. Ibid., p. 502, letter from Elizabeth Hamilton to Angelica Church, November 8, 1789.
54. Flexner, *Washington*, p. 219.
55. *PAH*, vol. 6, p. 334, *Greenleaf's New York Journal and Patriotic Register*, April 15, 1790.
56. MHi-TPP, reel 51, p. 153.
57. *PAH*, vol. 5, p. 348, "Eulogy on Nathanael Greene," July 4, 1789.
58. Ibid., p. 350.
59. Meleny, *Public Life of Aedanus Burke*, p. 193.
60. *PAH*, vol. 5, p. 351, "Eulogy on Nathanael Greene," July 4, 1789.
61. Lomask, *Aaron Burr: The Years from Princeton to Vice President*, p. 138.
62. Ibid., p. 139.
63. *PAH*, vol. 5, p. 360, letter from Robert Troup, July 12, 1789.
64. Custis, *Recollections and Private Memoirs of Washington*, pp. 349–50.
65. McDonald, *Alexander Hamilton*, p. 128.
66. Custis, *Recollections and Private Memoirs of Washington*, p. 351.

67. Mitchell, *Alexander Hamilton: The National Adventure*, p. 22.
68. LC-AHP, reel 31, "Additional Facts Relative to the Life and Character of General Hamilton," January 1, 1821.
69. *PAH*, vol. 21, p. 78, letter to William Hamilton, May 2, 1797.
70. Madison, *Papers of James Madison*, vol. 12, p. 185.
71. NYHS-MM, reel 4, letter from Abraham Bancker to Evert Bancker, July 16, 1789.
72. *PAH*, vol. 2, p. 417, letter to James Duane, September 3, 1780.
73. Cooke, *Alexander Hamilton*, p. 27.
74. *PAH*, vol. 9, p. 30, "Conversations with George Beckwith," August 12, 1791.
75. Ellis, *Founding Brothers*, p. 124.
76. *PAH*, vol. 25, p. 214, *Letter from Alexander Hamilton*, October 24, 1800.
77. Custis, *Recollections and Private Memoirs of George Washington*, p. 214.

Fifteen: Villainous Business

1. Callahan, *Henry Knox*, pp. 235–36.
2. Freeman, *Affairs of Honor*, p. 46.
3. *PAH*, vol. 5, p. 579, letter to Elizabeth Hamilton, November 1789.
4. Ibid., p. 422, letter to Jeremiah Wadsworth, October 3, 1789.
5. Ibid., vol. 18, p. 292, letter to Joseph Anthony, March 11, 1795.
6. Ibid., vol. 5, p. 369, letter to Samuel Meredith, September 13, 1789.
7. "William Duer and the Business of Government in the Era of the American Revolution," *The William and Mary Quarterly*, July 1975.
8. Ibid.
9. *PAH*, vol. 13, p. 526, "On James Blanchard," January 1793.
10. Ibid., vol. 5, p. 486, "Conversation with George Beckwith," October 1789.
11. Ibid., p. 482.
12. Ibid., p. 488.
13. Ibid., p. 482.
14. Ibid.
15. Ibid., p. 487.
16. Ibid., vol. 6, p. 53.
17. Ibid., p. 54.
18. Ibid., vol. 5, p. 464, letter from John Witherspoon, October 26, 1789.
19. Ibid., p. 439, letter to James Madison, October 12, 1789.
20. Elkins and McKitrick, *Age of Federalism*, p. 114.
21. *PAH*, vol. 5, p. 526, letter from James Madison, November 19, 1789.
22. Ibid., vol. 6, p. 69, *Report on Public Credit*, January 1790.
23. Ibid., p. 67.
24. Ibid., p. 96.
25. Ibid., p. 73.
26. Ibid., p. 78.
27. Knott, *Alexander Hamilton and the Persistence of Myth*, p. 95.
28. *PAH*, vol. 6, p. 98, *Report on Public Credit*, January 1790.
29. Ibid., p. 100.
30. Ibid., p. 106.
31. Ibid., vol. 12, p. 570, "Fact No. II," *National Gazette*, Philadelphia, October 16, 1792.
32. Ibid., vol. 18, p. 102, "Report on a Plan for the Further Support of the Public Credit," January 16, 1795.
33. Ibid.
34. *PAH*, vol. 6, p. 1, letter to Henry Lee, December 1, 1789.
35. Ibid., p. 50, letter to Angelica Church, January 7, 1790.
36. Gordon, *Hamilton's Blessing*, pp. 40–41.
37. *PAH*, vol. 18, p. 116, "Report on a Plan for the Further Support of the Public Credit," January 16, 1795.
38. Maclay, *Journal of William Maclay*, p. 177.
39. Ibid.
40. Ibid., p. 188.
41. *PAH*, vol. 12, p. 249, letter to George Washington, August 18, 1792.
42. Maclay, *Journal of William Maclay*, p. 332.
43. Burrows and Wallace, *Gotham*, p. 304.
44. Elkins and McKitrick, *Age of Federalism*, p. 141.
45. Mitchell, *Alexander Hamilton: The National Adventure*, p. 45.
46. Madison, *Papers of James Madison*, vol. 13, p. 98.
47. Gordon, *Hamilton's Blessing*, p. 28.
48. *PAH*, vol. 6, p. 436, letter to George Washington, May 28, 1790.
49. Maclay, *Journal of William Maclay*, p. 189.
50. Ibid., p. 194.
51. Hamilton, *Intimate Life of Alexander Hamilton*, p. 279.
52. Adams, *New Letters of Abigail Adams*, p. 37.
53. Maclay, *Journal of William Maclay*, p. 201.
54. Madison, *Papers of James Madison*, vol. 13, p. 147.
55. Ibid.
56. Ketcham, *James Madison*, p. 310.
57. Ellis, *Founding Brothers*, p. 84.
58. Hamilton, *Life of Alexander Hamilton*, vol. 4, p. 99.
59. Ellis, *Founding Brothers*, p. 114.
60. *New York Historical Society Quarterly*, October 1948.
61. *The New Yorker*, March 10, 2003.
62. *Greenleaf's New York Journal and Patriotic Register*, April 15, 1790.

63. Freeman, *Affairs of Honor*, p. 30.
64. Ibid., p. 29.
65. Ibid., p. 30.
66. Ames, *Sketch of the Character of Alexander Hamilton*, p. 8.
67. Meleny, *Public Life of Aedanus Burke*, p. 194.
68. Ibid., p. 196.
69. *PAH*, vol. 6, pp. 333–34, letter to Aedanus Burke, April 1, 1790.
70. Ibid., p. 336, letter from Aedanus Burke, April 1, 1790.
71. Maclay, *Journal of William Maclay*, p. 227.

Sixteen: Dr. Pangloss

1. Wilson and Stanton, *Jefferson Abroad*, p. 205.
2. Ibid., p. 210.
3. Ibid., p. 279.
4. Maclay, *Journal of William Maclay*, p. 272.
5. Malone, *Jefferson and His Time*, vol. 1, p. 69.
6. Ibid., p. 55.
7. Ibid., vol. 2, p. 77.
8. Bailyn, *Ideological Origins of the American Revolution*, p. 236.
9. Bobrick, *Angel in the Whirlwind*, p. 359.
10. McCullough, *John Adams*, p. 633.
11. Hamilton, *Life of Alexander Hamilton*, vol. 2, p. 168.
12. "Phocion No. IX," *Gazette of the United States*, October 21, 1796.
13. Wilson and Stanton, *Jefferson Abroad*, p. 11.
14. Malone, *Jefferson and His Time*, vol. 1, p. 201.
15. Ibid., vol. 2, p. 204.
16. Wilson and Stanton, *Jefferson Abroad*, p. 42.
17. Malone, *Jefferson and His Time*, vol. 2, p. 171.
18. Ibid., p. 46.
19. Brodie, *Thomas Jefferson*, p. 216.
20. Ibid., p. 227.
21. Jefferson, *Papers of Thomas Jefferson*, vol. 14, p. 554.
22. Ibid., p. 261.
23. Malone, *Jefferson and His Time*, vol. 2, p. 142.
24. *PAH*, vol. 4, p. 294.
25. Brodie, *Thomas Jefferson*, p. 228.
26. Wilson and Stanton, *Jefferson Abroad*, p. 268.
27. Elkins and McKitrick, *Age of Federalism*, p. 314.
28. Wilson and Stanton, *Jefferson Abroad*, p. 283.
29. Schama, *Citizens*, p. 326.
30. Ibid., p. 436.
31. Wilson and Stanton, *Jefferson Abroad*, p. 292.
32. Ibid., pp. 290–91.
33. *PAH*, vol. 5, p. 425, letter to the marquis de Lafayette, October 6, 1789.
34. Ibid., vol. 11, p. 439, letter to Edward Carrington, May 26, 1792.
35. Wilson and Stanton, *Jefferson Abroad*, p. 215.

36. Ibid., p. 73.
37. Ibid., p. 270.
38. Ferling, *John Adams*, p. 306.
39. Jefferson, *Papers of Thomas Jefferson*, vol. 16, p. 549.
40. Malone, *Jefferson and His Time*, vol. 2, p. 170.
41. Hamilton, *Intimate Life of Alexander Hamilton*, p. 49.
42. Jefferson, *Anas of Thomas Jefferson*, p. 30.
43. Ibid., p. 91.
44. Ibid.
45. *The William and Mary Quarterly*, January 1992.
46. Ellis, *Passionate Sage*, p. 64.
47. Ibid., p. 115.
48. Ellis, *Founding Brothers*, p. 53.
49. Jefferson, *Complete Anas of Thomas Jefferson*, p. 32.
50. Ellis, *Founding Brothers*, p. 57.
51. *PAH*, vol. 11, p. 428, letter to Edward Carrington, May 26, 1792.
52. Madison, *Papers of James Madison*, vol. 16, p. 248.
53. *PAH*, vol. 11, p. 440, letter to Edward Carrington, May 26, 1792.
54. Ketcham, *James Madison*, p. 473.
55. Ellis, *Founding Brothers*, p. 149.
56. Ketcham, *James Madison*, p. 360.
57. *PAH*, vol. 12, p. 238, letter to George Washington, August 18, 1792.
58. Ibid., vol. 19, p. 39, "The Defence of the Funding System," July 1795.
59. Ibid., vol. 12, p. 256, letter to George Washington, August 18, 1792.
60. Flexner, *Washington*, p. 232.
61. Cooke, *Alexander Hamilton*, pp. 225–26.
62. Freeman, *Affairs of Honor*, pp. 27, 234; McCullough, *John Adams*, p. 407.
63. McCullough, *John Adams*, p. 407.
64. Madison, *Papers of James Madison*, vol. 13, p. 146.
65. Maclay, *Journal of William Maclay*, p. 234.
66. Bowen, *Miracle at Philadelphia*, p. 210.
67. *PAH*, vol. 5, p. 209, letter to William Livingston, August 29, 1788.
68. Ibid., pp. 276–77.
69. Maclay, *Journal of William Maclay*, p. 178.
70. Madison, *Papers of James Madison*, vol. 13, p. 145.
71. Elkins and McKitrick, *Age of Federalism*, p. 170.
72. Ellis, *Founding Brothers*, p. 58.
73. Jefferson, *Anas of Thomas Jefferson*, p. 32.
74. NYPL-PSP, reel 17, letter from Philip Schuyler to Stephen Van Rensselaer, May 16, 1790.
75. Maclay, *Journal of William Maclay*, p. 273.
76. Ibid., p. 292.
77. Freeman, *Affairs of Honor*, p. 51.

78. Maclay, *Journal of William Maclay*, p. 299.
79. Elkins and McKitrick, *Age of Federalism*, p. 155.
80. Jefferson, *Anas of Thomas Jefferson*, p. 32.
81. Ibid.
82. Ellis, *Founding Brothers*, p. 49.
83. Freeman, *Affairs of Honor*, p. 49.
84. Malone, *Jefferson and His Time*, vol. 2, p. 303.
85. Maclay, *Journal of William Maclay*, p. 304.
86. Ibid., p. 310.
87. Ibid., p. 331.
88. Freeman, *Affairs of Honor*, p. 32.
89. CU-HPPP, box 262.
90. Mitchell, *Alexander Hamilton: The National Adventure*, p. 83.
91. Ibid.
92. Jefferson, *Anas of Thomas Jefferson*, p. 35.
93. *Gazette of the United States*, September 1, 1790.

Seventeen: The First Town in America

1. *PAH*, vol. 7, p. 608, letter to Angelica Church, January 31, 1791.
2. Hamilton, *Intimate Life of Alexander Hamilton*, pp. 42–43.
3. *PAH*, vol. 9, p. 404, letter from Henry Lee, October 18, 1791.
4. CU-HPPP, letter from Tench Coxe to William Duer, September 6, 1791.
5. LC-AHP, reel 29, letter from Angelica Church to Elizabeth Hamilton, April 25, 1792.
6. "Life Portraits of Alexander Hamilton," *The William and Mary Quarterly*, April 1955.
7. Ibid.
8. Sullivan, *Public Men of the Revolution*, pp. 261–62.
9. *PAH*, vol. 12, p. 571, "Fact No. II," *National Gazette*, October 16, 1792.
10. Freeman, *Affairs of Honor*, p. 106.
11. Hamilton, *Intimate Life of Alexander Hamilton*, p. 241.
12. *PAH*, vol. 24, p. 64, letter from James Wilkinson, November 21, 1799.
13. Ibid., vol. 6, p. 511, letter from Morgan Lewis, July 26, 1790.
14. Ibid., vol. 13, p. 480, letter from James Tillary, January 14, 1793.
15. Ibid., vol. 7, p. 132, letter to Tobias Lear, October 29, 1790.
16. Baxter, *Godchild of Washington*, p. 224.
17. Steiner, *Life and Correspondence of James McHenry*, p. 129.
18. NYHS-NPP, letter from Elizabeth Hamilton to George Cabot, September 20, 1804.
19. Hamilton, *Intimate Life of Alexander Hamilton*, p. 227.
20. Ibid., p. 216.
21. *PAH*, vol. 15, p. 432, letter to Angelica Hamilton, November 1793.
22. Menz, *Historic Furnishing Report*, p. 13.
23. *PAH*, vol. 3, p. 468, letter to George Clinton, October 3, 1783.
24. Ibid., vol. 19, p. 460, "Draft of George Washington's Seventh Annual Address to Congress," November 28–December 7, 1795.
25. Ibid., pp. 146–47, "Hamilton-Oneida Academy Mortgage," August 15, 1795.
26. Burrows and Wallace, *Gotham*, p. 305.
27. Furnas, *Americans*, p. 197.
28. St. Méry, *Moreau de St. Méry's American Journey*, p. 135.
29. *PAH*, vol. 6, p. 545, letter to Walter Stewart, August 5, 1790.
30. Ibid., p. 297, letter to Benjamin Lincoln, March 10, 1790.
31. Ibid., p. 469, letter to George Washington, June 21, 1790.
32. Ibid., vol. 7, p. 31, letter to George Washington, September 10, 1790.
33. Ibid., vol. 6, p. 408, "Treasury Department Circular to the Collectors of the Customs," June 1, 1791.
34. Ibid., vol. 8, p. 432, "Treasury Department Circular to the Captains of the Revenue Cutters," June 4, 1791.
35. Freeman, *Affairs of Honor*, p. 88.
36. *PAH*, vol. 9, p. 370, letter to Otho Williams, October 11, 1791.
37. Madison, *Papers of James Madison*, vol. 13, p. 143.
38. *PAH*, vol. 7, p. 197, letter from Benjamin Lincoln, December 4, 1790.
39. Madison, *Papers of James Madison*, vol. 13, p. 344.
40. Ibid., p. 366.
41. Maclay, *Journal of William Maclay*, p. 385.
42. Ibid., p. 387.
43. *PAH*, vol. 8, p. 375, "Treasury Department Circular to the Collectors of the Customs," May 26, 1791.
44. Ibid., vol. 11, p. 77, "Report on the Difficulties in the Execution of the Act Laying Duties on Distilled Spirits," March 5, 1792.
45. Ibid., vol. 19, p. 41, "The Defence of the Funding System," July 1795.

Eighteen: Of Avarice and Enterprise

1. *The New York Review of Books*, April 13, 2000.
2. *PAH*, vol. 19, p. 190, "The Defence No. XI," August 28, 1795.
3. Ibid., p. 32, "The Defence of the Funding System," July 1795.
4. Mitchell, *Alexander Hamilton: The National Adventure*, p. 351.

5. Ibid., p. 61.

6. Marsh, *Monroe's Defense of Jefferson and Freneau Against Hamilton*, p. 31.

7. Ellis, *Passionate Sage*, p. 161.

8. *The William and Mary Quarterly*, April 1955.

9. Ellis, *Passionate Sage*, p. 136.

10. *PAH*, vol. 14, p. 112, "Report on the State of the Treasury at the Commencement of Each Quarter During the Years 1791 and 1792," February 19, 1793.

11. Ibid., vol. 2, p. 414, letter to James Duane, September 3, 1780.

12. Ibid., vol. 7, p. 305, "Report on the Bank," December 13, 1790.

13. Ibid., p. 308.

14. Ibid., p. 314.

15. Ibid., p. 315.

16. Ibid., p. 321.

17. Ibid., p. 327.

18. Ibid., p. 331.

19. *PAH*, vol. 8, p. 218, "Notes on the Advantages of a National Bank," March 27, 1791.

20. Miller, *Alexander Hamilton*, p. 272.

21. *PAH*, vol. 8, pp. 218, 221, letter to George Washington, March 27, 1791.

22. Ketcham, *James Madison*, p. 322.

23. Ammon, *James Monroe*, p. 86.

24. Mitchell, *Alexander Hamilton: The National Adventure*, p. 95.

25. *PAH*, vol. 8, p. 113, "Opinion on Constitutionality of Bank," February 23, 1791.

26. Ibid., p. 290.

27. Smith, *John Marshall*, p. 170.

28. Malone, *Jefferson and His Time*, vol. 2, p. 338.

29. Cooke, *Alexander Hamilton*, p. 77.

30. *PAH*, vol. 12, p. 85, letter from Thomas Jefferson to James Madison, October 1, 1792.

31. Cooke, *Alexander Hamilton*, p. 77.

32. *PAH*, vol. 8, p. 58, letter to George Washington, February 21, 1791.

33. Ibid., p. 62, letter to George Washington, February 23, 1791.

34. Mitchell, *Alexander Hamilton: The National Adventure*, p. 99.

35. *PAH*, vol. 8, p. 97, "Final Version of an Opinion on the Constitutionality of an Act to Establish a Bank," February 23, 1791.

36. Ibid., p. 98.

37. Ibid., p. 99.

38. Ibid., p. 132.

39. Lodge, *Alexander Hamilton*, p. 103.

40. Cooke, *Alexander Hamilton*, p. xvii.

41. *PAH*, vol. 7, p. 586, *Report on the Mint*, January 28, 1791.

42. Ibid., p. 601.

43. Ibid., p. 598.

44. Ibid., p. 577.

45. Ibid., p. 572.

46. *PAH*, vol. 7, p. 451, letter from Thomas Jefferson, January 24, 1791.

47. Mitchell, *Alexander Hamilton: The National Adventure*, p. 104.

48. *PAH*, vol. 7, p. 516, letter to Benjamin Goodhue, June 30, 1791.

49. *New York Historical Society Quarterly*, October 1948.

50. Smith, *Patriarch*, p. 108.

51. *New York Historical Society Quarterly*, October 1948.

52. *PAH*, vol. 8, p. 589, letter from Fisher Ames, July 31, 1791.

53. Ibid.

54. McDonald, *Alexander Hamilton*, p. 223.

55. Smith, *Patriarch*, p. 109.

56. *PAH*, vol. 9, p. 60, letter from Rufus King, August 15, 1791.

57. Ibid.

58. Ibid., p. 75, letter to Rufus King, August 17, 1791.

59. Ibid., p. 71, letter to William Seton, August 16, 1791.

60. Ibid., p. 74, letter to William Duer, August 17, 1791.

61. Ibid., p. 75.

62. Ibid., vol. 26, p. 617, letter from William Duer, August 16, 1791.

63. Davis, *Essays in the Earlier History of American Corporations*, p. 208.

64. Ibid.

Nineteen: City of the Future

1. Ketcham, *James Madison*, p. 385.

2. *PAH*, vol. 8, pp. 343–44, letter from Philip Schuyler, May 15, 1791.

3. Freeman, *Affairs of Honor*, p. 149; Cooke, *Alexander Hamilton*, p. 20; Latrobe, *Correspondence and Miscellaneous Papers of Benjamin Henry Latrobe*, p. 331.

4. *PAH*, vol. 8, pp. 522–23, letter to Mercy Warren, July 1, 1791.

5. Ibid., vol. 13, p. 385, letter to Susanna Livingston, December 29, 1792.

6. Ibid., vol. 8, p. 526, letter to Martha Walker, July 2, 1791.

7. Ibid., vol. 21, p. 250, "The Reynolds Pamphlet," August 1797.

8. Ibid.

9. Ibid., p. 251.

10. Ibid., p. 252.

11. Ibid., vol. 21, p. 187, letter to Jeremiah Wadsworth, July 28, 1797.

12. Ibid., pp. 189–90, Richard Folwell statement, August 12, 1797.

13. Ibid.

14. Ibid., p. 262, "The Reynolds Pamphlet," August 1797.
15. Ibid., vol. 9, pp. 6–7, letter to Elizabeth Hamilton, August 2, 1791.
16. Ibid., p. 69, letter to Elizabeth Hamilton, August 17, 1791.
17. Ibid., p. 87, letter to Elizabeth Hamilton, August 21, 1791.
18. Ibid., p. 172, letter to Elizabeth Hamilton, September 4, 1791.
19. Ibid., vol. 21, p. 264, "The Reynolds Pamphlet," August 1797.
20. Ibid., p. 252.
21. Ibid., vol. 10, pp. 378–79, letter from Maria Reynolds, December 15, 1791.
22. Ibid., p. 376, letter from James Reynolds, December 15, 1791.
23. Ibid., vol. 21, p. 253, "The Reynolds Pamphlet," August 1797.
24. Ibid., vol. 10, p. 388, letter from James Reynolds, December 17, 1791.
25. Ibid., pp. 389–90, letter to an unnamed correspondent, December 18, 1791.
26. Ibid, vol. 21, p. 253, "The Reynolds Pamphlet," August 1797.
27. Ibid.
28. Cooke, *Alexander Hamilton*, p. 148.
29. Gordon, *Business of America*, p. 16.
30. *PAH*, vol. 26, p. 520, letter from Tench Coxe, February 1790.
31. "Tench Coxe, Alexander Hamilton, and the Encouragement of American Manufactures," *The William and Mary Quarterly*, July 1975.
32. Ibid.
33. Ibid.
34. Passaic County Historical Society, Gledhill Collection, SEUM, box 2, prospectus for the Society for Establishing Useful Manufactures, April 29, 1791.
35. McDonald, *Alexander Hamilton*, p. 231.
36. Passaic County Historical Society, Gledhill Collection, SEUM, box 2, prospectus for the Society for Establishing Useful Manufactures, April 29, 1791.
37. Ibid.
38. "Tench Coxe, Alexander Hamilton, and the Encouragement of American Manufactures," *The William and Mary Quarterly*, July 1975.
39. *PAH*, vol. 8, p. 571, letter from Thomas Marshall, July 24–31, 1791.
40. Flexner, *Young Hamilton*, p. 437.
41. *PAH*, vol. 10, p. 13.
42. Ibid., p. 291, *Report on Manufactures*, December 5, 1791.
43. Ibid., vol. 8, p. 497, "Treasury Department Circular to the Supervisors of the Revenue," June 22, 1791.
44. Ibid., vol. 19, p. 97, letter to Oliver Wolcott, Jr., August 5, 1795.
45. Wilson and Stanton, *Jefferson Abroad*, p. 249.
46. *PAH*, vol. 10, p. 236, *Report on Manufactures*, December 5, 1791.
47. Ibid., p. 246.
48. Ibid., p. 249.
49. Ibid., p. 253.
50. Ibid., p. 255.
51. Ibid., vol. 25, p. 467, "The Examination," no. 3. *New-York Evening Post*, December 24, 1801.
52. Ibid., vol. 10, p. 266, *Report on Manufactures*, December 5, 1791.
53. Ibid., p. 268.
54. *The New York Review of Books*, December 21, 2000.
55. *PAH*, vol. 10, p. 268, *Report on Manufactures*, December 5, 1791.
56. Ibid., p. 321.
57. Ibid., p. 317.
58. Ibid., p. 338.
59. Ibid., p. 302.
60. Malone, *Thomas Jefferson and His Time*, vol. 2, p. 430.
61. Jefferson, *Anas of Thomas Jefferson*, p. 55.
62. Mitchell, *Alexander Hamilton: The National Adventure*, p. 170.
63. Ibid.
64. "Tench Coxe, Alexander Hamilton, and the Encouragement of American Manufactures," *The William and Mary Quarterly*, July 1975.
65. *PAH*, vol. 11, p. 110, letter from James Tillary, March 6, 1792.
66. Ibid., vol. 10, p. 525, letter to William Seton, January 18, 1792.
67. Ibid., p. 528, letter from William Seton, January 22, 1792.
68. Ibid., vol. 11, p. 28, letter to William Seton, February 10, 1792.
69. Ibid.
70. Jefferson, *Anas of Thomas Jefferson*, p. 55.
71. Malone, *Jefferson and His Time*, vol. 3, p. 17.
72. *PAH*, vol. 14, p. 100, "Report on the State of the Treasury at the Commencement of Each Quarter," February 19, 1793.
73. "Tench Coxe, Alexander Hamilton, and the Encouragement of American Manufactures," *The William and Mary Quarterly*, July 1975.
74. *PAH*, vol. 11, p. 156, letter from Robert Troup, March 19, 1792.
75. Ibid., p. 126, letter from William Duer, March 12, 1792.
76. Ibid., pp. 131–32, letter to William Duer, March 14, 1792.
77. Brodie, *Thomas Jefferson*, p. 267.

78. *PAH*, vol. 11, p. 273, letter to William Seton, April 12, 1792.

79. Ibid., p. 190, letter to William Seton, March 25, 1792.

80. Ibid., p. 156, letter from Robert Troup, March 19, 1792.

81. Gordon, *Business of America*, p. 169.

82. *The Diary; or, Loudon's Register*, April 20, 1792.

83. *PAH*, vol. 11, pp. 218–19, letter to Philip Livingston, April 2, 1792.

84. Malone, *Jefferson and His Time*, vol. 2, p. 436.

85. Mitchell, *Alexander Hamilton: The National Adventure*, pp. 175–76.

86. *PAH*, vol. 11, p. 434, letter to Edward Carrington, May 26, 1792.

87. Adams, *New Letters of Abigail Adams*, p. 83.

88. *PAH*, vol. 10, p. 482, letter to Roger Alden et al., January 15, 1792.

89. Ibid., vol. 11, p. 171, letter to William Duer, March 23, 1792.

90. Ibid., p. 247, letter from Archibald Mercer, April 6, 1792.

91. Ibid., p. 425, letter to William Seton, May 25, 1792.

92. Ibid., vol. 14, p. 303, letter to Peter Colt, April 10, 1793.

93. Ibid., p. 549, "To the Directors of the Society for Establishing Useful Manufactures," October 12, 1792.

94. Mitchell, *Alexander Hamilton: The National Adventure*, p. 172.

95. *PAH*, vol. 12, p. 369, letter from Elisha Boudinot, September 13, 1792.

96. Ibid., vol. 14, p. 283, letter to John Brown, April 5, 1793.

97. Ibid., vol. 26, p. 764, letter from William Duer, February 16, 1799.

Twenty: Corrupt Squadrons

1. Hamilton, *Life of Alexander Hamilton*, vol. 5, p. 49.

2. Elkins and McKitrick, *Age of Federalism*, p. 241.

3. Malone, *Jefferson and His Time*, vol. 2, p. 362.

4. Elkins and McKitrick, *Age of Federalism*, p. 77.

5. Malone, *Jefferson and His Time*, vol. 4, p. 430.

6. McCullough, *John Adams*, p. 346.

7. *PAH*, vol. 13, p. 393, "The Defence No. I," [1792–1795].

8. Kent, *Memoirs and Letters of James Kent*, p. 207.

9. *PAH*, vol. 4, p. 432, "Federalist No. 26," December 22, 1787.

10. Ibid., p. 435, "Federalist No. 27," December 25, 1787.

11. Malone, *Jefferson and His Time*, vol. 3, pp. 364–65.

12. Elkins and McKitrick, *Age of Federalism*, p. 24.

13. Flexner, *Washington*, p. 241.

14. Wilson and Stanton, *Jefferson Abroad*, p. 73.

15. *PAH*, vol. 25, p. 201, *Letter from Alexander Hamilton*, October 24, 1800.

16. Brookhiser, *Alexander Hamilton*, p. 104.

17. Smith, *John Marshall*, p. 38.

18. Malone, *Jefferson and His Time*, vol. 1, p. 212.

19. *PAH*, vol. 10, p. 373, "Conversation with George Hammond," December 15–16, 1791.

20. Ibid.

21. Malone, *Jefferson and His Time*, vol. 2, p. 413.

22. Elkins and McKitrick, *Age of Federalism*, p. 254.

23. Ibid., p. 255.

24. Malone, *Jefferson and His Time*, vol. 2, p. 424.

25. Smith, *Patriarch*, p. 83.

26. Bobrick, *Angel in the Whirlwind*, p. 149.

27. *PAH*, vol. 12, p. 101.

28. Ibid., p. 192, "An American No. II," *Gazette of the United States*, August 11, 1792.

29. Parton, *Life and Times of Aaron Burr*, p. 224.

30. McDonald, *Sermon on the Premature and Lamented Death of General Alexander Hamilton*, p. 31.

31. Freeman, *Affairs of Honor*, p. 146.

32. Ketcham, *James Madison*, p. 327.

33. Jefferson, *Anas of Thomas Jefferson*, p. 97.

34. Brodie, *Thomas Jefferson*, p. 267.

35. Jefferson, *Anas of Thomas Jefferson*, p. 44.

36. Brodie, *Thomas Jefferson*, pp. 318–19.

37. Knott, *Alexander Hamilton and the Persistence of Myth*, p. 253.

38. Jefferson, *Anas of Thomas Jefferson*, p. 51.

39. Jefferson, *Anas of Thomas Jefferson*, p. 71.

40. McDonald, *Alexander Hamilton*, p. 251.

41. Wills, *James Madison*, p. 44.

42. Ketcham, *James Madison*, p. 329.

43. Elkins and McKitrick, *Age of Federalism*, p. 277.

44. Adams, *New Letters of Abigail Adams*, pp. 80–81.

45. Ketcham, *James Madison*, p. 333.

46. McDonald, *Alexander Hamilton*, p. 241.

47. Malone, *Jefferson and His Time*, vol. 2, p. 446.

48. Smith, *Patriarch*, p. 132.

49. *PAH*, vol. 11, p. 429, letter to Edward Carrington, May 26, 1792.

50. Ibid., p. 440.

51. Ibid., p. 432.

52. Ibid., p. 443.

53. Ibid., p. 444.

54. Ibid.

55. Maclay, *Journal of William Maclay*, p. 375.

56. Malone, *Jefferson and His Time*, vol. 3, p. 271.

57. Elkins and McKitrick, *Age of Federalism*, p. 497.

58. Malone, *Jefferson and His Time*, vol. 2, p. 460.
59. Jefferson, *Anas of Thomas Jefferson*, p. 104.
60. Smith, *Patriarch*, p. 139.
61. *PAH*, vol. 12, p. 107, *Gazette of the United States*, July 25, 1792.
62. Ibid., p. 124, *National Gazette*, July 28, 1792.
63. Ibid., p. 131, letter from George Washington, July 29, 1792.
64. Ibid., p. 137, letter to George Washington, August 3, 1792.
65. Ibid., p. 160, "An American No. I," *Gazette of the United States*, August 4, 1792.
66. Ibid., p. 191, "An American No. II," *Gazette of the United States*, August 11, 1792.
67. Ibid., p. 228, letter to George Washington, August 18, 1792.
68. Ibid., p. 247.
69. Ibid., p. 249.
70. Ibid., p. 248.
71. Ibid., pp. 276–77, letter from George Washington, August 26, 1792.
72. *Gazette of the United States*, September 8, 1792.
73. *PAH*, vol. 12, p. 347, letter to George Washington, September 9, 1792.
74. Ibid., p. 348.
75. Ibid., p. 349.
76. Ibid., p. 348.
77. Malone, *Jefferson and His Time*, vol. 2, pp. 466–67.
78. *National Gazette*, September 12, 1792.
79. Ibid., p. 365.
80. Ibid., p. 505, "Catullus No. III," *Gazette of the United States*, September 29, 1792.
81. Ibid., p. 504.
82. Ketcham, *James Madison*, p. 331.
83. Freeman, *Affairs of Honor*, p. 78.
84. Jefferson, *Anas of Thomas Jefferson*, p. 90.
85. Ibid.
86. Ibid., p. 91.
87. Freeman, *Affairs of Honor*, p. 76.

Twenty-one: Exposure
1. *PAH*, vol. 21, p. 272, "The Reynolds Pamphlet," Jacob Clingman affidavit, December 13, 1792.
2. *PAH*, vol. 10, p. 557, letter from Maria Reynolds, January 23–March 18, 1792.
3. Ibid., vol. 11, p. 177, letter from Maria Reynolds, March 24, 1792.
4. Ibid., p. 176, letter from James Reynolds, March 24, 1792.
5. Ibid., p. 222, letter from James Reynolds, April 3, 1792.
6. Ibid., p. 254, letter to James Reynolds, April 7, 1792.

7. Ibid., vol. 21, p. 244, "The Reynolds Pamphlet," August 1797.
8. Ibid., p. 246.
9. Ibid., vol. 11, p. 297, letter from James Reynolds, April 17, 1792.
10. Ibid., p. 330, letter from James Reynolds, April 23, 1792.
11. Ibid., p. 354, letter from James Reynolds, May 2, 1792.
12. Ibid., p. 354, "The Reynolds Pamphlet," August 1797.
13. Ibid., p. 481, letter from Maria Reynolds, June 2, 1792.
14. Ibid., p. 482, letter to James Reynolds, June 3–22, 1792.
15. Ibid., p. 491, letter to David Ross, September 26, 1792.
16. Ibid., vol. 26, p. 682, letter to Tobias Lear, September 6, 1792.
17. Ibid., vol. 12, p. 543, letter to Charles Cotesworth Pinckney, October 10, 1792.
18. Mitchell, *Alexander Hamilton: The National Adventure*, p. 403.
19. *PAH*, vol. 21, p. 264, "The Reynolds Pamphlet," August 1797.
20. Ibid., p. 130.
21. Ibid., p. 268.
22. Ibid., p. 269.
23. Jefferson, *Papers of Thomas Jefferson*, vol. 18, p. 635.
24. Callender, *History of the United States for 1796*, p. 216.
25. Ibid.
26. *PAH*, vol. 21, p. 257, "The Reynolds Pamphlet," August 1797.
27. Ibid., p. 258.
28. Ibid.
29. Ibid., p. 135.
30. Callender, *History of the United States for 1796*, p. 218.
31. *PAH*, vol. 21, p. 134.
32. *Gazette of the United States*, January 5, 1793.
33. *PAH*, vol. 14, p. 267, "For *Gazette of the United States*," March–April 1793.

Twenty-two: Stabbed in the Dark
1. Smith, *Patriarch*, p. 135.
2. *PAH*, vol. 12, p. 567, letter to John Steele, October 15, 1792.
3. McCullough, *John Adams*, p. 434.
4. Malone, *Jefferson and His Time*, vol. 2, p. 457.
5. *PAH*, vol. 12, p. 342, letter to John Adams, September 9, 1792.
6. Ferling, *John Adams*, p. 318.
7. Ibid.
8. Kaminski, *George Clinton*, p. 230.

9. *PAH,* vol. 12, p. 387, letter from Rufus King, September 17, 1792.
10. Ellis, *Founding Brothers,* p. 175.
11. Tripp, "Robert Troup," p. 105.
12. *PAH,* vol. 12, p. 408, letter to an unnamed correspondent, September 21, 1792.
13. Ibid., p. 480, letter to an unnamed correspondent, September 26, 1792.
14. Mitchell, *Alexander Hamilton: The National Adventure,* p. 209.
15. Ibid.
16. Ammon, *James Monroe,* p. 44.
17. *PAH,* vol. 13, p. 227, letter from David Ross, November 23, 1792.
18. Ibid., vol. 12, p. 573, letter from John F. Mercer, October 16[−28], 1792.
19. Ibid., vol. 13, p. 513, letter from John F. Mercer, January 31, 1793.
20. Jefferson, *Anas of Thomas Jefferson,* p. 186.
21. *Gazette of the United States,* December 8, 1792.
22. Smith, *Patriarch,* p. 152.
23. McCullough, *John Adams,* p. 441.
24. *PAH,* vol. 13, p. 338, letter to John Jay, December 18, 1792.
25. Smith, *Patriarch,* p. 157.
26. Ibid.
27. Mitchell, *Alexander Hamilton: The National Adventure,* p. 255.
28. *PAH,* vol. 11, p. 432, letter to Edward Carrington, May 26, 1792.
29. Malone, *Jefferson and His Time,* vol. 3, p. 18.
30. *PAH,* vol. 14, p. 58, "Report Relative to the Loans Negotiated under the Acts of the Fourth and Twelfth of August, 1790," February 13–14, 1793.
31. *The William and Mary Quarterly,* October 1992.
32. Mitchell, *Alexander Hamilton: The National Adventure,* p. 260.
33. Elkins and McKitrick, *Age of Federalism,* p. 301.
34. King, *Life and Correspondence of Rufus King,* vol. 1, p. 483.
35. *PAH,* vol. 14, p. 276, letter to Rufus King, April 2, 1793.
36. Ibid., vol. 13, p. 523, "On James Blanchard," January 1793.
37. Ibid.
38. Ibid., vol. 21, p. 132, letter from Henry Lee, May 6, 1793.
39. *PAH,* vol. 14, p. 466, letter from John Beckley to an unnamed recipient, June 22, 1793.
40. Ibid.
41. Ibid.
42. Freeman, *Affairs of Honor,* p. 102.
43. *PAH,* vol. 14, p. 467, letter from John Beckley to an unknown recipient, July 2, 1793.
44. Ibid., vol. 15, p. 165, letter to Andrew G. Fraunces, August 2, 1793.

45. Ibid., p. 171, letter to Andrew G. Fraunces, August 3, 1793.
46. *The Diary,* October 11, 1793.
47. *The Daily Advertiser,* October 12, 1793.

Twenty-three: Citizen Genêt

1. Hamilton, *Life of Alexander Hamilton,* vol. 5, p. 213.
2. Elkins and McKitrick, *Age of Federalism,* p. 312.
3. Hamilton, *Intimate Life of Alexander Hamilton,* p. 300.
4. Elkins and McKitrick, *Age of Federalism,* p. 316.
5. Schama, *Citizens,* p. 615.
6. McCullough, *John Adams,* p. 438.
7. Ibid.
8. Schama, *Citizens,* p. 687.
9. Malone, *Jefferson and His Time,* vol. 3, p. 61.
10. Hamilton, *Life of Alexander Hamilton,* vol. 5, p. 222.
11. McCullough, *John Adams,* p. 444.
12. Elkins and McKitrick, *Age of Federalism,* p. 357.
13. Ketcham, *James Madison,* pp. 337, 338–39.
14. Ibid., p. 341.
15. Hamilton, *Life of Alexander Hamilton,* vol. 6, p. 222.
16. *PAH,* vol. 14, pp. 85–86, letter from Gouverneur Morris, February 6, 1793.
17. Jefferson, *Anas of Thomas Jefferson,* p. 69.
18. Ketcham, *James Madison,* p. 338.
19. Ellis, *Founding Brothers,* p. 170.
20. *PAH,* vol. 21, p. 450, letter to the marquis de Lafayette, April 28, 1798.
21. Ibid., vol. 14, p. 386, letter from Alexander Hamilton and Henry Knox to George Washington, May 2, 1793.
22. Ibid., p. 371.
23. Ibid., vol. 17, pp. 586–87, "The French Revolution," unpublished fragment, 1794.
24. Ibid., p. 588.
25. Ibid., vol. 14, p. 291, letter to George Washington, April 5, 1793.
26. Malone, *Jefferson and His Time,* vol. 3, p. 67.
27. *PAH,* vol. 14, p. 504, "Defence of the President's Neutrality Proclamation," May 1793.
28. Ibid., p. 328, "Cabinet Meeting: Opinion on a Proclamation of Neutrality and on Receiving the French Minister," April 19, 1793.
29. Ketcham, *James Madison,* p. 342.
30. Lodge, *Alexander Hamilton,* p. 161.
31. Malone, *Jefferson and His Time,* vol. 3, p. 70.
32. *Political Science Quarterly,* March 1956.
33. Ketcham, *James Madison,* p. 342.
34. Brookhiser, *Gentleman Revolutionary,* pp. 139–40.
35. *PAH,* vol. 15, p. 246, "No Jacobin No. V," Au-

gust 14, 1793, *Dunlap's American Daily Adver-tiser;* vol. 19, p. 519, "American Jacobins," [1795–1796].

36. Elkins and McKitrick, *Age of Federalism,* p. 357.
37. Ketcham, *James Madison,* p. 342.
38. Malone, *Jefferson and His Time,* vol. 3, p. 83.
39. Brookhiser, *Gentleman Revolutionary,* p. 140.
40. Elkins and McKitrick, *Age of Federalism,* p. 360.
41. Adams, *Correspondence Between the Hon. John Adams, and the Late Wm. Cunningham,* p. 35.
42. Parton, *Life and Times of Aaron Burr,* p. 220.
43. Mitchell, *Alexander Hamilton: The National Adventure,* p. 299.
44. Elkins and McKitrick, *Age of Federalism,* p. 344.
45. Mitchell, *Alexander Hamilton: The National Adventure,* p. 227.
46. *PAH,* vol. 15, p. 74, "Reasons for the Opinion of the Secretary of the Treasury and the Secretary at War Respecting the Brigantine *Little Sarah,*" July 8, 1793.
47. Elkins and McKitrick, *Age of Federalism,* p. 348.
48. Malone, *Jefferson and His Time,* vol. 3, p. 114.
49. *PAH,* vol. 15, p. 77, "Reasons for the Opinion of the Secretary of the Treasury and the Secretary at War Respecting the Brigantine *Little Sarah,*" July 8, 1793.
50. Ibid., vol. 15, p. 34, "Pacificus No. I," June 29, 1793.
51. Ibid., p. 67, "Pacificus No. III," July 6, 1793.
52. Ibid., p. 94, "Pacificus No. V," July 13–17, 1793.
53. Ibid., p. 92.
54. Ibid., pp. 103, 106, "Pacificus No. VI," July 17, 1793.
55. Hamilton, *Federalist,* p. c.
56. Elkins and McKitrick, *Age of Federalism,* p. 362.
57. Ketcham, *James Madison,* pp. 345–46.
58. *Political Science Quarterly,* March 1956.
59. Ketcham, *James Madison,* p. 436.
60. Flexner, *Washington,* p. 288.
61. Jefferson, *Anas of Thomas Jefferson,* p. 150.
62. *PAH,* vol. 15, p. 145, "No Jacobin No. I," *American Daily Advertiser,* July 31, 1793.
63. Ibid., p. 282, "No Jacobin No. VIII," *American Daily Advertiser,* August 26, 1793.
64. Jefferson, *Anas of Thomas Jefferson,* p. 157.
65. Ibid.
66. Ibid., p. 158.
67. Ibid., p. 157.
68. Ibid., p. 158.
69. Mitchell, *Alexander Hamilton: The National Adventure,* p. 242.
70. Jefferson, *Anas of Thomas Jefferson,* p. 162.
71. Malone, *Jefferson and His Time,* vol. 3, p. 125.

72. *PAH,* vol. 15, p. 234, letter from Edmond Charles Genêt to George Washington, August 13, 1793.
73. Freeman, *Affairs of Honor,* p. 97.
74. Ketcham, *James Madison,* p. 344.

Twenty-four: A Disagreeable Trade

1. McCullough, *John Adams,* p. 133.
2. Colimore, *The* Philadelphia Inquirer's *Guide to Historic Philadelphia,* p. 46.
3. Mitchell, *Alexander Hamilton: The National Adventure,* p. 282.
4. *PAH,* vol. 15, p. 324, letter from George Washington, September 6, 1793.
5. Ibid., p. 325, in editorial note.
6. Ibid., p. 331, "To the College of Physicians," September 11, 1793.
7. Smith, *Patriarch,* p. 180.
8. Day, *Edward Stevens,* p. 81.
9. Ibid., pp. 80–81.
10. CU-HPPP, box 267, letter from Philip Schuyler to Abraham Yates, Jr., September 25, 1793.
11. *PAH,* vol. 15, p. 347, letter to Abraham Yates, Jr., September 26, 1793.
12. Ibid., p. 360, letter from Tobias Lear, October 10, 1793.
13. Ibid., p. 361, letter from George Washington, October 14, 1793.
14. Ibid., p. 374, letter to George Washington, October 24, 1793.
15. Day, *Edward Stevens,* p. 82.
16. *PAH,* vol. 15, p. 455, letter to Thomas Jefferson, December 11, 1793.
17. Ibid., p. 593, letter to Angelica Church, December 27, 1793.
18. McCullough, *John Adams,* p. 448.
19. Jefferson, *Papers of Thomas Jefferson,* vol. 26, p. 215.
20. Ibid., vol. 27, p. 449.
21. Malone, *Jefferson and His Time,* vol. 3, p. 182.
22. Brodie, *Thomas Jefferson,* p. 263.
23. Ibid.
24. *PAH,* vol. 11, p. 441, letter to Edward Carrington, May 26, 1792.
25. CU-JCHP, box 20.
26. *PAH,* vol. 15, p. 593, letter to Angelica Church, December 27, 1793.
27. Ibid., vol. 16, p. 356, letter to ——, April–May 1794.
28. Ibid., vol. 15, p. 465, letter to Frederick A. C. Muhlenberg, December 16, 1793.
29. Ibid., vol. 16, p. 49, letter to John Adams, February 22, 1794.
30. Ibid., p. 249, letter from George Washington, April 8, 1794.
31. Ibid., p. 249, letter from James Madison to Thomas Jefferson, April 14, 1794.

32. Ibid., p. 252, letter to George Washington, April 8, 1794.
33. Ibid., p. 495.
34. Ibid., vol. 21, pp. 241–42, "The Reynolds Pamphlet," August 1797.
35. NYPL-JAHP, box 1, letter from Alexander Hamilton to Angelica Church, April 4, 1794.

Twenty-five: Seas of Blood

1. Hamilton, *Life of Alexander Hamilton*, vol. 5, p. 450.
2. *PAH*, vol. 15, p. 671, "Americanus No. I," January 31, 1794.
3. Hamilton, *Life of Alexander Hamilton*, vol. 5, pp. 532–33.
4. *PAH*, vol. 16, p. 134, letter to George Washington, March 8, 1794.
5. Ketcham, *James Madison*, p. 351.
6. Hamilton, *Life of Alexander Hamilton*, vol. 5, pp. 532–33.
7. McDonald, *Alexander Hamilton*, p. 291.
8. *PAH*, vol. 16, p. 264.
9. Mitchell, *Alexander Hamilton: The National Adventure*, p. 332.
10. Malone, *Jefferson and His Time*, vol. 3, p. 184.
11. *PAH*, vol. 16, p. 273, letter to George Washington, April 14, 1794.
12. Ibid.
13. Ibid.
14. Ibid.
15. Ibid., vol. 3, p. 295, "Remarks on the Provisional Peace Treaty," March 19, 1783.
16. Ibid., vol. 16, p. 281, "Conversation with George Hammond," April 15–16, 1794.
17. Ibid.
18. Ibid., p. 381, letter to John Jay, May 6, 1794.
19. Ketcham, *James Madison*, p. 352.
20. Ellis, *Founding Brothers*, p. 142.
21. Elkins and McKitrick, *Age of Federalism*, p. 409.
22. *PAH*, vol. 26, p. 738, "Views on the French Revolution," [1794].
23. Ibid., p. 739.
24. *The Pennsylvania Magazine of History and Biography*, July 1967.
25. Baxter, *Godchild of Washington*, p. 224.
26. St. Méry, *Moreau de St. Méry's American Journey*, p. 138.
27. Harcourt, *Memoirs of Madame de la Tour du Pin*, p. 273.
28. Hamilton, *Intimate Life of Alexander Hamilton*, p. 36.
29. *PAH*, vol. 17, p. 428, letter to Angelica Church, December 8, 1794.
30. Ibid., vol. 15, p. 600, "List of French Distressed Persons," 1793.
31. Brookhiser, *Gentleman Revolutionary*, p. 106.

32. Cooper, *Talleyrand*, p. 28.
33. Schama, *Citizens*, p. 678.
34. *PAH*, vol. 16, p. 380, letter from Angelica Church to Elizabeth Hamilton, February 4, 1794.
35. Hamilton, *Life of Alexander Hamilton*, vol. 7, p. 134.
36. *PAH*, vol. 16, p. 387, letter from George Washington, May 6, 1794.
37. Baxter, *Godchild of Washington*, p. 224.
38. Flexner, *Young Hamilton*, p. 449.
39. Hamilton, *Life of Alexander Hamilton*, vol. 6, p. 251.
40. Cooper, *Talleyrand*, p. 73.
41. Talleyrand, *Memoirs of the Prince de Talleyrand*, p. 185.
42. Hamilton, *Intimate Life of Alexander Hamilton*, p. 239.

Twenty-six: The Wicked Insurgents of the West

1. *PAH*, vol. 4, p. 348, "The Federalist No. 12," November 27, 1787.
2. *National Gazette*, June 18, 1792.
3. *PAH*, vol. 12, p. 306, letter from John Neville to George Clymer, August 23, 1792.
4. CU-HPPP, box 265.
5. Mitchell, *Alexander Hamilton: The National Adventure*, p. 317.
6. *PAH*, vol. 12, pp. 311–12, letter to George Washington, September 1, 1792.
7. Ibid., p. 390, letter from George Washington, September 17, 1792.
8. Ibid., vol. 16, p. 591, letter to George Washington, July 11, 1794.
9. Ibid., p. 616, letter to George Washington, July 23, 1794.
10. Ibid., vol. 17, p. 16, letter to George Washington, August 2, 1794.
11. Elkins and McKitrick, *Age of Federalism*, p. 475.
12. *The Journal of American History*, December 1972; Elkins and McKitrick, *Age of Federalism*, p. 479.
13. *PAH*, vol. 22, p. 552, letter to James McHenry, March 18, 1799.
14. *The Journal of American History*, December 1972.
15. *PAH*, vol. 17, pp. 76–77, letter to William Bradford, August 8, 1794.
16. *The Journal of American History*, December 1972.
17. *PAH*, vol. 17, pp. 14–15, letter to Elizabeth Hamilton, August 2, 1794.
18. Ibid.
19. Ibid., p. 85, letter to Elizabeth Hamilton, August 12, 1794.
20. Ibid., p. 148, "Tully No. II," *Claypoole's American Daily Advertiser*, August 26, 1794.

21. Ibid., p. 159, "Tully No. III," *Claypoole's American Daily Advertiser,* August 28, 1794.
22. Smith, *Patriarch,* p. 214.
23. *PAH,* vol. 17, p. 285, letter to George Gale, September 28, 1794.
24. Ibid., p. 241, letter to Rufus King, September 17, 1794.
25. Ibid., p. 255, letter to George Washington, September 19, 1794.
26. Hamilton, *Life of Alexander Hamilton,* vol. 6, p. 101.
27. *PAH,* vol. 17, p. 287, letter to Philip A. and Alexander Hamilton, Jr., September 29, 1794.
28. Ibid., p. 309, letter to Samuel Hodgdon, October 7, 1794.
29. Findley, *History of the Insurrection in the Four Western Counties of Pennsylvania,* p. 142.
30. Hamilton, *Life of Alexander Hamilton,* vol. 6, p. 106.
31. Ibid.
32. Ibid., p. 108.
33. *PAH,* vol. 22, p. 453, letter to Theodore Sedgwick, February 2, 1799.
34. Rakove, *James Madison and the Creation of the American Republic,* p. 135.
35. *PAH,* vol. 17, p. 340, letter to Angelica Church, October 23, 1794.
36. *Aurora General Advertiser,* November 8, 1794.
37. *PAH,* vol. 17, p. 366, letter to George Washington, November 11, 1794.
38. Ibid., p. 348, letter to Rufus King, October 30, 1794.
39. Findley, *History of the Insurrection in the Four Western Counties of Pennsylvania,* p. 228.
40. *PAH,* vol. 17, p. 383, "Examination of Hugh Henry Brackenridge," November 18–19, 1794.
41. Findley, *History of the Insurrection in the Four Western Counties of Pennsylvania,* p. 236.
42. Ibid., p. 238.
43. Ibid., p. 245.
44. Ketcham, *James Madison,* p. 354.
45. Rakove, *James Madison and the Creation of the American Republic,* p. 136.
46. Madison, *Papers of James Madison,* vol. 16, p. 440.
47. Ellis, *Founding Brothers,* p. 140.
48. MHi-TPP, reel 47, p. 180.
49. NYHS-MM, reel 64, letter from Angelica Church to Elizabeth Hamilton, December 11, 1794.
50. *PAH,* vol. 17, p. 392, letter from Henry Knox, November 24, 1794.
51. Ibid., p. 428, letter to Angelica Church, December 8, 1794.
52. LC-AHP, reel 29, letter from Angelica Church to Elizabeth Hamilton, January 25, 1795.
53. Hamilton, *Intimate Life of Alexander Hamilton,* p. 164.
54. LC-AHP, reel 30, memo of Timothy Pickering, talk with John Marshall, February 13, 1811.
55. *PAH,* vol. 18, p. 248, letter from George Washington, February 2, 1795.
56. Ibid., p. 58, *Report on a Plan for the Further Support of Public Credit,* January 16, 1795.
57. *PAH,* vol. 19, p. 56, "The Defence of the Funding System," July 1795.
58. Malone, *Jefferson and His Time,* vol. 3, p. 35.
59. *PAH,* vol. 18, p. 278, letter to Rufus King, February 21, 1795.
60. Ibid., pp. 278–79.
61. Knott, *Alexander Hamilton and the Persistence of Myth,* p. 238.
62. Lodge, *Alexander Hamilton,* p. 184.

Twenty-seven: Sugar Plums and Toys

1. *The Daily Advertiser,* February 28, 1795.
2. Hamilton, *Intimate Life of Alexander Hamilton,* p. 205.
3. *PAH,* vol. 18, p. 344, letter to Richard Varick, May 12, 1795.
4. Ibid., p. 196, letter from David Campbell, January 27, 1795.
5. Ibid., vol. 17, p. 428, letter to Angelica Church, December 8, 1794.
6. Ibid., vol. 16, p. 356, letter to Angelica Church, April–May 1794.
7. Hamilton, *Life of Alexander Hamilton,* vol. 6, p. 213.
8. Custis, *Recollections and Private Memoirs of Washington,* p. 352.
9. LC-AHP, reel 31, Robert Troup, "Additional Facts Relative to the Life, and Character, of General Hamilton," January 1, 1821.
10. *PAH,* vol. 18, p. 310, letter from Robert Troup, March 31, 1795.
11. Ibid., pp. 328–29, letter to Robert Troup, April 13, 1795.
12. NYSL, letter from Alexander Hamilton to Elizabeth Schuyler Hamilton, April 8, 1795.
13. *PAH,* vol. 16, p. 609, letter from John Jay, July 18[–August 5], 1794.
14. Ibid.
15. *Political Science Quarterly,* March 1956.
16. Rakove, *James Madison and the Creation of the American Republic,* p. 137.
17. Ellis, *Founding Brothers,* p. 136.
18. *PAH,* vol. 18, p. 383, letter to Rufus King, June 20, 1795.
19. Ibid., p. 391.
20. Ellis, *Founding Brothers,* p. 137.
21. Lomask, *Aaron Burr: The Years from Princeton to Vice President,* p. 182.
22. Elkins and McKitrick, *Age of Federalism,* p. 375.
23. *PAH,* vol. 18, p. 531.
24. Ellis, *Founding Brothers,* p. 137.

25. *PAH*, vol. 18, p. 399, letter from George Washington, July 3, 1795.
26. Ibid., p. 451, letter to George Washington, July 9–11, 1795.
27. Ibid., p. 461, letter from George Washington, July 13, 1795.
28. Ibid., p. 512, letter to Oliver Wolcott, Jr., June 18, 1795.
29. Madison, *Papers of James Madison*, vol. 16, p. 9.
30. Mitchell, *Alexander Hamilton: The National Adventure*, p. 341.
31. *The Argus, or Greenleaf's New Daily Advertiser*, July 20, 1795.
32. Ibid.
33. Mitchell, *Alexander Hamilton: The National Adventure*, p. 342.
34. King, *Life and Correspondence of Rufus King*, vol. 2, p. 20.
35. Malone, *Jefferson and His Time*, vol. 3, p. 248.
36. Ibid., p. 383.
37. *The Minerva, and Mercantile Evening Advertiser*, December 12, 1796.
38. *PAH*, vol. 20, p. 42.
39. Ibid.
40. Freeman, *Affairs of Honor*, p. xiv.
41. *PAH*, vol. 18, p. 471, letter to James Nicholson, July 20, 1795.
42. Ibid., p. 473, letter to James Nicholson, July 20, 1795.
43. Ibid., vol. 21, p. 143.
44. Ibid., vol. 14, p. 537, letter from James Hamilton, June 12, 1793.
45. Ibid., vol. 18, p. 503, letter to Robert Troup, July 25, 1795.
46. Ibid.
47. Ibid., p. 505.
48. King, *Life and Correspondence of Rufus King*, vol. 2, p. 13.
49. LC-AHP, letter from James Kent to Elizabeth Hamilton, December 20, 1832.
50. *PAH*, vol. 18, p. 481, "The Defence No. I," July 22, 1795.
51. Ibid., p. 478, letter from George Washington, July 29, 1795.
52. Ibid., p. 524, letter from George Washington, July 20, 1795.
53. Ibid., p. 493, "The Defence No. II," July 25, 1795.
54. Ibid., p. 498.
55. Ibid., vol. 19, p. 75, "Horatius No. II," July 1795.
56. Ibid., vol. 18, p. 526, "Address on the Jay Treaty," July 30, 1795.
57. Ibid., p. 527, letter from Oliver Wolcott, Jr., July 30, 1795.
58. Ibid., p. 513, "The Defence No. III," July 29, 1795.
59. Ibid.
60. Ibid., vol. 19, p. 102, "Philo Camillus No. II," August 7, 1795.
61. Ibid., p. 96, "The Defence No. V," August 5, 1795.
62. Ketcham, *James Madison*, p. 357.
63. *PAH*, vol. 19, p. 172, "The Defence No. X," August 26, 1795.
64. Ibid, p. 174.
65. Elkins and McKitrick, *Age of Federalism*, p. 436.
66. *PAH*, vol. 18, p. 478.
67. Ibid.
68. Wills, *James Madison*, p. 42.
69. Hamilton, *Life of Alexander Hamilton*, vol. 6, p. 454.
70. *PAH*, vol. 20, p. 13, "The Defence No. XXX," January 6, 1796.
71. McCullough, *John Adams*, p. 459.
72. Hamilton, *Life of Alexander Hamilton*, vol. 6, p. 315.
73. Ellis, *Founding Brothers*, p. 143.
74. *PAH*, vol. 20, p. 68, letter to George Washington, March 7, 1796.
75. Ibid., p. 83, letter to George Washington, March 28, 1796.
76. Ibid., p. 89, letter to George Washington, March 29, 1796.
77. Ibid., p. 113, letter to Rufus King, April 15, 1796.
78. Smith, *Patriarch*, p. 264.
79. *PAH*, vol. 20, p. 133, "To the Citizens Who Shall Be Convened This Day in the Fields in the City of New York," April 22, 1796.
80. Ellis, *Founding Brothers*, p. 138.
81. Mitchell, *Alexander Hamilton: The National Adventure*, p. 350.
82. Wills, *James Madison*, p. 42.
83. Ketcham, *James Madison*, p. 364.
84. Ellis, *Founding Brothers*, p. 138.
85. *PAH*, vol. 20, p. 104, letter from George Washington, March 31, 1796.

Twenty-eight: Spare Cassius

1. *PAH*, vol. 20, p. 515, letter to Rufus King, February 15, 1797.
2. CU-JCHP, box 20.
3. *PAH*, vol. 18, p. 397, letter from William Bradford, July 2, 1795.
4. Hamilton, *Life of Alexander Hamilton*, vol. 6, p. 343.
5. Mitchell, *Alexander Hamilton: The National Adventure*, p. 381.
6. King, *Life and Correspondence of Rufus King*, vol. 2, p. 98.
7. *PAH*, vol. 20, p. 353, letter to Elizabeth Hamilton, October 25, 1796.
8. Baxter, *Godchild of Washington*, p. 225.
9. Gottschalk, *Letters of Lafayette to Washington*, p. 363.

10. *PAH,* vol. 21, p. 451, letter to the marquis de Lafayette, April 28, 1798.

11. Ibid., vol. 18, p. 324, letter to Oliver Wolcott, Jr., April 10, 1795.

12. Ibid., p. 511, letter from Oliver Wolcott, Jr., July 28, 1795.

13. Ibid., vol. 19, p. 295, letter from Oliver Wolcott, Jr., September 26, 1795.

14. Ibid., vol. 19, p. 236, letter to George Washington, September 4, 1795.

15. LC-WPP, reel 2, letter from William Plumer to Jeremiah Smith, February 19, 1796.

16. *PAH,* vol. 19, p. 356, letter from George Washington, October 29, 1795.

17. Ibid., p. 395, letter to George Washington, November 5, 1795.

18. Smith, *Patriarch,* p. 252.

19. Ketcham, *James Madison,* p. 359.

20. *PAH,* vol. 20, p. 239, letter from George Washington, June 26, 1796.

21. Cooke, *Alexander Hamilton,* p. 111.

22. *PAH,* vol. 20, pp. 173–74, letter from George Washington, May 10, 1796.

23. Smith, *Patriarch,* p. 267.

24. *PAH,* vol. 20, p. 293, letter from George Washington, August 10, 1796.

25. Grafton, *Declaration of Independence and Other Great Documents of American History,* p. 53.

26. *PAH,* vol. 20, p. 164, letter from George Washington, May 8, 1796.

27. Ibid., p. 282, "Draft of Washington's Farewell Address," July 30, 1796.

28. Ibid., p. 280.

29. Cooke, *Alexander Hamilton,* p. 119.

30. Ellis, *Founding Brothers,* p. 160.

31. Ibid., p. 126.

32. *PAH,* vol. 20, p. 172.

33. Ibid., p. 173.

34. Ibid., p. 172.

35. Brodie, *Thomas Jefferson,* p. 303.

36. Wills, *James Madison,* p. xvii.

37. Madison, *Papers of James Madison,* vol. 16, p. 440.

38. Callender, *History of the United States for 1796,* p. 208.

39. Ferling, *John Adams,* p. 326.

40. *PAH,* vol. 20, p. 376, letter to an unnamed recipient, November 8, 1796.

41. Ibid., vol. 25, p. 193, *Letter from Alexander Hamilton,* October 24, 1800.

42. MHi-TPP, reel 51, p. 133.

43. *PAH,* vol. 25, p. 196, *Letter from Alexander Hamilton,* October 24, 1800.

44. Elkins and McKitrick, *Age of Federalism,* p. 540.

45. Emery, *Alexander Hamilton,* p. 176.

46. McCullough, *John Adams,* p. 463.

47. *PAH,* vol. 25, p. 195.

48. Ellis, *Passionate Sage,* p. 27.

49. Smith, *Patriarch,* p. 284.

50. *PAH,* vol. 12, pp. 504–5, "Catullus No. III," *Gazette of the United States,* September 29, 1792.

51. "Phocion No. IV," *Gazette of the United States,* October 19, 1796.

52. "Phocion No. IX," *Gazette of the United States,* October 25, 1796.

53. Brodie, *Thomas Jefferson,* p. 287.

54. Ibid., p. 296.

55. "Phocion No. I," *Gazette of the United States,* October 14, 1796.

56. Ibid.

57. "Phocion No. II," *Gazette of the United States,* October 15, 1796.

58. Brodie, *Thomas Jefferson,* p. 158.

59. "Phocion No. I," *Gazette of the United States,* October 14, 1796.

60. "Phocion No. II," *Gazette of the United States,* October 15, 1796.

61. Brodie, *Thomas Jefferson,* p. 352.

62. "Phocion No. II," *Gazette of the United States,* October 15, 1796.

63. Ibid.

64. "Phocion No. VI," *Gazette of the United States,* October 21, 1796.

65. *PAH,* vol. 12, p. 510, "Catullus No. III," *Gazette of the United States,* September 29, 1792.

66. "Phocion No. VIII," *Gazette of the United States,* October 24, 1796.

67. Mitchell, *Alexander Hamilton: The National Adventure,* p. 394.

68. Malone, *Jefferson and His Time,* vol. 4, pp. 163–64.

69. McCullough, *John Adams,* p. 464.

70. Madison, *Papers of James Madison,* vol. 16, p. 440.

71. Ibid.

72. *PAH,* vol. 20, p. 515, letter to Rufus King, February 15, 1797.

73. Ibid., p. 465, letter from Stephen Higginson, January 12, 1797.

Twenty-nine: The Man in the Glass Bubble

1. McCullough, *John Adams,* p. 414.

2. Ellis, *Passionate Sage,* p. 50.

3. Ferling, *John Adams,* p. 98.

4. McCullough, *John Adams,* p. 106.

5. Ferling, *John Adams,* p. 203.

6. Rosenfeld, *American Aurora,* p. 440.

7. Van Doren, *Benjamin Franklin,* p. 695.

8. Morgan, *Benjamin Franklin,* p. 293.

9. Bailyn, *To Begin the World Anew,* p. 64.

10. Brookhiser, *America's First Dynasty,* p. 67.

11. Ketcham, *James Madison,* p. 123.

12. Wilson and Stanton, *Jefferson Abroad*, p. 122.
13. Brookhiser, *America's First Dynasty*, p. 46.
14. Ellis, *Founding Brothers*, p. 207.
15. Ferling, *John Adams*, p. 440.
16. Bobrick, *Angel in the Whirlwind*, p. 97.
17. Ferling, *John Adams*, p. 159.
18. Ibid., p. 19.
19. Ibid., p. 233.
20. Ellis, *Passionate Sage*, p. 60.
21. Hamilton, *Life of Alexander Hamilton*, vol. 3, p. 598.
22. Ellis, *Founding Brothers*, p. 217; Adams, *Old Family Letters*, p. 164.
23. Brookhiser, *America's First Dynasty*, p. 53.
24. Freeman, *Affairs of Honor*, p. 138.
25. Ellis, *Passionate Sage*, p. 57.
26. McCullough, *John Adams*, p. 373.
27. Ellis, *Passionate Sage*, p. 146.
28. Ferling, *John Adams*, p. 312.
29. Ibid.
30. McCullough, *John Adams*, p. 48.
31. Ellis, *Passionate Sage*, p. 116.
32. Cooke, *Alexander Hamilton*, p. vii.
33. Knott, *Alexander Hamilton and the Persistence of Myth*, p. 19.
34. Brookhiser, *Alexander Hamilton*, p. 31; Adams, *Statesman and Friend*, p. 116; Gerlach, *Proud Patriot*, p. 400.
35. Pickering, *Review of the Correspondence Between the Hon. John Adams and the Late Wm. Cunningham*, p. 156.
36. Adams, *Old Family Letters*, pp. 163–64.
37. Ferling, *John Adams*, p. 360.
38. Flexner, *Young Hamilton*, p. 62.
39. Adams, *Old Family Letters*, pp. 163–64.
40. Adams, *Statesman and Friend*, pp. 157–58.
41. Ferling, *John Adams*, p. 429.
42. Ellis, *Founding Brothers*, p. 166.
43. Ibid., p. 176.
44. Ellis, *Passionate Sage*, p. 62.
45. Emery, *Alexander Hamilton*, p. 183.
46. McCullough, *John Adams*, p. 471.
47. *PAH*, vol. 25, p. 214, *Letter from Alexander Hamilton*, October 24, 1800.
48. Hamilton, *Life of Alexander Hamilton*, vol. 7, p. 598.
49. Ferling, *John Adams*, p. 424.
50. *PAH*, vol. 25, p. 183.
51. *The Boston Patriot*, May 29, 1809.
52. Hamilton, *Life of Alexander Hamilton*, vol. 7, p. 329.
53. Ferling, *John Adams*, pp. 316–17.
54. Hamilton, *Life of Alexander Hamilton*, vol. 7, p. 326.
55. Brookhiser, *Alexander Hamilton*, p. 131.
56. McCullough, *John Adams*, p. 526.

Thirty: Flying Too Near the Sun

1. *PAH*, vol. 21, p. 79, letter to William Hamilton, May 2, 1797.
2. Ibid., pp. 78–79.
3. Ibid., p. 78.
4. Hamilton, *Intimate Life of Alexander Hamilton*, p. 227.
5. *PAH*, vol. 18, p. 287, letter to Angelica Church, March 6, 1795.
6. LC-AHP, reel 29, letter from Angelica Church to Elizabeth Hamilton, January 24, 1795.
7. Menz, *Historic Furnishing Report*, p. 65.
8. *PAH*, vol. 20, p. 56, letter from Angelica Church, February 19, 1796.
9. Hamilton, *Intimate Life of Alexander Hamilton*, p. 108.
10. *PAH*, vol. 20, p. 236, letter to Angelica Church, June 25, 1796.
11. Ibid.
12. Ibid., vol. 9, p. 266, letter to Angelica Church, October 2, 1791.
13. LC-AHP, reel 29, letter from Angelica Church to Elizabeth Hamilton, July 9, 1796.
14. NYHS-RTP, letter from Robert Troup to Rufus King, June 3, 1797.
15. *PAH*, vol. 21, p. 259, "The Reynolds Pamphlet," August 1797.
16. Ibid., p. 149, letter to John Fenno, July 6, 1797.
17. Malone, *Jefferson and His Time*, vol. 3, p. 331.
18. Ibid., p. 470.
19. Brodie, *Thomas Jefferson*, p. 319; Brookhiser, *Alexander Hamilton*, p. 132.
20. Callender, *History of the United States for 1796*, p. 204.
21. Ibid., p. 205.
22. Ibid.
23. Ibid.
24. Ibid., p. 220.
25. Ibid., p. 222.
26. Ibid., p. 207.
27. "Phocion No. IV," *Gazette of the United States*, October 19, 1796.
28. *PAH*, vol. 21, p. 132.
29. Ibid.
30. Ibid., p. 133.
31. Hamilton, *Life of Alexander Hamilton*, vol. 5, p. 30.
32. Ketcham, *James Madison*, p. 335.
33. Brodie, *Thomas Jefferson*, p. 317.
34. *PAH*, vol. 21, p. 145, letter from Oliver Wolcott, Jr., July 3, 1797.
35. Ibid., p. 194, letter from Jeremiah Wadsworth, August 2, 1797.
36. *The* [Philadelphia] *Merchants' Daily Advertiser*, July 12, 1797.
37. CU-HPPP, box 272, letter from William Loughton Smith to Rufus King, December 14, 1797.

38. *PAH*, vol. 21, p. 238, "The Reynolds Pamphlet," August 1797.
39. Ibid.
40. Ibid., p. 240.
41. Ibid., p. 243.
42. Ibid., pp. 244–45.
43. Ibid., p. 239.
44. Ibid., pp. 243–44.
45. Ibid., p. 267.
46. Ames, *Sketch of the Character of Alexander Hamilton*, p. 12.
47. Lomask, *Aaron Burr: The Years from Princeton to Vice President*, p. 208.
48. NYHS-RTP, letter from Robert Troup to Rufus King, September 3, 1797.
49. CU-HPPP, box 272, letter from William Loughton Smith to Rufus King, December 14, 1797.
50. Mitchell, *Alexander Hamilton: The National Adventure*, p. 408.
51. *PAH*, vol. 21, p. 140.
52. Rosenfeld, *American Aurora*, p. 33.
53. Mitchell, *Alexander Hamilton: The National Adventure*, p. 713.
54. Rosenfeld, *American Aurora*, p. 33.
55. *PAH*, vol. 21, p. 139.
56. McCullough, *John Adams*, p. 480.
57. MHi-TPP, reel 51, pp. 164–65.
58. McCullough, *John Adams*, p. 493.
59. Adams, *Correspondence Between the Hon. John Adams, and the Late Wm. Cunningham*, p. 159.
60. Fleming, *Duel*, p. 360.
61. Lomask, *Aaron Burr: The Years from Princeton to Vice President*, pp. 208–9.
62. Adams, *Correspondence Between the Hon. John Adams, and the Late Wm. Cunningham*, p. 161.
63. *PAH*, vol. 21, p. 214, letter from George Washington, August 21, 1797.
64. Hamilton, *Intimate Life of Alexander Hamilton*, p. 59.
65. *PAH*, vol. 21, p. 259, "The Reynolds Pamphlet," August 1797.
66. Ibid., p. 159, letter from Abraham B. Venable, July 10, 1797.
67. Ibid., p. 157, letter to James Monroe, July 10, 1797.
68. Ammon, *James Monroe*, p. 30.
69. Knott, *Alexander Hamilton and the Persistence of Myth*, p. 12.
70. Ammon, *James Monroe*, p. 106.
71. Ibid., p. 168.
72. *PAH*, vol. 21, p. 160, "David Gelston Account of a Meeting Between Alexander Hamilton and James Monroe," July 11, 1797.
73. Ibid.
74. Ibid.
75. Ibid.
76. Ibid.
77. *Aurora General Advertiser*, July 17, 1797.
78. *PAH*, vol. 21, pp. 180–81, letter to James Monroe, July 21, 1797.
79. Ibid., p. 186, letter to James Monroe, July 25, 1797.
80. *PAH*, vol. 21, p. 201.
81. Ibid., p. 202.
82. Ibid., p. 211.
83. Ibid., p. 317.
84. Davis, *Memoirs of Aaron Burr*, vol. 2, p. 434.
85. *PAH*, vol. 21, p. 286, letter to George Washington, August 28, 1797.
86. *Aurora General Advertiser*, September 19, 1797.
87. *PAH*, vol. 21, p. 163, letter from John B. Church, July 13, 1797. The word *scoundrels* appears in brackets because Hamilton's editors guessed at the difficult-to-decipher word.
88. *Aurora General Advertiser*, September 19, 1797.
89. *PAH*, vol. 21, p. 164, letter from John B. Church, July 13, 1797.
90. Ibid., p. 175, letter to Elizabeth Hamilton, July 19, 1797.
91. Ibid., p. 177, letter to Elizabeth Hamilton, July 21, 1797.
92. Mitchell, *Alexander Hamilton: The National Adventure*, pp. 417–18.
93. Ibid.
94. *PAH*, vol. 21, p. 295.
95. Ibid., vol. 21, p. 294, letter to Elizabeth Hamilton, September 12, 1797.
96. LC-AHP, reel 30, letter from Dr. David Hosack to Elizabeth Hamilton, January 1, 1833.
97. Ibid.
98. *PAH*, vol. 25, p. 436.
99. Ibid.

Thirty-one: An Instrument of Hell

1. *PAH*, vol. 20, p. 492, "The Warning No. I," January 27, 1797.
2. Ibid., p. 509, "The Warning No. II," February 7, 1797.
3. Ibid., p. 545, letter to Timothy Pickering, March 22, 1797.
4. Ibid., p. 568, letter to Oliver Wolcott, Jr., March 30, 1797.
5. Ibid., vol. 21, p. 99, letter to Oliver Wolcott, Jr., June 6, 1797.
6. Ibid., p. 21, letter to William Loughton Smith, April 5, 1797.
7. Elkins and McKitrick, *Age of Federalism*, p. 545.
8. *PAH*, vol. 21, p. 26, letter to Rufus King, April 8, 1797.
9. Elkins and McKitrick, *Age of Federalism*, p. 566.
10. Smith, *John Marshall*, p. 190.
11. McCullough, *John Adams*, p. 484.
12. *Aurora General Advertiser*, July 14, 1797.

13. Ellis, *Founding Brothers,* pp. 188–89.
14. *PAH,* vol. 21, p. 99, letter to Oliver Wolcott, Jr., June 6, 1797.
15. Ibid., vol. 20, p. 558, letter to Timothy Pickering, March 30, 1797.
16. Harcourt, *Memoirs of Madame de la Tour du Pin,* p. 248.
17. Hamilton, *Intimate Life of Alexander Hamilton,* p. 75.
18. Ibid., p. 195.
19. Smith, *John Marshall,* p. 198.
20. Ibid., p. 226.
21. *PAH,* vol. 21, p. 365, letter to Timothy Pickering, March 17, 1798.
22. Ibid.
23. Ferling, *John Adams,* p. 354.
24. *PAH,* vol. 21, p. 371, letter to Timothy Pickering, March 25, 1798.
25. *The New Republic,* July 2, 2001.
26. King, *Life and Correspondence of Rufus King,* vol. 2, p. 329.
27. Ellis, *Founding Brothers,* p. 196.
28. Elkins and McKitrick, *Age of Federalism,* p. 588.
29. Smith, *John Marshall,* p. 227.
30. Rakove, *James Madison and the Creation of the American Republic,* p. 149; Ketcham, *James Madison,* p. 392.
31. Rosenfeld, *American Aurora,* p. 67.
32. *PAH,* vol. 21, p. 432, "The Stand No. V," *The* [New York] *Commercial Advertiser,* April 16, 1798.
33. Ibid., p. 442, "The Stand No. VII," *The* [New York] *Commercial Advertiser,* April 21, 1798.
34. Ellis, *Founding Brothers,* p. 186.
35. *PAH,* vol. 21, p. 436, "The Stand No. VI," *The* [New York] *Commercial Advertiser,* April 19, 1798.
36. Wood, *American Revolution,* p. 106.
37. Isaacson, *Benjamin Franklin,* p. 456.
38. Wills, *James Madison,* p. 62.
39. Ferling, *John Adams,* p. 355.
40. *The Boston Patriot,* May 29, 1809.
41. Lind, *Hamilton's Republic,* p. 136.
42. *PAH,* vol. 21, p. 462, letter to James McHenry, May 17, 1798.
43. Hamilton, *Life of Alexander Hamilton,* vol. 7, p. 169.
44. *PAH,* vol. 21, p. 435, "The Stand No. VI," *The* [New York] *Commercial Advertiser,* April 19, 1798.
45. King, *Life and Correspondence of Rufus King,* vol. 2, p. 330.
46. *PAH,* vol. 21, p. 482, letter to Elizabeth Hamilton, June 3, 1798.
47. Ibid., p. 496, letter to Elizabeth Hamilton, June 8, 1798.
48. Ibid., p. 434, letter from John Jay, April 19, 1798.
49. Ames, *Sketch of the Character of Alexander Hamilton,* p. 14.
50. NYHS-RTP, letter from Robert Troup to Rufus King, June 10, 1797.
51. Ferling, *John Adams,* p. 133.
52. *PAH,* vol. 21, p. 468, letter to George Washington, May 19, 1798.
53. Ibid., p. 470, letter from George Washington, May 27, 1798.
54. Ibid., p. 479, letter to George Washington, June 2, 1798.
55. Ibid., p. 486, letter to Oliver Wolcott, Jr., June 5, 1798.
56. Hamilton, *Intimate Life of Alexander Hamilton,* p. 323.
57. Ibid.
58. *PAH,* vol. 21, p. 535.
59. Ibid., p. 534, letter to George Washington, July 8, 1798.
60. Ibid.
61. Elkins and McKitrick, *Age of Federalism,* p. 602.
62. Malone, *Jefferson and His Time,* vol. 3, p. 426.
63. *PAH,* vol. 22, p. 83, letter to James McHenry, August 19, 1798.
64. Ibid., vol. 17, p. 312, letter from Henry Knox, October 8, 1794.
65. Rosenfeld, *American Aurora,* p. 198.
66. Ibid., p. 431.
67. Elkins and McKitrick, *Age of Federalism,* p. 603.
68. *PAH,* vol. 22, p. 10.
69. Elkins and McKitrick, *Age of Federalism,* p. 605.
70. Ibid.
71. Ferling, *John Adams,* p. 362.
72. Smith, *Patriarch,* p. 331.
73. CU-HPPP, box 273, letter from George Washington to John Adams, September 25, 1798.
74. Smith, *Patriarch,* p. 332.
75. *PAH,* vol. 22, p. 202.
76. CU-HPPP, box 273, letter from George Washington to Timothy Pickering, September 9, 1798.
77. CU-FFP, letter from Timothy Pickering to Nicholas Fish, December 5, 1823.
78. Ibid.
79. Ferling, *John Adams,* p. 361.
80. *PAH,* vol. 24, p. 524, letter to John Adams, May 24, 1800.
81. Ibid., p. 593, letter from John Adams, June 20, 1800.
82. King, *Life and Correspondence of Rufus King,* vol. 3, p. 263.
83. Ibid., vol. 2, p. 346.
84. Parton, *Life and Times of Aaron Burr,* p. 237.
85. *PAH,* vol. 21, p. 521, letter to Oliver Wolcott, Jr., June 28, 1798.
86. Lomask, *Aaron Burr: The Years from Princeton to Vice President,* p. 216.

87. Parton, *Life and Times of Aaron Burr*, p. 235.
88. Ibid.
89. *PAH*, vol. 24, p. 136, "Battle Plans," December 1799–March 1800.
90. Ibid., vol. 22, p. 478, letter to James Wilkinson, February 12, 1799.
91. Ibid., p. 368, letter to James McHenry, December 16, 1798.
92. Ibid., vol. 24, p. 229, letter to Elizabeth Hamilton, February 10, 1800.
93. Ibid., vol. 22, p. 161, letter to John Adams, August 24, 1798.
94. Ibid., vol. 24, p. 127, letter to James McHenry, December 1799.
95. Ibid., vol. 23, p. 493, letter to James McHenry, October 3, 1799.
96. Ibid., vol. 24, p. 143, "Elements of the Tactics of the Infantry," 1799.
97. Ibid., vol. 22, p. 252, letter to John Jay, November 19, 1798.
98. Ibid., p. 29, letter to Louis le Bègue du Portail, July 23, 1798.
99. Ibid., vol. 24, p. 70, letter to James McHenry, November 23, 1799.
100. Ibid., vol. 23, p. 433, letter to James McHenry, September 17, 1799.
101. Ibid., vol. 22, p. 65, letter from Oliver Wolcott, Jr., August 9, 1798.
102. Ibid., p. 62, letter from George Washington, August 9, 1798.
103. Ibid., p. 38, letter to George Washington, July 29[–August 1], 1798.
104. Smith, *Patriarch*, p. 340.
105. *PAH*, vol. 21, p. 345, letter to James McHenry, January 27–February 11, 1798.
106. Robertson, *Life of Miranda*, vol. 1, p. 177.
107. *PAH*, vol. 22, p. 155, letter to Francisco de Miranda, August 22, 1798.
108. Ibid.
109. Ibid., p. 154, letter to Rufus King, August 22, 1798.
110. Ibid., p. 345, letter from George Washington to James McHenry, December 13, 1798.
111. Ibid., p. 441, letter to Harrison Gray Otis, January 26, 1799.
112. Emery, *Alexander Hamilton*, p. 180.
113. Elkins and McKitrick, *Age of Federalism*, p. 671.
114. Morison, *Harrison Gray Otis*, p. 158.
115. Lomask, *Aaron Burr: The Conspiracy and Years of Exile*, p. 180.
116. *PAH*, vol. 23, p. 383, letter from James Wilkinson, September 6, 1799.

Thirty-two: Reign of Witches

1. *PAH*, vol. 21, p. 506, *Gazette of the United States*, June 13, 1798.
2. Malone, *Jefferson and His Time*, vol. 3, p. 360.
3. Smith, *John Marshall*, p. 239.
4. Rosenfeld, *American Aurora*, p. 43.
5. Bailyn, *To Begin the World Anew*, p. 156.
6. Rosenfeld, *American Aurora*, p. 235.
7. Ferling, *John Adams*, p. 366.
8. Ellis, *Founding Brothers*, p. 191.
9. Ibid.
10. Rosenfeld, *American Aurora*, p. 132.
11. *PAH*, vol. 21, p. 468, *The Time Piece*, May 21, 1798.
12. Ibid., May 22, 1798.
13. *The Boston Patriot*, May 29, 1809.
14. *The Review of Politics*, July 1954.
15. *PAH*, vol. 21, p. 522, letter to Oliver Wolcott, Jr., June 29, 1798.
16. Ibid., vol. 23, p. 604, letter to Jonathan Dayton, October–November, 1799.
17. *Speeches at Full Length of Mr. Van Ness*, p. 76.
18. Rosenfeld, *American Aurora*, pp. 128, 136.
19. Ibid., p. 136.
20. Jefferson, *Anas of Thomas Jefferson*, p. 38.
21. Ibid., p. 381.
22. Ibid., vol. 4, p. 155.
23. Wills, *James Madison*, p. 49.
24. Rakove, *James Madison and the Creation of the American Republic*, p. 151.
25. Wills, *James Madison*, p. 49.
26. Ketcham, *James Madison*, p. 397.
27. Knott, *Alexander Hamilton and the Persistence of Myth*, p. 48.
28. Brookhiser, *Alexander Hamilton*, p. 142.
29. *PAH*, vol. 22, p. 452, letter to Theodore Sedgwick, February 2, 1799.
30. Ibid.
31. Ibid., p. 465, letter to Rufus King, February 6, 1799.
32. *The New York Times*, July 3, 2001.
33. Brodie, *Thomas Jefferson*, p. 321.
34. *The Review of Politics*, July 1954.
35. Rosenfeld, *American Aurora*, p. 689.
36. *The Argus, or Greenleaf's New Daily Advertiser*, November 6, 1799.
37. *PAH*, vol. 24, p. 5, letter to Josiah Ogden Hoffman, November 6, 1799.
38. *Greenleaf's New York Journal and Patriotic Register*, December 11, 1799.
39. *Aurora*, November 25, 1799.
40. Rosenfeld, *American Aurora*, p. 716.
41. *Greenleaf's New York Journal and Patriotic Register*, November 20, 1799.
42. Rosenfeld, *American Aurora*, p. 547.
43. *PAH*, vol. 22, p. 394, letter to Harrison Gray Otis, December 27, 1798.
44. Ibid., p. 415, letter from William Heth, January 14, 1799.

45. Ibid., p. 453, letter to Theodore Sedgwick, February 2, 1799.
46. Malone, *Jefferson and His Time,* vol. 3, p. 440.
47. *PAH,* vol. 22, p. 532.
48. Ibid., vol. 23, p. 7, letter to George Washington, April 3, 1799.
49. Ibid., p. 1, letter from Oliver Wolcott, Jr., April 1, 1799.
50. Brookhiser, *America's First Dynasty,* p. 197.
51. *The Boston Patriot,* May 29, 1809.
52. Ellis, *Founding Brothers,* pp. 206–7.

Thirty-three: Works Godly and Ungodly

1. NYHS-NYCMS, reel 2, "Minutes of the Standing Committee," March 7 [?], 1799.
2. LC-AHP, reel 30, Alexander Hamilton, Jr., memo about Elizabeth Hamilton.
3. Hamilton, *Reminiscences of James A. Hamilton,* p. 65.
4. Pettit, "Women, Sunday Schools, and Politics," p. 37.
5. Bethune, *Memoirs of Mrs. Joanna Bethune,* p. 112.
6. Rosenfeld, *American Aurora,* p. 725.
7. *PAH,* vol. 22, p. 313, letter to Elizabeth Hamilton, November 1798.
8. Ibid., p. 251, letter to Elizabeth Hamilton, November 19, 1798.
9. Ibid., p. 236, letter to Elizabeth Hamilton, November 11, 1798.
10. *PAH,* vol. 24, p. 211, letter to Angelica Church, January 22, 1800.
11. King, *Life and Correspondence of Rufus King,* vol. 3, p. 34.
12. *PAH,* vol. 22, p. 232, letter to Elizabeth Hamilton, November 10, 1798.
13. Ibid., vol. 24, p. 212, letter to Angelica Church, January 22, 1800.
14. Ibid., vol. 22, p. 450, letter from Philip Schuyler, January 31, 1799.
15. Hamilton, *Intimate Life of Alexander Hamilton,* p. 349.
16. *PAH,* vol. 22, p. 450.
17. Ibid., p. 451.
18. Pettit, "Women, Sunday Schools, and Politics," p. 44.
19. King, *Life and Correspondence of Rufus King,* vol. 2, p. 429.
20. *Political Science Quarterly,* December 1957.
21. *PAH,* vol. 21, p. 481, letter to Oliver Wolcott, Jr., June 2, 1798.
22. Lomask, *Aaron Burr: The Years from Princeton to Vice President,* p. 226.
23. *PAH,* vol. 22, p. 447.
24. Ibid., vol. 25, p. 321, letter to James A. Bayard, January 16, 1801.
25. Burr, *Political Correspondence and Public Papers of Aaron Burr,* vol. 1, p. 402.
26. Ibid., p. 399.
27. Ibid., p. 403.
28. *The New-York Gazette and General Advertiser,* September 14, 1799.
29. Burr, *Political Correspondence and Public Papers of Aaron Burr,* vol. 2, p. 410.
30. *PAH,* vol. 21, p. 481, letter to Oliver Wolcott, Jr., June 2, 1798.
31. Biddle, *Autobiography of Charles Biddle,* p. 303.
32. Davis, *Memoirs of Aaron Burr,* vol. 1, p. 417.
33. Burr, *Political Correspondence and Public Papers of Aaron Burr,* vol. 2, p. 410.

Thirty-four: In an Evil Hour

1. Brookhiser, *America's First Dynasty,* p. 49.
2. *The Boston Patriot,* May 29, 1809.
3. *PAH,* vol. 22, p. 405.
4. Ibid., p. 472, letter from James McHenry, February 8, 1799.
5. Ibid., p. 482, letter to George Washington, February 15, 1799.
6. Ibid., p. 471, letter from Theodore Sedgwick, February 7, 1799.
7. McCullough, *John Adams,* p. 523.
8. Ferling, *John Adams,* p. 370.
9. *PAH,* vol. 22, p. 500, letter from Timothy Pickering, February 25, 1799.
10. Ferling, *John Adams,* p. 390.
11. MHi-TPP, reel 15, p. 267, letter from Timothy Pickering to Richard Stockton, December 31, 1821.
12. *PAH,* vol. 22, p. 494, letter from Theodore Sedgwick, February 22, 1799.
13. Ibid., p. 493, letter to Theodore Sedgwick, February 21, 1799.
14. Ibid., vol. 25, p. 207, *Letter from Alexander Hamilton,* October 24, 1800.
15. Ibid., vol. 22, p. 493, letter to Theodore Sedgwick, February 21, 1799.
16. Malone, *Jefferson and His Time,* vol. 3, p. 437.
17. *PAH,* vol. 22, p. 507, letter from George Washington, February 25, 1799.
18. Ibid., p. 586, letter from George Washington, March 25, 1799.
19. Ibid., vol. 23, p. 122, letter to James McHenry, May 18, 1799.
20. Ibid., pp. 186–87, letter to James McHenry, June 14, 1799.
21. Ibid., p. 223, letter from James McHenry, June 26, 1799.
22. Ibid., p. 227, letter to James McHenry, June 27, 1799.
23. Ibid.
24. Ibid., p. 313, letter to James McHenry, August 13, 1799.
25. Ibid.
26. Ferling, *John Adams,* p. 381.

27. Ibid., p. 384.
28. Brodie, *Thomas Jefferson*, p. 334.
29. Ferling, *John Adams*, p. 386.
30. Elkins and McKitrick, *Age of Federalism*, p. 640.
31. Mitchell, *Alexander Hamilton: The National Adventure*, p. 482.
32. *PAH*, vol. 25, p. 22, *Letter from Alexander Hamilton*, October 24, 1800.
33. Ibid., vol. 23, p. 546.
34. McCullough, *John Adams*, p. 531.
35. *PAH*, vol. 23, p. 547.
36. Ibid.
37. Ibid., p. 545, letter to George Washington, October 21, 1799.
38. Ibid., p. 574, letter from George Washington, October 27, 1799.
39. Elkins and McKitrick, *Age of Federalism*, p. 730.
40. *PAH*, vol. 23, p. 100.
41. Ibid., vol. 23, p. 602, letter to Jonathan Dayton, October–November 1799.
42. Ibid., p. 604.
43. Ibid.
44. Ibid., vol. 24, p. 99, letter from George Washington, December 12, 1799.
45. Ibid., p. 116, letter to Charles Cotesworth Pinckney, December 22, 1799.
46. Ibid., p. 155, letter to Tobias Lear, January 2, 1800.
47. Ibid., p. 184, letter to Martha Washington, January 12, 1800.
48. McCullough, *John Adams*, p. 533.
49. Ellis, *Passionate Sage*, p. 67.
50. *PAH*, vol. 24, p. 168, letter to Rufus King, January 5, 1800.
51. Baxter, *Godchild of Washington*, p. 226.
52. *The New York Review of Books*, April 25, 2002.
53. *PAH*, vol. 24, p. 267, letter to George Izard, February 27, 1800.
54. Rosenfeld, *American Aurora*, p. 791.
55. McCullough, *John Adams*, p. 540.
56. Elkins and McKitrick, *Age of Federalism*, p. 719.
57. Adams, *New Letters of Abigail Adams*, p. 252.

Thirty-five: Gusts of Passion

1. *LPAH*, vol. 1, p. 721.
2. Ibid., pp. 693–94.
3. Lomask, *Aaron Burr: The Years from Princeton to Vice President*, p. 90; *LPAH*, vol. 1, p. 706.
4. *LPAH*, vol. 1, p. 694.
5. Lomask, *Aaron Burr: The Years from Princeton to Vice President*, p. 91.
6. *LPAH*, vol. 1, p. 747.
7. Lodge, *Alexander Hamilton*, p. 239.
8. Parton, *Life and Times of Aaron Burr*, p. 148.
9. *LPAH*, vol. 1, p. 761.
10. Lomask, *Aaron Burr: The Years from Princeton to Vice President*, p. 93; *LPAH*, vol. 1, p. 704.
11. *LPAH*, vol. 1, p. 774.
12. Hamilton, *Intimate Life of Alexander Hamilton*, p. 186.
13. Rosenfeld, *American Aurora*, p. 751.
14. King, *Life and Correspondence of Rufus King*, vol. 3, p. 208.
15. Lomask, *Aaron Burr: The Years from Princeton to Vice President*, p. 240.
16. Freeman, *Affairs of Honor*, p. 209.
17. Lomask, *Aaron Burr: The Years from Princeton to Vice President*, p. 239.
18. *The New York Times Book Review*, February 13, 2000.
19. Freeman, *Affairs of Honor*, p. 232.
20. Ibid.
21. Lomask, *Aaron Burr: The Years from Princeton to Vice President*, p. 244.
22. Ammon, *James Monroe*, p. 185.
23. Lomask, *Aaron Burr: The Years from Princeton to Vice President*, p. 246.
24. Ibid.
25. Knott, *Alexander Hamilton and the Persistence of Myth*, p. 89.
26. Rosenfeld, *American Aurora*, p. 785.
27. Ibid.
28. *PAH*, vol. 24, p. 465, letter to John Jay, May 7, 1800.
29. Ibid.
30. Ibid.
31. Lodge, *Alexander Hamilton*, p. 224.
32. *PAH*, vol. 24, p. 467.
33. Ellis, *American Sphinx*, p. 212.
34. Jefferson, *Anas of Thomas Jefferson*, p. 227.
35. Ibid., pp. 227–28.
36. Parton, *Life and Times of Aaron Burr*, p. 255.
37. Ferling, *John Adams*, p. 310.
38. *PAH*, vol. 25, p. 5.
39. Ibid.
40. Ellis, *Passionate Sage*, p. 37.
41. Ibid.
42. *PAH*, vol. 25, p. 71, letter from James A. Bayard, August 18, 1800.
43. Ellis, *American Sphinx*, p. 222.
44. Rosenfeld, *American Aurora*, p. 804; *Aurora.General Advertiser*, June 3, 1800.
45. *PAH*, vol. 24, p. 452, letter to Theodore Sedgwick, May 4, 1800.
46. Freeman, *Affairs of Honor*, p. 105.
47. *PAH*, vol. 24, p. 555, letter from James McHenry, June 2, 1800.
48. Ibid, p. 557.
49. McCullough, *John Adams*, p. 538.
50. Steiner, *Life and Correspondence of James McHenry*, p. 454; *PAH*, vol. 24, p. 508, letter from James McHenry, May 20, 1800.
51. *PAH*, vol. 25, p. 222, *Letter from Alexander Hamilton*, October 24, 1800.

52. Steiner, *Life and Correspondence of James McHenry,* p. 569.
53. *PAH,* vol. 20, p. 374, letter to George Washington, November 5, 1796.
54. Adams, *Correspondence Between the Hon. John Adams and the Late Wm. Cunningham,* p. 50.
55. Ibid., p. 39.
56. Ibid.
57. MHi-TPP, reel 55, p. 208.
58. King, *Life and Correspondence of Rufus King,* vol. 3, p. 262.
59. MHi-TPP, reel 55, p. 47.
60. Ibid., reel 15, p. 267, letter from Timothy Pickering to Richard Stockton, December 31, 1821.
61. *PAH,* vol. 24, p. 485.
62. Ibid., p. 573, letter to James McHenry, June 6, 1800.
63. Elkins and McKitrick, *Age of Federalism,* p. 740.
64. *The* [Boston] *Independent Chronicle and Universal Advertiser,* July 28–31, 1800.
65. *PAH,* vol. 25, p. 88, letter to William Jackson, August 26, 1800.
66. Ibid., p. 89.
67. Ibid., p. 111, letter from James McHenry, September 4, 1800.
68. *J. Russell's Gazette Commercial and Political,* June 23, 1800.
69. Ibid.
70. *PAH,* vol. 24, p. 584.
71. Ibid., p. 580.
72. Ibid., p. 576.
73. Ellis, *Passionate Sage,* p. 33.
74. McCullough, *John Adams,* p. 545.
75. *PAH,* vol. 24, p. 574.
76. Ibid., p. 575.
77. Ibid., p. 4, letter to Oliver Wolcott, Jr., July 1, 1800.
78. Ibid., p. 596, "Conversation with Arthur Fenner," June 25–26, 1800.
79. Ibid.
80. Ibid., vol. 25, p. 30, letter from John Rutledge, Jr., July 17, 1800.

Thirty-six: In a Very Belligerent Humor
1. Sparks, *Life of Gouverneur Morris,* pp. 260–61.
2. NYHS-NPP, n.d.
3. Rogow, *Fatal Friendship,* p. 275.
4. *PAH,* vol. 24, p. 487, letter to Timothy Pickering, May 14, 1800.
5. Ibid., p. 491, letter from Timothy Pickering, May 15, 1800.
6. Ibid., p. 573, letter to James McHenry, June 6, 1800.
7. CU-HPPP, box 276, letter from Oliver Wolcott, Jr., to Fisher Ames, August 10, 1800.
8. *PAH,* vol. 25, p. 15, letter from Oliver Wolcott, Jr., July 7, 1800.
9. Ferling, *John Adams,* p. 397.
10. *PAH,* vol. 25, p. 15, letter from Oliver Wolcott, Jr., July 7, 1800.
11. Adams, *Correspondence Between the Hon. John Adams, and the Late Wm. Cunningham,* p. 40.
12. Freeman, *Affairs of Honor,* p. 137.
13. *Aurora.General Advertiser,* July 12, 1800.
14. *PAH,* vol. 25, p. 54, letter to Oliver Wolcott, Jr., August 3, 1800.
15. Ibid., p. 51, letter to John Adams, August 1, 1800.
16. Ibid., p. 125, letter to John Adams, October 1, 1800.
17. Ibid., p. 74, letter from George Cabot, August 21, 1800.
18. CU-HPPP, box 276, letter from John Beckley to Ephraim King, October 25, 1800.
19. Ibid., letter from William S. Shaw to William Smith, November 8, 1800.
20. Elkins and McKitrick, *Age of Federalism,* p. 739.
21. Parton, *Life and Times of Aaron Burr,* p. 257.
22. Fleming, *Duel,* p. 78.
23. Lodge, *Alexander Hamilton,* p. 229.
24. *PAH,* vol. 25, p. 186, *Letter from Alexander Hamilton,* October 24, 1800.
25. Ibid., p. 190.
26. Ibid., p. 202.
27. Ibid., p. 223.
28. Ibid., p. 228.
29. Ibid., p. 233.
30. Ellis, *Passionate Sage,* p. 24.
31. *PAH,* vol. 25, p. 238, letter from Benjamin Goodhue, November 15, 1800.
32. Ibid., p. 242, quoted in letter from James McHenry, November 19, 1800.
33. LC-WPP, reel 2, letter from William Plumer to Jeremiah Smith, December 10, 1800.
34. King, *Life and Correspondence of Rufus King,* vol. 3, p. 331.
35. Ibid.
36. CU-HPPP, box 276, letter from George Cabot to Oliver Wolcott, Jr., November 28, 1800.
37. King, *Life and Correspondence of Rufus King,* vol. 3, p. 350.
38. *PAH,* vol. 25, p. 137, letter to Timothy Pickering, November 13, 1800.
39. Ibid., p. 182.
40. "Hamilton's Quarrel with Washington, 1781," *The William and Mary Quarterly,* April 1955.
41. Adams, *New Letters of Abigail Adams,* p. 255.
42. Freeman, *Affairs of Honor,* p. 108.
43. *The Boston Patriot,* May 29, 1809.
44. McCullough, *John Adams,* p. 556.
45. Parton, *Life and Times of Aaron Burr,* p. 258.
46. Ferling, *John Adams,* p. 404.
47. Freeman, *Affairs of Honor,* p. 119.
48. Adams, *Correspondence Between the Hon. John Adams, and the Late Wm. Cunningham,* p. 28.

49. Emery, *Alexander Hamilton,* p. 186.
50. Freeman, *Affairs of Honor,* pp. 90–91.
51. Knott, *Alexander Hamilton and the Persistence of Myth,* p. 16.
52. CU-HPPP, box 276, letter from Harrison Gray Otis to John Rutledge, Jr., August 25, 1800.
53. Brookhiser, *America's First Dynasty,* p. 67.
54. Brodie, *Thomas Jefferson,* p. 338.
55. Ibid., p. 101.

Thirty-seven: Deadlock

1. *PAH,* vol. 25, p. 307.
2. Mitchell, *Alexander Hamilton: The National Adventure,* p. 462.
3. Ferling, *John Adams,* p. 449; Ellis, *Passionate Sage,* p. 76.
4. Ellis, *Passionate Sage,* p. 78.
5. LC-WPP, reel 1, diary entry of March 15, 1806.
6. CU-HPPP, box 276, letter from Aaron Burr to Samuel Smith, December 16, 1800.
7. *PAH,* vol. 25, p. 257, letter to Oliver Wolcott, Jr., December 16, 1800.
8. Ibid.
9. Ibid., p. 323, letter to James A. Bayard, January 16, 1801.
10. McCullough, *John Adams,* p. 558.
11. Bergh, *Writings of Thomas Jefferson,* vol. 11, p. 191.
12. CU-HPPP, box 276, letter from Aaron Burr to John Taylor, October 23, 1800.
13. Ibid., letter from Fisher Ames to Theodore Sedgwick, December 31, 1800.
14. *PAH,* vol. 25, p. 286, letter to Oliver Wolcott, Jr., December 1800.
15. Ibid., p. 270, letter to Theodore Sedgwick, December 22, 1800.
16. Ibid., p. 272, letter to Gouverneur Morris, December 24, 1800.
17. *The William and Mary Quarterly,* April 1947.
18. *PAH,* vol. 25, p. 292, letter to James McHenry, January 4, 1801.
19. Fleming, *Duel,* p. 92.
20. *PAH,* vol. 25, p. 319, letter to James A. Bayard, January 16, 1801.
21. Ellis, *Founding Brothers,* p. 202.
22. *PAH,* vol. 25, p. 320, letter to James A. Bayard, January 16, 1801.
23. Lomask, *Aaron Burr: The Years from Princeton to Vice President,* p. 288.
24. Malone, *Jefferson and His Time,* vol. 3, p. 495.
25. *PAH,* vol. 25, p. 608, letter to James A. Bayard, April [16–21], 1802.
26. *Washington Federalist,* February 12, 1801.
27. Brodie, *Thomas Jefferson,* p. 335.
28. King, *Life and Correspondence of Rufus King,* vol. 3, p. 391.
29. *PAH,* vol. 25, p. 272, letter to Gouverneur Morris, December 24, 1800.

30. Freeman, *Affairs of Honor,* p. 248.
31. Rufus King, *Life and Correspondence of Rufus King,* vol. 4, p. 160.
32. Malone, *Jefferson and His Time,* vol. 4, p. 11.
33. Brookhiser, *America's First Dynasty,* p. 70.
34. *PAH,* vol. 25, p. 321, letter to James A. Bayard, January 16, 1801.
35. Lomask, *Aaron Burr: The Years from Princeton to Vice President,* p. 291.
36. MHi-TPP, reel 47, p. 57.
37. *The New York Times,* August 11, 2000.
38. Lomask, *Aaron Burr: The Years from Princeton to Vice President,* p. 297.
39. Brookhiser, *Gentleman Revolutionary,* p. 167.
40. *PAH,* vol. 25, p. 365, "An Address to the Electors of the State of New York," March 21, 1801.

Thirty-eight: A World Full of Folly

1. *PAH,* vol. 24, p. 220, letter to Elizabeth Hamilton, January 26, 1800.
2. Ibid., vol. 22, p. 251, letter to Elizabeth Hamilton, November 19, 1798.
3. Ibid., vol. 26, p. 69, letter to Richard Peters, December 29, 1802.
4. Ibid., vol. 25, p. 481, letter to Elizabeth Hamilton, possibly February 19, 1801.
5. Ibid., vol. 24, p. 588, letter to Elizabeth Hamilton, June 8, 1800.
6. *The New York Times,* March 26, 1965.
7. *PAH,* vol. 26, p. 69, letter to Richard Peters, December 29, 1802.
8. Ibid., pp. 182–83, "Plan for a Garden," 1803.
9. Ibid., vol. 25, p. 388, letter to William Beekman, June 15, 1801.
10. NYHS-NPP, letter from Elizabeth Hamilton to Nathaniel Pendleton, September 29, 1804.
11. *PAH,* vol. 26, p. 95, letter to Elizabeth Hamilton, March 20, 1803.
12. King, *Life and Correspondence of Rufus King,* vol. 3, p. 459.
13. *PAH,* vol. 25, p. 339, letter to Elizabeth Hamilton, February 20, 1801.
14. Ibid., p. 348, letter to Elizabeth Hamilton, March 16, 1801.
15. Ibid., p. 354, "An Address to the Electors of the State of New York," March 21, 1801.
16. McDonald, *Alexander Hamilton,* p. 353.
17. [Newark] *Centinel of Freedom,* April 28, 1801.
18. *PAH,* vol. 25, p. 376.
19. King, *Life and Correspondence of Rufus King,* vol. 3, p. 459.
20. Ellis, *American Sphinx,* p. 201.
21. Malone, *Jefferson and His Time,* vol. 3, p. 486.
22. Hamilton, *Reminiscences of James A. Hamilton,* p. 23.
23. *Pennsylvania Magazine of History and Biography,* July 1937.

24. Knott, *Alexander Hamilton and the Persistence of Myth,* p. 244.
25. CU-HPPP, box 276, letter from Thomas Jefferson to Joseph Vanmetre, September 4, 1800.
26. Smith, *John Marshall,* p. 303.
27. Ibid.
28. Ibid., p. 11.
29. Ibid.
30. Brookhiser, *Alexander Hamilton,* p. 10.
31. Knott, *Alexander Hamilton and the Persistence of Myth,* p. 17.
32. Lomask, *Aaron Burr: The Conspiracy and Years of Exile,* p. 126.
33. *PAH,* vol. 25, pp. 550–51, "The Examination," no. 14, *New-York Evening Post,* March 2, 1802.
34. Ibid., p. 549.
35. Ibid., pp. 529–30, "The Examination," no. 12, *New-York Evening Post,* February 23, 1802.
36. Ibid., p. 450.
37. MHi-TPP, reel 44, letter from William Coleman to Octavius Pickering, February 15, 1829.
38. Ibid., reel 15, letter from Timothy Pickering to Nicholas Fish, July 30, 1822.
39. CU-HPPP, box 277, letter from William Coleman to Thomas Jefferson, 1801.
40. Nevins, *Evening Post,* p. 17.
41. *Columbia University Quarterly,* March 1938.
42. *New-York Evening Post,* November 25, 1801.
43. Mitchell, *Alexander Hamilton: The National Adventure,* p. 495.
44. Nevins, *Evening Post,* p. 20.
45. Hamilton, *Intimate Life of Alexander Hamilton,* p. 72.
46. Ibid., p. 212.
47. Ibid., p. 103.
48. McDonald, *Alexander Hamilton,* p. 356.
49. King, *Life and Correspondence of Rufus King,* vol. 4, p. 28.
50. Hamilton, *Intimate Life of Alexander Hamilton,* p. 217.
51. Fleming, *Duel,* p. 7.
52. *PAH,* vol. 25, p. 428, letter to Elizabeth Hamilton, October 21, 1801.
53. Mitchell, *Alexander Hamilton: The National Adventure,* p. 496.
54. *American Citizen,* November 26, 1802.
55. *New-York Evening Post,* November 24, 1801.
56. *PAH,* vol. 25, p. 436.
57. *The Historical Magazine,* October 1867.
58. Ibid.
59. *PAH,* vol. 25, p. 437.
60. LC-AHP, reel 30, letter from Dr. David Hosack to John C. Hamilton, January 1, 1833.
61. King, *Life and Correspondence of Rufus King,* vol. 4, p. 28.
62. *The Historical Magazine,* October 1867.
63. Hamilton, *Intimate Life of Alexander Hamilton,* p. 213.
64. Ibid., p. 218.
65. *New-York Evening Post,* November 24, 1801.
66. Ibid.
67. *PAH,* vol. 26, p. 71, letter to Charles Cotesworth Pinckney, December 29, 1802.
68. Kent, *Memoirs and Letters of James Kent,* p. 143.
69. Menz, *Historic Furnishing Report,* p. 20.
70. CU-HFP, box 3, letter from Elizabeth H. Holly to Catharine Cochran, December 16, ca. 1856.
71. King, *Life and Correspondence of Rufus King,* vol. 4, p. 28.
72. *PAH,* vol. 25, p. 584, letter to Benjamin Rush, March 29, 1802.
73. McDonald, *Alexander Hamilton,* p. 356.

Thirty-nine: Pamphlet Wars

1. King, *Life and Correspondence of Rufus King,* vol. 4, p. 103.
2. *PAH,* vol. 25, p. 544, letter to Gouverneur Morris, February 27, 1802.
3. Ibid., p. 496, "The Examination," no. 8, *New-York Evening Post,* January 12, 1802.
4. Ibid., p. 494, "The Examination," no. 7, *New-York Evening Post,* January 7, 1702.
5. Ibid., p. 576, "The Examination," no. 17, *New-York Evening Post,* March 20, 1802.
6. Ibid., p. 605, letter to James A. Bayard, April [16–21], 1802.
7. *PAH,* vol. 2, p. 168, letter to John Laurens, September 11, 1779.
8. Ibid., vol. 17, p. 585, "The Cause of France," 1794, unpublished fragment.
9. "Phocion No. X," *Gazette of the United States,* October 27, 1796.
10. Ibid.
11. *PAH,* vol. 25, p. 583, letter to John Dickinson, March 29, 1802.
12. Ibid., vol. 26, p. 219, letter to an unknown recipient, April 13, 1804.
13. CU-JCHP, box 20.
14. Ibid.
15. Ibid.
16. Davis, *Memoirs of Aaron Burr,* vol. 2, p. 185.
17. Fleming, *Duel,* p. 79.
18. Lomask, *Aaron Burr: The Years from Princeton to Vice President,* p. 307.
19. Ibid., p. 313.
20. *PAH,* vol. 25, p. 587, letter to James A. Bayard, April 6, 1802.
21. Ibid., p. 559, letter to Gouverneur Morris, March 4, 1802.
22. Fleming, *Duel,* p. 83.
23. Mitchell, *Alexander Hamilton: The National Adventure,* p. 525.

24. Latrobe, *Correspondence and Miscellaneous Papers of Benjamin Henry Latrobe*, vol. 2, p. 331.
25. *American Citizen*, April 22, 1803.
26. *PAH*, vol. 26, p. 114.
27. Davis, *Memoirs of Aaron Burr*, vol. 2, p. 316.
28. King, *Life and Correspondence of Rufus King*, vol. 4, p. 121.
29. Cheetham, *Narrative of the Suppression by Col. Burr*, p. 52.
30. Ibid., p. 54.
31. Ibid., p. 18.
32. Freeman, *Affairs of Honor*, p. 167.
33. Lomask, *Aaron Burr: The Years from Princeton to Vice President*, p. 319.
34. Hamilton, *Intimate Life of Alexander Hamilton*, p. 72.
35. Schachner, *Alexander Hamilton*, p. 1.
36. *PAH*, vol. 26, p. 37.
37. McCullough, *John Adams*, p. 578; Brodie, *Thomas Jefferson*, p. 349.
38. Malone, *Jefferson and His Time*, vol. 4, p. 212.
39. Brodie, *Thomas Jefferson*, p. 352.
40. Ibid., p. 360.
41. Malone, *Jefferson and His Time*, vol. 4, p. 231; Brodie, *Thomas Jefferson*, p. 353.
42. Brodie, *Thomas Jefferson*, p. 352.
43. Brookhiser, *America's First Dynasty*, p. 55.
44. Ellis, *Passionate Sage*, p. 115.
45. Brodie, *Thomas Jefferson*, p. 353.
46. *PAH*, vol. 26, p. 36, letter from Philip Schuyler, August 19, 1802.
47. *The William and Mary Quarterly*, 1955.
48. Brodie, *Thomas Jefferson*, p. 356.
49. Ibid., p. 350.
50. Ibid., p. 356.

Forty: The Price of Truth

1. King, *Life and Correspondence of Rufus King*, vol. 4, p. 326.
2. Hamilton, *Federalist*, p. cxi.
3. Kent, *Memoirs and Letters of James Kent*, p. 143.
4. Ibid., p. 317.
5. Ibid., p. 328.
6. Ibid., p. 143.
7. Ibid., p. 33.
8. *PAH*, vol. 26, p. 93, letter to Elizabeth Hamilton, March 13, 1803.
9. Ibid., pp. 94–95, letter to Elizabeth Hamilton, March [16–17], 1803.
10. King, *Life and Correspondence of Rufus King*, vol. 4, p. 135.
11. *The New York Times*, July 3, 2001.
12. Knott, *Alexander Hamilton and the Persistence of Myth*, p. 21; Bailyn, *To Begin the World Anew*, p. 53.
13. *LPAH*, vol. 1, p. 776.
14. Fleming, *Duel*, p. 167.
15. Malone, *Jefferson and His Time*, vol. 4, p. 232.
16. *LPAH*, vol. 1, p. 784.
17. Hamilton, *Intimate Life of Alexander Hamilton*, p. 178.
18. *Speeches at Full Length of Mr. Van Ness*, p. 62.
19. Ibid., p. 64.
20. Ibid., p. 65.
21. Ibid.
22. Ibid., p. 69.
23. Ibid., p. 70.
24. Ibid., p. 76.
25. Ibid., p. 72.
26. Ibid., p. 77.
27. Fleming, *Duel*, p. 175.
28. MHi-TPP, reel 16, p. 340, letter from Thomas Pickering to William Coleman, September 11, 1827.
29. LC-AHP, reel 30, letter from James Kent to Elizabeth Hamilton, December 20, 1832.
30. *The New Criterion*, May 1999.
31. Malone, *Jefferson and His Time*, vol. 4, p. 331.
32. *New-York Evening Post*, February 8, 1803.
33. Ibid., July 5, 1803.
34. Jefferson, *Anas of Thomas Jefferson*, p. 224.
35. Ibid.
36. Jefferson, *Works of Thomas Jefferson*, p. 378.
37. Lomask, *Aaron Burr: The Years from Princeton to Vice President*, p. 341.
38. Biddle, *Autobiography of Charles Biddle*, p. 302.
39. Fleming, *Duel*, p. 209.
40. *American Citizen*, January 6, 1804.
41. Ibid., January 14, 1804.
42. *PAH*, vol. 26, p. 187, "Speech at a Meeting of Federalists in Albany," February 10, 1804.
43. Davis, *Memoirs of Aaron Burr*, vol. 2, p. 277.
44. *American Citizen*, March 1, 1804.
45. *PAH*, vol. 26, p. 193, letter to Robert G. Harper, February 19, 1804.
46. Davis, *Memoirs of Aaron Burr*, vol. 2, p. 293.
47. Strong, *Letters of George W. Strong*, p. 218.
48. *PAH*, vol. 26, p. 200, letter to George Clinton, February 27, 1804.
49. Ibid., p. 210, letter from George Clinton, March 6, 1804.
50. Fleming, *Duel*, p. 228.
51. Lomask, *Aaron Burr: The Years from Princeton to Vice President*, p. 343.
52. Parton, *Life and Times of Aaron Burr*, p. 364.
53. NYPL-KVB, p. v.4.
54. Ibid.
55. Ibid.
56. Ibid.
57. Ibid.
58. Davis, *Memoirs of Aaron Burr*, vol. 2, p. 281.

59. Ibid.
60. Ibid.
61. Steiner, *Life and Correspondence of James McHenry,* p. 530.
62. *PAH,* vol. 26, p. 225, letter to Philip Jeremiah Schuyler, April 20, 1804.
63. Fleming, *Duel,* p. 235.
64. Ellis, *Founding Brothers,* pp. 46–47.
65. Biddle, *Autobiography of Charles Biddle,* p. 309.
66. Parton, *Life and Times of Aaron Burr,* p. 335.
67. Burr, *Political Correspondence and Public Papers of Aaron Burr,* vol. 2, p. 839.
68. Davis, *Memoirs of Aaron Burr,* vol. 2, p. 285.
69. LC-AHP, reel 30, letter from Adam Hoops to James A. Hamilton, March 30, 1829.
70. Ibid.
71. Ibid.
72. Morris, *Diary and Letters of Gouverneur Morris,* p. 454.
73. Malone, *Jefferson and His Time,* vol. 4, p. 403.
74. LC-AHP, reel 30, letter from Major James Fairlie to John Church Hamilton, March 21, 1829.
75. Malone, *Jefferson and His Time,* vol. 4, p. 430.
76. *PAH,* vol. 26, p. 310.

Forty-one: A Despicable Opinion

1. CU-DWCP, reel 1, letter from John Tayler to De Witt Clinton, April 8, 1804.
2. *American Citizen,* July 23, 1804.
3. Fleming, *Duel,* p. 232.
4. NYPL-KVB, p. v.4, letter from Charles D. Cooper to Philip Schuyler, April 23, 1804, quoted in an anonymous handbill.
5. Ibid.
6. *New-York Evening Post,* October 13, 1802.
7. *PAH,* vol. 26, p. 240.
8. Freeman, *Affairs of Honor,* p. 188.
9. Biddle, *Autobiography of Charles Biddle,* p. 305.
10. Lomask, *Aaron Burr: The Years from Princeton to Vice President,* p. 326.
11. Fleming, *Duel,* p. 283.
12. *PAH,* vol. 26, p. 237.
13. Van Doren, *Benjamin Franklin,* p. 711.
14. Sullivan, *Public Men of the Revolution,* p. 266.
15. *PAH,* vol. 24, p. 5, letter to Josiah Ogden Hoffman, November 6, 1799.
16. Biddle, *Autobiography of Charles Biddle,* p. 302.
17. Ogden, *Four Letters on the Death of Alexander Hamilton,* p. 9.
18. *Speeches at Full Length of Mr. Van Ness,* p. 67.
19. NYHS-MM, reel 11, Nathaniel Pendleton, obituary notice for Alexander Hamilton.
20. *PAH,* vol. 26, p. 243, letter from Aaron Burr, June 18, 1804.
21. Ibid., p. 247, "William P. Van Ness's Narrative of the Events of June 18–21, 1804."

22. Ibid.
23. Ibid., p. 248, letter to Aaron Burr, June 20, 1804.
24. Ibid.
25. Ibid., p. 249.
26. Ibid., p. 250, letter from Aaron Burr, June 21, 1804.
27. Ibid., p. 251, "William P. Van Ness's Narrative of the Events of June 22, 1804."
28. Ibid.
29. Ibid., p. 252.
30. Davis, *Memoirs of Aaron Burr,* vol. 2, p. 303.
31. *PAH,* vol. 26, p. 252, "Nathaniel Pendleton's Narrative of the Events of June 22, 1804."
32. Ibid., p. 264, "William P. Van Ness's Narrative of Later Events of June 25, 1804."
33. Ibid., p. 253, letter to Aaron Burr, June 22, 1804.
34. Ibid., vol. 19, p. 397, letter to George Washington, November 5, 1795.
35. Fleming, *Duel,* p. 347.
36. LC-WPP, reel 1, diary entry of March 15, 1806.
37. *PAH,* vol. 26, pp. 255–56, letter from Aaron Burr, June 22, 1804.
38. Ibid., p. 260, "Nathaniel Pendleton's Narrative of the Events of June 23–25, 1804."
39. Ibid., p. 257, "Aaron Burr's Instructions to William P. Van Ness," June 22–23, 1804.
40. Ibid., p. 261, "Nathaniel Pendleton's First Account of Alexander Hamilton's Conversation at John Tayler's House," June 25, 1804.
41. Ibid., p. 264, "William P. Van Ness's Narrative of the Events of June 25, 1804"; ibid., p. 265, letter from Aaron Burr to William P. Van Ness, June 25, 1804.
42. Ibid, p. 271, letter from Nathaniel Pendleton to William P. Van Ness, June 26, 1804.
43. Ibid., p. 278, "Remarks on the Letter of June 27, 1804."
44. *New-York Evening Post,* November 28, 1801.
45. Freeman, *Affairs of Honor,* p. 163.
46. King, *Life and Correspondence of Rufus King,* vol. 4, p. 396.
47. Knott, *Alexander Hamilton and the Persistence of Myth,* p. 17.
48. *The William and Mary Quarterly,* April 1996.
49. Kennedy, *Burr, Hamilton, and Jefferson,* p. 12.
50. Ellis, *Founding Brothers,* p. 23.
51. Ogden, *Four Letters on the Death of Alexander Hamilton,* p. 15.
52. *The William and Mary Quarterly,* April 1996.
53. *PAH,* vol. 24, p. 299, letter to Henry Lee, March 7, 1800.
54. LC-AHP, reel 30, letter from Robert Troup to Timothy Pickering, March 31, 1828.
55. Ibid.
56. *The Balance and Columbian Repository,* August 14, 1804.
57. Van Vechten, *Memoirs of John Mason,* p. 187.

58. J. P. Morgan Chase Archives, RG 11, letter from John B. Church to Philip Church, July 16, 1804, New York, N.Y.
59. Biddle, *Autobiography of Charles Biddle*, p. 303.
60. Strong, *Letters of George W. Strong*, p. 16.
61. Biddle, *Autobiography of Charles Biddle*, p. 303.
62. Ellis, *Founding Brothers*, p. 36.
63. Parton, *Life and Times of Aaron Burr*, p. 348.
64. *PAH*, vol. 26, p. 281, letter to James A. Hamilton, June 1804.
65. Ibid., p. 282.
66. CU-JCHP, box 20.
67. *PAH*, vol. 26, p. 288, "Statement of My Property and Debts, July 1, 1804."
68. Ibid., p. 289.
69. Ibid.
70. Ibid., p. 280, "Statement on Impending Duel with Aaron Burr," June 28–July 10, 1804.
71. Ibid., p. 279.
72. Ibid.
73. Ibid., p. 280.
74. Parton, *Life and Times of Aaron Burr*, p. 617.

Forty-two: Fatal Errand

1. *PAH*, vol. 26, p. 310.
2. Ibid., p. 311.
3. Ibid., p. 305, "Last Will and Testament of Alexander Hamilton," July 9, 1804.
4. Ibid.
5. Ibid.
6. Ibid., p. 300, letter from Aaron Burr to William P. Van Ness, July 9, 1804.
7. Ibid., p. 301.
8. Mitchell, *Alexander Hamilton: The National Adventure*, p. 533.
9. L. Tom Perry Special Collections Library, Brigham Young University, Provo, Utah, Weir Family Papers, Vault Manuscripts 51, box 1, folder 11, letter from Dirck Ten Broeck to Abraham Ten Broeck, July 12, 1804.
10. *PAH*, vol. 26, p. 311.
11. LC-AHP, reel 31, "Robert Troup Memoir of General Hamilton," March 22, 1821.
12. *New-York Evening Post*, July 19, 1804.
13. *PAH*, vol. 26, p. 309, letter to Theodore Sedgwick, July 10, 1804.
14. Ibid.
15. Ibid., p. 307, letter to Elizabeth Hamilton, July 10, 1804.
16. Ibid., p. 308.
17. Ibid.
18. Hamilton, *Life of Alexander Hamilton*, vol. 7, p. 802.
19. Parton, *Life and Times of Aaron Burr*, p. 347.
20. Davis, *Memoirs of Aaron Burr*, vol. 2, p. 322.
21. Ibid.

22. Biddle, *Autobiography of Charles Biddle*, p. 309.
23. Freeman, *Affairs of Honor*, p. 192.
24. CU-JCHP, box 24.
25. Ogden, *Four Letters on the Death of Alexander Hamilton*, p. 8.
26. CU-JCHP, box 24.
27. Mitchell, *Alexander Hamilton: The National Adventure*, p. 534.
28. Lomask, *Aaron Burr: The Years from Princeton to Vice President*, p. 354.
29. *New-York Evening Post*, July 19, 1804.
30. NYHS-WVNP, "Duel Papers," letter from William Van Ness to Charles Biddle, n.d.
31. Ibid.
32. Parton, *Life and Times of Aaron Burr*, p. 617.
33. Burr, *Political Correspondence and Public Papers of Aaron Burr*, vol. 2, p. 887.
34. Ellis, *Founding Brothers*, p. 40.
35. Burr, *Political Correspondence and Public Papers of Aaron Burr*, vol. 2, p. 884.
36. Ibid., p. 887.
37. NYHS-WVNP, "Duel Papers," letter from William Van Ness to Charles Biddle, n.d.
38. LC-AHP, reel 33, letter from William Van Ness to an unnamed recipient, n.d.
39. Parton, *Life and Times of Aaron Burr*, p. 617.
40. *PAH*, vol. 26, p. 344, letter from David Hosack to William Coleman, August 17, 1804.
41. Ibid., p. 345.
42. Ibid.
43. Fleming, *Duel*, p. 325.
44. *PAH*, vol. 26, p. 345, letter from David Hosack to William Coleman, August 17, 1804.
45. Ibid.
46. Parton, *Life and Times of Aaron Burr*, p. 346.
47. L. Tom Perry Special Collections Library, Brigham Young University, Provo, Utah, Weir Family Papers, Vault Manuscripts 51, box 1, folder 11, letter from Dirck Ten Broeck to Abraham Ten Broeck, July 12, 1804.
48. Ogden, *Four Letters on the Death of Alexander Hamilton*, p. 7.
49. *PAH*, vol. 26, p. 317.
50. Ibid., p. 346, letter from David Hosack to William Coleman, August 17, 1804.
51. Ibid., p. 345.
52. Ogden, *Four Letters on the Death of Alexander Hamilton*, pp. 9–10.
53. Phelan, *Man Who Owned the Pistols*, p. 111.
54. Hamilton, *Intimate Life of Alexander Hamilton*, p. 404.
55. *PAH*, vol. 25, p. 403, letter to Rufus King, July 28, 1801.
56. Van Vechten, *Memoirs of John Mason*, p. 182.
57. Ibid.
58. Ibid., p. 183.

59. Ibid.
60. Ibid., p. 184.
61. Ogden, *Four Letters on the Death of Alexander Hamilton*, p. 8.
62. *PAH*, vol. 26, p. 315, letter from Benjamin Moore to William Coleman, July 12, 1804.
63. Ibid.
64. Ibid., p. 316.
65. Ibid., p. 347, letter from David Hosack to William Coleman, August 17, 1804.
66. Ogden, *Four Letters on the Death of Alexander Hamilton*, p. 11.
67. Fleming, *Duel*, p. 331.
68. Brookhiser, *Gentleman Revolutionary*, p. 173.
69. Hamilton, *Federalist*, p. lxxxix.
70. Hamilton, *Intimate Life of Alexander Hamilton*, pp. 405–6.
71. Ogden, *Four Letters on the Death of Alexander Hamilton*, p. 12.
72. *PAH*, vol. 26, p. 293, letter to Elizabeth Hamilton, July 4, 1804.

Forty-three: The Melting Scene

1. King, *Life and Correspondence of Rufus King*, vol. 4, p. 575.
2. Biddle, *Autobiography of Charles Biddle*, p. 302.
3. McDonald, *Sermon on the Premature and Lamented Death of General Alexander Hamilton*, p. 14.
4. Knott, *Alexander Hamilton and the Persistence of Myth*, p. 49.
5. Brookhiser, *Gentleman Revolutionary*, p. 173.
6. Knott, *Alexander Hamilton and the Persistence of Myth*, p. 2.
7. Ogden, *Four Letters on the Death of Alexander Hamilton*, p. 13.
8. Freeman, *Affairs of Honor*, p. 191.
9. Morris, *Diary and Letters of Gouverneur Morris*, pp. 456–57.
10. Ibid., p. 458.
11. Ibid., p. 457.
12. *PAH*, vol. 26, p. 324.
13. *New-York Evening Post*, July 17, 1804.
14. *American Citizen*, July 16, 1804.
15. Knott, *Alexander Hamilton and the Persistence of Myth*, p. 2.
16. Bowen, *Miracle at Philadelphia*, p. 111.
17. Van Vechten, *Memoirs of John Mason*, p. 187.
18. Hamilton, *Intimate Life of Alexander Hamilton*, p. 422.
19. Malone, *Jefferson and His Time*, vol. 4, p. 426.
20. Knott, *Alexander Hamilton and the Persistence of Myth*, p. 19.
21. Ibid., p. 13.
22. Malone, *Jefferson and His Time*, vol. 4, p. 425.
23. Parton, *Life and Times of Aaron Burr*, p. 364.
24. Biddle, *Autobiography of Charles Biddle*, p. 305.

25. L. Tom Perry Special Collections Library, Brigham Young University, Provo, Utah, Weir Family Papers, Vault Manuscripts 51, box 1, folder 11, letter from Dirck Ten Broeck to Abraham Ten Broeck, July 12, 1804.
26. *The Balance and Columbian Repository*, August 14, 1804.
27. Parton, *Life and Times of Aaron Burr*, p. 358.
28. LC-AHP, reel 31, "Remembrancer," New York *Mirror*, n.d.
29. *Journal of the Early Republic*, spring 1995.
30. Ibid.
31. Davis, *Memoirs of Aaron Burr*, vol. 2, p. 327.
32. Burr, *Political Correspondence and Public Papers of Aaron Burr*, vol. 2, p. 885.
33. Ibid., p. 884.
34. Davis, *Memoirs of Aaron Burr*, vol. 2, p. 328.
35. Lomask, *Aaron Burr: The Years from Princeton to Vice President*, p. 357.
36. Lomask, *Aaron Burr: The Conspiracy and Years of Exile*, p. 29.
37. Parton, *Life and Times of Aaron Burr*, p. 358.
38. Lomask, *Aaron Burr: The Years from Princeton to Vice President*, p. 358.
39. Fleming, *Duel*, p. 352.
40. Lomask, *Aaron Burr: The Years from Princeton to Vice President*, p. 360.
41. Ibid., p. 361.
42. Fleming, *Duel*, p. 357.
43. Burr, *Political Correspondence and Public Papers of Aaron Burr*, vol. 2, p. 818.
44. Freeman, *Affairs of Honor*, p. 178.
45. Burr, *Political Correspondence and Public Papers of Aaron Burr*, vol. 2, p. 899.
46. Ibid., p. 896.
47. Adams, *Diary of John Quincy Adams*, p. 32.
48. Fleming, *Duel*, p. 369.
49. Lomask, *Aaron Burr: The Conspiracy and Years of Exile*, p. 48.
50. Davis, *Memoirs of Aaron Burr*, vol. 2, p. 365.
51. Smith, *John Marshall*, p. 362.
52. Hamilton, *Intimate Life of Alexander Hamilton*, p. 427.
53. Lomask, *Aaron Burr: The Conspiracy and Years of Exile*, p. 309.
54. "Life Portraits of Alexander Hamilton," *The William and Mary Quarterly*, April 1955.
55. Lomask, *Aaron Burr: The Conspiracy and Years of Exile*, p. 364.
56. Ibid., p. 372.
57. Kent, *Memoirs and Letters of James Kent*, p. 36.
58. Hamilton, *Intimate Life of Alexander Hamilton*, pp. 427–28.
59. Knott, *Alexander Hamilton and the Persistence of Myth*, p. 50.
60. Parton, *Life and Times of Aaron Burr*, p. 616.

61. Fleming, *Duel,* p. 404.
62. *The New Republic,* June 13, 1983.

Epilogue: Eliza

1. Hamilton, *Intimate Life of Alexander Hamilton,* p. 411.
2. LC-AHP, reel 30, letter from Elizabeth Hamilton to William S. Smith, August 11, 1804.
3. NYHS-NPP, letter from Elizabeth Hamilton to Nathaniel Pendleton, September 20, 1804.
4. King, *Life and Correspondence of Rufus King,* vol. 4, pp. 403–4.
5. NYHS-NPP.
6. *PAH,* vol. 3, p. 506, "Petition to the New York Legislature," February 4, 1784.
7. NYHS-MM, letter from Elizabeth Hamilton to Philip Schuyler, January 9, 1813; Hamilton, *Intimate Life of Alexander Hamilton,* p. 140.
8. NYHS-NPP, letter from Elizabeth Hamilton to George Cabot, September 20, 1804.
9. Ibid., letter from Elizabeth Hamilton to Nathaniel Pendleton, September 17, 1804.
10. Emery, *Alexander Hamilton,* p. 246.
11. Bethune, *Memoirs of Mrs. Joanna Bethune,* p. 116.
12. Hamilton, *Intimate Life of Alexander Hamilton,* p. 115.
13. Ibid., p. 116.
14. Ibid., p. 117.
15. Ibid.
16. Matthews, *Short History of the Orphan Asylum Society in the City of New York,* p. 12.
17. Frémont, *Souvenirs of My Time,* p. 117.
18. Hamilton, *Reminiscences of James A. Hamilton,* p. 65.
19. Bethune, *Memoirs of Mrs. Joanna Bethune,* p. 111.
20. Frémont, *Souvenirs of My Time,* p. 117.
21. Ibid., p. 120.
22. Ibid., p. 118.
23. Ibid., p. 115.
24. Knott, *Alexander Hamilton and the Persistence of Myth,* p. 242.
25. Baxter, *Godchild of Washington,* p. 222.
26. NYHS-DGFP, letter from Elizabeth Hawley to her aunt, January 4, 1853.
27. LC-AHP, reel 32.

Bibliography

Selected Books, Pamphlets, and Dissertations

Abercrombie, James. *A Sermon, Occasioned by the Death of Major Gen. Alexander Hamilton.* Philadelphia: H. Maxwell, 1804.

An Account of the Late Dreadful Hurricane, Which Happened on the 31st of August, 1772. St. Christopher: Thomas Howe, 1772.

Adams, Abigail. *New Letters of Abigail Adams, 1788–1801.* Ed. Stewart Mitchell. Boston: Houghton Mifflin, 1947.

Adams, John. *Correspondence Between the Hon. John Adams, and the Late Wm. Cunningham, Esq.* Boston: True and Greene, 1823.

———. *Old Family Letters: Series A. Letters from John Adams to Dr. Benjamin Rush.* Philadelphia: J. B. Lippincott, 1892.

———. *Statesman and Friend: Correspondence of John Adams with Benjamin Waterhouse, 1784–1822.* Ed. Worthington Chauncey Ford. Boston: Little, Brown, 1927.

Adams, John Quincy. *The Diary of John Quincy Adams, 1794–1845.* Ed. Allan Nevins. New York: Charles Scribner's Sons, 1951.

Ames, Fisher. *A Sketch of the Character of Alexander Hamilton.* Boston: Repertory Office, 1804.

Ammon, Harry. *James Monroe: The Quest for National Identity.* Charlottesville: University Press of Virginia, 1990 [1971].

Anderson, James R. *The Provosts of Glasgow from 1609 to 1832.* Glasgow: James Hedderwick and Sons, [n.d.]. Copy in the Mitchell Library, Glasgow, Scotland.

Andrews, Evangeline Walker, ed. *Journal of a Lady of Quality; Being the Narrative of a Journey from Scotland to the West Indies, North Carolina, and Portugal, in the Years 1774 to 1776.* New Haven: Yale University Press, 1921.

Aptheker, Herbert. *American Negro Slave Revolts.* New York: International Publishers, 1983.

Atherton, Gertrude. *Adventures of a Novelist.* New York: Liveright, 1932.

Bailyn, Bernard. *The Ideological Origins of the American Revolution.* Cambridge, Mass.: Harvard University Press, 1992 [1967].

———. *To Begin the World Anew: The Genius and Ambiguities of the American Founders.* New York: Alfred A. Knopf, 2003.

Baxter, Katharine Schuyler. *A Godchild of Washington.* London: F. Tennyson Neely, 1898.

Ben-Atar, Doron, and Barbara B. Oberg. *Federalists Reconsidered.* Charlottesville: University Press of Virginia, 1998.

Bentham, Jeremy. *The Correspondence of Jeremy Bentham.* Vols. 7 and 8. Ed. J. R. Dinwiddy, Stephen Conway, et al. Oxford: Clarendon Press, 1988.

Bergh, Albert Ellery, ed. *The Writings of Thomas Jefferson.* Vol. 11. Washington, D.C.: Thomas Jefferson Memorial Association, 1907.

Berkin, Carol. *A Brilliant Solution: Inventing the American Constitution.* New York: Harcourt, 2002.

Berrian, William. *Recollections of Departed Friends.* New York: Stanford and Sword, 1850.

Bethune, George W. *Memoirs of Mrs. Joanna Bethune.* New York: Harper and Brothers, 1863.

Biddle, Charles. *Autobiography of Charles Biddle, Vice-President of the Supreme Executive Council of Pennsylvania.* Philadelphia: E. Claxton, 1883.

Bobrick, Benson. *Angel in the Whirlwind: The Triumph of the American Revolution.* New York: Simon & Schuster, 1997.

Bowen, Catherine Drinker. *Miracle at Philadelphia: The Story of the Constitutional Convention May to September 1787.* Boston: Back Bay Books, 1986 [1966].

Boyd, Julian P. *Number 7: Alexander Hamilton's Secret Attempt to Control American Foreign Policy.* Princeton, N.J.: Princeton University Press, 1964.

Brandt, Clare. *An American Aristocracy: The Livingstons.* Poughkeepsie, N.Y: n.p., 1990 [1986].

Brodie, Fawn M. *Thomas Jefferson: An Intimate History.* New York: W. W. Norton, 1974.

Brookhiser, Richard. *Alexander Hamilton, American.* New York: Free Press, 1999.

———. *America's First Dynasty: The Adamses, 1735–1918.* New York: Free Press, 2002.

———. *Gentleman Revolutionary: Gouverneur Morris, the Rake Who Wrote the Constitution.* New York: Free Press, 2003.

Brooks, Geraldine. *Dames and Daughters of Colonial Days.* New York: Thomas Y. Crowell, 1900.

Burke, Edmund. *Reflections on the Revolution in France.* Indianapolis: Hackett, 1987 [1790].

Burr, Aaron. *Political Correspondence and Public Papers of Aaron Burr.* 2 vols. Ed. Mary-Jo Kline et al. Princeton, N.J.: Princeton University Press, 1983.

Burrows, Edwin G., and Mike Wallace. *Gotham: A History of New York City to 1898.* New York: Oxford University Press, 1999.

Butzner, Jane, ed. *Constitutional Chaff—Rejected Suggestions of the Constitutional Convention of 1787.* New York: Columbia University Press, 1941.

Callahan, North. *Henry Knox: General Washington's General.* New York: Rinehart, 1958.

———. *Royal Raiders: The Tories of the American Revolution.* New York: Bobbs-Merrill, 1963.

Callender, James Thomson. *The History of the United States for 1796.* Philadelphia: Snowden and McCorkle, 1797.

Callender, Tom (probably James Thomson Callender). *Letters to Alexander Hamilton, King of the Feds.* New York: Richard Reynolds, 1802.

Castle, Colin M. *John Glassford of Douglaston.* Glasgow: Milngavie and Bearsden Historical Society, 1989.

Chastellux, marquis de. *Travels in North America in the Years 1780, 1781, and 1782.* Vol. 1. New York: Arno Press, 1968.

Cheetham, James. *A Narrative of the Suppression by Col. Burr, of the History of the Administration of John Adams, Late President of the United States.* New York: Denniston and Cheetham, 1802.

Colimore, Edward. *The* Philadelphia Inquirer's *Guide to Historic Philadelphia.* Philadelphia: Camino Books, 2001.

Cooke, Jacob E. *Alexander Hamilton: A Profile.* New York: Hill and Wang, 1967.

Cooper, Duff. *Talleyrand.* New York: Grove Press, 1997 [1932].

Cunningham, Anna K. *Schuyler Mansion: A Critical Catalogue of the Furnishings and Decorations.* Albany: New York State Education Department, 1955.

Cunningham, William. *A Letter to an Ex-President of the United States.* Leominster, Mass.: Salmon Wilder, 1812.

Custis, George Washington Parke. *Recollections and Private Memoirs of Washington.* Philadelphia: J. W. Bradley, 1861.

Daiches, David. *Glasgow.* London: Andre Deutsch, 1977.

Dasent, Sir John Roche. *A West Indian Planter's Family: Its Rise and Fall.* Edinburgh: David Douglas, 1914.

Davis, Joseph Stancliffe. *Essays in the Earlier History of American Corporations.* New York: Russell and Russell, 1965.

Davis, Matthew L. *Memoirs of Aaron Burr: With Miscellaneous Selections from His Correspondence.* 2 vols. Freeport, N.Y.: Books for Libraries Press, 1970 [1836].

Day, Stacey B. *Edward Stevens: Gastric Physiologist, Physician, and American Statesman.* Cincinnati: Cultural and Educational Productions, 1969.

de Beaufort, Raphael, trans. *Memoirs of the Prince de Talleyrand.* Vol. 1. New York: AMS Press, 1973.

Devine, T. M. *The Tobacco Lords: A Study of the Tobacco Merchants of Glasgow and Their Trading Activities c. 1740–90.* Edinburgh: John Donald, 1975.

Domett, Henry W. *A History of the Bank of New York, 1784–1884.* New York: Greenwood Press, 1884.

Drinker, Elizabeth. *The Diary of Elizabeth Drinker.* Vols. 2 and 3. Ed. Elaine Forman Crane et al. Boston: Northeastern University Press, 1991.

Duncan, William Cary. *The Amazing Madame Jumel.* New York: Frederick A. Stokes, 1935.

Elkins, Stanley, and Eric McKitrick. *The Age of Federalism: The Early American Republic, 1788–1800.* New York: Oxford University Press, 1995 [1993].

Ellis, Joseph J. *American Sphinx: The Character of Thomas Jefferson.* New York: Vintage Books, 1998 [1996].

———. *Founding Brothers: The Revolutionary Generation.* New York: Alfred A. Knopf, 2000.

———. *Passionate Sage: The Character and Legacy of John Adams.* New York: W. W. Norton, 1994 [1993].

Emery, Noemie. *Alexander Hamilton.* New York: G. P. Putnam's Sons, 1982.

Ernst, Robert. *Rufus King: American Federalist.* Chapel Hill: University of North Carolina Press, 1968.

Extract from the Proceedings of the New-York State Society, of the Cincinnati, Convened on the 4th of July, 1786. New York: n.p., 1786.

Ferling, John. *John Adams: A Life.* New York: Henry Holt, 1996 [1992].

Findley, William. *History of the Insurrection in the Four Western Counties of Pennsylvania: In the Year M.DCC.XCIV.* Philadelphia: Samuel Harrison Smith, 1796.

Fleming, Thomas. *Duel: Alexander Hamilton, Aaron Burr, and the Future of America.* New York: Basic Books, 1999.

Fleming, Thomas, introd. In *Rags to Riches: The Financing of America, 1776–1836.* New York: Museum of American Financial History, 1998.

Flexner, James Thomas. *Washington: The Indispensable Man.* Boston: Back Bay Books, 1974 [1969].

———. *The Young Hamilton: A Biography.* New York: Fordham University Press, 1997 [1978].

Foreman, Amanda. *Georgiana: Duchess of Devonshire.* New York: Random House, 1998.

Freeman, Joanne B. *Affairs of Honor: National Politics in the New Republic.* New Haven: Yale University Press, 2001.

Frémont, Jessie Benton. *Souvenirs of My Time.* Boston: D. Lothrop, 1887.

Furnas, J. C. *The Americans: A Social History of the United States, 1587–1914.* New York: G. P. Putnam's Sons, 1969.

Gerlach, Don R. *Proud Patriot: Philip Schuyler and the War of Independence, 1775–1783.* Syracuse, N.Y.: Syracuse University Press, 1987.

Gibson, John. *The History of Glasgow.* Glasgow: Rob. Chapman and Alex. Duncan, 1777.

Gordon, John Steele. *The Business of America.* New York: Walker, 2001.

———. *Hamilton's Blessing: The Extraordinary Life and Times of Our National Debt.* New York: Walker, 1997.

Gottschalk, Louis, ed. *The Letters of Lafayette to Washington, 1777–1799.* New York: H. F. Hubbard, 1944.

Grafton, John. *The Declaration of Independence and Other Great Documents of American History, 1775–1865.* Mineola, N.Y.: Dover, 2000.

Graydon, Alexander. *Memoirs of His Own Time.* Philadelphia: Lindsay and Blakiston, 1846.

Hamilton, Alexander. *The Law Practice of Alexander Hamilton: Documents and Commentary.* 5 vols. Ed. Julius Goebel, Jr., et al. New York: Columbia University Press, 1964–1981.

———. *The Papers of Alexander Hamilton.* 27 vols. Ed. Harold C. Syrett and Jacob E. Cooke. New York: Columbia University Press, 1961–1987.

———. *Writings.* Ed. Joanne B. Freeman. New York: Library of America, 2001.

Hamilton, Allan McLane. *The Intimate Life of Alexander Hamilton.* New York: Charles Scribner's Sons, 1911.

———. *Recollections of an Alienist, Personal and Professional.* New York: George H. Doran, 1916.

Hamilton, George. *A History of the House of Hamilton.* Edinburgh: J. Skinner, 1933.

Hamilton, James A. *Reminiscences of James A. Hamilton.* New York: Charles Scribner, 1869.

Hamilton, John C. *Life of Alexander Hamilton.* 7 vols. Boston: Houghton, Osgood, 1879 [1841–1864].

Hamilton, John C., ed. *The Federalist: A Commentary on the Constitution of the United States.* Washington, D.C.: Regnery, 1947.

Harcourt, Felice, ed. and trans. *Memoirs of Madame de la Tour du Pin (1770–1853).* London: Harvill Press, 1969 [1913].

Hibbert, Christopher. *George III: A Personal History.* New York: Basic Books, 1998.

Howell, T. B., ed. *A Complete Collection of State Trials and Proceedings for High Treason and Other Crimes and Misdemeanors.* Vol. 18, *1743–1753.* London: T. C. Hansard, 1813.

Hubbard, Vincent K. *Swords, Ships, and Sugar: History of Nevis to 1900.* Corvallis, Oreg.: Premiere Editions International, 1998.

Humphreys, Mary Gay. *Catherine Schuyler.* New York: Charles Scribner's Sons, 1897.

Isaacson, Walter. *Benjamin Franklin: An American Life.* New York: Simon & Schuster, 2003.

Jay, John. *An Address to the People of the State of New-York, on the Subject of the Constitution, Agreed upon at Philadelphia, the 17th of September, 1787.* New York: Samuel and John Loudon, 1797.

Jefferson, Thomas. *The Anas of Thomas Jefferson.* Ed. Franklin B. Sawvel. New York: Da Capo Press, 1970.

———. *The Papers of Thomas Jefferson.* Vol. 2, *January 1 to August 6, 1787.* Ed. Julian Boyd. Princeton, N.J.: Princeton University Press, 1955.

———. *The Papers of Thomas Jefferson.* Vol. 18, *November 4 , 1790, to January 24, 1791.* Ed. Julian Boyd. Princeton, N.J.: Princeton University Press, 1976.

———. *The Papers of Thomas Jefferson.* Vol. 24, *June 1 to December 31, 1792.* Ed. John Catanzariti. Princeton, N.J.: Princeton University Press, 1990.

———. *The Works of Thomas Jefferson.* Vol. 1. Ed. Paul Leicester Ford. New York: G. P. Putnam's Sons, 1904.

Jouve, Daniel. *Paris: Birthplace of the U.S.A., a Walking Guide.* Paris: Grund, 1995.

Kaminski, John P. *George Clinton: Yeoman Politician of the New Republic.* Madison, Wisc.: Madison House, 1993.

Kennedy, Roger G. *Burr, Hamilton, and Jefferson: A*

Study in Character. New York: Oxford University Press, 2000 [1999].

Kent, James. *Anniversary Discourse, Delivered before the New-York Historical Society.* New York: G. and C. Carvill, 1829.

Kent, William, ed. *Memoirs and Letters of James Kent.* Boston: Little, Brown, 1898.

Ketcham, Ralph. *James Madison: A Biography.* Charlottesville: University Press of Virginia, 1990 [1971].

King, Rufus. *The Life and Correspondence of Rufus King.* Vols. 1–6. Ed. Charles R. King. New York: G. P. Putnam's Sons, 1894.

Knott, Stephen F. *Alexander Hamilton and the Persistence of Myth.* Lawrence: University Press of Kansas, 2002.

Knox, Hugh. *Letter to the Rev. Mr. Jacob Green, of New Jersey.* New York: T. and J. Swords, 1809.

Lafayette, marquis de. *Lafayette in the American Revolution: Selected Letters and Papers, 1776–1790.* Vols. 3–5. Ed. Stanley J. Idzerda et al. Ithaca: Cornell University Press, 1980, 1981, 1983.

Latrobe, Benjamin Henry. *The Correspondence and Miscellaneous Papers of Benjamin Henry Latrobe.* 2 vols. Ed. John C. Van Horne et al. New Haven: Yale University Press, 1984.

———. *The Virginia Journals of Benjamin Henry Latrobe.* 3 vols. Ed. Edward C. Carter II et al. New Haven: Yale University Press, 1977.

Laurens, Henry. *The Papers of Henry Laurens.* Vols. 7, 8, and 11. Ed. George C. Rogers, Jr., and David R. Chesnutt. Columbia: University of South Carolina Press, 1979.

Lawaetz, Erik J. *St. Croix: 500 Years, Pre-Columbus to 1900.* Herning, Denmark: Poul Kristensen, 1991.

Lee, Charles. *The Charles Lee Papers.* Vol. 3, *1778–1782. Collections of the New-York Historical Society for the Year 1873.* New York: printed for the Society, 1874.

Lind, Michael, ed. *Hamilton's Republic: Readings in the American Democratic Nationalist Tradition.* New York: Free Press, 1997.

Livingston, William. *The Papers of William Livingston.* 5 vols. Ed. Carl E. Prince et al. New Brunswick, N.J.: Rutgers University Press, 1979–1988.

Lodge, Henry Cabot. *Alexander Hamilton.* American Statesmen Series. New York: Chelsea House, 1980.

Lomask, Milton. *Aaron Burr: The Conspiracy and Years of Exile, 1805–1836.* New York: Farrar, Straus and Giroux, 1982.

———. *Aaron Burr: The Years from Princeton to Vice President, 1756–1805.* New York: Farrar, Straus and Giroux, 1979.

Lossing, Benson J. *Hours with the Living Men and Women of the Revolution.* New York: Funk and Wagnalls, 1889.

McCullough, David. *John Adams.* New York: Simon & Schuster, 2001.

McDonald, Forrest. *Alexander Hamilton: A Biography.* New York: W. W. Norton, 1982 [1979].

McDonald, John. *Sermon on the Premature and Lamented Death of General Alexander Hamilton.* Boston: John Barber, 1804.

McDonough, Daniel J. *Christopher Gadsden and Henry Laurens: The Parallel Lives of Two American Patriots.* Sellinsgrove, Pa.: Susquehanna University Press, 2000.

Maclay, William. *Journal of William Maclay: United States Senator from Pennsylvania, 1789–1791.* Ed. Edgar S. Maclay. New York: D. Appleton, 1890.

McNamara, Peter. *Political Economy and Statesmanship: Smith, Hamilton, and the Foundation of the Commercial Republic.* DeKalb: Northern Illinois University Press, 1998.

Madison, James. *The Papers of James Madison: Presidential Series.* Vol. 1, *March 1–September 30, 1809.* Ed. Robert A. Rutland, Robert J. Brugger, et al. Charlottesville: University Press of Virginia, 1984.

———. *The Papers of James Madison: Presidential Series.* Vol. 2, *October 1, 1809–November 2, 1810.* Ed. J.C.A. Stagg, Jeanne Kerr Cross, and Susan Holbrook Perdue. Charlottesville: University Press of Virginia, 1992.

———. *The Papers of James Madison.* Vol. 10. Ed. Robert A. Rutland et al. Chicago: University of Chicago Press, 1977.

———. *The Papers of James Madison.* Vol. 11. Ed. Robert A. Rutland et al. Charlottesville: University Press of Virginia, 1977.

———. *The Papers of James Madison,* Vols. 12 and 13. Ed. Charles F. Hobson et al. Charlottesville: University Press of Virginia, 1979, 1981.

———. *The Papers of James Madison.* Vol. 16. Ed. J.C.A. Stagg et al. Charlottesville: University Press of Virginia, 1989.

Maier, Pauline. *American Scripture: Making the Declaration of Independence.* New York: Random House, 1998 [1997].

Malone, Dumas. *Jefferson and His Time.* 6 vols. Boston: Little, Brown, 1948–81.

Marsh, Philip M., ed. *Monroe's Defense of Jefferson and Freneau Against Hamilton.* Oxford, Ohio: self-published, 1948.

Matthews, Joanna H. *A Short History of the Orphan Asylum Society in the City of New York.* New York: Anson D. F. Randolph, 1893.

Mead, Walter Russell. *Special Providence: American Foreign Policy and How It Changed the World.* New York: Alfred A. Knopf, 2001.

Meleny, John C. *The Public Life of Aedanus Burke: Revolutionary Republican in Post-Revolutionary South Carolina.* Columbia: University of South Carolina Press, 1989.

Menz, Katherine B. *Historic Furnishing Report, Hamilton Grange National Monument.* Harpers Ferry Center: National Park Service, U.S. Department of the Interior, 1986.

Miller, John C. *Alexander Hamilton: Portrait in Paradox.* New York: Harper and Brothers, 1959.

Miller, Samuel. *Memoirs of the Rev. John Rodgers, D.D.* New York: Whiting and Watson, 1813.

Mitchell, Broadus. *Alexander Hamilton: The National Adventure, 1788–1804.* New York: Macmillan, 1962.

———. *Alexander Hamilton: Youth to Maturity, 1755–1788.* New York: Macmillan, 1957.

Monaghan, Frank. *John Jay.* New York: Bobbs-Merrill, 1935.

Morgan, Edmund S. *Benjamin Franklin.* New Haven: Yale University Press, 2002.

Morison, Samuel Eliot. *Harrison Gray Otis: The Urbane Federalist.* Boston: Houghton Mifflin, 1969.

Morris, Anne Cary, ed. *The Diary and Letters of Gouverneur Morris.* Vol. 2. New York: Da Capo Press, 1970.

Muldoon, Sylvan J. *Alexander Hamilton's Pioneer Son: The Life and Times of Colonel William Stephen Hamilton, 1797–1850.* Harrisburg, Pa.: Aurand Press, 1930.

Nevins, Allan. *The Evening Post: A Century of Journalism.* New York: Boni and Liveright, 1922.

———. *History of the Bank of New York and Trust Company 1784 to 1934.* New York: privately printed, 1934.

Oakley, C. A. *Our Illustrious Forebears.* London: Blackie and Son, 1980.

O'Brien, Michael J. *Hercules Mulligan: Confidential Correspondent of General Washington.* New York: P. J. Kennedy and Sons, 1937.

Odell, Mrs. Jonathan, et al. *Origin and History of the Orphan Asylum Society in the City of New York, 1806–1896.* Vol. 1. New York: Bonnell, Silver, n.d.

Ogden, David B. *Four Letters on the Death of Alexander Hamilton, 1804; Found in the Papers of William Meredith of Philadelphia.* Portland, Me.: Anthoensen Press, 1980.

Oliver, Vere Langford. *Caribbeana: Relating to the History, Genealogy, Topography, and Antiquities of the British West Indies.* 6 vols. London: Mitchell Hughes and Clarke, 1910–1919.

Otis, Harrison G. *Eulogy on Alexander Hamilton Pronounced at the Request of the Citizens of Boston, July 26, 1804.* Boston: Manning and Loring, 1804.

Parker, Cortlandt. *Alexander Hamilton and William Paterson.* Philadelphia: E. C. Markley and Sons, 1880.

Parton, James. *The Life and Times of Aaron Burr.* New York: Mason Brothers, 1858.

Pasquin, Anthony [John Williams]. *The Hamiltoniad.* New York: printed for the Hamilton Club, 1865 [1804].

Paterson, James. *History of the County of Ayr: With a Genealogical Account of the Families of Ayrshire.* Vol. 2. Edinburgh: T. G. Stevenson, 1852.

Pettit, Marilyn Hilley. "Women, Sunday Schools, and Politics: Early National New York City, 1797–1827." Ph.D. diss. New York University, 1991.

Phelan, Helene. *The Man Who Owned the Pistols: John Barker Church and His Family.* Interlaken, N.Y.: Heart of the Lake Publishing, 1981.

Pickering, Timothy. *Review of the Correspondence Between the Hon. John Adams and the Late Wm. Cunningham, Esq.* Salem, Mass.: Cushing and Appleton, 1824.

Pidgin, Charles Felton. *Theodosia: The First Gentlewoman of Her Time.* Boston: C. M. Clark, 1907.

Pilkington, Walter. *The Journals of Samuel Kirkland.* Clinton, N.Y.: Hamilton College, 1980.

Powell, J. H. *Bring Out Your Dead: The Great Plague of Yellow Fever in Philadelphia in 1793.* Philadelphia: University of Pennsylvania Press, 1949.

Ragatz, Lowell Joseph. *The Fall of the Planter Class in the British Caribbean, 1763–1833.* New York: Century, 1928.

Rakove, Jack N. *James Madison and the Creation of the American Republic.* New York: Longman, 2002 [1947].

Ramsing, Holger Utke. *Alexander Hamilton's Birth and Parentage.* Trans. Solvejg Vahl. Copenhagen: n.p., 1939. Manuscript in the New York Public Library, New York, N.Y.

Randolph, Edmund. *A Vindication of Mr. Randolph's Resignation.* Philadelphia: Samuel H. Smith, 1795.

Renwick, James. *Lives of John Jay and Alexander Hamilton.* New York: Harper and Brothers, 1840.

A Reply to Alexander Hamilton's Letter, Concerning the Public Conduct and Character of John Adams, Esq., President of the United States. By a Federal Republican. New York: L. Nichols, 1800.

Riedesel, Madame de. *Letters and Memoirs Relating to the War of American Independence, and the Capture of the German Troops at Saratoga.* Trans. New York: G. and C. Carvill, 1827.

Robertson, William Spence. *The Life of Miranda.* Vol. 1. New York: Cooper Square, 1969.

Rogow, Arnold A. *A Fatal Friendship: Alexander Hamilton and Aaron Burr.* New York: Hill and Wang, 1998.

Rosenfeld, Richard N. *American Aurora: A Democratic-Republican Returns.* New York: St. Martin's Press, 1997.

Sabine, Lorenzo. *Notes on Duels and Duelling.* Boston: Crosby, Nichols, 1855.

St. Méry, Moreau de. *Moreau de St. Méry's American Journey.* Trans. and ed. Kenneth Roberts and

Anna M. Roberts. Garden City, N.Y.: Doubleday, 1947.

Schachner, Nathan. *Alexander Hamilton*. New York: Thomas Yoseloff, 1946.

Schama, Simon. *Citizens: A Chronicle of the French Revolution*. New York: Vintage Books, 1990 [1989].

Schecter, Barnet. *The Battle for New York: The City at the Heart of the American Revolution*. New York: Walker, 2002.

Schuyler, George W. *Colonial New York: Philip Schuyler and His Family*. Vol. 2. New York: Charles Scribner's Sons, 1885.

Scigliano, Robert, ed. *The Federalist: A Commentary on the Constitution of the United States by Alexander Hamilton, James Madison, and John Jay*. New York: Modern Library, 2000.

Sedgwick, Theodore, Jr. *A Memoir of the Life of William Livingston*. New York: J. and J. Harper, 1833.

Shephard, Charles. *An Historical Account of the Island of Saint Vincent*. London: Frank Cass, 1997 [1871].

Smith, Jean Edward. *John Marshall: Definer of a Nation*. New York: Henry Holt, 1998 [1996].

Smith, Richard Norton. *Patriarch: George Washington and the New American Nation*. Boston: Houghton Mifflin, 1993.

Sparks, Jared. *The Life of Gouverneur Morris with Selections from His Correspondence and Miscellaneous Papers*. Vol. 3. Boston: Gray and Bowen, 1832.

The Speeches at Full Length of Mr. Van Ness, Mr. Caines, the Attorney-General, Mr. Harrison, and General Hamilton, in the Great Cause of the People, against Harry Croswell, on an Indictment for a Libel on Thomas Jefferson, President of the United States. New York: G. and R. Waite, 1804.

Steiner, Bernard C. *The Life and Correspondence of James McHenry*. New York: Arno Press, 1979.

Stevens, John Austin, Jr. *Colonial Records of the New York Chamber of Commerce, 1768–1784*. New York: John F. Trow, 1867.

Stewart, George. *Curiosities of Glasgow Citizenship*. Glasgow: James Maclehose, 1881.

Strong, George W. *Letters of George W. Strong*. Ed. John R. Strong. New York: G. P. Putnam's Sons, 1922.

Sullivan, William. *The Public Men of the Revolution*. Philadelphia: Carey and Hart, 1847.

Taft, Henry W. *A Century and a Half at the New York Bar*. New York: privately printed, 1938. Copy in New-York Historical Society, New York, N.Y.

Tappan, Lewis. *The Life of Arthur Tappan*. Westport, Conn.: Negro Universities Press, 1970 [1871].

Thomas, Milton Halsey, ed. *The Black Book or Book of Misdemeanors in King's College, New-York,*

1771–1775. New York: Columbia University Press, 1931.

Thorne, R. G. *The House of Commons, 1790–1820*. Vol. 3. London: Secker and Warburg, 1986.

Tripp, Wendell Edward, Jr. "Robert Troup: A Quest for Security in a Turbulent New Nation, 1775–1832." Ph.D. diss. Columbia University, 1973.

Tuchman, Barbara W. *The First Salute*. New York: Ballantine Books, 1989 [1988].

Tyler, Moses Coit. *The Literary History of the American Revolution, 1763–1783*. Vol. 1, *1763–1776*. New York: Frederick Ungar, 1957.

Tyson, George F., and Arnold R. Highfield, eds. *The Kamina Folk: Slavery and Slave Life in the Danish West Indies*. U.S. Virgin Islands: Virgin Islands Humanities Council, 1994.

Valentine, Alan. *Lord Stirling*. New York: Oxford University Press, 1969.

Van Amringe, John H., and Munroe Smith. *A History of Columbia University 1754–1904*. New York: Columbia University Press, 1904.

Van Doren, Carl. *Benjamin Franklin*. New York: Viking Press, 1938.

———. *Secret History of the American Revolution*. New York: Viking Press, 1968.

Van Vechten, Jacob, ed. *Memoirs of John Mason, D.D., S.T.P., with Portions of His Correspondence*. New York: Robert Carter and Brothers, 1856.

Vidal, Gore. *Burr*. New York: Vintage Books, 2000 [1971].

Wallace, David Duncan. *The Life of Henry Laurens*. New York: Russell and Russell, 1967 [1915].

Warville, J. P. Brissot de. *New Travels in the United States of America, 1788*. Cambridge, Mass.: Belknap Press, Harvard University Press, 1964.

Waters, Ivor. *The Unfortunate Valentine Morris*. Chepstow, Monmouthshire (Great Britain): Chepstow Society, 1964.

Westergaard, Waldemar. *The Danish West Indies under Company Rule (1671–1754)*. New York: Macmillan, 1917.

William Myers, A. J. *Long Hammering: Essays on the Forging of an African American Presence in the Hudson River Valley to the Early Twentieth Century*. Trenton: Africa World Press, 1994.

Williams, Eric. *From Columbus to Castro: The History of the Caribbean*. New York: Vintage Books, 1984 [1970].

Wills, Garry. *Explaining America: The Federalist*. New York: Penguin, 1982 [1981].

———. *James Madison*. New York: Times Books, 2002.

Wilson, Douglas L., and Lucia Stanton. *Jefferson Abroad*. New York: Modern Library, 1999.

Wood, Gordon S. *The American Revolution*. New York: Modern Library, 2002.

Woodcock, Henry Iles. *A History of Tobago.* Hertford, England: Stephen Austin and Sons, 1971 [1871].

Wright, Robert E. *Hamilton Unbound: Finance and the Creation of the American Republic.* Westport, Conn.: Greenwood Press, 2002.

Selected Articles

Adair, Douglas, and Marvin Harvey. "Was Alexander Hamilton a Christian Statesman?" *The William and Mary Quarterly,* 3d series, 12, 1955.

Atherton, Gertrude. "The Hunt for Hamilton's Mother." *The North American Review* 175, no. 2, August 1902.

Bland, Harry MacNeill, and Virginia W. Northcott. "Life Portraits of Alexander Hamilton." *The William and Mary Quarterly* 12, no. 2, April 1955.

Bowman, Albert H. "Jefferson, Hamilton, and American Foreign Policy." *Political Science Quarterly* 71, no. 1, March 1956.

Brooks, Robin. "Alexander Hamilton, Melancton Smith, and the Ratification of the Constitution in New York." *The William and Mary Quarterly* 24, no. 3, July 1967.

Bruchey, Stuart. "Alexander Hamilton and the State Banks." *The William and Mary Quarterly* 27, no. 3, July 1970.

Butler, George Hamilton. "The Student Days of Alexander Hamilton." *The Columbia Monthly* 1, no. 1, February 1904.

Butler, Nicholas Murray. "Address at the Unveiling of the Statue of Alexander Hamilton in the City of Paterson, May 30, 1907." Copy in Columbia University Library.

———. "This World Needs Another Alexander Hamilton." *Columbia University Quarterly* 26, no. 3, September 1934.

Carnahan, James. "The Pennsylvania Insurrection of 1794, Commonly Called the Whiskey Insurrection." *Proceedings of the New Jersey Historical Society* 6, no. IV, 1853.

Charles, Joseph. "Hamilton and Washington: The Origins of the American Party System." *The William and Mary Quarterly* 12, no. 2, April 1955.

"The Church Pistols: Historical Relics of the Burr-Hamilton Duel." The Chase Manhattan Bank, New York, n.d. Copy in New-York Historical Society, New York, N.Y.

Cooke, Jacob E. "Tench Coxe, Alexander Hamilton, and the Encouragement of American Manufactures." *The William and Mary Quarterly* 32, no. 3, July 1975.

Cunningham, Noble. "John Beckley: An Early American Party Manager." *The William and Mary Quarterly* 13, no. 1, January 1956.

Dawson, Henry B. "The Duels Between Price and Philip Hamilton, and George I. Eacker." *The Historical Magazine,* 2d series, 2, October 1867.

Earl, John L., III. "Talleyrand in Philadelphia, 1794–1796." *The Pennsylvania Magazine of History and Biography* 91, no. 3, July 1967.

Elkins, Stanley, and Eric McKitrick. "The Founding Fathers: Young Men of the Revolution." *Political Science Quarterly* 76, no. 2, June 1961.

Estabrook, Henry D. "The Lawyer Hamilton." Speech delivered to the American Bar Association, Denver, August 22, 1901.

Freeman, Joanne B. "Dueling as Politics: Reinterpreting the Burr-Hamilton Duel." *The William and Mary Quarterly* 53, no. 2, April 1996.

Gerlach, Don R. "After Saratoga: The General, His Lady and 'Gentleman Johnny' Burgoyne." *New York History* 52, 1971.

Govan, Thomas P. "The Rich, the Well-born, and Alexander Hamilton." *The Mississippi Valley Historical Review* 36, no. 4, March 1950.

Harper, John L. "Mentor for a Hegemon: The Rising Fortune of Alexander Hamilton." *The National Interest,* fall 2000.

Hawley, George M. B. "The Hamilton-Burr Duel Pistols." Pamphlet in J. P. Morgan Chase Archives, record group 11, "Art & Artifacts," New York, N.Y.

Jennings, Robert M., Donald F. Swanson, and Andrew P. Trout. "Alexander Hamilton's Tontine Proposal." *The William and Mary Quarterly* 45, no. 1, January 1988.

Jones, A. Leroy. "Myles Cooper, LL.D." *Columbia University Quarterly,* September 1899.

Jones, Robert F. "William Duer and the Business of Government in the Era of the American Revolution." *The William and Mary Quarterly* 32, no. 3, July 1975.

Kenyon, Cecilia M. "Men of Little Faith: The Anti-Federalists on the Nature of Representative Government." *The William and Mary Quarterly* 12, no. 1, January 1955.

"Kerelaw House." *Kilmarnock Standard,* April 5, 1924. Article signed H.W.C.

Kohn, Richard H. "The Washington Administration's Decision to Crush the Whiskey Rebellion." *The Journal of American History* 59, no. 3, December 1972.

Larson, Harold. "Alexander Hamilton: The Fact and Fiction of His Early Years." *The William and Mary Quarterly* 9, no. 2, April 1952.

———. "The Birth and Parentage of Alexander Hamilton." *The American Genealogist* 21, no. 3, January 1945.

"The Last Hours of Alexander Hamilton." *Columbia University Quarterly* 29, no. 1, March 1937.

"Letters of Toussaint L'Ouverture and of Edward

Stevens, 1798-1800." *The American Historical Review* 16, no. 1, October 1910.

Livingston, John C. "Alexander Hamilton and the American Tradition." *Midwest Journal of Political Science* 1, no. 3/4, November 1957.

Lund, Nelson. "Taking the Second Amendment Seriously." *The Weekly Standard,* July 24, 2000.

McCarthy, Callahan J. "Lieut. Col. Francis Barber of Elizabethtown." *The New Jersey Historical Proceedings* 50, no. 3, July 1932.

Malone, Dumas. "The Threatened Prosecution of Alexander Hamilton under the Sedition Act." *The American Historical Review* 29, no. 1, October 1923.

Marsh, Philip. "Hamilton and Monroe." *The Mississippi Historical Review* 34, no. 3, December 1947.

———. "Hamilton's Neglected Essays, 1791–1793." *New York Historical Society Quarterly* 32, no. 4, October 1948.

———. "John Beckley: Mystery Man of the Early Jeffersonians." *Pennsylvania Magazine of History and Biography* 72, no. 1, January 1948.

Meyer, Freeman W. "A Note on the Origins of the 'Hamiltonian System.'" *The William and Mary Quarterly* 21, no. 4, October 1964.

Mitchell, Broadus. "Hamilton's Quarrel with Washington, 1781." *The William and Mary Quarterly* 12, no. 2, April 1955.

———. "The Man Who Discovered Hamilton." *Proceedings of the New Jersey Historical Society* 69, no. 2, April 1951.

Morse, Anson D. "Alexander Hamilton." *Political Science Quarterly* 5, no. 1, March 1890.

Nelson, John R., Jr. "Alexander Hamilton and American Manufacturing: A Reexamination." *The Journal of American History* 65, no. 4, March 1979.

Panagopoulos, E. P. "Hamilton's Notes in His Pay Book of the New York State Artillery Company." *The American Historical Review* 62, no. 2, January 1957.

"Reminiscences of Mrs. Alexander Hamilton." *Atlantic Monthly,* vol. 78, no. 466, August 1896.

Reubens, Beatrice G. "Burr, Hamilton, and the Manhattan Company. Part 1: Gaining the Charter." *Political Science Quarterly* 72, no. 4, December 1957.

———. "Burr, Hamilton, and the Manhattan Company. Part 2: Launching a Bank." *Political Science Quarterly* 73, no. 1, March 1958.

"R. F. Cutting, '71, Relates Story about Alexander Hamilton's Death." *Columbia Alumni News* 21, no. 14, January 17, 1930.

Roberts, Russell. "Hamilton's Great Experiment: The SUM." *Financial History,* no. 65, 1999.

Rorabaugh, W. J. "The Political Duel in the Early Republic: Burr v. Hamilton." *Journal of the Early Republic* 15, no. 1, spring 1995.

Schachner, Nathan. "Alexander Hamilton Viewed by His Friends: The Narratives of Robert Troup and Hercules Mulligan." *The William and Mary Quarterly* 4, no. 2, April 1947.

Sheridan, Eugene R. "Thomas Jefferson and the Giles Resolutions." *The William and Mary Quarterly* 49, no. 4, October 1992.

Smith, James Morton. "Alexander Hamilton, the Alien Law, and Seditious Libel." *The Review of Politics* 16, no. 3, July 1954.

Swan, Robert J. "Prelude and Aftermath of the Doctors' Riot of 1788: A Religious Interpretation of White and Black Reaction to Grave Robbing." *New York History* 81, no. 4, October 2000.

Swanson, Donald F., and Andrew P. Trout. "Alexander Hamilton's Hidden Sinking Fund." *The William and Mary Quarterly* 49, no. 1, January 1992.

Torrey, Raymond H. "Hamilton Grange." *Scenic and Historic America* 3, no. 3, April 1934.

Tugwell, Rexford, and Joseph Dorfman. "Alexander Hamilton: Nation-Maker. Part 1." *Columbia University Quarterly* 29, no. 4, December 1937.

———. "Alexander Hamilton: Nation-Maker. Part 2." *Columbia University Quarterly* 30, no. 1, March 1938.

Wadsworth, Eliot. "Alexander Hamilton, First Secretary of the Treasury." *Columbia Alumni News* 16, no. 12, December 19, 1924.

Walker, G.P.J. "Murder at Frigate Bay." *London Magazine,* August 1753.

Webb, James. "The Fateful Encounter." *American Heritage* 26, no. 5, August 1975.

Westergaard, Waldemar. "Account of the Negro Rebellion on St. Croix, Danish West Indies, 1859." *Journal of Negro History* 11, no. 1, January 1926.

———. "A St. Croix Map of 1766: With a Note on Its Significance in West Indian Plantation Economy." *Journal of Negro History* 23, April 1938.

Wetterau, James O. "New Light on the First Bank of the United States." *Pennsylvania Magazine of History and Biography* 61, no. 3, July 1937.

Whitson, Agnes M. "The Outlook of the Continental American Colonies on the British West Indies, 1760–1775." *Political Science Quarterly* 43, no. 1, March 1930.

Williams, D. "The Westchester Farmer." *Magazine of American History* 8, no. 2, February 1882.

Williams, William Appleman. "The Age of Mercantilism: An Interpretation of the American Political Economy, 1763 to 1828." *The William and Mary Quarterly* 15, no. 4, October 1958.

Wilson, R. Jackson. "The Founding Father." *The New Republic* 188, no. 23, issue 3, June 13, 1983.

Wood, Gordon S. "An Affair of Honor." *The New York Review of Books,* April 13, 2000.

———. "The American Love Boat." *The New York Review of Books,* October 7, 1999.

———. "Debt and Democracy." *The New York Review of Books,* June 12, 2003.

———. "Early American Get-Up-and-Go." *The New York Review of Books,* June 29, 2000.

———. "Give Me Diversity or Give Me Death." *The New Republic,* June 12, 2000.

———. "The Revenge of Aaron Burr." *The New York Review of Books,* February 2, 1984.

Illustration Permissions

IN ORDER OF APPEARANCE

Frontispiece

Alexander Hamilton (1755–1804), by John Trumbull (1756–1843)
Oil on canvas, 1832
Yale University Art Gallery, Trumbull Collection (1832.11)

Illustration Insert

Alexander Hamilton (1755–1804), by John Trumbull (1756–1843)
Oil on canvas, 1792
Collection of Credit Suisse First Boston
Myles Cooper, D.D. (1737–1785), by John Singleton Copley (1738–1815)
Oil on canvas, ca. 1768
Columbia University, gift of The New-York Historical Society, 1820 (COO.735)
Courtesy of the Frick Art Reference Library
View of Columbia College in the City of New York, by Cornelius Tiebout (ca. 1773–1832) after J. Anderson
Copper engraving from the *New-York Magazine,* May 1790
Collection of The New-York Historical Society (PR 020 Geographic File, negative #20415)
George Washington at Princeton, by Charles Willson Peale (1741–1827)
Oil on canvas, 1779
Pennsylvania Academy of Fine Arts, Philadelphia; gift of Maria McKean Allen and Phebe Warren Downes through the bequest of their mother, Elizabeth Wharton McKean
John Laurens (1754–1782), by Charles Willson Peale (1741–1827)
Watercolor on ivory, set in gold with enamel and gemstones, ca. 1784
Independence National Historical Park

Marquis de Lafayette (1757–1834), by Joseph Boze (1745–1826)
Oil on canvas, 1790
Massachusetts Historical Society
Elizabeth Schuyler Hamilton, Mrs. Alexander Hamilton (1757–1854), by Ralph Earl (1751–1801)
Oil on canvas, 1787
Museum of the City of New York, gift of Mrs. Alexander Hamilton and General Pierpont Morgan Hamilton (1971.31.2)
Major General Philip John Schuyler (1733–1804), by John Trumbull (1756–1843)
Oil on wood panel, 1792
Collection of The New-York Historical Society, bequest of Philip Schuyler (1915.13, negative #29012)
Mrs. John Barker Church (Angelica Schuyler Church), with Child and Servant, by John Trumbull (1756–1843)
Oil on canvas, ca. 1785
Belvidere Trust Collection through Mr. and Mrs. Robert Bromeley
Philip Schuyler Mansion, Albany, New York, by Philip Hooker (1766–1836)
Ink and watercolor on paper, 1818
Collection of The New-York Historical Society (1961.13, negative #38794)
James Madison (1751–1836), by Charles Willson Peale (1741–1827)
Oil on canvas, 1792
Collection of the Gilcrease Museum, Tulsa, Oklahoma
John Jay (1745–1829), by Joseph Wright (1756–1793)
Oil on canvas, 1786
Collection of The New-York Historical Society, gift of John Pintard (1817.5, negative #6066)

The Federalist *number 1*
From the *New-York Independent Journal,* October 27, 1787
Collection of The New-York Historical Society (negative #52128)
George Clinton (1739–1812), by Ezra Ames (1768–1836)
Oil on canvas, 1814
Collection of The New-York Historical Society, gift of George Clinton Tallmadge (1858.84, negative #6108)
Thomas Jefferson (1743–1826), by Mather Brown (1761–1831)
Oil on canvas, 1786
National Portrait Gallery, Smithsonian Institution (99.66)/Art Resource, New York
Thomas Jefferson (1743–1826), by James Sharples, Sr. (ca. 1751–1811), from life
Pastel on paper, 1796–1797
Independence National Historical Park
Philip Morin Freneau (1752–1832)
Reprinted from Philip Morin Freneau, *Poems Relating to the American Revolution* (New York: W. J. Widdleton, 1865)
James Monroe (1758–1831), by Jean-Baptiste-Claude Sené, (1748–1803)
Watercolor on ivory, 1794
Courtesy of James Monroe Museum and Memorial Library, Fredericksburg, Virginia
William Branch Giles (1762–1830), after Gilbert Stuart (1755–1828)
Photogravure, n.d.
Collection of The New-York Historical Society (PR 052 Portrait File, negative #75966)
Edmond Charles Genêt (1763–1834), by Gilles-Louis Chrétien (1754–1811) after Jean Fouquet (active 1793–1798)
Engraving, restrike from the original copper plate of 1793
Albany Institute of History and Art, bequest of George Clinton Genet through the estate of Augusta G. K. C. Genet (1912.2.4)
Charles-Maurice de Talleyrand-Périgord (1754–1838), by Pierre-Paul Prud'hon (1758–1823)
Oil on canvas, 1817
Metropolitan Museum of Art, purchase, Mrs. Charles Wrightsman, gift in memory of Jacqueline Bouvier Kennedy Onassis (1994.190)
John Adams (1735–1826), by Charles Willson Peale (1741–1827), from life
Oil on canvas 1791–1794
Independence National Historical Park
Letter from Alexander Hamilton, Concerning the Public Conduct and Character of John Adams, Esq., President of the United States
New York: printed for John Lang by George F. Hopkins, 1800
Collection of The New-York Historical Society, gift of Gulian E. Verplanck, 1809 (negative #51097)

Timothy Pickering (1745–1829), by Hezekiah W. Smith after Gilbert Stuart (1755–1828)
Engraving, ca. 1860
Collection of The New-York Historical Society, gift of Henry O. Havemeyer (PR 025, negative #75964)
Oliver Wolcott, Jr. (1760–1833), by Joseph Andrews (1806–1837) and W. H. Tappan after John Trumbull (1756–1843)
Engraving, ca. 1850
Collection of The New-York Historical Society, gift of Henry O. Havemeyer (PR 025, negative #75965)
James McHenry (1753–1816), by James Sharples, Sr. (ca. 1751–1811), from life
Pastel on paper, ca. 1796–1800
Independence National Historical Park
Aaron Burr (1756–1836), attributed to Gilbert Stuart (1755–1828)
Oil on canvas, ca. 1792
Collection of The New Jersey Historical Society, Newark, New Jersey, gift of David A. Hayes for John Chetwood (1854.1)
Aaron Burr (1756–1836), by John Vanderlyn (1775–1852)
Oil on canvas, 1802
Collection of The New-York Historical Society, gift of Dr. John E. Stillwell (1931.58, negative #6227)
Aaron Burr (1756–1836), by James Van Dyck (active nineteenth century)
Oil on canvas, 1834
Collection of The New-York Historical Society, gift of Dr. John E. Stillwell (1931.57, negative #6832)
Philip Hamilton (1782–1801)
Reprinted from Allan McLane Hamilton, *The Intimate Life of Alexander Hamilton* (New York: Charles Scribner's Sons, 1911)
Alexander Hamilton (1755–1804), by Ezra Ames (1768–1836)
Oil on canvas, 1810
Special Collections, Schaffer Library, Union College, gift of General Alexander Hamilton, 1875
Elizabeth Schuyler Hamilton, Mrs. Alexander Hamilton (1757–1854), attributed to John D. Martin
Charcoal and chalk on paper, 1851
Museum of the City of New York, gift of Mrs. Alexander Hamilton and General Pierpont Morgan Hamilton (1971.31.6)
Alexander Hamilton (1755–1804), by Giuseppe Ceracchi (1751–1802)
Marble, ca. 1793
Collection of The New-York Historical Society, gift of James Gore King (1928.18, negative #50044)
Hamilton Grange, New York, by Randall Comfort
Photograph, 1891
Collection of The New-York Historical Society (PR 020 Geographic File, negative #75963)

Index

AVAILABLE FROM PENGUIN

Winner of the 2011 Pulitzer Prize for Biography

Washington
A Life

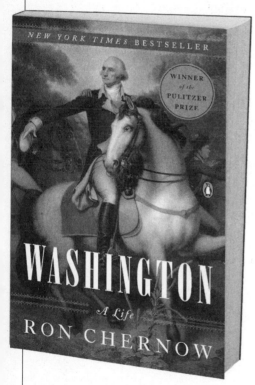

Celebrated biographer Ron Chernow provides a richly nuanced portrait of the father of our nation. With a breadth and depth matched by no other one-volume biography of George Washington, this narrative carries the reader through his adventurous early years, his heroic exploits with the Continental Army during the Revolutionary War, his presiding over the Constitutional Convention, and his magnificent performance as America's first president. Chernow shatters Washington's stereotype as a stolid, unemotional figure and brings to life a dashing, passionate man of fiery opinions and many moods.

ISBN 978-0-14-311996-8

"Truly magnificent… [a] well-researched, well-written and absolutely definitive biography."
—Andrew Roberts, The Wall Street Journal

**PENGUIN
BOOKS**